LSAT® 2015
WORKBOOK

PUBLISHING

New York

Special thanks to those who made this book possible:

Matthew Belinkie, Kim Bowers, Jack Chase, David Cohen, Cailin Emmett, John Fritschie, Christopher George, Joseph Gordon, Joanna Graham, Craig Harman, Gar Hong, Rebecca Houck, Michael Kermmoade, Terrence McGovern, Greg Mitchell, Joseph Moulden, Walt Neidner, Christine Novello, Rachel Pearsall, Anne Peterson, Rachel Reina, Larry Rudman, Amjed Saffarini, Jessica Smith, Glen Stohr, Sascha Strelka, Jay Thomas

10 9 8 7 6 5 4 3 2 1

ISBN: 978-1-62523-003-4

Preface: About Your Kaplan Resources vii

Introduction: About the LSAT 1

Why the LSAT? 1

What the LSAT Tests 1

Structure of the LSAT 2

How the LSAT Is Scored 4

Registration for and Administration of the LSAT 6

LSAT Study Skills 7

PART ONE: LSAT REASONING

CHAPTER 1: LSAT Reasoning 11

Levels of Truth 11

Determining What Must Be True, What Must Be False,
and What Could Be True or False from a Set of Statements 16

Formal Logic: Conditional Statements 22

Formal Logic: Contrapositives 44

Formal Logic: Numerical Deductions from Conditional Statements 67

Perform 72

Reflection 78

PART TWO: LOGIC GAMES

CHAPTER 2: The Kaplan Logic Games Method 81

Reflection 111

CHAPTER 3: Logic Games: Overviews, Sketches, and Game Types 113

Step 1 of the Logic Games Method: Working with Game Overviews 115

Step 2 of the Logic Games Method: Making a Sketch 120

Game Types 126

Perform: LSAT Logic Games Overviews and Sketches 161

Review. 171

CHAPTER 4: Logic Games: Rules and Deductions **175**

Step 3 of the Logic Games Method: Analyze and Draw the Rules 175

Step 4 of the Logic Games Method: Combine the Rules
and Restrictions to Make Deductions. 221

LSAT Game Practice 252

Reflection 271

CHAPTER 5: Logic Games: The Questions **273**

Logic Games Question Types 273

Acceptability Questions. 275

Completely Determine Questions 294

Must Be/Could Be Questions 299

New-"If" Questions 315

Other Logic Games Question Types 352

Reflection 357

CHAPTER 6: Logic Games Practice **359**

Notes on Logic Games Practice. 359

Question Pool 1 360

Question Pool 2 374

Answer Key 400

CHAPTER 7: Logic Games: Managing the Section **401**

Timing and Section Management 401

Taking the Timing Section 403

Answer Key 412

PART THREE: LOGICAL REASONING

Chapter 8: The Kaplan Logical Reasoning Method **415**

Logical Reasoning Question Format and the Kaplan
Logical Reasoning Method 416

Wrong Answers in Logical Reasoning Questions 433

Reflection 434

CHAPTER 9: Argument-Based Questions **435**

Conclusions and Main Point Questions 436

Evidence and Arguments: Role of a Statement,
Point at Issue, and Method of Argument Questions 463

Reflection 509

Question Pool...510

Answer Key 514

CHAPTER 10: Assumption Family Questions **515**

Mismatched Concepts 518

Overlooked Possibilities 532

Untangling and Analyzing LSAT Arguments 544

Assumption Questions 552

Flaw Questions...585

Strengthen and Weaken Questions 622

Argument-Based Principle Questions.....................................656

Parallel Reasoning and Parallel Flaw Questions 668

Identify and Apply the Principle Questions 698

Reflection 701

Question Pools...702

Answer Key 731

CHAPTER 11: Non-Argument Questions 733

Making Deductions and Inference Questions 734

Principle Questions Asking for Inferences 786

Resolving Discrepancies and Paradox Questions 802

Identifying Question Stems...827

Reflection 831

Summary 831

Question Pools...832

Answer Key 842

CHAPTER 12: Logical Reasoning: Managing the Section **843**

Timing and Section Management...843

Taking the Timing Section 845

Answer Key 862

PART FOUR: READING COMPREHENSION

CHAPTER 13: The Kaplan Reading Comprehension Method **865**

A Strategic Approach to Reading Comprehension 865

Reflection 889

CHAPTER 14: Reading Comprehension: Passage Types and Question Types **893**

Strategic Reading and Reading Comprehension Passage Types. 894

Reading Comprehension Question Strategies 924

Full Passage Practice 948

Reflection 956

Answer Key 957

CHAPTER 15: Reading Comprehension Practice **959**

Notes on Reading Comprehension Practice 959

Question Pool. 960

Answer Key 980

CHAPTER 16: Reading Comprehension: Managing the Section. **981**

Timing and Section Management 981

Taking the Timing Section 983

Answer Key 992

PART FIVE: COUNTDOWN TO TEST DAY

CHAPTER 17: Test Day **995**

The Week Before the Test 995

The Day Before the Test. 998

The Morning of the Test 999

At the Test Site and During the Test 1000

After the Test 1004

PART SIX: PRACTICE TESTS

PrepTest 63: PrepTest 63 (June 2011) **1011**

PrepTest 55: PrepTest 55 (October 2008) **1047**

PrepTest 53: PrepTest 53 (December 2007). **1083**

PrepTest 47: PrepTest 47 (October 2005) **1119**

About Your Kaplan Resources

Welcome to Kaplan's *LSAT Workbook*! Your Kaplan LSAT resources will be all you need to prepare for the LSAT. Included with the book is your Online Center—more on that in a bit. Let's start with how you should use this book.

HOW TO USE THIS BOOK

First—Get Acquainted with the LSAT

Start by reading the "Introduction to the LSAT" chapter, which will introduce you to the details about the test, including structure, scoring, registration info, and how best to study.

Second—Start Becoming an LSAT Warrior

In the subsequent chapters, you'll work on the skills needed for LSAT success. We've broken down each of the skills into discrete **Learning Objectives**. Each section of the book will inform you of the Learning Objectives you're about to master, and you'll be provided with an opportunity to prepare, practice, and perform. This may involve full LSAT questions or it may simply involve drills that will prepare you to tackle full LSAT questions. All the full questions presented in this book are from real LSATs. Each year, there are four major dates on which the LSAT is given, and three of those exams are *released* by the Law School Admission Council. This means that all of the questions that were on the scored portion of that exam are available to use as study material.

Each released exam contains four scored sections and is called a **PrepTest**. This book contains every question from PrepTests 47, 49, 51, 53, 55, 57, 59, 61, 63, and 65—this is all recent material that came out between 2005 and 2011, over 1,000 questions! Beneath each LSAC-released question in this book, you'll see a Source ID (e.g., *PrepTest61 Sec2 Q2* which means that question appears in the released LSAT from PrepTest 61 in October 2010, in Section 2, as the second question).

Throughout this book, you'll see how LSAT experts—Kaplan teachers who have scored in the 99th percentile—analyze questions, games, and passages from recent LSAT exams. Study these "worked examples" carefully; they provide a chance for you to think along with an LSAT expert as he or she attacks the LSAT efficiently and accurately. Expert analysis is always laid out with the test material in the left-hand column, and with the expert's thinking immediately to the right or beneath. Where the LSAT expert demonstrates a multistep method, we've included the steps to help you train to take the most effective route through the question.

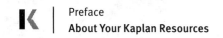
Here are a few things to be aware of whenever you study expert analyses:

This column contains test material; always read it first, so you know what the expert is analyzing.

In this column, you'll see the LSAT expert's analysis of each part of the test question—here's your coach "thinking out loud" for your benefit.

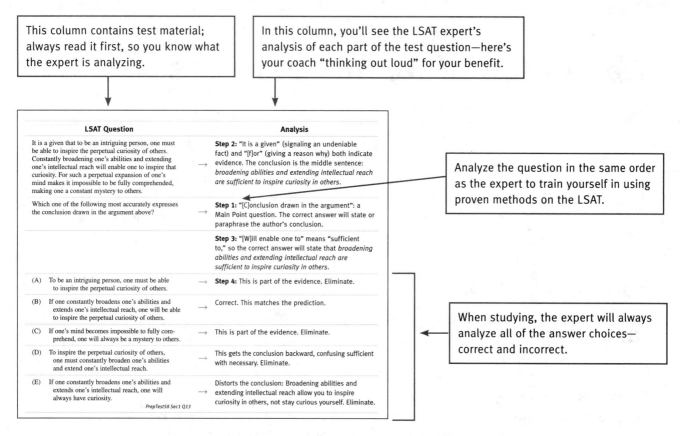

Analyze the question in the same order as the expert to train yourself in using proven methods on the LSAT.

When studying, the expert will always analyze all of the answer choices—correct and incorrect.

From time to time, you'll have practice exercises in which you'll have the chance to analyze a question. Use the spaces in the right-hand column to record your own analysis. On the following pages, we'll always provide expert analysis so that you can compare your thinking to that of an LSAT expert.

The format of our expert analysis is the result of work by leading academics in learning science. Merely doing LSAT questions and checking to see when you got the right answer is good for you, but studies indicate that practicing questions by studying expert thinking alongside actual test material produces better results and is a more effective—and faster—way to master LSAT skills. As you complete the questions, don't just check to see if you got them right or wrong. If you use each question as an opportunity to better understand the patterns of the test as well as your own strengths and weaknesses, you will see improved performance. The explanations for questions in the "Question Pools" are located in a PDF accessible in your Online Center.

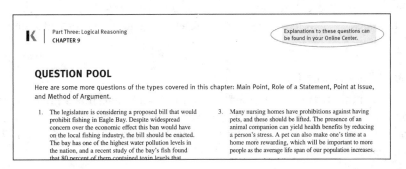

The explanations break each question down step-by-step and provide detailed reasons why the one credited answer is correct and each of the others is wrong. The explanations also include information about the relative difficulty of the question you just attempted. That way, you can see how you're performing on easy vs. difficult content. Each question is rated on a star system: one-star questions are the easiest, four-star questions are the hardest. These star rankings have come from thousands of Kaplan students who have used our products and studied for the LSAT just as you are about to do.

Third—Test Out Your LSAT Skills

In the back of the book, there are four 4-section tests, along with five testing grids. The additional grid is for the full LSAT sections in Chapters 7, 12, and 16. You've got several options for best using these tests. Some future test takers like to take a test as the first thing they do to get a baseline idea of what their performance is before they've started their practice. Other people will want to dive into the material, learn what they can, and then try their hand at a test. Either way is acceptable, but it is recommended that you save two of the tests to take in the last of couple weeks before your actual test as a dry run and final rehearsal. You can use the other two as a couple of midterms or as a baseline and midterm depending on your preference. Although the answer key and scoring scale are contained at the back of each test, we recommend entering your answers into Smart Reports® (see Online Center info below).

Do I Have to Go through This Whole Book?

You may have already noticed that there's a lot of material in this book, and that's great for those who have the time and determination to maximize their preparation. However, other people may want just some targeted practice before the exam, or they may not have the opportunity to finish up everything. Here's a quick rundown on which chapters may be considered prerequisites for the others.

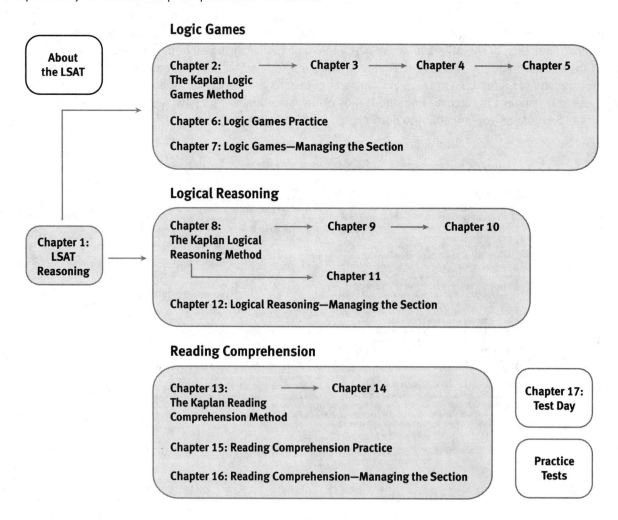

Also, if there's anything you want to approach without instruction, the question pools contained in Chapters 6 and 15, and at the end of Chapters 9, 10, and 11, serve as quick access to individual question practice material. The four tests and three Managing the Section chapters (7, 12, and 16) serve as comprehensive or individual section practice material.

If You Also Have Kaplan's *LSAT Premier* or *Strategies, Practice, and Review* (*SPR*) Book

Some of you may have purchased this book in conjunction with or after using another Kaplan LSAT book. You'll see that the Table of Contents for the *LSAT Workbook* is identical to that in both our *LSAT Premier* book and *LSAT Strategies, Practice, and Review* book (*SPR*). However, all of the question content—exercises, LSAT questions, tests, etc.—are different in the *Workbook* than in those other books. This book features more material, but does not have as much explanatory text as the other books. It doesn't matter which order you use the books in: you could complete *Premier* or *SPR* and then use the *Workbook* for more practice, or you could use the *Workbook* and then consult *Premier* or *SPR* for more explanation on certain concepts as well as more LSAT content. By aligning the Tables of Contents we've made using the books in conjunction easy. However, this single book may be sufficient for your practice—it just depends on how much time you plan to put in to your preparation. Your online resources will be largely the same regardless of which book you purchased.

HOW TO USE THE ONLINE RESOURCES

First—Register for Your Online Center

The Online Center gives you access to even more test prep, including question explanations, Smart Reports® (our data analysis of your performance), and more!

Register for your Online Center using these simple steps:

1. Go to http://kaptest.com/lsatworkbook2015

2. Enter the password as directed. Instructions for the password are given in the registration form.

3. Click on "Register Now" and follow the on-screen instructions.

4. Once registered, click on the "Go to your Student Homepage" link to access your online companion materials.

Please have a copy of your book with you because you will need information from the book to access your account.

Access to the Online Center is limited to the original owner of this book and is nontransferable. Kaplan is not responsible for providing access to the Online Center for customers who purchase or borrow used copies of this book. Access to the Online Center expires one year after you register.

Second—Study Plans

This is a big book, and you might not have the time to approach everything in it. That's where our online study plans come in. In your Online Center, you'll find several study plans to review that provide you guidance on how best to use the resources depending on the hours/days/weeks/months you have available to study.

Third—Scoring Your Tests in Smart Reports®

For each 4-section test taken from the back of the book, you can see how you scored by section and by individual question/passage/game type where applicable. You can also review your responses and the Kaplan explanations to each question. In Smart Reports®, you can view your performance on an individual test or section, or look at your overall performance as you progress through the four tests.

LOOKING FOR MORE?

At Kaplan, we're thrilled you've chosen us to help you on your journey to law school. Beyond this book, there's a wealth of additional resources accessible to you that we invite you to check out to aid you with your LSAT preparation and your law school application.

- · – Our blog, the180.com, featuring several articles a week on the nuances of LSAT preparation and applying to law school, authored by Kaplan instructors and admissions experts.

- · – "The 180–Live" is our monthly talk show exclusively for pre-law students. Free to attend, The 180–Live is the perfect place to meet and interact with law school admissions officers, law students, attorneys, and LSAT experts. Join us for a new and unique show each and every month. Show information and highlights from past episodes are available at the180.com.

- · – Facebook, Twitter, YouTube—Kaplan is wherever you are. Like us. Follow us. Subscribe to us. Get regular tips all throughout the course of your study.

- · Kaplanlsat.com – Of course, we'd be remiss if we did not mention the world's most popular LSAT preparation courses. Visit our website to learn about our comprehensive prep options. Choose from Classroom On Site, Classroom Anywhere™ (Live Online), On Demand (Recording Online) and Private Tutoring options depending on your needs and learning style.

As you can plainly see, you have so much you can do. Ready to get started? Let's do this!

About the LSAT

WHY THE LSAT?

Each year, Kaplan surveys law school admissions officials, and consistently, over 60 percent say that the LSAT is their number-one consideration as they evaluate applications. Why do they put so much emphasis on this test? A breakdown of the components in the application offers the best explanation.

- **5** components of the standard law school application: LSAT score, undergraduate GPA, personal statement, letters of recommendation, and "resume factors," such as work experience, extra-curricular activities, and so on
- **2** quantitative measures: LSAT score and undergraduate GPA
- **1** quantitative measure comparable for all applicants: LSAT score

The LSAT doesn't care what you majored in or where you went to school. It's the one element of the law school application that measures all applicants on a level playing field.

WHAT THE LSAT TESTS

While the LSAT offers a standard, quantitative measure of all applicants, law school admissions officers would not value it so highly if the LSAT did not test skills relevant to—indeed, central to—an applicant's law school potential. Studies have consistently shown that LSAT score is more strongly correlated with law school performance, especially in a student's first year, than any other factor in the application.

THE FOUR CORE LSAT SKILLS

Reading Strategically—understanding the structure of a piece of text and the author's purpose for writing it

Analyzing Arguments—distinguishing an author's conclusion from her evidence and identifying the implicit assumptions the author has made

Understanding Formal Logic—determining what must, can, or cannot be true on the basis of conditional "If/then" statements

Making Deductions—determining what follows logically from a set of statements or rules

Law schools know that these skills are crucial to a student's success as a law student and in the practice of law later on. Because they are so fundamental to the test, these four core skills underlie all of the learning objectives found in this workbook.

STRUCTURE OF THE LSAT

The LSAT consists of five multiple-choice sections: two Logical Reasoning sections, one Logic Games section, one Reading Comprehension section, and one unscored "experimental" section that will look exactly like one of the other multiple-choice sections. With the exception of the Writing Sample, which will always be last, the five multiple-choice sections can appear in any order on Test Day. A 10- or 15-minute break will come between the third and fourth sections of the test.

Aligning the four core LSAT skills to the section of the test demonstrates why the LSAT is structured as it is.

FOUR CORE LSAT SKILLS BY SECTION

Core Skill	Primary Section Tested	Secondary Section Tested
Reading Strategically	Reading Comprehension	Logical Reasoning
Analyzing Arguments	Logical Reasoning	Reading Comprehension
Understanding Formal Logic	Logical Reasoning	Logic Games
Making Deductions	Logic Games	Logical Reasoning

Note that Logical Reasoning is the primary section for two of the core skills and the secondary section for the other two. Reading Comprehension and Logic Games are the primary section and secondary section one time each. This helps explain why the LSAT features two scored Logical Reasoning sections, one scored Reading Comprehension section, and one scored Logic Games section per test.

Section	Number of Questions	Minutes
Logical Reasoning	24–26	35
Logical Reasoning	24–26	35
Reading Comprehension	26–28	35
Logic Games	22–24	35
"Experimental"	22–28	35
Writing Sample	n/a	35

Familiarize yourself with the content of each section.

LSAT Scored Sections

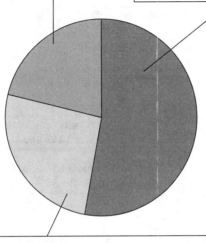

Logic Games

One section with four games and 22–24 questions

Logic Games reward you for sequencing, matching, distributing, or selecting entities on the basis of rules that combine to limit the acceptable arrangements.

Logical Reasoning

Two sections with 24–26 questions each

Logical Reasoning rewards you for analyzing arguments to strengthen or weaken them or to identify their assumptions and flaws. Other LR questions require you to draw valid inferences from a set of facts.

Reading Comprehension

One section with four passages and 26–28 questions

Reading Comp questions reward you for identifying the author's purpose and main idea, drawing valid inferences from the passage, and determining how and why the author uses certain details.

LSAT Unscored Sections

Experimental

The Experimental section is an additional, unscored section of Logical Reasoning, Reading Comprehension, or Logic Games. You will not know what type of section you will get, and it can show up anywhere, including after the break. You'll have to bring your A-game for the entire test, as there is no reliable way to determine which section is experimental while you're taking the test. The LSAT testmaker uses the unscored section to test questions for use as scored items on upcoming exams.

The Writing Sample

After you complete the five multiple-choice sections of the test, you'll write a short essay choosing between two possible courses of action. While unscored, your Writing Sample is submitted to all law schools to which you apply, and law schools use it as part of the evaluation process.

HOW THE LSAT IS SCORED

The LSAT is measured on three different scoring scales: raw score (the number of correct answers), scaled score, and percentile.

Percentile (Scaled score)	10th (139)	20th (143)	30th (146)	40th (149)	50th (151)	60th (154)	70th (156)	80th (160)	90th (164)	95th (167)	99th (172)
# Correct	38	45	50	55	58	64	67	72	80	85	91

Source – PrepTest 68 (December 2012)

LSAT Score Breakdown

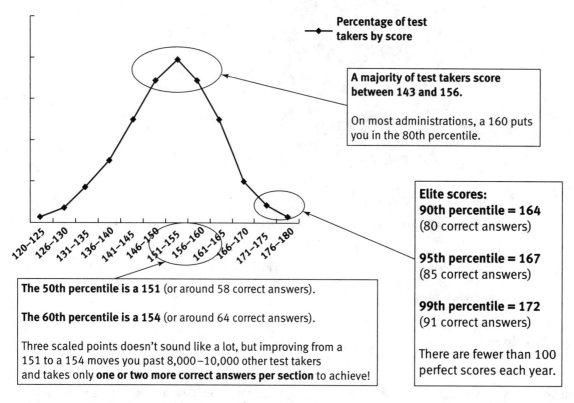

Percentage of test takers by score

A majority of test takers score between 143 and 156.

On most administrations, a 160 puts you in the 80th percentile.

Elite scores:
90th percentile = 164 (80 correct answers)

95th percentile = 167 (85 correct answers)

99th percentile = 172 (91 correct answers)

There are fewer than 100 perfect scores each year.

The 50th percentile is a 151 (or around 58 correct answers).

The 60th percentile is a 154 (or around 64 correct answers).

Three scaled points doesn't sound like a lot, but improving from a 151 to a 154 moves you past 8,000–10,000 other test takers and takes only **one or two more correct answers per section** to achieve!

Raw score is simply the number of questions answered correctly.

Scaled score, the familiar 120–180 number, is a conversion of the raw score. Here, a raw score of 67—that is, 67 correct answers—converts to a scaled score of 156. A raw score of 58—meaning 58 correct answers—converts to a 151. On a different test, a raw score of 58 might convert to a 150 or a 152. To account for differences in overall difficulty, each test has a slightly different raw score-to-scaled score conversion table.

Percentile score indicates how a test taker performed relative to other test takers over a three-year period. The conversion from scaled score to percentile score remains relatively stable, with only minor variations over the years. Test after test, a 151 scaled score is approximately a 50th percentile score.

The way in which the LSAT is scored has three important implications for your performance:

- First, only the number of *right* answers determines your score. There is no guessing penalty. Never leave a question blank on the LSAT.
- Second, every question is worth the same, regardless of how hard it is. Learn to spot difficult questions and leave them for the end of each section. Find the easy questions and rack up points. If you're going to run out of time or need to guess, you want to do so on the tough stuff.
- Third, every additional correct answer can leapfrog you ahead of hundreds—or even thousands—of other test takers, your competition. How's that for inspiration?

What's a Good LSAT Score?

What you consider a good LSAT score depends on your own expectations and goals, but here are a few interesting statistics:

Getting about half of all of the scored questions right (a raw score of roughly 50) will earn a scaled score of roughly 146 or 147, around the 30th percentile—not a great performance. However, getting only one additional question right every 10 minutes (of the scored sections) would produce a raw score of 64, or a scaled score of approximately 154, around the 60th percentile—a huge improvement.

So you don't have to be perfect to do well. On a typical LSAT, you can still get 25 wrong and end up in the 160s, or about 20 wrong and get a 164, typically a 90th percentile score. Even a perfect score of 180 often allows for a question or two to be missed.

Here is a chart detailing some top law schools and the scores of their admitted students:

Rank*	School	25th–75th %ile LSAT* (Scaled)	25th–75th %ile UGPA*	25th–75th %ile LSAT** (Raw)
1	Yale University	170–176	3.82–3.97	89–95
6	New York University	168–172	3.57–3.85	86–91
9	University of California—Berkeley	163–169	3.66–3.89	79–88
10	Duke University	165–170	3.59–3.84	82–89
15	University of Texas—Austin	163–168	3.43–3.82	79–86
20	George Washington University	159–167	3.42–3.82	72–85
27	Boston University	161–166	3.44–3.77	76–84
31	University of Wisconsin—Madison	156–163	3.21–3.70	67–79
46	Tulane University	156–162	3.12–3.60	67–77
49	University of Utah	155–161	3.31–3.68	65–76
61	University of Miami (FL)	155–160	3.16–3.60	65–74
87	Seattle University	153–158	3.03–3.55	62–70
93	St. Louis University	151–158	3.15–3.66	58–70

* U.S. News & World Report, 2015 Law School Rankings
** LSAT PrepTest 68, December 2012 Exam

REGISTRATION FOR AND ADMINISTRATION OF THE LSAT

The LSAT is administered by the Law School Admission Council (LSAC) (www.lsac.org) four times each year.

LSAT FACTS

Each year, the LSAT is administered on:

- A Saturday morning in February
- A Monday afternoon in June
- A Saturday morning in late September or early October
- A Saturday morning in December

There are some exceptions. For example, Saturday Sabbath observers have the option to take the test on a specified weekday following a typical Saturday administration. Dates and times may also be different for tests administered outside the United States, Canada, and the Caribbean.

How do I register for the LSAT? Register for the LSAT online at www.lsac.org. Check the LSAC website for details on the procedures, deadlines, and fee schedules.

When should I register? Register as soon as you have chosen your test date. Test sites may fill up quickly. Registration is typically due about five weeks before Test Day, with an additional week of registration allowed subject to a "Late Registration" fee.

Can I change my test date or location? You can change your test dates or locations (subject to an additional "change" fee) via the LSAC website. Timely changes of test date are not reported to schools; "no shows" are reported, however.

What is the CAS? Upon signing up for the LSAT, you also need to register with the Credential Assembly Service (CAS) as part of the application process required by every ABA-approved law school. CAS receives your undergraduate transcripts and distributes a summary of your undergraduate performance, along with your letters of recommendation, evaluations, and LSAT score report to each of the law schools to which you apply. www.lsac.org lists the fees and sign-up details for CAS.

When are law schools' application deadlines? All law schools provide their application deadlines on their websites. Some schools require the LSAT be taken by December for admission the following fall; others will accept a February LSAT score. Because most schools use a "rolling admissions" process, taking the test in June or September/October is preferable; also, taking the test earlier gives the test taker a chance to repeat the LSAT prior to most application deadlines.

Can I repeat the LSAT? The LSAT can be taken up to three times in a two-year period. This limit includes tests that have been canceled. More on that in the Test Day chapter. Any test taker who wishes to take the test a second time will need to reregister for the test.

How do law schools view multiple LSAT scores? This varies from school to school. Few schools now average multiple scores as was the policy in the past, but most consider *all scores from a five-year period* when evaluating applications. Applicants cannot choose which scores to report with their application. Find more information on repeating the test at www.lsac.org/jd/lsat/about-the-lsat.

Can I receive accommodations? The LSAC grants accommodation testing for physical, learning, and cognitive impairments, and there are a wide variety of accommodations available. A test taker must be registered for a test date before requesting accommodations. Full information about accommodated testing is available at www.lsac.org/jd/lsat/accommodated-testing.

LSAT STUDY SKILLS

The LSAT is a skills-based test. For this reason, improving your score is, in some ways, more like mastering a musical instrument or an athletic skill than it is like learning a subject in school. The LSAT is very practical, testing what you can do above what you know. As such, it is also practice-able and coachable. Expect Kaplan to show you the best ways to practice. Whether you are using this Workbook as part of a comprehensive Kaplan course, in conjunction with another Kaplan LSAT book, or on its own, we'll show you the patterns of the test and how to tackle every question type. Expect us to show you how to manage every section. Expect us to show you how, when, and why to use your resources. In return, you're going to need to work—hard. Reaching your full potential on the LSAT takes lots of practice. We will show you precisely what you need to do, but ultimately it's up to you to do it.

LSAT Strategy and the Three Levels of Practice

On Test Day, you'll be asked to deal with stringent testing policies and procedures, answer approximately 125 multiple-choice questions (of which typically 101 will count toward your score), and write a short essay. It's a grueling and intense four hours. Moreover, depending on how efficient your test proctors are, that four-hour process may end up lasting five hours or more.

A strategic approach to the LSAT means increasing your speed only to the extent you can do so without sacrificing accuracy. Your goal is not to attempt as many questions as possible; your goal is to get as many questions right as possible. If you had unlimited time to take this test, you'd likely perform quite well. But you don't. You have a strict 35 minutes to complete each section, and many students are not able to tackle every question in the time allotted. For you, this means three things:

- It's important that you learn not only how to answer the questions effectively, but also how to answer them efficiently.
- It's important to approach each section strategically, knowing which questions to attack first and which questions to save for last.
- It's important that you prepare for the rigors of 3½–4 hours of testing. You'll want to maintain your focus in the final section as well as you did in the first.

To achieve your goals, you'll want to work on three key levels: Mastery, Timing, and Endurance.

Mastery is about learning the patterns of the exam and how to identify them in new questions. Kaplan provides a proven method for the questions in each section of the test. You will gain command of the method and master efficient, effective strategies and tactics through repeated practice on skill-based drills and individual questions. You'll study the answers and explanations to learn how the testmaker builds questions and answer choices. You'll identify why right answers are right and why wrong answers are wrong, what traps you consistently fall into, and how to avoid them. That's what Mastery practice is for.

Once you've learned the skills, you'll try full-length section practice, or **Timing** practice. At 3½ hours, the LSAT can seem like a marathon, but it's really a series of sprints—five 35-minute tests, plus the writing sample. Learning section management—how to recognize and apply the patterns you've learned efficiently, maximizing the number of questions you get correct—is what Timing practice teaches you to do.

Finally, there's **Endurance** practice. Can you maintain your ability to identify and apply these patterns efficiently throughout the whole exam? Some test takers lose focus after two hours or so, and then struggle through the last two sections of the test. Others need warm-up time and underperform on the first section. Taking practice tests will help you build your stamina and focus. A word of warning, however: Repeated testing without practice and review can be counterproductive. Think about it like learning a musical instrument. If you're trying to learn the piano, do you schedule a recital every other day? No, of course not. It's piano *practice*—even the most routine parts, such as playing scales—that allows you to improve. While practice tests are important, they should be spaced out and taken only when you're sure you've made some improvement through your Mastery and Timing practice.

By approaching your practice in this way—starting with Mastery and then layering in first Timing and then Endurance—you'll be fully and properly prepared by Test Day.

LSAT Attitude

In the main chapters, you'll learn, practice, and master the methods, strategies, and tactics that lead to Test Day success. Nevertheless, two students with equal LSAT proficiency still might not produce the same score. Of those two "equal" test takers, the one with greater confidence and less stress will likely outperform the other. You can develop these positive psychological characteristics just as you can your LSAT skill set.

Stay Positive

Those who approach the LSAT as an obstacle and rail against the necessity of taking it generally don't fare as well as those who see the LSAT as an opportunity, a chance to show law schools one's proficiency with the four core skills. A great LSAT score will distinguish your application from those of your competition.

- Look at the LSAT as a challenge, but try not to obsess over it; you certainly don't want to psych yourself out of the game.
- Remember that the LSAT is important, but this one test will not single-handedly determine the outcome of your life.
- Try to have fun with the test. Learning how to unlock the patterns of the test and approach the content in the way the testmakers have crafted the exam can be very satisfying, and the skills you'll acquire will benefit you in law school and your career.

Confidence and Stress Management

Confidence in your ability leads to quick, sure answers and a sense of well-being that translates into more points. Confidence feeds on itself; unfortunately, so does self-doubt. If you lack confidence, you end up reading sentences and answer choices two, three, or four times, until you confuse yourself and get off-track. This leads to timing difficulties that perpetuate a downward spiral of anxiety, rushing, and poor performance. If you subscribe to the proper LSAT mind-set, however, you'll gear all of your practice toward taking control of the test. When you've achieved that goal—armed with the principles, techniques, strategies, and methods Kaplan has to offer—you'll be ready to face the LSAT with confidence. Your Online Center has more good information, explanations, and other resources to help you minimize test anxiety, manage stress, and maximize your performance.

PART ONE

LSAT
Reasoning

CHAPTER 1

LSAT Reasoning

Welcome to your LSAT studies! By the time you reach the end of this book, you'll have practiced all of the skills and strategies necessary to master the LSAT. While it is common to divide the LSAT into sections and further divide those sections into question types, there are core thinking, reading, and reasoning skills rewarded throughout the test. In this chapter, you'll build important critical thinking and reasoning skills that lay the groundwork for all that is to come.

LEVELS OF TRUTH

Every section of the LSAT rewards an ability to distinguish correct answers based on what must be true, what is possible (could be true or false), and what must be false.

LEARNING OBJECTIVES

In this section, you'll learn to:

· Characterize the levels of truth in statements (and thus of the correct and incorrect answers in various LSAT question stems)
· Determine what must be true, what could be true or false, and what must be false given a set of statements

The following chart shows how central this skill is to your LSAT performance.

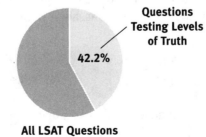

Questions Testing Levels of Truth

42.2%

All LSAT Questions
PrepTests 57–71; released 2009–2013.

Characterizing Levels of Truth

Review how an LSAT expert characterizes the truth value of the correct and incorrect answers in two standard LSAT question stems.

Question Stem		Analysis
Which one of the following must be true?	→	Right answers: Must be true Wrong answers: Could be false or must be false
Each of the following must be false EXCEPT	→	Right answers: Could be true or must be true Wrong answers: Must be false

To understand how the expert characterized the answer choices, look at this chart.

Degree of Certainty	→	"Charge"
Must		True
Could		False

For all LSAT questions that ask for what *must be true, could be true, could be false,* or *must be false*, the correct answer combines one degree of certainty with one of the charges. The incorrect answers will combine the other degree of certainty to the other charge.

TEST DAY TIP

Any statement that must be true, could be true. Any statement that must be false, could be false. If the LSAT asks for a correct answer that *must be false*, you know the four wrong answers *could be true*, and thus, any answer that *must be true* is a wrong answer in that question.

Learning to characterize the correct and incorrect answer choices is the LSAT's most direct way of testing your ability to distinguish levels of truth, but the testmaker rewards this skill on statements made by the authors of Logical Reasoning arguments and Reading Comprehension passages as well.

LSAT STRATEGY

The LSAT always gives you exactly one right answer, so there's only ever one answer that falls into the level of truth targeted by the question stem.

Practice

For each of the following, make a note of which level or levels of truth the correct answer must display. Then make a note of which level or levels of truth the wrong answer choices will display.

Question Stem		My Analysis
[Example] Which of the following could be true?	→	Correct answer: Could be true Wrong answers: Must be false
[Example] Each of the following could be true EXCEPT	→	Correct answer: Must be false Wrong answers: Could be true
1. Which of the following could be false?	→	Correct: Could be false Wrong: Must be true
2. Manny must accept each of the following contract bids EXCEPT	→	Correct: Manny does not have to accept Wrong: Manny must accept
3. Rich could attend each of the following lectures EXCEPT	→	Correct: A lecture Rich could not attend Wrong: A lecture Rich could attend
4. Each of the following conflicts with the company guidelines EXCEPT	→	Correct: Does not conflict with guidelines Wrong: Conflicts with company guidelines
5. Which of the following must be the chairperson assigned to speak fourth?	→	Correct: Chairperson who must speak 4th Wrong: Chairperson who could not speak 4th
6. Which of the following pieces CANNOT be included in the performance?	→	Correct: Piece cannot be included Wrong: Could be included
7. Which of the following is an acceptable arrangement of the items, from left to right?	→	Correct: Acceptable arrangement Wrong: Unacceptable arrangement
8. If the statements above are true, each of the following could also be true EXCEPT	→	Correct: Must be false Incorrect: Could be true
9. Which of the following entrees CANNOT be served at the dinner party?	→	Correct - Cannot be served Incorrect - Could be served
10. Which of the following CANNOT be properly inferred from the statements above?	→	Correct: Cannot be properly inferred Wrong: Could be inferred
11. If Kate joins the study, each of the following must also join the study EXCEPT	→	Correct: Could not join study Wrong: Must join the study
12. If Nina does not go to the park, then which of the following could be false?	→	Correct: Could be false Wrong: Must be true
13. If the statements above are true, which of the following must also be true?	→	Correct: Must be true Wrong: Could be false
14. Each of the following must be false EXCEPT	→	Correct: must be true Wrong: must be false
15. Each of the following could be false EXCEPT	→	Correct: must be true Wrong: Could be false

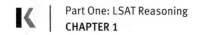
Expert Analysis

Here's how an LSAT expert would characterize those question stems.

Question Stem	Analysis
1. Which of the following could be false?	→ Correct answer: Could be false Wrong answers: Must be true
2. Manny must accept each of the following contract bids EXCEPT	→ Correct answer: A bid Manny could refuse Wrong answers: Bids Manny must accept
3. Rich could attend each of the following lectures EXCEPT	→ Correct answer: A lecture Rich cannot attend Wrong answers: Lectures Rich could attend
4. Each of the following conflicts with the company guidelines EXCEPT	→ Correct answer: An action that does not conflict with the company guidelines Wrong answers: Actions that conflict with the company guidelines
5. Which of the following must be the chairperson assigned to speak fourth?	→ Correct answer: The chairperson who must speak fourth Wrong answers: Chairpersons who could speak in a spot other than the fourth spot
6. Which of the following pieces CANNOT be included in the performance?	→ Correct answer: A piece that that cannot be included in the performance Wrong answers: Pieces that that could be included in the performance
7. Which of the following is an acceptable arrangement of the items, from left to right?	→ Correct answer: An arrangement that could be true Wrong answers: Arrangements that must be false
8. If the statements above are true, each of the following could also be true EXCEPT	→ Correct answer: Must be false Wrong answers: Could be true
9. Which of the following entrees CANNOT be served at the dinner party?	→ Correct answer: An entree that must not be served Wrong answers: Entrees that could be served
10. Which of the following CANNOT be properly inferred from the statements above?	→ Correct answer: Could be false Wrong answers: Must be true
11. If Kate joins the study, each of the following must also join the study EXCEPT	→ Correct answer: Someone who could decline to join the study Wrong answers: Individuals who must join the study
12. If Nina does not go to the park, then which of the following could be false?	→ Correct answer: Could be false Wrong answers: Must be true
13. If the statements above are true, which of the following must also be true?	→ Correct answer: Must be true Wrong answers: Could be false
14. Each of the following must be false EXCEPT	→ Correct answer: Could be true Wrong answers: Must be false
15. Each of the following could be false EXCEPT	→ Correct answer: Must be true Wrong answers: Could be false

Reflection

Every time you practice LSAT problems in this book, pause afterward and look over your practice to learn more. Don't speed through this step. Carefully reviewing your practice can enrich your understanding of:

- Why is a right answer right? Maybe you got a question right for the wrong reasons, and you need to clarify your understanding.
- Why are the wrong answers wrong? Maybe your intuition told you an answer was wrong, but you couldn't explain why or replicate your thinking.
- Which of your LSAT skills are strong and which do you still need to work on?
- What patterns do the LSAT questions display? The best thing you can do on the LSAT is to spot its patterns; through frequent and thorough review you'll likely be able to do so.

For the exercises you just completed, look back at your work and think about these questions:

- Where was it easier to correctly identify the level of truth being asked for?
- Once the level of truth in the correct answer had been identified, did you always take a moment to think about and characterize the levels of truth that would be displayed by the wrong answers?
- What was challenging about this exercise?

TEST DAY TIP

On the LSAT, never confuse *true* and *false* statements with *right* and *wrong* answers. Always characterize what you're looking for before you evaluate the answer choices.

DETERMINING WHAT MUST BE TRUE, WHAT MUST BE FALSE, AND WHAT COULD BE TRUE OR FALSE FROM A SET OF STATEMENTS

In all sections of the LSAT, you will be asked to deduce what must, could, and cannot be true based on statements or rules presented by the testmaker. Often, you will need to combine statements to make the relevant inferences. Take a look at a brief example.

Set of Premises	Analysis
(1) Ainsley owns at least two red shirts.	
(2) Ainsley has worn every shirt she owns.	
Determine the level of truth for each of the following statements:	
Ainsley owns a blue shirt.	⟶ Could Be True: No information has been given on blue shirts.
Ainsley has never worn a red shirt.	⟶ Must Be False: She owns red shirts and has worn every shirt she owns.
Ainsley owns four red shirts.	⟶ Could Be True: The statement does not specify she owns *exactly* two red shirts—she could own more.
Ainsley owns red shirts she has never worn.	⟶ Must Be False: She owns red shirts and has worn every shirt she owns.

LSAT STRATEGY

When two statements contain the same term(s), ask how the statements are related and how information in one defines or limits the information in the other.

Practice

In the following exercise, you are given a set of premises and a set of statements that may or may not be valid deductions given those premises. Note whether each would-be deduction must be true, must be false, or could be either true or false based on the premises.

Exercise 1

Premises and Possible Deductions	My Analysis
(1) Bob's fruit stand sells blueberries but not kiwis.	
(2) Every time I buy blueberries, I also buy kiwis. →	
(3) Today, I bought blueberries and strawberries.	

Determine the level of truth for each of the following statements:
Must be true; could be true or false; or must be false

16. Today, I bought fruit from Bob's fruit stand. →	Could be true
17. Today, I bought fruit from some place other than Bob's fruit stand. →	Must be true
18. Today, I bought kiwis. →	Must be true
19. Bob's fruit stand sells kiwis. →	Must be false
20. Bob's fruit stand sells strawberries. →	Could be true

Expert Analysis

Here's how an LSAT expert would have analyzed the premises and determined the levels of truth for the statements in the preceding exercise.

Premises and Possible Deductions	Analysis
(1) Bob's fruit stand sells blueberries but not kiwis. (2) Every time I buy blueberries, I also buy kiwis. (3) Today, I bought blueberries and strawberries.	Deductions: Today, I bought blueberries and every time I buy blueberries, I buy kiwis. Thus, I must have bought kiwis today. Since Bob's fruit stand does not sell kiwis, I must have bought fruit from a location other than Bob's fruit stand. I may have purchased my blueberries and strawberries from Bob's (the first statement doesn't say blueberries are the only fruit Bob's sells), or I may have gotten all of my fruit elsewhere.

Determine the level of truth for each of the following statements:
Must be true; could be true or false; or must be false

16. Today, I bought fruit from Bob's fruit stand.	This could be true or false. No statement says I have to purchase all of my fruit from the same place, and Bob's fruit stand does NOT sell at least one of the items purchased (kiwis).
17. Today, I bought fruit from some place other than Bob's fruit stand.	This must be true. I purchased blueberries today, which means I also purchased kiwis; however, Bob's fruit stand does not sell kiwis, which means I must have purchased them some place other than Bob's fruit stand.
18. Today, I bought kiwis.	This must be true. Since I purchased blueberries today, it must be true that I also purchased kiwis.
19. Bob's fruit stand sells kiwis.	This must be false. This conflicts with the first statement. Bob's fruit stand does not sell kiwis.
20. Bob's fruit stand sells strawberries.	This could be true or false. No statement defines whether Bob's fruit stand sells strawberries. The first statement says that Bob's fruit stand sells blueberries (and not kiwis), but is silent on whether Bob's fruit stand sells other fruit.

In the following exercise, you are given a set of premises and a set of statements that may or may not be valid deductions given those premises. Note whether each would-be deduction is true (that is, a valid deduction), false, or merely possible (could be true/could be false).

Exercise 2

Premises and Possible Deductions	My Analysis
(1) A city's budget committee will vote on all new initiatives covering education, parks and recreation, and highways.	
(2) Approval of a new initiative requires a majority vote of the budget committee.	
(3) The budget committee will not approve any new education initiatives this year.	$\longrightarrow$
(4) The committee will vote on any highway initiatives the same way it votes on any education initiative.	
(5) The teachers' union has proposed a new education initiative requesting 300 additional textbooks.	
(6) The new parks initiative requesting safer playground equipment will be approved.	

Determine the level of truth for each of the following statements:

Must be true; could be true or false; or must be false

21. There is not enough room in the city's budget to subsidize more than one new initiative this year.	$\longrightarrow$ Could be true
22. There will not be 300 additional textbooks in the city's classrooms this year.	$\longrightarrow$ Could not be true ~~Could be true~~ ~~Could not be true~~
23. The teachers' union initiative, requesting 300 additional textbooks, will not be approved by the budget committee.	$\longrightarrow$ ~~Must be true~~ could be true
24. The budget committee may approve a popular initiative to provide urgent repairs to a bridge on the local highway.	$\longrightarrow$ ~~Must be~~ False
25. At least one new parks initiative received a majority vote by the budget committee.	$\longrightarrow$ True
26. At least two-thirds of the budget committee will vote in favor of the new parks initiative for safer playground equipment.	$\longrightarrow$ Could be true
27. The budget committee will fail to pass at least some initiatives that are popular with city residents.	$\longrightarrow$ Could be true

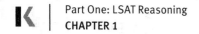
Expert Analysis

Here's how an LSAT expert would analyze the statements and how she would evaluate each of the possible deductions.

Premises and Possible Deductions	Analysis
(1) A city's budget committee will vote on all new initiatives covering education, parks and recreation, and highways.	The budget committee will not approve any education initiatives and, thus, will not approve any highway initiatives either. Because it will approve no education initiatives, the committee will not approve the teachers' union's initiative for 300 additional textbooks. However, it will approve the new parks initiative requesting safer playground equipment, which means that initiative must not count as an education or highway initiative and must have received a majority vote by the budget committee.
(2) Approval of a new initiative requires a majority vote of the budget committee.	
(3) The budget committee will not approve any new education initiatives this year.	
(4) The committee will vote on any highway initiatives the same way it votes on any education initiative.	
(5) The teachers' union has proposed a new education initiative requesting 300 additional textbooks.	
(6) The new parks initiative requesting safer playground equipment will be approved.	

Determine the level of truth for each of the following statements:
Must be true; could be true or false; or must be false

21. There is not enough room in the city's budget to subsidize more than one new initiative this year.	This could be true or false. The statements provide no information about how much room there is in the city's budget.
22. There will not be 300 additional textbooks in the city's classrooms this year.	This could be true or false. While statement (3) makes clear that the budget committee will deny the teachers' union's proposal, it does not rule out other ways (e.g., donations or fundraising efforts) in which the city's schools might obtain new textbooks.
23. The teachers' union initiative, requesting 300 additional textbooks, will not be approved by the budget committee.	This must be true. Statement (5) makes clear that the teachers' union's proposal is an education initiative, and statement (3) makes clear that the budget committee will not approve any education initiatives.

Premises and Possible Deductions (cont.)	**Analysis (cont.)**
24. The budget committee may approve a popular initiative to provide urgent repairs to a bridge on the local highway. →	This must be false. Statement (4) indicates that the committee will vote identically on highway and education initiatives. Because statement (3) rules out approval of any education initiative, it is clear that all highway initiatives will fail as well.
25. At least one new parks initiative received a majority vote by the budget committee. →	This must be true. Statement (6) says that the budget committee will approve the new parks initiative for safer playgrounds, and statement (2) says approval of an initiative requires a majority vote.
26. At least two-thirds of the budget committee will vote in favor of the new parks initiative for safer playground equipment. →	This could be true or false. Statement (6) says that this initiative will pass. Statement (2) says that a majority vote is needed to pass initiatives. None of the statements, however, says anything about the fraction of the committee that will vote for or against a particular initiative.
27. The budget committee will fail to pass at least some initiatives that are popular with city residents. →	This could be true or it could be false. No statement here has anything to say about which initiatives are popular with city residents or whether the committee will take popularity into account when voting.

FORMAL LOGIC: CONDITIONAL STATEMENTS

Frequently on the LSAT, the premises from which you make deductions are conditional statements—statements that can be expressed in "If ... then" form (though, as you will see, not all conditional statements take that form).

LEARNING OBJECTIVES

In this section, you'll learn to:

- Identify what is and is not a conditional statement (that is, understand what it means for a statement to be a conditional statement)
- Understand conditional statements that include *and* or *or*
- Translate a sentence that expresses a conditional relationship into If-Then format
- Make deductions on the basis of conditional statements

Conditional statements will appear in LSAT questions in all three sections of the test, but are most important in Logical Reasoning and Logic Games. The following chart shows the relative importance of Formal Logic in the sections of the test.

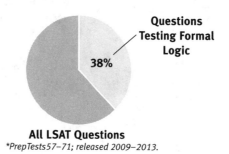

All LSAT Questions
PrepTests 57–71; released 2009–2013.

LSAT STRATEGY

Although Formal Logic appears in a minority of LSAT questions, its importance is heightened by two considerations:

1. Most test takers have not refined the skill of understanding Formal Logic prior to preparing for the LSAT. Familiarity with Formal Logic will give you a competitive advantage.
2. Expertise in understanding and applying Formal Logic makes the correct answer to many LSAT questions unequivocal. There is little room for doubt or error if you have analyzed conditional statements correctly.

Identifying Conditional Statements

Before you can work with conditional statements to make valid deductions and inferences (and answer LSAT questions), you must be able to identify such statements.

> **LSAT STRATEGY**
>
> Every conditional statement has two parts:
>
> 1. A *sufficient term*, also known as the "trigger" or "if" term.
> 2. A *necessary term*, also known as the "result" or "then" term.

Consider this conditional statement:

> If you are in Australia, then you are south of the Equator.

Knowing that you are in Australia is *sufficient* to know that you are south of the Equator. Likewise, being south of the Equator is *necessary* to being in Australia. But be careful: Being in Australia is not necessary to being south of the Equator (after all, you might be in Madagascar or Argentina). Similarly, knowing that you are south of the Equator is not sufficient to know that you are in Australia.

The following conditional statement takes a different form, but has the same features:

> All dogs are mammals.

Can you identify the sufficient and necessary terms here? If you reversed the terms, would the statement still make sense? How would you write this statement in "If...then" form?

If you are a dog, then you are a mammal

LSAT questions contain conditional statements exactly like those on the previous page.

> If the letter is addressed to Rini, then the postcard is
> addressed to Jana.
>
> *PrepTest49 Sec1 Qs8–12*

> All lyrical composers are poets.
>
> *PrepTest59 Sec2 Q16*

Make sure you can distinguish the *sufficient* and *necessary* terms in all such statements. Confusion between sufficiency and necessity is the basis of many wrong answers on the LSAT.

Conditional relationships can be expressed in many ways other than the "If ... then" or "All ... are" sentence structures. Take a look at how an LSAT expert identifies the conditional statements among the following statements.

Premises		Analysis
Is each of the following a conditional statement?		
The State of Pennsylvania requires a building permit for structures larger than 100 square feet.	→	Yes. Because a building permit is a *requirement* for structures larger than 100 square feet, it's a necessary condition.
Whenever Bill eats cereal, he also drinks coffee.	→	Yes. The word *whenever* indicates that Bill will drink coffee *every* time he eats cereal. Eating cereal is the trigger, or the sufficient condition.
Patty stopped to smell the flowers by the side of the road.	→	No. This is just an action that Patty performed.
All of the jelly beans in this jar are either red or blue.	→	Yes. Because this concerns *all* of the jelly beans in the jar, we know that each jelly bean in the jar *must* be either red or blue.

Practice

In the following exercise, read each statement and decide whether it expresses a conditional relationship. If it does, which term is *sufficient* and which is *necessary*?

Premises		My Analysis
28. Every person in this room is a doctor. _S_ _N_	→	Yes.
29. The scientists should consider running another experiment. _S_	→	No
30. It's impossible to turn on this computer unless it's plugged in. _N_ _S_	→	Yes
31. I'm going to go to the family reunion only if my brother goes as well. _S_ _N_	→	Yes
32. To stay healthy, you need to exercise at least twice a week. _N_	→	No
33. There are times when I think I'm going crazy. _N_	→	No
34. Only competitors with a signed medical waiver are eligible for the event. _N_	→	Yes
35. You can vote for chapter president only if your dues are paid. _N_ _S_	→	Yes

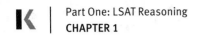

Expert Analysis

Here's how an LSAT expert would analyze those statements.

Premises	Analysis
28. Every person in this room is a doctor.	Yes. This could be written: *All people in this room are doctors*. Being a person in this room is *sufficient* to establish that one is a doctor. It is *necessary* that one is a doctor for him or her to be a person in this room.
29. The scientists should consider running another experiment.	No. This is a recommendation. The scientists have no obligation to run another experiment.
30. It's impossible to turn on this computer unless it's plugged in.	Yes. This could be written: *If the computer can be turned on, then it is plugged in*. The computer's being turned on is *sufficient* to know that it is plugged in, and it's being plugged in is *necessary* for it to be turned on.
31. I'm going to go to the family reunion only if my brother goes as well.	Yes. This could be written: *If I go to the family reunion, then my brother will go to the family reunion*. My attendance at the family reunion is *sufficient* to establish my brother's attendance. And, my brother's going to the reunion is *necessary* for me to go.
32. To stay healthy, you need to exercise at least twice a week.	Yes. This could be written: *If you are to stay healthy, then you must exercise at least twice a week*. According to this statement, a person's staying healthy is *sufficient* to establish that she exercises at least twice per week, and her exercising at least twice per week is *necessary* to her continued health.
33. There are times when I think I'm going crazy.	No. This is an assertion of fact. There is neither a sufficient nor a necessary term in this statement.
34. Only competitors with a signed medical waiver are eligible for the event.	Yes. This could be written: *If a competitor is eligible for the event, he has a signed medical waiver*. A competitor's eligibility is *sufficient* evidence that he has a signed medical waiver; a signed medical waiver is *necessary* for eligibility.
35. You can vote for chapter president only if your dues are paid.	Yes. This could be written: *If you can vote for chapter president, then your dues are paid*. Being able to vote is *sufficient* to know that your dues are paid. Having your dues paid is *necessary* to be able to vote.

A Note about Cause-and-Effect Relationships

Cause and effect are important concepts in the law and affect the outcome of many legal cases. Thus, the reasoning underlying cause and effect is tested regularly on the LSAT. The reasoning errors of confusing correlation for causation, or of assuming that some result has only one cause when, in fact, there are multiple factors at work, are often found in the arguments of Logical Reasoning questions.

Some conditional Formal Logic statements reflect a cause-and-effect relationship, but not all. And not all cause-and-effect statements can be expressed in "If ... then" terms. It is important not to confuse the two. Here's a handy way to categorize the relationships between causal statements and conditional statements.

Statements in Which the Cause Is Sufficient, but Not Necessary, for the Result

In this type of statement, the result is guaranteed any and every time that the cause occurs. For example: *If you drop this television from the top of the building, then it will smash.*

But the television could get smashed in other ways, too, right? So while dropping it off of the building is sufficient to smash the TV, it is not necessary. If someone told you their TV got smashed, you wouldn't know for certain that it had been dropped from a great height.

Statements in Which the Cause Is Necessary, but Not Sufficient, for the Result

In this type of statement, the trigger could not happen without the result. You may know, for example, that certain types of ulcers are caused by exposure to the bacteria *Helicobacter pylori*. Thus, we could say: *If a person develops a duodenal ulcer, he has been infected by* H. pylori.

But not everyone who is exposed to the bacteria develops ulcers. Other factors are at work as well. The ulcer is sufficient evidence of exposure to the bacteria, but not the other way around.

Statements in Which the Cause Is Both Necessary and Sufficient, for the Result

In this type of statement, the result occurs if, and only if, the cause is present. For example: *Water will freeze into ice if, and only if, it is kept below 32° Fahrenheit.*

Water will always freeze when it is below 32° Fahrenheit, and only under that condition.

Statements That Reflect Causation but Are Not Conditional Statements

Some statements reflect causality but are not strong enough or certain enough to be written in "If . . .then" form. For example: *Texting while driving may cause you to get into an accident.*

The word *may* makes this statement too uncertain to translate into conditional Formal Logic terms. In a particular case, we may know that texting while driving was the direct cause of an accident, but we cannot say: *If a person texts while driving, then he will get into an accident.* Nor can we say: *If a person got into an accident, then he was texting while driving.* The best we could say here is: *Texting while driving increases your chances of getting into an accident.*

Understanding Conditional Statements with "And" or "Or"

Some conditional statements will also contain the words *and* or *or*. The two terms have quite different effects in conditional statements.

LSAT STRATEGY

In Formal Logic:

· *And* means both terms are needed for a sufficient condition to trigger a result or for a necessary condition to be fulfilled.

· *Or* means that at least one of the terms (the first or the second or both) is needed for a sufficient condition to trigger a result or for a necessary condition to be fulfilled.

Note how an LSAT expert analyzes conditional statements containing *and* or *or*.

Conditional Statement		Analysis
If Amy and Jairus join the dance troupe, then Hector will also join.	→	One way to guarantee Hector's joining the dance troupe is to have Amy and Jairus join. Having either Amy or Jairus join without the other does not guarantee that Hector will join.
If potatoes are selected, then so are onions and carrots.	→	When potatoes are selected, you are guaranteed to have both onions and carrots as well. It's not possible to select potatoes and then select only one of onions or carrots—if potatoes are selected, it must be that all three are selected.
If Saul finishes the race in second or seventh place, then Maria finishes first.	→	If Saul finishes in either second or seventh place, then Maria is guaranteed to finish the race in first place. If Saul finishes in some other position, then it's still possible that Maria finishes first.
If the pet store does not sell lizards, then it sells either dogs or cats.	→	If the pet store does not sell lizards, then it's guaranteed that it sells dogs or cats. It's also possible that if the pet store doesn't sell lizards, it sells *both* dogs and cats. If the pet store sells lizards, then nothing is known about whether the store also sells dogs or cats—it's possible that the store sells all three species.

Practice

Check your understanding by analyzing the following conditional statements. For the purposes of this exercise, assume that only one person can present per day.

Conditional Statement	My Analysis
If Patel or Beatrice presents on Day 3, then Darius will present on Day 4.	
36. What do we know if we are told that Patel presents on Day 4?	→ ~~Pat~~ Beatrice does not present on day 3.
37. What do we know if we are told that both Patel and Beatrice present on Day 3?	→ Darius will present day 4.
38. What do we know if we are told that Darius presents on Day 4?	→ Either Patel or Beatrice presented day 3.
If Nancy and Bill are ranked in the top three, then Jim is ranked last (seventh).	
39. What do we know if Nancy is ranked third?	→ Nothing
40. What do we know if Nancy and Bill are ranked first and second, respectively?	→ Jim is ranked last
41. What do we know if Jim is ranked sixth?	→ ~~No~~ Either Nancy or Bill is not top 3.
If the lake contains bluegill, then it contains bass and walleye.	
42. What do we know if the lake contains bass and walleye?	→ Nothing
43. What do we know if the lake doesn't contain bluegill?	→ Nothing
44. What do we know if the lake doesn't contain bass?	→ No bluegill
If the store stocks red pants, then it also stocks green pants or blue pants.	
45. What do we know if the store stocks green pants and blue pants?	→ Nothing
46. What do we know if the store stocks red pants?	→ Stocks green or blue pants
47. What do we know if the store stocks yellow pants?	→ nothing

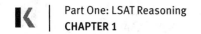
Expert Analysis

Here's how an LSAT expert would analyze the questions about each conditional statement in the exercise.

Conditional Statement		Analysis

If Patel or Beatrice presents on Day 3, then Darius will present on Day 4.

36. What do we know if we are told that Patel presents on Day 4?	⟶	Nothing concrete. Patel presenting on Day 4 triggers nothing.
37. What do we know if we are told that both Patel and Beatrice present on Day 3?	⟶	Darius must present on Day 4.
38. What do we know if we are told that Darius presents on Day 4?	⟶	Nothing additional. Though it's possible that Patel or Beatrice (or both) presents on Day 3, we don't know for sure.

If Nancy and Bill are ranked in the top three, then Jim is ranked last (seventh).

39. What do we know if Nancy is ranked third?	⟶	Nothing additional. We need both sufficient conditions to be true to trigger the necessary condition.
40. What do we know if Nancy and Bill are ranked first and second, respectively?	⟶	Both of those positions are in the top three, so that triggers the result. We know that Jim is ranked seventh.
41. What do we know if Jim is ranked sixth?	⟶	Jim being ranked seventh is necessary for Nancy and Bill to both finish among the top three. If he is ranked elsewhere, the necessary condition is not fulfilled, and it is not possible that both Nancy and Bill are ranked in the top three. If they were, then Jim would be ranked seventh, which he's not.

If the lake contains bluegill, then it contains bass and walleye.

42. What do we know if the lake contains bass and walleye?	⟶	Nothing additional. It might or might not also contain bluegill.
43. What do we know if the lake doesn't contain bluegill?	⟶	Nothing additional. The lake could still contain bass or walleye (or both).
44. What do we know if the lake doesn't contain bass?	⟶	If the lake doesn't contain bass, then there's no way it could also contain bluegill, since bluegill triggers bass being in the lake.

If the store stocks red pants, then it also stocks green pants or blue pants.

45. What do we know if the store stocks green pants and blue pants?	⟶	Nothing additional.
46. What do we know if the store stocks red pants?	⟶	The store must also stock green pants or blue pants. It's possible that the store stocks both green and blue pants.
47. What do we know if the store stocks yellow pants?	⟶	Nothing additional. Yellow pants are outside the scope of this statement.

Translating Conditional Statements into If-Then Format

Conditional statements can be phrased in many different ways; you'll see that some of those are more common than others on the LSAT, but they all appear from time to time. You will need to learn to quickly distill the prose into a notation like the following.

Formal Logic Statement	Analysis		
If A, then B	If A	→	B
All C are D	If C	→	D
Every E is F	If E	→	F
If G, then not H	If G	→	~H
No I are J	If I	→	~J
Only K are L	If L	→	K
M only if N	If M	→	N
The only O are P	If O	→	P
No Q unless R	If Q	→	R
S unless T	If ~S	→	T
No U without V	If U	→	V
Without W, no X	If X	→	W
Y if, but only if, Z	If Y	→	Z
	If Z	→	Y
AA if, and only if, BB	If AA	→	BB
	If BB	→	AA
If CC, then neither DD nor EE	If CC	→	~DD AND ~EE
FF if GG	If GG	→	FF
HH is always II	If HH	→	II

It's okay if your shorthand is different from what is shown here, but it must be consistent and accurate to ensure your success on the test.

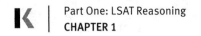
Practice

Using the previous statements as reference, translate each of the following statements, each of which expresses a sufficient and necessary relationship, into simple shorthand.

Formal Logic Statement	My Analysis
48. Kelly always takes her vacation in August.	Kelly Vacation → August
49. Bob cuts the grass only when it's more than three inches tall.	~~If~~ Bob cut grass → ~~~~ >3 inches
50. I'll take a bike ride if it doesn't rain.	No rain → bike ride
51. No one involved in the crash sustained any injuries.	Crash → No injuries
52. Chloe refuses to move into a house without a second bathroom.	No second bathroom → No Chloe
53. Every bag of chips in this case is smashed to smithereens.	~~Every~~ bag of chips → smithereens
54. Carl won't get a good job unless he starts getting up before 11 A.M.	No getting up < 11AM → No good job
55. All pets must be registered with the rental office.	Pet → registered
56. The only permissible form of identification is a driver's license.	Permissible ID → Driver Lic
57. Johanna won't take karate unless Ellie and Michael agree to take it with her.	Johanna Karate → Ellie + Michael Karate

Formal Logic Statement	My Analysis
58. My car will pass inspection if, but only if, I get a new muffler.	pass inspection → get a muffler
59. Any student who masters Formal Logic will have an advantage on the LSAT.	Master formal logic → adv. LSAT
60. Whenever Melanie makes salsa, she includes freshly minced garlic and cilantro.	Make salsa → garli + cil.
61. All students registering for Crafting 201 must have completed either Basket Weaving 101 or Pottery 101.	Reg 201 → Weaving or Pott.
62. If I'm not mistaken, this lo mein contains MSG.	Not mistaken → contains Msg
63. Unless the river has already crested, the town will definitely flood.	town not flooded → river has crestd
64. Paul will be able to afford his dream car only if he gives up his weekly laser-tag matches.	Give up laser tag → afford dream car
65. Every plant that I've bought at Brown Thumb Nurseries has died.	Plnt bought at Brown thumb → dead
66. Only applicants with flawless driving records and no convictions will be considered for the position.	Cons. fr position → flw. dri. No conviction
67. No snack food can be considered nutritious unless it contains either whole grains or essential vitamins.	Considere nut. → either whole grains or v.t.

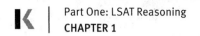
Expert Analysis

This is how an LSAT expert might abbreviate each of the statements from the exercise.

	Formal Logic Statement	Analysis		
48.	Kelly always takes her vacation in August.	If Kelly's vacation	→	August
49.	Bob cuts the grass only when it's more than three inches tall.	If Bob cuts grass	→	over 3"
50.	I'll take a bike ride if it doesn't rain.	If NOT rain	→	bike ride
51.	No one involved in the crash sustained any injuries.	If in crash	→	NO injuries
52.	Chloe refuses to move into a house without a second bathroom.	If Chloe move	→	second bathroom
53.	Every bag of chips in this case is smashed to smithereens.	If chips in case	→	smashed
54.	Carl won't get a good job unless he starts getting up before 11 A.M.	If Carl gets good job	→	up before 11
55.	All pets must be registered with the rental office.	If pet	→	registered
56.	The only permissible form of identification is a driver's license.	If permissible ID	→	driver's license
57.	Johanna won't take karate unless Ellie and Michael agree to take it with her.	If Johanna karate	→	Ellie karate AND Michael karate

Formal Logic Statement	Analysis		
58. My car will pass inspection if, but only if, I get a new muffler.	If car passes inspection	→	get new muffler
	If get new muffler	→	car passes inspection
59. Any student who masters Formal Logic will have an advantage on the LSAT.	If master FL	→	advantage on LSAT
60. Whenever Melanie makes salsa, she includes freshly minced garlic and cilantro.	If Melanie makes salsa	→	includes garlic AND cilantro
61. All students registering for Crafting 201 must have completed either Basket Weaving 101 or Pottery 101.	If registering for Crafting 201	→	taken Basket Weaving 101 OR taken Pottery 101
62. If I'm not mistaken, this lo mein contains MSG.	If NOT mistaken	→	MSG in lo mein
63. Unless the river has already crested, the town will definitely flood.	If river has NOT crested or	→	town will flood
	If town NOT flooded	→	river has crested
64. Paul will be able to afford his dream car only if he gives up his weekly laser-tag matches.	If Paul can afford car	→	gives up weekly laser tag
65. Every plant that I've bought at Brown Thumb Nurseries has died.	If plant bought at BTN	→	plant died
66. Only applicants with flawless driving records and no convictions will be considered for the position.	If considered for position	→	flawless driving record AND no convictions
67. No snack food can be considered nutritious unless it contains either whole grains or essential vitamins.	If snack food considered nutritious	→	whole grains OR essential vitamins

Exercise: Recognizing Equivalent Statements

In this exercise, enter the appropriate terms or phrases from the bolded conditional statement into the blanks in the statements beneath such that all of the statements are equivalent in meaning.

If Joey goes to the movies, then Jane goes to the movies.

68. Every time ___Joey___ goes to the movies, ___Jane___ must also go to the movies.

69. ___Joey___ does not go to the movies unless ___Jane___ also goes to the movies.

70. ___Joey___ goes to the movies only if ___Jane___ also goes to the movies.

71. ___Jane___ going to the movies is necessary for ___Joey___ to go to the movies.

Miguel plays hockey if Cindy goes to the movies.

72. ___Cindy goes to movies___ only if ___Miguel plays hockey___

73. If ___Cindy goes to movies___, then ___Miguel plays hockey___

74. ___Cindy___ will not ___go to movies___ unless ___Miguel plays hockey___

75. Knowing that ___Miguel plays hockey___ is sufficient to know that ___Cindy goes to movies___.

All mollusks are invertebrates.

76. If a creature is a(n) ___mollusk___, then it is a(n) ___invertebrate___.

77. A creature is a(n) ___mollusk___ only if it is a(n) ___invertebrate___

78. Only ___invertebrates___ are ___mollusk___.

79. A creature is not a(n) ___mollusk___ unless it a(n) ___invertebrate___

Only patrons at least 21 years of age will be admitted to the concert.

80. ___21___ is necessary for a patron ___to be admitted to concert___.

81. If a patron is ___admitted___, then s/he is ___21___.

82. A patron ___admitted___ only if s/he ___is 21 years___.

83. A patron will not ___be admitted___ unless s/he ___21___.

Being a good lawyer requires strong writing skills.

84. If someone ___is a lawyer___, then s/he will ___writing skills___

85. ___strong skills___ is/are necessary for a person ___to be a lawyer___.

86. A person cannot ___be a good lawyer___ unless s/he ___strong writing skills___

87. Only a person who ___strong writing skills___ can ___be a good lawyer___

Running the school's summer program depends upon receiving generous contributions from the community.

88. Only if _a school recieve gen, conts. from commu_ will _run summer program_.

89. _A school's summer_ will _not run_ unless _it recieves gen, conti_.

90. If _generous donations_ are not _given from community_, then _schools summer program will not run_.

91. _running summer program_ necessitates _generous conts. fro community._

Only if it is sunny will Gail go to the beach.

92. Gail _will go to beach_ only if _it it is sunny_.

93. Gail does not _go to bech_ unless _it is sunny_.

94. If Gail _goes to beach_, then _it is sunny_.

95. Gail's _going to beach_ requires _it to be sunny_.

Unless she plays the viola, Linda cannot join the band.

96. If Linda _____, then _____.

97. Linda _____ only if _____.

98. If Linda does not _____, then _____.

99. Linda's _____ depends upon _____.

Every winning game included the team's all-star player.

100. If _____, then _____.

101. A _____ needs _____.

102. Only when _____ does _____.

103. The team _____ unless _____.

Whenever June eats a salty snack, she eats pretzels.

104. June _____ only if _____.

105. June does not _____ unless_____.

106. If June _____, then _____.

107. Every _____ she _____.

Expert Analysis

Check your work against that of an LSAT expert.

If Joey goes to the movies, then Jane goes to the movies.

68. Every time *Joey* goes to the movies, *Jane* must also go to the movies.

69. *Joey* does not go to the movies unless *Jane* also goes to the movies.

70. *Joey* goes to the movies only if *Jane* also goes to the movies.

71. *Jane's* going to the movies is necessary for *Joey* to go to the movies.

Miguel plays hockey if Cindy goes to the movies.

72. *Cindy goes to the movies* only if *Miguel plays hockey.*

73. If *Cindy goes to the movies* then *Miguel plays hockey.*

74. *Cindy* will not *go to the movies* unless *Miguel plays hockey.*

75. Knowing that *Cindy goes to the movies* is sufficient to know that *Miguel plays hockey.*

All mollusks are invertebrates.

76. If a creature is a *mollusk*, then it is an *invertebrate.*

77. A creature is a *mollusk* only if it is an *invertebrate.*

78. Only *invertebrates* are *mollusks.*

79. A creature is not a *mollusk* unless it is an *invertebrate.*

Only patrons at least 21 years of age will be admitted to the concert.

80. *Being at least 21* is necessary for a patron *to be admitted to the concert.*

81. If a patron is *admitted to the concert*, then s/he *is at least 21.*

82. A patron *will be admitted to the concert* only if s/he *is at least 21.*

83. A patron will not *be admitted to the concert* unless s/he *is at least 21.*

Being a good lawyer requires strong writing skills.

84. If someone *is a good lawyer* then s/he *has strong writing skills.*

85. *Strong writing skills* are necessary for a person *to be a good lawyer.*

86. A person cannot *be a good lawyer* unless s/he *has strong writing skills.*

87. Only a person who *has strong writing skills* can *be a good lawyer.*

Running the school's summer program depends upon receiving generous contributions from the community.

88. Only if *the school receives generous contributions from the community* will *the school's summer program run.*

89. *The school's summer program* will *not run* unless *it receives generous contributions from the community.*

90. If *contributions from the community* are not *generous*, then *the school's summer program will not run.* (Or If *generous contributions from the community* are not *received*, then *the school's summer program will not run.*)

91. *Running the school's summer program* necessitates *receiving generous contributions from the community.*

Only if it is sunny will Gail go to the beach.

92. Gail *goes to the beach* only if *it is sunny.*

93. Gail does not *go to the beach* unless *it is sunny.*

94. If Gail *goes to the beach*, then *it is sunny.*

95. Gail's *going to the beach* requires *it to be sunny.*

Unless she plays the viola, Linda cannot join the band.

96. If Linda *joins the band,* then *she plays the viola.*

97. Linda *joins the band* only if *she plays the viola.*

98. If Linda does not *play the viola*, then *she does not join the band.*

99. Linda's *joining the band* depends upon *her playing the viola.*

Every winning game included the team's all-star player.

100. If *the team wins a game*, then *it included the team's all-star player.*

101. A *winning game* needs *the team's all-star player.*

102. Only when *the team includes the all-star player* does *it win.*

103. The team *will not win* unless *it includes the team's all-star player.*

Whenever June eats a salty snack, she eats pretzels.

104. June *eats a salty snack* only if she eats *pretzels.*

105. June does not *eat a salty snack* unless *she eats pretzels.*

106. If June *eats a salty snack*, then *she eats pretzels.*

107. Every *time June eats a salty snack,* she *eats pretzels.*

Making Valid Deductions from Conditional Statements

Now that you understand conditional relationships and how to spot them, you're ready to think about how to combine them to make new deductions.

Formal Logic Statements	Analysis
If A then B If B then C	If A → B → C Deduction: If A → C
If D then E If F then E	If D OR F → E
If G then H If G then I	If G → H AND I

LSAT STRATEGY

Anytime the necessary or "result" clause of one statement matches the sufficient or "If" clause of another, the two statements can be combined. For example:

> If N → ~P
>
> If ~P → ~Q
>
> If N → ~P → ~Q

Deduction:

> If N → ~Q

Practice

Translate the given conditional statements and use them to create a chain of logic. Then, answer questions about what we must know, given the chain.

Formal Logic Statements	**My Analysis**
(1) If Patrick is selected, then so is Jane.	
(2) If Jane is selected, then so is Eloise.	
(3) If Eloise is selected, then so is Grace.	

What do we know if ...

108. Patrick is selected?	$\longrightarrow$
109. Jane is selected?	$\longrightarrow$
110. Grace is selected?	$\longrightarrow$

Formal Logic Statements	**My Analysis**
(1) If a store stocks bicycles, then it also stocks sofas.	
(2) If a store stocks sofas, then it also stocks televisions and mattresses.	
(3) If a store stocks televisions, then it also stocks dishwashers.	
(4) If a store doesn't stock dishwashers, then it doesn't stock computers.	

What do we know if ...

111. the store stocks sofas?	$\longrightarrow$
112. the store stocks televisions?	$\longrightarrow$
113. the store stocks dishwashers?	$\longrightarrow$

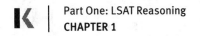
Expert Analysis

Here's how an LSAT expert would translate and combine the conditional statements in the previous exercise.

Formal Logic Statements	Analysis
(1) If Patrick is selected, then so is Jane.	If P → J
(2) If Jane is selected, then so is Eloise.	If J → E
(3) If Eloise is selected, then so is Grace.	If E → G
	If P → J → E → G

What do we know if ...	
108. Patrick is selected?	→ If Patrick is selected, then Jane is selected, Eloise is selected, and Grace is selected. If P → J → E → G
109. Jane is selected?	→ If Jane is selected, then Eloise is selected and Grace is selected. Patrick may or may not be selected. If J → E → G
110. Grace is selected?	→ If Grace is selected, then it's not certain whether anyone else is selected. Selecting Grace does not trigger any other conditions.

Formal Logic Statements	**Analysis**
(1) If a store stocks bicycles, then it also stocks sofas.	If B → S
(2) If a store stocks sofas, then it also stocks televisions and mattresses.	If S → T AND M
(3) If a store stocks televisions, then it also stocks dishwashers.	If T → D
(4) If a store doesn't stock dishwashers, then it doesn't stock computers.	If ~D → ~C
	If B → S → T AND M

What do we know if ...

111. the store stocks sofas?	→ If a store stocks sofas, then it also stocks televisions and mattresses. And stores that stock televisions also stock dishwashers.

$$S \rightarrow T \; AND \; M \nearrow^{D}$$

112. the store stocks televisions?	→ A store that stocks televisions also stocks dishwashers.

$$T \rightarrow D$$

113. the store stocks dishwashers?	→ Nothing else can be determined if all that is known is that a store stocks dishwashers.

FORMAL LOGIC: CONTRAPOSITIVES

Despite the many ways to express conditional statements, the logic underlying conditional statements is remarkably consistent. One more feature of these statements that is crucial for making deductions is the contrapositive.

LEARNING OBJECTIVES

In this section, you'll learn to:

- Translate a conditional statement into its contrapositive
- Make valid deductions from the contrapositive of a conditional statement
- Analyze correctly the implications of conditional statements containing "and" and "or"
- Analyze correctly the implications of conditional statements containing an "exclusive or"

Translating "If ... Then" Statements into Contrapositives

The contrapositive of a conditional statement is just another way of phrasing the sufficient/necessary relationship described in that statement. Take the following statement as an example:

> All overnight campers are required to obtain a permit from the park ranger.

It's clear from this statement that obtaining a permit is a *necessary* condition for camping overnight at this particular park. We can abbreviate the statement as

> If *camp overnight* → *obtain ranger permit*

Now, what happens if you cannot obtain a permit from the ranger? Well, you can't camp overnight. That's the contrapositive of the statement. It looks like this:

> If NOT *obtain ranger permit* → NOT *camp overnight*

That's the basis for the contrapositive: What happens if the *necessary* condition is negated, if it cannot happen? In that case, the sufficient condition cannot happen either. Every contrapositive is formed in exactly that way.

> ## LSAT STRATEGY
>
> To form the contrapositive:
>
> · Reverse the sufficient and necessary terms.
> · Negate each term.
> · Change *and* to *or* and change *or* to *and* (whenever applicable).

To understand the last point in the strategy box, consider a conditional statement with two terms in the necessary condition:

> No application will be processed unless it is accompanied by a signed form BE101 and the applicant presents valid identification.

Abbreviate that statement in Formal Logic shorthand:

> If application processed   →   signed BE101 AND valid ID

Now, what happens if either one of the two necessary conditions is not met?

> If NO signed BE101   →   application NOT processed
>
> If NO valid ID   →   application NOT processed

Thus, to form the contrapositive of the first statement, the *and* in the necessary condition must become *or* in the sufficient condition of the contrapositive:

> If NO signed BE101 OR NO valid ID   →   application NOT processed

It is important to remember to change *and* and *or* whenever they appear in conditional statements. Imagine the following rule in a logic game:

> If Maria is selected, then Annabelle and Tobias are also selected.

What do you know if one of the game's questions tells you that Tobias is not selected?

Here is a chart of the most common Formal Logic statements and their contrapositives.

Formal Logic Statements		Analysis	
All A are B	If A	→	B
	If ~B	→	~A
No C are D	If C	→	~D
	If D	→	~C
E unless F	If ~E	→	F
	If ~F	→	E
If G then neither H nor I	If G	→	~H AND ~I
	If H OR I	→	~G
If J or K, then no L	If J OR K	→	~L
	If L	→	~J AND ~K

Practice

Translate each of the following statements into simple shorthand, and form the correct contrapositive of each.

Formal Logic Statement	My Analysis
114. All new counselors are required to undergo two weeks of training.	
115. The company will consider purchasing any new technology that is proven to increase the productivity of its workers.	
116. Every bed sold today comes with free delivery.	
117. Due to statistical anomalies, each vote from district nine was recounted.	
118. Deborah will agree to go kayaking if Jesse and Sara go as well.	
119. Whenever James plays tennis, Kay goes rock climbing.	
120. Megan only listens to hip-hop.	
121. The car will run only if the radiator is replaced.	
122. The only candidates admitted by the committee this year applied before April.	
123. No Liberty Head nickels were officially authorized for production in 1913.	
124. Patrick never attends classes on Tuesdays.	
125. The watch is not on the nightstand.	
126. None of the diners ordered today's special.	
127. Anna will not go sledding unless Paul and Reid go with her.	
128. Scott doesn't go anywhere without a banjo.	
129. The LSAT is a prerequisite for law school.	
130. If the Lions win or the Trojans lose, then the Eagles will advance to the playoffs.	
131. Her record will do well on the charts if and only if it is popular with her key demographic.	

Expert Analysis

Here's how an LSAT expert might abbreviate the statements and form the contrapositives.

	Formal Logic Statement	Analysis		
114.	All new counselors are required to undergo two weeks of training.	If new counselor	→	2 wks train
		If ~2 wks train	→	~new counselor
115.	The company will consider purchasing any new technology that is proven to increase the productivity of its workers.	If tech increases prod	→	co consider
		If ~co consider	→	~tech increases prod
116.	Every bed sold today comes with free delivery.	If bed sold today	→	free delivery
		If ~free delivery	→	~bed sold today
117.	Due to statistical anomalies, each vote from district nine was recounted.	If vote dist 9	→	recounted
		If ~recounted	→	~vote dist 9
118.	Deborah will agree to go kayaking if Jesse and Sara go as well.	If S kayaking AND J kayaking	→	D kayaking
		If ~D kayaking	→	~S kayaking OR ~J kayaking
119.	Whenever James plays tennis, Kay goes rock climbing.	If J tennis	→	K rock climbing
		If ~K rock climbing	→	~J tennis
120.	Megan only listens to hip-hop.	If M	→	hip-hop
		If ~hip-hop	→	~M
121.	The car will run only if the radiator is replaced.	If car run	→	radiator replaced
		If ~radiator replaced	→	~car run
122.	The only candidates admitted by the committee this year applied before April.	If candidate admitted by committee	→	applied before Apr
		If ~applied before Apr	→	~candidate admitted by committee
123.	No Liberty Head nickels were officially authorized for production in 1913.	If 1913	→	~LHN auth
		If LHN auth	→	~1913

Formal Logic Statement (cont.)	Analysis (cont.)		
124. Patrick never attends classes on Tuesdays.	If P attends classes	→	~Tues
	If Tues	→	~P attend classes
125. The watch is not on the nightstand.	If watch	→	~nightstand
	If nightstand	→	~watch
126. None of the diners ordered today's special.	If diner	→	~special
	If special	→	~diner
127. Anna will not go sledding unless Paul and Reid go with her.	If A sleds	→	P sleds AND R sleds
	If P ~sled OR R ~sled	→	A ~sled
128. Scott doesn't go anywhere without a banjo.	If Scott	→	banjo
	If ~banjo	→	~Scott
129. The LSAT is a prerequisite for law school.	If law school	→	LSAT
	If ~LSAT	→	~law school
130. If the Lions win or the Trojans lose, then the Eagles will advance to the playoffs.	If Lions win OR Trojans lose	→	Eagles advance
	If ~Eagles advance	→	~Lions win AND ~Trojans lose
131. Her record will do well on the charts if and only if it is popular with her key demographic.	If rec does well on charts	→	pop key demo
	If ~pop key demo	→	rec ~do well on charts
	If pop key demo	→	rec do well on charts
	If rec ~do well on charts	→	~pop key demo

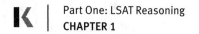
Exercise: Recognizing Equivalent Statements

In this exercise, enter the appropriate terms or phrases from the bolded conditional statement into the blanks in the statements beneath such that all of the statements are equivalent in meaning.

Ike's shopping trip is successful if he buys a book and reads a magazine.

132. If _____, then _____.

133. Ike does not _____ unless _____.

134. If Ike does not _____, then _____.

135. Only _____ include _____.

Phillip bakes cookies any time Sally goes to the mall.

136. Sally _____ only if _____.

137. If Phillip does not _____, then Sally _____.

138. Sally does not _____ unless _____.

139. Sally's _____ depends upon _____.

If John is elected, either Stan moves or Allison is appointed.

140. John cannot _____ unless _____.

141. If _____ and _____, then _____.

142. Knowing _____ is sufficient to determine _____.

143. Only if _____ does _____.

Sadie walks the dog only when Harry is not home or Julie is at work.

144. Sadie _____ only if _____.

145. If Sadie _____, then _____.

146. Sadie does not _____ unless_____.

147. It is necessary for _____ in order to have _____.

No pennies are purple.

148. If _____, then _____.

149. Something is not _____ unless _____.

150. All _____ are not _____.

151. Something _____ is not _____.

It takes time to heal.

152. If there is not _____, then there is not _____.

153. No _____ unless _____.

154. If _____, then _____.

155. _____ only if _____.

Tree growth depends upon proper maintenance.

156. If _____, then _____.

157. _____ only if _____.

158. A tree cannot _____ unless _____.

159. If no _____, then no _____.

All comets have an extended, gravitationally unbound atmosphere surrounding their central nucleus.

160. If there is not _____, then it is not _____.

161. It is not _____ unless _____.

162. If it _____, then it _____.

163. An object _____ only if it _____.

To prove an intentional tort, you must show that the defendant is liable for damages as the result of a willful act.

164. If _____, then _____.

165. _____ only if _____.

166. _____ unless _____.

167. If not _____, then not _____.

Unless a gastropod is bilaterally symmetrical, it is not nudibranch.

168. If _____ is not _____, then it is not _____.

169. If _____ is _____, then _____.

170. All _____ are _____.

171. A _____ is a _____ only if it is _____.

Expert Analysis

Check your work against that of an LSAT expert.

Ike's shopping trip is successful if he buys a book and reads a magazine.

132. If *Ike buys a book and reads a magazine*, then *he had a successful shopping trip*.

133. Ike does not *buy a book or does not read a magazine* unless *he has a successful shopping trip*.

134. If Ike does not *have a successful shopping trip*, then *he did not buy a book or he did not read a magazine*.

135. Only *successful shopping trips* include *Ike buying a book and reading a magazine*.

Phillip bakes cookies anytime Sally goes to the mall.

136. Sally *goes to the mall* only if *Phillip bakes cookies*.

137. If Phillip does not *bake cookies*, then Sally *does not go to the mall*.

138. Sally does not *go to the mall* unless *Phillip bakes cookies*.

139. Sally's *going to the mall* depends upon *Phillip baking cookies*.

If John is elected, either Stan moves or Allison is appointed.

140. John cannot *be elected* unless *Stan moves or Allison is appointed*.

141. If *Stan does* not *move* and *Allison does* not *get appointed*, then *John is not elected*.

142. Knowing *John is elected* is sufficient to determine *that Stan moves or Allison is appointed*.

143. Only if *Stan moves or Allison is appointed* does John *get elected*.

Sadie walks the dog only when Harry is not home or Julie is at work.

144. Sadie *walks the dog* only if Harry *is not home or Julie is at work*.

145. If Sadie *walks the dog*, then *Harry is not home or Julie is at work*.

146. Sadie does not *walk the dog* unless *Harry is not home or Julie is at work*.

147. It is necessary for *Harry to be not home or Julie to be at work* in order to have *Sadie walk the dog*.

No pennies are purple.

148. If *something is a penny*, then *it is not purple*.

149. Something is not *a penny* unless *it is not purple*.

150. All *pennies* are not *purple*.

151. Something *purple* is not *a penny*.

It takes time to heal.

152. If there is not *time* then there is not *healing*.

153. No *healing* unless *time*.

154. If *healing* then *time*.

155. *Healing* only if *time*.

Tree growth depends upon proper maintenance.

156. If *a tree grows*, then *there is proper maintenance*.

157. A *tree grows* only if *there is proper maintenance*.

158. A tree cannot *grow* unless *there is proper maintenance*.

159. If no *proper maintenance*, then no *tree growth occurs*.

All comets have an extended, gravitationally unbound atmosphere surrounding their central nucleus.

160. If there is not *an extended, gravitationally unbound atmosphere surrounding the central nucleus*, then it is not *a comet*.

161. It is not *a comet* unless *it has an extended, gravitationally unbound atmosphere surrounding the central nucleus*.

162. If it is *a comet*, then it *has an extended, gravitationally unbound atmosphere surrounding the central nucleus*.

163. An object *is a comet* only if it *has an extended, gravitationally unbound atmosphere surrounding the central nucleus*.

To prove an intentional tort, you must show that the defendant is liable for damages as the result of a willful act.

164. If *you prove an intentional tort,* then *the defendant is liable for damages and the defendant acted willfully*.

165. *You can prove an intentional tort* only if *the defendant is liable for damages and the defendant acted willfully*.

166. *You cannot prove an intentional tort* unless *the defendant is liable for damages and the defendant acted willfully*.

167. If *the defendant is not liable for damages or the defendant did not act willfully,* then *you have not proved an intentional tort*.

Unless a gastropod is bilaterally symmetrical, it is not a nudibranch.

168. If *a gastropod* is not *bilaterally symmetrical,* then it is not a *nudibranch*.

169. If a *gastropod* is *a nudibranch,* then it is *bilaterally symmetrical*.

170. All *nudibranches* are *bilaterally symmetrical*.

171. A *gastropod* is *a nudibranch* only if it is *bilaterally symmetrical*.

Making Valid Deductions from the Contrapositive of a Conditional Statement

Being able to form the contrapositive of a conditional statement (and being able to understand its implications) broadens your ability to make deductions from a set of conditional statements.

Review the deduction exercise you tried earlier, and then complete the practice on the next page.

Formal Logic Statements	Analysis
If Patrick is selected, then so is Jane.	If P $\rightarrow$ J
If Jane is selected, then so is Eloise.	If J $\rightarrow$ E
If Eloise is selected, then so is Grace.	If E $\rightarrow$ G
	If P $\rightarrow$ J $\rightarrow$ E $\rightarrow$ G

What do we know if...

Patrick is selected?	$\rightarrow$ If Patrick is selected, then Jane is selected, Eloise is selected, and Grace is selected.
	If P $\rightarrow$ J $\rightarrow$ E $\rightarrow$ G
Jane is selected?	$\rightarrow$ If Jane is selected, then Eloise is selected and Grace is selected. Patrick may or may not be selected.
	If J $\rightarrow$ E $\rightarrow$ G
Grace is selected?	$\rightarrow$ If Grace is selected, then it's not certain whether anyone else is selected. Selecting Grace does not trigger any other conditions.

Practice

For each of the following statements, form the contrapositive of the statement and add it to the My Analysis column. Then answer the questions that follow.

Formal Logic Statements	My Analysis
If Patrick is selected, then so is Jane.	If P → J
If Jane is selected, then so is Eloise.	If J → E
If Eloise is selected, then so is Grace.	If E → G
	If P → J → E → G

What do we know if ...

172. Grace is not selected?

    ⟶

173. Eloise is not selected?

    ⟶

174. Jane is not selected?

    ⟶

175. Patrick is not selected?

    ⟶

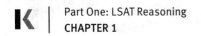

Expert Analysis

Here's how an LSAT expert would analyze the previous statements and answer the associated questions.

Formal Logic Statements	Analysis		
If Patrick is selected, then so is Jane.	If P	→	J
	If ~J	→	~P
If Jane is selected, then so is Eloise.	If J	→	E
	If ~E	→	~J
If Eloise is selected, then so is Grace.	If E	→	G
	If ~G	→	~E
	If P → J → E → G		
	If ~G → ~E → ~J → ~P		

What do we know if ...

172. Grace is not selected?	→	If Grace is not selected, then Eloise, Jane, and Patrick will also not be selected.
173. Eloise is not selected?	→	If Eloise is not selected, then Jane and Patrick will also not be selected. We cannot determine whether Grace will or will not be selected based on Eloise's not being selected.
174. Jane is not selected?	→	If Jane is not selected, then Patrick will not be selected. Jane's not being selected, however, tells us nothing about Eloise or Grace.
175. Patrick is not selected?	→	We do not know anything additional from the fact that Patrick is not selected.

In the practice sets on the following pages, you will need to make the initial translations and abbreviations for the conditional statements, and then form the contrapositives before moving on to answer the questions.

Practice

For each of the following statements, turn it into shorthand, form the contrapositive, and then make notes about how each can be combined with other conditional statements in the same set to make deductions.

Formal Logic Statements	My Analysis
If Devin goes to the lecture, then he will not go to the movies.	
If Devin goes to the movies, then he will buy popcorn.	
If Devin does not get soda, then he will not buy popcorn.	

What do we know if ...

176. Devin does not purchase popcorn?	$\longrightarrow$
177. Devin does not go to the movies?	$\longrightarrow$
178. Devin does not get soda?	$\longrightarrow$
179. Devin does not go to the lecture?	$\longrightarrow$
180. Devin goes to the movies?	$\longrightarrow$

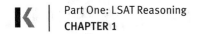

Expert Analysis

Here's how an LSAT expert would analyze the previous statements and answer the associated questions.

Formal Logic Statements	Analysis		
If Devin goes to the lecture, then he will not go to the movies.	If lecture	→	~movies
	If movies	→	~lecture
If Devin goes to the movies, then he will buy popcorn.	If movies	→	popcorn
	If ~popcorn	→	~movies
If Devin does not get soda, then he will not buy popcorn.	If ~soda	→	~popcorn
	If popcorn	→	soda
	If movies → popcorn → soda		
	If ~soda → ~popcorn → ~movies		

What do we know if ...

176. Devin does not purchase popcorn?	He did not go to the movies.
177. Devin does not go to the movies?	Nothing
178. Devin does not get soda?	He did not purchase popcorn, and he did not go to the movies.
179. Devin does not go to the lecture?	Nothing
180. Devin goes to the movies?	He does not go to the lecture, he purchases popcorn, and he gets soda.

Practice

For each of the following statements, turn it into shorthand, form the contrapositive, and then make notes about how each can be combined with other conditional statements in the same set to make deductions.

Formal Logic Statements	My Analysis
If Rosa doesn't purchase a television, then she will purchase a microwave.	
If Rosa purchases a television, then she will also purchase a DVD player.	
If Rosa visits the electrician, then she will not purchase a microwave.	
If Rosa doesn't visit the electrician, then she will go grocery shopping and will not get the car serviced.	

What do we know if . . .

181. Rosa purchases a television?	$\longrightarrow$
182. Doesn't purchase a microwave?	$\longrightarrow$
183. Rosa gets the car serviced?	$\longrightarrow$
184. Rosa does not visit the electrician?	$\longrightarrow$
185. Rosa does not purchase a DVD player?	$\longrightarrow$

Expert Analysis

Here's how an LSAT expert would analyze the previous statements and answer the associated questions.

Formal Logic Statements	Analysis		
If Rosa doesn't purchase a television, then she will purchase a microwave.	If ~television	→	microwave
	If ~microwave	→	television
If Rosa purchases a television, then she will also purchase a DVD player.	If television	→	DVD
	If ~DVD	→	~television
If Rosa visits the electrician, then she will not purchase a microwave.	If electrician	→	~microwave
	If microwave	→	~electrician
If Rosa doesn't visit the electrician, then she will go grocery shopping and will not get the car serviced.	If ~electrician	→	groceries AND ~car serviced
	If car serviced OR ~groceries	→	electrician

If car serviced OR ~groceries → electrician → ~microwave → television → DVD

If ~DVD → ~television → microwave → ~electrician → groceries AND ~car serviced

What do we know if ...

181. Rosa purchases a television? →	She will also purchase a DVD player.
182. Doesn't purchase a microwave? →	She purchases a television and a DVD player.
183. Rosa gets the car serviced? →	She visits the electrician, does not purchase a microwave, and purchases a television and a DVD player.
184. Rosa does not visit the electrician? →	She goes grocery shopping, and does not get the car serviced.
185. Rosa does not purchase a DVD player? →	She does not purchase a television, purchases a microwave, does not visit the electrician, goes grocery shopping and does not get the car serviced.

Making Valid Deductions from Conditional Statements Containing *And* and *Or*

Earlier in the chapter, you learned that when a conditional statement includes an *and* or an *or* in one of its conditions, you must swap *and* for *or* (and vice versa) when forming the contrapositive. Here's another example to refresh your memory.

> Whenever the country singer Joe Samson's mother is in the audience at one of his concerts, he always sings either "Mama Tried" or "Will the Circle Be Unbroken" during the encore.

In a Formal Logic abbreviation, that statement would become:

> If mother is in audience → MT OR WTCBU

To form the contrapositive, reverse and negate the terms and swap the *or* for *and*.

> If ~MT AND ~WTCBU → mother ~in audience

So, consider what you know in each of the following cases:

- When Joe's mother is in the audience
- When Joe's mother is not in the audience
- When Joe sings "Mama Tried" but does not sing "Will the Circle Be Unbroken"
- When Joe sings "Will the Circle Be Unbroken" but does not sing "Mama Tried"
- When Joe sings both "Mama Tried" and "Will the Circle Be Unbroken"
- When Joe sings neither "Mama Tried" nor "Will the Circle Be Unbroken"

Compare your thinking to that of an LSAT expert. Did you analyze each possibility accurately?

- When Joe's mother is in the audience, then Joe sings "Mama Tried," "Will the Circle Be Unbroken," or both during the encore. REMEMBER: *Or* is not exclusive in conditional statements unless you're told that it is.
- When Joe's mother is not in the audience, we don't know what he sings during the encore. He may still sing one or both of the songs, but he might not.
- When Joe sings "Mama Tried" but does not sing "Will the Circle Be Unbroken," we cannot deduce whether his mother is in the audience. Singing one of the songs is necessary, but not sufficient, to establish that she is in the audience.
- When Joe sings "Will the Circle Be Unbroken" but does not sing "Mama Tried," we cannot deduce whether his mother is in the audience. Singing one of the songs is necessary, but not sufficient, to establish that she is in the audience.
- When Joe sings both "Mama Tried" and "Will the Circle Be Unbroken," we cannot deduce whether his mother is in the audience. He might sing both songs when she is in the audience, or even when she is not. We just know he sings at least one when she is there.
- When Joe sings neither "Mama Tried" nor "Will the Circle Be Unbroken," we know his mother is not in the audience.

Here is a chart of the standard translations for conditional statements containing *and* and *or* along with their contrapositives.

	Formal Logic Statement			Contrapositive		
If A	→	B OR C		If ~B AND ~C	→	~A
If D	→	E AND F		If ~E OR ~F	→	~D
If G OR H	→	J		If ~J	→	~G AND ~H
If K AND L	→	M		If ~M	→	~K OR ~L
If N AND O	→	P AND R		If ~P OR ~R	→	~N OR ~O
If S OR T	→	U AND V		If ~U OR ~V	→	~S AND ~T
If W AND X	→	Y OR Z		If ~Y AND ~Z	→	~W OR ~X
If AA OR BB	→	CC OR DD		If ~CC AND ~DD	→	~AA AND ~BB

Make sure to consider the implications of these statements carefully. The following example illustrates the implications of a conditional statement containing *and* in the result clause.

Conditional Statement		Analysis		
Whenever Claudia goes to the health club, then Ann and Becky go as well.	→	If C	→	A AND B
		If ~A OR ~B	→	~C

Is each of the following an acceptable group of visitors to the health club?		
Ann, Becky, and Claudia together	→	Yes
Ann and Becky, but not Claudia	→	Yes
Ann and Claudia, but not Becky	→	No
Becky and Claudia, but not Ann	→	No
Ann alone	→	Yes
Becky alone	→	Yes
Claudia alone	→	No

Practice

In this exercise, translate each of the conditional statements to Formal Logic abbreviations and form the correct contrapositive of each statement. Then, answer the questions beneath the statement using your work.

Conditional Statement		My Analysis
The forestry bill will not pass without the support of both Senator Brown and Senator Mendoza.	$\longrightarrow$	
186. If both Senator Brown and Senator Mendoza support the forestry bill, will it pass?	$\longrightarrow$	
187. If Senator Brown supports the forestry bill, but Senator Mendoza opposes it, will the bill pass?	$\longrightarrow$	
188. If the forestry bill passes, what do you know?	$\longrightarrow$	
If Tomoko sings and Garrett plays drums, then Juniper must play the saxophone solo.		
189. If Tomoko sings, but Garrett does not play the drums, can Juniper play the saxophone solo?	$\longrightarrow$	
190. If Juniper does not play the saxophone, what do you know?	$\longrightarrow$	
191. If Juniper does play the saxophone solo, what do you know?	$\longrightarrow$	
All members of the policy panel have either a J.D. or a Ph.D.		
192. What do you know about someone who has neither a J.D. nor a Ph.D.?	$\longrightarrow$	
193. Could a member of the policy panel have both a J.D. and a Ph.D.?	$\longrightarrow$	
194. Could a member of the policy panel have an M.B.A. degree?	$\longrightarrow$	

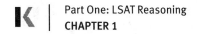
Expert Analysis

Here's how an LSAT expert would analyze the previous statements and answer the questions.

Conditional Statement		Analysis
The forestry bill will not pass without the support of both Senator Brown and Senator Mendoza.	→	If bill passes → Brown supports AND Mendoza supports If Brown ~support OR Mendoza ~support → bill ~pass
186. If both Senator Brown and Senator Mendoza support the forestry bill, will it pass?	→	We don't know. Their mutual support is necessary, but not sufficient, to ensure passage.
187. If Senator Brown supports the forestry bill, but Senator Mendoza opposes it, will the bill pass?	→	No. The support of both Senators is necessary to passage.
188. If the forestry bill passes, what do you know?	→	Both Senators supported it. The support of both is necessary to passage.
If Tomoko sings and Garrett plays drums, then Juniper must play the saxophone solo.	→	If T sings AND G drums → J sax solo If J ~sax solo → T ~sing OR G ~drum
189. If Tomoko sings, but Garrett does not play the drums, can Juniper play the saxophone solo?	→	Yes. She is required to play the sax solo when BOTH sufficient conditions apply, but she may play it without those conditions.
190. If Juniper does not play the saxophone, what do you know?	→	Either Tomoko did not sing OR Garrett did not play the drums.
191. If Juniper does play the saxophone solo, what do you know?	→	Nothing. She might play the sax solo in any case; she's required to when Tomoko sings AND Garrett drums.
All members of the policy panel have either a J.D. or a Ph.D.	→	If p.p. member → J.D. OR Ph.D. If ~J.D. AND ~Ph.D. → ~p.p. member
192. What do you know about someone who has neither a J.D. nor a Ph.D.?	→	That person is NOT a member of the policy panel.
193. Could a member of the policy panel have both a J.D. and a Ph.D.?	→	Yes. They must have one OR the other, but nothing prevents them from having both.
194. Could a member of the policy panel have an M.B.A. degree?	→	Yes, provided that she also has either a J.D. or a Ph.D.

Making Valid Deductions from Conditional Statements Containing an "Exclusive Or" Provision

So far, you've learned the fact that *or*, by itself, does not denote a relationship of mutual exclusivity in conditional Formal Logic statements. However, if the LSAT adds a phrase such as "but not both," then, and only then, does it become a case of mutual exclusivity. Such statements are rare on the LSAT, but they warrant enough practice that you won't be thrown by them on Test Day.

Formal Logic Statements	Analysis		
If X, then Y or Z, but not both	If X	$\rightarrow$	Y OR Z
	If ~Y AND ~Z	$\rightarrow$	~X
	If Y AND Z	$\rightarrow$	~X

Practice

Record each of the following statements in "If …then" format, and form both parts of their contrapositive.

Formal Logic Statements	My Analysis
195. The radio edit of this song will feature either the drum solo or the guitar solo, but not both.	
196. Every Family Budget Pass includes admission to exactly one of the IMAX movie experience or the water park.	

Expert Analysis

Here's how an LSAT expert might analyze the statements on the previous page.

Formal Logic Statements		Analysis		
195. The radio edit of this song will feature either the drum solo or the guitar solo, but not both.		If radio edit	→	drum solo OR guitar solo
	→	If ~drum solo AND ~guitar solo	→	~radio edit
		If drum solo AND guitar solo	→	~radio edit
196. Every Family Budget Pass includes admission to exactly one of the IMAX movie experience or the water park.		If FBP	→	IMAX OR water park
		If ~IMAX AND ~water park	→	~FBP
	→	If IMAX AND water park	→	~FBP

FORMAL LOGIC: NUMERICAL DEDUCTIONS FROM CONDITIONAL STATEMENTS

Numerical deductions are often rewarded on the LSAT, especially in Logic Games. This section highlights two such deductions that frequently arise from conditional Formal Logic statements.

LEARNING OBJECTIVES

In this section, you'll learn to:

- Determine the valid deduction from If X → ~Y
- Determine the valid deduction from If ~X → Y

Determining the Valid Deduction from If X → ~Y

The trigger involves something that *does* happen, and the result is something else that *cannot* happen. This reduces the number of terms by at least one.

In this case, the deduction is this: You cannot have both. (And you might have neither.)

Determining the Valid Deduction from If ~X → Y

The trigger involves something that *doesn't* happen, and the result is something that *must* happen. This increases the number of terms chosen by at least one.

In this case, the deduction is this: You must have at least one. (And you might have both.)

Formal Logic Statements	Analysis
No X are Y	→ If X → ~Y You cannot have both X and Y. You may have X without Y, Y without X, or neither Y nor X.
R unless S	→ If ~R → S You must have at least one of R and S. You can either have just R, just S, or both R and S.

Practice

For each of the following statements, write out the statement in shorthand, and indicate whether a numerical deduction can be made based on the statement.

Formal Logic Statements	My Analysis
197. Sylvia will serve either veggie burgers or falafel at her cookout. →	
198. If Vernon eats the potato salad, he won't eat the macaroni and cheese. →	
199. I can't meet my friend for lunch unless I skip my exercise class. →	
200. If the customer purchases the door, she will purchase at least two matching windows as well. →	
201. Any flowerbed that isn't planted with petunias must be planted with impatiens. →	
202. Keith bought six tickets to the concert, but if Darren doesn't go, then neither will Charles, so Keith could end up with extra tickets. →	
203. If Joanna is not selected for the varsity team, then Megan is selected for the varsity team. →	
204. Any bin that contains potatoes cannot contain onions. →	

Expert Analysis

Here's how an LSAT expert might translate and analyze the statements in the exercise.

Formal Logic Statements		Analysis
197. Sylvia will serve either veggie burgers or falafel at her cookout.	→	If ~veggie burger → falafel If ~falafel → veggie burger This statement establishes a minimum of one of these menu options. Sylvia must serve at least one of the two foods; she may serve both.
198. If Vernon eats the potato salad, he won't eat the macaroni and cheese.	→	If potato salad → ~mac & cheese If mac & cheese → ~potato salad In simpler terms: Vernon cannot eat both the potato salad and the mac & cheese. **Vernon never potato salad and mac & cheese** This statement reduces Vernon's maximum number of food choices by one.
199. I can't meet my friend for lunch unless I skip my exercise class.	→	If lunch w/friend → ~exercise class If exercise class → ~lunch w/friend *Or* **Never lunch and exercise class** This rule decreases my maximum number of activities by one, because either of my activities definitively excludes another of my activities.

Formal Logic Statements	Analysis
200. If the customer purchases the door, she will purchase at least two matching windows as well.	If purchase door → purchase 2+ windows If ~purchase 2+ windows → ~purchase door → This statement does not set a minimum or maximum because the purchase of windows *depends* on the purchase of a door. The customer could purchase neither a window nor a door, or the customer could purchase one or more windows, without triggering this rule.
201. Any flowerbed that isn't planted with petunias must be planted with impatiens.	If ~petunias → impatiens If ~impatiens → petunias → At least one of petunias and impatiens must be included in each flower bed: This statement establishes a minimum of one of these flower types.
202. Keith bought six tickets to the concert, but if Darren doesn't go, then neither will Charles, so Keith could end up with extra tickets.	If ~Darren go to concert → ~Charles go to concert If Charles go to concert → Darren go to concert → This rule does not affect the minimum or maximum number of concert attendees, because we don't know at this point whether Charles is going or Darren is not going.
203. If Joanna is not selected for the varsity team, then Megan is selected for the varsity team.	If ~J varsity → M varsity → If ~M varsity → J varsity At least one of Joanna or Megan will make the varsity team; it's possible that both do.
204. Any bin that contains potatoes cannot contain onions.	If potatoes → ~onions If onions → ~potatoes This reduces by one the maximum number of vegetables that can be stored in a bin; no bin may have potatoes and onions.

PERFORM

Translate the following statements into shorthand format and contrapose the statement. If numerical deductions can be made, what is the deduction? If there are multiple statements, can they be chained together?

Formal Logic Statement		My Analysis
205. No one will be admitted without both a valid photo ID and an event badge.	$\longrightarrow$	
206. The Wi-Fi in this building requires a username and password.	$\longrightarrow$	
207. Anyone planning to travel on the BQE this afternoon should plan for significant delays due to traffic.	$\longrightarrow$	
208. Every type of frog in that region is on the endangered species list.	$\longrightarrow$	
209. Each passenger on Flight 434 will receive a complimentary voucher for $200 toward a future flight with our airline.	$\longrightarrow$	
210. We will stop to take pictures in Badlands National Park if and only if we are making good time.	$\longrightarrow$	
211. The court cannot proceed unless all members of the jury are present.	$\longrightarrow$	
212. Students enrolling after July 31 must visit the registrar in person and will not be allowed to sign up for classes until August 15.	$\longrightarrow$	
213. Polyamines are essential for cellular function.	$\longrightarrow$	
214. If Kelly goes to the river, she will bring either a towel or sunscreen, or both.	$\longrightarrow$	

Formal Logic Statement		**My Analysis**
215. Our employees will not be allowed to work more than 40 hours a week this quarter.	$\longrightarrow$	
216. The only people eligible for a flu shot today are children under the age of 3 or adults 65 or older.	$\longrightarrow$	
217. Travel to Mars will be possible only if scientists can devise a way to transform the hydrogen found in water into an alternate fuel source.	$\longrightarrow$	
218. Empty the recycling bin before you leave.	$\longrightarrow$	
219. All the current top 40 songs will be played during today's broadcast.	$\longrightarrow$	
220. No children under the age of 17 will be allowed to see this film in theaters.	$\longrightarrow$	
221. Forest will get a dog only if it is a corgi.	$\longrightarrow$	
222. Erik's homeowners' insurance policy covers neither flood nor wind damage.	$\longrightarrow$	
223. None of the bodegas in that neighborhood are stocked with shaving cream.	$\longrightarrow$	
224. If Nirmal moves to Boston, he will either teach or write for the local paper.	$\longrightarrow$	

Expert Analysis

Here's the LSAT expert's analysis. Compare your work.

Formal Logic Statement	Analysis
205. No one will be admitted without both a valid photo ID and an event badge.	If admitted → valid ID AND event badge → If ~event badge OR ~valid ID → ~admitted ["No" indicates Formal Logic here.]
206. The Wi-Fi in this building requires a username and password.	If Wi-Fi → username AND password → If ~username OR ~password → ~Wi-Fi ["[R]equires" indicates that a username and password are both necessary.]
207. Anyone planning to travel on the BQE this afternoon should plan for significant delays due to traffic.	If BQE → Should plan for delays → If ~should plan for delays → ~BQE [The word "[a]nyone" indicates sufficiency.]
208. Every type of frog in that region is on the endangered species list.	If frog in region → end species list → If ~end species list → ~frog in region ["Every" indicates sufficiency.]
209. Each passenger on Flight 434 will receive a complimentary voucher for $200 toward a future flight with our airline.	If 434 passenger → $200 voucher → If ~$200 voucher → ~434 passenger ["Each" indicates sufficiency.]
210. We will stop to take pictures in Badlands National Park if and only if we are making good time.	If pics in Badlands → good time If ~good time → ~pics in Badlands If good time → pics in Badlands → If ~pics in Badlands → ~good time ["[I]f and only if" indicates that making good time and taking pictures are equivalent and that each are, therefore, both sufficient and necessary to each other.]

Formal Logic Statement	Analysis

211. The court cannot proceed unless all members of the jury are present.

→

If court proceed   →   jury present

If ~jury present   →   ~court proceed

["[C]annot" and "unless" indicate Formal Logic here.]

212. Students enrolling after July 31 must visit the registrar in person and will not be allowed to sign up for classes until August 15.

If after July 31   →   visit registrar AND ~sign up until Aug 15

If ~visit registrar OR sign up before Aug 15   →   before August 1

→ ["[M]ust" indicates the necessity of visiting the registrar. "[N]ot" also indicates necessity, though negated necessity. Be careful negating the statement "not be allowed to sign up … until August 15." If students cannot sign up *until* the 15th, then they cannot sign up *before* August 15th, but they will be able to on the 15th. Additionally, "not after July 31" can also be written "before August 1."]

213. Polyamines are essential for cellular function.

→

If cell function   →   polyamines

If ~polyamines   →   ~cell function

[The word "essential" indicates that polyamines are necessary.]

214. If Kelly goes to the river, she will bring either a towel or sunscreen, or both.

→

If K river   →   towel OR sunscreen

If ~towel AND ~sunscreen   →   ~K river

[Remember: In Formal Logic, "or" is assumed to be inclusive, so if Kelly goes to the river she could bring both a towel and sunscreen, which means the "or both" is redundant.]

Formal Logic Statement		Analysis
215. Our employees will not be allowed to work more than 40 hours a week this quarter.		If our employee → ~more than 40/wk
	→	If more than 40/wk → ~our employee
		["[N]ot" indicates mutual exclusion and negated necessity.]
216. The only people eligible for a flu shot today are children under the age of 3 or adults 65 or older.		If eligible for flu shot → under 3 OR 65 or older
	→	If ~65 or older AND ~under 3 → ~eligible for flu shot
		["The only" indicates sufficiency.]
217. Travel to Mars will be possible only if scientists can devise a way to transform the hydrogen found in water into an alternate fuel source.		If Mars → turn H to fuel
	→	If ~turn H to fuel → ~Mars
		["[O]nly if" indicates necessity.]
218. Empty the recycling bin before you leave.	→	[This is a command and is therefore not a Formal Logic statement.]
219. All the current top 40 songs will be played during today's broadcast.		If top 40 → played during bc
	→	If ~played during bc → ~top 40
		["All" indicates sufficiency.]
220. No children under the age of 17 will be allowed to see this film in theaters.		If see film in theater → ~under 17
	→	If under 17 → ~see film in theater
		["No" indicates mutual exclusion and negated necessity.]
221. Forest will get a dog only if it is a corgi.		If F dog → corgi
	→	If ~corgi → ~F dog
		["[O]nly if" indicates necessity.]

Formal Logic Statement	Analysis
222. Erik's homeowners' insurance policy covers neither flood nor wind damage. $\longrightarrow$	If E's insurance policy $\longrightarrow$ ~flood AND ~wind If wind OR flood $\longrightarrow$ ~E's insurance policy ["[N]either … nor … " indicates Formal Logic and should be translated "~… AND ~… "]
223. None of the bodegas in that neighborhood are stocked with shaving cream. $\longrightarrow$	If Bodega in that $\longrightarrow$ ~stocked with neighborhood shaving cream If stocked with $\longrightarrow$ ~bodega in that shaving cream neighborhood ["None" indicates mutual exclusion and negated necessity.]
224. If Nirmal moves to Boston he will either teach or write for the local paper. $\longrightarrow$	If N moves to Boston $\longrightarrow$ teach OR write If ~teach AND ~write $\longrightarrow$ ~N moves to Boston ["If" indicates sufficiency.]

REFLECTION

Look back over your practice.

- · Did you take the time to understand each conditional statement before noting it down in shorthand?
- · If you couldn't immediately see how to write it down in one sentence, did you translate it into If-Then form and make the contrapositive? (If so, that's great!)
- · Did you tend to get confused about the side of the arrow on which *not* should appear?
- · Did you always remember that the result (the necessary condition) can occur without the trigger (the sufficient condition), but not vice versa?

Now, take a moment to look back over all of Chapter 1. You may not have been thinking about it as you did your work, but you've now successfully employed a great many essential LSAT skills, skills you will continue to use in law school and in the practice of law. Now that you've built this foundation, you are ready for work in all of the other sections of the LSAT.

Come back to Chapter 1 any time you need a refresher on the fundamentals of LSAT reasoning.

Logic Games

CHAPTER 2

The Kaplan Logic Games Method

Every administration of the LSAT features one scored Logic Games section. A majority of test takers consider it the most difficult section on the test—at least they do before beginning their LSAT preparation. While logic games may initially appear abstract and irrelevant to the skills necessary for a legal career, they actually test core LSAT skills. The ability to interpret, deconstruct, and combine individual rules to deduce what must, can, or cannot be true under various conditions is central to the work you'll do in law school.

If you've already done the work in Chapter 1, "LSAT Reasoning," then much of what the Logic Games section rewards will already be familiar. Looking at a typical Logic Games question illustrates this.

If Griseldi's session is on the 5th, then which one of the following must be true?

- (A)   Farnham's session is on the 3rd.
- (B)   Heany's session is on the 7th.
- (C)   Juarez's session is on the 4th.
- (D)   Lightfoot's session is on the 1st.
- (E)   Moreau's session is on the 2nd.

PrepTest61 Sec3 Q22

Notice that the question stem starts by providing a condition, just like the opening clause of a Formal Logic statement. It then asks you about the level of certainty, in this case what "must be true."

In this chapter, you'll see the Kaplan Logic Games Method, the approach an LSAT expert uses.

THE KAPLAN LOGIC GAMES METHOD

Step 1: Overview

Step 2: Sketch

Step 3: Rules

Step 4: Deductions

Step 5: Questions

Chapters 3–5 focus on each step of the method: breaking down a Logic Game's overview, creating a master sketch to organize the information, translating rules and combining them to make deductions, and answering questions quickly and effectively.

3 **3** **3** **3** **3**

Questions 18–23

From the 1st through the 7th of next month, seven nurses—Farnham, Griseldi, Heany, Juarez, Khan, Lightfoot, and Moreau—will each conduct one information session at a community center. Each nurse's session will fall on a different day. The nurses' schedule is governed by the following constraints:

> At least two of the other nurses' sessions must fall in between Heany's session and Moreau's session.
> Griseldi's session must be on the day before Khan's.
> Juarez's session must be on a later day than Moreau's.
> Farnham's session must be on an earlier day than Khan's but on a later day than Lightfoot's.
> Lightfoot cannot conduct the session on the 2nd.

---

18. Which one of the following could be the order of the nurses' sessions, from first to last?

(A) Farnham, Griseldi, Khan, Moreau, Juarez, Lightfoot, Heany

(B) Heany, Lightfoot, Farnham, Moreau, Juarez, Griseldi, Khan

(C) Juarez, Heany, Lightfoot, Farnham, Moreau, Griseldi, Khan

(D) Lightfoot, Moreau, Farnham, Juarez, Griseldi, Khan, Heany

(E) Moreau, Lightfoot, Heany, Juarez, Farnham, Griseldi, Khan

---

The opening paragraph is called the Overview. It describes the game and presents the game's action(s).

These are the rules of the game. They establish what must, might, or cannot be true in the game.

F G H J K L M

$$\overline{1}\ \overline{2}\ \overline{3}\ \overline{4}\ \overline{5}\ \overline{6}\ \overline{7}$$

~K ~L ~K ~L ~L ~L ~L
~G ~K ~G ~K   ~F ~F
~F ~G   ~G
~J   ~M

H/M _ _ ... M/H
L ... F ... G K
M ... J

An LSAT expert creates a master sketch that visually displays the game's action(s) and restrictions.

Experts translate the game's rules into a consistent visual shorthand.

PrepTest61 Sec3 Qs 18–23

3   3   3   3   **3**

19. Juarez's session CANNOT be on which one of the following days?

   ✗ CBT

  (A) the 2nd
  (B) the 3rd
  (C) the 5th
  (D) the 6th
  (E) the 7th

20. If Juarez's session is on the 3rd, then which one of the following could be true?

  (A) Moreau's session is on the 1st.
  (B) Khan's session is on the 5th.
  (C) Heany's session is on the 6th.
  (D) Griseldi's session is on the 5th.
  (E) Farnham's session is on the 2nd.

21. If Khan's session is on an earlier day than Moreau's, which one of the following could conduct the session on the 3rd?

  (A) Griseldi
  (B) Heany
  (C) Juarez
  (D) Lightfoot
  (E) Moreau

L ...F... GK ...M...J
~2   H

22. If Griseldi's session is on the 5th, then which one of the following must be true?

  (A) Farnham's session is on the 3rd.
  (B) Heany's session is on the 7th.
  (C) Juarez's session is on the 4th.

> Experts know that it is important to characterize the correct and incorrect answer choices in Logic Games.

  (A) the 3rd
  (B) the 4th
  (C) the 5th
  (D) the 6th
  (E) the 7th

> Experts don't try to keep all of the rules and deductions in their heads. They depict relationships on the page and continue to add new information.

S T O P

IF YOU FINISH BEFORE TIME IS CALLED, YOU MAY CHECK YOUR WORK ON THIS SECTION ONLY.
DO NOT WORK ON ANY OTHER SECTION IN THE TEST.

20. L M J   F...GK
    1 2 3 4 5 6 7
          H

22.   M J E
      F M J
      m F J
 L   G K H
 1 2 3 4 5 6 7
 M J L E G K H

> Use the available space to create new sketches for questions that ask you to consider new information.

Step 1: Overview

The first thing an LSAT expert does is read a game's opening paragraph to understand the game's moving parts. The expert asks four questions while conducting this overview: the SEAL questions.

STEP 1: OVERVIEW—THE SEAL QUESTIONS

Situation—What is the real-world scenario being described? What is the deliverable information—an ordered list, a calendar, a chart showing what's matched up?

Entities—Who or what are the "moving parts," the people or things I'm distributing, selecting, sequencing, or matching?

Action—What is the specific action—distribution, selection, sequencing, matching, or a combination of those—that I'm performing on the entities?

Limitations—Does the game state parameters (e.g., select four of seven, sequence the entities one per day, etc.) that restrict how I'll set up and sketch the game?

Read through the following overview, and then answer the SEAL questions that follow:

From the 1st through the 7th of next month, seven nurses—
Farnham, Griseldi, Heany, Juarez, Khan, Lightfoot, and
Moreau—will each conduct one information session at
a community center. Each nurse's session will fall on a
different day. The nurses' schedule is governed by the
following constraints

PrepTest61 Sec3 Qs 18–23

What is this game's **Situation?** _____

What **Entities** are involved in this game? _____

What is this game's **Action?** _____

Are there any **Limitations** to this game? _____

Step 2: Sketch

After conducting the overview, an LSAT expert creates a sketch based on the game's action (or actions) and limitations. Instead of trying to keep information in her head, the expert uses her sketch to record concrete rules and deductions. A strong sketch is simple, easy to read, and often based on something familiar: If a game's action involves scheduling, for example, the sketch may mimic a calendar, or if the game involves putting people or items into different groups, the sketch might be a table.

STEP 2: THE SKETCH

- Create a sketch that depicts the game's action(s) and limitations.
- Aim for a sketch that is easy to read, quick to replicate, and able to account for what is certain and uncertain based on the game's rules.

Revisit the overview of the game you've seen before and create an appropriate sketch.

From the 1st through the 7th of next month, seven nurses—Farnham, Griseldi, Heany, Juarez, Khan, Lightfoot, and Moreau—will each conduct one information session at a community center. Each nurse's session will fall on a different day. The nurses' schedule is governed by the following constraints:

PrepTest61 Sec3 Qs 18–23

My Sketch:

How an LSAT Expert Sees It

Step 1: Overview

Revisit the overview of the game you've seen before and create an appropriate sketch.

From the 1st through the 7th of next month, seven nurses—Farnham, Griseldi, Heany, Juarez, Khan, Lightfoot, and Moreau—will each conduct one information session at a community center. Each nurse's session will fall on a different day. The nurses' schedule is governed by the following constraints:

PrepTest61 Sec3 Qs 18–23

What is this game's **Situation?** *A schedule of nursing information sessions over the course of a week*

What **Entities** are involved in this game? *The nurses—F, G, H, J, K, L, and M*

What is this game's **Action?** *Sequencing: Determine the order of nurses' sessions*

Are there any **Limitations** to this game? *One nurse per day*

Step 2: Sketch

In this Sequencing game, the order of the sessions matters. Create a sketch of seven horizontal dashes. The earliest session will be day 1, the latest will be day 7. When the placement of nurses is determined, that information can be added directly to the sketch.

F G H J K L M

__ __ __ __ __ __ __
1 2 3 4 5 6 7

Step 3: Rules

The rules limit the possible permutations of a game by establishing restrictions on the placement, order, or selection of entities, or by establishing relationships between entities.

> ### STEP 3: RULES
>
> · Whenever possible, add information directly to your master sketch.
> · Write the rules in a way that matches the style and conventions of the master sketch.
> · Consider both the positive and negative implications of a rule.
> · Write similar rules consistently, the same way from game to game.

For clarity and certainty, the LSAT expert always seeks to add the information from a rule directly into the master sketch framework. If he cannot add the information directly to the master sketch, he will translate the rule into shorthand and place it next to or beneath the master sketch. Experts check a rule's positive *and* negative implications to determine where the entity or entities must, can, or cannot be placed.

Try your hand at analyzing and writing rules on the next page.

Read through each of the rules to the Nurses' Information Session game. Use the questions and spaces on the facing page to record your analyses.

From the 1st through the 7th of next month, seven nurses—Farnham, Griseldi, Heany, Juarez, Khan, Lightfoot, and Moreau—will each conduct one information session at a community center. Each nurse's session will fall on a different day. The nurses' schedule is governed by the following constraints:

At least two of the other nurses' sessions must fall in between Heany's session and Moreau's session.

Griseldi's session must be on the day before Khan's.

Juarez's session must be on a later day than Moreau's.

Farnham's session must be on an earlier day than Khan's but on a later day than Lightfoot's.

Lightfoot cannot conduct the session on the 2nd.

PrepTest61 Sec3 Qs 18–23

Rule 1: At least two of the other nurses' sessions must fall in between Heany's session and Moreau's session.

Can the information in this rule be placed directly into the sketch?

If the answer is no, write this rule in shorthand that is appropriate for the sketch:

Rule 2: Griseldi's session must be on the day before Khan's.

Can the information in this rule be placed directly into the sketch?

If the answer is no, write this rule in shorthand that is appropriate for the sketch:

Rule 3: Juarez's session must be on a later day than Moreau's.

Can the information in this rule be placed directly into the sketch?

If the answer is no, write this rule in shorthand that is appropriate for the sketch:

Rule 4: Farnham's session must be on an earlier day than Khan's but on a later day than Lightfoot's.

Can the information in this rule be placed directly into the sketch?

If the answer is no, write this rule in a shorthand that is appropriate for the sketch:

Rule 5: Lightfoot cannot conduct the session on the 2nd.

Can the information in this rule be placed directly into the sketch?

If the answer is no, write this rule in shorthand that is appropriate for the sketch:

PrepTest61 Sec3 Qs 18–23

How an LSAT Expert Sees It

Step 3: Rules

Rule 1: At least two of the other nurses' sessions must fall in between Heany's session and Moreau's session.

Can the information in this rule be placed directly into the sketch? NO

H/M __ __ . . . M/H
Or
H __ __ . . . M or M __ __ . . . H

Rule 2: Griseldi's session must be on the day before Khan's.

Can the information in this rule be placed directly into the sketch? NO

<u>G</u> K

Rule 3: Juarez's session must be on a later day than Moreau's.

Can the information in this rule be placed directly into the sketch? NO

M . . . J

Rule 4: Farnham's session must be on an earlier day than Khan's but on a later day than Lightfoot's.

Can the information in this rule be placed directly into the sketch? NO

L . . . F . . . K

Rule 5: Lightfoot cannot conduct the session on the 2nd.

Can the information in this rule be placed directly into the sketch? YES

F G H J K L M

__ __ __ __ __ __ __
1 2 3 4 5 6 7
  ~L

PrepTest61 Sec3 Qs 18–23

Step 4: Deductions

This is the step that the majority of untrained test takers overlook. Even those who instinctively understand the value of making a sketch or depicting the rules visually often don't take the time to determine what must be true or must be false beyond what the rules explicitly state.

An LSAT expert, however, knows that in most games, it is possible to combine the rules with each other (or with the game's overall limitations) in a way that reveals greater certainty when she goes to tackle the questions. As you practice, you'll start to make valuable deductions almost instinctively, but learn to be systematic and rigorous in this step so that you get all of a game's potential deductions quickly and accurately.

The vast majority of deductions come from one of five patterns, easily remembered with the mnemonic BLEND. Use this as a checklist, not a series of steps. You don't look for Blocks of Entities first, necessarily.

STEP 4: DEDUCTIONS

Blocks of Entities—Two or more players who are always grouped together

Limited Options—Rules or restrictions that limit the overall setup to one of two acceptable arrangements

Established Entities—A player locked into a specific space or group

Number Restrictions—Rules or limitations that provide guidance about the number of entities assigned to a group or space

Duplications—Entities that appear in two or more rules and allow the rules to be combined

As you gain familiarity with the various game types, you'll recognize that certain types of deductions are associated more often with certain actions. Not every game will feature all of the BLEND restrictions, but using the checklist is a good way to make sure no available deductions slip through your fingers.

On the following pages, practice making the deductions available in the Nurses' Information Sessions game you've been studying.

See what deductions you can make in the Nurses' Information Sessions game. Here is the game's opening paragraph and rules, along with the expert sketch and rule analyses.

LSAT Question	Analysis
From the 1st through the 7th of next month, seven nurses—Farnham, Griseldi, Heany, Juarez, Khan, Lightfoot, and Moreau—will each conduct one information session at a community center. Each nurse's session will fall on a different day. The nurses' schedule is governed by the following constraints: At least two of the other nurses' sessions must fall in between Heany's session and Moreau's session. Griseldi's session must be on the day before Khan's. Juarez's session must be on a later day than Moreau's. Farnham's session must be on an earlier day than Khan's but on a later day than Lightfoot's. Lightfoot cannot conduct the session on the 2nd. *PrepTest61 Sec3 Qs 18–23* →	F G H J K L M __ __ __ __ __ __ __ 1 2 3 4 5 6 7 ~L H/M __ __ … M/H G K M … J L … F … K

Go through the BLEND checklist and determine which, if any, of those restrictions you see here. How can those provide additional certainty in this game?

HINT: Which of the rules share common entities? How can those rules be combined?

Make sure to consider both the positive and negative implications of any of the rules or deductions. Which of the rules are most restrictive? Which of the entities are most restricted?

Use the space on this page to record any deductions you make. Incorporate all deductions into your master sketch.

LSAT Question	Analysis

From the 1st through the 7th of next month, seven nurses—Farnham, Griseldi, Heany, Juarez, Khan, Lightfoot, and Moreau—will each conduct one information session at a community center. Each nurse's session will fall on a different day. The nurses' schedule is governed by the following constraints:

At least two of the other nurses' sessions must fall in between Heany's session and Moreau's session.

Griseldi's session must be on the day before Khan's.

Juarez's session must be on a later day than Moreau's.

Farnham's session must be on an earlier day than Khan's but on a later day than Lightfoot's.

Lightfoot cannot conduct the session on the 2nd.

PrepTest61 Sec3 Qs 18–23

→

F G H J K L M

1	2	3	4	5	6	7
	~L					

H/M ___ ___ ... M/H

G K

M ... J

L ... F ... K

My Deductions:

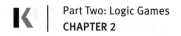
How an LSAT Expert Sees It

Step 4: Deductions

LSAT Question	Analysis

From the 1st through the 7th of next month, seven nurses—Farnham, Griseldi, Heany, Juarez, Khan, Lightfoot, and Moreau—will each conduct one information session at a community center. Each nurse's session will fall on a different day. The nurses' schedule is governed by the following constraints:

At least two of the other nurses' sessions must fall in between Heany's session and Moreau's session.

Griseldi's session must be on the day before Khan's.

Juarez's session must be on a later day than Moreau's.

Farnham's session must be on an earlier day than Khan's but on a later day than Lightfoot's.

Lightfoot cannot conduct the session on the 2nd.

PrepTest61 Sec3 Qs 18–23

Analysis:

F G H J K L M

 ___ ___ ___ ___ ___ ___ ___
  1   2   3   4   5   6   7
      ~L

→   H/M ___ ___ ... M/H

        G   K

     M ... J

     L ... F ... K

Deductions:

Duplication: Rules 1 and 3 share Moreau.

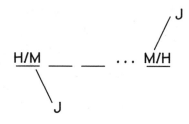

Duplication: Rules 2 and 4 share Khan.

L ... F ... G K

Deductions (cont.)

The string created by combining Rules 2 and 4 restricts four entities: L, F, G, and K. Given the order in the string, it has strong negative implications: K cannot conduct a session on days 1, 2, or 3; G cannot conduct a session on days 1, 2, or 7; F cannot conduct a session on days 1, 6, or 7; and L cannot conduct a session on days 5, 6, or 7 (and is forbidden already by Rule 5 from conducting a session on day 2).

1	2	3	4	5	6	7
~K	~L	~K		~L	~F	~G
~G	~K				~L	~F
~F	~G					~L

Rule 3's negative implications can likewise be entered into the sketch.

1	2	3	4	5	6	7
~K	~L	~K		~L	~F	~G
~G	~K				~L	~F
~F	~G					~L
~J						~M

Because the L-F-GK string accounts for four days and because Rule 1 requires at least two days between H and M, it is impossible for either L or K to conduct a session on day 4. If either of them did so, there would be insufficient space for H and M to be properly spaced.

F G H J K L M

1	2	3	4	5	6	7
~K	~L	~K	~L	~L	~L	~L
~G	~K	~G	~K		~F	~F
~F	~G					~G
~J						~M

Note too, that since K cannot conduct a session on day 4, G cannot conduct a session on day 3. That is your final sketch.

Step 5: Questions

Making a useful sketch, writing out the rules, and making available deductions are necessary, but not sufficient for success in the Logic Games section. Experts know that the ultimate goal is to answer the questions correctly—and not just correctly, but also quickly. To get through the questions quickly and effectively, experts keep a few things in mind.

STEP 5: THE QUESTIONS

· Be able to characterize both correct and incorrect answer choices.
· Know the different question types and how to approach each one.
· Don't hesitate to draw a new sketch in "If" questions.
· Use deductions and past work to eliminate wrong answers quickly.

In Chapter 5, you'll see strategies for all of the question types you may encounter in the Logic Games section. For the remainder of this chapter, work through the questions associated with the Nurses' Information Sessions game, and explore how an LSAT expert would tackle each of them efficiently and effectively.

Acceptability Question

The first question for this game (and the first question in most games' question sets) is an Acceptability question. In these questions, the correct answer is the one that breaks none of the rules. All four wrong answers break one or more of the rules. The expert's strategy is simple: Check the answers rule-by-rule, and eliminate choices that break the rules. If an answer choice breaks a rule, cross it out.

LSAT Question	My Analysis
From the 1st through the 7th of next month, seven nurses—Farnham, Griseldi, Heany, Juarez, Khan, Lightfoot, and Moreau—will each conduct one information session at a community center. Each nurse's session will fall on a different day. The nurses' schedule is governed by the following constraints: At least two of the other nurses' sessions must fall in between Heany's session and Moreau's session. Griseldi's session must be on the day before Khan's. Juarez's session must be on a later day than Moreau's. Farnham's session must be on an earlier day than Khan's but on a later day than Lightfoot's. Lightfoot cannot conduct the session on the 2nd.	Rule 1 broken by answer choice: _____ Rule 2 broken by answer choice: _____ Rule 3 broken by answer choice: _____ → Rule 4 broken by answer choice: _____ Rule 5 broken by answer choice: _____

18. Which one of the following could be the order of the nurses' sessions, from first to last?

    (A) Farnham, Griseldi, Khan, Moreau, Juarez, Lightfoot, Heany   →

    (B) Heany, Lightfoot, Farnham, Moreau, Juarez, Griseldi, Khan   →

    (C) Juarez, Heany, Lightfoot, Farnham, Moreau, Griseldi, Khan   →

    (D) Lightfoot, Moreau, Farnham, Juarez, Griseldi, Khan, Heany   →

    (E) Moreau, Lightfoot, Heany, Juarez, Farnham, Griseldi, Khan

    PrepTest61 Sec3 Q18 →

How an LSAT Expert Sees It

Acceptability Question

LSAT Question	Analysis
From the 1st through the 7th of next month, seven nurses—Farnham, Griseldi, Heany, Juarez, Khan, Lightfoot, and Moreau—will each conduct one information session at a community center. Each nurse's session will fall on a different day. The nurses' schedule is governed by the following constraints: At least two of the other nurses' sessions must fall in between Heany's session and Moreau's session. Griseldi's session must be on the day before Khan's. Juarez's session must be on a later day than Moreau's. Farnham's session must be on an earlier day than Khan's but on a later day than Lightfoot's. Lightfoot cannot conduct the session on the 2nd.	Rule 1 broken by answer choice: **(E)** Rule 2 broken by answer choice: **None** Rule 3 broken by answer choice: **(C)** Rule 4 broken by answer choice: **(A)** Rule 5 broken by answer choice: **(B)**

18. Which one of the following could be the order of the nurses' sessions, from first to last?

(A)	Farnham, Griseldi, Khan, Moreau, Juarez, Lightfoot, Heany	Violates Rule 4. Eliminate.
(B)	Heany, Lightfoot, Farnham, Moreau, Juarez, Griseldi, Khan	Violates Rule 5. Eliminate.
(C)	Juarez, Heany, Lightfoot, Farnham, Moreau, Griseldi, Khan	Violates Rule 3. Eliminate.
(D)	Lightfoot, Moreau, Farnham, Juarez, Griseldi, Khan, Heany	Correct.
(E)	Moreau, Lightfoot, Heany, Juarez, Farnham, Griseldi, Khan	Violates Rule 1. Eliminate.

PrepTest61 Sec3 Q18 ⟶

Must Be False Question

This next question is called a Must be False question. The correct answer will be the one that cannot be true in any situation. The four incorrect answer choices, then, all could be true. Check the final master sketch and eliminate any answer that could be true, or select the answer choice that must be false.

LSAT Question	**My Analysis**

From the 1st through the 7th of next month, seven nurses—Farnham, Griseldi, Heany, Juarez, Khan, Lightfoot, and Moreau—will each conduct one information session at a community center. Each nurse's session will fall on a different day. The nurses' schedule is governed by the following constraints:

    At least two of the other nurses' sessions must fall in between Heany's session and Moreau's session.
    Griseldi's session must be on the day before Khan's.
    Juarez's session must be on a later day than Moreau's.
    Farnham's session must be on an earlier day than Khan's but on a later day than Lightfoot's.
    Lightfoot cannot conduct the session on the 2nd.

→

```
        F G H J K L M                              J
                                                  /
 __   __   __   __   __   __   __     H/M __  __ ...M/H
 1    2    3    4    5    6    7           \
~K   ~L   ~K   ~L   ~L   ~L   ~L            J
~G   ~K   ~G   ~K        ~F   ~F
~F   ~G        ~K        ~G          L...F... G  K
~J                            ~G
                              ~M
```

19. Juarez's session CANNOT be on which one of the following days?   →

  (A) the 2nd

    →

  (B) the 3rd

    →

  (C) the 5th

    →

  (D) the 6th

    →

  (E) the 7th

               PrepTest61 Sec3 Q19   →

HINT: Why might the LSAT expert skip this question temporarily and return to it after completing the other questions in the set?

How an LSAT Expert Sees It
Must Be False Question

Because this question potentially requires testing four of the answers before arriving at the correct answer, the LSAT expert may choose to skip it and complete the rest of the question set. Then, he can check his notes for the remaining questions and eliminate any answer containing a day on which he found it was acceptable for Juarez to conduct a session.

LSAT Question	Analysis
From the 1st through the 7th of next month, seven nurses—Farnham, Griseldi, Heany, Juarez, Khan, Lightfoot, and Moreau—will each conduct one information session at a community center. Each nurse's session will fall on a different day. The nurses' schedule is governed by the following constraints: At least two of the other nurses' sessions must fall in between Heany's session and Moreau's session. Griseldi's session must be on the day before Khan's. Juarez's session must be on a later day than Moreau's. Farnham's session must be on an earlier day than Khan's but on a later day than Lightfoot's. Lightfoot cannot conduct the session on the 2nd.	F G H J K L M 1 2 3 4 5 6 7 ~K ~L ~K ~L ~L ~L ~L ~G ~K ~G ~K ~F ~F ~F ~G ~G ~J ~M H/M ___ ___ ... M/H J L...F... G K
19. Juarez's session CANNOT be on which one of the following days?	Rule 3 eliminates Juarez from day 1, but that doesn't help with any of the answer choices.
(A) the 2nd	M-J-L-F-H-G-K and M-J-L-H-F-G-K are acceptable. Eliminate. Question 22 also proves that Juarez could be second.
(B) the 3rd	L-M-J-F-H-G-K is acceptable. Eliminate. Question 20 also proves that Juarez could be third.
(C) the 5th	Correct.
(D) the 6th	L-F-M-G-K-J-H and L-M-F-G-K-J-H are acceptable. Eliminate.
(E) the 7th *PrepTest61 Sec3 Q19*	L-H-F-G-K-M-J, L-F-H-G-K-M-J, L-M-F-G-K-H-J, and L-F-M-G-K-H-J are all acceptable. Eliminate. Question 21 also proves that Juarez could be seventh.

New-"If"/Could Be True Question

This next question is a New-"If" question. An LSAT expert knows to redraw the master sketch, add J to the third session, and make any available deductions. The correct answer could be true under this question's condition. The four wrong answers must be false under this question's condition.

LSAT Question	My Analysis

From the 1st through the 7th of next month, seven nurses—Farnham, Griseldi, Heany, Juarez, Khan, Lightfoot, and Moreau—will each conduct one information session at a community center. Each nurse's session will fall on a different day. The nurses' schedule is governed by the following constraints:

At least two of the other nurses' sessions must fall in between Heany's session and Moreau's session.
Griseldi's session must be on the day before Khan's.
Juarez's session must be on a later day than Moreau's.
Farnham's session must be on an earlier day than Khan's but on a later day than Lightfoot's.
Lightfoot cannot conduct the session on the 2nd.

$\longrightarrow$

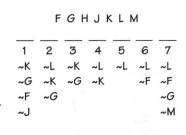

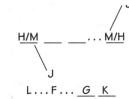

20. If Juarez's session is on the 3rd, then which one of the following could be true?

$\longrightarrow$

(A)   Moreau's session is on the 1st.

$\longrightarrow$

(B)   Khan's session is on the 5th.

$\longrightarrow$

(C)   Heany's session is on the 6th.

$\longrightarrow$

(D)   Griseldi's session is on the 5th.

$\longrightarrow$

(E)   Farnham's session is on the 2nd.

PrepTest61 Sec3 Q20

$\longrightarrow$

HINT: How does this question's stem help you answer question 19?

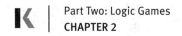
How an LSAT Expert Sees It
New-"If"/Could Be True Question

LSAT Question	Analysis

From the 1st through the 7th of next month, seven nurses—Farnham, Griseldi, Heany, Juarez, Khan, Lightfoot, and Moreau—will each conduct one information session at a community center. Each nurse's session will fall on a different day. The nurses' schedule is governed by the following constraints:

At least two of the other nurses' sessions must fall in between Heany's session and Moreau's session.

Griseldi's session must be on the day before Khan's.

Juarez's session must be on a later day than Moreau's.

Farnham's session must be on an earlier day than Khan's but on a later day than Lightfoot's.

Lightfoot cannot conduct the session on the 2nd.

→

F G H J K L M

1	2	3	4	5	6	7
~K	~L	~K	~L	~L	~L	~L
~G	~K	~G	~K		~F	~F
~F	~G					~G
~J						~M

H/M __ __ __ ... M/H   / J

       \ J

L...F... <u>G</u> <u>K</u>

---

20. If Juarez's session is on the 3rd, then which one of the following could be true?

→

Redraw the master sketch, and add J to spot 3:

__ __ <u>J</u> __ __ __ __

With J placed, Rule 3 forces M into day 1 or 2. And, according to Rule 1, H must go at least 3 days later than M, and so, later than J. Now, work in the L-F-GK string. L must go earlier than J, but can't take day 2 (Rule 5), and so must take day 1. To obey Rule 1, F must take day 4. So, there are two possible arrangements.

<u>L</u> <u>M</u> <u>J</u> <u>F</u> <u>H</u> <u>G</u> <u>K</u>

<u>L</u> <u>M</u> <u>J</u> <u>F</u> <u>G</u> <u>K</u> <u>H</u>

(A)	Moreau's session is on the 1st.	→ Must be false. Moreau takes day 2. Eliminate.
(B)	Khan's session is on the 5th.	→ Must be false. Khan takes day 6 or 7. Eliminate.
(C)	Heany's session is on the 6th.	→ Must be false. Heany takes day 5 or 7. Eliminate.
(D)	Griseldi's session is on the 5th.	→ Correct.
(E)	Farnham's session is on the 2nd.	→ Must be false. Farnham takes day 4. Eliminate.

PrepTest61 Sec3 Q20

Note that, in this question's sketch, J can acceptably conduct a session on day 3. Return to question 19 and eliminate **(B)**.

New-"If"/Could Be True Question

Here is another New-"If" question. Again, the expert will account for the new information in a sketch and make any available deductions. NOTE: New-"If" conditions apply only to the question in which they appear. Do not carry over one question's New-"If" to another question. Keep your question-specific notes distinct and clearly labeled.

LSAT Question	My Analysis

From the 1st through the 7th of next month, seven nurses— Farnham, Griseldi, Heany, Juarez, Khan, Lightfoot, and Moreau—will each conduct one information session at a community center. Each nurse's session will fall on a different day. The nurses' schedule is governed by the following constraints:

At least two of the other nurses' sessions must fall in between Heany's session and Moreau's session.
Griseldi's session must be on the day before Khan's.
Juarez's session must be on a later day than Moreau's.
Farnham's session must be on an earlier day than Khan's but on a later day than Lightfoot's.
Lightfoot cannot conduct the session on the 2nd.

$\longrightarrow$

```
    F G H J K L M                                J
                                                /
 __  __  __  __  __  __  __     H/M __  __ ...M/H
  1   2   3   4   5   6   7             \
 ~K  ~L  ~K  ~L  ~L  ~L  ~L              J
 ~G  ~K  ~G  ~K      ~F  ~F    L...F... G  K
 ~F  ~G          ~G            ‾  ‾
 ~J              ~M
```

21. If Khan's session is on an earlier day than Moreau's, which one of the following could conduct the session on the 3rd? $\longrightarrow$

   (A) Griseldi $\longrightarrow$

   (B) Heany $\longrightarrow$

   (C) Juarez $\longrightarrow$

   (D) Lightfoot $\longrightarrow$

   (E) Moreau

   PrepTest61 Sec3 Q21 $\longrightarrow$

HINT: How is the new condition in this question stem different from the one in question 20? What will you do differently in your notes?

How an LSAT Expert Sees It
New-"If"/Could Be True Question

LSAT Question	Analysis

From the 1st through the 7th of next month, seven nurses—Farnham, Griseldi, Heany, Juarez, Khan, Lightfoot, and Moreau—will each conduct one information session at a community center. Each nurse's session will fall on a different day. The nurses' schedule is governed by the following constraints:

At least two of the other nurses' sessions must fall in between Heany's session and Moreau's session.
Griseldi's session must be on the day before Khan's.
Juarez's session must be on a later day than Moreau's.
Farnham's session must be on an earlier day than Khan's but on a later day than Lightfoot's.
Lightfoot cannot conduct the session on the 2nd.

→

F G H J K L M

1	2	3	4	5	6	7
~K	~L	~K	~L	~L	~L	~L
~G	~K	~G	~K		~F	~F
~F	~G					~G
~J						~M

```
          J
         /
H/M __ __ ...M/H
         \
          J

L...F... G K
```

---

21. If Khan's session is on an earlier day than Moreau's, which one of the following could conduct the session on the 3rd?

→

Deductions:

Adding the new info to the L-F-GK string produces:

L...F...GK...M...J

The only entity not accounted for is H, which must be separated from M by at least two days (Rule 1).

L	H/F	F/H	G	K	M	J
~L						

The correct answer could be true, while the four wrong answer choices all must be false under these conditions.

(A) Griseldi → Must be on day 4. Eliminate.

(B) Heany → Correct.

(C) Juarez → Must be on day 7. Eliminate.

(D) Lightfoot → Must be on day 1. Eliminate.

(E) Moreau → Must be on day 6. Eliminate.

PrepTest61 Sec3 Q21

Note that, in this New-"If" sketch, J can conduct a session on day 7. Return to question 19 and eliminate **(E)**.

New-"If"/Must Be True Question

Question 22 is another New-"If" question.

LSAT Question	My Analysis

From the 1st through the 7th of next month, seven nurses—Farnham, Griseldi, Heany, Juarez, Khan, Lightfoot, and Moreau—will each conduct one information session at a community center. Each nurse's session will fall on a different day. The nurses' schedule is governed by the following constraints:

> At least two of the other nurses' sessions must fall in between Heany's session and Moreau's session.
> Griseldi's session must be on the day before Khan's.
> Juarez's session must be on a later day than Moreau's.
> Farnham's session must be on an earlier day than Khan's but on a later day than Lightfoot's.
> Lightfoot cannot conduct the session on the 2nd.

$\longrightarrow$

F G H J K L M

```
 __   __   __   __   __   __   __
 1    2    3    4    5    6    7
~K   ~L   ~K   ~L   ~L   ~L   ~L
~G   ~K   ~G   ~K        ~F   ~F
~F   ~G                       ~G
~J                            ~M
```

```
         J
        /
H/M __ __ ... M/H
    \
     J

L...F... G  K
```

22. If Griseldi's session is on the 5th, then which one of the following must be true? $\longrightarrow$

(A) Farnham's session is on the 3rd. $\longrightarrow$

(B) Heany's session is on the 7th. $\longrightarrow$

(C) Juarez's session is on the 4th. $\longrightarrow$

(D) Lightfoot's session is on the 1st. $\longrightarrow$

(E) Moreau's session is on the 2nd.
PrepTest61 Sec3 Q22 $\longrightarrow$

HINT: What is the characteristic of the one correct answer? How about the characteristics of the four wrong answers?

How an LSAT Expert Sees It
New-"If"/Must Be True Question

LSAT Question	Analysis

From the 1st through the 7th of next month, seven nurses—Farnham, Griseldi, Heany, Juarez, Khan, Lightfoot, and Moreau—will each conduct one information session at a community center. Each nurse's session will fall on a different day. The nurses' schedule is governed by the following constraints:

At least two of the other nurses' sessions must fall in between Heany's session and Moreau's session.

Griseldi's session must be on the day before Khan's.

Juarez's session must be on a later day than Moreau's.

Farnham's session must be on an earlier day than Khan's but on a later day than Lightfoot's.

Lightfoot cannot conduct the session on the 2nd.

⟶

```
        F G H J K L M                                          J
                                                              /
___ ___ ___ ___ ___ ___ ___     H/M ___ ___ ___ ...M/H
 1   2   3   4   5   6   7                          \
~K  ~L  ~K  ~L  ~L  ~L  ~L                           J
~G  ~K  ~G  ~K      ~F  ~F
~F  ~G              ~G              L...F... G  K
~J                  ~M
```

22. If Griseldi's session is on the 5th, then which one of the following must be true?

⟶ Placing G on day 5 affects the L-F-GK string.

```
    L...F...
___ ___ ___ ___ G  K  ___
 ~L
```

⟶ Now, which of H, J, or M could take day 7? Not M (Rule 3). And not J, because either H and M would run afoul of Rule 1, or L would violate Rule 5. So, H takes day 7.

```
    M...J...
    L...F...
___ ___ ___ ___ G  K  H
 ~L
```

(A)	Farnham's session is on the 3rd.	⟶	Could be false—F could take days 2 or 4. Eliminate.
(B)	Heany's session is on the 7th.	⟶	Correct.
(C)	Juarez's session is on the 4th.	⟶	Could be false—J could take days 2 or 3. Eliminate.
(D)	Lightfoot's session is on the 1st.	⟶	Could be false—L could take day 3. Eliminate.
(E)	Moreau's session is on the 2nd.	⟶	Could be false—M could take days 1 or 3. Eliminate.

PrepTest61 Sec3 Q22

Note that, in this New-"If" sketch, J can teach session 2. Return to question 19 and eliminate **(A)**.

Could Be True Question

This next question is a Could be True question. Characterize the answer choices, consult the master sketch, and identify the correct answer.

LSAT Question	**My Analysis**

From the 1st through the 7th of next month, seven nurses—Farnham, Griseldi, Heany, Juarez, Khan, Lightfoot, and Moreau—will each conduct one information session at a community center. Each nurse's session will fall on a different day. The nurses' schedule is governed by the following constraints:

At least two of the other nurses' sessions must fall in between Heany's session and Moreau's session.

Griseldi's session must be on the day before Khan's.

Juarez's session must be on a later day than Moreau's.

Farnham's session must be on an earlier day than Khan's but on a later day than Lightfoot's.

Lightfoot cannot conduct the session on the 2nd.

F G H J K L M

```
 __   __   __   __   __   __   __
 1    2    3    4    5    6    7
~K   ~L   ~K   ~L   ~L   ~L   ~L
~G   ~K   ~G   ~K        ~F   ~F
~F   ~G             ~G
~J                  ~M
```

$$H/M \underline{\quad} \underline{\quad} \underline{\quad} \ldots M/H$$

$$J$$

$$J$$

$$L \ldots F \ldots \underline{G} \ \underline{K}$$

23. Lightfoot's session could be on which one of the following days?

   (A)   the 3rd

   (B)   the 4th

   (C)   the 5th

   (D)   the 6th

   (E)   the 7th

PrepTest61 Sec3 Q23

HINT: Where can you find help in answering this question? What alternative approaches are available to determine the correct answer or eliminate incorrect answers?

How an LSAT Expert Sees It
Could Be True Question

LSAT Question	Analysis

From the 1st through the 7th of next month, seven nurses—
Farnham, Griseldi, Heany, Juarez, Khan, Lightfoot, and
Moreau—will each conduct one information session at
a community center. Each nurse's session will fall on a
different day. The nurses' schedule is governed by the
following constraints:

At least two of the other nurses' sessions must fall in
between Heany's session and Moreau's session.

Griseldi's session must be on the day before Khan's.

Juarez's session must be on a later day than Moreau's.

Farnham's session must be on an earlier day than Khan's
but on a later day than Lightfoot's.

Lightfoot cannot conduct the session on the 2nd.

F G H J K L M

1	2	3	4	5	6	7
~K	~L	~K	~L	~L	~L	~L
~G	~K	~G	~K		~F	~F
~F	~G					~G
~J						~M

```
          J
         /
H/M ___ ___ ... M/H
         \
          J

L...F... G K
```

23. Lightfoot's session could be on which one of the
following days?

You know from the master sketch that Lightfoot
cannot conduct a session on day 4, 5, 6, or 7.
That leaves only one possibility among the answer
choices.

(A) the 3rd

Correct.

(B) the 4th

Must be false. Eliminate.

(C) the 5th

Must be false. Eliminate.

(D) the 6th

Must be false. Eliminate.

(E) the 7th

Must be false. Eliminate.

PrepTest61 Sec3 Q23

This question illustrates the value of making all available deductions in Step 4. With the complete master sketch in
place, answering this question correctly takes only a few seconds.

Back to Question 19

As you completed the other questions in this set, you were able to eliminate three of the wrong answers in question 19. Finish the game by returning to determine which of the remaining answers in question 19 is correct.

LSAT Question	My Analysis

From the 1st through the 7th of next month, seven nurses—Farnham, Griseldi, Heany, Juarez, Khan, Lightfoot, and Moreau—will each conduct one information session at a community center. Each nurse's session will fall on a different day. The nurses' schedule is governed by the following constraints:

At least two of the other nurses' sessions must fall in between Heany's session and Moreau's session.

Griseldi's session must be on the day before Khan's.

Juarez's session must be on a later day than Moreau's.

Farnham's session must be on an earlier day than Khan's but on a later day than Lightfoot's.

Lightfoot cannot conduct the session on the 2nd.

→

F G H J K L M

1	2	3	4	5	6	7
~K	~L	~K	~L	~L	~L	~L
~G	~K	~G	~K		~F	~F
~F	~G					~G
~J						~M

H/M __ __ __ ... M/H   J /

→ J \

L...F... G K

19. Juarez's session CANNOT be on which one of the following days?

→ Rule 3 eliminates Juarez from day 1, but that doesn't help with any of the answer choices.

(A) the 2nd

→ Question 22 proved that Juarez could be second. Eliminate.

(B) the 3rd

→ Question 20 proved that Juarez could be third. Eliminate.

(C) the 5th

→

(D) the 6th

→

(E) the 7th

PrepTest61 Sec3 Q19

→ Question 21 proved that Juarez could be seventh. Eliminate.

HINT: How many of the remaining answers will you need to check before completing the question?

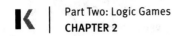

How an LSAT Expert Sees It
Could Be True Question

LSAT Question	Analysis

From the 1st through the 7th of next month, seven nurses—Farnham, Griseldi, Heany, Juarez, Khan, Lightfoot, and Moreau—will each conduct one information session at a community center. Each nurse's session will fall on a different day. The nurses' schedule is governed by the following constraints:

   At least two of the other nurses' sessions must fall in between Heany's session and Moreau's session.
   Griseldi's session must be on the day before Khan's.
   Juarez's session must be on a later day than Moreau's.
   Farnham's session must be on an earlier day than Khan's but on a later day than Lightfoot's.
   Lightfoot cannot conduct the session on the 2nd.

F G H J K L M

1	2	3	4	5	6	7
~K	~L	~K	~L	~L	~L	~L
~G	~K	~G	~K		~F	~F
~F	~G					~G
~J						~M

H/M __ __ __ . . . M/H

        J
       /
L . . . F . . . G K

J
 \
H/M

19. Juarez's session CANNOT be on which one of the following days?

Rule 3 eliminates Juarez from day 1, but that doesn't help with any of the answer choices.

(A) the 2nd

Question 22 proved that Juarez could be second. Eliminate.

(B) the 3rd

Question 20 proved that Juarez could be third. Eliminate.

(C) the 5th

Correct—must be false. With J on day 5, a problem arises for the GK block. If G and K take days 6 and 7, H and M would need to take days 1 and 4, but that violates Rule 5 by placing L on day 2.

H/M ~L̸ F M/H J G K

If the L-F-GK string takes days 1–4, H and M are forced to take days 6 and 7, violating Rule 1.

L F G K J H/M̸ M/H̸

(D) the 6th

For the record: L-F-M-G-K-J-H and L-M-F-G-K-J-H are acceptable. Eliminate.

(E) the 7th

PrepTest61 Sec3 Q19

Question 21 also proved that Juarez could be seventh. Eliminate.

The LSAT expert is finished with the questions in this set and is ready to confidently move on to the next game or the next section.

REFLECTION

Now that you've seen the Logic Games Method, take a few minutes to reflect on the following questions.

- Did any part of the Logic Games Method surprise you?
- Are there specific steps in the Logic Games Method that excite you?
- Were any of the steps confusing? How will you get additional practice with those steps?
- How will you approach Logic Games differently the next time you practice them?
- What techniques did you see applied to the game in this chapter that you can immediately put to use the next time you practice Logic Games?

As you practice Logic Games further, review the explanations thoroughly. The explanations will cover each step in the Logic Games Method and help make clear how every game can be done most efficiently and effectively.

The remaining chapters of this section will delve deeper into the steps of the Logic Games Method and apply it to all of the game types that regularly appear on the LSAT.

- Chapter 3 covers Steps 1 and 2—Overview and Sketch.
- Chapter 4 takes you deeper into Steps 3 and 4—Rules and Deductions.
- Chapter 5 examines Step 5—Questions.
- Chapter 6 contains 20 recent Logic Games for further practice.
- Chapter 7 has a recent Logic Games section for timing and section management practice.

Logic Games: Overviews, Sketches, and Game Types

Now that you've seen how an expert tackles an entire game, focus on just the first two steps: assessing a game's overview and making a useful sketch. In this chapter, you will practice Steps 1 and 2 of the Logic Games Method on all of the common game actions. Knowing the different types of games will help you make sketches quickly and efficiently.

LEARNING OBJECTIVES

In this chapter, you'll learn to:

- Characterize a game's action and limitations given various game setups
- Create a valid sketch based on a game's action and limitations
- Identify and differentiate among game types

Start with Step 1 of the Logic Games Method: understanding the game's overview. By "overview" we mean just the part that is highlighted here.

> A clown will select a costume consisting of two pieces and no others: a jacket and overalls. One piece of the costume will be entirely one color, and the other piece will be plaid. Selection is subject to the following restrictions:
>
>   If the jacket is plaid, then there must be exactly three colors in it.
>   If the overalls are plaid, then there must be exactly two colors in them.
>   The jacket and overalls must have exactly one color in common.
>   Green, red, and violet are the only colors that can be in the jacket.
>   Red, violet, and yellow are the only colors that can be in the overalls.

PrepTest51 Sec4 Qs 1–5

We will discuss the indented part—the rules—in depth in Chapter 4.

As you read through the overview, focus specifically on answering the four key questions—the SEAL questions—introduced in Chapter 2.

STEP 1: OVERVIEW—THE SEAL QUESTIONS

Situation—What is the real-world scenario being described? What is the deliverable information—an ordered list, a calendar, a chart showing what's matched up?

Entities—Who or what are the "moving parts," the people or things I'm distributing, selecting, sequencing, or matching?

Action—What is the specific action—distribution, selection, sequencing, matching, or a combination of those—that I'm performing on the entities?

Limitations—Does the game state parameters (e.g., select four of seven, sequence the entities one per day, etc.) that restrict how I'll set up and sketch the game?

The most important of the SEAL questions is the one that asks for the game's action. Are you arranging entities in order? Distributing them into groups? Choosing some and not others? Once you determine the game's action, you can create the appropriate sketch in which to organize the game's entities, restrictions, and rules.

STEP 1 OF THE LOGIC GAMES METHOD: WORKING WITH GAME OVERVIEWS

There are four* main game actions in LSAT Logic Games.

- Sequencing (putting entities in order)
- Selection (choosing a select group of entities from a larger group)
- Matching (assigning attributes to entities)
- Distribution (organizing entities into groups)

*There are also Hybrid games, which combine more than one of the four game actions.

Take another look at the overview from the Nurses' Information Sessions game discussed in Chapter 2. Note how an LSAT expert quickly identifies the four key components of the overview.

LSAT Question	Analysis
From the 1st through the 7th of next month, seven nurses—Farnham, Griseldi, Heany, Juarez, Khan, Lightfoot, and Moreau—will each conduct one information session at a community center. Each nurse's session will fall on a different day. The nurses' schedule is governed by the following constraints: *PrepTest61 Sec3 Qs 18–23*	**Step 1:** **Situation:** Nurses conducting different information sessions–this is a calendaring task **Entities:** The seven nurses—F, G, H, J, K, L, and M **Action:** Schedule the nurses' sessions by determining their order (note the language "Each ... session will fall on a different day"). **Limitations:** Different nurse on each day

Practice

Now, try some yourself. For each one of the following game-like overviews, answer the SEAL questions to get a feel for the game. Pay special attention to the words and phrases that provide clues to the game's task or action (Sequencing, Matching, Distribution, Selection, or Hybrid, a combination of two or more).

Game	My Analysis
1. Exactly five runners—A, B, C, D, and E—are ranked according to their speed at the end of a race from first place to last place. There are no ties. The ranking must be consistent with the following conditions: →	**Step 1:** **Situation:** **Entities:** **Action:** **Limitations:**

Game	My Analysis
2. From a group of seven auditioning actors—A, B, C, D, E, F, and G—exactly four will be cast in speaking roles. Selection must conform to the following specifications: →	**Step 1:** **Situation:** **Entities:** **Action:** **Limitations:**

Game	My Analysis
3. Exactly four bakers—P, Q, R, and S—will each bake at least one of the following kinds of bread: cornbread, frybread, pumpernickel, sourdough, and whole wheat. The bakers will bake bread according to the following conditions:	**Step 1:** **Situation:** **Entities:** **Action:** **Limitations:**

Game	My Analysis
4. At a sailing camp, each of six children—Q, R, S, T, X, and Z—will be assigned to exactly one of two vessels—a catamaran or a dinghy. Each vessel can hold a maximum of four people. The assignments must conform to the following conditions:	**Step 1:** **Situation:** **Entities:** **Action:** **Limitations:**

Game	My Analysis
5. At the start of a race, exactly five bicyclists—A, B, C, D, and E—are lined up in positions 1 through 5, from left to right. Each bicyclist is wearing a green, a red, or a white shirt.	**Step 1:** **Situation:** **Entities:** **Action:** **Limitations:**

Expert Analysis

Here's how an LSAT expert would look at each of those game scenarios.

Game	Analysis
1. Exactly five runners—A, B, C, D, and E—are ranked according to their speed at the end of a race from first place to last place. There are no ties. The ranking must be consistent with the following conditions: →	**Step 1:** **Situation:** Runners at a race **Entities:** The five runners—A, B, C, D, and E **Action:** Sequencing. Rank the runners from first to fifth. **Limitations:** No ties, so each position needs to be filled by exactly one runner

Game	Analysis
2. From a group of seven auditioning actors—A, B, C, D, E, F, and G—exactly four will be cast in speaking roles. Selection must conform to the following specifications: →	**Step 1:** **Situation:** Actors auditioning for parts **Entities:** The seven auditioning actors—A, B, C, D, E, F, and G **Action:** Selection. Determine which four of the seven actors are being selected for speaking parts. **Limitations:** Must pick four exactly

Game	Analysis
3. Exactly four bakers—P, Q, R, and S—will each bake at least one of the following kinds of bread: cornbread, frybread, pumpernickel, sourdough, and whole wheat. The bakers will bake bread according to the following conditions: →	**Step 1:** **Situation:** Bakers baking breads **Entities:** The four bakers—P, Q, R, and S—and the different types of bread—c, f, p, s, w **Action:** Matching. Determine which type[s] of bread each baker will bake. **Limitations:** Each baker bakes at least one type of bread, but no limit to maximum number of bread types he can bake

Game	Analysis
4. At a sailing camp, each of six children—Q, R, S, T, X, and Z—will be assigned to exactly one of two vessels—a catamaran or a dinghy. Each vessel can hold a maximum of four people. The assignments must conform to the following conditions: →	**Step 1:** **Situation:** Children assigned to vessels at sailing camp **Entities:** The six children—Q, R, S, T, X, and Z **Action:** Distribution. Assign the children to one of the two vessels: the catamaran or the dinghy. **Limitations:** Maximum of four children in each vessel; by deduction, then, a minimum of two in each vessel

Game	Analysis
5. At the start of a race, exactly five bicyclists—A, B, C, D, and E—are lined up in positions 1 through 5, from left to right. Each bicyclist is wearing a green, a red, or a white shirt. →	**Step 1:** **Situation:** Five bicyclists at the start of a race **Entities:** The bicyclists—A, B, C, D, and E—and the color of their shirts—green, red, or white **Action:** Hybrid—Sequencing/Matching. Determine the order in which the bicyclists are arranged, and match a color to the shirt of each bicyclist. **Limitations:** Exactly one bicyclist per position; no limitation on the number of shirts that can be a specific color

STEP 2 OF THE LOGIC GAMES METHOD: MAKING A SKETCH

After reading the overview and answering the SEAL questions, move on to Step 2: creating a sketch. Steps 1 and 2 are intertwined: The game's action and limitations will dictate your sketch for that game.

As a quick refresher, here's how the LSAT expert created the sketch for the Nurses' Information Sessions game.

LSAT Question	Analysis
From the 1st through the 7th of next month, seven nurses—Farnham, Griseldi, Heany, Juarez, Khan, Lightfoot, and Moreau—will each conduct one information session at a community center. Each nurse's session will fall on a different day. The nurses' schedule is governed by the following constraints: *PrepTest61 Sec3 Qs 18–23*	**Step 1:** **Situation:** Nurses conducting different information sessions—this is a calendaring task **Entities:** The seven nurses—F, G, H, J, K, L, and M **Action:** Schedule the nurses' sessions by determining their order (note the language "Each ... session will fall on a different day"). **Limitations:** A different nurse on each day **Step 2:** **Sketch:**

$$\begin{array}{ccccccc} \text{F} & \text{G} & \text{H} & \text{J} & \text{K} & \text{L} & \text{M} \\ \underline{} & \underline{} & \underline{} & \underline{} & \underline{} & \underline{} & \underline{} \\ 1 & 2 & 3 & 4 & 5 & 6 & 7 \end{array}$$

STEP 2: THE SKETCH

· Create a sketch that depicts the game's action(s) and limitations.
· Aim for a sketch that is easy to read, quick to replicate, and able to account for what is certain and uncertain based on the game's rules.

Practice

Revisit the overviews you've just analyzed. For each, create sketches that depict the situation, entities, action, and limitations present.

Game	My Analysis
6. Exactly five runners—A, B, C, D, and E—are ranked according to their speed at the end of a race from first place to last place. There are no ties. The ranking must be consistent with the following conditions:	**Action(s):** **Sketch:** $\longrightarrow$

Game	My Analysis
7. From a group of seven auditioning actors—A, B, C, D, E, F, and G—exactly four will be cast in speaking roles. Selection must conform to the following specifications:	**Action(s):** **Sketch:** $\longrightarrow$

Game	My Analysis
8. Exactly four bakers—P, Q, R, and S—will each bake at least one of the following kinds of bread: cornbread, frybread, pumpernickel, sourdough, and whole wheat. The bakers will bake bread according to the following conditions: $\longrightarrow$	**Action(s):** **Sketch:**

Game	My Analysis
9. At a sailing camp, each of six children—Q, R, S, T, X, and Z—will be assigned to exactly one of two vessels—a catamaran or a dinghy. Each vessel can hold a maximum of four people. The assignments must conform to the following conditions: $\longrightarrow$	**Action(s):** **Sketch:**

Game	My Analysis
10. At the start of a race, exactly five bicyclists—A, B, C, D, and E—are lined up in positions 1 through 5, from left to right. Each bicyclist is wearing a green, red, or white shirt. $\longrightarrow$	**Action(s):** **Sketch:**

Expert Analysis

Here are the sketches an LSAT expert might make for the games in the preceding exercise.

Game	Analysis
6. Exactly five runners—A, B, C, D, and E—are ranked according to their speed at the end of a race from first place to last place. There are no ties. The ranking must be consistent with the following conditions:	**Action(s):** Sequencing. Rank the runners from first to fifth. **Sketch:** A B C D E ⎯ ⎯ ⎯ ⎯ ⎯ 1 2 3 4 5

Game	Analysis
7. From a group of seven auditioning actors—A, B, C, D, E, F and G—exactly four will be cast in speaking roles. Selection must conform to the following specifications:	**Action(s):** Selection. Determine which four of the seven actors are being selected for speaking parts. **Sketch:** A B C D E F G (pick 4) Or A B C D E F G in ⎪ out ⎯ ⎯ ⎯ ⎯ ⎪ ⎯ ⎯ ⎯

	Game	**Analysis**

Game

8. Exactly four bakers—P, Q, R, and S—will each bake at least one of the following kinds of bread: cornbread, frybread, pumpernickel, sourdough, and whole wheat. The bakers will bake bread according to the following conditions:

Analysis

Action: Matching. Determine which bread types each baker will bake.

Sketch: As a table:

breads: c f p s w

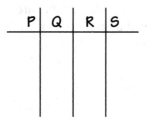

P	Q	R	S

→ Or as a grid:

	P	Q	R	S
c				
f				
p				
s				
w				

Game	Analysis

9. At a sailing camp, each of six children—Q, R, S, T, X, and Z—will be assigned to exactly one of two vessels—a catamaran or a dinghy. Each vessel can hold a maximum of four people. The assignments must conform to the following conditions:

Action: Distribution. Assign the children to one of the two vessels: the catamaran or the dinghy.

Sketch:

Children: Q R S T X Z

$\longrightarrow$ (2–4)   (2–4)

cat | ding

Game	Analysis

10. At the start of a race, exactly five bicyclists—A, B, C, D, and E—are lined up in positions 1 through 5, from left to right. Each bicyclist is wearing a green, a red, or a white shirt.

Action: Hybrid–Sequencing/Matching. Determine the order in which the bicyclists are arranged, and match a color to the shirt of each bicyclist.

Sketch:

$\longrightarrow$

__ __ __ __ __ A B C D E

__ __ __ __ __ grn/red/wht

   1   2   3   4   5

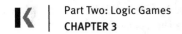
GAME TYPES

When we say that there are a limited number of game types, we really mean that there are a limited number of *actions* used in Logic Games. That's because the action determines the types of sketches you'll use to account for the entities, rules, and restrictions.

Sequencing Games

By far, the most common Logic Game action is Sequencing. Because these games ask you to put entities in order, the sketch for a Sequencing game is most often a series of horizontal dashes representing the open positions. Occasionally, a game will use language indicating that you are placing entities "above," "below," "higher," or "lower" than one another. When this happens, it may be more effective to arrange the dashes vertically. One variant among Sequencing games—the Loose Sequencing game, discussed further a little later—requires no framework (no dashes) at all. In Loose Sequencing, you'll account for the positions of entities relative to one another.

Here's the expert analysis on a standard Sequencing game you saw earlier in the chapter.

Game	Analysis
Exactly five runners—A, B, C, D, and E—are ranked according to their speed at the end of a race from first place to last place. There are no ties. The ranking must be consistent with the following conditions:	**Step 1:** **Situation:** Runners at a race **Entities:** The five runners—A, B, C, D, and E **Action:** Sequencing. Rank the runners from first to fifth. → **Limitations:** No ties, so each position needs to be filled by exactly one runner **Step 2:** **Sketch:** A B C D E — — — — — 1 2 3 4 5

Practice

Now it's your turn. Take a look at these basic overviews. Answer the SEAL questions and generate a master sketch for each.

Game	My Analysis
11. Exactly five students—L, M, N, O, and P— are being lined up for a school picture. The students are arranged by height from tallest (first) to shortest (last). Their order must be consistent with the following conditions:	**Step 1:** **Situation:** **Entities:** **Action:** **Limitations:** → **Step 2:** **Sketch:**

Game	My Analysis
12. Professor Jones is scheduling his office hour appointments for next week. During the week he needs to meet with exactly four students—H, J, K, and L. He has one available spot on each day from Monday through Friday. He meets with each student exactly once. The meetings must be consistent with the following conditions:	**Step 1:** **Situation:** **Entities:** **Action:** **Limitations:** → **Step 2:** **Sketch:**

Game	My Analysis

13. A conference center is arranging its schedule for the following week. It has available rooms on Monday, Tuesday, and Wednesday. On each day, there is a morning reservation and an afternoon reservation. Six companies will be making appointments: A, B, C, D, E, and F. No two companies can share the same reservation. The schedule must conform to the following conditions:

→

Step 1:

Situation:

Entities:

Action:

Limitations:

Step 2:

Sketch:

Game	My Analysis

14. Shady Glen Apartments is a residential building with exactly six open apartments. At least one of the apartments on each of the building's four floors is open. At the beginning of the month, exactly six renters—G, H, J, K, L, and M—will move into Shady Glen. Each renter will occupy exactly one of the open apartments. The following conditions apply:

→

Step 1:

Situation:

Entities:

Action:

Limitations:

Step 2:

Sketch:

Expert Analysis: Sequencing Games

Here's how an LSAT expert might analyze and diagram those game scenarios.

Game	Analysis
11. Exactly five students—L, M, N, O, and P—are being lined up for a school picture. The students are arranged by height from tallest (first) to shortest (last). Their order must be consistent with the following conditions:	**Step 1:** **Situation:** Students in a classroom **Entities:** The students—L, M, N, O, and P **Action:** Sequencing. Order the students by height from tallest to shortest. → **Limitations:** No limitations **Step 2:** **Sketch:** L M N O P (tall) ‾1‾ ‾2‾ ‾3‾ ‾4‾ ‾5‾ (short)

Game	Analysis
12. Professor Jones is scheduling his office hour appointments for next week. During the week he needs to meet with exactly four students—H, J, K, and L. He has one available spot on each day from Monday through Friday. He meets with each student exactly once. The meetings must be consistent with the following conditions:	**Step 1:** **Situation:** Professor meeting with students **Entities:** The students—H, J, K, and L **Action:** Sequencing. Schedule each of four students on one of five days. **Limitations:** Only one available spot on each day, so there is no overlap. On one of the days, there will be no appointment. **Step 2:** **Sketch:**

H J K L

—— —— —— —— ——
M   Tu   W   Th   Fr

Game	Analysis
13. A conference center is arranging its schedule for the following week. It has available rooms on Monday, Tuesday, and Wednesday. On each day there is a morning reservation and an afternoon reservation. Six companies will be making appointments: A, B, C, D, E, and F. No two companies can share the same reservation. The schedule must conform to the following conditions:	**Step 1:** **Situation:** Companies reserving rooms at specific times

Entities: The companies—A, B, C, D, E, and F—the days—Monday, Tuesday, and Wednesday—and the time of day—morning and afternoon

Action: Sequencing. Determine the order in which the companies reserve the rooms.

→ **Limitations:** Only one company can reserve rooms at a time—no overlap

Step 2:

Sketch:

Companies: A B C D E F

	Mon	Tues	Wed
Morning			
Afternoon			

Game	Analysis

14. Shady Glen Apartments is a residential building with exactly six open apartments. At least one of the apartments on each of the building's four floors is open. At the beginning of the month, exactly six renters—G, H, J, K, L, and M—will move into Shady Glen. Each renter will occupy exactly one of the open apartments. The following conditions apply:

Step 1:

Situation: Renters moving into different apartments in a four-story building

Entities: The renters—G, H, J, K, L, and M

Action: Sequencing. Figure out which floor each renter moves into.

Limitations: Each floor has at least one apartment. This means that either two floors have two apartments each and two floors have one apartment each OR one floor has three apartments and three floors have one apartment each. Each renter occupies exactly one apartment.

Step 2:

Sketch:

G H J K L M

4 ___

3 ___   (___)

2 ___   (___) [2 apts, floor unknown]

1 ___

(Apts/floor: 2 × 2 and 2 × 1
          OR
          1 × 3 and 3 × 1)

Loose Sequencing Games

Loose Sequencing is a variant of Sequencing games in which the preponderance of the rules determines the positions of entities relative to one another—e.g., "A is earlier than B" or "C is ranked higher than F but lower than K." Unlike the rules in standard Strict Sequencing games, Loose Sequencing rules *never* establish definite relationships—e.g., "A and B are in consecutive spaces" or "C is ranked exactly two positions higher than F." Moreover, Loose Sequencing games do *not* contain rules that place entities into specific positions—e.g., "B is seated in chair 7" or "M is ranked third." An effective sketch for these games captures the relative relationships between and among entities. No framework of numbered spaces is necessary because nothing is known about the specific positions of the entities.

> ## LSAT STRATEGY
>
> To distinguish Strict Sequencing from Loose Sequencing, check the indented rules. Loose Sequencing rules:
>
> · Give only relative relationships between or among entities
> · Never define the precise number of spaces between two entities, and
> · Never place entities into specific, numbered spaces in the sequence

The opening paragraphs of Strict Sequencing and Loose Sequencing games may appear identical. After all, both task you with arranging entities in some sort of order. Here's an example:

Jolie is creating a mix tape for a friend. She will include six songs—M, N, P, Q, R, and S. She will arrange the order of the songs according to the following restrictions:
    P will play before N.
    N will play before M and Q.
    M will play after R.
    S will play after Q.

It's not until you see that all of the indented rules give only relative relationships that you realize that this is a classic Loose Sequencing game. In Chapter 4, you'll have much more practice with the Rules and Deductions steps of the Logic Games Method. By then, you'll spot the differences between Strict and Loose Sequencing almost automatically. For now, just know that Loose Sequencing, when you spot it, rewards a slightly different kind of sketch.

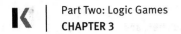
Take a look at how an LSAT expert might analyze and sketch the Loose Sequencing setup you saw on the preceding page.

Situation	Analysis

Jolie is creating a mix tape for a friend. She will include six songs—M, N, P, Q, R, and S. She will arrange the order of the songs according to the following restrictions:
    P will play before N.
    N will play before M and Q.
    M will play after R.
    S will play after Q.
	Step 1:
	
	Situation: Arranging the songs on a mix tape
	
	Entities: The songs—M, N, P, Q, R, and S
	
	Action: Sequencing. Determine the order of the songs.
	
	Limitations: [Implicit: The songs go onto the tape one at a time.]
	
	Step 2:
	
	Sketch:
	
	(A vertical arrangement like a family tree:)
	
	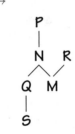
	
	(Or, a horizontal web of Loose Sequencing rules:)
	
	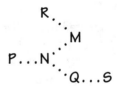

TEST DAY TIP

Loose Sequencing rules almost always account for all of the entities in the game. Thus, your sketch will show the relative relationship of every entity with at least one of the other entities in the game.

Practice

Here's another Loose Sequencing overview. How do you know this is a Loose Sequencing game? How would you create the master sketch, and what would it look like?

Game	My Analysis

15. Seven runners—P, Q, R, S, T, U, and W—are running a race. They are ranked in order from first to last, with no ties, according to the following conditions:
  Q places earlier than R but later than S.
  P places later than R.
  Both R and W place earlier than U.
  T places earlier than Q.
	Step 1:
	
	Situation:
	
	Entities:
	
	Action:
	
	Limitations:
	
	Step 2:
	
	Sketch:

$\longrightarrow$

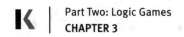

Expert Analysis: Loose Sequencing Games

Here's how an LSAT expert might analyze and sketch the Loose Sequencing example.

Game	Analysis
15. Seven runners—P, Q, R, S, T, U, and W—are running a race. They are ranked in order from first to last, with no ties, according to the following conditions: Q places earlier than R but later than S. P places later than R. Both R and W place earlier than U. T places earlier than Q.	**Step 1:** **Situation:** Runners in a race **Entities:** The seven runners—P, Q, R, S, T, U, and W **Action:** Sequencing. Rank the runners in order from first to last. **Limitations:** No ties $\rightarrow$ **Step 2:** **Sketch:** [Because all of the rules establish relative positions between entities, a Loose Sequencing sketch is appropriate.] P Q R S T U W S...........P T...Q...R...U ....W

We'll revisit this sketch when we discuss deductions in Chapter 4. For now, take a moment to reflect on Sequencing games.

Selection Games

Some games ask you to simply select a subset of entities from a larger group of entities. These games, called Selection games, are dominated by rules containing conditional Formal Logic statements.

The Selection game you saw earlier in this chapter is reprinted here. A sketch for a Selection game is often just the list of entities; you can circle those selected and/or cross out those rejected as you encounter the rules, deductions, and New-"If" conditions in the questions. If the game stipulates the number of entities to be selected, you may choose to use an "in/out" sketch instead.

Game	Analysis
From a group of seven auditioning actors—A, B, C, D, E, F, and G—exactly four will be cast in speaking roles. Selection must conform to the following specifications:	**Step 1:** **Situation:** Actors auditioning for parts **Entities:** The seven auditioning actors—A, B, C, D, E, F, and G **Action:** Selection. Determine which four of the seven actors are being selected for speaking parts. **Limitations:** Must pick four exactly $\longrightarrow$ **Step 2:** **Sketch:** A B C D E F G (pick 4) Or A B C D E F G in | out — — — —|— — —

TEST DAY TIP

Selection games may:

- Define the exact number of entities to be selected (e.g., choose four of seven)
- Define a minimum number of entities to be selected (e.g., hire at least three of the applicants), or
- Tell you only that some entities are selected (e.g., Jane is considering eight items she might buy for her house. Her purchase decisions will conform to the following...). In the latter case, anticipate questions about the minimum or maximum that may be selected.

Practice

Now, take a look at these basic overviews. Answer the SEAL questions and generate a master sketch for each.

Game	My Analysis
16. A landscape designer is creating a garden plan for a homeowner who wishes to plant exactly four annual and exactly two perennial plants. The designer will choose annuals from among species G, H, J, L, M and N, and perennials from among species S, T, U, V, and W. The following conditions must apply:	**Step 1:** **Situation:** **Entities:** **Action:** **Limitations:** **Step 2:** **Sketch:** $\longrightarrow$

Game	My Analysis
17. A real estate agent visits a bakery to purchase at least one kind of treat for his upcoming open house. The bakery carries the following items: B, C, E, F, G, and J. The bakery does not carry any other items. The real estate agent's selection of treats must conform to the following conditions:	**Step 1:** **Situation:** **Entities:** **Action:** **Limitations:** → **Step 2:** **Sketch:**

Game	My Analysis
18. A pet shelter has a number of dogs and cats (but no other animals) available for adoption. The dogs are of breeds B, C, D, G, and J; the cats are of breeds M, P, S, and T. At least one animal will be adopted, according to the following guidelines:	**Step 1:** **Situation:** **Entities:** **Action:** **Limitations:** **Step 2:** → **Sketch:**

Expert Analysis: Selection Games

Compare your analyses to those of an LSAT expert.

Game	Analysis
16. A landscape designer is creating a garden plan for a homeowner who wishes to plant exactly four annual and exactly two perennial plants. The designer will choose annuals from among species G, H, J, L, M, and N, and perennials from among species S, T, U, V, and W. The following conditions must apply:	**Step 1:** **Situation:** A landscape designer picking plants for a garden **Entities:** The various plants: six types of annuals—G, H, J, L, M, N—and five types of perennials—s, t, u, v, w **Action:** While there are two different types of plants here, we're still just picking some of each, indicating that this is a pure Selection game. **Limitations:** Here, both the number and the types of plants are specified. Of the six plants chosen, four must be annuals and two must be perennials. → **Step 2:** **Sketch:** This Selection sketch must reflect the fact that there are two different types of entities. *ann. (4)* *peren. (2)* G H J L M N s t u v w Or Ann. In Out ___ ___ ___ ___｜___ ___ Peren. In ｜ Out ___ ___｜___ ___ ___

Game	Analysis
17. A real estate agent visits a bakery to purchase at least one kind of treat for his upcoming open house. The bakery carries the following items: B, C, E, F, G, and J. The bakery does not carry any other items. The real estate agent's selection of treats must conform to the following conditions:	**Step 1:**

Situation: A real estate agent is choosing baked treats to serve at an open house.

Entities: The treats—B, C, E, F, G, J

Action: Selection. One or more types of treats must be chosen from a larger group.

→ **Limitations:** A minimum of one treat out of the six must be chosen. If this limitation were not included, it would be possible, though unlikely, that a question could provide a condition under which nothing is selected.

Step 2:

Sketch: A simple list of entities will suffice for this game's sketch.

B C E F G J

Game	Analysis

18. A pet shelter has a number of dogs and cats (but no other animals) available for adoption. The dogs are of breeds B, C, D, G, and J; the cats are of breeds M, P, S, and T. At least one animal will be adopted, according to the following guidelines:	**Step 1:**
	
	Situation: Cats and dogs up for adoption at an animal shelter
	
	Entities: Dogs of five breeds—B, C, D, G, J—and cats of four breeds—m, p, s, t
	
	Action: Selection. Pick at least one animal from among the available breeds.
	
	Limitations: In this overview, the only limitation is at least one animal is chosen. There is as yet no limitation on the number of dogs or cats, or on the number of animals of a particular breed that may be adopted. It's possible, for example, that two dogs of breed B and one dog of breed J, and no cats, are adopted. Anticipate that the rules will impose restrictions along these lines.
	
	Step 2:
	
	Sketch: The two types of entities in this sketch should be distinguished.
	
	    dog breeds (#?) **cat breeds (#?)**
	    B C D G J m p s t

Matching Games

In Matching games, you'll be given two types of entities: One set of entities will be more concrete or tangible, while the other set will be made up of possible traits or characteristics of the members of the first set. To create a master sketch for a Matching game, place the information in a table or grid.

Here is the LSAT expert's analysis of the Matching game you saw earlier in the chapter.

Game	Analysis
Exactly four bakers—P, Q, R, and S—will each bake at least one of the following kinds of bread: cornbread, frybread, pumpernickel, sourdough, and whole wheat. The bakers will bake bread according to the following conditions:	**Step 1:** **Situation:** Bakers baking breads **Entities:** The four bakers—P, Q, R, and S—and the types of bread—c, f, p, s, and w **Action:** Matching. Determine which bread types each baker will bake. **Limitations:** Each baker bakes at least one type of bread, but no limit to maximum number of bread types he can bake **Step 2:** **Sketch:** As a table:

breads: c f p s w

$$\rightarrow \quad \frac{P \mid Q \mid R \mid S}{}$$

Or as a grid:

	P	Q	R	S
c				
f				
p				
s				
w				

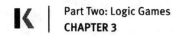

Practice

Now, take a look at these basic overviews. Answer the SEAL questions and generate a master sketch for each.

Game	My Analysis
19. Each of exactly five newly created types of cell phones—J, K, L, M, and N—will contain at least one of the following features: conferencing, GPS, touch screen, voice command, and web browsing. Features will be matched to cell phones according to the following restrictions:	**Step 1:** **Situation:** **Entities:** **Action:** **Limitations:** **Step 2:** **Sketch:**

$\longrightarrow$

Game	My Analysis
20. Two new houses, 1 and 2, are being built. Each house's front door, garage door, and window frames will be painted. The colors available for painting are blue, green, and yellow. No color will be used more than once in each house. Paint colors will be assigned according to the following conditions:	**Step 1:** **Situation:** **Entities:** **Action:** **Limitations:** → **Step 2:** **Sketch:**

Game	My Analysis
21. A minting company is tasked with manufacturing new coins for currency. Coins will be one of three sizes—small, medium, and large. Each coin minted will consist entirely of one of the following kinds of materials: copper, gold, and nickel. The company will manufacture coins in accordance with the following restrictions:	**Step 1:** **Situation:** **Entities:** **Action:** **Limitations:** → **Step 2:** **Sketch:**

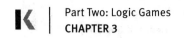
Expert Analysis: Matching Games

Here's how an LSAT expert might analyze and sketch the game tasks from this exercise.

LSAT Question	Analysis
19. Each of exactly five newly created types of cell phones—J, K, L, M, and N—will contain at least one of the following features: conferencing, GPS, touch screen, voice command, and web browsing. Features will be matched to cell phones according to the following restrictions:	**Step 1:** **Situation:** Cell phone manufacturer **Entities:** Types of cell phones—J, K, L, M, and N—and their features—Conferencing, GPS, touch screen, voice command, and web browsing **Action:** Matching the types of cell phones to their features **Limitations:** Each type of cell phone has at least one of the five features. **Step 2:** **Sketch:** Features: c g t v w

$$\begin{array}{|c|c|c|c|c|} \hline J & K & L & M & N \\ \hline & & & & \\ & & & & \\ \hline \end{array}$$

LSAT Question	**Analysis**
20. Two new houses, 1 and 2, are being built. Each house's front door, garage door, and window frames will be painted. The colors available for painting are blue, green, and yellow. No color will be used more than once in each house. Paint colors will be assigned according to the following conditions:	**Step 1:** **Situation:** Construction site building houses **Entities:** The houses—1 and 2; the parts of the houses to be painted—front door, garage door, and window frames; and the available paint colors—blue, green, and yellow **Action:** Matching each house's part to the color used for painting it → **Limitations:** One color per house part; different colors across each row **Step 2:** **Sketch:**

Colors: b g y

	FD	GD	WF
1			
2			

LSAT Question	**Analysis**

21. A minting company is tasked with manufacturing new coins for currency. Coins will be one of three sizes—small, medium, and large. Each coin minted will consist entirely of one of the following kinds of materials: copper, gold, and nickel. The company will manufacture coins in accordance with the following restrictions:

$\longrightarrow$

Step 1:

Situation: Minting company making coins

Entities: The size of the coins—small, medium, and large—and their material—copper, gold, and nickel

Action: Matching coin size to material used

Limitations: Each coin minted is made of only one type of material

Step 2:

Sketch:

	c	g	n
S			
M			
L			

Distribution Games

The next game action, Distribution, is similar to Matching, with one big difference: In Matching games, the traits or characteristics can be shared by more than one fixed entity. For example, in a Matching game where your task is to assign colors to bicycles, it's possible that more than one bicycle is red. In Distribution games, you are being asked to place fixed entities into groups, and once an entity is placed, it cannot be used again. Distribution games can ask you to divvy up entities among (typically) two or three groups. The game's setup may or may not tell you the exact number of entities assigned to each group.

Revisit the Expert's Analysis of the Distribution game you saw earlier in the chapter.

LSAT Question	Analysis
At a sailing camp, each of six children—Q, R, S, T, X, and Z—will be assigned to exactly one of two vessels: a catamaran or a dinghy. Each vessel can hold a maximum of four people. The assignments must conform to the following conditions:	**Situation:** Children assigned to vessels at sailing camp **Entities:** The six children—Q, R, S, T, X, and Z **Action:** Distribution. Assign the children to one of the two vessels: the catamaran or the dinghy. **Limitations:** Maximum of four children in each vessel; by deduction, then, a minimum of two in each vessel **Sketch:** Children: Q R S T X Z (2–4) (2–4) cat | ding

Practice

Now, take a look at these basic overviews. Answer the SEAL questions and generate a master sketch for each.

LSAT Question	My Analysis
22. A local library has exactly seven volumes needing to be shelved—J, K, L, M, N, O, and P. There are three open shelves available, and each volume will occupy only one shelf. The following conditions must apply:	**Step 1:** **Situation:** **Entities:** **Action:** **Limitations:** **Step 2:** → **Sketch:**

LSAT Question	My Analysis
23. At a wedding reception, seven family members—A, B, C, D, E, F, and H—will be seated at three tables, numbered 1, 2, and 3. A, C, E, and H are from the bride's family. B, D, and F are from the groom's family. The seating arrangements are subject to the following conditions:	**Step 1:** **Situation:** **Entities:** **Action:** **Limitations:** → **Step 2:** **Sketch:**

LSAT Question	My Analysis
24. At a business retreat, eight managers—George, Heather, Ian, Janet, Katie, Lars, Maggie, and Nan—will be assigned to exactly one of two strategy teams: branding or sales. Each team will have four members. Each manager will participate on one team throughout the retreat. The following conditions apply:	**Step 1:** **Situation:** **Entities:** **Action:** **Limitations:** → **Step 2:** **Sketch:**

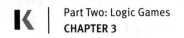
Expert Analysis: Distribution Games

Compare your work on those game scenarios to that of an LSAT expert.

Game	Analysis
22. A local library has exactly seven volumes needing to be shelved—J, K, L, M, N, O, and P. There are three open shelves available, and each volume will occupy only one shelf. The following conditions must apply:	**Step 1:** **Situation:** Volumes in a library needing to be shelved **Entities:** The seven volumes—J, K, L, M, N, O, and P—and three shelves **Action:** Distribute volumes onto shelves **Limitations:** Each volume occupies only one shelf → **Step 2:** **Sketch:** J K L M N O P 1	2	3

LSAT Question	**Analysis**
23. At a wedding reception, seven family members—A, B, C, D, E, F, and H—will be seated at three tables, numbered 1, 2, and 3. A, C, E, and H are from the bride's family. B, D, and F are from the groom's family. The seating arrangements are subject to the following conditions:	**Step 1:** **Situation:** Seating arrangements at a wedding reception. **Entities:** Seven family members—A, C, E, and H from the bride's family and b, d, and f from the groom's family **Action:** Distribute the family members among three tables **Limitations:** No explicit limitations, but anticipate that rules or questions will introduce restrictions on how many members of each family may or may not sit at a given table **Step 2:** **Sketch:** Bride: A C E H Groom: b d f

$$\begin{array}{c|c|c} 1 & 2 & 3 \\ \hline & & \\ & & \end{array}$$

Game	Analysis
24. At a business retreat, eight managers—George, Heather, Ian, Janet, Katie, Lars, Maggie, and Nan—will be assigned to exactly one of two strategy teams: branding or sales. Each team will have four members. Each manager will participate on one team throughout the retreat. The following conditions apply:	**Step 1:** **Situation:** Team membership at a business retreat **Entities:** Eight managers—G, H, I, J, K, L, M, and N **Action:** Distribute the managers between two strategy teams **Limitations:** Each strategy team has exactly four members, and once assigned, no managers will switch teams. **Step 2:** **Sketch:**

$\longrightarrow$

G H I J K L M N

Branding	Sales
—	—
—	—
—	—
—	—

Hybrid Games

A typical LSAT Logic Games section features one or two Hybrid games, mixing two or, rarely, three of the standard game actions. The most common Hybrid combines Sequencing and Matching actions. For example, a Sequencing/Matching Hybrid game might ask you to determine the order of speakers at a conference and then match the topic of the speech to each speaker. As you practice games from recent LSAT tests, you'll see several other Hybrid variations, such as Distribution/Sequencing, Selection/Distribution, and Selection/Matching.

Take another look at the following game, a Hybrid task you saw earlier in the chapter.

LSAT Question	Analysis
At the start of a race, exactly five bicyclists—A, B, C, D, and E—are lined up in positions 1 through 5, from left to right. Each bicyclist is wearing a green, a red, or a white shirt.	**Step 1:**
	Situation: Five bicyclists at the start of a race
	Entities: The bicyclists—A, B, C, D, and E—and the color of their shirts—green, red, or white
	Action: Hybrid—Sequencing/Matching. Determine the order in which the bicyclists are arranged, and match a color to the shirt of each bicyclist.
	→ **Limitations:** Exactly one bicyclist per position; no limitation on the number of shirts that can be a specific color
	Step 2:
	Sketch:
	__ __ __ __ __ A B C D E
	__ __ __ __ __ grn/red/wht
	1 2 3 4 5

LSAT STRATEGY

Don't be intimidated by Hybrid games. While Hybrids combine two or three actions, they usually present very simple versions of the individual tasks.

Practice

Now, take a look at these basic overviews. Answer the SEAL questions and generate a master sketch for each.

Game	My Analysis
25. At a summer camp, two teams of three campers each will participate in a swim relay. The two teams—Team 1 and Team 2—will be composed of the following six campers—F, G, H, J, K, and L. Each swimmer will swim either the first, second, or third leg of the relay.	**Step 1:** **Situation:** **Entities:** **Action:** **Limitations:** **Step 2:** → **Sketch:**

Game	My Analysis
26. Each of five advertising firms—A, B, C, D, and E—will occupy one of the first five floors of a new office building. Each floor will hold exactly one firm, and each firm will specialize in one of three advertising media: online, print, or television.	**Step 1:** **Situation:** **Entities:** **Action:** **Limitations:** ⟶ **Step 2:** **Sketch:**

Game	My Analysis
27. A local garden center is deciding which five of eight plants—M, N, O, P, Q, R, S, and T—to display in the center's greenhouse. Each of the plants produces a flower that is completely blue, completely yellow, or both blue and yellow.	**Step 1:** **Situation:** **Entities:** **Action:** **Limitations:** ⟶ **Step 2:** **Sketch:**

Expert Analysis: Hybrid Games

Here's how an LSAT expert might analyze and sketch the games from the Hybrid game exercise.

Game	Analysis
25. At a summer camp, two teams of three campers each will participate in a swim relay. The two teams—Team 1 and Team 2—will be composed of the following six campers—F, G, H, J, K, and L. Each swimmer will swim either the first, second, or third leg of the relay.	**Step 1:** **Situation:** Swimmers at a summer camp **Entities:** The two teams—1 and 2—and the campers—F, G, H, J, K, and L **Action:** Divide the campers into two teams, and then place them in order. This is a Hybrid game—Distribution and Sequencing. **Limitations:** Each swimmer assigned to one spot only **Step 2:** **Sketch:**

$\longrightarrow$

F G H J K L

	Team 1	Team 2
first:	___	___
second:	___	___
third:	___	___

or

F G H J K L
1st 2nd 3rd

Team 1   ___ ___ ___

Team 2   ___ ___ ___

Game	Analysis
26. Each of five advertising firms—A, B, C, D, and E—will occupy one of the first five floors of a new office building. Each floor will hold exactly one firm, and each firm will specialize in one of three advertising media: online, print, or television.	**Step 1:** **Situation:** Advertising firms occupying a building **Entities:** The ad firms—A, B, C, D, and E—and the different areas of specialty—o, p, and t **Action:** Assign the firms to floors and match them to a specialty. This is a Hybrid game—Sequencing and Matching. **Limitations:** One firm per floor; one speciality per firm **Step 2:** **Sketch:**

$\longrightarrow$

Floor Firm Spec.

5   __   __

4   __   __

3   __   __

2   __   __

1   __   __

Game	Analysis
27. A local garden center is deciding which five of eight plants—M, N, O, P, Q, R, S, and T—to display in the center's greenhouse. Each of the plants produces a flower that is completely blue, completely yellow, or both blue and yellow.	**Step 1:** **Situation:** Garden center display **Entities:** The eight plants—M, N, O, P, Q, R, S, and T—and the different colors—blue, yellow, or mix **Action:** Select five of eight plants and match a color to each. This is a Selection/Matching Hybrid game. **Limitations:** Pick only five plants; no limit on the number of plants of a certain color **Step 2:** **Sketch:** (A list for selection—circle selected entities and cross out rejected—and slots beneath each entity to account for the matching of color to plant)

→

(Choose 5)

M N O P Q R S T

— — — — — — — — blu/yel/mix

Or

(Two rows of slots: one to account for the plants that are in/out and one to account for the flower color)

In   Out

— — — — — | — — — M N O P Q R S T

— — — — — | — — — blu/yel/mix

PERFORM: LSAT LOGIC GAMES OVERVIEWS AND SKETCHES

Now that you're more familiar with Steps 1 and 2 of the Kaplan Method, try your hand at breaking down some actual LSAT game overviews. For each of these, answer the SEAL questions, and then create a sketch that is appropriate for the game's action(s) and limitations.

LSAT Question	My Analysis
28. A summer program offers at least one of the following seven courses: geography, history, literature, mathematics, psychology, sociology, zoology. The following restrictions on the program must apply: *PrepTest49 Sec1 Qs 13–17*	**Step 1:** **Situation:** **Entities:** **Action:** **Limitations:** **Step 2:** → **Sketch:**

LSAT Question	**My Analysis**
29. A museum curator is arranging seven photographs—*Fence, Gardenias, Hibiscus, Irises, Katydid, Lotus,* and *Magnolia*—on a gallery wall in accordance with the photographer's requirements. The photographs are to be hung along the wall in a row, in seven positions sequentially numbered from first to seventh. The photographer's requirements are as follows: *PrepTest59 Sec1 Qs 6–10*	**Step 1:** **Situation:** **Entities:** **Action:** **Limitations:** → **Step 2:** **Sketch:**

LSAT Question	**My Analysis**
30. A courier delivers exactly eight parcels—G, H, J, K, L, M, N, and O. No two parcels are delivered at the same time, nor is any parcel delivered more than once. The following conditions must apply: *PrepTest51 Sec4 Qs 16–22*	**Step 1:** **Situation:** **Entities:** **Action:** **Limitations:** → **Step 2:** **Sketch:**

LSAT Question	**My Analysis**
31. A clown will select a costume consisting of two pieces and no others: a jacket and overalls. One piece of the costume will be entirely one color, and the other piece will be plaid. Selection is subject to the following restrictions:	**Step 1:**
	Situation:
	Entities:
	Action:
PrepTest51 Sec4 Qs 1–5	**Limitations:**
$\longrightarrow$	**Step 2:**
	Sketch:

LSAT Question	**My Analysis**
32. Exactly six workers—Faith, Gus, Hannah, Juan, Kenneth, and Lisa—will travel to a business convention in two cars—car 1 and car 2. Each car must carry at least two of the workers, one of whom will be assigned to drive. For the entire trip, the workers will comply with an assignment that also meets the following constraints:	**Step 1:**
	Situation:
	Entities:
	Action:
PrepTest61 Sec3 Qs 1–5	**Limitations:**
$\longrightarrow$	**Step 2:**
	Sketch:

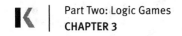
LSAT Question	**My Analysis**
33. A locally known guitarist's demo CD contains exactly seven different songs—S, T, V, W, X, Y, and Z. Each song occupies exactly one of the CD's seven tracks. Some of the songs are rock classics; the others are new compositions. The following conditions must hold: *PrepTest51 Sec4 Qs 11–15*	**Step 1:** **Situation:** **Entities:** **Action:** **Limitations:** **Step 2:** ⟶ **Sketch:**

Expert Analysis: LSAT Logic Games Overviews and Sketches

Here's how an LSAT expert might analyze and sketch each of the Logic Games' setups in that exercise.

LSAT Question	Analysis
28. A summer program offers at least one of the following seven courses: geography, history, literature, mathematics, psychology, sociology, zoology. The following restrictions on the program must apply: *PrepTest49 Sec1 Qs 13–17*	**Step 1:** **Situation:** Summer program offering classes **Entities:** The classes—G, H, L, M, P, S, Z **Action:** "Offers at least one ..." indicates that this is a Selection game. Which courses are offered is what needs to be determined. **Limitations:** Need to select at least one of the courses **Step 2:** **Sketch:** For a Selection game that does not have a specified number of selected entities, the sketch can simply be the roster: G H L M P S Z

LSAT Question	**Analysis**

29. A museum curator is arranging seven photographs—*Fence, Gardenias, Hibiscus, Irises, Katydid, Lotus,* and *Magnolia*—on a gallery wall in accordance with the photographer's requirements. The photographs are to be hung along the wall in a row, in seven positions sequentially numbered from first to seventh. The photographer's requirements are as follows:

PrepTest59 Sec1 Qs 6–10

→

Step 1:

Situation: Arranging photographs on a wall

Entities: The photographs—F, G, H, I, K, L, M

Action: "Hung along the wall in a row . . ." indicates that order matters. This is a Sequencing game.

Limitations: Each photograph gets its own spot

Step 2:

Sketch: Without seeing the rules, this could be either a Strict or Loose Sequencing game. If it's a Loose one, build a tree or web in accordance with the indented rules. If it's Strict, then:

F G H I K L M

___ ___ ___ ___ ___ ___ ___
1   2   3   4   5   6   7

LSAT Question	Analysis
30. A courier delivers exactly eight parcels—G, H, J, K, L, M, N, and O. No two parcels are delivered at the same time, nor is any parcel delivered more than once. The following conditions must apply: *PrepTest51 Sec4 Qs 16–22*	**Step 1:** **Situation:** Courier delivering packages **Entities:** Parcels—G, H, J, K, L, M, N, O **Action:** "No two parcels are delivered at the same time … " indicates that if they're not delivered at the same time, then they're delivered at different times, and the order matters. This is a Sequencing game.

$\longrightarrow$ **Limitations:** Each package delivered separately, used only once

Step 2:

Sketch: Without seeing the rules, this could be either a Strict or Loose Sequencing game. If it's a Loose one, draw a tree or web according to the indented rules. If it's Strict, then:

G H J K L M N O

__	__	__	__	__	__	__	__
1	2	3	4	5	6	7	8

LSAT Question	Analysis

LSAT Question

31.   A clown will select a costume consisting
      of two pieces and no others: a jacket and
      overalls. One piece of the costume will be
      entirely one color, and the other piece will
      be plaid. Selection is subject to the following
      restrictions:

                              PrepTest51 Sec4 Qs 1–5

Analysis

Step 1:

Situation: Clown picking clothes to wear

Entities: The two pieces of clothing—jacket
and overalls—and two possible patterns—uniform
color or plaid

Action: Determine the pattern of each piece
of clothing. This is a Matching game.

Limitation: No limitations so far

Step 2:

→ **Sketch:** A table is an easy sketch for Matching
games. We know that one piece of clothing will be
plaid and the other uniform, but we can't depict this
in the sketch until we get more information about
colors from the rules in this game.

jacket	overalls

LSAT Question	Analysis

32. Exactly six workers—Faith, Gus, Hannah, Juan, Kenneth, and Lisa—will travel to a business convention in two cars—car 1 and car 2. Each car must carry at least two of the workers, one of whom will be assigned to drive. For the entire trip, the workers will comply with an assignment that also meets the following constraints:

PrepTest61 Sec3 Qs 1–5

Step 1:

Situation: Workers traveling in two different cars

Entities: The two cars—1 and 2—and the six workers—F, G, H, J, K, and L

Action: Determine which workers ride or drive in each car. This is a Distribution game.

Limitations: Minimum of two and maximum of four workers in each car; each car has a driver

Step 2:

→ **Sketch:** Tables make great sketches for Distribution games.

	car 1	car 2
driver:	___	___
riders:	___	___
	...	...
	...	...

LSAT Question	Analysis

33. A locally known guitarist's demo CD contains exactly seven different songs—S, T, V, W, X, Y, and Z. Each song occupies exactly one of the CD's seven tracks. Some of the songs are rock classics; the others are new compositions. The following conditions must hold:

PrepTest51 Sec4 Qs 11–15

Step 1:

Situation: A demo CD with seven songs

Entities: The seven songs—S, T, V, W, X, Y, and Z—and the two styles—rock classics and new compositions

Action: Put the songs in order from first to seventh. Additionally, determine the style of each song. This is a Sequencing/Matching Hybrid game.

→ **Limitations:** Each song is exactly one track, so there are no ties. There's no limit on the number of songs that can be either rock or new.

Step 2:

Sketch:

```
__  __  __  __  __  __  __    S T V W X Y Z

__  __  __  __  __  __  __    r n
 1   2   3   4   5   6   7
```

REVIEW

There are four basic game actions that inform how we make sketches: Sequencing (putting entities in order); Selection (choosing some entities and rejecting others); Matching (matching attributes to entities); and Distribution (putting entities into groups). Sketches should be easy to read and understand, quick to replicate, and able to accommodate ambiguity.

> ## LSAT STRATEGY
>
> As you practice Logic Games, develop and maintain a library of common sketch formats for each game type. There are a limited number of game actions and basic sketch templates are useful time after time.

Here are the basic sketches Kaplan recommends for each standard game action. Your individual sketches may vary, of course, but the examples here provide a tested foundation that should be useful for all test takers.

Strict Sequencing

$$A \quad B \quad C \quad D \quad E \quad F$$

$$\overline{\quad} \quad \overline{\quad} \quad \overline{\quad} \quad \overline{\quad} \quad \overline{\quad} \quad \overline{\quad}$$
$$1 \quad 2 \quad 3 \quad 4 \quad 5 \quad 6$$

Loose Sequencing

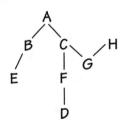

or

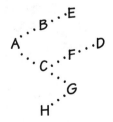

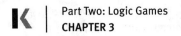
Matching Games

x y z

$$\underline{A} \mid \underline{B} \mid \underline{C} \mid \underline{D} \mid \underline{E} \mid \underline{F}$$

or

	A	B	C	D	E	F
x						
y						
z						

Distribution Games

L M N O P R S

$$\underline{A} \mid \underline{B} \mid \underline{C}$$

Selection Games

A̶ B̶ Ⓒ D E̶ F Ⓖ

For Selection games defining a specific number of entities, some test takers prefer:

A B C D E F

In | Out

__ __ __ __ | __ __

Sequencing/Matching Hybrid Games

__ __ __ __ __ __ A B C D E F

__ __ __ __ __ __ g/h

1   2   3   4   5   6

CHAPTER 4

Logic Games: Rules and Deductions

Once you have conducted an overview and created an initial sketch, it's on to Steps 3 and 4 of the Logic Games Method. In Step 3, you analyze and draw the rules. In Step 4, you make additional deductions by combining the rules and restrictions to determine what must, cannot, and could be true.

STEP 3 OF THE LOGIC GAMES METHOD: ANALYZE AND DRAW THE RULES

Here's the game you analyzed in Chapter 2. You can see the setup and the indented rules.

From the 1st through the 7th of next month, seven nurses—
Farnham, Griseldi, Heany, Juarez, Khan, Lightfoot, and
Moreau—will each conduct one information session at
a community center. Each nurse's session will fall on a
different day. The nurses' schedule is governed by the
following constraints:

    At least two of the other nurses' sessions must fall in
      between Heany's session and Moreau's session.
    Griseldi's session must be on the day before Khan's.
    Juarez's session must be on a later day than Moreau's.
    Farnham's session must be on an earlier day than Khan's
      but on a later day than Lightfoot's.
    Lightfoot cannot conduct the session on the 2nd.

PrepTest61 Sec3 Qs 18–23

When you draw out the rules, depict them clearly, in a way that matches and fits into the framework of the sketch. Account for what the rule does and does not determine.

LEARNING OBJECTIVES

In this section, you'll learn to:

- Determine accurately what a rule restricts and what it leaves undetermined
- Determine whether to draw a rule into the sketch framework or to display it off to the side
- Analyze and sketch rules
- Decide whether a rule is more helpful drawn in positive or negative terms

---

In the first part of this chapter, you'll see how an LSAT expert depicts the typical rules of each common game type using the sketch frameworks introduced in Chapter 3.

Take another look at the Nurses' Information Sessions game. Here, you see how an LSAT expert might depict the rules to match the standard Strict Sequencing sketch.

LSAT Question	Analysis
From the 1st through the 7th of next month, seven nurses—Farnham, Griseldi, Heany, Juarez, Khan, Lightfoot, and Moreau—will each conduct one information session at a community center. Each nurse's session will fall on a different day. The nurses' schedule is governed by the following constraints:	**Steps 1 and 2:** F G H J K L M __ __ __ __ __ __ __ 1 2 3 4 5 6 7
At least two of the other nurses' sessions must fall in between Heany's session and Moreau's session.	**Step 3:** H/M __ __ ... M/H Or H__ __ ... M or M __ __ ... H
Griseldi's session must be on the day before Khan's.	GK
Juarez's session must be on a later day than Moreau's.	M ... J
Farnham's session must be on an earlier day than Khan's but on a later day than Lightfoot's.	L ... F ... K
Lightfoot cannot conduct the session on the 2nd.	F G H J K L M __ __ __ __ __ __ __ 1 2 3 4 5 6 7 ~L

How did the LSAT expert ensure that the rules matched her sketch? Why is that valuable on Test Day?

Rules in Sequencing Games

Sequencing games are, by far, the most common games on recent LSATs. The testmaker uses several variations on Sequencing, so practice with the rules of these games is essential to Logic Games mastery.

LSAT STRATEGY

Sequencing rules basically tell you one or more of the following:

· The order in which two or more entities are placed
· The number of spaces between two or more entities
· The slot(s) in which a given entity can or cannot be placed

---

Here's the overview of a Sequencing game you saw in Chapter 3. This time, look at how an expert considers the rules and writes them in shorthand.

Sequencing Game	Analysis

Exactly five runners—A, B, C, D, and E—are ranked according to their speed at the end of a race from first place to last place. There are no ties. The ranking must be consistent with the following conditions:
  A ranks behind D.
  D and E finish next to each other.
  Exactly two runners finish between A and E.
	Steps 1 and 2:
	
	A B C D E
	— — — — —
	1 2 3 4 5

A ranks behind D.	**Step 3:** This states that D ranks ahead of A, but not how many spots ahead of A. D ... A
D and E finish next to each other.	D and E finish next to each other, but the order of the two runners is not stated. D/E E/D or DE or ED
Exactly two runners finish between A and E.	The rule states the number of runners between A and E, but not the order in which A and E appear. A/E __ __ E/A

Common Sequencing Rules

Now, take a look at more rules commonly found in Sequencing games. Note how an expert turns the rules into clear and consistent shorthand.

Sequencing Rule		Analysis
A is ranked ahead of B.	$\longrightarrow$	A ... B
C teaches a session on the day immediately before the day on which D teaches a session.	$\longrightarrow$	CD
E arrives exactly two days after F arrives.	$\longrightarrow$	F __ E
G finishes ahead of H, but after J.	$\longrightarrow$	J ... G ... H
In a Strict Sequencing game that doesn't allow ties and in which there are six open positions: K finishes either first or sixth.	$\longrightarrow$	$\underline{}\ \underline{}\ \underline{}\ \underline{}\ \underline{}\ \underline{}$ 1 2 3 4 5 6 K
L and M present on consecutive days.	$\longrightarrow$	L/M M/L or LM *or* ML
N arrives before both P and Q.	$\longrightarrow$	N ⋰ P ⋱ Q

Practice

Try some more on your own right now. Imagine each of the following is a rule listed for a game that uses the following basic Strict Sequencing sketch:

$$\overline{1} \ \overline{2} \ \overline{3} \ \overline{4} \ \overline{5}$$

Translate each rule in the space provided. If the rule can be placed directly into the sketch, redraw the blank sketch with the rule inserted.

Sequencing Rules	My Analysis
1. A must be scheduled for the day before B. $\longrightarrow$	
2. Q must be scheduled for some day before R. $\longrightarrow$	
3. D must be scheduled exactly one day after E. $\longrightarrow$	
4. G and H must be scheduled on consecutive days. $\longrightarrow$	
5. K cannot be scheduled for Day 4. $\longrightarrow$	
6. S is scheduled exactly three days before O. $\longrightarrow$	
7. C must be scheduled before both F and J. $\longrightarrow$	
8. X must be scheduled for either Day 1 or Day 5. $\longrightarrow$	
9. T must be scheduled at least two days before U and V. $\longrightarrow$	
10. If R is scheduled for Day 1, then W must be scheduled for Day 4. $\longrightarrow$	
11. M must come before N or before P, but not both. $\longrightarrow$	

Expert Analysis

Here's how an LSAT expert might depict each of the rules in the exercise.

Sequencing Rules		Analysis
1. A must be scheduled for the day before B.	$\rightarrow$	AB
2. Q must be scheduled for some day before R.	$\rightarrow$	Q ... R
3. D must be scheduled exactly one day after E.	$\rightarrow$	ED
4. G and H must be scheduled on consecutive days.	$\rightarrow$	GH or HG

5. K cannot be scheduled for Day 4.

$\rightarrow$

$$\underline{\hspace{1em}}\ \ \underline{\hspace{1em}}\ \ \underline{\hspace{1em}}\ \ \underline{\hspace{1em}}\ \ \underline{\hspace{1em}}$$
$$1\quad 2\quad 3\quad 4\quad 5$$
$${\sim}K$$

6. S is scheduled exactly three days before O. $\rightarrow$ S __ __ O

7. C must be scheduled before both F and J.

$\rightarrow$

$$C \begin{smallmatrix} \cdots F \\ \cdots J \end{smallmatrix}$$

8. X must be scheduled for either Day 1 or Day 5.

$\rightarrow$

X

$$\underline{\hspace{1em}}\ \ \underline{\hspace{1em}}\ \ \underline{\hspace{1em}}\ \ \underline{\hspace{1em}}\ \ \underline{\hspace{1em}}$$
$$1\quad 2\quad 3\quad 4\quad 5$$

9. T must be scheduled at least two days before U and V.

$\rightarrow$

$$T \underline{\hspace{1em}} \begin{smallmatrix} \cdots U \\ \cdots V \end{smallmatrix}$$

10. If R is scheduled for Day 1, then W must be scheduled for Day 4.

$\rightarrow$

If $R_1 \rightarrow W_4$

If ${\sim}W_4 \rightarrow {\sim}R_1$

11. M must come before N or before P, but not both. $\rightarrow$ N ... M ... P or P ... M ... N

Loose Sequencing Rules

Loose Sequencing games are comprised of "loose" sequencing rules. These rules establish the relative relationships between or among entities, but do not place entities into specific slots and do not define the precise number of spaces between or among entities. In Loose Sequencing games, build your sketch by combining rules together in a web. Take another look at the game below, which you first saw in Chapter 3. Follow the expert as he works through the rules, and note how he combines the information as he goes.

Loose Sequencing Game		Analysis

Seven runners are running a race: P, Q, R, S, T, U, and W. They are ranked in order according to the following conditions, and there are no ties:
     Q places earlier than R, but later than S.
     P places later than R.
     Both R and W place earlier than U.
     T places earlier than Q.
	$\longrightarrow$	**Steps 1 and 2:** The overview allows for either a Strict or Loose Sequencing sketch. A glance at the rules confirms this is a Loose Sequencing game, so the sketch will be built as we work through the rules.

Q places earlier than R, but later than S.	$\longrightarrow$	**Step 3:** Q places before R, but it's not known how far in front of R. And Q places later than S, but it's not known how many spaces after S.
		
		             S ... Q ... R
		                 or
		                  S
		                  |
		                  Q
		                  |
		                  R

Loose Sequencing Game	Analysis
P places later than R.	This rule defines the relationship between P and R.

$$R \ldots P$$

or

$$\begin{array}{c} R \\ | \\ P \end{array}$$

→ Combine with the previous rule:

$$S \ldots Q \ldots R \ldots P$$

or

$$\begin{array}{c} S \\ | \\ Q \\ | \\ R \\ | \\ P \end{array}$$

Both R and W place earlier than U.

or

Combine with previous rules:

→

or

Loose Sequencing Game	**Analysis**
T places earlier than Q.	T ... Q

or

T
|
Q

Combine with previous rules:

Or

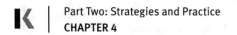
Regardless of the game type, there are a handful of principles that will help you make consistently strong depictions of the rules. Familiarize yourself with this list of questions and apply it throughout your Logic Games practice.

> ## LSAT STRATEGY
>
> When analyzing and drawing rules, always ask the following:
>
> · What does the rule restrict?
> · What does the rule leave undetermined?
> · Is the rule stated in affirmative or negative terms?
> · If stated affirmatively, can I learn something concrete from its negative implications (or vice versa)?
> · Can I place the rule directly into the sketch framework?
> · If not, how can I best draw the rule to account for what it does and does not restrict?

Practice

Now it's your turn. Turn these Sequencing rules into consistent, repeatable shorthand.

Sequencing Rule		My Analysis
12. P is ranked either immediately above or immediately below R.	$\longrightarrow$	
13. B arrives at some point before D.	$\longrightarrow$	
14. E and F are not assigned to consecutive positions.	$\longrightarrow$	

In a game with seven meetings:

15. The meeting with S will be scheduled either fifth or sixth.	$\longrightarrow$	

In a game where six runners compete in a race:

16. If H finishes first or second, P will not finish in the top three.	$\longrightarrow$	
17. There are exactly two appointments between A and T.	$\longrightarrow$	

In a game that does not allow ties:

18. If U is ranked fifth, then Z will rank ahead of Y.	$\longrightarrow$	

In a game that schedules meetings on days of the week, Monday through Friday:

19. Either C or K will be scheduled for the Tuesday meeting.	$\longrightarrow$	
20. X before Y or after Z but not both.	$\longrightarrow$	
21. M after L or after T but not both.	$\longrightarrow$	

Expert Analysis

How did you do? Compare your work to that of an LSAT expert.

Sequencing Rule		Analysis
12. P is ranked either immediately above or immediately below R.	$\longrightarrow$	PR or RP or <u>P/R</u> <u>R/P</u>
13. B arrives at some point before D.	$\longrightarrow$	B ... D
14. E and F are not assigned to consecutive positions.	$\longrightarrow$	Never EF and Never FE or E/F __ ... F/E
In a game with seven meetings: 15. The meeting with S will be scheduled either fifth or sixth.	$\longrightarrow$	
In a game where six runners compete in a race: 16. If H finishes first or second, P will not finish in the top three.	$\longrightarrow$	If H in 1 – 2 $\longrightarrow$ P in 4 – 6 If P in 1 – 3 $\longrightarrow$ H NOT in 1 – 2
17. There are exactly two appointments between A and T.	$\longrightarrow$	A __ __ T or T __ __ A or A/T __ __ T/A
In a game that does not allow ties: 18. If U is ranked fifth, then Z will rank ahead of Y.	$\longrightarrow$	If U_5 $\longrightarrow$ Z ... Y If Y ... Z $\longrightarrow$ ~U_5

Sequencing Rule	Analysis

In a game that schedules meetings on days of the week, Monday through Friday:

$\longrightarrow$

$$\frac{}{M} \quad \frac{C/K}{Tu} \quad \frac{}{W} \quad \frac{}{Th} \quad \frac{}{F}$$

19. Either C or K will be scheduled for the Tuesday meeting.

20. X before Y or after Z but not both.

$\longrightarrow$

X ... Y
or
Z ... X

Never
Z ... X ... Y

or

X : Y
Z

or

Z : X
Y

21. M after L or after T but not both.

$\longrightarrow$

L ... M
or
T ... M

Never
L : M
T

or

L ... M ... T
or
T ... M ... L

Rules in Selection Games

Selection games are less common than Sequencing games and do not appear on every test. Because these games always involve choosing some entities and rejecting others, almost all Selection rules involve conditional Formal Logic statements.

LSAT STRATEGY

Selection rules tell you one or more of the following:

- At least one of two entities must be rejected.
- At least one of two entities must be selected.
- Two entities must be selected or rejected as a pair (one cannot be selected or rejected without the other).

Use Selection game practice as an opportunity to polish your Formal Logic skills. Translate each rule into Formal Logic shorthand, and always determine and record its contrapositive.

Here is a Selection game you saw in Chapter 3, this time with rules. Note how the LSAT expert evaluates and creates shorthand for each rule.

Selection Game	Analysis

A real estate agent visits a bakery to purchase at least one kind of treat for his upcoming open house. The bakery carries the following items: B, C, E, F, G and J. The bakery does not carry any other items. The real estate agent's selection of treats must conform to the following conditions:
 	
    If the real estate agent selects a B, he will also select an F.
    If the real estate agent does not select any G, he will select a B.
    The real estate agent will not select a J if he selects an F.
    The real estate agent selects an E if but only if he selects a C.
	Steps 1 and 2: A simple list of entities will suffice for this game's sketch.
	
	  B C E F G J
	Circle selected entities and cross out rejected ones.

If the real estate agent selects a B, he will also select an F.	**Step 3:** If Ⓑ → Ⓕ If ~F → ~B
If the real estate agent does not select any G, he will select a B.	If ~G → Ⓑ If ~B → Ⓖ or ≥1 of B or G (possibly both)
The real estate agent will not select a J if he selects an F.	If Ⓕ → ~J If Ⓙ → ~F or Never F and J together
The real estate agent selects an E if, but only if, he selects a C.	If Ⓔ → Ⓒ If Ⓒ → Ⓔ If ~C → ~E If ~E → ~C or EC—in together or out together

Common Selection Rules

Take a look at more rules commonly found in Selection games. Study the wording of each rule and see if you can translate it into a standard "If ... then" statement. Then, note how an LSAT expert turns the rules into clear and consistent shorthand.

Selection Rule	Analysis
If G is selected for the committee, so is T.	If Ⓖ → Ⓣ
	→ If ~T → ~G
	Reminder: This allows for a selection in which T is selected and G is not selected.
R plays in every game in which P plays.	→ If Ⓟ → Ⓡ
	If ~R → ~P
If A is not selected, then Y is selected.	If ~A → Ⓨ
	→ If ~Y → Ⓐ
	One of A or Y must be selected; it is possible that A and Y are both included.
Either J or S or both will be selected.	~J → Ⓢ
	→ ~S → Ⓙ
	One of J or S must be selected; it is possible that J and S are both included.
If L is selected, then either B or C will also be selected.	If Ⓛ → Ⓑ or Ⓒ
	If ~B and ~C → ~L
	→ It is possible that L, B, and C are all selected. It is also possible to select one or both of B or C and to reject L.
Whenever D is included, H is not included.	If Ⓓ → ~H
	→ If Ⓗ → ~D
	D and H can never be included together. It is possible that both are excluded.
Exactly one of N or F is included.	If Ⓝ → ~F
	If Ⓕ → ~N
	If ~N → Ⓕ
	→ If ~F → Ⓝ
	You can never have a selection without one of these entities, and can never have a selection with both of them.
If either X or Q is included, E is included.	If Ⓧ or Ⓠ → Ⓔ
	If ~E → ~X and ~Q
	→ or
	If Ⓧ → Ⓔ If Ⓠ → Ⓔ
	If ~E → ~X If ~E → ~Q

Practice

Now it's your turn to try depicting some Selection rules. Read the rules carefully and analyze what they do and do not restrict.

Selection Rule	My Analysis
22. If A is included, then neither B nor D is included.	$\longrightarrow$
23. Either E or F or both are selected.	$\longrightarrow$
24. If G is selected, then H is also selected.	$\longrightarrow$
25. J is not selected unless K is selected.	$\longrightarrow$
26. L is included only if M and N are included.	$\longrightarrow$
27. If P is not included, then Q is included.	$\longrightarrow$
28. R and S are selected if, but only if, T is also selected.	List the acceptable selections among R, S, and T: $\longrightarrow$

Selection Rule		**My Analysis**

In a game that asks you to select four activities from among four sports—A, B, C, and D—, and four musical instruments—f, g, h, and j: $\longrightarrow$

29. If a student participates in two or more sports, she can play at most one musical instrument.

30. Either U or V must be selected, but U and V cannot both be selected.

$\longrightarrow$

31. If either X or Y is selected, the other must also be selected.

$\longrightarrow$

32. If A is selected, then B is selected or C is selected.

$\longrightarrow$

33. If either of C or D is included, then E must also be included.

$\longrightarrow$

34. If F and G are selected, then H cannot be selected.

$\longrightarrow$

Expert Analysis

How did you do? Compare your work to that of an LSAT expert.

Selection Rule	**Analysis**
22. If A is included, then neither B nor D is included.	If Ⓐ → ~B AND ~D If ⒷOR Ⓓ→ ~A or If Ⓐ → ~B → If Ⓑ → ~A If Ⓐ → ~D If Ⓓ → ~A or Never AB Never AD
23. Either E or F or both are selected.	If ~E → Ⓕ IF ~F → Ⓔ or → E/F: at least one or ≥1 (E/F)
24. If G is selected, then H is also selected.	→ If Ⓖ → Ⓗ If ~H → ~G
25. J is not selected unless K is selected.	→ If Ⓙ → Ⓚ If ~K → ~J
26. L is included only if M and N are included.	If Ⓛ → Ⓜ AND Ⓝ If ~M OR ~N → ~L or → If Ⓛ → Ⓜ If ~M → ~L If Ⓛ → Ⓝ If ~N → ~L

Selection Rule		**Analysis**
27. If P is not included, then Q is included.		If ~P → ⓠ If ~Q → ⓟ or P/Q: at least one or ≥1 (P/Q)
28. R and S are selected if, but only if, T is also selected.	→	If ⓣ → Ⓡ and ⓢ If ~R or ~S → ~T If Ⓡ and ⓢ → ⓣ If ~T → ~R or ~S Acceptable selections among R, S, and T: T R S R alone S alone None of the three
In a game that asks you to select four activities from among four sports—A, B, C, and D—and four musical instruments—f, g, h, and j: 29. If a student participates in two or more sports, she can play at most one musical instrument.	→	If ≥ 2 sports → ≤ 1 instrument If > 1 instrument → < 2 sports or If 2+ of [A B C D], then 0 or 1 of [f g h j] If 2+ of [f g h j], then 0 or 1 of [A B C D]
30. Either U or V must be selected, but U and V cannot both be selected.	→	If ⓤ → ~V If ⓥ → ~U If ~U → ⓥ If ~V → ⓤ or ⓤ or ⓥ but not both U/V: exactly 1 or 1 (U/V)

Selection Rule		**Analysis**
31. If either X or Y is selected, the other must also be selected.	$\longrightarrow$	If Ⓧ →Ⓨ If ~Y → ~X If Ⓨ →Ⓧ If ~X → ~Y or XY : both or neither
32. If A is selected, then B is selected or C is selected.	$\longrightarrow$	IfⒶ →Ⓑ orⒸ If ~B and ~C → ~A NOTE: Having A, B, and C all selected is acceptable. Having none of the three selected is also acceptable.
33. If either of C or D is included, then E must also be included.	$\longrightarrow$	IfⒸ orⒹ →Ⓔ If ~E → ~C and ~D or IfⒸ →Ⓔ If ~E → ~C IfⒹ →Ⓔ If ~E → ~D
34. If F and G are selected, then H cannot be selected.	$\longrightarrow$	IfⒻ andⒼ → ~H IfⒽ → ~F or ~G NOTE: Having H and F selected is acceptable, provided G is not selected. Having H and G selected is acceptable, provided F is not selected.

Rules in Matching and Distribution Games

The rules in Matching and Distribution games are similar. The primary difference between the two games is that entities, attributes, and characteristics can be used more than once in Matching games. Typically in Distribution games, once an entity is placed into a group, it cannot be placed into any other groups.

LSAT STRATEGY

Distribution rules tell you one or more of the following:

- Entities that must or cannot be assigned to the same group
- The number of entities that must, can, or cannot be assigned to a group, or the relative sizes among groups (e.g., the Blue Group must have more members than the Green Group)
- Conditions triggering the assignment of an entity to a particular group (e.g., if Rachel joins the marketing team, then Gar joins the service team)

Matching rules tell you one or more of the following:

- Attributes that must or cannot be matched to the same entity
- The number of attributes that must, can, or cannot be assigned to an entity, or the relative numbers among entities (e.g., Sascha must be assigned more of the tasks than Craig is assigned)
- Conditions triggering the assignment of an attribute to a particular entity (e.g., if Rebecca is assigned copyediting, then Jesse is assigned layout)

Let's revisit the Distribution game you saw from Chapter 3. This time, the game has rules. Note how an expert evaluates and creates shorthand for each rule.

Distribution Game	Analysis
At a sailing camp, each of six children—Q, R, S, T, X, and Z—will be assigned to exactly one of two vessels—a catamaran or a dinghy. Each vessel can hold a maximum of four people. The assignments must conform to the following conditions: S and T are assigned to the same vessel. Q and X are assigned to different vessels. If S is in the catamaran, then R is in the dinghy.	**Steps 1 and 2:** Q R S T X Z (2–4) (2–4) Cat | Din
S and T are assigned to the same vessel.	**Step 3:** Don't know to which vessel they're assigned, but they must be together. Combine as a Block of Entities. S T
Q and X are assigned to different vessels.	Don't know the assignment of either Q or X, but can determine that either Q or X is in 1, and the other one is in 2. Can add to sketch: (2–4) (2–4) Cat Din Q/X X/Q
If S is in the catamaran, then R is in the dinghy.	Formal Logic rule: If $S_{CAT} \rightarrow R_{DIN}$ If $R_{CAT} \rightarrow S_{DIN}$ Though at first glance it may appear as though R and S cannot be in the same vessel, this rule only says that they can't be in the catamaran together. They could both be in the dinghy.

Now take a look at a Matching game from Chapter 3.

Matching Game	**Analysis**

Each of exactly five newly created types of cell phones—J, K, L, M, and N—will contain at least one of the following features: conferencing, GPS, touch screen, voice command, and web browsing. Features will be matched to cell phones according to the following restrictions:

    K has conferencing and GPS, and has no other features.

    L has more features than K has.

    L and M have no features in common.

    Exactly three cell phones have GPS.

Steps 1 and 2:

Features: *c g t v w*

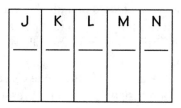

K has conferencing and GPS, and has no other features.

Step 3: Can add this information directly to the sketch:

Features: *c g t v w*

L has more features than K has.

Nothing definitive about the features that L has. However, because K has exactly two features, then L must have three, four, or five features. Note that above the sketch:

Features: *c g t v w*

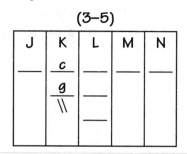

Matching Game (cont.)	**Analysis (cont.)**
L and M have no features in common.	Nothing definitive about the features that L or M has. Because every cell phone, including M, has at least one of the features, L cannot have all five features. L can only have 3 or 4 features, which means M will have either 1 or 2 features.

Features: c g t v w

$\longrightarrow$

(3–4) (1–2)

J	K	L	M	N
—	c	—	—	—
	g	—		
	\\\\			

L ≠ M

Exactly three cell phones have GPS.	Nothing definitive about which cell phones (besides K) have GPS. Note this rule above or below the roster of features:

$\longrightarrow$

3

Features: c g t v w

Practice 1

Now it's your turn. Take a look at more rules commonly found in Distribution and Matching games. Translate these rules into clear and consistent shorthand.

Distribution or Matching Rule	**My Analysis**
In a game where you have to determine the color and size of different boats: $\longrightarrow$	
35. Boat P is painted red and is a medium-sized boat.	
In a game where every person decides to go to either Jamaica or Alaska for vacation: $\longrightarrow$	
36. R and T do not go on vacation together.	
In a game where runners will wear either green, blue, or yellow shorts: $\longrightarrow$	
37. Runner H does not wear blue shorts.	

Distribution or Matching Rule (cont.)	My Analysis (cont.)
In a game where horses will be placed into one of two fields:	
38. If horse J is in field 1, then horse P will also be in field 1.	
In a game that asks us to match musical instruments to people: $\longrightarrow$	
39. If Jim plays the tuba, then Mary plays the flute.	
In a game that asks us to match musical instruments to people, and the only instruments available to play are the tuba, flute, and drums: $\longrightarrow$	
40. If Jim plays the tuba, then Mary plays the flute.	
In a game where people are hired to one of three departments (Sales, Accounts, or Marketing) within a company: $\longrightarrow$	
41. If H is hired in the Sales Department, then P is not hired in the Accounts Department.	

Expert Analysis

Now take a look at how an expert analyzed the same rules.

Distribution or Matching Rule	Analysis
In a game where you have to determine the color and size of different boats: 35. Boat P is painted red and is a medium-sized boat.	$\dfrac{\dfrac{\text{P}}{\text{r}}}{\text{m}}$ In a Matching game, block together an entity with that entity's characteristics.
In a game where every person decides to go to either Jamaica or Alaska for vacation: 36. R and T do not go on vacation together.	J | A R/T | T/R Because every person goes on vacation, it's possible to add this rule directly to the sketch. Either R or T goes to Jamaica, and the other one goes to Alaska.
In a game where runners will wear either green, blue, or yellow shorts: 37. Runner H does not wear blue shorts.	$\dfrac{\text{H}}{\text{g/y}}$ In Matching games, it's common for a type of entity to only have three possible options. When one of those options is removed, make the positive deduction that one of the remaining two options must be present. Here, H must wear green or yellow shorts.

Distribution or Matching Rule (cont.)	Analysis (cont.)
In a game where horses will be placed into one of two fields: 38. If horse J is in field 1, then horse P will also be in field 1.	If $J_1 \rightarrow P_1$ If $P_2 \rightarrow J_2$ When making the contrapositive, turn "P not in field 1" into a positive: "P in field 2." Also keep in mind that this rule *does not say* that P and J must be in the same field as each other. It's possible that P is in field 1 and J is in field 2.
In a game that asks us to match musical instruments to people: 39. If Jim plays the tuba, then Mary plays the flute.	$\boxed{\dfrac{J}{t}} \rightarrow \boxed{\dfrac{M}{f}}$ $\sim\boxed{\dfrac{M}{f}} \rightarrow \sim\boxed{\dfrac{J}{t}}$ This rule does not mean that if Mary plays the flute then Jim must play the tuba. But it does mean that if Mary doesn't play the flute, then Jim can't play the tuba.
In a game that asks us to match musical instruments to people, and the only instruments available to play are the tuba, flute, and drums: 40. If Jim plays the tuba, then Mary plays the flute.	$\boxed{\dfrac{J}{t}} \rightarrow \boxed{\dfrac{M}{f}}$ $\boxed{\dfrac{M}{t/d}} \rightarrow \boxed{\dfrac{J}{f/d}}$ The same rule as before, with one big difference: here, we know that there are only three instruments. That allows us to turn the contrapositive into a positive deduction.
In a game where people are hired to one of three departments (Sales, Accounts, or Marketing) within a company: 41. If H is hired in the Sales Department, then P is not hired in the Accounts Department.	If $H_{sal} \rightarrow \sim P_{acc}$ If $P_{acc} \rightarrow \sim H_{sal}$ Alternatively: If $H_{sal} \rightarrow P_{sal/mar}$ If $P_{acc} \rightarrow H_{acc/mar}$ In this game, because there are three groups instead of two, it's not possible to definitively know where a person goes if that person is not selected for a particular group. Instead, either list where the person cannot go, or denote that that person could go to one of two departments.

Practice 2

Try some more on your own right now. Imagine each of the following rules is listed for a game that uses the following basic Matching sketch. Translate each rule in the space provided. If the rule can be placed directly into the sketch, redraw the blank sketch with the rule inserted.

Matching Rules		**My Analysis**
In a game where each of Q, P, and R is matched with at least one of a, b, c, and d:	$\longrightarrow$	
42. Q is matched with a.		
43. Anything R is matched with is not matched with P.	$\longrightarrow$	
44. Q is matched with more things than R is.	$\longrightarrow$	

Matching Rules		**My Analysis**
In a game where each of Q, P, and R is matched with at least one of j, k, m, and n:	$\longrightarrow$	
45. If R is matched with m, then Q is matched with n.		
46. P is matched with exactly two attributes.	$\longrightarrow$	
47. Anything matched to P is also matched to Q.	$\longrightarrow$	

Try some more on your own right now. This time, imagine each of the following rules is listed for the following basic Distribution sketch. Translate each rule in the space provided. If the rule can be placed directly into the sketch, redraw the blank sketch with the rule inserted.

$$1 \mid 2$$

Distribution Rules		My Analysis
In a game where each of five players—A, B, C, D, and E—is assigned to one of two teams:	$\rightarrow$	
48. A and B are on different teams.		
49. B and C are on the same team.	$\rightarrow$	
50. If D is on Team 1, then E is on Team 2.	$\rightarrow$	

Distribution Rules		My Analysis
In a game where each of five players—J, K, L, M, and N—is assigned to one of two teams, and each team has at least one player:	$\rightarrow$	
51. If J is on Team 1, then L is on Team 1.		
52. If K is on Team 2, then M is on Team 1.	$\rightarrow$	
53. Team 2 has more players than Team 1.	$\rightarrow$	

Why is it important to note that there are only two groups in this model game?

Now imagine each of the following rules is listed for a game that asks you to place each of six entities—P, Q, R, S, T, and U—into one of *three* teams. Using the following basic Distribution sketch, translate each rule in the space provided. If the rule can be placed directly into the sketch, redraw the blank sketch with the rule inserted.

P Q R S T U

1	2	3

Distribution Rules	**My Analysis**
54. P and Q cannot be on the same team.	$\longrightarrow$
55. If R is on Team 1, then S is on Team 2.	$\longrightarrow$
56. Each team has at least one player, and Team 1 has more players than Team 2.	$\longrightarrow$
57. If T is on Team 2, then U is on Team 2.	$\longrightarrow$

How is this model game, with three groups, different than the preceding model with two groups? How does the difference affect the ways in which you depict rules?

Expert Analysis

Now take a look at how an LSAT expert might translate the Matching and Distribution rules in that exercise. The first set of rules refer to this Matching sketch.

$$\begin{array}{c|c|c} Q & P & R \end{array}$$

Matching Rules		Analysis
In a game where each of Q, P, and R is matched with at least one of a, b, c, and d: 42. Q is matched with a.	$\longrightarrow$	Add this information directly to the sketch. a b c d $$\begin{array}{c|c|c} Q & P & R \\ \hline a & \rule{1em}{0.4pt} & \rule{1em}{0.4pt} \end{array}$$
43. Anything R is matched with is not matched with P.	$\longrightarrow$	If R $\longrightarrow$ ~P If P $\longrightarrow$ ~R In other words, no entity can be matched to both P and R. This affects number limitations: It is impossible for either P or R to have all four entities.
44. Q is matched with more things than R is.	$\longrightarrow$	Q > R This affects number limitations. Q must have two to four entities, while R must have one to three entities.

The following examples refer to this Matching sketch.

$$Q \mid P \mid R$$

Matching Rules	Analysis
In a game where each of Q, P, and R is matched with at least one of j, k, m, and n:	Write these rules like they are blocks of entities:

45. If R is matched with m, then Q is matched with n. →

$$\boxed{\frac{R}{m}} \rightarrow \boxed{\frac{Q}{n}}$$

$$\sim\boxed{\frac{Q}{n}} \rightarrow \sim\boxed{\frac{R}{m}}$$

46. P is matched with exactly two attributes.

Add this directly to the sketch by drawing two dashes underneath P.

→

$$Q \mid P \mid R$$

47. Anything matched to P is also matched to Q.

If with P → with Q

If ~with Q → ~with P

→ In other words, combined with the previous rule, the two entities that are assigned to P must also be assigned to Q. This does not mean that Q has only two entities matched to it, though. Q could also have all four.

The following examples refer to this two-group Distribution sketch.

$$1 \mid 2$$

Distribution Rules	Analysis
In a game where each of five players—A, B, C, D, and E—is assigned to one of two teams:	Add this information directly to the sketch. One of A or B is on Team 1, while one of A or B is on Team 2.

48. A and B are on different teams. $\longrightarrow$

$$A \ B \ C \ D \ E$$

$$\begin{array}{c|c} 1 & 2 \\ \hline A/B & B/A \end{array}$$

49. B and C are on the same team. $\longrightarrow$ Block together B and C. They are on the same team, but it is not known which team.

$$\boxed{\begin{array}{c} B \\ C \end{array}}$$

50. If D is on Team 1, then E is on Team 2. $\longrightarrow$ Write this rule in Formal Logic, but remember that not being on Team 1 is the same as being on Team 2, and vice versa.

If $D_1 \rightarrow E_2$

If $E_1 \rightarrow D_2$

The following examples refer to this two-group Distribution sketch.

$$1 \mid 2$$

Distribution Rules	Analysis
In a game where each of five players—J, K, L, M, and N—is assigned to one of two teams, and each team has at least one player: 51. If J is on Team 1, then L is on Team 1.	If $J_1 \rightarrow L_1$ If $L_2 \rightarrow J_2$ Be careful that you don't misread this rule. This rule does not say that J and L are on the same team: it is possible that L is on Team 1 and J is on Team 2.
52. If K is on Team 2, then M is on Team 1.	If $K_2 \rightarrow M_1$ If $M_2 \rightarrow K_1$ Be careful that you don't misread this rule. This rule does not say that K and M are on different teams: it is possible that M and K are both on Team 1.
53. Team 2 has more players than Team 1.	This affects the number limitations of the game. Because each team must have at least one player, Team 1 will have 1–2 players and Team 2 will have 3–4 players. Add this information to the sketch. J K L M N (1–2) (3–4) $1 \mid 2$

The following examples refer to this three-group Distribution sketch.

$$P \ Q \ R \ S \ T \ U$$

1	2	3

Distribution Rules	Analysis
54. P and Q cannot be on the same team.	**Never PQ together** or $\sim[PQ]$ This rule cannot be added directly to the sketch, because there are three groups instead of just two.
55. If R is on Team 1, then S is on Team 2.	Write this rule in Formal Logic, but be careful when creating the contrapositive. Because there are three groups instead of two, "not Team 1" no longer means "on Team 2." Instead, "not Team 1" means "either Team 2 or Team 3." If $R_1 \rightarrow S_2$ If $\sim S_2 \rightarrow \sim R_1$ or If $R_1 \rightarrow S_2$ If $S_{(1 \text{ or } 3)} \rightarrow R_{(2 \text{ or } 3)}$

Distribution Rules	**Analysis**
56. Each team has at least one player, and Team 1 has more players than Team 2.	A number limitation rule. Add this information directly to the sketch if possible. If each team has at least one player, and Team 1 has more than Team 2, then Team 1 has a minimum of 2 and a maximum of 4.

$$P \quad Q \quad R \quad S \quad T \quad U$$

$\longrightarrow$

(2–4)	(1–2)	(1–3)
1	2	3

57. If T is on Team 2, then U is on Team 2.	If $T_2 \rightarrow U_2$
	If $\sim U_2 \rightarrow \sim T_2$
	or
$\longrightarrow$	If $T_2 \rightarrow U_2$
	If $U_{(1 \text{ or } 3)} \rightarrow T_{(1 \text{ or } 3)}$
	Be careful about what this rule does and does not say. It does not say that T and U are on the same team together. If U is on Team 2, T can be on any team.

Rules in Hybrid Games

The rules in Hybrid games will be of the same type that you see in single-action games. The only difference is that within a Hybrid game, you will see a mix of different types of rules. For example, in a Distribution/Sequencing game, some rules will restrict or define which entities can go in which group (Distribution rules), while other rules will restrict or define the order in which entities can go (Sequencing rules).

> ## LSAT STRATEGY
>
> Hybrid rules tell you one of the following:
>
> · How the first of the actions is restricted
> · How the second of the actions is restricted
> · How the actions are restricted simultaneously

NOTE: Rarely, a Hybrid game will include three actions. The function of the rules is identical in that case.

Let's revisit a game you saw in Chapter 3, this time with its rules. Note how an LSAT expert evaluates and creates shorthand for each rule.

Hybrid Game	Analysis
At a summer camp, two teams of three campers each will participate in a swim relay. The two teams—Team 1 and Team 2—will be composed of the following six campers—F, G, H, J, K, and L. Each swimmer will swim either the first, second, or third leg of the relay. F and G are on the same team. Neither F nor J swims the first leg of the relay. K swims the second leg of the relay. H swims in an earlier position than G.	**Steps 1 and 2:** F G H J K L Team 1 | Team 2 first: ___ | ___ second: ___ | ___ third: ___ | ___

Hybrid Game (cont.)	**Analysis (cont.)**
F and G are on the same team.	**Step 3:**

$\rightarrow$ $\boxed{FG}$

F and G will be together, but their specific team is not known, nor is their order. This cannot be drawn into the sketch. Note it out to the side.

Hybrid Game (cont.)	**Analysis (cont.)**
Neither F nor J swims the first leg of the relay.	Not sure whether F or J swims second or third, but it's confirmed they don't swim first. Add that information to the sketch:

$\rightarrow$

	Team 1	Team 2	
first:	___	___	~F ~J
second:	___	___	
third:	___	___	

Hybrid Game (cont.)	**Analysis (cont.)**
K swims the second leg of the relay.	Not sure whether K swims on Team 1 or Team 2, but it's confirmed she doesn't swim first or last. Add that information to the sketch:

$\rightarrow$

	Team 1	Team 2	
first:	___	___	~F ~J ~K
second:	___	___	K
third:	___	___	~K

Hybrid Game (cont.)	**Analysis (cont.)**
H swims in an earlier position than G.	H swimming earlier than G means that G cannot be first. Adding that information to the sketch reveals that only two entities can go first—H and L. Because there are two teams, H and L are the campers who swim first. Add that information directly to the sketch:

$\rightarrow$

	Team 1	Team 2	
first:	H/L	H/L	~F ~J ~K ~G
second:	___	___	K
third:	___	___	~K

Common Hybrid Game Rules

Now, take a look at more rules you might find in a Hybrid game. Note how an expert turns the rules into clear and consistent shorthand.

Hybrid Rule	Analysis
In a Selection/Matching game where cars of different colors will be selected for display: If the sedan is selected, it will be purple.	If $S \rightarrow \boxed{\frac{S}{P}}$ If $\sim\boxed{\frac{S}{P}} \rightarrow \sim S$ Because a sedan may not be selected this rule needs to be conditional. If no purple cars are displayed, then no sedans will be displayed.
In a Sequencing/Matching game where six runners —M, N, O, P, Q, and R— are finishing a race, and each runner is from either England, France, or Brazil: Paul, who finishes fourth, is not from England.	$$\begin{array}{cccccc} \_\_ & \_\_ & \_\_ & \mathrm{F/B} & \_\_ & \_\_ \quad \mathrm{E\,F\,B} \\ \_\_ & \_\_ & \_\_ & \mathrm{P} & \_\_ & \_\_ \quad \mathrm{m\,n\,o\,p\,q\,r} \\ 1 & 2 & 3 & 4 & 5 & 6 \end{array}$$ In a Sequencing/Matching Hybrid, create a two-layered Strict Sequencing sketch.
In a Selection/Sequencing game that asks you to display five of seven possible flowers in order from left to right: T is not chosen for display unless S is placed in the third vase from the left.	If $T \rightarrow S_3$ If $\sim S_3 \rightarrow \sim T$ If T is in the game, then S must be in the game in spot 3. If S is not in the game, or is in any spot other than 3, then T is not in the game.

Hybrid Rule (cont.)	**Analysis (cont.)**

In a Distribution/Sequencing game where six tennis players—A, B, C, D, E, and F—will be divided into two teams of three, and each player is ranked first, second, or third on each team:

If A is on Team 1, then B and C are both on Team 2, with C ranking higher than B. $\longrightarrow$

If A_1 $\rightarrow C_2 \ldots B_2$

If $\sim[C_2 \ldots B_2]$ $\rightarrow A_2$

or

$$\text{If } A_1 \rightarrow \begin{array}{c} C_2 \\ | \\ B_2 \end{array}$$

$$\text{If } \sim \begin{array}{c} C_2 \\ | \\ B_2 \end{array} \rightarrow \sim A_1$$

When you are drawing the rules for Hybrid games, add another question to the list of questions you should always ask as you analyze the rules.

LSAT STRATEGY

When analyzing and drawing a rule in a Hybrid game, always ask:

· **Does the rule affect one or both of the actions in the Hybrid? If only one, which one?**
· What does the rule restrict?
· What does the rule leave undetermined?
· Is the rule stated in affirmative or negative terms?
· If stated affirmatively, can I learn something concrete from its negative implications (or vice versa)?
· Can I place the rule directly into the sketch framework?
· If not, how can I best draw the rule to account for what it does and does not restrict?

Practice

Now it's your turn. Analyze the following rules carefully and decide how best to draw them.

Hybrid Rules	My Analysis
In a Selection/Sequencing game where four of six toys are chosen for review, then ranked from safest to least safe:	
58. If the dinosaur is selected for review, it will be ranked the second safest toy. →	
In a Selection/Matching game where four of six cakes—A, B, C, D, E, and F—are chosen for a taste test and matched to a color of icing—blue, white, and yellow: →	
59. Cake B is chosen only if it is yellow.	
In a Distribution/Sequencing/Selection game where six of seven runners—A, B, C, D, E, F, and G—are placed on one of two relay teams—H and J. Each team has a first, second, and third relay runner: →	
60. If F is chosen for a team, she will run the first leg of the relay.	
In the same game:	
61. B is not chosen to run on a team unless C is chosen to run the second leg of the relay on Team H. →	

Hybrid Rules	**My Analysis**

In a Distribution/Sequencing game where six people—A, B, C, D, E, and F—attended one of two high schools—G and H—at different times:

62. B graduated later than C, and they attended different high schools. $\longrightarrow$

In a Sequencing/Selection/Matching game where four of five automobiles—A, B, C, D, and E—will be selected for a parade; each automobile will be either a convertible, sedan, or truck, and the automobiles will be placed in order from first to fourth: $\longrightarrow$

63. If B is not selected to be the first automobile in the parade, then C will not be selected at all.

In the same game:

64. At least two trucks are selected for the parade, but no trucks are in consecutive places.

$\longrightarrow$

Expert Analysis

Now take a look at how an expert broke these rules down:

Hybrid Rule	Analysis
In a Selection/Sequencing game where four of six toys are chosen for review, then ranked from safest to least safe:	$$\underline{}\ \underline{}\ \underline{}\ \underline{}\Big\vert\ \underline{}\ \underline{}$$ $$1\quad 2\quad 3\quad 4\qquad \text{out}$$
58. If the dinosaur is selected for review, it will be ranked the second safest toy.	$$D \rightarrow \frac{D}{2}$$
$\rightarrow$	$$\sim\frac{D}{2} \rightarrow \sim D$$
	If D is in the game, then it will be in spot 2. The contrapositive states that if D is not in spot 2—in other words, if anything else is in spot 2—then D is not selected, and we can put D in one of the "out" slots.
In a Selection/Matching game where four of six cakes—A, B, C, D, E, and F—are chosen for a taste test and matched to a color of icing—blue, white, and yellow:	A B C D E F $$\underline{}\ \underline{}\ \underline{}\ \underline{}\Big\vert\ \underline{}\ \underline{}$$ $$\text{out}$$
59. Cake B is chosen only if it is yellow.	b/w/y $\underline{}\ \underline{}\ \underline{}\ \underline{}$
$\rightarrow$	$$B \rightarrow \frac{B}{y}$$ $$\sim\frac{B}{y} \rightarrow \sim B$$
	Remember that "only if" signifies a necessary condition will follow. Turn "only if" into "then" in standard Formal Logic translation. Here, if B is in the game, then it will be Y (order doesn't matter—it will just be in one of the four "in" spots). The contrapositive states that if B is not yellow, then B is not selected, and we can put B in one of the "out" slots.

Hybrid Rule	**Analysis**

In a Distribution/Sequencing/Selection game where six of seven runners—A, B, C, D, E, F, and G—are placed on one of two relay teams—H and J. Each team has a first, second, and third relay runner:

60. If F is chosen for a team, she will run the first leg of the relay.

$\longrightarrow$

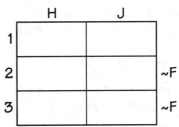

The tendency here is to put F next to spot 1 in some way, but because this game has a selection element, it's not certain that F is selected at all. What is certain is that F CANNOT run the second or third leg of the relay for either team.

In the same game:

61. B is not chosen to run on a team unless C is chosen to run the second leg of the relay on Team H.

$\longrightarrow$

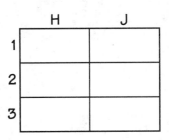

If B in game $\longrightarrow C_{second}H$

If $\sim C_{second}H \longrightarrow$ B out

If C does not take the second leg on Team H, B is not selected. That determines the six runners: A, C, D, E, F, and G.

In a Distribution/Sequencing game where six people—A, B, C, D, E, and F—attended one of two high schools—G and H—at different times:

62. B graduated later than C, and they attended different high schools.

$\longrightarrow$

A B C D E F

Earlier $\dfrac{\quad G \mid H \quad}{\qquad \quad \sim B}$

$\dfrac{\quad\quad}{\quad\quad}$

Later $\cdots \mid \cdots$ $\bigcirc\!\!\!\!\!\!\dfrac{C}{B}$ $\begin{matrix}C\\ \mid \\ B\end{matrix}$

B cannot be the first person who graduated at either G or H. Additionally, because B and C did not go to the same school, at least one person went to G and at least one person went to H. Signify the two parts of the rule separately.

Hybrid Rule	**Analysis**

In a Sequencing/Selection/Matching game where four of five automobiles—A, B, C, D, and E—will be selected for a parade; each automobile is either a convertible, sedan, or truck, and the automobiles selected for the parade will be placed in order from first to fourth:

$$\underline{\quad}\ \underline{\quad}\ \underline{\quad}\ \underline{\quad}\ |\ \underline{\quad}\ A\ B\ C\ D\ E$$

$$\underline{\quad}\ \underline{\quad}\ \underline{\quad}\ \underline{\quad}\ |\ \underline{\quad}\ c\ s\ t$$

$$\ \ 1\quad 2\quad 3\quad 4\quad \text{out}$$

63. If B is not selected to be the first automobile in the parade, then C will not be selected at all.

$\longrightarrow$
If $\sim B_1 \longrightarrow \sim C$
If $C \longrightarrow B_1$

If any car besides B is in Spot 1, then C is not selected (which means that all of the other cars are selected). If C is in the game, then B must be in the first position.

In the same game:

$$\underline{\quad}\ \underline{\quad}\ \underline{\quad}\ \underline{\quad}\ |\ \underline{\quad}\ A\ B\ C\ D\ E$$

$$\underline{\quad}\ \underline{\quad}\ \underline{\quad}\ \underline{\quad}\ |\ \underline{\quad}\ tt + cc/cs/ss$$

$$\ \ 1\quad 2\quad 3\quad 4\quad \text{out}$$

64. At least two trucks are selected for the parade, but no trucks are in consecutive places.

$\sim[tt]$

$\longrightarrow$ If trucks cannot be consecutive, then there can be a maximum of two trucks. The rule states that there is a minimum of two trucks. Therefore there must be exactly two trucks in the parade. The first truck must show up in either Spot 1 or Spot 2: if it shows up in Spot 2, then the second truck would definitely be in Spot 4. The other vehicles could be two convertibles, two sedans, or one convertible and one sedan. No rule requires that each vehicle type be chosen.

STEP 4 OF THE LOGIC GAMES METHOD: COMBINE THE RULES AND RESTRICTIONS TO MAKE DEDUCTIONS

After you understand, analyze, and sketch the rules, it's time for Step 4 of the Kaplan Method: making deductions. Deductions occur when you combine rules and restrictions to determine what else must, cannot, and could be true in each game. Making appropriate deductions is key to Logic Games success.

LEARNING OBJECTIVES

In this section, you'll learn to:

· Identify the points of greatest restriction within a logic game
· Use the BLEND checklist to make all available deductions within a logic game
· Identify Floaters (unrestricted entities) after making all available deductions
· Know when all available deductions have been made (and it is time to move on to answering the questions)

As an example, take a look at a couple of the rules you saw in the Nurses' Information Sessions game.

LSAT Rule		Analysis
Griseldi's session must be on the day before Khan's.	$\rightarrow$	GK
Farnham's session must be on an earlier day than Khan's but on a later day than Lightfoot's.	$\rightarrow$	L … F … K
PrepTest61 Sec3 Qs 18–23		

Instead of considering each of these rules separately, consider them together. Notice that K is an entity in both rules. Can you combine them and make a deduction?

   L … F … GK

Combined, we now know that both L and F must come before G (which must come immediately before K).

Making good deductions isn't the result of blind luck, or magic. Like the rest of the LSAT, it's the result of following a specific approach and recognizing common patterns. In fact, most deductions will come from a combination of five types of rules. Remember them by memorizing the mnemonic BLEND:

LSAT STRATEGY

Blocks of Entities—Two or more players who are always grouped together

Limited Options—Rules or restrictions that limit the overall setup to one of two acceptable arrangements

Established Entities—A player locked into a specific space or group

Numbers Restrictions—Rules or limitations that provide guidance about the number of entities assigned to a group or space

Duplications—Entities that appear in two or more rules, thus allowing the rules to be combined

---

NOTE: BLEND is not a series of steps. You needn't go through it in order. It is a checklist to help ensure that you check for all of the possible deductions in each game.

Deductions in Sequencing Games

As you practice, take note of the types of rules and restrictions that tend to produce deductions most often in various game types. Here are the most likely sources of deductions in Sequencing games.

LSAT STRATEGY

In Sequencing games, deductions are likely to stem from:

· **Blocks of Entities**—Two or more entities that are linked together; when one is placed, the other's movement is determined or restricted

· **Duplications**—Entities shared by two or more rules; duplications are almost always at the heart of Loose Sequencing games

· **Established Entities**—Entities placed into a specific space; even if no rule directly provides for an Established Entity, you may be able to determine an entity's exact position by combining other rules

In Sequencing games, deductions may involve:

· **Limited Options**—The situation arises when a Block of Entities or a key player (an entity affecting the positions of other entities) can take either of two positions; when this occurs, create Limited Options sketches

· **Numbers Restrictions**—Limitations or rules affecting the number of entities that can be placed in a given position; this is rare in Sequencing games—typically, the limitation is one per space

---

Practice

Practice by working through some deductions common to Sequencing games.

These practice examples apply to the following basic Strict Sequencing model. For each example, translate both rules. Then, combine the rules and find all possible deductions. Keep in mind that some deductions will be "negative," i.e., they will determine where a given entity cannot be placed. Analyze each pair of statements independently; the examples are **not** cumulative.

$$\begin{array}{cccccc} P & Q & R & S & T & U \\ \hline \overline{1} & \overline{2} & \overline{3} & \overline{4} & \overline{5} & \overline{6} \end{array}$$

Sequencing Rule	**My Analysis**
65. P must be scheduled before R. S must be scheduled for the day before T.	$\longrightarrow$
66. Q must be scheduled for Day 3. S must be scheduled for the day before T.	$\longrightarrow$
67. R must be scheduled for some day after P. R must be scheduled for the day before T.	$\longrightarrow$
68. R must be scheduled for some day before U. P must be scheduled for some day after U.	$\longrightarrow$
69. U must be scheduled for Day 3. P must be scheduled for exactly three days before Q.	$\longrightarrow$
70. R must be scheduled for some time before Q. Q must be scheduled for some time after T.	$\longrightarrow$

The following examples apply to a Loose Sequencing sketch. Translate each rule into its shorthand, and combine the rules in one chain. Then, answer each of the questions.

A B C D E F

Loose Sequencing Rule		My Analysis
C must be earlier than D.	$\longrightarrow$	
D must be earlier than F.	$\longrightarrow$	
B must be earlier than D.	$\longrightarrow$	
E must be later than F.	$\longrightarrow$	
A must be later than B.	$\longrightarrow$	

Combined Rules:

Answer each of the following deductive questions or write "Impossible to know."

71. Who comes earlier, B or E?	$\longrightarrow$
72. Who comes earlier, C or F?	$\longrightarrow$
73. Who comes earlier, A or F?	$\longrightarrow$
74. Who comes earlier, A or C?	$\longrightarrow$
75. How many entities must come before D?	$\longrightarrow$
76. How many entities must come after C?	$\longrightarrow$
77. Which entities could possibly go first?	$\longrightarrow$
78. Which entities could possibly go last?	$\longrightarrow$

Expert Analysis

Now, take a look at how an expert evaluated each of the Sequencing deductions you just saw.

All of these practice examples apply to the following basic Strict Sequencing game.

$$P \quad Q \quad R \quad S \quad T \quad U$$

$$\overline{1} \quad \overline{2} \quad \overline{3} \quad \overline{4} \quad \overline{5} \quad \overline{6}$$

Sequencing Rule	Analysis
65. P must be scheduled before R. S must be scheduled for the day before T.	$\underline{P \dots R}$ $\boxed{S \ T}$ **Deductions:** The negative implications of each rule mean that R and T can't be on Day 1, and P and S can't be on Day 6. The two rules do not share any entities, and so do not combine for further deductions. **Sketch:** $\overline{\quad} \ \overline{\quad} \ \overline{\quad} \ \overline{\quad} \ \overline{\quad} \ \overline{\quad}$ 1　2　3　4　5　6 ~R　　　　　　~P ~T　　　　　　~S

All of these practice examples apply to the following basic Strict Sequencing game.

P Q R S T U

___ ___ ___ ___ ___ ___
1   2   3   4   5   6

Sequencing Rule	**Analysis**

66. Q must be scheduled for Day 3.
    S must be scheduled for the day before T.

Add the first rule directly to the sketch.

| S T |

The ST block can only go in spaces 1 and 2, spaces 4 and 5, or spaces 5 and 6.

→ **Sketch:**

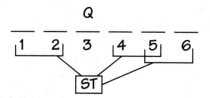

67. R must be scheduled for some day after P.
    R must be scheduled for the day before T.

P...R

| R T |

Combine them:

P...R T

→ **Deductions:** R cannot be first or last; P has at least two entities after it; and T has at least two entities before it.

Sketch:

___ ___ ___ ___ ___ ___
1   2   3   4   5   6
~R   ~T   ~P   ~P
~T   ~R

All of these practice examples apply to the following basic Strict Sequencing game.

P Q R S T U

__ __ __ __ __ __
1 2 3 4 5 6

Sequencing Rule	**Analysis**
68. R must be scheduled for some day before U. P must be scheduled for some day after U.	R...U U...P Then combine: R...U...P → **Sketch:** __ __ __ __ __ __ 1 2 3 4 5 6 ~U ~P ~R ~U ~P ~R
69. U must be scheduled for Day 3. P must be scheduled for exactly three days before Q.	Put the first rule in the sketch. P __ __ Q Combine the two rules: P __ __ Q can only go in spaces 1 and 4 or in spaces → 2 and 5. **Sketch:** P __ __ U Q __ __ 1 2 3 4 5 6 __ P U __ Q __ 1 2 3 4 5 6

All of these practice examples apply to the following basic Strict Sequencing game.

P Q R S T U

—— —— —— —— —— ——
1   2   3   4   5   6

Sequencing Rule		Analysis
70. R must be scheduled for some time before Q. Q must be scheduled for some time after T.		R ... Q T ... Q

Both rules discuss Q. Combine these rules:

$\longrightarrow$

T··.
    ·.·Q
R···

Impact on sketch:

—— —— —— —— —— ——
1   2   3   4   5   6
~Q   ~Q   ~T
                        ~R

The following rules apply to a Loose Sequencing sketch incorporating the following entities.

A   B   C   D   E   F

Loose Sequencing Rule		Analysis
C must be earlier than D.	$\rightarrow$	C...D or C | D
D must be earlier than F.	$\rightarrow$	D...F or D | F
B must be earlier than D.	$\rightarrow$	B...D or B | D
E must be later than F.	$\rightarrow$	F...E or F | E
A must be later than B.	$\rightarrow$	B...A or B | A

Combined Rules

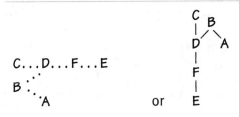

C...D...F...E
B
  A   or

C
\|
D   B
\| ╱ \
F   A
\|
E

Answer each of the following deductive questions or write "Impossible to know."

71. Who comes earlier, B or E?	$\rightarrow$	B
72. Who comes earlier, C or F?	$\rightarrow$	C
73. Who comes earlier, A or F?	$\rightarrow$	Impossible to know
74. Who comes earlier, A or C?	$\rightarrow$	Impossible to know
75. How many entities must come before D?	$\rightarrow$	2 (C and B)
76. How many entities must come after C?	$\rightarrow$	3 (D, E, and F)
77. Which entities could possibly go first?	$\rightarrow$	B or C
78. Which entities could possibly go last?	$\rightarrow$	A or E

Deductions in Selection Games

Because the great majority of Selection rules involve Formal Logic, simply noting the valid contrapositive of each rule is a great source of deductions. Having the contrapositives down also helps you to see which rules trigger others.

LSAT STRATEGY

In Selection games, deductions are likely to stem from:

- **Duplications**—Entities shared by two or more rules; Selection games often feature "chains," or duplications of Formal Logic linked by shared entities.
- **Numbers Restrictions**—Restrictions or limitations on the number of entities to be selected or determinations of the minimum and maximum numbers that can be selected given the game's rules.

In Selection games, deductions may involve:

- **Limited Options**—The situation that arises when a rule specifies only one of two selection patterns is acceptable (e.g., G is selected and F is not selected, or F is selected and G is not selected)
- **Blocks of Entities**—Two or more entities that must be selected or rejected as a pair
- **Established Entities**—Entities that must be selected or rejected; this is very rare in Selection games where all or most rules are conditional; occasionally, the Numbers Restrictions will allow you to determine that a specific entity can never be selected

---

Practice

Let's take a look at some common deductions in Selection games. Translate the following rules into consistent, repeatable shorthand—and be on the lookout for Formal Logic!

Selection Rule	$\longrightarrow$	**My Analysis**
A bakery sells six types of treats—B, C, E, F, G, and J.		
79. If J is not purchased, then G is purchased.	$\longrightarrow$	
80. If C is purchased, then E or F or both are also purchased.	$\longrightarrow$	
81. E cannot be purchased unless B is purchased.	$\longrightarrow$	
82. F and G cannot both be purchased.	$\longrightarrow$	

Selection Rule	**My Analysis**

Entities of two types: G, H, J, L, M, and N (select four of these); and s, t, u, v, and w (select two of these)

83. If M is selected, *v* must be selected but G cannot be selected.

$\longrightarrow$

84. If *s* is selected, G must be selected.

$\longrightarrow$

85. If either J or L is selected, the other must also be selected.

$\longrightarrow$

Expert Analysis

Now, take a look at how an LSAT expert might handle these rules.

Selection Rule	Analysis
A bakery sells six types of treats—B, C, E, F, G, and J.	
79. If J is not purchased, then G is purchased.	If ~J → Ⓖ If ~G → Ⓙ → This rule means that you must select J or G or both. The only thing forbidden is to have both J and G rejected. This establishes a minimum of one treat selected.
80. If C is purchased, then E or F or both are also purchased.	If Ⓒ → Ⓔ or Ⓕ If ~E and ~F → ~C → Either E or F may be excluded and C can still be selected; only the exclusion of both E and F takes out C. Finally, because *or* is inclusive in Formal Logic, the "or both" portion of this rule is redundant and is accounted for by the rule as written.
81. E cannot be purchased unless B is purchased.	→ If Ⓔ → Ⓑ If ~B → ~E
82. F and G cannot both be purchased.	If Ⓕ → ~G If Ⓖ → ~F or **Never FG** The rule reduces by one the maximum number of treats that may be selected. Use the duplicated entity G to combine this with the rule in #79. If Ⓕ → ~G → Ⓙ If ~J → Ⓖ → ~F

Selection Rule	Analysis
Entities of two types: G, H, J, L, M, and N (select four of these); and s, t, u, v, and w (select two of these)	In this Selection game, the number of entities that will be chosen is specified. You can set up a sketch with slots for entities that are selected and for those that are excluded:

$\longrightarrow$

G H J L M N   s t u v w
in   out   in   out
— — — —|— —|— —|— — —

83. If M is selected, *v* must be selected but G cannot be selected.

If   Ⓜ → Ⓥ and ~G
If Ⓖ or ~v → ~M

or

If Ⓜ   → Ⓥ
If ~v   → ~M

Never MG

$\longrightarrow$

A "never pair" in a Selection game with specified numbers is noteworthy, because one member of the pair will take one of the "out" spots.

G H J L M N   s t u v w
in   out   in   out
— — — —|M/G —|— —|— — —

Selection Rule	**Analysis**

84. If *s* is selected, G must be selected.

→

If ⑤→Ⓖ

If ~G → ~s

This rule shares an entity with the first rule. Because the selection of *s* triggers the selection of G and the selection of G triggers the rejection of M, you can deduce:

If ⑤ → ~M

If Ⓜ → ~s

---

85. If either J or L is selected, the other must also be selected.

→

If Ⓙ → Ⓛ

If ~L → ~J

If Ⓛ → Ⓙ

If ~J → ~L

or

J ↔ L

or

JL: Both or neither

Again, because you must select exactly four of G, H, J, L, M, and N, this rule takes on special significance. J and L must both be in or both be out. However, because of rule #83, one of G and M must also be out. Thus, only one "out" spot remains, and there isn't room for both J and L to be out. Thus, J and L are both selected.

```
G H J L M N              s t u v w
in          out          in       out
 J  L __ __|M/G__       __ __|__ __ __
```

Deductions in Matching Games

Matching game rules tend to produce many deductions at the intersection of Numbers Restrictions and Duplications. These deductions can be very powerful. For example, a game in which children are being given different kinds of toys might tell you that Matt gets exactly two toys while another rule tells you that Oliver gets more toys than Matt. You now know that Oliver receives three or more of the toys.

Here are the deductions most commonly associated with Matching games. Be on the lookout for these patterns as you practice.

LSAT STRATEGY

In Matching games, deductions are likely to stem from:

- **Duplications**—Entities shared by two or more rules; one rule might match a certain attribute to entity X, and another might tell you that entity Y has more attributes matched to it than X does.

- **Numbers Restrictions**—Limitations on the number of attributes that can be assigned to a given entity or limitations on the number of entities to which an attribute can be matched.

- **Established Entities**—Matches between entities and attributes that must be maintained throughout the game (e.g., Entity X wears the red jacket); Established Entities are quite common in Matching games.

In Matching games, deductions may involve:

- **Blocks of Entities**—Two or more entities that must be assigned a given attribute or two or more attributes that must be assigned to the same entity or entities; Blocks are somewhat rare in Matching games.

- **Limited Options**—The situation that arises when a rule or combination of rules makes all acceptable arrangements fall into one of two patterns; Limited Options is a rare deduction to find in Matching games.

Practice

Get some practice now by making some deductions commonly found in Matching games. Each of the following practice examples applies to the following basic Matching sketch. The italicized text in each example states the task and is followed by two or three rules. For each exercise, translate the rules and combine them to make deductions.

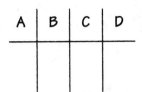

Matching Rules		**My Analysis**
86. *Each of entities A, B, C, and D will be given at least one object of types x, y, and z.*		
An object of type *x* is given to three of the entities.	$\longrightarrow$	
Any object matched with A is not matched with B.		

Matching Rules	**My Analysis**

87. *Each of entities A, B, C, and D will be assigned exactly two of tasks r, s, and t.*

Any task assigned to C will be assigned to D.

Task *r* is assigned to only one of the entities. $\longrightarrow$

88. *At least one of attributes m, n, and p will be matched with each of entities A, B, C, and D.*

More attributes are matched to entity B than to entity A.

More attributes are matched to entity C than to entity B. $\longrightarrow$

Any attribute matched to entity A will be matched to entity D.

Expert Analysis

Take a look at the way an LSAT expert translates rules and makes appropriate deductions in each of the previous examples. Each of these practice examples applies to the following basic Matching sketch.

$$\begin{array}{c|c|c|c} A & B & C & D \\ \hline & & & \end{array}$$

Matching Rules	**Analysis**
86. *Each of entities A, B, C, and D will be given at least one object of types x, y, and z.* An object of type *x* is given to three of the entities. Any object matched with A is not matched with B.	The two rules can be added to the space above the sketch. Note the object types and note that there are exactly three *x*'s to be placed on the sketch. The second rule states that any object matched with A is not matched with B. In Formal Logic, you could write that as: If with A → ~ with B If with B → ~ with A or AB never same This affects the number restrictions. It is not possible for either A or B to have all three of *x*, *y*, and *z*. Combine the rules: Where can the three *x*'s go? If A has an *x*, then B cannot, and vice versa. Therefore, both C and D must have *x*. **Sketch:** (x x x) y z (1–2)(1–2) $$\begin{array}{c|c|c|c} A & B & C & D \\ \hline & & x & x \end{array}$$ AB never same

Matching Rules	**Analysis**

87. *Each of entities A, B, C, and D will be assigned exactly two of tasks r, s, and t.*

Any task assigned to C will be assigned to D.

Task *r* is assigned to only one of the entities.

Account for the task by placing two slots under each of A, B, C, and D. Jot the two rules to the side of the sketch in shorthand, and consider their combined implications.

Because C and D must be assigned identical tasks, and since task *r* can be assigned to only one entity, entity C cannot do task *r*. Thus, C and D must both tackle tasks *s* and *t*.

$\longrightarrow$ **Sketch:**

```
                    r s t

              A   B   C   D
If with C → with D  ___ ___ s   s
   only one r
              ___ ___ t   t
```

88. *At least one of attributes m, n, and p will be matched with each of entities A, B, C, and D.*

More attributes are matched to entity B than to entity A.

More attributes are matched to entity C than to entity B.

Any attribute matched to entity A will be matched to entity D.

Jot down all three rules in shorthand and consider their implications. The first two rules deal with the number limitations on entities A, B, C, and D. There are three attributes, so the number of attributes matched to each of A, B, and C is now clear: C must have 3, B must have 2, and A can have only 1.

$\longrightarrow$ **Sketch:**

```
                        m n p

              1   2   3  (1–3)
              A   B   C   D
more B than A
more C than B         m
with A → with D  //  ___ ___ ___
                      //    n
                           p
                          //
```

Be careful with the third rule: That any attribute matched with A will be matched with D does not mean that any attribute matched with D must be matched with A. D could have anywhere from 1 to 3 of *m*, *n*, and *p* matched to it, and A will be matched with one of the attributes matched to D.

Deductions in Distribution Games

While Distribution games have much in common with Matching games, remember that, in Distribution tasks, once you assign an entity to a group, you typically cannot assign it to any other group. This fundamental restriction places a huge premium on the Numbers Restrictions in the game. Once you identify your task as Distribution, make absolutely sure you understand how the numbers must work out. That's the basis of a strategic approach here.

LSAT STRATEGY

In Distribution games, deductions are likely to stem from:

- **Numbers Restrictions**—Limitations on the number of entities per group or determinations of the minimum and maximum numbers of entities per group; in Distribution games, rules preventing entities from being assigned to the same group may act as de facto Numbers Restrictions (e.g., B and F must see different events; ergo, each event has at least one attendee).
- **Blocks of Entities**—These are two or more entities that must be placed in the same group.
- **Limited Options**—The situation that arises when the game specifies only two possible patterns for the number of entities per group (e.g., Group A contains four students and Group B contains five students, or Group A contains five students and Group B contains four students); in Distribution games, you can sometimes determine a Limited Options numbers scenario by applying other rules to the game's overall framework.
- **Duplications**—Entities shared by two or more rules; a common occurrence in Distribution games is one rule that says A and B will be in the same group and another rule that says A and C cannot be in the same group—from this, you can deduce that B and C cannot be in the same group.

In Distribution games, deductions may involve:

- **Established Entities**—Entities that are assigned to one group for the entire game; this is not very common in Distribution games.

Practice

Now, get some practice by making some of the deductions most commonly associated with Distribution games. In each exercise, examine the task in italics and decide how to set up a simple sketch. Analyze and draw each of the numbered rules. Then, see if combining the rules provides additional deductions about what must, can, or cannot be true in each case.

Distribution Rule	My Analysis
Each of five students—A, B, C, D, and E—will be placed on Team 1 or Team 2.	
89. A and B are on the same team.	

$\longrightarrow$

90. C and D are on different teams.

$\longrightarrow$

91. Team 1 has fewer players than Team 2.

$\longrightarrow$

Distribution Rule	**My Analysis**

Each of five cards—F, G, H, J, and K—will be placed in pile 1 or pile 2.

92. If F is in pile 1, then G is in pile 2.

$\longrightarrow$

93. If H is in pile 2, then J is in pile 2.

$\longrightarrow$

94. If J is in pile 2, then F is in pile 1.

$\longrightarrow$

95. J and K are in different piles.

$\longrightarrow$

Each of six mugs—L, M, N, P, Q, and R—will be placed in cabinet 1, cabinet 2, or cabinet 3.

96. Cabinet 2 contains at least two more mugs than cabinet 1 contains.

$\longrightarrow$

97. L and M are in different cabinets.

$\longrightarrow$

98. L and N are in the same cabinet.

$\longrightarrow$

99. If P is in cabinet 1, then Q is in cabinet 2.

$\longrightarrow$

Expert Analysis

Now, take a look at how an LSAT expert might have approached these exercises.

Distribution Rule		Analysis
Each of five students—A, B, C, D, and E—will be placed on Team 1 or Team 2.	→	A B C D E 1 | 2
89. A and B are on the same team.	→	A B
90. C and D are on different teams.	→	Add this rule directly to the sketch: One of C or D will be on Team 1 and one of C or D will be on Team 2. [See final sketch.]
91. Team 1 has fewer players than Team 2.	→	Rule #90 makes it clear that each team will have at least one student. Based on that, Rule #91 establishes that team 1 will have either 1 or 2 students, while Team 2 will have either 3 or 4 students.

Deductions:

The A-B block runs into restrictions in the numbers. The A-B block cannot go on Team 1 because one of C or D is already taking a spot there. A and B join Team 2. Student E is a Floater and can be on either team.

Sketch:

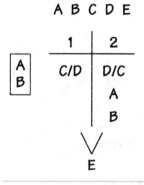

Distribution Rule		**Analysis**

Each of five cards—F, G, H, J, and K—will be placed in pile 1 or pile 2.	$\rightarrow$	F G H J K
		
		  1 $\vert$ 2
		  $\vert$
		  $\vert$
		  $\vert$
		
		While translating the rules, remember that, with exactly two groups, the condition "<u>not</u> in pile 1" is equivalent to "must be in pile 2."

92. If F is in pile 1, then G is in pile 2.	$\rightarrow$	If F1 $\rightarrow$ G2 If G1 $\rightarrow$ F2 NOTE: F and G need not always be in separate groups. They could both be in pile 2 (and at least one of them must be in pile 2).
93. If H is in pile 2, then J is in pile 2.	$\rightarrow$	If H2 $\rightarrow$ J2 If J1 $\rightarrow$ H1
94. If J is in pile 2, then F is in pile 1.	$\rightarrow$	If J2 $\rightarrow$ F1 If F2 $\rightarrow$ J1
95. J and K are in different piles.	$\rightarrow$	Add directly to the sketch: One of J/K in pile 1 and one of J/K in pile 2. [See final sketch.]

Deductions:

All of the rules contain conditional Formal Logic statements. When given a series of Formal Logic statements, look for duplicate entities. Some test takers find it helpful to write out Formal Logic deduction chains:

If H2 $\rightarrow$ J2 $\rightarrow$ F1 $\rightarrow$ G2

If G1 $\rightarrow$ F2 $\rightarrow$ J1 $\rightarrow$ H1

Sketch:

F G H J K

1	2
J/K	K/J

If $F_1 \rightarrow G_2$

If $G_1 \rightarrow F_2$

If $H_2 \rightarrow J_2$

If $J_1 \rightarrow H_1$

If $J_2 \rightarrow F_1$

If $F_2 \rightarrow J_1$

Distribution Rule	Analysis

Each of six mugs (L, M, N, P, Q, and R) will be placed in cabinet 1, cabinet 2, or cabinet 3.

→

L M N P Q R

1	2	3

NOTE: No rule prescribes a minimum number of mugs per cabinet. It's possible that a cabinet has all of the mugs, or no mugs.

---

96. Cabinet 2 contains at least two more mugs than cabinet 1 contains.

→

Cab 2 > Cab 1

(2+)

Flesh out the implications of this rule. Because cabinet 1 might contain no mugs, the minimum number possible in cabinet 2 is two. Likewise, the maximum number of mugs possible in cabinet 1 is two, because that would require cabinet 2 to have four (thus using up all of the mugs). Because cabinet 2 must have at least two mugs, the maximum number cabinet 3 could have is four. Add all of this to the sketch.

L M N P Q R

(0–2)	(2–6)	(0–4)
1	2	3

___
___

---

97. L and M are in different cabinets.

→

Never ML or $\begin{array}{c} M \\ \diagup \\ L \end{array}$

NOTE: Because no cabinet may have all six mugs, the number range for cabinet 2 is now 2–5. Change that in the sketch.

Distribution Rule	Analysis
98. L and N are in the same cabinet.	$\boxed{\begin{array}{c} L \\ N \end{array}}$
$\longrightarrow$ Combining Rule #98 with Rule #97 produces:	
Never MN or $\boxed{\begin{array}{c} \cancel{M} \\ N \end{array}}$	

99. If P is in cabinet 1, then Q is in cabinet 2.	If $P_1 \longrightarrow Q_2$ If $\sim Q_2 \longrightarrow \sim P_1$ or If $Q_{(1 \text{ or } 3)} \longrightarrow P_{(2 \text{ or } 3)}$

Deductions:

In this case, all deductions were made as rules were added one by one.

Sketch:

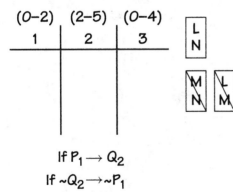

Deductions in Hybrid Games

In Hybrid games, expect to see the same types of deductions you saw earlier in the chapter centering around individual game actions.

LSAT STRATEGY

In Hybrid games, deductions are likely to stem from:

- **BLEND**—Because Hybrid games may involve any of the standard logic games actions, all five of the BLEND elements are on the table.
- **"Cross Over" rules**—In Hybrid games, keep an eye out for rules that provide restrictions to both of the actions in the game.

Remember that, in the section of this chapter on rules, you learned to ask about rules in Hybrid games, "Does this rule affect the first action? The second? Both?" As you turn to the deduction step, keep your eyes open for situations in which rules targeting one of the Hybrid game's actions allows you to make deductions about the other action.

Practice

Now, practice by making deductions commonly found in Hybrid games. Apply the rules in the scenarios on the facing page to the Sequencing/Matching Hybrid model that follows. Treat A, B, C, D, and E as entities to be sequenced, and treat x, y, and z as attributes to be matched to each entity. Analyze and draw each of the rules. Then, consider how the rules can be combined to produce additional deductions.

$$\underline{\quad}\ \underline{\quad}\ \underline{\quad}\ \underline{\quad}\ \underline{\quad}\ \text{A B C D E}$$
$$\ \ 1\quad 2\quad 3\quad 4\quad 5$$
$$\underline{\quad}\ \underline{\quad}\ \underline{\quad}\ \underline{\quad}\ \underline{\quad}\ \text{x y z}$$

Hybrid Rule		My Analysis
Scenario I		
100. A cannot be matched with x.	$\longrightarrow$	
101. Exactly two people are matched with x, and they are consecutive.	$\longrightarrow$	
102. C is matched with z.		
103. There are exactly two spaces between C and A.	$\longrightarrow$	

Deductions:

Hybrid Rule		My Analysis
Scenario II		
104. C is placed immediately before D.	$\longrightarrow$	
105. Exactly two people matched with y are placed after D.	$\longrightarrow$	
106. Nobody matched with y is next to another person matched with y.	$\longrightarrow$	

Deductions:

Expert Analysis

Here's how an expert might analyze the scenarios in the practice exercise.

$$\underline{\quad}\ \underline{\quad}\ \underline{\quad}\ \underline{\quad}\ \underline{\quad}\ A\ B\ C\ D\ E$$
$$\ 1\quad 2\quad 3\quad 4\quad 5$$

$$\underline{\quad}\ \underline{\quad}\ \underline{\quad}\ \underline{\quad}\ \underline{\quad}\ x\ y\ z$$

Hybrid Rule		Analysis
Scenario I		Turn this rule into a positive deduction:
100. A cannot be matched with *x*.	$\longrightarrow$	$\dfrac{A}{y/z}$
101. Exactly two people are matched with *x*, and they are consecutive.	$\longrightarrow$	$\dfrac{\underline{\ }\ \underline{\ }}{x\quad x}$
102. C is matched with *z*.	$\longrightarrow$	$\dfrac{C}{z}$
103. There are exactly two spaces between C and A.	$\longrightarrow$	A/C __ __ C/A

Deductions:

The A-C block will fit only in spaces 1 and 4 or in spaces 2 and 5. That creates Limited Options. Because neither A nor C may be matched with *x*, the *x-x* block must take the spaces between A and C.

Sketch:

A/C __ __ C/A __ A B C D E
1   2   3   4   5

__ x x __ __ x y z

__ A/C __ __ C/A A B C D E
1   2   3   4   5

__ __ x x __ x y z

Hybrid Rule		**Analysis**

Scenario II

104. C is placed immediately before D. $\longrightarrow$

105. Exactly two people matched with *y* are placed after D.

Because the preceding rule also dealt with D, combine this rule with that rule:

$\longrightarrow$

106. Nobody matched with *y* is next to another person matched with *y*. $\longrightarrow$

Deductions:

Combine the last rule with the second rule: The two *y*'s that are placed after D cannot be next to each other. Because there are only five positions in the sketch, the C-D block will take spots 1 and 2, and the two *y*'s will be matched to the entities in spots 3 and 5.

Sketch:

$$\underline{\ C\ }\ \underline{\ D\ }\ \underline{\ \ \ }\ \underline{\ \ \ }\ \underline{\ \ \ }\quad A\ B\ C\ D\ E$$
$$\ \ 1\quad 2\quad 3\quad 4\quad 5$$
$$\underline{\ \ \ }\ \underline{\ \ \ }\ \underline{\ y\ }\ \underline{\ \ \ }\ \underline{\ y\ }\quad x\ v\ z$$

LSAT GAME PRACTICE

Now that you are familiar with Steps 3 and 4 of the Logic Games Method, try setting up the official LSAT games you saw in Chapter 3 all the way through the Deduction step. To get you started, we've provided summaries of an LSAT expert's thinking on Steps 1 and 2. For each rule, determine whether you can add the information to the sketch, or how you would write the rule in shorthand. Then, make deductions using the BLEND checklist.

Summary Program Classes

LSAT Question	My Analysis
A summer program offers at least one of the following seven courses: geography, history, literature, mathematics, psychology, sociology, zoology. The following restrictions on the program must apply:	**Step 1: Overview** **Situation:** Summer program offering classes **Entities:** The classes—G, H, L, M, P, S, Z **Action:** "Offers at least one … " indicates that this is a Selection game. Determine which courses are offered. ⟶ **Limitations:** Select at least one of the courses. **Step 2: Sketch** For a Selection game that does not have a specified number of selected entities, the sketch can simply be the roster of entities: G H L M P S Z
If mathematics is offered, then either literature or sociology (but not both) is offered.	⟶ **Step 3: Rules**
If literature is offered, then geography is also offered but psychology is not.	⟶
If sociology is offered, then psychology is also offered but zoology is not.	
If geography is offered, then both history and zoology are also offered. *PrepTest49 Sec 1 Qs 13–17*	⟶

My Analysis (cont.)

Step 4: Deductions (make any deductions here, and add to your master sketch)

Museum Photographs

LSAT Question	My Analysis

A museum curator is arranging seven photographs—*Fence, Gardenias, Hibiscus, Irises, Katydid, Lotus,* and *Magnolia*—on a gallery wall in accordance with the photographer's requirements. The photographs are to be hung along the wall in a row, in seven positions sequentially numbered from first to seventh. The photographer's requirements are as follows:

→

Step 1: Overview
Situation: Arranging photographs on a wall
Entities: The photos—F, G, H, I, K, L, M
Action: "Hung along the wall in a row ... " indicates that order matters. This is a Sequencing game.
Limitations: Each photo gets its own spot.

Step 2: Sketch

F G H I K L M

— — — — — — —
1 2 3 4 5 6 7

Gardenias must be immediately before *Katydid.*

→

Step 3: Rules

Hibiscus must be somewhere before *Katydid* but cannot be the first photograph.

→

Irises and *Lotus* must be next to one another.

→

Magnolia must be one of the first three photographs.

→

Fence must be either first or seventh.

PrepTest59 Sec1 Qs 6–10 →

Step 4: Deductions (make any deductions here, and add to your master sketch)

Parcel Delivery

LSAT Question	My Analysis
A courier delivers exactly eight parcels—G, H, J, K, L, M, N, and O. No two parcels are delivered at the same time, nor is any parcel delivered more than once. The following conditions must apply:	**Step 1: Overview** **Situation:** Courier delivering packages **Entities:** Parcels—G, H, J, K, L, M, N, O **Action:** "No two parcels are delivered at the same time ... " Sequencing game. **Limitations:** Each package delivered separately, used only once. **Step 2: Sketch** Look at the rules. This is a Loose Sequencing game. Build the sketch as you go.
L is delivered later than H.	**Step 3: Rules**
K is delivered earlier than O.	
H is delivered earlier than M.	
O is delivered later than G.	
M is delivered earlier than G.	
Both N and J are delivered earlier than M. *PrepTest51 Sec4 Qs 16–22*	

Step 4: Deductions (make any deductions here, and add to your master sketch)

Clown Costume

LSAT Question	My Analysis
A clown will select a costume consisting of two pieces and no others: a jacket and overalls. One piece of the costume will be entirely one color, and the other piece will be plaid. Selection is subject to the following restrictions:	**Step 1: Overview** **Situation:** Clown picking clothes to wear **Entities:** Two pieces of clothing—jacket and overalls; two patterns—uniform color or plaid **Action:** Determine the pattern of each piece of clothing. This is a Matching game. **Limitation:** There are no limitations so far. **Step 2: Sketch** A table is an easy sketch for Matching games. jacket | overalls
If the jacket is plaid, then there must be exactly three colors in it.	**Step 3: Rules**
If the overalls are plaid, then there must be exactly two colors in them.	
The jacket and overalls must have exactly one color in common.	
Green, red, and violet are the only colors that can be in the jacket.	
Red, violet, and yellow are the only colors that can be in the overalls. *PrepTest51 Sec4 Qs 1–5*	

Step 4: Deductions (make any deductions here, and add to your master sketch)

Convention Car Pool

LSAT Question	My Analysis
Exactly six workers—Faith, Gus, Hannah, Juan, Kenneth, and Lisa—will travel to a business convention in two cars—car 1 and car 2. Each car must carry at least two of the workers, one of whom will be assigned to drive. For the entire trip, the workers will comply with an assignment that also meets the following constraints:	**Step 1: Overview** **Situation:** Workers traveling in two different cars **Entities:** The two cars—1 and 2—and the six workers—F, G, H, J, K, and L **Action:** Determine which workers drive and which ride in each car; a Distribution game. **Limitations:** Minimum of two and maximum of four workers in each car; the driver of each car is specified.

$\longrightarrow$ **Step 2: Sketch**
Use a table for Distribution games.

	car 1	car 2
driver:	___	___
riders:	___	___
	. . .	. . .
	. . .	. . .

Either Faith or Gus must drive the car in which Hannah travels. $\longrightarrow$	**Step 3: Rules**
Either Faith or Kenneth must drive the car in which Juan travels. $\longrightarrow$	
Gus must travel in the same car as Lisa. *PrepTest61 Sec3 Qs 1–5* $\longrightarrow$	

Step 4: Deductions (make any deductions here, and add to your master sketch)

Guitarist's Demo CD

LSAT Question	My Analysis
A locally known guitarist's demo CD contains exactly seven different songs—S, T, V, W, X, Y, and Z. Each song occupies exactly one of the CD's seven tracks. Some of the songs are rock classics; the others are new compositions. The following conditions must hold:	**Step 1: Overview** **Situation:** A demo CD with seven songs. **Entities:** The seven songs—S, T, V, W, X, Y, and Z—and the two styles—rock classics and new **Action:** Order the songs, first to seventh. Determine the style of each song; a Sequencing/Matching Hybrid game. **Limitations:** Each song occupies exactly one track, so no ties. The number of rock songs and new songs is undefined.

Step 2: Sketch

— — — — — — — S T V W X Y Z

— — — — — — — r n

1   2   3   4   5   6   7

S occupies the fourth track of the CD.	**Step 3: Rules**
Both W and Y precede S on the CD.	
T precedes W on the CD.	
A rock classic occupies the sixth track of the CD.	
Each rock classic is immediately preceded on the CD by a new composition.	
Z is a rock classic. *PrepTest51 Sec4 Qs 11–15*	

Step 4: Deductions (make any deductions here, and add to your master sketch)

Expert Analysis

Here is an LSAT expert's analysis on each of those practice games.

Summer Program Classes

LSAT Question	Analysis
A summer program offers at least one of the following seven courses: geography, history, literature, mathematics, psychology, sociology, zoology. The following restrictions on the program must apply:	**Step 1: Overview** **Situation:** Summer program offering classes **Entities:** The classes—G, H, L, M, P, S, Z **Action:** "Offers at least one … " indicates that this is a Selection game. Need to determine which courses are offered. **Limitations:** Need to select at least one of the courses. **Step 2: Sketch** For a Selection game that does not have a specified number of selected entities, the sketch can simply be the roster of entities: G H L M P S Z
If mathematics is offered, then either literature or sociology (but not both) is offered.	**Step 3: Rules** If Ⓜ → [exactly one of Ⓛ/Ⓢ] If ~[exactly one of L/S] → ~M
If literature is offered, then geography is also offered but psychology is not.	If Ⓛ → Ⓖ If ~G → ~L If Ⓛ → ~P If Ⓟ → ~L } Never LP together
If sociology is offered, then psychology is also offered but zoology is not.	If Ⓢ → Ⓟ If ~P → ~S If Ⓢ → ~Z If Ⓩ → ~S } Never SZ together

Summer Program Classes (cont.)

LSAT Question	Analysis
If geography is offered, then both history and zoology are also offered. *PrepTest49 Sec1 Qs 13–17* →	If Ⓖ → Ⓗ If ~H → ~G If Ⓖ → Ⓩ If ~Z → ~G

Step 4: Deductions

In a Selection game, look to key entities and Floaters. Here, all entities are represented in the rules, so there are no Floaters.

We do know that L and P can never be offered together and that S and Z can never be offered together.

Some test takers like to create chains of deductions before heading into the rest of the game. For example:

Museum Photographs

LSAT Question	Analysis
A museum curator is arranging seven photographs—*Fence, Gardenias, Hibiscus, Irises, Katydid, Lotus,* and *Magnolia*—on a gallery wall in accordance with the photographer's requirements. The photographs are to be hung along the wall in a row, in seven positions sequentially numbered from first to seventh. The photographer's requirements are as follows:	**Step 1: Overview** **Situation:** Arranging photographs on a wall **Entities:** The photos—F, G, H, I, K, L, M **Action:** "Hung along the wall in a row … " indicates that order matters. This is a Sequencing game. **Limitations:** Each photo gets its own spot.

Step 2: Sketch

$$F\ G\ H\ I\ K\ L\ M$$

$$\underline{\quad}\ \ \underline{\quad}\ \ \underline{\quad}\ \ \underline{\quad}\ \ \underline{\quad}\ \ \underline{\quad}\ \ \underline{\quad}$$
$$1\quad 2\quad 3\quad 4\quad 5\quad 6\quad 7$$

LSAT Question	Analysis
Gardenias must be immediately before *Katydid.*	**Step 3: Rules** GK
Hibiscus must be somewhere before *Katydid* but cannot be the first photograph.	__ … H … K
Irises and *Lotus* must be next to one another.	I/L L/I
Magnolia must be one of the first three photographs.	M over positions 1–3 (bracket) $\underline{1}\ \ \underline{2}\ \ \underline{3}\ \ \underline{4}\ \ \underline{5}\ \ \underline{6}\ \ \underline{7}$
Fence must be either first or seventh. *PrepTest59 Sec1 Qs 6–10*	F pointing to positions 1 and 7 $\underline{1}\ \ \underline{2}\ \ \underline{3}\ \ \underline{4}\ \ \underline{5}\ \ \underline{6}\ \ \underline{7}$

Step 4: Deductions

Rules 1 and 2 contain a duplicate entity: K. Combine them and record their negative implications in the master sketch.

__ . . . H . . . GK

Rules 4 and 5 can both be written on the master sketch. Record their negative implications if it is helpful to you.

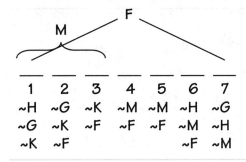

1	2	3	4	5	6	7
~H	~G	~K	~M	~M	~H	~G
~G	~K	~F	~F	~F	~M	~H
~K	~F				~F	~M

Parcel Delivery

LSAT Question	Analysis
A courier delivers exactly eight parcels—G, H, J, K, L, M, N, and O. No two parcels are delivered at the same time, nor is any parcel delivered more than once. The following conditions must apply:	**Step 1: Overview** **Situation:** Courier delivering packages **Entities:** Parcels—G, H, J, K, L, M, N, O **Action:** "No two parcels are delivered at the same time ... " Sequencing game. **Limitations:** Each package delivered separately, used only once **Step 2: Sketch** Look at the rules. This is a Loose Sequencing game. Build the sketch as you go.
L is delivered later than H.	**Step 3: Rules** $$H\ldots L \quad \text{or} \quad \begin{array}{c} H \\ | \\ L \end{array}$$
K is delivered earlier than O.	$$K\ldots O \quad \text{or} \quad \begin{array}{c} K \\ | \\ O \end{array}$$
H is delivered earlier than M.	$$H\ldots M \quad \text{or} \quad \begin{array}{c} H \\ | \\ M \end{array}$$
O is delivered later than G.	$$G\ldots O \quad \text{or} \quad \begin{array}{c} G \\ | \\ O \end{array}$$
M is delivered earlier than G.	$$M\ldots G \quad \text{or} \quad \begin{array}{c} M \\ | \\ G \end{array}$$
Both N and J are delivered earlier than M. *PrepTest51 Sec4 Qs 16–22*	$$\begin{array}{c} N\cdots \\ \quad\ \, M \\ J\cdots \end{array} \quad \text{or} \quad \begin{array}{c} N\quad J \\ \diagdown\diagup \\ M \end{array}$$

Parcel Delivery (cont.)

Deductions (make any deductions here, and add to your master sketch)

Every entity is included in at least one of the rules, and every rule shares an entity with at least one other rule. Combining the rules produces a standard Loose Sequencing sketch. Either a horizontal web:

```
        ..L
   H.·.
   J..:M...G..
   N·'        ·:O
          K·'
```

Or a vertical tree:

```
N    J    H
 \   |   /\
   M      L
   |
   G
K  |
 \ O
```

Clown Costume

LSAT Question	Analysis
A clown will select a costume consisting of two pieces and no others: a jacket and overalls. One piece of the costume will be entirely one color, and the other piece will be plaid. Selection is subject to the following restrictions:	**Step 1: Overview** **Situation:** Clown picking clothes to wear **Entities:** Two pieces of clothing—jacket and overalls; two patterns—uniform color or plaid **Action:** Determine the pattern of each piece of clothing; a Matching game. **Limitation:** No limitations so far **Step 2: Sketch** A table is an easy sketch for Matching games. jacket | overalls
If the jacket is plaid, then there must be exactly three colors in it.	J_{plaid} jacket | overalls
If the overalls are plaid, then there must be exactly two colors in them.	O_{plaid} jacket | overalls This rule, combined with the first rule, creates Limited Options.
The jacket and overalls must have exactly one color in common.	$J = O$ exact 1x
Green, red, and violet are the only colors that can be in the jacket.	J colors = g, r, v NOTE: When the jacket is plaid, the three colors are completely determined. When the overalls are plaid, the jacket cannot be green (see Rules 3 and 5).
Red, violet, and yellow are the only colors that can be in the overalls. *PrepTest51 Sec4 Qs 1–5*	O colors = r, v, y NOTE: When the jacket is plaid, the overalls cannot be yellow (see Rules 3 and 4).

Clown Costume (cont.)

Step 4: Deductions

This game presents a classic Limited Options scenario, based on Rules 1 and 2.

Option 1

jacket	overalls
G	R/V
R	
V	

Because the jacket and the overalls must have a color in common, the color in the overalls must be either red or violet.

Option 2

jacket	overalls
R/V	___
	___

(G/R/V)　　(R/V/Y)

The jacket and the overalls must have one color in common. The only colors that are common to both are red and violet. That means that the jacket's color cannot be green—it must be either red or violet.

Convention Car Pool

LSAT Question	Analysis
Exactly six workers—Faith, Gus, Hannah, Juan, Kenneth, and Lisa—will travel to a business convention in two cars—car 1 and car 2. Each car must carry at least two of the workers, one of whom will be assigned to drive. For the entire trip, the workers will comply with an assignment that also meets the following constraints:	**Step 1: Overview** **Situation:** Workers traveling in two different cars **Entities:** The two cars (1 and 2) and the six workers (F, G, H, J, K, and L) **Action:** Determine which workers drive and which ride in each car; a Distribution game. **Limitations:** Minimum of two and maximum of four workers in each car; the driver of each car is specified.

Step 2: Sketch

Use a table for Distribution games.

	car 1	car 2
driver:	___	___
riders:	___	___
	. . .	. . .
	. . .	. . .

Either Faith or Gus must drive the car in which Hannah travels.	Drv: F/G H NOTE: H can never be one of the drivers.
Either Faith or Kenneth must drive the car in which Juan travels.	Drv: F/K J NOTE: J can never be one of the drivers.
Gus must travel in the same car as Lisa. *PrepTest61 Sec3 Qs 1–5*	G L NOTE: No indication whether G, L, or neither is the driver.

Convention Car Pool (cont.)

Step 4: Deductions

Note first that nothing in the rules or restrictions makes any distinction between the cars. So, we can use Car 1 and Car 2 for convenience, but the passengers in each could be swapped without changing anything in the car. The rules and restrictions all hinge on who's together in a car and who is driving.

This game has one concrete Block of Entities: **G and L** must be in the same car.

There are two Duplications: F and G appear in multiple rules, but do not, in this case, combine to produce further concrete deductions.

To find further deductions, look for the greatest restrictions within the game. Together, the Numbers Restrictions (2 to 4 workers per car) and the G–L Block leave little wiggle room. Note that Rule 2, which dictates J's driver, includes entities other than G and L. Place the G–L block with J, and then place G and L in a different car than J. The result is a helpful Limited Options scenario.

Opt 1:

	Car 1	Car 2
Drv:	F/K	___
	G	___
	L	
	J	

Opt 2:

	Car 1	Car 2
Drv:	___	K/F
	___	J
	G/L	

In Option 1, Car 1 is full. H will have to go in Car 2. Because H requires F or G as a driver, F will have to drive Car 2. So, when the G–L block rides with J, the passenger assignments are determined.

In Option 2, there is less to deduce. H could be a passenger in Car 2 with F driving. H could also be a passenger in Car 1 with either G or F driving.

Opt 1:

	Car 1	Car 2
Drv:	K	F
	G	H
	L	
	J	

Opt 2:

	Car 1	Car 2
Drv:	___	K/F
	___	J
	G/L	

NOTE: The numbers on the cars do not matter. In Option 1, for example, K, G, L, and J could take Car 2 and F and H Car 1. But, when G and L ride with J, the division of passengers and the assignment of drivers is established.

Guitarist's Demo CD

LSAT Question	Analysis
A locally known guitarist's demo CD contains exactly seven different songs—S, T, V, W, X, Y, and Z. Each song occupies exactly one of the CD's seven tracks. Some of the songs are rock classics; the others are new compositions. The following conditions must hold:	**Step 1: Overview** **Situation:** A demo CD with seven songs **Entities:** The seven songs—S, T, V, W, X, Y, and Z— and the two styles—rock classics and new. **Action:** Order the songs, first to seventh. Determine the style of each song; a Sequencing/Matching Hybrid game. → **Limitations:** Each song is exactly one track, so no ties. The number of rock songs and new songs is undefined.

Step 2: Sketch

__ __ __ __ __ __ __ S T V W X Y Z
_____ r n
1 2 3 4 5 6 7

S occupies the fourth track of the CD.	→	__ __ __ S __ __ __ S T V W X Y Z 1 2 3 4 5 6 7 r n
Both W and Y precede S on the CD.	→	W⋅⋅., 　　.S Y⋅⋅⋅
T precedes W on the CD.	→	T . . . W
A rock classic occupies the sixth track of the CD.	→	__ __ __ S __ __ __ S T V W X Y Z 　　　　　　r 1 2 3 4 5 6 7 r n
Each rock classic is immediately preceded on the CD by a new composition.	→	If r → nr If ~nr → ~r Record the implications of this rule in the sketch. __ __ __ S __ __ __ S T V W X Y Z n　　　　　n r n r n 1 2 3 4 5 6 7
Z is a rock classic. *PrepTest51 Sec4 Qs 11–15*	→	Z r

Guitarist's Demo CD (cont.)

Step 4: Deductions

Rules 2 and 3 provide information relating to W. Combine them.

$$T \ldots W \ldots$$
$$Y \ldots : S$$

Because we know that S must be in position 4, then T, W, and Y must all be in positions 1 through 3. The other songs (V, X, Z) must then be in positions 5 through 7:

			S				S T V W X Y Z
n				n	r	n	r n
1	2	3	4	5	6	7	

Y, T ... W   V, X, Z

The last rule states that Z must be a rock classic. Of spots 5, 6, and 7, only 6 is a rock classic. So Z is on track 6, while X and V will be in 5 and 7 (in any order):

			S	V/X	Z	X/V	S T V W X Y Z
n				n	r	n	r n
1	2	3	4	5	6	7	

Y, T ... W

REFLECTION

Think back over the work you did in this chapter. Consider what you learned about Steps 3 and 4 of the Logic Games Method. Here are a few specific questions to reflect upon.

Rules

- How do I look at Logic Games rules differently?
- Can I consistently understand the negative implications of positive rules and vice versa?
- Can I consistently spot rules that can be drawn directly into the sketch, as distinct from those that need to be drawn below or beside the sketch?
- When I depict rules, do the style and size of my drawings match those of the sketch?

Deductions

- Do I know the BLEND checklist, and can I spot rules and restrictions that fit the various deduction types in BLEND?
- Can I identify the spaces or entities that are most restricted within a game? How about those that are least restricted?
- Can I spot the rules and restrictions most likely to produce deductions in various game types?
- Am I confident that I have made all of the available deductions?

We actually do the kind of thinking required by Logic Games all the time in our jobs, schooling, and various "real life" obligations. In the coming days and weeks, take note of tasks in real life that resemble those in Logic Games: deciding who to include or exclude from a work group or sports team; making a seating arrangement for a wedding reception; distributing photos among various albums; etc. Notice how the criteria you use to complete those tasks resemble the rules in Logic Games. When multiple criteria apply to the task, how do you combine those criteria to make deductions? You can actually "practice" LSAT skills 24/7 when you remain aware of what the various sections of the exam are designed to test.

In the next chapter, you'll complete your preparation in the Logic Games Method by learning about and practicing Step 5: Questions. That's where all of the work you've done so far pays off with quick, confident, and correct answers to the Logic Games questions.

CHAPTER 5

Logic Games: The Questions

The first four steps of the Logic Games Method deal with analyzing a game's setup: understanding the overview, making a sketch, understanding the rules, and making deductions. Step 5 is the payoff for all of that work—answering the questions quickly, confidently, and above all, correctly.

With a strong setup and accurate, thorough deductions, it may shock you how easy it is to answer many of the questions. Nevertheless, some questions will remain difficult unless you know exactly what the testmaker is asking for and have solid strategies for how to approach the question. That's why knowing the Logic Games question types is so helpful.

LOGIC GAMES QUESTION TYPES

Here's Kaplan's taxonomy of question types for the Logic Games section.

LSAT STRATEGY

Logic Games Question Types

- Acceptability Questions
- Must Be/Could Be Questions
- New-"If" Questions
- Other Question Types
  - Complete and Accurate List Questions
  - Completely Determine Questions
  - Numerical Questions
    - Minimum/Maximum Questions
    - Earliest/Latest Questions
    - "How Many" Questions
  - Rule Alteration Questions
    - Rule Change Questions
    - Rule Substitution Questions
  - Supply the "If" Questions

While that looks like quite a list, keep in mind that those question types basically represent a variety of ways of asking what must, can, and cannot be true given the task, rules, and restrictions in the game. In that way, the Logic Games section rewards the same underlying reasoning skills rewarded on the other sections of the test.

Being able to recognize the question types and learning the most effective strategies and tactics to apply to each type is, of course, extremely valuable to your score in the Logic Games section. But not all Logic Games question types are of equal importance.

The majority of points in the Logic Games section come from Must Be/Could Be and New-"If" questions. You'll practice more on those types than all of the others combined.

That said, we'll start this chapter by examining Acceptability questions. These questions are almost always the first in the question set, and by learning one targeted strategy, you'll soon be able to answer Acceptability questions in a matter of seconds.

Logic Games Question Types

PrepTests 57–71; released 2009–2013

ACCEPTABILITY QUESTIONS

Most likely, you will see one Acceptability question per game*, and it will almost always be the first question in the question set associated with the game.

*Occasionally, a game will appear without an Acceptability question; even more rarely, a game may have two Acceptability questions (with the second being a Partial Acceptability question asking for an acceptable arrangement of just part of the overall game task).

Acceptability questions ask for an acceptable arrangement of the entities in the game, one possible solution to the puzzle, as it were. Here are some typical Acceptability question stems.

Acceptability Questions

17.2%

Logic Games Question Types

PrepTests 57–71; released 2009–2013

> Which one of the following could be the order of the nurses' sessions, from first to last?
>
> *PrepTest61 Sec3 Q18*

> Which one of the following is a possible assignment of the workers to the cars?
>
> *PrepTest61 Sec3 Q1*

> Which one of the following could be a complete and accurate list of the colors in the costume?
>
> *PrepTest51 Sec4 Q1*

Think about the negative implications of those question stems. If the correct answer is an acceptable list, what characteristic will all four wrong answers share?

Right. All of the wrong answers are unacceptable. That is, all four wrong answers will break one or more of the rules. This shared characteristic of the wrong answers is the key to the strategy for answering Acceptability questions: Apply each rule to the answer choices and eliminate any answer that breaks the rule. Training yourself to check rules against answer choices (instead of the other way around) will allow you to answer Acceptability questions quickly and accurately every time.

LEARNING OBJECTIVES

In this section, you'll learn to:

· Answer Acceptability questions strategically

In Chapter 2, you saw how an LSAT expert would work through one Acceptability question from the Nurses' Information Sessions game. Go back through that step-by-step analysis on the following pages to refresh your memory and prepare you to try more Acceptability questions on your own.

Notice that the final sketch produced by Steps 1–4 is included here but that the LSAT expert has no real need to consult it for the Acceptability question.

LSAT Question	Analysis

From the 1st through the 7th of next month, seven nurses—Farnham, Griseldi, Heany, Juarez, Khan, Lightfoot, and Moreau—will each conduct one information session at a community center. Each nurse's session will fall on a different day. The nurses' schedule is governed by the following constraints:

At least two of the other nurses' sessions must fall in between Heany's session and Moreau's session.

Griseldi's session must be on the day before Khan's.

Juarez's session must be on a later day than Moreau's.

Farnham's session must be on an earlier day than Khan's but on a later day than Lightfoot's.

Lightfoot cannot conduct the session on the 2nd.

Steps 1–4:

F G H J K L M

1	2	3	4	5	6	7
~F	~L	~G	~L	~L	~L	~L
~G	~G	~K	~K		~F	~F
~K	~K					~G
~J						~M

L . . . F . . . GK

J

H/M ___ ___ . . . M/H

J

Which one of the following could be the order of the nurses' sessions, from first to last?

Step 5: The correct answer is an acceptable sequence. Each wrong answer violates one or more rules. Check each rule against the answer choices and eliminate violators.

(A) Farnham, Griseldi, Khan, Moreau, Juarez, Lightfoot, Heany

(B) Heany, Lightfoot, Farnham, Moreau, Juarez, Griseldi, Khan

(C) Juarez, Heany, Lightfoot, Farnham, Moreau, Griseldi, Khan

(D) Lightfoot, Moreau, Farnham, Juarez, Griseldi, Khan, Heany

(E) Moreau, Lightfoot, Heany, Juarez, Farnham, Griseldi, Khan

PrepTest61 Sec3 Q18

Check Rule 1.

LSAT Question	Analysis

From the 1st through the 7th of next month, seven nurses—Farnham, Griseldi, Heany, Juarez, Khan, Lightfoot, and Moreau—will each conduct one information session at a community center. Each nurse's session will fall on a different day. The nurses' schedule is governed by the following constraints:

> At least two of the other nurses' sessions must fall in between Heany's session and Moreau's session.
> Griseldi's session must be on the day before Khan's.
> Juarez's session must be on a later day than Moreau's.
> Farnham's session must be on an earlier day than Khan's but on a later day than Lightfoot's.
> Lightfoot cannot conduct the session on the 2nd.

Steps 1–4:

F G H J K L M

1	2	3	4	5	6	7
~F	~L	~G	~L	~L	~L	~L
~G	~G	~K	~K		~F	~F
~K	~K					~G
~J						~M

L . . . F . . . GK

J

H/M __ __ . . . M/H

J

⟶

Which one of the following could be the order of the nurses' sessions, from first to last?	**Step 5:** The correct answer is an acceptable sequence. Each wrong answer violates one or more rules. Check each rule against the answer choices and eliminate violators.

(A) Farnham, Griseldi, Khan, Moreau, Juarez, Lightfoot, Heany ⟶

(B) Heany, Lightfoot, Farnham, Moreau, Juarez, Griseldi, Khan ⟶

(C) Juarez, Heany, Lightfoot, Farnham, Moreau, Griseldi, Khan ⟶

(D) Lightfoot, Moreau, Farnham, Juarez, Griseldi, Khan, Heany ⟶

(E) ~~Moreau, Lightfoot, Heany, Juarez, Farnham, Griseldi, Khan~~ ⟶ Breaks Rule 1. Only one session separates Heany and Moreau. Eliminate.

PrepTest61 Sec3 Q18

Checking Rule 2 reveals no violations among the remaining answer choices. Check Rule 3.

LSAT Question	Analysis
From the 1st through the 7th of next month, seven nurses—Farnham, Griseldi, Heany, Juarez, Khan, Lightfoot, and Moreau—will each conduct one information session at a community center. Each nurse's session will fall on a different day. The nurses' schedule is governed by the following constraints:	**Steps 1–4:**

F G H J K L M

1	2	3	4	5	6	7
—	—	—	—	—	—	—
~F	~L	~G	~L	~L	~L	~L
~G	~G	~K	~K		~F	~F
~K	~K					~G
~J						~M

At least two of the other nurses' sessions must fall in between Heany's session and Moreau's session.

Griseldi's session must be on the day before Khan's.

Juarez's session must be on a later day than Moreau's.

Farnham's session must be on an earlier day than Khan's but on a later day than Lightfoot's.

Lightfoot cannot conduct the session on the 2nd.

L . . . F . . . GK

    / J

H/M __ __ . . . M/H

       \ J

Which one of the following could be the order of the nurses' sessions, from first to last?

Step 5: The correct answer is an acceptable sequence. Each wrong answer violates one or more rules. Check each rule against the answer choices and eliminate violators.

(A) Farnham, Griseldi, Khan, Moreau, Juarez, Lightfoot, Heany

(B) Heany, Lightfoot, Farnham, Moreau, Juarez, Griseldi, Khan

(C) ~~Juarez, Heany, Lightfoot, Farnham, Moreau, Griseldi, Khan~~ → Breaks Rule 3. Juarez comes before Moreau. Eliminate.

(D) Lightfoot, Moreau, Farnham, Juarez, Griseldi, Khan, Heany

(E) ~~Moreau, Lightfoot, Heany, Juarez, Farnham, Griseldi, Khan~~ → Breaks Rule 1. Only one session separates Heany and Moreau. Eliminate.

PrepTest61 Sec3 Q18

Check Rule 4.

LSAT Question	Analysis

From the 1st through the 7th of next month, seven nurses—Farnham, Griseldi, Heany, Juarez, Khan, Lightfoot, and Moreau—will each conduct one information session at a community center. Each nurse's session will fall on a different day. The nurses' schedule is governed by the following constraints:

> At least two of the other nurses' sessions must fall in between Heany's session and Moreau's session.
> Griseldi's session must be on the day before Khan's.
> Juarez's session must be on a later day than Moreau's.
> Farnham's session must be on an earlier day than Khan's but on a later day than Lightfoot's.
> Lightfoot cannot conduct the session on the 2nd.

Steps 1–4:

F G H J K L M

1	2	3	4	5	6	7
~F	~L	~G	~L	~L	~L	~L
~G	~G	~K	~K		~F	~F
~K	~K					~G
~J						~M

L . . . F . . . GK

J

H/M ___ ___ . . . M/H

J

Which one of the following could be the order of the nurses' sessions, from first to last?

Step 5: The correct answer is an acceptable sequence. Each wrong answer violates one or more rules. Check each rule against the answer choices and eliminate violators.

(A) ~~Farnham, Griseldi, Khan, Moreau, Juarez, Lightfoot, Heany~~ — Breaks Rule 4. Lightfoot is later than Farnham. Eliminate.

(B) Heany, Lightfoot, Farnham, Moreau, Juarez, Griseldi, Khan —

(C) ~~Juarez, Heany, Lightfoot, Farnham, Moreau, Griseldi, Khan~~ — Breaks Rule 3. Juarez comes before Moreau. Eliminate.

(D) Lightfoot, Moreau, Farnham, Juarez, Griseldi, Khan, Heany —

(E) ~~Moreau, Lightfoot, Heany, Juarez, Farnham, Griseldi, Khan~~ — Breaks Rule 1. Only one session separates Heany and Moreau. Eliminate.

PrepTest61 Sec3 Q18

One rule remains unchecked. One of the remaining choices will break the rule. The other will obey it, and that one is the correct answer.

LSAT Question	Analysis

From the 1st through the 7th of next month, seven nurses—Farnham, Griseldi, Heany, Juarez, Khan, Lightfoot, and Moreau—will each conduct one information session at a community center. Each nurse's session will fall on a different day. The nurses' schedule is governed by the following constraints:

At least two of the other nurses' sessions must fall in between Heany's session and Moreau's session.
Griseldi's session must be on the day before Khan's.
Juarez's session must be on a later day than Moreau's.
Farnham's session must be on an earlier day than Khan's but on a later day than Lightfoot's.
Lightfoot cannot conduct the session on the 2nd.

Steps 1–4:

F G H J K L M

1	2	3	4	5	6	7
~F	~L	~G	~L	~L	~L	~L
~G	~G	~K	~K		~F	~F
~K	~K					~G
~J						~M

L . . . F . . . GK

Which one of the following could be the order of the nurses' sessions, from first to last?

Step 5: The correct answer is an acceptable sequence. Each wrong answer violates one or more rules. Check each rule against the answer choices and eliminate violators.

(A) ~~Farnham, Griseldi, Khan, Moreau, Juarez, Lightfoot, Heany~~ → Breaks Rule 4. Lightfoot is later than Farnham. Eliminate.

(B) ~~Heany, Lightfoot, Farnham, Moreau, Juarez, Griseldi, Khan~~ → Breaks Rule 5.

(C) ~~Juarez, Heany, Lightfoot, Farnham, Moreau, Griseldi, Khan~~ → Breaks Rule 3. Juarez comes before Moreau. Eliminate.

(D) Lightfoot, Moreau, Farnham, Juarez, Griseldi, Khan, Heany → Correct.

(E) ~~Moreau, Lightfoot, Heany, Juarez, Farnham, Griseldi, Khan~~ → Breaks Rule 1. Only one session separates Heany and Moreau. Eliminate.

PrepTest61 Sec3 Q18

TEST DAY TIP

In Acceptability questions:

· There may be rules that are not broken by any of the answer choices, but
· Every wrong answer will break at least one of the rules

Cross off wrong answers and once they are eliminated, don't bother to check other rules against them. The correct answer is the only one that breaks none of the rules.

Practice

Now, apply that strategic approach to some more Acceptability questions from games you've worked with in earlier chapters. Check the rules one-by-one against the answer choices. Eliminate any and all answers that violate a rule until you are left with the one correct answer. [NOTE: The final sketches produced by Steps 1–4 are included for your convenience.]

LSAT Question	My Analysis

Exactly six workers—Faith, Gus, Hannah, Juan, Kenneth, and Lisa—will travel to a business convention in two cars—car 1 and car 2. Each car must carry at least two of the workers, one of whom will be assigned to drive. For the entire trip, the workers will comply with an assignment that also meets the following constraints:

    Either Faith or Gus must drive the car in which Hannah travels.

    Either Faith or Kenneth must drive the car in which Juan travels.

    Gus must travel in the same car as Lisa.

Steps 1–4:

F G H J K L

2–4/Car

Opt. I   Opt. II

(1) (2)   (1) (2)

Driver: K | F   ___ | F/K
         J | H   ___ | J
         G | (___)(___)
         L | (___)(___)

                G
                L

                (__H__)?

Driver: F/G
        H

Driver: F/K
        J
        G
        L

1. Which one of the following is a possible assignment of the workers to the cars?

    Step 5:

(A)   car 1: Faith (driver), Hannah, and Juan
       car 2: Gus (driver), Kenneth, and Lisa

(B)   car 1: Faith (driver), Hannah, and Kenneth
       car 2: Lisa (driver), Gus, and Juan

(C)   car 1: Faith (driver), Juan, Kenneth, and Lisa
       car 2: Gus (driver) and Hannah

(D)   car 1: Faith (driver) and Juan
       car 2: Kenneth (driver), Gus, Hannah, and Lisa

(E)   car 1: Gus (driver), Hannah, and Lisa
       car 2: Juan (driver), Faith, and Kenneth

PrepTest61 Sec3 Q1

HINT: There are only three rules. At least one of them will be violated by two or more answer choices.

LSAT Question	**My Analysis**

A museum curator is arranging seven photographs—*Fence, Gardenias, Hibiscus, Irises, Katydid, Lotus,* and *Magnolia*— on a gallery wall in accordance with the photographer's requirements. The photographs are to be hung along the wall in a row, in seven positions sequentially numbered from first to seventh. The photographer's requirements are as follows:

Steps 1–4:

F G H I K L M

> *Gardenias* must be immediately before *Katydid*.
> *Hibiscus* must be somewhere before *Katydid* but cannot be the first photograph.
> *Irises* and *Lotus* must be next to one another.
> *Magnolia* must be one of the first three photographs.
> *Fence* must be either first or seventh.

1	2	3	4	5	6	7
~H	~F	~F	~F	~F	~F	~M
~G	~G	~K	~M	~M	~M	~H
~K	~K				~H	~G

__ ... H ... G K

I L or L I

2. Which one of the following could be the positions, from first to seventh, in which the photographs are hung?

Step 5:

(A) *Fence, Hibiscus, Gardenias, Magnolia, Katydid, Irises, Lotus*

(B) *Hibiscus, Magnolia, Gardenias, Katydid, Irises, Lotus, Fence*

(C) *Irises, Lotus, Magnolia, Hibiscus, Gardenias, Katydid, Fence*

(D) *Lotus, Magnolia, Irises, Hibiscus, Gardenias, Katydid, Fence*

(E) *Magnolia, Fence, Hibiscus, Gardenias, Katydid, Lotus, Irises*

PrepTest59 Sec1 Q6

LSAT Question	My Analysis

A clown will select a costume consisting of two pieces and no others: a jacket and overalls. One piece of the costume will be entirely one color, and the other piece will be plaid. Selection is subject to the following restrictions:

> If the jacket is plaid, then there must be exactly three colors in it.
> If the overalls are plaid, then there must be exactly two colors in them.
> The jacket and overalls must have exactly one color in common.
> Green, red, and violet are the only colors that can be in the jacket.
> Red, violet, and yellow are the only colors that can be in the overalls.

→

Steps 1–4:

[*exactly 1 color in common*]

Opt. I   *Opt. II*

Jacket	Overalls	Jacket	Overalls
g	r/v	r/v	r/v
v	~~y~~	~~g~~	___
r			r/v/y

---

3. Which one of the following could be a complete and accurate list of the colors in the costume?

→ **Step 5:**

	Jacket	Overalls	
(A)	red	red	→
(B)	red	violet, yellow	→
(C)	violet	green, violet	→
(D)	violet	red, violet	→
(E)	violet	red, violet, yellow	→

PrepTest51 Sec4 Q1 →

HINT: Occasionally, an answer choice will violate a restriction from the opening paragraph rather than one of the rules. How do the answer choices signal whether the jacket or the overalls are intended to be the plaid piece of clothing? What if you are unable to tell?

LSAT Question		**My Analysis**

A courier delivers exactly eight parcels—G, H, J, K, L, M, N, and O. No two parcels are delivered at the same time, nor is any parcel delivered more than once. The following conditions must apply:

    L is delivered later than H.
    K is delivered earlier than O.
    H is delivered earlier than M.
    O is delivered later than G.
    M is delivered earlier than G.
    Both N and J are delivered earlier than M.

$\longrightarrow$

Steps 1–4:

4. Which one of the following could be the order of deliveries from first to last?

$\longrightarrow$ **Step 5:**

(A)   N, H, K, M, J, G, O, L

$\longrightarrow$

(B)   H, N, J, K, G, O, L, M

$\longrightarrow$

(C)   J, H, N, M, K, O, G, L

$\longrightarrow$

(D)   N, J, H, L, M, K, G, O

$\longrightarrow$

(E)   K, N, J, M, G, H, O, L

PrepTest51 Sec4 Q16 $\longrightarrow$

HINT: There are six rules, but only four wrong answers. What can you expect?

LSAT Question	**My Analysis**

A locally known guitarist's demo CD contains exactly seven different songs—S, T, V, W, X, Y, and Z. Each song occupies exactly one of the CD's seven tracks. Some of the songs are rock classics; the others are new compositions. The following conditions must hold:

>   S occupies the fourth track of the CD.
>   Both W and Y precede S on the CD.
>   T precedes W on the CD.
>   A rock classic occupies the sixth track of the CD.
>   Each rock classic is immediately preceded on the CD by a new composition.
>   Z is a rock classic.

Steps 1–4:

Y; T . . . W

			S	X/V	Z	V/X	~~S~~ T V W X Y ~~Z~~
1	2	3	4	5	6	7	
n				n	r	n	n r

always __n__ before any __r__

5. Which one of the following could be the order of the songs on the CD, from the first track through the seventh?

Step 5:

(A) T, W, V, S, Y, X, Z

(B) V, Y, T, S, W, Z, X

(C) X, Y, W, S, T, Z, S

(D) Y, T, W, S, X, Z, V

(E) Z, T, X, W, V, Y, S

PrepTest51 Sec4 Q11

HINT: This is a Partial Acceptability question—the answer choices only address the Sequencing action in this Hybrid game. Which rules will likely be helpful in determining the correct answer?

LSAT Question	**My Analysis**
A summer program offers at least one of the following seven courses: geography, history, literature, mathematics, psychology, sociology, zoology. The following restrictions on the program must apply:	**Steps 1–4:**

G H L M P S Z

If Ⓜ   → exactly 1 of Ⓛ or Ⓢ
If Ⓛ and Ⓢ → M̸
If L̸ and S̸ → M̸
If Ⓛ   → Ⓖ and P̸
If G̸ or Ⓟ → L̸
If Ⓢ   → Ⓟ and Z̸
If P̸ or Ⓩ → S̸
If Ⓖ   → Ⓗ and Ⓩ
If H̸ or Z̸ → G̸

If mathematics is offered, then either literature or sociology (but not both) is offered.

If literature is offered, then geography is also offered but psychology is not.

If sociology is offered, then psychology is also offered but zoology is not.

If geography is offered, then both history and zoology are also offered.

6. Which one of the following could be a complete and accurate list of the courses offered by the summer program?   **Step 5:**

(A) history, psychology

(B) geography, history, literature

(C) history, mathematics, psychology

(D) literature, mathematics, psychology

(E) history, literature, mathematics, sociology
        PrepTest49 Sec1 Q13

HINT: Sometimes, it's easier to spot a violation of a rule's contrapositive than it is to spot a violation of the rule as written.

Expert Analysis

Take a look at an LSAT expert's approach to those same Acceptability questions.

LSAT Question	**Analysis**

Exactly six workers—Faith, Gus, Hannah, Juan, Kenneth, and Lisa—will travel to a business convention in two cars—car 1 and car 2. Each car must carry at least two of the workers, one of whom will be assigned to drive. For the entire trip, the workers will comply with an assignment that also meets the following constraints:

  Either Faith or Gus must drive the car in which Hannah travels.

  Either Faith or Kenneth must drive the car in which Juan travels.

  Gus must travel in the same car as Lisa.

→

Steps 1–4:

1. Which one of the following is a possible assignment of the workers to the cars?

→ **Step 5:** The correct answer is an acceptable distribution. Each wrong answer violates one or more rules. Check each rule against the answer choices and eliminate violators.

(A) car 1: Faith (driver), Hannah, and Juan
car 2: Gus (driver), Kenneth, and Lisa

→ Correct.

(B) car 1: Faith (driver), Hannah, and Kenneth
car 2: Lisa (driver), Gus, and Juan

→ Breaks Rule 2. Here, Juan is in a car that Lisa is driving. Eliminate.

(C) car 1: Faith (driver), Juan, Kenneth, and Lisa
car 2: Gus (driver) and Hannah

→ Breaks Rule 3. Here, Gus and Lisa are in different cars. Eliminate.

(D) car 1: Faith (driver) and Juan
car 2: Kenneth (driver), Gus, Hannah, and Lisa

→ Breaks Rule 1. Here, Hannah is in a car that Kenneth is driving. Eliminate.

(E) car 1: Gus (driver), Hannah, and Lisa
car 2: Juan (driver), Faith, and Kenneth

→ Breaks Rule 2. Here, Juan is driving! Eliminate.

PrepTest61 Sec3 Q1

LSAT Question	**Analysis**

A museum curator is arranging seven photographs—*Fence, Gardenias, Hibiscus, Irises, Katydid, Lotus,* and *Magnolia*—on a gallery wall in accordance with the photographer's requirements. The photographs are to be hung along the wall in a row, in seven positions sequentially numbered from first to seventh. The photographer's requirements are as follows:

    Gardenias must be immediately before *Katydid.*
    Hibiscus must be somewhere before *Katydid* but cannot be the first photograph.
    Irises and *Lotus* must be next to one another.
    Magnolia must be one of the first three photographs.
    Fence must be either first or seventh.

$\longrightarrow$

Steps 1–4:

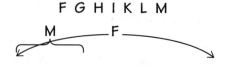

1	2	3	4	5	6	7
~H	~F	~F	~F	~F	~F	~M
~G	~G	~K	~M	~M	~M	~H
~K	~K				~H	~G

    __ . . . __H__ . . . __G__ __K__

    __I__ __L__ or __L__ __I__

---

2. Which one of the following could be the positions, from first to seventh, in which the photographs are hung?

$\longrightarrow$

Step 5: The correct answer is an acceptable sequence. Each wrong answer violates one or more rules. Check each rule against the answer choices and eliminate violators.

(A)	*Fence, Hibiscus, Gardenias, Magnolia, Katydid, Irises, Lotus*	$\longrightarrow$	Breaks Rule 1. G is not immediately before K here. M is in between. Eliminate.
(B)	*Hibiscus, Magnolia, Gardenias, Katydid, Irises, Lotus, Fence*	$\longrightarrow$	Breaks Rule 2. H is first here. Eliminate.
(C)	*Irises, Lotus, Magnolia, Hibiscus, Gardenias, Katydid, Fence*	$\longrightarrow$	Correct.
(D)	*Lotus, Magnolia, Irises, Hibiscus, Gardenias, Katydid, Fence*	$\longrightarrow$	Breaks Rule 3. I and L are not consecutive. M is in between here. Eliminate.
(E)	*Magnolia, Fence, Hibiscus, Gardenias, Katydid, Lotus, Irises*	$\longrightarrow$	Breaks Rule 5. F is second, not first or last, here. Eliminate.

PrepTest59 Sec1 Q6

LSAT Question	Analysis

A clown will select a costume consisting of two pieces and no others: a jacket and overalls. One piece of the costume will be entirely one color, and the other piece will be plaid. Selection is subject to the following restrictions:

    If the jacket is plaid, then there must be exactly three colors in it.

    If the overalls are plaid, then there must be exactly two colors in them.

    The jacket and overalls must have exactly one color in common.

    Green, red, and violet are the only colors that can be in the jacket.

    Red, violet, and yellow are the only colors that can be in the overalls.

Steps 1–4:

[exactly 1 color in common]

Opt. I		Opt. II	
Jacket	Overalls	Jacket	Overalls
g	r/v	r/v	r/v
v	~~y~~	~~g~~	___
r			r/v/y

3. Which one of the following could be a complete and accurate list of the colors in the costume?

Step 5: The correct answer is an acceptable matching of colors to pieces of clothing. Each wrong answer violates one or more rules. Check each rule against the answer choices and eliminate violators.

	Jacket	Overalls	
(A)	red	red	Breaks the restriction from the opening paragraph: "One piece of the costume . . . will be plaid." Neither is plaid here. Eliminate.
(B)	red	violet, yellow	Breaks Rule 3. The jacket and overalls have nothing in common here. Eliminate.
(C)	violet	green, violet	Breaks Rule 5. The overalls have green in them here. Eliminate.
(D)	violet	red, violet	Correct.
(E)	violet	red, violet, yellow	Breaks Rule 2. The overalls are plaid, but have three colors here. Eliminate.

PrepTest51 Sec4 Q1

LSAT Question	**Analysis**

A courier delivers exactly eight parcels—G, H, J, K, L, M, N, and O. No two parcels are delivered at the same time, nor is any parcel delivered more than once. The following conditions must apply:
 	
L is delivered later than H.
K is delivered earlier than O.
H is delivered earlier than M.
O is delivered later than G.
M is delivered earlier than G.
Both N and J are delivered earlier than M.
	Steps 1–4:
	
	→
	
	J N H
	  \ | /\\
	    M L
	    |
	K G
	  \ |
	    O

4. Which one of the following could be the order of deliveries from first to last?	**Step 5:** The correct answer is an acceptable sequence. Each wrong answer violates one or more rules. Check each rule against the answer choices and eliminate violators.
(A) N, H, K, M, J, G, O, L	→ Breaks Rule 6. J is delivered later than M here. Eliminate.
(B) H, N, J, K, G, O, L, M	→ Breaks Rule 5. M is delivered later than G here. Eliminate.
(C) J, H, N, M, K, O, G, L	→ Breaks Rule 4. O is delivered earlier than G here. Eliminate.
(D) N, J, H, L, M, K, G, O	→ Correct.
(E) K, N, J, M, G, H, O, L *PrepTest51 Sec4 Q16*	→ Breaks Rule 3. H is delivered later than M here. Eliminate.

LSAT Question	Analysis

A locally known guitarist's demo CD contains exactly seven different songs—S, T, V, W, X, Y, and Z. Each song occupies exactly one of the CD's seven tracks. Some of the songs are rock classics; the others are new compositions. The following conditions must hold:

    S occupies the fourth track of the CD.

    Both W and Y precede S on the CD.

    T precedes W on the CD.

    A rock classic occupies the sixth track of the CD.

    Each rock classic is immediately preceded on the CD by a new composition.

    Z is a rock classic.

Steps 1–4:

$\rightarrow$

Y; T . . . W

			S	X/V	Z	V/X	~~S~~ T V W X Y ~~Z~~
1	2	3	4	5	6	7	
n				n	r	n	n r

always __n__ before any __r__

---

5. Which one of the following could be the order of the songs on the CD, from the first track through the seventh?

$\rightarrow$

Step 5: The correct answer is an acceptable sequence (the Matching part of the Hybrid is not tested here). Each wrong answer violates one or more rules. Check each rule against the answer choices and eliminate violators.

  (A) T, W, V, S, Y, X, Z

$\rightarrow$

Breaks Rule 2. Song Y follows Song S here. Eliminate.

  (B) V, Y, T, S, W, Z, X

$\rightarrow$

Breaks Rule 2. Song W follows Song S here. Eliminate.

  (C) X, Y, W, S, T, Z, S

$\rightarrow$

Breaks Rule 3. Song T follows Song W here. Eliminate.

  (D) Y, T, W, S, X, Z, V

$\rightarrow$

Correct.

  (E) Z, T, X, W, V, Y, S

PrepTest51 Sec4 Q11

$\rightarrow$

Breaks Rule 1. Song S is not the fourth song here. Eliminate.

HINT: The two rules dealing with the Matching part of this Hybrid—Rules 4, 5, and 6 about the genres of songs—are not relevant to this Partial Acceptability question about the order of the songs.

LSAT Question	**Analysis**

A summer program offers at least one of the following seven courses: geography, history, literature, mathematics, psychology, sociology, zoology. The following restrictions on the program must apply:

>If mathematics is offered, then either literature or sociology (but not both) is offered.

>If literature is offered, then geography is also offered but psychology is not.

>If sociology is offered, then psychology is also offered but zoology is not.

>If geography is offered, then both history and zoology are also offered.

Steps 1–4:

G H L M P S Z

If Ⓜ   → exactly 1 of Ⓛ or Ⓢ
If Ⓛ and Ⓢ → M̶
If L̶ and S̶ → M
If Ⓛ   → Ⓖ and P̶
If G̶ or Ⓟ → L̶
If Ⓢ   → Ⓟ and Z̶
If P̶ or Ⓩ → S̶
If Ⓖ   → Ⓗ and Ⓩ
If H̶ or Z̶ → G̶

6. Which one of the following could be a complete and accurate list of the courses offered by the summer program?

Step 5: The correct answer is an acceptable selection. Each wrong answer violates one or more rules. Check each rule against the answer choices and eliminate violators.

(A) history, psychology

Correct.

(B) geography, history, literature

Breaks Rule 4. Geography is offered here, but zoology is not. Eliminate.

(C) history, mathematics, psychology

Breaks Rule 1. Mathematics is offered here, but neither literature nor sociology is. Eliminate.

(D) literature, mathematics, psychology

Breaks Rule 2. Literature is offered here, but geography is not, and psychology is. Eliminate.

(E) history, literature, mathematics, sociology

PrepTest49 Sec1 Q13

Breaks Rule 1. Mathematics is offered here, but so are both literature and sociology. Eliminate.

A Note on Complete and Accurate List Questions

Two of the Acceptability questions you just reviewed had the following question stems.

Which one of the following could be a complete and
accurate list of the colors in the costume?

PrepTest51 Sec4 Q1

Which one of the following could be a complete and
accurate list of the courses offered by the summer
program?

PrepTest49 Sec1 Q13

The wording in those stems amounts to asking for an acceptable matching or selection, and the correct answers presented one possible "solution" to the game.

It's worth noting, however, that rarely the testmaker will use the phrase "complete and accurate list" for a question that focuses on a narrower part of the game. Here are a couple of examples.

Which one of the following is a complete and
accurate list of the days, any one of which is a day on
which a film in Italian could be shown?

PrepTest49 Sec1 Q4

Which one of the following is a complete and accurate
list of the pieces of mail, any one of which could be the
only piece of mail addressed to Jana?

PrepTest49 Sec1 Q9

For Complete and Accurate List questions such as these, the correct answer must contain any and all of the acceptable slots or entities called for by the question stem. In other words, the wrong answers will be *incomplete*—they will exclude an acceptable slot or entity—or *inaccurate*—they will include an unacceptable slot or entity.

Don't spend too much time trying to hunt down examples of this rare question type. (There were none in the games you've studied so far and only four such questions among the 40 games contained in this book.)

When you do come across Complete and Accurate List questions, don't panic or change your strategic approach to Logic Games. Simply characterize the answer choices and eliminate answer choices that are *incomplete* or *inaccurate*.

COMPLETELY DETERMINE QUESTIONS

Completely Determine questions are relatively rare. Among the 40 games in this book, there are only eight Completely Determine questions. And among the games you've studied so far, there is just one. You'll practice it in a moment.

In a Completely Determine question, the correct answer is a condition that, once established, forces all of the entities in the game into fixed positions. Thus, the four wrong answers will provide conditions that, even if established, would leave at least some of the entities' positions, placements, or selections undetermined.

There is exactly one possible order in which the cities are used if which one of the following is true?

PrepTest59 Sec1 Q19

The question of which runners will be chosen to run in the track meet and in what races they will run can be completely resolved if which one of the following is true?

PrepTest61 Sec3 Q14

It is fully determined which grants are awarded for each quarter of a particular calendar year if which one of the following is true that year?

PrepTest57 Sec1 Q23

Your instinct, when you see these question stems, might be to test every answer choice in order from (A) to (E). The more strategic approach, however, is to concentrate on the entities or spaces least restricted by the game's setup. Because the correct answer will need to establish a single, fixed assignment for each entity, take a moment to consider which entities are least restricted by the game's setup. Locking down a Floater, for example, may determine the placement of the remaining entities. Often, this kind of analysis will take you directly to the correct answer, or will at least allow you to ignore two or three of the choices.

Practice

Try that now with this Completely Determine question from the Seven Photographs game.

LSAT Question	**My Analysis**

A museum curator is arranging seven photographs—*Fence, Gardenias, Hibiscus, Irises, Katydid, Lotus,* and *Magnolia*—on a gallery wall in accordance with the photographer's requirements. The photographs are to be hung along the wall in a row, in seven positions sequentially numbered from first to seventh. The photographer's requirements are as follows:

Gardenias must be immediately before *Katydid.*

Hibiscus must be somewhere before *Katydid* but cannot be the first photograph.

Irises and *Lotus* must be next to one another.

Magnolia must be one of the first three photographs.

Fence must be either first or seventh.

→

Steps 1–4:

F G H I K L M

M ⟶ F

1	2	3	4	5	6	7
~H	~F	~F	~F	~F	~F	~M
~G	~G	~K	~M	~M	~M	~H
~K	~K				~H	~G

___ ...H... G K

_I_ _L_ or _L_ _I_

---

7. Where each photograph is hung is fully determined if which one of the following is true?   → **Step 5:**

(A) *Gardenias* is fourth.   →

(B) *Hibiscus* is second.   →

(C) *Irises* is second.   →

(D) *Lotus* is first.   →

(E) *Magnolia* is third.   →

PrepTest59 Sec1 Q8

HINT: Which are the least restricted entities in this game? There is one pair of photographs restricted only with respect to how close they must be to one another, not by order. Spot that pair and you need only evaluate two of the answer choices here.

Expert Analysis

Now take a look at how an expert attacks this Completely Determine question.

LSAT Question	Analysis
A museum curator is arranging seven photographs—*Fence, Gardenias, Hibiscus, Irises, Katydid, Lotus,* and *Magnolia*—on a gallery wall in accordance with the photographer's requirements. The photographs are to be hung along the wall in a row, in seven positions sequentially numbered from first to seventh. The photographer's requirements are as follows: *Gardenias* must be immediately before *Katydid.* *Hibiscus* must be somewhere before *Katydid* but cannot be the first photograph. *Irises* and *Lotus* must be next to one another. *Magnolia* must be one of the first three photographs. *Fence* must be either first or seventh	**Steps 1–4:**

F G H I K L M

M ⟵⟍ F ⟍⟶

	1	2	3	4	5	6	7
	~H	~F	~F	~F	~F	~F	~M
	~G	~G	~K	~M	~M	~M	~H
	~K	~K				~H	~G

___ ... H ... G K

_I_ _L_ or _L_ _I_

7. Where each photograph is hung is fully determined if which one of the following is true?	**Step 5:** A Completely Determine question—the correct answer will allow for only one arrangement and account for every entity's position. Here, I and L are the least restricted entities. I and L must be next to each other (Rule 3), but nothing establishes their order. Even if all other entities are placed, the overall order will not be determined until the relative positions of I and L are locked down.
(A) *Gardenias* is fourth.	Does not account for I and L. Eliminate.
(B) *Hibiscus* is second.	Does not account for I and L. Eliminate.
(C) *Irises* is second.	This choice mentions I, but placing I second would allow L to be either first or third, with M taking the other slot among the first three positions. This does not completely determine the order. Eliminate.
(D) *Lotus* is first.	Correct. With L first, there is only one acceptable order.

L	I	M	H	G	K	F
1	2	3	4	5	6	7

(E) *Magnolia* is third.	Does not account for I and L. Eliminate.

PrepTest59 Sec1 Q8

Characterizing the Answer Choices in Acceptability, Complete and Accurate List, and Completely Determine Questions

Now that you've seen a handful of Logic Games question types, make sure that you can distinguish among Acceptability, Complete and Accurate List, and Completely Determine questions.

Practice

For each question stem, identify the question type and characterize the one correct and four incorrect answer choices.

Question Stem	My Analysis
8. Which of the following is an acceptable placement of trophies in the two display cases?	Question Type: 1 Right: 4 Wrong:
9. Which of the following is an acceptable pairing of wines to entrees?	Question Type: 1 Right: 4 Wrong:
10. Each of the following could be an accurate ordering of the carpenters EXCEPT:	Question Type: 1 Right: 4 Wrong:
11. Which of the following could be a complete and accurate ordering of the marbles, from left to right?	Question Type: 1 Right: 4 Wrong:
12. Which of the following, if true, would establish the complete list of candidates for the election?	Question Type: 1 Right: 4 Wrong:
13. Which of the following is a complete and accurate list of the days that Senator R can visit?	Question Type: 1 Right: 4 Wrong:
14. Which of the following, if true, would cause the ranking of the swimmers to be completely determined?	Question Type: 1 Right: 4 Wrong:
15. Which one of the following could be the order in which the bands perform, from first through sixth?	Question Type: 1 Right: 4 Wrong:

Expert Analysis

Note how an LSAT expert would analyze each of the question stems you just saw.

Question Stem	Analysis
8. Which of the following is an acceptable placement of trophies in the two display cases?	**Question Type:** Acceptability **1 Right:** An acceptable distribution of trophies **4 Wrong:** Each violates at least one of the rules
9. Which of the following is an acceptable pairing of wines to entrees?	**Question Type:** Acceptability **1 Right:** An acceptable matching **4 Wrong:** Each violates at least one of the rules
10. Each of the following could be an accurate ordering of the carpenters EXCEPT:	**Question Type:** Acceptability EXCEPT **1 Right:** Violates at least one of the rules **4 Wrong:** Each presents an acceptable sequence
11. Which of the following could be a complete and accurate ordering of the marbles, from left to right?	**Question Type:** Acceptability **1 Right:** An acceptable sequence **4 Wrong:** Each violates at least one of the rules
12. Which of the following, if true, would establish the complete list of candidates for the election?	**Question Type:** Completely Determine **1 Right:** A condition that establishes exactly one acceptable selection **4 Wrong:** Each allows some ambiguity about which candidates are/are not selected
13. Which of the following is a complete and accurate list of the days that Senator R can visit?	**Question Type:** Complete and Accurate List **1 Right:** A list of any and all days that Senator R can visit **4 Wrong:** Each will 1) omit a day on which Senator R can visit, 2) include a day on which Senator R cannot visit, or 3) both
14. Which of the following, if true, would cause the ranking of the swimmers to be completely determined?	**Question Type:** Completely Determine **1 Right:** A condition that establishes exactly one acceptable sequence **4 Wrong:** Each allows for two or more of the entities' places to remain uncertain
15. Which one of the following could be the order in which the bands perform, from first through sixth?	**Question Type:** Acceptability **1 Right:** An acceptable sequence **4 Wrong:** Each violates at least one of the rules

MUST BE/COULD BE QUESTIONS

Must Be/Could Be questions account for just under 25 percent of the questions you'll see in a Logic Games section, but your practice with these questions is more important than that. When you add in the New-"If" questions that provide a new condition and then ask a Must Be/Could Be question about the circumstances the new condition creates, about 70 percent of your Logic Games score is at stake.

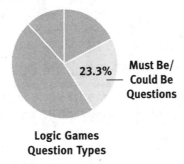

23.3% — **Must Be/ Could Be Questions**

Logic Games Question Types

PrepTests57–71; released 2009–2013

These questions ask you what must, could, or cannot be true in a game, based on the game's limitations, rules, and deductions. Some of these question stems are generic and straightforward.

Which one of the following CANNOT be true?

PrepTest57 Sec1 Q3

Which one of the following must be true?

PrepTest51 Sec4 Q17

Each of the following could be true EXCEPT:

PrepTest51 Sec4 Q20

Other Must Be/Could Be questions ask what must, can, or cannot be true of a specific entity or space within the game.

Which one of the following CANNOT be the assignment for any of the floors?

PrepTest59 Sec1 Q3

Which one of the following runners must the coach select to run in the track meet?

PrepTest61 Sec3 Q13

Lightfoot's session could be on which one of the following days?

PrepTest61 Sec3 Q23

In this section, you'll learn several strategies for answering Must Be/Could Be questions accurately and efficiently, but keep this fact in mind: The test always gives you all of the information you need to answer the question correctly (even if that isn't always obvious at first glance). If you have a strong setup with all of the rules, restrictions, and deductions drawn out clearly and accurately, you can get the right answer to any Must Be/Could Be question.

LEARNING OBJECTIVES

In this section, you'll learn to:

· Identify and answer Must Be/Could Be questions
· Characterize accurately the correct and incorrect answer choices in Must Be/Could Be questions

Characterizing Answer Choices in Must Be/Could Be Questions

To answer Must Be/Could Be questions correctly, you must answer the right question! That is, you need to appropriately characterize the one right and the four wrong answer choices. This goes back to the work you did in Chapter 1 on understanding levels of truth.

Before we turn to full Must Be/Could Be questions, refresh your skills at characterizing answer choices.

Question Stem	Analysis
Which of the following must be true?	**Question Type:** Must Be True **1 Right:** Must be true in every acceptable arrangement **4 Wrong:** Could be false
Which of the following could be false?	**Question Type:** Could Be False **1 Right:** Could be false in at least one acceptable arrangement **4 Wrong:** Must be true
Each of the following must be false EXCEPT:	**Question Type:** Could Be True (Must Be False EXCEPT) **1 Right:** Could be true in at least one acceptable arrangement **4 Wrong:** Must be false
Which of the following cannot be true?	**Question Type:** Must Be False **1 Right:** Must be false in every acceptable arrangement **4 Wrong:** Could be true
Which of the following could be true?	**Question Type:** Could Be True **1 Right:** Could be true in at least one acceptable arrangement **4 Wrong:** Must be false

TEST DAY TIP

· Be very careful not to hastily confuse a *true* statement with a *right* answer. Characterize the answer choices before evaluating them as correct or incorrect.

Practice

Now it's your turn. For each question stem, characterize correct and incorrect answer choices.

Question Stem		My Analysis
16. Which of the following must be true?	→	**Question Type:** **1 Right:** **4 Wrong:**
17. Bob CANNOT present on day	→	**Question Type:** **1 Right:** **4 Wrong:**
18. The bean dip recipe must include which of the following?	→	**Question Type:** **1 Right:** **4 Wrong:**
19. Jerrod must perform on either	→	**Question Type:** **1 Right:** **4 Wrong:**
20. Which of the following could be false?	→	**Question Type:** **1 Right:** **4 Wrong:**
21. The picnic basket could include each of the following EXCEPT:	→	**Question Type:** **1 Right:** **4 Wrong:**
22. Which of the following could be scheduled for Day 4?	→	**Question Type:** **1 Right:** **4 Wrong:**
23. It could be true that the jacket is	→	**Question Type:** **1 Right:** **4 Wrong:**

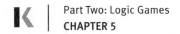
Expert Analysis

Take a look at how an LSAT Expert characterizes the question stems you just saw:

Question Stem	Analysis
16. Which of the following must be true?	**Question Type:** Must Be True ⟶ **1 Right:** Must be true in every acceptable arrangement **4 Wrong:** Could be false
17. Bob CANNOT present on day	**Question Type:** Must Be False ⟶ **1 Right:** A day on which Bob may not acceptably present **4 Wrong:** Days on which Bob could present
18. The bean dip recipe must include which of the following?	**Question Type:** Must Be True ⟶ **1 Right:** An ingredient the bean dip must include **4 Wrong:** Ingredients the bean dip need not include
19. Jerrod must perform on either	**Question Type:** Must Be True ⟶ **1 Right:** A pair of days at least one of which Jerrod must perform on **4 Wrong:** Two days Jerrod need not perform on
20. Which of the following could be false?	**Question Type:** Could Be False ⟶ **1 Right:** Could be false in at least one acceptable arrangement **4 Wrong:** Must be true
21. The picnic basket could include each of the following EXCEPT:	**Question Type:** Must Be False ⟶ **1 Right:** A food that cannot be in the basket **4 Wrong:** Foods that could be in the basket
22. Which of the following could be scheduled for Day 4?	**Question Type:** Could Be True ⟶ **1 Right:** An entity that could go on Day 4 **4 Wrong:** Entities that cannot go on Day 4
23. It could be true that the jacket is	**Question Type:** Could Be True **1 Right:** A color or characteristic that the jacket could have ⟶ **4 Wrong:** Colors or characteristics that the jacket must not have

Answering Must Be/Could Be Questions

As you read earlier, the test will always provide you with enough information to answer any Must Be/Could Be question you might encounter. At times, questions like these directly reward your ability to make the available deductions.

Take a look at a question you first encountered in Chapter 2. Take your time and be sure you remember how the LSAT expert reached all of the deductions reflected in the final sketch.

LSAT Question	Analysis

From the 1st through the 7th of next month, seven nurses—Farnham, Griseldi, Heany, Juarez, Khan, Lightfoot, and Moreau—will each conduct one information session at a community center. Each nurse's session will fall on a different day. The nurses' schedule is governed by the following constraints:
 	
    At least two of the other nurses' sessions must fall in between Heany's session and Moreau's session.
    Griseldi's session must be on the day before Khan's.
    Juarez's session must be on a later day than Moreau's.
    Farnham's session must be on an earlier day than Khan's but on a later day than Lightfoot's.
    Lightfoot cannot conduct the session on the 2nd.
	Steps 1–4:
	
	F G H J K L M
	
	1 2 3 4 5 6 7
	~F ~L ~G ~L ~L ~L ~L
	~G ~G ~K ~K ~F ~F
	~K ~K ~G
	~J ~M
	
	L . . . F . . . GK
	
	       / J
	H/M __ __ . . . M/H
	                  \ J

Lightfoot's session could be on which one of the following days?	**Step 5:** The correct answer is a day on which L can go. The four wrong answers are all days on which L cannot go. Evaluate the answer choices in light of the final sketch. L can only go on Day 1 or Day 3.
(A) the 3rd	→ Correct. An acceptable day for L.
(B) the 4th	→ L cannot go on Day 4. Eliminate.
(C) the 5th	→ L cannot go on Day 5. Eliminate.
(D) the 6th	→ L cannot go on Day 6. Eliminate.
(E) the 7th	→ L cannot go on Day 7. Eliminate.

PrepTest61 Sec3 Q23

Not every Must Be/Could Be question can be answered with a glance at the sketch. You may recall, in this question from Chapter 2, that the LSAT expert was able to use her work on other questions to identify choices that *could be true*, and were therefore *incorrect* in this Must Be False question.

LSAT Question	Analysis
From the 1st through the 7th of next month, seven nurses—Farnham, Griseldi, Heany, Juarez, Khan, Lightfoot, and Moreau—will each conduct one information session at a community center. Each nurse's session will fall on a different day. The nurses' schedule is governed by the following constraints: At least two of the other nurses' sessions must fall in between Heany's session and Moreau's session. Griseldi's session must be on the day before Khan's. Juarez's session must be on a later day than Moreau's. Farnham's session must be on an earlier day than Khan's but on a later day than Lightfoot's. Lightfoot cannot conduct the session on the 2nd.	**Steps 1–4:** F G H J K L M

Juarez's session CANNOT be on which one of the following days?	The correct answer is a day on which J cannot go. The four wrong answers are all days on which it is acceptable for J to go. Rule 3 eliminates Juarez from week 1, but that doesn't help with any of the answer choices.
(A) the 2nd	M-J-L-F-H-G-K and M-J-L-H-F-G-K are acceptable. Eliminate. Question 22 from this game also proves that Juarez could be second.
(B) the 3rd	L-M-J-F-H-G-K is acceptable. Eliminate. Question 20 from this game also proves that Juarez could be third.
(C) the 5th	Correct. If J is in 5, then G-K will have to take 6 and 7. That leaves spaces 1 and 4 for H and M. L and F would be forced into spaces 2 and 3, in that order, but that would put L in day 2, violating Rule 5. Must be false.
(D) the 6th	L-F-M-G-K-J-H and L-M-F-G-K-J-H are acceptable. Eliminate.
(E) the 7th	L-H-F-G-K-M-J, L-F-H-G-K-M-J, L-M-F-G-K-H-J, and L-F-M-G-K-H-J are all acceptable. Eliminate. Question 21 from this game also proves that Juarez could be seventh.

PrepTest61 Sec3 Q19

Be strategic. Eliminate any choices you can by consulting the final sketch. If that doesn't single out the correct answer, decide whether to test the remaining choices one-by-one or to come back to the question after completing the remaining questions in the set and consulting them for help.

Practice

Now practice by completing the Must Be/Could Be questions from some of the games you worked with in Chapters 3 and 4. The LSAT expert's final sketches are included for your convenience.

Clown Costume

LSAT Question	My Analysis

A clown will select a costume consisting of two pieces and no others: a jacket and overalls. One piece of the costume will be entirely one color, and the other piece will be plaid. Selection is subject to the following restrictions:

- If the jacket is plaid, then there must be exactly three colors in it.
- If the overalls are plaid, then there must be exactly two colors in them.
- The jacket and overalls must have exactly one color in common.
- Green, red, and violet are the only colors that can be in the jacket.
- Red, violet, and yellow are the only colors that can be in the overalls.

→

Steps 1–4:

[exactly 1 color in common]

Opt. I   Opt. II

Jacket	Overalls	Jacket	Overalls
g	r/v	r/v	r/v
v	~~y~~	~~g~~	_____
r			r/v/y

---

24. Which one of the following must be false? → **Step 5:**

   (A) Both green and red are colors used in the costume. →

   (B) Both green and violet are colors used in the costume. →

   (C) Both green and yellow are colors used in the costume. →

   (D) Both red and violet are colors used in the costume. →

   (E) Both violet and yellow are colors used in the costume. →

   PrepTest51 Sec4 Q4

HINT: This game uses Limited Options sketches. Think about how best to use those sketches to determine what must be false.

Guitarist's Demo CD

LSAT Question	My Analysis

A locally known guitarist's demo CD contains exactly seven different songs—S, T, V, W, X, Y, and Z. Each song occupies exactly one of the CD's seven tracks. Some of the songs are rock classics; the others are new compositions. The following conditions must hold:

    S occupies the fourth track of the CD.
    Both W and Y precede S on the CD.
    T precedes W on the CD.
    A rock classic occupies the sixth track of the CD.
    Each rock classic is immediately preceded on the CD by a new composition.
    Z is a rock classic.

→ **Steps 1–4:**

Y; T . . . W

__	__	__	S	X/V	Z	V/X	S̶TVWXYZ̶
1	2	3	4	5	6	7	
n	__	__	__	n	r	n	n r

always __n__ before any __r__

---

25. Which one of the following is a pair of songs that must occupy consecutive tracks on the CD?

→ **Step 5:**

    (A)   S and V   →

    (B)   S and W   →

    (C)   T and Z   →

    (D)   T and Y   →

    (E)   V and Z   →

PrepTest51 Sec4 Q12

---

26. Which one of the following songs must be a new composition?

→ **Step 5:**

    (A)   S   →

    (B)   T   →

    (C)   W   →

    (D)   X   →

    (E)   Y   →

PrepTest51 Sec4 Q13

Parcel Delivery

LSAT Question	My Analysis

A courier delivers exactly eight parcels—G, H, J, K, L, M, N, and O. No two parcels are delivered at the same time, nor is any parcel delivered more than once. The following conditions must apply:

> L is delivered later than H.
> K is delivered earlier than O.
> H is delivered earlier than M.
> O is delivered later than G.
> M is delivered earlier than G.
> Both N and J are delivered earlier than M.

Steps 1–4:

27. Which one of the following must be true?

Step 5:

   (A) At least one parcel is delivered earlier than K is delivered.

   (B) At least two parcels are delivered later than G is delivered.

   (C) At least four parcels are delivered later than H is delivered.

   (D) At least four parcels are delivered later than J is delivered.

   (E) At least four parcels are delivered earlier than M is delivered.

   PrepTest51 Sec4 Q17

28. Each of the following could be true EXCEPT:

Step 5:

   (A) H is delivered later than K.

   (B) J is delivered later than G.

   (C) L is delivered later than O.

   (D) M is delivered later than L.

   (E) N is delivered later than H.

   PrepTest51 Sec4 Q20

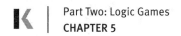

Convention Car Pool

LSAT Question	My Analysis

Exactly six workers—Faith, Gus, Hannah, Juan, Kenneth, and Lisa—will travel to a business convention in two cars—car 1 and car 2. Each car must carry at least two of the workers, one of whom will be assigned to drive. For the entire trip, the workers will comply with an assignment that also meets the following constraints:

    Either Faith or Gus must drive the car in which Hannah travels.

    Either Faith or Kenneth must drive the car in which Juan travels.

    Gus must travel in the same car as Lisa.

Steps 1–4:

F G H J K L

2–4/Car   Driver: F/G

Opt. I   Opt. II   H

                                       Driver: F/K

(1) | (2)   (1) | (2)   J

Driver: K | F | F/K

        J | H | J   G

        G   (__)(__)   L

        L   (__)(__)

                       G

                       L

               (__H__)?

29. The two workers who drive the cars CANNOT be

    Step 5:

    (A)   Faith and Gus

    (B)   Faith and Kenneth

    (C)   Faith and Lisa

    (D)   Gus and Kenneth

    (E)   Kenneth and Lisa

PrepTest61 Sec3 Q2

30. Which one of the following CANNOT be true?

    Step 5:

    (A)   Gus is the only person other than the driver in one of the cars.

    (B)   Hannah is the only person other than the driver in one of the cars.

    (C)   Juan is the only person other than the driver in one of the cars.

    (D)   Kenneth is the only person other than the driver in one of the cars.

    (E)   Lisa is the only person other than the driver in one of the cars.

PrepTest61 Sec3 Q5

HINT: Remember that, in the final sketch, the cars are numbered only for convenience. As you evaluate the answers, check for who must be in the same car, and for who must drive, but remember that the numbering on the cars could be swapped.

Summer Program Courses

LSAT Question	My Analysis
A summer program offers at least one of the following seven courses: geography, history, literature, mathematics, psychology, sociology, zoology. The following restrictions on the program must apply: If mathematics is offered, then either literature or sociology (but not both) is offered. If literature is offered, then geography is also offered but psychology is not. If sociology is offered, then psychology is also offered but zoology is not. If geography is offered, then both history and zoology are also offered.	**Steps 1–4:** G H L M P S Z If Ⓜ → exactly 1 of Ⓛ or Ⓢ If Ⓛ and Ⓢ → M̶ If L̶ and S̶ → M̶ If Ⓛ → Ⓖ and P̶ If G̶ or Ⓟ → L̶ If Ⓢ → Ⓟ and Z̶ If P̶ or Ⓩ → S̶ If Ⓖ → Ⓗ and Ⓩ If H̶ or Z̶ → G̶

31. Which one of the following must be false of the summer program?   **Step 5:**

   (A) Both geography and psychology are offered.

   (B) Both geography and mathematics are offered.

   (C) Both psychology and mathematics are offered.

   (D) Both history and mathematics are offered.

   (E) Both geography and sociology are offered.

   PrepTest49 Sec1 Q17

HINT: In Selection games, where all of the rules are conditional, either test the choices one-by-one or look to your work on other questions to help you spot acceptable selections.

Expert Analysis

Now take a look at how an LSAT expert tackled those same questions.

Clown Costume

LSAT Question	Analysis
A clown will select a costume consisting of two pieces and no others: a jacket and overalls. One piece of the costume will be entirely one color, and the other piece will be plaid. Selection is subject to the following restrictions: If the jacket is plaid, then there must be exactly three colors in it. If the overalls are plaid, then there must be exactly two colors in them. The jacket and overalls must have exactly one color in common. Green, red, and violet are the only colors that can be in the jacket. Red, violet, and yellow are the only colors that can be in the overalls.	**Steps 1–4:**

[exactly 1 color in common]

Opt. I		Opt. II	
Jacket	Overalls	Jacket	Overalls
g	r/v	r/v	r/v
v	~~y~~	~~g~~	____
r			r/v/y

24. Which one of the following must be false?	**Step 5:** Must Be False. The correct answer cannot ever occur in an acceptable costume. The four wrong answers can be true of at least one acceptable color combination.
(A) Both green and red are colors used in the costume.	Could be true in Opt I. Eliminate.
(B) Both green and violet are colors used in the costume.	Could be true in Opt I. Eliminate.
(C) Both green and yellow are colors used in the costume.	Correct.
(D) Both red and violet are colors used in the costume.	Could be true in either option. Eliminate.
(E) Both violet and yellow are colors used in the costume.	Could be true in Opt II. Eliminate.

PrepTest51 Sec4 Q4

Guitarist's Demo CD

LSAT Question	Analysis
A locally known guitarist's demo CD contains exactly seven different songs—S, T, V, W, X, Y, and Z. Each song occupies exactly one of the CD's seven tracks. Some of the songs are rock classics; the others are new compositions. The following conditions must hold:	**Steps 1–4:**

Steps 1–4:

Y; T . . . W

			S	X/V	Z	V/X	$\cancel{S}$ T V W X Y $\cancel{Z}$
1	2	3	4	5	6	7
n				n	r	n	n r

always __n__ before any __r__

LSAT Question (continued):

S occupies the fourth track of the CD.
Both W and Y precede S on the CD.
T precedes W on the CD.
A rock classic occupies the sixth track of the CD.
Each rock classic is immediately preceded on the CD by a new composition.
Z is a rock classic.

LSAT Question	Analysis
25. Which one of the following is a pair of songs that must occupy consecutive tracks on the CD?	**Step 5:** The correct answer lists two songs that must be back-to-back. The four wrong answers are pairs of songs that could be separated.
(A) S and V	S is always in spot 4. V could be in spot 7. Eliminate.
(B) S and W	S is always in spot 4. W could be in spot 2. Eliminate.
(C) T and Z	T is always in spots 1–3. Z is always in spot 6. Eliminate.
(D) T and Y	T could be in spot 1. Y could be in spot 3. Eliminate.
(E) V and Z *PrepTest51 Sec4 Q12*	Correct. V is always either spot 5 or spot 7. Z is always spot 6. V and Z must be consecutive.
26. Which one of the following songs must be a new composition?	**Step 5:** The correct answer must be a new song. The four wrong answers could be classic rock songs. The final sketch and deductions show that V and X must be new songs.
(A) S	S could be a classic rock song. Eliminate.
(B) T	T could be a classic rock song. Eliminate.
(C) W	W could be a classic rock song. Eliminate.
(D) X	Correct. X must be a new song.
(E) Y *PrepTest51 Sec4 Q13*	Y could be a classic rock song. Eliminate.

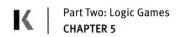

Parcel Delivery

LSAT Question	Analysis

A courier delivers exactly eight parcels—G, H, J, K, L, M, N, and O. No two parcels are delivered at the same time, nor is any parcel delivered more than once. The following conditions must apply:
    L is delivered later than H.
    K is delivered earlier than O.
    H is delivered earlier than M.
    O is delivered later than G.
    M is delivered earlier than G.
    Both N and J are delivered earlier than M.
	Steps 1–4:
	
	J N H
	        M L
	
	K G
	     O

27. Which one of the following must be true?	**Step 5:** Correct answer must be true in every case. The four wrong answers could be false.
(A) At least one parcel is delivered earlier than K is delivered.	Could be false: K could be delivered anywhere from first through seventh. Eliminate.
(B) At least two parcels are delivered later than G is delivered.	Could be false: O might be the only delivery after G. Eliminate.
(C) At least four parcels are delivered later than H is delivered.	Correct. G, L, M, and O must be delivered after H. Must be true.
(D) At least four parcels are delivered later than J is delivered.	Could be false: M, G, and O might be the only deliveries after J. Eliminate.
(E) At least four parcels are delivered earlier than M is delivered. *PrepTest51 Sec4 Q17*	Could be false: H, J, and N might be the only deliveries to precede M's delivery. Eliminate.
28. Each of the following could be true EXCEPT:	**Step 5:** Correct answer must be false in any acceptable arrangement. The four wrong answers could be true.
(A) H is delivered later than K.	Could be true. H and K do not restrict each other. Eliminate.
(B) J is delivered later than G.	Correct. J must be delivered earlier than M, and M must be delivered earlier than G. (B) must be false.
(C) L is delivered later than O.	Could be true. L and O do not restrict each other. Eliminate.
(D) M is delivered later than L.	Could be true. L and M do not restrict each other. Eliminate.
(E) N is delivered later than H. *PrepTest51 Sec4 Q20*	Could be true. H and N do not restrict each other. Eliminate.

Convention Car Pool

LSAT Question	Analysis

Exactly six workers—Faith, Gus, Hannah, Juan, Kenneth, and Lisa—will travel to a business convention in two cars—car 1 and car 2. Each car must carry at least two of the workers, one of whom will be assigned to drive. For the entire trip, the workers will comply with an assignment that also meets the following constraints:

    Either Faith or Gus must drive the car in which Hannah travels.

    Either Faith or Kenneth must drive the car in which Juan travels.

    Gus must travel in the same car as Lisa.

Steps 1–4:

F G H J K L

2–4/Car   Driver: F/G

    Opt. I   Opt. II   H

                      Driver: F/K

   (1) | (2)   (1) | (2)   J

Driver: K | F   F/K   G

      J | H   J   L

      G | (—)(—)

      L | (—)(—)

           G

           L

          (H)?

---

29. The two workers who drive the cars CANNOT be

Step 5: The right answer has a pair of workers who may not both drive in the same arrangement. The four wrong answers have pairs who could both drive. Rules 1 and 2 are the keys here.

  (A) Faith and Gus

→ F could drive H and J, or F could drive H and G could drive J. Eliminate.

  (B) Faith and Kenneth

→ F could drive H and J, or F could drive H and K could drive J. Eliminate.

  (C) Faith and Lisa

→ F could drive H and J while L drives the other car. Eliminate.

  (D) Gus and Kenneth

→ G could drive H, and K could drive J. Eliminate.

  (E) Kenneth and Lisa

               PrepTest61 Sec3 Q2

→ Correct. H's car has no acceptable driver here (Rule 1). Must be false.

---

30. Which one of the following CANNOT be true?

Step 5: The right answer must be false in both options. The four wrong answers could be true in at least one of the options.

  (A) Gus is the only person other than the driver in one of the cars.

→ Could be true in Opt II. L would be the driver. Eliminate.

  (B) Hannah is the only person other than the driver in one of the cars.

→ Could be true in Opt I. Eliminate.

  (C) Juan is the only person other than the driver in one of the cars.

→ Could be true in Opt II. Either F or K would be the driver. Eliminate.

  (D) Kenneth is the only person other than the driver in one of the cars.

→ Correct. K is the driver in Opt I. In Opt II, either K drives or K is a passenger along with J or along with G and L. Must be false.

  (E) Lisa is the only person other than the driver in one of the cars.

               PrepTest61 Sec3 Q5

→ Could be true in Opt II. G would be the driver. Eliminate.

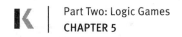

Summer Program Courses

LSAT Question	Analysis

A summer program offers at least one of the following seven courses: geography, history, literature, mathematics, psychology, sociology, zoology. The following restrictions on the program must apply:
If mathematics is offered, then either literature or sociology (but not both) is offered.
If literature is offered, then geography is also offered but psychology is not.
If sociology is offered, then psychology is also offered but zoology is not.
If geography is offered, then both history and zoology are also offered.
	Steps 1–4:
	G H L M P S Z
	If (M) → *exactly 1 of (L) or (S)*
	If (L) and (S) → ~~M~~
	If ~~L~~ and ~~S~~ → ~~M~~
	If (L) → (G) and ~~P~~
	If ~~G~~ or (P) → ~~L~~
	If (S) → (P) and ~~Z~~
	If ~~P~~ or (Z) → ~~S~~
	If (G) → (H) and (Z)
	If ~~H~~ or ~~Z~~ → ~~G~~

31. Which one of the following must be false of the summer program?	**Step 5:** The correct answer must be false in any acceptable selection. The four wrong answers each could be possible in at least one acceptable selection. Look for pairs of entities the selection of which would contradict the rules.
(A) Both geography and psychology are offered.	Could be true. Offering G triggers offering H and Z (Rule 4). Offering P triggers rejecting S (Rule 3). No conflict. Eliminate.
(B) Both geography and mathematics are offered.	Could be true. Offering G triggers offering H and Z (Rule 4). Offering M triggers offering either L or S (Rule 1). No conflict. Eliminate.
(C) Both psychology and mathematics are offered.	Could be true. Offering P triggers rejecting S (Rule 3). Offering M triggers offering L or S (Rule 1). Since offering P allows for offering L, there's no conflict. Eliminate.
(D) Both history and mathematics are offered.	Could be true. Offering H does not trigger anything, so there can be no conflict with offering M. Eliminate.
(E) Both geography and sociology are offered. *PrepTest49 Sec1 Q17*	Correct. Offering G triggers offering Z (Rule 4). Offering S means rejecting Z (Rule 3). There is the conflict. Must be false.

NEW-"IF" QUESTIONS

New-"If" questions account for nearly half of all of the questions in the Logic Games section. Mastering this question type is crucial to your Logic Games performance.

New-"If" questions ask you to consider a new condition, or new information, that has not yet been established in the rules or limitations of the game.

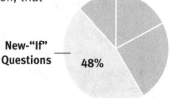

New-"If" Questions — 48%

Logic Games Question Types

PrepTests 57–71; released 2009–2013

If Gombrich auditions on both Wednesday and Saturday, then which one of the following could be true?

PrepTest57 Sec1 Q11

If Lisa drives one of the cars, then which one of the following could be true?

PrepTest61 Sec3 Q3

If K is the seventh parcel delivered, then each of the following could be true EXCEPT:

PrepTest51 Sec4 Q21

NOTE: After the New-"If" condition, each of these questions asked what must, can, or cannot be true. That means that you'll be using exactly the same skills you employed to answer Must Be/Could Be questions, but now you'll be analyzing the answer choices in light of the new condition or restriction given by the question stem.

TEST DAY TIP

· The new conditions or restrictions in New-"If" questions apply only to that question. When you make a new sketch, label it as applying to that question number, and do not carry the restrictions over to a subsequent question.

This section covers all you need to know to become a New-"If" question expert.

LEARNING OBJECTIVES

In this section, you'll learn to:

- Identify and answer New-"If" questions
- Create new sketches to account for the "If" condition in New-"If" questions, and make additional deductions applicable to the question

Generally speaking, the most efficient and effective way to approach these questions is to copy your master sketch, add the new information, and then make further deductions.

Take another look at how the LSAT expert analyzed and answered the New-"If" questions from the Nurses' Information Sessions game you first saw in Chapter 2.

LSAT Question	**Analysis**

From the 1st through the 7th of next month, seven nurses—Farnham, Griseldi, Heany, Juarez, Khan, Lightfoot, and Moreau—will each conduct one information session at a community center. Each nurse's session will fall on a different day. The nurses' schedule is governed by the following constraints:

At least two of the other nurses' sessions must fall in between Heany's session and Moreau's session.
Griseldi's session must be on the day before Khan's.
Juarez's session must be on a later day than Moreau's.
Farnham's session must be on an earlier day than Khan's but on a later day than Lightfoot's.
Lightfoot cannot conduct the session on the 2nd.

→

Steps 1–4:

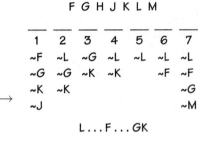

If Juarez's session is on the 3rd, then which one of the following could be true?

→

Step 5: "If": Redraw master sketch, and add J to spot 3:

With J placed, Rule 3 forces M into week 1 or 2. And, according to Rule 1, H must go at least 3 weeks later than M, and so later than J. Now, work in the L-F-GK string. L must go earlier than J, but can't take week 2 (Rule 5), and so must take week 1. To obey Rule 1, F must take week 4. So, there are two possible arrangements.

L	M	J	F	H	G	K
L	M	J	F	G	K	H

(A)	Moreau's session is on the 1st.	→	Must be false. Moreau takes week 2. Eliminate.
(B)	Khan's session is on the 5th.	→	Must be false. Khan takes week 6 or 7. Eliminate.
(C)	Heany's session is on the 6th.	→	Must be false. Heany takes week 5 or 7. Eliminate.
(D)	Griseldi's session is on the 5th.	→	Correct. This could be true.
(E)	Farnham's session is on the 2nd.	→	Must be false. Farnham takes week 4. Eliminate.

PrepTest61 Sec3 Q20

LSAT Question	**Analysis**
From the 1st through the 7th of next month, seven nurses—Farnham, Griseldi, Heany, Juarez, Khan, Lightfoot, and Moreau—will each conduct one information session at a community center. Each nurse's session will fall on a different day. The nurses' schedule is governed by the following constraints:	**Steps 1–4:**

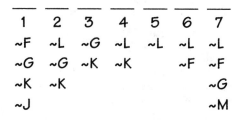

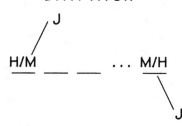

> At least two of the other nurses' sessions must fall in between Heany's session and Moreau's session.
> Griseldi's session must be on the day before Khan's.
> Juarez's session must be on a later day than Moreau's.
> Farnham's session must be on an earlier day than Khan's but on a later day than Lightfoot's.
> Lightfoot cannot conduct the session on the 2nd.

If Khan's session is on an earlier day than Moreau's, which one of the following could conduct the session on the 3rd?	**Step 5: "If":** Adding the new info to the L-F-GK string produces:

$$L \ldots F \ldots GK \ldots M \ldots J$$

The only entity not accounted for is H, which must be separated from M by at least two spaces (Rule 1).

L	H/F	F/H	G	K	M	J
~L						

The correct answer could be true, while the four wrong answer choices all must be false under these conditions.

(A)	Griseldi	→	Must be in week 4. Eliminate.
(B)	Heany	→	Correct.
(C)	Juarez	→	Must be in week 7. Eliminate.
(D)	Lightfoot	→	Must be in week 1. Eliminate.
(E)	Moreau	→	Must be in week 6. Eliminate.

PrepTest61 Sec3 Q21

LSAT Question	Analysis

From the 1st through the 7th of next month, seven nurses—Farnham, Griseldi, Heany, Juarez, Khan, Lightfoot, and Moreau—will each conduct one information session at a community center. Each nurse's session will fall on a different day. The nurses' schedule is governed by the following constraints:

At least two of the other nurses' sessions must fall in between Heany's session and Moreau's session.

Griseldi's session must be on the day before Khan's.

Juarez's session must be on a later day than Moreau's.

Farnham's session must be on an earlier day than Khan's but on a later day than Lightfoot's.

Lightfoot cannot conduct the session on the 2nd.

Steps 1–4:

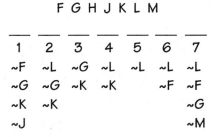

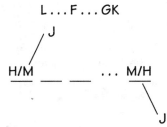

If Griseldi's session is on the 5th, then which one of the following must be true?

Step 5: "If": Placing G in week 5 affects the L-F-GK string.

L . . . F . . .

___ ___ ___ ___ G K ___
~L

Now, which of H, J, or M could take week 7? Not M (Rule 3). And not J, because either H and M would run afoul of Rule 1, or L would violate Rule 5. So, H takes week 7.

L . . . F . . .

___ ___ ___ ___ G K H
~L

(A)	Farnham's session is on the 3rd.	Could be false—F could take weeks 2 or 4. Eliminate.
(B)	Heany's session is on the 7th.	Correct.
(C)	Juarez's session is on the 4th.	Could be false—J could take weeks 2 or 3. Eliminate.
(D)	Lightfoot's session is on the 1st.	Could be false—L could take week 3. Eliminate.
(E)	Moreau's session is on the 2nd.	Could be false—M could take weeks 1 or 3. Eliminate.

PrepTest61 Sec3 Q22

Notice how, in each case, the LSAT expert read the "If" condition and depicted it as a new rule or restriction for that specific question. She then made all of the deductions available under that new condition. Only after doing that did she analyze the rest of the question stem and evaluate the answer choices.

LSAT STRATEGY

New-"If" Question Checklist:

- Read up to the comma.
- Ask: Is there new info here that is not in the master sketch?
- If "yes," then copy the master sketch and add the "If" condition.
- Make all available deductions, and add this new information to the sketch.
- When you have made the available deductions, read the rest of the question stem, characterize the one right and four wrong answers, and evaluate the choices.

Practice approaching New-"If" questions with this list until it is second nature. Once you have the hang of New-"If" questions, you may use additional information at the end of a question stem to dictate when you can stop making deductions. For example, if a question stem ends with "then who must be in the fourth position?" you can stop once you have figured out who must be fourth.

You'll also see, later in this section, how New-"If" questions can be answered quickly and precisely in games with Limited Options sketches.

For now, practice this approach deliberately. You'll see the benefit of sketching the "If" condition and making deductions when you realize how directly you can determine the correct answer to the questions.

New-"If" Question Practice: Stopping at the Comma

Here are two New-"If" question stems from the Museum Photographs game. Read the new condition, copy your master sketch, add the new condition, and make all available deductions. After this, you'll review how an LSAT expert would have analyzed these conditions. Then, you can answer the full questions.

LSAT Question	My Analysis

A museum curator is arranging seven photographs—*Fence, Gardenias, Hibiscus, Irises, Katydid, Lotus,* and *Magnolia*—on a gallery wall in accordance with the photographer's requirements. The photographs are to be hung along the wall in a row, in seven positions sequentially numbered from first to seventh. The photographer's requirements are as follows:

> *Gardenias* must be immediately before *Katydid*.
> *Hibiscus* must be somewhere before *Katydid* but cannot be the first photograph.
> *Irises* and *Lotus* must be next to one another.
> *Magnolia* must be one of the first three photographs.
> *Fence* must be either first or seventh.

Steps 1–4:

F G H I K L M

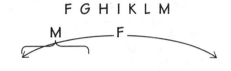

1	2	3	4	5	6	7
~H	~F	~F	~F	~F	~F	~M
~G	~G	~K	~M	~M	~M	~H
~K	~K				~H	~G

___ . . . H . . . G K

___ I L or L I

---

32. If *Irises* is immediately before *Gardenias,* which one of the following could be true?

PrepTest59 Sec1 Q7

Step 5:

---

33. If *Magnolia* is second, which one of the following CANNOT be true?

PrepTest59 Sec1 Q9

Step 5:

Expert Analysis

Here's how an LSAT expert might analyze those question stems.

LSAT Question	Analysis

Steps 1–4:

A museum curator is arranging seven photographs—*Fence, Gardenias, Hibiscus, Irises, Katydid, Lotus,* and *Magnolia*—on a gallery wall in accordance with the photographer's requirements. The photographs are to be hung along the wall in a row, in seven positions sequentially numbered from first to seventh. The photographer's requirements are as follows:

  Gardenias must be immediately before *Katydid*.
  Hibiscus must be somewhere before *Katydid* but cannot be the first photograph.
  Irises and *Lotus* must be next to one another.
  Magnolia must be one of the first three photographs.
  Fence must be either first or seventh.

F G H I K L M

	1	2	3	4	5	6	7
	~H	~F	~F	~F	~F	~F	~M
	~G	~G	~K	~M	~M	~M	~H
	~K	~K					~H	~G

___ ... H ... G K

I L or L I

32. If *Irises* is immediately before *Gardenias,* which one of the following could be true?

PrepTest59 Sec1 Q7

Step 5: "If": Placing I right before G means that L will come right before I (Rule 3), and K will come right after G (Rule 1).

L	I	G	K

H must come before that newly created block (Rule 2).

H ... | L | I | G | K |

M, which must take one of the first three spaces (Rule 4), will come right before or right after H, and F will be either first or seventh (Rule 5).

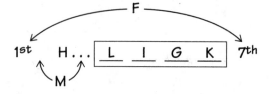

That produces the following possibilities:

F	H/M	M/H	L	I	G	K
1	2	3	4	5	6	7

M	H	L	I	G	K	F
1	2	3	4	5	6	7

LSAT Question	**Analysis**

33. If *Magnolia* is second, which one of the following CANNOT be true?

PrepTest59 Sec1 Q9

Step 5: "If": Placing M in the second spot restricts who can take the first spot. No one in the G-K or I-L blocks can go there because they must be in consecutive spaces as pairs (Rules 1 and 3). H cannot go there at all (Rule 2). So, the first spot must go to F.

F	M					
1	2	3	4	5	6	7

→ With that much established, there are now only three ways to accommodate both the G-K and I-L blocks.

F	M	H	G	K	I/L	L/I
1	2	3	4	5	6	7

F	M	H	I/L	L/I	G	K
1	2	3	4	5	6	7

F	M	I/L	L/I	H	G	K
1	2	3	4	5	6	7

This process may appear time-consuming at first, but expert test takers realize that it is a tremendous time-saver. Get in the habit of going through your New-"If" checklist. As soon as you determine that the new information in the question stem is not in your master sketch, decide immediately to create a new sketch.

New-"If" Practice: Full Questions

Now, apply the work you just did to the full questions. Read the part of the question stem following the New-"If" condition; characterize the one right and four wrong answers; and then, use the deductions that followed from the New-"If" conditions to evaluate the answer choices.

LSAT Question	My Analysis

34. If *Irises* is immediately before *Gardenias*, which one of the following could be true?

Step 5: "If": Placing I right before G means that L will come right before I (Rule 3), and K will come right after G (Rule 1).

$$\boxed{\underline{L} \quad \underline{I} \quad \underline{G} \quad \underline{K}}$$

H must come before that newly created block, but cannot be first (Rule 2).

$$H \ldots \boxed{\underline{L} \quad \underline{I} \quad \underline{G} \quad \underline{K}}$$

→ M, which must take one of the first three spaces (Rule 4), will come right before or right after H, and F will be either first or seventh (Rule 5).

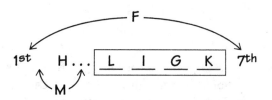

That produces the following possibilities.

F	H/M	M/H	L	I	G	K
1	2	3	4	5	6	7

M	H	L	I	G	K	F
1	2	3	4	5	6	7

(A) *Gardenias* is fourth. →

(B) *Hibiscus* is fourth. →

(C) *Irises* is third. →

(D) *Lotus* is second. →

(E) *Magnolia* is third. →

PrepTest59 Sec1 Q7

LSAT Question	**My Analysis**
35. If *Magnolia* is second, which one of the following CANNOT be true?	**Step 5:** "If": Placing M in the second spot restricts who can take the first spot. No one in the G-K or I-L blocks can go there because they must be in consecutive spaces as pairs (Rules 1 and 3). H cannot go there at all (Rule 2). So, the first spot must go to F.

$$\begin{array}{ccccccc} F & M & \_\_ & \_\_ & \_\_ & \_\_ & \_\_ \\ 1 & 2 & 3 & 4 & 5 & 6 & 7 \end{array}$$

→ With that much established, there are now only three ways to accommodate both the G-K and I-L blocks.

$$\begin{array}{ccccccc} F & M & H & G & K & I/L & L/I \\ 1 & 2 & 3 & 4 & 5 & 6 & 7 \end{array}$$

$$\begin{array}{ccccccc} F & M & H & I/L & L/I & G & K \\ 1 & 2 & 3 & 4 & 5 & 6 & 7 \end{array}$$

$$\begin{array}{ccccccc} F & M & I/L & L/I & H & G & K \\ 1 & 2 & 3 & 4 & 5 & 6 & 7 \end{array}$$

(A)	*Hibiscus* is third.	→
(B)	*Hibiscus* is fourth.	→
(C)	*Hibiscus* is fifth.	→
(D)	*Gardenias* is fourth.	→
(E)	*Gardenias* is sixth.	→

PrepTest59 Sec1 Q9

Expert Analysis

Here's how an LSAT expert might have used the New-"If" sketches to evaluate the answer choices in those questions.

LSAT Question	Analysis

34. If *Irises* is immediately before *Gardenias*, which one of the following could be true?

→

Step 5: "If": Placing I right before G means that L will come right before I (Rule 3), and K will come right after G (Rule 1).

L	I	G	K

H must come before that newly created block, but cannot be first (Rule 2).

H . . . | L | I | G | K |

M, which must take one of the first three spaces (Rule 4), will come right before or right after H, and F will be either first or seventh (Rule 5).

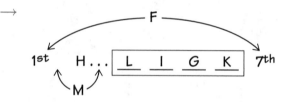

That produces the following possibilities.

F	H/M	M/H	L	I	G	K
1	2	3	4	5	6	7

M	H	L	I	G	K	F
1	2	3	4	5	6	7

The correct answer could be true under this question's conditions; the four wrong answers must be false.

(A) *Gardenias* is fourth.

→ Must be false. G is either fifth or sixth here. Eliminate.

(B) *Hibiscus* is fourth.

→ Must be false. H is either second or third here. Eliminate.

(C) *Irises* is third.

→ Must be false. I is either fourth or fifth here. Eliminate.

(D) *Lotus* is second.

→ Must be false. L is either third or fourth here. Eliminate.

(E) *Magnolia* is third.

→ Correct. This could be true: F-H-M-L-I-G-K.

PrepTest59 Sec1 Q7

LSAT Question	Analysis
35. If *Magnolia* is second, which one of the following CANNOT be true?	**Step 5:** "If": Placing M in the second spot restricts who can take the first spot. No one in the G-K or I-L blocks can go there because they must be in consecutive spaces as pairs (Rules 1 and 3). H cannot go there at all (Rule 2). So, the first spot must go to F.

$$\frac{\text{F} \quad \text{M} \quad \underline{} \quad \underline{} \quad \underline{} \quad \underline{} \quad \underline{}}{1 \quad 2 \quad 3 \quad 4 \quad 5 \quad 6 \quad 7}$$

With that much established, there are now only three ways to accommodate both the G-K and I-L blocks.

$$\frac{\text{F} \quad \text{M} \quad \text{H} \quad \text{G} \quad \text{K} \quad \text{I/L} \quad \text{L/I}}{1 \quad 2 \quad 3 \quad 4 \quad 5 \quad 6 \quad 7}$$

$$\frac{\text{F} \quad \text{M} \quad \text{H} \quad \text{I/L} \quad \text{L/I} \quad \text{G} \quad \text{K}}{1 \quad 2 \quad 3 \quad 4 \quad 5 \quad 6 \quad 7}$$

$$\frac{\text{F} \quad \text{M} \quad \text{I/L} \quad \text{L/I} \quad \text{H} \quad \text{G} \quad \text{K}}{1 \quad 2 \quad 3 \quad 4 \quad 5 \quad 6 \quad 7}$$

The correct answer must be false under this question's conditions. The four wrong answers could be true.

(A)	*Hibiscus* is third.	Could be true. H can take third or fifth here. Eliminate.
(B)	*Hibiscus* is fourth.	Correct. H cannot take the fourth position under this question stem's condition. Must be false.
(C)	*Hibiscus* is fifth.	Could be true. H can take third or fifth here. Eliminate.
(D)	*Gardenias* is fourth.	Could be true. G can take either fourth or sixth here. Eliminate.
(E)	*Gardenias* is sixth.	Could be true. G can take either fourth or sixth here. Eliminate.

PrepTest59 Sec1 Q9

More New-"If" Practice

Now, try your hand at the questions from another game you've been working with. Read the question stem; stop after the comma; integrate the New-"If" condition into a sketch; make all of the available deductions; read the rest of the question; characterize the one right and four wrong answers; then, use the deductions that followed from the New-"If" conditions to evaluate the answer choices.

Guitarist's Demo CD

LSAT Question	My Analysis
A locally known guitarist's demo CD contains exactly seven different songs—S, T, V, W, X, Y, and Z. Each song occupies exactly one of the CD's seven tracks. Some of the songs are rock classics; the others are new compositions. The following conditions must hold:	**Steps 1–4:**

A locally known guitarist's demo CD contains exactly seven different songs—S, T, V, W, X, Y, and Z. Each song occupies exactly one of the CD's seven tracks. Some of the songs are rock classics; the others are new compositions. The following conditions must hold:

> S occupies the fourth track of the CD.
> Both W and Y precede S on the CD.
> T precedes W on the CD.
> A rock classic occupies the sixth track of the CD.
> Each rock classic is immediately preceded on the CD by a new composition.
> Z is a rock classic.

Steps 1–4:

Y; T . . . W

			S	X/V	Z	V/X	$\not{S}$ T V W X Y $\not{Z}$
1	2	3	4	5	6	7	
n				n	r	n	n r

always _n_ before any _r_

36. If W precedes Y on the CD, then which one of the following must be true?

→ **Step 5:**

(A) S is a rock classic.

→

(B) V is a rock classic.

→

(C) Y is a rock classic.

→

(D) T is a new composition.

→

(E) W is a new composition.

PrepTest51 Sec4 Q14 →

LSAT Question	**My Analysis**
37. If there are exactly two songs on the CD that both precede V and are preceded by Y, then which one of the following could be true?	**Step 5:**
	$\longrightarrow$
(A) V occupies the seventh track of the CD.	$\longrightarrow$
(B) X occupies the fifth track of the CD.	$\longrightarrow$
(C) Y occupies the third track of the CD.	$\longrightarrow$
(D) T is a rock classic.	$\longrightarrow$
(E) W is a rock classic.	$\longrightarrow$
PrepTest51 Sec4 Q15	

Expert Analysis

Here's how an LSAT expert might have approached those two New-"If" questions. Compare your work. Did you fully analyze the condition in the question stem and make all available deductions before you turned to the answer choices?

Guitarist's Demo CD

LSAT Question	Analysis

A locally known guitarist's demo CD contains exactly seven different songs—S, T, V, W, X, Y, and Z. Each song occupies exactly one of the CD's seven tracks. Some of the songs are rock classics; the others are new compositions. The following conditions must hold:
    S occupies the fourth track of the CD.
    Both W and Y precede S on the CD.
    T precedes W on the CD.
    A rock classic occupies the sixth track of the CD.
    Each rock classic is immediately preceded on the CD by a new composition.
    Z is a rock classic.
	Steps 1–4:
	
	Y; T . . . W
	
	___ ___ ___ S X/V Z V/X S̸ T V W X Y Z̸
	 1 2 3 4 5 6 7
	 n ___ ___ ___ n r n n r
	
	always _n_ before any _r_

36. If W precedes Y on the CD, then which one of the following must be true?	**Step 5:** "If": Adding the condition that W precedes Y to the information in the final sketch establishes the order of the first four songs. T W Y S V/X Z X/V 1 2 3 4 5 6 7 n ___ ___ ___ n r n The correct answer must be true under these conditions; the four wrong answers could be false.
(A) S is a rock classic.	Could be false. S is always fourth, and the fourth song could be new or it could be a rock classic. Eliminate.
(B) V is a rock classic.	False. V is always a new song, whether it comes fifth or seventh on the CD. Eliminate.
(C) Y is a rock classic.	Could be false. Y now falls third on the CD. The third song could be a new composition or it could be a rock classic. Eliminate
(D) T is a new composition.	Correct. T is now the first song, and the first song is always a new composition.
(E) W is a new composition. <div align="right">*PrepTest51 Sec4 Q14*</div>	Could be false. W now falls second on the CD. The second song could be new or it could be a rock classic. Eliminate.

LSAT Question	Analysis

37. If there are exactly two songs on the CD that both precede V and are preceded by Y, then which one of the following could be true?

Step 5: "If": create a new sketch with the condition from the question stem. The only way to accommodate the new condition given here is to make V the fifth song on the CD and to make Y the second song.

T . . . W

	Y		S	V	Z	X
1	2	3	4	5	6	7
n				n	r	n

Now, T must be the first song and W the third song to abide by Rule 3.

T	Y	W	S	V	Z	X
1	2	3	4	5	6	7
n				n	r	n

The correct answer could be true under these conditions; the four wrong answers must be false.

(A) V occupies the seventh track of the CD. → Must be false. V is now the fifth song, and X must be the seventh song, on the CD. Eliminate.

(B) X occupies the fifth track of the CD. → Must be false. V is now the fifth song, and X must be the seventh song, on the CD. Eliminate.

(C) Y occupies the third track of the CD. → Must be false. Y is now the second song on the CD. Eliminate.

(D) T is a rock classic. → Must be false. T is now the first song, and the first song is always a new song. Eliminate.

(E) W is a rock classic.
    PrepTest51 Sec4 Q15 → Correct. W is now the third song, and the third song could be a rock classic.

New-"If" Questions in Loose Sequencing

Master sketches for Loose Sequencing games are best drawn as "family trees" or "webs" that visually represent the relative positioning of the entities in the game. New-"If" question stems, however, often supply conditions that allow you to specifically place one or more of the entities. When this happens, you may find it most helpful to draw a Strict Sequencing sketch to analyze the new condition. As an example, look at how an expert analyzed this question from the Parcel Delivery game.

LSAT Question	Analysis

A courier delivers exactly eight parcels—G, H, J, K, L, M, N, and O. No two parcels are delivered at the same time, nor is any parcel delivered more than once. The following conditions must apply:
L is delivered later than H.
K is delivered earlier than O.
H is delivered earlier than M.
O is delivered later than G.
M is delivered earlier than G.
Both N and J are delivered earlier than M.
	Steps 1–4:
	
	J N H
	 \ \ /\
	   M L
	   |
	K G
	  \ /
	   O

If H is the fourth parcel delivered, then each of the following could be true EXCEPT:	**Step 5: "If":** Make a Strict Sequencing-style sketch and place H in space 4. $$\underline{\hphantom{1}}\ \underline{\hphantom{2}}\ \underline{\hphantom{3}}\ \underset{1\quad 2\quad 3\quad 4\quad 5\quad 6\quad 7\quad 8}{\underline{H}\ \underline{\hphantom{5}}\ \underline{\hphantom{6}}\ \underline{\hphantom{7}}\ \underline{\hphantom{8}}}$$ J, K, and N will take spaces 1–3 in any order, which means L and the M-G-O string will take spaces 5–8. J/K/N⎤ L, M—G—O The correct answer must be false under these conditions; the four wrong answers could be true.
(A) K is the fifth parcel delivered.	Correct. K is among the first three parcels delivered here. Must be false.
(B) L is the sixth parcel delivered.	Could be true. L could be anywhere from the fifth to the eighth parcel delivered here. Eliminate.
(C) M is the sixth parcel delivered.	Could be true. M could be the fifth or sixth parcel delivered here. Eliminate.
(D) G is the seventh parcel delivered.	Could be true. G could be the sixth or seventh parcel delivered here. Eliminate.
(E) O is the seventh parcel delivered. *PrepTest51 Sec4 Q19*	Could be true. O could be the seventh or eighth parcel delivered here. Eliminate.

New-"If" Practice: Loose Sequencing

Now, try the remaining New-"If" questions from the same game. Read the question stem; stop after the comma; integrate the New-"If" conditions into a sketch; make all of the available deductions; read the rest of the question; characterize the one right and four wrong answers; and then, use the deductions that followed from the New-"If" conditions to evaluate the answer choices.

LSAT Question	My Analysis
A courier delivers exactly eight parcels—G, H, J, K, L, M, N, and O. No two parcels are delivered at the same time, nor is any parcel delivered more than once. The following conditions must apply:	**Steps 1–4:**
L is delivered later than H.	$\rightarrow$
K is delivered earlier than O.	
H is delivered earlier than M.	
O is delivered later than G.	
M is delivered earlier than G.	
Both N and J are delivered earlier than M.	

```
J   N   H
 \  |  / \
    M    L
K   G
 \  |
    O
```

38. If M is the fourth parcel delivered, then which one of the following must be true?	**Step 5:**
	$\rightarrow$
(A) G is the fifth parcel delivered.	$\rightarrow$
(B) O is the seventh parcel delivered.	$\rightarrow$
(C) J is delivered later than H.	$\rightarrow$
(D) K is delivered later than N.	$\rightarrow$
(E) G is delivered later than L.	$\rightarrow$

PrepTest51 Sec4 Q18

LSAT Question		**My Analysis**

A courier delivers exactly eight parcels—G, H, J, K, L, M, N, and O. No two parcels are delivered at the same time, nor is any parcel delivered more than once. The following conditions must apply:

> L is delivered later than H.
> K is delivered earlier than O.
> H is delivered earlier than M.
> O is delivered later than G.
> M is delivered earlier than G.
> Both N and J are delivered earlier than M.

Steps 1–4:

$\longrightarrow$

```
J   N   H
 \  |  / \
    M     L
 /  |
K   G
 \  |
    O
```

39. If K is the seventh parcel delivered, then each of the following could be true EXCEPT:

Step 5:

$\longrightarrow$

   (A)   G is the fifth parcel delivered. $\longrightarrow$

   (B)   M is the fifth parcel delivered. $\longrightarrow$

   (C)   H is the fourth parcel delivered. $\longrightarrow$

   (D)   L is the fourth parcel delivered. $\longrightarrow$

   (E)   J is the third parcel delivered. $\longrightarrow$

PrepTest51 Sec4 Q 21

40. If L is delivered earlier than K, then which one of the following must be false?

Step 5:

$\longrightarrow$

   (A)   N is the second parcel delivered. $\longrightarrow$

   (B)   L is the third parcel delivered. $\longrightarrow$

   (C)   H is the fourth parcel delivered. $\longrightarrow$

   (D)   K is the fifth parcel delivered. $\longrightarrow$

   (E)   M is the sixth parcel delivered. $\longrightarrow$

PrepTest51 Sec4 Q22

Expert Analysis

Here's how an LSAT expert might have approached those two New-"If" questions. Compare your work. Did you fully analyze the condition in the question stem and make all available deductions before you turned to the answer choices?

LSAT Question	Analysis
A courier delivers exactly eight parcels—G, H, J, K, L, M, N, and O. No two parcels are delivered at the same time, nor is any parcel delivered more than once. The following conditions must apply: L is delivered later than H. K is delivered earlier than O. H is delivered earlier than M. O is delivered later than G. M is delivered earlier than G. Both N and J are delivered earlier than M.	**Steps 1–4:**
38. If M is the fourth parcel delivered, then which one of the following must be true?	**Step 5:** "If": Make a Strict Sequencing-style sketch and place M in space 4. H, J, and N will take spaces 1–3 in any order, which means L and the K-G-O block will take spaces (with K and G earlier than O) 5–8. The correct answer must be true under these conditions; the four wrong answers could be false.
(A) G is the fifth parcel delivered.	Could be false. G could be fifth, sixth, or seventh here. Eliminate.
(B) O is the seventh parcel delivered.	Could be false. O could be seventh or eighth here. Eliminate.
(C) J is delivered later than H.	Could be false. H could go earlier than J here. Eliminate.
(D) K is delivered later than N.	Correct. K goes after M (in either space 5 or 6) while N goes earlier than M (in spaces 1–3). Must be true.
(E) G is delivered later than L. *PrepTest51 Sec4 Q18*	Could be false. G could go in spaces 5, 6, and 7, while L could go as late as eighth here. Eliminate.

LSAT Question	Analysis

A courier delivers exactly eight parcels—G, H, J, K, L, M, N, and O. No two parcels are delivered at the same time, nor is any parcel delivered more than once. The following conditions must apply:

    L is delivered later than H.
    K is delivered earlier than O.
    H is delivered earlier than M.
    O is delivered later than G.
    M is delivered earlier than G.
    Both N and J are delivered earlier than M.

Steps 1–4:

$$\longrightarrow$$

```
J  N  H
 \ | / \
   M    L
   |
K  G
 \ /
  O
```

39. If K is the seventh parcel delivered, then each of the following could be true EXCEPT:

Step 5: "If": Make a Strict Sequencing-style sketch and place K in space 7.

$$\underline{\quad}\ \underline{\quad}\ \underline{\quad}\ \underline{\quad}\ \underline{\quad}\ \underline{\quad}\ \overset{K}{\underline{\quad}}\ \underline{\quad}$$
$$1\quad 2\quad 3\quad 4\quad 5\quad 6\quad 7\quad 8$$

Now, O must take space 8. The remaining entities maintain their restrictions from the final sketch.

$$\longrightarrow$$

```
  H   L
   \ /
N→ M—G
  J
```

$$\underline{\quad}\ \underline{\quad}\ \underline{\quad}\ \underline{\quad}\ \underline{\quad}\ \underline{\quad}\ \overset{K}{\underline{\quad}}\ \overset{O}{\underline{\quad}}$$
$$1\quad 2\quad 3\quad 4\quad 5\quad 6\quad 7\quad 8$$

The correct answer must be false under these conditions; the four wrong answers could be true.

(A)	G is the fifth parcel delivered.	$\longrightarrow$ Could be true. G could be delivered fifth or sixth in this case. Eliminate.
(B)	M is the fifth parcel delivered.	$\longrightarrow$ Could be true. M could be delivered fourth or fifth in this case. Eliminate.
(C)	H is the fourth parcel delivered.	$\longrightarrow$ Correct. K and O are seventh and eighth here. H must also be followed by M-G and L. The latest H could be delivered here is third. Must be false.
(D)	L is the fourth parcel delivered.	$\longrightarrow$ Could be true. L could be delivered anywhere from second through sixth in this case. Eliminate.
(E)	J is the third parcel delivered.	$\longrightarrow$ Could be true. J could be delivered anywhere from first through fourth in this case. Eliminate.

PrepTest51 Sec4 Q21

LSAT Question	Analysis
40. If L is delivered earlier than K, then which one of the following must be false?	**Step 5:** "If": The condition in this question does not establish any entities in exact positions. Adapt the Loose Sequencing sketch to accommodate the new restriction. Redraw the final sketch to include "L earlier than K":

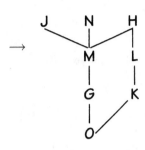

The correct answer must be false under these conditions; the four wrong answers could be true.

(A)	N is the second parcel delivered.	→	Could be true. N could be delivered anywhere from first through fifth in this case. Eliminate.
(B)	L is the third parcel delivered.	→	Could be true. L could be delivered anywhere from second through sixth in this case. Eliminate.
(C)	H is the fourth parcel delivered.	→	Correct. Under this question's conditions, H is followed by L-K and M-G-O. The latest H could be delivered is third. Must be false.
(D)	K is the fifth parcel delivered.	→	Could be true. K could be delivered anywhere from third through seventh in this case. Eliminate.
(E)	M is the sixth parcel delivered. *PrepTest51 Sec4 Q22*	→	Could be true. M could be delivered anywhere from fourth through sixth in this case. Eliminate.

New-"If" Questions in Selection Games

New-"If" questions are generally easy to deal with in Selection games. Because most (if not all) of the rules are conditional, the new condition in the question stem is virtually guaranteed to trigger one or more of the primary rules. Moreover, the sketch itself is usually little more than a list of the entities, so it is very easy to recreate multiple times. Take a look at how an LSAT expert deals with one of the New-"If" questions from the Summer Program Classes game.

LSAT Question	Analysis

A summer program offers at least one of the following seven courses: geography, history, literature, mathematics, psychology, sociology, zoology. The following restrictions on the program must apply:
 	
    If mathematics is offered, then either literature or sociology (but not both) is offered.
    If literature is offered, then geography is also offered but psychology is not.
    If sociology is offered, then psychology is also offered but zoology is not.
    If geography is offered, then both history and zoology are also offered.
	Steps 1–4:
	
	  G H L M P S Z
	
	If Ⓜ → exactly 1 of Ⓛ or Ⓢ
	If Ⓛ and Ⓢ → M̸
	If L̸ and S̸ → M̸
	If Ⓛ → Ⓖ and P̸
	If G̸ or Ⓟ → L̸
	If Ⓢ → Ⓟ and Z̸
	If P̸ or Ⓩ → S̸
	If Ⓖ → Ⓗ and Ⓩ
	If H̸ or Z̸ → G̸

If history is not offered by the summer program, then which one of the following is another course that CANNOT be offered?	**Step 5: "If":** Recopy the roster and cross off H to account for the new condition.
	
	  G H̸ L M P S Z
	
	Rejecting H means rejecting G (Rule 4), and rejecting G means rejecting L (Rule 2).
	
	  G̸ H̸ L̸ M P S Z
	
	Rejecting L doesn't trigger any additional deductions.
	
	The correct answer here must be false under these conditions; the four wrong answers could be true.

(A) literature	Correct. L is rejected in this case. Must be false.
(B) mathematics	Could be selected here. Eliminate.
(C) psychology	Could be selected here. Eliminate.
(D) sociology	Could be selected here. Eliminate.
(E) zoology	Could be selected here. Eliminate.

PrepTest49 Sec1 Q15

New-"If" Practice: Selection

Now, try the remaining New-"If" questions from the same game. Read the question stem; stop after the comma; integrate the New-"If" condition into a sketch; make all of the available deductions; read the rest of the question; characterize the one right and four wrong answers; then, use the deductions that followed from the New-"If" conditions to evaluate the answer choices.

Consult the final sketch from the previous page.

LSAT Question	My Analysis
41. If the summer program offers literature, then which one of the following could be true?	Step 5:
	$\longrightarrow$
(A) Sociology is offered. $\longrightarrow$	
(B) History is not offered. $\longrightarrow$	
(C) Mathematics is not offered. $\longrightarrow$	
(D) A total of two courses are offered. $\longrightarrow$	
(E) Zoology is not offered. $\longrightarrow$	
PrepTest49 Sec1 Q 14	
42. If the summer program offers mathematics, then which one of the following must be true?	Step 5:
	$\longrightarrow$
(A) Literature is offered. $\longrightarrow$	
(B) Psychology is offered. $\longrightarrow$	
(C) Sociology is offered. $\longrightarrow$	
(D) At least three courses are offered. $\longrightarrow$	
(E) At most four courses are offered. $\longrightarrow$	
PrepTest49 Sec1 Q16	

Expert Analysis

Here's how an LSAT expert might have approached those New-"If" questions. Compare your work. Did you fully analyze the condition in the question stem and make all available deductions before you turned to the answer choices?

LSAT Question	Analysis
A summer program offers at least one of the following seven courses: geography, history, literature, mathematics, psychology, sociology, zoology. The following restrictions on the program must apply: If mathematics is offered, then either literature or sociology (but not both) is offered. If literature is offered, then geography is also offered but psychology is not. If sociology is offered, then psychology is also offered but zoology is not. If geography is offered, then both history and zoology are also offered.	**Steps 1–4:** G H L M P S Z If Ⓜ → exactly 1 of Ⓛ or Ⓢ If Ⓛ and Ⓢ → M̸ If L̸ and S̸ → M̸ If Ⓛ → Ⓖ and P̸ If G̸ or Ⓟ → L̸ If Ⓢ → Ⓟ and Z̸ If P̸ or Ⓩ → S̸ If Ⓖ → Ⓗ and Ⓩ If H̸ or Z̸ → G̸
41. If the summer program offers literature, then which one of the following could be true?	**Step 5:** "If": Recopy the roster and circle L to account for the new condition. G H Ⓛ M P S Z Selecting L means selecting G and rejecting P (Rule 2), and rejecting P means rejecting S (Rule 3). Ⓖ H Ⓛ M P̸ S̸ Z Selecting G means selecting H and Z (Rule 4). Ⓖ Ⓗ Ⓛ M P̸ S̸ Ⓩ The correct answer here could be true under these conditions; the four wrong answers must be false.
(A) Sociology is offered.	Must be false. S is rejected here. Eliminate.
(B) History is not offered.	Must be false. H is selected here. Eliminate.
(C) Mathematics is not offered.	Correct. M may be selected or rejected here. Could be true.
(D) A total of two courses are offered.	Must be false. At least 4 courses are selected. Eliminate.
(E) Zoology is not offered.	Must be false. Z is selected here. Eliminate.

PrepTest49 Sec1 Q14

LSAT Question	Analysis
42. If the summer program offers mathematics, then which one of the following must be true?	**Step 5:** "If": Recopy the roster and circle M to account for the new condition.

G H L Ⓜ P S Z

Selecting M means selecting exactly one of L or S (Rule 1). Try both ways. If M and L are selected, S is rejected. From there, G is selected and P is rejected (Rule 2). Finally, selecting G means selecting H and Z (Rule 4).

→ (I) Ⓖ Ⓗ Ⓛ Ⓜ P̶ S̶ Ⓩ

In the other scenario, if M and S are selected, then L is rejected. From there, P is selected and Z is rejected (Rule 3). Finally, rejecting Z means rejecting G (Rule 4).

(II) G̶ H L̶ Ⓜ Ⓟ Ⓢ Z̶

The correct answer here must be true under these conditions; the four wrong answers could be false.

(A) Literature is offered.	→ Could be false. L will be rejected if M and S are selected. Eliminate.
(B) Psychology is offered.	→ Could be false. P will be rejected if M and L are selected. Eliminate.
(C) Sociology is offered.	→ Could be false. S will be rejected if M and L are selected. Eliminate.
(D) At least three courses are offered.	→ Correct. In either scenario, at least 3 courses are selected. Must be true.
(E) At most four courses are offered.	→ Could be false. In the scenario in which M and L are selected, 5 courses will be offered. Eliminate.

PrepTest49 Sec1 Q16

New-"If" Questions in Limited Options

In games with Limited Options sketches, you may be able to evaluate the answer choices without having to draw a new sketch. That's because the New-"If" condition may simply restrict you to one option or the other. As an example, take a look at how the LSAT expert was able to use the Limited Options final sketch to quickly answer this question from the Clown Costume game.

LSAT Question	Analysis

A clown will select a costume consisting of two pieces and no others: a jacket and overalls. One piece of the costume will be entirely one color, and the other piece will be plaid. Selection is subject to the following restrictions:

> If the jacket is plaid, then there must be exactly three colors in it.
>
> If the overalls are plaid, then there must be exactly two colors in them.
>
> The jacket and overalls must have exactly one color in common.
>
> Green, red, and violet are the only colors that can be in the jacket.
>
> Red, violet, and yellow are the only colors that can be in the overalls.

Steps 1–4:

[*exactly 1 color in common*]

	Opt. I			Opt. II	
	Jacket	Overalls		Jacket	Overalls
	g	r/v		r/v	r/v
	v	~~y~~		~~g~~	____
	r				r/v/y

If there are exactly three colors in the costume, the overalls must be

Step 5: "If": Three colors in the costume puts us in Option I.

⟶ The correct answer must be true of the overalls in Option I. The four wrong answers could be false of the overalls in Option I. The overalls in Option I must be one color, either red or violet.

(A)	entirely red or else red and violet plaid	⟶	False in Option I. Eliminate.
(B)	entirely yellow or else violet and yellow plaid	⟶	False in Option I. Eliminate.
(C)	entirely violet or else red and violet plaid	⟶	False in Option I. Eliminate.
(D)	entirely red or else entirely yellow	⟶	False in Option I. Eliminate.
(E)	entirely red or else entirely violet	⟶	Correct. Must be true.

PrepTest51 Sec4 Q5

New-"If" Practice: Limited Options

Now, try the remaining New-"If" questions from the games you've worked on previously. Read the question stem; stop after the comma; consider whether the new condition applies to one or both options; read the rest of the question; characterize the one right and four wrong answers; and then, use the Limited Options sketches to evaluate the answer choices.

The first two questions come from the Clown Costume game, so consult the final sketch on the previous page.

LSAT Question	My Analysis
43. If there are exactly two colors in the costume, then which one of the following must be false? $\longrightarrow$	**Step 5:**
(A) At least part of the jacket is green. $\longrightarrow$	
(B) At least part of the jacket is red. $\longrightarrow$	
(C) The overalls are red and violet. $\longrightarrow$	
(D) The overalls are red and yellow. $\longrightarrow$	
(E) The overalls are violet and yellow. $\longrightarrow$ *PrepTest51 Sec4 Q2*	
44. If at least part of the jacket is green, then which one of the following could be true? $\longrightarrow$	**Step 5:**
(A) The overalls are plaid. $\longrightarrow$	
(B) No part of the jacket is red. $\longrightarrow$	
(C) No part of the jacket is violet. $\longrightarrow$	
(D) At least part of the overalls are yellow. $\longrightarrow$	
(E) At least part of the overalls are violet. $\longrightarrow$ *PrepTest51 Sec4 Q3*	

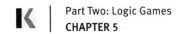

Sometimes, even with a Limited Options sketch, the condition in the question stem will be so specific that it necessitates a new sketch. The next two questions are from the Convention Car Pool game. In both, after you read the question stem and determine which option is called for, decide how you can create a new sketch based on that option that will facilitate further deductions.

LSAT Question	My Analysis

Exactly six workers—Faith, Gus, Hannah, Juan, Kenneth, and Lisa—will travel to a business convention in two cars—car 1 and car 2. Each car must carry at least two of the workers, one of whom will be assigned to drive. For the entire trip, the workers will comply with an assignment that also meets the following constraints:

> Either Faith or Gus must drive the car in which Hannah travels.
> Either Faith or Kenneth must drive the car in which Juan travels.
> Gus must travel in the same car as Lisa.

Steps 1–4:

F G H J K L

2–4/Car   Driver: F/G
Opt. I   Opt. II   H

Driver: F/K
J

(1) | (2)   (1) | (2)
Driver: K | F   ___ | F/K   G
         J | H   ___ | J   L
         G | (__)(__)
         L | (__)(__)
                    G
                    L
                  (__H__)?

45. If Lisa drives one of the cars, then which one of the following could be true?

Step 5:

(A) Faith travels in the same car as Kenneth.

(B) Faith travels in the same car as Lisa.

(C) Gus travels in the same car as Hannah.

(D) Gus travels in the same car as Juan.

(E) Hannah travels in the same car as Lisa.

PrepTest61 Sec3 Q3

	LSAT Question	**My Analysis**

46. If Faith travels with two other workers in car 1, and if Faith is not the driver, then the person in car 1 other than Faith and the driver must be

Step 5:

$\longrightarrow$

(A) Gus

$\longrightarrow$

(B) Hannah

$\longrightarrow$

(C) Juan

$\longrightarrow$

(D) Kenneth

$\longrightarrow$

(E) Lisa

PrepTest61 Sec3 Q4 $\longrightarrow$

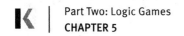

Expert Analysis

Here's how an LSAT expert might have approached those New-"If" questions. Compare your work. Did you use the Limited Options sketches efficiently to evaluate the answer choices?

LSAT Question	Analysis
A clown will select a costume consisting of two pieces and no others: a jacket and overalls. One piece of the costume will be entirely one color, and the other piece will be plaid. Selection is subject to the following restrictions: If the jacket is plaid, then there must be exactly three colors in it. If the overalls are plaid, then there must be exactly two colors in them. The jacket and overalls must have exactly one color in common. Green, red, and violet are the only colors that can be in the jacket. Red, violet, and yellow are the only colors that can be in the overalls.	**Steps 1–4:** [exactly 1 color in common] Opt. I Opt. II | Jacket	Overalls		Jacket	Overalls
---	---	---	---	---
g	r/v		r/v	r/v
v	y̶		g̶	___
r				r/v/y	

43.	If there are exactly two colors in the costume, then which one of the following must be false?	**Step 5: "If":** Two colors in the costume indicates Option II. The correct answer must be false in Option II; the four wrong answers could be true in Option II.
(A)	At least part of the jacket is green.	Correct. Green cannot be used in Option II. Must be false.
(B)	At least part of the jacket is red.	Could be true. Red or violet are acceptable in Option II. Eliminate.
(C)	The overalls are red and violet.	Could be true. Red, violet, and yellow are acceptable in Option II. Eliminate.
(D)	The overalls are red and yellow.	Could be true. Red, violet, and yellow are acceptable in Option II. Eliminate.
(E)	The overalls are violet and yellow. *PrepTest51 Sec4 Q2*	Could be true. Red, violet, and yellow are acceptable in Option II. Eliminate.

LSAT Question		Analysis
44. If at least part of the jacket is green, then which one of the following could be true?	$\longrightarrow$	**Step 5:** "If": Having green in the jacket means Option I. The correct answer could be true in Option I; the four wrong answers must be false in Option I.
(A) The overalls are plaid.	$\longrightarrow$	Must be false. The overalls are a single color in Option I. Eliminate.
(B) No part of the jacket is red.	$\longrightarrow$	Must be false. The jacket has to be green, red, and violet plaid in Option I. Eliminate.
(C) No part of the jacket is violet.	$\longrightarrow$	Must be false. The jacket has to be green, red, and violet plaid in Option I. Eliminate.
(D) At least part of the overalls are yellow.	$\longrightarrow$	Must be false. Yellow cannot be used in Option I. Eliminate.
(E) At least part of the overalls are violet. *PrepTest51 Sec4 Q3*	$\longrightarrow$	Correct. The overalls could be red or violet in Option I. Could be true.

LSAT Question	**Analysis**

Exactly six workers—Faith, Gus, Hannah, Juan, Kenneth, and Lisa—will travel to a business convention in two cars—car 1 and car 2. Each car must carry at least two of the workers, one of whom will be assigned to drive. For the entire trip, the workers will comply with an assignment that also meets the following constraints:

Either Faith or Gus must drive the car in which Hannah travels.

Either Faith or Kenneth must drive the car in which Juan travels.

Gus must travel in the same car as Lisa.

Steps 1–4:

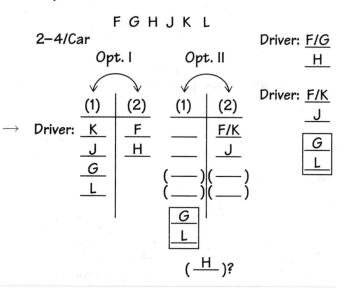

45. If Lisa drives one of the cars, then which one of the following could be true?

Step 5: "If": Lisa can only be the driver in Option II. G has to ride along with her (Rule 3).

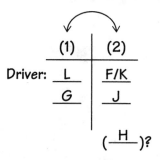

→   With L driving, H and J both have to ride in the other car (see Rules 1 and 2). Because H needs F or G to drive, F will be the driver of that car.

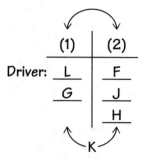

The only unanswered question is where K rides.

The correct answer could be true in this scenario; the four wrong answers must be false here.

LSAT Question		Analysis
(A)	Faith travels in the same car as Kenneth. →	Correct. K could ride along with F, H, and J. Could be true.
(B)	Faith travels in the same car as Lisa. →	Must be false. With L driving, F must drive the other car. Eliminate.
(C)	Gus travels in the same car as Hannah. →	Must be false. The new condition here is that L drives. G rides with L no matter what (Rule 3), and H can never ride in a car driven by L (Rule 1). Eliminate.
(D)	Gus travels in the same car as Juan. →	Must be false. Option II is based on the idea that G and L are in a different car than J. Eliminate.
(E)	Hannah travels in the same car as Lisa. *PrepTest61 Sec3 Q3* →	Must be false. H must ride in a car driven by F or G (Rule 1). If L is driving, H cannot be in that car. Eliminate.

LSAT Question	Analysis
46. If Faith travels with two other workers in car 1, and if Faith is not the driver, then the person in car 1 other than Faith and the driver must be	**Step 5:** "If": Only in option II can F travel with two others and be a passenger. Put F as the passenger in one car with a blank for the driver and another passenger.

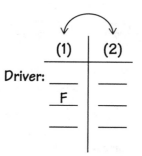

The car F is in cannot be the one G and L are in, as that would leave no driver for H (Rule 1). So, F will go with J and K. K must drive (Rule 2). Fill that in.

	(1)	(2)
Driver:	K	G
	F	L
	J	H

G, H, and L will take the other car, with G driving (Rule 1).

The correct answer will be the other passenger in F's car. That's J.

(A)	Gus	$\longrightarrow$	
(B)	Hannah	$\longrightarrow$	
(C)	Juan	$\longrightarrow$	Correct
(D)	Kenneth	$\longrightarrow$	
(E)	Lisa	$\longrightarrow$	

PrepTest61 Sec3 Q4

Using Previous Work to Answer Logic Games Questions

Be strategic when answering Logic Games questions. Some Must Be/Could Be questions may appear extremely difficult to answer without testing the choices one-by-one, and in the process, creating a number of new sketches. Before drawing, look through the other questions you've answered. The correct answer to the Acceptability question always provides at least one "could be true" scenario. In addition, the sketches you create for New-"If" questions may help you eliminate wrong answer choices. In some situations, previous work might even lead you right to the correct answer.

You saw this illustrated in Chapter 2 on the second question from the Nurses' Information Sessions game.

OTHER LOGIC GAMES QUESTION TYPES

The vast majority of questions in a Logic Games section will be examples of the question types you've already worked through in this chapter: Acceptability, Must Be/Could Be, and New-"If." In addition to those, though, there are a handful of other question types that you may see from time to time.

We talked a bit about Complete and Accurate List and Completely Determine questions earlier in the chapter. Here's a quick outline of what the remaining question types ask for accompanied by examples of their question stems.

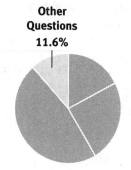

Other Questions 11.6%

Logic Games Question Types

PrepTests 57–71; released 2009–2013

Numerical Questions

Minimum/Maximum questions show up occasionally in Selection and Distribution games. These questions ask you to determine either the minimum or the maximum number of entities that can be selected or assigned to a particular group.

> What is the maximum number of courses the student could take during the summer school session?
>
> *PrepTest58 Sec3 Q19*

Earliest/Latest questions may appear in games with a sequencing element. These questions ask for the earliest or latest spot in which an entity could appear.

> What is the latest year in which L could have been begun?
>
> *PrepTest58 Sec3 Q2*

"How Many" questions can appear in any game type. These questions are straightforward: They ask how many entities could appear on a specific day, in a specific location, or within a specific group.

> Exactly how many of the artifacts are there any one of which could be first?
>
> *PrepTest61 Sec3 Q7*

> If the plaque is first, then exactly how many artifacts are there any one of which could be second?
>
> *PrepTest61 Sec3 Q10*

Note that the second stem represented there is a New-"If" question that asks a "How Many" question. All numerical questions could be preceded by New-"If" clauses.

Rule Alteration Questions

Rule Substitution questions did not make their debut on the LSAT until PrepTest 57, so if you study with older materials, there's a good chance you'd never see one. Since PrepTest 57, however, there has been exactly one of these questions on every released exam except for PrepTests 60, 67, and 68 (on which there were none) and PrepTest 71 (on which there were two).

The correct answer in Rule Substitution questions supplies a rule that would have precisely the same impact on the game as the rule cited in the question stem. The four wrong answers will be either too strong or too weak to substitute exactly for the rule in the stem. By chance, one of these questions accompanied the Arranging Photographs game. Take a look at how the LSAT expert analyzed and answered it.

LSAT Question	Analysis

A museum curator is arranging seven photographs—*Fence, Gardenias, Hibiscus, Irises, Katydid, Lotus,* and *Magnolia*—on a gallery wall in accordance with the photographer's requirements. The photographs are to be hung along the wall in a row, in seven positions sequentially numbered from first to seventh. The photographer's requirements are as follows:

> *Gardenias* must be immediately before *Katydid.*
> *Hibiscus* must be somewhere before *Katydid* but cannot be the first photograph.
> *Irises* and *Lotus* must be next to one another.
> *Magnolia* must be one of the first three photographs.
> *Fence* must be either first or seventh.

Steps 1–4:

1	2	3	4	5	6	7
~H	~F	~F	~F	~F	~F	~M
~G	~G	~K	~M	~M	~M	~H
~K	~K				~H	~G

___ ... <u>H</u> ... <u>G</u> <u>K</u>

<u>I</u> <u>L</u> or <u>L</u> <u>I</u>

Which one of the following, if substituted for the condition that *Hibiscus* must be hung somewhere before *Katydid* but cannot be the first photograph, would have the same effect in determining the arrangement of the photographs?

Step 5: The correct answer will state a rule exactly equivalent to Rule 2. The four wrong answers will state rules that do not have the same impact as Rule 2 does.

(A) If *Fence* is seventh, *Hibiscus* is second.

This rule is conditional and not always true. Eliminate.

(B) *Gardenias* is somewhere after *Hibiscus,* and either *Fence* or *Magnolia* is first.

This is too strong. In the game, I or L could be first. Eliminate.

(C) *Hibiscus* must be somewhere between the first and sixth photographs.

This is too weak. It doesn't require H to be before K. Eliminate.

(D) Unless *Hibiscus* is second, it must be somewhere between *Magnolia* and *Gardenias.*

Correct. Because G and K are a block, this rule keeps H earlier than K. Because M is always among the first three photos, this also keeps H out of first.

(E) *Katydid* is somewhere after *Hibiscus,* which must be somewhere after *Fence.*

PrepTest59 Sec1 Q10

This is too strong. In the game, F could be last, but Rule 2 is still in force. Eliminate.

Rule Change questions used to appear occasionally, but in recent years, they have become almost extinct. In the 60 games found in tests released from 2009–2013, there was only one Rule Change question. Rule Change questions are similar to New-"If" questions, but instead of adding a new restriction to the game, they alter or suspend one of the original rules. In the highly unlikely chance that you run into a Rule Change question, the best strategy is to make a new sketch to account for the altered conditions, and use that sketch to evaluate the choices.

Supply the "If" Questions

Supply the "If" questions are also quite rare. Among the 60 games to appear in tests released from 2009–2013, there were only three Supply the "If" questions. If you do encounter one of these, think of it as a New-"If" question in reverse. The question stem provides the *result*, while the correct answer supplies the condition that forces that result.

L must be the monument that was begun in 602 if which one of the following is true?

PrepTest58 Sec3 Q5

Consider what would compel the result cited in the stem, and then evaluate the choices by looking for the one condition that would trigger that result.

FOR FURTHER PRACTICE

You can find examples of these questions in the following games:

Complete and Accurate List:
pp. 383 (#65), 395 (#100), 397 (#105), 1076 (#18), 1077 (#20*)

Completely Determine:
pp. 377 (#47), 381 (#58), 383 (#64), 391 (#91), 405 (#4), 1076 (#16), 1094 (#4)

Minimum/Maximum:
pp. 1147 (#9*), 1147 (#11), 1075 (#8), 1075 (#12*)

Earliest/Latest:
p. 399 (#112*)

How Many:
pp. 375 (#40), 375 (#43*), 377 (#50*), 405 (#5), 411 (#18*), 1074 (#4*), 1097 (#21*)

Rule Substitution:
pp. 375 (#44), 385 (#73), 411 (#23), 1022 (#5)

Rule Change:
p. 381 (#61)

Supply the If:
p. 381 (#59)

*Question is with New-"If"

We suggest that you wait to practice these questions within the context of the full games.

Exercise: Characterizing the Answer Choices in "Other" Questions

Now it's your turn. For each question stem, identify the question type and then characterize the one correct and four incorrect answer choices.

Question Stem	My Analysis
47. The minimum number of dressings that could be offered at the salad bar is	→ **Question type:** **1 Right:** **4 Wrong:**
48. If the peach is chosen, then the maximum number of fruits that are also chosen is	→ **Question type:** **1 Right:** **4 Wrong:**
49. Suppose that the condition stating that the German car is sold on Thursday is replaced with a condition that the French car is sold on Thursday. If all other conditions remain the same, which of the following could be true?	→ **Question type:** **1 Right:** **4 Wrong:**
50. Which of the following, if substituted for the condition that Beatrice is in a higher grade than Tony, would have the same effect in determining the students in each grade?	→ **Question type:** **1 Right:** **4 Wrong:**
51. Judy must be a physician if which of the following contestants is a lawyer?	→ **Question type:** **1 Right:** **4 Wrong:**
52. What is the latest time at which Jamaal could be scheduled for a dentist appointment?	→ **Question type:** **1 Right:** **4 Wrong:**
53. If Rebecca sings the seventh solo, how many vocalists are there any one of whom could sing the second solo?	→ **Question type:** **1 Right:** **4 Wrong:**
54. The lemonade stand ranks second in sales if which of the following is false?	→ **Question type:** **1 Right:** **4 Wrong:**

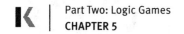
Expert Analysis

Take a look at how an LSAT expert characterizes the question stems you just saw:

Question Stem	Analysis
47. The minimum number of dressings that could be offered at the salad bar is	**Question type:** Minimum/Maximum **1 Right:** The minimum number of dressings the salad bar could offer **4 Wrong:** A number greater or smaller than the minimum number of dressings
48. If the peach is chosen, then the maximum number of fruits that are also chosen is	**Question type:** New-"If"/Maximum **1 Right:** The maximum number of fruits that could be chosen if the peach is chosen **4 Wrong:** A number greater or smaller than the maximum number of fruits that could be chosen along with the peach
49. Suppose that the condition stating that the German car is sold on Thursday is replaced with a condition that the French car is sold on Thursday. If all other conditions remain the same, which of the following could be true?	**Question type:** Rule Change **1 Right:** Could be true under the new rule **4 Wrong:** Must be false under the new rule
50. Which of the following, if substituted for the condition that Beatrice is in a higher grade than Tony, would have the same effect in determining the students in each grade?	**Question type:** Rule Substitution **1 Right:** A rule that has the same effect as the one cited in the stem **4 Wrong:** A rule more or less restrictive than the one cited in the stem
51. Judy must be a physician if which of the following contestants is a lawyer?	**Question type:** Supply the "If" **1 Right:** A condition guaranteeing that Judy is a physician **4 Wrong:** A condition insufficient to guarantee that Judy is a physician
52. What is the latest time at which Jamaal could be scheduled for a dentist appointment?	**Question type:** Earliest/Latest **1 Right:** The latest time for which Jamal's appointment may be scheduled **4 Wrong:** A time earlier or later than the latest time for which Jamal's appointment may be scheduled
53. If Rebecca sings the seventh solo, how many vocalists are there any one of whom could sing the second solo?	**Question type:** New-"If"/How Many **1 Right:** The number of singers who could sing second when Rebecca sings seventh **4 Wrong:** A number either greater or less than the number of singers who could sing second when Rebecca sings seventh
54. The lemonade stand ranks second in sales if which of the following is false?	**Question type:** Supply the "If" **1 Right:** A condition the falsity of which is sufficient to guarantee that the lemonade stand ranks second **4 Wrong:** Conditions the falsity of which do not guarantee that the lemonade stand ranks second

REFLECTION

Congratulations! You've made it through the lessons on all five steps of the Logic Games Method. Your performance will continue to improve as you practice the Method and all of the associated strategies and tactics to which you've been introduced.

Take a few minutes and go back over the work you did in this chapter. Consider how your approach to Logic Games questions has changed. Here are some questions to ask yourself as you reflect:

- · How will I approach Logic Games questions differently in the future?
- · How does characterizing the "truth value" of both the one right and the four wrong answers help me answer more effectively?
- · How does understanding the question types reinforce the importance of Steps 1–4 (the setup and deductions) of the Logic Games Method?
- · How does having a solid sketch help answer the questions more accurately?
- · How does having a solid sketch help answer the questions more quickly?
- · When should I consider skipping a question and coming back to it? How can the work I do on subsequent questions help me to answer one that I skipped?

The kind of thinking rewarded in the Logic Games section goes on all the time in the real world. In the coming days—at work, school, even at home—pay attention to the kinds of tasks you are asked to complete. Which ones resemble Logic Games actions, such as Sequencing, Matching, Selection, and Distribution? Do you sometimes have to consider how to proceed in light of various conditions? Anytime your boss says something along the lines of "If Carter comes in from Chicago on Thursday, we'll have to reschedule the conference call with WidgetCo," you're answering a New-"If" question. Take note of how often Logic Games thinking is present in your day-to-day life. In fact, notice how often you solve logical puzzles far more complex than those on the LSAT. It will help you build confidence that you can answer these questions on Test Day.

Logic Games Practice

The earlier chapters in the Logic Games section covered the Logic Games Method and demonstrated the skills and strategies rewarded by the testmaker. This chapter gives you the opportunity to work with full games. It contains all of the games from PrepTests 49, 51, 57, 59, and 61.

NOTES ON LOGIC GAMES PRACTICE

Use the Logic Games Method Consistently—Continue to use the Logic Games Method as you practice full games. Pay close attention to your work with Steps 1–4. Many test takers underestimate the importance of these steps; they impede their progress on the Logic Games section as a result.

THE KAPLAN LOGIC GAMES METHOD

Step 1: Overview—Ask the SEAL questions to understand your task and get a mental picture of the actions and limitations.

Step 2: Sketch—Create a simple, helpful framework in which you can record the game's rules and restrictions.

Step 3: Rules—Analyze each rule; build it into the framework or jot it down in shorthand just to the side.

Step 4: Deductions—Combine rules and restrictions to determine what must be true or false about the arrangement of entities in the game.

Step 5: Questions—Use your understanding of the game and your master sketch to attack the questions efficiently and confidently.

Review Your Work Thoroughly—Complete explanations for the games in this chapter are found in your Online Center. Review them completely, even if you get all of the questions correct. Each question's difficulty—from ★ (easiest) to ★ ★ ★ ★ (hardest)—is indicated in the explanations.

Practice and Timing—On Test Day, you will have about 8 1/2 minutes per game, a pace that can make even routine games feel challenging. As you work on individual games, however, keep your focus on the successful implementation of the Logic Games Method. Your greatest gains in speed will come with familiarity, practice, and (ironically) patience. When you practice full tests or 35-minute Logic Games sections, time yourself strictly.

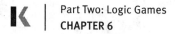

Part Two: Logic Games
CHAPTER 6

Explanations for these questions
can be found in your Online Center.

QUESTION POOL 1

The seven games in this pool appeared as examples and practice in Chapters 2–5. They are presented in their entirety here for your reference and convenience. The games in this pool are arranged by type.

Strict Sequencing

Questions 1–6

From the 1st through the 7th of next month, seven nurses—Farnham, Griseldi, Heany, Juarez, Khan, Lightfoot, and Moreau—will each conduct one information session at a community center. Each nurse's session will fall on a different day. The nurses' schedule is governed by the following constraints:

At least two of the other nurses' sessions must fall in between Heany's session and Moreau's session.
Griseldi's session must be on the day before Khan's.
Juarez's session must be on a later day than Moreau's.
Farnham's session must be on an earlier day than Khan's but on a later day than Lightfoot's.
Lightfoot cannot conduct the session on the 2nd.

1. Which one of the following could be the order of the nurses' sessions, from first to last?

(A) Farnham, Griseldi, Khan, Moreau, Juarez, Lightfoot, Heany
(B) Heany, Lightfoot, Farnham, Moreau, Juarez, Griseldi, Khan
(C) Juarez, Heany, Lightfoot, Farnham, Moreau, Griseldi, Khan
(D) Lightfoot, Moreau, Farnham, Juarez, Griseldi, Khan, Heany
(E) Moreau, Lightfoot, Heany, Juarez, Farnham, Griseldi, Khan

GO ON TO THE NEXT PAGE.

Explanations for these questions can be found in your Online Center.

Part Two: Logic Games
Logic Games Practice   K

2. Juarez's session CANNOT be on which one of the following days?

   (A) the 2nd
   (B) the 3rd
   (C) the 5th
   (D) the 6th
   (E) the 7th

3. If Juarez's session is on the 3rd, then which one of the following could be true?

   (A) Moreau's session is on the 1st.
   (B) Khan's session is on the 5th.
   (C) Heany's session is on the 6th.
   (D) Griseldi's session is on the 5th.
   (E) Farnham's session is on the 2nd.

4. If Khan's session is on an earlier day than Moreau's, which one of the following could conduct the session on the 3rd?

   (A) Griseldi
   (B) Heany
   (C) Juarez
   (D) Lightfoot
   (E) Moreau

5. If Griseldi's session is on the 5th, then which one of the following must be true?

   (A) Farnham's session is on the 3rd.
   (B) Heany's session is on the 7th.
   (C) Juarez's session is on the 4th.
   (D) Lightfoot's session is on the 1st.
   (E) Moreau's session is on the 2nd.

6. Lightfoot's session could be on which one of the following days?

   (A) the 3rd
   (B) the 4th
   (C) the 5th
   (D) the 6th
   (E) the 7th

PrepTest61 Sec3 Qs 18–23

GO ON TO THE NEXT PAGE.

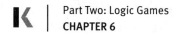
Explanations for these questions can be found in your Online Center.

Questions 7–11

A museum curator is arranging seven photographs—*Fence, Gardenias, Hibiscus, Irises, Katydid, Lotus,* and *Magnolia*—on a gallery wall in accordance with the photographer's requirements. The photographs are to be hung along the wall in a row, in seven positions sequentially numbered from first to seventh. The photographer's requirements are as follows:

> *Gardenias* must be immediately before *Katydid.*
> *Hibiscus* must be somewhere before *Katydid* but cannot be the first photograph.
> *Irises* and *Lotus* must be next to one another.
> *Magnolia* must be one of the first three photographs.
> *Fence* must be either first or seventh.

7. Which one of the following could be the positions, from first to seventh, in which the photographs are hung?

(A) *Fence, Hibiscus, Gardenias, Magnolia, Katydid, Irises, Lotus*

(B) *Hibiscus, Magnolia, Gardenias, Katydid, Irises, Lotus, Fence*

(C) *Irises, Lotus, Magnolia, Hibiscus, Gardenias, Katydid, Fence*

(D) *Lotus, Magnolia, Irises, Hibiscus, Gardenias, Katydid, Fence*

(E) *Magnolia, Fence, Hibiscus, Gardenias, Katydid, Lotus, Irises*

GO ON TO THE NEXT PAGE.

Explanations for these questions can be found in your Online Center.

Part Two: Logic Games
Logic Games Practice

8. If *Irises* is immediately before *Gardenias*, which one of the following could be true?

    (A) *Gardenias* is fourth.
    (B) *Hibiscus* is fourth.
    (C) *Irises* is third.
    (D) *Lotus* is second.
    (E) *Magnolia* is third.

9. Where each photograph is hung is fully determined if which one of the following is true?

    (A) *Gardenias* is fourth.
    (B) *Hibiscus* is second.
    (C) *Irises* is second.
    (D) *Lotus* is first.
    (E) *Magnolia* is third.

10. If *Magnolia* is second, which one of the following CANNOT be true?

    (A) *Hibiscus* is third.
    (B) *Hibiscus* is fourth.
    (C) *Hibiscus* is fifth.
    (D) *Gardenias* is fourth.
    (E) *Gardenias* is sixth.

11. Which one of the following, if substituted for the condition that *Hibiscus* must be hung somewhere before *Katydid* but cannot be the first photograph, would have the same effect in determining the arrangement of the photographs?

    (A) If *Fence* is seventh, *Hibiscus* is second.
    (B) *Gardenias* is somewhere after *Hibiscus*, and either *Fence* or *Magnolia* is first.
    (C) *Hibiscus* must be somewhere between the first and sixth photographs.
    (D) Unless *Hibiscus* is second, it must be somewhere between *Magnolia* and *Gardenias*.
    (E) *Katydid* is somewhere after *Hibiscus*, which must be somewhere after *Fence*.

PrepTest59 Sec1 Qs 6–10

GO ON TO THE NEXT PAGE.

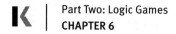

Explanations for these questions
can be found in your Online Center.

Loose Sequencing

Questions 12–18

A courier delivers exactly eight parcels—G, H, J, K, L, M, N, and O. No two parcels are delivered at the same time, nor is any parcel delivered more than once. The following conditions must apply:

L is delivered later than H.
K is delivered earlier than O.
H is delivered earlier than M.
O is delivered later than G.
M is delivered earlier than G.
Both N and J are delivered earlier than M.

12. Which one of the following could be the order of deliveries from first to last?

(A)   N, H, K, M, J, G, O, L
(B)   H, N, J, K, G, O, L, M
(C)   J, H, N, M, K, O, G, L
(D)   N, J, H, L, M, K, G, O
(E)   K, N, J, M, G, H, O, L

GO ON TO THE NEXT PAGE.

Explanations for these questions can be found in your Online Center.

Part Two: Logic Games
Logic Games Practice

K

13. Which one of the following must be true?

(A) At least one parcel is delivered earlier than K is delivered.
(B) At least two parcels are delivered later than G is delivered.
(C) At least four parcels are delivered later than H is delivered.
(D) At least four parcels are delivered later than J is delivered.
(E) At least four parcels are delivered earlier than M is delivered.

14. If M is the fourth parcel delivered, then which one of the following must be true?

(A) G is the fifth parcel delivered.
(B) O is the seventh parcel delivered.
(C) J is delivered later than H.
(D) K is delivered later than N.
(E) G is delivered later than L.

15. If H is the fourth parcel delivered, then each of the following could be true EXCEPT:

(A) K is the fifth parcel delivered.
(B) L is the sixth parcel delivered.
(C) M is the sixth parcel delivered.
(D) G is the seventh parcel delivered.
(E) O is the seventh parcel delivered.

16. Each of the following could be true EXCEPT:

(A) H is delivered later than K.
(B) J is delivered later than G.
(C) L is delivered later than O.
(D) M is delivered later than L.
(E) N is delivered later than H.

17. If K is the seventh parcel delivered, then each of the following could be true EXCEPT:

(A) G is the fifth parcel delivered.
(B) M is the fifth parcel delivered.
(C) H is the fourth parcel delivered.
(D) L is the fourth parcel delivered.
(E) J is the third parcel delivered.

18. If L is delivered earlier than K, then which one of the following must be false?

(A) N is the second parcel delivered.
(B) L is the third parcel delivered.
(C) H is the fourth parcel delivered.
(D) K is the fifth parcel delivered.
(E) M is the sixth parcel delivered.

PrepTest51 Sec4 Qs 16–22

GO ON TO THE NEXT PAGE.

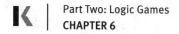
Explanations for these questions can be found in your Online Center.

Selection

Questions 19–23

A summer program offers at least one of the following seven courses: geography, history, literature, mathematics, psychology, sociology, zoology. The following restrictions on the program must apply:

> If mathematics is offered, then either literature or sociology (but not both) is offered.
>
> If literature is offered, then geography is also offered but psychology is not.
>
> If sociology is offered, then psychology is also offered but zoology is not.
>
> If geography is offered, then both history and zoology are also offered.

19. Which one of the following could be a complete and accurate list of the courses offered by the summer program?

(A) history, psychology
(B) geography, history, literature
(C) history, mathematics, psychology
(D) literature, mathematics, psychology
(E) history, literature, mathematics, sociology

GO ON TO THE NEXT PAGE.

Explanations for these questions can be found in your Online Center.

Part Two: Logic Games
Logic Games Practice

K

20. If the summer program offers literature, then which one of the following could be true?

    (A)   Sociology is offered.
    (B)   History is not offered.
    (C)   Mathematics is not offered.
    (D)   A total of two courses are offered.
    (E)   Zoology is not offered.

21. If history is not offered by the summer program, then which one of the following is another course that CANNOT be offered?

    (A)   literature
    (B)   mathematics
    (C)   psychology
    (D)   sociology
    (E)   zoology

22. If the summer program offers mathematics, then which one of the following must be true?

    (A)   Literature is offered.
    (B)   Psychology is offered.
    (C)   Sociology is offered.
    (D)   At least three courses are offered.
    (E)   At most four courses are offered.

23. Which one of the following must be false of the summer program?

    (A)   Both geography and psychology are offered.
    (B)   Both geography and mathematics are offered.
    (C)   Both psychology and mathematics are offered.
    (D)   Both history and mathematics are offered.
    (E)   Both geography and sociology are offered.

PrepTest49 Sec1 Qs 13–17

GO ON TO THE NEXT PAGE.

Explanations for these questions
can be found in your Online Center.

Matching

<u>Questions 24–28</u>

A clown will select a costume consisting of two pieces and
no others: a jacket and overalls. One piece of the costume
will be entirely one color, and the other piece will be plaid.
Selection is subject to the following restrictions:

> If the jacket is plaid, then there must be exactly three
> colors in it.
>
> If the overalls are plaid, then there must be exactly two
> colors in them.
>
> The jacket and overalls must have exactly one color in
> common.
>
> Green, red, and violet are the only colors that can be in
> the jacket.
>
> Red, violet, and yellow are the only colors that can be in
> the overalls.

24. Which one of the following could be a complete and
accurate list of the colors in the costume?

	Jacket	Overalls
(A)	red	red
(B)	red	violet, yellow
(C)	violet	green, violet
(D)	violet	red, violet
(E)	violet	red, violet, yellow

GO ON TO THE NEXT PAGE.

Explanations for these questions
can be found in your Online Center.

Part Two: Logic Games
Logic Games Practice

K

25. If there are exactly two colors in the costume, then which one of the following must be false?

    (A)   At least part of the jacket is green.
    (B)   At least part of the jacket is red.
    (C)   The overalls are red and violet.
    (D)   The overalls are red and yellow.
    (E)   The overalls are violet and yellow.

26. If at least part of the jacket is green, then which one of the following could be true?

    (A)   The overalls are plaid.
    (B)   No part of the jacket is red.
    (C)   No part of the jacket is violet.
    (D)   At least part of the overalls are yellow.
    (E)   At least part of the overalls are violet.

27. Which one of the following must be false?

    (A)   Both green and red are colors used in the costume.
    (B)   Both green and violet are colors used in the costume.
    (C)   Both green and yellow are colors used in the costume.
    (D)   Both red and violet are colors used in the costume.
    (E)   Both violet and yellow are colors used in the costume.

28. If there are exactly three colors in the costume, the overalls must be

    (A)   entirely red or else red and violet plaid
    (B)   entirely yellow or else violet and yellow plaid
    (C)   entirely violet or else red and violet plaid
    (D)   entirely red or else entirely yellow
    (E)   entirely red or else entirely violet

PrepTest51 Sec4 Qs 1–5

GO ON TO THE NEXT PAGE.

Distribution

Questions 29–33

Exactly six workers—Faith, Gus, Hannah, Juan, Kenneth, and Lisa—will travel to a business convention in two cars— car 1 and car 2. Each car must carry at least two of the workers, one of whom will be assigned to drive. For the entire trip, the workers will comply with an assignment that also meets the following constraints:

> Either Faith or Gus must drive the car in which Hannah travels.
> Either Faith or Kenneth must drive the car in which Juan travels.
> Gus must travel in the same car as Lisa.

29. Which one of the following is a possible assignment of the workers to the cars?

  (A) car 1: Faith (driver), Hannah, and Juan
           car 2: Gus (driver), Kenneth, and Lisa

  (B) car 1: Faith (driver), Hannah, and Kenneth
           car 2: Lisa (driver), Gus, and Juan

  (C) car 1: Faith (driver), Juan, Kenneth, and Lisa
           car 2: Gus (driver) and Hannah

  (D) car 1: Faith (driver) and Juan
           car 2: Kenneth (driver), Gus, Hannah, and Lisa

  (E) car 1: Gus (driver), Hannah, and Lisa
           car 2: Juan (driver), Faith, and Kenneth

GO ON TO THE NEXT PAGE.

Explanations for these questions can be found in your Online Center.

Part Two: Logic Games
Logic Games Practice | K

30. The two workers who drive the cars CANNOT be

    (A) Faith and Gus
    (B) Faith and Kenneth
    (C) Faith and Lisa
    (D) Gus and Kenneth
    (E) Kenneth and Lisa

31. If Lisa drives one of the cars, then which one of the following could be true?

    (A) Faith travels in the same car as Kenneth.
    (B) Faith travels in the same car as Lisa.
    (C) Gus travels in the same car as Hannah.
    (D) Gus travels in the same car as Juan.
    (E) Hannah travels in the same car as Lisa.

32. If Faith travels with two other workers in car 1, and if Faith is not the driver, then the person in car 1 other than Faith and the driver must be

    (A) Gus
    (B) Hannah
    (C) Juan
    (D) Kenneth
    (E) Lisa

33. Which one of the following CANNOT be true?

    (A) Gus is the only person other than the driver in one of the cars.
    (B) Hannah is the only person other than the driver in one of the cars.
    (C) Juan is the only person other than the driver in one of the cars.
    (D) Kenneth is the only person other than the driver in one of the cars.
    (E) Lisa is the only person other than the driver in one of the cars.

    PrepTest61 Sec3 Qs 1–5

GO ON TO THE NEXT PAGE.

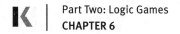
Explanations for these questions
can be found in your Online Center.

Hybrid

Questions 34–38

A locally known guitarist's demo CD contains exactly seven different songs—S, T, V, W, X, Y, and Z. Each song occupies exactly one of the CD's seven tracks. Some of the songs are rock classics; the others are new compositions. The following conditions must hold:

> S occupies the fourth track of the CD.
> Both W and Y precede S on the CD.
> T precedes W on the CD.
> A rock classic occupies the sixth track of the CD.
> Each rock classic is immediately preceded on the CD by a new composition.
> Z is a rock classic.

34. Which one of the following could be the order of the songs on the CD, from the first track through the seventh?

(A) T, W, V, S, Y, X, Z
(B) V, Y, T, S, W, Z, X
(C) X, Y, W, S, T, Z, S
(D) Y, T, W, S, X, Z, V
(E) Z, T, X, W, V, Y, S

GO ON TO THE NEXT PAGE.

Explanations for these questions can be found in your Online Center.

Part Two: Logic Games
Logic Games Practice

35. Which one of the following is a pair of songs that must occupy consecutive tracks on the CD?

   (A) S and V
   (B) S and W
   (C) T and Z
   (D) T and Y
   (E) V and Z

36. Which one of the following songs must be a new composition?

   (A) S
   (B) T
   (C) W
   (D) X
   (E) Y

37. If W precedes Y on the CD, then which one of the following must be true?

   (A) S is a rock classic.
   (B) V is a rock classic.
   (C) Y is a rock classic.
   (D) T is a new composition.
   (E) W is a new composition.

38. If there are exactly two songs on the CD that both precede V and are preceded by Y, then which one of the following could be true?

   (A) V occupies the seventh track of the CD.
   (B) X occupies the fifth track of the CD.
   (C) Y occupies the third track of the CD.
   (D) T is a rock classic.
   (E) W is a rock classic.

PrepTest51 Sec4 Qs 11–15

GO ON TO THE NEXT PAGE.

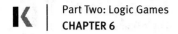

Explanations for these questions can be found in your Online Center.

QUESTION POOL 2

Try out some practice on games that have not appeared in earlier chapters. These games are arranged chronologically, from most to least recent.

Questions 39–44

An archaeologist has six ancient artifacts—a figurine, a headdress, a jar, a necklace, a plaque, and a tureen—no two of which are the same age. She will order them from first (oldest) to sixth (most recent). The following has already been determined:

> The figurine is older than both the jar and the headdress.
> The necklace and the jar are both older than the tureen.
> Either the plaque is older than both the headdress and the necklace, or both the headdress and the necklace are older than the plaque.

39. Which one of the following could be the artifacts in the order of their age, from first to sixth?

(A) figurine, headdress, jar, necklace, plaque, tureen
(B) figurine, jar, plaque, headdress, tureen, necklace
(C) figurine, necklace, plaque, headdress, jar, tureen
(D) necklace, jar, figurine, headdress, plaque, tureen
(E) plaque, tureen, figurine, necklace, jar, headdress

GO ON TO THE NEXT PAGE.

Explanations for these questions can be found in your Online Center.

Part Two: Logic Games
Logic Games Practice | **K**

40. Exactly how many of the artifacts are there any one of which could be first?

 (A) one
 (B) two
 (C) three
 (D) four
 (E) five

41. Which one of the following artifacts CANNOT be fourth?

 (A) figurine
 (B) headdress
 (C) jar
 (D) necklace
 (E) plaque

42. If the figurine is third, which one of the following must be second?

 (A) headdress
 (B) jar
 (C) necklace
 (D) plaque
 (E) tureen

43. If the plaque is first, then exactly how many artifacts are there any one of which could be second?

 (A) one
 (B) two
 (C) three
 (D) four
 (E) five

44. Which one of the following, if substituted for the information that the necklace and the jar are both older than the tureen, would have the same effect in determining the order of the artifacts?

 (A) The tureen is older than the headdress but not as old as the figurine.
 (B) The figurine and the necklace are both older than the tureen.
 (C) The necklace is older than the tureen if and only if the jar is.
 (D) All of the artifacts except the headdress and the plaque must be older than the tureen.
 (E) The plaque is older than the necklace if and only if the plaque is older than the tureen.

PrepTest61 Sec3 Qs 6–11

GO ON TO THE NEXT PAGE.

Part Two: Logic Games
CHAPTER 6

Explanations for these questions
can be found in your Online Center.

Questions 45–50

The coach of a women's track team must determine which
four of five runners—Quinn, Ramirez, Smith, Terrell, and
Uzoma—will run in the four races of an upcoming track
meet. Each of the four runners chosen will run in exactly
one of the four races—the first, second, third, or fourth. The
coach's selection is bound by the following constraints:

> If Quinn runs in the track meet, then Terrell runs in the
> race immediately after the race in which Quinn runs.
> Smith does not run in either the second race or the
> fourth race.
> If Uzoma does not run in the track meet, then Ramirez
> runs in the second race.
> If Ramirez runs in the second race, then Uzoma does not
> run in the track meet.

45. Which one of the following could be the order in which
the runners run, from first to fourth?

(A) Uzoma, Ramirez, Quinn, Terrell
(B) Terrell, Smith, Ramirez, Uzoma
(C) Smith, Ramirez, Terrell, Quinn
(D) Ramirez, Uzoma, Smith, Terrell
(E) Quinn, Terrell, Smith, Ramirez

GO ON TO THE NEXT PAGE.

Explanations for these questions can be found in your Online Center.

Part Two: Logic Games
Logic Games Practice

K

46. Which one of the following runners must the coach select to run in the track meet?

(A) Quinn
(B) Ramirez
(C) Smith
(D) Terrell
(E) Uzoma

47. The question of which runners will be chosen to run in the track meet and in what races they will run can be completely resolved if which one of the following is true?

(A) Ramirez runs in the first race.
(B) Ramirez runs in the second race.
(C) Ramirez runs in the third race.
(D) Ramirez runs in the fourth race.
(E) Ramirez does not run in the track meet.

48. Which one of the following CANNOT be true?

(A) Ramirez runs in the race immediately before the race in which Smith runs.
(B) Smith runs in the race immediately before the race in which Quinn runs.
(C) Smith runs in the race immediately before the race in which Terrell runs.
(D) Terrell runs in the race immediately before the race in which Ramirez runs.
(E) Uzoma runs in the race immediately before the race in which Terrell runs.

49. If Uzoma runs in the first race, then which one of the following must be true?

(A) Quinn does not run in the track meet.
(B) Smith does not run in the track meet.
(C) Quinn runs in the second race.
(D) Terrell runs in the second race.
(E) Ramirez runs in the fourth race.

50. If both Quinn and Smith run in the track meet, then how many of the runners are there any one of whom could be the one who runs in the first race?

(A) one
(B) two
(C) three
(D) four
(E) five

PrepTest61 Sec3 Qs 12–17

GO ON TO THE NEXT PAGE.

Explanations for these questions
can be found in your Online Center.

Questions 51–55

A law firm has seven departments—family law, health law, injury law, labor law, probate, securities, and tax law. The firm is to occupy a building with three floors—the bottom floor, the middle floor, and the top floor. Each floor can accommodate up to four departments, and no department is to be on more than one floor. Assignment of departments to floors is subject to the following constraints:

Probate must be on the same floor as tax law.

Health law must be on the floor immediately above injury law.

Labor law must occupy an entire floor by itself.

51. Which one of the following could be the assignment of departments to floors?

(A)   top floor: labor law
        middle floor: injury law, probate, tax law
        bottom floor: family law, health law, securities

(B)   top floor: family law, health law, probate
        middle floor: injury law, securities, tax law
        bottom floor: labor law

(C)   top floor: health law, probate, tax law
        middle floor: family law, injury law, securities
        bottom floor: labor law

(D)   top floor: health law, probate, tax law
        middle floor: injury law, securities
        bottom floor: family law, labor law

(E)   top floor: family law, health law, probate, tax law
        middle floor: labor law
        bottom floor: injury law, securities

GO ON TO THE NEXT PAGE.

Explanations for these questions can be found in your Online Center.

Part Two: Logic Games
Logic Games Practice

52. If injury law and probate are both assigned to the middle floor, which one of the following could be true?

   (A)   Family law is assigned to the middle floor.
   (B)   Health law is assigned to the middle floor.
   (C)   Labor law is assigned to the top floor.
   (D)   Securities is assigned to the bottom floor.
   (E)   Tax law is assigned to the top floor.

53. Which one of the following CANNOT be the assignment for any of the floors?

   (A)   family law, health law, probate, and tax law
   (B)   family law, injury law, probate, and tax law
   (C)   family law, probate, securities, and tax law
   (D)   health law, probate, securities, and tax law
   (E)   injury law, probate, securities, and tax law

54. If family law is assigned to the same floor as securities, which one of the following could be true?

   (A)   Exactly one department is assigned to the middle floor.
   (B)   Exactly four departments are assigned to the middle floor.
   (C)   Exactly two departments are assigned to the bottom floor.
   (D)   Exactly three departments are assigned to the bottom floor.
   (E)   Exactly four departments are assigned to the bottom floor.

55. If probate is assigned to the middle floor along with exactly two other departments, then which one of the following must be true?

   (A)   Family law is assigned to the floor immediately above health law.
   (B)   Family law is assigned to the floor immediately below labor law.
   (C)   Family law is assigned to the same floor as securities.
   (D)   Probate is assigned to the same floor as health law.
   (E)   Probate is assigned to the same floor as injury law.

Preptest59 Sec1 Qs 1–5

GO ON TO THE NEXT PAGE.

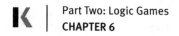
Explanations for these questions can be found in your Online Center.

Questions 56–61

Alicia will take exactly four courses this semester. She must choose from the following seven courses—Geography, Japanese, Macroeconomics, Psychology, Russian, Statistics (which is offered twice, once each on Tuesdays at 9 A.M. and 3 P.M.), and World History. No one is allowed to take any course more than once per semester. Because of university requirements and time conflicts, the following restrictions apply to Alicia's choices:

> She must take Japanese if she does not take Russian.
> She cannot take Japanese if she takes Macroeconomics.
> She cannot take World History if she takes Statistics at 9 A.M.
> She must take Statistics at 9 A.M. if she takes Psychology.
> She must take either Geography or World History but cannot take both.

56. Which one of the following could be the list of the four courses Alicia takes?

(A) Geography, Japanese, Psychology, Russian
(B) Geography, Macroeconomics, Psychology, Statistics
(C) Geography, Japanese, Macroeconomics, Russian
(D) Geography, Psychology, Russian, Statistics
(E) Macroeconomics, Psychology, Russian, Statistics

GO ON TO THE NEXT PAGE.

Explanations for these questions can be found in your Online Center.

Part Two: Logic Games
Logic Games Practice

K

57. Which one of the following could be an accurate list of three of the courses Alicia takes?

(A) Geography, Statistics, World History
(B) Japanese, Macroeconomics, Statistics
(C) Japanese, Psychology, World History
(D) Psychology, Russian, World History
(E) Russian, Statistics, World History

58. Which courses Alicia takes is fully determined if she takes Russian and which one of the following?

(A) World History
(B) Statistics
(C) Psychology
(D) Macroeconomics
(E) Japanese

59. Alicia could take Statistics at either of the available times if she takes which one of the following pairs of courses?

(A) Geography and Japanese
(B) Geography and Psychology
(C) Japanese and World History
(D) Psychology and Russian
(E) Russian and World History

60. If Alicia takes Statistics at 3 P.M. and Geography, then which one of the following courses must she also take?

(A) Japanese
(B) Macroeconomics
(C) Psychology
(D) Russian
(E) World History

61. Suppose that Alicia must take Statistics if she takes Psychology, but rather than being restricted to taking Statistics at 9 A.M. she can take it at either 9 A.M. or at 3 P.M. If all the other restrictions remain the same, then which one of the following could be the list of the four courses Alicia takes?

(A) Psychology, Russian, Statistics, World History
(B) Macroeconomics, Psychology, Statistics, World History
(C) Macroeconomics, Psychology, Russian, World History
(D) Geography, Psychology, Russian, World History
(E) Geography, Macroeconomics, Russian, World History

PrepTest59 Sec1 Qs 11–16

GO ON TO THE NEXT PAGE.

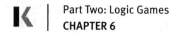
Explanations for these questions
can be found in your Online Center.

Questions 62–68

An organization will hold its first six annual meetings in
exactly six cities—Los Angeles, Montreal, New York,
Toronto, Vancouver, and Washington—using each city only
once. The following conditions govern the order in which the
cities are used:

> Los Angeles must be used in some year after the year in
> which Toronto is used.
> Vancouver must be used either immediately before or
> immediately after Washington.
> The meeting in Toronto must be separated from the
> meeting in Montreal by meetings in exactly two other
> cities.
> The meeting in Vancouver must be separated from the
> meeting in Los Angeles by meetings in exactly two other
> cities.

62. Which one of the following lists the cities in an order in
which they could be used for the meetings, from the first
year through the sixth?

(A) Toronto, Vancouver, Washington, Montreal,
     Los Angeles, New York

(B) Vancouver, Washington, Montreal, Los Angeles,
     New York, Toronto

(C) Vancouver, Washington, Toronto, New York,
     Los Angeles, Montreal

(D) Washington, Montreal, Vancouver, New York,
     Toronto, Los Angeles

(E) Washington, Vancouver, New York, Toronto,
     Los Angeles, Montreal

GO ON TO THE NEXT PAGE.

Explanations for these questions can be found in your Online Center.

Part Two: Logic Games
Logic Games Practice | **K**

63. Which one of the following must be true?

   (A)   Toronto is used in the first year.
   (B)   Montreal is used in the fourth year.
   (C)   Toronto is used at some time before Montreal is used.
   (D)   New York is used either immediately before or immediately after Vancouver.
   (E)   The meeting in New York is separated from the meeting in Washington by meetings in exactly two other cities.

64. There is exactly one possible order in which the cities are used if which one of the following is true?

   (A)   Los Angeles is used in the fifth year.
   (B)   Montreal is used in the sixth year.
   (C)   New York is used in the fifth year.
   (D)   Vancouver is used in the first year.
   (E)   Washington is used in the second year.

65. Which one of the following is a complete and accurate list of the years in which Washington could be used?

   (A)   1, 3, 5
   (B)   2, 3, 4, 5
   (C)   2, 3, 4, 6
   (D)   1, 2, 4, 6
   (E)   1, 2, 3, 4, 5, 6

66. If Montreal is used in the first year, which one of the following CANNOT be true?

   (A)   Washington is used in the third year.
   (B)   Vancouver is used in the third year.
   (C)   Toronto is used in the fourth year.
   (D)   New York is used in the fifth year.
   (E)   Los Angeles is used in the third year.

67. Which one of the following could be true?

   (A)   Los Angeles is used in the first year.
   (B)   New York is used in the second year.
   (C)   Montreal is used in the third year.
   (D)   Vancouver is used in the fourth year.
   (E)   Toronto is used in the sixth year.

68. Which one of the following must be false?

   (A)   Los Angeles is used either immediately before or immediately after New York.
   (B)   Los Angeles is used either immediately before or immediately after Washington.
   (C)   New York is used either immediately before or immediately after Toronto.
   (D)   Toronto is used either immediately before or immediately after Vancouver.
   (E)   Toronto is used either immediately before or immediately after Washington.

PrepTest59 Sec1 Qs 17–23

GO ON TO THE NEXT PAGE.

K | Part Two: Logic Games
CHAPTER 6

Explanations for these questions
can be found in your Online Center.

Questions 69–73

On a particular Saturday, a student will perform six activities—grocery shopping, hedge trimming, jogging, kitchen cleaning, laundry, and motorbike servicing. Each activity will be performed once, one at a time. The order in which the activities are performed is subject to the following conditions:

Grocery shopping has to be immediately after hedge trimming.

Kitchen cleaning has to be earlier than grocery shopping.

Motorbike servicing has to be earlier than laundry.

Motorbike servicing has to be either immediately before or immediately after jogging.

69. Which one of the following could be the order, from first to last, of the student's activities?

(A) jogging, kitchen cleaning, hedge trimming, grocery shopping, motorbike servicing, laundry

(B) jogging, motorbike servicing, laundry, hedge trimming, grocery shopping, kitchen cleaning

(C) kitchen cleaning, hedge trimming, grocery shopping, laundry, motorbike servicing, jogging

(D) kitchen cleaning, jogging, motorbike servicing, laundry, hedge trimming, grocery shopping

(E) motorbike servicing, jogging, laundry, hedge trimming, kitchen cleaning, grocery shopping

GO ON TO THE NEXT PAGE.

Explanations for these questions can be found in your Online Center.

Part Two: Logic Games
Logic Games Practice | **K**

70. Which one of the following activities CANNOT be third?

    (A) grocery shopping
    (B) hedge trimming
    (C) jogging
    (D) kitchen cleaning
    (E) motorbike servicing

71. Which one of the following CANNOT be true?

    (A) Hedge trimming is fourth.
    (B) Jogging is fourth.
    (C) Kitchen cleaning is second.
    (D) Laundry is third.
    (E) Motorbike servicing is second.

72. Which one of the following activities CANNOT be fifth?

    (A) grocery shopping
    (B) hedge trimming
    (C) jogging
    (D) laundry
    (E) motorbike servicing

73. Which one of the following, if substituted for the condition that motorbike servicing has to be earlier than laundry, would have the same effect in determining the order of the student's activities?

    (A) Laundry has to be one of the last three activities.
    (B) Laundry has to be either immediately before or immediately after jogging.
    (C) Jogging has to be earlier than laundry.
    (D) Laundry has to be earlier than hedge trimming.
    (E) Laundry has to be earlier than jogging.

PrepTest57 Sec1 Qs 1–5

GO ON TO THE NEXT PAGE.

K | Part Two: Logic Games
CHAPTER 6

Explanations for these questions
can be found in your Online Center.

<u>Questions 74–79</u>

Each of exactly three actors—Gombrich, Otto, and Raines—
auditions for parts on exactly two of the following days of a
particular week: Wednesday, Thursday, Friday, and Saturday.
On each of these days at least one of the actors auditions for
parts. The order of that week's auditions must meet the
following conditions:

> The first day on which Otto auditions is some day before
> the first day on which Raines auditions.
> There is at least one day on which both Gombrich and
> Raines audition.
> At least one of the actors auditions on both Thursday and
> Saturday.

74. Which one of the following could be an accurate
matching of the actors to the days on which they
audition?

(A) Gombrich: Thursday, Friday
Otto: Wednesday, Saturday
Raines: Friday, Saturday

(B) Gombrich: Thursday, Saturday
Otto: Wednesday, Friday
Raines: Friday, Saturday

(C) Gombrich: Friday, Saturday
Otto: Thursday, Saturday
Raines: Wednesday, Friday

(D) Gombrich: Wednesday, Thursday
Otto: Wednesday, Saturday
Raines: Thursday, Saturday

(E) Gombrich: Wednesday, Friday
Otto: Wednesday, Thursday
Raines: Thursday, Saturday

GO ON TO THE NEXT PAGE.

Explanations for these questions can be found in your Online Center.

Part Two: Logic Games
Logic Games Practice   K

75. If Otto auditions on both Thursday and Saturday, then Gombrich could audition on both

(A) Wednesday and Thursday
(B) Wednesday and Friday
(C) Thursday and Friday
(D) Thursday and Saturday
(E) Friday and Saturday

76. Which one of the following CANNOT be true of the week's auditions?

(A) Gombrich's last audition is on Thursday.
(B) Gombrich's last audition is on Friday.
(C) Otto's last audition is on Saturday.
(D) Raines's last audition is on Friday.
(E) Raines's last audition is on Thursday.

77. Which one of the following pairs of days CANNOT be the two days on which Otto auditions?

(A) Wednesday and Thursday
(B) Wednesday and Friday
(C) Wednesday and Saturday
(D) Thursday and Friday
(E) Thursday and Saturday

78. Which one of the following could be true?

(A) All three actors audition on Wednesday.
(B) All three actors audition on Friday.
(C) All three actors audition on Saturday.
(D) Otto auditions on Friday and on Saturday.
(E) Raines auditions on Wednesday and on Friday.

79. If Gombrich auditions on both Wednesday and Saturday, then which one of the following could be true?

(A) Otto auditions on both Wednesday and Thursday.
(B) Otto auditions on both Wednesday and Friday.
(C) Otto auditions on both Wednesday and Saturday.
(D) Raines auditions on both Wednesday and Saturday.
(E) Raines auditions on both Thursday and Friday.

PrepTest57 Sec1 Qs 6–11

GO ON TO THE NEXT PAGE.

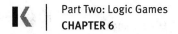
Explanations for these questions can be found in your Online Center.

Questions 80–85

Each of seven toy dinosaurs—an iguanadon, a lambeosaur, a plateosaur, a stegosaur, a tyrannosaur, an ultrasaur, and a velociraptor—is completely colored either green, mauve, red, or yellow. A display is to consist entirely of exactly five of these toys. The display must meet the following specifications:

    Exactly two mauve toys are included.
    The stegosaur is red and is included.
    The iguanadon is included only if it is green.
    The plateosaur is included only if it is yellow.
    The velociraptor is included only if the ultrasaur is not.
    If both the lambeosaur and the ultrasaur are included, at least one of them is not mauve.

80. Which one of the following could be the toys included in the display?

    (A)   the lambeosaur, the plateosaur, the stegosaur, the ultrasaur, the velociraptor

    (B)   the lambeosaur, the plateosaur, the stegosaur, the tyrannosaur, the ultrasaur

    (C)   the iguanadon, the lambeosaur, the plateosaur, the stegosaur, the ultrasaur

    (D)   the iguanadon, the lambeosaur, the plateosaur, the tyrannosaur, the velociraptor

    (E)   the iguanadon, the lambeosaur, the stegosaur, the ultrasaur, the velociraptor

GO ON TO THE NEXT PAGE.

Explanations for these questions can be found in your Online Center.

Part Two: Logic Games
Logic Games Practice

81. If the tyrannosaur is not included in the display, then the display must contain each of the following EXCEPT:

(A) a green iguanadon
(B) a mauve velociraptor
(C) a mauve lambeosaur
(D) a mauve ultrasaur
(E) a yellow plateosaur

82. Which one of the following is a pair of toys that could be included in the display together?

(A) a green lambeosaur and a mauve velociraptor
(B) a green lambeosaur and a yellow tyrannosaur
(C) a green lambeosaur and a yellow ultrasaur
(D) a yellow tyrannosaur and a green ultrasaur
(E) a yellow tyrannosaur and a red velociraptor

83. If the display includes a yellow tyrannosaur, then which one of the following must be true?

(A) The iguanadon is included in the display.
(B) The plateosaur is not included in the display.
(C) The display includes two yellow toy dinosaurs.
(D) The display contains a green lambeosaur.
(E) The display contains a mauve velociraptor.

84. If both the iguanadon and the ultrasaur are included in the display, then the display must contain which one of the following?

(A) a mauve tyrannosaur
(B) a mauve ultrasaur
(C) a yellow lambeosaur
(D) a yellow plateosaur
(E) a yellow ultrasaur

85. If the display includes two green toys, then which one of the following could be true?

(A) There is exactly one yellow toy included in the display.
(B) The tyrannosaur is included in the display and it is green.
(C) Neither the lambeosaur nor the velociraptor is included in the display.
(D) Neither the tyrannosaur nor the velociraptor is included in the display.
(E) Neither the ultrasaur nor the velociraptor is included in the display.

PrepTest57 Sec1 Qs 12–17

GO ON TO THE NEXT PAGE.

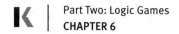

Explanations for these questions can be found in your Online Center.

Questions 86–91

A charitable foundation awards grants in exactly four areas—medical services, theater arts, wildlife preservation, and youth services—each grant being in one of these areas. One or more grants are awarded in each of the four quarters of a calendar year. Additionally, over the course of a calendar year, the following must obtain:

Grants are awarded in all four areas.
No more than six grants are awarded.
No grants in the same area are awarded in the same quarter or in consecutive quarters.
Exactly two medical services grants are awarded.
A wildlife preservation grant is awarded in the second quarter.

86. Which one of the following is a possible allocation of grants in a particular calendar year?

(A) first quarter: theater arts
     second quarter: wildlife preservation
     third quarter: medical services, youth services
     fourth quarter: theater arts

(B) first quarter: wildlife preservation
     second quarter: medical services
     third quarter: theater arts
     fourth quarter: medical services, youth services

(C) first quarter: youth services
     second quarter: wildlife preservation, medical services
     third quarter: theater arts
     fourth quarter: medical services, youth services

(D) first quarter: medical services, theater arts
     second quarter: theater arts, wildlife preservation
     third quarter: youth services
     fourth quarter: medical services

(E) first quarter: medical services, theater arts
     second quarter: wildlife preservation, youth services
     third quarter: theater arts
     fourth quarter: medical services, youth services

GO ON TO THE NEXT PAGE.

Explanations for these questions can be found in your Online Center.

Part Two: Logic Games
Logic Games Practice | K

87. Which one of the following CANNOT be true in a particular calendar year?

    (A) In each of the two quarters in which a medical services grant is awarded, no other grant is awarded.
    (B) Exactly two theater arts grants are awarded, one in the second quarter and one in the fourth quarter.
    (C) Exactly two youth services grants are awarded, one in the first quarter and one in the third quarter.
    (D) Two wildlife preservation grants and two youth services grants are awarded.
    (E) Three grants are awarded in the fourth quarter.

88. If a wildlife preservation grant and a youth services grant are awarded in the same quarter of a particular calendar year, then any of the following could be true that year EXCEPT:

    (A) A medical services grant is awarded in the second quarter.
    (B) A theater arts grant is awarded in the first quarter.
    (C) A theater arts grant is awarded in the second quarter.
    (D) A wildlife preservation grant is awarded in the fourth quarter.
    (E) A youth services grant is awarded in the third quarter.

89. If exactly two grants are awarded in just one of the four quarters of a particular calendar year, then which one of the following could be true that year?

    (A) Two youth services grants are awarded.
    (B) Neither a medical services grant nor a youth services grant is awarded in the first quarter.
    (C) A wildlife preservation grant is awarded in the fourth quarter.
    (D) Both a youth services grant and a theater arts grant are awarded in the first quarter.
    (E) A youth services grant is awarded in the first quarter and a theater arts grant is awarded in the second quarter.

90. Which one of the following CANNOT be true in a particular calendar year?

    (A) Three grants are awarded in a quarter, none of which is a medical services grant.
    (B) Exactly two grants are awarded in the first quarter and exactly two in the third quarter.
    (C) Exactly two grants are awarded in the first quarter and exactly two in the fourth quarter.
    (D) Theater arts grants are awarded in the first and fourth quarters, and no other grants are awarded in those two quarters.
    (E) Wildlife preservation grants are awarded in the second and fourth quarters, and no other grants are awarded in those two quarters.

91. It is fully determined which grants are awarded for each quarter of a particular calendar year if which one of the following is true that year?

    (A) Two theater arts grants are awarded.
    (B) Two youth services grants are awarded.
    (C) Three grants are awarded in the first quarter.
    (D) Three grants are awarded in the second quarter.
    (E) Three grants are awarded in the third quarter.

PrepTest57 Sec1 Qs 18–23

GO ON TO THE NEXT PAGE.

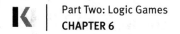

Explanations for these questions
can be found in your Online Center.

Questions 92–96

Six hotel suites—F, G, H, J, K, L—are ranked from most expensive (first) to least expensive (sixth). There are no ties. The ranking must be consistent with the following conditions:

> H is more expensive than L.
> If G is more expensive than H, then neither K nor L is more expensive than J.
> If H is more expensive than G, then neither J nor L is more expensive than K.
> F is more expensive than G, or else F is more expensive than H, but not both.

92. Which one of the following could be the ranking of the suites, from most expensive to least expensive?

(A) G, F, H, L, J, K
(B) H, K, F, J, G, L
(C) J, H, F, K, G, L
(D) J, K, G, H, L, F
(E) K, J, L, H, F, G

GO ON TO THE NEXT PAGE.

Explanations for these questions can be found in your Online Center.

Part Two: Logic Games
Logic Games Practice | **K**

93. If G is the second most expensive suite, then which one of the following could be true?

   (A)   H is more expensive than F.
   (B)   H is more expensive than G.
   (C)   K is more expensive than F.
   (D)   K is more expensive than J.
   (E)   L is more expensive than F.

94. Which one of the following CANNOT be the most expensive suite?

   (A)   F
   (B)   G
   (C)   H
   (D)   J
   (E)   K

95. If L is more expensive than F, then which one of the following could be true?

   (A)   F is more expensive than H.
   (B)   F is more expensive than K.
   (C)   G is more expensive than H.
   (D)   G is more expensive than J.
   (E)   G is more expensive than L.

96. If H is more expensive than J and less expensive than K, then which one of the following could be true?

   (A)   F is more expensive than H.
   (B)   G is more expensive than F.
   (C)   G is more expensive than H.
   (D)   J is more expensive than L.
   (E)   L is more expensive than K.

PrepTest51 Sec4 Qs 6–10

GO ON TO THE NEXT PAGE.

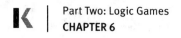

Explanations for these questions can be found in your Online Center.

Questions 97–103

During an international film retrospective lasting six consecutive days—day 1 through day 6—exactly six different films will be shown, one each day. Twelve films will be available for presentation, two each in French, Greek, Hungarian, Italian, Norwegian, and Turkish. The presentation of the films must conform to the following conditions:

> Neither day 2 nor day 4 is a day on which a film in Norwegian is shown.
>
> A film in Italian is not shown unless a film in Norwegian is going to be shown the next day.
>
> A film in Greek is not shown unless a film in Italian is going to be shown the next day.

97. Which one of the following is an acceptable order of films for the retrospective, listed by their language, from day 1 through day 6?

(A)   French, Greek, Italian, Turkish, Norwegian, Hungarian

(B)   French, Hungarian, Italian, Norwegian, French, Hungarian

(C)   Hungarian, French, Norwegian, Greek, Norwegian, Italian

(D)   Norwegian, Turkish, Hungarian, Italian, French, Turkish

(E)   Turkish, French, Norwegian, Hungarian, French, Turkish

GO ON TO THE NEXT PAGE.

Explanations for these questions can be found in your Online Center.

Part Two: Logic Games
Logic Games Practice | K

98. If two films in Italian are going to be shown, one on day 2 and one on day 5, then the film shown on day 1 could be in any one of the following languages EXCEPT:

(A) French
(B) Greek
(C) Hungarian
(D) Norwegian
(E) Turkish

99. If two films in Italian are shown during the retrospective, which one of the following must be false?

(A) A film in French is shown on day 3.
(B) A film in Greek is shown on day 1.
(C) A film in Hungarian is shown on day 6.
(D) A film in Norwegian is shown on day 5.
(E) A film in Turkish is shown on day 4.

100. Which one of the following is a complete and accurate list of the days, any one of which is a day on which a film in Italian could be shown?

(A) day 1, day 3, day 5
(B) day 2, day 4, day 5
(C) day 2, day 5, day 6
(D) day 1, day 3
(E) day 2, day 4

101. If two films in French are going to be shown, one on day 3 and one on day 5, which one of the following is a pair of films that could be shown on day 1 and day 6, respectively?

(A) a film in French, a film in Turkish
(B) a film in Greek, a film in Hungarian
(C) a film in Italian, a film in Norwegian
(D) a film in Norwegian, a film in Turkish
(E) a film in Turkish, a film in Greek

102. If neither a film in French nor a film in Italian is shown during the retrospective, which one of the following must be true?

(A) A film in Norwegian is shown on day 1.
(B) A film in Norwegian is shown on day 5.
(C) A film in Turkish is shown on day 4.
(D) A film in Hungarian or else a film in Norwegian is shown on day 3.
(E) A film in Hungarian or else a film in Turkish is shown on day 2.

103. If a film in Greek is going to be shown at some time after a film in Norwegian, then a film in Norwegian must be shown on

(A) day 1
(B) day 3
(C) day 5
(D) day 1 or else day 3
(E) day 3 or else day 5

PrepTest49 Sec1 Qs 1–7

GO ON TO THE NEXT PAGE.

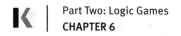
Explanations for these questions can be found in your Online Center.

Questions 104–108

There are exactly five pieces of mail in a mailbox: a flyer, a letter, a magazine, a postcard, and a survey. Each piece of mail is addressed to exactly one of three housemates: Georgette, Jana, or Rini. Each housemate has at least one of the pieces of mail addressed to her. The following conditions must apply:

> Neither the letter nor the magazine is addressed to Georgette.
>
> If the letter is addressed to Rini, then the postcard is addressed to Jana.
>
> The housemate to whom the flyer is addressed has at least one of the other pieces of mail addressed to her as well.

104. Which one of the following could be a complete and accurate matching of the pieces of mail to the housemates to whom they are addressed?

(A) Georgette: the flyer, the survey
  Jana: the letter
  Rini: the magazine

(B) Georgette: the flyer, the postcard
  Jana: the letter, the magazine
  Rini: the survey

(C) Georgette: the magazine, the survey
  Jana: the flyer, the letter
  Rini: the postcard

(D) Georgette: the survey
  Jana: the flyer, the magazine
  Rini: the letter, the postcard

(E) Georgette: the survey
  Jana: the letter, the magazine, the postcard
  Rini: the flyer

GO ON TO THE NEXT PAGE. ·

Explanations for these questions can be found in your Online Center.

Part Two: Logic Games
Logic Games Practice

K

105. Which one of the following is a complete and accurate list of the pieces of mail, any one of which could be the only piece of mail addressed to Jana?

(A) the postcard
(B) the letter, the postcard
(C) the letter, the survey
(D) the magazine, the survey
(E) the letter, the magazine, the postcard

106. Which one of the following CANNOT be a complete and accurate list of the pieces of mail addressed to Jana?

(A) the flyer, the letter, the magazine
(B) the flyer, the letter, the postcard
(C) the flyer, the letter, the survey
(D) the flyer, the magazine, the postcard
(E) the flyer, the magazine, the survey

107. Which one of the following CANNOT be a complete and accurate list of the pieces of mail addressed to Rini?

(A) the magazine, the postcard
(B) the letter, the survey
(C) the letter, the magazine
(D) the flyer, the magazine
(E) the flyer, the letter

108. If the magazine and the survey are both addressed to the same housemate, then which one of the following could be true?

(A) The survey is addressed to Georgette.
(B) The postcard is addressed to Rini.
(C) The magazine is addressed to Jana.
(D) The letter is addressed to Rini.
(E) The flyer is addressed to Jana.

PrepTest49 Sec1 Qs 8–12

GO ON TO THE NEXT PAGE.

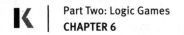
Explanations for these questions
can be found in your Online Center.

Questions 109–113

Exactly eight computer processor chips—F, G, H, J, K, L, M, and O—are ranked according to their speed from first (fastest) to eighth (slowest). The ranking must be consistent with the following:

> There are no ties.
> Either F or G is ranked first.
> M is not the slowest.
> H is faster than J, with exactly one chip intermediate in speed between them.
> K is faster than L, with exactly two chips intermediate in speed between them.
> O is slower than both J and L.

109. Which one of the following could be true?

(A)   F is ranked first and M is ranked eighth.
(B)   G is ranked fifth and O is ranked eighth.
(C)   J is ranked third and L is ranked seventh.
(D)   K is ranked second and H is ranked third.
(E)   M is ranked seventh and L is ranked eighth.

GO ON TO THE NEXT PAGE.

Explanations for these questions can be found in your Online Center.

Part Two: Logic Games
Logic Games Practice K

110. H CANNOT be ranked

   (A)   second
   (B)   third
   (C)   fourth
   (D)   fifth
   (E)   sixth

111. If O is faster than F, then which one of the following chips could be ranked second?

   (A)   G
   (B)   H
   (C)   M
   (D)   J
   (E)   L

112. If M is faster than J, then the fastest ranking J could have is

   (A)   second
   (B)   third
   (C)   fourth
   (D)   fifth
   (E)   sixth

113. Which one of the following must be true?

   (A)   J is ranked no faster than fifth.
   (B)   K is ranked no faster than third.
   (C)   L is ranked no faster than fifth.
   (D)   M is ranked no faster than third.
   (E)   O is ranked no faster than eighth.

PrepTest49 Sec1 Qs 18–22

ANSWER KEY

Question Pool 1

Game 1–Nurses

1. D
2. C
3. D
4. B
5. B
6. A

Game 2–Museum Photographs

7. C
8. E
9. D
10. B
11. D

Game 3–Parcel Delivery

12. D
13. C
14. D
15. A
16. B
17. C
18. C

Game 4–Summer Courses

19. A
20. C
21. A
22. D
23. E

Game 5–Clown Costumes

24. D
25. A
26. E
27. C
28. E

Game 6–Convention Car Pool

29. A
30. E
31. A
32. C
33. D

Game 7–Guitarist's Demo CD

34. D
35. E
36. D
37. D
38. E

Question Pool 2

Game 8–Ancient Artifacts

39. A
40. C
41. A
42. C
43. B
44. D

Game 9–Track Team

45. D
46. D
47. B
48. A
49. E
50. B

Game 10–Law Firm Departments

51. C
52. A
53. C
54. D
55. C

Game 11–Alicia's Courses

56. D
57. E
58. C
59. A
60. D
61. A

Game 12–Organization Meetings

62. A
63. E
64. D
65. E
66. E
67. B
68. B

Game 13–Student Activities

69. D
70. B
71. C
72. D
73. C

Game 14–Acting Auditions

74. B
75. B
76. E
77. D
78. C
79. B

Game 15–Toy Dinosaurs

80. B
81. D
82. A
83. E
84. A
85. B

Game 16–Charitable Foundation Grants

86. C
87. D
88. E
89. B
90. D
91. E

Game 17–Hotel Suites

92. B
93. C
94. A
95. D
96. D

Game 18–International Films

97. E
98. D
99. A
100. B
101. D
102. E
103. D

Game 19–Housemates and Mail

104. B
105. B
106. E
107. B
108. E

Game 20–Computer Processor Chips

109. B
110. E
111. B
112. D
113. C

Complete explanations for all of these questions can be found in your Online Center.

CHAPTER 7

Logic Games: Managing the Section

The bulk of this chapter consists of a complete Logic Games section. Taking full timed practice sections helps you maximize your score by learning to improve section management. Perfecting your timing in LSAT sections involves much more than just "getting faster." Indeed, in many cases, hurrying through the overview, setup, and deduction steps of the Logic Games Method may wind up costing you time by causing you to do extra work in each of the questions, as well as costing you points directly when incomplete deductions lead to wrong answers.

TIMING AND SECTION MANAGEMENT

Here are a few of the principles of great section management that LSAT experts use to their advantage. Learn them and put them into practice whenever you undertake timed section or full test practice.

Logic Games Section Timing: The Basics

The facts: Every Logic Games section has four games, each with 5–7 questions, for a total of 22–24 questions to be completed in 35 minutes.

The strategy: On average, then, you should take between eight and nine minutes for each game. Of that time, you'll usually take between three and four minutes to set up the game, analyze the rules, and make deductions, and then utilize the remaining four to five minutes to answer the questions. Don't rush steps 1–4 of the Logic Games Method. Approached strategically, the easiest games may take less than eight minutes. Bank that extra time for tougher games. When a game threatens to drag on much longer than nine minutes, however, be prepared to guess on its toughest questions and move on with ample time to solve the next game and answer its questions.

Efficiency, Not Speed

The facts: You actually have more time per question in Logic Games than you do in any other section of the LSAT. A complete and accurate setup with all available deductions made up front will allow you to answer the questions much more quickly than you could with an incomplete setup.

The strategy: Follow the Logic Games Method. In the preceding chapters, you've seen how a clear overview, useful sketch, properly analyzed rules, and thorough deductions provide everything you need to answer questions quickly and accurately. Don't let "clock anxiety" tempt you into abandoning the most efficient approach to games and questions. Being methodical does not mean being slow. When you have practiced enough that the Logic Games Method is second nature, you'll find that it provides the shortest and most direct route to correct answers, the single goal of all the work you do on the LSAT.

Triage: Take Control of the Section

The facts: You are under no obligation to do the games or questions in the order in which they are presented. The first game in the section is most often the easiest for most test takers. Either the third or fourth game is most often the hardest for most test takers.

The strategy: Triage is a term used in the medical profession to refer to the process of determining priorities in an emergency. You can "triage" the Logic Games section by looking for and prioritizing the games and questions most likely to turn into correct answers for you. Some LSAT experts triage the section by taking a minute or less at the start of the section to look at all four games and choose an optimal order in which to address them. These experts prioritize games that are simple, concrete (look for strong, unequivocal terms such as *exactly, only, precisely*, or *always*), and familiar. Other experts follow a predetermined order (1-2-4-3 is a reasonable rule of thumb), but they are willing to skip and come back to a game or to rearrange their order of attack immediately upon determining that a game is particularly difficult.

Similarly, you can triage the questions within a game. When a game has an Acceptability question, it is usually the first (and easiest) question in the set. After that, you may choose to complete the New-"If" questions before more open-ended Must/Could Be True/False questions, especially in games that provided few deductions up front. In games with strong deduction patterns (for example, those with Limited Options), taking the questions in order may be the most efficient approach.

Whether you are triaging a section or a set of questions, follow the best practices of a great doctor triaging an emergency: Be decisive and remember that you are in control of the situation.

Skip and Guess Strategically

The facts: You do not need to answer every question in order to get a great score. Certain time-consuming questions (e.g., Rule Substitution questions) almost always appear at the end of a question set. There is no bonus for solving the hardest question(s) in the section.

The strategy: Remember that you are in control of how much time and effort you dedicate to any particular game or question. Allowing yourself to get into an "ego battle" with particular games or questions—"I *will* figure this one out no matter what!"—can take precious minutes away from other questions you could be answering quickly and accurately. Be willing to skip one or two difficult or very time-consuming questions if doing so will allow you to get more questions correct on subsequent games. Preempt situations in which you are guessing out of frustration—"Okay, I give up. I've already given this two minutes; I'll never get it!"—by learning to guess strategically—"I'll guess on this Rule Substitution question and give myself an extra two minutes for the next two games." In other words, guess when it is to your benefit to do so. Stay in control of the section and the test.

TAKING THE TIMING SECTION

The Logic Games section that follows was originally Section 2 in PrepTest 65, administered in December 2011.

Proctoring

Complete this section under timed test-like conditions. Give yourself 35 minutes for the section and finish it in one uninterrupted sitting. If you are taking the section as part of a class, follow the proctor's instructions strictly. If you are taking the section on your own, use the LSAT Proctor Anywhere app.

Record your answer selections using one of the answer grids found at the back of this book.

Scoring

After you finish the section, record your answers in the appropriate webgrid (PrepTest 65, Section 2) found in your Online Center. This will make your results and percent correct easy to see, and the score report will contain links to the explanations for each game and question.

NOTE: Chapters 12 and 16 contain the other three scored sections from PrepTest 65. After completing those sections (under timed, proctored conditions), you may enter your answers from all four sections into the webgrid for PrepTest 65 to receive a score for the entire test.

Review

For your convenience, an answer key is included at the end of this chapter. For complete answers and explanations, consult the explanations PDF in your Online Center. Check that you consistently followed the Logic Games Method, set up each game with a helpful sketch, and made all of the available deductions as well.

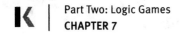

Explanations for these questions can be found in your Online Center.

PrepTest 65, Section 2

Time—35 minutes

23 Questions

Directions: Each group of questions in this section is based on a set of conditions. In answering some of the questions, it may be useful to draw a rough diagram. Choose the response that most accurately and completely answers each question and blacken the corresponding space on your answer sheet.

Questions 1–5

A professor must determine the order in which five of her students—Fernando, Ginny, Hakim, Juanita, and Kevin—will perform in an upcoming piano recital. Each student performs one piece, and no two performances overlap. The following constraints apply:

Ginny must perform earlier than Fernando.
Kevin must perform earlier than Hakim and Juanita.
Hakim must perform either immediately before or immediately after Fernando.

1. Which one of the following could be the order, from first to last, in which the students perform?

(A) Ginny, Fernando, Hakim, Kevin, Juanita
(B) Ginny, Juanita, Kevin, Hakim, Fernando
(C) Ginny, Kevin, Hakim, Juanita, Fernando
(D) Kevin, Ginny, Juanita, Fernando, Hakim
(E) Kevin, Juanita, Fernando, Hakim, Ginny

GO ON TO THE NEXT PAGE.

Explanations for these questions can be found in your Online Center.

Part Two: Logic Games
Logic Games: Managing the Section

2. If Juanita performs earlier than Ginny, then which one of the following could be true?

    (A) Fernando performs fourth.
    (B) Ginny performs second.
    (C) Hakim performs third.
    (D) Juanita performs third.
    (E) Kevin performs second.

3. Which one of the following CANNOT be true?

    (A) Fernando performs immediately before Juanita.
    (B) Ginny performs immediately before Hakim.
    (C) Hakim performs immediately before Ginny.
    (D) Juanita performs immediately before Ginny.
    (E) Kevin performs immediately before Hakim.

4. The order in which the students perform is fully determined if which one of the following is true?

    (A) Fernando performs immediately before Hakim.
    (B) Ginny performs immediately before Fernando.
    (C) Hakim performs immediately before Juanita.
    (D) Juanita performs immediately before Hakim.
    (E) Kevin performs immediately before Fernando.

5. How many of the students are there any one of whom could perform fourth?

    (A) one
    (B) two
    (C) three
    (D) four
    (E) five

GO ON TO THE NEXT PAGE.

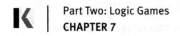
Explanations for these questions can be found in your Online Center.

Questions 6–11

As part of an open house at a crafts studio, three teachers—Jiang, Kudrow, and Lanning—will give six consecutive presentations on six different subjects. Jiang will present on needlework and origami; Kudrow on pottery, stenciling, and textile making; and Lanning on woodworking. The order of their presentations will meet the following conditions:

> Kudrow cannot give two presentations in a row.
> The presentation on stenciling must be given earlier than the one on origami.
> The presentation on textile making must be given earlier than the one on woodworking.

6. Which one of the following could be the order of the presentations, from first to sixth?

(A) stenciling, origami, needlework, textile making, pottery, woodworking

(B) stenciling, origami, pottery, woodworking, needlework, textile making

(C) stenciling, origami, textile making, woodworking, needlework, pottery

(D) textile making, origami, stenciling, woodworking, needlework, pottery

(E) textile making, stenciling, woodworking, needlework, pottery, origami

GO ON TO THE NEXT PAGE.

Explanations for these questions can be found in your Online Center.

Part Two: Logic Games
Logic Games: Managing the Section

K

7. If textile making is presented fifth, which one of the following could be true?

   (A) Needlework is presented sixth.
   (B) Pottery is presented fourth.
   (C) Stenciling is presented second.
   (D) Stenciling is presented third.
   (E) Woodworking is presented second.

8. If needlework is presented first, which one of the following could be true?

   (A) Origami is presented sixth.
   (B) Pottery is presented second.
   (C) Stenciling is presented third.
   (D) Textile making is presented fifth.
   (E) Woodworking is presented third.

9. Jiang CANNOT give both

   (A) the first and third presentations
   (B) the first and fourth presentations
   (C) the first and fifth presentations
   (D) the second and third presentations
   (E) the second and fourth presentations

10. If needlework is presented sixth, which one of the following must be true?

   (A) Origami is presented fourth.
   (B) Pottery is presented fifth.
   (C) Stenciling is presented third.
   (D) Textile making is presented first.
   (E) Woodworking is presented fourth.

11. Which one of the following CANNOT be the subject of the second presentation?

   (A) needlework
   (B) origami
   (C) pottery
   (D) textile making
   (E) woodworking

GO ON TO THE NEXT PAGE.

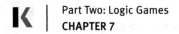

Explanations for these questions can
be found in your Online Center.

Questions 12–16

The organizer of a luncheon will select exactly five
foods to be served from among exactly eight foods: two
desserts—F and G; three main courses—N, O, and P;
three side dishes—T, V, and W. Only F, N, and T are hot
foods. The following requirements will be satisfied:

> At least one dessert, at least one main course, and at
> least one side dish must be selected.
> At least one hot food must be selected.
> If either P or W is selected, both must be selected.
> If G is selected, O must be selected.
> If N is selected, V cannot be selected.

12. Which one of the following is a list of foods that
could be the foods selected?

(A) F, N, O, T, V
(B) F, O, P, T, W
(C) G, N, P, T, W
(D) G, O, P, T, V
(E) G, O, P, V, W

GO ON TO THE NEXT PAGE.

Explanations for these questions can
be found in your Online Center.

Part Two: Logic Games
Logic Games: Managing the Section

K

13. Which one of the following is a pair of foods of which
the organizer of the luncheon must select at least
one?

(A) F, T
(B) G, O
(C) N, T
(D) O, P
(E) V, W

14. If O is the only main course selected, then which one of
the following CANNOT be selected?

(A) F
(B) G
(C) T
(D) V
(E) W

15. If F is not selected, which one of the following could
be true?

(A) P is the only main course selected.
(B) T is the only side dish selected.
(C) Exactly two hot foods are selected.
(D) Exactly three main courses are selected.
(E) Exactly three side dishes are selected.

16. If T and V are the only side dishes selected, then which
one of the following is a pair of foods each of which
must be selected?

(A) F and G
(B) F and N
(C) F and P
(D) N and O
(E) O and P

GO ON TO THE NEXT PAGE.

Explanations for these questions can be found in your Online Center.

<u>Questions 17–23</u>

A television programming director is scheduling a three-hour block of programs beginning at 1 P.M. The programs that are to fill this time block include an hour-long program called *Generations* and four half-hour programs: *Roamin'*, *Sundown*, *Terry*, and *Waterloo*. The programs will be shown one after the other, each program shown exactly once. The schedule must meet the following constraints:

> *Generations* starts on the hour rather than the half hour.
> *Terry* starts on the half hour rather than the hour.
> *Roamin'* is shown earlier than *Sundown*.
> If *Waterloo* is shown earlier than *Terry*, it is shown immediately before *Terry*.

17. Which one of the following could be the order in which the programs are shown, from earliest to latest?

(A) *Generations, Roamin', Waterloo, Terry, Sundown*
(B) *Roamin', Sundown, Waterloo, Terry, Generations*
(C) *Roamin', Terry, Waterloo, Generations, Sundown*
(D) *Waterloo, Roamin', Sundown, Terry, Generations*
(E) *Waterloo, Terry, Sundown, Roamin', Generations*

GO ON TO THE NEXT PAGE.

Explanations for these questions can be found in your Online Center.

Part Two: Logic Games
Logic Games: Managing the Section K

18. If *Waterloo* is the first program, then how many orders are there in which the remaining programs could be shown?

    (A) one
    (B) two
    (C) three
    (D) four
    (E) five

19. If *Roamin'* is the second program, then each of the following could be true EXCEPT:

    (A) *Sundown* is the third program.
    (B) *Sundown* is the fourth program.
    (C) *Terry* is the fifth program.
    (D) *Waterloo* is the third program.
    (E) *Waterloo* is the fifth program.

20. If *Sundown* is the third program, then which one of the following must be true?

    (A) *Generations* is the first program.
    (B) *Roamin'* is the first program.
    (C) *Roamin'* is the second program.
    (D) *Terry* is the fifth program.
    (E) *Waterloo* is the fourth program.

21. If *Generations* is the third program, then which one of the following could be true?

    (A) *Roamin'* is the second program.
    (B) *Roamin'* is the fifth program.
    (C) *Sundown* is the fourth program.
    (D) *Terry* is the fourth program.
    (E) *Waterloo* is the second program.

22. Which one of the following CANNOT be true?

    (A) *Sundown* is shown immediately before *Generations*.
    (B) *Waterloo* is shown immediately before *Roamin'*.
    (C) *Generations* is shown immediately before *Sundown*.
    (D) *Roamin'* is shown immediately before *Terry*.
    (E) *Terry* is shown immediately before *Waterloo*.

23. Which one of the following, if substituted for the constraint that *Generations* starts on the hour rather than the half hour, would have the same effect in determining the order in which the programs are shown?

    (A) *Generations* is not shown immediately before *Terry*.
    (B) *Generations* is either the first program or the fifth.
    (C) *Generations* is neither the second program nor the fourth.
    (D) If *Generations* is shown third, then *Roamin'* is shown first.
    (E) If *Generations* is not shown first, then it is shown later than *Terry*.

S T O P

IF YOU FINISH BEFORE TIME IS CALLED, YOU MAY CHECK YOUR WORK ON THIS SECTION ONLY.
DO NOT WORK ON ANY OTHER SECTION IN THE TEST.

ANSWER KEY

Game 1–Piano Recital

1. D
2. A
3. C
4. E
5. B

Game 2–Crafts Presentations

6. C
7. D
8. E
9. B
10. B
11. C

Game 3–Selecting Luncheon Foods

12. B
13. D
14. E
15. D
16. A

Game 4–TV Scheduling

17. B
18. B
19. D
20. E
21. C
22. B
23. C

Complete explanations for all of these questions can be found in your Online Center.

Logical Reasoning

CHAPTER 8

The Kaplan Logical Reasoning Method

The Logical Reasoning sections of the LSAT test your ability to analyze and critique short arguments and to evaluate and apply factual statements. The skills associated with Logical Reasoning are the most important to your LSAT score. The reason is clear.

Logical Reasoning accounts for roughly half of your LSAT score. Every administration of the LSAT contains exactly two scored Logical Reasoning sections of between 24 and 26 questions apiece. Among the 50 or so Logical Reasoning questions you'll see on each test, you will learn to identify the following question types, grouped here into the families of questions covered in the next three chapters.

LSAT Score Distribution by Section

LOGICAL REASONING QUESTION TYPES

Argument-Based Questions (Ch. 9)
- Main Point
- Role of a Statement
- Method of Argument
- Point at Issue

Assumption Family Questions (Ch. 10)
- Assumption
- Flaw
- Strengthen/Weaken
- Principle (Assumption/ Strengthen)
- Parallel Reasoning

Non-Argument Questions (Ch. 11)
- Inference
- Paradox
- Principle (Inference)

Before turning to the best strategies for each question type, this chapter will focus on two features common to all Logical Reasoning questions: 1) their overall structure and 2) the way their incorrect answer choices are devised. In the remainder of this chapter, you'll see how an LSAT expert uses these universal features to apply a fast, effective, methodical approach to every Logical Reasoning question.

LOGICAL REASONING QUESTION FORMAT AND THE KAPLAN LOGICAL REASONING METHOD

Although Logical Reasoning questions ask for several different kinds of analyses, the LSAT expert uses a consistent approach on all of the questions.

THE KAPLAN LOGICAL REASONING METHOD

Step 1: Identify the Question Type
Step 2: Untangle the Stimulus
Step 3: Predict the Correct Answer
Step 4: Evaluate the Answer Choices

There is nothing abstract about this method. Take a look at it mapped onto a Logical Reasoning question. This is how the well-trained expert sees it.

5. Studies reveal that <u>most people select the foods they eat primarily on the basis of flavor, and that nutrition is usually a secondary concern at best.</u> This suggests that <health experts would have more success in encouraging people to eat wholesome foods if they emphasized how flavorful those foods truly are rather than how nutritious they are.>

Which one of the following, if true, most strengthens the argument above?

(A) Most people currently believe that wholesome foods are more flavorful, on average, than unwholesome foods are.

(B) Few people, when given a choice between foods that are flavorful but not nutritious and foods that are nutritious but not flavorful, will choose the foods that are nutritious but not flavorful.

(C) Health experts' attempts to encourage people to eat wholesome foods by emphasizing how nutritious those foods are have been moderately successful.

(D) The studies that revealed that people choose the foods they eat primarily on the basis of flavor also revealed that people rated as most flavorful those foods that were least nutritious.

(E) In a study, subjects who were told that a given food was very flavorful were more willing to try the food and more likely to enjoy it than were subjects who were told that the food was nutritious.

PrepTest57 Sec2 Q5

Step 1: Identify the Question Type
Start here, so you know what to look for in the stimulus.

Step 2: Untangle the Stimulus
Zero in on what is relevant. Here, the underlined and bracketed text helps you to predict the correct answer.

Step 3: Predict the Correct Answer
In your own words, state what the correct answer must say.

Step 4: Evaluate the Answer Choices
Identify the answer that matches your prediction. Eliminate those that do not.

Now, try applying the Logical Reasoning Method to that question one step at a time. What is this question asking for?

LSAT Question	My Analysis
Studies reveal that most people select the foods they eat primarily on the basis of flavor, and that nutrition is usually a secondary concern at best. This suggests that health experts would have more success in encouraging people to eat wholesome foods if they emphasized how flavorful those foods truly are rather than how nutritious they are. $\longrightarrow$	**Step 2:**
Which one of the following, if true, most strengthens the argument above? $\longrightarrow$	**Step 1:**
	Step 3:
(A) Most people currently believe that wholesome foods are more flavorful, on average, than unwholesome foods are. $\longrightarrow$	**Step 4:**
(B) Few people, when given a choice between foods that are flavorful but not nutritious and foods that are nutritious but not flavorful, will choose the foods that are nutritious but not flavorful. $\longrightarrow$	
(C) Health experts' attempts to encourage people to eat wholesome foods by emphasizing how nutritious those foods are have been moderately successful. $\longrightarrow$	
(D) The studies that revealed that people choose the foods they eat primarily on the basis of flavor also revealed that people rated as most flavorful those foods that were least nutritious. $\longrightarrow$	
(E) In a study, subjects who were told that a given food was very flavorful were more willing to try the food and more likely to enjoy it than were subjects who were told that the food was nutritious. $\longrightarrow$	

PrepTest57 Sec2 Q5

Don't worry that you don't know all of the names and terminology that go along with various Logical Reasoning question types. You'll pick that up in subsequent chapters. At this point, just concentrate on what each step accomplishes and how it helps you anticipate what to look for in the subsequent step.

Here's how an LSAT expert might analyze the question stem in the LSAT question you're working on.

LSAT Question	Analysis
Studies reveal that most people select the foods they eat primarily on the basis of flavor, and that nutrition is usually a secondary concern at best. This suggests that health experts would have more success in encouraging people to eat wholesome foods if they emphasized how flavorful those foods truly are rather than how nutritious they are.	**Step 2:**
Which one of the following, if true, most strengthens the argument above?	**Step 1:** The correct answer will be a fact that makes the argument stronger. That is, it will make the conclusion more likely to follow from the evidence.
	Step 3:
(A) Most people currently believe that wholesome foods are more flavorful, on average, than unwholesome foods are.	**Step 4:**
(B) Few people, when given a choice between foods that are flavorful but not nutritious and foods that are nutritious but not flavorful, will choose the foods that are nutritious but not flavorful.	
(C) Health experts' attempts to encourage people to eat wholesome foods by emphasizing how nutritious those foods are have been moderately successful.	
(D) The studies that revealed that people choose the foods they eat primarily on the basis of flavor also revealed that people rated as most flavorful those foods that were least nutritious.	
(E) In a study, subjects who were told that a given food was very flavorful were more willing to try the food and more likely to enjoy it than were subjects who were told that the food was nutritious.	

PrepTest57 Sec2 Q5

The correct answer makes the argument stronger. What does that tell you about what you need to read for as you untangle the stimulus?

LSAT Question	My Analysis
Studies reveal that most people select the foods they eat primarily on the basis of flavor, and that nutrition is usually a secondary concern at best. This suggests that health experts would have more success in encouraging people to eat wholesome foods if they emphasized how flavorful those foods truly are rather than how nutritious they are. →	**Step 2:**
Which one of the following, if true, most strengthens the argument above? →	**Step 1:** The correct answer will be a fact that makes the argument stronger. That is, it will make the conclusion more likely to follow from the evidence.
	Step 3:
(A) Most people currently believe that wholesome foods are more flavorful, on average, than unwholesome foods are. →	**Step 4:**
(B) Few people, when given a choice between foods that are flavorful but not nutritious and foods that are nutritious but not flavorful, will choose the foods that are nutritious but not flavorful. →	
(C) Health experts' attempts to encourage people to eat wholesome foods by emphasizing how nutritious those foods are have been moderately successful. →	
(D) The studies that revealed that people choose the foods they eat primarily on the basis of flavor also revealed that people rated as most flavorful those foods that were least nutritious. →	
(E) In a study, subjects who were told that a given food was very flavorful were more willing to try the food and more likely to enjoy it than were subjects who were told that the food was nutritious. →	

PrepTest57 Sec2 Q5

Compare your analysis to that of an LSAT expert. As you work through the exercises and practice in Chapters 9 and 10, your analyses will become just as targeted and efficient.

LSAT Question	Analysis
Studies reveal that most people select the foods they eat primarily on the basis of flavor, and that nutrition is usually a secondary concern at best. This suggests that health experts would have more success in encouraging people to eat wholesome foods if they emphasized how flavorful those foods truly are rather than how nutritious they are. $\longrightarrow$	**Step 2:** Conclusion—Experts will have more success selling people on how good a healthy food tastes than on how good it is for them. Evidence—Studies show people choose food based on taste more than on nutrition. Assumption—The author takes for granted that people will respond favorably to expert suggestions that correspond to their own preferences (flavor over nutrition).
Which one of the following, if true, most strengthens the argument above? $\longrightarrow$	**Step 1:** The correct answer will be a fact that makes the argument stronger. That is, it will make the conclusion more likely to follow from the evidence. **Step 3:**
(A) Most people currently believe that wholesome foods are more flavorful, on average, than unwholesome foods are. $\longrightarrow$	**Step 4:**
(B) Few people, when given a choice between foods that are flavorful but not nutritious and foods that are nutritious but not flavorful, will choose the foods that are nutritious but not flavorful. $\longrightarrow$	
(C) Health experts' attempts to encourage people to eat wholesome foods by emphasizing how nutritious those foods are have been moderately successful. $\longrightarrow$	
(D) The studies that revealed that people choose the foods they eat primarily on the basis of flavor also revealed that people rated as most flavorful those foods that were least nutritious. $\longrightarrow$	
(E) In a study, subjects who were told that a given food was very flavorful were more willing to try the food and more likely to enjoy it than were subjects who were told that the food was nutritious. $\longrightarrow$	

PrepTest57 Sec2 Q5

Given the author's conclusion, and the evidence she has provided for it, what would make the argument stronger? What kind of fact will the correct answer need to contain?

LSAT Question	My Analysis
Studies reveal that most people select the foods they eat primarily on the basis of flavor, and that nutrition is usually a secondary concern at best. This suggests that health experts would have more success in encouraging people to eat wholesome foods if they emphasized how flavorful those foods truly are rather than how nutritious they are. $\longrightarrow$	**Step 2:** Conclusion—Experts will have more success selling people on how good a healthy food tastes than on how good it is for them. Evidence—Studies show people choose food based on taste more than on nutrition. Assumption—The author takes for granted that people will respond favorably to expert suggestions that correspond to their own preferences (flavor over nutrition).
Which one of the following, if true, most strengthens the argument above? $\longrightarrow$	**Step 1:** The correct answer will be a fact that makes the argument stronger. That is, it will make the conclusion more likely to follow from the evidence. **Step 3:**

(A)	Most people currently believe that wholesome foods are more flavorful, on average, than unwholesome foods are. $\longrightarrow$	**Step 4:**
(B)	Few people, when given a choice between foods that are flavorful but not nutritious and foods that are nutritious but not flavorful, will choose the foods that are nutritious but not flavorful. $\longrightarrow$	
(C)	Health experts' attempts to encourage people to eat wholesome foods by emphasizing how nutritious those foods are have been moderately successful. $\longrightarrow$	
(D)	The studies that revealed that people choose the foods they eat primarily on the basis of flavor also revealed that people rated as most flavorful those foods that were least nutritious. $\longrightarrow$	
(E)	In a study, subjects who were told that a given food was very flavorful were more willing to try the food and more likely to enjoy it than were subjects who were told that the food was nutritious. $\longrightarrow$	

PrepTest57 Sec2 Q5

421

Compare your prediction to that of the LSAT expert. Are you ready to evaluate the answer choices?

LSAT Question	Analysis
Studies reveal that most people select the foods they eat primarily on the basis of flavor, and that nutrition is usually a secondary concern at best. This suggests that health experts would have more success in encouraging people to eat wholesome foods if they emphasized how flavorful those foods truly are rather than how nutritious they are. $\longrightarrow$	**Step 2:** Conclusion—Experts will have more success selling people on how good a healthy food tastes than on how good it is for them. Evidence—Studies show people choose food based on taste more than on nutrition. Assumption—The author takes for granted that people will respond favorably to expert suggestions that correspond to their own preferences (flavor over nutrition).
Which one of the following, if true, most strengthens the argument above? $\longrightarrow$	**Step 1:** The correct answer will be a fact that makes the argument stronger. That is, it will make the conclusion more likely to follow from the evidence.
	Step 3: The correct answer needs to supply a fact suggesting that people are more likely to be convinced by claims about flavor than by those about nutrition.
(A) Most people currently believe that wholesome foods are more flavorful, on average, than unwholesome foods are. $\longrightarrow$	**Step 4:**
(B) Few people, when given a choice between foods that are flavorful but not nutritious and foods that are nutritious but not flavorful, will choose the foods that are nutritious but not flavorful. $\longrightarrow$	
(C) Health experts' attempts to encourage people to eat wholesome foods by emphasizing how nutritious those foods are have been moderately successful. $\longrightarrow$	
(D) The studies that revealed that people choose the foods they eat primarily on the basis of flavor also revealed that people rated as most flavorful those foods that were least nutritious. $\longrightarrow$	
(E) In a study, subjects who were told that a given food was very flavorful were more willing to try the food and more likely to enjoy it than were subjects who were told that the food was nutritious. $\longrightarrow$	

PrepTest57 Sec2 Q5

Step 4 is the payoff for your methodical approach. Zero in on the only choice that makes the argument stronger. Which is the only choice that makes it more likely that people will follow the experts' recommendations?

LSAT Question	My Analysis
Studies reveal that most people select the foods they eat primarily on the basis of flavor, and that nutrition is usually a secondary concern at best. This suggests that health experts would have more success in encouraging people to eat wholesome foods if they emphasized how flavorful those foods truly are rather than how nutritious they are.	**Step 2:** Conclusion—Experts will have more success selling people on how good a healthy food tastes than on how good it is for them. Evidence—Studies show people choose food based on taste more than on nutrition. Assumption—The author takes for granted that people will respond favorably to expert suggestions that correspond to their own preferences (flavor over nutrition).
Which one of the following, if true, most strengthens the argument above?	**Step 1:** The correct answer will be a fact that makes the argument stronger. That is, it will make the conclusion more likely to follow from the evidence.
	Step 3: The correct answer needs to supply a fact suggesting that people are more likely to be convinced by claims about flavor than by those about nutrition.
(A) Most people currently believe that wholesome foods are more flavorful, on average, than unwholesome foods are.	**Step 4:**
(B) Few people, when given a choice between foods that are flavorful but not nutritious and foods that are nutritious but not flavorful, will choose the foods that are nutritious but not flavorful.	
(C) Health experts' attempts to encourage people to eat wholesome foods by emphasizing how nutritious those foods are have been moderately successful.	
(D) The studies that revealed that people choose the foods they eat primarily on the basis of flavor also revealed that people rated as most flavorful those foods that were least nutritious.	
(E) In a study, subjects who were told that a given food was very flavorful were more willing to try the food and more likely to enjoy it than were subjects who were told that the food was nutritious.	

PrepTest57 Sec2 Q5

Compare your analysis to that of an LSAT expert. Did you select the correct answer? Was it clear to you why each wrong answer did not strengthen the argument?

LSAT Question	Analysis
Studies reveal that most people select the foods they eat primarily on the basis of flavor, and that nutrition is usually a secondary concern at best. This suggests that health experts would have more success in encouraging people to eat wholesome foods if they emphasized how flavorful those foods truly are rather than how nutritious they are. →	**Step 2:** Conclusion—Experts will have more success selling people on how good a healthy food tastes than on how good it is for them. Evidence—Studies show people choose food based on taste more than on nutrition. Assumption—The author takes for granted that people will respond favorably to expert suggestions that correspond to their own preferences (flavor over nutrition).
Which one of the following, if true, most strengthens the argument above? →	**Step 1:** The correct answer will be a fact that makes the argument stronger. That is, it will make the conclusion more likely to follow from the evidence.
	Step 3: The correct answer needs to supply a fact suggesting that people are more likely to be convinced by claims about flavor than by those about nutrition.
(A) Most people currently believe that wholesome foods are more flavorful, on average, than unwholesome foods are. →	**Step 4:** 180. If people already believe nutritious foods to be better tasting, then experts telling them so isn't likely to make them more successful. Eliminate.
(B) Few people, when given a choice between foods that are flavorful but not nutritious and foods that are nutritious but not flavorful, will choose the foods that are nutritious but not flavorful. →	Out of Scope. The argument is about telling people that nutritious foods are tasty, not about foods that are wholesome but bad tasting. Eliminate.
(C) Health experts' attempts to encourage people to eat wholesome foods by emphasizing how nutritious those foods are have been moderately successful. →	Out of Scope. The argument is about encouraging people to choose wholesome foods by telling them that these foods taste good. Eliminate.
(D) The studies that revealed that people choose the foods they eat primarily on the basis of flavor also revealed that people rated as most flavorful those foods that were least nutritious. →	180. This choice makes it less likely that people will be persuaded by the experts' suggestions. Eliminate.
(E) In a study, subjects who were told that a given food was very flavorful were more willing to try the food and more likely to enjoy it than were subjects who were told that the food was nutritious. →	Correct. This introduces a new study that found that people were more likely to try and to like foods they are *told* are flavorful, exactly what the experts would be telling people in the author's conclusion.

PrepTest57 Sec2 Q5

Practice

Try applying the Logical Reasoning Method to a few more questions. As you complete each step, think about how it prepares you to tackle the subsequent step more efficiently and effectively.

LSAT Question		My Analysis
1. Some political thinkers hope to devise a form of government in which every citizen's rights are respected. But such a form of government is impossible. For any government must be defined and controlled by laws that determine its powers and limits; and it is inevitable that some individuals will learn how to interpret these laws to gain a greater share of political power than others have.	→	**Step 2:**
Which one of the following is an assumption required by the argument?	→	**Step 1:**
		Step 3:
(A) In any form of government that leads to unequal distribution of political power, the rights of the majority of people will be violated.	→	**Step 4:**
(B) A government can ensure that every citizen's rights are respected by keeping the citizens ignorant of the laws.	→	
(C) Not all the laws that define a government's power and limits can be misinterpreted.	→	
(D) In any form of government, if anybody gains a greater share of political power than others have, then somebody's rights will be violated.	→	
(E) People who have more political power than others have tended to use it to acquire an even greater share of political power.	→	

PrepTest51 Sec3 Q2

LSAT Question		My Analysis
2. Politician: Most of those at the meeting were not persuaded by Kuyler's argument, nor should they have been, for Kuyler's argument implied that it would be improper to enter into a contract with the government; and yet—as many people know—Kuyler's company has had numerous lucrative contracts with the government.	→	**Step 2:**
Which one of the following describes a flaw in the politician's argument?	→	**Step 1:**
		Step 3:
(A) It concludes that an argument is defective merely on the grounds that the argument has failed to persuade anyone of the truth of its conclusion.	→	**Step 4:**
(B) It relies on testimony that is likely to be biased.	→	
(C) It rejects an argument merely on the grounds that the arguer has not behaved in a way that is consistent with the argument.	→	
(D) It rejects a position merely on the grounds that an inadequate argument has been given for it.	→	
(E) It rejects an argument on the basis of an appeal to popular opinion. *PrepTest57 Sec3 Q2*	→	

LSAT Question	My Analysis
3. Engineers are investigating the suitability of Wantastiquet Pass as the site of a new bridge. Because one concern is whether erosion could eventually weaken the bridge's foundations, they contracted for two reports on erosion in the region. Although both reports are accurate, one claims that the region suffers relatively little erosion, while the other claims that regional erosion is heavy and a cause for concern.	**Step 2:**
Which one of the following, if true, most helps to explain how both reports could be accurate?	**Step 1:**
	Step 3:
(A) Neither report presents an extensive chemical analysis of the soil in the region.	**Step 4:**
(B) Both reports include computer-enhanced satellite photographs.	
(C) One report was prepared by scientists from a university, while the other report was prepared by scientists from a private consulting firm.	
(D) One report focuses on regional topsoil erosion, while the other report focuses on riverbank erosion resulting from seasonal floods.	
(E) One report cost nearly twice as much to prepare as did the other report.	

PrepTest51 Sec3 Q8

LSAT Question	My Analysis
4. Over the last five years, every new major alternative-energy initiative that initially was promised government funding has since seen that funding severely curtailed. In no such case has the government come even close to providing the level of funds initially earmarked for these projects. Since large corporations have made it a point to discourage alternative-energy projects, it is likely that the corporations' actions influenced the government's funding decisions. $\longrightarrow$	**Step 2:**
Which one of the following, if true, most strengthens the reasoning above? $\longrightarrow$	**Step 1:**
	Step 3:
(A) For the past two decades, most alternative-energy initiatives have received little or no government funding. $\longrightarrow$	**Step 4:**
(B) The funding initially earmarked for a government project is always subject to change, given the mechanisms by which the political process operates. $\longrightarrow$	
(C) The only research projects whose government funding has been severely curtailed are those that large corporations have made it a point to discourage. $\longrightarrow$	
(D) Some projects encouraged by large corporations have seen their funding severely curtailed over the last five years. $\longrightarrow$	
(E) All large corporations have made it a point to discourage some forms of research. $\longrightarrow$	

PrepTest61 Sec2 Q6

Expert Analysis

Compare your work to that of an LSAT expert. As you review the following analysis, pay special attention to how the expert characterized each of the wrong answers.

LSAT Question	Analysis
1. Some political thinkers hope to devise a form of government in which every citizen's rights are respected. But such a form of government is impossible. For any government must be defined and controlled by laws that determine its powers and limits; and it is inevitable that some individuals will learn how to interpret these laws to gain a greater share of political power than others have.	**Step 2:** Conclusion—A form of government respecting every citizen's rights is impossible. → Evidence—1) Government must be defined and controlled by laws, and 2) some people will learn how to use the laws to gain more political power than others.
Which one of the following is an assumption required by the argument?	**Step 1:** The correct answer will be an unstated premise ("assumption") that must be true in order for the conclusion to be drawn from the evidence.
	Step 3: The author must assume that if some people have more political power, then not every citizen's rights can be respected.
(A) In any form of government that leads to unequal distribution of political power, the rights of the majority of people will be violated.	**Step 4:** Extreme. The argument assumes only that some citizen's rights will be violated, not that a majority of people's rights will. Eliminate.
(B) A government can ensure that every citizen's rights are respected by keeping the citizens ignorant of the laws.	Distortion. The author makes clear that some individuals will learn how to manipulate the laws. Moreover, there is no assumption about how to make sure everyone's rights are respected because the argument concludes that it is impossible to do so. Eliminate.
(C) Not all the laws that define a government's power and limits can be misinterpreted.	Extreme/Distortion. The evidence states that individuals will learn to distort laws to their own advantage. Whether that involves some or all of the laws is irrelevant. Eliminate.
(D) In any form of government, if anybody gains a greater share of political power than others have, then somebody's rights will be violated.	Correct. This assumption is necessary to the argument. If (D) is not true, then the evidence in the argument does not support the conclusion.
(E) People who have more political power than others have tend to use it to acquire an even greater share of political power. *PrepTest51 Sec3 Q2*	Outside the Scope. Whether an initial imbalance in political power leads to greater imbalance is beyond the purview of the argument. Eliminate.

LSAT Question	Analysis
2. Politician: Most of those at the meeting were not persuaded by Kuyler's argument, nor should they have been, for Kuyler's argument implied that it would be improper to enter into a contract with the government; and yet—as many people know—Kuyler's company has had numerous lucrative contracts with the government.	**Step 2:** Conclusion—Kuyler is wrong to imply that entering into a government contract would be improper. Evidence—Kuyler's company has entered into many lucrative government contracts.
Which one of the following describes a flaw in the politician's argument?	**Step 1:** The correct answer describes a mistake in the politician's reasoning.
	Step 3: The author assumes that Kuyler's conclusion is incorrect because Kuyler is a hypocrite.
(A) It concludes that an argument is defective merely on the grounds that the argument has failed to persuade anyone of the truth of its conclusion.	**Step 4:** Distortion. The politician states that "*most of those at the meeting were not persuaded.*" Moreover, the politician doesn't attack Kuyler for his failure to persuade but for his hypocrisy. Eliminate.
(B) It relies on testimony that is likely to be biased.	Outside the Scope. The politician's argument is not supported by any testimony. Eliminate.
(C) It rejects an argument merely on the grounds that the arguer has not behaved in a way that is consistent with the argument.	Correct. This summarizes the flaw of arguing ad hominem. Kuyler's conclusion may be right even though his behavior is hypocritical.
(D) It rejects a position merely on the grounds that an inadequate argument has been given for it.	Outside the Scope. The politician doesn't even say what Kuyler's argument was; he just attacks Kuyler's conclusion because of Kuyler's behavior. Eliminate.
(E) It rejects an argument on the basis of an appeal to popular opinion. *PrepTest57 Sec3 Q2*	Outside the Scope. There is no suggestion that the notion that Kuyler is a hypocrite is a popular opinion. Eliminate.

TEST DAY TIP

On Test Day, when you are confident that an answer matches your prediction and is correct, circle it and move on. In practice, however, reviewing every answer choice is recommended.

LSAT Question	Analysis
3. Engineers are investigating the suitability of Wantastiquet Pass as the site of a new bridge. Because one concern is whether erosion could eventually weaken the bridge's foundations, they contracted for two reports on erosion in the region. Although both reports are accurate, one claims that the region suffers relatively little erosion, while the other claims that regional erosion is heavy and a cause for concern.	**Step 2:** Two studies looked at erosion near a bridge. Both are accurate. Report 1—Relatively little erosion Report 2—Heavy erosion
Which one of the following, if true, most helps to explain how both reports could be accurate?	**Step 1:** The correct answer will provide a fact that explains how two (apparently contradictory) reports can both be true.
	Step 3: For two reports to be accurate, and yet reach opposite conclusions, they must be studying different things. The correct answer will explain this.
(A) Neither report presents an extensive chemical analysis of the soil in the region.	**Step 4:** 180. This is yet another way in which the studies are similar. Eliminate.
(B) Both reports include computer-enhanced satellite photographs.	180. This is yet another way in which the studies are similar. Eliminate.
(C) One report was prepared by scientists from a university, while the other report was prepared by scientists from a private consulting firm.	Irrelevant Comparison. The fact that different people ran the two studies doesn't explain how both can be accurate. Eliminate.
(D) One report focuses on regional topsoil erosion, while the other report focuses on riverbank erosion resulting from seasonal floods.	Correct. If the reports studied two different kinds of erosion, they may reach opposite conclusions without one being incorrect.
(E) One report cost nearly twice as much to prepare as did the other report. *PrepTest51 Sec3 Q8*	Irrelevant Comparison. The fact that the reports cost a different amount doesn't explain how both can be correct. Eliminate.

LSAT Question	Analysis
4. Over the last five years, every new major alternative-energy initiative that initially was promised government funding has since seen that funding severely curtailed. In no such case has the government come even close to providing the level of funds initially earmarked for these projects. Since large corporations have made it a point to discourage alternative-energy projects, it is likely that the corporations' actions influenced the government's funding decisions.	**Step 2:** Conclusion—Corporate influence is the reason the government has cut alternative energy funding. → Evidence—Corporations have worked to discourage alternative energy projects, and funding for those projects has been cut.
Which one of the following, if true, most strengthens the reasoning above?	**Step 1:** The correct answer provides a fact that strengthens the argument; it will make the conclusion more likely to follow from the evidence.
	Step 3: The author assumes that corporate influence (and not some other factor) is the cause of the reduction in government funding. The correct answer will make it more likely that corporate influence was the cause of the funding cuts, or will rule out some other possible reason.
(A) For the past two decades, most alternative-energy initiatives have received little or no government funding.	**Step 4:** Outside the Scope. The argument is about *why* alternative energy research has been cut. The fact that it has not been funded for a long time doesn't make the author's assertion that corporate opposition is the cause any more or any less likely. Eliminate.
(B) The funding initially earmarked for a government project is always subject to change, given the mechanisms by which the political process operates.	Outside the Scope. A general statement about the uncertainties of government funding doesn't make the author's assertion about the cause of alternative energy program funding cuts any more or any less likely. Eliminate.
(C) The only research projects whose government funding has been severely curtailed are those that large corporations have made it a point to discourage.	Correct. If research projects not opposed by corporations have continued to be funded, it is less likely that the alternative energy programs were simply victims of overall cost cutting measures.
(D) Some projects encouraged by large corporations have seen their funding severely curtailed over the last five years.	180. This suggests that corporate influence is not all powerful. If even projects that corporations support have been cut, maybe the alternative energy programs were cut for other reasons, too. Eliminate.
(E) All large corporations have made it a point to discourage some forms of research. *PrepTest61 Sec2 Q6*	Extreme. This blanket statement about corporate behavior does not make it more likely that corporate influence was the cause of these research cuts. Eliminate.

WRONG ANSWERS IN LOGICAL REASONING QUESTIONS

As you reviewed the analysis of the practice questions, you probably noticed that certain wrong-answer types appeared several times. While not every wrong answer fits neatly into one of the following types identified (and, arguably, some wrong answers fit into more than one category), an LSAT expert can use the common wrong-answer types to quickly and confidently eliminate dozens of wrong answers on Test Day.

LOGICAL REASONING: WRONG ANSWER TYPES

- **Outside the Scope**—A choice containing a statement that is too broad, too narrow, or beyond the purview of the stimulus, making the statement in the choice irrelevant
- **Irrelevant Comparison**—A choice that compares two items or attributes in a way not germane to the author's argument or statements
- **Extreme**—A choice containing language too emphatic to be supported by the stimulus; Extreme choices are often (though not always) characterized by words such as *all*, *never*, *every*, or *none*
- **Distortion**—A choice that mentions details from the stimulus but mangles or misstates the relationship between those details as implied by the author
- **180**—A choice that directly contradicts what the correct answer must say (for example, a choice that strengthens the argument in a Weaken question)
- **Faulty Use of Detail**—A choice that accurately states something from the stimulus but in a manner that answers the question incorrectly; this type is rarely used

The bottom line is that every wrong answer is wrong because it does not answer the question posed by the question stem. As you continue to study, practice, and review, make a point of explaining in your own words *why* each wrong answer is incorrect.

LSAT STRATEGY

Some wrong answers apply to specific question types. In Assumption and Main Point questions, for example, it is common to see wrong answers that simply repeat the author's evidence. You'll see more question-specific wrong answers as you move through the following chapters and learn why they are incorrect on the exam.

REFLECTION

Take a moment and look back over the work you did in this chapter. Reflect on the following questions:

- How does the Logical Reasoning Method help you tackle questions more efficiently?
- Were you consistently predicting what the correct answer would say before evaluating the choices?
- How does predicting the correct answer help you to eliminate wrong answer choices?
- If you have practiced LSAT Logical Reasoning questions before now, how will your approach to these questions change going forward?

In the following chapters, you will learn how to identify and answer all of the questions in the Logical Reasoning sections of the LSAT. Along the way, you'll build the skills that these questions are designed to reward. Some Logical Reasoning questions zero in on one skill, but most test several reading and thinking skills in combination. Chapters 9 and 10 are arranged so that you begin with the most fundamental skills and work your way to some of the most challenging and complex problems on the test.

CHAPTER 9

Argument-Based Questions

On the LSAT, the word *argument* does not refer to a dispute between two people. An LSAT argument is one person's attempt to convince the reader that some assertion is true or that some action is advisable. LSAT arguments are defined by two explicit components: the *conclusion* and the *evidence*.

LSAT STRATEGY

Every LSAT argument contains:

- A conclusion—The assertion, evaluation, or recommendation about which the author is trying to convince his readers
- Evidence—The facts, studies, or contentions the author believes support or establish the conclusion

The question types covered in this chapter—Main Point, Role of a Statement, Method of Argument, and Point at Issue questions—directly reward your ability to identify, paraphrase, and describe the explicit parts of the argument.

The Assumption Family questions covered in Chapter 10 add your ability to determine the implicit part of an argument—the assumption—to the skills. This is the most important group of Logical Reasoning question types.

Taken together, Argument-Based and Assumption Family questions account for over 75 percent of Logical Reasoning questions on recent LSATs. That's more than one-third of your score on the entire test.

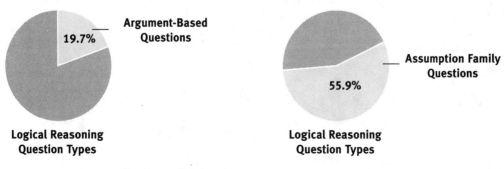

PrepTests 57–71; released 2009–2013

CONCLUSIONS AND MAIN POINT QUESTIONS

LEARNING OBJECTIVES

In this section, you'll learn to:

· Identify the conclusion in an LSAT argument
· Characterize and paraphrase the conclusion
· Identify and answer Main Point questions

All Argument-Based and Assumption Family questions reward your ability to identify an argument's conclusion. Main Point questions, like the one that follows, test this skill directly.

Editorial: Almost every year the Smithfield River floods the coastal fishing community of Redhook, which annually spends $3 million on the cleanup. Some residents have proposed damming the river, which would cost $5 million but would prevent the flooding. However, their position is misguided. A dam would prevent nutrients in the river from flowing into the ocean. Fish that now feed on those nutrients would start feeding elsewhere. The loss of these fish would cost Redhook $10 million annually.

Which one of the following most accurately expresses the main conclusion of the editorial's argument?

(A) The Smithfield River should be dammed to prevent flooding.
(B) Nutrients from the Smithfield River are essential to the local fish population.
(C) Damming the Smithfield River is not worth the high construction costs for such a project.
(D) For Redhook to build a dam on the Smithfield River would be a mistake.
(E) The Smithfield River floods cost Redhook $3 million every year.

PrepTest51 Sec1 Q1

Identify the Conclusion

The conclusion of an argument is the author's main point: the statement she hopes to convince the reader is true.

Conclusion Keywords
Many LSAT arguments include Keywords that highlight the conclusion.

LSAT Question	Analysis
Vanwilligan: Some have argued that professional athletes receive unfairly high salaries. But in an unrestricted free market, such as the market these athletes compete in, salaries are determined by what someone else is willing to pay for their services. These athletes make enormous profits for their teams' owners, and that is why owners are willing to pay them extraordinary salaries. Thus the salaries they receive are fair. *PrepTest49 Sec2 Q19*	*Thus* signals the author's conclusion: *The salaries professional athletes receive are fair.*

LSAT STRATEGY

Conclusion Keywords include:

- Thus
- Therefore
- As a result
- It follows that

- Consequently
- So
- [Evidence] is evidence that [conclusion]

Now, you try it. Circle the conclusion Keyword and mark the conclusion in the following argument.

> Editorial: Clearly, during the past two years, the unemployment situation in our city has been improving. Studies show that the number of unemployed people who are actively looking for jobs has steadily decreased during that period.
>
> *PrepTest49 Sec4 Q1*

Clearly is a conclusion Keyword. The argument's main point is: Unemployment in our city has been improving over the past two years.

TEST DAY TIP

Bracket the conclusion of an argument in your test booklet. Get in the habit of doing this on all Argument-Based and Assumption Family questions.

Subsidiary conclusions

Not every conclusion Keyword signals the author's main point or final conclusion. Some arguments on the LSAT contain subsidiary or intermediate conclusions.

LSAT Question	Analysis
Economist: As should be obvious, raising the minimum wage significantly would make it more expensive for businesses to pay workers for minimum-wage jobs. Therefore, businesses could not afford to continue to employ as many workers for such jobs. So raising the minimum wage significantly will cause an increase in unemployment. *PrepTest57 Sec3 Q6*	Conclusion: *So* signals the author's main point: *Significantly increasing the minimum wage will increase unemployment.* *Therefore* signals a subsidiary conclusion that serves as evidence for the main point.

What is a subsidiary conclusion?

How can you distinguish a subsidiary conclusion from the argument's main point?

Evidence Keywords

In other LSAT arguments, evidence Keywords signal the support for the author's conclusion.

LSAT Question	Analysis
In a poll of a representative sample of a province's residents, the provincial capital was the city most often selected as the best place to live in that province. Since the capital is also the largest of that province's many cities, the poll shows that most residents of that province generally prefer life in large cities to life in small cities.	The Keyword *Since* signals the evidence in the argument. The conclusion begins after the comma in that sentence:
PrepTest51 Sec1 Q18	*The poll shows that most in the province prefer life in big cities to life in small cities.*

LSAT STRATEGY

Evidence Keywords include:

- Because
- Since
- [Evidence] is evidence of [conclusion]
- After all
- For

Now you try it. Circle the evidence Keyword(s) and mark the conclusion in the following argument.

There is a difference between beauty and truth. After all, if there were no difference, then the most realistic pieces of art would be the best as well, since the most realistic pieces are the most truthful. But many of the most realistic artworks are not among the best.

PrepTest49 Sec4 Q16

After all and [S]*ince* are evidence Keywords. The argument's main point is the first sentence: Beauty and truth are not the same.

Conclusion from context
Still other LSAT arguments contain neither conclusion nor evidence Keywords.

LSAT Question	Analysis
It is due to a misunderstanding that most modern sculpture is monochromatic. When ancient sculptures were exhumed years ago, they were discovered to be uncolored. No one at the time had reason to believe, as we now do, that the sculptures had originally been colorfully painted, but that centuries of exposure to moisture washed away the paint. *PrepTest49 Sec4 Q13*	Conclusion: *Modern sculpture is monochromatic due to a mistaken understanding.* $\longrightarrow$ The facts in the rest of the argument are offered to support the first sentence.

How can you identify a conclusion when there are no Keywords to signal evidence or conclusion in an argument? Is the author's main point still clear?

Conclusion as a negation of opponent's point
In one other case, the author's conclusion is an assertion that another person's position is incorrect.

LSAT Question	Analysis
Musicologist: Many critics complain of the disproportion between text and music in Handel's *da capo* arias. These texts are generally quite short and often repeated well beyond what is needed for literal understanding. Yet such criticism is refuted by noting that repetition serves a vital function: it frees the audience to focus on the music itself, which can speak to audiences whatever their language. *PrepTest61 Sec 4 Q6*	Conclusion: Those who say that the disproportion between text and music is a weakness in Handel's *da capo* arias are wrong. $\longrightarrow$ The author's conclusion says that "such criticism is refuted," referring to those who criticize the disproportion between text and music in Handel's *da capo* arias.

How do you incorporate the author's opponent's position into a statement of the author's conclusion?

Practice

Circle conclusion and evidence Keywords and mark the conclusion in each of the following arguments.

LSAT Question	My Analysis
1. 1990 editorial: Local pay phone calls have cost a quarter apiece ever since the 1970s, when a soft drink from a vending machine cost about the same. The price of a soft drink has more than doubled since, so phone companies should be allowed to raise the price of pay phone calls too. $\longrightarrow$ *PrepTest49 Sec2 Q8*	
2. Scientist: A controversy in paleontology centers on the question of whether prehistoric human ancestors began to develop sophisticated tools before or after they came to stand upright. I argue that they stood upright first, simply because advanced toolmaking requires free use of the hands, and standing upright makes this possible. $\longrightarrow$ *PrepTest49 Sec2 Q14*	
3. Eating garlic reduces the levels of cholesterol and triglycerides in the blood and so helps reduce the risk of cardiovascular disease. Evidence that eating garlic reduces these levels is that a group of patients taking a garlic tablet each day for four months showed a 12 percent reduction in cholesterol and a 17 percent reduction in triglycerides; over the same period, a group of similar patients taking a medically inert tablet showed only a 2 percent reduction in triglycerides and a 3 percent reduction in cholesterol. $\longrightarrow$ *PrepTest49 Sec4 Q2*	
4. Letter to the editor: Middle-class families in wealthy nations are often criticized for the ecological damage resulting from their lifestyles. This criticism should not be taken too seriously, however, since its source is often a movie star or celebrity whose own lifestyle would, if widely adopted, destroy the environment and deplete our resources in a short time. $\longrightarrow$ *PrepTest49 Sec2 Q5*	

Expert Analysis

Here's how an LSAT expert might identify the conclusion in each of the previous arguments.

LSAT Question	Analysis
1. 1990 editorial: Local pay phone calls have cost a quarter apiece ever since the 1970s, when a soft drink from a vending machine cost about the same. The price of a soft drink has more than doubled since, so phone companies should be allowed to raise the price of pay phone calls too. *PrepTest49 Sec2 Q8*	*So* identifies the conclusion: Phone companies should be allowed to raise the price of pay phone calls.
2. Scientist: A controversy in paleontology centers on the question of whether prehistoric human ancestors began to develop sophisticated tools before or after they came to stand upright. I argue that they stood upright first, simply because advanced toolmaking requires free use of the hands, and standing upright makes this possible. *PrepTest49 Sec2 Q14*	*I argue that* signals the conclusion: Human ancestors stood upright before developing sophisticated tools.
3. Eating garlic reduces the levels of cholesterol and triglycerides in the blood and so helps reduce the risk of cardiovascular disease. Evidence that eating garlic reduces these levels is that a group of patients taking a garlic tablet each day for four months showed a 12 percent reduction in cholesterol and a 17 percent reduction in triglycerides; over the same period, a group of similar patients taking a medically inert tablet showed only a 2 percent reduction in triglycerides and a 3 percent reduction in cholesterol. *PrepTest49 Sec4 Q2*	[A]nd so signals the author's main point: Eating garlic helps reduce the risk of cardiovascular disease. The first part of the sentence gives the author's reason, and the word [e]vidence at the start of the second sentence indicates that the rest of the argument supports that reason.
4. Letter to the editor: Middle-class families in wealthy nations are often criticized for the ecological damage resulting from their lifestyles. This criticism should not be taken too seriously, however, since its source is often a movie star or celebrity whose own lifestyle would, if widely adopted, destroy the environment and deplete our resources in a short time. *PrepTest49 Sec2 Q5*	The letter writer negates a common criticism. The idea that middle-class lifestyles damage the environment, the author says, "should not be taken too seriously."

Paraphrase and Characterize the Conclusion

Once you can spot conclusions, the next skill is understanding what they mean. LSAT arguments don't always use the simplest or most succinct language. Paraphrasing the conclusion is important because, in some questions, the LSAT will paraphrase the author's conclusion in the answer choices. Moreover, paraphrasing simplifies the argument and makes it easier to zero in on the author's main point.

Here's how an LSAT expert might simplify a fairly complex conclusion.

LSAT Question	Analysis
From the fact that people who studied music as children frequently are quite proficient at mathematics, it cannot be concluded that the skills required for mathematics are acquired by studying music: it is equally likely that proficiency in mathematics and studying music are both the result of growing up in a family that encourages its children to excel at all intellectual and artistic endeavors. *PrepTest49 Sec4 Q17*	A colon usually signals evidence, because it leads to further explanation or examples. The author's conclusion is the first sentence. *Being good at music is correlated with being good at math, but that doesn't mean that the person's math skills came from studying music.*

Paraphrasing is made easier by knowing that nearly all LSAT conclusions fall into one of six categories.

LSAT STRATEGY

The conclusions of LSAT arguments almost always match one of these six types:

1. Prediction (X *will* or *will not* happen in the future)
2. Recommendation (we *should* or *should not* do X)
3. Comparison (X is taller/shorter/more common/less common/etc. than Y)
4. Assertion of Fact (X is true or X is false)
5. If/Then (a conditional prediction, recommendation, or assertion; e.g., If X is true, then so is Y or If you are an M, you should do N)
6. Value Judgment (an evaluative statement; e.g., Action X is unethical or Y's recital was poorly sung)

Identify the conclusion type in each of the following examples.

Conclusion		My Analysis
a.	It is likely, therefore, that the level of carbon dioxide in the atmosphere was significantly higher than it is today.	→ *[H]igher than* makes this conclusion a[n]
b.	Obviously, our society values sports more than it values education.	→ *[M]ore than* makes this conclusion a[n]
c.	It is time to put a halt to this trivial journalism.	→ *It is time to* makes this conclusion a[n]
d.	I maintain, however, that to save lives, automobile manufacturers ought to stop equipping cars with them.	→ *[O]ught* makes this conclusion a[n]
e.	Therefore, criminal organizations will undoubtedly try to become increasingly involved in these areas.	→ *[W]ill* makes this conclusion a[n]
f.	This shows that a decrease in humidity can make people ill.	→ *[A] … can* makes this conclusion a[n]
g.	However, the editorial is unfair.	→ *[U]nfair* makes this conclusion a[n]
h.	So if the screen is to be a hedge, it will be a hemlock hedge.	→ *[I]f … will* makes this conclusion a[n]

a. Comparison; b. Comparison; c. Recommendation; d. Recommendation; e. Prediction; f. Assertion of fact; g. Value Judgment; h. If/Then, Prediction

Practice

Identify, characterize, and paraphrase the conclusion in each of the following arguments.

LSAT Question	My Analysis
5. Ecologists predict that the incidence of malaria will increase if global warming continues or if the use of pesticides is not expanded. But the use of pesticides is known to contribute to global warming, so it is inevitable that we will see an increase in malaria in the years to come. *PrepTest51 Sec3 Q24*	Paraphrase: Type:
6. Bethany: Psychologists have discovered a technique for replacing one's nightmares with pleasant dreams, and have successfully taught it to adults suffering from chronic nightmares. Studies have found that nightmare-prone children are especially likely to suffer from nightmares as adults. Thus, psychologists should direct efforts toward identifying nightmare-prone children so that these children can be taught the technique for replacing their nightmares with pleasant dreams. *PrepTest59 Sec2 Q13*	Paraphrase: Type:
7. Pundit: The average salary for teachers in our society is lower than the average salary for athletes. Obviously, our society values sports more than it values education. *PrepTest51 Sec3 Q4*	Paraphrase: Type:
8. A recent study confirms that nutritious breakfasts make workers more productive. For one month, workers at Plant A received free nutritious breakfasts every day before work, while workers in Plant B did not. The productivity of Plant A's workers increased, while that of Plant B's workers did not. *PrepTest59 Sec 2 Q22*	Paraphrase: Type:
9. Team captain: Winning requires the willingness to cooperate, which in turn requires motivation. So you will not win if you are not motivated. *PrepTest57 Sec2 Q19*	Paraphrase: Type:

LSAT Question	**My Analysis**
10. Sometimes one reads a poem and believes that the poem expresses contradictory ideas, even if it is a great poem. So it is wrong to think that the meaning of a poem is whatever the author intends to communicate to the reader by means of the poem. No one who is writing a great poem intends it to communicate contradictory ideas. *PrepTest57 Sec2 Q24*	Paraphrase: Type:
11. Engineer: Thermophotovoltaic generators are devices that convert heat into electricity. The process of manufacturing steel produces huge amounts of heat that currently go to waste. So if steel-manufacturing plants could feed the heat they produce into thermophotovoltaic generators, they would greatly reduce their electric bills, thereby saving money. *PrepTest61 Sec2 Q16*	Paraphrase: Type:
12. Scientist: A controversy in paleontology centers on the question of whether prehistoric human ancestors began to develop sophisticated tools before or after they came to stand upright. I argue that they stood upright first, simply because advanced toolmaking requires free use of the hands, and standing upright makes this possible. *PrepTest49 Sec2 Q14*	Paraphrase: Type:
13. Archaeologist: After the last ice age, groups of paleohumans left Siberia and crossed the Bering land bridge, which no longer exists, into North America. Archaeologists have discovered in Siberia a cache of Clovis points—the distinctive stone spear points made by paleohumans. This shows that, contrary to previous belief, the Clovis point was not invented in North America. *PrepTest57 Sec2 Q22*	Paraphrase: Type:

LSAT Question	**My Analysis**
14. In a poll of a representative sample of a province's residents, the provincial capital was the city most often selected as the best place to live in that province. Since the capital is also the largest of that province's many cities, the poll shows that most residents of that province generally prefer life in large cities to life in small cities. *PrepTest51 Sec1 Q18*	Paraphrase: → Type:
15. Essayist: Lessing contended that an art form's medium dictates the kind of representation the art form must employ in order to be legitimate; painting, for example, must represent simultaneous arrays of colored shapes, while literature, consisting of words read in succession, must represent events or actions occurring in sequence. The claim about literature must be rejected, however, if one regards as legitimate the imagists' poems, which consist solely of amalgams of disparate images. *PrepTest57 Sec2 Q7*	Paraphrase: → Type:
16. The typological theory of species classification, which has few adherents today, distinguishes species solely on the basis of observable physical characteristics, such as plumage color, adult size, or dental structure. However, there are many so-called "sibling species," which are indistinguishable on the basis of their appearance but cannot interbreed and thus, according to the mainstream biological theory of species classification, are separate species. Since the typological theory does not count sibling species as separate species, it is unacceptable. *PrepTest51 Sec1 Q15*	Paraphrase: → Type:

Expert Analysis

Here's how an LSAT expert might paraphrase and categorize the conclusions in the previous arguments.

LSAT Question	Analysis
5. Ecologists predict that the incidence of malaria will increase if global warming continues or if the use of pesticides is not expanded. But the use of pesticides is known to contribute to global warming, so it is inevitable that we will see an increase in malaria in the years to come. *PrepTest51 Sec3 Q24*	Paraphrase: A rise in malaria is inevitable. Type: Prediction
6. Bethany: Psychologists have discovered a technique for replacing one's nightmares with pleasant dreams, and have successfully taught it to adults suffering from chronic nightmares. Studies have found that nightmare-prone children are especially likely to suffer from nightmares as adults. Thus, psychologists should direct efforts toward identifying nightmare-prone children so that these children can be taught the technique for replacing their nightmares with pleasant dreams. *PrepTest59 Sec2 Q13*	Paraphrase: Psychologists should focus on identifying nightmare-prone children (so that the kids can benefit from the new technique). Type: Recommendation
7. Pundit: The average salary for teachers in our society is lower than the average salary for athletes. Obviously, our society values sports more than it values education. *PrepTest51 Sec3 Q4*	Paraphrase: Our society values sports more than it does education. Type: Comparison
8. A recent study confirms that nutritious breakfasts make workers more productive. For one month, workers at Plant A received free nutritious breakfasts every day before work, while workers in Plant B did not. The productivity of Plant A's workers increased, while that of Plant B's workers did not. *PrepTest59 Sec 2 Q22*	Paraphrase: Eating a nutritious breakfast causes an increase in worker productivity. Type: Assertion of fact
9. Team captain: Winning requires the willingness to cooperate, which in turn requires motivation. So you will not win if you are not motivated. *PrepTest57 Sec2 Q19*	Paraphrase: Motivation is necessary for winning. If win → motivated. If not motivated → not win. Type: If/Then, Assertion of fact

LSAT Question	Analysis
10. Sometimes one reads a poem and believes that the poem expresses contradictory ideas, even if it is a great poem. So it is wrong to think that the meaning of a poem is whatever the author intends to communicate to the reader by means of the poem. No one who is writing a great poem intends it to communicate contradictory ideas. *PrepTest57 Sec2 Q24*	Paraphrase: A poem's meaning is *not* determined by the author's intent. → Type: Assertion of fact
11. Engineer: Thermophotovoltaic generators are devices that convert heat into electricity. The process of manufacturing steel produces huge amounts of heat that currently go to waste. So if steel-manufacturing plants could feed the heat they produce into thermophotovoltaic generators, they would greatly reduce their electric bills, thereby saving money. *PrepTest61 Sec2 Q16*	Paraphrase: If steel plants could cycle heat into TP generators, then they would save money on electricity. → Type: If/Then, Prediction
12. Scientist: A controversy in paleontology centers on the question of whether prehistoric human ancestors began to develop sophisticated tools before or after they came to stand upright. I argue that they stood upright first, simply because advanced toolmaking requires free use of the hands, and standing upright makes this possible. *PrepTest49 Sec2 Q14*	Paraphrase: Human ancestors stood upright before they developed sophisticated tools. → Type: Assertion of fact
13. Archaeologist: After the last ice age, groups of paleohumans left Siberia and crossed the Bering land bridge, which no longer exists, into North America. Archaeologists have discovered in Siberia a cache of Clovis points—the distinctive stone spear points made by paleohumans. This shows that, contrary to previous belief, the Clovis point was not invented in North America. *PrepTest57 Sec2 Q22*	Paraphrase: The Clovis point was not invented in North America. → Type: Assertion of fact

LSAT Question	Analysis
14. In a poll of a representative sample of a province's residents, the provincial capital was the city most often selected as the best place to live in that province. Since the capital is also the largest of that province's many cities, the poll shows that most residents of that province generally prefer life in large cities to life in small cities. *PrepTest51 Sec1 Q18*	Paraphrase: Most residents of the province prefer big-city life to life in small cities. Type: Comparison
15. Essayist: Lessing contended that an art form's medium dictates the kind of representation the art form must employ in order to be legitimate; painting, for example, must represent simultaneous arrays of colored shapes, while literature, consisting of words read in succession, must represent events or actions occurring in sequence. The claim about literature must be rejected, however, if one regards as legitimate the imagists' poems, which consist solely of amalgams of disparate images. *PrepTest57 Sec2 Q7*	Paraphrase: Literature does not have to depict events in sequence. Type: Assertion of fact, If/Then
16. The typological theory of species classification, which has few adherents today, distinguishes species solely on the basis of observable physical characteristics, such as plumage color, adult size, or dental structure. However, there are many so-called "sibling species," which are indistinguishable on the basis of their appearance but cannot interbreed and thus, according to the mainstream biological theory of species classification, are separate species. Since the typological theory does not count sibling species as separate species, it is unacceptable. *PrepTest51 Sec1 Q15*	Paraphrase: The typological theory is unacceptable. Type: Value judgment

Identify and Answer Main Point Questions

Separating an author's main conclusion from her evidence is so critical on the LSAT that there is even a question type—Main Point questions—that asks you to do only that.

You can identify Main Point questions from question stems such as these:

Which one of the following most accurately expresses the main conclusion of the argument?

PrepTest59 Sec2 Q10

Which one of the following sentences best expresses the main point of the musicologist's reasoning?

PrepTest61 Sec4 Q6

Which one of the following most accurately expresses the conclusion of the argument as a whole?

PrepTest57 Sec3 Q3

MAIN POINT AT A GLANCE

Task: Identify the argument's main conclusion.

Strategies: Use conclusion Keywords, evidence Keywords, subsidiary conclusions, and/or the argument's structure to distinguish the author's main point from her supporting evidence.

Main Point questions are not prevalent; on LSAT tests released from 2009 through 2013, there were an average of 2.5 Main Point questions per test. But remember that being able to identify and understand an argument's conclusion is a skill involved in more than 75 percent of Logical Reasoning questions.

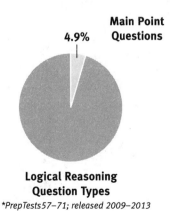

Main Point Questions

4.9%

**Logical Reasoning
Question Types**
PrepTests57–71; released 2009–2013

Here's how an LSAT expert might apply the Logical Reasoning Method to a Main Point question.

LSAT Question	Analysis
Editorial: Almost every year the Smithfield River floods the coastal fishing community of Redhook, which annually spends $3 million on the cleanup. Some residents have proposed damming the river, which would cost $5 million but would prevent the flooding. However, their position is misguided. A dam would prevent nutrients in the river from flowing into the ocean. Fish that now feed on those nutrients would start feeding elsewhere. The loss of these fish would cost Redhook $10 million annually.	**Step 2:** Conclusion: Their [some residents'] position [damming the river] is misguided. The rest of the facts are offered to support the author's rebuttal of those who advocate for a dam or as background context to the debate.
Which one of the following most accurately expresses the main conclusion of the editorial's argument?	**Step 1:** A Main Point question: The correct answer will paraphrase the argument's final conclusion.
	Step 3: The correct answer will paraphrase the main point: Damming the river is a bad idea.
(A) The Smithfield River should be dammed to prevent flooding.	**Step 4:** 180. The author's conclusion rejects this view. Eliminate.
(B) Nutrients from the Smithfield River are essential to the local fish population.	This is part of the author's evidence for why building a dam would be a bad idea. Eliminate.
(C) Damming the Smithfield River is not worth the high construction costs for such a project.	The author mentions the cost of construction when describing "some residents'" argument, but his discussion of costs is in the evidence. Eliminate.
(D) For Redhook to build a dam on the Smithfield River would be a mistake.	Correct. This matches the conclusion of the stimulus argument.
(E) The Smithfield River floods cost Redhook $3 million every year. *PrepTest51 Sec1 Q1*	This is background to the debate over damming the river. Eliminate.

Practice

Follow the Logical Reasoning Method to answer each of the following Main Point questions.

LSAT Question	My Analysis
17. Musicologist: Classification of a musical instrument depends on the mechanical action through which it produces music. So the piano is properly called a percussion instrument, not a stringed instrument. Even though the vibration of the piano's strings is what makes its sound, the strings are caused to vibrate by the impact of hammers.	Step 2:
Which one of the following most accurately expresses the main conclusion of the musicologist's argument?	Step 1:
	Step 3:
(A) Musical instruments should be classified according to the mechanical actions through which they produce sound.	Step 4:
(B) Musical instruments should not be classified based on the way musicians interact with them.	
(C) Some people classify the piano as a stringed instrument because of the way the piano produces sound.	
(D) The piano should be classified as a stringed instrument rather than as a percussion instrument.	
(E) It is correct to classify the piano as a percussion instrument rather than as a stringed instrument.	

PrepTest61 Sec2 Q9

LSAT Question	My Analysis

18. Chemical fertilizers not only create potential health hazards, they also destroy earthworms, which are highly beneficial to soil. For this reason alone the use of chemical fertilizers should be avoided. The castings earthworms leave behind are much richer than the soil they ingest, thus making a garden rich in earthworms much more fertile than a garden without them.

$\longrightarrow$ **Step 2:**

Which one of the following most accurately expresses the main conclusion of the argument? $\longrightarrow$ **Step 1:**

Step 3:

(A) Earthworms are highly beneficial to soil. **Step 4:**

$\longrightarrow$

(B) Chemical fertilizers destroy earthworms.

$\longrightarrow$

(C) The castings that earthworms leave behind are much richer than the soil they ingest.

$\longrightarrow$

(D) The use of chemical fertilizers should be avoided.

$\longrightarrow$

(E) A garden rich in earthworms is much more fertile than a garden that is devoid of earthworms.

$\longrightarrow$

PrepTest59 Sec2 Q10

LSAT Question	My Analysis

19. Although free international trade allows countries to specialize, which in turn increases productivity, such specialization carries risks. After all, small countries often rely on one or two products for the bulk of their exports. If those products are raw materials, the supply is finite and can be used up. If they are foodstuffs, a natural disaster can wipe out a season's production overnight.

$\longrightarrow$

Step 2:

Which one of the following most accurately expresses the conclusion of the argument as a whole?

$\longrightarrow$

Step 1:

Step 3:

(A) Specialization within international trade comes with risks.

$\longrightarrow$

Step 4:

(B) A natural disaster can destroy a whole season's production overnight, devastating a small country's economy.

$\longrightarrow$

(C) A small country's supply of raw materials can be used up in a short period.

$\longrightarrow$

(D) Some countries rely on a small number of products for the export-based sectors of their economies.

$\longrightarrow$

(E) When international trade is free, countries can specialize in what they export.

$\longrightarrow$

PrepTest57 Sec3 Q3

455

LSAT Question		My Analysis
20. Manager: There is no good reason to suppose that promoting creativity is a proper goal of an employee training program. Many jobs require little or no creativity and, in those positions, using creativity is more likely to be disruptive than innovative. Furthermore, even if creativity were in demand, there is no evidence that it can be taught.	⟶	**Step 2:**
Which one of the following most accurately expresses the main conclusion drawn in the manager's argument?	⟶	**Step 1:**
		Step 3:
(A) Using creativity in jobs that require little or no creativity can be disruptive.	⟶	**Step 4:**
(B) Employee training programs are not able to teach employees creativity.	⟶	
(C) Many jobs require little or no creativity.	⟶	
(D) There is no good reason to suppose that employee training programs should promote creativity.	⟶	
(E) Creativity is in demand, but there is no evidence that it can be taught.	⟶	

PrepTest59 Sec3 Q9

LSAT Question	My Analysis
21. Musicologist: Many critics complain of the disproportion between text and music in Handel's *da capo* arias. These texts are generally quite short and often repeated well beyond what is needed for literal understanding. Yet such criticism is refuted by noting that repetition serves a vital function: it frees the audience to focus on the music itself, which can speak to audiences whatever their language. $\longrightarrow$	**Step 2:**
Which one of the following sentences best expresses the main point of the musicologist's reasoning? $\longrightarrow$	**Step 1:**
	Step 3:
(A) Handel's *da capo* arias contain a disproportionate amount of music. $\longrightarrow$	**Step 4:**
(B) Handel's *da capo* arias are superior to most in their accessibility to diverse audiences. $\longrightarrow$	
(C) At least one frequent criticism of Handel's *da capo* arias is undeserved. $\longrightarrow$	
(D) At least some of Handel's *da capo* arias contain unnecessary repetitions. $\longrightarrow$	
(E) Most criticism of Handel's *da capo* arias is unwarranted. $\longrightarrow$	

PrepTest61 Sec4 Q6

Note: You saw the stimulus for this question in an earlier exercise.

Expert Analysis

Here's how an LSAT expert might use the Logical Reasoning Method to answer the previous practice questions.

LSAT Question	Analysis
17. Musicologist: Classification of a musical instrument depends on the mechanical action through which it produces music. So the piano is properly called a percussion instrument, not a stringed instrument. Even though the vibration of the piano's strings is what makes its sound, the strings are caused to vibrate by the impact of hammers.	**Step 2:** *So* signals the conclusion: the piano is properly categorized as a percussion instrument, not a string instrument. The rest of the argument explains why the author agrees with this categorization.
Which one of the following most accurately expresses the main conclusion of the musicologist's argument?	**Step 1:** A Main Point question: The correct answer will paraphrase the argument's final conclusion.
	Step 3: The piano is properly categorized as a percussion instrument, not a string instrument.
(A) Musical instruments should be classified according to the mechanical actions through which they produce sound.	**Step 4:** This is the rule about how to categorize instruments. The author applies the rule in order to reach his conclusion. Eliminate.
(B) Musical instruments should not be classified based on the way musicians interact with them.	Outside the Scope. Not only is this not the author's conclusion, it actually disagrees with the rule he states in the evidence. Eliminate.
(C) Some people classify the piano as a stringed instrument because of the way the piano produces sound.	Outside the Scope. How others classify the piano is not relevant to the author's conclusion, which expresses how it should be categorized. Eliminate.
(D) The piano should be classified as a stringed instrument rather than as a percussion instrument.	180. The author concludes the opposite. Eliminate.
(E) It is correct to classify the piano as a percussion instrument rather than as a stringed instrument. *PrepTest61 Sec2 Q9*	Correct. This paraphrases the author's main point.

LSAT Question	Analysis
18. Chemical fertilizers not only create potential health hazards, they also destroy earthworms, which are highly beneficial to soil. For this reason alone the use of chemical fertilizers should be avoided. The castings earthworms leave behind are much richer than the soil they ingest, thus making a garden rich in earthworms much more fertile than a garden without them.	**Step 2:** *[T]his reason* refers to the first sentence, so the first sentence must be evidence, and not the main point. What follows *For this reason* is a recommendation. When the argument includes a recommendation, the recommendation is nearly always the author's main point. The final sentence contains another reason to avoid chemical fertilizers, so it must be a subsidiary conclusion.
Which one of the following most accurately expresses the main conclusion of the argument?	**Step 1:** A Main Point question: The correct answer will paraphrase the argument's final conclusion.
	Step 3: Chemical fertilizers should not be used.
(A) Earthworms are highly beneficial to soil.	**Step 4:** Part of the first sentence, which is evidence. Eliminate.
(B) Chemical fertilizers destroy earthworms.	Part of the first sentence. Evidence. Eliminate.
(C) The castings that earthworms leave behind are much richer than the soil they ingest.	Part of the third sentence, which helps to explain why we should not use chemical fertilizers. Evidence. Eliminate.
(D) The use of chemical fertilizers should be avoided.	Correct. States the argument's conclusion word for word.
(E) A garden rich in earthworms is much more fertile than a garden that is devoid of earthworms. *PrepTest59 Sec2 Q10*	The subsidiary conclusion. This choice is attractive to someone who jumps at the word *thus* without considering the author's main idea. Eliminate.

LSAT Question	Analysis
19. Although free international trade allows countries to specialize, which in turn increases productivity, such specialization carries risks. After all, small countries often rely on one or two products for the bulk of their exports. If those products are raw materials, the supply is finite and can be used up. If they are foodstuffs, a natural disaster can wipe out a season's production overnight.	**Step 2:** *After all* at the beginning of the second sentence signals the evidence. That indicates that the conclusion is the first sentence: The specialization enabled by international free trade carries risks. Everything following *After all* explains and provides examples of the risks the author recognizes in her conclusion.
Which one of the following most accurately expresses the conclusion of the argument as a whole?	**Step 1:** A Main Point question: The correct answer will paraphrase the argument's final conclusion.
	Step 3: The specialization enabled by international free trade carries risks.
(A) Specialization within international trade comes with risks.	**Step 4:** Correct. This closely paraphrases the conclusion in the argument.
(B) A natural disaster can destroy a whole season's production overnight, devastating a small country's economy.	This is one of the hypothetical scenarios in the author's evidence. Eliminate.
(C) A small country's supply of raw materials can be used up in a short period.	This is one of the hypothetical scenarios in the author's evidence. Eliminate.
(D) Some countries rely on a small number of products for the export-based sectors of their economies.	This is the author's basic premise (or evidence) for why she believes her conclusion. Eliminate.
(E) When international trade is free, countries can specialize in what they export. *PrepTest57 Sec3 Q3*	While the author would agree with this statement, it doesn't contain the author's negative opinion about specialization, and so does not match her main point. Eliminate.

LSAT Question		Analysis
20. Manager: There is no good reason to suppose that promoting creativity is a proper goal of an employee training program. Many jobs require little or no creativity and, in those positions, using creativity is more likely to be disruptive than innovative. Furthermore, even if creativity were in demand, there is no evidence that it can be taught.	→	**Step 2:** There are no Keywords in the argument, but the first sentence is an opinion supported by the facts in the second and third sentences. So the first sentence is the author's main point: There is no support for the notion that employee training programs should have promoting creativity as a goal.
Which one of the following most accurately expresses the main conclusion drawn in the manager's argument?	→	**Step 1:** A Main Point question: The correct answer will paraphrase the argument's final conclusion.
		Step 3: There is no support for the notion that employee training programs should have promoting creativity as a goal.
(A) Using creativity in jobs that require little or no creativity can be disruptive.	→	**Step 4:** Part of the evidence. Eliminate.
(B) Employee training programs are not able to teach employees creativity.	→	A slight overstatement of part of the evidence ("there is no evidence that it can be taught"), but definitely not the conclusion. Eliminate.
(C) Many jobs require little or no creativity.	→	Part of the evidence. Eliminate.
(D) There is no good reason to suppose that employee training programs should promote creativity.	→	Correct. It's not word-for-word, but this is a close and accurate paraphrase of the author's conclusion.
(E) Creativity is in demand, but there is no evidence that it can be taught. *PrepTest59 Sec3 Q9*	→	The author states this conditionally in the evidence ("even if creativity were in demand . . ."), but it is not his main point. Eliminate.

LSAT Question	Analysis
21. Musicologist: Many critics complain of the disproportion between text and music in Handel's *da capo* arias. These texts are generally quite short and often repeated well beyond what is needed for literal understanding. Yet such criticism is refuted by noting that repetition serves a vital function: it frees the audience to focus on the music itself, which can speak to audiences whatever their language.	**Step 2:** Conclusion: Those who say that the disproportion between text and music is a weakness in Handel's *da capo* arias are wrong. The author's conclusion says that "such criticism is refuted" referring to those who criticize the disproportion between text and music in Handel's *da capo* arias.
Which one of the following sentences best expresses the main point of the musicologist's reasoning?	**Step 1:** A Main Point question: The correct answer will paraphrase the argument's final conclusion.
	Step 3: Those who say that the disproportion between text and music is a weakness in Handel's *da capo* arias are wrong.
(A) Handel's *da capo* arias contain a disproportionate amount of music.	**Step 4:** Distortion. The author agrees with this statement, but his conclusion is about whether the arias should be criticized for their repetitiveness. Eliminate.
(B) Handel's *da capo* arias are superior to most in their accessibility to diverse audiences.	Outside the Scope. The author doesn't compare Handel's arias to those of any other composer. Eliminate.
(C) At least one frequent criticism of Handel's *da capo* arias is undeserved.	Correct. This paraphrases the author's conclusion by substituting [a]t least one for the specific criticism the author rejects.
(D) At least some of Handel's *da capo* arias contain unnecessary repetitions.	180. This is part of the author's opponents' position. The author's evidence, however, actually finds merit in the repetition. Eliminate.
(E) Most criticism of Handel's *da capo* arias is unwarranted. *PrepTest61 Sec4 Q6*	Extreme. The author rejects one criticism of the arias. He may or may not agree with *most* of the others. Eliminate.

EVIDENCE AND ARGUMENTS: ROLE OF A STATEMENT, POINT AT ISSUE, AND METHOD OF ARGUMENT QUESTIONS

On the LSAT, you will never be asked to defend the author's evidence. Frequently, however, you will need to analyze an argument's structure and characterize how the evidence interacts with the author's conclusion. Those skills are most directly rewarded on questions like these:

Role of a Statement

It would not be surprising to discover that the trade routes between China and the West were opened many centuries, even millennia, earlier than 200 B.C., contrary to what is currently believed. After all, what made the Great Silk Road so attractive as a trade route linking China and the West—level terrain, easily traversable mountain passes, and desert oases—would also have made it an attractive route for the original emigrants to China from Africa and the Middle East, and this early migration began at least one million years ago.

That a migration from Africa and the Middle East to China occurred at least one million years ago figures in the above reasoning in which one of the following ways?

(A) It is cited as conclusive evidence for the claim that trade links between China and the Middle East were established long before 200 B.C.

(B) It is an intermediate conclusion made plausible by the description of the terrain along which the migration supposedly took place.

(C) It is offered as evidence in support of the claim that trade routes between China and the West could easily have been established much earlier than is currently believed.

(D) It is offered as evidence against the claim that trade routes between China and Africa preceded those eventually established between China and the Middle East.

(E) It is the main conclusion that the argument attempts to establish about intercourse between China and the West.

PrepTest51 Sec1 Q14

Point at Issue

Talbert: Chess is beneficial for school-age children. It is enjoyable, encourages foresight and logical thinking, and discourages carelessness, inattention, and impulsiveness. In short, it promotes mental maturity.

Sklar: My objection to teaching chess to children is that it diverts mental activity from something with societal value, such as science, into something that has no societal value.

Talbert's and Sklar's statements provide the strongest support for holding that they disagree with each other over whether

(A) chess promotes mental maturity
(B) many activities promote mental maturity just as well as chess does
(C) chess is socially valuable and science is not
(D) children should be taught to play chess
(E) children who neither play chess nor study science are mentally immature

PrepTest61 Sec2 Q7

Method of Argument

Hernandez: I recommend that staff cars be replaced every four years instead of every three years. Three-year-old cars are still in good condition and this would result in big savings.

Green: I disagree. Some of our salespeople with big territories wear out their cars in three years.

Hernandez: I meant three-year-old cars subjected to normal use.

In the conversation, Hernandez responds to Green's objection in which one of the following ways?

(A) by explicitly qualifying a premise used earlier
(B) by criticizing salespeople who wear out their cars in three years
(C) by disputing the accuracy of Green's evidence
(D) by changing the subject to the size of sales territories
(E) by indicating that Green used a phrase Ambiguously

PrepTest57 Sec3 Q5

Evidence and Role of a Statement Questions

Once you've learned to identify the conclusion, the next step in analyzing an argument is to distinguish the relevant evidence from the conclusion and from any general background information.

> ### LEARNING OBJECTIVES
>
> In this section, you'll learn to:
>
> · Distinguish evidence from background information
> · Identify and answer Role of a Statement Questions

As a strategic reader, you should be able to describe the way each statement serves the argument. Take a look at how an LSAT expert might distinguish among the roles of various statements in an argument you've already seen.

LSAT Question	Analysis
Editorial: Almost every year the Smithfield River floods the coastal fishing community of Redhook, which annually spends $3 million on the cleanup. Some residents have proposed damming the river, which would cost $5 million but would prevent the flooding. However, their position is misguided. A dam would prevent nutrients in the river from flowing into the ocean. Fish that now feed on those nutrients would start feeding elsewhere. The loss of these fish would cost Redhook $10 million annually. *PrepTest51 Sec1 Q1*	**Step 2:** Sentence 1—**Background—the impetus for a debate:** Flood cleanup costs $3 million. Sentence 2—**Some residents' (not the author's) recommendation:** Build a dam for $5 million. Sentence 3—**The author's conclusion:** *some residents'* recommendation is a mistake. Sentences 4, 5, and 6—**The author's evidence:** · A dam would stop nutrients. · Fish that need the nutrients would leave the area. · Losing the fish costs $10 million.

> ### LSAT STRATEGY
>
> One sentence does not always contain one "statement." A single sentence might contain two pieces of evidence or an evidentiary premise and the conclusion.

Practice

Identify how each statement functions in the following LSAT arguments. Identify the conclusion first, and then describe the roles played by the other statements.

LSAT Question	My Analysis
[Example] Most of the employees of the Compujack Corporation are computer programmers. Since most computer programmers receive excellent salaries from their employers, at least one Compujack employee must receive an excellent salary from Compujack. *PrepTest49 Sec4 Q24*	[Example] **Conclusion:** [last part of sentence 2] *At least one CJ employee receives an excellent salary from CJ.* Sentence 1 and first part of sentence 2—**Two separate pieces of evidence:** · Most employees of CJ are programmers · Most programmers have great salaries
22. An art critic, by ridiculing an artwork, can undermine the pleasure one takes in it; conversely, by lavishing praise upon an artwork, an art critic can render the experience of viewing the artwork more pleasurable. So an artwork's artistic merit can depend not only on the person who creates it but also on those who critically evaluate it. *PrepTest61 Sec4 Q13*	**Conclusion:**
23. Vanwilligan: Some have argued that professional athletes receive unfairly high salaries. But in an unrestricted free market, such as the market these athletes compete in, salaries are determined by what someone else is willing to pay for their services. These athletes make enormous profits for their teams' owners, and that is why owners are willing to pay them extraordinary salaries. Thus the salaries they receive are fair. *PrepTest49 Sec2 Q19*	**Conclusion:**
24. Chiu: The belief that a person is always morally blameworthy for feeling certain emotions, such as unjustifiable anger, jealousy, or resentment, is misguided. Individuals are responsible for only what is under their control, and whether one feels such an emotion is not always under one's control. *PrepTest51 Sec1 Q16*	**Conclusion:**

LSAT Question	My Analysis
25. Scientist: A controversy in paleontology centers on the question of whether prehistoric human ancestors began to develop sophisticated tools before or after they came to stand upright. I argue that they stood upright first, simply because advanced toolmaking requires free use of the hands, and standing upright makes this possible. → *PrepTest49 Sec2 Q14*	**Conclusion:**
26. Bethany: Psychologists have discovered a technique for replacing one's nightmares with pleasant dreams, and have successfully taught it to adults suffering from chronic nightmares. Studies have found that nightmare-prone children are especially likely to suffer from nightmares as adults. Thus, psychologists should direct efforts toward identifying nightmare-prone children so that these children can be taught the technique for replacing their nightmares with pleasant dreams. → *PrepTest59 Sec2 Q13*	**Conclusion:**
27. Columnist: It has been noted that attending a live musical performance is a richer experience than is listening to recorded music. Some say that this is merely because we do not see the performers when we listen to recorded music. However, there must be some other reason, for there is relatively little difference between listening to someone read a story over the radio and listening to someone in the same room read a story. → *PrepTest59 Sec2 Q7*	**Conclusion:**
28. It is primarily by raising interest rates that central bankers curb inflation, but an increase in interest rates takes up to two years to affect inflation. Accordingly, central bankers usually try to raise interest rates before inflation becomes excessive, at which time inflation is not yet readily apparent either. But unless inflation is readily apparent, interest rate hikes generally will be perceived as needlessly restraining a growing economy. Thus, central bankers' success in temporarily restraining inflation may make it harder for them to ward off future inflation without incurring the public's wrath. → *PrepTest49 Sec2 Q12*	**Conclusion:**

Expert Analysis

Here's how an LSAT expert might characterize the roles of the statements in those practice arguments.

LSAT Question	Analysis
22. An art critic, by ridiculing an artwork, can undermine the pleasure one takes in it; conversely, by lavishing praise upon an artwork, an art critic can render the experience of viewing the artwork more pleasurable. So an artwork's artistic merit can depend not only on the person who creates it but also on those who critically evaluate it. *PrepTest61 Sec4 Q13*	**Conclusion:** [second sentence] A work's artistic merit can depend on both the artist and the critics. Sentence 1—**Two contrasting pieces of evidence:** · Critics can decrease pleasure in art. · But critics can increase pleasure, too.
23. Vanwilligan: Some have argued that professional athletes receive unfairly high salaries. But in an unrestricted free market, such as the market these athletes compete in, salaries are determined by what someone else is willing to pay for their services. These athletes make enormous profits for their teams' owners, and that is why owners are willing to pay them extraordinary salaries. Thus the salaries they receive are fair. *PrepTest49 Sec2 Q19*	**Conclusion:** [fourth sentence] Professional athletes' salaries are fair. Sentence 1—**Author's opponents' position:** Pro athletes' salaries are unfair. Sentence 2—**A rule for testing the issue:** Free markets set fair salaries at what employers are willing to pay. Sentence 3—**Author's evidence:** Owners are willing to pay pro athletes' salaries.
24. Chiu: The belief that a person is always morally blameworthy for feeling certain emotions, such as unjustifiable anger, jealousy, or resentment, is misguided. Individuals are responsible for only what is under their control, and whether one feels such an emotion is not always under one's control. *PrepTest51 Sec1 Q16*	**Conclusion:** [first sentence] People are not always blameworthy for feeling negative emotions. Sentence 2—**Two related pieces of evidence:** · People are responsible only for things under their control. · Feeling emotions is not always under a person's control.

LSAT Question	Analysis
25. Scientist: A controversy in paleontology centers on the question of whether prehistoric human ancestors began to develop sophisticated tools before or after they came to stand upright. I argue that they stood upright first, simply because advanced toolmaking requires free use of the hands, and standing upright makes this possible. *PrepTest49 Sec2 Q14*	**Conclusion:** [first part of Sentence 2] Humans stood upright before making advanced tools. Sentence 1—**Background description of a scientific debate:** Which came first—standing upright or making advanced tools? Second part of Sentence 2—**Author's evidence:** · Need free hands to make advanced tools. · Standing up frees up the hands.
26. Bethany: Psychologists have discovered a technique for replacing one's nightmares with pleasant dreams, and have successfully taught it to adults suffering from chronic nightmares. Studies have found that nightmare-prone children are especially likely to suffer from nightmares as adults. Thus, psychologists should direct efforts toward identifying nightmare-prone children so that these children can be taught the technique for replacing their nightmares with pleasant dreams. *PrepTest59 Sec2 Q13*	**Conclusion:** [first part of Sentence 3] Psychologists should focus on nightmare-prone kids. Sentence 1—**A scientific discovery that gives rise to the author's argument:** successful nightmare treatments Sentence 2—**A second discovery that makes the first important for one group:** nightmare-prone kids Second part of Sentence 3—**The reason for the recommendation in the author's conclusion**
27. Columnist: It has been noted that attending a live musical performance is a richer experience than is listening to recorded music. Some say that this is merely because we do not see the performers when we listen to recorded music. However, there must be some other reason, for there is relatively little difference between listening to someone read a story over the radio and listening to someone in the same room read a story. *PrepTest59 Sec2 Q7*	**Conclusion:** [first part of Sentence 3] Seeing the musicians is *not* the reason live music is richer (my opponents' explanation is wrong). Sentence 1—**Background observation:** Live music is a richer experience than recorded music. Sentence 2—**The author's opponents' explanation for the observation:** Live music is richer because we see the musicians. Second part of Sentence 3—**Author's evidence:** An analogy showing why the opponents' explanation must be wrong.
28. It is primarily by raising interest rates that central bankers curb inflation, but an increase in interest rates takes up to two years to affect inflation. Accordingly, central bankers usually try to raise interest rates before inflation becomes excessive, at which time inflation is not yet readily apparent either. But unless inflation is readily apparent, interest rate hikes generally will be perceived as needlessly restraining a growing economy. Thus, central bankers' success in temporarily restraining inflation may make it harder for them to ward off future inflation without incurring the public's wrath. *PrepTest49 Sec2 Q12*	**Conclusion:** [fourth sentence] Temporary success in halting inflation makes it harder to prevent future inflation without causing public anger. Sentences 1, 2, and 3 **are three related pieces of the author's evidence:** · The main way bankers try to halt inflation is by raising interest rates. · Bankers usually raise interest rates early, before it becomes apparent. · If inflation isn't apparent, the public gets angry at steps that slow the economy.

Identify and Answer Role of a Statement Questions

Role of a Statement questions, which ask how a statement functions in an argument, reward your ability to identify the argument's conclusion, evidence, and other components.

You can identify Role of a Statement questions from question stems like these:

> The statement that the educational use of computers enables schools to teach far more courses with far fewer teachers figures in the argument in which one of the following ways?
>
> *PrepTest57 Sec2 Q13*

> The statement that human food-producing capacity has increased more rapidly than human population plays which one of the following roles in the argument?
>
> *PrepTest59 Sec2 Q18*

> Which one of the following most accurately describes the role played in the argument by the claim that it is primarily by raising interest rates that central bankers curb inflation?
>
> *PrepTest49 Sec2 Q12*

ROLE OF A STATEMENT AT A GLANCE

Task: Identify how a specified statement or idea functions within the argument.

Strategy: Note the statement cited in the question stem; then, analyze the argument to characterize the role played by the statement.

Released LSATs between 2009 and 2013 featured an average of 2.1 Role of a Statement questions.

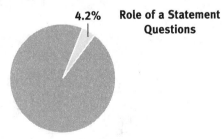

4.2% **Role of a Statement Questions**

Logical Reasoning Question Types

*PrepTests 57–71; released 2009–2013

Here's how an expert LSAT test taker might proceed through a Role of a Statement question.

LSAT Question	Analysis
It would not be surprising to discover that the trade routes between China and the West were opened many centuries, even millennia, earlier than 200 B.C., contrary to what is currently believed. After all, what made the Great Silk Road so attractive as a trade route linking China and the West—level terrain, easily traversable mountain passes, and desert oases—would also have made it an attractive route for the original emigrants to China from Africa and the Middle East, and this early migration began at least one million years ago.	**Step 2:** Conclusion: Trade routes between China and the West may very well have opened long before 200 B.C. Evidence: *After all* is the evidence signal. · What made the GSR a desirable route would've made it desirable for the original emigrants to China. · The original emigrant migration began a million years ago or more.
That a migration from Africa and the Middle East to China occurred at least one million years ago figures in the above reasoning in which one of the following ways?	**Step 1:** "Figures … in which one of the following ways"—Role of a Statement question.
	Step 3: One of two pieces of evidence included to support the conclusion.
(A) It is cited as conclusive evidence for the claim that trade links between China and the Middle East were established long before 200 B.C.	**Step 4:** The statement is one of two parts of evidence, so by itself it cannot be "conclusive evidence." Eliminate.
(B) It is an intermediate conclusion made plausible by the description of the terrain along which the migration supposedly took place.	The *and* before the statement means that it is another evidentiary fact, not a conclusion. Eliminate.
(C) It is offered as evidence in support of the claim that trade routes between China and the West could easily have been established much earlier than is currently believed.	Correct. The choice has the right role—"offered as evidence"—and the correct conclusion.
(D) It is offered as evidence against the claim that trade routes between China and Africa preceded those eventually established between China and the Middle East.	The author does not claim that routes between China and Africa came before those between China and the Middle East. Eliminate.
(E) It is the main conclusion that the argument attempts to establish about intercourse between China and the West.	The main conclusion is the first sentence, not the statement in question. Eliminate.

PrepTest51 Sec1 Q14

Practice

Apply the Logical Reasoning Method steps to answer each of the following Role of a Statement questions.

LSAT Question	My Analysis
29. Ethicist: It would be a mistake to say that just because someone is not inclined to do otherwise, she or he does not deserve to be praised for doing what is right, for although we do consider people especially virtuous if they successfully resist a desire to do what is wrong, they are certainly no less virtuous if they have succeeded in extinguishing all such desires. →	**Step 2:**
The assertion that people are considered especially virtuous if they successfully resist a desire to do what is wrong plays which one of the following roles in the ethicist's argument. →	**Step 1:**
	Step 3:
(A) It is a claim for which the argument attempts to provide justification. →	**Step 4:**
(B) It makes an observation that, according to the argument, is insufficient to justify the claim that the argument concludes is false. →	
(C) It is a claim, acceptance of which, the argument contends, is a primary obstacle to some people's having an adequate conception of virtue. →	
(D) It is, according to the argument, a commonly held opinion that is nevertheless false. →	
(E) It reports an observation that, according to the argument, serves as evidence for the truth of its conclusion. →	

PrepTest51 Sec3 Q23

LSAT Question		**My Analysis**
30. Administrators of educational institutions are enthusiastic about the educational use of computers because they believe that it will enable schools to teach far more courses with far fewer teachers than traditional methods allow. Many teachers fear computers for the same reason. But this reason is mistaken. Computerized instruction requires more, not less, time of instructors, which indicates that any reduction in the number of teachers would require an accompanying reduction in courses offered.	$\longrightarrow$	**Step 2:**
The statement that the educational use of computers enables schools to teach far more courses with far fewer teachers figures in the argument in which one of the following ways?	$\longrightarrow$	**Step 1:**
		Step 3:
(A) It is presented as a possible explanation for an observation that follows it.	$\longrightarrow$	**Step 4:**
(B) It is a statement of the problem the argument sets out to solve.	$\longrightarrow$	
(C) It is a statement that the argument is designed to refute.	$\longrightarrow$	
(D) It is a statement offered in support of the argument's main conclusion.	$\longrightarrow$	
(E) It is the argument's main conclusion.	$\longrightarrow$	
PrepTest57 Sec2 Q13		

LSAT Question	My Analysis
31. Librarian: Some argue that the preservation grant we received should be used to restore our original copy of our town's charter, since if the charter is not restored, it will soon deteriorate beyond repair. But this document, although sentimentally important, has no scholarly value. Copies are readily available. Since we are a research library and not a museum, the money would be better spent preserving documents that have significant scholarly value.	**Step 2:**
The claim that the town's charter, if not restored, will soon deteriorate beyond repair plays which one of the following roles in the librarian's argument?	**Step 1:**
	Step 3:
(A) It is a claim that the librarian's argument attempts to show to be false.	**Step 4:**
(B) It is the conclusion of the argument that the librarian's argument rejects.	
(C) It is a premise in an argument whose conclusion is rejected by the librarian's argument.	
(D) It is a premise used to support the librarian's main conclusion.	
(E) It is a claim whose truth is required by the librarian's argument.	

PrepTest61 Sec4 Q22

LSAT Question	**My Analysis**

32. It is primarily by raising interest rates that central bankers curb inflation, but an increase in interest rates takes up to two years to affect inflation. Accordingly, central bankers usually try to raise interest rates before inflation becomes excessive, at which time inflation is not yet readily apparent either. But unless inflation is readily apparent, interest rate hikes generally will be perceived as needlessly restraining a growing economy. Thus, central bankers' success in temporarily restraining inflation may make it harder for them to ward off future inflation without incurring the public's wrath. → **Step 2:**

Which one of the following most accurately describes the role played in the argument by the claim that it is primarily by raising interest rates that central bankers curb inflation? → **Step 1:**

Step 3:

(A) It is presented as a complete explanation of the fact that central bankers' success in temporarily restraining inflation may make it harder for them to ward off future inflation without incurring the public's wrath. → **Step 4:**

(B) It is a description of a phenomenon for which the claim that an increase in interest rates takes up to two years to affect inflation is offered as an explanation. →

(C) It is a premise offered in support of the conclusion that central bankers' success in temporarily restraining inflation may make it harder for them to ward off future inflation without incurring the public's wrath. →

(D) It is a conclusion for which the statement that an increase in interest rates takes up to two years to affect inflation is offered as support. →

(E) It is a premise offered in support of the conclusion that unless inflation is readily apparent, interest rate hikes generally will be perceived as needlessly restraining a growing economy. →

PrepTest49 Sec2 Q12

	LSAT Question	**My Analysis**
33.	Software reviewer: Dictation software allows a computer to produce a written version of sentences that are spoken to it. Although dictation software has been promoted as a labor-saving invention, it fails to live up to its billing. The laborious part of writing is in the thinking and the editing, not in the typing. And proofreading the software's error-filled output generally squanders any time saved in typing. →	**Step 2:**
	Which one of the following most accurately describes the role played in the software reviewer's argument by the claim that dictation software fails to live up to its billing? →	**Step 1:**
		Step 3:
	(A) It is the argument's main conclusion but not its only conclusion. →	**Step 4:**
	(B) It is the argument's only conclusion. →	
	(C) It is an intermediate conclusion that is offered as direct support for the argument's main conclusion. →	
	(D) It is a premise offered in support of the argument's conclusion. →	
	(E) It is a premise offered as direct support for an intermediate conclusion of the argument. →	

PrepTest57 Sec2 Q16

LSAT Question	**My Analysis**

34. Columnist: It has been noted that attending a live musical performance is a richer experience than is listening to recorded music. Some say that this is merely because we do not see the performers when we listen to recorded music. However, there must be some other reason, for there is relatively little difference between listening to someone read a story over the radio and listening to someone in the same room read a story. → **Step 2:**

Which one of the following most accurately expresses the role played in the argument by the observation that attending a live musical performance is a richer experience than is listening to recorded music? → **Step 1:**

Step 3:

(A) It is what the columnist's argument purports to show. → **Step 4:**

(B) It is the reason given for the claim that the columnist's argument is attempting to undermine. →

(C) It is what the columnist's argument purports to explain. →

(D) It is what the columnist's argument purports to refute. →

(E) It is what the position that the columnist tries to undermine is purported to explain. →

PrepTest59 Sec2 Q7

Expert Analysis

Here's how an LSAT expert might have approached those practice questions.

LSAT Question	Analysis
29. Ethicist: It would be a mistake to say that just because someone is not inclined to do otherwise, she or he does not deserve to be praised for doing what is right, for although we do consider people especially virtuous if they successfully resist a desire to do what is wrong, they are certainly no less virtuous if they have succeeded in extinguishing all such desires.	**Step 2:** One sentence, three statements. First statement—Conclusion: A person deserves praise for doing right even if she or he has no desire to do wrong. The rest is evidence, signaled by *for*.
	Second statement—the one in the question stem—[*a*]*lthough* signals that it *seems to be* evidence against the conclusion.
	Third part—author's evidence showing why second statement is not strong enough to refute the conclusion.
The assertion that people are considered especially virtuous if they successfully resist a desire to do what is wrong plays which one of the following roles in the ethicist's argument.	**Step 1:** Role of a Statement question—the correct answer will describe how the statement fits into the argument.
	Step 3: A statement that appears to be against the conclusion, but which the author believes isn't strong enough.
(A) It is a claim for which the argument attempts to provide justification.	**Step 4:** 180. The argument attempts to counter this claim. Eliminate.
(B) It makes an observation that, according to the argument, is insufficient to justify the claim that the argument concludes is false.	Correct. The statement in question appears to counter the author's conclusion, but the author tries to demonstrate that it isn't strong enough.
(C) It is a claim, acceptance of which, the argument contends, is a primary obstacle to some people's having an adequate conception of virtue.	Distortion. The author makes no claim about what, if anything, is the primary obstacle to understanding virtue. Eliminate.
(D) It is, according to the argument, a commonly held opinion that is nevertheless false.	180. The author actually says the belief is true, just not strong enough to refute his conclusion. Eliminate.
(E) It reports an observation that, according to the argument, serves as evidence for the truth of its conclusion.	180. It is an apparent contradiction to the author's conclusion. Eliminate.

PrepTest51 Sec3 Q23

LSAT Question	Analysis
30. Administrators of educational institutions are enthusiastic about the educational use of computers because they believe that it will enable schools to teach far more courses with far fewer teachers than traditional methods allow. Many teachers fear computers for the same reason. But this reason is mistaken. Computerized instruction requires more, not less, time of instructors, which indicates that any reduction in the number of teachers would require an accompanying reduction in courses offered.	**Step 2:** Conclusion: It isn't true that computers will let schools teach many more courses with way fewer teachers. Evidence: Computerized instruction needs more time from teachers, so if we lose teachers we would also lose courses. The statement in question is neither the conclusion nor the evidence. It's a belief that the author claims is wrong.
The statement that the educational use of computers enables schools to teach far more courses with far fewer teachers figures in the argument in which one of the following ways?	**Step 1:** "[F]igures in the argument in which of the following ways" signals a Role of a Statement question.
	Step 3: Statement that the author attempts to contradict.
(A) It is presented as a possible explanation for an observation that follows it.	**Step 4:** The statement in question is a belief; it doesn't explain or support anything. Eliminate.
(B) It is a statement of the problem the argument sets out to solve.	There is no problem mentioned in the argument, merely a possible innovation. Eliminate.
(C) It is a statement that the argument is designed to refute.	Correct. The author's conclusion and evidence try to prove that the belief is wrong.
(D) It is a statement offered in support of the argument's main conclusion.	The statement cannot support a main conclusion that claims it is wrong! Eliminate.
(E) It is the argument's main conclusion. *PrepTest57 Sec2 Q13*	The argument's main conclusion is the sentence that follows the statement in the question stem. Eliminate.

LSAT Question	Analysis
31. Librarian: Some argue that the preservation grant we received should be used to restore our original copy of our town's charter, since if the charter is not restored, it will soon deteriorate beyond repair. But this document, although sentimentally important, has no scholarly value. Copies are readily available. Since we are a research library and not a museum, the money would be better spent preserving documents that have significant scholarly value.	**Step 2:** A library received a grant. The author's conclusion (last part of fourth sentence) is that the grant money is better spent on scholarly documents than on preserving the town charter. The first sentence—which contains the statement in the question stem—is the librarian's opponents' argument. *Since* signals that the statement in question is the opponents' evidence.
The claim that the town's charter, if not restored, will soon deteriorate beyond repair plays which one of the following roles in the librarian's argument?	**Step 1:** Role of a Statement question—the correct answer will describe how the statement fits into the argument.
	Step 3: The author's opponents' evidence.
(A) It is a claim that the librarian's argument attempts to show to be false.	**Step 4:** Distortion. The author doesn't say the claim that the charter will deteriorate is false (indeed, she appears to agree). What she says is that there are better places to spend the grant money. Eliminate.
(B) It is the conclusion of the argument that the librarian's argument rejects.	Distortion. It is the *evidence* of the argument she rejects. Eliminate.
(C) It is a premise in an argument whose conclusion is rejected by the librarian's argument.	Correct. *Premise* means evidence, and the statement in question is the author's opponents' evidence.
(D) It is a premise used to support the librarian's main conclusion.	Distortion. It is the evidence used by the librarian's opponents to support *their* conclusion. Eliminate.
(E) It is a claim whose truth is required by the librarian's argument. *PrepTest61 Sec4 Q22*	180/Distortion. It is a claim the *opponents* believe is *sufficient* to support their conclusion. The author doesn't doubt the truth of their claim, but rejects the idea that it leads to their recommendation for how to spend the grant money. Eliminate.

LSAT Question	Analysis
32. It is primarily by raising interest rates that central bankers curb inflation, but an increase in interest rates takes up to two years to affect inflation. Accordingly, central bankers usually try to raise interest rates before inflation becomes excessive, at which time inflation is not yet readily apparent either. But unless inflation is readily apparent, interest rate hikes generally will be perceived as needlessly restraining a growing economy. Thus, central bankers' success in temporarily restraining inflation may make it harder for them to ward off future inflation without incurring the public's wrath.	**Step 2:** Conclusion: [fourth sentence] Temporary success in halting inflation makes it harder to prevent future inflation without causing public anger. Sentences 1, 2, and 3 are three related pieces of the author's evidence: · The main way bankers try to halt inflation is by raising interest rates. [This is the statement in the question stem.] · Bankers usually raise interest rates early, before it becomes apparent. · If inflation isn't apparent, the public gets angry at steps that slow the economy.
Which one of the following most accurately describes the role played in the argument by the claim that it is primarily by raising interest rates that central bankers curb inflation?	**Step 1:** Role of a Statement question—the correct answer will describe how the statement fits into the argument.
	Step 3: One of the statements given as evidence for the author's conclusion.
(A) It is presented as a complete explanation of the fact that central bankers' success in temporarily restraining inflation may make it harder for them to ward off future inflation without incurring the public's wrath.	**Step 4:** Extreme. The statement in question is one of three pieces of evidence offered for the conclusion. *Complete explanation* is too strong. Eliminate.
(B) It is a description of a phenomenon for which the claim that an increase in interest rates takes up to two years to affect inflation is offered as an explanation.	Distortion. The *claim* referred to in this choice is just a detail about the statement in question, not an explanation of it. Eliminate.
(C) It is a premise offered in support of the conclusion that central bankers' success in temporarily restraining inflation may make it harder for them to ward off future inflation without incurring the public's wrath.	Correct. *Premise* means the same as evidence, and the paraphrase of the author's conclusion here is accurate. The statement in question was just evidence for the conclusion.
(D) It is a conclusion for which the statement that an increase in interest rates takes up to two years to affect inflation is offered as support.	Distortion. The statement in question was actually the first piece in a string of evidence. Eliminate.
(E) It is a premise offered in support of the conclusion that unless inflation is readily apparent, interest rate hikes generally will be perceived as needlessly restraining a growing economy.	Distortion. What this answer identifies as the conclusion is actually another piece of evidence for the author's main point. Eliminate.

PrepTest49 Sec2 Q12

LSAT Question	Analysis
33. Software reviewer: Dictation software allows a computer to produce a written version of sentences that are spoken to it. Although dictation software has been promoted as a labor-saving invention, it fails to live up to its billing. The laborious part of writing is in the thinking and the editing, not in the typing. And proofreading the software's error-filled output generally squanders any time saved in typing.	**Step 2:** Conclusion (second part of second sentence): Dictation software hasn't lived up to the hype. [This is the statement from the question stem.] Everything else supports the conclusion: First sentence—background: a definition of dictation software → First part of second sentence—more background: what was hyped about dictation software (it makes writing easier) Third and fourth sentences—two related pieces of evidence: · What makes writing hard · Why dictation software doesn't make it any easier
Which one of the following most accurately describes the role played in the software reviewer's argument by the claim that dictation software fails to live up to its billing?	→ **Step 1:** Role of a Statement question—the correct answer will describe how the statement fits into the argument.
	Step 3: It is the argument's main point, the conclusion.
(A) It is the argument's main conclusion but not its only conclusion.	→ **Step 4:** Distortion. There are no subsidiary conclusions here. Eliminate.
(B) It is the argument's only conclusion.	→ Correct. There are no subsidiary conclusions and the statement in question is the author's main point.
(C) It is an intermediate conclusion that is offered as direct support for the argument's main conclusion.	→ There are no subsidiary conclusions. The statement in question *is* the main point. Eliminate.
(D) It is a premise offered in support of the argument's conclusion.	→ Distortion. It *is* the main point. The rest of the argument is evidence. Eliminate.
(E) It is a premise offered as direct support for an intermediate conclusion of the argument. *PrepTest57 Sec2 Q16*	→ Distortion. The statement in question is the main point, and there are no intermediate conclusions. Eliminate.

LSAT Question	Analysis
34. Columnist: It has been noted that attending a live musical performance is a richer experience than is listening to recorded music. Some say that this is merely because we do not see the performers when we listen to recorded music. However, there must be some other reason, for there is relatively little difference between listening to someone read a story over the radio and listening to someone in the same room read a story. $\longrightarrow$	**Step 2: Conclusion:** [first part of sentence 3] Seeing the musicians is *not the reason* live music is richer (my opponents' explanation is wrong). Sentence 1—**background observation:** Live music is a richer experience than recorded music. [This is the statement in the question stem.] Sentence 2—**the author's opponents' explanation for the observation:** Live music is richer because we see the musicians. Second part of sentence 3—**author's evidence:** an analogy showing why the opponents' explanation must be wrong.
Which one of the following most accurately expresses the role played in the argument by the observation that attending a live musical performance is a richer experience than is listening to recorded music? $\longrightarrow$	**Step 1:** Role of a Statement question—the correct answer will describe how the statement fits into the argument.
	Step 3: The statement in question stipulates a fact. The author and his opponents fight about *the reason* it is true.
(A) It is what the columnist's argument purports to show. $\longrightarrow$	**Step 4:** Distortion. The author wants to show that someone else's explanation for the statement is wrong. Eliminate.
(B) It is the reason given for the claim that the columnist's argument is attempting to undermine. $\longrightarrow$	Distortion. The statement in question is not the reason for the claim; it *is* the claim. Moreover, the author is not trying to undermine the claim, but rather, his opponents' explanation of it. Eliminate.
(C) It is what the columnist's argument purports to explain. $\longrightarrow$	Distortion. The author never offers his own explanation for why live music is richer; he just wants to show that his opponents' explanation is wrong. Eliminate.
(D) It is what the columnist's argument purports to refute. $\longrightarrow$	The author does not want to refute the claim that live music is richer. Implicitly, he accepts that. He wants to show that seeing the musicians is not the reason it is richer. Eliminate.
(E) It is what the position that the columnist tries to undermine is purported to explain. *PrepTest59 Sec2 Q7* $\longrightarrow$	Correct. The author and his opponents agree that live music is a richer experience. The opponents try to explain this by saying, "It is true because you see the musicians." Their explanation is what the author rejects.

Outlining Complete Arguments and Point at Issue Questions

All LSAT arguments—even those written in the most complicated prose—can be reduced to the pattern of "conclusion *because* evidence."

LEARNING OBJECTIVES

In this section, you'll learn to:

· Outline complete arguments
· Identify and answer Point at Issue questions

When you distill an LSAT argument down to its essence, accept the background information as given, and focus on the conclusion and the evidence the author offers in direct support of her main point.

Here's how an LSAT expert might outline one of the complete arguments you saw earlier.

LSAT Question	Analysis
The typological theory of species classification, which has few adherents today, distinguishes species solely on the basis of observable physical characteristics, such as plumage color, adult size, or dental structure. However, there are many so-called "sibling species," which are indistinguishable on the basis of their appearance but cannot interbreed and thus, according to the mainstream biological theory of species classification, are separate species. Since the typological theory does not count sibling species as separate species, it is unacceptable.	Conclusion: The typological theory of species classification is unacceptable. *because* Evidence: The typological theory of species classification does not count sibling species as separate species (while the mainstream theory does).
PrepTest51 Sec1 Q15	

An expert reader uses the background information—such as the definition of sibling species—to get the context she needs, but her analysis of the argument zeroes in on the author's conclusion and evidence.

LSAT STRATEGY

When a Logical Reasoning question includes two arguments, or when a single argument involves the author's response to someone else's position, paraphrase both arguments and be sure you understand how they relate to one another.

Practice

Outline the argument structure, using the "conclusion because evidence" format, in each of the following LSAT stimuli.

LSAT Question	My Analysis
35. A survey of clerical workers' attitudes toward their work identified a group of secretaries with very positive attitudes. They responded "Strongly agree" to such statements as "I enjoy word processing" and "I like learning new secretarial skills." These secretaries had been rated by their supervisors as excellent workers—far better than secretaries whose attitudes were identified as less positive. Clearly these secretaries' positive attitudes toward their work produced excellent job performance. *PrepTest49 Sec2 Q13*	Conclusion: *because* Evidence:
36. There can be no individual freedom without the rule of law, for there is no individual freedom without social integrity, and pursuing the good life is not possible without social integrity. *PrepTest61 Sec4 Q25*	Conclusion: *because* Evidence:
37. Letter to the editor: Middle-class families in wealthy nations are often criticized for the ecological damage resulting from their lifestyles. This criticism should not be taken too seriously, however, since its source is often a movie star or celebrity whose own lifestyle would, if widely adopted, destroy the environment and deplete our resources in a short time. *PrepTest49 Sec2 Q5*	Conclusion: *because* Evidence:
38. Ilana: Carver's stories are somber and pessimistic, which is a sure sign of inferior writing. I have never read a single story of his that ends happily. Gustav: Carver was one of the finest writers of the past 30 years. Granted, his stories are characterized by somberness and pessimism, but they are also wryly humorous, compassionate, and beautifully structured. *PrepTest49 Sec2 Q1*	**[Ilana]** Conclusion: *because* Evidence: **[Gustav]** Conclusion: *because* Evidence:

LSAT Question		My Analysis
39. Vanwilligan: Some have argued that professional athletes receive unfairly high salaries. But in an unrestricted free market, such as the market these athletes compete in, salaries are determined by what someone else is willing to pay for their services. These athletes make enormous profits for their teams' owners, and that is why owners are willing to pay them extraordinary salaries. Thus the salaries they receive are fair. *PrepTest49 Sec2 Q19*	$\longrightarrow$	Conclusion: *because* Evidence:
40. A development company has proposed building an airport near the city of Dalton. If the majority of Dalton's residents favor the proposal, the airport will be built. However, it is unlikely that a majority of Dalton's residents would favor the proposal, for most of them believe that the airport would create noise problems. Thus, it is unlikely that the airport will be built. *PrepTest61 Sec4 Q11*	$\longrightarrow$	Conclusion: *because* Evidence:
41. Politician: The huge amounts of money earned by oil companies elicit the suspicion that the regulations designed to prevent collusion need to be tightened. But just the opposite is true. If the regulations designed to prevent collusion are not excessively burdensome, then oil companies will make profits sufficient to motivate the very risky investments associated with exploration that must be made if society is to have adequate oil supplies. But recent data show that the oil industry's profits are not the highest among all industries. Clearly, the regulatory burden on oil companies has become excessive. *PrepTest49 Sec4 Q12*	$\longrightarrow$	Conclusion: *because* Evidence:
42. Talbert: Chess is beneficial for school-age children. It is enjoyable, encourages foresight and logical thinking, and discourages carelessness, inattention, and impulsiveness. In short, it promotes mental maturity. Sklar: My objection to teaching chess to children is that it diverts mental activity from something with societal value, such as science, into something that has no societal value. *PrepTest61 Sec2 Q7*	$\longrightarrow$	[Talbert] Conclusion: *because* Evidence: [Sklar] Conclusion: *because* Evidence:

Expert Analysis

Here's how an LSAT expert might outline the argument structure in each of those LSAT stimuli.

LSAT Question	Analysis
35. A survey of clerical workers' attitudes toward their work identified a group of secretaries with very positive attitudes. They responded "Strongly agree" to such statements as "I enjoy word processing" and "I like learning new secretarial skills." These secretaries had been rated by their supervisors as excellent workers—far better than secretaries whose attitudes were identified as less positive. Clearly these secretaries' positive attitudes toward their work produced excellent job performance. *PrepTest49 Sec2 Q13*	Conclusion: The positive attitudes of secretaries in the positive group caused their excellent job performance. *because* Evidence: Secretaries in the positive group were rated excellent workers by their supervisors. Secretaries not in the positive group were rated lower.
36. There can be no individual freedom without the rule of law, for there is no individual freedom without social integrity, and pursuing the good life is not possible without social integrity. *PrepTest61 Sec4 Q25*	Conclusion: Individual freedom requires the rule of law. *because* Evidence: Individual freedom requires social integrity.
37. Letter to the editor: Middle-class families in wealthy nations are often criticized for the ecological damage resulting from their lifestyles. This criticism should not be taken too seriously, however, since its source is often a movie star or celebrity whose own lifestyle would, if widely adopted, destroy the environment and deplete our resources in a short time. *PrepTest49 Sec2 Q5*	Conclusion: The criticism that middle-class lifestyles cause ecological damage should not be taken seriously. *because* Evidence: Those making the criticism are often celebrities who live worse lifestyles.
38. Ilana: Carver's stories are somber and pessimistic, which is a sure sign of inferior writing. I have never read a single story of his that ends happily. Gustav: Carver was one of the finest writers of the past 30 years. Granted, his stories are characterized by somberness and pessimism, but they are also wryly humorous, compassionate, and beautifully structured. *PrepTest49 Sec2 Q1*	[Ilana] Conclusion: Carver's writing is inferior. *because* Evidence: 1) Somberness and pessimism are signs of inferior writing. 2) I've never read a happy Carver story. [Gustav] Conclusion: Carver was one of the best writers of the last three decades. *because* Evidence: Carver's stories are funny, compassionate, and well-structured (even if they are somber and pessimistic).

LSAT Question	Analysis
39. Vanwilligan: Some have argued that professional athletes receive unfairly high salaries. But in an unrestricted free market, such as the market these athletes compete in, salaries are determined by what someone else is willing to pay for their services. These athletes make enormous profits for their teams' owners, and that is why owners are willing to pay them extraordinary salaries. Thus the salaries they receive are fair. *PrepTest49 Sec2 Q19*	Conclusion: Professional athletes' salaries are fair. *because* Evidence: 1) The free market sets salaries at what employers are willing to pay, and 2) team owners are willing to pay professional athletes' salaries.
40. A development company has proposed building an airport near the city of Dalton. If the majority of Dalton's residents favor the proposal, the airport will be built. However, it is unlikely that a majority of Dalton's residents would favor the proposal, for most of them believe that the airport would create noise problems. Thus, it is unlikely that the airport will be built. *PrepTest61 Sec4 Q11*	Conclusion: The proposed Dalton airport probably will not be built. *because* Evidence: A majority of Dalton residents probably won't support building the proposed airport.
41. Politician: The huge amounts of money earned by oil companies elicit the suspicion that the regulations designed to prevent collusion need to be tightened. But just the opposite is true. If the regulations designed to prevent collusion are not excessively burdensome, then oil companies will make profits sufficient to motivate the very risky investments associated with exploration that must be made if society is to have adequate oil supplies. But recent data show that the oil industry's profits are not the highest among all industries. Clearly, the regulatory burden on oil companies has become excessive. *PrepTest49 Sec4 Q12*	Conclusion: Oil companies are excessively burdened by regulation. *because* Evidence: Oil companies' profits are not the highest among all industries.
42. Talbert: Chess is beneficial for school-age children. It is enjoyable, encourages foresight and logical thinking, and discourages carelessness, inattention, and impulsiveness. In short, it promotes mental maturity. Sklar: My objection to teaching chess to children is that it diverts mental activity from something with societal value, such as science, into something that has no societal value. *PrepTest61 Sec2 Q7*	**[Talbert]** Conclusion: Chess is good for school kids. *because* Evidence: Chess promotes mental maturity (in three specific ways). **[Sklar]** Conclusion: Teaching chess to school kids is objectionable. *because* Evidence: Chess diverts mental activity away from things with social value to something without social value.

Identify and Answer Point at Issue Questions

Once you are able to summarize complete arguments, you have the skill necessary to answer Point at Issue questions. These questions require you to pinpoint the specific issue about which two speakers disagree. In rare cases, they will ask for a point of agreement between the speakers.

Point at Issue questions always present a dialogue stimulus, but not every dialogue stimulus represents a Point at Issue question. You can identify Point at Issue questions from question stems like these:

The dialogue most strongly supports the claim that
Constance and Brigita disagree with each other about
which one of the following?

PrepTest51 Sec1 Q23

Megan and Channen disagree over whether

PrepTest49 Sec2 Q10

On the basis of their statements, Price and Albrecht are
committed to disagreeing about whether

PrepTest59 Sec2 Q2

POINT AT ISSUE AT A GLANCE

Task: Identify the specific claim, statement, or recommendation about which two speakers disagree (or rarely, about which they agree).

Strategy: Analyze both speakers' arguments and determine the point at issue between them, or use the Point at Issue Tree approach to identify the correct answer.

On LSAT tests released from 2009 through 2013, there were an average of 1.7 Point at Issue questions.

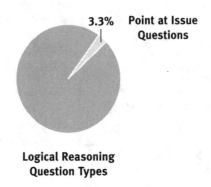

3.3% **Point at Issue Questions**

**Logical Reasoning
Question Types**

PrepTests57–71; released 2009–2013

Point at Issue Tree

In Point at Issue questions, one (and only one) answer choice will contain a statement about which the two speakers disagree. This provides a built-in way to evaluate the answer choices efficiently and effectively. It is depicted in the "decision tree" model that follows.

> **TEST DAY TIP**
>
> A great way to evaluate the answer choices in Point at Issue questions is to apply the questions from the Point at Issue Tree to the answer choices to identify the right answer.

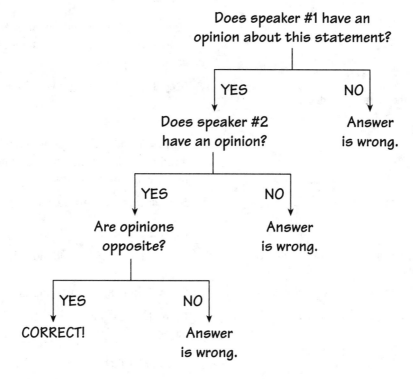

What are the characteristics of wrong answers in Point at Issue questions?

Here is how an LSAT expert might analyze a Point at Issue question.

LSAT Question	Analysis
Talbert: Chess is beneficial for school-age children. It is enjoyable, encourages foresight and logical thinking, and discourages carelessness, inattention, and impulsiveness. In short, it promotes mental maturity. Sklar: My objection to teaching chess to children is that it diverts mental activity from something with societal value, such as science, into something that has no societal value.	**Step 2:** [Talbert] Conclusion: Chess is good for school kids. *because* Evidence: Chess promotes mental maturity (in three specific ways). [Sklar] Conclusion: Teaching chess to school kids is objectionable. *because* Evidence: Chess diverts mental activity away from things with social value to something without social value.
Talbert's and Sklar's statements provide the strongest support for holding that they disagree with each other over whether	**Step 1:** [D]*isagree* signals a Point at Issue question.
	Step 3: T and S disagree about whether chess is good for school children. The Point at Issue Tree helps evaluate each answer choice.
(A) chess promotes mental maturity	**Step 4:** Does Talbert have an opinion? Yes. Does Sklar have an opinion? No. Eliminate.
(B) many activities promote mental maturity just as well as chess does	Does Talbert have an opinion? No. Eliminate.
(C) chess is socially valuable and science is not	Does Talbert have an opinion? No. Eliminate.
(D) children should be taught to play chess	Correct. Does Talbert have an opinion? Yes. He agrees. Does Sklar have an opinion? Yes. He disagrees. Are the opinions opposite? Yes.
(E) children who neither play chess nor study science are mentally immature *PrepTest61 Sec2 Q7*	Does Talbert have an opinion? No. Eliminate.

Practice

Use the Logical Reasoning Method and the Point at Issue Tree to complete the following questions.

LSAT Question	My Analysis
43. Ilana: Carver's stories are somber and pessimistic, which is a sure sign of inferior writing. I have never read a single story of his that ends happily.	**Step 2:**
Gustav: Carver was one of the finest writers of the past 30 years. Granted, his stories are characterized by somberness and pessimism, but they are also wryly humorous, compassionate, and beautifully structured. $\longrightarrow$	
On the basis of their statements, Ilana and Gustav are committed to disagreeing over whether $\longrightarrow$	**Step 1:**
	Step 3:
(A) Carver's stories are truly compassionate $\longrightarrow$	**Step 4:**
(B) Carver's stories are pessimistic in their vision $\longrightarrow$	
(C) stories that are characterized by somberness and pessimism can appropriately be called humorous $\longrightarrow$	
(D) stories that are well written can be somber and pessimistic $\longrightarrow$	
(E) there are some characteristics of a story that are decisive in determining its aesthetic value $\longrightarrow$	

PrepTest49 Sec2 Q1

LSAT Question	My Analysis
44. Megan: People pursue wealth beyond what their basic needs require only if they see it as a way of achieving high status or prestige.	**Step 2:**
Channen: Not everybody thinks that way. After all, money is the universal medium of exchange. So, if you have enough of it, you can exchange it for whatever other material goods you may need or want even if you are indifferent to what others think of you. $\longrightarrow$	
Megan and Channen disagree over whether $\longrightarrow$	**Step 1:**
	Step 3:
(A) people ever pursue wealth beyond what is required for their basic needs $\longrightarrow$	**Step 4:**
(B) it is irrational to try to achieve high status or prestige in the eyes of one's society $\longrightarrow$	
(C) the pursuit of monetary wealth is irrational only when it has no further purpose $\longrightarrow$	
(D) it is rational to maximize one's ability to purchase whatever one wants only when the motive for doing so is something other than the desire for prestige $\longrightarrow$	
(E) the motive for pursuing wealth beyond what one's basic needs require is ever anything other than the desire for prestige or high status $\longrightarrow$	

PrepTest49 Sec2 Q10

LSAT Question		My Analysis
45. Wong: Although all countries are better off as democracies, a transitional autocratic stage is sometimes required before a country can become democratic.		**Step 2:**
Tate: The freedom and autonomy that democracy provides are of genuine value but the simple material needs of people are more important. Some countries can better meet these needs as autocracies than as democracies.	$\longrightarrow$	
Wong's and Tate's statements provide the most support for the claim that they disagree over the truth of which one of the following?	$\longrightarrow$	**Step 1:**
		Step 3:
(A) There are some countries that are better off as autocracies than as democracies.	$\longrightarrow$	**Step 4:**
(B) Nothing is more important to a country than the freedom and autonomy of the individuals who live in that country.	$\longrightarrow$	
(C) In some cases, a country cannot become a democracy.	$\longrightarrow$	
(D) The freedom and autonomy that democracy provides are of genuine value.	$\longrightarrow$	
(E) All democracies succeed in meeting the simple material needs of people.	$\longrightarrow$	

PrepTest61 Sec4 Q18

Expert Analysis

Here's how an LSAT expert might have approached those practice questions.

LSAT Question	Analysis
43. Ilana: Carver's stories are somber and pessimistic, which is a sure sign of inferior writing. I have never read a single story of his that ends happily. Gustav: Carver was one of the finest writers of the past 30 years. Granted, his stories are characterized by somberness and pessimism, but they are also wryly humorous, compassionate, and beautifully structured.	**Step 2:** [Ilana] Conclusion: Carver's writing is inferior. *because* Evidence: 1) Somberness and pessimism are signs of inferior writing. 2) I've never read a happy Carver story. **[Gustav]** Conclusion: Carver was one of the best writers of the last three decades. *because* Evidence: Carver's stories are funny, compassionate, and well-structured (even if they are somber and pessimistic).
On the basis of their statements, Ilana and Gustav are committed to disagreeing over whether	**Step 1:** "[C]ommitted to disagreeing" signals a Point at Issue question.
	Step 3: I & G disagree about whether Carver's somberness and pessimism make him a bad writer. The Point at Issue Tree helps evaluate each answer choice.
(A) Carver's stories are truly compassionate	**Step 4:** Ilana expresses no opinion on this. Eliminate.
(B) Carver's stories are pessimistic in their vision	180. Ilana and Gustav *agree* that Carver's stories are pessimistic. Eliminate.
(C) stories that are characterized by somberness and pessimism can appropriately be called humorous	Ilana expresses no opinion about this. Eliminate.
(D) stories that are well written can be somber and pessimistic	Correct. Ilana has an opinion (she disagrees). Gustav has an opinion (he agrees). The two opinions are opposite.
(E) there are some characteristics of a story that are decisive in determining its aesthetic value *PrepTest49 Sec2 Q1*	Ilana would agree with this statement, but Gustav seems to think that stories can be good despite or because of various characteristics. Eliminate.

LSAT Question	Analysis
44. Megan: People pursue wealth beyond what their basic needs require only if they see it as a way of achieving high status or prestige.	**Step 2: [Megan]** Conclusion: If people pursue wealth beyond their needs, then they see wealth as a means to status or prestige. [No evidence.]
Channen: Not everybody thinks that way. After all, money is the universal medium of exchange. So, if you have enough of it, you can exchange it for whatever other material goods you may need or want even if you are indifferent to what others think of you.	**[Channen]** Conclusion: Status and prestige aren't the only motivations for acquiring wealth beyond one's needs. *because* Evidence: Wealth is money, and with enough, you buy anything you want.
Megan and Channen disagree over whether	**Step 1:** "[D]isagree over whether" signals a Point at Issue question.
	Step 3: M & C disagree about whether status and prestige are the only reasons people seek excess wealth. The Point at Issue Tree will help evaluate the answer choices.
(A) people ever pursue wealth beyond what is required for their basic needs	**Step 4:** 180. At least implicitly, the two speakers *agree* that people pursue excess wealth. Eliminate.
(B) it is irrational to try to achieve high status or prestige in the eyes of one's society	Neither speaker expresses an opinion on this statement. Eliminate.
(C) the pursuit of monetary wealth is irrational only when it has no further purpose	Neither speaker opines on whether the pursuit of wealth is *irrational* in any case. Eliminate.
(D) it is rational to maximize one's ability to purchase whatever one wants only when the motive for doing so is something other than the desire for prestige	Megan says nothing about whether the pursuit of excess wealth is ever *rational*. Eliminate.
(E) the motive for pursuing wealth beyond what one's basic needs require is ever anything other than the desire for prestige or high status *PrepTest49 Sec2 Q10*	Correct. Megan would disagree (status and prestige are the *only* motivators). Channen would agree (sometimes it's just about "things"). The two opinions are opposite.

LSAT Question	Analysis
45. Wong: Although all countries are better off as democracies, a transitional autocratic stage is sometimes required before a country can become democratic.	**Step 2:** [Wong] Conclusion: Sometimes, a transitional autocratic stage is needed for a country to become democratic, but democracies are always better off. [No evidence.]
Tate: The freedom and autonomy that democracy provides are of genuine value, but the simple material needs of people are more important. Some countries can better meet these needs as autocracies than as democracies.	[Tate] Conclusion: Some countries can better meet the *more important* material needs of their people as autocracies than they can as democracies.
Wong's and Tate's statements provide the most support for the claim that they disagree over the truth of which one of the following?	**Step 1:** "[D]isagree over the truth of which one" signals a Point at Issue question.
	Step 3: W & T disagree about whether all countries are better off as democracies. The Point at Issue Tree will help evaluate the answer choices.
(A) There are some countries that are better off as autocracies than as democracies.	**Step 4:** Correct. Both speakers express an opinion, and their opinions are opposites.
(B) Nothing is more important to a country than the freedom and autonomy of the individuals who live in that country.	Wong doesn't express an opinion on this point. He thinks democracies are always better off, but doesn't say why he thinks so. Eliminate.
(C) In some cases, a country cannot become a democracy.	Neither speaker expresses an opinion on this statement. Eliminate.
(D) The freedom and autonomy that democracy provides are of genuine value.	Tate explicitly agrees with this point. While Wong prefers democracy, he doesn't say why. Perhaps the speakers agree on this point, but Wong is not explicit enough to know for sure. Eliminate.
(E) All democracies succeed in meeting the simple material needs of people.	Wong expresses no opinion on this statement. Eliminate.

PrepTest61 Sec4 Q18

Describing Argument Strategies and Method of Argument Questions

Now that you have some practice outlining argument structures, you're ready to learn how to describe authors' argumentative strategies, that is, to summarize *how* an author tries to convince the reader.

LEARNING OBJECTIVES

In this section, you'll learn to:

- Describe an author's argumentative strategy
- Identify and answer Method of Argument questions

Describing an author's method of argument may, at first, seem somewhat generic and abstract. Instead of focusing on the content of the argument, you have to summarize the author's technique. Keywords help keep your focus on what the author does rather than what she says. Here's how an LSAT expert might describe the argumentative strategy in an argument you saw earlier in the chapter.

LSAT Question	Analysis
Columnist: It has been noted that attending a live musical performance is a richer experience than is listening to recorded music. Some say that this is merely because we do not see the performers when we listen to recorded music. However, there must be some other reason, for there is relatively little difference between listening to someone read a story over the radio and listening to someone in the same room read a story. *PrepTest59 Sec2 Q7*	The author offers an analogy (stories on the radio are like recorded music) as a supposed counterexample to a claim (live music is richer because you see the musicians).

It is impossible to anticipate exactly the argumentative strategies you'll see on Test Day, but a few methods of argument appear more regularly on the LSAT than others.

LSAT STRATEGY

Methods of argument common on the LSAT include:

- Analogy, in which an author draws parallels between two unrelated (but purportedly similar) situations
- Example, in which an author cites specific cases in order to justify a generalization
- Counterexamples, in which an author seeks to discredit an opponent's argument by citing a specific case in which the opponent's conclusion appears to be invalid
- Appeal to authority, in which an author cites an expert or another figure as support for her conclusion
- Elimination of alternatives, in which an author lists possibilities and discredits all but one
- Ad hominem attack, in which an author attacks her opponent's personal credibility rather than the substance of her opponent's argument
- Means/Requirements, in which the author argues that something is needed to achieve a desired result

Practice

Describe the method of argument used in each of the following stimuli.

LSAT Question	My Analysis
46. The more modern archaeologists learn about Mayan civilization, the better they understand its intellectual achievements. Not only were numerous scientific observations and predictions made by Mayan astronomers, but the people in general seem to have had a strong grasp of sophisticated mathematical concepts. We know this from the fact that the writings of the Mayan religious scribes exhibit a high degree of mathematical competence. $\longrightarrow$	
PrepTest59 Sec3 Q8	
47. Archaeologist: After the last ice age, groups of paleohumans left Siberia and crossed the Bering land bridge, which no longer exists, into North America. Archaeologists have discovered in Siberia a cache of Clovis points—the distinctive stone spear points made by paleohumans. This shows that, contrary to previous belief, the Clovis point was not invented in North America. $\longrightarrow$	
PrepTest57 Sec2 Q22	
48. To predict that a device will be invented, one must develop a conception of the device that includes some details at least about how it will function and the consequences of its use. But clearly, then, the notion of predicting an invention is self-contradictory, for inventing means developing a detailed conception, and one cannot predict what has already taken place. $\longrightarrow$	
PrepTest59 Sec3 Q23	
49. Letter to the editor: Middle-class families in wealthy nations are often criticized for the ecological damage resulting from their lifestyles. This criticism should not be taken too seriously, however, since its source is often a movie star or celebrity whose own lifestyle would, if widely adopted, destroy the environment and deplete our resources in a short time. $\longrightarrow$	
PrepTest49 Sec2 Q5	

LSAT Question	**My Analysis**
50. Gilbert: This food label is mistaken. It says that these cookies contain only natural ingredients, but they contain alphahydroxy acids that are chemically synthesized by the cookie company at their plant. Sabina: The label is not mistaken. After all, alphahydroxy acids also are found occurring naturally in sugarcane. *PrepTest59 Sec2 Q5*	→
51. In modern deep-diving marine mammals, such as whales, the outer shell of the bones is porous. This has the effect of making the bones light enough so that it is easy for the animals to swim back to the surface after a deep dive. The outer shell of the bones was also porous in the ichthyosaur, an extinct prehistoric marine reptile. We can conclude from this that ichthyosaurs were deep divers. *PrepTest61 Sec4 Q21*	→

Expert Analysis

Here's how an LSAT expert might analyze those arguments.

LSAT Question	Analysis
46. The more modern archaeologists learn about Mayan civilization, the better they understand its intellectual achievements. Not only were numerous scientific observations and predictions made by Mayan astronomers, but the people in general seem to have had a strong grasp of sophisticated mathematical concepts. We know this from the fact that the writings of the Mayan religious scribes exhibit a high degree of mathematical competence. *PrepTest59 Sec3 Q8*	Examples. The author cites the knowledge of Mayan astronomers and the general population in order to reach a conclusion about Mayan religious scribes.
47. Archaeologist: After the last ice age, groups of paleohumans left Siberia and crossed the Bering land bridge, which no longer exists, into North America. Archaeologists have discovered in Siberia a cache of Clovis points—the distinctive stone spear points made by paleohumans. This shows that, contrary to previous belief, the Clovis point was not invented in North America. *PrepTest57 Sec2 Q22*	The author offers a supposed counterexample that he claims undermines a previous belief.
48. To predict that a device will be invented, one must develop a conception of the device that includes some details at least about how it will function and the consequences of its use. But clearly, then, the notion of predicting an invention is self-contradictory, for inventing means developing a detailed conception, and one cannot predict what has already taken place. *PrepTest59 Sec3 Q23*	The author uses two definitions to show that a certain type of prediction is a contradiction in terms.
49. Letter to the editor: Middle-class families in wealthy nations are often criticized for the ecological damage resulting from their lifestyles. This criticism should not be taken too seriously, however, since its source is often a movie star or celebrity whose own lifestyle would, if widely adopted, destroy the environment and deplete our resources in a short time. *PrepTest49 Sec2 Q5*	Ad hominem attack. The author concludes that a social critique need not be taken seriously because many who make the critique act hypocritically.

LSAT Question	Analysis
50. Gilbert: This food label is mistaken. It says that these cookies contain only natural ingredients, but they contain alphahydroxy acids that are chemically synthesized by the cookie company at their plant. Sabina: The label is not mistaken. After all, alphahydroxy acids also are found occurring naturally in sugarcane. *PrepTest59 Sec2 Q5*	[Gilbert] Means/Requirement. Argues that an ingredient does not fit a definition. [Sabina] Means/Requirement. Argues that the ingredient does fit the definition.
51. In modern deep-diving marine mammals, such as whales, the outer shell of the bones is porous. This has the effect of making the bones light enough so that it is easy for the animals to swim back to the surface after a deep dive. The outer shell of the bones was also porous in the ichthyosaur, an extinct prehistoric marine reptile. We can conclude from this that ichthyosaurs were deep divers. *PrepTest61 Sec4 Q21*	Analogy. From the fact that a modern animal displays a characteristic, the author concludes that ancient animals with the same characteristic must have behaved in the same way.

Identify and Answer Method of Argument Questions

Method of Argument questions, like many Reading Comprehension questions, focus on the argument's structure more than on its content. The correct answer will describe the author's argumentative strategy, usually in generic, abstract terms.

You can identify Method of Argument questions from question stems such as these.

Which one of the following most accurately describes
the technique of reasoning employed by the argument?

PrepTest59 Sec3 Q23

In the conversation, Hernandez responds to Green's
objection in which one of the following ways?

PrepTest57 Sec3 Q5

The argument proceeds by

PrepTest49 Sec4 Q15

Note how all of those question stems, despite their different wording, ask you describe *how* the author makes her argument.

METHOD OF ARGUMENT AT A GLANCE

Task: Describe the author's argumentative strategy, *how* she argues (not necessarily what she says).

Strategy: Identify the author's conclusion and evidence; take note of Keywords indicating the author's purpose; and summarize the author's strategy in generic, descriptive terms.

Method of Argument questions are relatively rare in the Logical Reasoning sections of the test. LSAT tests released from 2009 through 2013 had an average of 1.7 Method of Argument questions.

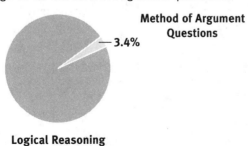

Method of Argument Questions

— 3.4%

Logical Reasoning Question Types

*PrepTests57–71; released 2009–2013

Here's how an LSAT expert would attack a Method of Argument question.

LSAT Question	Analysis
Hernandez: I recommend that staff cars be replaced every four years instead of every three years. Three-year-old cars are still in good condition and this would result in big savings. Green: I disagree. Some of our salespeople with big territories wear out their cars in three years. Hernandez: I meant three-year-old cars subjected to normal use.	**Step 2:** Hernandez's response begins with "I meant," which suggests that she has to clarify something that she's said. Examining her original statement, we see that she is clarifying her comment regarding three-year-old cars.
In the conversation, Hernandez responds to Green's objection in which one of the following ways?	**Step 1:** "[R]esponds ... in which ... way" means the right answer will describe how Hernandez responds (not *what* she says in response). This is a Method of Argument question.
	Step 3: Clarifying an earlier statement
(A) by explicitly qualifying a premise used earlier	**Step 4:** Correct. Hernandez clarifies her original evidence, so "explicitly qualifying a premise" is a perfect description of *how* she responds.
(B) by criticizing salespeople who wear out their cars in three years	Hernandez doesn't criticize anyone. Moreover, she clarifies her statement to exclude the salespeople with big territories. Eliminate.
(C) by disputing the accuracy of Green's evidence	Hernandez seems to agree with Green's evidence; that's why she clarifies her statement to exclude cars driven by people with big territories. Eliminate.
(D) by changing the subject to the size of sales territories	Hernandez does not change the subject; Green is the one who mentions territory size. Eliminate.
(E) by indicating that Green used a phrase ambiguously *PrepTest57 Sec3 Q5*	Hernandez says nothing about how Green *used* a phrase (although she implies something about how Green may have understood the phrase Hernandez used). Eliminate.

Practice

Use the Logical Reasoning Method to complete the following Method of Argument questions.

LSAT Question	My Analysis
52. Economist: A country's trade deficit may indicate weakness in its economy, but it does not in itself weaken that economy. So restricting imports to reduce a trade deficit would be like sticking a thermometer into a glass of cold water in the hope of bringing down a patient's feverish temperature. $\longrightarrow$	**Step 2:**
The economist's argument employs which one of the following techniques? $\longrightarrow$	**Step 1:**
	Step 3:
(A) claiming that a crucial assumption entails a falsehood $\longrightarrow$	**Step 4:**
(B) demonstrating that an analogy explicitly used to establish a certain conclusion is faulty $\longrightarrow$	
(C) appealing to an analogy in order to indicate the futility of a course of action $\longrightarrow$	
(D) calling into question the authority on the basis of which a claim is made $\longrightarrow$	
(E) showing that a recommended course of action would have disastrous consequences $\longrightarrow$ *PrepTest59 Sec3 Q14*	

LSAT Question	**My Analysis**

53. To predict that a device will be invented, one must develop a conception of the device that includes some details at least about how it will function and the consequences of its use. But clearly, then, the notion of predicting an invention is self-contradictory, for inventing means developing a detailed conception, and one cannot predict what has already taken place. $\longrightarrow$

Step 2:

Which one of the following most accurately describes the technique of reasoning employed by the argument? $\longrightarrow$

Step 1:

Step 3:

(A) constructing a counterexample to a general hypothesis about the future

Step 4:

$\longrightarrow$

(B) appealing to definitions to infer the impossibility of a kind of occurrence

$\longrightarrow$

(C) countering a hypothesis by indicating the falsehood of the implications of that hypothesis

$\longrightarrow$

(D) pointing out how a problem is widely thought to be scientific yet is really conceptual

$\longrightarrow$

(E) attempting to show that predicting any event implies that it has in fact already taken place

PrepTest59 Sec3 Q23 $\longrightarrow$

Expert Analysis

Here's how an LSAT expert might approach those practice questions.

LSAT Question	Analysis
52. Economist: A country's trade deficit may indicate weakness in its economy, but it does not in itself weaken that economy. So restricting imports to reduce a trade deficit would be like sticking a thermometer into a glass of cold water in the hope of bringing down a patient's feverish temperature. →	**Step 2:** Conclusion: Restricting imports to fix a trade deficit is like chilling a thermometer to reduce a sick person's fever. *because* Evidence: A trade deficit reveals (but does not cause) economic weakness. The author uses an analogy to make her point.
The economist's argument employs which one of the following techniques? →	**Step 1:** "[E]mploys which … techniques": a Method of Argument question. The correct answer will accurately describe how the author makes her case.
	Step 3: The author uses an analogy to show why an action is misguided.
(A) claiming that a crucial assumption entails a falsehood →	**Step 4:** Distortion. The author says nothing about another argument's assumption. Eliminate.
(B) demonstrating that an analogy explicitly used to establish a certain conclusion is faulty →	180. It is the author who uses the analogy; she apparently thinks it is an apt one. Eliminate.
(C) appealing to an analogy in order to indicate the futility of a course of action →	Correct. This describes the author's argumentative strategy precisely: just as chilling the thermometer won't help the patient, slowing imports won't help the economy.
(D) calling into question the authority on the basis of which a claim is made →	The author doesn't question anyone's authority or expertise. Eliminate.
(E) showing that a recommended course of action would have disastrous consequences *PrepTest59 Sec3 Q14* →	Extreme. The author simply says the action won't work, not that it would be disastrous. Eliminate.

LSAT Question	Analysis
53. To predict that a device will be invented, one must develop a conception of the device that includes some details at least about how it will function and the consequences of its use. But clearly, then, the notion of predicting an invention is self-contradictory, for inventing means developing a detailed conception, and one cannot predict what has already taken place. $\longrightarrow$	**Step 2:** Conclusion: The idea of predicting an invention is self-contradictory. *because* Evidence: 1) predicting an invention has to include details about the device's function and use, and 2) detailing a device's function and use is inventing. In short, if you've predicted an invention, then you have invented it, so you cannot *predict* what's already happened.
Which one of the following most accurately describes the technique of reasoning employed by the argument? $\longrightarrow$	**Step 1:** "[D]escribes the technique of reasoning" signals a Method of Argument question. The correct answer will accurately describe how the author makes his case.
	Step 3: The author shows how two definitions make it a contradiction to say you've done something.
(A) constructing a counterexample to a general hypothesis about the future $\longrightarrow$	**Step 4:** Outside the Scope. No general hypothesis about the future is discussed, and the author presents no counterexamples to anything. Eliminate.
(B) appealing to definitions to infer the impossibility of a kind of occurrence $\longrightarrow$	Correct. The author infers that one cannot predict an invention, because by the time one has sufficiently predicted it, then it is, by definition, invented.
(C) countering a hypothesis by indicating the falsehood of the implications of that hypothesis $\longrightarrow$	Distortion. Nothing indicates that to "predict a device will be invented" is anyone's hypothesis, and the author appeals to the definitions of terms (not the implications of a hypothesis) to make his case. Eliminate.
(D) pointing out how a problem is widely thought to be scientific yet is really conceptual $\longrightarrow$	Outside the Scope. The author does not say that most people treat the idea of predicting an invention as scientific. Eliminate.
(E) attempting to show that predicting any event implies that it has in fact already taken place *PrepTest59 Sec3 Q23* $\longrightarrow$	Extreme. The author's argument is about predicting inventions, not about predicting *any event*. Eliminate.

REFLECTION

Look back over the arguments you saw in the chapter. Consider the various analytical skills that the LSAT rewarded.

- How do you now look at arguments differently?
- When you see an argument, can you zero in on the conclusion directly?
- Is it easier to spot what the author considers to be the direct and relevant evidence for the conclusion?
- Are you able to spot the actual points of disagreement between two speakers?
- Can you separate the author's argumentative strategy from the content of the argument? Do you think you could spot arguments with similar argumentative strategies even if they are on different subjects?

Arguments occur everywhere in the real world: television news and commentary, advertisements, debate over music, and claims about sports teams. In the coming days, read and listen to arguments very carefully. Apply the analytical skills you practiced in this chapter.

- What is the author's main point? Does she offer any subsidiary conclusions in the argument?
- What kind of conclusion is the author offering: a recommendation? a prediction? a comparison? an assertion of fact?
- Is the conclusion conditional?
- What is the author's evidence? Is it relevant to the conclusion?
- If two people are arguing, what is their actual disagreement over? Do they have points of agreement? Are the two actually making different points?
- What argumentative strategies are being used? Does the speaker or advertiser offer an analogy? A counterexample?
- What is the role of necessity and sufficiency in the arguments you read or hear?

In the next chapter, you'll take your analytical skills to the next level, learning to identify the assumption(s) an author is making (of which he or she may not even be aware). The skill of identifying assumptions opens the door to several of the most important—and most challenging—question types on the LSAT: Assumption, Strengthen/Weaken, Flaw, and Parallel Reasoning.

K | Part Three: Logical Reasoning
CHAPTER 9

Explanations to these questions can
be found in your Online Center.

QUESTION POOL

Here are some more questions of the types covered in this chapter: Main Point, Role of a Statement, Point at Issue, and Method of Argument.

1. The legislature is considering a proposed bill that would prohibit fishing in Eagle Bay. Despite widespread concern over the economic effect this ban would have on the local fishing industry, the bill should be enacted. The bay has one of the highest water pollution levels in the nation, and a recent study of the bay's fish found that 80 percent of them contained toxin levels that exceed governmental safety standards. Continuing to permit fishing in Eagle Bay could thus have grave effects on public health.

   The argument proceeds by presenting evidence that

   (A) the toxic contamination of fish in Eagle Bay has had grave economic effects on the local fishing industry
   (B) the moral principle that an action must be judged on the basis of its foreseeable effects is usually correct
   (C) the opponents of the ban have failed to weigh properly its foreseeable negative effects against its positive ones
   (D) failure to enact the ban would carry with it unacceptable risks for the public welfare
   (E) the ban would reduce the level of toxins in the fish in Eagle Bay

   PrepTest61 Sec2 Q4

2. Herbalist: While standard antibiotics typically have just one active ingredient, herbal antibacterial remedies typically contain several. Thus, such herbal remedies are more likely to retain their effectiveness against new, resistant strains of bacteria than are standard antibiotics. For a strain of bacteria, the difficulty of developing resistance to an herbal antibacterial remedy is like a cook's difficulty in trying to prepare a single meal that will please all of several dozen guests, a task far more difficult than preparing one meal that will please a single guest.

   In the analogy drawn in the argument above, which one of the following corresponds to a standard antibiotic?

   (A) a single guest
   (B) several dozen guests
   (C) the pleasure experienced by a single guest
   (D) a cook
   (E) the ingredients available to a cook

   PrepTest61 Sec2 Q17

3. Many nursing homes have prohibitions against having pets, and these should be lifted. The presence of an animal companion can yield health benefits by reducing a person's stress. A pet can also make one's time at a home more rewarding, which will be important to more people as the average life span of our population increases.

   Which one of the following most accurately expresses the conclusion drawn in the argument above?

   (A) As the average life span increases, it will be important to more people that life in nursing homes be rewarding.
   (B) Residents of nursing homes should enjoy the same rewarding aspects of life as anyone else.
   (C) The policy that many nursing homes have should be changed so that residents are allowed to have pets.
   (D) Having a pet can reduce one's stress and thereby make one a healthier person.
   (E) The benefits older people derive from having pets need to be recognized, especially as the average life span increases.

   PrepTest61 Sec4 Q16

4. Near many cities, contamination of lakes and rivers from pollutants in rainwater runoff exceeds that from industrial discharge. As the runoff washes over buildings and pavements, it picks up oil and other pollutants. Thus, water itself is among the biggest water polluters.

   The statement that contamination of lakes and rivers from pollutants in rainwater runoff exceeds that from industrial discharge plays which one of the following roles in the argument?

   (A) It is a conclusion for which the claim that water itself should be considered a polluter is offered as support.
   (B) It is cited as evidence that pollution from rainwater runoff is a more serious problem than pollution from industrial discharge.
   (C) It is a generalization based on the observation that rainwater runoff picks up oil and other pollutants as it washes over buildings and pavements.
   (D) It is a premise offered in support of the conclusion that water itself is among the biggest water polluters.
   (E) It is stated to provide an example of a typical kind of city pollution.

   PrepTest61 Sec4 Q17

Explanations to these questions can be found in your Online Center.

Part Three: Logical Reasoning
Argument-Based Questions

5. Pat: E-mail fosters anonymity, which removes barriers to self-revelation. This promotes a degree of intimacy with strangers that would otherwise take years of direct personal contact to attain.

   Amar: Frankness is not intimacy. Intimacy requires a real social bond, and social bonds cannot be formed without direct personal contact.

   The dialogue most strongly supports the claim that Pat and Amar disagree with each other about whether

   (A) barriers to self-revelation hinder the initial growth of intimacy
   (B) e-mail can increase intimacy between friends
   (C) intimacy between those who communicate with each other solely by e-mail is possible
   (D) real social bonds always lead to intimacy
   (E) the use of e-mail removes barriers to self-revelation

   PrepTest57 Sec2 Q11

6. Editorial: It is a travesty of justice, social critics say, that we can launch rockets into outer space but cannot solve social problems that have plagued humanity. The assumption underlying this assertion is that there are greater difficulties involved in a space launch than are involved in ending long-standing social problems, which in turn suggests that a government's failure to achieve the latter is simply a case of misplaced priorities. The criticism is misplaced, however, for rocket technology is much simpler than the human psyche, and until we adequately understand the human psyche we cannot solve the great social problems.

   The statement that rocket technology is much simpler than the human psyche plays which one of the following roles in the editorial's argument?

   (A) It is cited as a possible objection to the argument's conclusion.
   (B) According to the argument, it is a fact that has misled some social critics.
   (C) It is the argument's conclusion.
   (D) It is claimed to be a false assumption on which the reasoning that the argument seeks to undermine rests.
   (E) It is used by the argument to attempt to undermine the reasoning behind a viewpoint.

   PrepTest57 Sec2 Q21

7. Sociologist: The more technologically advanced a society is, the more marked its members' resistance to technological innovations. This is not surprising, because the more technologically advanced a society is, the more aware its members are of technology's drawbacks. Specifically, people realize that sophisticated technologies deeply affect the quality of human relations.

   The claim that the more technologically advanced a society is, the more aware its members are of technology's drawbacks plays which one of the following roles in the sociologist's argument?

   (A) It is a conclusion supported by the claim that people realize that sophisticated technologies deeply affect the quality of human relations.
   (B) It is offered as an explanation of why people's resistance to technological innovations is more marked the more technologically advanced the society in which they live is.
   (C) It is a premise in support of the claim that the quality of human relations in technologically advanced societies is extremely poor.
   (D) It is a generalization based on the claim that the more people resist technological innovations, the more difficult it is for them to adjust to those innovations.
   (E) It is an example presented to illustrate the claim that resistance to technological innovations deeply affects the quality of human relations.

   PrepTest57 Sec3 Q21

8. It is a mistake to think, as ecologists once did, that natural selection will eventually result in organisms that will be perfectly adapted to their environments. After all, perfect adaptation of an individual to its environment is impossible, for an individual's environment can vary tremendously; no single set of attributes could possibly prepare an organism to cope with all the conditions that it could face.

   Which one of the following most accurately expresses the main conclusion of the argument?

   (A) It is not possible for an individual to be perfectly adapted to its environment.
   (B) Natural selection will never result in individuals that will be perfectly adapted to their environments.
   (C) No single set of attributes could enable an individual organism to cope with all of the conditions that it might face.
   (D) Because an individual's environment can vary tremendously, no individual can be perfectly adapted to its environment.
   (E) Ecologists once believed that natural selection would eventually result in individuals that will be perfectly adapted to their environments.

   PrepTest51 Sec1 Q13

K | Part Three: Logical Reasoning
CHAPTER 9

Explanations to these questions can
be found in your Online Center.

9. Constance: The traditional definition of full
employment as a 5 percent unemployment rate is
correct, because at levels below 5 percent,
inflation rises.

Brigita: That traditional definition of full employment
was developed before the rise of temporary and
part-time work and the fall in benefit levels.
When people are juggling several part-time jobs
with no benefits, or working in a series of
temporary assignments, as is now the case,
5 percent unemployment is not full employment.

The dialogue most strongly supports the claim that
Constance and Brigita disagree with each other about
which one of the following?

(A) what definition of full employment is applicable
under contemporary economic conditions

(B) whether it is a good idea, all things considered,
to allow the unemployment level to drop below
5 percent

(C) whether a person with a part-time job should
count as fully employed

(D) whether the number of part-time and temporary
workers has increased since the traditional
definition of full employment was developed

(E) whether unemployment levels above 5 percent
can cause inflation levels to rise

PrepTest51 Sec1 Q23

10. When a major record label signs a contract with a
band, the label assumes considerable financial risk. It
pays for videos, album art, management, and
promotions. Hence, the band does not need to assume
nearly as much risk as it would if it produced its own
records independently. For this reason, it is only fair
for a major label to take a large portion of the profits
from the record sales of any band signed with it.

Which one of the following most accurately describes
the role played in the argument by the claim that a
band signed with a major label does not need to
assume nearly as much risk as it would if it produced
its own records independently?

(A) It is the only conclusion that the argument
attempts to establish.

(B) It is one of two unrelated conclusions, each of
which the same premises are used to support.

(C) It is a general principle from which the
argument's conclusion follows as a specific
instance.

(D) It describes a phenomenon for which the rest of
the argument offers an explanation.

(E) Premises are used to support it, and it is used to
support the main conclusion.

PrepTest51 Sec3 Q11

11. Publisher: The new year is approaching, and with it the
seasonal demand for books on exercise and
fitness. We must do whatever it takes to ship
books in that category on time; our competitors
have demonstrated a high level of organization,
and we cannot afford to be outsold.

Which one of the following most accurately expresses
the main conclusion drawn in the publisher's
argument?

(A) The company should make shipping books its
highest priority.

(B) By increasing its efficiency, the company can
maintain its competitive edge.

(C) The company will be outsold if it does not
maintain its competitors' high level of
organization.

(D) It is imperative that the company ship fitness
and exercise books on time.

(E) The company should do whatever is required in
order to adopt its competitors' shipping
practices.

PrepTest51 Sec3 Q16

12. Editorialist: There would seem to be little hazard for
consumers associated with chemicals used in
treated lumber because the lumber is used outside
where fumes cannot accumulate. However,
immediate steps should be taken to determine the
safety of these chemicals since consumers could
ingest them. If the lumber is used for children's
playground equipment, youngsters could put their
mouths on the wood, and if it is used to contain
soil in a vegetable garden, the chemicals could
leach into the soil.

Which one of the following most accurately expresses
the main conclusion of the editorialist's argument?

(A) The chemicals used in treated lumber are
apparently not dangerous to the consumer.

(B) Treated lumber is as dangerous when used
outdoors as it is when used indoors.

(C) The effects on humans from the chemicals in
treated lumber should be studied.

(D) Parents should not allow children to put their
mouths on playground equipment.

(E) Treated lumber is more dangerous than was
once believed.

PrepTest49 Sec4 Q7

Explanations to these questions can be found in your Online Center.

Part Three: Logical Reasoning
Argument-Based Questions

K

13. According to the proposed Factory Safety Act, a company may operate an automobile factory only if that factory is registered as a class B factory. In addressing whether a factory may postpone its safety inspections, this Act also stipulates that no factory can be class B without punctual inspections. Thus, under the Factory Safety Act, a factory that manufactures automobiles would not be able to postpone its safety inspections.

The argument proceeds by

(A) pointing out how two provisions of the proposed Factory Safety Act jointly entail the unacceptability of a certain state of affairs

(B) considering two possible interpretations of a proposed legal regulation and eliminating the less plausible one

(C) showing that the terms of the proposed Factory Safety Act are incompatible with existing legislation

(D) showing that two different provisions of the proposed Factory Safety Act conflict and thus cannot apply to a particular situation

(E) pointing out that if a provision applies in a specific situation, it must apply in any analogous situation

PrepTest49 Sec4 Q15

14. Contrary to Malthus's arguments, human food-producing capacity has increased more rapidly than human population. Yet, agricultural advances often compromise biological diversity. Therefore, Malthus's prediction that insufficient food will doom humanity to war, pestilence, and famine will likely be proven correct in the future, because a lack of biodiversity will eventually erode our capacity to produce food.

The statement that human food-producing capacity has increased more rapidly than human population plays which one of the following roles in the argument?

(A) It is a hypothesis the argument provides reasons for believing to be presently false.

(B) It is a part of the evidence used in the argument to support the conclusion that a well-known view is misguided.

(C) It is an observation that the argument suggests actually supports Malthus's position.

(D) It is a general fact that the argument offers reason to believe will eventually change.

(E) It is a hypothesis that, according to the argument, is accepted on the basis of inadequate evidence.

PrepTest59 Sec2 Q18

15. Price: A corporation's primary responsibility is to its shareholders. They are its most important constituency because they take the greatest risks. If the corporation goes bankrupt, they lose their investment.

Albrecht: Shareholders typically have diversified investment portfolios. For employees, however, the well-being of the corporation for which they have chosen to work represents their very livelihood. The corporation's primary responsibility should be to them.

On the basis of their statements, Price and Albrecht are committed to disagreeing about whether

(A) corporations have a responsibility to their shareholders

(B) corporations are responsible for the welfare of their employees

(C) means should be provided for a corporation's investors to recoup their losses if the corporation goes bankrupt

(D) a corporation's shareholders have more at stake than anyone else does in the corporation's success or failure

(E) the livelihood of some of the shareholders depends on the corporation's success

PrepTest59 Sec2 Q2

ANSWER KEY

1. D
2. A
3. C
4. D
5. C
6. E
7. B
8. B
9. A
10. E
11. D
12. C
13. A
14. D
15. D

Complete explanations for all of these questions can be found in your Online Center.

Assumption Family Questions

This chapter builds on Chapter 9 by adding another layer to your skills in the analysis of arguments: determining the author's assumption(s), or unstated premise(s). With the exception of a handful of Parallel Reasoning questions, every argument you'll encounter in this chapter is incomplete as written. There is an essential premise that the author has left unsaid. Developing an ability to quickly, calmly, and accurately put your finger on an author's key assumption is the foundational skill tested by more than half of all Logical Reasoning questions, and thus accounts for more than one-quarter of your LSAT score.

LSAT STRATEGY

Every Assumption Family argument contains the following:

- A conclusion—The author's main point: an assertion, evaluation, or recommendation
- Evidence—The facts and information the author presents in support of the conclusion
- An assumption—The unstated premise that logically connects the evidence to the conclusion

As you analyzed the explicit parts of arguments in Chapter 9, it's likely that you felt that most of these arguments were not entirely convincing. Here's a good example:

Pundit: The average salary for teachers in our society is lower than the average salary for athletes. Obviously, our society values sports more than it values education.

PrepTest51 Sec3 Q4

Assumption Family Questions

55.9%

Logical Reasoning Question Types

PrepTests57–71; released 2009–2013

As you see it again now, what's your reaction? Do you have the sense that there is more to this argument than what the author has presented? Can you think of things the author may be overlooking or failing to take into account? Can you think of other facts that would strengthen or weaken this argument, or that you would at least like to know to evaluate it? If so, you are anticipating all of the key question types in the Assumption Family of Logical Reasoning questions.

On LSAT tests released from 2009 to 2013, there were approximately 28 Assumption Family questions per test.

LEARNING OBJECTIVES

In this section, you'll learn to:

· Identify Mismatched Concepts in an argument
· Identify Overlooked Possibilities in an argument
· Identify the assumption in both types of arguments
· Use an argument's assumption to predict the correct answer in each Assumption Family question type

There are three main Assumption Family question types:

Assumption Questions: These ask directly for an unstated premise in the argument.

Flaw Questions: These ask you to describe the error in the author's reasoning; the error is most often related to what the author has overlooked, or how the evidence fails to establish the conclusion.

Strengthen/Weaken Questions: These ask for facts that, if true, would make the argument more or less likely to be valid; you'll need to understand what the author is assuming to answer most of these questions accurately and efficiently.

Here are examples of each of those question types:

Assumption Question

There can be no individual freedom without the rule of law, for there is no individual freedom without social integrity, and pursuing the good life is not possible without social integrity.

The conclusion drawn above follows logically if which one of the following is assumed?

(A) There can be no rule of law without social integrity.
(B) There can be no social integrity without the rule of law.
(C) One cannot pursue the good life without the rule of law.
(D) Social integrity is possible only if individual freedom prevails.
(E) There can be no rule of law without individual freedom.

PrepTest61 Sec4 Q25

Flaw Question

The more modern archaeologists learn about Mayan civilization, the better they understand its intellectual achievements. Not only were numerous scientific observations and predictions made by Mayan astronomers, but the people in general seem to have had a strong grasp of sophisticated mathematical concepts. We know this from the fact that the writings of the Mayan religious scribes exhibit a high degree of mathematical competence.

The argument's reasoning is most vulnerable to criticism on the grounds that the argument

(A) fails to provide an adequate definition of the term "intellectual achievement"
(B) bases a generalization on a sample that is likely to be unrepresentative
(C) overlooks the impressive achievements of other past civilizations
(D) relies on two different senses of the term "scientific"
(E) takes a mere correlation to be evidence of a causal relationship

PrepTest59 Sec3 Q8

Weaken Question

We can now dismiss the widely held suspicion that sugar consumption often exacerbates hyperactivity in children with attention deficit disorder. A scientific study of the effects of three common sugars— sucrose, fructose, and glucose—on children who have attention deficit disorder, with experimental groups each receiving a type of sugar in their diets and a control group receiving a sugar substitute instead of sugar, showed no statistically significant difference between the groups in thinking or behavior.

Which one of the following, if true, would most weaken the argument above?

(A) Only one of the three types of sugar used in the study was ever widely suspected of exacerbating hyperactivity.

(B) The consumption of sugar actually has a calming effect on some children.

(C) The consumption of some sugar substitutes exacerbates the symptoms of hyperactivity.

(D) The study included some observations of each group in contexts that generally tend to make children excited and active.

(E) Some children believe that they can tell the difference between the taste of sugar and that of sugar substitutes.

PrepTest51 Sec1 Q8

Strengthen Question

A recent study confirms that nutritious breakfasts make workers more productive. For one month, workers at Plant A received free nutritious breakfasts every day before work, while workers in Plant B did not. The productivity of Plant A's workers increased, while that of Plant B's workers did not.

Which one of the following, if true, most strengthens the argument?

(A) Few workers in Plant B consumed nutritious breakfasts during the month of the study.

(B) Workers in the study from Plant A and Plant B started work at the same time of day.

(C) During the month before the study, workers at Plant A and Plant B were equally productive.

(D) Workers from Plant A took fewer vacation days per capita during the month than did workers from Plant B.

(E) Workers in Plant B were more productive during the month of the study than were workers from Plant A.

PrepTest59 Sec2 Q22

As you examine these questions, notice that they focus on the author's *reasoning*. Even in Strengthen/Weaken questions, the LSAT will never ask you to contradict facts stipulated in the evidence or to decide which of two experts is the more believable witness. On Test Day, don't spend time trying to pull in "real world" examples or facts. Analyze the argument given, understanding its explicit and implicit components, and answer the specific question asked.

TEST DAY TIP

Do not confuse the truth of a conclusion with the validity of an argument. Remember:

· A conclusion can be true even if the evidence for it is incomplete or the argument's reasoning is flawed.

· A valid argument can produce a false conclusion.

By the end of this chapter, you'll have learned and practiced all of the fundamental skills and strategies rewarded by these all-important questions, and you'll have gone a long way toward improving your LSAT score. In addition, you'll learn to identify and answer other questions—Parallel Reasoning, Parallel Flaw, and certain Principle questions—which apply the Assumption Family skills in slightly different ways.

MISMATCHED CONCEPTS

There are two broad categories of assumptions in LSAT arguments: Mismatched Concepts and Overlooked Possibilities. The categories are not mutually exclusive. As you will see, some arguments can be described in both ways. The first broad category of LSAT arguments is one in which the author assumes a relationship between terms or concepts of two different *kinds*; we'll refer to these assumptions as Mismatched Concepts.

Mismatched Concepts: The Basics

Have you ever made an argument like one of these?

> "She likes bananas, so she will like plantains, too."
> "Joseph must watch his diet. All professional dancers are diet conscious."

If so, you've made an argument with a Mismatched Concepts assumption. You've assumed (and perhaps your audience has, too) that two terms or concepts were related in such a way that you could draw a conclusion about something different than what is in your evidence. Your argument may have been right, but without an unstated premise, it was incomplete.

LSAT STRATEGY

How can you tell an argument contains mismatched concepts?

· The terms or concepts in the evidence appear unrelated to those in the conclusion.
· A new term or concept—not related to the evidence—appears in the conclusion.

Most arguments containing Mismatched Concepts fall into one of two patterns. In the first, the evidence and conclusion make different claims about the same subject.

> Socrates is human. Therefore, Socrates is mortal.

Here, the author assumes that what is claimed in the conclusion is entailed by what is claimed in the evidence: "Humans are mortal." In the second pattern, the same claim is made about two different subjects.

> Humans are mortal. Therefore, Socrates is mortal.

In this type of Mismatched Concepts argument, the author assumes that the subject of the conclusion is logically related to the subject of the evidence: "Socrates is human." Although LSAT arguments are longer, wordier, and more complex than those examples, you may be surprised to find that many of them boil down to one of those two patterns.

LSAT STRATEGY

When tackling an argument containing Mismatched Concepts:

· Separate concepts in the evidence from concepts in the conclusion.
· Identify the mismatched concepts that the author *assumes* are related.
· Find the assumption by forming a sentence that logically bridges the mismatched concepts—this sentence serves to make the evidence relevant to the conclusion.

Mismatched Concepts: Sample Arguments

Here are a handful of representative examples of Mismatched Concepts arguments.

Argument	Analysis
Bobby is a championship swimmer. Hence, he trains every day.	**Conclusion:** Bobby trains every day. *because* **Evidence:** Bobby is a championship swimmer. **Assumption:** Championship swimmers train every day.
Cats are cleaner animals than dogs. Therefore, cats make better pets than dogs make.	**Conclusion:** Cats make better pets than dogs make. *because* **Evidence:** Cats are cleaner animals than dogs are. **Assumption:** Cleaner animals make better pets.
Every kid loves ice cream, so Judy loves ice cream.	**Conclusion:** Judy loves ice cream. *because* **Evidence:** Every kid loves ice cream. **Assumption:** Judy is a kid.
Susan doesn't eat her vegetables. So Susan will not grow big and strong.	**Conclusion:** Susan will not grow big and strong. *because* **Evidence:** Susan doesn't eat her vegetables. **Assumption:** Susan needs to eat her vegetables to grow big and strong.
This package weighs more than 50 pounds. Therefore, the post office cannot ship it.	**Conclusion:** The post office cannot ship this package. *because* **Evidence:** This package weighs more than 50 pounds. **Assumption:** The post office cannot ship packages that weigh more than 50 pounds.

Practice

Now, analyze some arguments similar to those in the preceding examples. When you're done, compare your work to that of an LSAT expert on the pages following this exercise.

Argument	My Analysis
1. Lena has final exams so she must not be an English major.	**Conclusion:** *because* → **Evidence:** **Assumption:**
2. Jeremy can afford only $500 per month for rent. Therefore, Jeremy cannot afford to rent an apartment in Brentwood.	**Conclusion:** *because* → **Evidence:** **Assumption:**
3. Since tigers are heavy animals, they cannot run fast.	**Conclusion:** *because* → **Evidence:** **Assumption:**
4. This tree fell in the woods with no one around to hear it. So this tree fell without making a sound.	**Conclusion:** *because* → **Evidence:** **Assumption:**
5. Julie's handbag costs more than Karen's handbag. Clearly, Julie's handbag is softer to the touch.	**Conclusion:** *because* → **Evidence:** **Assumption:**

Argument	My Analysis
6. This raspberry lemonade is a very sour drink. Hence, it will not pair well with the pasta dish.	**Conclusion:** *because* → **Evidence:** **Assumption:**
7. Sam will not eat at least three plates of food. Therefore, the buffet option will not be worth it for Sam.	**Conclusion:** *because* → **Evidence:** **Assumption:**
8. Digital flashcards are a more convenient study aid than traditional textbooks. Consequently, Sophia prefers digital flashcards for studying.	**Conclusion:** *because* → **Evidence:** **Assumption:**
9. Airport security will not allow any passenger carrying more than 3 ounces of liquid to board the plane. Clearly, Sandra will not be permitted to board the plane.	**Conclusion:** *because* → **Evidence:** **Assumption:**
10. On Friday night, the local newspaper surveyed moviegoers and found that 75 percent of them were seeing an action movie or a romantic comedy. This proves that action and romantic comedy are the most popular movie genres.	**Conclusion:** *because* → **Evidence:** **Assumption:**

Expert Analysis

Here's how an LSAT expert would analyze those arguments. Were you able to accurately determine the author's assumption in each case?

Argument	Analysis
1. Lena has final exams so she must not be an English major.	**Conclusion:** Lena must not be an English major. *because* **Evidence:** Lena has final exams. **Assumption:** "English majors do not have final exams." The phrases "English major" and "have final exams" are mutually exclusive.
2. Jeremy can afford only $500 per month for rent. Therefore, Jeremy cannot afford to rent an apartment in Brentwood.	**Conclusion:** Jeremy cannot afford to rent an apartment in Brentwood. *because* **Evidence:** Jeremy can afford $500 per month for rent. **Assumption:** "An apartment in Brentwood costs more than $500 per month to rent." The phrases "apartment in Brentwood" and "$500 or less per month" are mutually exclusive. (Or, the phrases "apartment in Brentwood" and "more than $500 per month" are equivalent.)
3. Since tigers are heavy animals, they cannot run fast.	**Conclusion:** Tigers cannot run fast. *because* **Evidence:** Tigers are heavy animals. **Assumption:** "Heavy animals cannot run fast." The terms "heavy animals" and "run fast" are mutually exclusive.

Argument	Analysis
4. This tree fell in the woods with no one around to hear it. So this tree fell without making a sound.	**Conclusion:** This tree fell without making a sound. *because* **Evidence:** This tree fell in the woods with no one around. **Assumption:** "If a tree falls in the woods with no one around, then it doesn't make a sound." The phrases "falls in the woods with no one around" and "makes a sound" are mutually exclusive.
5. Julie's handbag costs more than Karen's handbag. Clearly, Julie's handbag is softer to the touch.	**Conclusion:** Julie's handbag is softer to the touch. *because* **Evidence:** Julie's handbag costs more than Karen's handbag. **Assumption:** "Handbags that cost more are softer to the touch." The terms "cost more" and "softer to the touch" are equivalent.
6. This raspberry lemonade is a very sour drink. Hence, it will not pair well with the pasta dish.	**Conclusion:** This raspberry lemonade will not pair well with the pasta dish. *because* **Evidence:** This raspberry lemonade is a very sour drink. **Assumption:** "A very sour drink will not pair well with the pasta dish." The terms "very sour drink" and "pair well with the pasta" are mutually exclusive.
7. Sam will not eat at least three plates of food. Therefore, the buffet option will not be worth it for Sam.	**Conclusion:** The buffet option will not be worth it for Sam. *because* **Evidence:** Sam will not eat at least three plates of food. **Assumption:** "A diner needs to eat at least three plates of food to make the buffet worth it." The evidence term is necessary for the conclusion.

Argument	Analysis
8. Digital flashcards are a more convenient study aid than traditional textbooks. Consequently, Sophia prefers digital flashcards for studying.	**Conclusion:** Sophia prefers digital flashcards for studying.
	because
	→ **Evidence:** Digital flashcards are a more convenient study aid than traditional textbooks.
	Assumption: "Sophia prefers to study with study aids that are more convenient." The terms "prefers" and "more convenient" are equivalent (at least in Sophia's case).
9. Airport security will not allow any passenger carrying more than 3 ounces of liquid to board the plane. Clearly, Sandra will not be permitted to board the plane.	**Conclusion:** Sandra will not be permitted to board the plane.
	because
	→ **Evidence:** Airport security will not allow any passenger carrying more than 3 ounces of liquid to board the plane.
	Assumption: "Sandra is a passenger carrying more than 3 ounces of liquid." The term "Sandra" is equivalent to the phrase "a passenger carrying more than 3 ounces of liquid" (at least right now).
10. On Friday night, the local newspaper surveyed moviegoers and found that 75 percent of them were seeing an action movie or a romantic comedy. This proves that action and romantic comedy are the most popular movie genres.	**Conclusion:** Action movies and romantic comedies are the most popular movie genres.
	because
	→ **Evidence:** Seventy-five percent of moviegoers on Friday were seeing an action movie or a romantic comedy.
	Assumption: "Moviegoers on Friday night are representative of all moviegoers." The sample in the evidence is representative of that in the conclusion.

Going Deeper: Common Relationships between Mismatched Concepts

You may have noticed that the sample arguments in the preceding exercise demonstrated a handful of relationships in their assumptions. That's not by chance. LSAT arguments containing Mismatched Concepts tend to feature four common relationships.

LSAT STRATEGY

The most commonly assumed relationships between mismatched concepts are:

· The terms or concepts are alike/equivalent
· The terms or concepts are mutually exclusive
· One term or concept is needed for the other
· One term or concept represents the other

Being able to characterize the relationship in an argument with Mismatched Concepts will help you answer Assumption Family questions about those arguments. Take a little deeper look at each common relationship.

Alike/Equivalent is the assumption that two terms/concepts are similar enough to justify the conclusion. *Example*: "This house is decorated with antiques and memorabilia. It will, therefore, appeal to a sentimental person." The assumption here is that antiques and memorabilia appeal to sentimental people.

Mutually Exclusive is the assumption that two terms/concepts are incompatible.

Example: "These dwellings are built using adobe materials. Thus, while they are excellent examples of adobe construction, they cannot be said to represent the native architecture of the region." The assumption here is that the native architecture of the region *did not* use adobe materials.

NOTE: Neither of those arguments is inherently flawed. Both, however, are incomplete because each lacks a premise that would logically tie the evidence to the conclusion. When Alike/Equivalent or Mutually Exclusive arguments appear in Flaw questions, they nearly always contain terms and concepts in the evidence so different from those in the conclusion that the author's assumption is unwarranted. Kaplan explanations often refer to these as "Scope Shift" flaws. You'll see several examples later in the chapter and in the Question Pools that accompany the chapter.

One Term/Concept Needed for the Other is the assumption that A cannot happen without B. In other words, B is necessary for A.

Example: "I cannot vote because I am not registered." The assumption here is that voting *requires* registration.

LSAT arguments sometimes present a closely related argument with this structure: Something is necessary for something else; therefore, something else won't happen.

Example: "Voters are required to register. Therefore, I cannot vote." The assumption here is that a necessary condition (registration) was not fulfilled.

NOTE: Neither of these examples contains flawed *reasoning*. If registration is a requirement for voting in this district or state, then the arguments are correct. This pattern will not appear in a Flaw question. However, arguments in which the author confuses a sufficient condition for a necessary one are quite common in Flaw questions. You'll see these arguments in the next section on Overlooked Possibilities arguments.

One Term/Concept Representative of the Other is the assumption that the group or sample in the evidence is representative of the group or sample in the conclusion.

Example: "Doctors are unlikely to prescribe the new drug. We know this from a survey of recent medical school graduates in which over 70 percent of those surveyed said they would not prescribe the new drug." The assumption here is recent medical school graduates are representative of doctors in general.

NOTE: The LSAT will include Representativeness arguments in Flaw questions. When you see them, be on the lookout for reasons that the sample or group in the evidence does not provide strong evidence for the sample or group in the conclusion.

Practice: Mismatched Concepts

Analyze the following LSAT arguments. Identify the conclusion and evidence, and determine the author's assumption. Categorize the assumption according to the common relationships on the previous page. NOTE: You first saw some of these arguments in Chapter 9.

LSAT Argument	My Analysis
11. Chiu: The belief that a person is always morally blameworthy for feeling certain emotions, such as unjustifiable anger, jealousy, or resentment, is misguided. Individuals are responsible for only what is under their control, and whether one feels such an emotion is not always under one's control. *PrepTest51 Sec1 Q16*	**Conclusion:** *because* **Evidence:** **Assumption:** **Assumption type:**
12. Critic: Photographers, by deciding which subjects to depict and how to depict them, express their own worldviews in their photographs, however realistically those photographs may represent reality. Thus, photographs are interpretations of reality. *PrepTest61 Sec2 Q13*	**Conclusion:** *because* **Evidence:** **Assumption:** **Assumption type:**
13. Essayist: Lessing contended that an art form's medium dictates the kind of representation the art form must employ in order to be legitimate; painting, for example, must represent simultaneous arrays of colored shapes, while literature, consisting of words read in succession, must represent events or actions occurring in sequence. The claim about literature must be rejected, however, if one regards as legitimate the imagists' poems, which consist solely of amalgams of disparate images. *PrepTest57 Sec2 Q7*	**Conclusion:** *because* **Evidence:** **Assumption:** **Assumption type:**
14. The more modern archaeologists learn about Mayan civilization, the better they understand its intellectual achievements. Not only were numerous scientific observations and predictions made by Mayan astronomers, but the people in general seem to have had a strong grasp of sophisticated mathematical concepts. We know this from the fact that the writings of the Mayan religious scribes exhibit a high degree of mathematical competence. *PrepTest59 Sec3 Q8*	**Conclusion:** *because* **Evidence:** **Assumption:** **Assumption type:**

Expert Analysis: Mismatched Concepts

Here's how an LSAT expert would analyze the arguments from that exercise. Compare your work.

LSAT Argument	Analysis
11. Chiu: The belief that a person is always morally blameworthy for feeling certain emotions, such as unjustifiable anger, jealousy, or resentment, is misguided. Individuals are responsible for only what is under their control, and whether one feels such an emotion is not always under one's control. *PrepTest51 Sec1 Q16* $\longrightarrow$	**Conclusion:** A person is not always blameworthy for feeling certain emotions. *because* **Evidence:** 1) Feeling emotions is not always under one's control, and 2) a person is responsible only for what is under his control. **Assumption:** If a person is not responsible for something, he isn't blameworthy for doing it. (Blameworthiness *requires* responsibility.) **Assumption type:** Mismatched Concepts—Need
12. Critic: Photographers, by deciding which subjects to depict and how to depict them, express their own worldviews in their photographs, however realistically those photographs may represent reality. Thus, photographs are interpretations of reality. *PrepTest61 Sec2 Q13* $\longrightarrow$	**Conclusion:** Photographs are interpretations of reality. *because* **Evidence:** Photographers express their worldviews in photographs. **Assumption:** The expression of a worldview is an interpretation of reality. **Assumption type:** Mismatched Concepts—Alike/ Equivalent

LSAT Argument	Analysis
13. Essayist: Lessing contended that an art form's medium dictates the kind of representation the art form must employ in order to be legitimate; painting, for example, must represent simultaneous arrays of colored shapes, while literature, consisting of words read in succession, must represent events or actions occurring in sequence. The claim about literature must be rejected, however, if one regards as legitimate the imagists' poems, which consist solely of amalgams of disparate images. *PrepTest57 Sec2 Q7*	**Conclusion:** Literature does not have to represent events in sequence. *because* **Evidence:** If imagist poems are literature, they are just amalgams of disparate images. **Assumption:** An amalgam of disparate images does not represent events in sequence. **Assumption type:** Mismatched Concepts—Mutually Exclusive
14. The more modern archaeologists learn about Mayan civilization, the better they understand its intellectual achievements. Not only were numerous scientific observations and predictions made by Mayan astronomers, but the people in general seem to have had a strong grasp of sophisticated mathematical concepts. We know this from the fact that the writings of the Mayan religious scribes exhibit a high degree of mathematical competence. *PrepTest59 Sec3 Q8*	**Conclusion:** Mayan people in general had a strong understanding of mathematical concepts. *because* **Evidence:** Mayan religious scribes exhibited strong mathematical competence. **Assumption:** What's true of Mayan religious scribes is likely to be true of the Mayan people in general. **Assumption type:** Mismatched Concepts—Representativeness

Formal Logic in Mismatched Concepts

You may have noticed already that many of the arguments containing Mismatched Concepts are, or could easily be, expressed in conditional Formal Logic statements. The argument about photographs is a good example. It might sound awkward to say:

> If a work is a photograph, then it expresses the artist's worldview. Therefore, if a work is a photograph, it is an interpretation of reality.

Nevertheless, the reasoning in the argument, and thus, the author's assumption, is exactly the same.

The advantage of recognizing Formal Logic in Assumption Family questions is that it highlights the mismatched concepts very clearly.

	Sample Argument			Analysis		
Evidence	If photograph	→	**express artist's worldview**	If A	→	**B**
Conclusion	If photograph	→	**interpretation of reality**	If A	→	**C**

This provides a neat visual depiction of the argument that makes the author's assumption clear.

	Sample Argument			Analysis		
Evidence	If photograph	→	**express artist's worldview**	If A	→	**B**
Assumption	**If express artist's worldview**	→	**interpretation of reality**	**If B**	→	**C**
Conclusion	If photograph	→	**interpretation of reality**	If A	→	**C**

TEST DAY TIP

LSAT experts differ on how much of the Formal Logic they actually write out on Test Day: Some jot down shorthand nearly every time they encounter Formal Logic while others do it only in the most complex arguments. Practice both approaches to find which works best for you. You may find that being more explicit with Formal Logic initially helps you spot patterns that you'll better analyze in your head later on.

Making It More Difficult: Adding an Extra Concept in the Evidence

Many LSAT arguments with Mismatched Concepts feature two evidentiary statements that can be combined to help you determine the author's assumption. Consider this argument:

> Every member of my research team is an honors student, and every honors student has completed the Great Ideas course. Thus, every member of my research team has read Plato's *Symposium*.

When you combine the two statements in the evidence, this argument takes exactly the same form as the argument about photographs.

	Sample Argument			Analysis
Evidence 1	If research team	→	honors	If A → X
Evidence 2	If honors	→	Great Ideas course	If X → B
Evidence [combined]	If research team	→	**Great Ideas course**	If A → **B**
Assumption	**If Great Ideas course**	→	**read Plato's Symposium**	If **B** → **C**
Conclusion	If research team	→	**read Plato's Symposium**	If A → **C**

Whenever you see two statements in the evidence of an argument containing Mismatched Concepts, consider whether you can combine them into a single, relevant piece of evidence.

Same Necessary Term

So far, the examples you've seen have had the mismatched terms in the necessary (or "then") clause of the Formal Logic statements. Occasionally, you'll see LSAT examples in which the mismatched terms are in the sufficient (or "If") clause. For example:

> Those who are nostalgic for the 1960s love the theater's new musical. So, Ella is going to love the new musical.

	Sample Argument			Analysis		
Evidence	**If nostalgic for the 1960s**	→	love the new musical	If **A**	→	B
Assumption	**If Ella**	→	**nostalgic for the 1960s**	If **C**	→	**A**
Conclusion	If **Ella**	→	love the new musical	If **C**	→	B

NOTE: Compare the argument about the photographs and this one about Ella to the two examples on the mortality of Socrates at the beginning of the chapter. Do you recognize the similarity in patterns?

Mismatched Concepts in the Evidence—Rare

Very rarely, the LSAT will feature an argument with Mismatched Concepts in which the "gap" is between two pieces of evidence rather than between the evidence and the conclusion. Here's an example:

> On extremely cold days, people are more physically uncomfortable. Moreover, people who are less aware of danger are more likely to jaywalk. From this it can be concluded that on extremely cold days, people are more likely to jaywalk.

	Sample Argument			Analysis
Evidence 1	If extremely cold day	→	**more physically uncomfortable**	If A → **B**
Assumption	**If more physically uncomfortable**	→	**unaware of danger**	If **B → C**
Evidence 2	**If unaware of danger**	→	more likely to jaywalk	If **C** → D
Conclusion	If extremely cold day	→	more likely to jaywalk	If A → D

OVERLOOKED POSSIBILITIES

The other common pattern in LSAT arguments involves those in which the author assumes a difference in *scale*, *degree*, or *level of certainty*, rather than a difference of kind; we'll refer to these assumptions as containing Overlooked Possibilities.

Overlooked Possibilities: The Basics

Have you ever made an argument like this, maybe to a sibling or a roommate?

> The sandwich I was saving is gone. You must have eaten it.

Now, it is certainly possible that the accused party ate your sandwich. But, by concluding that he or she *must* have eaten it, you're overlooking several possibilities. Maybe someone else ate the sandwich. Maybe it wasn't eaten at all, but was thrown out because it was getting moldy. Maybe something was accidentally spilled on it and your roommate kindly disposed of it for you.

LSAT STRATEGY

You can identify Overlooked Possibilities as follows:

· The terms or concepts in the evidence are related to the conclusion.
· The conclusion reached is too strong or extreme to follow logically from the evidence.
· The author has failed to consider possible objections to the conclusion.

What sort of overlooked possibilities do you spot in this argument?

> The city budget surplus is large enough to build a new park or to repave streets in the financial district. A recent study shows that the city has an abundance of parks, so the only viable project on which to spend the surplus is the repaving of streets in the financial district.

Here, the author has given a false dichotomy. There may be any number of other projects that are viable and perhaps even preferable to his recommendation.

LSAT STRATEGY

When tackling an argument with Overlooked Possibilities:

· Focus on the conclusion.
· Determine the objections to that conclusion.
· Understand the assumptions in negative terms: the author assumes that the objections are not present or did not happen.

Overlooked Possibilities: Sample Arguments

Argument	Analysis
Samson does not have a movie stub so he must have sneaked into the movie without paying.	**Conclusion:** Samson must have sneaked into the movie. *because* **Evidence:** Samson has no ticket stub. **Assumption:** Since Samson doesn't have a ticket, he must have sneaked in; the *only way* to be in the theater without a ticket is to have sneaked in.
Sarah was late to work this morning and her boss fired her. Therefore, she must have been fired over her lateness.	**Conclusion:** Lateness is the reason for Sarah's firing. *because* **Evidence:** Sarah was late and got fired. **Assumption:** There was no other reason for Sarah's firing; lateness is the *only* reason Sarah got fired.
George is a better race car driver than Jeff. Clearly, George will beat Jeff in the upcoming car race.	**Conclusion:** George will beat Jeff in the car race. *because* **Evidence:** George is a better driver than Jeff. **Assumption:** There is no other factor that could cause George to lose; driver skill is the *only* relevant factor in who will win. (In Mismatched Concepts terminology: The better driver will win the upcoming race.)
Jonah's marketing plan will save the company money. Therefore, the company should adopt Jonah's plan.	**Conclusion:** The company should adopt Jonah's plan. *because* **Evidence:** Jonah's plan has one advantage: It saves money. **Assumption:** There are no overlooked disadvantages to Jonah's plan; saving money is the *only* relevant factor in the company's decision. (In Mismatched Concepts terminology: The company should adopt plans that save money.)

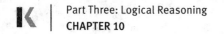

Overlooked Possibilities: Sample Arguments (cont.)

Argument	Analysis
Linda worked neither Tuesday nor Thursday of this week. Hence, Linda must not have worked this week.	**Conclusion:** Linda must not have worked this week. *because* → **Evidence:** Linda did not work Tues or Thurs. **Assumption:** Linda could not have worked any other day this week; Tues and Thurs are the *only* days on which Linda could have worked.

Practice

Now, analyze some arguments similar to those in the preceding examples. When you're done, compare your work to that of an LSAT expert on the pages following this exercise.

Argument	My Analysis
15. Roger is not playing on the swing set today. Therefore, he must be in the sandbox.	**Conclusion:** → *because* **Evidence:** **Assumption:**
16. The house on the near side of the street has better lighting than the house on the far side of the street. Clearly, Inga should buy the house on the near side of the street.	**Conclusion:** → *because* **Evidence:** **Assumption:**
17. Beth has been working for ABG Corp. longer than Antonio. Obviously, Beth will make assistant manager before Antonio does.	**Conclusion:** → *because* **Evidence:** **Assumption:**
18. Jules held a commanding lead over Esteban in the first 20 minutes of the race. Clearly, Jules will defeat Esteban in this race.	**Conclusion:** → *because* **Evidence:** **Assumption:**

Argument	**My Analysis**
19. My doctor charged me 35 percent more for an X-ray this year than last. As the X-ray procedure hasn't changed over the last year, my doctor must be overcharging me out of greed. →	Conclusion: *because* Evidence: Assumption:
20. To qualify for the university's science prize, a student must publish original research. Neither Becky nor Ahmed have published original research this year, so unfortunately, none of Dr. Iglesias's students will receive the university science prize. →	Conclusion: *because* Evidence: Assumption:
21. Infant mortality rates are lower in country M than they are in county N. Country M must have a better medical system and better doctors than country N has. →	Conclusion: *because* Evidence: Assumption:
22. Taking the school bus ensures that one gets to school on time. Jason missed the bus this morning, so he will definitely be late to school. →	Conclusion: *because* Evidence: Assumption:
23. My snow blower refuses to start this morning, so I must have forgotten to charge the batteries. →	Conclusion: *because* Evidence: Assumption:
24. In May, gasoline prices skyrocketed, driving up transportation costs. Shortly thereafter, produce prices at local grocery stores spiked. Rising transportation costs must have caused the spike in produce prices. →	Conclusion: *because* Evidence: Assumption:

Expert Analysis

Here's how an LSAT expert would analyze those arguments. Were you able to accurately determine the author's assumption in each case?

Argument	Analysis
15. Roger is not playing on the swing set today. Therefore, he must be in the sandbox.	**Conclusion:** Roger *must* be in the sandbox. *because* → **Evidence:** Roger is not playing on the swing set. **Assumption:** There is no place other than the sandbox or the swing set that Roger could be; there are *only* two places Roger could be.
16. The house on the near side of the street has better lighting than the house on the far side of the street. Clearly, Inga should buy the house on the near side of the street.	**Conclusion:** Inga should buy the house on the near side of the street. *because* → **Evidence:** The house on the near side of the street has better lighting than the house on the far side of the street. **Assumption:** There is no other factor that should sway Inga's decision; lighting is the *only* factor Inga should consider when buying the house.
17. Beth has been working for ABG Corp. longer than Antonio. Obviously, Beth will make assistant manager before Antonio does.	**Conclusion:** Beth *will* make assistant manager before Antonio does. *because* → **Evidence:** Beth has been working for ABG Corp. longer than Antonio. **Assumption:** There is no other factor that could influence the promotion to assistant manager; seniority is the *only* factor relevant to the promotion to assistant manager.

Argument	Analysis
18. Jules held a commanding lead over Esteban in the first 20 minutes of the race. Clearly, Jules will defeat Esteban in this race.	**Conclusion:** Jules *will* defeat Esteban in this race.
	because
→	**Evidence:** Jules held a commanding lead over Esteban in the first 20 minutes of the race.
	Assumption: Nothing could happen that would allow Esteban to defeat Jules; *only* the runner with the commanding lead early in the race can win.
19. My doctor charged me 35 percent more for an X-ray this year than last. As the X-ray procedure hasn't changed over the last year, my doctor must be overcharging me out of greed.	**Conclusion:** My doctor *must* be overcharging me out of greed.
	because
→	**Evidence:** 1) My doctor charged me 35 percent more for an X-ray this year than last. 2) The X-ray procedure hasn't changed over the last year.
	Assumption: There is no reason other than greed for the X-ray to cost 35 percent more this year than last year; greed is the *only* reason to charge that much more than last year.
20. To qualify for the university's science prize, a student must publish original research. Neither Becky nor Ahmed have published original research this year, so unfortunately, none of Dr. Iglesias's students will receive the university science prize.	**Conclusion:** *None* of Dr. Iglesias's students will receive the university's science prize.
	because
→	**Evidence:** 1) The university's science prize requires publication of original research, and 2) neither Becky nor Ahmed have published original research.
	Assumption: Dr. Iglesias has no students other than Becky or Ahmed who might have published original research; Becky and Ahmed are the *only* students of Dr. Iglesias who might have published original research.

Argument	Analysis
21. Infant mortality rates are lower in country M than they are in country N. Country M must have a better medical system and better doctors than country N has.	**Conclusion:** Country M must have a better medical system and better doctors than country N has. *because* → **Evidence:** Infant mortality rates are lower in country M than they are in country N. **Assumption:** Nothing other than a better medical system or better doctors could be responsible for a lower infant mortality rate; a better medical system or better doctors are the *only* reasons for a lower infant mortality rate.
22. Taking the school bus ensures that one gets to school on time. Jason missed the bus this morning, so he will definitely be late to school.	**Conclusion:** Jason will not be at school on time. *because* **Evidence:** 1) Taking the bus is *sufficient* to get one to school on time, and 2) Jason did not take the bus. → **Assumption:** The author has confused a sufficient condition for a necessary one. That means she overlooks the possibility of any other condition sufficient to get Jason to school on time; the author (perhaps mistakenly) assumes that taking the bus is the *only* way to get to school on time.
23. My snow blower refuses to start this morning, so I must have forgotten to charge the batteries.	**Conclusion:** I must have forgotten to charge the snow blower's batteries. *because* → **Evidence:** The snow blower won't start this morning. **Assumption:** There is no reason other than an uncharged battery for my snow blower to refuse to start; a dead battery is the *only* reason my snow blower won't start.

Argument	Analysis
24. In May, gasoline prices skyrocketed, driving up transportation costs. Shortly thereafter, produce prices at local grocery stores spiked. Rising transportation costs must have caused the spike in produce prices.	**Conclusion:** Rising transportation costs caused the spike in produce prices. *because* $\rightarrow$ **Evidence:** Produce prices rose shortly after transportation costs shot up. **Assumption:** No factor other than transportation costs caused the spike in produce prices; increased transportation costs are the *only* reason produce prices went up.

Going Deeper: Common Patterns and Relationships in Overlooked Possibilities Arguments

You may have noticed that the sample arguments in the preceding exercise demonstrated a handful of relationships in their assumptions. That's not by chance. On the LSAT, arguments featuring Overlooked Possibilities tend to feature six common relationships.

LSAT STRATEGY

Overlooked Possibilities arguments tend to fit one of the following patterns:

- Fails to consider other explanations, reasons, or outcomes based on the evidence
- Confuses sufficient and necessary terms
- Does not consider potential advantages or disadvantages when offering a recommendation
- Assumes that something will occur simply because it could occur
- Arrives at a claim of causation based on evidence of correlation
- Makes a prediction by assuming that circumstances will or will not change

Being able to characterize the relationship in an Overlooked Possibilities argument will help you answer Assumption Family questions about those arguments. Overlooked Possibilities arguments are especially common in Weaken and Flaw questions. Take a little deeper look at each common relationship, presented in rough order of frequency on the test.

Assuming There is No Other Explanation, Reason, or Outcome

Example: "Sheila has enough money for a comfortable retirement. She must have regularly put a portion of her salary into savings." The assumption here is that regularly putting a portion of her salary is the *only* way Sheila could have enough money for a comfortable retirement. The author has overlooked any number of possible objections to this argument. Finding an alternative method of acquiring money for retirement would weaken this argument.

Assuming That What Is Sufficient Is Actually Necessary or Vice Versa

Example: "Booking during the week of February 1st ensures a stateroom on the summer jazz cruise. Nathan did not book during the week of February 1st, so he won't be able to get a stateroom on the summer jazz cruise." The author mistakes a condition sufficient to book a stateroom for one necessary to get a stateroom. The author (perhaps mistakenly) assumes that there is no other way to book a stateroom.

Assuming That a Correlation Proves Causation

Example: "I notice that whenever the store has a poor sales month, employee tardiness is higher. It must be that employee tardiness causes the store to lose sales." The author assumes no factor other than tardiness causes the store's lost sales.

There are three ways in which an argument conflating correlation with causation could be wrong. Think of a correlation versus causation argument like this: *X and Y are correlated, so X must cause Y.*

1) It could be that the author confuses an effect for a cause. *Maybe Y causes X.* (In the example above, maybe employees are showing up late because sales are so poor.)

2) It could be that a third factor is responsible for both the author's purported cause and effect. *Maybe Z causes both X and Y.* (In the previous example, maybe the manager goes on vacation or is out of the store during months when sales decrease and employees are tardy.)

3) It could be that the correlation is simply a coincidence. *Maybe X and Y are unrelated.* (In the previous example, maybe it is just by chance that poor sales and tardiness have happened to occur at the same time.)

Pointing out facts that suggest any of those three possibilities will weaken an Overlooked Possibilities—Causation versus Correlation argument.

Assuming Changed or Unchanged Circumstances to Make a Prediction

Example: "For the past ten years, the winner of *Moviestar*'s best actor award has starred in a serious political drama. Hap Studley only appeared in romantic comedies this year, so he will not be named *Moviestar*'s best actor." The author assumes that the past trend will continue, thus overlooking any possibility that *Moviestar* could break from it. He assumes that the same conditions that have applied for the past decade *will* apply again this year.

Assuming That There Are No Overlooked Advantages or Disadvantages to a Recommendation

Example: "You really ought to buy the new Brand Q minivan. After all, it is the safest family vehicle currently produced." The author assumes that there are no factors that could trump safety in her listener's buying decision. She overlooks any number of considerations: price, appearance, gas mileage, and so on. Pointing out any one of those as a possible concern of the listener would weaken this argument.

Assuming That Something That Can Occur, Will (or Should) Occur

Example: "A popular proposal before the city council has the potential to balance the city's budget next fiscal year. Thus, for the first time in nearly a decade, the city will not run a budget deficit next year." Not only does the author assume that the popular proposal will be enacted, but also assumes that nothing else will happen that could cause the city to run a deficit even with the proposal in place.

Practice: Overlooked Possibilities

Analyze the following LSAT arguments. Identify the conclusion and evidence, and determine the author's assumption. Categorize the assumption according to the common relationships on the previous page. NOTE: You first saw some of these arguments in Chapter 9.

LSAT Argument	My Analysis
25. Scientist: While studying centuries-old Antarctic ice deposits, I found that several years of relatively severe atmospheric pollution in the 1500s coincided with a period of relatively high global temperatures. So it is clear in this case that atmospheric pollution did cause global temperatures to rise. *PrepTest59 Sec2 Q4*	**Conclusion:** *because* **Evidence:** **Assumption:** **Assumption type:**
26. Economist: As should be obvious, raising the minimum wage significantly would make it more expensive for businesses to pay workers for minimum-wage jobs. Therefore, businesses could not afford to continue to employ as many workers for such jobs. So raising the minimum wage significantly will cause an increase in unemployment. *PrepTest57 Sec3 Q6*	**Conclusion:** *because* **Evidence:** **Assumption:** **Assumption type:**
27. Recently discovered bird fossils are about 20 million years older than the fossils of the birdlike dinosaurs from which the birds are generally claimed to have descended. So these newly discovered fossils show, contrary to the account espoused by most paleontologists, that no bird descended from any dinosaur. *PrepTest51 Sec3 Q6*	**Conclusion:** *because* **Evidence:** **Assumption:** **Assumption type:**
28. Scientist: A controversy in paleontology centers on the question of whether prehistoric human ancestors began to develop sophisticated tools before or after they came to stand upright. I argue that they stood upright first, simply because advanced toolmaking requires free use of the hands, and standing upright makes this possible. *PrepTest49 Sec2 Q14*	**Conclusion:** *because* **Evidence:** **Assumption:** **Assumption type:**

Expert Analysis: Overlooked Possibilities

Here's how an LSAT expert would analyze the arguments from that exercise. Compare your work.

LSAT Argument	Analysis
25. Scientist: While studying centuries-old Antarctic ice deposits, I found that several years of relatively severe atmospheric pollution in the 1500s coincided with a period of relatively high global temperatures. So it is clear in this case that atmospheric pollution did cause global temperatures to rise. *PrepTest59 Sec2 Q4* ⟶	**Conclusion:** In the 1500s, air pollution caused global warming. *because* **Evidence:** In the 1500s, air pollution coincided with (was correlated with) global warming. **Assumption:** In the 1500s: 1) Global warming did not cause air pollution; 2) there was no third factor that caused both air pollution and global warming; and 3) air pollution and global warming were not merely coincidental. **Assumption type:** Overlooked Possibilities—Correlation versus Causation
26. Economist: As should be obvious, raising the minimum wage significantly would make it more expensive for businesses to pay workers for minimum-wage jobs. Therefore, businesses could not afford to continue to employ as many workers for such jobs. So raising the minimum wage significantly will cause an increase in unemployment. *PrepTest57 Sec3 Q6*	**Conclusion:** Raising the minimum wage will increase unemployment. *because* **Evidence:** 1) Raising the minimum wage will make paying minimum-wage workers more expensive, and so 2) businesses will cut the number of minimum-wage jobs. ⟶ **Assumption:** There is no way other than by keeping minimum-wage job numbers steady for businesses to keep employment numbers steady. The author overlooks both an increase in the number of non-minimum wage jobs and other ways in which businesses might afford to keep employment numbers up. **Assumption type:** Overlooked Possibilities—No Other Outcome/No Change in Circumstances

LSAT Argument	**Analysis**
27. Recently discovered bird fossils are about 20 million years older than the fossils of the birdlike dinosaurs from which the birds are generally claimed to have descended. So these newly discovered fossils show, contrary to the account espoused by most paleontologists, that no bird descended from any dinosaur. *PrepTest51 Sec3 Q6* $\longrightarrow$	**Conclusion:** No bird descended from any dinosaur. *because* **Evidence:** Scientists have discovered bird fossils older than those of one dinosaur thought to be the ancestor of birds. **Assumption:** 1) The existence of the dinosaur claimed to be the ancestor of birds does not predate the earliest known fossils of that dinosaur. 2) There is no other dinosaur that might have been the ancestor of birds; this one dinosaur is the only dinosaur that might have been the ancestor of birds. **Assumption type:** Overlooked Possibilities—No Other Explanation
28. Scientist: A controversy in paleontology centers on the question of whether prehistoric human ancestors began to develop sophisticated tools before or after they came to stand upright. I argue that they stood upright first, simply because advanced toolmaking requires free use of the hands, and standing upright makes this possible. *PrepTest49 Sec2 Q14* $\longrightarrow$	**Conclusion:** Early humans stood upright prior to developing sophisticated tools. *because* **Evidence:** 1) Free use of the hands is necessary for making sophisticated tools, and 2) standing upright is sufficient for free use of the hands. **Assumption:** There is no way other than standing upright to allow for free use of the hands; standing upright is the *only* way to allow for free use of the hands. **Assumption type:** Overlooked Possibilities—Necessary versus Sufficient

UNTANGLING AND ANALYZING LSAT ARGUMENTS

Now, put together all of the work you've done on Assumptions. In the following exercise, you'll see a mixture of Mismatched Concepts and Overlooked Possibilities arguments. Some, but not all, of the arguments here will neatly fit the common patterns you learned, so analyze each argument carefully.

Practice

Analyze each of the following arguments. Identify the author's conclusion and evidence. Use them to determine the key assumption(s). Note the type of argument, and where applicable, the common pattern to which it conforms.

LSAT Argument		My Analysis
29. A recent study confirms that nutritious breakfasts make workers more productive. For one month, workers at Plant A received free nutritious breakfasts every day before work, while workers in Plant B did not. The productivity of Plant A's workers increased, while that of Plant B's workers did not. *Prep59 Sec2 Q22*	→	**Conclusion:** *because* **Evidence:** **Assumption:** **Assumption type:**
30. A development company has proposed building an airport near the city of Dalton. If the majority of Dalton's residents favor the proposal, the airport will be built. However, it is unlikely that a majority of Dalton's residents would favor the proposal, for most of them believe that the airport would create noise problems. Thus, it is unlikely that the airport will be built. *PrepTest61 Sec4 Q11*	→	**Conclusion:** *because* **Evidence:** **Assumption:** **Assumption type:**
31. Although Jaaks is a respected historian, her negative review of Yancey's new book on the history of coastal fisheries in the region rests on a mistake. Jaaks's review argues that the book inaccurately portrays the lives of fishery workers. However, Yancey used the same research methods in this book as in her other histories, which have been very popular. This book is also very popular in local bookstores. *PrepTest59 Sec2 Q6*	→	**Conclusion:** *because* **Evidence:** **Assumption:** **Assumption type:**

LSAT Argument		**My Analysis**
32.	1990 editorial: Local pay phone calls have cost a quarter apiece ever since the 1970s, when a soft drink from a vending machine cost about the same. The price of a soft drink has more than doubled since, so phone companies should be allowed to raise the price of pay phone calls too. *PrepTest49 Sec2 Q8*	**Conclusion:** *because* **Evidence:** **Assumption:** **Assumption type:**
33.	Sometimes one reads a poem and believes that the poem expresses contradictory ideas, even if it is a great poem. So it is wrong to think that the meaning of a poem is whatever the author intends to communicate to the reader by means of the poem. No one who is writing a great poem intends it to communicate contradictory ideas. *PrepTest57 Sec2 Q24*	**Conclusion:** *because* **Evidence:** **Assumption:** **Assumption type:**
34.	A survey of clerical workers' attitudes toward their work identified a group of secretaries with very positive attitudes. They responded "Strongly agree" to such statements as "I enjoy word processing" and "I like learning new secretarial skills." These secretaries had been rated by their supervisors as excellent workers—far better than secretaries whose attitudes were identified as less positive. Clearly these secretaries' positive attitudes toward their work produced excellent job performance. *PrepTest49 Sec2 Q13*	**Conclusion:** *because* **Evidence:** **Assumption:** **Assumption type:**
35.	There can be no individual freedom without the rule of law, for there is no individual freedom without social integrity, and pursuing the good life is not possible without social integrity. *PrepTest61 Sec4 Q25*	**Conclusion:** *because* **Evidence:** **Assumption:** **Assumption type:**

LSAT Argument		**My Analysis**
36. Vanwilligan: Some have argued that professional athletes receive unfairly high salaries. But in an unrestricted free market, such as the market these athletes compete in, salaries are determined by what someone else is willing to pay for their services. These athletes make enormous profits for their teams' owners, and that is why owners are willing to pay them extraordinary salaries. Thus the salaries they receive are fair. *PrepTest49 Sec2 Q19*	$\longrightarrow$	**Conclusion:** *because* **Evidence:** **Assumption:** **Assumption type:**
37. Eating garlic reduces the levels of cholesterol and triglycerides in the blood and so helps reduce the risk of cardiovascular disease. Evidence that eating garlic reduces these levels is that a group of patients taking a garlic tablet each day for four months showed a 12 percent reduction in cholesterol and a 17 percent reduction in triglycerides; over the same period, a group of similar patients taking a medically inert tablet showed only a 2 percent reduction in triglycerides and a 3 percent reduction in cholesterol. *PrepTest49 Sec4 Q2*	$\longrightarrow$	**Conclusion:** *because* **Evidence:** **Assumption:** **Assumption type:**
38. To cut costs, a high school modified its air-conditioning system to increase its efficiency. The modified system, however, caused the humidity in the school air to decrease by 18 percent. Twenty-four hours after the decrease in air humidity, a 25 percent increase in the number of visits to the school nurse was reported. This shows that a decrease in humidity can make people ill. *PrepTest59 Sec3 Q12*	$\longrightarrow$	**Conclusion:** *because* **Evidence:** **Assumption:** **Assumption type:**

Expert Analysis

Here's how an LSAT expert would analyze the arguments from that exercise. Compare your work.

LSAT Argument	Analysis
29. A recent study confirms that nutritious breakfasts make workers more productive. For one month, workers at Plant A received free nutritious breakfasts every day before work, while workers in Plant B did not. The productivity of Plant A's workers increased, while that of Plant B's workers did not. *Prep59 Sec2 Q22* $\longrightarrow$	**Conclusion:** Nutritious breakfasts make workers more productive. *because* **Evidence:** A study: Plant A workers given free nutritious breakfast; Plant B workers not. Result: Plant A workers more productive; Plant B workers not. **Assumption:** More Plant A workers than Plant B workers *ate* a nutritious breakfast. **Assumption type:** Mismatched Concepts— Representativeness (You could say the author overlooks the possibility that Plant B workers ate breakfast as often as Plant A workers did and get at the same assumption.)
30. A development company has proposed building an airport near the city of Dalton. If the majority of Dalton's residents favor the proposal, the airport will be built. However, it is unlikely that a majority of Dalton's residents would favor the proposal, for most of them believe that the airport would create noise problems. Thus, it is unlikely that the airport will be built. *PrepTest61 Sec4 Q11* $\longrightarrow$	**Conclusion:** It is unlikely that the Dalton airport will be built. *because* **Evidence:** 1) A majority vote in favor of building the airport is sufficient for the Dalton airport to be built, but 2) it is unlikely that building the airport will receive a majority vote. **Assumption:** The author assumes that the airport will be built *only* if building the airport receives a majority vote. Said another way, the author assumes the airport won't be built without a majority vote in its favor. **Assumption type:** Overlooked Possibilities— Necessary versus Sufficient

547

LSAT Argument	**Analysis**
31. Although Jaaks is a respected historian, her negative review of Yancey's new book on the history of coastal fisheries in the region rests on a mistake. Jaaks's review argues that the book inaccurately portrays the lives of fishery workers. However, Yancey used the same research methods in this book as in her other histories, which have been very popular. This book is also very popular in local bookstores. *PrepTest59 Sec2 Q6*	**Conclusion:** Yancey's new book portrays the lives of fishery workers accurately (a reviewer who says otherwise is mistaken). *because* **Evidence:** 1) Yancey's new book is very popular, and 2) she used the same research methods in her other popular books. **Assumption:** The popularity of Yancey's new book assures its accuracy. **Assumption type:** Mismatched Concepts—Alike/Equivalent
32. 1990 editorial: Local pay phone calls have cost a quarter apiece ever since the 1970s, when a soft drink from a vending machine cost about the same. The price of a soft drink has more than doubled since, so phone companies should be allowed to raise the price of pay phone calls too. *PrepTest49 Sec2 Q8*	**Conclusion:** Phone companies should be allowed to raise pay phone call prices. *because* **Evidence:** 1) In 1970, pay phone calls and soft drinks were the same price, but 2) now, soft drink prices have doubled. **Assumption:** There are no relevant factors to account for the difference between the current price of soft drinks and that of pay phone calls. The current price of a soda is (for some reason) a good indication of what the price of a pay phone call should be. **Assumption type:** Overlooked Possibilities—No Other Reason or Explanation (You could also see this argument as an example of Mismatched Concepts—Alike/Equivalent.)

LSAT Argument	**Analysis**
33. Sometimes one reads a poem and believes that the poem expresses contradictory ideas, even if it is a great poem. So it is wrong to think that the meaning of a poem is whatever the author intends to communicate to the reader by means of the poem. No one who is writing a great poem intends it to communicate contradictory ideas. *PrepTest57 Sec2 Q24*	**Conclusion:** An author's intentions do not determine the meaning of a poem. *because* **Evidence:** 1) No author of a great poem intends it to have contradictory ideas, but 2) readers of great poems sometimes believe them to express contradictory ideas. **Assumption:** A reader's beliefs about what a poem expresses are a part of the poem's meaning. **Assumption type:** Mismatched Concepts—Alike/Equivalent
34. A survey of clerical workers' attitudes toward their work identified a group of secretaries with very positive attitudes. They responded "Strongly agree" to such statements as "I enjoy word processing" and "I like learning new secretarial skills." These secretaries had been rated by their supervisors as excellent workers—far better than secretaries whose attitudes were identified as less positive. Clearly these secretaries' positive attitudes toward their work produced excellent job performance. *PrepTest49 Sec2 Q13*	**Conclusion:** The positive attitudes of excellent secretaries caused their excellent performance. *because* **Evidence:** Secretaries with excellent performance were more likely to have positive attitudes. **Assumption:** 1) The excellent performance did not cause the positive attitudes; 2) there was no third factor that caused both excellent performance and positive attitudes; and 3) the excellent performance and positive attitudes are not merely coincidental. **Assumption type:** Overlooked Possibilities—Correlation versus Causation

LSAT Argument	**Analysis**
35. There can be no individual freedom without the rule of law, for there is no individual freedom without social integrity, and pursuing the good life is not possible without social integrity.	**Conclusion:** Individual freedom requires the rule of law. If **individual freedom** → **rule of law**
PrepTest61 Sec4 Q25	*because*
→	**Evidence:** Individual freedom requires social integrity. If **individual freedom** → **social integrity**
	Assumption: Social integrity requires the rule of law. If **social integrity** → **rule of law**
	Assumption type: Mismatched Concepts—One Concept Needed for the Other
36. Vanwilligan: Some have argued that professional athletes receive unfairly high salaries. But in an unrestricted free market, such as the market these athletes compete in, salaries are determined by what someone else is willing to pay for their services. These athletes make enormous profits for their teams' owners, and that is why owners are willing to pay them extraordinary salaries. Thus the salaries they receive are fair.	**Conclusion:** Professional athletes' salaries are fair.
	because
PrepTest49 Sec2 Q19	**Evidence:** Owners are willing to pay professional athletes' salaries.
→	**Assumption:** What owners are willing to pay constitutes a fair salary.
	Assumption type: Mismatched Concepts—Alike/Equivalent

LSAT Argument	**Analysis**
37. Eating garlic reduces the levels of cholesterol and triglycerides in the blood and so helps reduce the risk of cardiovascular disease. Evidence that eating garlic reduces these levels is that a group of patients taking a garlic tablet each day for four months showed a 12 percent reduction in cholesterol and a 17 percent reduction in triglycerides; over the same period, a group of similar patients taking a medically inert tablet showed only a 2 percent reduction in triglycerides and a 3 percent reduction in cholesterol. *PrepTest49 Sec4 Q2*	**Conclusion:** Eating garlic reduces cholesterol and triglycerides in the blood. *because* **Evidence:** A study: Test group given a garlic tablet; control group given placebo. Results: The test group had a larger drop in cholesterol (12%) and triglycerides (17%) than did the control group, 2% and 3%, respectively. → **Assumption:** The groups were alike in every relevant respect other than the amount of garlic they consumed. The author overlooks 1) that the test group may have been different in terms of exercise, diet, smoking, etc., and 2) that the control group may have consumed garlic in another way. In drawing a conclusion about "eating garlic," the author also assumes that garlic has the same effect whether taken as a tablet or as food. **Assumption type:** Overlooked Possibilities—No Other Reason or Explanation
38. To cut costs, a high school modified its air conditioning system to increase its efficiency. The modified system, however, caused the humidity in the school air to decrease by 18 percent. Twenty-four hours after the decrease in air humidity, a 25 percent increase in the number of visits to the school nurse was reported. This shows that a decrease in humidity can make people ill. → *PrepTest59 Sec3 Q12*	**Conclusion:** A decrease in humidity can make people ill. *because* **Evidence:** A school decreased humidity and saw a subsequent spike in visits to the school nurse. **Assumption:** The visits to the nurse were due to illness (and not due to injury, accident, etc.). **Assumption type:** Overlooked Possibilities—No Other Cause or Explanation

ASSUMPTION QUESTIONS

The most direct application of the work you've been doing on the analysis of arguments is the Assumption question type. These questions reward you for being able to determine an author's unstated premise(s). While that task is relatively straightforward, Assumption questions are consistently among the hardest on the test.

You can identify Assumption questions from question stems like these:

The argument's conclusion follows logically if which one of the following is assumed? *PrepTest57 Sec3 Q24*	Which one of the following is an assumption on which the argument depends? *PrepTest51 Sec1 Q7*
Which one of the following, if assumed, enables the essayist's conclusion to be properly drawn? *PrepTest57 Sec2 Q7*	Which one of the following is an assumption required by the argument? *PrepTest49 Sec4 Q16*

Notice that the two question stems on the left ask for an assumption sufficient to establish the conclusion on the basis of the evidence, while the two on the right ask for assumptions necessary to the argument. We'll cover that distinction in more detail on the following pages. That small difference in wording has a huge impact on what constitutes a correct answer.

ASSUMPTION AT A GLANCE

Task: Determine the unstated premise that is either 1) sufficient to guarantee that the conclusion follows logically from the evidence or 2) necessary for the conclusion to follow logically from the evidence.

Strategy: Analyze the argument, identifying the author's conclusion and evidence. Consider what the author has taken for granted in making the argument.

LSAT tests released from 2009 to 2013 had an average of 7.5 Assumption questions per test.

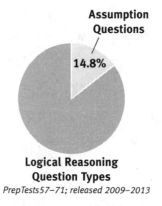

Assumption Questions

14.8%

Logical Reasoning Question Types
PrepTests57–71; released 2009–2013

On most tests, by the way, Assumption questions are split just about 60–40 between those calling for a necessary assumption and those asking for a sufficient assumption.

In this section, you'll learn to:

- Identify and answer Assumption questions
- Recognize Sufficient Assumption questions
- Recognize Necessary Assumption questions

Sufficient Assumption Questions

Look again at the question stems indicating Sufficient Assumption questions.

The argument's conclusion follows logically if which one of the following is assumed? *PrepTest57 Sec3 Q24*	Which one of the following, if assumed, enables the essayist's conclusion to be properly drawn? *PrepTest57 Sec2 Q7*

These questions seek an assumption strong enough to ensure that the conclusion is true on the basis of the evidence. The correct answer can, and often will, be stronger than what is merely necessary for the argument's validity. Consider a simple argument:

> Plovers are short-billed wading birds. Therefore, plovers hunt by sight, rather than by feel.

Now, examine two assumptions. Which one is sufficient to guarantee the conclusion in that argument?

    (1)   All short-billed wading birds hunt by sight.

    (2)   At least some short-billed wading birds hunt by sight.

Only statement (1) is sufficient to establish the conclusion in the previous argument. If, indeed, plovers are short-billed wading birds and all short-billed wading birds hunt by sight, then it is beyond doubt that plovers hunt by sight. It's worth noting that statement (1) is *not* necessary for the conclusion. It might be the case that short-billed wading birds hunt by feel, for example, while still being true that plovers use sight to find their food. Note, too, that statement (2) *is* necessary for the argument to be true. If you were asked a Necessary Assumption question about the plover argument, statement (2) would be the correct answer, and statement (1) would not.

Some facts to remember about Sufficient Assumption questions:

- Recognize these questions from the phrases "if assumed" or "the conclusion follows logically if" in the question stem.
- The correct answer, when added to the evidence, guarantees the conclusion.
- Mismatched Concepts arguments (often with Formal Logic) dominate the Sufficient Assumption question type, although other argument patterns appear as well.

Here's how an LSAT expert might identify, analyze, and answer a Sufficient Assumption question.

LSAT Question	Analysis
There can be no individual freedom without the rule of law, for there is no individual freedom without social integrity, and pursuing the good life is not possible without social integrity.	**Step 2:** Conclusion—The rule of law is necessary for individual freedom. **If individual freedom → rule of law** *because* Evidence—Social integrity is necessary for individual freedom **If individual freedom → social integrity** [NOTE: The statement that social integrity is necessary for pursuit of the good life is irrelevant to the conclusion.]
The conclusion drawn above follows logically if which one of the following is assumed?	**Step 1:** "[F]ollows logically if"—a Sufficient Assumption question. The correct answer will establish the conclusion on the basis of the evidence. The four wrong answers will not.
	Step 3: The author assumes that the rule of law is necessary for social integrity. **If social integrity → rule of law** **If ~rule of law → ~social integrity**
(A) There can be no rule of law without social integrity.	**Step 4:** Distortion. The author assumes that the rule of law is necessary to social integrity; this choice says the rule of law is sufficient. Eliminate.
(B) There can be no social integrity without the rule of law.	Correct. Adding this statement makes the argument complete and logical.
(C) One cannot pursue the good life without the rule of law.	Outside the Scope. This doesn't establish the relationship of the evidence to the conclusion, which is about social integrity. Eliminate.
(D) Social integrity is possible only if individual freedom prevails.	Distortion. This statement contains only terms from the evidence, so it cannot link the conclusion. Moreover, it mistakes the sufficient term for the necessary one in the evidence. Eliminate.
(E) There can be no rule of law without individual freedom. *PrepTest61 Sec4 Q25*	Distortion. This statement contains only terms from the conclusion, so it cannot link the evidence. Moreover, it mistakes the sufficient term for the necessary one in the conclusion. Eliminate.

Necessary Assumption Questions

Look again at the question stems indicating Necessary Assumption questions.

> Which one of the following is an assumption on which the argument depends?
>
> *PrepTest51 Sec1 Q7*

> Which one of the following is an assumption required by the argument?
>
> *PrepTest49 Sec4 Q16*

In these questions, the correct answer will be an unstated premise without which the conclusion cannot follow logically from the evidence. The author *needs* the correct answer to be true, although it might not, even when combined with the evidence, be sufficient to unequivocally establish the conclusion.

Mismatched Concepts in Necessary Assumption Questions

To understand how to predict the correct answer to a Necessary Assumption question with a Mismatched Concepts argument, consider the following:

> At State College, a freshman athlete who is on academic probation may not try out for one of the school's sports teams. Therefore, Mark, a freshman athlete at State College, may try out for the football team.

Here are two assumptions. Which is necessary for the argument above to be valid?

(1) Mark has the strongest academic record of any freshman athlete at State College.
(2) Mark is not on academic probation.

Assumption (2) is necessary to the argument. Statement (1) is too extreme to be necessary to the argument. Mark may be a mediocre student, but assuming he's a freshman athlete who is not on academic probation, he may be eligible to try out.

Here's how an LSAT expert might identify, analyze, and answer a Necessary Assumption question.

LSAT Question	Analysis
It is due to a misunderstanding that most modern sculpture is monochromatic. When ancient sculptures were exhumed years ago, they were discovered to be uncolored. No one at the time had reason to believe, as we now do, that the sculptures had originally been colorfully painted, but that centuries of exposure to moisture washed away the paint.	**Step 2:** Conclusion—Modern sculpture is monochromatic (all one color) due to a misunderstanding of historical sculpture. *because* Evidence—Ancient sculptures were originally painted, but by the time they were discovered, the paint had washed away.
Which one of the following is an assumption on which the argument depends?	**Step 1:** "[A]ssumption on which the argument depends"—the correct answer is a statement without which the conclusion cannot follow from the evidence. The four wrong answers are not needed for the argument.
	Step 3: The author must assume that modern sculptors were trying to imitate their ancient counterparts. If not, she couldn't claim that modern sculpture's monochromatic style was *due to* a misunderstanding of historical sculpture.
(A) The natural beauty of the materials out of which modern sculptures are made plays a part in their effect.	**Step 4:** Outside the Scope/180. This statement has no effect on the author's argument. If anything, it might harm the argument, suggesting that modern sculpture is monochromatic to show off its pretty materials. Eliminate.
(B) Modern sculpture has been influenced by beliefs about ancient sculpture.	Correct. Without this statement being true, the author's conclusion does not follow from the evidence.
(C) Ancient sculptures were more susceptible to moisture damage than are modern sculptures.	Irrelevant Comparison. Whether true or false, this statement has no impact on the argument. Eliminate.
(D) Some ancient paintings known to early archaeologists depicted sculptures.	180. This undermines the author's evidence ("[n]o one at the time had reason to believe"), so it is certainly not necessary to his argument. Eliminate.
(E) As modern sculptors come to believe that ancient sculpture was painted, they will begin to create polychromatic works.	Outside the Scope. Whether ancient sculpture's influence will continue in the future is irrelevant. Eliminate.

PrepTest49 Sec4 Q13

Overlooked Possibilities in Necessary Assumption Questions

For an author's Overlooked Possibilities argument to be valid, she must assume that any and all of the potential objections to her argument are not true. That means that it is necessary that each individual objection is not true. To see how that plays out in a Necessary Assumption question with an Overlooked Possibilities argument, consider the following:

> Since ServCo instituted its green energy program last quarter, the company's costs are down 8 percent. Cleary, the green energy program is saving ServCo money.

Here are two assumptions. Which one is necessary for the argument above to be valid?

(1) ServCo's reduction in expenses was not the result of reducing payroll.

(2) Every company instituting the green energy program used at ServCo has seen a cost reduction of at least 8 percent as a result.

Statement (1) is necessary. Analyzing the argument reveals that its author has overlooked other possible cost savings at ServCo. To establish the conclusion, it is necessary to rule out all other possible ways the company might have saved money. Statement (2), while it makes the green energy program sound great, is not necessary for the argument.

The Denial Test

Because the correct answer to a Necessary Assumption question must be true for the argument to be valid, it can be useful to evaluate the answer choices by denying them. When you deny the correct answer to a Necessary Assumption question, the argument falls apart. Denying an incorrect answer has no effect on the argument. See what happens when you deny the two statements associated with Mark.

(1)   Mark **does not have** the strongest academic record of any freshman athlete at State College.

(2)   Mark **is** ~~not~~ on academic probation.

When you deny statement (2), Mark's status makes him clearly ineligible to try out for a sports team. When you deny statement (1), however, all you know is that Mark isn't the best student; he may still be eligible to go out for football. Statement (2) is a necessary assumption.

Try it again on the two statements you just evaluated in light of the ServCo argument.

(1)   ServCo's reduction in expenses **was** ~~not~~ the result of reducing payroll.

(2)   **Not** every company instituting the green energy program used at ServCo has seen a cost reduction of at least 8 percent as a result.

When you deny the necessary assumption, statement (1), the conclusion falls apart. It was not the green energy program that saved the company money. When you deny the wrong answer, statement (2), the green energy program doesn't sound quite as impressive, but it is still possible that it saved money in ServCo's case.

You don't need to use the Denial Test on every Necessary Assumption question. If you have a strong prediction, you'll often spot the correct answer right away. The Denial Test may be helpful, though, when you are down to considering two or three choices and you want a clear way to distinguish among them. And, the Denial Test can be a good way to check the validity of your prediction.

LSAT STRATEGY

Some facts to remember about Necessary Assumption questions:

· Recognize these questions from the phrases "required by the argument" or "the argument depends on" in the question stem.

· The correct answer does not have to guarantee the conclusion, but the conclusion cannot logically follow from the evidence if the correct answer is not true.

· Both Mismatched Concepts and Overlooked Possibilities arguments will appear.

· The Denial Test can help distinguish the correct answer.

Assumption Question Practice

Practice the following Assumption questions. In Step 1, determine whether the question asks for an assumption sufficient or necessary to establish the conclusion. In Step 2, analyze the argument: Identify the conclusion and evidence. In Step 3, determine the author's assumption and use it as your prediction of the correct answer. In Step 4, evaluate the answer choices: Choose the answer that matches your prediction and/or eliminate those that do not state the author's assumption.

LSAT Question	My Analysis
39. It is widely believed that lancelets—small, primitive sea animals—do not have hearts. Each lancelet has a contracting vessel, but this vessel is considered an artery rather than a heart. However, this vessel is indeed a heart. After all, it strongly resembles the structure of the heart of certain other sea animals. Moreover, the muscular contractions in the lancelet's vessel closely resemble the muscular contractions of other animals' hearts.	**Step 2:** Conclusion— → *because* Evidence—
The argument's conclusion follows logically if which one of the following is assumed? →	**Step 1:**
	Step 3:
(A) Only animals that have contracting vessels have hearts. →	**Step 4:**
(B) Some primitive animals other than lancelets have what is widely held to be a heart. →	
(C) A vessel whose structure and actions closely resemble those of other animal hearts is a heart. →	
(D) For a vessel in an animal to be properly considered a heart, that vessel must undergo muscular contractions. →	
(E) No animal that has a heart lacks an artery. →	

PrepTest57 Sec3 Q24

LSAT Question	**My Analysis**

40. Global ecological problems reduce to the problem of balancing supply and demand. Supply is strictly confined by the earth's limitations. Demand, however, is essentially unlimited, as there are no limits on the potential demands made by humans. The natural tendency for there to be an imbalance between demand and sustainable supply is the source of these global problems. Therefore, any solutions require reducing current human demand.

⟶ **Step 2:** Conclusion—

because

Evidence—

Which one of the following is an assumption on which the argument depends?

⟶ **Step 1:**

Step 3:

(A) Supply and demand tend to balance themselves in the long run.

⟶ **Step 4:**

(B) It is possible to determine the limitations of the earth's sustainable supply. ⟶

(C) Actual human demand exceeds the earth's sustainable supply. ⟶

(D) It is never possible to achieve a balance between the environmental supply and human demand. ⟶

(E) Human consumption does not decrease the environmental supply. ⟶

PrepTest51 Sec1 Q7

LSAT Question	My Analysis
41. Essayist: Lessing contended that an art form's medium dictates the kind of representation the art form must employ in order to be legitimate; painting, for example, must represent simultaneous arrays of colored shapes, while literature, consisting of words read in succession, must represent events or actions occurring in sequence. The claim about literature must be rejected, however, if one regards as legitimate the imagists' poems, which consist solely of amalgams of disparate images.	**Step 2:** Conclusion— *because* Evidence—
Which one of the following, if assumed, enables the essayist's conclusion to be properly drawn?	**Step 1:**
	Step 3:
(A) An amalgam of disparate images cannot represent a sequence of events or actions.	**Step 4:**
(B) Poems whose subject matter is not appropriate to their medium are illegitimate.	
(C) Lessing was not aware that the imagists' poetry consists of an amalgam of disparate images.	
(D) All art, even the imagists' poetry, depicts or represents some subject matter.	
(E) All art represents something either as simultaneous or as successive.	

PrepTest57 Sec2 Q7

LSAT Question	My Analysis
42. To cut costs, a high school modified its air-conditioning system to increase its efficiency. The modified system, however, caused the humidity in the school air to decrease by 18 percent. Twenty-four hours after the decrease in air humidity, a 25 percent increase in the number of visits to the school nurse was reported. This shows that a decrease in humidity can make people ill. $\longrightarrow$	**Step 2:** Conclusion— *because* Evidence—
The argument depends on assuming which one of the following? $\longrightarrow$	**Step 1:**
	Step 3:
(A) At least some of the visits to the school nurse after the system was modified were due to illness. $\longrightarrow$	**Step 4:**
(B) Most of the students at the high school suffered from the decrease in air humidity. $\longrightarrow$	
(C) It takes 24 hours after a person is infected with a virus for that person to exhibit symptoms. $\longrightarrow$	
(D) A decrease of 18 percent in air humidity causes an increase of 25 percent in one's probability of becoming ill. $\longrightarrow$	
(E) Modifying the air-conditioning system proved to be an ineffective way to cut costs. $\longrightarrow$	

PrepTest59 Sec3 Q12

LSAT Question	My Analysis
43. Critic: Photographers, by deciding which subjects to depict and how to depict them, express their own worldviews in their photographs, however realistically those photographs may represent reality. Thus, photographs are interpretations of reality.	**Step 2:** Conclusion— → *because* Evidence—
The argument's conclusion is properly drawn if which one of the following is assumed?	→ **Step 1:**
	Step 3:
(A) Even representing a subject realistically can involve interpreting that subject.	→ **Step 4:**
(B) To express a worldview is to interpret reality.	→
(C) All visual art expresses the artist's worldview.	→
(D) Any interpretation of reality involves the expression of a worldview.	→
(E) Nonrealistic photographs, like realistic photographs, express the worldviews of the photographers who take them.	→

PrepTest61 Sec2 Q13

LSAT Question	My Analysis

44. An art critic, by ridiculing an artwork, can undermine the pleasure one takes in it; conversely, by lavishing praise upon an artwork, an art critic can render the experience of viewing the artwork more pleasurable. So an artwork's artistic merit can depend not only on the person who creates it but also on those who critically evaluate it.

→

Step 2: Conclusion—

because

Evidence—

The conclusion can be properly drawn if which one of the following is assumed?

→ **Step 1:**

Step 3:

(A) The merit of an artistic work is determined by the amount of pleasure it elicits.

→ **Step 4:**

(B) Most people lack the confidence necessary for making their own evaluations of art.

→

(C) Art critics understand what gives an artwork artistic merit better than artists do.

→

(D) Most people seek out critical reviews of particular artworks before viewing those works.

→

(E) The pleasure people take in something is typically influenced by what they think others feel about it.

→

PrepTest61 Sec4 Q13

LSAT Question	My Analysis
45. Chiu: The belief that a person is always morally blameworthy for feeling certain emotions, such as unjustifiable anger, jealousy, or resentment, is misguided. Individuals are responsible for only what is under their control, and whether one feels such an emotion is not always under one's control.	**Step 2:** Conclusion— → *because* Evidence—
Chiu's conclusion follows logically if which one of the following is assumed?	→ **Step 1:**
	Step 3:
(A) Individuals do not have control over their actions when they feel certain emotions.	→ **Step 4:**
(B) If a person is morally blameworthy for something, then that person is responsible for it.	→
(C) Although a person may sometimes be unjustifiably angry, jealous, or resentful, there are occasions when these emotions are appropriate.	→
(D) If an emotion is under a person's control, then that person cannot hold others responsible for it.	→
(E) The emotions for which a person is most commonly blamed are those that are under that person's control.	→

PrepTest51 Sec1 Q16

LSAT Question	My Analysis

46. Engineer: Thermophotovoltaic generators are devices that convert heat into electricity. The process of manufacturing steel produces huge amounts of heat that currently go to waste. So if steel-manufacturing plants could feed the heat they produce into thermophotovoltaic generators, they would greatly reduce their electric bills, thereby saving money.

⟶ **Step 2:** Conclusion—

because

Evidence—

Which one of the following is an assumption on which the engineer's argument depends?

⟶ **Step 1:**

Step 3:

(A) There is no other means of utilizing the heat produced by the steel-manufacturing process that would be more cost effective than installing thermophotovoltaic generators.

⟶ **Step 4:**

(B) Using current technology, it would be possible for steel-manufacturing plants to feed the heat they produce into thermophotovoltaic generators in such a way that those generators could convert at least some of that heat into electricity.

(C) The amount steel-manufacturing plants would save on their electric bills by feeding heat into thermophotovoltaic generators would be sufficient to cover the cost of purchasing and installing those generators.

(D) At least some steel-manufacturing plants rely on electricity as their primary source of energy in the steel-manufacturing process.

(E) There are at least some steel-manufacturing plants that could greatly reduce their electricity bills only if they used some method of converting wasted heat or other energy from the steel-manufacturing process into electricity.

PrepTest61 Sec2 Q16

LSAT Question	**My Analysis**
47. There is a difference between beauty and truth. After all, if there were no difference, then the most realistic pieces of art would be the best as well, since the most realistic pieces are the most truthful. But many of the most realistic artworks are not among the best. →	**Step 2:** Conclusion— *because* Evidence—
Which one of the following is an assumption required by the argument? →	**Step 1:**
	Step 3:
(A) The most beautiful artworks are the best artworks. →	**Step 4:**
(B) If an artwork contains nonrealistic elements, then it is not at all truthful. →	
(C) None of the best artworks are realistic. →	
(D) Only the best artworks are beautiful. →	
(E) An artwork's beauty is inherently subjective and depends on who is viewing it. →	

PrepTest49 Sec4 Q16

LSAT Question	**My Analysis**
48. Human beings can exhibit complex, goal-oriented behavior without conscious awareness of what they are doing. Thus, merely establishing that nonhuman animals are intelligent will not establish that they have consciousness.	**Step 2:** Conclusion— *because* ⟶ Evidence—
Which one of the following is an assumption on which the argument depends?	⟶ **Step 1:**
	Step 3:
(A) Complex, goal-oriented behavior requires intelligence.	⟶ **Step 4:**
(B) The possession of consciousness does not imply the possession of intelligence.	⟶
(C) All forms of conscious behavior involve the exercise of intelligence.	⟶
(D) The possession of intelligence entails the possession of consciousness.	⟶
(E) Some intelligent human behavior is neither complex nor goal-oriented.	⟶

PrepTest49 Sec2 Q17

LSAT Question	My Analysis
49. Any fruit that is infected is also rotten. No fruit that was inspected is infected. Therefore, any fruit that was inspected is safe to eat.	**Step 2:** Conclusion— *because* ⟶ Evidence—
The conclusion of the argument follows logically if which one of the following is assumed? ⟶	**Step 1:**
	Step 3:
(A) It is not safe to eat any fruit that is rotten. ⟶	**Step 4:**
(B) It is safe to eat any fruit that is not rotten. ⟶	
(C) It would have been safe to eat infected fruit if it had been inspected. ⟶	
(D) It is not safe to eat any fruit that is infected. ⟶	
(E) It is safe to eat any fruit that is uninfected. ⟶	

PrepTest49 Sec2 Q7

LSAT Question	**My Analysis**
50. Vanwilligan: Some have argued that professional athletes receive unfairly high salaries. But in an unrestricted free market, such as the market these athletes compete in, salaries are determined by what someone else is willing to pay for their services. These athletes make enormous profits for their teams' owners, and that is why owners are willing to pay them extraordinary salaries. Thus the salaries they receive are fair.	**Step 2:** Conclusion— ⟶ *because* Evidence—
Vanwilligan's conclusion follows logically if which one of the following is assumed? ⟶	**Step 1:**
	Step 3:
(A) The fairest economic system for a society is one in which the values of most goods and services are determined by the unrestricted free market. ⟶	**Step 4:**
(B) If professional athletes were paid less for their services, then the teams for which they play would not make as much money. ⟶	
(C) The high level of competition in the marketplace forces the teams' owners to pay professional athletes high salaries. ⟶	
(D) Any salary that a team owner is willing to pay for the services of a professional athlete is a fair salary. ⟶	
(E) If a professional athlete's salary is fair, then that salary is determined by what an individual is willing to pay for the athlete's services in an unrestricted free market. ⟶	

PrepTest49 Sec2 Q19

LSAT Question	**My Analysis**

51. Sometimes one reads a poem and believes that the poem expresses contradictory ideas, even if it is a great poem. So it is wrong to think that the meaning of a poem is whatever the author intends to communicate to the reader by means of the poem. No one who is writing a great poem intends it to communicate contradictory ideas. →

Step 2: Conclusion—

because

Evidence—

Which one of the following is an assumption on which the argument depends? → **Step 1:**

Step 3:

(A) Different readers will usually disagree about what the author of a particular poem intends to communicate by means of that poem. → **Step 4:**

(B) If someone writes a great poem, he or she intends the poem to express one primary idea. →

(C) Readers will not agree about the meaning of a poem if they do not agree about what the author of the poem intended the poem to mean. →

(D) Anyone reading a great poem can discern every idea that the author intended to express in the poem. →

(E) If a reader believes that a poem expresses a particular idea, then that idea is part of the meaning of the poem. →

PrepTest57 Sec2 Q24

Assumption Question Expert Analysis

Compare your work to that of an LSAT expert. Did you identify the type of assumption called for? Was your analysis of the argument thorough and accurate? Were you able to predict the correct answer? Which answer choices gave you trouble, and which were easier to evaluate?

LSAT Question	Analysis
39. It is widely believed that lancelets—small, primitive sea animals—do not have hearts. Each lancelet has a contracting vessel, but this vessel is considered an artery rather than a heart. However, this vessel is indeed a heart. After all, it strongly resembles the structure of the heart of certain other sea animals. Moreover, the muscular contractions in the lancelet's vessel closely resemble the muscular contractions of other animals' hearts.	**Step 2:** Conclusion—The lancelet's contracting vessel **is** a heart. *because* Evidence—(1) It **looks like** a heart found in other sea creatures, and (2) it **acts like** a heart.
The argument's conclusion follows logically if which one of the following is assumed?	**Step 1:** "[F]ollows logically if"—a Sufficient Assumption question. The correct answer will establish the conclusion on the basis of the evidence. The four wrong answers will not.
	Step 3: The author assumes that something that looks and acts like a heart is a heart, and not something else.
(A) Only animals that have contracting vessels have hearts.	**Step 4:** Distortion. The issue is whether the lancelet's vessel is a heart, not what else is required to have a heart. Eliminate.
(B) Some primitive animals other than lancelets have what is widely held to be a heart.	Outside the Scope. The anatomy of other primitive creatures is irrelevant. Eliminate.
(C) A vessel whose structure and actions closely resemble those of other animal hearts is a heart.	Correct. Taken together with the evidence, this statement guarantees the validity of the conclusion.
(D) For a vessel in an animal to be properly considered a heart, that vessel must undergo muscular contractions.	Distortion. Whether contraction is necessary for something to be considered a heart is irrelevant. Eliminate.
(E) No animal that has a heart lacks an artery. *PrepTest57 Sec3 Q24*	Outside the Scope. The definition of the lancelet's artery/heart is at issue, not whether arteries always accompany hearts. Eliminate.

LSAT Question	Analysis
40. Global ecological problems reduce to the problem of balancing supply and demand. Supply is strictly confined by the earth's limitations. Demand, however, is essentially unlimited, as there are no limits on the potential demands made by humans. The natural tendency for there to be an imbalance between demand and sustainable supply is the source of these global problems. Therefore, any solutions require reducing current human demand.	**Step 2:** Conclusion—Solutions to problems in supply and demand require reducing human demand. *because* Evidence—(1) Supply is limited by Earth's resources; (2) demand is essentially unlimited; and (3) it's natural to find imbalance between sustainable supply and demand.
Which one of the following is an assumption on which the argument depends?	**Step 1:** "[A]ssumption on which the argument depends"—the correct answer is a statement without which the conclusion cannot follow from the evidence. The four wrong answers are not needed for the argument.
	Step 3: The author must assume that the imbalance is because demand outstrips supply. If there were a glut of supply, he wouldn't conclude that reducing demand offered a solution to the imbalance.
(A) Supply and demand tend to balance themselves in the long run.	**Step 4:** Outside the Scope. Whether this is true or not doesn't impact the author's conclusion about what solutions to imbalance require.
(B) It is possible to determine the limitations of the earth's sustainable supply.	Extreme. It is not necessary to determine the overall supply in order to know what solutions to imbalance require. Eliminate.
(C) Actual human demand exceeds the earth's sustainable supply.	Correct. Without this statement being true, the author's conclusion would not be logical in light of his evidence. Eliminate.
(D) It is never possible to achieve a balance between the environmental supply and human demand.	Extreme. The author does not require complete, permanent balance. Eliminate.
(E) Human consumption does not decrease the environmental supply. *PrepTest51 Sec1 Q7*	180. If this were true, there would be no imbalance in supply and demand. Eliminate.

LSAT Question	Analysis
41. Essayist: Lessing contended that an art form's medium dictates the kind of representation the art form must employ in order to be legitimate; painting, for example, must represent simultaneous arrays of colored shapes, while literature, consisting of words read in succession, must represent events or actions occurring in sequence. The claim about literature must be rejected, however, if one regards as legitimate the imagists' poems, which consist solely of amalgams of disparate images.	**Step 2:** Conclusion—Literature need **not represent actions in sequence** (i.e., Lessing is wrong about literature). *because* Evidence—Imagist poems (for example) are literature, but they're just **"amalgams of disparate images."**
Which one of the following, if assumed, enables the essayist's conclusion to be properly drawn?	**Step 1:** "[I]f assumed … the … conclusion is properly drawn"–a Sufficient Assumption question. The correct answer will establish the conclusion on the basis of the evidence. The four wrong answers will not.
	Step 3: The author assumes that amalgams of disparate images do **not** represent actions in sequence.
(A) An amalgam of disparate images cannot represent a sequence of events or actions.	**Step 4:** Correct. Adding this statement completes the argument logically and unequivocally.
(B) Poems whose subject matter is not appropriate to their medium are illegitimate.	180. The author states that imagist poems must be taken as legitimate to work as his evidence. If they aren't legitimate, his evidence fails. Eliminate.
(C) Lessing was not aware that the imagists' poetry consists of an amalgam of disparate images.	Outside the Scope. The stimulus doesn't say whether Lessing knew about imagist poems or whether Lessing considered them legitimate literature. Eliminate.
(D) All art, even the imagists' poetry, depicts or represents some subject matter.	Extreme/Outside the Scope. Knowing this is true of *all* art (including, say, music) adds nothing to the argument. The argument is about form, *not* subject matter. Eliminate.
(E) All art represents something either as simultaneous or as successive. *PrepTest57 Sec2 Q7*	Extreme/Outside the Scope. Knowing this is true of *all* art (including, say, music) adds nothing to the argument. Whether Lessing had other criteria for other types of art is irrelevant. Eliminate.

LSAT Question	Analysis
42. To cut costs, a high school modified its air-conditioning system to increase its efficiency. The modified system, however, caused the humidity in the school air to decrease by 18 percent. Twenty-four hours after the decrease in air humidity, a 25 percent increase in the number of visits to the school nurse was reported. This shows that a decrease in humidity can make people ill.	**Step 2:** Conclusion—Reducing humidity can make people ill.

because

Evidence—Twenty-four hours after the school's modified air-conditioning lowered humidity, there was a 25 percent uptick in visits to the school nurse. |
The argument depends on assuming which one of the following?	**Step 1:** "[D]epends on assuming"—the correct answer is a statement without which the conclusion cannot follow from the evidence. The four wrong answers are not needed for the argument.
	Step 3: Overlooked Possibilities—The author must assume that nothing else was responsible for all these visits to the school nurse (e.g., sports injuries, a chemical spill in the chem lab, etc.).
(A) At least some of the visits to the school nurse after the system was modified were due to illness.	**Step 4:** Correct. If all of the visits to the nurse were due to injury or accident, the author's argument would fall apart.
(B) Most of the students at the high school suffered from the decrease in air humidity.	Extreme. The author's evidence is a 25 percent increase in visits to the nurse. He need not assume *most* students were impacted. Eliminate.
(C) It takes 24 hours after a person is infected with a virus for that person to exhibit symptoms.	Too specific to be necessary to the argument. First, the author doesn't claim that the illness was a virus. Second, 24 hours is the time after which people went to the nurse; they may have felt *symptoms* earlier. Eliminate.
(D) A decrease of 18 percent in air humidity causes an increase of 25 percent in one's probability of becoming ill.	Too specific to be necessary to the argument. The author claims only that reducing humidity *can* cause illness. Eliminate.
(E) Modifying the air-conditioning system proved to be an ineffective way to cut costs. *PrepTest59 Sec3 Q12*	Outside of the Scope. Cost cutting happened to be the initial impetus for the air-conditioning modifications. That has no impact on the argument about humidity and illness. Eliminate.

LSAT Question	Analysis
43. Critic: Photographers, by deciding which subjects to depict and how to depict them, express their own worldviews in their photographs, however realistically those photographs may represent reality. Thus, photographs are interpretations of reality.	**Step 2:** Conclusion—Photographs are **interpretations of reality**. *because* Evidence—Photographers **express their own worldviews** in photographs.
The argument's conclusion is properly drawn if which one of the following is assumed?	**Step 1:** "The ... conclusion is properly drawn if"—a Sufficient Assumption question. The correct answer will establish the conclusion on the basis of the evidence. The four wrong answers will not.
	Step 3: The author assumes that expressing one's worldview constitutes an interpretation of reality.
(A) Even representing a subject realistically can involve interpreting that subject.	**Step 4:** Distortion. This is not inconsistent with the argument, but doesn't complete it either. It doesn't link interpretation to the expression of a worldview. Eliminate.
(B) To express a worldview is to interpret reality.	Correct. Adding this statement completes the argument logically.
(C) All visual art expresses the artist's worldview.	Extreme/Outside the Scope. Knowing that the evidence applies to *all* visual artists doesn't help to establish the conclusion. Eliminate.
(D) Any interpretation of reality involves the expression of a worldview.	Distortion. This confuses necessity and sufficiency. The author assumes that expressing a worldview is always an interpretation of reality, but there may be interpretations of reality other than the expression of worldviews. Who knows? Eliminate.
(E) Nonrealistic photographs, like realistic photographs, express the worldviews of the photographers who take them. *PrepTest61 Sec2 Q13*	Distortion. This adds nothing to the evidence, which already covers all photographs "however realistic." It certainly doesn't link the evidence to the interpretation of reality. Eliminate.

LSAT Question	Analysis
44. An art critic, by ridiculing an artwork, can undermine the pleasure one takes in it; conversely, by lavishing praise upon an artwork, an art critic can render the experience of viewing the artwork more pleasurable. So an artwork's artistic merit can depend not only on the person who creates it but also on those who critically evaluate it.	**Step 2:** Conclusion—An artwork's **merit** depends on its creator and its critics. *because* Evidence—(1) A critics' ridicule can reduce a viewer's **pleasure** in an artwork. (2) A critic's praise can increase a viewer's **pleasure** in an artwork.
The conclusion can be properly drawn if which one of the following is assumed?	**Step 1:** "The conclusion can be properly drawn if"—a Sufficient Assumption question. The correct answer will establish the conclusion on the basis of the evidence. The four wrong answers will not.
	Step 3: The author assumes that the amount of pleasure viewers take in an artwork is the measure of the artwork's merit.
(A) The merit of an artistic work is determined by the amount of pleasure it elicits.	**Step 4:** Correct. Adding this to the argument establishes the conclusion absolutely from the evidence.
(B) Most people lack the confidence necessary for making their own evaluations of art.	Extreme/Outside the Scope. Whether some (let alone *most*) viewers trust their own judgment in evaluating art is beside the point. Eliminate.
(C) Art critics understand what gives an artwork artistic merit better than artists do.	Irrelevant Comparison. Which group *better* understands artistic merit is beside the point. The conclusion says both groups influence an artwork's value. Eliminate.
(D) Most people seek out critical reviews of particular artworks before viewing those works.	Extreme/Outside the Scope. Whether some (let alone *most*) viewers read reviews before viewing artworks is beside the point. Eliminate.
(E) The pleasure people take in something is typically influenced by what they think others feel about it. *PrepTest61 Sec4 Q13*	Extreme. The author stipulates that critics *can* influence perception. Whether people *typically* let other views influence them is too specific a point to affect the conclusion. Eliminate.

LSAT Question	Analysis
45. Chiu: The belief that a person is always morally blameworthy for feeling certain emotions, such as unjustifiable anger, jealousy, or resentment, is misguided. Individuals are responsible for only what is under their control, and whether one feels such an emotion is not always under one's control.	**Step 2:** Conclusion—People are not always **blameworthy** for feeling certain emotions. *because* Evidence—(1) Feeling certain emotions is not always under one's control, and (2) people are **responsible** only **for** what's under their control.
Chiu's conclusion follows logically if which one of the following is assumed?	**Step 1:** "[F]ollows logically if"—a Sufficient Assumption question. The correct answer will establish the conclusion on the basis of the evidence. The four wrong answers will not.
	Step 3: The author assumes that if a person's feelings are blameworthy, then the feelings are ones for which the person is responsible. Or, phrased negatively, if a feeling is not one for which a person is responsible, then the feeling cannot be blameworthy.
(A) Individuals do not have control over their actions when they feel certain emotions.	**Step 4:** Extreme/Outside the Scope. The author says that feeling emotions is *not always* under one's control. Moreover, the argument does not touch at all upon one's ability to control their *actions* when feeling certain emotions. Eliminate.
(B) If a person is morally blameworthy for something, then that person is responsible for it.	Correct. Adding this statement to the argument makes the argument complete and logical.
(C) Although a person may sometimes be unjustifiably angry, jealous, or resentful, there are occasions when these emotions are appropriate.	Distortion. The author's argument doesn't hinge on when certain emotions are appropriate, but on whether feeling them is blameworthy. Eliminate.
(D) If an emotion is under a person's control, then that person cannot hold others responsible for it.	Outside the Scope. When a person can blame others for emotions that person feels doesn't enter into this argument. Eliminate.
(E) The emotions for which a person is most commonly blamed are those that are under that person's control. *PrepTest51 Sec1 Q16*	Outside the Scope. How *often* someone is blamed for an action is irrelevant. Eliminate.

LSAT Question	Analysis
46. Engineer: Thermophotovoltaic generators are devices that convert heat into electricity. The process of manufacturing steel produces huge amounts of heat that currently go to waste. So if steel-manufacturing plants could feed the heat they produce into thermophotovoltaic generators, they would greatly reduce their electric bills, thereby saving money.	**Step 2:** Conclusion—If steel manufacturing plants could feed heat into TPV generators (to cut electricity costs), the plants would save money. *because* Evidence—Steel manufacturing plants waste a lot of heat.
Which one of the following is an assumption on which the engineer's argument depends?	**Step 1:** "[A]ssumption on which the argument depends"—the correct answer is a statement without which the conclusion cannot follow from the evidence. The four wrong answers are not needed for the argument.
	Step 3: The author must assume that the money saved in electricity would more than offset whatever costs are associated with TPV generators.
(A) There is no other means of utilizing the heat produced by the steel-manufacturing process that would be more cost effective than installing thermophotovoltaic generators.	**Step 4:** Irrelevant Comparison. The argument needs to prove that TPV generators would save money, not that they save the most money possible. Eliminate.
(B) Using current technology, it would be possible for steel-manufacturing plants to feed the heat they produce into thermophotovoltaic generators in such a way that those generators could convert at least some of that heat into electricity.	Not necessary because the author's conclusion is conditional: "[I]f steel-manufacturing plants could feed the heat they produce into thermophotovoltaic generators …" Current feasibility is not an issue for the author. Eliminate.
(C) The amount steel-manufacturing plants would save on their electric bills by feeding heat into thermophotovoltaic generators would be sufficient to cover the cost of purchasing and installing those generators.	Correct. If the cost of TPV generators is higher than the amount of money by which their use would reduce electric bills, the plants will not save money, and the author's conclusion is shot.
(D) At least some steel-manufacturing plants rely on electricity as their primary source of energy in the steel-manufacturing process.	Outside the Scope/Extreme. Whether electricity is the *primary source* of energy is irrelevant. Eliminate.
(E) There are at least some steel-manufacturing plants that could greatly reduce their electricity bills only if they used some method of converting wasted heat or other energy from the steel-manufacturing process into electricity. *PrepTest61 Sec2 Q16*	Extreme. The argument does not require that use of TPV generators be the *only* way steel plants can save money on electricity. Eliminate.

LSAT Question	Analysis
47. There is a difference between beauty and truth. After all, if there were no difference, then the most realistic pieces of art would be the best as well, since the most realistic pieces are the most truthful. But many of the most realistic artworks are not among the best.	**Step 2:** Conclusion—Beauty and truth are not the same thing (there's a difference between them). *because* Evidence—[Author attempts to show a contradiction if his conclusion were not true:] → If beauty and truth were the same, then most realistic art would be the best art. *and that's because* The most realistic art is the most truthful. *but* Most realistic (i.e., most truthful) art isn't always the best.
Which one of the following is an assumption required by the argument?	**Step 1:** "[A]n assumption required"—the correct → answer is a statement without which the conclusion cannot follow from the evidence. The four wrong answers are not needed for the argument.
	Step 3: The author has shown a contradiction between most truthful (most realistic) art and the best art, but his conclusion is that truth is distinct from beauty. He must be assuming that the *most beautiful* art is the best art.
(A) The most beautiful artworks are the best artworks.	**Step 4:** Correct. Without this connection, the → author's evidence (best art) doesn't relate to his conclusion (beauty).
(B) If an artwork contains nonrealistic elements, then it is not at all truthful.	Extreme. The author requires a connection between → beauty and quality. What makes art not at all truthful is irrelevant. Eliminate.
(C) None of the best artworks are realistic.	Extreme. The author's evidence has established that → the most realistic aren't always the best. Eliminate.
(D) Only the best artworks are beautiful.	Distortion. The argument doesn't require that only → the best art is beautiful, just that the most beautiful is the best. Eliminate.
(E) An artwork's beauty is inherently subjective and depends on who is viewing it. *PrepTest49 Sec4 Q16*	180. The author requires a relationship between → the most beautiful art and the best. This statement suggests that no consistent evaluation of beauty is possible. Eliminate.

LSAT Question	Analysis
48. Human beings can exhibit complex, goal-oriented behavior without conscious awareness of what they are doing. Thus, merely establishing that nonhuman animals are intelligent will not establish that they have consciousness.	**Step 2:** Conclusion—Knowing a creature is **intelligent** is not sufficient to know that the creature has consciousness. Why not? *because* Evidence—Humans exhibit **complex, goal-oriented behavior** without having conscious awareness of doing so.
Which one of the following is an assumption on which the argument depends?	**Step 1:** "[A]ssumption on which the argument depends"—the correct answer is a statement without which the conclusion cannot follow from the evidence. The four wrong answers are not needed for the argument.
	Step 3: The author must assume that intelligence is necessary for complex, goal-oriented behavior. If she doesn't, her evidence doesn't support her conclusion.
(A) Complex, goal-oriented behavior requires intelligence.	**Step 4:** Correct. Without this assumption, the evidence does not relate to the conclusion.
(B) The possession of consciousness does not imply the possession of intelligence.	Distortion. This is a mistaken paraphrase of the conclusion. It does not link to the evidence at all. Eliminate.
(C) All forms of conscious behavior involve the exercise of intelligence.	180. This contradicts the conclusion. Eliminate.
(D) The possession of intelligence entails the possession of consciousness.	180. This contradicts the conclusion. Eliminate.
(E) Some intelligent human behavior is neither complex nor goal-oriented. *PrepTest49 Sec2 Q17*	Distortion. The author must assume that complex, goal-oriented behavior requires intelligence. Whether there are other types of intelligent behavior is irrelevant. Eliminate.

LSAT Question	Analysis
49. Any fruit that is infected is also rotten. No fruit that was inspected is infected. Therefore, any fruit that was inspected is safe to eat.	**Step 2:** Conclusion—If a fruit was inspected, then that fruit is safe to eat.
	If inspected → safe
	because
	Evidence—If a fruit was inspected, then that fruit is not infected.
	If inspected → ~infected
	[NOTE: The terms in the statement that infected fruits are rotten are unrelated to the terms in the conclusion.]
The conclusion of the argument follows logically if which one of the following is assumed?	**Step 1:** "[F]ollows logically if"—a Sufficient Assumption question. The correct answer will establish the conclusion on the basis of the evidence. The four wrong answers will not.
	Step 3: The author assumes that any uninfected fruit is safe to eat.
	If ~infected → safe
(A) It is not safe to eat any fruit that is rotten.	**Step 4:** Outside the Scope. The author tells you what is safe (inspected, uninfected fruits). What is unsafe is not defined here, and many things could make fruit unsafe to eat. Eliminate.
(B) It is safe to eat any fruit that is not rotten.	Distortion. Knowing that fruit is not rotten means it is not infected, which means that it was not inspected. That, however, doesn't mean that inspected fruits are safe to eat, and so does not establish the conclusion. Eliminate.
(C) It would have been safe to eat infected fruit if it had been inspected.	Distortion. This introduces a contradiction into the argument, which tells you that inspected fruits are *not* infected, and therefore safe to eat. Eliminate.
(D) It is not safe to eat any fruit that is infected.	Outside the Scope. The argument is about fruits that *are* safe to eat. Eliminate.
(E) It is safe to eat any fruit that is uninfected.	Correct. This completes the argument logically.

PrepTest49 Sec2 Q7

	LSAT Question	**Analysis**
50.	Vanwilligan: Some have argued that professional athletes receive unfairly high salaries. But in an unrestricted free market, such as the market these athletes compete in, salaries are determined by what someone else is willing to pay for their services. These athletes make enormous profits for their teams' owners, and that is why owners are willing to pay them extraordinary salaries. Thus the salaries they receive are fair.	**Step 2:** Conclusion—Professional athletes' salaries are **fair**. *because* Evidence—**Owners are willing to pay** professional athletes' salaries.
	Vanwilligan's conclusion follows logically if which one of the following is assumed?	**Step 1:** "[F]ollows logically if"—a Sufficient Assumption question. The correct answer will establish the conclusion on the basis of the evidence. The four wrong answers will not.
		Step 3: Assuming that whatever owners are willing to pay is fair completes this argument unequivocally.
(A)	The fairest economic system for a society is one in which the values of most goods and services are determined by the unrestricted free market.	**Step 4:** Extreme/Outside the Scope. The author makes no claim that the free market is the *fairest* of all systems. He's interested in the definition of a *fair salary* within the free market system. Eliminate.
(B)	If professional athletes were paid less for their services, then the teams for which they play would not make as much money.	Distortion. If teams paid players less, they'd likely make more money, but that's beside the point. Given that players compete in a free market, the team owners are willing to pay. Eliminate.
(C)	The high level of competition in the marketplace forces the teams' owners to pay professional athletes high salaries.	Outside the Scope. The business reasons that influence owners to pay are irrelevant; it's their willingness to pay that constitutes fairness. Eliminate.
(D)	Any salary that a team owner is willing to pay for the services of a professional athlete is a fair salary.	Correct. Adding this assumption to the argument makes the author's conclusion follows ineluctably from his evidence.
(E)	If a professional athlete's salary is fair, then that salary is determined by what an individual is willing to pay for the athlete's services in an unrestricted free market. *PrepTest49 Sec2 Q19*	Distortion. The author assumes that the owner's willingness to pay is sufficient for fairness; this choice says the owner's willingness is necessary for fairness. Eliminate.

LSAT Question	**Analysis**
51. Sometimes one reads a poem and believes that the poem expresses contradictory ideas, even if it is a great poem. So it is wrong to think that the meaning of a poem is whatever the author intends to communicate to the reader by means of the poem. No one who is writing a great poem intends it to communicate contradictory ideas.	**Step 2:** Conclusion—A poem's **meaning is not** determined by the **author's intentions**. *because* Evidence—(1) A **reader can believe he's found contradictory ideas** in a great poem, and (2) **no author** of a great poem **intends contradictory ideas**.
Which one of the following is an assumption on which the argument depends?	**Step 1:** "[A]ssumption on which the argument depends"—the correct answer is a statement without which the conclusion cannot follow from the evidence. The four wrong answers are not needed for the argument.
	Step 3: The author must assume that a poem's meaning is determined, at least in part, by what a reader believes the poem says.
(A) Different readers will usually disagree about what the author of a particular poem intends to communicate by means of that poem.	**Step 4:** Extreme/Distortion. Whether readers will *usually* disagree is irrelevant. Moreover, this choice does not link the evidence to the poem's *meaning*. Eliminate.
(B) If someone writes a great poem, he or she intends the poem to express one primary idea.	Extreme. The authors of great poems do not intend contradictory ideas; that doesn't mean they're limited to "one primary idea." Eliminate.
(C) Readers will not agree about the meaning of a poem if they do not agree about what the author of the poem intended the poem to mean.	Distortion. Nothing in the argument hinges on the reader being aware of the author's intentions. Eliminate.
(D) Anyone reading a great poem can discern every idea that the author intended to express in the poem.	Extreme/Distortion. Whether *any* reader can discern *every* idea is irrelevant. Moreover, this choice does not link the evidence to the poem's *meaning*. Eliminate.
(E) If a reader believes that a poem expresses a particular idea, then that idea is part of the meaning of the poem. *PrepTest57 Sec2 Q24*	Correct. If this statement is not added to the argument, then the evidence about readers' beliefs cannot support the conclusion about a poem's meaning.

FLAW QUESTIONS

The second major Assumption Family question type is the Flaw question. These will directly reward your skills in understanding and summarizing the kinds of reasoning errors you've learned to identify in LSAT arguments.

You can identify Flaw questions from question stems such as these:

> The argument's reasoning is most vulnerable to criticism on the grounds that the argument
>
> *PrepTest59 Sec3 Q8*

> Which of the following identifies a reasoning error in the argument?
>
> *PrepTest49 Sec2 Q13*

> The reasoning in the pundit's argument is questionable because the argument
>
> *PrepTest51 Sec3 Q4*

Note that each of these questions asks you to *describe* the *flawed reasoning* in the argument. There are two important takeaways from that observation. First, your task is to describe the flaw. That means that the answers will be worded abstractly, in a way that covers the generic flaw committed by the author, rather than focusing on the details of the particular argument. More on that in a moment. Second, your task here is to describe the error in reasoning. That tells you that the answer choices describe logical missteps, not mistakes of fact. Both of those aspects of Flaw questions add difficulties for the test taker. Fortunately, there are patterns and strategies you can learn that will give you back the advantage.

FLAW AT A GLANCE

Task: Describe the author's reasoning error.

Strategy: Analyze the argument, identifying the author's conclusion and evidence; determine the author's assumption and use it to help you describe the logical fallacy or reasoning error the author has committed.

LSAT tests released from 2009 to 2013 had an average of 7.6 Flaw questions per test.

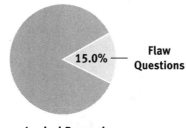

**Logical Reasoning
Question Types**

PrepTests57–71; released 2009–2013

LEARNING OBJECTIVES

In this section, you'll learn to:

· Identify and answer Flaw questions
· Recognize and characterize the most common flawed argument patterns
· Recognize an abstractly worded but correct answer choice in a Flaw question

Common Flaw Types

Your performance on Flaw questions will benefit from your familiarity with the common argument structures on the LSAT. In fact, the majority of Flaw questions feature a limited set of inherently flawed arguments.

LSAT STRATEGY

Flaw questions are dominated by these common argument types:

· Overlooked Possibilities (general)—A failure to consider alternative explanations or possible objections
· Overlooked Possibilities (correlation versus causation)—A conclusion of causation based on evidence of correlation
· Overlooked Possibilities (necessity versus sufficiency)—A conclusion treating a sufficient term in the evidence as if it were necessary
· Mismatched Concepts (including alike/equivalent, mutually exclusive, and representation)—A conclusion the scope or terms of which are unwarranted given the evidence

The way that Flaw question answer choices are worded provides evidence of just how common these reasoning errors are. As you practice, take note of answer choices like these, describing Overlooked Possibilities:

The argument is most vulnerable to the criticism that it

overlooks the possibility that …
ignores the possibility that …
fails to take into account the possibility that …

And note the difference between those and answer choices that describe arguments in which the author makes an unreasonable leap between Mismatched Concepts.

The argument is most vulnerable to the criticism that it

fails to justify its presumption that …
presumes, without providing justification …
presumes, without warrant …

Less Common Flaws

While the majority of arguments in Flaw questions fit into the categories on the previous page, you should be prepared to see examples of a few less common flaws as well.

Mismatched Concepts—Equivocation: This reasoning error occurs when someone uses the same word or term inconsistently in the conclusion and evidence. For example: "The president of Bill's wine club said that Bill is a discriminating individual. But the president must be mistaken. Bill would never discriminate against anyone." The correct answer will say something along the lines of "The argument allows a key term to shift meaning illicitly."

Mismatched Concepts—Part to Whole: When this flaw shows up on the LSAT, it usually involves the author assuming that what is true of something's parts is true of its whole. For example: "Each of the chapters in this novel is short, so the novel must be short." The correct answer usually describes this flaw clearly: "...assumes, without warrant, that what is true of an object's parts is true of the whole object."

Circular Reasoning: This form of argument goes wrong because the evidence provided simply assumes the truth of the conclusion. For example: "Without Jim, our team is incomplete, because even with everyone other than Jim on the team, it will still be incomplete." LSAT versions of the argument can be subtle, but you will recognize the correct answer from language like: "The purported evidence presumes the truth of the conclusion."

Evidence Contradicts Conclusion: This blatant flaw draws a conclusion that is the opposite of what its evidence implies. For example: "Management's position in the negotiations is strong. You can see this from the numerous concessions they've made to labor." The correct answer describes this error plainly: "The argument's conclusion conflicts with the evidence provided." Don't confuse this flaw with Overlooked Possibilities arguments in which the evidence is equally likely to support or contradict the conclusion. For example: "Our football team has a new quarterback. Therefore, the team must be stronger." Who knows? Maybe the new quarterback is weaker than the old one.

LSAT STRATEGY

Some extremely rare reasoning flaws you may see described on the LSAT:

- Conflating numerical values with percent values
- Using evidence of a belief to draw a conclusion of fact
- Attacking the person making the argument instead of the argument (ad hominem)
- Stating that an absence of evidence is evidence of absence
- Making an inappropriate appeal to authority ("Professor Y says it's true, so it must be.")
- Failing to address another speaker's point

Learning to recognize language describing rare flaws is valuable even when the argument in question is not flawed in one of these ways; you may find descriptions of these rare flaws among the *wrong answers*, and you will want to be confident that they do not match the argument in the stimulus.

Here's how an LSAT expert might analyze, predict, and answer a Flaw question.

LSAT Question	Analysis
The more modern archaeologists learn about Mayan civilization, the better they understand its intellectual achievements. Not only were numerous scientific observations and predictions made by Mayan astronomers, but the people in general seem to have had a strong grasp of sophisticated mathematical concepts. We know this from the fact that the writings of the Mayan religious scribes exhibit a high degree of mathematical competence.	**Step 2:** Conclusion—Mayan astronomers and lay people understood high-level math concepts. *because* Evidence—Mayan religious scribes' writings display high-level mathematical competence.
The argument's reasoning is most vulnerable to criticism on the grounds that the argument	**Step 1:** "[V]ulnerable to criticism on the grounds"—the correct answer will describe a flaw in the argument's reasoning.
	Step 3: Mismatched Concepts—The author draws a conclusion about astronomers and lay people from evidence about religious scribes. The group in the evidence may not be representative of those in the conclusion.
(A) fails to provide an adequate definition of the term "intellectual achievement"	**Step 4:** Distortion. The author's chief example—"mathematical competence"—fits the plain-language understanding of "intellectual achievement." Eliminate.
(B) bases a generalization on a sample that is likely to be unrepresentative	Correct. This points out the untenable shift in scope between the author's evidence and his conclusion.
(C) overlooks the impressive achievements of other past civilizations	Outside the Scope. Both conclusion and evidence are about the Mayans. Other groups are irrelevant. Eliminate.
(D) relies on two different senses of the term "scientific"	Distortion. "[S]cientific" is used just once in the argument, and nothing implies two understandings of that word. Eliminate.
(E) takes a mere correlation to be evidence of a causal relationship *PrepTest59 Sec3 Q8*	Distortion. The author makes no causal claim in the argument. Eliminate.

Which of the flaw types does this question represent?

Common Wording of Flaw Types in Answer Choices

A solid foundation for answering Flaw questions comes from knowing that you can identify the flaws common in LSAT arguments. It is also important that you are able to understand which flaws the answer choices are describing. This allows you not only to spot the correct answer, but also to quickly and confidently eliminate wrong answers, those describing flaws not made in this case.

LSAT STRATEGY

Common Flaw Question Answer Choices by Argument Pattern

Overlooked Possibilities— General	"overlooks the possibility that"/"ignores the possibility that"/"fails to consider"
	"assumes only one possibility when more exist"
	"treats one explanation of many as though it were the only one"
Overlooked Possibilities— Causation	"mistakes a correlation for causation"
	"presumes that because one event was followed by another, the first event caused the second"
	"ignores the possibility that two things that occur together may be only coincidentally related"
Overlooked Possibilities— Nec vs Suff	"confuses a result with a condition that is required to bring about that result"
	"mistakes something that is necessary for a particular outcome for something that is merely sufficient for that outcome"
	"ignores the possibility that a particular outcome may be sufficient but not necessary for another"
Mismatched Concepts— General	"relies on irrelevant evidence"
	"facts that are not directly related to the case are used to support a conclusion about it"
	"draws an analogy between two things that are not alike enough in the ways they would need to be in order for the conclusion to be properly drawn"
Mismatched Concepts— Representation	"draws a general conclusion from a few isolated instances"
	"generalizes from an unrepresentative sample"
	"treats the children living in County X as though they were representative of all children that age living in State Y"
Mismatched Concepts— Equivocation	"relies on an ambiguity in the term *plant*"
	"allows a key phrase to shift in meaning from one use to the next"
Circular Reasoning	"the conclusion is no more than a restatement of the evidence used to support it"
	"restates its conclusion without providing sufficient justification for accepting it"
	"presupposes the truth of what it seeks to establish"
Evidence Contradicts the Conclusion	"the evidence given actually undermines the argument's conclusion"
	"some of the evidence given is inconsistent with other evidence presented"
	"draws a recommendation that is inconsistent with the evidence given to support it"

Drill: Identifying Argument Types in Flaw Question Answer Choices

For each of the following, name the flaw described in the answer choice.

Answer Choices		My Analysis
The argument is vulnerable to criticism on the grounds that the argument:		
52. presumes, without justification, that retirement benefits are used primarily for purchases of essential goods	$\longrightarrow$	
53. treats a characteristic known to be true of one class of things as if that characteristic were unique to that class	$\longrightarrow$	
54. mistakes a condition sufficient for bringing about a result for a condition necessary for doing so	$\longrightarrow$	
55. takes the failure of evidence to establish the truth of a statement as evidence that that statement is false	$\longrightarrow$	
56. concludes that two things that occur at the same time have a common cause	$\longrightarrow$	
57. overlooks the possibility that most star systems are uninhabited	$\longrightarrow$	
58. treats as similar two cases that are different in a critical respect	$\longrightarrow$	
59. confuses the percentage of the budget spent on a program with the overall amount spent on the program	$\longrightarrow$	
60. assumes the truth of what it attempts to demonstrate	$\longrightarrow$	
61. bases its conclusion about a group on survey results that may not be representative of the group	$\longrightarrow$	
62. assumes that because something is true of each of an object's parts, it is true of the object	$\longrightarrow$	
63. improperly exploits an ambiguity in the phrase "public interest"	$\longrightarrow$	

Expert Analysis

Here's how an LSAT expert would denominate the flaws described by the answer choices in that exercise.

Answer Choices	Analysis
The argument is vulnerable to criticism on the grounds that the argument:	
52. presumes, without justification, that retirement benefits are used primarily for purchases of essential goods →	Mismatched Concepts. "Presumes, without justification" signals a problem in the author's assumption. The author's conclusion relies on the connection between retirement benefits and the purchase of essential goods, but the argument gives us no reason to know that this is true.
53. treats a characteristic known to be true of one class of things as if that characteristic were unique to that class →	Overlooked Possibility: Necessity versus Sufficiency. The author treats a characteristic necessary to a group of things as if it is sufficient to designate things as being in that group.
54. mistakes a condition sufficient for bringing about a result for a condition necessary for doing so →	Overlooked Possibility: Necessity versus Sufficiency. The author has treated a sufficient condition as though it were a necessary one.
55. takes the failure of evidence to establish the truth of a statement as evidence that that statement is false →	Overlooked Possibilities. The specific flaw here is often described as "an absence of evidence is the same as evidence of absence." For example, absence of evidence for the existence of aliens is NOT evidence for the absence of aliens.
56. concludes that two things that occur at the same time have a common cause →	Overlooked Possibilities: Correlation versus Causation
57. overlooks the possibility that most star systems are uninhabited →	Overlooked Possibilities. Arguments in which the author assumes only one possibility without giving a reason to rule out others are inherently flawed.
58. treats as similar two cases that are different in a critical respect →	Mismatched Concepts: Alike/Equivalent. The author assumes a shared property between two different things. The argument in this case might contain a faulty analogy.

Answer Choices (Cont.)		Analysis (Cont.)
59. confuses the percentage of the budget spent on a program with the overall amount spent on the program	→	Mismatched Concepts: Numbers versus Percents
60. assumes the truth of what it attempts to demonstrate	→	Circular Reasoning
61. bases its conclusion about a group on survey results that may not be representative of the group	→	Mismatched Concepts: Representativeness. The author relies on a sample that differs in some critical respect from the group in the conclusion.
62. assumes that because something is true of each of an object's parts, it is true of the object	→	Mismatched Concept: Part/Whole. The part or whole can have properties that are lacking in the other.
63. improperly exploits an ambiguity in the phrase "public interest"	→	Mismatched Concepts: Equivocation. This flaw occurs when one word or term is used in two incompatible senses in the argument.

LSAT STRATEGY

Some facts to remember about Flaw questions:

· The correct answer will describe the error in the author's reasoning.
· You will be tested on your ability to identify flaws in both Mismatched Concepts and Overlooked Possibilities arguments.
· Correct answer choices are often written in abstract terms; form a prediction and match it to the most appropriate answer choice.

Flaw Question Practice

Practice some Flaw questions. In each: Identify the question; analyze the argument—locate the conclusion and evidence; consider the author's assumption to help you spot the error in his reasoning; predict the correct answer; and evaluate the choices.

LSAT Question	My Analysis
64. Although Jaaks is a respected historian, her negative review of Yancey's new book on the history of coastal fisheries in the region rests on a mistake. Jaaks's review argues that the book inaccurately portrays the lives of fishery workers. However, Yancey used the same research methods in this book as in her other histories, which have been very popular. This book is also very popular in local bookstores. $\longrightarrow$	**Step 2:** Conclusion— *because* Evidence—
The reasoning above is flawed in that it $\longrightarrow$	**Step 1:**
	Step 3:
(A) relies on the word of a scholar who is unqualified in the area in question $\longrightarrow$	**Step 4:**
(B) attacks the person making the claim at issue rather than addressing the claim $\longrightarrow$	
(C) takes for granted that the popularity of a book is evidence of its accuracy $\longrightarrow$	
(D) bases a general conclusion on a sample that is likely to be unrepresentative $\longrightarrow$	
(E) presumes, without providing justification, that the methods used by Yancey are the only methods that would produce accurate results $\longrightarrow$	

PrepTest59 Sec2 Q6

LSAT Question	My Analysis

65. Deirdre: Many philosophers have argued that the goal of every individual is to achieve happiness—that is, the satisfaction derived from fully living up to one's potential. They have also claimed that happiness is elusive and can be achieved only after years of sustained effort. But these philosophers have been unduly pessimistic, since they have clearly exaggerated the difficulty of being happy. Simply walking along the seashore on a sunny afternoon causes many people to experience feelings of happiness.

$\longrightarrow$

Step 2: Conclusion—

because

Evidence—

Which one of the following most accurately describes a reasoning flaw in Deirdre's argument? $\longrightarrow$ **Step 1:**

Step 3:

(A) It dismisses a claim because of its source rather than because of its content. $\longrightarrow$ **Step 4:**

(B) It fails to take into account that what brings someone happiness at one moment may not bring that person happiness at another time. $\longrightarrow$

(C) It allows the key term "happiness" to shift in meaning illicitly in the course of the argument. $\longrightarrow$

(D) It presumes, without providing justification, that happiness is, in fact, the goal of life. $\longrightarrow$

(E) It makes a generalization based on the testimony of a group whose views have not been shown to be representative. $\longrightarrow$

PrepTest51 Sec1 Q6

LSAT Question	My Analysis
66. Editorial: Clearly, during the past two years, the unemployment situation in our city has been improving. Studies show that the number of unemployed people who are actively looking for jobs has steadily decreased during that period. $\longrightarrow$	**Step 2:** Conclusion— *because* Evidence—
The editorial's reasoning is most vulnerable to criticism on the grounds that it $\longrightarrow$	**Step 1:**
	Step 3:
(A) presumes, without providing justification, that the government is at least partly responsible for the improvement in the employment situation $\longrightarrow$	**Step 4:**
(B) relies on data from a period that is too short to justify an inference about a general trend $\longrightarrow$	
(C) fails to take into account the possibility that many unemployed workers who still desire jobs may have stopped looking for jobs $\longrightarrow$	
(D) fails to take into account that the sorts of governmental efforts that reduce unemployment may not be effective in creating more high-paying jobs $\longrightarrow$	
(E) ignores other economic indicators, which may not have improved during the past two years $\longrightarrow$	

PrepTest49 Sec4 Q1

LSAT Question	My Analysis
67. Pundit: The average salary for teachers in our society is lower than the average salary for athletes. Obviously, our society values sports more than it values education.	**Step 2:** Conclusion—

because

⟶ Evidence— |
The reasoning in the pundit's argument is questionable because the argument ⟶	**Step 1:**
	Step 3:
(A) presumes, without providing justification, that sports have some educational value ⟶	**Step 4:**
(B) fails to consider that the total amount of money spent on education may be much greater than the total spent on sports ⟶	
(C) fails to consider both that most teachers are not in the classroom during the summer and that most professional athletes do not play all year ⟶	
(D) compares teachers' salaries only to those of professional athletes rather than also to the salaries of other professionals ⟶	
(E) fails to compare salaries for teachers in the pundit's society to salaries for teachers in other societies ⟶	

PrepTest51 Sec3 Q4

LSAT Question	My Analysis
68. Scientist: While studying centuries-old Antarctic ice deposits, I found that several years of relatively severe atmospheric pollution in the 1500s coincided with a period of relatively high global temperatures. So it is clear in this case that atmospheric pollution did cause global temperatures to rise.	**Step 2:** Conclusion— *because* Evidence—
The reasoning in the scientist's argument is most vulnerable to criticism on the grounds that the argument	**Step 1:**
	Step 3:
(A) presumes, without providing justification, that a rise in global temperatures is harmful	**Step 4:**
(B) draws a general conclusion based on a sample that is likely to be unrepresentative	
(C) inappropriately generalizes from facts about a specific period of time to a universal claim	
(D) takes for granted that the method used for gathering data was reliable	
(E) infers, merely from a claim that two phenomena are associated, that one phenomenon causes the other	

PrepTest59 Sec2 Q4

LSAT Question	My Analysis
69. Recently discovered bird fossils are about 20 million years older than the fossils of the birdlike dinosaurs from which the birds are generally claimed to have descended. So these newly discovered fossils show, contrary to the account espoused by most paleontologists, that no bird descended from any dinosaur.	**Step 2:** Conclusion— *because* Evidence—
The reasoning in the argument is flawed in that the argument	**Step 1:**
	Step 3:
(A) draws a generalization that is broader than is warranted by the findings cited	**Step 4:**
(B) rejects the consensus view of experts in the field without providing any counterevidence	
(C) attacks the adherents of the opposing view personally instead of addressing any reason for their view	
(D) fails to consider the possibility that dinosaurs descended from birds	
(E) ignores the possibility that dinosaurs and birds descended from a common ancestor	

PrepTest51 Sec3 Q6

LSAT Question	My Analysis
70. A survey of clerical workers' attitudes toward their work identified a group of secretaries with very positive attitudes. They responded "Strongly agree" to such statements as "I enjoy word processing" and "I like learning new secretarial skills." These secretaries had been rated by their supervisors as excellent workers—far better than secretaries whose attitudes were identified as less positive. Clearly these secretaries' positive attitudes toward their work produced excellent job performance.	**Step 2:** Conclusion— *because* Evidence—
Which one of the following identifies a reasoning error in the argument?	**Step 1:**
	Step 3:
(A) It attempts to prove a generalization about job performance by using the single example of clerical workers.	**Step 4:**
(B) It restates the claim that the secretaries' positive attitudes produced their excellent job performance instead of offering evidence for it.	
(C) It does not consider the possibility that secretaries with very positive attitudes toward their work might also have had very positive attitudes toward other activities.	
(D) It uses the term "positive attitudes" to mean two different things.	
(E) It identifies the secretaries' positive attitudes as the cause of their excellent job performance although their attitudes might be an effect of their performance.	

PrepTest49 Sec2 Q13

LSAT Question	My Analysis
71. Letter to the editor: Middle-class families in wealthy nations are often criticized for the ecological damage resulting from their lifestyles. This criticism should not be taken too seriously, however, since its source is often a movie star or celebrity whose own lifestyle would, if widely adopted, destroy the environment and deplete our resources in a short time.	**Step 2:** Conclusion— *because* Evidence—
The reasoning in the letter to the editor is vulnerable to criticism in that it	**Step 1:**
	Step 3:
(A) criticizes a characteristic of the people giving an argument rather than criticizing the argument itself	**Step 4:**
(B) takes failure to act consistently with a belief as an indication of the sincerity with which that belief is held	
(C) presumes that a viewpoint must be unreasonable to accept simply because some of the grounds advanced to support it do not adequately do so	
(D) fails to recognize that evidence advanced in support of a conclusion actually undermines that conclusion	
(E) generalizes about the behavior of all people on the basis of the behavior of a few	

PrepTest49 Sec2 Q5

LSAT Question	My Analysis

72. In a poll of a representative sample of a province's residents, the provincial capital was the city most often selected as the best place to live in that province. Since the capital is also the largest of that province's many cities, the poll shows that most residents of that province generally prefer life in large cities to life in small cities.

$\longrightarrow$

Step 2: Conclusion—

because

Evidence—

The argument is most vulnerable to the criticism that it $\longrightarrow$

Step 1:

Step 3:

(A) overlooks the possibility that what is true of the residents of the province may not be true of other people $\longrightarrow$

Step 4:

(B) does not indicate whether most residents of other provinces also prefer life in large cities to life in small cities $\longrightarrow$

(C) takes for granted that when people are polled for their preferences among cities, they tend to vote for the city that they think is the best place to live $\longrightarrow$

(D) overlooks the possibility that the people who preferred small cities over the provincial capital did so not because of their general feelings about the sizes of cities, but because of their general feelings about capital cities $\longrightarrow$

(E) overlooks the possibility that most people may have voted for small cities even though a large city received more votes than any other single city $\longrightarrow$

PrepTest51 Sec1 Q18

LSAT Question	My Analysis
73. A development company has proposed building an airport near the city of Dalton. If the majority of Dalton's residents favor the proposal, the airport will be built. However, it is unlikely that a majority of Dalton's residents would favor the proposal, for most of them believe that the airport would create noise problems. Thus, it is unlikely that the airport will be built. →	**Step 2:** Conclusion— *because* Evidence—
The reasoning in the argument is flawed in that the argument →	**Step 1:**
	Step 3:
(A) treats a sufficient condition for the airport's being built as a necessary condition →	**Step 4:**
(B) concludes that something must be true, because most people believe it to be true →	
(C) concludes, on the basis that a certain event is unlikely to occur, that the event will not occur →	
(D) fails to consider whether people living near Dalton would favor building the airport →	
(E) overlooks the possibility that a new airport could benefit the local economy →	

PrepTest61 Sec4 Q11

LSAT Question	My Analysis
74. Politician: The huge amounts of money earned by oil companies elicit the suspicion that the regulations designed to prevent collusion need to be tightened. But just the opposite is true. If the regulations designed to prevent collusion are not excessively burdensome, then oil companies will make profits sufficient to motivate the very risky investments associated with exploration that must be made if society is to have adequate oil supplies. But recent data show that the oil industry's profits are not the highest among all industries. Clearly, the regulatory burden on oil companies has become excessive.	**Step 2:** Conclusion— *because* ⟶ Evidence—
The reasoning in the politician's argument is most vulnerable to criticism on the grounds that the argument	⟶ **Step 1:**
	⟶ **Step 3:**
(A) fails to justify its presumption that profits sufficient to motivate very risky investments must be the highest among all industries	⟶ **Step 4:**
(B) attacks the character of the oil companies rather than the substance of their conduct	⟶
(C) fails to justify its presumption that two events that are correlated must also be causally related	⟶
(D) treats the absence of evidence that the oil industry has the highest profits among all industries as proof that the oil industry does not have the highest profits among all industries	⟶
(E) illicitly draws a general conclusion from a specific example that there is reason to think is atypical	⟶

PrepTest49 Sec4 Q12

LSAT Question	My Analysis

75. The typological theory of species classification, which has few adherents today, distinguishes species solely on the basis of observable physical characteristics, such as plumage color, adult size, or dental structure. However, there are many so-called "sibling species," which are indistinguishable on the basis of their appearance but cannot interbreed and thus, according to the mainstream biological theory of species classification, are separate species. Since the typological theory does not count sibling species as separate species, it is unacceptable.

→ **Step 2:** Conclusion—

because

Evidence—

The reasoning in the argument is most vulnerable to criticism on the grounds that

→ **Step 1:**

Step 3:

(A) the argument does not evaluate all aspects of the typological theory

→ **Step 4:**

(B) the argument confuses a necessary condition for species distinction with a sufficient condition for species distinction

→

(C) the argument, in its attempt to refute one theory of species classification, presupposes the truth of an opposing theory

→

(D) the argument takes a single fact that is incompatible with a theory as enough to show that theory to be false

→

(E) the argument does not explain why sibling species cannot interbreed

→

PrepTest51 Sec1 Q15

LSAT Question	My Analysis
76. One is likely to feel comfortable approaching a stranger if the stranger is of one's approximate age. Therefore, long-term friends are probably of the same approximate age as each other since most long-term friendships begin because someone felt comfortable approaching a stranger. $\longrightarrow$	**Step 2:** Conclusion— *because* Evidence—
The reasoning in the argument is flawed in that it $\longrightarrow$	**Step 1:**
	Step 3:
(A) presumes, without warrant, that one is likely to feel uncomfortable approaching a person only if that person is a stranger $\longrightarrow$	**Step 4:**
(B) infers that a characteristic is present in a situation from the fact that that characteristic is present in most similar situations $\longrightarrow$	
(C) overlooks the possibility that one is less likely to feel comfortable approaching someone who is one's approximate age if that person is a stranger than if that person is not a stranger $\longrightarrow$	
(D) presumes, without warrant, that one never approaches a stranger unless one feels comfortable doing so $\longrightarrow$	
(E) fails to address whether one is likely to feel comfortable approaching a stranger who is not one's approximate age $\longrightarrow$	

PrepTest61 Sec4 Q24

	LSAT Question		**My Analysis**
77.	Counselor: Constantly comparing oneself to those one sees as more able or more successful almost invariably leads to self-disparagement. Conversely, constantly comparing oneself to those one sees as less able or less successful almost invariably leads to being dismissive of others. So, those who for the most part refrain from comparing themselves to others will most likely be, on the whole, self-accepting and accepting of others.	$\longrightarrow$	**Step 2:** Conclusion— *because* Evidence—
	The counselor's reasoning is most vulnerable to criticism because it	$\longrightarrow$	**Step 1:**
			Step 3:
(A)	overlooks the possibility that one can compare oneself both to those one perceives to be more able and more successful than oneself and to those one perceives to be less able and less successful than oneself	$\longrightarrow$	**Step 4:**
(B)	overlooks the possibility that constantly comparing oneself to others may have beneficial effects that those who refrain from making such comparisons are deprived of	$\longrightarrow$	
(C)	takes for granted that if one is both dismissive of others and self-disparaging, one will not be self-accepting and accepting of others	$\longrightarrow$	
(D)	overlooks the possibility that self-disparagement and being dismissive of others can result from something other than comparing oneself to others	$\longrightarrow$	
(E)	takes for granted that whenever one compares oneself to others one sees them as more successful and more able than oneself or less successful and less able than oneself	$\longrightarrow$	

PrepTest49 Sec4 Q23

Flaw Question Expert Analysis

Compare your work to that of an LSAT expert. After analyzing the argument, were you able to describe the author's error in reasoning? Where was your prediction helpful in spotting the correct answer? When it was less helpful, can you see how you could have better phrased it?

LSAT Question	Analysis
64. Although Jaaks is a respected historian, her negative review of Yancey's new book on the history of coastal fisheries in the region rests on a mistake. Jaaks's review argues that the book inaccurately portrays the lives of fishery workers. However, Yancey used the same research methods in this book as in her other histories, which have been very popular. This book is also very popular in local bookstores.	**Step 2:** Conclusion—Yancey's history is accurate (i.e., Jaaks is wrong to say Yancey's book is inaccurate). *because* Evidence—Yancey's book is popular and uses the same methods as her other popular books.
The reasoning above is flawed in that it	**Step 1:** "[F]lawed in that ... " The correct answer will describe the author's flaw.
	Step 3: The author assumes that the book's popularity is evidence of its accuracy—a classic mismatched concepts mistake.
(A) relies on the word of a scholar who is unqualified in the area in question	**Step 4:** Distortion. The author relies on no other scholar's opinion in the argument. Eliminate.
(B) attacks the person making the claim at issue rather than addressing the claim	180. The author is, in fact, respectful of Jaaks, but still feels her to be mistaken in this case. Eliminate.
(C) takes for granted that the popularity of a book is evidence of its accuracy	Correct. This matches the prediction and describes the flaw perfectly.
(D) bases a general conclusion on a sample that is likely to be unrepresentative	Extreme. The conclusion is specific, not general: it deals with one historian's opinion of one book. Eliminate.
(E) presumes, without providing justification, that the methods used by Yancey are the only methods that would produce accurate results *PrepTest59 Sec2 Q6*	Outside the Scope. The author asserts that Yancey's methods have been sound, but does not offer any opinion about other methods. Eliminate.

LSAT Question	Analysis
65. Deirdre: Many philosophers have argued that the goal of every individual is to achieve happiness—that is, the satisfaction derived from fully living up to one's potential. They have also claimed that happiness is elusive and can be achieved only after years of sustained effort. But these philosophers have been unduly pessimistic, since they have clearly exaggerated the difficulty of being happy. Simply walking along the seashore on a sunny afternoon causes many people to experience feelings of happiness.	**Step 2:** Conclusion—Philosophers exaggerate the difficulty of being happy (where "happy" is defined as "the satisfaction derived from fully living up to one's potential"). *because* Evidence—A walk on the beach can make people feel happy.
Which one of the following most accurately describes a reasoning flaw in Deirdre's argument?	**Step 1:** Flaw question—The correct answer "describes a reasoning flaw" in the argument.
	Step 3: Equivocation: The definition of happiness in the conclusion is far more specific than the "feelings of happiness" in the evidence.
(A) It dismisses a claim because of its source rather than because of its content.	**Step 4:** Distortion. The author doesn't say the philosophers are wrong because of *who* they are. Eliminate.
(B) It fails to take into account that what brings someone happiness at one moment may not bring that person happiness at another time.	180. Taking the statement here into account makes Deirdre's argument even more suspect. So, failing to take it into account cannot be a weakness of her argument. Eliminate.
(C) It allows the key term "happiness" to shift in meaning illicitly in the course of the argument.	Correct. The author equivocates over the meaning of "happiness."
(D) It presumes, without providing justification, that happiness is, in fact, the goal of life.	Outside the Scope. Neither the philosophers nor Deirdre make this claim. Eliminate.
(E) It makes a generalization based on the testimony of a group whose views have not been shown to be representative. *PrepTest51 Sec1 Q6*	Distortion. The evidence does not consist of testimony, and the author offers the experience of "many people" to counter a generalization, not to make one. Eliminate.

LSAT Question	Analysis
66. Editorial: Clearly, during the past two years, the unemployment situation in our city has been improving. Studies show that the number of unemployed people who are actively looking for jobs has steadily decreased during that period. ⟶	**Step 2:** Conclusion—The city's unemployment situation is better. *because* Evidence—Fewer unemployed people are actively seeking work.
The editorial's reasoning is most vulnerable to criticism on the grounds that it ⟶	**Step 1:** "[V]ulnerable to criticism on the grounds"—the correct answer will describe a flaw in the argument's reasoning.
	Step 3: The author assumes fewer people are looking for jobs because they now have jobs, but this overlooks the possibility that they have just given up on finding work, and so aren't actively searching for jobs.
(A) presumes, without providing justification, that the government is at least partly responsible for the improvement in the employment situation ⟶	**Step 4:** Outside the Scope. There is no claim—good or bad—about the government's role here. Eliminate.
(B) relies on data from a period that is too short to justify an inference about a general trend ⟶	Distortion. The conclusion is a specific comparison (not a general trend), and the data cover precisely the time period discussed in the conclusion. Eliminate.
(C) fails to take into account the possibility that many unemployed workers who still desire jobs may have stopped looking for jobs ⟶	Correct. This cites the overlooked possibility that makes the author's assumption questionable.
(D) fails to take into account that the sorts of governmental efforts that reduce unemployment may not be effective in creating more high-paying jobs ⟶	Outside the Scope. The argument doesn't make any claims about the government's role here; nor does it imply that people have been able to get high-paying jobs. Eliminate.
(E) ignores other economic indicators, which may not have improved during the past two years *PrepTest49 Sec4 Q1* ⟶	Outside the Scope. The conclusion is specifically about unemployment; the author need not examine other economic indicators. Eliminate.

LSAT Question	Analysis
67. Pundit: The average salary for teachers in our society is lower than the average salary for athletes. Obviously, our society values sports more than it values education. →	**Step 2:** Conclusion—Society values sports more than it values education. *because* Evidence—Professional athletes' salaries are higher on average than those of teachers.
The reasoning in the pundit's argument is questionable because the argument →	**Step 1:** "The reasoning is questionable because"—a Flaw question.
	Step 3: The author assumes that overall societal value placed on sports and education can be compared on the basis of athletes' and teachers' salaries. This overlooks all the other spending on the two institutions and any other factors related to how societal priorities could be measured.
(A) presumes, without providing justification, that sports have some educational value →	**Step 4:** Outside the Scope. The author makes no such claim. Eliminate.
(B) fails to consider that the total amount of money spent on education may be much greater than the total spent on sports →	Correct. This may be the most obvious of the many measures the author ignores.
(C) fails to consider both that most teachers are not in the classroom during the summer and that most professional athletes do not play all year →	Irrelevant Comparison. That both teachers and athletes have "off seasons" makes the two groups comparable, so the pundit's failure to mention this isn't a weakness in his argument. Eliminate.
(D) compares teachers' salaries only to those of professional athletes rather than also to the salaries of other professionals →	Irrelevant Comparison. The conclusion is only about sports and education, so the salaries of other professionals is a non-issue. Eliminate.
(E) fails to compare salaries for teachers in the pundit's society to salaries for teachers in other societies *PrepTest51 Sec3 Q4* →	Irrelevant Comparison. The conclusion is about "our society" (meaning the pundit's society), so he's under no obligation to consider other societies. Eliminate.

LSAT Question	Analysis
68. Scientist: While studying centuries-old Antarctic ice deposits, I found that several years of relatively severe atmospheric pollution in the 1500s coincided with a period of relatively high global temperatures. So it is clear in this case that atmospheric pollution did cause global temperatures to rise. →	**Step 2:** Conclusion—Atmospheric pollution caused global warming in the 1500s. *because* Evidence—Atmospheric pollution was correlated with global warming in the 1500s.
The reasoning in the scientist's argument is most vulnerable to criticism on the grounds that the argument →	**Step 1:** "[V]ulnerable to criticism on the grounds"—the correct answer will describe a flaw in the argument's reasoning.
	Step 3: The author assumes that because two phenomena coincided, one of them caused the other.
(A) presumes, without providing justification, that a rise in global temperatures is harmful →	**Step 4:** Outside the Scope. The author does not claim that global warming is harmful. Eliminate.
(B) draws a general conclusion based on a sample that is likely to be unrepresentative →	Extreme. The author draws a specific conclusion about the 1500s based on evidence about the 1500s. Eliminate.
(C) inappropriately generalizes from facts about a specific period of time to a universal claim →	Extreme. The author is careful to claim causation only "in this case," not universally. Eliminate.
(D) takes for granted that the method used for gathering data was reliable →	Outside the Scope. The argument's flaw is not in the reliability of its data. Even if its data are flawless, the author makes a reasoning error by claiming causation on the basis of correlation. Eliminate.
(E) infers, merely from a claim that two phenomena are associated, that one phenomenon causes the other →	Correct. This describes the "correlation versus causation" mistake that the author makes.

PrepTest59 Sec2 Q4

LSAT Question	Analysis
69. Recently discovered bird fossils are about 20 million years older than the fossils of the birdlike dinosaurs from which the birds are generally claimed to have descended. So these newly discovered fossils show, contrary to the account espoused by most paleontologists, that no bird descended from any dinosaur.	**Step 2:** Conclusion—*No* bird descended from *any* dinosaur. *because* Evidence—We've found bird fossils older than the fossils of birdlike dinosaurs thought generally to be birds' ancestors.
The reasoning in the argument is flawed in that the argument	**Step 1:** A straightforward Flaw question stem—the correct answer will describe an error in the author's reasoning.
	Step 3: The conclusion is a blanket statement: No bird came from any dinosaur. Period. But all the evidence suggests is that at least one type of bird didn't come from the dinosaurs thought to be the ancestors of birds in general. Even that assumption is questionable because the birdlike dinosaur may have existed earlier than its earliest known fossil. Overlooked Possibility: It may still be that some birds came from the later birdlike dinosaurs or even from entirely other dinosaurs.
(A) draws a generalization that is broader than is warranted by the findings cited	**Step 4:** Correct. The findings show an exception to what was generally thought; they don't prove a blanket rejection of the idea.
(B) rejects the consensus view of experts in the field without providing any counterevidence	180. The author provides counterevidence to the authorities; it's just not strong enough to support his blanket conclusion. Eliminate.
(C) attacks the adherents of the opposing view personally instead of addressing any reason for their view	Outside the Scope. The author doesn't attack the paleontologists personally and does provide evidence against their position. Eliminate.
(D) fails to consider the possibility that dinosaurs descended from birds	The author is under no obligation to consider this possibility; his conclusion is simply that birds didn't descend from dinosaurs. Eliminate.
(E) ignores the possibility that dinosaurs and birds descended from a common ancestor *PrepTest51 Sec3 Q6*	The author is under no obligation to consider this possibility; his conclusion is simply that birds didn't descend from dinosaurs. Eliminate.

LSAT Question	Analysis
70. A survey of clerical workers' attitudes toward their work identified a group of secretaries with very positive attitudes. They responded "Strongly agree" to such statements as "I enjoy word processing" and "I like learning new secretarial skills." These secretaries had been rated by their supervisors as excellent workers—far better than secretaries whose attitudes were identified as less positive. Clearly these secretaries' positive attitudes toward their work produced excellent job performance.	**Step 2:** Conclusion—Positive attitudes cause highly rated secretaries' excellent job performance. *because* Evidence—Secretaries with positive attitudes were more likely to be rated highly than those with less positive attitudes were.
Which one of the following identifies a reasoning error in the argument?	**Step 1:** The right answer "identifies a reasoning error"—Flaw question.
	Step 3: On the basis of a correlation (positive attitude and excellence) the author assumes causation (positive attitudes are the reason for the excellence). The author overlooks three possibilities: 1) the causation is reversed (excellent performance brings about positive attitudes); 2) alternative reasons for excellence; and 3) mere coincidence. The first seems most likely in this case; the third, least likely here.
(A) It attempts to prove a generalization about job performance by using the single example of clerical workers.	**Step 4:** Extreme. The author limits his conclusion to secretaries and does not try to prove a generalization. Eliminate.
(B) It restates the claim that the secretaries' positive attitudes produced their excellent job performance instead of offering evidence for it.	Distortion. The author offers evidence: the correlation between secretaries' survey results and their performance ratings. Eliminate.
(C) It does not consider the possibility that secretaries with very positive attitudes toward their work might also have had very positive attitudes toward other activities.	Irrelevant Comparison. The author has no need to investigate attitudes toward anything other than work; his conclusion is limited to the effect of positive attitudes on job performance. Eliminate.
(D) It uses the term "positive attitudes" to mean two different things.	Distortion. The term "positive attitudes" appears to be used the same way throughout the argument. Eliminate.
(E) It identifies the secretaries' positive attitudes as the cause of their excellent job performance although their attitudes might be an effect of their performance.	Correct. This describes the first of the three "causation versus correlation" overlooked possibilities.

PrepTest49 Sec2 Q13

LSAT Question	Analysis
71. Letter to the editor: Middle-class families in wealthy nations are often criticized for the ecological damage resulting from their lifestyles. This criticism should not be taken too seriously, however, since its source is often a movie star or celebrity whose own lifestyle would, if widely adopted, destroy the environment and deplete our resources in a short time.	**Step 2:** Conclusion—Criticism of middle-class families' lifestyles' impact on the environment should be ignored. *because* Evidence—The lifestyles of those making the criticism are often worse on the environment.
The reasoning in the letter to the editor is vulnerable to criticism in that it	**Step 1:** "[V]ulnerable to criticism in that it"—the correct answer will describe a flaw in the argument's reasoning.
	Step 3: The author wants us to ignore the criticism because those making it act hypocritically. This is the ad hominem flaw—attacking the person instead of the argument.
(A) criticizes a characteristic of the people giving an argument rather than criticizing the argument itself	**Step 4:** Correct. This describes the ad hominem flaw.
(B) takes failure to act consistently with a belief as an indication of the sincerity with which that belief is held	Distortion. The letter writer doesn't say the celebrities are insincere, just that they shouldn't be taken seriously. Eliminate.
(C) presumes that a viewpoint must be unreasonable to accept simply because some of the grounds advanced to support it do not adequately do so	Outside the Scope. We can't say the author claims that the celebrities' evidence is inadequate; he doesn't comment on their evidence at all. Eliminate.
(D) fails to recognize that evidence advanced in support of a conclusion actually undermines that conclusion	Outside the Scope. The author doesn't include anyone's substantive evidence, so there is no way to say what he does or does not recognize about it. Eliminate.
(E) generalizes about the behavior of all people on the basis of the behavior of a few *PrepTest49 Sec2 Q5*	Extreme. The author doesn't say all people behave hypocritically, just the ones making this argument. Eliminate.

LSAT Question	Analysis
72. In a poll of a representative sample of a province's residents, the provincial capital was the city most often selected as the best place to live in that province. Since the capital is also the largest of that province's many cities, the poll shows that most residents of that province generally prefer life in large cities to life in small cities.	**Step 2:** Conclusion—Most residents prefer life in large cities to life in small cities. *because* Evidence—The province's largest city received more "best place to live" votes than did any other city in the province.
The argument is most vulnerable to the criticism that it	**Step 1:** "[V]ulnerable to criticism in that it"—the correct answer will describe a flaw in the argument's reasoning.
	Step 3: The author bases her conclusion about "most residents" on evidence that the largest city received more votes than any other place. But what about all other places in aggregate? It's possible that *most* residents voted for small cities. To simplify this, imagine that the largest city received 100 votes, while 20 small cities received 10 votes apiece.
(A) overlooks the possibility that what is true of the residents of the province may not be true of other people	**Step 4:** Outside the Scope. The entire argument is about *this* province and its residents. Eliminate.
(B) does not indicate whether most residents of other provinces also prefer life in large cities to life in small cities	Outside the Scope. The entire argument is about *this* province. Eliminate.
(C) takes for granted that when people are polled for their preferences among cities, they tend to vote for the city that they think is the best place to live	180. The author does not take this for granted; she states it. Eliminate.
(D) overlooks the possibility that the people who preferred small cities over the provincial capital did so not because of their general feelings about the sizes of cities, but because of their general feelings about capital cities	Outside the Scope. *Why* residents felt or voted as they did is irrelevant. Eliminate.
(E) overlooks the possibility that most people may have voted for small cities even though a large city received more votes than any other single city	Correct. This summarizes the author's flaw nicely.

PrepTest51 Sec1 Q18

LSAT Question	Analysis
73. A development company has proposed building an airport near the city of Dalton. If the majority of Dalton's residents favor the proposal, the airport will be built. However, it is unlikely that a majority of Dalton's residents would favor the proposal, for most of them believe that the airport would create noise problems. Thus, it is unlikely that the airport will be built.	**Step 2:** Conclusion—The new Dalton airport probably won't be built. *because* Evidence—1) A majority vote is *sufficient* to get the new Dalton airport built. 2) The new airport probably won't get a majority vote.
The reasoning in the argument is flawed in that the argument	**Step 1:** "The reasoning is flawed in that ... "—the correct answer will describe a logical error in the argument.
	Step 3: The author confuses necessity and sufficiency. His conclusion treats a majority vote as *necessary* for airport construction although his evidence states only that a condition *sufficient* for construction is unlikely to occur.
(A) treats a sufficient condition for the airport's being built as a necessary condition	**Step 4:** Correct. This matches the prediction and describes the author's reasoning error.
(B) concludes that something must be true, because most people believe it to be true	Distortion. The conclusion is a prediction (something probably won't happen), not an assertion of fact (something is true). Eliminate.
(C) concludes, on the basis that a certain event is unlikely to occur, that the event will not occur	Distortion. The author *concludes* that airport construction is "unlikely" from evidence that something is "unlikely." Eliminate.
(D) fails to consider whether people living near Dalton would favor building the airport	180. The author explicitly states that a vote in favor of construction is unlikely to pass. Eliminate.
(E) overlooks the possibility that a new airport could benefit the local economy *PrepTest61 Sec4 Q11*	Outside the Scope. The reasons why voters should favor the airport are irrelevant to the argument about whether the airport is likely to be built. Eliminate.

LSAT Question	Analysis
74. Politician: The huge amounts of money earned by oil companies elicit the suspicion that the regulations designed to prevent collusion need to be tightened. But just the opposite is true. If the regulations designed to prevent collusion are not excessively burdensome, then oil companies will make profits sufficient to motivate the very risky investments associated with exploration that must be made if society is to have adequate oil supplies. But recent data show that the oil industry's profits are not the highest among all industries. Clearly, the regulatory burden on oil companies has become excessive.	**Step 2:** Conclusion—Regulation of oil companies is excessive. *because* Evidence—1) If regulation is not excessive, then oil companies will make profits high enough to motivate risky investment, but 2) the oil industry is not the most profitable of all industries.
The reasoning in the politician's argument is most vulnerable to criticism on the grounds that the argument	**Step 1:** "[V]ulnerable to criticism on the grounds"—the correct answer will describe a flaw in the argument's reasoning.
	Step 3: Mismatched Concepts in the evidence—the author assumes that in order to make profits sufficient to spark risky investments, oil must be the most profitable of all industries. That is an unwarranted leap of logic.
(A) fails to justify its presumption that profits sufficient to motivate very risky investments must be the highest among all industries	**Step 4:** Correct. This answer summarizes the author's unwarranted assumption.
(B) attacks the character of the oil companies rather than the substance of their conduct	180. The author is *supporting* the oil companies. Eliminate.
(C) fails to justify its presumption that two events that are correlated must also be causally related	Distortion. The author doesn't assume causation (excessive regulation is a disincentive to investment) from a correlation (investment declines when regulation is excessive). Rather, he infers excessive regulation from the fact that oil is not the most profitable industry. Eliminate.
(D) treats the absence of evidence that the oil industry has the highest profits among all industries as proof that the oil industry does not have the highest profits among all industries	Distortion. The author *has* data showing that oil is not the most profitable industry. The problem is his assumption that such data show excessive regulation. Eliminate.
(E) illicitly draws a general conclusion from a specific example that there is reason to think is atypical	Distortion. There's no reason to suspect the author's evidence is atypical. Eliminate.

PrepTest49 Sec4 Q12

LSAT Question	Analysis
75. The typological theory of species classification, which has few adherents today, distinguishes species solely on the basis of observable physical characteristics, such as plumage color, adult size, or dental structure. However, there are many so-called "sibling species," which are indistinguishable on the basis of their appearance but cannot interbreed and thus, according to the mainstream biological theory of species classification, are separate species. Since the typological theory does not count sibling species as separate species, it is unacceptable.	**Step 2:** Conclusion—The typological theory of species classification is unacceptable (a value judgment). *because* Evidence—The typological theory does not account for sibling species (as the mainstream theory does).
The reasoning in the argument is most vulnerable to criticism on the grounds that	**Step 1:** "[V]ulnerable to criticism on the grounds"— the correct answer will describe a flaw in the argument's reasoning.
	Step 3: The author concludes that typological theory is inadequate on the grounds that it doesn't account for one thing mainstream theory accounts for. But what makes mainstream theory right?
(A) the argument does not evaluate all aspects of the typological theory	**Step 4:** Extreme. The author need not find more reasons typological theory is inadequate; he needs to establish that his one reason is a decisive reason. Eliminate.
(B) the argument confuses a necessary condition for species distinction with a sufficient condition for species distinction	Distortion. The author assumes that accounting for sibling species is necessary and draws his conclusion in a way consistent with that. The problem is that his only reason for thinking this way is that mainstream theory does it. Eliminate.
(C) the argument, in its attempt to refute one theory of species classification, presupposes the truth of an opposing theory	Correct. The author just asserts the inadequacy of typological theory, but does nothing to establish the adequacy of mainstream theory.
(D) the argument takes a single fact that is incompatible with a theory as enough to show that theory to be false	Distortion. The author's problem isn't that he has too few criteria for evaluation, but that he has failed to establish the relevance of his criterion. Eliminate.
(E) the argument does not explain why sibling species cannot interbreed *PrepTest51 Sec1 Q15*	Outside the Scope. The author's conclusion is an evaluation of a theory, not an explanation of species. Eliminate.

LSAT Question	Analysis
76. One is likely to feel comfortable approaching a stranger if the stranger is of one's approximate age. Therefore, long-term friends are probably of the same approximate age as each other since most long-term friendships begin because someone felt comfortable approaching a stranger. ⟶	**Step 2:** Conclusion—Long-term friends are probably age mates. *because* Evidence—1) Long-term friendships start because one person is comfortable approaching a stranger, and 2) people are usually comfortable approaching their age mates.
The reasoning in the argument is flawed in that it ⟶	**Step 1:** "The reasoning is flawed in that … "—the correct answer will describe a logical error in the argument.
	Step 3: The author gives one reason we're comfortable approaching strangers, but couldn't there be others (similar dress, jobs, schooling, hobbies, tone of voice, facial expression, etc.)? Similar age is sufficient, but may not be necessary.
(A) presumes, without warrant, that one is likely to feel uncomfortable approaching a person only if that person is a stranger ⟶	**Step 4:** Outside the Scope. Why we might be uncomfortable with people we know (ex-spouses? known criminals?) is irrelevant. Eliminate.
(B) infers that a characteristic is present in a situation from the fact that that characteristic is present in most similar situations ⟶	Distortion. The author assumes that a sufficient characteristic (similar age) is the most common one. Eliminate.
(C) overlooks the possibility that one is less likely to feel comfortable approaching someone who is one's approximate age if that person is a stranger than if that person is not a stranger ⟶	Outside the Scope. Premise: Long-term friendships begin because someone approaches a stranger. Whether we're more comfortable approaching acquaintances is irrelevant. Eliminate.
(D) presumes, without warrant, that one never approaches a stranger unless one feels comfortable doing so ⟶	Extreme. The author starts from the premise that most long-term friendships start this way; she's not guilty of saying we *never* approach others unless we're comfortable. Eliminate.
(E) fails to address whether one is likely to feel comfortable approaching a stranger who is not one's approximate age *PrepTest61 Sec4 Q24* ⟶	Correct. Until the author rules out other reasons to feel comfortable approaching a stranger, her conclusion that age is the reason we start friendships is suspect.

LSAT Question	Analysis
77. Counselor: Constantly comparing oneself to those one sees as more able or more successful almost invariably leads to self-disparagement. Conversely, constantly comparing oneself to those one sees as less able or less successful almost invariably leads to being dismissive of others. So, those who for the most part refrain from comparing themselves to others will most likely be, on the whole, self-accepting and accepting of others.	**Step 2:** Conclusion—If a person does not compare herself to others, then she will likely be self-accepting and accepting of others. *because* Evidence—1) If a person compares herself negatively to others, then she will be self-disparaging. 2) If a person compares herself positively to others, then she will be disparaging of others.
The counselor's reasoning is most vulnerable to criticism because it	**Step 1:** "[V]ulnerable to criticism because"—the correct answer will describe a flaw in the argument's reasoning.
	Step 3: Classic *sufficient* evidence versus *necessary* conclusion flaw: the author overlooks the possibility that there are other sufficient reasons for disparaging oneself and others.
(A) overlooks the possibility that one can compare oneself both to those one perceives to be more able and more successful than oneself and to those one perceives to be less able and less successful than oneself	**Step 4:** 180. The author does *not* overlook this; indeed, the effects of these two types of comparisons *are* her two pieces of evidence. Eliminate.
(B) overlooks the possibility that constantly comparing oneself to others may have beneficial effects that those who refrain from making such comparisons are deprived of	Outside the Scope. The effects, good or bad, of comparison on characteristics other than the acceptance of self and others are irrelevant to the author's conclusion. Eliminate.
(C) takes for granted that if one is both dismissive of others and self-disparaging, one will not be self-accepting and accepting of others	180. The terms listed here *are* opposites; the author doesn't take this for granted. Eliminate.
(D) overlooks the possibility that self-disparagement and being dismissive of others can result from something other than comparing oneself to others	Correct. There may be other factors sufficient to make one self-disparaging or disparaging of others.
(E) takes for granted that whenever one compares oneself to others one sees them as more successful and more able than oneself or less successful and less able than oneself	Extreme. The author's evidence applies to cases of unequal comparison, and her conclusion is qualified ("most likely be, on the whole"). She's not guilty of ignoring neutral comparisons. Eliminate.

PrepTest49 Sec4 Q23

STRENGTHEN AND WEAKEN QUESTIONS

The third major Assumption Family question type is Strengthen and Weaken questions. These are very practical, "lawyerly" questions. The correct answer provides a piece of evidence that would help convince someone that the argument is more (Strengthen) or less (Weaken) likely to be true.

You can identify Strengthen and Weaken questions from question stems such as these:

Which one of the following, if true, most strengthens the argument above?	Which one of the following, if true, would most weaken the argument above?
PrepTest57 Sec2 Q5	*PrepTest51 Sec1 Q8*
Which one of the following, if true, most strongly supports the claim above?	Which one of the following, if true, most calls into question the claim above?
PrepTest59 Sec2 Q3	*PrepTest57 Sec2 Q9*

Notice that all of the question stems include "if true"; this tells you to treat the answer choices as facts. Don't argue with the choices. Rather, pick the answer that provides a fact you would like a jury to hear if you were arguing in favor of or against the argument. The correct answer need not prove or disprove the argument; it just needs to make the conclusion more or less likely to follow from the evidence.

STRENGTHEN/WEAKEN AT A GLANCE

Task: Provide a fact that would make the conclusion more (Strengthen) or less (Weaken) likely to follow from the evidence.

Strategy: Analyze the argument, determine the author's assumption, and then choose the answer containing a fact that supports or undermines the author's reasoning.

LSAT tests released from 2009 through 2013 had an average of 8.5 Strengthen/Weaken questions.

16.8% — Strengthen/ Weaken Questions

**Logical Reasoning
Question Types**
PrepTests57–71; released 2009–2013

Representation of Strengthen and Weaken questions is roughly equal on the test. On LSAT tests released from 2009 through 2013, Weaken questions made up 46.9 percent of the questions in this type. Strengthen questions accounted for 47.6 percent. Other Strengthen/Weaken questions, such as Evaluate questions, represented 5.5 percent (less than one per test, on average).

LEARNING OBJECTIVES

In this section, you'll learn to:

· Identify and answer Strengthen/Weaken questions
· Turn assumptions into accurate predictions of the correct answer
· Recognize answer choices that strengthen/weaken the author's assumption

Strengthening or Weakening Overlooked Possibilities

Overlooked Possibilities arguments are more common than Mismatched Concepts in Strengthen/Weaken questions. The characteristically overbroad conclusions in Overlooked Possibilities arguments lend themselves easily to Strengthen/Weaken questions. Consider the following argument:

The health of the city's economy is threatened by traffic congestion in the downtown business area. Petrucci's traffic plan would reduce congestion downtown. Therefore, the city should adopt Petrucci's plan.

Here are two facts. Which strengthens, and which weakens, the argument?

(1) Petrucci's plan would not increase the city's budget.

(2) Petrucci's plan would increase traffic and speed limits near schools and residential areas.

The author assumes that the advantage of reducing traffic downtown justifies a blanket endorsement of Petrucci's plan. He overlooks any potential disadvantages. Statement (1) strengthens the argument by ruling out a possible objection to the plan. Statement (2) weakens the argument by introducing a negative consideration that the author overlooked.

Strengthening or Weakening Mismatched Concepts

Mismatched Concepts are less common than Overlooked Possibilities, especially in Weaken questions. When you do encounter a Mismatched Concepts argument here, look for the fact that supports or undermines the assumed connection. Consider the following argument:

The team captain's primary goal is to enhance team morale and enthusiasm. Thus, one of the captain's responsibilities is the continual development and training of less skilled players.

Here are two facts. Which strengthens and which weakens the argument?

(1) The ability and performance of all players affects a team's morale and enthusiasm.

(2) A team's morale and enthusiasm typically follow from the example set by the team's most skilled players.

The author assumes that the development and training of the team's less skilled players affects the team's morale and enthusiasm. Statement (1) strengthens the argument by affirming the author's assumption. Statement (2) weakens the argument by undermining the assumption.

Here's how an LSAT expert might analyze, predict, and answer a Strengthen question.

LSAT Question	Analysis
Archaeologist: After the last ice age, groups of paleohumans left Siberia and crossed the Bering land bridge, which no longer exists, into North America. Archaeologists have discovered in Siberia a cache of Clovis points—the distinctive stone spear points made by paleohumans. This shows that, contrary to previous belief, the Clovis point was not invented in North America.	**Step 2:** Conclusion—Clovis points were not invented in North America. *because* Evidence—1) Clovis points have been found in Siberia, and 2) paleohumans left Siberia and crossed into North America after the last ice age.
Which one of the following, if true, would most strengthen the archaeologist's argument?	**Step 1:** "[S]trengthens"—the correct answer will make the author's conclusion more likely to follow from her evidence. The four wrong answers will weaken the argument *or* do nothing.
	Step 3: The author assumes that paleohumans invented the Clovis points in Siberia before leaving; she overlooks the possibility that the paleohumans invented the Clovis points in North America and carried them back to Siberia. The correct answer will help rule out this overlooked possibility.
(A) The Clovis points found in Siberia are older than any of those that have been found in North America.	**Step 4:** Correct. This makes it less likely that the paleohumans carried the Clovis points back to Siberia, and thus, more likely that the points were invented there.
(B) The Bering land bridge disappeared before any of the Clovis points found to date were made.	Outside the Scope. It's not clear how this affects the argument. If anything, it suggests that the Clovis point was independently invented in Siberia and North America. Eliminate.
(C) Clovis points were more effective hunting weapons than earlier spear points had been.	Outside the Scope. Without more information, this doesn't tell us anything about where the points were invented. Eliminate.
(D) Archaeologists have discovered in Siberia artifacts that date from after the time paleohumans left Siberia.	Outside the Scope. There's not enough information to know if this statement is even relevant to the argument. Did these later artifacts include Clovis points? Eliminate.
(E) Some paleohuman groups that migrated from Siberia to North America via the Bering land bridge eventually returned to Siberia. *PrepTest57 Sec2 Q22*	180. This weakens the author's argument, explaining how the points could have returned to Siberia even if they were invented in North America. Eliminate.

Here's how an LSAT expert might analyze, predict, and answer a Weaken question.

LSAT Question	Analysis
We can now dismiss the widely held suspicion that sugar consumption often exacerbates hyperactivity in children with attention deficit disorder. A scientific study of the effects of three common sugars—sucrose, fructose, and glucose—on children who have attention deficit disorder, with experimental groups each receiving a type of sugar in their diets and a control group receiving a sugar substitute instead of sugar, showed no statistically significant difference between the groups in thinking or behavior.	**Step 2:** Conclusion—Consuming sugar does not increase hyperactivity in children. *because* Evidence—A study. Methodology: Test groups—ADD children got three kinds of sugars. Control groups—ADD children got sugar substitutes. Result: No difference in thinking or behavior.
Which one of the following, if true, would most weaken the argument above?	**Step 1:** "[M]ost weakens"—the correct answer makes the conclusion less likely to follow from the evidence. The four wrong answers either strengthen or do nothing.
	Step 3: The author assumes that the study was sound. That means he thinks that if sugar exacerbates hyperactivity, the control group should have shown a difference in thinking and behavior from the test groups. So, the correct answer will suggest a reason that the two groups would act the same.
(A) Only one of the three types of sugar used in the study was ever widely suspected of exacerbating hyperactivity.	**Step 4:** Irrelevant Comparison. That test group, at least, should have shown differences in thinking and behavior if sugar makes hyperactivity worse. But they didn't. Eliminate.
(B) The consumption of sugar actually has a calming effect on some children.	Extreme/180. The author's claim is simply that sugar doesn't make hyperactivity worse. If anything, this helps the author's case. Eliminate.
(C) The consumption of some sugar substitutes exacerbates the symptoms of hyperactivity.	Correct. This undermines the validity of the study. If the sugar substitutes also make hyperactivity worse, then sugar may have made hyperactivity worse, too, without the groups showing any differences.
(D) The study included some observations of each group in contexts that generally tend to make children excited and active.	180. This makes the study even more sound as a test of the effects of sugar on hyperactivity. Eliminate.
(E) Some children believe that they can tell the difference between the taste of sugar and that of sugar substitutes.	Outside the Scope. Without more information, we can't tell what effect, if any, this had on the study's results. Eliminate.

PrepTest51 Sec1 Q8

Less Common Strengthen/Weaken Questions

Strengthen/Weaken EXCEPT Questions

These questions are quite rare. The key to answering these questions is to characterize the one right and four wrong answers before evaluating the choices.

Each of the following, if true, strengthens the
psychiatrist's argument EXCEPT:

PrepTest61 Sec2 Q22

LSAT STRATEGY

Some facts to remember about Strengthen and Weaken EXCEPT questions:

- Always slow down and characterize the one right and four wrong answer choices.
- The correct answer in a Strengthen EXCEPT question will either weaken the argument or have no impact.
- The correct answer in a Weaken EXCEPT question will either strengthen the argument or have no impact.

Evaluate Questions

Occasionally, the LSAT asks a question about a fact's relevance to the argument. Think of these as Strengthen-or-Weaken questions, because the disposition of the correct answer will impact the argument either positively or negatively. All four wrong answers will contain issues irrelevant to the argument.

It would be most important to determine which one of
the following in evaluating the argument?

PrepTest49 Sec4 Q2

LSAT STRATEGY

Some facts to remember about Evaluate questions:

- These questions are similar to Strengthen and Weaken questions.
- Untangle the stimulus; then find the assumption.
- The correct answer will often present a question, the answers to which have either a positive or a negative impact on the argument.

Principle-Application Stimuli

This unusual-looking question is really just a Strengthen question. Treat the Principle as evidence and the Application as the conclusion if you happen to see one of these.

Principle: When none of the fully qualified candidates for a new position at Arvue Corporation currently works for that company, it should hire the candidate who would be most productive in that position.

Application: Arvue should not hire Krall for the new position, because Delacruz is a candidate and is fully qualified.

Which one of the following, if true, justifies the above application of the principle?*

PrepTest61 Sec4 Q19

"Claim" Stimuli

From time to time, the testmaker asks you to weaken a "claim" rather than an argument. In these cases, treat the entire stimulus as a conclusion and seek the answer that directly attacks the author's claim.

Despite the enormous number of transactions processed daily by banks nowadays, if a customer's bank account is accidentally credited with a large sum of money, it is extremely unlikely that the error will not be detected by the bank's internal audit procedures.

Which one of the following, if true, most strongly supports the claim above?*

PrepTest59 Sec2 Q3

* The full question appears in the Question Pools at the end of this chapter.

LSAT STRATEGY

Some facts to remember about Strengthen and Weaken questions:

· A correct answer does not have to prove or disprove the conclusion; it just has to make the conclusion more or less likely to follow from the evidence.

· Overlooked Possibilities is the most common argument type, especially in Weaken questions.

· To strengthen an argument containing Overlooked Possibilities, choose the answer that rules out a possible objection; to weaken such an argument, look for a fact that introduces an overlooked objection.

· To strengthen an argument containing Mismatched Concepts, choose the answer that helps to affirm the author's assumption; to weaken such an argument, look for a fact that undermines the assumption.

Strengthen and Weaken Question Practice

Try the following Strengthen/Weaken questions. In each, read the question stem and characterize the one right and four wrong answers; analyze the argument by identifying the conclusion and evidence, and determine the author's assumption; consider the types of facts that would make the assumption more or less likely to be true and use that as your prediction; then, evaluate the answer choices.

LSAT Question	My Analysis
78. 1990 editorial: Local pay phone calls have cost a quarter apiece ever since the 1970s, when a soft drink from a vending machine cost about the same. The price of a soft drink has more than doubled since, so phone companies should be allowed to raise the price of pay phone calls too. $\longrightarrow$	**Step 2:** Conclusion— *because* Evidence—
Which one of the following, if true, most weakens the editorial's argument? $\longrightarrow$	**Step 1:**
	Step 3:
(A) A pay phone typically cost less than a soft-drink machine in the 1970s. $\longrightarrow$	**Step 4:**
(B) Due to inflation, the prices of most goods more than doubled between the 1970s and 1990. $\longrightarrow$	
(C) Government regulation of phone call prices did not become more stringent between the 1970s and 1990. $\longrightarrow$	
(D) Between the 1970s and 1990 the cost of ingredients for soft drinks increased at a greater rate than the cost of telephone equipment. $\longrightarrow$	
(E) Technological advances made telephone equipment more sophisticated between the 1970s and 1990. $\longrightarrow$	

PrepTest49 Sec2 Q8

LSAT Question	My Analysis
79. On the Caribbean island of Guadeloupe, a researcher examined 35 patients with atypical Parkinson's disease and compared their eating habits to those of 65 healthy adults. She found that all of the patients with atypical Parkinson's regularly ate the tropical fruits soursop, custard apple, and pomme cannelle, whereas only 10 of the healthy adults regularly ate these fruits. From this, she concluded that eating these fruits causes atypical Parkinson's.	**Step 2:** Conclusion— → *because* Evidence—
Which one of the following, if true, most strengthens the researcher's reasoning? →	**Step 1:**
	Step 3:
(A) For many of the atypical Parkinson's patients, their symptoms stopped getting worse, and in some cases actually abated, when they stopped eating soursop, custard apple, and pomme cannelle. →	**Step 4:**
(B) Of the healthy adults who did not regularly eat soursop, custard apple, and pomme cannelle, most had eaten each of these fruits on at least one occasion. →	
(C) In areas other than Guadeloupe, many people who have never eaten soursop, custard apple, and pomme cannelle have contracted atypical Parkinson's. →	
(D) The 10 healthy adults who regularly ate soursop, custard apple, and pomme cannelle ate significantly greater quantities of these fruits, on average, than did the 35 atypical Parkinson's patients. →	
(E) Soursop, custard apple, and pomme cannelle contain essential vitamins not contained in any other food that is commonly eaten by residents of Guadeloupe. →	

PrepTest59 Sec2 Q1

LSAT Question	My Analysis

80. Eating garlic reduces the levels of cholesterol and triglycerides in the blood and so helps reduce the risk of cardiovascular disease. Evidence that eating garlic reduces these levels is that a group of patients taking a garlic tablet each day for four months showed a 12 percent reduction in cholesterol and a 17 percent reduction in triglycerides; over the same period, a group of similar patients taking a medically inert tablet showed only a 2 percent reduction in triglycerides and a 3 percent reduction in cholesterol.

→ **Step 2:** Conclusion—

because

Evidence—

It would be most important to determine which one of the following in evaluating the argument?

→ **Step 1:**

Step 3:

(A) whether the garlic tablets are readily available to the public

→ **Step 4:**

(B) what the diets of the two groups were during the period →

(C) what effect taking the garlic tablets each day for a period of less than four months had on the levels of cholesterol and triglycerides →

(D) whether large amounts of garlic are well tolerated by all patients →

(E) whether the manufacturer of the garlic tablets cites the study in its advertising →

PrepTest49 Sec4 Q2

LSAT Question	My Analysis
81. Essayist: Politicians deserve protection from a prying press. No one wants his or her private life spread across the pages of the newspapers. Furthermore, the press's continual focus on politicians' private lives dissuades talented people from pursuing a career in politics and turns reporters into character cops who walk their beats looking for minute and inconsequential personality flaws in public servants. It is time to put a halt to this trivial journalism. $\longrightarrow$	**Step 2:** Conclusion— *because* Evidence—
Each of the following, if true, strengthens the essayist's argument EXCEPT: $\longrightarrow$	**Step 1:**
	Step 3:
(A) The press is unusually inaccurate when it reports on people's private lives. $\longrightarrow$	**Step 4:**
(B) Reporting on politicians' private lives distracts voters from more important issues in a campaign. $\longrightarrow$	
(C) Much writing on politicians' private lives consists of rumors circulated by opposing candidates. $\longrightarrow$	
(D) In recent elections, the best local politicians have refused to run for national office because of the intrusiveness of press coverage. $\longrightarrow$	
(E) Politicians' personality flaws often ultimately affect their performance on the job. $\longrightarrow$	

PrepTest49 Sec4 Q4

LSAT Question	**My Analysis**
82. Economist: As should be obvious, raising the minimum wage significantly would make it more expensive for businesses to pay workers for minimum-wage jobs. Therefore, businesses could not afford to continue to employ as many workers for such jobs. So raising the minimum wage significantly will cause an increase in unemployment.	**Step 2:** Conclusion— *because* Evidence—
Which one of the following, if true, most weakens the economist's argument?	**Step 1:**
	Step 3:
(A) Businesses typically pass the cost of increased wages on to consumers without adversely affecting profits.	**Step 4:**
(B) When the difference between minimum wage and a skilled worker's wage is small, a greater percentage of a business's employees will be skilled workers.	
(C) A modest increase in unemployment is acceptable because the current minimum wage is not a livable wage.	
(D) Most workers are earning more than the current minimum wage.	
(E) The unemployment rate has been declining steadily in recent years. *PrepTest57 Sec3 Q6*	

LSAT Question	My Analysis
83. Gilbert: This food label is mistaken. It says that these cookies contain only natural ingredients, but they contain alphahydroxy acids that are chemically synthesized by the cookie company at their plant. →	**Step 2:** Conclusion– *because* Evidence–
Sabina: The label is not mistaken. After all, alphahydroxy acids also are found occurring naturally in sugarcane.	
Which one of the following, if true, would most strengthen Sabina's argument? →	**Step 1:**
	Step 3:
(A) The cookie company has recently dropped alphahydroxy acids from its cookie ingredients. →	**Step 4:**
(B) Not all chemicals that are part of the manufacturing process are ingredients of the cookies. →	
(C) The label was printed before the cookie company decided to switch from sugarcane alphahydroxy acids to synthesized ones. →	
(D) Many other foods advertising all natural ingredients also contain some ingredients that are chemically synthesized. →	
(E) All substances except those that do not occur naturally in any source are considered natural. →	

PrepTest59 Sec2 Q5

LSAT Question	My Analysis
84. The cattle egret is a bird that lives around herds of cattle. The only available explanation of the fact that the cattle egret follows cattle herds is that the egrets consume the insects stirred up from the grasses as the cattle herds graze. $\longrightarrow$	**Step 2:** Conclusion— *because* Evidence—
Which one of the following, if true, would most seriously undermine the claim that the explanation given above is the only available one? $\longrightarrow$	**Step 1:**
	Step 3:
(A) Birds other than cattle egrets have been observed consuming insects stirred up by the movement of cattle. $\longrightarrow$	**Step 4:**
(B) Cattle egrets are known to follow other slow-moving animals, such as rhinoceroses and buffalo. $\longrightarrow$	
(C) The presence of cattle dissuades many would-be predators of the cattle egret. $\longrightarrow$	
(D) Cattle egrets are not generally known to live outside the range of large, slow-moving animals. $\longrightarrow$	
(E) Forests are generally inhospitable to cattle egrets because of a lack of insects of the kind egrets can consume. $\longrightarrow$	

PrepTest49 Sec2 Q6

LSAT Question	My Analysis
85. In modern deep-diving marine mammals, such as whales, the outer shell of the bones is porous. This has the effect of making the bones light enough so that it is easy for the animals to swim back to the surface after a deep dive. The outer shell of the bones was also porous in the ichthyosaur, an extinct prehistoric marine reptile. We can conclude from this that ichthyosaurs were deep divers.	**Step 2:** Conclusion— → *because* Evidence—
Which one of the following, if true, most weakens the argument? →	**Step 1:**
	Step 3:
(A) Some deep-diving marine species must surface after dives but do not have bones with porous outer shells. →	**Step 4:**
(B) In most modern marine reptile species, the outer shell of the bones is not porous. →	
(C) In most modern and prehistoric marine reptile species that are not deep divers, the outer shell of the bones is porous. →	
(D) In addition to the porous outer shells of their bones, whales have at least some characteristics suited to deep diving for which there is no clear evidence whether these were shared by ichthyosaurs. →	
(E) There is evidence that the bones of ichthyosaurs would have been light enough to allow surfacing even if the outer shells were not porous. →	

PrepTest61 Sec4 Q21

LSAT Question	My Analysis
86. The supernova event of 1987 is interesting in that there is still no evidence of the neutron star that current theory says should have remained after a supernova of that size. This is in spite of the fact that many of the most sensitive instruments ever developed have searched for the tell-tale pulse of radiation that neutron stars emit. Thus, current theory is wrong in claiming that supernovas of a certain size always produce neutron stars. $\longrightarrow$	**Step 2:** Conclusion— *because* Evidence—
Which one of the following, if true, most strengthens the argument? $\longrightarrow$	**Step 1:**
	Step 3:
(A) Most supernova remnants that astronomers have detected have a neutron star nearby. $\longrightarrow$	**Step 4:**
(B) Sensitive astronomical instruments have detected neutron stars much farther away than the location of the 1987 supernova. $\longrightarrow$	
(C) The supernova of 1987 was the first that scientists were able to observe in progress. $\longrightarrow$	
(D) Several important features of the 1987 supernova are correctly predicted by the current theory. $\longrightarrow$	
(E) Some neutron stars are known to have come into existence by a cause other than a supernova explosion. $\longrightarrow$	

PrepTest51 Sec1 Q24

LSAT Question	My Analysis
87. On average, corporations that encourage frequent social events in the workplace show higher profits than those that rarely do. This suggests that the EZ Corporation could boost its profits by having more staff parties during business hours. →	**Step 2:** Conclusion— *because* Evidence—
Which one of the following, if true, most weakens the argument above? →	**Step 1:**
	Step 3:
(A) The great majority of corporations that encourage frequent social events in the workplace do so at least in part because they are already earning above-average profits. →	**Step 4:**
(B) Corporations that have frequent staff parties after business hours sometimes have higher profits than do corporations that have frequent staff parties during business hours. →	
(C) The EZ Corporation already earns above-average profits, and it almost never brings play into the workplace. →	
(D) Frequent social events in a corporate workplace leave employees with less time to perform their assigned duties than they would otherwise have. →	
(E) At one time the EZ Corporation encouraged social events in the workplace more frequently than it currently does, but it has not always been one of the most profitable corporations of its size. →	

PrepTest51 Sec1 Q25

LSAT Question	My Analysis
88. Scientist: A controversy in paleontology centers on the question of whether prehistoric human ancestors began to develop sophisticated tools before or after they came to stand upright. I argue that they stood upright first, simply because advanced toolmaking requires free use of the hands, and standing upright makes this possible.	**Step 2:** Conclusion— *because* Evidence—
Which one of the following statements, if true, most weakens the scientist's argument?	**Step 1:**
	Step 3:
(A) Many animals that do not stand upright have learned to make basic tools.	**Step 4:**
(B) Advanced hunting weapons have been discovered among the artifacts belonging to prehistoric human ancestors who did not stand upright.	
(C) Many prehistoric human ancestors who stood upright had no sophisticated tools.	
(D) Those prehistoric human ancestors who first came to stand upright had no more dexterity with their hands than did those who did not stand upright.	
(E) Many of the earliest sophisticated tools did not require their users to be able to stand upright.	

PrepTest49 Sec2 Q14

LSAT Question	**My Analysis**
89. When people show signs of having a heart attack an electrocardiograph (EKG) is often used to diagnose their condition. In a study, a computer program for EKG diagnosis of heart attacks was pitted against a very experienced, highly skilled cardiologist. The program correctly diagnosed a significantly higher proportion of the cases that were later confirmed to be heart attacks than did the cardiologist. Interpreting EKG data, therefore, should be left to computer programs.	**Step 2:** Conclusion— *because* Evidence—
Which one of the following, if true, most weakens the argument?	**Step 1:**
	Step 3:
(A) Experts agreed that the cardiologist made few obvious mistakes in reading and interpreting the EKG data.	**Step 4:**
(B) The practice of medicine is as much an art as a science, and computer programs are not easily adapted to making subjective judgments.	
(C) The cardiologist correctly diagnosed a significantly higher proportion of the cases in which no heart attack occurred than did the computer program.	
(D) In a considerable percentage of cases, EKG data alone are insufficient to enable either computer programs or cardiologists to make accurate diagnoses.	
(E) The cardiologist in the study was unrepresentative of cardiologists in general with respect to skill and experience.	

PrepTest61 Sec2 Q20

LSAT Question	**My Analysis**
90. A recent study confirms that nutritious breakfasts make workers more productive. For one month, workers at Plant A received free nutritious breakfasts every day before work, while workers in Plant B did not. The productivity of Plant A's workers increased, while that of Plant B's workers did not. $\longrightarrow$	**Step 2:** Conclusion— *because* Evidence—
Which one of the following, if true, most strengthens the argument? $\longrightarrow$	**Step 1:**
	Step 3:
(A) Few workers in Plant B consumed nutritious breakfasts during the month of the study. $\longrightarrow$	**Step 4:**
(B) Workers in the study from Plant A and Plant B started work at the same time of day. $\longrightarrow$	
(C) During the month before the study, workers at Plant A and Plant B were equally productive. $\longrightarrow$	
(D) Workers from Plant A took fewer vacation days per capita during the month than did workers from Plant B. $\longrightarrow$	
(E) Workers in Plant B were more productive during the month of the study than were workers from Plant A. $\longrightarrow$	

PrepTest59 Sec2 Q22

LSAT Question	My Analysis

91. Poetry journal patron: Everybody who publishes in *The Brick Wall Review* has to agree in advance that if a poem is printed in one of its regular issues, the magazine also has the right to reprint it, without monetary compensation, in its annual anthology. *The Brick Wall Review* makes enough money from sales of its anthologies to cover most operating expenses. So, if your magazine also published an anthology of poems first printed in your magazine, you could depend less on donations. After all, most poems published in your magazine are very similar to those published in *The Brick Wall Review*.

→

Step 2: Conclusion—

because

Evidence—

Which one of the following, if true, most weakens the patron's argument?

→ **Step 1:**

Step 3:

(A) Neither *The Brick Wall Review* nor the other magazine under discussion depends on donations to cover most operating expenses.

→ **Step 4:**

(B) Many of the poets whose work appears in *The Brick Wall Review* have had several poems rejected for publication by the other magazine under discussion.

→

(C) The only compensation poets receive for publishing in the regular issues of the magazines under discussion are free copies of the issues in which their poems appear.

→

(D) *The Brick Wall Review* depends on donations to cover most operating expenses not covered by income from anthology sales.

→

(E) *The Brick Wall Review*'s annual poetry anthology always contains a number of poems by famous poets not published in the regular issues of the magazine.

→

PrepTest57 Sec2 Q17

Strengthen and Weaken Question Expert Analysis

Compare your work to that of an LSAT expert. Were you able to turn your understanding of the argument into a solid prediction of the type of fact the correct answer would contain? Did you remember to characterize the right and wrong answers before evaluating the answer choices?

LSAT Question	Analysis
78. 1990 editorial: Local pay phone calls have cost a quarter apiece ever since the 1970s, when a soft drink from a vending machine cost about the same. The price of a soft drink has more than doubled since, so phone companies should be allowed to raise the price of pay phone calls too.	**Step 2:** Conclusion—Phone companies should be allowed to increase the cost of pay phone calls (circa 1990). *because* Evidence—1) In the 1970s, vending-machine soft drinks and pay phone calls cost the same, and 2) vending-machine soft drinks are now (circa 1990) more expensive.
Which one of the following, if true, most weakens the editorial's argument?	**Step 1:** "[M]ost weakens"—the correct answer makes the conclusion less likely to follow from the evidence. The four wrong answers either strengthen or do nothing.
	Step 3: The author assumes that the overhead for providing pay phone calls has increased proportionately to that for providing soft drinks. Weaken this by finding a fact suggesting a way in which the increase in soft drink prices is justified that the increase in pay phone call prices is not.
(A) A pay phone typically cost less than a soft-drink machine in the 1970s.	**Step 4:** Outside the Scope. Equipment cost is one factor, but to be relevant, this would need to compare equipment costs circa 1990, too. Eliminate.
(B) Due to inflation, the prices of most goods more than doubled between the 1970s and 1990.	Outside the Scope/180. Are these other goods relevant to pay phone service? If anything, this strengthens the argument by pointing out an overall inflationary trend. Eliminate.
(C) Government regulation of phone call prices did not become more stringent between the 1970s and 1990.	Outside the Scope. The author doesn't care whether regulation is stricter or looser than it was, just that prices be allowed to increase now. Eliminate.
(D) Between the 1970s and 1990 the cost of ingredients for soft drinks increased at a greater rate than the cost of telephone equipment.	Correct. This damages the author's analogy between soft drinks and pay phone calls.
(E) Technological advances made telephone equipment more sophisticated between the 1970s and 1990. *PrepTest49 Sec2 Q8*	Outside the Scope. Did these advances make pay phone calls more or less expensive to deliver? Were there similar advances in vending machine technology? Who knows? Eliminate.

LSAT Question	Analysis
79. On the Caribbean island of Guadeloupe, a researcher examined 35 patients with atypical Parkinson's disease and compared their eating habits to those of 65 healthy adults. She found that all of the patients with atypical Parkinson's regularly ate the tropical fruits soursop, custard apple, and pomme cannelle, whereas only 10 of the healthy adults regularly ate these fruits. From this, she concluded that eating these fruits causes atypical Parkinson's.	**Step 2:** Conclusion—Eating certain fruits causes atypical Parkinson's disease. → *because* Evidence—Study: Thirty-five Parkinson's sufferers all ate the fruits. Of 65 unaffected adults, only 10 ate the fruits.
Which one of the following, if true, most strengthens the researcher's reasoning?	**Step 1:** "[S]trengthens"—the correct answer will make the author's conclusion more likely to follow from her evidence. The four wrong answers will weaken the argument *or* do nothing.
	Step 3: Correlation versus causation. To strengthen this argument, we need a fact that 1) *rules out* an alternative cause; 2) shows that the causation is *not* reversed (unlikely here); or 3) suggests the correlation is *not* coincidence.
(A) For many of the atypical Parkinson's patients, their symptoms stopped getting worse, and in some cases actually abated, when they stopped eating soursop, custard apple, and pomme cannelle.	**Step 4:** Correct. If the disease halted or reversed when the patients stopped eating these fruits, it is somewhat less likely that the correlation is mere coincidence.
(B) Of the healthy adults who did not regularly eat soursop, custard apple, and pomme cannelle, most had eaten each of these fruits on at least one occasion.	Extreme. The author doesn't claim that having eaten the fruits a few times would be enough to cause the disease. Eliminate.
(C) In areas other than Guadeloupe, many people who have never eaten soursop, custard apple, and pomme cannelle have contracted atypical Parkinson's.	Outside the Scope. The author's conclusion is that eating these fruits causes Parkinson's, not that it's the only cause. Eliminate.
(D) The 10 healthy adults who regularly ate soursop, custard apple, and pomme cannelle ate significantly greater quantities of these fruits, on average, than did the 35 atypical Parkinson's patients.	180. This makes it less likely that the fruits are the causal agents. Why aren't these 10 even worse off, after all? Eliminate.
(E) Soursop, custard apple, and pomme cannelle contain essential vitamins not contained in any other food that is commonly eaten by residents of Guadeloupe.	Outside the Scope. This might be a good reason to eat the fruits, but makes them no more or less likely to be the cause of Parkinson's. Eliminate.

PrepTest59 Sec2 Q1

LSAT Question	Analysis
80. Eating garlic reduces the levels of cholesterol and triglycerides in the blood and so helps reduce the risk of cardiovascular disease. Evidence that eating garlic reduces these levels is that a group of patients taking a garlic tablet each day for four months showed a 12 percent reduction in cholesterol and a 17 percent reduction in triglycerides; over the same period, a group of similar patients taking a medically inert tablet showed only a 2 percent reduction in triglycerides and a 3 percent reduction in cholesterol.	**Step 2:** Conclusion—Eating garlic helps reduce the risk of CV disease. *because* Evidence—1) Reducing the levels of cholesterol and triglycerides in the blood helps reduce the risk of CV disease, and 2) a study. Methodology: Test group took a garlic tablet every day; control group took placebo. Results: Test group—cholesterol down 12 percent and triglycerides down 17 percent; control group—cholesterol down 3 percent and triglycerides down 2 percent.
It would be most important to determine which one of the following in evaluating the argument?	**Step 1:** "[M]ost important ... in evaluating the argument"—the correct answer will be a fact relevant to the argument; the four wrong answers will be irrelevant.
	Step 3: The author's primary evidence is the study. The correct answer will cite information relevant to the validity of the study.
(A) whether the garlic tablets are readily available to the public	**Step 4:** Outside the Scope. How quickly the tablets could get to the general public has no impact on the study results. Eliminate.
(B) what the diets of the two groups were during the period	Correct. Knowing what else the two groups were eating is relevant to the legitimacy of the study.
(C) what effect taking the garlic tablets each day for a period of less than four months had on the levels of cholesterol and triglycerides	Irrelevant Comparison. Knowing this would tell us *how fast* the garlic treatment works, not whether it works. Eliminate.
(D) whether large amounts of garlic are well tolerated by all patients	Outside the Scope/Distortion. The argument does not address side effects. Moreover, we don't know whether the tablet contains "large amounts of garlic." Eliminate.
(E) whether the manufacturer of the garlic tablets cites the study in its advertising	Outside the Scope. The business implications of the study are irrelevant to the argument. Eliminate.

PrepTest49 Sec4 Q2

LSAT Question	Analysis
81. Essayist: Politicians deserve protection from a prying press. No one wants his or her private life spread across the pages of the newspapers. Furthermore, the press's continual focus on politicians' private lives dissuades talented people from pursuing a career in politics and turns reporters into character cops who walk their beats looking for minute and inconsequential personality flaws in public servants. It is time to put a halt to this trivial journalism.	**Step 2:** Conclusion—"Trivial" journalism focused on politicians' personal lives should end. *because* Evidence—Three negative effects of such journalism: 1) private lives exposed; 2) qualified people dissuaded from public service; and 3) journalists look for inconsequential character flaws.
Each of the following, if true, strengthens the essayist's argument EXCEPT:	**Step 1:** "[S]trengthens ... EXCEPT"—the right answer will either weaken the argument or will be irrelevant. The four wrong answers strengthen the argument.
	Step 3: The author points out three negatives of journalism that investigates politicians' private lives. What about the positives? The four wrong answers will add to the negatives or rule out potential positives. The correct answer is likely to point out one of the positives of such journalism the author has overlooked.
(A) The press is unusually inaccurate when it reports on people's private lives.	**Step 4:** Strengthener. This points out another negative aspect of journalism that investigates politicians' personal lives. Eliminate.
(B) Reporting on politicians' private lives distracts voters from more important issues in a campaign.	Strengthener. This points out another negative aspect of journalism that investigates politicians' personal lives. Eliminate.
(C) Much writing on politicians' private lives consists of rumors circulated by opposing candidates.	Strengthener. This points out another negative aspect of journalism that investigates politicians' personal lives. Eliminate.
(D) In recent elections, the best local politicians have refused to run for national office because of the intrusiveness of press coverage.	Strengthener. This points out another negative aspect of journalism that investigates politicians' personal lives. Eliminate.
(E) Politicians' personality flaws often ultimately affect their performance on the job. *PrepTest49 Sec4 Q4*	Correct. This answer points out a potential positive effect of journalism that investigates politicians' personal lives.

LSAT Question	Analysis
82. Economist: As should be obvious, raising the minimum wage significantly would make it more expensive for businesses to pay workers for minimum-wage jobs. Therefore, businesses could not afford to continue to employ as many workers for such jobs. So raising the minimum wage significantly will cause an increase in unemployment.	**Step 2:** Conclusion—Raising the minimum wage will increase unemployment. *because* Evidence—1) Raising the minimum wage makes it more expensive to pay minimum-wage workers, and 2) businesses could not afford as many minimum-wage workers.
Which one of the following, if true, most weakens the economist's argument?	**Step 1:** "[M]ost weakens"—the correct answer makes the conclusion less likely to follow from the evidence. The four wrong answers either strengthen or do nothing.
	Step 3: The author overlooks the possibilities that employers might find other ways to pay their minimum-wage workforce, or that they might increase their revenue to offset higher payroll. The right answer will point out one of these overlooked possibilities.
(A) Businesses typically pass the cost of increased wages on to consumers without adversely affecting profits.	**Step 4:** Correct. This describes one of the author's overlooked possibilities, thereby weakening his argument.
(B) When the difference between minimum wage and a skilled worker's wage is small, a greater percentage of a business's employees will be skilled workers.	Outside the Scope. It's unclear whether this situation has any effect on unemployment, or if so, what effect. Eliminate.
(C) A modest increase in unemployment is acceptable because the current minimum wage is not a livable wage.	Outside the Scope. This may be a good justification for raising the minimum wage, but it does not impact the author's argument about unemployment. Eliminate.
(D) Most workers are earning more than the current minimum wage.	Irrelevant Comparison. The author's argument is solely about minimum-wage workers and unemployment. Eliminate.
(E) The unemployment rate has been declining steadily in recent years. *PrepTest57 Sec3 Q6*	Outside the Scope. The author's argument is prospective, not retrospective. Eliminate.

LSAT Question	Analysis
83. Gilbert: This food label is mistaken. It says that these cookies contain only natural ingredients, but they contain alphahydroxy acids that are chemically synthesized by the cookie company at their plant.	**Step 2:** [Gilbert] Conclusion—These cookies do not contain all natural ingredients.
	because
Sabina: The label is not mistaken. After all, alphahydroxy acids also are found occurring naturally in sugarcane. →	Evidence—The alphahydroxy acids in these cookies are synthesized.
	[**Sabina**] Conclusion—The cookies do contain all natural ingredients.
	because
	Evidence—Alphahydroxy acids occur in nature.
Which one of the following, if true, would most strengthen Sabina's argument? →	**Step 1:** "[S]trengthen Sabina's argument"—the correct answer will present a fact that supports Sabina's conclusion or perhaps that weakens Gilbert's.
	Step 3: The two speakers argue over whether chemicals found in nature can be listed as "natural ingredients" even when they are synthesized in a particular case. Sabina says they can.
(A) The cookie company has recently dropped alphahydroxy acids from its cookie ingredients. →	**Step 4:** Outside the Scope. They're arguing about the cookie label from the time when the company included alphahydroxy acids. Eliminate.
(B) Not all chemicals that are part of the manufacturing process are ingredients of the cookies. →	Outside the Scope. Alphahydroxy acids *are* listed as an ingredient. Eliminate.
(C) The label was printed before the cookie company decided to switch from sugarcane alphahydroxy acids to synthesized ones. →	Irrelevant Comparison. Gilbert claims that the alphahydroxy acids in his cookies are synthesized. Sabina doesn't dispute that. Eliminate.
(D) Many other foods advertising all natural ingredients also contain some ingredients that are chemically synthesized. →	Outside the Scope. Gilbert and Sabina could have the same argument about those foods and their ingredients. Eliminate.
(E) All substances except those that do not occur naturally in any source are considered natural. *PrepTest59 Sec2 Q5* →	Correct. This statement supports Sabina's definition of "natural ingredients."

LSAT Question	Analysis
84. The cattle egret is a bird that lives around herds of cattle. The only available explanation of the fact that the cattle egret follows cattle herds is that the egrets consume the insects stirred up from the grasses as the cattle herds graze.	**Step 2:** This stimulus is a "claim," not an argument. The claim is that the only explanation for egrets following cattle is that they can eat the insects the cattle stir up when grazing.
Which one of the following, if true, would most seriously undermine the claim that the explanation given above is the only available one?	**Step 1:** The correct answer will suggest that other explanations are available. The four wrong answers will make it more likely that the explanation in the stimulus is the only one, or will do nothing.
	Step 3: The correct answer will suggest a benefit that the egret derives from following cattle herds other than having insects to eat.
(A) Birds other than cattle egrets have been observed consuming insects stirred up by the movement of cattle.	**Step 4:** 180. This makes the author's claim even more likely. Eliminate.
(B) Cattle egrets are known to follow other slow-moving animals, such as rhinoceroses and buffalo.	Irrelevant Comparison. Presumably, rhinos and buffalo stir up insects, too. Eliminate.
(C) The presence of cattle dissuades many would-be predators of the cattle egret.	Correct. Receiving protection is a distinct benefit for the egrets. Maybe having bugs stirred up isn't the only explanation.
(D) Cattle egrets are not generally known to live outside the range of large, slow-moving animals.	Outside the Scope. *Why* they follow cattle herds is the question, not whether they live elsewhere, too. Eliminate.
(E) Forests are generally inhospitable to cattle egrets because of a lack of insects of the kind egrets can consume.	Outside the Scope. The author claims to know why egrets follow cattle herds, not why they don't live in the forest. Eliminate.

PrepTest49 Sec2 Q6

LSAT Question	**Analysis**
85. In modern deep-diving marine mammals, such as whales, the outer shell of the bones is porous. This has the effect of making the bones light enough so that it is easy for the animals to swim back to the surface after a deep dive. The outer shell of the bones was also porous in the ichthyosaur, an extinct prehistoric marine reptile. We can conclude from this that ichthyosaurs were deep divers.	**Step 2:** Conclusion—Ichthyosaurs were deep divers. *because* Evidence—1) Ichthyosaurs had a porous outer shell of bone, and 2) modern deep-diving animals have a porous outer shell of bones (which make it easier to dive deep).
Which one of the following, if true, most weakens the argument?	**Step 1:** "[M]ost weakens"—the correct answer makes the conclusion less likely to follow from the evidence. The four wrong answers either strengthen or do nothing.
	Step 3: The author tells us that modern deep-diving animals have a porous outer shell of bone, but he doesn't tell us that *only* deep divers have this feature. If non-deep divers also have porous outer shells of bones, or if this feature has other benefits, the author's argument is suspect.
(A) Some deep-diving marine species must surface after dives but do not have bones with porous outer shells.	**Step 4:** Irrelevant Comparison. It must be harder for these deep divers to resurface, but that has no impact on the argument. The author needs to show that *only deep divers have porous outer shells*, not that only those with porous outer shells dive deep.
(B) In most modern marine reptile species, the outer shell of the bones is not porous.	Outside the Scope. Perhaps most modern reptiles are not deep divers. Eliminate.
(C) In most modern and prehistoric marine reptile species that are not deep divers, the outer shell of the bones is porous.	Correct. If non-deep divers have the same bone structure, then it is just as likely that ichthyosaurs were non-deep divers, too.
(D) In addition to the porous outer shells of their bones, whales have at least some characteristics suited to deep diving for which there is no clear evidence whether these were shared by ichthyosaurs.	Irrelevant Comparison. Whales may be better deep divers than ichthyosaurs, but that doesn't suggest that ichthyosaurs were not deep divers. Eliminate.
(E) There is evidence that the bones of ichthyosaurs would have been light enough to allow surfacing even if the outer shells were not porous. *PrepTest61 Sec4 Q21*	180. This makes it more likely that ichthyosaurs were deep divers, not less. Eliminate.

LSAT Question	Analysis
86. The supernova event of 1987 is interesting in that there is still no evidence of the neutron star that current theory says should have remained after a supernova of that size. This is in spite of the fact that many of the most sensitive instruments ever developed have searched for the tell-tale pulse of radiation that neutron stars emit. Thus, current theory is wrong in claiming that supernovas of a certain size always produce neutron stars. ⟶	**Step 2:** Conclusion—Supernovas of a certain size do not always produce neutron stars (the current theory is wrong). *because* Evidence—Despite searching with sensitive instruments, scientists have found no trace of a neutron star following from the 1987 supernova.
Which one of the following, if true, most strengthens the argument? ⟶	**Step 1:** "[S]trengthens"—the correct answer will make the author's conclusion more likely to follow from her evidence. The four wrong answers will weaken the argument *or* do nothing.
	Step 3: The author assumes an absence of evidence (we haven't found the neutron star) is evidence of absence (there was no neutron star). The correct answer will be a fact that makes it more likely that absence of evidence really proves that there was no neutron star.
(A) Most supernova remnants that astronomers have detected have a neutron star nearby. ⟶	**Step 4:** 180. This observation is the basis of the current theory that the author opposes. Eliminate.
(B) Sensitive astronomical instruments have detected neutron stars much farther away than the location of the 1987 supernova. ⟶	Correct. If the same instruments have discovered neutron stars even farther away, it is more likely that a failure to find a neutron star following the 1987 supernova means that there is no such star, and not that the instruments simply cannot search far enough.
(C) The supernova of 1987 was the first that scientists were able to observe in progress. ⟶	Outside the Scope. Without more information, this makes it neither more nor less likely that the neutron star exists. Eliminate.
(D) Several important features of the 1987 supernova are correctly predicted by the current theory. ⟶	180. This supports the current theory, and makes it more likely that the 1987 supernova produced a neutron star that hasn't been found. Eliminate.
(E) Some neutron stars are known to have come into existence by a cause other than a supernova explosion. ⟶	Outside the Scope. Other ways neutron stars can be produced are irrelevant. Eliminate.

PrepTest51 Sec1 Q24

LSAT Question	Analysis
87. On average, corporations that encourage frequent social events in the workplace show higher profits than those that rarely do. This suggests that the EZ Corporation could boost its profits by having more staff parties during business hours.	**Step 2:** Conclusion—More staff parties during business hours causes increased corporate profits. *because* Evidence—Frequent social events for employees correlate to higher profits.
Which one of the following, if true, most weakens the argument above?	**Step 1:** "[M]ost weakens"—the correct answer makes the conclusion less likely to follow from the evidence. The four wrong answers either strengthen or do nothing.
	Step 3: The author assumes a causal conclusion from evidence of correlation. This can be weakened by showing 1) alternate causes; 2) reversed causation (likely here); or 3) mere coincidence.
(A) The great majority of corporations that encourage frequent social events in the workplace do so at least in part because they are already earning above-average profits.	**Step 4:** Correct. This shows reversed causation. Already profitable companies are more likely to fete their employees.
(B) Corporations that have frequent staff parties after business hours sometimes have higher profits than do corporations that have frequent staff parties during business hours.	Outside the Scope. Maybe parties after work hours are *even better*, but that certainly doesn't damage the author's argument. Eliminate.
(C) The EZ Corporation already earns above-average profits, and it almost never brings play into the workplace.	Outside the Scope. The author concludes that more staff parties could *boost* profitability even more, not that EZ isn't profitable now. Eliminate.
(D) Frequent social events in a corporate workplace leave employees with less time to perform their assigned duties than they would otherwise have.	Irrelevant Comparison. We would need information about how employees' completion of their assigned duties affects profitability to assess the impact of this statement. Eliminate.
(E) At one time the EZ Corporation encouraged social events in the workplace more frequently than it currently does, but it has not always been one of the most profitable corporations of its size. *PrepTest51 Sec1 Q25*	Extreme. Many factors influence whether EZ is "*one of the most* profitable corporations." The relevant question for the author would be: Was EZ more profitable when it encouraged more parties than it is now? Eliminate.

LSAT Question	Analysis
88. Scientist: A controversy in paleontology centers on the question of whether prehistoric human ancestors began to develop sophisticated tools before or after they came to stand upright. I argue that they stood upright first, simply because advanced toolmaking requires free use of the hands, and standing upright makes this possible.	**Step 2:** Conclusion—Human ancestors stood upright before they made sophisticated tools. $\longrightarrow$ *because* Evidence—1) If advanced toolmaking, then free use of hands, and 2) if stand upright, then free use of hands.
Which one of the following statements, if true, most weakens the scientist's argument?	**Step 1:** "[M]ost weakens"—the correct answer $\longrightarrow$ makes the conclusion less likely to follow from the evidence. The four wrong answers either strengthen or do nothing.
	Step 3: The author assumes humans stood upright before making advanced tools because standing upright is sufficient to allow one characteristic (free use of hands) necessary for making advanced tools. The author overlooks other ways to get free use of the hands, like sitting down. The right answer will suggest that humans didn't need to stand upright to make advanced tools.
(A) Many animals that do not stand upright have learned to make basic tools.	**Step 4:** Outside the Scope. The argument is about $\longrightarrow$ *advanced* tools. Eliminate.
(B) Advanced hunting weapons have been discovered among the artifacts belonging to prehistoric human ancestors who did not stand upright.	Correct. If human ancestors who could not stand $\longrightarrow$ upright had advanced tools, they must have found another way to free up their hands.
(C) Many prehistoric human ancestors who stood upright had no sophisticated tools.	Distortion. The author stipulates that free use of $\longrightarrow$ hands is *necessary* (not sufficient) for advanced toolmaking. Eliminate.
(D) Those prehistoric human ancestors who first came to stand upright had no more dexterity with their hands than did those who did not stand upright.	Irrelevant Comparison. Without more information, $\longrightarrow$ we don't know how manual dexterity impacts the argument. Eliminate.
(E) Many of the earliest sophisticated tools did not require their users to be able to stand upright. *PrepTest49 Sec2 Q14*	Distortion. The author is arguing that standing $\longrightarrow$ enabled human ancestors to *make* the tools, not to *use* them. Eliminate.

LSAT Question	Analysis
89. When people show signs of having a heart attack an electrocardiograph (EKG) is often used to diagnose their condition. In a study, a computer program for EKG diagnosis of heart attacks was pitted against a very experienced, highly skilled cardiologist. The program correctly diagnosed a significantly higher proportion of the cases that were later confirmed to be heart attacks than did the cardiologist. Interpreting EKG data, therefore, should be left to computer programs.	**Step 2:** Conclusion—EKG data should be interpreted by computers, not by doctors. *because* Evidence—A study. Methodology: Computers and skilled, experienced doctors both interpreted EKG data. Result: Computer correctly diagnosed heart attacks more often than doctors did.
Which one of the following, if true, most weakens the argument?	**Step 1:** "[M]ost weakens"—the correct answer makes the conclusion less likely to follow from the evidence. The four wrong answers either strengthen or do nothing.
	Step 3: The study shows that computers are more accurate when patients did have heart attacks. But are doctors better at another aspect of interpreting EKGs, such as when patients' symptoms were due to something else? The correct answer will likely point out an overlooked advantage to having doctors interpret EKGs.
(A) Experts agreed that the cardiologist made few obvious mistakes in reading and interpreting the EKG data.	**Step 4:** 180. This suggests that it is really hard to know when the doctors are wrong, making computer interpretation more valuable. Eliminate.
(B) The practice of medicine is as much an art as a science, and computer programs are not easily adapted to making subjective judgments.	Outside the Scope. Without more information, we don't know that interpreting EKGs ever involves subjective judgments. Eliminate.
(C) The cardiologist correctly diagnosed a significantly higher proportion of the cases in which no heart attack occurred than did the computer program.	Correct. This supports the position that doctors, too, should review the EKG data.
(D) In a considerable percentage of cases, EKG data alone are insufficient to enable either computer programs or cardiologists to make accurate diagnoses.	Irrelevant Comparison. The author does not suggest that doctors should not also examine patients, just that they should not interpret EKG data. Eliminate.
(E) The cardiologist in the study was unrepresentative of cardiologists in general with respect to skill and experience. *PrepTest61 Sec2 Q20*	180. The doctors in the study were highly skilled and experienced, but were still less accurate than the computers. Imagine how poor unskilled, inexperienced doctors would be! Eliminate.

LSAT Question	Analysis
90. A recent study confirms that nutritious breakfasts make workers more productive. For one month, workers at Plant A received free nutritious breakfasts every day before work, while workers in Plant B did not. The productivity of Plant A's workers increased, while that of Plant B's workers did not. →	**Step 2:** Conclusion—Eating a nutritious breakfast increases productivity. *because* Evidence—A study. Methodology: Workers in Plant A received a free nutritious breakfast; workers in Plant B did not. Result: Workers' productivity increased in Plant A; workers' productivity in Plant B did not increase.
Which one of the following, if true, most strengthens the argument? →	**Step 1:** "[S]trengthens"—the correct answer will make the author's conclusion more likely to follow from her evidence. The four wrong answers will weaken the argument *or* do nothing.
	Step 3: The author concludes that *eating* breakfast increases productivity on the basis of evidence saying that one group *received* breakfast. He must be assuming that, during the study, more Plant A workers than Plant B workers *ate* breakfast.
(A) Few workers in Plant B consumed nutritious breakfasts during the month of the study. →	**Step 4:** Correct. The conclusion is about eating a nutritious breakfast (not receiving one free). To strengthen the argument, we need to know that more workers in Plant A ate breakfast than did workers in Plant B.
(B) Workers in the study from Plant A and Plant B started work at the same time of day. →	Outside the Scope. Whether this contributes to more workers at one plant eating breakfast is unclear. Eliminate.
(C) During the month before the study, workers at Plant A and Plant B were equally productive. →	Outside the Scope. The author doesn't care which group was more productive, but whether eating a nutritious breakfast made a particular group *more* productive than they were. Eliminate.
(D) Workers from Plant A took fewer vacation days per capita during the month than did workers from Plant B. →	Outside the Scope. This tells us nothing about the effects of eating breakfast on worker productivity. Eliminate.
(E) Workers in Plant B were more productive during the month of the study than were workers from Plant A. *PrepTest59 Sec2 Q22* →	Outside the Scope. The question is not which group was more productive, but whether a group eating breakfast was more productive than they had been when not eating breakfast. Eliminate.

LSAT Question	Analysis
91. Poetry journal patron: Everybody who publishes in *The Brick Wall Review* has to agree in advance that if a poem is printed in one of its regular issues, the magazine also has the right to reprint it, without monetary compensation, in its annual anthology. *The Brick Wall Review* makes enough money from sales of its anthologies to cover most operating expenses. So, if your magazine also published an anthology of poems first printed in your magazine, you could depend less on donations. After all, most poems published in your magazine are very similar to those published in *The Brick Wall Review*.	**Step 2:** Conclusion—If your magazine published an anthology of poems *first published in the magazine*, it would make money (you could depend less on donations). *because* Evidence—1) *BWR*'s anthology makes money, and 2) most of the poems in your magazine are very similar to those in *BWR*. [NOTE: Poets submitting to *BWR* sign a release allowing for reprint in *BWR*'s anthology, but that doesn't mean those are the poems in the anthology.]
Which one of the following, if true, most weakens the patron's argument?	**Step 1:** "[M]ost weakens"—the correct answer makes the conclusion less likely to follow from the evidence. The four wrong answers either strengthen or do nothing.
	Step 3: The author assumes that the poems in *BWR*'s anthology are poems first published in *BWR*. His analogous suggestion is that "your magazine" publish an anthology of "poems first printed in your magazine." The correct answer will weaken the argument by suggesting that either the assumption or the suggestion based on it is not true.
(A) Neither *The Brick Wall Review* nor the other magazine under discussion depends on donations to cover most operating expenses.	**Step 4:** Irrelevant Comparison/Extreme. The author's argument could still be true even if "your magazine" doesn't need donations for *most* of its expenses. Eliminate.
(B) Many of the poets whose work appears in *The Brick Wall Review* have had several poems rejected for publication by the other magazine under discussion.	180. If anything, this suggests that "your magazine's" poems are even better than those in *BWR* and that, as a result, your anthology might sell even better. Eliminate.
(C) The only compensation poets receive for publishing in the regular issues of the magazines under discussion are free copies of the issues in which their poems appear.	Outside the Scope. Without knowing whether the poets would receive compensation for being reprinted in an anthology, this has no impact on the argument. Eliminate.
(D) *The Brick Wall Review* depends on donations to cover most operating expenses not covered by income from anthology sales.	Outside the Scope. *BWR*'s anthology makes money. Where it gets additional money is irrelevant. Eliminate.
(E) *The Brick Wall Review*'s annual poetry anthology always contains a number of poems by famous poets not published in the regular issues of the magazine. *PrepTest57 Sec2 Q17*	Correct. If *BWR*'s anthology is successful because of the poems by famous poets that were not first printed in *BWR*, the author's analogous suggestion for "your magazine" is now suspect.

ARGUMENT-BASED PRINCIPLE QUESTIONS

Principle questions mimic other question types, including Assumption and Strengthen questions from the Assumption Family. These will be covered in this section. Later in this chapter, you'll see Principle questions that test Parallel Reasoning, and in Chapter 11, those that test Inference skills.

LEARNING OBJECTIVES

In this section, you'll learn to:

· Recognize Principle question stems
· Distinguish Identify the Principle questions from other Principle question types
· Use your knowledge of Assumption Family questions to answer Principle Assumption and Principle Strengthen questions

Recognizing Principle Question Stems

On the LSAT, think of a *principle* like you would a law, a general rule applicable to all relevant cases. A question that asks you to either identify or apply a general rule is a Principle question. These question stems often use the word *principle*, but they may also use *proposition* or *policy*. Be on the lookout for tasks such as "most closely conforms to," "best illustrates," and "helps to justify."

LSAT Principle Q Stem		Analysis
Which one of the following most accurately expresses the principle underlying the reasoning above? *PrepTest51 Sec3 Q7*	→	"[E]xpresses the principle underlying the reasoning" indicates a Principle question that acts like an Assumption question.
Which one of the following principles, if valid, most helps to justify drawing the conclusion in the argument above? *PrepTest49 Sec2 Q15*	→	"[P]rinciple ... most helps to justify"—a Principle question that acts like a Strengthen question.
The reasoning above most closely conforms to which one of the following principles? *PrepTest57 Sec2 Q1*	→	"[M]ost closely conforms ... principles" indicates that this is a Principle question that tests Inference skills.
Which one of the following is an example of efficiency as described above? *PrepTest49 Sec2 Q3*	→	A question that asks you to apply a definition to an example is a Principle question that tests Inference skills.
Of the following, which one illustrates a principle that is most similar to the principle illustrated by the passage? *PrepTest61 Sec2 Q2*	→	"[A] principle ... most similar to the principle illustrated by the passage" is a Principle question that rewards the analysis seen in Parallel Reasoning questions.

Distinguishing Types of Principle Questions

Identify the Principle questions will present a specific argument or set of events in the question stem, then ask you to identify a more general principle that underlies or strengthens the stimulus. These question types can mimic Assumption, Strengthen, or even Inference questions.

Apply the Principle questions operate in the opposite direction: They present a general rule or definition in the stimulus (often, but not always, expressed as a Formal Logic statement), then ask you to identify a specific situation that conforms to that rule or definition.

Identify and Apply the Principle questions ask you to perform both actions: Identify the general principle illustrated by the specific situation in the stimulus, and then match that same principle to a specific situation in the answer choices.

Practice

Classify the Principle question type in each of the following question stems. Pay attention to whether you're asked to find a specific situation from a general rule, a general rule from a specific situation, or both.

LSAT Question		My Analysis
92. Which one of the following principles, if valid, most helps to justify the reasoning above? *PrepTest61 Sec2 Q21*	$\longrightarrow$	
93. Which one of the following judgments conforms most closely to the principles described by the industrial adviser? *PrepTest51 Sec1 Q17*	$\longrightarrow$	
94. The situation described above most closely conforms to which one of the following generalizations? *PrepTest59 Sec2 Q23*	$\longrightarrow$	
95. Which one of the following most closely conforms to the principle to which the reasoning in the passage conforms? *PrepTest59 Sec3 Q6*	$\longrightarrow$	
96. Which one of the following most accurately expresses the principle underlying the argument above? *PrepTest59 Sec3 Q18*	$\longrightarrow$	

Expert Analysis

Here's how an LSAT expert would characterize each of the question stems in that exercise.

LSAT Question	Analysis
92. Which one of the following principles, if valid, most helps to justify the reasoning above? *PrepTest61 Sec2 Q21* $\longrightarrow$	"[M]ost helps to justify the reasoning" sounds a lot like a Strengthen question. Because the question asks for "the following principle," though, this is an Identify the Principle question that mimics a Strengthen question.
93. Which one of the following judgments conforms most closely to the principles described by the industrial adviser? *PrepTest51 Sec1 Q17* $\longrightarrow$	This question asks for a specific "judgment" that "conforms most closely to the principles described [above]." This is an Apply the Principle question similar to an Inference question.
94. The situation described above most closely conforms to which one of the following generalizations? *PrepTest59 Sec2 Q23* $\longrightarrow$	This question asks for a generalization that "most closely conforms to" the specific situation above. It is an Identify the Principle question that operates like an Inference question.
95. Which one of the following most closely conforms to the principle to which the reasoning in the passage conforms? *PrepTest59 Sec3 Q6* $\longrightarrow$	In this question, *both* the stimulus above *and* the correct answer "closely conform" to the same principle. This is an Identify and Apply the Principle question, much like Parallel Reasoning.
96. Which one of the following most accurately expresses the principle underlying the argument above? *PrepTest59 Sec3 Q18* $\longrightarrow$	"[P]rinciple underlying the argument above"—this is like an Assumption question. In this Identify the Principle question, the right answer states a general rule that connects the argument's evidence to its conclusion.

ASSUMPTION FAMILY PRINCIPLE AT A GLANCE

Task: Identify whether the question is asking for the principle that acts as the argument's assumption ("underlies the argument") or as a strengthener ("most justifies").

Strategy: Use the same skills you would to answer an Assumption or Strengthen question, but phrase your prediction of the correct answer as a broad general rule.

On LSAT tests released between 2008 and 2013, there were an average of 5.1 Principle questions per test.

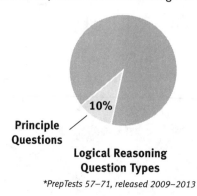

10%

Principle
Questions

**Logical Reasoning
Question Types**
PrepTests 57–71, released 2009–2013

Here's how an LSAT expert might analyze and answer a Principle question that acts as a Strengthen question.

LSAT Question	Analysis
Philosopher: Some of the most ardent philosophical opponents of democracy have rightly noted that both the inherently best and the inherently worst possible forms of government are those that concentrate political power in the hands of a few. Thus, since democracy is a consistently mediocre form of government, it is a better choice than rule by the few.	**Step 2:** Conclusion—Democracy is a better choice than rule by the few. *because* Evidence: The best and worst forms of government concentrate power in the hands of a few, and democracy is a consistently mediocre form of government.
Which one of the following principles, if valid, most helps to justify the philosopher's argument?	**Step 1:** The phrase "following principles" indicates an Identify the Principle question. The word "justify" signifies that this acts as a Strengthen question.
	Step 3: The correct answer will provide a broad, general rule that strengthens the author's reasoning. The author assumes that a mediocre form of government is preferable to one that could be the best but carries the risk of being the worst.
(A) A society should adopt a democratic form of government if and only if most members of the society prefer a democratic form of government.	**Step 4:** What most members of a society *prefer* is Outside the Scope. Eliminate.
(B) In choosing a form of government, it is better for a society to avoid the inherently worst than to seek to attain the best.	Correct. This choice summarizes the author's assumption: Don't risk the worst form of government, even if it might turn out to be the best; play it safe and go with mediocrity instead.
(C) The best form of government is the one that is most likely to produce an outcome that is on the whole good.	Distortion. The only criterion the philosopher gives for the best form of government is that it "concentrate[s] political power in the hands of the few." Eliminate.
(D) Democratic governments are not truly equitable unless they are designed to prevent interest groups from exerting undue influence on the political process.	Outside the Scope. The philosopher does not attempt to define *equitable* government. Eliminate.
(E) It is better to choose a form of government on the basis of sound philosophical reasons than on the basis of popular preference. *PrepTest51 Sec3 Q13*	Outside the Scope. The philosopher says nothing about the role of *popular preference* in choosing a form of government. Eliminate.

Assumption Family Principle Question Practice

Practice the following Assumption Family Principle questions. Use the question stem to identify whether the question acts like an Assumption or Strengthen question and then apply the same skills you would use for those. But keep in mind that the correct answer will be a broad rule rather than a specific statement of the assumption or a helpful fact.

	LSAT Question		My Analysis
97.	Bethany: Psychologists have discovered a technique for replacing one's nightmares with pleasant dreams, and have successfully taught it to adults suffering from chronic nightmares. Studies have found that nightmare-prone children are especially likely to suffer from nightmares as adults. Thus, psychologists should direct efforts toward identifying nightmare-prone children so that these children can be taught the technique for replacing their nightmares with pleasant dreams.		**Step 2:** Conclusion— *because* → Evidence—
	Which one of the following principles, if valid, most helps to justify drawing the conclusion in Bethany's argument?	→	**Step 1:**
			Step 3:
(A)	Psychologists should make an effort to determine why certain children are especially prone to nightmares while other children are not.	→	**Step 4:**
(B)	Any psychological technique that can be successfully taught to a child can also be successfully taught to an adult.	→	
(C)	Psychologists should do everything they can to minimize the number of adults troubled by chronic nightmares.	→	
(D)	Identifying nightmare-prone children is generally more difficult than teaching adults the technique for replacing nightmares with pleasant dreams.	→	
(E)	Psychologists should not teach the technique for replacing nightmares with pleasant dreams to children who are unlikely to suffer from nightmares as adults.	→	

PrepTest59 Sec2 Q13

LSAT Question	My Analysis
98. Those who claim that governments should not continue to devote resources to space exploration are wrong. Although most people's lives are relatively unaffected by the direct consequences of space exploration, many modern technologies that have a tremendous impact on daily life—e.g., fiber optics, computers, and lasers—are unexpected consequences of it. Society might have missed the benefits of these technologies if governments had not devoted resources to space exploration. →	**Step 2:** Conclusion— *because* Evidence—
Which one of the following most accurately expresses the principle underlying the argument above? →	**Step 1:**
	Step 3:
(A) Governments should not be prevented from allocating resources to projects whose intended consequences do not directly benefit most people. →	**Step 4:**
(B) One can never underestimate the beneficial consequences of government support of ambitious technological undertakings. →	
(C) The less practical the goal of a government-supported project, the more unexpected the consequences of that project. →	
(D) Governments should continue to support those projects that have, in the past, produced unintended benefits. →	
(E) In attempting to advance the welfare of society, governments should continue to dedicate resources to ambitious technological undertakings. →	

PrepTest59 Sec3 Q18

LSAT Question	My Analysis
99. A government study indicates that raising speed limits to reflect the actual average speeds of traffic on level, straight stretches of high-speed roadways reduces the accident rate. Since the actual average speed for level, straight stretches of high-speed roadways tends to be 120 kilometers per hour (75 miles per hour), that should be set as a uniform national speed limit for level, straight stretches of all such roadways. $\longrightarrow$	**Step 2:** Conclusion— *because* Evidence—
Which one of the following principles, if valid, most helps to justify the reasoning above? $\longrightarrow$	**Step 1:**
	Step 3:
(A) Uniform national speed limits should apply only to high-speed roadways. $\longrightarrow$	**Step 4:**
(B) Traffic laws applying to high-speed roadways should apply uniformly across the nation. $\longrightarrow$	
(C) A uniform national speed limit for high-speed roadways should be set only if all such roadways have roughly equal average speeds of traffic. $\longrightarrow$	
(D) Long-standing laws that are widely violated are probably not good laws. $\longrightarrow$	
(E) Any measure that reduces the rate of traffic accidents should be implemented. $\longrightarrow$	

PrepTest61 Sec2 Q21

LSAT Question	My Analysis
100. Ethicist: People who avoid alcoholic beverages simply because they regard them as a luxury beyond their financial means should not be praised for their abstinence. Similarly, those who avoid alcohol simply because they lack the desire to partake should not be praised, unless this disinclination has somehow resulted from an arduous process of disciplining oneself to refrain from acting indiscriminately on one's desires.	**Step 2:** Conclusion— *because* Evidence—
Which one of the following principles, if valid, most helps to justify the ethicist's claims?	**Step 1:**
	Step 3:
(A) Whether behavior should be regarded as praiseworthy is a function of both its consequences and the social context in which the agent acts.	**Step 4:**
(B) A person should be blamed for an action only if that action was not motivated by a desire to be virtuous or if the person did not have to overcome any obstacles in order to perform that action.	
(C) A person is praiseworthy for a particular behavior only if, in order to adopt that behavior, the person at some point had to overcome a desire to do something that she or he felt able to afford to do.	
(D) The extent to which the process of acquiring self-discipline is arduous for a person is affected by that person's set of desires and aversions.	
(E) The apportionment of praise and blame should be commensurate with the arduousness or ease of the lives of those who receive praise or blame.	

PrepTest49 Sec4 Q21

Expert Analysis: Assumption Family Principle Questions

Compare your work to that of an LSAT expert. Were you able to identify whether each of the questions acted like an Assumption or Strengthen question? Did you apply what you know about analyzing and evaluating LSAT arguments?

LSAT Question	Analysis
97. Bethany: Psychologists have discovered a technique for replacing one's nightmares with pleasant dreams, and have successfully taught it to adults suffering from chronic nightmares. Studies have found that nightmare-prone children are especially likely to suffer from nightmares as adults. Thus, psychologists should direct efforts toward identifying nightmare-prone children so that these children can be taught the technique for replacing their nightmares with pleasant dreams.	**Step 2:** Conclusion—Psychologists should identify nightmare-prone children so that these children can learn to replace nightmares with pleasant dreams. *because* Evidence—Nightmare-prone children are especially likely to suffer from nightmares as adults.
Which one of the following principles, if valid, most helps to justify drawing the conclusion in Bethany's argument?	**Step 1:** The phrase "following principles" indicates an Identify the Principle question, and "justify ... the conclusion" signals a Strengthen-type question.
	Step 3: Bethany concludes that nightmare-prone children should be identified because such children are likely to become nightmare-prone adults, and there are now ways to reduce nightmares in adults. The correct answer will contain a broad rule that supports this reasoning.
(A) Psychologists should make an effort to determine why certain children are especially prone to nightmares while other children are not.	**Step 4:** Outside the Scope. *Why* certain children are nightmare-prone is irrelevant to Bethany's argument about identifying them for treatment. Eliminate.
(B) Any psychological technique that can be successfully taught to a child can also be successfully taught to an adult.	180. If anything, Bethany assumes that a technique that can be taught to an adult can also be taught to a child. Eliminate.
(C) Psychologists should do everything they can to minimize the number of adults troubled by chronic nightmares.	Correct. If this broad rule is valid, then Bethany's assumption is justified. The reason she wants to identify childhood sufferers is to prevent them from becoming nightmare-prone adults.
(D) Identifying nightmare-prone children is generally more difficult than teaching adults the technique for replacing nightmares with pleasant dreams.	Irrelevant Comparison. The relative difficulty of these things has no bearing on Bethany's argument that nightmare-prone children should in fact be identified. Eliminate.
(E) Psychologists should not teach the technique for replacing nightmares with pleasant dreams to children who are unlikely to suffer from nightmares as adults.	180. Bethany's objective is to identify children who *are* likely to be nightmare-prone as adults. Eliminate.

PrepTest59 Sec2 Q13

LSAT Question	Analysis
98. Those who claim that governments should not continue to devote resources to space exploration are wrong. Although most people's lives are relatively unaffected by the direct consequences of space exploration, many modern technologies that have a tremendous impact on daily life—e.g., fiber optics, computers, and lasers—are unexpected consequences of it. Society might have missed the benefits of these technologies if governments had not devoted resources to space exploration.	**Step 2:** Conclusion—Governments *should* continue to devote resources to space exploration (those who say otherwise are wrong). *because* Evidence—Although people's lives are not affected by the direct consequences of space exploration, their lives are affected by technologies that have emerged as unexpected consequences of space exploration.
Which one of the following most accurately expresses the principle underlying the argument above?	**Step 1:** The word *principle* signals a Principle question, while the word *underlying* indicates that this acts as an Assumption question.
	Step 3: The author assumes that space exploration should receive continued support because it provides unexpected technological benefits to society. The correct answer will state this assumption as a broad, general rule.
(A) Governments should not be prevented from allocating resources to projects whose intended consequences do not directly benefit most people.	**Step 4:** Space exploration's *un*intended benefits, not its intended consequences, are at issue here. Eliminate.
(B) One can never underestimate the beneficial consequences of government support of ambitious technological undertakings.	Distortion. The author is concerned that we *have* underestimated (or even ignored) the unintended benefits of space exploration. Eliminate.
(C) The less practical the goal of a government-supported project, the more unexpected the consequences of that project.	Outside the Scope. A rule stating that the predictability of consequences is inversely related to the practicality of goals does not strengthen the argument. Eliminate.
(D) Governments should continue to support those projects that have, in the past, produced unintended benefits.	Correct. This choice broadly states the author's assumption about space exploration.
(E) In attempting to advance the welfare of society, governments should continue to dedicate resources to ambitious technological undertakings. *PrepTest59 Sec3 Q18*	Distortion. This choice misses the point: It is not the fact that a technological undertaking is *ambitious*, but rather the fact that it has produced unexpected benefits that is important. Eliminate.

LSAT Question	Analysis
99. A government study indicates that raising speed limits to reflect the actual average speeds of traffic on level, straight stretches of high-speed roadways reduces the accident rate. Since the actual average speed for level, straight stretches of high-speed roadways tends to be 120 kilometers per hour (75 miles per hour), that should be set as a uniform national speed limit for level, straight stretches of all such roadways. →	**Step 2:** Conclusion—The speed limit for all level, straight stretches of roadways should be 75 mph. *because* Evidence—A government study indicates that raising the speed limit to drivers' actual average speed on level, straight roadways reduces the accident rate. The actual average speed on such roadways is currently about 75 mph.
Which one of the following principles, if valid, most helps to justify the reasoning above? →	**Step 1:** The phrase "following principles" signals an Identify the Principle question. The word *justify* indicates that this is also a Strengthen question.
	Step 3: The argument assumes that an action that reduces the number of accidents should be taken. The correct answer will be in line with this assumption and will be phrased in broad, general terms.
(A) Uniform national speed limits should apply only to high-speed roadways. →	**Step 4:** Roadways other than high-speed roadways are Outside the Scope. Eliminate.
(B) Traffic laws applying to high-speed roadways should apply uniformly across the nation. →	General traffic laws are Outside the Scope. The only law the author is interested in is the speed limit on high-speed roadways. Eliminate.
(C) A uniform national speed limit for high–speed roadways should be set only if all such roadways have roughly equal average speeds of traffic. →	This choice commits a necessity-sufficiency error. The argument in the stimulus says that if (*not* only if) the speed limit on high-speed roadways tends to be the same, there should be a uniform speed limit. Eliminate.
(D) Long-standing laws that are widely violated are probably not good laws. →	The reference to "long-standing laws" is far too general. Eliminate.
(E) Any measure that reduces the rate of traffic accidents should be implemented. *PrepTest61 Sec2 Q21* →	Correct. In light of the evidence that a uniform speed limit would help reduce accidents, this principle supports the conclusion that the speed limit on level, straight roadways should be raised to 75 mph.

LSAT Question	Analysis
100. Ethicist: People who avoid alcoholic beverages simply because they regard them as a luxury beyond their financial means should not be praised for their abstinence. Similarly, those who avoid alcohol simply because they lack the desire to partake should not be praised, unless this disinclination has somehow resulted from an arduous process of disciplining oneself to refrain from acting indiscriminately on one's desires.	**Step 2:** [No argument; just two claims] Those who cannot afford alcoholic beverages should not be praised for abstaining from them. Likewise, those who do not desire alcohol should not be praised for abstinence, unless the lack of desire is the result of tough self-discipline.
Which one of the following principles, if valid, most helps to justify the ethicist's claims?	**Step 1:** The phrase "following principles" signals an Identify the Principle question. The word "justify" indicates that this is also a Strengthen question.
	Step 3: The correct answer will be a broad rule that strengthens the ethicist's claims. The ethicist allows praise only in cases where self-discipline has changed one's behavior, so the correct answer will state a rule to the effect that no behavior is praiseworthy unless there was self-discipline involved.
(A) Whether behavior should be regarded as praiseworthy is a function of both its consequences and the social context in which the agent acts.	**Step 4:** Consequences and social context are both Outside the Scope. Eliminate.
(B) A person should be blamed for an action only if that action was not motivated by a desire to be virtuous or if the person did not have to overcome any obstacles in order to perform that action.	Outside the Scope. The ethicist does not discuss blameworthy actions. He gives guidelines about praiseworthy actions. Eliminate.
(C) A person is praiseworthy for a particular behavior only if, in order to adopt that behavior, the person at some point had to overcome a desire to do something that she or he felt able to afford to do.	Correct. This general rule governs what the ethicist says about abstinence from alcohol: Praise is merited only for behavior produced through self-discipline.
(D) The extent to which the process of acquiring self-discipline is arduous for a person is affected by that person's set of desires and aversions.	Outside the Scope. This choice does not impact the concept of which behaviors are praiseworthy. Eliminate.
(E) The apportionment of praise and blame should be commensurate with the arduousness or ease of the lives of those who receive praise or blame. *PrepTest49 Sec4 Q21*	The general "arduousness or ease" of someone's *life* is Outside the Scope. What is important to the ethicist is the difficulty of performing a specific *action*. Eliminate.

PARALLEL REASONING AND PARALLEL FLAW QUESTIONS

One more way in which the LSAT tests your ability to recognize argument structures is through Parallel Reasoning and Parallel Flaw questions. Parallel Reasoning questions ask you to identify two arguments—on different subjects—that use the same pattern to reach the same kind of conclusion. Parallel Flaw questions ask you to identify two different arguments that commit the same reasoning error.

You can recognize Parallel Reasoning and Parallel Flaw questions from question stems such as these:

Parallel Reasoning	**Parallel Flaw**
The pattern of reasoning in which one of the following arguments is most parallel to that in the argument above?	The pattern of flawed reasoning exhibited by the argument above is most similar to that exhibited by which one of the following?
PrepTest49 Sec4 Q17	*PrepTest51 Sec1 Q20*
The reasoning in which one of the following is most similar to the reasoning in the argument above?	Which one of the following most closely parallels the questionable reasoning cited above?
PrepTest61 Sec4 Q9	*PrepTest57 Sec2 Q8*

The phrases "most closely parallels" or "most similar to" are associated with almost all Parallel Reasoning and Parallel Flaw questions. Parallel Flaw questions are always explicit about the fact that the stimulus argument is flawed.

LEARNING OBJECTIVES

In this section, you'll learn to:

- Rule out incorrect answers in Parallel Reasoning and Parallel Flaw questions based on conclusion type
- In Parallel Reasoning questions, identify similar argument structures
- In Parallel Flaw questions, find the answer choice in which the flaw type matches the flaw type in the stimulus

---

On LSAT tests released from 2009 through 2013, there were an average of 3.5 Parallel Reasoning and Parallel Flaw questions per test.

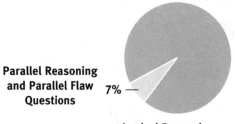

Parallel Reasoning and Parallel Flaw Questions 7%

Logical Reasoning Question Types
PrepTests 57–71, released 2009–2013

Parallel Flaw is more common than Parallel Reasoning. On LSAT tests released from 2009 through 2013, Parallel Flaw questions accounted for 56.6 percent of these questions, while Parallel Reasoning accounted for 43.3 percent.

Parallel Reasoning Questions

> ### PARALLEL REASONING AT A GLANCE
>
> **Task:** Identify the answer choice in which the argument has the same structure and reaches the same type of conclusion as the argument in the stimulus.
>
> **Strategy:** Use your knowledge of conclusion types, patterns of argument, Formal Logic, and/or principles to identify the answer containing an argument parallel to the one in the stimulus.

Parallel Reasoning questions are often very long; some have nearly as much text as a Reading Comprehension passage. Fortunately, there are a variety of tools and tactics to help you manage them efficiently and confidently.

Compare Conclusions. For two arguments to have parallel structures, they must reach the same kind of conclusion. For example, consider this conclusion:

> The company should decline the merger offer.

Here are the conclusions of two other arguments. Which one comes from an argument that could be parallel to the argument from the which the sample conclusion was drawn?

> (1) Further consolidation will lead to layoffs at the plant.
>
> (2) The patient should avoid high cholesterol foods.

Conclusion (2) is a negative recommendation, parallel to the example. Statement (1) is a prediction. Its argument could not be parallel to that from which the example came.

Compare Formal Logic. When a Parallel Reasoning argument features a clear application of Formal Logic, the best approach is often to abstract the argument into an "A, B, C" shorthand, and evaluate the answer choices by doing the same to them. Consider the following argument:

> Amanda is a strong legal writer. All strong legal writers are good analysts. So,
> Amanda must be a good analyst.

Here are two other arguments. Which is parallel to the argument in the example?

> (1) Bruno is a well-trained Labrador retriever. All well-trained Labrador retrievers are sweet tempered. So, Bruno is a good dog for a family with children.
>
> (2) Erika must have good balance. After all, excellent surfers always have good balance, and Erika is an excellent surfer.

Argument (2) has the structure "If A, then B. C is an A. Therefore, C is a B." That matches the sample argument's structure. Argument (1) introduces a new term in its conclusion. It's "If A, then B. C is an A. Therefore, C is a *D*" structure is not parallel to that in the sample argument.

TEST DAY TIP

Parallel arguments will have the same argument structure, but the pieces of the argument need NOT appear in the same order.

Compare Evidence. Evidence is not as easily categorized as are conclusions, but you can still compare features in the evidence of the stimulus argument to features of the evidence in each answer choice and eliminate answers in which the evidence is clearly not parallel. For example, imagine that you see a stimulus argument with the following evidence:

> The larger a nation's manufacturing base, the more likely it is that its middle class will have economic mobility.

Here are pieces of evidence from two arguments. Which could be parallel to the argument from which the sample evidence came?

> (1) Chicago has a larger manufacturing base than Omaha does.

> (2) Greater artistic innovation is likely to be found in areas with greater population density.

Statement (2) is a rule of proportionality, matching the evidence in the example. Statement (1), even though it touches on the same subject matter, is simply a comparison, and not parallel to the example.

Compare Principles. Rarely, a Parallel Reasoning argument illustrates an easily identifiable principle. Consider an argument like this one:

> Policy A will strengthen the economy. Policy B will not. One goal of good government is to strengthen the economy. Therefore, Congress should vote for Policy A.

Here are two other arguments. Which is parallel to that in the example?

> (1) Destination Q will be educational, but not relaxing. Destination P will be relaxing. Since the goal of a good family vacation is relaxation, the Miller family should choose Destination P.

> (2) School X offers many in-state employment opportunities. School Y does not. Susan should choose School X because, above all, she wants in-state employment opportunities.

The principle underlying the sample argument is "Government should support policies that meet the goals of good government." Statement (1)'s underlying principle is parallel: "A family should choose a vacation destination that meets the goals of a good family vacation." Statement (2), if it can be said to illustrate a principle at all, seems to follow the principle "A student should choose the school that gives her what she wants most."

TEST DAY TIP

Parallel Reasoning questions sometimes feature complete, unflawed arguments.

Before practicing on full Parallel Reasoning questions, refresh your conclusion types. You first learned the standard conclusion types in Chapter 9. Take that work a step farther here, by accounting for the strength and "charge" (positive/negative) of conclusions, as well.

Practice: Characterizing Conclusions

For each of the following, identify the conclusion type; where applicable, characterize it as positive or negative; and designate each as "strong" or "qualified."

LSAT Argument Conclusion		My Analysis
101. [M]erely establishing that nonhuman animals are intelligent will not establish that they have consciousness. *PrepTest49 Sec2 Q17*	$\longrightarrow$	Type: +/–: Strength:
102. [T]he driver of the second vehicle is not liable for the accident. *PrepTest51 Sec1 Q2*	$\longrightarrow$	Type: +/–: Strength:
103. [T]he marks are probably the traces of geological processes rather than of worms. *PrepTest61 Sec2 Q14*	$\longrightarrow$	Type: +/–: Strength:
104. [T]here is very little difference between what a typical doughnut eater and typical bagel eater each consumes at one sitting. *PrepTest59 Sec2 Q14*	$\longrightarrow$	Type: +/–: Strength:
105. [T]here are circumstances in which it is not immoral to ask for money or a favor while making a threat. *PrepTest59 Sec3 Q15*	$\longrightarrow$	Type: +/–: Strength:
106. [A]ny fruit that was inspected is safe to eat. *PrepTest49 Sec2 Q7*	$\longrightarrow$	Type: +/–: Strength:

LSAT Argument Conclusion		**My Analysis**
107. Malthus's prediction that insufficient food will doom humanity to war, pestilence, and famine will likely be proven correct in the future. *PrepTest59 Sec2 Q18*	→	Type: +/−: Strength:
108. [P]sychologists should direct efforts toward identifying nightmare-prone children so that these children can be taught the technique for replacing their nightmares with pleasant dreams. *PrepTest59 Sec2 Q13*	→	Type: +/−: Strength:
109. [T]he artist has considerably more control over the composition and subject of a still-life painting than over those a landscape painting or portrait. *PrepTest57 Sec3 Q13*	→	Type: +/−: Strength:
110. [Y]ou will not win if you are not motivated. *PrepTest57 Sec2 Q19*	→	Type: +/−: Strength:
111. [T]he EZ Corporation could boost its profits by having more staff parties during business hours. *PrepTest51 Sec1 Q25*	→	Type: +/−: Strength:
112. [75 miles per hour] should be set as a uniform national speed limit for level, straight stretches of all such roadways. *PrepTest61 Sec2 Q21*	→	Type: +/−: Strength:

Expert Analysis: Characterizing Conclusions

Here's how an LSAT expert would characterize the conclusions in the preceding exercise. Compare your characterizations to those of the LSAT expert on the pages following this exercise. Make sure you accurately determined not only the conclusion type, but also the strength and "charge" of each conclusion.

LSAT Argument Conclusion	Analysis
101. [M]erely establishing that nonhuman animals are intelligent will not establish that they have consciousness. *PrepTest49 Sec2 Q17* →	Type: Prediction +/−: Negative (will not) Strength: Strong
102. [T]he driver of the second vehicle is not liable for the accident. *PrepTest51 Sec1 Q2* →	Type: Assertion of fact +/−: Negative Strength: Strong
103. [T]he marks are probably the traces of geological processes rather than of worms. *PrepTest61 Sec2 Q14* →	Type: Assertion of fact +/−: Positive Strength: Qualified (probably)
104. [T]here is very little difference between what a typical doughnut eater and typical bagel eater each consumes at one sitting. *PrepTest59 Sec2 Q14* →	Type: Comparison +/−: Negative (no difference) Strength: Strong
105. [T]here are circumstances in which it is not immoral to ask for money or a favor while making a threat. *PrepTest59 Sec3 Q15* →	Type: Value judgment (not immoral) +/−: Positive Strength: Qualified (circumstances)
106. [A]ny fruit that was inspected is safe to eat. *PrepTest49 Sec2 Q7* →	Type: Conditional, Assertion of fact (any *x* is *y*) +/−: Positive Strength: Strong

LSAT Argument Conclusion	Analysis
107. Malthus's prediction that insufficient food will doom humanity to war, pestilence, and famine will likely be proven correct in the future. *PrepTest59 Sec2 Q18* →	Type: Prediction (will likely be) +/−: Positive Strength: Qualified (likely)
108. [P]sychologists should direct efforts toward identifying nightmare-prone children so that these children can be taught the technique for replacing their nightmares with pleasant dreams. *PrepTest59 Sec2 Q13* →	Type: Recommendation (should direct) +/−: Positive Strength: Strong
109. [T]he artist has considerably more control over the composition and subject of a still-life painting than over those a landscape painting or portrait. *PrepTest57 Sec3 Q13* →	Type: Comparison (more ... than) +/−: Positive Strength: Strong (considerably more control)
110. [Y]ou will not win if you are not motivated. *PrepTest57 Sec2 Q19* →	Type: Prediction, Conditional +/−: Negative (if not x, then not y) Strength: Strong
111. [T]he EZ Corporation could boost its profits by having more staff parties during business hours. *PrepTest51 Sec1 Q25* →	Type: Assertion of fact +/−: Positive Strength: Qualified (could boost)
112. [75 miles per hour] should be set as a uniform national speed limit for level, straight stretches of all such roadways. *PrepTest61 Sec2 Q21* →	Type: Recommendation (should be set) +/−: Positive Strength: Strong

Here's how an LSAT expert might analyze and answer a Parallel Reasoning question. Note: Italics indicate where the answer choices' arguments' structures differ from that of the stimulus argument.

LSAT Question	Analysis
Ecologists predict that the incidence of malaria will increase if global warming continues or if the use of pesticides is not expanded. But the use of pesticides is known to contribute to global warming, so it is inevitable that we will see an increase in malaria in the years to come. →	**Step 2:** Conclusion: A *strong positive prediction* ("it is inevitable") that there will be an increase in malaria incidence. *because* Evidence (if needed): If global warming continues or if pesticide use is not expanded, then malaria incidence will increase. Pesticide use contributes to global warming.
The pattern of reasoning in which one of the following is most similar to that in the argument above? →	**Step 1:** The phrase "most similar to" indicates a Parallel Reasoning question.
	Step 3: Rule out choices in which the conclusion is not a strong positive prediction that something will get worse and/or compare the overall argument structure: If A or not B, then C; but if B, then A. Therefore, C.
(A) The crime rate will increase if the economy does not improve or if we do not increase the number of police officers. But we will be able to hire more police officers if the economy does improve. Therefore, the crime rate will not increase. →	**Step 4:** Conclusion is a *negative* prediction: the crime rate *will not* go up. Structure: If *not* A or not B, then C; but if *A*, then *D*. Therefore, *not* C. Eliminate.
(B) If educational funds remain at their current level or if we fail to recruit qualified teachers, student performance will worsen. But we will fail to recruit qualified teachers. Therefore, student performance will worsen. →	Conclusion is parallel, a strong positive prediction that student performance will get worse. Structure: If A or not B, then C; but *not B will happen*. Therefore, C. The second part of the evidence does not match. Eliminate.
(C) If interest rates increase or demand for consumer goods does not decline, inflation will rise. But if there is a decline in the demand for consumer goods that will lead to higher interest rates. Therefore, inflation will rise. →	Correct. Conclusion is a strong prediction that inflation will get worse. Structure: If A or not B, then C; but if B, then A. Therefore, C.
(D) If global warming continues or if the rate of ozone depletion is not reduced, there will be an increase in the incidence of skin cancer. But reduced use of aerosols ensures both that global warming will not continue and that ozone depletion will be reduced. Thus, the incidence of skin cancer will not increase. →	Conclusion is a *negative* prediction: Skin cancer *will not* get worse. Structure: If A or not B, then C; but if B, then *not A and not D*. Therefore, *not* C. Eliminate.

LSAT Question (cont.)	→	Analysis (cont.)

(E)   If deforestation continues at the current rate and the use of chemicals is not curtailed, wildlife species will continue to become extinct. But because of increasing population worldwide, it is inevitable that the current rate of deforestation will continue and that the use of chemicals will not be curtailed. Thus, wildlife species will continue to become extinct.

PrepTest51 Sec3 Q24

→   Conclusion is a prediction that extinction will continue, not that it will get worse. Structure: If A *and* not B, then C; but *A and not B will happen.* Therefore, C. Eliminate.

Parallel Reasoning Question Practice

Now, practice some Parallel Reasoning questions. Use any of the tools and tactics discussed earlier in this section. When you're finished, compare your work to that of an LSAT expert.

LSAT Question	My Analysis
113. Team captain: Winning requires the willingness to cooperate, which in turn requires motivation. So you will not win if you are not motivated. $\longrightarrow$	**Step 2:**
The pattern of reasoning in which one of the following is most similar to that in the argument above? $\longrightarrow$	**Step 1:**
	Step 3:
(A) Being healthy requires exercise. But exercising involves risk of injury. So, paradoxically, anyone who wants to be healthy will not exercise. $\longrightarrow$	**Step 4:**
(B) Learning requires making some mistakes. And you must learn if you are to improve. So you will not make mistakes without there being a noticeable improvement. $\longrightarrow$	
(C) Our political party will retain its status only if it raises more money. But raising more money requires increased campaigning. So our party will not retain its status unless it increases its campaigning. $\longrightarrow$	
(D) You can repair your own bicycle only if you are enthusiastic. And if you are enthusiastic, you will also have mechanical aptitude. So if you are not able to repair your own bicycle, you lack mechanical aptitude. $\longrightarrow$	
(E) Getting a ticket requires waiting in line. Waiting in line requires patience. So if you do not wait in line, you lack patience. $\longrightarrow$	

PrepTest57 Sec2 Q19

LSAT Question	My Analysis
114. Judicial punishment's power to deter people from committing crimes is a function of the severity of the penalty and the likelihood of one's actually receiving the penalty. Occasionally, juries decide that a crime's penalty is too severe and so refuse to convict a person they are convinced has committed that crime. Thus, increasing the penalty may decrease the deterrent power of judicial punishment.	**Step 2:**
The pattern of reasoning in which one of the following arguments is most similar to the pattern of reasoning in the argument above?	**Step 1:**
	Step 3:
(A) Success in attaining one's first academic job depends on the quality of one's dissertation and the amount of time spent working on it in graduate school. But sometimes, so much time is spent on a dissertation that it becomes too lengthy to be coherent and its quality suffers. So spending more time working on a dissertation can lead to less success in attaining a first academic job.	**Step 4:**
(B) People who drive cars having many safety features are likely to drive more aggressively than do people who drive cars having few safety features. Thus, the people who drive the safest cars are likely to be the most dangerous drivers on the road.	
(C) A new surgical technique is developed to treat a dangerous condition. This technique enables people to live longer than does an older form of surgery. But the new surgery's mortality rate is also slightly higher. Thus, if more people choose to undergo the new surgery, more people may die from the dangerous condition than previously.	
(D) To be attractive to tourists, it is best for a city to have both wide appeal and sufficient hotel space. Though a sufficient number of hotel rooms alone cannot attract tourists, it is much harder for city governments to affect the appeal of their city than for them to affect its amount of hotel space. Thus, governments of cities that want to increase their attractiveness to tourists should put their energies into increasing their hotel space.	
(E) Many young, talented artists, because they are unknown, decide to charge low prices for their work. As their reputations grow, the prices they can charge for their work increase. Thus, raising the price of an artist's work can improve that artist's reputation.	

PrepTest49 Sec2 Q24

LSAT Question	My Analysis
115. From the fact that people who studied music as children frequently are quite proficient at mathematics, it cannot be concluded that the skills required for mathematics are acquired by studying music: it is equally likely that proficiency in mathematics and studying music are both the result of growing up in a family that encourages its children to excel at all intellectual and artistic endeavors. →	**Step 2:**
The pattern of reasoning in which one of the following arguments is most parallel to that in the argument above? →	**Step 1:**
	Step 3:

(A)	Although children who fail to pay attention tend to perform poorly in school, it should not necessarily be thought that their poor performance is caused by their failure to pay attention, for it is always possible that their failure to pay attention is due to undiagnosed hearing problems that can also lead to poor performance in school. →	**Step 4:**
(B)	People who attend a university in a foreign country are usually among the top students from their native country. It would therefore be wrong to conclude from the fact that many foreign students perform better academically than others in this country that secondary schools in other countries are superior to those in this country; it may be that evaluation standards are different. →	
(C)	People whose diet includes relatively large quantities of certain fruits and vegetables have a slightly lower than average incidence of heart disease. But it would be premature to conclude that consuming these fruits and vegetables prevents heart disease, for this correlation may be merely coincidental. →	
(D)	Those who apply to medical school are required to study biology and chemistry. It would be a mistake, however, to conclude that those who have mastered chemistry and biology will succeed as physicians, for the practical application of knowledge is different from its acquisition. →	
(E)	Those who engage in vigorous exercise tend to be very healthy. But it would be silly to conclude that vigorous exercise is healthful simply because people who are healthy exercise vigorously, since it is possible that exercise that is less vigorous also has beneficial results. →	

PrepTest49 Sec4 Q17

LSAT Question	My Analysis
116. Landscape architect: If the screen between these two areas is to be a hedge, that hedge must be of either hemlocks or Leyland cypress trees. However, Leyland cypress trees cannot be grown this far north. So if the screen is to be a hedge, it will be a hemlock hedge.	**Step 2:**
In which one of the following is the pattern of reasoning most similar to that in the landscape architect's argument?	**Step 1:**
	Step 3:
(A) If there is to be an entrance on the north side of the building, it will have to be approached by a ramp. However, a ramp would become impossibly slippery in winter, so there will be no entrance on the north side.	**Step 4:**
(B) If visitors are to travel to this part of the site by automobile, there will be a need for parking spaces. However, no parking spaces are allowed for in the design. So if visitors are likely to come by automobile, the design will be changed.	
(C) The subsoil in these five acres either consists entirely of clay or consists entirely of shale. Therefore, if one test hole in the area reveals shale, it will be clear that the entire five acres has a shale subsoil.	
(D) Any path along this embankment must be either concrete or stone. But a concrete path cannot be built in this location. So if there is to be a path on the embankment, it will be a stone path.	
(E) A space the size of this meadow would be suitable for a playground or a picnic area. However, a playground would be noisy and a picnic area would create litter. So it will be best for the area to remain a meadow.	

PrepTest51 Sec1 Q5

Expert Analysis: Parallel Reasoning Questions

Compare your work to that of an LSAT expert. Which tools did you use to evaluate the answer choices? Where did the expert use a different tool?

LSAT Question	Analysis
113. Team captain: Winning requires the willingness to cooperate, which in turn requires motivation. So you will not win if you are not motivated.	**Step 2:** Conclusion is conditional (*If/Then*): If you are not motivated, then you won't win.
	because
	Evidence (if needed): If you win, then you cooperated; and if you cooperated, then you had motivation.
The pattern of reasoning in which one of the following is most similar to that in the argument above?	**Step 1:** The phrase "most similar to" indicates a Parallel Reasoning question.
	Step 3: A scan of the choices reveals that all have conditional conclusions, so compare the Formal Logic structures: If A (win), then B (cooperate); if B, then C (motivation). Therefore, if no C, then no A.
(A) Being healthy requires exercise. But exercising involves risk of injury. So, paradoxically, anyone who wants to be healthy will not exercise.	**Step 4:** Structure: If A (healthy), then B (exercise); but if B, then *risk of C* (injury). Therefore, if *want* A, then *not B*. Eliminate.
(B) Learning requires making some mistakes. And you must learn if you are to improve. So you will not make mistakes without there being a noticeable improvement.	Structure: If A (improve), then B (learn). If B, then C (make mistakes). Therefore, *if not A, then not C*. Eliminate.
(C) Our political party will retain its status only if it raises more money. But raising more money requires increased campaigning. So our party will not retain its status unless it increases its campaigning.	Correct. The structure is identical to that in the stimulus: if A (retain status), then B (raise more money); if B, then C (more campaigning); therefore, if not C, then not A.
(D) You can repair your own bicycle only if you are enthusiastic. And if you are enthusiastic, you will also have mechanical aptitude. So if you are not able to repair your own bicycle, you lack mechanical aptitude.	Structure: If A (repair bike), then B (enthusiastic); if B, then C (mechanical aptitude). Therefore, *if not A, then not C*. Eliminate.
(E) Getting a ticket requires waiting in line. Waiting in line requires patience. So if you do not wait in line, you lack patience. *PrepTest57 Sec2 Q19*	Structure: If A (get ticket), then B (wait in line); if B, then C (patience). Therefore, *If not B, then not C*. Eliminate.

LSAT Question	Analysis
114. Judicial punishment's power to deter people from committing crimes is a function of the severity of the penalty and the likelihood of one's actually receiving the penalty. Occasionally, juries decide that a crime's penalty is too severe and so refuse to convict a person they are convinced has committed that crime. Thus, increasing the penalty may decrease the deterrent power of judicial punishment.	**Step 2:** Conclusion—*A weak assertion* that an increase in one thing (the severity of a penalty) may cause a decrease in another (deterrence). *because* Evidence—*Two requirements* (deterrence needs severity of penalty and chance of receiving penalty) *subject to a dilemma* (if severity of penalty increases, chance of receiving penalty may decrease).
The pattern of reasoning in which one of the following arguments is most similar to the pattern of reasoning in the argument above?	**Step 1:** "Most similar to" indicates a Parallel Reasoning question.
	Step 3: Start by ruling out choices in which the conclusion is not a weak assertion that an increase in one thing may cause a decrease in something else; if necessary, compare the evidence.
(A) Success in attaining one's first academic job depends on the quality of one's dissertation and the amount of time spent working on it in graduate school. But sometimes, so much time is spent on a dissertation that it becomes too lengthy to be coherent and its quality suffers. So spending more time working on a dissertation can lead to less success in attaining a first academic job.	**Step 4:** Correct. Conclusion is a weak assertion that increasing time spent on dissertation may lower chances of success. (No other choice has a matching conclusion!) Evidence is two requirements subject to a dilemma.
(B) People who drive cars having many safety features are likely to drive more aggressively than do people who drive cars having few safety features. Thus, the people who drive the safest cars are likely to be the most dangerous drivers on the road.	Conclusion is a weak assertion, but the superlatives "safest" and "most dangerous" make it different from the stimulus. The evidence presents neither requirements nor a dilemma. Eliminate.

LSAT Question (cont.)	Analysis (cont.)
(C) A new surgical technique is developed to treat a dangerous condition. This technique enables people to live longer than does an older form of surgery. But the new surgery's mortality rate is also slightly higher. Thus, if more people choose to undergo the new surgery, more people may die from the dangerous condition than previously.	Conclusion is a conditional If/Then statement. The evidence presents a dilemma, but not one between two requirements. Eliminate.
(D) To be attractive to tourists, it is best for a city to have both wide appeal and sufficient hotel space. Though a sufficient number of hotel rooms alone cannot attract tourists, it is much harder for city governments to affect the appeal of their city than for them to affect its amount of hotel space. Thus, governments of cities that want to increase their attractiveness to tourists should put their energies into increasing their hotel space.	Conclusion is a recommendation, a piece of advice to city governments that want to increase their attractiveness to tourists. The evidence presents a comparison, not a dilemma. Eliminate.
(E) Many young, talented artists, because they are unknown, decide to charge low prices for their work. As their reputations grow, the prices they can charge for their work increase. Thus, raising the price of an artist's work can improve that artist's reputation. *PrepTest49 Sec2 Q24*	Conclusion is a weak assertion that an increase in one thing (price) can lead to an *increase,* not a decrease, in something else (reputation). The conclusion presents neither requirements nor a dilemma. Eliminate.

LSAT Question	Analysis
115. From the fact that people who studied music as children frequently are quite proficient at mathematics, it cannot be concluded that the skills required for mathematics are acquired by studying music: it is equally likely that proficiency in mathematics and studying mus ic are both the result of growing up in a family that encourages its children to excel at all intellectual and artistic endeavors. →	**Step 2:** Conclusion—A *strong negative assertion* that correlation does not prove causation—specifically, math skills are not necessarily acquired by studying music. *because* Evidence (if needed)—Proficiency in math and music may both be the result of growing up in a certain type of family.
The pattern of reasoning in which one of the following arguments is most parallel to that in the argument above? →	**Step 1:** The phrase "most parallel to" identifies this as a Parallel Reasoning question.
	Step 3: The argument's structure is easily summarized: A (musical ability) and B (math skills) are correlated, but both A and B may be the result of C (family encouragement). Therefore, A cannot be said to cause B. Compare the argument structures in the answer choices.
(A) Although children who fail to pay attention tend to perform poorly in school, it should not necessarily be thought that their poor performance is caused by their failure to pay attention, for it is always possible that their failure to pay attention is due to undiagnosed hearing problems that can also lead to poor performance in school. →	**Step 4:** Correct. This argument has a structure identical to that in the stimulus. A (poor attention) and B (poor performance) are correlated, but A and B may be the result of C (hearing problems). Therefore, A cannot be said to cause B.
(B) People who attend a university in a foreign country are usually among the top students from their native country. It would therefore be wrong to conclude from the fact that many foreign students perform better academically than others in this country that secondary schools in other countries are superior to those in this country; it may be that evaluation standards are different. →	This argument includes too many terms. A (attend foreign university) and B (top scholar in home country) are correlated, but C (foreign evaluation standards may be different). Therefore, *D* (the fact that foreign students outperform some domestic students) *does not imply* E (superiority of foreign high schools). Eliminate.
(C) People whose diet includes relatively large quantities of certain fruits and vegetables have a slightly lower than average incidence of heart disease. But it would be premature to conclude that consuming these fruits and vegetables prevents heart disease, for this correlation may be merely coincidental. →	This argument is parallel but for one problem: instead of introducing a possible third factor, it says the correlation may be mere coincidence. Eliminate.
(D) Those who apply to medical school are required to study biology and chemistry. It would be a mistake, however, to conclude that those who have mastered chemistry and biology will succeed as physicians, for the practical application of knowledge is different from its acquisition. →	This argument does not attempt to refute a correlation versus causation argument. Rather, it says that the fact that A (apply to med school) requires B (study chem and bio) does not mean that B is sufficient for C (being a doctor). Eliminate.

LSAT Question (cont.)	Analysis (cont.)
(E) Those who engage in vigorous exercise tend to be very healthy. But it would be silly to conclude that vigorous exercise is healthful simply because people who are healthy exercise vigorously, since it is possible that exercise that is less vigorous also has beneficial results. *PrepTest49 Sec4 Q17*	$\longrightarrow$ The conclusion is a strong assertion that correlation does not prove causation. But the evidence is all wrong: instead of proposing a third factor that might cause both A (vigorous exercise) and B (health), the author states that another type of A (less vigorous exercise) might be generally beneficial. Eliminate.

LSAT Question	Analysis
116. Landscape architect: If the screen between these two areas is to be a hedge, that hedge must be of either hemlocks or Leyland cypress trees. However, Leyland cypress trees cannot be grown this far north. So if the screen is to be a hedge, it will be a hemlock hedge.	**Step 2:** Conclusion—A *strong conditional prediction*—if A (the screen is a hedge), then it must be B (hemlock). *because* Evidence (if needed)—If A (the screen is a hedge), then it must be B (hemlock) or C (cypress), but C is impossible (cypress doesn't grow this far north).
In which one of the following is the pattern of reasoning most similar to that in the landscape architect's argument?	**Step 1:** The phrase "most similar to" identifies this as a Parallel Reasoning question.
	Step 3: Compare conclusions and/or overall structures of the answer choices with those in the stimulus.
(A) If there is to be an entrance on the north side of the building, it will have to be approached by a ramp. However, a ramp would become impossibly slippery in winter, so there will be no entrance on the north side.	**Step 4:** Conclusion is a strong negative prediction ("there will be no entrance … "), but is not conditional. Eliminate.
(B) If visitors are to travel to this part of the site by automobile, there will be a need for parking spaces. However, no parking spaces are allowed for in the design. So if visitors are likely to come by automobile, the design will be changed.	Conclusion is a conditional prediction, but it introduces a qualifier in the sufficient condition: "likely" is not parallel to the stimulus. Moreover, the evidence does not match the "B or C, but C is impossible" structure of the stimulus. Eliminate.
(C) The subsoil in these five acres either consists entirely of clay or consists entirely of shale. Therefore, if one test hole in the area reveals shale, it will be clear that the entire five acres has a shale subsoil.	Conclusion lacks the structure "If there will be X then it will be a special kind of X." Moreover, the evidence does not match the "B or C, but C is impossible" structure of the stimulus. Eliminate.
(D) Any path along this embankment must be either concrete or stone. But a concrete path cannot be built in this location. So if there is to be a path on the embankment, it will be a stone path.	Correct. Only this choice has a conclusion that is parallel to the one in the stimulus: "If there's a path then it will be a special kind of path." The evidence also matches the "B or C, but C is impossible" structure of the stimulus.
(E) A space the size of this meadow would be suitable for a playground or a picnic area. However, a playground would be noisy and a picnic area would create litter. So it will be best for the area to remain a meadow. *PrepTest51 Sec1 Q5*	Conclusion is a recommendation: "it will be best … " Moreover, the evidence does not match the "B or C, but C is impossible" structure of the stimulus. Eliminate.

Parallel Flaw Questions

Compared to Parallel Reasoning questions, the strategy for Parallel Flaw questions is relatively straightforward. That's because you already know from the question stem that the argument will be flawed. When attacking Parallel Flaw questions, use one of these approaches.

Compare Flaws. After all of the work you did earlier in the section on Flaw questions, this tactic should feel familiar. Analyze the argument in the stimulus and describe the error in reasoning. Evaluate the answer choices by looking for the only one that contains exactly the same flaw. Consider this argument:

> A certain species of otter lives only in the vicinity of Midland Bay, which is also the only place a particular species of mussel grows. It must be the case that the otter of this specific species eats the mussels of this specific species.

Here are two other arguments. Which one is parallel to that in the example?

> (1) If two species are found exclusively in proximity to one another, then they must be part of an interconnected ecosystem. A certain bird and a certain snake are part of an interconnected wetlands ecosystem; therefore, the bird and the snake must be found exclusively in proximity to one another.

> (2) We can conclude that a certain species of snail consumes a certain species of mushroom from the fact that this species of mushroom grows exclusively in the shade of oak trees which are the exclusive home of the snail.

Argument (2) is an Overlooked Possibilities argument in which the author has failed to consider other reasons that the snail and the mushroom may be found together with the oak trees. That is parallel to the example argument. Argument (1) confuses sufficiency for necessity. That's a different flaw, and therefore, a wrong answer.

TEST DAY TIP

A Parallel Flaw argument may commit more than one reasoning error. If that's the case, then the argument in the correct answer will commit all of the same flaws.

Compare Conclusions. This is the same technique used in Parallel Reasoning questions. Keep in mind that qualifying or softening a conclusion often makes an Overlooked Possibilities argument's reasoning sound. That is, softening the conclusion removes the flaw.

Compare Formal Logic. Just as in Parallel Reasoning, when a Parallel Flaw argument is easily diagrammed in Formal Logic shorthand, comparing the argument structures can be even more efficient than describing the conclusion. Consider this argument:

> Whenever Craig goes shopping, Anne goes shopping too. Craig isn't shopping today, so Anne must not be shopping either.

Here are two more arguments. Which one is flawed in exactly the same way as the one in the example?

(1) The zookeeper must not be feeding the penguins. This is obvious from the fact that he is not feeding the seals. Whenever the zookeeper feeds the seals, he also feeds the penguins.

(2) Joan is not taking calculus this semester. Joan will take only classes also taken by Barbara, and Barbara is not taking calculus this semester.

The original argument confuses sufficiency for necessity: If C, then A; not C; therefore, not A. Although written differently, argument (1) is parallel: If S, then P; not S. Therefore, not P. Argument (2) is not flawed, and so cannot be parallel to the example argument.

TEST DAY TIP

If an answer choice contains an argument with sound reasoning, it cannot be the correct answer to a Parallel Flaw question.

PARALLEL FLAW AT A GLANCE

Task: Identify the answer choice in which the argument makes the same error(s) in reasoning that the argument in the stimulus commits.

Strategy: Analyze the argument in the stimulus and identify the author's reasoning error(s). Evaluate the answer choices to find the one containing an argument in which the author commits the same error(s) as did the author of the stimulus.

Here's how an LSAT expert might analyze and answer a Parallel Flaw question.

LSAT Question	Analysis
Most of the employees of the Compujack Corporation are computer programmers. Since most computer programmers receive excellent salaries from their employers, at least one Compujack employee must receive an excellent salary from Compujack.	**Step 2:** Conclusion—A *strong assertion of fact* that at least one CJ employee must receive an excellent salary. *because* Evidence—(1) Most CJ employees are computer programmers, and (2) most computer programmers receive excellent salaries.
Which one of the following arguments exhibits a flawed pattern of reasoning most similar to the flawed pattern of reasoning exhibited by the argument above?	**Step 1:** The words "most similar to" and "flawed" identify this question as a Parallel Flaw question.
	Step 3: The stimulus wrongly assumes that at least one excellently salaried computer programmer works for CJ. Argument is structured like this: Most A are B; most B are C. Thus, at least one A is C.
(A) Most gardeners are people with a great deal of patience. Since most of Molly's classmates are gardeners, at least one of Molly's classmates must be a person with a great deal of patience.	**Step 4:** Correct. This choice has a structure identical to the one in the stimulus: most A (classmates) are B (gardeners); most B are C (patient). Thus, at least one A is C.
(B) Most of Molly's classmates are gardeners. Since most gardeners are people with a great deal of patience, some of Molly's classmates could be people with a great deal of patience.	Conclusion is qualified ("could be") in a way that removes any flaws. Most A are B; most B are C. Thus, *some* A *could be* C. Eliminate.
(C) Most gardeners are people with a great deal of patience. Since most of Molly's classmates are gardeners, at least one of Molly's classmates who is a gardener must be a person with a great deal of patience.	The conclusion does not match: Most A (classmates) are B (gardeners); most B are C (patient). Thus, at least one A is *B and C*. Eliminate.
(D) Most gardeners are people with a great deal of patience. Since most of Molly's classmates who garden are women, at least one female classmate of Molly's must be a person with a great deal of patience.	This choice introduces an additional term: women/female. Diagram the structure here and you need a D term. Eliminate.
(E) Most of Molly's classmates are gardeners with a great deal of patience. Since most of Molly's classmates are women, at least one female classmate of Molly's must be a gardener with a great deal of patience.	Most A (classmates) are B (patient gardeners); most A are C (female). [*That piece of evidence doesn't match.*] Thus, at least one C and A is B. [*Conclusion doesn't match, either.*] Eliminate.

PrepTest49 Sec4 Q24

Parallel Flaw Question Practice

Practice some Parallel Flaw questions. In each, analyze the argument in the stimulus to determine if you want to evaluate the choices by comparing flaws, comparing structures, or a combination of the two.

LSAT Question	My Analysis
117. A psychiatrist argued that there is no such thing as a multiple personality disorder on the grounds that in all her years of clinical practice, she had never encountered one case of this type. →	**Step 2:** Conclusion— *because* Evidence—
Which one of the following most closely parallels the questionable reasoning cited above? →	**Step 1:**
	Step 3:
(A) Anton concluded that colds are seldom fatal on the grounds that in all his years of clinical practice, he never had a patient who died of a cold. →	**Step 4:**
(B) Lyla said that no one in the area has seen a groundhog and so there are probably no groundhogs in the area. →	
(C) Sauda argued that because therapy rarely had an effect on her patient's type of disorder, therapy was not warranted. →	
(D) Thomas argued that because Natasha has driven her car to work every day since she bought it, she would probably continue to drive her car to work. →	
(E) Jerod had never spotted a deer in his area and concluded from this that there are no deer in the area. *PrepTest57 Sec2 Q8* →	

LSAT Question	My Analysis
118. There are circumstances in which it is not immoral to make certain threats, and there are circumstances in which it is not immoral to ask for money or some other favor. Therefore, there are circumstances in which it is not immoral to ask for money or a favor while making a threat.	**Step 2:** Conclusion— *because* Evidence—
Which one of the following exhibits a flawed pattern of reasoning most similar to that in the argument above?	**Step 1:**
	Step 3:
(A) There are many business events for which casual dress is appropriate, and there are many social events for which casual dress is appropriate; therefore, if an occasion is neither a business event nor a social event, casual dress is not likely to be appropriate.	**Step 4:**
(B) It is usually easy to move a piano after you have convinced five people to help you, provided that you do not need to take it up or down stairs. Therefore, it is usually easy to move a piano.	
(C) It is healthful to take drug A for a headache, and it is healthful to take drug B for a headache; therefore, it is healthful to take drug A together with drug B for a headache.	
(D) Heavy trucks are generally operated in a safe manner, but the ability to drive a truck safely can be impaired by certain prescription drugs. Therefore, heavy trucks cannot be operated safely while the driver is under the effect of a prescription drug.	
(E) The mountain roads are treacherous after it rains, and the mountain streams are full after a rain. So, if the roads in the mountains are treacherous, and the mountain streams are full, it surely has rained recently.	

PrepTest59 Sec3 Q15

LSAT Question	My Analysis
119. Only experienced salespeople will be able to meet the company's selling quota. Thus, I must not count as an experienced salesperson, since I will be able to sell only half the quota. $\longrightarrow$	**Step 2:** Conclusion— *because* Evidence—
The pattern of flawed reasoning exhibited by the argument above is most similar to that exhibited by which one of the following? $\longrightarrow$	**Step 1:**
	Step 3:
(A) Only on Fridays are employees allowed to dress casually. Today is Friday but Hector is dressed formally. So he must not be going to work. $\longrightarrow$	**Step 4:**
(B) Only music lovers take this class. Thus, since Hillary is not taking this class, she apparently does not love music. $\longrightarrow$	
(C) Only oceanographers enjoy the Atlantic in midwinter. Thus, we may expect that Gerald does not enjoy the Atlantic in midwinter, since he is not an oceanographer. $\longrightarrow$	
(D) As this tree before us is a giant redwood, it follows that we must be in a northern latitude, since it is only in northern latitudes that one finds giant redwoods. $\longrightarrow$	
(E) Only accomplished mountain climbers can scale El Capitan. Thus, Michelle must be able to scale El Capitan, since she is an accomplished mountain climber. $\longrightarrow$	

PrepTest51 Sec1 Q20

LSAT Question	My Analysis
120. Food that is very high in fat tends to be unhealthy. These brownies are fat-free, while those cookies contain a high percentage of fat. Therefore, these fat-free brownies are healthier than those cookies are. →	**Step 2:** Conclusion— *because* Evidence—
Which one of the following exhibits flawed reasoning most similar to the flawed reasoning exhibited by the argument above? →	**Step 1:**
	Step 3:
(A) Canned foods always contain more salt than frozen foods do. Therefore, these canned peas contain more salt than those frozen peas do. →	**Step 4:**
(B) Vegetables that are overcooked generally have few vitamins. Therefore, these carrots, which are overcooked, contain fewer vitamins than those peas, which are uncooked. →	
(C) The human body needs certain amounts of many minerals to remain healthy. Therefore, this distilled water, which has no minerals, is unhealthy. →	
(D) Some types of nuts make Roy's throat itch. These cookies contain a greater percentage of nuts than that pie contains. Therefore, these cookies are more likely to make Roy's throat itch. →	
(E) Eating at a restaurant costs more than eating food prepared at home. Therefore, this home-cooked meal is less expensive than a restaurant meal of the same dishes would be. →	

PrepTest51 Sec3 Q22

Expert Analysis: Parallel Flaw Questions

Compare your work to that of an LSAT expert. Where did your approaches align? Were you as efficient and confident in eliminating wrong answers as you could have been?

LSAT Question	Analysis
117. A psychiatrist argued that there is no such thing as a multiple personality disorder on the grounds that in all her years of clinical practice, she had never encountered one case of this type.	**Step 2:** Conclusion—The psychiatrist concludes that there is no such thing as a multiple personality disorder. This is a *strong assertion of fact.* *because* Evidence—The psychiatrist has never seen a case of multiple personality disorder.
Which one of the following most closely parallels the questionable reasoning cited above?	**Step 1:** The words "parallels" and "questionable" signal a Parallel Flaw question.
	Step 3: The flaw boils down to "I've never seen it, so it doesn't exist."
(A) Anton concluded that colds are seldom fatal on the grounds that in all his years of clinical practice, he never had a patient who died of a cold.	**Step 4:** Conclusion is not parallel: "seldom fatal" is qualified. Eliminate.
(B) Lyla said that no one in the area has seen a groundhog and so there are probably no groundhogs in the area.	Conclusion is qualified ("probably"). Eliminate.
(C) Sauda argued that because therapy rarely had an effect on her patient's type of disorder, therapy was not warranted.	Conclusion is a recommendation: therapy is "not warranted," that is, it should not be done. Eliminate.
(D) Thomas argued that because Natasha has driven her car to work every day since she bought it, she would probably continue to drive her car to work.	Conclusion is a weak prediction that Natasha will "probably" continue to drive her car to work. Eliminate.
(E) Jerod had never spotted a deer in his area and concluded from this that there are no deer in the area. *PrepTest57 Sec2 Q8*	Correct. This is the only choice with a conclusion that is a strong assertion ("there are no deer in this area"). The flaw is the same: Jerod hasn't seen a deer in the area, so deer must not exist there.

LSAT Question	Analysis
118. There are circumstances in which it is not immoral to make certain threats, and there are circumstances in which it is not immoral to ask for money or some other favor. Therefore, there are circumstances in which it is not immoral to ask for money or a favor while making a threat.	**Step 2:** Conclusion—A *strong assertion* that it is not immoral to ask for money or a favor while making a threat. *because* Evidence—There are circumstances in which it is not immoral to make a threat, and there are circumstances in which it is not immoral to ask for money or a favor.
Which one of the following exhibits a flawed pattern of reasoning most similar to that in the argument above?	**Step 1:** The phrase "most similar to" indicates a Parallel Reasoning question. The word "flawed" identifies this question more specifically as a Parallel Flaw question.
	Step 3: The flawed assumption is that if two things are each okay to do independently, it is okay to do them in combination. The correct answer will contain this same faulty assumption.
(A) There are many business events for which casual dress is appropriate, and there are many social events for which casual dress is appropriate; therefore, if an occasion is neither a business event nor a social event, casual dress is not likely to be appropriate.	**Step 4:** Conclusion is phrased as a conditional statement. Eliminate.
(B) It is usually easy to move a piano after you have convinced five people to help you, provided that you do not need to take it up or down stairs. Therefore, it is usually easy to move a piano.	Conclusion contains the qualifier "usually." Eliminate.
(C) It is healthful to take drug A for a headache, and it is healthful to take drug B for a headache; therefore, it is healthful to take drug A together with drug B for a headache.	Correct. This argument contains the same flawed assumption as the argument in the stimulus: if two things are okay individually, then combining them must also be okay.
(D) Heavy trucks are generally operated in a safe manner, but the ability to drive a truck safely can be impaired by certain prescription drugs. Therefore, heavy trucks cannot be operated safely while the driver is under the effect of a prescription drug.	Conclusion states that combining two things (operating a truck and taking prescription medication) is *not* a good idea. Eliminate.
(E) The mountain roads are treacherous after it rains, and the mountain streams are full after a rain. So, if the roads in the mountains are treacherous, and the mountain streams are full, it surely has rained recently. *PrepTest59 Sec3 Q15*	Conclusion is phrased as a conditional statement. Eliminate.

LSAT Question	Analysis
119. Only experienced salespeople will be able to meet the company's selling quota. Thus, I must not count as an experienced salesperson, since I will be able to sell only half the quota.	**Step 2:** Conclusion—*Strong assertion* that I must not be an experienced salesperson. *because* Evidence—I will only be able to sell half the quota, and only experienced salespeople will be able to meet the quota.
The pattern of flawed reasoning exhibited by the argument above is most similar to that exhibited by which one of the following?	**Step 1:** The words "flawed" and "most similar to" indicate a Parallel Flaw question.
	Step 3: The author confuses necessity for sufficiency. The fact that only experienced salespeople can meet the quota does not imply that all experienced salespeople can do so. Nevertheless, in concluding that he does not count as an experienced salesperson, the author assumes that all experienced salespeople can meet the quota.
(A) Only on Fridays are employees allowed to dress casually. Today is Friday but Hector is dressed formally. So he must not be going to work.	**Step 4:** Assumes that Hector would be dressing casually for work at any time he was permitted to do so. This is not the same necessity-sufficiency error in the stimulus. Eliminate.
(B) Only music lovers take this class. Thus, since Hillary is not taking this class, she apparently does not love music.	Correct. This argument assumes that all music lovers will take the class Hillary has chosen to skip.
(C) Only oceanographers enjoy the Atlantic in midwinter. Thus, we may expect that Gerald does not enjoy the Atlantic in midwinter, since he is not an oceanographer.	This argument contains no flaw, just a properly formed contrapositive. Eliminate.
(D) As this tree before us is a giant redwood, it follows that we must be in a northern latitude, since it is only in northern latitudes that one finds giant redwoods.	This argument contains no flaw, just properly analyzed Formal Logic. Eliminate.
(E) Only accomplished mountain climbers can scale El Capitan. Thus, Michelle must be able to scale El Capitan, since she is an accomplished mountain climber. *PrepTest51 Sec1 Q20*	Assumes that all accomplished mountain climbers can scale El Capitan, but unlike the stimulus, this choice concludes that Michelle must be able to do something based on the group she is a member of, rather than concluding that she is *not* a member of that group based on evidence of something that she *cannot* do. Eliminate.

LSAT Question	Analysis
120. Food that is very high in fat tends to be unhealthy. These brownies are fat-free, while those cookies contain a high percentage of fat. Therefore, these fat-free brownies are healthier than those cookies are.	**Step 2:** Conclusion—These fat-free brownies are healthier than those cookies. This is a *strong comparison*. *because* Evidence—Food high in fat tends to be unhealthy. These brownies are fat-free; those cookies are high in fat.
Which one of the following exhibits flawed reasoning most similar to the flawed reasoning exhibited by the argument above?	**Step 1:** The phrases "most similar to" and "flawed reasoning" signal a Parallel Flaw question.
	Step 3: The author overlooks the possibility that there might be some other factor that might make the brownies less healthy overall than the cookies, despite their respective fat contents.
(A) Canned foods always contain more salt than frozen foods do. Therefore, these canned peas contain more salt than those frozen peas do.	**Step 4:** The problem with this argument is that we don't know the relative quantities of the two foods. If the quantities of canned and frozen peas are the same, there is no flaw. But there's no way to establish this. Eliminate.
(B) Vegetables that are overcooked generally have few vitamins. Therefore, these carrots, which are overcooked, contain fewer vitamins than those peas, which are uncooked.	Correct. This argument overlooks the possibility that the overcooked carrots actually have more vitamins than the uncooked peas for some reason that has nothing to do with cooking (such as freshness or growing conditions).
(C) The human body needs certain amounts of many minerals to remain healthy. Therefore, this distilled water, which has no minerals, is unhealthy.	Conclusion is not a comparison. Eliminate.
(D) Some types of nuts make Roy's throat itch. These cookies contain a greater percentage of nuts than that pie contains. Therefore, these cookies are more likely to make Roy's throat itch.	This choice distinguishes between different types of nuts, only "some" of which make Roy's throat itch. The stimulus does not distinguish different types of fat, only *some* of which are unhealthy. The evidence here is not parallel to that in the stimulus. Eliminate.
(E) Eating at a restaurant costs more than eating food prepared at home. Therefore, this home-cooked meal is less expensive than a restaurant meal of the same dishes would be. *PrepTest51 Sec3 Q22*	There is no flaw in this argument. Eliminate.

IDENTIFY AND APPLY THE PRINCIPLE QUESTIONS

Identify and Apply the Principle questions (also called Parallel Principle questions) ask you to identify the principle underlying the argument in the stimulus, and then, find the answer in which the argument has a similar principle underlying it. Much like Parallel Reasoning, the answer choices are likely to contain subject matter different than that in the stimulus argument.

You can identify Identify and Apply the Principle questions from question stems such as these:

Of the following, which one illustrates a principle that is most similar to the principle illustrated by the passage?

PrepTest61 Sec2 Q2

Which one of the following most closely conforms to the principle to which the reasoning in the passage conforms?

PrepTest59 Sec3 Q6

IDENTIFY AND APPLY THE PRINCIPLE AT A GLANCE

Task: Identify the principle underlying the argument in the stimulus and use that principle to distinguish the one answer containing an argument with a similar principle underlying it.

Strategy: Analyze the stimulus argument and identify the principle underlying its assumption. Evaluate the choices by spotting the one with a principle paralleling that of the argument in the stimulus.

Identify and Apply the Principle questions are extremely rare. On LSAT tests released between 2008 and 2013, there was an average of less than one per test.

Practice

Try an Identify and Apply the Principle Question. Analyze the argument in the stimulus. Consider the principle that underlies the author's assumption and use that principle to evaluate the answer choices.

LSAT Question		My Analysis
121. Since there is no survival value in an animal's having an organ that is able to function when all its other organs have broken down to such a degree that the animal dies, it is a result of the efficiency of natural selection that no organ is likely to evolve in such a way that it greatly outlasts the body's other organs.	→	**Step 2:**
Of the following, which one illustrates a principle that is most similar to the principle illustrated by the passage?	→	**Step 1:**
		Step 3:
(A) A store in a lower-income neighborhood finds that it is unable to sell its higher-priced goods and so stocks them only when ordered by a customer.	→	**Step 4:**
(B) The body of an animal with a deficient organ is often able to compensate for that deficiency when other organs perform the task the deficient one normally performs.	→	
(C) One car model produced by an automobile manufacturer has a life expectancy that is so much longer than its other models that its great popularity requires the manufacturer to stop producing some of the other models.	→	
(D) Athletes occasionally overdevelop some parts of their bodies to such a great extent that other parts of their bodies are more prone to injury as a result.	→	
(E) Automotive engineers find that it is not cost-effective to manufacture a given automobile part of such high quality that it outlasts all other parts of the automobile, as doing so would not raise the overall quality of the automobile.	→	

PrepTest61 Sec2 Q2

Expert Analysis

Here's how an LSAT expert might have approached that question. Compare your work. Did you adequately paraphrase the principle underlying the author's argument before you evaluated the answer choices?

LSAT Question	Analysis
121. Since there is no survival value in an animal's having an organ that is able to function when all its other organs have broken down to such a degree that the animal dies, it is a result of the efficiency of natural selection that no organ is likely to evolve in such a way that it greatly outlasts the body's other organs.	**Step 2:** Conclusion—No animal organ likely to evolve to outlast the other organs. *because* Evidence—Having one organ that outlasts the others doesn't increase survival value.
Of the following, which one illustrates a principle that is most similar to the principle illustrated by the passage?	**Step 1:** The stimulus illustrates a principle. The correct answer illustrates the same principle. This is an Identify and Apply the Principle question. It works much like Parallel Reasoning.
	Step 3: The right answer will argue that there is no reason to have one part outlast other parts if the part in question doesn't add value in outlasting others.
(A) A store in a lower-income neighborhood finds that it is unable to sell its higher-priced goods and so stocks them only when ordered by a customer.	**Step 4:** Outside the Scope. Having a plan for when to deploy overpriced items has nothing in common with the argument in the stimulus. Eliminate.
(B) The body of an animal with a deficient organ is often able to compensate for that deficiency when other organs perform the task the deficient one normally performs.	Distortion. This is about compensating for an underdeveloped organ, not whether there is an advantage to having an overdeveloped one. Eliminate.
(C) One car model produced by an automobile manufacturer has a life expectancy that is so much longer than its other models that its great popularity requires the manufacturer to stop producing some of the other models.	Distortion/180. This argument is about different models, not parts of a whole. Moreover, the overdeveloped part is beneficial. Eliminate.
(D) Athletes occasionally overdevelop some parts of their bodies to such a great extent that other parts of their bodies are more prone to injury as a result.	180. Here the overdevelopment of one part is detrimental to the other parts. Eliminate.
(E) Automotive engineers find that it is not cost-effective to manufacture a given automobile part of such high quality that it outlasts all other parts of the automobile, as doing so would not raise the overall quality of the automobile.	Correct. There is no reason to design one part to outlast others since it isn't cost effective to do so. This matches the original argument's principle in a different context.

PrepTest61 Sec2 Q2

REFLECTION

Look back over the arguments you saw in the chapter. Consider the various analytical skills that the LSAT rewarded.

- How do you now look at arguments differently?
- When you see an argument, can you determine the author's assumption?
- Are you able to determine the type of assumption the author is making?
- Once you have determined the author's assumption, can you establish the types of facts that would make his reasoning more or less likely to be valid?
- Can you identify and describe the flaws in an author's argument more efficiently and effectively?

Arguments occur everywhere in the real world: television news and commentary, advertisements, debate over music, and claims about sports teams. In the coming days, read and listen to arguments very carefully. Apply the analytical skills you practiced in this chapter.

- What is the author's assumption?
- What assumptions are necessary for her conclusion to follow from her evidence?
- What assumption would be sufficient to establish her conclusion from her evidence?
- Is the author's argument sound? If flawed, does her error in reasoning match one or more of the flaws commonly tested on the LSAT?
- Can I describe her flaw in general language without reference to the argument's content?
- Am I able to think of facts that would strengthen or weaken the reasoning in the argument?

In the next chapter, you'll leave argument-based questions behind temporarily and focus on LSAT questions that ask you to make valid inferences from one or more statements. Essentially, you'll be given evidence and then asked for a conclusion that can be deduced from it. Making valid inferences from pieces of text is also an important skill in the Reading Comprehension section, so as you work in Chapter 11, remember that you are building strengths that will add to your LSAT score even beyond the specific Logical Reasoning questions you are learning.

K | Part Three: Logical Reasoning
CHAPTER 10

Explanations for these questions
can be found in your Online Center.

QUESTION POOLS

Assumption Questions

This pool consists of Assumption questions you have not seen in earlier chapters. They are arranged in reverse chronological order—from most to least recent.

1. Historian: It is unlikely that someone would see history as the working out of moral themes unless he or she held clear and unambiguous moral beliefs. However, one's inclination to morally judge human behavior decreases as one's knowledge of history increases. Consequently, the more history a person knows, the less likely that person is to view history as the working out of moral themes.

The conclusion of the argument is properly drawn if which one of the following is assumed?

(A) Historical events that fail to elicit moral disapproval are generally not considered to exemplify a moral theme.

(B) The less inclined one is to morally judge human behavior, the less likely it is that one holds clear and unambiguous moral beliefs.

(C) Only those who do not understand human history attribute moral significance to historical events.

(D) The more clear and unambiguous one's moral beliefs, the more likely one is to view history as the working out of moral themes.

(E) People tend to be less objective regarding a subject about which they possess extensive knowledge than regarding a subject about which they do not possess extensive knowledge.

PrepTest61 Sec2 Q24

2. At one sitting, a typical doughnut eater consumes 4 doughnuts containing a total of 680 calories and 40 grams of fat. The typical bagel eater consumes exactly one bagel, at 500 calories and one or two grams of fat per sitting, though the addition of spreads can raise calorie and fat content to the four-doughnut range. Thus, as far as total calorie content is concerned, there is very little difference between what a typical doughnut eater and a typical bagel eater each consumes at one sitting.

The argument depends on assuming which one of the following?

(A) The calories and fat in bagels have the same health impact on bagel eaters as the calories and fat in doughnuts have on doughnut eaters.

(B) Most bagel eaters are not fully aware of the calorie and fat content of a bagel.

(C) Eating bagels instead of eating doughnuts provides no real health benefit.

(D) The typical doughnut eater does not add to doughnuts any substances that increase the total caloric intake.

(E) Most typical doughnut eaters are not also bagel eaters.

PrepTest59 Sec2 Q14

3. Commentator: For a free market to function properly, each prospective buyer of an item must be able to contact a large number of independent prospective sellers and compare the prices charged for the item to what the item is worth. Thus, despite advertised prices and written estimates available from many of its individual businesses, the auto repair industry does not constitute a properly functioning free market.

The conclusion of the commentator's argument follows logically if which one of the following is assumed?

(A) People do not usually shop for auto repairs but instead take their autos to their regular repair shop out of habit.

(B) Some persons who are shopping for auto repairs cannot determine what these repairs are worth.

(C) Not all auto repair shops give customers written estimates.

(D) Many auto repair shops charge more for auto repairs than these repairs are worth.

(E) Because it is not regulated, the auto repair industry does not have standardized prices.

PrepTest59 Sec2 Q26

Explanations for these questions can be found in your Online Center.

Part Three: Logical Reasoning

Assumption Family Questions

K

4. Science writer: All scientists have beliefs and values that might slant their interpretations of the data from which they draw their conclusions. However, serious scientific papers are carefully reviewed by many other scientists before publication. These reviewers are likely to notice and object to biases that they do not share. Thus, any slanted interpretations of scientific data will generally have been removed before publication.

Which one of the following is an assumption required by the science writer's argument?

(A) The scientists reviewing serious scientific papers for publication do not always have biases likely to slant their interpretations of the data in those papers.

(B) In general, biases that slant interpretations of data in serious scientific papers being reviewed for publication are not shared among all scientists.

(C) Biases that are present in published scientific papers and shared by most scientists, including those who review the papers, are unlikely to impair the scientific value of those papers.

(D) The interpretation of data is the only part of a serious scientific paper that is sometimes slanted by the beliefs and values of scientists.

(E) Slanted interpretations of data in a scientific paper can be removed only through careful review by scientists who do not share the biases of the author or authors of the paper.

PrepTest59 Sec3 Q25

5. Criminologist: The main purpose of most criminal organizations is to generate profits. The ongoing revolutions in biotechnology and information technology promise to generate enormous profits. Therefore, criminal organizations will undoubtedly try to become increasingly involved in these areas.

The conclusion of the criminologist's argument is properly inferred if which one of the following is assumed?

(A) If an organization tries to become increasingly involved in areas that promise to generate enormous profits, then the main purpose of that organization is to generate profits.

(B) At least some criminal organizations are or will at some point become aware that the ongoing revolutions in biotechnology and information technology promise to generate enormous profits.

(C) Criminal organizations are already heavily involved in every activity that promises to generate enormous profits.

(D) Any organization whose main purpose is to generate profits will try to become increasingly involved in any technological revolution that promises to generate enormous profits.

(E) Most criminal organizations are willing to become involved in legal activities if those activities are sufficiently profitable.

PrepTest57 Sec2 Q12

6. Editorial: To qualify as an effective law, as opposed to merely an impressive declaration, a command must be backed up by an effective enforcement mechanism. That is why societies have police. The power of the police to enforce a society's laws makes those laws effective. But there is currently no international police force. Hence, what is called "international law" is not effective law.

Which one of the following is an assumption required by the editorial's argument?

(A) No one obeys a command unless mechanisms exist to compel obedience.

(B) If an international police force were established, then so-called international law would become effective law.

(C) The only difference between international law and the law of an individual society is the former's lack of an effective enforcement mechanism.

(D) The primary purpose of a police force is to enforce the laws of the society.

(E) Only an international police force could effectively enforce international law.

PrepTest57 Sec3 Q12

7. Consumer: If you buy a watch at a department store and use it only in the way it was intended to be used, but the watch stops working the next day, then the department store will refund your money. So by this very reasonable standard, Bingham's Jewelry Store should give me a refund even though they themselves are not a department store, since the watch I bought from them stopped working the very next day.

The consumer's argument relies on the assumption that

(A) one should not sell something unless one expects that it will function in the way it was originally designed to function

(B) a watch bought at a department store and a watch bought at Bingham's Jewelry Store can both be expected to keep working for about the same length of time if each is used only as it was intended to be used

(C) a seller should refund the money that was paid for a product if the product does not perform as the purchaser expected it to perform

(D) the consumer did not use the watch in a way contrary to the way it was intended to be used

(E) the watch that was purchased from Bingham's Jewelry Store was not a new watch

PrepTest57 Sec3 Q17

703

Part Three: Logical Reasoning

CHAPTER 10

Explanations for these questions can be found in your Online Center.

8. Geneticist: Genes, like viruses, have a strong tendency to self-replicate; this has led some biologists to call genes "selfish." This term is, in this instance, intended to be defined behaviorally: it describes what genes do without ascribing intentions to them. But even given that genes are ascribed no intentions, the label "selfish" as applied to genes is a misnomer. Selfishness only concerns bringing about the best conditions for oneself; creating replicas of oneself is not selfish.

Which one of the following, if assumed, allows the geneticist's conclusion to be properly drawn?

(A) Bringing about the best conditions for oneself is less important than doing this for others.

(B) Creating replicas of oneself does not help bring about the best conditions for oneself.

(C) The behavioral definition of "selfish" is incompatible with its everyday definition.

(D) To ignore the fact that self-replication is not limited to genes is to misunderstand genetic behavior.

(E) Biologists have insufficient evidence about genetic behavior to determine whether it is best described as selfish.

PrepTest51 Sec1 Q19

9. Whoever murdered Jansen was undoubtedly in Jansen's office on the day of the murder, and both Samantha and Herbert were in Jansen's office on that day. If Herbert had committed the murder, the police would have found either his fingerprints or his footprints at the scene of the crime. But if Samantha was the murderer, she would have avoided leaving behind footprints or fingerprints. The police found fingerprints but no footprints at the scene of the crime. Since the fingerprints were not Herbert's, he is not the murderer. Thus Samantha must be the killer.

Which one of the following, if assumed, allows the conclusion that Samantha was the killer to be properly inferred?

(A) If there had been footprints at the scene of the crime, the police would have found them.

(B) Jansen's office was the scene of the crime.

(C) No one but Herbert and Samantha was in Jansen's office on the day of the murder.

(D) The fingerprints found at the scene of the crime were not Jansen's.

(E) The fingerprints found at the scene of the crime were not Samantha's.

PrepTest51 Sec3 Q20

10. A mathematical theorem proved by one mathematician should not be accepted until each step in its proof has been independently verified. Computer-assisted proofs generally proceed by conducting a vast number of calculations—surveying all the possible types of instances in which the theorem could apply and proving that the theorem holds for each type. In most computer-assisted proofs there are astronomically many types of instances to survey, and no human being could review every step in the proof. Hence, computer-assisted proofs involving astronomically many types of instances should not be accepted.

Which one of the following is an assumption on which the argument relies?

(A) The use of the computer to assist in the proof of mathematical theorems has greatly simplified the mathematician's task.

(B) Most attempts to construct proofs of mathematical theorems do not result in demonstrations that the theorems are true.

(C) Computers cannot be used to assist in generating proofs of mathematical theorems that involve only a very limited number of steps.

(D) Any mathematical proof that does not rely on the computer cannot proceed by surveying all possible types of instances to which the candidate theorem might apply.

(E) The use of an independent computer program does not satisfy the requirement for independent verification of each step in a proof that is extended enough to be otherwise unverifiable.

PrepTest49 Sec2 Q22

Explanations for these questions can be found in your Online Center.

Part Three: Logical Reasoning
Assumption Family Questions

K

Flaw Questions

This pool consists of Flaw questions you have not seen in earlier chapters. They are arranged in reverse chronological order—from most to least recent.

11. Marcia: Not all vegetarian diets lead to nutritional deficiencies. Research shows that vegetarians can obtain a full complement of proteins and minerals from nonanimal foods.

    Theodora: You are wrong in claiming that vegetarianism cannot lead to nutritional deficiencies. If most people became vegetarians, some of those losing jobs due to the collapse of many meat-based industries would fall into poverty and hence be unable to afford a nutritionally adequate diet.

    Theodora's reply to Marcia's argument is most vulnerable to criticism on the grounds that her reply

    (A) is directed toward disproving a claim that Marcia did not make
    (B) ignores the results of the research cited by Marcia
    (C) takes for granted that no meat-based industries will collapse unless most people become vegetarians
    (D) uses the word "diet" in a nontechnical sense whereas Marcia's argument uses this term in a medical sense
    (E) takes for granted that people losing jobs in meat-based industries would become vegetarians

    PrepTest61 Sec2 Q8

12. To find out how barn owls learn how to determine the direction from which sounds originate, scientists put distorting lenses over the eyes of young barn owls before the owls first opened their eyes. The owls with these lenses behaved as if objects making sounds were farther to the right than they actually were. Once the owls matured, the lenses were removed, yet the owls continued to act as if they misjudged the location of the source of sounds. The scientists consequently hypothesized that once a barn owl has developed an auditory scheme for estimating the point from which sounds originate, it ceases to use vision to locate sounds.

    The scientists' reasoning is vulnerable to which one of the following criticisms?

    (A) It fails to consider whether the owls' vision was permanently impaired by their having worn the lenses while immature.
    (B) It assumes that the sense of sight is equally good in all owls.
    (C) It attributes human reasoning processes to a nonhuman organism.
    (D) It neglects to consider how similar distorting lenses might affect the behavior of other bird species.
    (E) It uses as evidence experimental results that were irrelevant to the conclusion.

    PrepTest61 Sec2 Q18

13. Though ice cream is an excellent source of calcium, dairy farmers report that during the past ten years there has been a sharp decline in ice cream sales. And during the same period, sales of cheddar cheese have nearly doubled. Therefore, more and more people must be choosing to increase their intake of calcium by eating cheddar cheese rather than ice cream.

    The reasoning above is most vulnerable to criticism on the grounds that it

    (A) fails to produce statistical evidence supporting the dairy farmers' claims
    (B) fails to consider alternative explanations of the decline in sales of ice cream
    (C) relies solely on the testimony of individuals who are likely to be biased
    (D) presumes, without providing justification, that ice cream is a better source of calcium than is cheddar cheese
    (E) presumes, without providing justification, that people who eat cheddar cheese never eat ice cream

    PrepTest59 Sec2 Q8

14. Quality control investigator: Upon testing samples of products from our supplier that were sent by our field inspectors from various manufacturing locations, our laboratory discovered that over 20 percent of the samples were defective. Since our supplier is contractually required to limit the rate of defects among items it manufactures for us to below 5 percent, it has violated its contract with us.

    The reasoning in the quality control investigator's argument is flawed in that the argument

    (A) bases its conclusion on too small a sample of items tested by the laboratory
    (B) presumes, without providing justification, that the field inspectors were just as likely to choose a defective item for testing as they were to choose a nondefective item
    (C) overlooks the possibility that a few of the manufacturing sites are responsible for most of the defective items
    (D) overlooks the possibility that the field inspectors tend to choose items for testing that they suspect are defective
    (E) presumes, without providing justification, that the field inspectors made an equal number of visits to each of the various manufacturing sites of the supplier

    PrepTest59 Sec2 Q20

K Part Three: Logical Reasoning
CHAPTER 10

Explanations for these questions
can be found in your Online Center.

15. Challenger: The mayor claims she has vindicated those
who supported her in the last election by fulfilling
her promise to increase employment opportunities
in our city, citing the 8 percent increase in the
number of jobs in the city since she took office.
But during her administration, the national
government relocated an office to our city,
bringing along nearly the entire staff from the
outside. The 8 percent increase merely represents
the jobs held by these newcomers.

Mayor: Clearly my opponent does not dispute the
employment statistics. The unemployed voters in
this city want jobs. The 8 percent increase in the
number of jobs during my term exceeds that of
any of my predecessors.

As a response to the challenger, the mayor's answer is
flawed in that it

(A) takes for granted that those who supported the
mayor in the last election believed job
availability to be a significant city issue

(B) does not consider whether the number of
unemployed persons within the city represents
more than 8 percent of the eligible voters

(C) fails to address the challenger's objection that
the 8 percent increase did not result in an
increase in job availability for those who lived
in the city at the time of the last election

(D) ignores the challenger's contention that the
influx of newcomers during the mayor's
administration has increased the size of the
voting public and altered its priorities

(E) explicitly attributes to the challenger beliefs that
the challenger has neither asserted nor implied

PrepTest59 Sec3 Q5

16. The peppered moth avoids predators by blending into its
background, typically the bark of trees. In the late
nineteenth century, those peppered moths with the
lightest pigmentation had the greatest contrast with their
backgrounds, and therefore were the most likely to be
seen and eaten by predators. It follows, then, that the
darkest peppered moths were the least likely to be seen
and eaten.

Which one of the following most accurately describes a
flaw in the reasoning of the argument?

(A) The argument overlooks the possibility that
light peppered moths had more predators than
dark peppered moths.

(B) The argument takes for granted that peppered
moths are able to control the degree to which
they blend into their backgrounds.

(C) The argument presumes, without providing
justification, that all peppered moths with the
same coloring had the same likelihood of
being seen and eaten by a predator.

(D) The argument overlooks the possibility that
there were peppered moths of intermediate
color that contrasted less with their backgrounds
than the darkest peppered moths did.

(E) The argument presumes, without providing
justification, that the only defense mechanism
available to peppered moths was to blend into
their backgrounds.

PrepTest59 Sec3 Q20

Explanations for these questions can be found in your Online Center.

Part Three: Logical Reasoning
Assumption Family Questions

17. Since anyone who makes an agreement has an obligation to fulfill the terms of that agreement, it follows that anyone who is obligated to perform an action has agreed to perform that action. Hence, saying that one has a legal obligation to perform a given action is the same as saying that one is required to fulfill one's agreement to perform that action.

Which one of the following statements most accurately characterizes the argument's reasoning flaws?

(A) The argument fails to make a crucial distinction between an action one is legally obligated to perform and an action with good consequences, and it takes for granted that everything true of legal obligations is true of obligations generally.

(B) The argument takes for granted that there are obligations other than those resulting from agreements made, and it fails to consider the possibility that actions that uphold agreements made are sometimes performed for reasons other than to uphold those agreements.

(C) The argument contains a premise that is logically equivalent to its conclusion, and it takes for granted that there are only certain actions that one should agree to perform.

(D) The argument treats a condition that is sufficient to make something an obligation as also a requirement for something to be an obligation, and it takes for granted that any obligation to perform an action is a legal obligation.

(E) The argument rests on an ambiguous use of the term "action," and it fails to consider the possibility that people are sometimes unwilling to perform actions that they have agreed to perform.

PrepTest59 Sec3 Q22

18. Professor: A guest speaker recently delivered a talk entitled "The Functions of Democratic Governments" to a Political Ideologies class at this university. The talk was carefully researched and theoretical in nature. But two students who disagreed with the theory hurled vicious taunts at the speaker. Several others applauded their attempt to humiliate the speaker. This incident shows that universities these days do not foster fair-minded and tolerant intellectual debate.

The professor's reasoning is flawed in that it

(A) draws a conclusion based on the professor's own opinion rather than on that of the majority of the students present at the talk

(B) is inconsistent in advocating tolerance while showing intolerance of the dissenting students' views

(C) relies primarily on an emotional appeal

(D) draws a general conclusion based on too small a sample

(E) incorrectly focuses on the behavior of the dissenting students rather than relating the reasons for that behavior

PrepTest57 Sec2 Q4

19. Studies show that individuals with a high propensity for taking risks tend to have fewer ethical principles to which they consciously adhere in their business interactions than do most people. On the other hand, individuals with a strong desire to be accepted socially tend to have more such principles than do most people. And, in general, the more ethical principles to which someone consciously adheres, the more ethical is that person's behavior. Therefore, business schools can promote more ethical behavior among future businesspeople by promoting among their students the desire to be accepted socially and discouraging the propensity for taking risks.

The reasoning in the argument is flawed because the argument

(A) infers from the fact that something is usually true that it is always true

(B) takes for granted that promoting ethical behavior is more important than any other goal

(C) concludes merely from the fact that two things are correlated that one causes the other

(D) takes for granted that certain actions are morally wrong simply because most people believe that they are morally wrong

(E) draws a conclusion that simply restates a claim presented in support of that conclusion

PrepTest57 Sec2 Q6

20. Carla: Professors at public universities should receive
paid leaves of absence to allow them to engage in
research. Research not only advances human
knowledge, but also improves professors'
teaching by keeping them abreast of the latest
information in their fields.

David: But even if you are right about the beneficial
effects of research, why should our limited
resources be devoted to supporting professors
taking time off from teaching?

David's response to Carla is most vulnerable to criticism
on the grounds that it

(A) ignores the part of Carla's remarks that could
provide an answer to David's question
(B) takes for granted that the only function of a
university professor is teaching
(C) incorrectly takes Carla's remarks as claiming
that all funding for professors comes from
tax money
(D) takes for granted that providing the opportunity
for research is the only function of paid leaves
of absence
(E) presumes, without providing justification, that
professors do not need vacations

PrepTest57 Sec2 Q15

21. Columnist: A recent research report suggests that by
exercising vigorously, one significantly lowers
one's chances of developing certain cardio-
respiratory illnesses. But exercise has this effect,
the report concludes, only if the exercise is
vigorous. Thus, one should not heed older studies
purporting to show that nonstrenuous walking
yields the same benefits.

The reasoning in the columnist's argument is most
vulnerable to criticism on the grounds that this
argument

(A) fails to consider the possibility that the risk of
developing certain cardio-respiratory illnesses
can be reduced by means other than exercise
(B) fails to consider that those who exercise
vigorously are at increased risk of physical
injury caused by exercise
(C) overlooks the possibility that vigorous exercise
may prevent life-endangering diseases that
have little to do with the cardio-respiratory
system
(D) fails to consider the possibility that those who
engage in vigorous physical exercise are more
likely than others to perceive themselves as
healthy
(E) fails to show that a certain conclusion of the
recent report is better justified than an
opposing conclusion reached in older studies

PrepTest51 Sec1 Q10

22. The number of different synthetic chemical compounds
that are known to be carcinogenic but are nonetheless
used as pesticides, preservatives, or food additives is
tiny compared to the number of nonsynthetic
carcinogenic compounds widely found in plants and
animals. It is therefore absurd to suppose that the rise
in the cancer rate in recent decades is due to synthetic
carcinogens.

The reasoning above is most vulnerable to criticism on
the grounds that it overlooks the possibility that

(A) the rise in the cancer rate in recent decades is
due to increased exposure to nonsynthetic
pollutants
(B) the rise in the cancer rate in recent decades is
due to something other than increased exposure
to carcinogens
(C) some synthetic chemical compounds that are not
known to be carcinogenic are in other respects
toxic
(D) people undergo significantly less exposure to
carcinogens that are not synthetic than to those
that are synthetic
(E) people can vary greatly in their susceptibility to
cancers caused by nonsynthetic carcinogens

PrepTest51 Sec1 Q12

23. Advertiser: There's nothing wrong with a tool that has
ten functions until you need a tool that can
perform an eleventh function! The VersaTool can
perform more functions than any other tool. If
you use the VersaTool, therefore, you will need
additional tools less often than you would using
any other multiple-function tool.

The reasoning in the advertiser's argument is most
vulnerable to criticism on the grounds that the
VersaTool might

(A) include some functions that are infrequently or
never needed
(B) include a number of functions that are difficult
to perform with any tool
(C) cost more than the combined cost of two other
multiple-function tools that together perform
more functions than the VersaTool
(D) be able to perform fewer often-needed functions
than some other multiple-function tool
(E) not be able to perform individual functions as
well as single-function tools

PrepTest51 Sec3 Q17

Explanations for these questions can be found in your Online Center.

Part Three: Logical Reasoning
Assumption Family Questions | K

24. New Age philosopher: Nature evolves organically and nonlinearly. Furthermore, it can best be understood as a whole; its parts are so interconnected that none could exist without support from many others. Therefore, attaining the best possible understanding of nature requires an organic, holistic, nonlinear way of reasoning rather than the traditional linear reasoning of science, which proceeds through experiments on deliberately isolated parts of nature.

The reasoning in the New Age philosopher's argument is most vulnerable to criticism on the grounds that the argument

(A) takes for granted that if a statement must be true for the argument's conclusion to be true, then that statement's truth is sufficient for the truth of the conclusion

(B) overlooks the possibility that the overall structure of a phenomenon is not always identical to the overall structure of the reasoning that people do about that phenomenon

(C) fails to distinguish adequately between the characteristics of a phenomenon as a whole and those of the deliberately isolated parts of that phenomenon

(D) takes for granted that what is interconnected cannot, through abstraction, be thought of as separate

(E) takes for granted that a phenomenon that can best be understood as having certain properties can best be understood only through reasoning that shares those properties

PrepTest49 Sec2 Q18

25. Commentator: Human behavior cannot be fully understood without inquiring into nonphysical aspects of persons. As evidence of this, I submit the following: suppose that we had a complete scientific account of the physical aspects of some particular human action—every neurological, physiological, and environmental event involved. Even with all that we would obviously still not truly comprehend the action or know why it occurred.

Which one of the following most accurately describes a flaw in the argument's reasoning?

(A) No support is offered for its conclusion other than an analogy that relates only superficially to the issue at hand.

(B) The purported evidence that it cites in support of its conclusion presumes that the conclusion is true.

(C) It concludes that a proposition must be true merely on the grounds that it has not been proven false.

(D) It fails to indicate whether the speaker is aware of any evidence that could undermine the conclusion.

(E) It presumes, without providing justification, that science can provide a complete account of any physical phenomenon.

PrepTest49 Sec2 Q23

K | Part Three: Logical Reasoning
CHAPTER 10

Explanations for these questions
can be found in your Online Center.

Strengthen/Weaken Questions

This pool consists of Strengthen/Weaken questions you have not seen in earlier chapters. They are arranged in reverse chronological order—from most to least recent.

26. Psychiatrist: In treating first-year students at this university, I have noticed that those reporting the highest levels of spending on recreation score at about the same level on standard screening instruments for anxiety and depression as those reporting the lowest levels of spending on recreation. This suggests that the first-year students with high levels of spending on recreation could reduce that spending without increasing their anxiety or depression.

    Each of the following, if true, strengthens the psychiatrist's argument EXCEPT:

    (A) At other universities, first-year students reporting the highest levels of spending on recreation also show the same degree of anxiety and depression as do those reporting the lowest levels of such spending.

    (B) Screening of first-year students at the university who report moderate levels of spending on recreation reveals that those students are less anxious and depressed than both those with the highest and those with the lowest levels of spending on recreation.

    (C) Among adults between the ages of 40 and 60, increased levels of spending on recreation are strongly correlated with decreased levels of anxiety and depression.

    (D) The screening instruments used by the psychiatrist are extremely accurate in revealing levels of anxiety and depression among university students.

    (E) Several of the psychiatrist's patients who are first-year students at the university have reduced their spending on recreation from very high levels to very low levels without increasing their anxiety or depression.

    PrepTest61 Sec2 Q22

27. Programmer: We computer programmers at Mytheco are demanding raises to make our average salary comparable with that of the technical writers here who receive, on average, 20 percent more in salary and benefits than we do. This pay difference is unfair and intolerable.

    Mytheco executive: But many of the technical writers have worked for Mytheco longer than have many of the programmers. Since salary and benefits at Mytheco are directly tied to seniority, the 20 percent pay difference you mention is perfectly acceptable.

    Evaluating the adequacy of the Mytheco executive's response requires a clarification of which one of the following?

    (A) whether any of the technical writers at Mytheco once worked as programmers at the company

    (B) how the average seniority of programmers compares with the average seniority of technical writers

    (C) whether the sorts of benefits an employee of Mytheco receives are tied to the salary of that employee

    (D) whether the Mytheco executive was at one time a technical writer employed by Mytheco

    (E) how the Mytheco executive's salary compares with that of the programmers

    PrepTest61 Sec4 Q2

28. In polluted industrial English cities during the Industrial Revolution, two plant diseases—black spot, which infects roses, and tar spot, which infects sycamore trees—disappeared. It is likely that air pollution eradicated these diseases.

    Which one of the following, if true, most strengthens the reasoning above?

    (A) Scientists theorize that some plants can develop a resistance to air pollution.

    (B) Certain measures help prevent infection by black spot and tar spot, but once infection occurs, it is very difficult to eliminate.

    (C) For many plant species, scientists have not determined the effects of air pollution.

    (D) Black spot and tar spot returned when the air in the cities became less polluted.

    (E) Black spot and tar spot were the only plant diseases that disappeared in any English cities during the Industrial Revolution.

    PrepTest61 Sec4 Q4

Explanations for these questions
can be found in your Online Center.

Part Three: Logical Reasoning
Assumption Family Questions

29. Principle: When none of the fully qualified candidates
for a new position at Arvue Corporation currently
works for that company, it should hire the candidate
who would be most productive in that position.

Application: Arvue should not hire Krall for the new
position, because Delacruz is a candidate and is
fully qualified.

Which one of the following, if true, justifies the above
application of the principle?

(A) All of the candidates are fully qualified for the
new position, but none already works for Arvue.

(B) Of all the candidates who do not already work
for Arvue, Delacruz would be the most
productive in the new position.

(C) Krall works for Arvue, but Delacruz is the
candidate who would be most productive in
the new position.

(D) Several candidates currently work for Arvue,
but Krall and Delacruz do not.

(E) None of the candidates already works for Arvue,
and Delacruz is the candidate who would be
most productive in the new position.

PrepTest61 Sec4 Q19

30. Despite the enormous number of transactions processed
daily by banks nowadays, if a customer's bank account
is accidentally credited with a large sum of money, it is
extremely unlikely that the error will not be detected by
the bank's internal audit procedures.

Which one of the following, if true, most strongly
supports the claim above?

(A) Banks initially process all transactions using
one set of computer programs, but then use a
different set of programs to double-check large
transactions.

(B) Recent changes in banking standards require
that customers present identification both when
making deposits into their accounts and when
making withdrawals from their accounts.

(C) Banks are required by law to send each
customer a monthly statement detailing every
transaction of the previous month.

(D) The average ratio of bank auditors to customer
accounts has slowly increased over the past
100 years.

(E) The development of sophisticated security
software has rendered bank computers nearly
impervious to tampering by computer hackers.

PrepTest59 Sec2 Q3

31. Essayist: When the first prehistoric migrations of
humans from Asia to North America took place,
the small bands of new arrivals encountered many
species of animals that would be extinct only
2,000 years later. Since it is implausible that
hunting by these small bands of humans could
have had such an effect, and since disease-causing
microorganisms not native to North America were
undoubtedly borne by the new arrivals as well as
by the animals that followed them, these
microorganisms were probably the crucial factor
that accounts for the extinctions.

Which one of the following, if true, most weakens the
essayist's argument?

(A) Animals weakened by disease are not only less
able to avoid hunters but are also less able to
avoid their other predators.

(B) Human beings generally have a substantial
degree of biological immunity to the diseases
carried by other species.

(C) Very few species of North American animals
not hunted by the new arrivals from Asia were
extinct 2,000 years after the first migrations.

(D) Individual humans and animals can carry a
disease-causing microorganism without
themselves suffering from the disease.

(E) Some species of North American animals
became extinct more than 2,000 years after the
arrival in North America of the first prehistoric
human migrants from Asia.

PrepTest59 Sec2 Q21

32. A recent study of 10,000 people who were involved in
automobile accidents found that a low percentage of
those driving large automobiles at the time of their
accidents were injured, but a high percentage of those
who were driving small automobiles at the time of their
accidents were injured. Thus, one is less likely to be
injured in an automobile accident if one drives a large
car rather than a small car.

Which one of the following, if true, most seriously
weakens the argument?

(A) Most of the accidents analyzed in the study
occurred in areas with very high speed limits.

(B) Most people who own small cars also drive
large cars on occasion.

(C) Half of the study participants drove
medium-sized cars at the time of their
accidents.

(D) A large automobile is far more likely to be
involved in an accident than is a small
automobile.

(E) Only a small percentage of those people
involved in an automobile accident are injured
as a result.

PrepTest59 Sec3 Q13

711

33. Even if many more people in the world excluded meat
from their diet, world hunger would not thereby be
significantly reduced.

Which one of the following, if true, most calls into
question the claim above?

(A)   Hunger often results from natural disasters like
      typhoons or hurricanes, which sweep away
      everything in their path.
(B)   Both herds and crops are susceptible to
      devastating viral and other diseases.
(C)   The amount of land needed to produce enough
      meat to feed one person for a week can grow
      enough grain to feed more than ten people for
      a week.
(D)   Often people go hungry because they live in
      remote barren areas where there is no efficient
      distribution for emergency food relief.
(E)   Most historical cases of famine have been due
      to bad social and economic policies or
      catastrophes such as massive crop failure.

PrepTest57 Sec2 Q9

34. Scientists have shown that older bees, which usually
forage outside the hive for food, tend to have larger
brains than do younger bees, which usually do not
forage but instead remain in the hive to tend to newly
hatched bees. Since foraging requires greater cognitive
ability than does tending to newly hatched bees, it
appears that foraging leads to the increased brain size
of older bees.

Which one of the following, if true, most seriously
weakens the argument above?

(A)   Bees that have foraged for a long time do not
      have significantly larger brains than do bees
      that have foraged for a shorter time.
(B)   The brains of older bees that stop foraging to
      take on other responsibilities do not become
      smaller after they stop foraging.
(C)   Those bees that travel a long distance to find
      food do not have significantly larger brains
      than do bees that locate food nearer the hive.
(D)   In some species of bees, the brains of older
      bees are only marginally larger than those of
      younger bees.
(E)   The brains of older bees that never learn to
      forage are the same size as those of their
      foraging counterparts of the same age.

PrepTest57 Sec2 Q14

35. In the past, when there was no highway speed limit, the
highway accident rate increased yearly, peaking a
decade ago. At that time, the speed limit on highways
was set at 90 kilometers per hour (kph) (55 miles per
hour). Every year since the introduction of the highway
speed limit, the highway accident rate has been at least
15 percent lower than that of its peak rate. Thus, setting
the highway speed limit at 90 kph (55 mph) has reduced
the highway accident rate by at least 15 percent.

Which one of the following, if true, most seriously
weakens the argument?

(A)   In the years prior to the introduction of the
      highway speed limit, many cars could go faster
      than 90 kph (55 mph).
(B)   Ten years ago, at least 95 percent of all
      automobile accidents in the area occurred
      on roads with a speed limit of under
      80 kph (50 mph).
(C)   Although the speed limit on many highways is
      officially set at 90 kph (55 mph), most people
      typically drive faster than the speed limit.
(D)   Thanks to changes in automobile design in the
      past ten years, drivers are better able to maintain
      control of their cars in dangerous situations.
(E)   It was not until shortly after the introduction of
      the highway speed limit that most cars were
      equipped with features such as seat belts and
      airbags designed to prevent harm to passengers.

PrepTest57 Sec2 Q20

Explanations for these questions can be found in your Online Center.

Part Three: Logical Reasoning
Assumption Family Questions | **K**

36. Many vaccines create immunity to viral diseases by introducing a certain portion of the disease-causing virus's outer coating into the body. Exposure to that part of a virus is as effective as exposure to the whole virus in stimulating production of antibodies that will subsequently recognize and kill the whole virus. To create a successful vaccine of this type, doctors must first isolate in the disease-causing virus a portion that stimulates antibody production. Now that a suitable portion of the virus that causes hepatitis E has been isolated, doctors claim they can produce a vaccine that will produce permanent immunity to that disease.

Which one of the following, if true, most strongly counters the doctors' claim?

(A) Most of the people who contract hepatitis E are young adults who were probably exposed to the virus in childhood also.

(B) Some laboratory animals exposed to one strain of the hepatitis virus developed immunity to all strains of the virus.

(C) Researchers developed a successful vaccine for another strain of hepatitis, hepatitis B, after first isolating the virus that causes it.

(D) The virus that causes hepatitis E is very common in some areas, so the number of people exposed to that virus is likely to be quite high in those areas.

(E) Many children who are exposed to viruses that cause childhood diseases such as chicken pox never develop those diseases.

PrepTest57 Sec3 Q11

37. In ancient Greece, court witnesses were not cross-examined and the jury, selected from the citizenry, received no guidance on points of law; thus, it was extremely important for litigants to make a good impression on the jurors. For this reason, courtroom oratory by litigants is a good source of data on the common conceptions of morality held by the citizens of ancient Greece.

Which one of the following, if true, would most strengthen the argument?

(A) Litigants believed jurors were more likely to be impressed by litigants whose personality they preferred.

(B) Litigants believed jurors were more likely to subject the litigants' personal moral codes to close critical scrutiny than were people who did not sit on juries.

(C) Litigants believed jurors were likely to be impressed by litigants whose professed moral code most resembled their own.

(D) Litigants believed jurors to be more impressed by litigants who were of the same economic class as the jurors.

(E) Litigants believed jurors were likely to render their decisions based on a good understanding of the law.

PrepTest51 Sec3 Q25

38. Cholesterol, which is a known factor in coronary heart disease and stroke, needs a carrier, known as a lipoprotein, to transport it through the bloodstream. Low-density lipoproteins (LDLs) increase the risk of coronary heart disease and stroke, but we can tentatively conclude that high-density lipoproteins (HDLs) help prevent coronary heart disease and stroke. First, aerobic exercise increases one's level of HDLs. Second, HDL levels are higher in women than in men. And both aerobic exercise and being female are positively correlated with lower risk of coronary heart disease and stroke.

Each of the following, if true, strengthens the argument EXCEPT:

(A) HDLs, unlike LDLs, help the body excrete cholesterol.

(B) Persons who are overweight tend to have a higher risk of early death due to coronary heart disease and stroke, and tend to have low levels of HDLs.

(C) HDLs are less easily removed from the bloodstream than are LDLs.

(D) A high level of HDLs mitigates the increased health risks associated with LDLs.

(E) Men whose level of HDLs is equal to the average level for women have been found to have a lower risk of coronary heart disease and stroke than that of most men.

PrepTest49 Sec2 Q11

K | Part Three: Logical Reasoning
CHAPTER 10

Explanations for these questions can be found in your Online Center.

Mixed Practice: Assumption, Flaw, and Strengthen/Weaken Questions

This pool consists of a mix of Assumption, Flaw, and Strengthen/Weaken questions you have not seen in earlier chapters or question pools.

39. Mary to Jamal: You acknowledge that as the legitimate owner of this business I have the legal right to sell it whenever I wish. But also you claim that because loyal employees will suffer if I sell it, I therefore have no right to do so. Obviously, your statements taken together are absurd.

    Mary's reasoning is most vulnerable to the criticism that she

    (A) overlooks the possibility that when Jamal claims that she has no right to sell the business, he simply means she has no right to do so at this time

    (B) overlooks the possibility that her employees also have rights related to the sale of the business

    (C) provides no evidence for the claim that she does have a right to sell the business

    (D) overlooks the possibility that Jamal is referring to two different kinds of right

    (E) attacks Jamal's character rather than his argument

    PrepTest61 Sec2 Q1

40. Psychologists observing a shopping mall parking lot found that, on average, drivers spent 39 seconds leaving a parking space when another car was quietly waiting to enter it, 51 seconds if the driver of the waiting car honked impatiently, but only 32 seconds leaving a space when no one was waiting. This suggests that drivers feel possessive of their parking spaces even when leaving them, and that this possessiveness increases in reaction to indications that another driver wants the space.

    Which one of the following, if true, most weakens the reasoning?

    (A) The more pressure most drivers feel because others are waiting for them to perform maneuvers with their cars, the less quickly they are able to perform them.

    (B) The amount of time drivers spend entering a parking space is not noticeably affected by whether other drivers are waiting for them to do so, nor by whether those other drivers are honking impatiently.

    (C) It is considerably more difficult and time-consuming for a driver to maneuver a car out of a parking space if another car waiting to enter that space is nearby.

    (D) Parking spaces in shopping mall parking lots are unrepresentative of parking spaces in general with respect to the likelihood that other cars will be waiting to enter them.

    (E) Almost any driver leaving a parking space will feel angry at another driver who honks impatiently, and this anger will influence the amount of time spent leaving the space.

    PrepTest61 Sec2 Q11

Explanations for these questions can be found in your Online Center.

Part Three: Logical Reasoning
Assumption Family Questions

K

41. Geologists recently discovered marks that closely resemble worm tracks in a piece of sandstone. These marks were made more than half a billion years earlier than the earliest known traces of multicellular animal life. Therefore, the marks are probably the traces of geological processes rather than of worms.

Which one of the following, if true, most weakens the argument?

(A) It is sometimes difficult to estimate the precise age of a piece of sandstone.

(B) Geological processes left a substantial variety of marks in sandstone more than half a billion years before the earliest known multicellular animal life existed.

(C) There were some early life forms other than worms that are known to have left marks that are hard to distinguish from those found in the piece of sandstone.

(D) At the place where the sandstone was found, the only geological processes that are likely to mark sandstone in ways that resemble worm tracks could not have occurred at the time the marks were made.

(E) Most scientists knowledgeable about early animal life believe that worms are likely to have been among the earliest forms of multicellular animal life on Earth, but evidence of their earliest existence is scarce because they are composed solely of soft tissue.

PrepTest61 Sec2 Q14

42. The giant Chicxulub crater in Mexico provides indisputable evidence that a huge asteroid, about six miles across, struck Earth around the time many of the last dinosaur species were becoming extinct. But this catastrophe was probably not responsible for most of these extinctions. Any major asteroid strike kills many organisms in or near the region of the impact, but there is little evidence that such a strike could have a worldwide effect. Indeed, some craters even larger than the Chicxulub crater were made during times in Earth's history when there were no known extinctions.

Which one of the following, if true, would most weaken the argument?

(A) The vast majority of dinosaur species are known to have gone extinct well before the time of the asteroid impact that produced the Chicxulub crater.

(B) The size of a crater caused by an asteroid striking Earth generally depends on both the size of that asteroid and the force of its impact.

(C) Fossils have been discovered of a number of dinosaurs that clearly died as a result of the asteroid impact that produced the Chicxulub crater.

(D) There is no evidence that any other asteroid of equal size struck Earth at the same time as the asteroid that produced the Chicxulub crater.

(E) During the period immediately before the asteroid that produced the Chicxulub crater struck, most of the world's dinosaurs lived in or near the region of the asteroid's impending impact.

PrepTest61 Sec4 Q8

43. Legislator: My staff conducted a poll in which my constituents were asked whether they favor high taxes. More than 97 percent answered "no." Clearly, then, my constituents would support the bill I recently introduced, which reduces the corporate income tax.

The reasoning in the legislator's argument is most vulnerable to criticism on the grounds that the argument

(A) fails to establish that the opinions of the legislator's constituents are representative of the opinions of the country's population as a whole

(B) fails to consider whether the legislator's constituents consider the current corporate income tax a high tax

(C) confuses an absence of evidence that the legislator's constituents oppose a bill with the existence of evidence that the legislator's constituents support that bill

(D) draws a conclusion that merely restates a claim presented in support of that conclusion

(E) treats a result that proves that the public supports a bill as a result that is merely consistent with public support for that bill

PrepTest61 Sec4 Q15

K Part Three: Logical Reasoning
CHAPTER 10

Explanations for these questions
can be found in your Online Center.

44. Many important types of medicine have been developed from substances discovered in plants that grow only in tropical rain forests. There are thousands of plant species in these rain forests that have not yet been studied by scientists, and it is very likely that many such plants also contain substances of medicinal value. Thus, if the tropical rain forests are not preserved, important types of medicine will never be developed.

Which one of the following is an assumption required by the argument?

(A) There are substances of medicinal value contained in tropical rain forest plants not yet studied by scientists that differ from those substances already discovered in tropical rain forest plants.

(B) Most of the tropical rain forest plants that contain substances of medicinal value can also be found growing in other types of environment.

(C) The majority of plant species that are unique to tropical rain forests and that have been studied by scientists have been discovered to contain substances of medicinal value.

(D) Any substance of medicinal value contained in plant species indigenous to tropical rain forests will eventually be discovered if those species are studied by scientists.

(E) The tropical rain forests should be preserved to make it possible for important medicines to be developed from plant species that have not yet been studied by scientists.

PrepTest61 Sec4 Q20

45. Teachers should not do anything to cause their students to lose respect for them. And students can sense when someone is trying to hide his or her ignorance. Therefore, a teacher who does not know the answer to a question a student has asked should not pretend to know the answer.

The conclusion is properly drawn if which one of the following is assumed?

(A) A teacher cannot be effective unless he or she retains the respect of students.

(B) Students respect honesty above all else.

(C) Students' respect for a teacher is independent of the amount of knowledge they attribute to that teacher.

(D) Teachers are able to tell when students respect them.

(E) Students lose respect for teachers whenever they sense that the teachers are trying to hide their ignorance.

PrepTest59 Sec2 Q17

46. About 3 billion years ago, the Sun was only 80 percent as luminous as it is currently. Such conditions today would result in the freezing of Earth's oceans, but geological evidence shows that water rather than ice filled the oceans at that time. Heat is trapped within Earth's atmosphere through the presence of carbon dioxide, which, like methane, is a "greenhouse gas." Only if the level of greenhouse gases were higher 3 billion years ago than it is today would Earth have retained enough heat to keep the oceans from freezing. It is likely, therefore, that the level of carbon dioxide in the atmosphere was significantly higher then than it is today.

Which one of the following, if true, weakens the argument?

(A) Sufficient heat to keep the oceans liquid 3 billion years ago could not have been generated through geological processes such as volcanic activity.

(B) Geological studies indicate that there is much less methane in Earth's atmosphere today than there was 3 billion years ago.

(C) Geological evidence indicates that the oceans contained greater amounts of dissolved minerals 3 billion years ago, but not enough to alter their freezing points significantly.

(D) The increase in the Sun's luminosity over the past 3 billion years roughly coincided with an increasing complexity of life forms on Earth.

(E) Because the distance from Earth to the Sun has not changed significantly over the last 3 billion years, the increase in the Sun's luminosity has resulted in more radiation reaching Earth.

PrepTest59 Sec2 Q25

Explanations for these questions can be found in your Online Center.

Part Three: Logical Reasoning
Assumption Family Questions

K

47. A university psychology department received a large donation from a textbook company after agreeing to use one of the company's books for a large introductory course. The department chair admitted that the department would not have received the donation if it used another company's textbook, but insisted that the book was chosen solely for academic reasons. As proof, she noted that the department's textbook committee had given that textbook its highest rating.

Which one of the following, if true, most weakens the case for the department chair's position?

(A) The members of the textbook committee were favorably influenced toward the textbook by the prospect of their department receiving a large donation.

(B) The department has a long-standing policy of using only textbooks that receive the committee's highest rating.

(C) In the previous year, a different textbook from the same company was used in the introductory course.

(D) The department chair is one of the members of the textbook committee.

(E) The textbook company does not routinely make donations to academic departments that use its books.

PrepTest59 Sec3 Q2

48. Producer: It has been argued that, while the government should not censor television shows, the public should boycott the advertisers of shows that promote violence and erode our country's values. But this would be censorship nonetheless, for if the public boycotted the advertisers, then they would cancel their advertisements, causing some shows to go off the air; the result would be a restriction of the shows that the public can watch.

The producer's conclusion is properly inferred if which one of the following is assumed?

(A) If there is neither government censorship nor boycotting of advertisers, there will be no restriction of the television shows that the public can watch.

(B) Public boycotts could force some shows off the air even though the shows neither promote violence nor erode values.

(C) For any television show that promotes violence and erodes values, there will be an audience.

(D) There is widespread public agreement about which television shows promote violence and erode values.

(E) Any action that leads to a restriction of what the public can view is censorship.

PrepTest59 Sec3 Q10

49. Predictions that printed books will soon be replaced by books in electronic formats such as CD-ROM are exaggerated. While research libraries may find an electronic format more convenient for scholars and scientists, bookstores and public libraries will stock books in the format desired by the general public, which will be something other than an electronic format.

Which one of the following, if true, most strengthens the argument?

(A) Scholars and scientists find an electronic format for books the most convenient one for quick searching and cross-referencing.

(B) Publishers will continue to print books in the format stocked by bookstores and public libraries.

(C) Scholars and scientists do not usually conduct their research in public libraries.

(D) At some bookstores and libraries, the popularity of books on tape and of videos is beginning to rival that of printed books.

(E) Some members of the general public prefer to purchase books in an electronic format rather than borrow them from the library.

PrepTest59 Sec3 Q11

50. A common genetic mutation that lowers levels of the enzyme cathepsin C severely reduces a person's ability to ward off periodontitis, or gum disease. The enzyme triggers immunological reactions that destroy diseased cells and eliminate infections in the mouth. But researchers are developing ways to restore the enzyme to normal levels. Once that happens, we will be able to eliminate periodontitis.

Which one of the following is an assumption on which the argument depends?

(A) Restoring cathepsin C to normal levels is the only way to eliminate periodontitis.

(B) Genetic mutation is the only cause of lowered levels of cathepsin C.

(C) Researchers will soon succeed in finding means of restoring cathepsin C to normal levels.

(D) Persons who do not have the genetic mutation that lowers levels of cathepsin C do not get gum disease.

(E) A person whose cathepsin C level has been restored to normal will not suffer from periodontitis.

PrepTest59 Sec3 Q16

Part Three: Logical Reasoning
CHAPTER 10

Explanations for these questions
can be found in your Online Center.

51. Eighteenth-century European aesthetics was reasonably successful in providing an understanding of all art, including early abstract art, until the 1960s, when artists self-consciously rebelled against earlier notions of art. Since the work of these rebellious artists is quite beautiful but outside the bounds of the aesthetic theory then current, there can be no complete theory of aesthetics.

The reasoning above is most vulnerable to criticism in that it

(A) takes for granted that it is more important for a complete aesthetic theory to account for the beauty of traditional art than for it to account for the beauty of self-consciously rebellious art

(B) presumes, without providing justification, that artists' rebellion in the 1960s against earlier notions of art was not guided by their knowledge of eighteenth-century European aesthetic theory

(C) presumes, without providing justification, that an aesthetic theory developed in one part of the world cannot be applied in another

(D) presumes, without providing justification, that art from the 1960s is the only art that cannot be adequately addressed by eighteenth-century European aesthetics

(E) presumes, without providing justification, that eighteenth-century European aesthetics is as encompassing as an aesthetic theory can be

PrepTest59 Sec3 Q24

52. Historian: Flavius, an ancient Roman governor who believed deeply in the virtues of manual labor and moral temperance, actively sought to discourage the arts by removing state financial support for them. Also, Flavius was widely unpopular among his subjects, as we can conclude from the large number of satirical plays that were written about him during his administration.

The historian's argumentation is most vulnerable to criticism on the grounds that it

(A) fails to consider the percentage of plays written during Flavius's administration that were not explicitly about Flavius

(B) treats the satirical plays as a reliable indicator of Flavius's popularity despite potential bias on the part of the playwrights

(C) presumes, without providing evidence, that Flavius was unfavorably disposed toward the arts

(D) takes for granted that Flavius's attempt to discourage the arts was successful

(E) fails to consider whether manual labor and moral temperance were widely regarded as virtues in ancient Rome

PrepTest57 Sec2 Q26

53. City council member: The Senior Guild has asked for a temporary exception to the ordinance prohibiting automobiles in municipal parks. Their case does appear to deserve the exception. However, if we grant this exception, we will find ourselves granting many other exceptions to this ordinance, some of which will be undeserved. Before long, we will be granting exceptions to all manner of other city ordinances. If we are to prevent anarchy in our city, we must deny the Senior Guild's request.

The city council member's argument is most vulnerable to criticism on the grounds that it

(A) distorts an argument and then attacks this distorted argument

(B) dismisses a claim because of its source rather than because of its content

(C) presumes, without sufficient warrant, that one event will lead to a particular causal sequence of events

(D) contains premises that contradict one another

(E) fails to make a needed distinction between deserved exceptions and undeserved ones

PrepTest57 Sec3 Q8

54. Physician: In comparing our country with two other countries of roughly the same population size, I found that even though we face the same dietary, bacterial, and stress-related causes of ulcers as they do, prescriptions for ulcer medicines in all socioeconomic strata are much rarer here than in those two countries. It's clear that we suffer significantly fewer ulcers, per capita, than they do.

Which one of the following, if true, most strengthens the physician's argument?

(A) The two countries that were compared with the physician's country had approximately the same ulcer rates as each other.

(B) The people of the physician's country have a cultural tradition of stoicism that encourages them to ignore physical ailments rather than to seek remedies for them.

(C) Several other countries not covered in the physician's comparisons have more prescriptions for ulcer medication than does the physician's country.

(D) A person in the physician's country who is suffering from ulcers is just as likely to obtain a prescription for the ailment as is a person suffering from ulcers in one of the other two countries.

(E) The physician's country has a much better system for reporting the number of prescriptions of a given type that are obtained each year than is present in either of the other two countries.

PrepTest57 Sec3 Q9

Explanations for these questions can be found in your Online Center.

Part Three: Logical Reasoning
Assumption Family Questions

55. Columnist: The failure of bicyclists to obey traffic regulations is a causal factor in more than one quarter of the traffic accidents involving bicycles. Since inadequate bicycle safety equipment is also a factor in more than a quarter of such accidents, bicyclists are at least partially responsible for more than half of the traffic accidents involving bicycles.

The columnist's reasoning is flawed in that it

(A) presumes, without providing justification, that motorists are a factor in less than half of the traffic accidents involving bicycles
(B) improperly infers the presence of a causal connection on the basis of a correlation
(C) fails to consider the possibility that more than one factor may contribute to a given accident
(D) fails to provide the source of the figures it cites
(E) fails to consider that the severity of injuries to bicyclists from traffic accidents can vary widely

PrepTest57 Sec3 Q10

56. A study found that patients referred by their doctors to psychotherapists practicing a new experimental form of therapy made more progress with respect to their problems than those referred to psychotherapists practicing traditional forms of therapy. Therapists practicing the new form of therapy, therefore, are more effective than therapists practicing traditional forms.

Which one of the following most accurately describes a flaw in the argument?

(A) It ignores the possibility that therapists trained in traditional forms of therapy use the same techniques in treating their patients as therapists trained in the new form of therapy do.
(B) It ignores the possibility that the patients referred to therapists practicing the new form of therapy had problems more amenable to treatment than did those referred to therapists practicing traditional forms.
(C) It presumes, without providing justification, that any psychotherapist trained in traditional forms of therapy is untrained in the new form of therapy.
(D) It ignores the possibility that therapists practicing the new form of therapy systematically differ from therapists practicing traditional forms of therapy with regard to some personality attribute relevant to effective treatment.
(E) It presumes, without providing justification, that the personal rapport between therapist and patient has no influence on the effectiveness of the treatment the patient receives.

PrepTest57 Sec3 Q18

57. To win democratic elections that are not fully subsidized by the government, nonwealthy candidates must be supported by wealthy patrons. This makes plausible the belief that these candidates will compromise their views to win that support. But since the wealthy are dispersed among the various political parties in roughly equal proportion to their percentage in the overall population, this belief is false.

The argument is vulnerable to criticism on the grounds that it fails to consider that

(A) the primary function of political parties in democracies whose governments do not subsidize elections might not be to provide a means of negating the influence of wealth on elections
(B) in democracies in which elections are not fully subsidized by the government, positions endorsed by political parties might be much less varied than the positions taken by candidates
(C) in democracies, government-subsidized elections ensure that the views expressed by the people who run for office might not be overly influenced by the opinions of the wealthiest people in those countries
(D) in democracies in which elections are not fully subsidized by the government, it might be no easier for a wealthy person to win an election than it is for a nonwealthy person to win an election
(E) a democracy in which candidates do not compromise their views in order to be elected to office might have other flaws

PrepTest57 Sec3 Q22

58. We already knew from thorough investigation that immediately prior to the accident, either the driver of the first vehicle changed lanes without signaling or the driver of the second vehicle was driving with excessive speed. Either of these actions would make a driver liable for the resulting accident. But further evidence has proved that the first vehicle's turn signal was not on, though the driver of that vehicle admits to having changed lanes. So the driver of the second vehicle is not liable for the accident.

Which one of the following would be most important to know in evaluating the conclusion drawn above?

(A) whether the second vehicle was being driven at excessive speed
(B) whether the driver of the first vehicle knew that the turn signal was not on
(C) whether any other vehicles were involved in the accident
(D) whether the driver of the first vehicle was a reliable witness
(E) whether the driver of the second vehicle would have seen the turn signal flashing had it been on

PrepTest51 Sec1 Q2

K

Part Three: Logical Reasoning
CHAPTER 10

Explanations for these questions
can be found in your Online Center.

59. Advertisement: Seventy-five percent of dermatologists surveyed prefer Dermactin to all other brands of skin cream. Why? We consulted dermatologists during the development of Dermactin to ensure that you have the best skin cream on the market. So if you need a skin cream, use Dermactin.

The reasoning in the advertisement is questionable because the advertisement

(A) overlooks the possibility that other types of doctors have cause to use Dermactin, which would render the sample unrepresentative

(B) fails to state the number of dermatologists surveyed, which leaves open the possibility that the sample of doctors is too small to be reliable

(C) presumes, without providing justification, that some dermatologists are less qualified than others to evaluate skin cream

(D) relies on an inappropriate appeal to the opinions of consumers with no special knowledge of skin care

(E) overlooks the possibility that for a few people, using no skin cream is preferable to using even the best skin cream

PrepTest51 Sec1 Q4

60. Studies have shown that treating certain illnesses with treatment X produces the same beneficial changes in patients' conditions as treating the same illnesses with treatment Y. Furthermore, treatment X is quicker and less expensive than treatment Y. Thus, in treating these illnesses, treatment X should be preferred to treatment Y.

Which one of the following, if true, would most weaken the argument above?

(A) Unlike treatment Y, treatment X has produced harmful side effects in laboratory animals.

(B) There are other illnesses for which treatment Y is more effective than treatment X.

(C) Until recently, treatment X was more expensive than treatment Y.

(D) Treatment Y is prescribed more often by physicians than treatment X.

(E) A third treatment, treatment Z, is even quicker and less expensive than treatment X.

PrepTest51 Sec3 Q1

61. Safety considerations aside, nuclear power plants are not economically feasible. While the cost of fuel for nuclear plants is significantly lower than the cost of conventional fuels, such as coal and oil, nuclear plants are far more expensive to build than are conventional power plants.

Which one of the following, if true, most strengthens the argument?

(A) Safety regulations can increase the costs of running both conventional and nuclear power plants.

(B) Conventional power plants spend more time out of service than do nuclear power plants.

(C) The average life expectancy of a nuclear power plant is shorter than that of a conventional one.

(D) Nuclear power plants cost less to build today than they cost to build when their technology was newly developed.

(E) As conventional fuels become scarcer their cost will increase dramatically, which will increase the cost of running a conventional power plant.

PrepTest51 Sec3 Q3

62. Letter to the editor: I have never seen such flawed reasoning and distorted evidence as that which you tried to pass off as a balanced study in the article "Speed Limits, Fatalities, and Public Policy." The article states that areas with lower speed limits had lower vehicle-related fatality rates than other areas. However, that will not be true for long, since vehicle-related fatality rates are rising in the areas with lower speed limits. So the evidence actually supports the view that speed limits should be increased.

The reasoning in the letter writer's argument is flawed because the argument

(A) bases its conclusion on findings from the same article that it is criticizing

(B) fails to consider the possibility that automobile accidents that occur at high speeds often result in fatalities

(C) fails to consider the possibility that not everyone wants to drive faster

(D) fails to consider the possibility that the vehicle-related fatality rates in other areas are also rising

(E) does not present any claims as evidence against the opposing viewpoint

PrepTest51 Sec3 Q9

Explanations for these questions can be found in your Online Center.

Part Three: Logical Reasoning
Assumption Family Questions   K

63. Sociologist: A contention of many of my colleagues—that the large difference between the wages of the highest- and lowest-paid workers will inevitably become a source of social friction—is unfounded. Indeed, the high differential should have an opposite effect, for it means that companies will be able to hire freely in response to changing conditions. Social friction arises not from large wage differences, but from wage levels that are static or slow changing.

Which one of the following is an assumption required by the sociologist's argument?

(A) When companies can hire freely in response to changing conditions, wage levels do not tend to be static or slow changing.

(B) People who expect their wages to rise react differently than do others to obvious disparities in income.

(C) A lack of financial caution causes companies to expand their operations.

(D) A company's ability to respond swiftly to changing conditions always benefits its workers.

(E) Even relatively well-paid workers may become dissatisfied with their jobs if their wages never change.

PrepTest51 Sec3 Q15

64. The flagellum, which bacteria use to swim, requires many parts before it can propel a bacterium at all. Therefore, an evolutionary ancestor of bacteria that had only a few of these parts would gain no survival advantage from them.

Which one of the following is an assumption on which the argument depends?

(A) Any of bacteria's evolutionary ancestors that had only a few of the parts of the flagellum would be at a disadvantage relative to similar organisms that had none of these parts.

(B) For parts now incorporated into the flagellum to have aided an organism's survival, they would have had to help it swim.

(C) All parts of the flagellum are vital to each of its functions.

(D) No evolutionary ancestor of bacteria had only a few of the parts of the flagellum.

(E) Any of bacteria's evolutionary ancestors that lacked a flagellum also lacked the capacity to swim.

PrepTest51 Sec3 Q18

65. Child psychologist: Some studies in which children have been observed before and after playing video games with violent content have shown that young children tend to behave more aggressively immediately after playing the games. This suggests that the violence in such video games leads young children to believe that aggressive behavior is acceptable.

Each of the following, if true, strengthens the child psychologist's argument EXCEPT:

(A) Young children tend to be more accepting of aggressive behavior in others immediately after playing video games with violent content.

(B) Many young children who have never played video games with violent content believe that aggressive behavior is acceptable.

(C) Other studies have shown no increase in aggressive behavior in young children who have just played nonviolent video games.

(D) Older children are less likely before playing video games with violent content than they are afterwards to believe that aggressive behavior is acceptable.

(E) Young children tend to behave more aggressively immediately after being told that aggressive behavior is acceptable than they did beforehand.

PrepTest49 Sec2 Q4

66. Cecile's association requires public disclosure of an officer's investments in two cases only: when an officer is authorized to disburse association funds, and when an officer sits on the board of a petrochemical company. Cecile, an officer who is not authorized to disburse funds, sits on the board of just one company, a small timber business. Therefore, there is no reason for Cecile to publicly disclose her investments at this time.

The conclusion of the argument follows logically if which one of the following is assumed?

(A) Cecile will not be appointed to a position in the association that authorizes her to disburse funds.

(B) Cecile's office and her position on the timber business's board create no conflicts of interest.

(C) The association's requirements provide the only reasons there might be for Cecile to disclose her investments.

(D) The timber business on whose board Cecile sits is owned by a petrochemical company.

(E) Cecile owns no investments in the petrochemical industry.

PrepTest49 Sec2 Q25

K

Part Three: Logical Reasoning

CHAPTER 10

Explanations for these questions can be found in your Online Center.

67. The simultaneous and apparently independent development in several ancient cultures of a myth of creatures who were half human and half horse parallels the increased use of horses in these cultures. But despite the nobility and gentleness traditionally ascribed to the horse, the mythical half-horse, half-humans were frequently portrayed as violent and savage. Many human cultures use myth to express unconscious thoughts, so these mythical creatures obviously reflect people's unconscious fear of the horse.

The reasoning in the argument is flawed because the argument

(A) fails to show that the mythical creature mentioned represents the horse in people's minds

(B) fails to consider that people might have good reason to fear horses

(C) confuses the expression of unconscious thoughts with the suppression of them

(D) fails to demonstrate that the myth was not borrowed from one of the cultures by the others

(E) fails to explain why people use myth for the expression of unconscious thoughts

PrepTest49 Sec4 Q6

68. One good clue as to which geographical regions an ancient relic was moved through in the past involves the analysis of pollen that clings to the surface of the relic. A relic is linked to a geographical area by the identification of pollen from plants that are known to have been unique to that area.

Which one of the following, if true, casts the most doubt on the reliability of the method described above?

(A) Pollens are often transported from one region to another by wind or human movement.

(B) There are several less complicated methods of determining the history of the movement of an object than the analysis and identification of pollen.

(C) Many types of pollen were common to several geographical regions in the ancient world.

(D) Data are scarce as to the geographical distribution of the pollens of many ancient plants.

(E) Pollen analysis is a painstaking process that is also expensive to conduct.

PrepTest49 Sec4 Q8

69. A physician has a duty to see to the health and best medical interests of the patient. On the other hand, the patient has a right to be fully informed about any negative findings concerning the patient's health. When this duty conflicts with this right, the right should prevail since it is a basic right. Anything else carries the risk of treating the patient as a mere object, not as a person.

The conclusion drawn above follows logically if which one of the following is assumed?

(A) All persons have a right to accept or reject any medical procedures proposed by a physician.

(B) Some actions are right independently of the consequences that might ensue.

(C) Because only persons have rights, objects do not have rights.

(D) A person's basic rights should never be violated.

(E) In medicine, the patient's basic right to information is stronger than most other rights.

PrepTest49 Sec4 Q18

70. Magazine article: Sugar consumption may exacerbate attention deficit disorder (ADD) in children. A recent study found that children produce large amounts of adrenaline within hours after consuming large amounts of sugar. This increase in adrenaline is especially noticeable if the source of sugar is candy, in which case the sugar's effects are not ameliorated by the ingestion of other foodstuffs.

Which one of the following is an assumption on which the argument in the magazine article depends?

(A) The adrenaline level of children who do not have ADD is not increased by excessive sugar consumption.

(B) Overproduction of adrenaline causes ADD in children.

(C) The most effective way to treat ADD in children is to restrict their intake of sugars.

(D) Increased adrenaline production can make ADD more severe in children.

(E) Sugar consumed with food substances other than candy does not substantially increase the level of adrenaline in the bloodstream of children with ADD.

PrepTest49 Sec4 Q20

Explanations for these questions can be found in your Online Center.

Part Three: Logical Reasoning
Assumption Family Questions

71. Economist: Some people argue that when large countries split into several small countries, the world economy is harmed by increased barriers to free trade in the form of an increased number of national tariffs. But small countries do not think of themselves as economically self-sufficient. Therefore, such division of large countries does not increase barriers to free trade.

Which one of the following, if assumed, enables the economist's conclusion to be properly drawn?

(A) A country has the right to split into smaller countries even if some of the economic consequences of division would harm the world economy.

(B) Increasing the number of countries in the world would strengthen rather than weaken the world economy.

(C) All countries that impose national tariffs or other barriers to free trade think of themselves as economically self-sufficient.

(D) There is strong evidence that national tariffs and other barriers to free trade harm the world economy.

(E) Large countries tend to be more economically self-sufficient than small countries.

PrepTest49 Sec4 Q22

72. Bowers: A few theorists hold the extreme view that society could flourish in a condition of anarchy, the absence of government. Some of these theorists have even produced interesting arguments to support that position. One writer, for example, contends that anarchy is laissez-faire capitalism taken to its logical extreme. But these theorists' views ignore the fundamental principle of social philosophy—that an acceptable social philosophy must promote peace and order. Any social philosophy that countenances chaos, i.e., anarchy, accordingly deserves no further attention.

The reasoning in Bowers's argument is most vulnerable to criticism on the grounds that

(A) the meaning of a key term shifts illicitly during the course of the argument

(B) the argument fails to show that laissez-faire capitalism deserves to be rejected as a social philosophy

(C) the truth or falsity of a view is not determined by the number of people who accept it as true

(D) the argument presumes, without providing justification, that any peaceful society will flourish

(E) it is unreasonable to reject a view merely because it can be described as extreme

PrepTest59 Sec2 Q15

K | Part Three: Logical Reasoning
CHAPTER 10

Explanations for these questions
can be found in your Online Center.

Principle Questions

This pool consists of Assumption Family Principle questions and Identify and Apply the Principle questions you have not seen in earlier chapters. They are arranged in reverse chronological order—from most to least recent.

73. Vandenburg: This art museum is not adhering to its purpose. Its founders intended it to devote as much attention to contemporary art as to the art of earlier periods, but its collection of contemporary art is far smaller than its other collections.

    Simpson: The relatively small size of the museum's contemporary art collection is appropriate. It's an art museum, not an ethnographic museum designed to collect every style of every period. Its contemporary art collection is small because its curators believe that there is little high-quality contemporary art.

    Which one of the following principles, if valid, most helps to justify the reasoning in Simpson's response to Vandenburg?

    (A) An art museum should collect only works that its curators consider to be of high artistic quality.
    (B) An art museum should not collect any works that violate the purpose defined by the museum's founders.
    (C) An art museum's purpose need not be to collect every style of every period.
    (D) An ethnographic museum's purpose should be defined according to its curators' beliefs.
    (E) The intentions of an art museum's curators should not determine what is collected by that museum.

    PrepTest61 Sec2 Q5

74. Columnist: Although much has been learned, we are still largely ignorant of the intricate interrelationships among species of living organisms. We should, therefore, try to preserve the maximum number of species if we have an interest in preserving any, since allowing species toward which we are indifferent to perish might undermine the viability of other species.

    Which one of the following principles, if valid, most helps to justify the columnist's argument?

    (A) It is strongly in our interest to preserve certain plant and animal species.
    (B) We should not take any action until all relevant scientific facts have been established and taken into account.
    (C) We should not allow the number of species to diminish any further than is necessary for the flourishing of present and future human populations.
    (D) We should not allow a change to occur unless we are assured that that change will not jeopardize anything that is important to us.
    (E) We should always undertake the course of action that is likely to have the best consequences in the immediate future.

    PrepTest61 Sec4 Q23

Explanations for these questions
can be found in your Online Center.

Part Three: Logical Reasoning
Assumption Family Questions

K

75. A recent magazine editorial criticizes psychologists for not attempting to establish the order in which different areas of the brain are activated during a cognitive task such as imagining the face of a friend. However, the editorial is unfair because there is currently no technology that can detect the order of activation of brain areas.

Which one of the following most closely conforms to the principle to which the reasoning in the passage conforms?

(A) Construction companies have been unfairly criticized for using fewer layers of heating insulation in new houses than the number of layers used in previous years. Recent technology has made insulation more efficient, so fewer layers are required.

(B) Utility companies have been unfairly criticized for not using nuclear fusion to meet the nation's electricity needs. There is no way to harness fusion that could produce enough electricity to supply even one small town.

(C) The food industry has been unfairly criticized for attempting to preserve food longer by treating it with radiation. If food remained edible for longer, the cost of food would decrease substantially.

(D) The school system has been unfairly criticized for not making familiarity with computer technology a requirement. Computer studies could not be added to the curriculum without sacrificing some other subject.

(E) CEOs of large companies have been unfairly criticized for not always using their knowledge of economic theory to run their companies. Economic theory is sometimes irrelevant to making wise corporate decisions.

PrepTest59 Sec3 Q6

76. Essayist: One of the drawbacks of extreme personal and political freedom is that free choices are often made for the worst. To expect people to thrive when they are given the freedom to make unwise decisions is frequently unrealistic. Once people see the destructive consequences of extreme freedom, they may prefer to establish totalitarian political regimes that allow virtually no freedom. Thus, one should not support political systems that allow extreme freedom.

Which one of the following principles, if valid, most helps to justify the essayist's reasoning?

(A) One should not support any political system that will inevitably lead to the establishment of a totalitarian political regime.

(B) One should not expect everyone to thrive even in a political system that maximizes people's freedom in the long run.

(C) One should support only those political systems that give people the freedom to make wise choices.

(D) One should not support any political system whose destructive consequences could lead people to prefer totalitarian political regimes.

(E) One should not support any political system that is based on unrealistic expectations about people's behavior under that system.

PrepTest57 Sec3 Q19

K | Part Three: Logical Reasoning
CHAPTER 10

Explanations for these questions
can be found in your Online Center.

77. The greater the number of people who regularly use a product, the greater the number whose health is potentially at risk due to that product. More people regularly use household maintenance products such as cleaning agents and lawn chemicals than regularly use prescription medicines. Therefore, it is even more important for such household products to be carefully tested to ensure their safety than it is for prescription medicines to be so tested.

Which one of the following principles, if valid, most helps to justify drawing the conclusion in the argument above?

(A) Whether or not it is important for a given product to be carefully tested depends mainly on the number of people who regularly use that product.

(B) It is very important for any product that is regularly used by a large number of people to be carefully tested to ensure its safety.

(C) The more people whose health might be at risk from the regular use of a particular product, the more important it is for that product to be carefully tested to ensure its safety.

(D) If one type of medicine must be taken in more frequent doses than another type of medicine, it is more important for the former to be carefully tested than for the latter.

(E) It is generally more important for a medicine than it is for a nonmedical product to be carefully tested to ensure its safety unless more people's health would be at risk from the nonmedical product than from the medicine.

PrepTest49 Sec2 Q15

78. Whether one is buying men's or women's clothing, it pays to consider fashion trends. A classic suit may stay in style for as long as five years, so it is worthwhile to pay more to get a well-constructed one. A trendy hat that will go out of style in a year or two should be purchased as cheaply as possible.

Which one of the following most accurately expresses the principle underlying the reasoning above?

(A) Formal attire tends to be designed and constructed to last longer than casual attire.

(B) The amount of money one spends on a garment should be roughly proportionate to the length of time one plans to keep wearing it.

(C) One should not buy a cheaply made garment when a well-constructed garment is available.

(D) The amount of money one spends on clothing should be roughly the same whether one is purchasing men's or women's attire.

(E) It is more appropriate to spend money on office attire than on casual attire.

PrepTest51 Sec3 Q7

Explanations for these questions
can be found in your Online Center.

Part Three: Logical Reasoning
Assumption Family Questions

Parallel Reasoning and Parallel Flaw Questions

This pool consists of Parallel Reasoning and Parallel Flaw questions you have not seen in earlier chapters. They are arranged in reverse chronological order — from most to least recent.

79. Every brick house on River Street has a front yard. Most of the houses on River Street that have front yards also have two stories. So most of the brick houses on River Street have two stories.

    Which one of the following is most appropriate as an analogy demonstrating that the reasoning in the argument above is flawed?

    (A) By that line of reasoning, we could conclude that most politicians have run for office, since all legislators are politicians and most legislators have run for office.

    (B) By that line of reasoning, we could conclude that most public servants are legislators, since most legislators have run for office and most politicians who have run for office are public servants.

    (C) By that line of reasoning, we could conclude that not every public servant has run for office, since every legislator is a public servant but some public servants are not legislators.

    (D) By that line of reasoning, we could conclude that most legislators have never run for office, since most public servants have never run for office and all legislators are public servants.

    (E) By that line of reasoning, we could conclude that most legislators are not public servants, since most public servants have not run for office and most legislators have run for office.

    PrepTest61 Sec2 Q23

80. In a sample containing 1,000 peanuts from lot A and 1,000 peanuts from lot B, 50 of the peanuts from lot A were found to be infected with *Aspergillus*. Two hundred of the peanuts from lot B were found to be infected with *Aspergillus*. Therefore, infection with *Aspergillus* is more widespread in lot B than in lot A.

    The reasoning in which one of the following is most similar to the reasoning in the argument above?

    (A) Every one of these varied machine parts is of uniformly high quality. Therefore, the machine that we assemble from them will be of equally high quality.

    (B) If a plant is carelessly treated, it is likely to develop blight. If a plant develops blight, it is likely to die. Therefore, if a plant is carelessly treated, it is likely to die.

    (C) In the past 1,000 experiments, whenever an experimental fungicide was applied to coffee plants infected with coffee rust, the infection disappeared. The coffee rust never disappeared before the fungicide was applied. Therefore, in these experiments, application of the fungicide caused the disappearance of coffee rust.

    (D) Three thousand registered voters—1,500 members of the Liberal party and 1,500 members of the Conservative party—were asked which mayoral candidate they favored. Four hundred of the Liberals and 300 of the Conservatives favored Pollack. Therefore, Pollack has more support among Liberals than among Conservatives.

    (E) All of my livestock are registered with the regional authority. None of the livestock registered with the regional authority are free-range livestock. Therefore, none of my livestock are free-range livestock.

    PrepTest61 Sec4 Q9

K | Part Three: Logical Reasoning
CHAPTER 10

Explanations for these questions
can be found in your Online Center.

81. Economist: Countries with an uneducated population are destined to be weak economically and politically, whereas those with an educated population have governments that display a serious financial commitment to public education. So any nation with a government that has made such a commitment will avoid economic and political weakness.

The pattern of flawed reasoning in which one of the following arguments is most similar to that in the economist's argument?

(A) Animal species with a very narrow diet will have more difficulty surviving if the climate suddenly changes, but a species with a broader diet will not; for changes in the climate can remove the traditional food supply.

(B) People incapable of empathy are not good candidates for public office, but those who do have the capacity for empathy are able to manipulate others easily; hence, people who can manipulate others are good candidates for public office.

(C) People who cannot give orders are those who do not understand the personalities of the people to whom they give orders. Thus, those who can give orders are those who understand the personalities of the people to whom they give orders.

(D) Poets who create poetry of high quality are those who have studied traditional poetry, because poets who have not studied traditional poetry are the poets most likely to create something shockingly inventive, and poetry that is shockingly inventive is rarely fine poetry.

(E) People who dislike exercise are unlikely to lose weight without sharply curtailing their food intake; but since those who dislike activity generally tend to avoid it, people who like to eat but dislike exercise will probably fail to lose weight.

PrepTest61 Sec4 Q26

82. No member of the Richardson Theater Group is both a performer and an administrator. Since Leon and Marta are both members of the Richardson Theater Group but neither is an administrator, it follows that both are performers.

Which one of the following arguments displays a flawed pattern of reasoning most similar to that in the argument above?

(A) Not all of the employees of the Tedenco Company are salaried employees of that company. Since Mr. López and Ms. Allen are both salaried employees of the Tedenco Company, it follows that they are not the only employees of the Tedenco Company.

(B) No employee of the Tedenco Company is both an accountant and a corporate attorney. Since Ms. Walsh is both an accountant and a corporate attorney, it follows that she is not an employee of the Tedenco Company.

(C) No company can have its headquarters in both Canada and Mexico. Since neither the Dumone Company nor the Tedenco Company has its headquarters in Mexico, it follows that both have their headquarters in Canada.

(D) No corporate attorney represents both the Dumone Company and the Tedenco Company. Since Ms. Tseung is a corporate attorney who represents the Dumone Company, it follows that she does not also represent the Tedenco Company.

(E) No member of the board of directors of the Dumone Company is also a member of the board of directors of the Tedenco Company. Since neither company has fewer than five board members, it follows that both boards together include at least ten members.

PrepTest59 Sec2 Q9

Explanations for these questions can be found in your Online Center.

Part Three: Logical Reasoning
Assumption Family Questions | K

83. All poets, aside from those who write only epigrams, have wit. All lyrical composers are poets. Azriel does not write epigrams, though he is a lyrical composer. So Azriel has wit.

The pattern of reasoning in which one of the following is most similar to that in the argument above?

(A) All squeeze toys, except those designed for cats, are safe for infants. All squeeze toys are sold prewrapped. This item is not designed for cats, and it is sold prewrapped. So it must be safe for infants.

(B) Aside from the dogcatcher and the police chief, all of the politicians in town are lawyers. All of the politicians in town have websites. Sal is a politician in town, but is neither the dogcatcher nor the police chief. Since Sal is a politician in town he must have a website.

(C) All visas are assigned by this office, except for those that are issued through diplomatic channels. All visit permits are visas. Thus, the visit permit in Will's passport was assigned through diplomatic channels.

(D) All of this store's winter garments are on sale, except for the designer clothes. None of the shirts in this store are designer clothes. This shirt, therefore, since it is on sale, is a winter garment.

(E) All residential buildings are subject to the original fire code, except for those built last year. All townhouses are residential buildings. Bloom House was not built last year, and it is a townhouse, so it is subject to the original fire code.

PrepTest59 Sec2 Q16

84. Medical ethicist: Assuming there is a reasonable chance for a cure, it is acceptable to offer experimental treatments for a disease to patients who suffer from extreme symptoms of that disease. Such patients are best able to weigh a treatment's risks against the benefits of a cure. Therefore, it is never acceptable to offer experimental treatments to patients who experience no extreme symptoms of the relevant disease.

The flawed reasoning in which one of the following is most similar to the flawed reasoning in the medical ethicist's argument?

(A) Even a geological engineer with a background in economics can lose money investing in mineral extraction. So, those who are less knowledgeable about geology or economics should not expect to make money in every investment in mineral extraction.

(B) One is always in a better position to judge whether an automobile would be worth its cost if one has test-driven that automobile. Therefore, if an automobile proves to be not worth its cost, it is likely that it was not test-driven.

(C) Someone born and raised in a country, who has lived abroad and then returned, is exceptionally qualified to judge the merits of living in that country. That is why someone who has not lived in that country should not form judgments about the merits of living there.

(D) One can never eliminate all of the risks of daily life, and even trying to avoid every risk in life is costly. Therefore, anyone who is reasonable will accept some of the risks of daily life.

(E) Almost any industrial development will have unwelcome environmental side effects. Therefore, it is not worthwhile to weigh the costs of potential environmental side effects since such side effects are unavoidable.

PrepTest57 Sec3 Q15

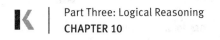

Part Three: Logical Reasoning
CHAPTER 10

Explanations for these questions
can be found in your Online Center.

85. Ethicist: Every moral action is the keeping of an agreement, and keeping an agreement is nothing more than an act of securing mutual benefit. Clearly, however, not all instances of agreement-keeping are moral actions. Therefore, some acts of securing mutual benefit are not moral actions.

The pattern of reasoning in which one of the following arguments is most similar to that in the ethicist's argument?

(A) All calculators are kinds of computers, and all computers are devices for automated reasoning. However, not all devices for automated reasoning are calculators. Therefore, some devices for automated reasoning are not computers.

(B) All exercise is beneficial, and all things that are beneficial promote health. However, not all things that are beneficial are forms of exercise. Therefore, some exercise does not promote health.

(C) All metaphors are comparisons, and not all comparisons are surprising. However, all metaphors are surprising. Therefore, some comparisons are not metaphors.

(D) All architecture is design and all design is art. However, not all design is architecture. Therefore, some art is not design.

(E) All books are texts, and all texts are documents. However, not all texts are books. Therefore, some documents are not books.

PrepTest57 Sec3 Q20

86. The obesity invariably associated with some high-fat diets is caused by an absence in these diets of certain nutrients that are necessary for an active metabolism, not by excessive caloric intake. Hence, people on these high-fat diets do not consume too many calories.

The questionable pattern of reasoning in the argument above is most similar to that in which one of the following?

(A) Electrical storms are strongly correlated with precipitous drops in barometric pressure. So, electrical storms are caused by such drops in pressure, rather than by air turbulence.

(B) The impression that most viewers of sports programming are beer drinkers is due not to mere stereotyping but to the vast number of beer commercials broadcast during televised sports. Hence, most beer drinkers are avid fans of sports programs.

(C) The disorientation observed in airline pilots after transoceanic flights is caused not by sleep deprivation but by disruption in their exposure to daylight. Hence, transoceanic pilots do not suffer from sleep deprivation.

(D) Stock market crashes are due, not to panic in the face of predicted economic downturns, but to mere rumormongering without any basis in fact. Hence, economic downturns cannot be accurately predicted.

(E) The preponderance of mathematics graduates among professional computer programmers is due not to the intelligence of mathematicians but to the appropriateness of mathematical training for computer programming. Hence, most computer programmers have mathematical training.

PrepTest49 Sec2 Q26

Answer Key

Assumption Questions

1. B
2. D
3. B
4. B
5. D
6. E
7. D
8. B
9. C
10. E

Flaw Questions

11. A
12. A
13. B
14. D
15. C
16. D
17. D
18. D
19. C
20. A
21. E
22. D
23. D
24. E
25. B

Strengthen/Weaken Questions

26. C
27. B
28. D
29. E
30. A
31. C
32. D
33. C
34. E
35. D
36. A
37. C
38. C

Mixed Practice: Assumption, Flaw, Strengthen/Weaken Questions

39. D
40. A
41. D
42. E
43. B
44. A
45. E
46. B
47. A
48. E
49. B
50. E
51. E
52. B
53. C
54. D
55. C
56. B
57. B
58. A
59. B
60. A
61. C
62. D
63. A
64. B
65. B
66. C
67. A
68. A
69. D
70. D
71. C
72. A

Principle Questions

73. A
74. D
75. B
76. D
77. C
78. B

Parallel Reasoning and Parallel Flaw Questions

79. D
80. D
81. B
82. C
83. E
84. C
85. E
86. C

Complete explanations for these questions can be found in your Online Center.

Non-Argument Questions

Though most Logical Reasoning questions test your ability to analyze arguments, a significant number do not. Instead, these Non-Argument questions reward your ability to make valid deductions and inferences from a set of statements (Inference questions and some Principle questions) or to resolve an apparent discrepancy (Paradox questions). The best way to see the fundamental difference between Argument-Based and Non-Argument questions is to set questions of each type side by side.

Inference Question

Baxe Interiors, one of the largest interior design companies in existence, currently has a near monopoly in the corporate market. Several small design companies have won prestigious awards for their corporate work, while Baxe has won none. Nonetheless, the corporate managers who solicit design proposals will only contract with companies they believe are unlikely to go bankrupt, and they believe that only very large companies are unlikely to go bankrupt.

The statements above, if true, most strongly support which one of the following?

(A)   There are other very large design companies besides Baxe, but they produce designs that are inferior to Baxe's.

(B)   Baxe does not have a near monopoly in the market of any category of interior design other than corporate interiors.

(C)   For the most part, designs that are produced by small companies are superior to the designs produced by Baxe.

(D)   At least some of the corporate managers who solicit design proposals are unaware that there are designs that are much better than those produced by Baxe.

(E)   The existence of interior designs that are superior to those produced by Baxe does not currently threaten its near monopoly in the corporate market.

PrepTest61 Sec4 Q7

Strengthen Question

A recent study confirms that nutritious breakfasts make workers more productive. For one month, workers at Plant A received free nutritious breakfasts every day before work, while workers in Plant B did not. The productivity of Plant A's workers increased, while that of Plant B's workers did not.

Which one of **the following, if true**, most strengthens the argument?

(A)   Few workers in Plant B consumed nutritious breakfasts during the month of the study.

(B)   Workers in the study from Plant A and Plant B started work at the same time of day.

(C)   During the month before the study, workers at Plant A and Plant B were equally productive.

(D)   Workers from Plant A took fewer vacation days per capita during the month than did workers from Plant B.

(E)   Workers in Plant B were more productive during the month of the study than were workers from Plant A.

PrepTest59 Sec2 Q22

Notice that in the Non-Argument Inference question, the statements in the stimulus lead to the correct answer; in the Assumption Family Strengthen question, on the other hand, the correct answer supplements the argument in the stimulus. This pattern holds true for all questions in these families.

MAKING DEDUCTIONS AND INFERENCE QUESTIONS

Inference questions present a stimulus containing a number of related factual statements; then, you are asked to find an answer choice that must, could, or cannot be true based on those statements.

You can recognize Inference questions from question stems such as these:

If all of the statements above are true, then which one of the following must be true?

PrepTest61 Sec2 Q3

Which one of the following can be properly inferred from the information above?

PrepTest61 Sec2 Q10

Which one of the following is most strongly supported by the information above?

PrepTest59 Sec3 Q3

The statements above, if true, most support which one of the following?

PrepTest49 Sec2 Q9

The large majority of Inference questions, like those shown here, call for a correct answer that must be true based on the statements in the stimulus or that is most strongly supported by those statements. A handful of Inference questions, however, will ask for the answer that must be false or that receives no support from the stimulus.

The statements above, if true, provide support for each of the following EXCEPT:

PrepTest61 Sec4 Q3

If the statements above are true, then each of the following could also be true EXCEPT:

PrepTest49 Sec2 Q21

The facts described above provide the strongest evidence against which one of the following?

PrepTest57 Sec2 Q23

We'll analyze Inference question stems in more detail shortly.

INFERENCE QUESTIONS AT A GLANCE

Task: Identify the statement that must, could, or cannot be true based on a set of statements.

Strategy: Catalogue the statements in the stimulus: Identify the most concrete statement; combine related statements; note relationships indicated by Keywords; and/or use Formal Logic to evaluate the answer choices.

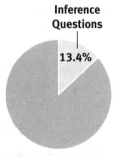

Inference Questions

13.4%

Logical Reasoning Question Types

PrepTests57–71; released 2009–2013

LSAT tests released from 2009 to 2013 had an average of 6.8 Inference questions per test.

Incidentally, on most tests, the Inference questions are split just about 50-50 between those calling for a correct answer that must be true based on the stimulus and those calling for the answer most strongly supported by the stimulus.

LEARNING OBJECTIVES

In this section, you'll learn to:

- Make valid inferences from single statements of fact
- Combine two or more statements to make valid inferences
- Recognize and use Keywords to make valid inferences
- Recognize and use Formal Logic to make valid inferences
- Recognize and use uncertain statements to make valid inferences
- Identify and answer Inference questions

If the Inference question stems on the previous page reminded you of Logic Games questions, your instincts are correct. Your task in Inference questions is much like that in the Logic Games section, except here, you are working with sets of statements rather than with rules.

TEST DAY TIP

Just as it does in Logic Games, the test gives you everything you need to distinguish the one correct answer from the four wrong answers in Inference questions.

Apply the same discipline to Inference questions that you've learned to exercise in Logic Games. Answer the question directly from the statements. Make sure you consider what the statements do and do not mean. Consider the following:

> Most members of Alpha Beta Chi are in-state students, and most members of Alpha Beta Chi enjoy playing basketball.

Which of the following statements is a valid inference based on those statements?

> (1) Most members of Alpha Beta Chi are in-state students who enjoy playing basketball.
> (2) At least one member of Alpha Beta Chi is an in-state student who enjoys playing basketball.

While statement (1) is possible, only statement (2) follows logically from the statements. There is no way to deduce how great the overlap between the two categories is. Be very careful of Extreme wrong answer choices in Inference questions.

In Inference questions, it is essential that you avoid adding statements based on outside knowledge or on your own assumptions. What is your first reaction to the following statements?

> The school cafeteria managers surveyed 500 female and 500 male students on their preference between honeydew melon and cantaloupe. The results were surprising. The female students overwhelmingly preferred honeydew.

After reading that, was your first thought that the male students must have overwhelmingly favored cantaloupe? If so, be careful. You cannot infer anything about the male students' response from those statements. Wrong answers in Inference questions will often target test takers' reasonable but unsupported assumptions.

What Inference Question Stems Ask For

As we said, Inference questions ask either for a valid deduction—something that must be true or must be false—made only from the facts in the stimulus, or for the answer that receives or does not receive support from the stimulus. Those tasks make Inference yet another LSAT question type in which it is crucial that you accurately characterize the one correct and four incorrect answer choices.

Practice

Use your knowledge of truth values from Chapter 1 to characterize the correct and incorrect answer choices called for by each of the following question stems. The expert analysis is on the facing page, so cover that page if you want to characterize all of the question stems before comparing your work.

LSAT Question Stem		My Analysis
1. If all of the statements above are true, then which one of the following must be true? *PrepTest61 Sec2 Q3*	→	**1 Right:** **4 Wrong:**
2. Which one of the following can be properly inferred from the information above? *PrepTest61 Sec2 Q10*	→	**1 Right:** **4 Wrong:**
3. Which one of the following is most strongly supported by the information above? *PrepTest59 Sec3 Q3*	→	**1 Right:** **4 Wrong:**
4. Which one of the following statements would most reasonably complete the argument? *PrepTest57 Sec2 Q18*	→	**1 Right:** **4 Wrong:**
5. If all of the statements above are true, which one of the following CANNOT be true? *PrepTest49 Sec4 Q5*	→	**1 Right:** **4 Wrong:**
6. The statements above, if true, provide support for each of the following EXCEPT: *PrepTest61 Sec4 Q3*	→	**1 Right:** **4 Wrong:**
7. If the statements above are true, then each of the following could also be true EXCEPT: *PrepTest49 Sec2 Q21*	→	**1 Right:** **4 Wrong:**
8. The facts described above provide the strongest evidence against which one of the following? *PrepTest57 Sec2 Q23*	→	**1 Right:** **4 Wrong:**

LSAT Question Stem	**Analysis**
1. If all of the statements above are true, then which one of the following must be true? *PrepTest61 Sec2 Q3* →	**1 Right:** Must be true **4 Wrong:** Could be false
2. Which one of the following can be properly inferred from the information above? *PrepTest61 Sec2 Q10* →	**1 Right:** Must be true **4 Wrong:** Could be false
3. Which one of the following is most strongly supported by the information above? *PrepTest59 Sec3 Q3* →	**1 Right:** Is supported by the stimulus **4 Wrong:** Is not supported by the stimulus
4. Which one of the following statements would most reasonably complete the argument? *PrepTest57 Sec2 Q18* →	**1 Right:** Must be true; represents the conclusion that follows from the stimulus's evidence **4 Wrong:** Could be false; is not a valid conclusion from the stimulus's evidence
5. If all of the statements above are true, which one of the following CANNOT be true? *PrepTest49 Sec4 Q5* →	**1 Right:** Must be false **4 Wrong:** Could be true
6. The statements above, if true, provide support for each of the following EXCEPT: *PrepTest61 Sec4 Q3* →	**1 Right:** Is NOT supported by the stimulus **4 Wrong:** Is supported by the stimulus
7. If the statements above are true, then each of the following could also be true EXCEPT: *PrepTest49 Sec2 Q21* →	**1 Right:** Must be false **4 Wrong:** Could be true
8. The facts described above provide the strongest evidence against which one of the following? *PrepTest57 Sec2 Q23* →	**1 Right:** Is WEAKENED by the stimulus **4 Wrong:** Is not weakened by the stimulus (could be strengthened by or outside the scope of the stimulus)

LSAT STRATEGY

Some facts to remember about LSAT inferences:

· An inference follows only from the facts given. No outside knowledge is required.

· An inference need not be mind-blowing. Sometimes it will be simple, even obvious.

· An inference may come from a single fact, or it may require combining multiple facts. It may not be necessary to take into account all the facts given in the stimulus.

Cataloging and Paraphrasing Statements in the Stimulus

Without an argument in the stimulus to analyze, untrained test takers may have difficulty knowing where to focus their attention in Inference stimuli. Expert test takers read strategically, paraphrasing the statements, and then catalog them according to five criteria.

To make valid inferences, LSAT experts:

1. Note the most concrete statements

2. Combine statements

3. Use Keywords

4. Use Formal Logic

5. Use uncertain statements

Note the Most Concrete Statements

Inferences and deductions are more likely to follow from strong assertions than from weak or qualified statements. In some Inference questions, the correct answer is just a summary of one of the concrete statements in the stimulus.

Review an LSAT expert's analysis of Steps 1 and 2 from an Inference question.

LSAT Question	Analysis
Commentator: Recently, articles criticizing the environmental movement have been appearing regularly in newspapers. According to Winslow, this is due not so much to an antienvironmental bias among the media as to a preference on the part of newspaper editors for articles that seem "daring" in that they seem to challenge prevailing political positions. It is true that editors like to run antienvironmental pieces mainly because they seem to challenge the political orthodoxy. But serious environmentalism is by no means politically orthodox, and antienvironmentalists can hardly claim to be dissidents, however much they may have succeeded in selling themselves as renegades.	**Step 2:** Background: 1) Newspapers' anti-EM articles ↑ 2) Winslow's reason: editors want to *appear* "daring"/unorthodox Commentator's view: 3) Winslow is right! *but* 4) Serious EM is not orthodox, and 5) Anti-EM aren't dissidents (even if they convince people they are)
The commentator's statements, if true, most strongly support which one of the following? *PrepTest51 Sec3 Q12*	**Step 1:** The statements above "most strongly support" the correct answer—Inference question.

What are the commentator's strongest assertions? What specific opinions does the commentator express? What do the commentator's statements *not* say? Does the commentator state that the newspaper editors believe what they're saying? Does she express any agreement with the environmental movement or the antienvironmentalists?

Now, take a look at the full question accompanying that stimulus. Evaluate the answer choices in light of your reflection on the expert's analysis.

LSAT Question	My Analysis
Commentator: Recently, articles criticizing the environmental movement have been appearing regularly in newspapers. According to Winslow, this is due not so much to an antienvironmental bias among the media as to a preference on the part of newspaper editors for articles that seem "daring" in that they seem to challenge prevailing political positions. It is true that editors like to run antienvironmental pieces mainly because they seem to challenge the political orthodoxy. But serious environmentalism is by no means politically orthodox, and antienvironmentalists can hardly claim to be dissidents, however much they may have succeeded in selling themselves as renegades.	**Step 2:** Background: 1) Newspapers' anti-EM articles ↑ 2) Winslow's reason: Editors want to *appear* "daring"/unorthodox Commentator's view: 3) Winslow is right! *but* 4) Serious EM is not orthodox, and 5) Anti-EM aren't dissidents (even if they convince people they are)
The commentator's statements, if true, most strongly support which one of the following?	**Step 1:** The statements above "most strongly support" the correct answer—Inference question.
	Step 3: The commentator agrees with Winslow—editors attack EM to appear "daring"; but "serious" EM is not orthodox, and anti-EM isn't daring or unorthodox. The right answer follows from those views.
(A) Winslow is correct about the preference of newspaper editors for controversial articles.	**Step 4:**
(B) Critics of environmentalism have not successfully promoted themselves as renegades.	
(C) Winslow's explanation is not consonant with the frequency with which critiques of environmentalism are published.	
(D) The position attacked by critics of environmentalism is actually the prevailing political position.	
(E) Serious environmentalism will eventually become a prevailing political position.	

PrepTest51 Sec3 Q12

Here's how the LSAT expert evaluated the answer choices.

LSAT Question	Analysis
Commentator: Recently, articles criticizing the environmental movement have been appearing regularly in newspapers. According to Winslow, this is due not so much to an antienvironmental bias among the media as to a preference on the part of newspaper editors for articles that seem "daring" in that they seem to challenge prevailing political positions. It is true that editors like to run antienvironmental pieces mainly because they seem to challenge the political orthodoxy. But serious environmentalism is by no means politically orthodox, and antienvironmentalists can hardly claim to be dissidents, however much they may have succeeded in selling themselves as renegades. $\longrightarrow$	**Step 2:** Background: 1) Newspapers' anti-EM articles ↑ 2) Winslow's reason: Editors want to *appear* "daring"/unorthodox Commentator's view: 3) Winslow is right! *but* 4) Serious EM is not orthodox, and 5) Anti-EM aren't dissidents (even if they convince people they are)
The commentator's statements, if true, most strongly support which one of the following? $\longrightarrow$	**Step 1:** The statements above "most strongly support" the correct answer—Inference question.
	Step 3: The commentator agrees with Winslow—editors attack EM to appear "daring"; but "serious" EM is not orthodox, and anti-EM isn't daring or unorthodox. The right answer follows from those views.
(A) Winslow is correct about the preference of newspaper editors for controversial articles. $\longrightarrow$	**Step 4:** Correct. One of the definitive statements confirms this preference.
(B) Critics of environmentalism have not successfully promoted themselves as renegades. $\longrightarrow$	180. This contradicts the last clause: Antienvironmentalists may have succeeded at least a little bit. Eliminate.
(C) Winslow's explanation is not consonant with the frequency with which critiques of environmentalism are published. $\longrightarrow$	180. In fact, Winslow is right about why the critiques are so common. Eliminate.
(D) The position attacked by critics of environmentalism is actually the prevailing political position. $\longrightarrow$	180/Distortion. The commentator thinks "serious" environmentalism is unorthodox. However, it's not clear whether the anti-EM critics are attacking the "serious" position. Either way, eliminate.
(E) Serious environmentalism will eventually become a prevailing political position. *PrepTest51 Sec3 Q12* $\longrightarrow$	Outside the Scope. The commentator makes no predictions about future events. Eliminate.

NOTE: The correct answer came directly from the commentator's clearest position: Winslow is right. Three of the wrong answers contradicted or distorted one or more of the commentator's stronger statements.

Practice

Practice this approach on another Inference question. Paraphrase and catalogue the statements in the stimulus. Use the author's most concrete statements to evaluate the answer choices.

LSAT Question	My Analysis
9. Hemoglobin, a substance in human blood, transports oxygen from the lungs to the rest of the body. With each oxygen molecule it picks up, a hemoglobin molecule becomes more effective at picking up additional oxygen molecules until its maximum capacity of four oxygen molecules is reached. Grabbing an oxygen molecule changes the shape of the hemoglobin molecule, each time causing it literally to open itself to receive more oxygen. $\longrightarrow$	**Step 2:**
Which one of the following is most strongly supported by the information above? $\longrightarrow$	**Step 1:**
	Step 3:
(A) A hemoglobin molecule that has picked up three oxygen molecules will probably acquire a fourth oxygen molecule. $\longrightarrow$	**Step 4:**
(B) The only factor determining how effective a hemoglobin molecule is at picking up oxygen molecules is how open the shape of that hemoglobin molecule is. $\longrightarrow$	
(C) A hemoglobin molecule that has picked up three oxygen molecules will be more effective at picking up another oxygen molecule than will a hemoglobin molecule that has picked up only one oxygen molecule. $\longrightarrow$	
(D) A hemoglobin molecule that has picked up four oxygen molecules will have the same shape as a hemoglobin molecule that has not picked up any oxygen molecules $\longrightarrow$	
(E) Each hemoglobin molecule in human blood picks up between one and four oxygen molecules in or near the lungs and transports them to some other part of the body. $\longrightarrow$	

PrepTest59 Sec3 Q3

Expert Analysis

Compare your work to that of an LSAT expert.

LSAT Question	Analysis
9. Hemoglobin, a substance in human blood, transports oxygen from the lungs to the rest of the body. With each oxygen molecule it picks up, a hemoglobin molecule becomes more effective at picking up additional oxygen molecules until its maximum capacity of four oxygen molecules is reached. Grabbing an oxygen molecule changes the shape of the hemoglobin molecule, each time causing it literally to open itself to receive more oxygen.	**Step 2:** Three definitive statements: 1) Hemoglobin transports oxygen through the body. 2) More oxygen molecules = hemoglobin more effective at getting oxygen molecules (max 4). 3) Hemoglobin changes shape each time it grabs an oxygen molecule.
Which one of the following is most strongly supported by the information above?	**Step 1:** "[M]ost supported by the information above" indicates an Inference question.
	Step 3: Each statement is definitive and clear. Check each answer choice against the statements: The four wrong answer choices are not supported by the statements; the correct answer choice is.
(A) A hemoglobin molecule that has picked up three oxygen molecules will probably acquire a fourth oxygen molecule.	**Step 4:** Close, but Extreme. The second statement does not say how likely it is that hemoglobin will reach its maximum of four molecules. Maybe there aren't that many available molecules to grab. Eliminate.
(B) The only factor determining how effective a hemoglobin molecule is at picking up oxygen molecules is how open the shape of that hemoglobin molecule is.	The word *only* makes this Extreme. There could be factors other than shape. Eliminate.
(C) A hemoglobin molecule that has picked up three oxygen molecules will be more effective at picking up another oxygen molecule than will a hemoglobin molecule that has picked up only one oxygen molecule.	Correct. This follows directly from the author's second statement.
(D) A hemoglobin molecule that has picked up four oxygen molecules will have the same shape as a hemoglobin molecule that has not picked up any oxygen molecules.	180. The last sentence states that the hemoglobin molecule changes shape each time it picks up an oxygen molecule. Eliminate.
(E) Each hemoglobin molecule in human blood picks up between one and four oxygen molecules in or near the lungs and transports them to some other part of the body. *PrepTest59 Sec3 Q3*	Extreme. It's reasonable to infer that some hemoglobin molecules follow this trajectory, but to say that "each" molecule does so goes too far. Eliminate.

Combine Statements to Make Valid Inferences

In most Inference questions, the correct answer does not follow from a single statement. In such cases, you will need to combine statements to make a deduction. As you paraphrase and catalogue the statements, take note of terms or concepts that appear multiple times in the stimulus. Then, if possible, combine information to determine what must or could be true. (Once again, this is not so different from how you make deductions from Logic Games rules.)

Review an LSAT expert's analysis of Steps 1 and 2 from an Inference question.

LSAT Question	Analysis
Market analyst: According to my research, 59 percent of consumers anticipate paying off their credit card balances in full before interest charges start to accrue, intending to use the cards only to avoid carrying cash and writing checks. This research also suggests that in trying to win business from their competitors, credit card companies tend to concentrate on improving the services their customers are the most interested in. Therefore, my research would lead us to expect that _____. $\longrightarrow$	**Step 2:** Two statements: 1) Research shows that most credit card customers intend to pay off cards before they begin to accrue interest. 2) "This research also suggests" that, to win customers, credit card companies tend to focus on services in which customers are most interested.
Which one of the following most logically completes the market analyst's argument? *PrepTest59 Sec2 Q24* $\longrightarrow$	**Step 1:** The correct answer "completes the . . . argument." It serves as a conclusion to the stimulus's evidence, so this is an Inference question.

Reflect on the expert's analysis.

What are the terms shared by the two statements? What phrase(s) in the stimulus indicates how the statements may be combined to make a valid inference?

Are you able to predict the correct answer precisely in this case?

Now, take a look at the full question accompanying that stimulus. Evaluate the answer choices in light of your reflection on the expert's analysis.

LSAT Question	My Analysis
Market analyst: According to my research, 59 percent of consumers anticipate paying off their credit card balances in full before interest charges start to accrue, intending to use the cards only to avoid carrying cash and writing checks. This research also suggests that in trying to win business from their competitors, credit card companies tend to concentrate on improving the services their customers are the most interested in. Therefore, my research would lead us to expect that _____.	**Step 2:** Two statements: 1) Research shows that most credit card customers intend to pay off cards before they begin to accrue interest. 2) "This research also suggests" that, to win customers, credit card companies tend to focus on services in which customers are most interested.
Which one of the following most logically completes the market analyst's argument?	**Step 1:** The correct answer "completes the . . . argument." It serves as a conclusion to the stimulus's evidence, so this is an Inference question.
	Step 3: Consumers don't plan to carry balances, so they likely aren't too concerned with interest rates. Because credit card companies tend to focus on features in which customers are interested, *they will focus on something other than interest rates.*
(A) most customers would be indifferent about which company's credit card they use	**Step 4:**
(B) credit card companies would not make the interest rates they charge on cards the main selling point	
(C) most consumers would prefer paying interest on credit card debts over borrowing money from banks	
(D) most consumers would ignore the length of time a credit card company allows to pay the balance due before interest accrues	
(E) the most intense competition among credit card companies would be over the number of places that they can get to accept their credit card	

PrepTest59 Sec2 Q24

Here's how the LSAT expert evaluated the answer choices.

LSAT Question	Analysis
Market analyst: According to my research, 59 percent of consumers anticipate paying off their credit card balances in full before interest charges start to accrue, intending to use the cards only to avoid carrying cash and writing checks. This research also suggests that in trying to win business from their competitors, credit card companies tend to concentrate on improving the services their customers are the most interested in. Therefore, my research would lead us to expect that _____.	**Step 2:** Two statements: 1) Research shows that most credit card customers intend to pay off cards before they begin to accrue interest. 2) "This research also suggests" that, to win customers, credit card companies tend to focus on services in which customers are most interested.
Which one of the following most logically completes the market analyst's argument?	**Step 1:** The correct answer "completes the . . . argument." It serves as a conclusion to the stimulus's evidence, so this is an Inference question.
	Step 3: Consumers don't plan to carry balances, so they likely aren't too concerned with interest rates. Because credit card companies tend to focus on features in which customers are interested, *they will focus on something other than interest rates.*
(A) most customers would be indifferent about which company's credit card they use	**Step 4:** 180. This contradicts the research findings that customers decide which credit card to carry based on the features in which they are interested. Eliminate.
(B) credit card companies would not make the interest rates they charge on cards the main selling point	Correct. This is the answer that follows from combining the analyst's two findings.
(C) most consumers would prefer paying interest on credit card debts over borrowing money from banks	Irrelevant Comparison. The stimulus does not discuss preferences in *paying* interest (rather, a desire to *avoid* interest) and says nothing at all about borrowing from banks. Eliminate.
(D) most consumers would ignore the length of time a credit card company allows to pay the balance due before interest accrues	Outside the Scope. The length of time allowed before interest begins to accrue is not discussed. Eliminate.
(E) the most intense competition among credit card companies would be over the number of places that they can get to accept their credit card	Outside the Scope. The stimulus does not even hint at a discussion of places where a credit card is accepted. Eliminate.

PrepTest59 Sec2 Q24

Practice

Practice this approach on two Inference questions. Paraphrase and catalogue the statements in the stimulus. Keep an eye out for statements that can be combined to lead to additional inferences.

LSAT Question	My Analysis
10. In a vast ocean region, phosphorus levels have doubled in the past few decades due to agricultural runoff pouring out of a large river nearby. The phosphorus stimulates the growth of plankton near the ocean surface. Decaying plankton fall to the ocean floor, where bacteria devour them, consuming oxygen in the process. Due to the resulting oxygen depletion, few fish can survive in this region. $\longrightarrow$	**Step 2:**
Which one of the following can be properly inferred from the information above? $\longrightarrow$	**Step 1:**
	Step 3:
(A) The agricultural runoff pouring out of the river contributes to the growth of plankton near the ocean surface. $\longrightarrow$	**Step 4:**
(B) Before phosphorus levels doubled in the ocean region, most fish were able to survive in that region. $\longrightarrow$	
(C) If agricultural runoff ceased pouring out of the river, there would be no bacteria on the ocean floor devouring decaying plankton. $\longrightarrow$	
(D) The quantity of agricultural runoff pouring out of the river has doubled in the past few decades. $\longrightarrow$	
(E) The amount of oxygen in a body of water is in general inversely proportional to the level of phosphorus in that body of water. $\longrightarrow$	

PrepTest61 Sec2 Q10

LSAT Question	**My Analysis**
11. Members of large-animal species must consume enormous amounts of food to survive. When climatic conditions in their environment deteriorate, such animals are often unable to find enough food. This fact helps make large-animal species more vulnerable to extinction than small-animal species, which can maintain greater populations on smaller amounts of food.	**Step 2:**
The statements above, if true, most support which one of the following?	**Step 1:**
	Step 3:
(A) The maximum population size that an animal species could maintain on any given amount of food is the main factor determining whether that species will become extinct.	**Step 4:**
(B) The vulnerability of an animal species to extinction depends at least in part on how much food individuals of that species must consume to survive.	
(C) When conditions deteriorate in a given environment, no small-animal species will become extinct unless some large-animal species also becomes extinct.	
(D) Within any given species, the prospects for survival of any particular individual depend primarily on the amount of food that individual requires.	
(E) Whenever climatic conditions in a given environment are bad enough to threaten large-animal species with extinction, small-animal species are able to find enough food to survive.	

PrepTest49 Sec2 Q9

Expert Analysis

Compare your work to that of an LSAT expert.

LSAT Question	Analysis
10. In a vast ocean region, phosphorus levels have doubled in the past few decades due to agricultural runoff pouring out of a large river nearby. The phosphorus stimulates the growth of plankton near the ocean surface. Decaying plankton fall to the ocean floor, where bacteria devour them, consuming oxygen in the process. Due to the resulting oxygen depletion, few fish can survive in this region. $\longrightarrow$	**Step 2:** The statements in the stimulus describe a chain of events: 1) Agricultural runoff from a nearby river causes phosphorus levels to rise. 2) The phosphorous causes plankton to grow near the ocean surface. 3) Increased plankton leads to less oxygen. 4) Less oxygen leads to fewer fish.
Which one of the following can be properly inferred from the information above? $\longrightarrow$	**Step 1:** "[C]an be properly inferred from the information above" indicates an Inference question.
	Step 3: The correct answer must be true based on the statements above.
(A) The agricultural runoff pouring out of the river contributes to the growth of plankton near the ocean surface. $\longrightarrow$	**Step 4:** Correct. This inference is supported by combining the information in the first two sentences.
(B) Before phosphorus levels doubled in the ocean region, most fish were able to survive in that region. $\longrightarrow$	Outside the Scope. What happened before the phosphorous levels doubled is not discussed. Other problems could have killed fish, too. Eliminate.
(C) If agricultural runoff ceased pouring out of the river, there would be no bacteria on the ocean floor devouring decaying plankton. $\longrightarrow$	Outside the Scope. What happens once the agricultural runoff stops pouring out of the river is not discussed. Eliminate.
(D) The quantity of agricultural runoff pouring out of the river has doubled in the past few decades. $\longrightarrow$	This is a distortion of the first sentence. Phosphorous levels have doubled, but that doesn't mean that runoff has doubled. Eliminate.
(E) The amount of oxygen in a body of water is in general inversely proportional to the level of phosphorus in that body of water. *PrepTest61 Sec2 Q10* $\longrightarrow$	A tempting answer choice, but be careful: The statements in the stimulus refer to one river flowing into a particular part of the ocean. Drawing an inference about bodies of water *in general* goes too far. Eliminate.

LSAT Question	Analysis
11. Members of large-animal species must consume enormous amounts of food to survive. When climatic conditions in their environment deteriorate, such animals are often unable to find enough food. This fact helps make large-animal species more vulnerable to extinction than small-animal species, which can maintain greater populations on smaller amounts of food.	**Step 2:** Four related statements: 1) Large animals need a lot of food to survive. 2) Changes in climate make it hard for large animals to find food. 3) Small animals need less food. 4) Statement 2 makes large animals more vulnerable to extinction than small animals are.
The statements above, if true, most support which one of the following?	**Step 1:** Statements in the stimulus "support" the correct answer choice—an Inference question.
	Step 3: The correct answer is supported by the statements above.
(A) The maximum population size that an animal species could maintain on any given amount of food is the main factor determining whether that species will become extinct.	**Step 4:** Outside the Scope/Extreme. The stimulus never discusses maximum population, only greater population size. Moreover, calling food availability the *main* factor in extinction goes too far. Eliminate.
(B) The vulnerability of an animal species to extinction depends at least in part on how much food individuals of that species must consume to survive.	Correct. This is a summary of all four statements in the stimulus. "[A]t least in part" ensures that this answer is not too extreme to follow from the stimulus.
(C) When conditions deteriorate in a given environment, no small-animal species will become extinct unless some large-animal species also becomes extinct.	Extreme. Small-animal species don't need as much food, but there could be other factors leading to a small-animal species's extinction happening before any large-animal species's extinctions. Eliminate.
(D) Within any given species, the prospects for survival of any particular individual depend primarily on the amount of food that individual requires.	This choice narrows the scope to individual animals within specific species. The stimulus compares only small- and large-animal species, not individual animals. Eliminate.
(E) Whenever climatic conditions in a given environment are bad enough to threaten large-animal species with extinction, small-animal species are able to find enough food to survive. *PrepTest49 Sec2 Q9*	Extreme. If conditions were severe enough, perhaps no species could find enough food to survive. Eliminate.

Use Keywords to Make Valid Inferences

Throughout the LSAT, Keywords help you understand the author's purpose and main point. In Inference questions, Keywords are especially helpful in seeing clearly how an author intends two or more statements to relate to one another. As you saw in Argument-Based and Assumption Family questions, Keywords also signal pertinent shifts within arguments. LSAT experts use Keywords—especially contrast words—to predict possible inferences.

Review an LSAT expert's analysis of Steps 1 and 2 from an Inference question.

LSAT Question	Analysis
Baxe Interiors, one of the largest interior design companies in existence, currently has a near monopoly in the corporate market. Several small design companies have won prestigious awards for their corporate work, while Baxe has won none. Nonetheless, the corporate managers who solicit design proposals will only contract with companies they believe are unlikely to go bankrupt, and they believe that only very large companies are unlikely to go bankrupt.	**Step 2:** Three facts about Baxe: 1) It's large; 2) it has a near-monopoly on the corporate market; and 3) it hasn't won any design awards. One fact about small design companies: Several have won design awards. *Nonetheless* Corporate managers will only use large companies, the only ones they believe are unlikely to go bankrupt.
The statements above, if true, most strongly support which one of the following? *PrepTest61 Sec4 Q7*	**Step 1:** The statements above "strongly support" an answer choice below—an Inference question.

Reflect on the expert's analysis. Doing so will provide a "prediction" that will help you distinguish the one right answer from the four wrong answers.

What does the word [n]onetheless tell you about how the author thinks the facts stated at the start of the stimulus relate to the situation described at the end of the stimulus?

How does the Keyword help you predict what the one right and four wrong answers are likely to contain?

Now, take a look at the full question accompanying that stimulus. Evaluate the answer choices in light of your reflection on the expert's analysis.

LSAT Question	**My Analysis**
Baxe Interiors, one of the largest interior design companies in existence, currently has a near monopoly in the corporate market. Several small design companies have won prestigious awards for their corporate work, while Baxe has won none. Nonetheless, the corporate managers who solicit design proposals will only contract with companies they believe are unlikely to go bankrupt, and they believe that only very large companies are unlikely to go bankrupt. →	**Step 2:** Three facts about Baxe: 1) It's large; 2) it has a near monopoly on the corporate market; and 3) it hasn't won any design awards. One fact about small design companies: Several have won design awards. *Nonetheless* Corporate managers will only use large companies, the only ones they believe are unlikely to go bankrupt.
The statements above, if true, most strongly support which one of the following? →	**Step 1:** The statements above "strongly support" an answer choice below—an Inference question.
	Step 3: The author explicitly contrasts his belief that corporate managers will continue to use large companies with the fact that Baxe (a large company) has no design awards while several small companies have won such awards. These statements support the correct answer.
(A) There are other very large design companies besides Baxe, but they produce designs that are inferior to Baxe's. →	**Step 4:**
(B) Baxe does not have a near monopoly in the market of any category of interior design other than corporate interiors. →	
(C) For the most part, designs that are produced by small companies are superior to the designs produced by Baxe. →	
(D) At least some of the corporate managers who solicit design proposals are unaware that there are designs that are much better than those produced by Baxe. →	
(E) The existence of interior designs that are superior to those produced by Baxe does not currently threaten its near monopoly in the corporate market. →	

PrepTest61 Sec4 Q7

Here's how the LSAT expert evaluated the answer choices.

LSAT Question	Analysis
Baxe Interiors, one of the largest interior design companies in existence, currently has a near monopoly in the corporate market. Several small design companies have won prestigious awards for their corporate work, while Baxe has won none. Nonetheless, the corporate managers who solicit design proposals will only contract with companies they believe are unlikely to go bankrupt, and they believe that only very large companies are unlikely to go bankrupt.	**Step 2:** Three facts about Baxe: 1) It's large; 2) it has a near monopoly on the corporate market; and 3) it has *not* won any design awards. One fact about small design companies: Several have won design awards. *Nevertheless* Corporate managers will only use large companies, the only ones they believe are unlikely to go bankrupt.
The statements above, if true, most strongly support which one of the following?	**Step 1:** The statements above "strongly support" an answer choice below—an Inference question.
	Step 3: The author explicitly contrasts his belief that corporate managers will continue to use large companies with the fact that Baxe (a large company) has no design awards while several small companies have won such awards. These statements support the correct answer.
(A) There are other very large design companies besides Baxe, but they produce designs that are inferior to Baxe's.	**Step 4:** The stimulus states only that Baxe is one of the largest interior design companies; there is no information about other large companies or the quality of their designs. Eliminate.
(B) Baxe does not have a near monopoly in the market of any category of interior design other than corporate interiors.	Outside the Scope. The stimulus says nothing about categories of interior design other than corporate interiors. Eliminate.
(C) For the most part, designs that are produced by small companies are superior to the designs produced by Baxe.	Extreme. Several small companies have won awards for their corporate work, but this says nothing about small companies overall. Eliminate.
(D) At least some of the corporate managers who solicit design proposals are unaware that there are designs that are much better than those produced by Baxe.	Outside the Scope. Corporate managers may or may not be aware of design quality; even if they are, they contract with companies they consider stable. Eliminate.
(E) The existence of interior designs that are superior to those produced by Baxe does not currently threaten its near monopoly in the corporate market. *PrepTest61 Sec4 Q7*	Correct. Baxe should continue to get business from corporate managers because of its large size (and perceived stability), and should thus hold onto its monopoly despite not winning awards.

Practice

Practice this approach on another Inference question. Paraphrase and catalogue the statements in the stimulus. Be on the lookout for Keywords that hint at an important inference.

LSAT Question	My Analysis
12. A theoretical framework facilitates conceptual organization of material and fruitful expansions of research. Many historians argue that historical analysis is therefore done best within a theoretical framework. But the past is too complex for all of its main trends to be captured within a theoretical framework. Therefore, _____. $\longrightarrow$	**Step 2:**
Which one of the following most logically completes the argument? $\longrightarrow$	**Step 1:**
	Step 3:
(A) there is no benefit ever to be gained in recommending to historians that they place their work within a theoretical framework $\longrightarrow$	**Step 4:**
(B) theoretical frameworks are less useful in history than they are in any other discipline $\longrightarrow$	
(C) even the best historical analysis done within a theoretical framework fails to capture all of history's main trends $\longrightarrow$	
(D) the value of theoretical work in extending research has been emphasized by historians who recommend doing historical analysis within a theoretical framework $\longrightarrow$	
(E) there is no difference between historical analysis that is placed within a theoretical framework and historical analysis that is not $\longrightarrow$	

PrepTest59 Sec2 Q12

Expert Analysis

Compare your work to that of an LSAT expert.

LSAT Question	Analysis
12. A theoretical framework facilitates conceptual organization of material and fruitful expansions of research. Many historians argue that historical analysis is therefore done best within a theoretical framework. But the past is too complex for all of its main trends to be captured within a theoretical framework. Therefore, _____.	**Step 2:** Background about theoretical frameworks followed by two contrasting assertions: 1) Many historians say that historical analysis is best done within a theoretical framework. *but* 2) The past is too complex for all of its main trends to be captured in a theoretical framework. *So,* _____.
Which one of the following most logically completes the argument?	**Step 1:** "[M]ost logically completes the argument" indicates an Inference question. This stimulus ends with "Therefore, _____," so the correct answer represents the conclusion of an argument based on the evidence in the stimulus.
	Step 3: Predict the author's conclusion. The Keyword *but* indicates that the author disagrees with historians who prefer a theoretical framework because such frameworks cannot capture all of history's main trends.
(A) there is no benefit ever to be gained in recommending to historians that they place their work within a theoretical framework	**Step 4:** Extreme. Just because it has one disadvantage (it can't capture all main trends) does not mean that a theoretical framework has *no* benefit. Eliminate.
(B) theoretical frameworks are less useful in history than they are in any other discipline	Irrelevant Comparison/Extreme. Whether (and to what extent) theoretical frameworks are useful in other disciplines is irrelevant here. Eliminate.
(C) even the best historical analysis done within a theoretical framework fails to capture all of history's main trends	Correct. If the author's statements are accurate, this must be true.
(D) the value of theoretical work in extending research has been emphasized by historians who recommend doing historical analysis within a theoretical framework	This combines the background information about theoretical frameworks with the statement that some historians like them. However, it misses entirely the statement following [b]*ut* in the stimulus, so it cannot be the author's conclusion. Eliminate.
(E) there is no difference between historical analysis that is placed within a theoretical framework and historical analysis that is not *PrepTest59 Sec2 Q12*	Irrelevant Comparison. The stimulus does not discuss other types of analyses. They may or may not differ from theoretical frameworks. Eliminate.

Using Formal Logic to Make Valid Inferences

On occasion, an Inference question will present a stimulus that includes Formal Logic statements. When Formal Logic is present, use your knowledge of conditional statements to analyze the stimulus and predict the correct answer. As you know from your work in Chapter 1 and elsewhere, when one conditional statement's necessary ("then") clause shares a term with another statement's sufficient ("If") clause, the two statements can be combined to produce a valid deduction. The pattern "If A → B" and "If B → C" producing the deduction "If A → C" is just one of several patterns you know now.

Moreover, a conditional statement may combine with a concrete assertion of fact to produce an inference. Imagine, for example, a stimulus reads "No one can become a successful prospector unless he or she has at least a rudimentary understanding of geology" and "Joshua is a successful prospector." From those statements, you can deduce Joshua has at least a rudimentary understanding of geology.

It is important that you know how to spot Formal Logic in all of its forms, including those that use terms such as *only, only if,* and *unless*. It's also important to be comfortable making Formal Logic contrapositives. Formal Logic appears in many forms in Inference stimuli. Conditional statements in Inference questions are often long and complex.

Review the following examples of conditional statements in Inference stimuli, convert them to Formal Logic abbreviations, and determine their contrapositives.

Sentence from LSAT stimulus	My Analysis
13. No one with a serious medical problem would rely on the average person to prescribe treatment. *PrepTest57 Sec2 Q18* →	
14. To be great, an artwork must express a deep emotion, such as sorrow or love. *PrepTest49 Sec4 Q10* →	
15. Any adequate set of criteria for determining a substance's addictiveness must embody the view, held by these medical experts, that a substance is addictive only if withdrawal from its habitual use causes most users extreme psychological and physiological difficulty. *PrepTest51 Sec3 Q14* →	

Here's how an LSAT expert might translate these sentences into Formal Logic shorthand.

Sentence from LSAT Stimulus	Analysis
13. No one with a serious medical problem would rely on the average person to prescribe treatment. *PrepTest57 Sec2 Q18* →	If person w/serious med. problem → not rely on avg. person to prescribe If rely on avg. person to prescribe → not person w/ serious med. problem
14. To be great, an artwork must express a deep emotion, such as sorrow or love. *PrepTest49 Sec4 Q10* →	If great art → express deep emotion If not express deep emotion → not great art
15. Any adequate set of criteria for determining a substance's addictiveness must embody the view, held by these medical experts, that a substance is addictive only if withdrawal from its habitual use causes most users extreme psychological and physiological difficulty. *PrepTest51 Sec3 Q14* →	If criteria adequate to determine substance's addictiveness → embodies view (if substance addictive, withdrawal extremely difficult) If not embody view (if substance addictive, withdrawal extremely difficult) → criteria not adequate to determine substance's addictiveness

TEST DAY TIP

LSAT experts vary in how much Formal Logic they write out in their test booklets. In practice, get used to jotting down translations and contrapositives so that you'll be ready to do so when it is helpful on Test Day.

Take a look at how an LSAT expert would translate and combine the Formal Logic statements to answer the following question.

LSAT Question	Analysis
To be great, an artwork must express a deep emotion, such as sorrow or love. But an artwork cannot express an emotion that the artwork's creator is incapable of experiencing.	**Step 2:** Two Formal Logic statements: 1) If **great art** → **express a deep emotion** If **not express a deep emotion** → **not great art** 2) If **art expresses an emotion** → **creator capable of experiencing that emotion** If **creator incapable of experiencing an emotion** → **art cannot express that emotion**
Which one of the following can be properly inferred from the statements above? *PrepTest49 Sec4 Q10*	**Step 1:** The correct answer is "properly inferred" from the statements above—Inference question. The correct answer must be true based on the stimulus.

Reflect on the expert's analysis. How can the statements in the stimulus be combined? Use the combined statements as your prediction of the correct answer.

Now, take a look at the full question accompanying that stimulus. Evaluate the answer choices in light of your reflection on the expert's analysis.

LSAT Question	My Analysis
To be great, an artwork must express a deep emotion, such as sorrow or love. But an artwork cannot express an emotion that the artwork's creator is incapable of experiencing. $\longrightarrow$	**Step 2:** Two Formal Logic statements: 1) If great art $\longrightarrow$ express a deep emotion If not express a deep emotion $\longrightarrow$ not great art 2) If art expresses an emotion $\longrightarrow$ creator capable of experiencing that emotion If creator incapable of experiencing an emotion $\longrightarrow$ art cannot express that emotion
Which one of the following can be properly inferred from the statements above? $\longrightarrow$	**Step 1:** The correct answer is "properly inferred" from the statements above—Inference question. The correct answer must be true based on the stimulus.
	Step 3: Combine the statements: If a creator is incapable of experiencing deep emotion $\longrightarrow$ art cannot be great
(A) A computer can create an artwork that expresses sorrow or love only if it has actually experienced such an emotion. $\longrightarrow$	**Step 4:**
(B) The greatest art is produced by those who have experienced the deepest emotions. $\longrightarrow$	
(C) An artwork that expresses a deep emotion of its creator is a great artwork. $\longrightarrow$	
(D) As long as computers are constructed so as to be incapable of experiencing emotions they will not create great artworks. $\longrightarrow$	
(E) Only artworks that succeed in expressing deep emotions are the products of great artists. $\longrightarrow$	

PrepTest49 Sec4 Q10

Here's how the LSAT expert evaluated the answer choices in that question.

	LSAT Question		Analysis
(A)	A computer can create an artwork that expresses sorrow or love only if it has actually experienced such an emotion.	$\longrightarrow$	**Step 4:** If computer can $\longrightarrow$ has experienced that create art expressing emotion sorrow/love For art to express an emotion, its creator must be *capable* of experiencing an emotion. This answer choice distorts that into "*has* experienced" an emotion. Eliminate.
(B)	The greatest art is produced by those who have experienced the deepest emotions.	$\longrightarrow$	Extreme. The stimulus says nothing about the *greatest* art. Eliminate.
(C)	An artwork that expresses a deep emotion of its creator is a great artwork.	$\longrightarrow$	If art expresses $\longrightarrow$ great art deep emotion This flips the necessary and sufficient terms in the Formal Logic of the first sentence. Being able to express deep emotion is necessary, not sufficient, for great artwork. Eliminate.
(D)	As long as computers are constructed so as to be incapable of experiencing emotions they will not create great artworks.	$\longrightarrow$	Correct. If incapable of $\longrightarrow$ won't create great art experiencing emotions This matches the prediction perfectly.
(E)	Only artworks that succeed in expressing deep emotions are the products of great artists. *PrepTest49 Sec4 Q10*	$\longrightarrow$	*Only* signifies a necessary condition. If product of great $\longrightarrow$ succeeds in expressing artist deep emotion Outside the Scope. Great art must express deep emotions, but perhaps not everything produced by a great artist is great art. Eliminate.

Practice

Practice this approach on two Inference questions. Paraphrase and catalogue the statements in the stimulus. When you encounter conditional statements: Translate them into Formal Logic shorthand, note their contrapositives, and look for opportunities to combine them to make deductions.

LSAT Question	My Analysis
16. Commentator: If a political administration is both economically successful and successful at protecting individual liberties, then it is an overall success. Even an administration that fails to care for the environment may succeed overall if it protects individual liberties. So far, the present administration has not cared for the environment but has successfully protected individual liberties. $\longrightarrow$	**Step 2:**
If all of the statements above are true, then which one of the following must be true? $\longrightarrow$	**Step 1:**
	Step 3:
(A) The present administration is economically successful. $\longrightarrow$	**Step 4:**
(B) The present administration is not an overall success. $\longrightarrow$	
(C) If the present administration is economically successful, then it is an overall success. $\longrightarrow$	
(D) If the present administration had been economically successful, it would have cared for the environment. $\longrightarrow$	
(E) If the present administration succeeds at environmental protection, then it will be an overall success $\longrightarrow$	

PrepTest61 Sec2 Q3

LSAT Question	My Analysis
17. At a gathering at which bankers, athletes, and lawyers are present, all of the bankers are athletes and none of the lawyers are bankers.	**Step 2:**
$\longrightarrow$	
If the statements above are true, which one of the following statements must also be true? $\longrightarrow$	**Step 1:**
	Step 3:
(A) All of the athletes are bankers. $\longrightarrow$	**Step 4:**
(B) Some of the lawyers are not athletes. $\longrightarrow$	
(C) Some of the athletes are not lawyers. $\longrightarrow$	
(D) All of the bankers are lawyers. $\longrightarrow$	
(E) None of the lawyers are athletes. $\longrightarrow$	

PrepTest59 Sec2 Q19

Expert Analysis

Compare your work to that of an LSAT expert.

LSAT Question	Analysis
16. Commentator: If a political administration is both economically successful and successful at protecting individual liberties, then it is an overall success. Even an administration that fails to care for the environment may succeed overall if it protects individual liberties. So far, the present administration has not cared for the environment but has successfully protected individual liberties. →	**Step 2:** A principle expressed in Formal Logic and an assessment of the current administration: If political admin. → overall success successful at econ. AND at protecting indiv. liberties Present administration: successful at protecting indiv. liberties The second sentence makes the present administration's failure to care for the environment irrelevant to an assessment of overall success.
If all of the statements above are true, then which one of the following must be true? →	**Step 1:** The correct answer "must be true" based on the stimulus—a classic Inference question stem.
	Step 3: Combine the Formal Logic statement and the statement in the last sentence: The present administration has met one of two conditions sufficient for overall success. The correct answer must be true based on these statements.
(A) The present administration is economically successful. →	**Step 4:** This cannot be inferred from the statements above. Eliminate.
(B) The present administration is not an overall success. →	This depends on whether the present administration is economically successful, and that is unknown here. Eliminate.
(C) If the present administration is economically successful, then it is an overall success. →	Correct. If this is true, then both sufficient conditions have been met, and the administration would be an overall success.
(D) If the present administration had been economically successful, it would have cared for the environment. →	Outside the Scope. We do not know what would have made the administration care or not care for the environment. Eliminate.
(E) If the present administration succeeds at environmental protection, then it will be an overall success.	The second half of the sufficient condition is a successful economy, not success protecting the environment. Eliminate.

PrepTest61 Sec2 Q3

LSAT Question	**Analysis**
17. At a gathering at which bankers, athletes, and lawyers are present, all of the bankers are athletes and none of the lawyers are bankers.	**Step 2:** Two Formal Logic statements about a meeting at which bankers, athletes, and lawyers are present:

$\longrightarrow$

If banker	$\longrightarrow$ athlete
If ~athlete	$\longrightarrow$ ~banker
If lawyer	$\longrightarrow$ ~banker
If banker	$\longrightarrow$ ~lawyer

If the statements above are true, which one of the following statements must also be true? $\longrightarrow$	**Step 1:** The correct answer must be true if the statements in the stimulus are true—an Inference question.

Step 3: None of the necessary terms in either statement matches a sufficient term in the other, so the statements cannot be combined to remove a redundant term.

But note that *banker* is a sufficient term in both statements, thus: All of the bankers at the gathering are athletes and *not* lawyers.

Because bankers are present at the gathering, there is at least one person in attendance who is a banker, an athlete, and not a lawyer.

(A) All of the athletes are bankers. $\longrightarrow$	**Step 4:** The fact that all the bankers are athletes doesn't mean that all the athletes are bankers. This confuses sufficient and necessary terms. Eliminate.
(B) Some of the lawyers are not athletes. $\longrightarrow$	The only thing we know about lawyers is that they are not bankers. But we don't know anything about people who are not bankers. Eliminate.
(C) Some of the athletes are not lawyers. $\longrightarrow$	Correct. Based on the statements, you can deduce that there is at least one banker-athlete who is not a lawyer attending the gathering. This answer choice describes (at least) that person.
(D) All of the bankers are lawyers. $\longrightarrow$	180. The bankers are *not* lawyers. Eliminate.
(E) None of the lawyers are athletes. *PrepTest59 Sec2 Q19* $\longrightarrow$	The fact that some of the athletes in the crowd (those who are bankers) are not lawyers does not mean that all lawyers in attendance are not athletes. Eliminate.

Using Uncertain Statements to Make Valid Inferences

Not all Inference question stimuli present concrete, or even conditional, statements. Terms such as *most, many, often, several,* and *some* indicate statements that lack absolute certainty.

Consider the following statements:

- Many of the birds that live near this lake are ducks.
- Some of the marbles in this jar are cracked.
- I go running often.
- Most of the restaurants in this town close before midnight.

Uncertain statements can't always be combined to make deductions. The LSAT will test you on your knowledge of when it is appropriate to combine information and when it is not appropriate.

In this set of statements, can you combine the information to make a further deduction?

> Some of the books in this library were written by French authors.
> Some of the books in this library were written on a typewriter.

What about these statements—can you combine them to make a further deduction?

> Most of the cars in this parking lot are red.
> Most of the cars in this parking lot are over ten years old.

LSAT STRATEGY

Levels of Certainty

Here are the types of statements you'll encounter in Inference stimuli, arranged from most concrete to least:

- **Unqualified Assertions** (e.g., *Bob is an attorney* or *Monday will be a rainy day*)
- **Conditional Statements/Formal Logic** (e.g., *If the company hopes to meet its budget, then it must cut travel costs* or *McLaren will lose the election unless the county sees record voter turnout*)
- **Statements with *most***—This means *more than half* but could include *all* (e.g., *Most of Company Y's employees are college graduates* or *A majority of the respondents preferred the new logo*).
- **Statement with *some* or *few***—This means anywhere from one to all, just not zero (e.g., *Some architects are painters*).

Take a look at how an LSAT expert would translate and combine the Formal Logic statements to answer the following question.

LSAT Question	Analysis
Most veterinarians, and especially those at university veterinary research centers, have a devoted interest in the biological sciences. But most veterinarians choose their profession primarily because they love animals. Among persons who are seriously interested in biological science but lack any special love for animals, one does not find any prominent veterinarians. $\longrightarrow$	**Step 2:** Two uncertain statements followed by a conditional statement: 1) Most (over half of) vets are devoted to bio. 2) Most (over half of) vets love animals. 3) If **devoted to bio AND ~love animals** $\longrightarrow$ **~prominent vet** If **prominent vet** $\longrightarrow$ **~devoted to bio OR love animals**
If all of the statements above are true, which one of the following CANNOT be true? $\longrightarrow$ *PrepTest49 Sec4 Q5*	**Step 1:** Based on the statements, the correct answer cannot be true—a negative Inference question. The correct answer will directly contradict the stimulus; the four wrong answers could be true in light of the stimulus.

What do the uncertain statements have in common?

Now, take a look at the full question accompanying that stimulus. Evaluate the answer choices in light of your reflection on the expert's analysis.

LSAT Question	My Analysis

Most veterinarians, and especially those at university veterinary research centers, have a devoted interest in the biological sciences. But most veterinarians choose their profession primarily because they love animals. Among persons who are seriously interested in biological science but lack any special love for animals, one does not find any prominent veterinarians. $\longrightarrow$	**Step 2:** Two uncertain statements followed by a conditional statement:
	
	1) Most (over half of) vets are devoted to bio.
	
	2) Most (over half of) vets love animals.
	
	3) **If devoted to** $\longrightarrow$ **~prominent vet**
	   bio AND ~love
	   animals
	
	   If prominent vet $\longrightarrow$ **~devoted to bio**
	   OR love animals

If all of the statements above are true, which one of the following CANNOT be true? $\longrightarrow$	**Step 1:** Based on the statements, the correct answer cannot be true—a negative Inference question. The correct answer will directly contradict the stimulus; the four wrong answers could be true in light of the stimulus.
	Step 3: Because both uncertain statements involve over half of the vet population, there must be some overlap. At least one vet must be devoted to bio and love animals. The Formal Logic statement applies to any *prominent* vet.
(A) Some veterinarians have a greater love for biological science than for individual animals. $\longrightarrow$	**Step 4:**
(B) Most veterinarians love animals and have an interest in biological science. $\longrightarrow$	
(C) Prominent veterinarians at some veterinary research centers are intensely devoted to the biological sciences but do not feel any pronounced affection for animals. $\longrightarrow$	
(D) Few veterinarians at university research centers chose their profession primarily because they love animals. $\longrightarrow$	
(E) Most veterinarians who are not prominent regard an understanding of the biological sciences as the most important quality for success in their profession. $\longrightarrow$	

PrepTest49 Sec4 Q5

Here's how the LSAT expert evaluated the answer choices in that question.

LSAT Question	Analysis
Most veterinarians, and especially those at university veterinary research centers, have a devoted interest in the biological sciences. But most veterinarians choose their profession primarily because they love animals. Among persons who are seriously interested in biological science but lack any special love for animals, one does not find any prominent veterinarians. $\longrightarrow$	**Step 2:** Two uncertain statements followed by a conditional statement: 1) Most (over half of) vets are devoted to bio. 2) Most (over half of) vets love animals. 3) If **devoted to** $\longrightarrow$ **~prominent vet** **bio AND ~love** **animals** If **prominent** $\longrightarrow$ **~devoted to bio** **vet** **OR love animals**
If all of the statements above are true, which one of the following CANNOT be true? $\longrightarrow$	**Step 1:** Based on the statements, the correct answer cannot be true—a negative Inference question. The correct answer will directly contradict the stimulus; the four wrong answers could be true in light of the stimulus.
	Step 3: Because both uncertain statements involve over half of the vet population, there must be some overlap. At least one vet must be devoted to bio and love animals. The Formal Logic statement applies to any *prominent* vet.
(A) Some veterinarians have a greater love for biological science than for individual animals. $\longrightarrow$	**Step 4:** Irrelevant Comparison. Most vets have at least one of these characteristics; the stimulus doesn't compare between them, however. Eliminate.
(B) Most veterinarians love animals and have an interest in biological science. $\longrightarrow$	Could be true. Most vets have one of these characteristics; it might be true that most have both. Eliminate.
(C) Prominent veterinarians at some veterinary research centers are intensely devoted to the biological sciences but do not feel any pronounced affection for animals. $\longrightarrow$	Correct. This choice contradicts the final sentence: There are no prominent vets who are seriously interested in bio but don't care intensely for animals.
(D) Few veterinarians at university research centers chose their profession primarily because they love animals. $\longrightarrow$	Could be true. Most vets overall choose their profession primarily because of their love of animals. This may not be true of those at research centers. Eliminate.
(E) Most veterinarians who are not prominent regard an understanding of the biological sciences as the most important quality for success in their profession. *PrepTest49 Sec4 Q5* $\longrightarrow$	Could be true. The stimulus is silent on vets' opinions about what leads to *success* in the profession. Eliminate.

Practice

Practice this approach on two Inference questions. Paraphrase and catalogue the statements in the stimulus. If you see uncertain statements, consider whether they can be combined to make valid deductions.

LSAT Question	My Analysis
18. Most opera singers who add demanding roles to their repertoires at a young age lose their voices early. It has been said that this is because their voices have not yet matured and hence lack the power for such roles. But young singers with great vocal power are the most likely to ruin their voices. The real problem is that most young singers lack the technical training necessary to avoid straining their vocal cords— especially when using their full vocal strength. Such misuse of the cords inevitably leads to a truncated singing career. $\longrightarrow$	**Step 2:**
Which one of the following does the information above most strongly support? $\longrightarrow$	**Step 1:**
	Step 3:
(A) Young opera singers without great vocal power are unlikely to ruin their voices by singing demanding roles. $\longrightarrow$	**Step 4:**
(B) Some young opera singers ruin their voices while singing demanding roles because their vocal cords have not yet matured. $\longrightarrow$	
(C) Only opera singers with many years of technical training should try to sing demanding roles. $\longrightarrow$	
(D) Only mature opera singers can sing demanding roles without undue strain on their vocal cords. $\longrightarrow$	
(E) Most young opera singers who sing demanding roles strain their vocal cords. $\longrightarrow$	

PrepTest51 Sec3 Q21

LSAT Question	**My Analysis**
19. Forester: The great majority of the forests remaining in the world are only sickly fragments of the fully functioning ecosystems they once were. These fragmented forest ecosystems have typically lost their ability to sustain themselves in the long term, yet they include the last refuges for some of the world's most endangered species. To maintain its full complement of plant and animal species, a fragmented forest requires regular interventions by resource managers. $\longrightarrow$	**Step 2:**
The forester's statements, if true, most strongly support which one of the following? $\longrightarrow$	**Step 1:**
	Step 3:
(A) Most of the world's forests will lose at least some of their plant or animal species if no one intervenes. $\longrightarrow$	**Step 4:**
(B) Unless resource managers regularly intervene in most of the world's remaining forests, many of the world's most endangered species will not survive. $\longrightarrow$	
(C) A fragmented forest ecosystem cannot sustain itself in the long term if it loses any of its plant or animal species. $\longrightarrow$	
(D) A complete, fully functioning forest ecosystem can always maintain its full complement of plant and animal species even without interventions by resource managers. $\longrightarrow$	
(E) At present, resource managers intervene regularly in only some of the world's fragmented forest ecosystems. $\longrightarrow$	

PrepTest49 Sec4 Q19

Expert Analysis

Compare your work to that of an LSAT expert.

LSAT Question	Analysis
18. Most opera singers who add demanding roles to their repertoires at a young age lose their voices early. It has been said that this is because their voices have not yet matured and hence lack the power for such roles. But young singers with great vocal power are the most likely to ruin their voices. The real problem is that most young singers lack the technical training necessary to avoid straining their vocal cords—especially when using their full vocal strength. Such misuse of the cords inevitably leads to a truncated singing career. →	**Step 2:** Catalogue the statements: 1) [uncertain] Most (over half of) young opera singers with demanding roles will lose voice prematurely. 2) [a popular explanation] Some say this is because they don't have the power for the roles. *but* 3) [author's observation] Those with the most power are the ones most likely to ruin their voices. 4) [author's reason—"the real problem"] Most (over half of) young singers lack technical training *and* 5) [Formal Logic] Training is *necessary* to avoid straining the vocal cords. *and* 6) Strained vocal cords shorten singing careers.
Which one of the following does the information above most strongly support? →	**Step 1:** The information above strongly supports the correct answer—an Inference question.
	Step 3: Combine statements and make deductions: Most young opera singers with demanding roles lack the training *necessary* to avoid vocal strain. The correct answer is supported by these statements.
(A) Young opera singers without great vocal power are unlikely to ruin their voices by singing demanding roles. →	**Step 4:** Young singers with great vocal power are *most likely* to ruin their voices. Young singers without power may ruin their voices, too. Eliminate.
(B) Some young opera singers ruin their voices while singing demanding roles because their vocal cords have not yet matured. →	Distortion. This is what "has been said" by others. The author disagrees and presents an alternative theory (the "real problem"). Eliminate.
(C) Only opera singers with many years of technical training should try to sing demanding roles. →	Extreme. The author does not say technical training requires many years. Eliminate.
(D) Only mature opera singers can sing demanding roles without undue strain on their vocal cords. →	Extreme. Young singers *could* take on demanding roles without straining their vocal cords if they were properly trained. Eliminate.
(E) Most young opera singers who sing demanding roles strain their vocal cords. *PrepTest51 Sec3 Q21* →	Correct. The "real problem" is that most young singers lack the training required to avoid straining vocal cords when singing demanding roles.

LSAT Question	Analysis
19. Forester: The great majority of the forests remaining in the world are only sickly fragments of the fully functioning ecosystems they once were. These fragmented forest ecosystems have typically lost their ability to sustain themselves in the long term, yet they include the last refuges for some of the world's most endangered species. To maintain its full complement of plant and animal species, a fragmented forest requires regular interventions by resource managers. →	**Step 2:** Catalogue the statements: 1) [uncertain] Most (over half of) remaining forests are just fragments of what they once were. 2) [uncertain] These fragmented forests have "typically" lost their ability to sustain themselves. 3) [uncertain] Fragmented forests are refuges for some of the world's endangered species. 4) [Formal Logic] Regular intervention by resource managers is *necessary* for fragmented forest to maintain all plant/animal species.
The forester's statements, if true, most strongly support which one of the following? →	**Step 1:** The correct answer is supported by the statements in the stimulus—an Inference question.
	Step 3: The Formal Logic statement is the strongest here: If ~regular intervention by resource managers → fragmented forests will lose some plant/ animal species. Combined with the first sentence, you can deduce: Without regular intervention by resource managers, most forests will lose *some* species.
(A) Most of the world's forests will lose at least some of their plant or animal species if no one intervenes. →	**Step 4:** Correct. This matches the deduction above.
(B) Unless resource managers regularly intervene in most of the world's remaining forests, many of the world's most endangered species will not survive. →	Extreme. Fragmented forests contain *some* of the world's most endangered species. It is impossible to determine whether many such species would be lost without intervention in *most* of these forests. Eliminate.
(C) A fragmented forest ecosystem cannot sustain itself in the long term if it loses any of its plant or animal species. →	Distortion. It is not clear that the loss of a single plant or animal species would make a forest unsustainable. Eliminate.
(D) A complete, fully functioning forest ecosystem can always maintain its full complement of plant and animal species even without interventions by resource managers. →	Extreme ("always") and Outside the Scope. It's not known what complete, fully functioning forest ecosystems can do. Eliminate.
(E) At present, resource managers intervene regularly in only some of the world's fragmented forest ecosystems. →	Outside the Scope. We have no way of knowing what resource managers are currently doing. Eliminate.

PrepTest49 Sec4 Q19

Practice: Inference Questions

Now, practice some Inference questions. In each of the following, look for opportunities to use any or all of the strategies you've learned in this section. Make inferences from concrete statements, combined statements, Keywords, Formal Logic, and uncertain statements.

LSAT Question		My Analysis
20. Although most people know what their bad habits are and want to rid themselves of them, a majority of these people find it very difficult to do so. This is because cessation of habitual behavior is immediately and vividly painful, while whatever benefit is to be gained by the absence of the habit is perceived only dimly because it is remote.	→	**Step 2:**
The information above most strongly supports the statement that the people who are most successful at ending their bad habits are those who	→	**Step 1:**
		Step 3:
(A) can vividly imagine remote but attainable benefit	→	**Step 4:**
(B) can vividly imagine their present pain being felt in the future	→	
(C) have succeeded in the past at modifying their behavior	→	
(D) are relatively unaware of their own behavioral characteristics	→	
(E) can vividly remember the pain caused them in the past by their bad habits	→	

PrepTest59 Sec3 Q7

LSAT Question	My Analysis

21. Cable TV stations have advantages that enable them to attract many more advertisers than broadcast networks attract. For example, cable stations are able to target particular audiences with 24-hour news, sports, or movies, whereas broadcast networks must offer a variety of programming. Cable can also offer lower advertising rates than any broadcast network can, because it is subsidized by viewers through subscriber fees. Additionally, many cable stations have expanded worldwide with multinational programming.

Step 2:

$\longrightarrow$

The statements above, if true, provide support for each of the following EXCEPT:

Step 1:

$\longrightarrow$

Step 3:

(A) Some broadcast networks can be viewed in several countries.

Step 4:

$\longrightarrow$

(B) Broadcast networks do not rely on subscriber fees from viewers.

$\longrightarrow$

(C) Low costs are often an important factor for advertisers in selecting a station or network on which to run a TV ad.

$\longrightarrow$

(D) Some advertisers prefer to have the opportunity to address a worldwide audience.

$\longrightarrow$

(E) The audiences that some advertisers prefer to target watch 24-hour news stations.

PrepTest61 Sec4 Q3 $\longrightarrow$

LSAT Question	**My Analysis**
22. Often a type of organ or body structure is the only physically feasible means of accomplishing a given task, so it should be unsurprising if, like eyes or wings, that type of organ or body structure evolves at different times in a number of completely unrelated species. After all, whatever the difference of heritage and habitat, as organisms animals have fundamentally similar needs and so _____. $\longrightarrow$	**Step 2:**
Which one of the following most logically completes the last sentence of the passage? $\longrightarrow$	**Step 1:**
	Step 3:
(A) will often live in the same environment as other species quite different from themselves $\longrightarrow$	**Step 4:**
(B) will in many instances evolve similar adaptations enabling them to satisfy these needs $\longrightarrow$	
(C) will develop adaptations allowing them to satisfy these needs $\longrightarrow$	
(D) will resemble other species having different biological needs $\longrightarrow$	
(E) will all develop eyes or wings as adaptations $\longrightarrow$ *PrepTest61 Sec2 Q15*	

LSAT Question	**My Analysis**

23. The law of the city of Weston regarding contributions to mayoral campaigns is as follows: all contributions to these campaigns in excess of $100 made by nonresidents of Weston who are not former residents of Weston must be registered with the city council. Brimley's mayoral campaign clearly complied with this law since it accepted contributions only from residents and former residents of Weston.

Step 2: →

If all the statements above are true, which one of the following statements must be true?

Step 1: →

Step 3:

(A) No nonresident of Weston contributed in excess of $100 to Brimley's campaign.

Step 4: →

(B) Some contributions to Brimley's campaign in excess of $100 were registered with the city council.

→

(C) No contributions to Brimley's campaign needed to be registered with the city council.

→

(D) All contributions to Brimley's campaign that were registered with the city council were in excess of $100.

→

(E) Brimley's campaign did not register any contributions with the city council.

PrepTest57 Sec2 Q25 →

LSAT Question	My Analysis

24. Most successful entrepreneurs work at least 18 hours a day, and no one who works at least 18 hours a day has time for leisure activities. But all happy entrepreneurs have time for leisure activities.   →

Step 2:

If the statements above are true, each of the following could be true EXCEPT: →

Step 1:

Step 3:

(A) Anyone who has no time for leisure activities works at least 18 hours a day.   →

Step 4:

(B) Some entrepreneurs who work at least 18 hours a day are successful.   →

(C) Some happy entrepreneurs are successful.   →

(D) Some entrepreneurs who work at least 18 hours a day are happy.   →

(E) Some successful entrepreneurs work less than 18 hours a day.

PrepTest49 Sec2 Q16   →

LSAT Question	My Analysis

25. Art historian: More than any other genre of representational painting, still-life painting lends itself naturally to art whose goal is the artist's self-expression, rather than merely the reflection of a preexisting external reality. This is because in still-life painting, the artist invariably chooses, modifies, and arranges the objects to be painted. Thus, the artist has considerably more control over the composition and subject of a still-life painting than over those of a landscape painting or portrait, for example.

$\longrightarrow$

Step 2:

Which one of the following is most strongly supported by the art historian's statements?

$\longrightarrow$

Step 1:

Step 3:

(A) Landscape painting and portraiture are the artistic genres that lend themselves most naturally to the mere reflection of a preexisting external reality. $\longrightarrow$

Step 4:

(B) The only way in which artists control the composition and subject of a painting is by choosing, modifying, and arranging the objects to be represented in that painting. $\longrightarrow$

(C) Nonrepresentational painting does not lend itself as naturally as still-life painting does to the goal of the artist's self-expression. $\longrightarrow$

(D) In genres of representational painting other than still-life painting, the artist does not always choose, modify, and arrange the objects to be painted. $\longrightarrow$

(E) When painting a portrait, artists rarely attempt to express themselves through the choice, modification, or arrangement of the background elements against which the subject of the portrait is painted. $\longrightarrow$

PrepTest57 Sec3 Q13

LSAT Question	**My Analysis**

26. Historian: The standard "QWERTY" configuration of the keys on typewriters and computer keyboards was originally designed to be awkward and limit typing speed. This was because early typewriters would jam frequently if adjacent keys were struck in quick succession. Experiments have shown that keyboard configurations more efficient than QWERTY can double typing speed while tremendously reducing typing effort. However, the expense and inconvenience of switching to a new keyboard configuration prevent any configuration other than QWERTY from attaining widespread use.

Step 2:

→

Which one of the following is most strongly supported by the historian's statements?

Step 1:

→

Step 3:

(A) Most people who have tried typing with non-QWERTY keyboards have typed significantly more quickly using those keyboards than they usually have done using QWERTY keyboards.

Step 4:

→

(B) Early QWERTY typewriters were less likely to jam than were at least some more recent typewriters if adjacent keys were struck in quick succession.

→

(C) If the designers of early typewriters had foreseen the possibility that technology would make it possible for adjacent keyboard keys to be struck in rapid succession without jamming, then they would not have proposed the QWERTY configuration.

→

(D) The benefit to society that would result from switching to a keyboard configuration other than QWERTY is significantly greater than the overall cost of such a switch.

→

(E) If the keyboard had been designed for computers, then it would not have been designed to limit typing speed.

→

PrepTest59 Sec3 Q21

Expert Analysis: Inference Questions

Compare your work to that of an LSAT expert. Note the strategies the expert employed in each of these questions. Were you able to make inferences from concrete statements, combined statements, Keywords, Formal Logic, and uncertain statements?

LSAT Question	Analysis
20. Although most people know what their bad habits are and want to rid themselves of them, a majority of these people find it very difficult to do so. This is because cessation of habitual behavior is immediately and vividly painful, while whatever benefit is to be gained by the absence of the habit is perceived only dimly because it is remote.	**Step 2**: Two uncertain statements and an explanation: 1) Most (over half of) people know their bad habits and want to end them. 2) Most (over half of) people find it hard to end their bad habits. *This is because* 3) The pain of ending bad habits is tangible. *but* 4) The benefits of ending bad habits are remote and hard to perceive.
The information above most strongly supports the statement that the people who are most successful at ending their bad habits are those who	**Step 1**: The stimulus "strongly supports" the correct answer—an Inference question. Here, the correct answer will define the characteristic(s) of people successful at ending bad habits.
	Step 3: Those who succeed at breaking bad habits must be either less susceptible to the pain of withdrawal or better at perceiving distant/hard to imagine benefits. The correct answer will follow from these statements.
(A) can vividly imagine remote but attainable benefit	**Step 4**: Correct. This follows directly from statement 4 in the stimulus.
(B) can vividly imagine their present pain being felt in the future	Distortion. It is withdrawal that causes pain. And it is the future benefit of quitting that must be imagined. Eliminate.
(C) have succeeded in the past at modifying their behavior	Outside the Scope. The stimulus says nothing about those who have modified their behavior previously. Eliminate.
(D) are relatively unaware of their own behavioral characteristics	Distortion/180. The stimulus says that most people are aware of their bad habits and the difficulty of ending them, but says nothing to suggest that being unaware would help a person succeed in quitting. Eliminate.
(E) can vividly remember the pain caused them in the past by their bad habits *PrepTest59 Sec3 Q7*	Distortion. The stimulus mentions the pain of *withdrawal*, not pain caused by engaging in bad habits. Eliminate.

LSAT Question	Analysis
21. Cable TV stations have advantages that enable them to attract many more advertisers than broadcast networks attract. For example, cable stations are able to target particular audiences with 24-hour news, sports, or movies, whereas broadcast networks must offer a variety of programming. Cable can also offer lower advertising rates than any broadcast network can, because it is subsidized by viewers through subscriber fees. Additionally, many cable stations have expanded worldwide with multinational programming.	**Step 2:** An assertion illustrated by thee examples: [assertion] Cable TV stations have advantages over broadcast networks in attracting advertisers. *Examples:* 1) Cable can target specific demographics *better* than broadcast. 2) Cable can offer advertising rates *lower* than broadcast (because cable charges subscribers and broadcast doesn't). 3) Many cable stations are global.
The statements above, if true, provide support for each of the following EXCEPT:	**Step 1:** Inference question: the stimulus "provide[s] support" for each of the four wrong answers; the stimulus either contradicts or is irrelevant to the correct answer.
	Step 3: The wrong answers follow from the stimulus. The correct answer does not, so what is unknown is important. NOTE: The only example that is not comparative is the third; it implies, but does not state, that broadcast networks are not global.
(A) Some broadcast networks can be viewed in several countries.	**Step 4:** Correct. This contradicts the implication of the third example. If global reach is an advantage for cable stations, then it's unlikely that networks are multinational.
(B) Broadcast networks do not rely on subscriber fees from viewers.	This is supported by the second example. Eliminate.
(C) Low costs are often an important factor for advertisers in selecting a station or network on which to run a TV ad.	The second example of cable's advantages in attracting advertisers is low rates, so it must be a factor in advertisers' decisions. Eliminate.
(D) Some advertisers prefer to have the opportunity to address a worldwide audience.	Cable's global reach is the third example of cable's advantages in attracting advertisers. Eliminate.
(E) The audiences that some advertisers prefer to target watch 24-hour news stations.	The first example advantage supports this statement. Eliminate.

PrepTest61 Sec4 Q3

LSAT Question	Analysis
22. Often a type of organ or body structure is the only physically feasible means of accomplishing a given task, so it should be unsurprising if, like eyes or wings, that type of organ or body structure evolves at different times in a number of completely unrelated species. After all, whatever the difference of heritage and habitat, as organisms animals have fundamentally similar needs and so _____. →	**Step 2**: Two statements describing a phenomenon and a statement of similarity: 1) Often an organ/body part is the only way to accomplish a task, *so* 2) different species naturally evolve similar organs/ body parts. *Since* 3) animals have similar needs, *It follows that _____.*
Which one of the following most logically completes the last sentence of the passage? →	**Step 1**: "[L]ogically completes" indicates an Inference question. The correct answer will provide a conclusion to the stimulus's evidence.
	Step 3: The statements build on one another and point to the conclusion that animals will likely develop similar organs/body parts.
(A) will often live in the same environment as other species quite different from themselves →	**Step 4**: Outside the Scope. The stimulus doesn't address whether those living in the same environment all have similar needs. Eliminate.
(B) will in many instances evolve similar adaptations enabling them to satisfy these needs →	Correct. This matches the prediction, substituting the word "adaptations" for "organs/body parts."
(C) will develop adaptations allowing them to satisfy these needs →	This is already implied by the evidence. The conclusion logically entails the development of *similar* adaptations, not just any adaptation. Eliminate.
(D) will resemble other species having different biological needs →	180. The stimulus suggests that similar needs produce similar adaptations. If anything, this implies that animals with different needs will develop different body parts. Eliminate.
(E) will all develop eyes or wings as adaptations *PrepTest61 Sec2 Q15* →	Distortion. This would work if the stimulus said "all animals need either to see or to fly," but it is nowhere near that specific. Eliminate.

LSAT Question	Analysis
23. The law of the city of Weston regarding contributions to mayoral campaigns is as follows: all contributions to these campaigns in excess of $100 made by nonresidents of Weston who are not former residents of Weston must be registered with the city council. Brimley's mayoral campaign clearly complied with this law since it accepted contributions only from residents and former residents of Weston.	**Step 2**: A principle and a purported application: 1) [principle/Formal Logic] Weston campaign law: Registration with the city council is *required* for contributions >$100 from nonresidents who are not former residents. 2) [application] Brimley accepted contributions only from residents and former residents, and so complies with the law.
If all the statements above are true, which one of the following statements must be true?	**Step 1**: The correct answer "must be true" based on the stimulus—an Inference question.
	Step 3: If the stimulus contains the complete law and the facts it provides about Brimley are correct, then he adhered to the law and need not register any contributions with the city council. The correct answer must be true based on these statements.
(A) No nonresident of Weston contributed in excess of $100 to Brimley's campaign.	**Step 4**: Distortion. No nonresident *who is not a former resident* contributed >$100 to Brimley. This choice is too broad. Eliminate.
(B) Some contributions to Brimley's campaign in excess of $100 were registered with the city council.	Outside the Scope. Brimley was not *required* to register any contributions; he may have registered some anyway, but that's beside the point. Eliminate.
(C) No contributions to Brimley's campaign needed to be registered with the city council.	Correct. Registration is required for $100+ contributions from nonresidents who are not former residents. Brimley had no contributors in that category.
(D) All contributions to Brimley's campaign that were registered with the city council were in excess of $100.	Distortion. From the stimulus, it's unclear that any of Brimley's contributions were registered. None needed to be. Eliminate.
(E) Brimley's campaign did not register any contributions with the city council. *PrepTest57 Sec2 Q25*	Outside the Scope. Brimley was not *required* to register any contributions; he may have registered some anyway, but that's beside the point. Eliminate.

LSAT Question	Analysis
24. Most successful entrepreneurs work at least 18 hours a day, and no one who works at least 18 hours a day has time for leisure activities. But all happy entrepreneurs have time for leisure activities.	**Step 2:** One uncertain statement and two conditional statements: 1) Most (over half of) successful entrepreneurs work ≥ 18 hours/day. 2) If work ≥ 18 hours/day → no time for leisure If time for leisure → work < 18 hours/day 3) If happy entrepreneur → time for leisure If no time for leisure → not happy entrepreneur
If the statements above are true, each of the following could be true EXCEPT:	**Step 1:** An Inference question: Based on the stimulus, the correct answer must be false, while each of the four wrong answers could be true.
	Step 3: The two conditional statements combine to tell you that no happy entrepreneurs work ≥ 18 hours/day. Combine that with the first statement about most successful entrepreneurs—they are not happy. Remember, the correct answer must be false given these statements.
(A) Anyone who has no time for leisure activities works at least 18 hours a day.	**Step 4:** This confuses necessity and sufficiency. Working ≥ 18 hours/day is one reason you may not have time for leisure, but there could be any number of other reasons. Eliminate.
(B) Some entrepreneurs who work at least 18 hours a day are successful.	Must be true based on the first statement in the stimulus. Eliminate.
(C) Some happy entrepreneurs are successful.	Could be true. Most successful entrepreneurs work too much to be happy, but that means that a minority may work less. Eliminate.
(D) Some entrepreneurs who work at least 18 hours a day are happy.	Correct. The two conditional statements combine to say: "If a person works ≥ 18 hours/day, then he or she is not a happy entrepreneur." The statement in this answer must be false.
(E) Some successful entrepreneurs work less than 18 hours a day. *PrepTest49 Sec2 Q16*	Could be true. Most successful entrepreneurs work more, so it's possible that some work less. Eliminate.

LSAT Question	Analysis
25. Art historian: More than any other genre of representational painting, still-life painting lends itself naturally to art whose goal is the artist's self-expression, rather than merely the reflection of a preexisting external reality. This is because in still-life painting, the artist invariably chooses, modifies, and arranges the objects to be painted. Thus, the artist has considerably more control over the composition and subject of a still-life painting than over those of a landscape painting or portrait, for example.	**Step 2**: A concrete statement and a two-part explanation for it: 1) Still-life painting lends itself to self-expression (as opposed to reflecting reality) more than any other representational genre does. *because* 2) In still-life, the painter *always* chooses, modifies, and arranges the objects. *and so* 3) The artist has more control over the composition of a still-life than over, for example, a landscape or a portrait.
Which one of the following is most strongly supported by the art historian's statements?	**Step 1**: The correct answer is "strongly supported by" the stimulus—an Inference question.
	Step 3: For the author's explanation to apply to the concrete statement, it must be the case that still-life is unique in having the painter invariably choose, modify, and arrange the subject matter, and that doing those things is tantamount to self-expression.
(A) Landscape painting and portraiture are the artistic genres that lend themselves most naturally to the mere reflection of a preexisting external reality.	**Step 4**: Outside the Scope. The stimulus does not address what, if anything, landscape and portraiture are best for. Eliminate.
(B) The only way in which artists control the composition and subject of a painting is by choosing, modifying, and arranging the objects to be represented in that painting.	Extreme. There may be other ways in which artists can control a painting's composition; the author finds still-life better for self-expression because, in still-life, painters *always* choose, modify, and arrange the objects. Eliminate.
(C) Nonrepresentational painting does not lend itself as naturally as still-life painting does to the goal of the artist's self-expression.	Outside the Scope. The stimulus is concerned exclusively with representational painting. Eliminate.
(D) In genres of representational painting other than still-life painting, the artist does not always choose, modify, and arrange the objects to be painted.	Correct. If this is the quality that explains still-life's superiority, it follows that other representational painting styles do not share this quality.
(E) When painting a portrait, artists rarely attempt to express themselves through the choice, modification, or arrangement of the background elements against which the subject of the portrait is painted. *PrepTest57 Sec3 Q13*	Distortion. Artists' attempts to control some or all of the composition in portraits need not be *rare* in order for still-life to be a superior genre for self-expression. After all, painters *always* choose, modify, and arrange the objects in a still-life. Eliminate.

LSAT Question	Analysis
26. Historian: The standard "QWERTY" configuration of the keys on typewriters and computer keyboards was originally designed to be awkward and limit typing speed. This was because early typewriters would jam frequently if adjacent keys were struck in quick succession. Experiments have shown that keyboard configurations more efficient than QWERTY can double typing speed while tremendously reducing typing effort. However, the expense and inconvenience of switching to a new keyboard configuration prevent any configuration other than QWERTY from attaining widespread use.	**Step 2:** Five related statements: 1) QWERTY keyboards originally designed to make typing slower and harder. *because* 2) Old typewriters would jam. 3) Faster, easier keyboards could be designed for computers now. *but* 4) They probably won't be used. *because* 5) Everyone is familiar with QWERTY keyboards, and switching is expensive and difficult.
Which one of the following is most strongly supported by the historian's statements?	**Step 1:** The correct answer is "strongly supported by" the stimulus—an Inference question.
	Step 3: The statements combine to allow for several possible inferences focusing on the differences between old typewriters and computers. The correct answer will follow from the stimulus statements.
(A) Most people who have tried typing with non-QWERTY keyboards have typed significantly more quickly using those keyboards than they usually have done using QWERTY keyboards.	**Step 4:** Extreme. Faster typing is possible with new keyboards, but that doesn't mean that over half of those who have used them typed significantly faster. Eliminate.
(B) Early QWERTY typewriters were less likely to jam than were at least some more recent typewriters if adjacent keys were struck in quick succession.	Distortion/180. Because all typewriters used QWERTY, which was designed to prevent jamming, there's no reason to believe this statement. If anything, one would suspect that newer typewriters solved jamming problems in other ways. Eliminate.
(C) If the designers of early typewriters had foreseen the possibility that technology would make it possible for adjacent keyboard keys to be struck in rapid succession without jamming, then they would not have proposed the QWERTY configuration.	Distortion. The need for a keyboard that worked well with old typewriters might still have prompted the use of QWERTY; it's unlikely that the world would have gone decades without typing. The stimulus doesn't give us enough information to draw this inference. Eliminate.
(D) The benefit to society that would result from switching to a keyboard configuration other than QWERTY is significantly greater than the overall cost of such a switch.	180. The passage suggests that the difficulty of learning a new keyboard will deter a switch to new faster, easier keyboards. Eliminate.
(E) If the keyboard had been designed for computers, then it would not have been designed to limit typing speed. *PrepTest59 Sec3 Q21*	Correct. Computers don't have problems with jamming, so faster, easier keyboards can be used, and so we wouldn't have developed the familiarity with QWERTY that deters the use of faster, easier keyboards now.

PRINCIPLE QUESTIONS ASKING FOR INFERENCES

Some Principle question stems—those you learned about in Chapter 10—mimic the skills associated with Assumption, Strengthen, and Parallel Reasoning questions. Other Principle questions test Inference question skills. These Principle questions ask you either to identify a general rule from a specific case or to determine which specific case follows from a general rule.

You can identify Principle questions that ask for inferences from question stems such as these:

Identify the Principle	Apply the Principle
Which one of the following is best illustrated by the examples presented above? *PrepTest51 Sec3 Q5*	Which one of the following judgments conforms most closely to the principles described by the industrial adviser? *PrepTest51 Sec1 Q17*
The situation described above most closely conforms to which of the following generalizations? *PrepTest59 Sec2 Q23*	Which of the following situations violates the food labeling regulation? *PrepTest57 Sec3 Q14*

NOTE: The two stems on the left indicate questions in which the stimulus presents a specific situation or example and you are asked for the answer stating the broad principle the stimulus illustrates. The two stems on the right, however, indicate questions in which the stimulus presents a broad principle and you are asked to choose the answer stating a specific situation or example that follows from the principle.

PRINCIPLE QUESTIONS ASKING FOR INFERENCES AT A GLANCE

Task: Identify the principle illustrated by the specific case in the stimulus, or apply the principle stated in the stimulus to the specific case in the correct answer.

Strategy: In Identify the Principle questions, summarize the broad rule illustrated by the situation or example and use your summary to find the answer choice with a matching principle; in Apply the Principle questions, note each element in the principle and find the situation or example that conforms to each and every element.

LSAT tests released from 2008 to 2013 had an average of 5.1 Principle questions per test.

Out of those, the typical test featured two or three Principle questions asking for inferences, usually one Apply the Principle and one or two Identify the Principle questions of this type.

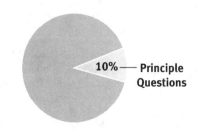

**Logical Reasoning
Question Types**

PrepTests57–71; released 2009–2013

LEARNING OBJECTIVES

In this section, you'll learn to:

· Infer a principle (general rule) from a specific case that illustrates it
· Identify a specific case that appropriately applies a principle (general rule)
· Identify and answer Identify the Principle—Inference question
· Identify and answer Apply the Principle question

Infer a Principle (General Rule) from a Specific Case That Illustrates It

When your task is to infer a general, law-like rule from a specific case, the stimulus tends to fall into one of two categories. Examine an LSAT expert's work in Steps 1 and 2 in an example of each and try to predict the correct answers:

Cases That Describe Actions and Outcomes: In these questions, the stimulus describes a specific, detailed example that you can broaden to fit similar scenarios.

LSAT Question	Analysis
Among Trinidadian guppies, males with large spots are more attractive to females than are males with small spots, who consequently are presented with less frequent mating opportunities. Yet guppies with small spots are more likely to avoid detection by predators, so in waters where predators are abundant only guppies with small spots live to maturity.	**Step 2:** The Keyword "yet" is central to the rule this situation illustrates: While large spots help male guppies mate, the large spots can also cause the guppies to be detected by predators.
The situation described above most closely conforms to which one of the following generalizations? *PrepTest61 Sec4 Q1*	**Step 1:** "Generalizations" is an LSAT synonym for principles. The "situation described above" means that the stimulus is a specific situation, while the answer choices will be broader in scope.

Cases That Make Recommendations: In these questions, the stimulus makes a recommendation and gives reasons to support that recommendation.

LSAT Question	Analysis
Many doctors cater to patients' demands that they be prescribed antibiotics for their colds. However, colds are caused by viruses, and antibiotics have no effect on viruses, and so antibiotics have no effect on colds. Such treatments are also problematic because antibiotics can have dangerous side effects. So doctors should never prescribe antibiotics to treat colds.	**Step 2:** The author recommends that doctors never prescribe antibiotics for colds, because antibiotics have no effect on colds and can even have dangerous side effects.
The reasoning above most closely conforms to which one of the following principles? *PrepTest57 Sec2 Q1*	**Step 1:** The phrase "conforms to which of the following principles" is a giveaway. The reasoning above is specific; the correct answer choice will state the reasoning in more general terms.

Now that you've considered the expert's analysis in Steps 1 and 2, use the predictions outlined here to evaluate the answer choices in those questions.

LSAT Question	My Analysis
Among Trinidadian guppies, males with large spots are more attractive to females than are males with small spots, who consequently are presented with less frequent mating opportunities. Yet guppies with small spots are more likely to avoid detection by predators, so in waters where predators are abundant only guppies with small spots live to maturity.	**Step 2:** The Keyword *yet* is central to the rule this situation illustrates: While large spots help male guppies mate, the large spots can also cause the guppies to be detected by predators.
The situation described above most closely conforms to which one of the following generalizations?	**Step 1:** "Generalizations" is an LSAT synonym for principles. The "situation described above" means that the stimulus is a specific situation, while the answer choices will be broader in scope.
	Step 3: The correct answer will take the specific situation in the stimulus and broaden the scope beyond the specific case of guppies: A physical feature that helps an animal mate might also end up causing that animal harm.
(A) A trait that helps attract mates is sometimes more dangerous to one sex than to another.	**Step 4:**
(B) Those organisms that are most attractive to the opposite sex have the greatest number of offspring.	
(C) Those organisms that survive the longest have the greatest number of offspring.	
(D) Whether a trait is harmful to the organisms of a species can depend on which sex possesses it.	
(E) A trait that is helpful to procreation can also hinder it in certain environments.	

PrepTest61 Sec4 Q1

LSAT Question	My Analysis
Many doctors cater to patients' demands that they be prescribed antibiotics for their colds. However, colds are caused by viruses, and antibiotics have no effect on viruses, and so antibiotics have no effect on colds. Such treatments are also problematic because antibiotics can have dangerous side effects. So doctors should never prescribe antibiotics to treat colds. $\longrightarrow$	**Step 2:** The author recommends that doctors never prescribe antibiotics for colds, because antibiotics have no effect on colds and can even have dangerous side effects.
The reasoning above most closely conforms to which one of the following principles? $\longrightarrow$	**Step 1:** The phrase "conforms to which of the following principles" is a giveaway. The reasoning above is specific; the correct answer choice will state the reasoning in more general terms.
	Step 3: Strip out the specificity of the argument and broaden it beyond doctors, colds, and antibiotics: Group x shouldn't perform action y if y has no positive effect and could cause harm.
(A) A doctor should not prescribe a drug for a condition if it cannot improve that condition and if the drug potentially has adverse side effects. $\longrightarrow$	**Step 4:**
(B) A doctor should not prescribe any drug that might have harmful effects on the patient even if the drug might have a positive effect on the patient. $\longrightarrow$	
(C) A doctor should attempt to prescribe every drug that is likely to affect the patient's health positively. $\longrightarrow$	
(D) A doctor should withhold treatment from a patient if the doctor is uncertain whether the treatment will benefit the patient. $\longrightarrow$	
(E) A doctor should never base the decision to prescribe a certain medication for a patient on the patient's claims about the effectiveness of that medication. $\longrightarrow$	

PrepTest57 Sec2 Q1

Here's how an LSAT expert would evaluate the answer choices for those two Principle questions.

LSAT Question	Analysis
Among Trinidadian guppies, males with large spots are more attractive to females than are males with small spots, who consequently are presented with less frequent mating opportunities. Yet guppies with small spots are more likely to avoid detection by predators, so in waters where predators are abundant only guppies with small spots live to maturity.	**Step 2:** The Keyword *yet* is central to the rule this situation illustrates: While large spots help male guppies mate, the large spots can also cause the guppies to be detected by predators.
The situation described above most closely conforms to which one of the following generalizations?	**Step 1:** "Generalizations" is an LSAT synonym for principles. The "situation described above" means that the stimulus is a specific situation, while the answer choices will be broader in scope.
	Step 3: The correct answer will take the specific situation in the stimulus and broaden the scope beyond the specific case of guppies: A physical feature that helps an animal mate might also end up causing that animal harm.
(A) A trait that helps attract mates is sometimes more dangerous to one sex than to another.	**Step 4:** Irrelevant Comparison. The stimulus says nothing about females facing more or less danger than the males due to large spots. Eliminate.
(B) Those organisms that are most attractive to the opposite sex have the greatest number of offspring.	Distortion. This may be true, but it is not the general rule illustrated in the stimulus. Eliminate.
(C) Those organisms that survive the longest have the greatest number of offspring.	Outside the Scope. The stimulus doesn't mention a relationship between life span and reproductive success, let alone illustrate a principle about it. Eliminate.
(D) Whether a trait is harmful to the organisms of a species can depend on which sex possesses it.	Irrelevant Comparison. The stimulus makes no sex-based distinction about the dangers of large spots. Eliminate.
(E) A trait that is helpful to procreation can also hinder it in certain environments. *PrepTest61 Sec4 Q1*	Correct. This general rule matches the specific example above.

LSAT Question	**Analysis**
Many doctors cater to patients' demands that they be prescribed antibiotics for their colds. However, colds are caused by viruses, and antibiotics have no effect on viruses, and so antibiotics have no effect on colds. Such treatments are also problematic because antibiotics can have dangerous side effects. So doctors should never prescribe antibiotics to treat colds. →	**Step 2:** The author recommends that doctors never prescribe antibiotics for colds, because antibiotics have no effect on colds and can even have dangerous side effects.
The reasoning above most closely conforms to which one of the following principles? →	**Step 1:** The phrase "conforms to which of the following principles" is a giveaway. The reasoning above is specific; the correct answer choice will state the reasoning in more general terms.
	Step 3: Strip out the specificity of the argument and broaden it to cover cases beyond colds and antibiotics: Doctors should not perform an action that has no positive effect and could cause harm.
(A) A doctor should not prescribe a drug for a condition if it cannot improve that condition and if the drug potentially has adverse side effects. →	**Step 4:** Correct. Spot on! If we apply this rule to the scenario about colds and antibiotics, it would lead to the recommendation in the stimulus.
(B) A doctor should not prescribe any drug that might have harmful effects on the patient even if the drug might have a positive effect on the patient. →	Distortion. This choice doesn't apply to the stimulus case, since antibiotics do *not* have a positive effect on patients with colds. Eliminate.
(C) A doctor should attempt to prescribe every drug that is likely to affect the patient's health positively. →	Outside the Scope. Nothing in the stimulus scenario is likely to affect a patient's health positively. Eliminate.
(D) A doctor should withhold treatment from a patient if the doctor is uncertain whether the treatment will benefit the patient. →	Distortion. In the stimulus, doctors are certain that antibiotics will not benefit the patient. Moreover, this principle says nothing about potential negative side effects. Eliminate.
(E) A doctor should never base the decision to prescribe a certain medication for a patient on the patient's claims about the effectiveness of that medication. *PrepTest57 Sec2 Q1* →	Distortion. This choice plays upon the first sentence in the stimulus, but the general rule here does not match the recommendation in the stimulus. Eliminate.

Identify a Specific Case That Applies a Principle (General Rule)

When your task is to apply a principle, the stimulus generally contains a rule, a set of rules, or a definition. Analyze the principle (or general rule) by identifying each of its elements. The correct answer will provide a specific case that matches the principle element-by-element; your task is to choose a specific example that conforms to the given condition(s). In addition to focusing on what a definition or rule allows, pay attention to what is not allowed.

Here is an example of an LSAT expert's work in Steps 1 and 2 on an Apply the Principle question asking for an inference.

LSAT Question	Analysis
Most employees spend their time completing unimportant tasks for which they have been given firm schedules and deadlines. Efficient employees know how to ignore such demands and instead spend their time on projects that will yield big rewards for their employers if successful, even when such projects carry the risk of significant loss if unsuccessful.	**Step 2:** The stimulus defines "efficiency" as: 1) Ignoring unimportant tasks with firm schedules and deadlines, and 2) spending time on high-risk, high-reward projects.
Which one of the following is an example of efficiency as described above? *PrepTest49 Sec2 Q3*	**Step 1:** The correct answer is an "example of" a definition in the stimulus—an Apply the Principle question asking for an inference.

Reflect for a moment on the expert's analysis.

How many elements are there in the definition/rule in the stimulus?

What type of employee behavior will be described in the correct answer? How about in the four wrong answers?

Now, use your reflection on the expert's analysis as a prediction of the right answer and evaluate the answer choices in this question.

LSAT Question		My Analysis
Most employees spend their time completing unimportant tasks for which they have been given firm schedules and deadlines. Efficient employees know how to ignore such demands and instead spend their time on projects that will yield big rewards for their employers if successful, even when such projects carry the risk of significant loss if unsuccessful.	→	**Step 2:** The stimulus defines "efficiency" as: 1) Ignoring unimportant tasks with firm schedules and deadlines, and 2) spending time on high-risk, high-reward projects.
Which one of the following is an example of efficiency as described above?	→	**Step 1:** The correct answer is an "example of" a definition in the stimulus—an Apply the Principle question asking for an inference.
		Step 3: The answer choices will describe employee actions. The correct answer will describe "efficient" behavior as defined in the stimulus. The four wrong answers will describe inefficient behaviors.
(A) spending the entire afternoon working on a report that a supervisor has ordered completed by the following day	→	**Step 4:**
(B) instead of working on a report that a supervisor has ordered completed by the following day, spending the entire afternoon completing routine correspondence that could be delayed	→	
(C) deciding to take an urgent call from a major customer instead of being punctual at a monthly sales meeting	→	
(D) meeting daily with other staff members to discuss workloads and schedules	→	
(E) spending time each morning scheduling tasks according to the most immediate deadlines	→	

PrepTest49 Sec2 Q3

Here's how the LSAT expert evaluated the answer choices in that question.

LSAT Question	Analysis
Most employees spend their time completing unimportant tasks for which they have been given firm schedules and deadlines. Efficient employees know how to ignore such demands and instead spend their time on projects that will yield big rewards for their employers if successful, even when such projects carry the risk of significant loss if unsuccessful.	**Step 2:** The stimulus defines "efficiency" as: 1) Ignoring unimportant tasks with firm schedules and deadlines, and 2) spending time on high-risk, high-reward projects.
Which one of the following is an example of efficiency as described above?	**Step 1:** The correct answer is an "example of" a definition in the stimulus—an Apply the Principle question asking for an inference.
	Step 3: The answer choices will describe employee actions. The correct answer will describe "efficient" behavior as defined in the stimulus. The four wrong answers will describe inefficient behaviors.
(A) spending the entire afternoon working on a report that a supervisor has ordered completed by the following day	**Step 4:** 180. Focusing on a menial task with a hard deadline is what an efficient employee should ignore. Eliminate.
(B) instead of working on a report that a supervisor has ordered completed by the following day, spending the entire afternoon completing routine correspondence that could be delayed	180. Routine correspondence that could be delayed is an example of a menial task with little reward. Eliminate.
(C) deciding to take an urgent call from a major customer instead of being punctual at a monthly sales meeting	Correct. The employee here is putting off a menial task so she can focus on a potentially high-yield project.
(D) meeting daily with other staff members to discuss workloads and schedules	180. This fits the "unimportant tasks" category defined in the stimulus as inefficient and best ignored. Eliminate.
(E) spending time each morning scheduling tasks according to the most immediate deadlines *PrepTest49 Sec2 Q3*	180. This employee is not ignoring trivial, deadline-driven work in order to focus on a high-yield project. Eliminate.

Identify the Principle—Inference and Apply the Principle Questions

When you're dealing with a Principle question that rewards a valid inference, you will first need to determine your task. Either you'll be asked to identify or infer a broad principle from a specific example in the stimulus (Identify the Principle—Inference) or you'll be asked to apply a broad rule or definition to a specific situation in the answer choices (Apply the Principle).

Use the following stems, along with their analysis, to check your ability to make this important distinction.

LSAT Question Stem	My Analysis
i. The situation described above most closely conforms to which one of the following generalizations? $\longrightarrow$ *PrepTest59 Sec2 Q23*	
ii. Which one of the following judgments most closely conforms to the principle cited by the philosopher? $\longrightarrow$ *PrepTest51 Sec1 Q9*	
iii. The executive's reasoning most closely conforms to which one of the following generalizations? $\longrightarrow$ *PrepTest49 Sec4 Q9*	
iv. Which of the following situations violates the food labeling regulation? $\longrightarrow$ *PrepTest57 Sec3 Q14*	

The correct analyses are: i. Identify the Principle—Inference; ii. Apply the Principle; iii. Identify the Principle—Inference; iv. Apply the Principle (NOTE: In example iv., you are asked to find the one case that violates the principle; the wrong answers in this case will either conform to the principle, or will be irrelevant to it.)

Practice: Principle Questions Asking for Inferences

Now, practice some Principle questions that ask you to make inferences. For each question below: Determine whether you are asked to identify the principle illustrated by the stimulus or to apply the principle in the stimulus to a matching case in the correct answer.

LSAT Question		My Analysis
27. Executive: In order to add to our profits, I was planning to promote and distribute herbal tinctures. However, some members of my advisory staff questioned the medical efficacy of such products. So I have consulted a variety of reliable medical publications, and these likewise claim that herbal tinctures are ineffective. Therefore, I must conclude that marketing such products would not produce the result I intended.	$\longrightarrow$	**Step 2:**
The executive's reasoning most closely conforms to which one of the following generalizations?	$\longrightarrow$	**Step 1:**
		Step 3:
(A) To be reliable, a medical publication that evaluates consumer products must include at least some independent evidence.	$\longrightarrow$	**Step 4:**
(B) If a majority of reliable sources conclude that a particular substance is medically ineffective, then that substance almost certainly is medically ineffective.	$\longrightarrow$	
(C) Consulting reliable publications is not, by itself, a reliable basis for determining whether or not the promotion of a new line of products will be profitable.	$\longrightarrow$	
(D) It would not be profitable to promote and distribute a new line of products if these products have adverse medical effects.	$\longrightarrow$	
(E) The promotion and distribution of a new line of products will not prove profitable if a number of reliable authorities declare them to be ineffective.	$\longrightarrow$	

PrepTest49 Sec4 Q9

LSAT Question	My Analysis
28. Philosopher: An action is morally good if it both achieves the agent's intended goal and benefits someone other than the agent. $\longrightarrow$	**Step 2:**
Which one of the following judgments most closely conforms to the principle cited by the philosopher? $\longrightarrow$	**Step 1:**
	Step 3:

(A) Colin chose to lie to the authorities questioning him, in an attempt to protect his friends. The authorities discovered his deception and punished Colin and his friends severely. But because he acted out of love for his friends, Colin's action was morally good. $\longrightarrow$ **Step 4:**

(B) Derek prepared a steak dinner to welcome his new neighbors to the neighborhood. When they arrived for dinner, Derek found out that the newcomers were strict vegetarians. Though the new neighbors were still grateful for Derek's efforts to welcome them, Derek's action was not morally good. $\longrightarrow$

(C) Ellen worked overtime hoping to get a promotion. The extra money she earned allowed her family to take a longer vacation that year, but she failed to get the promotion. Nevertheless, Ellen's action was morally good. $\longrightarrow$

(D) Louisa tried to get Henry into serious trouble by making it appear that he stole some expensive clothes from a store. But the store's detective realized what Louisa did, and so Louisa was punished rather than Henry. Since she intended to harm Henry, Louisa's action was not morally good. $\longrightarrow$

(E) Yolanda took her children to visit their grandfather because she wanted her children to enjoy their vacation and she knew they adored their grandfather. The grandfather and the children all enjoyed the visit. Though Yolanda greatly enjoyed the visit, her action was morally good. $\longrightarrow$

PrepTest51 Sec1 Q9

LSAT Question	My Analysis

29. Critic: As modern methods of communication and transportation have continued to improve, the pace of life today has become faster than ever before. This speed has created feelings of impermanence and instability, making us feel as if we never have enough time to achieve what we want—or at least what we think we want. $\longrightarrow$ **Step 2:**

The critic's statements most closely conform to which one of the following assessments? $\longrightarrow$ **Step 1:**

Step 3:

(A) The fast pace of modern life has made it difficult for people to achieve their goals. $\longrightarrow$ **Step 4:**

(B) The disadvantages of technological progress often outweigh the advantages. $\longrightarrow$

(C) Changes in people's feelings about life can result from technological changes. $\longrightarrow$

(D) The perception of impermanence in contemporary life makes it more difficult for people to know what they want. $\longrightarrow$

(E) Changes in people's feelings fuel the need for technological advancement. $\longrightarrow$

PrepTest57 Sec3 Q16

Expert Analysis: Principle Questions Asking for Inferences

LSAT Question	Analysis
27. Executive: In order to add to our profits, I was planning to promote and distribute herbal tinctures. However, some members of my advisory staff questioned the medical efficacy of such products. So I have consulted a variety of reliable medical publications, and these likewise claim that herbal tinctures are ineffective. Therefore, I must conclude that marketing such products would not produce the result I intended.	**Step 2:** Break the executive's argument into its pieces: Conclusion: Marketing herbal tinctures *will not be profitable*. *because* Evidence: Reliable medical publications *claim* that herbal tinctures are ineffective.
The executive's reasoning most closely conforms to which one of the following generalizations?	**Step 1:** "Generalization" is another word for "principle" on the LSAT. Here, the correct answer will state the general rule illustrated by the specific example—the executive's argument—in the stimulus.
	Step 3: Generalize the executive's argument: If a reliable authority *says* that a product is ineffective, then marketing that product will not be profitable.
(A) To be reliable, a medical publication that evaluates consumer products must include at least some independent evidence.	**Step 4:** Outside the Scope. This stimulus does not outline what makes a publication reliable. Eliminate.
(B) If a majority of reliable sources conclude that a particular substance is medically ineffective, then that substance almost certainly is medically ineffective.	Distortion. It is the authorities' *claims* of ineffectiveness that will make the product unprofitable, not whether the product is, in fact, ineffective. Eliminate.
(C) Consulting reliable publications is not, by itself, a reliable basis for determining whether or not the promotion of a new line of products will be profitable.	180. The executive reasons that a product will not be profitable precisely because of what reliable publications say about the product. Eliminate.
(D) It would not be profitable to promote and distribute a new line of products if these products have adverse medical effects.	Outside the Scope. This argument is about ineffective products, not adverse medical effects. Eliminate.
(E) The promotion and distribution of a new line of products will not prove profitable if a number of reliable authorities declare them to be ineffective.	Correct. This matches each element of the argument in the stimulus.

PrepTest49 Sec4 Q9

LSAT Question	Analysis
28. Philosopher: An action is morally good if it both achieves the agent's intended goal and benefits someone other than the agent.	**Step 2:** A conditional statement: If an action achieves the agent's intended goal AND the action benefits someone other than the agent → the action is morally good If an action is not morally good → the action did not achieve the agent's goal OR the action didn't benefit anyone else besides the agent
Which one of the following judgments most closely conforms to the principle cited by the philosopher?	**Step 1:** The correct answer is a specific judgment that "conforms to the principle cited" in the stimulus—an Apply the Principle question.
	Step 3: The correct answer will correctly apply the Formal Logic rule; the four wrong answers will misapply or fall outside the scope of the rule.
(A) Colin chose to lie to the authorities questioning him, in an attempt to protect his friends. The authorities discovered his deception and punished Colin and his friends severely. But because he acted out of love for his friends, Colin's action was morally good.	**Step 4:** Colin's action did not achieve its intended goal, so it does not fulfill the conditions sufficient to establish an action as morally good. Eliminate.
(B) Derek prepared a steak dinner to welcome his new neighbors to the neighborhood. When they arrived for dinner, Derek found out that the newcomers were strict vegetarians. Though the new neighbors were still grateful for Derek's efforts to welcome them, Derek's action was not morally good.	Outside the Scope. The stimulus rule does not define actions or outcomes sufficient to make an action *not* morally good. Eliminate.
(C) Ellen worked overtime hoping to get a promotion. The extra money she earned allowed her family to take a longer vacation that year, but she failed to get the promotion. Nevertheless, Ellen's action was morally good.	Ellen's action did not achieve its intended goal and did not benefit anyone else, so the conditions sufficient to make her action morally good were not met. Eliminate.
(D) Louisa tried to get Henry into serious trouble by making it appear that he stole some expensive clothes from a store. But the store's detective realized what Louisa did, and so Louisa was punished rather than Henry. Since she intended to harm Henry, Louisa's action was not morally good.	Outside the Scope. The stimulus rule does not define actions or outcomes sufficient to make an action *not* morally good. Eliminate.

LSAT Question	Analysis
(E) Yolanda took her children to visit their grandfather because she wanted her children to enjoy their vacation and she knew they adored their grandfather. The grandfather and the children all enjoyed the visit. Though Yolanda greatly enjoyed the visit, her action was morally good. *PrepTest51 Sec1 Q9*	Correct. Yolanda's action achieved its intended goal AND it benefited someone other than Yolanda, so according to the rule presented in the stimulus, it is a morally good action.

LSAT Question	Analysis
29. Critic: As modern methods of communication and transportation have continued to improve, the pace of life today has become faster than ever before. This speed has created feelings of impermanence and instability, making us feel as if we never have enough time to achieve what we want—or at least what we think we want.	**Step 2:** The statements describe a chain of causes and effects: Improved communication and transportation *caused* faster pace of life *causing* feelings of impermanence and instability *causing* the feeling that we don't have the time to achieve what we think we want.
The critic's statements most closely conform to which one of the following assessments?	**Step 1:** The stimulus statements "most closely conform to" the correct answer—an Identify the Principle question asking for an inference.
	Step 3: The correct answer must take into account all of the statements. Connect the first statement to the last: Technological improvements can cause people to have different feelings about their lives and goals.
(A) The fast pace of modern life has made it difficult for people to achieve their goals.	**Step 4:** Distortion. The last sentence in the stimulus says that the fast pace of life has caused us to *feel* as though we don't have time to achieve what we want. Eliminate.
(B) The disadvantages of technological progress often outweigh the advantages.	Outside the Scope. The statements in the stimulus never talk about the advantages of technological progress. Eliminate.
(C) Changes in people's feelings about life can result from technological changes.	Correct. This ties together all of the statements in the stimulus and sums them up succinctly.
(D) The perception of impermanence in contemporary life makes it more difficult for people to know what they want.	Distortion. Feelings of impermanence and instability have led to the feeling that we don't have time to achieve what we think we want. This choice says we don't know what we want. Eliminate.
(E) Changes in people's feelings fuel the need for technological advancement. *PrepTest57 Sec3 Q16*	Outside the Scope. The argument never discusses what fuels the need for technological advancement. Eliminate.

RESOLVING DISCREPANCIES AND PARADOX QUESTIONS

Paradox questions present two facts that appear to be in conflict, and then ask you to select the answer presenting information that, if true, helps to resolve or reconcile the apparent contradiction.

You can identify Paradox questions from question stems such as these:

Which one of the following, if true, most helps to explain how both reports could be accurate?

PrepTest51 Sec3 Q8

Which one of the following, if true, most helps to resolve the apparent conflict in the consumer activist's statements?

PrepTest49 Sec4 Q11

Each of the following, if true, would contribute to an explanation of the apparent discrepancy in the information above EXCEPT:

PrepTest59 Sec3 Q17

Which one of the following, if true, most helps to account for the apparent discrepancy in the students' preferences?

PrepTest61 Sec2 Q25

The most common verbs used to describe your task in Paradox questions are *explain, resolve,* or *reconcile*. Notice that the question stems always refer to an *apparent* conflict or discrepancy. In other cases, the testmaker might use a term such as "seeming discrepancy" or "unexpected result" to signal the presence of a paradox in the stimulus.

PARADOX QUESTIONS AT A GLANCE

Task: Select the one answer containing a fact that would help explain or resolve an apparent discrepancy.

Strategy: Identify the apparent contradiction or inexplicable situation in the stimulus. Use your description of the paradox to evaluate the answer choices.

On LSAT tests released from 2009 through 2013, there were an average of 3.7 Paradox questions per test.

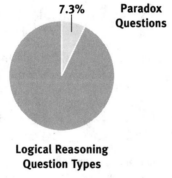

7.3% **Paradox Questions**

Logical Reasoning Question Types

PrepTests57–71; released 2009–2013

Incidentally, Paradox EXCEPT questions are fairly common; make sure they are part of your practice.

LEARNING OBJECTIVES

In this section, you'll learn to:

- Identify and paraphrase an apparent contradiction
- Infer what must be true to resolve an apparent contradiction
- Identify and answer Paradox questions
- Identify and answer Paradox EXCEPT questions

Identify and Paraphrase an Apparent Contradiction and Infer What Must Be True to Resolve It

Before you can find the answer choice that reconciles an apparent contradiction, you'll need to understand the contradiction. Once you've identified a question as calling for an explanation or resolution to an apparent paradox, look for the contrast Keyword that almost always highlights the conflict. After you've identified the two seemingly contradictory facts present in the stimulus, paraphrase the discrepancy in the form of a question, "How is it that fact 1 and fact 2 can both be true?"

Here, an LSAT expert identifies and paraphrases the apparent contradiction. Note how the paraphrase will allow the expert to anticipate the sort of fact that might resolve the paradox.

LSAT Question	Analysis
Human settlement of previously uninhabited areas tends to endanger species of wildlife. However, the Mississippi kite, a bird found on the prairies of North America, flourishes in areas that people have settled. In fact, during the five years since 1985 its population has risen far more rapidly in towns than in rural areas. *PrepTest51 Sec3 Q10* ⟶	"However" indicates the conflicting ideas. Fact 1: New human settlement usually endangers wildlife. *but* Fact 2: The Mississippi kite (a prairie bird) seems to do better in settled than in unsettled areas. Paradox: Even though most species are negatively affected by human settlement, the Mississippi kite seems to thrive in settled areas. Why would this prairie bird do better in town?

The correct answer will provide a fact that explains why settled environments are preferable for the Mississippi kite. Maybe there is more food or better protection around human environments.

You will revisit this stimulus along with its full question in a Practice exercise later in this section. Before moving into full-question practice, though, try identifying and paraphrasing some more apparent discrepancies from Paradox question stimuli.

Practice

Identify and paraphrase the anomaly in the following LSAT Paradox stimuli, and anticipate the kind of fact that would help provide a resolution for each one.

LSAT Question	**My Analysis**
30. Engineers are investigating the suitability of Wantastiquet Pass as the site of a new bridge. Because one concern is whether erosion could eventually weaken the bridge's foundations, they contracted for two reports on erosion in the region. Although both reports are accurate, one claims that the region suffers relatively little erosion, while the other claims that regional erosion is heavy and a cause for concern. $\longrightarrow$	
PrepTest51 Sec3 Q8	

LSAT Question	**My Analysis**
31. Scientists removed all viruses from a seawater sample and then measured the growth rate of the plankton population in the water. They expected the rate to increase dramatically, but the population actually got smaller. $\longrightarrow$	
PrepTest57 Sec3 Q7	

LSAT Question	**My Analysis**
32. Consumer activist: When antilock brakes were first introduced, it was claimed that they would significantly reduce the incidence of multiple-car collisions, thereby saving lives. Indeed, antilock brakes have reduced the incidence of multiple-car collisions. I maintain, however, that to save lives, automobile manufacturers ought to stop equipping cars with them. $\longrightarrow$	
PrepTest49 Sec4 Q11	

LSAT Question	**My Analysis**

33. The number of automobile thefts has declined steadily during the past five years, and it is more likely now than it was five years ago that someone who steals a car will be convicted of the crime.

          PrepTest61 Sec4 Q14

$\longrightarrow$

LSAT Question	**My Analysis**

34. A recent study of major motion pictures revealed that the vast majority of their plots were simply variations on plots that had been used many times before. Despite this fact, many people enjoy seeing several new movies each year.

          PrepTest59 Sec3 Q17

$\longrightarrow$

Expert Analysis

How do your analyses compare to those of an LSAT expert?

LSAT Question	Analysis
30. Engineers are investigating the suitability of Wantastiquet Pass as the site of a new bridge. Because one concern is whether erosion could eventually weaken the bridge's foundations, they contracted for two reports on erosion in the region. Although both reports are accurate, one claims that the region suffers relatively little erosion, while the other claims that regional erosion is heavy and a cause for concern. *PrepTest51 Sec3 Q8* $\longrightarrow$	*Although* and *while* reveal contradictory ideas: Fact 1: Both reports on erosion in the region are accurate. *but* Fact 2: One says that the region suffers little erosion, and the other says that the region suffers heavy erosion. How could it be that studies with contradictory results are both accurate?

Resolve this paradox by showing that the studies looked at two different kinds of erosion, or at erosion in two different contexts.

LSAT Question	Analysis
31. Scientists removed all viruses from a seawater sample and then measured the growth rate of the plankton population in the water. They expected the rate to increase dramatically, but the population actually got smaller. *PrepTest57 Sec3 Q7* $\longrightarrow$	[B]ut indicates the conflict: Fact 1: Scientists expected plankton population to grow rapidly upon removal of viruses from seawater. *instead* Fact 2: The plankton population shrank. Why would removing viruses from seawater cause the plankton population to decline?

Resolve this unexpected result by providing evidence that the plankton unexpectedly benefit from the viruses.

LSAT Question	Analysis
32. Consumer activist: When antilock brakes were first introduced, it was claimed that they would significantly reduce the incidence of multiple-car collisions, thereby saving lives. Indeed, antilock brakes have reduced the incidence of multiple-car collisions. I maintain, however, that to save lives, automobile manufacturers ought to stop equipping cars with them. *PrepTest49 Sec4 Q11* $\longrightarrow$	[H]owever indicates the conflict: Fact 1: Antilock brakes have reduced the incidence of multi-car collisions. *but* Fact 2: [author's assertion] To save lives, automakers should stop equipping cars with antilock brakes. Why would the author maintain that ceasing use of something that reduces the number of multi-car accidents would save lives?

Resolve this with evidence that equipping cars with anti-lock brakes makes a car or its driver less safe.

LSAT Question	**My Analysis**
33. The number of automobile thefts has declined steadily during the past five years, and it is more likely now than it was five years ago that someone who steals a car will be convicted of the crime. *PrepTest61 Sec4 Q14* →	Here, the facts are not necessarily in conflict; *and* indicates the relevant relationship: Fact 1: The number of auto thefts is down over the past five years. *and* Fact 2: Car thieves are more likely to be convicted now than they were five years ago. What would account for a higher conviction rate for car thieves despite a decline in the number of car thefts?

To explain both facts, provide a reason that car thieves are now more likely to be apprehended or why the cases against them are more likely to result in convictions.

LSAT Question	**Analysis**
34. A recent study of major motion pictures revealed that the vast majority of their plots were simply variations on plots that had been used many times before. Despite this fact, many people enjoy seeing several new movies each year. *PrepTest59 Sec3 Q17* →	"Despite this fact" indicates the conflict: Fact 1: Most motion pictures have derivative plots that have been used many times before. *but* Fact 2: People enjoy seeing several new movies per year. Why would people enjoy seeing movies that just recycle well-worn plots?

Resolve this paradox by showing that people enjoy familiar plots, that they are unaware that the plots of new movies have been used before, or that other factors are more important than plot.

Paradox Questions

Anticipating the sort(s) of fact that would resolve an apparent discrepancy provides the prediction you'll use to evaluate the answer choices.

Review an LSAT expert's work on the question featuring apparently contradictory erosion reports.

LSAT Question	Analysis
Engineers are investigating the suitability of Wantastiquet Pass as the site of a new bridge. Because one concern is whether erosion could eventually weaken the bridge's foundations, they contracted for two reports on erosion in the region. Although both reports are accurate, one claims that the region suffers relatively little erosion, while the other claims that regional erosion is heavy and a cause for concern. →	**Step 2:** "Although" and "while" reveal contradictory ideas: Fact 1: Both reports on erosion in the region are accurate. *but* Fact 2: One says that the region suffers little erosion, and the other says that the region suffers heavy erosion.
Which one of the following, if true, most helps to explain how both reports could be accurate? →	**Step 1:** "Most helps to explain" indicates that a contradiction needs resolution.
	Step 3: How could it be that studies with contradictory results are both accurate? Resolve this paradox by showing that the studies looked at two different kinds of erosion or at erosion in two different contexts.
(A) Neither report presents an extensive chemical analysis of the soil in the region. →	**Step 4:** 180. This states a similarity between the studies, making it even harder to understand how both could be accurate and yet report seemingly opposite findings. Eliminate.
(B) Both reports include computer-enhanced satellite photographs. →	180. This states a similarity between the studies, making it even harder to understand how both could be accurate and yet report seemingly opposite findings. Eliminate.
(C) One report was prepared by scientists from a university, while the other report was prepared by scientists from a private consulting firm. →	A difference in researchers' employers doesn't explain how both reports could be accurate while giving apparently contradictory results. Eliminate.
(D) One report focuses on regional topsoil erosion, while the other report focuses on riverbank erosion resulting from seasonal floods. →	Correct. If true, this explains why the reports, while both correct, got different results.
(E) One report cost nearly twice as much to prepare as did the other report. *PrepTest51 Sec3 Q8* →	A difference in cost does nothing to explain how both reports could be accurate while giving apparently contradictory results. Eliminate.

Practice: Paradox Questions

In each of the following Paradox questions, separate Fact A from Fact B in the stimulus, paraphrase the apparent contradiction, and predict what could be true to resolve it.

LSAT Question		My Analysis
35. After the rush-hour speed limit on the British M25 motorway was lowered from 70 miles per hour (115 kilometers per hour) to 50 miles per hour (80 kilometers per hour), rush-hour travel times decreased by approximately 15 percent.	⟶	**Step 2:**
Which one of the following, if true, most helps to explain the decrease in travel times described above?	⟶	**Step 1:**
		Step 3:
(A) After the decrease in the rush-hour speed limit, the average speed on the M25 was significantly lower during rush hours than at other times of the day.	⟶	**Step 4:**
(B) Travel times during periods other than rush hours were essentially unchanged after the rush-hour speed limit was lowered.	⟶	
(C) Before the rush-hour speed limit was lowered, rush-hour accidents that caused lengthy delays were common, and most of these accidents were caused by high-speed driving.	⟶	
(D) Enforcement of speed limits on the M25 was quite rigorous both before and after the rush-hour speed limit was lowered.	⟶	
(E) The number of people who drive on the M25 during rush hours did not increase after the rush-hour speed limit was lowered.	⟶	

PrepTest61 Sec4 Q12

LSAT Question	My Analysis
36. New technologies that promise to extend life and decrease pain involve innovations that require extensive scientific research. Therefore, investment in such technologies is very risky, because innovations requiring extensive scientific research also require large amounts of capital but are unlikely to provide any financial return. Nonetheless, some people are willing to invest in these new technologies. $\longrightarrow$	**Step 2:**
Which one of the following, if true, most helps to explain why some people are willing to invest in new technologies that promise to extend life and decrease pain? $\longrightarrow$	**Step 1:**
	Step 3:
(A) When investments in new technologies that promise to extend life and decrease pain do provide financial return, they generally return many times the original investment, which is much more than the return on safer investments. $\longrightarrow$	**Step 4:**
(B) A large variety of new technologies that promise to extend life and decrease pain have been developed in the last decade. $\longrightarrow$	
(C) The development of certain new technologies other than those that promise to extend life and decrease pain is also very risky, because these technologies require large amounts of capital but are unlikely to provide any financial return. $\longrightarrow$	
(D) Some investments that initially seem likely to provide reasonably large financial return ultimately provide no financial return. $\longrightarrow$	
(E) The scientific research necessary to develop new technologies that promise to extend life and decrease pain sometimes leads to no greater understanding of the natural world. $\longrightarrow$	

PrepTest59 Sec3 Q1

	LSAT Question		**My Analysis**
37.	A recent poll revealed that most students at our university prefer that the university, which is searching for a new president, hire someone who has extensive experience as a university president. However, in the very same poll, the person most students chose from among a list of leading candidates as the one they would most like to see hired was someone who has never served as a university president.	$\longrightarrow$	**Step 2:**
	Which one of the following, if true, most helps to account for the apparent discrepancy in the students' preferences?	$\longrightarrow$	**Step 1:**
			Step 3:
(A)	Because several of the candidates listed in the poll had extensive experience as university presidents, not all of the candidates could be differentiated on this basis alone.	$\longrightarrow$	**Step 4:**
(B)	Most of the candidates listed in the poll had extensive experience as university presidents.	$\longrightarrow$	
(C)	Students taking the poll had fewer candidates to choose from than were currently being considered for the position.	$\longrightarrow$	
(D)	Most of the students taking the poll did not know whether any of the leading candidates listed in the poll had ever served as a university president.	$\longrightarrow$	
(E)	Often a person can be well suited to a position even though they have relatively little experience in such a position.	$\longrightarrow$	

PrepTest61 Sec2 Q25

LSAT Question		My Analysis
38. Human settlement of previously uninhabited areas tends to endanger species of wildlife. However, the Mississippi kite, a bird found on the prairies of North America, flourishes in areas that people have settled. In fact, during the five years since 1985 its population has risen far more rapidly in towns than in rural areas.	→	**Step 2:**
Which one of the following, if true, most helps to explain why the Mississippi kite population does not follow the usual pattern?	→	**Step 1:**
		Step 3:
		⋅
(A) Residents of prairie towns have been setting off loud firecrackers near kites' roosting spots because of the birds' habit of diving at people and frightening them.	→	**Step 4:**
(B) Towns on the prairies tend to be small, with a low density of human population and large numbers of wild birds and animals	→	
(C) Since the international migratory bird protection treaty of 1972, it has been illegal to shoot kites, and the treaty has been effectively enforced.	→	
(D) Wildlife such as pigeons and raccoons had already adapted successfully to towns and cities long before there were towns on the North American prairies.	→	
(E) Trees are denser in towns than elsewhere on the prairie, and these denser trees provide greater protection from hail and windstorms for kites' nests and eggs.	→	

PrepTest51 Sec3 Q10

LSAT Question	My Analysis

39. Consumer activist: When antilock brakes were first introduced, it was claimed that they would significantly reduce the incidence of multiple-car collisions, thereby saving lives. Indeed, antilock brakes have reduced the incidence of multiple-car collisions. I maintain, however, that to save lives, automobile manufacturers ought to stop equipping cars with them.

→ **Step 2:**

Which one of the following, if true, most helps to resolve the apparent conflict in the consumer activist's statements?

→ **Step 1:**

Step 3:

(A) Drivers and passengers in automobiles with antilock brakes feel less vulnerable, and are thus less likely to wear seat belts.

→ **Step 4:**

(B) Under some circumstances, automobiles with traditional brakes stop just as quickly as do automobiles with antilock brakes.

→

(C) For inexperienced drivers, antilock brakes are easier to use correctly than are traditional brakes.

→

(D) Antilock brakes are considerably more expensive to manufacture than are traditional brakes.

→

(E) Antilock brakes are no more effective in preventing multiple-car accidents than in preventing other kinds of traffic accidents.

→

PrepTest49 Sec4 Q11

813

LSAT Question		My Analysis

40. Scientists removed all viruses from a seawater sample and then measured the growth rate of the plankton population in the water. They expected the rate to increase dramatically, but the population actually got smaller.

$\longrightarrow$ **Step 2:**

Which one of the following, if true, most helps to explain the unexpected result described above?

$\longrightarrow$ **Step 1:**

Step 3:

(A) Viruses in seawater help to keep the plankton population below the maximum level that the resources in the water will support.

$\longrightarrow$ **Step 4:**

(B) Plankton and viruses in seawater compete for some of the same nutrients.

$\longrightarrow$

(C) Plankton utilize the nutrients released by the death of organisms killed by viruses.

$\longrightarrow$

(D) The absence of viruses can facilitate the flourishing of bacteria that sometimes damage other organisms.

$\longrightarrow$

(E) At any given time, a considerable portion of the plankton in seawater are already infected by viruses.

PrepTest57 Sec3 Q7

LSAT Question	My Analysis

41. The number of automobile thefts has declined steadily during the past five years, and it is more likely now than it was five years ago that someone who steals a car will be convicted of the crime. → **Step 2:**

Which one of the following, if true, most helps to explain the facts cited above? → **Step 1:**

Step 3:

(A) Although there are fewer car thieves now than there were five years ago, the proportion of thieves who tend to abandon cars before their owners notice that they have been stolen has also decreased. → **Step 4:**

(B) Car alarms are more common than they were five years ago, but their propensity to be triggered in the absence of any criminal activity → has resulted in people generally ignoring them when they are triggered.

(C) An upsurge in home burglaries over the last five years has required police departments to → divert limited resources to investigation of these cases.

(D) Because of the increasingly lucrative market for stolen automobile parts, many stolen cars are → quickly disassembled and the parts are sold to various buyers across the country.

(E) There are more adolescent car thieves now than there were five years ago, and the sentences given to young criminals tend to be far more → lenient than those given to adult criminals.

PrepTest61 Sec4 Q14

LSAT Question	My Analysis
42. A study conducted over a 6-month period analyzed daily attendance and average length of visit at the local art museum. The results showed that when the museum was not featuring a special exhibition, attendance tended to be lower but patrons spent an average of 45 minutes longer in the museum than when it was featuring a special exhibition. $\longrightarrow$	**Step 2:**
Each of the following, if true, could help to explain the differing average lengths of visits to the museum EXCEPT: $\longrightarrow$	**Step 1:**
	Step 3:
(A) Visitors to the museum during special exhibitions tend to have narrower artistic interests, and do not view as many different exhibits during their visit. $\longrightarrow$	**Step 4:**
(B) A plan to extend normal museum hours during special exhibitions was considered but not enacted during the period studied. $\longrightarrow$	
(C) Many people who go to special exhibitions go simply for the prestige of having been there. $\longrightarrow$	
(D) Admission tickets to the special exhibitions at the museum are issued for a specific 1-hour period on a specific day. $\longrightarrow$	
(E) Many people who go to special exhibitions are on organized tours and do not have the opportunity to browse. $\longrightarrow$	

PrepTest49 Sec4 Q25

LSAT Question		My Analysis
43. A recent study of major motion pictures revealed that the vast majority of their plots were simply variations on plots that had been used many times before. Despite this fact, many people enjoy seeing several new movies each year.	$\longrightarrow$	**Step 2:**
Each of the following, if true, would contribute to an explanation of the apparent discrepancy in the information above EXCEPT:	$\longrightarrow$	**Step 1:**
		Step 3:
(A) Movies based on standard plots are more likely to be financially successful than are ones based on original plots.	$\longrightarrow$	**Step 4:**
(B) If the details of their stories are sufficiently different, two movies with the same basic plot will be perceived by moviegoers as having different plots.	$\longrightarrow$	
(C) Because of the large number of movies produced each year, the odds of a person seeing two movies with the same general plot structure in a five-year period are fairly low.	$\longrightarrow$	
(D) A certain aesthetic pleasure is derived from seeing several movies that develop the same plot in slightly different ways.	$\longrightarrow$	
(E) Although most modern movie plots have been used before, most of those previous uses occurred during the 1940s and 1950s.	$\longrightarrow$	

PrepTest59 Sec3 Q17

Expert Analysis: Paradox Questions

LSAT Question	Analysis
35. After the rush-hour speed limit on the British M25 motorway was lowered from 70 miles per hour (115 kilometers per hour) to 50 miles per hour (80 kilometers per hour), rush-hour travel times decreased by approximately 15 percent.	**Step 2:** Two facts, the second the result of the first: Fact 1: The rush-hour speed limit was lowered on the M25 motorway. *but then* Fact 2: Rush-hour travel times on the M25 decreased.
Which one of the following, if true, most helps to explain the decrease in travel times described above?	**Step 1:** "[M]ost helps to explain" indicates a Paradox question. The correct answer will explain or resolve the apparent discrepancy above.
	Step 3: How is it that speed limits were reduced (with cars presumably going slower), yet travel time has gone down? The correct answer will help explain the strange result. Perhaps fewer people are taking the road, or the decrease in the speed limit has increased the efficiency of driving on that road.
(A) After the decrease in the rush-hour speed limit, the average speed on the M25 was significantly lower during rush hours than at other times of the day.	**Step 4:** Irrelevant Comparison. Differences between average speed and rush hour speed don't explain why a lower speed limit at rush hour is making for a faster rush-hour commute. Eliminate.
(B) Travel times during periods other than rush hours were essentially unchanged after the rush-hour speed limit was lowered.	Outside the Scope. Travel times during other periods of the day don't help explain why rush-hour travel time has decreased. Eliminate.
(C) Before the rush-hour speed limit was lowered, rush-hour accidents that caused lengthy delays were common, and most of these accidents were caused by high-speed driving.	Correct. This explains why rush-hour travel time is down despite slower speeds: The road is no longer clogged by accidents caused by faster drivers.
(D) Enforcement of speed limits on the M25 was quite rigorous both before and after the rush-hour speed limit was lowered.	180. Showing a similarity between conditions before and after the new speed limit makes it even more confusing why there would have been a decrease in travel time. Eliminate.
(E) The number of people who drive on the M25 during rush hours did not increase after the rush-hour speed limit was lowered. *PrepTest61 Sec4 Q12*	Distortion. Knowing that the number of people who drive on the M25 during rush hour *did not* increase does not explain why travel time has decreased. Eliminate.

LSAT Question	Analysis
36. New technologies that promise to extend life and decrease pain involve innovations that require extensive scientific research. Therefore, investment in such technologies is very risky, because innovations requiring extensive scientific research also require large amounts of capital but are unlikely to provide any financial return. Nonetheless, some people are willing to invest in these new technologies.	**Step 2:** "Nonetheless" signals the seemingly contradictory facts: Fact 1: Investing in new technologies that promise to extend life and decrease pain is risky, because such investments require much capital and are unlikely to be profitable. *but* Fact 2: There are people who do invest in these technologies.
Which one of the following, if true, most helps to explain why some people are willing to invest in new technologies that promise to extend life and decrease pain?	**Step 1:** "[M]ost helps to explain" indicates that this is a Paradox question. Select an answer choice that explains or resolves the apparent discrepancy above.
	Step 3: Why are some people investing in technology that appears to carry significant financial risk? Find an answer choice that helps explain the strange result. Perhaps people are investing for reasons other than monetary gain, or there is something that justifies investment despite the slim chance of profit.
(A) When investments in new technologies that promise to extend life and decrease pain do provide financial return, they generally return many times the original investment, which is much more than the return on safer investments.	**Step 4:** Correct. This provides a reason why people would be willing to assume the risk of the investment: high-risk, but high reward. The potential payout is much greater than on safer investments.
(B) A large variety of new technologies that promise to extend life and decrease pain have been developed in the last decade.	Outside the Scope. According to the stimulus, all such technology is high-risk, so variety doesn't explain why people would invest. Eliminate.
(C) The development of certain new technologies other than those that promise to extend life and decrease pain is also very risky, because these technologies require large amounts of capital but are unlikely to provide any financial return.	Outside the Scope. The fact that other technologies carry similar risks doesn't help explain why people are investing in these technologies. Eliminate.
(D) Some investments that initially seem likely to provide reasonably large financial return ultimately provide no financial return.	Outside the Scope. The fact that some seemingly safe investments don't pan out doesn't explain why some people are investing in these high-risk technologies. Eliminate.
(E) The scientific research necessary to develop new technologies that promise to extend life and decrease pain sometimes leads to no greater understanding of the natural world.	180. This just deepens the paradox, because it removes a possible alternative reason why people would invest in this technology. Eliminate.

PrepTest59 Sec3 Q1

LSAT Question	Analysis
37. A recent poll revealed that most students at our university prefer that the university, which is searching for a new president, hire someone who has extensive experience as a university president. However, in the very same poll, the person most students chose from among a list of leading candidates as the one they would most like to see hired was someone who has never served as a university president.	**Step 2:** *However* signals the paradox: Fact 1: Recently polled students said they wanted the new university president to have previous experience as a university president. *but* Fact 2: The same students' top choice on a list of candidates was someone with no experience as a university president.
Which one of the following, if true, most helps to account for the apparent discrepancy in the students' preferences?	**Step 1:** The correct answer "helps to account for the apparent discrepancy" in the stimulus—a Paradox question.
	Step 3: Why would the students pick a candidate with no experience when they said they preferred candidates with experience? The correct answer will resolve this paradox. Maybe none of the candidates on the list had experience, or perhaps some other criterion trumps experience in students' minds.
(A) Because several of the candidates listed in the poll had extensive experience as university presidents, not all of the candidates could be differentiated on this basis alone.	**Step 4:** 180. The students went with a candidate who had no experience. Knowing that other candidates did deepens the paradox. Eliminate.
(B) Most of the candidates listed in the poll had extensive experience as university presidents.	180. The students went with a candidate who had no experience. Knowing what other candidates did deepens the paradox. Eliminate.
(C) Students taking the poll had fewer candidates to choose from than were currently being considered for the position.	Without knowing whether any candidate had experience, this does not explain the students' seemingly contradictory choice. Eliminate.
(D) Most of the students taking the poll did not know whether any of the leading candidates listed in the poll had ever served as a university president.	Correct. This essentially matches the first prediction. If students don't know that any candidate on the list has experience, then experience cannot be a differentiator among those on the list.
(E) Often a person can be well suited to a position even though they have relatively little experience in such a position. *PrepTest61 Sec2 Q25*	This may be true, but it doesn't explain why students seemingly ignored their own criteria in choosing a favorite candidate from the list. Eliminate.

LSAT Question	**Analysis**
38. Human settlement of previously uninhabited areas tends to endanger species of wildlife. However, the Mississippi kite, a bird found on the prairies of North America, flourishes in areas that people have settled. In fact, during the five years since 1985 its population has risen far more rapidly in towns than in rural areas.	**Step 2:** *However* indicates the conflicting ideas. Fact 1: New human settlement usually endangers wildlife. *but* Fact 2: The Mississippi kite (a prairie bird) seems to do better in settled than in unsettled areas.
Which one of the following, if true, most helps to explain why the Mississippi kite population does not follow the usual pattern?	**Step 1:** The correct answer helps explain a deviation from the "usual pattern"—a Paradox question.
	Step 3: Most species are negatively affected by human settlement, so why would this prairie bird do better in town? The correct answer will provide a fact that explains why settled environments are preferable for the Mississippi kite. Maybe there is more food or better protection around humans.
(A) Residents of prairie towns have been setting off loud firecrackers near kites' roosting spots because of the birds' habit of diving at people and frightening them.	**Step 4:** 180. This is a reason that the kites would not want to live near humans. Eliminate.
(B) Towns on the prairies tend to be small, with a low density of human population and large numbers of wild birds and animals.	Outside the Scope. This may be true, but it does not explain why kites are the exception to the rule that settlement tends to decrease animal and bird populations. Eliminate.
(C) Since the international migratory bird protection treaty of 1972, it has been illegal to shoot kites, and the treaty has been effectively enforced.	Outside the Scope. This might explain an overall increase in the kite population, but not a disproportionate rise near human settlements. Eliminate.
(D) Wildlife such as pigeons and raccoons had already adapted successfully to towns and cities long before there were towns on the North American prairies.	Irrelevant Comparison. To resolve the paradox, the answer must show a benefit to kites from living near humans. The fact that other species did it, too, doesn't explain *this* exception to the general rule. Eliminate.
(E) Trees are denser in towns than elsewhere on the prairie, and these denser trees provide greater protection from hail and windstorms for kites' nests and eggs.	Correct. Protection is the benefit that the kites get from living near humans. This explains why they are exceptions to the usual pattern.

PrepTest51 Sec3 Q10

LSAT Question	Analysis
39. Consumer activist: When antilock brakes were first introduced, it was claimed that they would significantly reduce the incidence of multiple-car collisions, thereby saving lives. Indeed, antilock brakes have reduced the incidence of multiple-car collisions. I maintain, however, that to save lives, automobile manufacturers ought to stop equipping cars with them.	**Step 2**: [*H*]*owever* indicates the conflict: Fact 1: Antilock brakes have reduced the incidence of multi-car collisions. *but* Fact 2: [author's assertion] To save lives, automakers should stop equipping cars with antilock brakes.
Which one of the following, if true, most helps to resolve the apparent conflict in the consumer activist's statements?	**Step 1**: The correct answer "helps to resolve the apparent conflict" in the activist's statements—a Paradox question.
	Step 3: Why would the author maintain that ceasing use of something that reduces the number of multi-car accidents would save lives? Resolve this with evidence that equipping cars with antilock brakes make a car or its driver less safe.
(A) Drivers and passengers in automobiles with antilock brakes feel less vulnerable, and are thus less likely to wear seat belts.	**Step 4**: Correct. If drivers and passengers behave less safely when in cars with antilock brakes, it helps explain why the activist might think removing them would save lives.
(B) Under some circumstances, automobiles with traditional brakes stop just as quickly as do automobiles with antilock brakes.	Irrelevant Comparison. This gives us no reason to think removing antilock brakes from cars would save lives. Eliminate.
(C) For inexperienced drivers, antilock brakes are easier to use correctly than are traditional brakes.	180. This is a reason to think cars with antilock brakes are safer. Eliminate.
(D) Antilock brakes are considerably more expensive to manufacture than are traditional brakes.	Irrelevant Comparison. We might save money this way, but the answer needs to explain why the activist thinks we will save *lives*. Eliminate.
(E) Antilock brakes are no more effective in preventing multiple-car accidents than in preventing other kinds of traffic accidents. *PrepTest49 Sec4 Q11*	Irrelevant Comparison/180. Knowing that antilock brakes help prevent other kinds of accidents doesn't explain why removing them would save lives. If anything, it just makes them seem safer overall. Eliminate.

LSAT Question	Analysis
40. Scientists removed all viruses from a seawater sample and then measured the growth rate of the plankton population in the water. They expected the rate to increase dramatically, but the population actually got smaller. $\longrightarrow$	**Step 2**: [B]*ut* indicates the conflict: Fact 1: Scientists expected plankton population to grow rapidly upon removal of viruses from seawater. *instead* Fact 2: The plankton population shrank.
Which one of the following, if true, most helps to explain the unexpected result described above? $\longrightarrow$	**Step 1**: The correct answer will "explain the unexpected results" described in the stimulus—a Paradox question.
	Step 3: Why would removing viruses from seawater cause the plankton population to decline? Resolve this unexpected result by providing evidence that the plankton unexpectedly benefit from the viruses.
(A) Viruses in seawater help to keep the plankton population below the maximum level that the resources in the water will support. $\longrightarrow$	**Step 4**: 180. If this were true, then at least initially, the plankton population would increase when the viruses were removed. Eliminate.
(B) Plankton and viruses in seawater compete for some of the same nutrients. $\longrightarrow$	180. If this were true, then the plankton population, which would no longer have to compete for resources, would increase when the viruses were removed. Eliminate.
(C) Plankton utilize the nutrients released by the death of organisms killed by viruses. $\longrightarrow$	Correct. If plankton use nutrients provided by viruses, then it is reasonable that plankton would decrease after viruses are removed.
(D) The absence of viruses can facilitate the flourishing of bacteria that sometimes damage other organisms. $\longrightarrow$	Without more information, it's not clear that bacteria harm plankton, so this doesn't clear up the unexpected results. Eliminate.
(E) At any given time, a considerable portion of the plankton in seawater are already infected by viruses. *PrepTest57 Sec3 Q7* $\longrightarrow$	180. Presuming that infection is bad for plankton, this provides a reason to expect the plankton population to rise once viruses are removed. Eliminate.

LSAT Question	Analysis
41. The number of automobile thefts has declined steadily during the past five years, and it is more likely now than it was five years ago that someone who steals a car will be convicted of the crime.	**Step 2:** [A]nd indicates the relevant relationship: Fact 1: The number of auto thefts is down over the past five years. *and* Fact 2: Car thieves are more likely to be convicted now than they were five years ago.
Which one of the following, if true, most helps to explain the facts cited above?	**Step 1:** The correct answer helps "explain the facts . . . above"—a Paradox question (although here, the two facts may not appear contradictory).
	Step 3: There are fewer thefts, but a greater rate of convictions. To explain both facts, provide a reason that car thieves are now more likely to be apprehended or why the cases against them are more likely to result in convictions.
(A) Although there are fewer car thieves now than there were five years ago, the proportion of thieves who tend to abandon cars before their owners notice that they have been stolen has also decreased.	**Step 4:** Correct. This provides an explanation for the increased conviction rate despite the overall decline in thefts.
(B) Car alarms are more common than they were five years ago, but their propensity to be triggered in the absence of any criminal activity has resulted in people generally ignoring them when they are triggered.	This explains neither the lower number of thefts nor the increased conviction rate. Eliminate.
(C) An upsurge in home burglaries over the last five years has required police departments to divert limited resources to investigation of these cases.	180. If anything, this would provide a reason why fewer car thieves are caught, making an increased conviction rate even more inexplicable. Eliminate.
(D) Because of the increasingly lucrative market for stolen automobile parts, many stolen cars are quickly disassembled and the parts are sold to various buyers across the country.	This does not explain the decline in the number of thefts nor why a higher rate of thieves is convicted. Eliminate.
(E) There are more adolescent car thieves now than there were five years ago, and the sentences given to young criminals tend to be far more lenient than those given to adult criminals. *PrepTest61 Sec4 Q14*	Without more evidence, there is no reason to believe that adolescent thieves are caught or convicted more often. Eliminate.

LSAT Question	Analysis
42. A study conducted over a 6-month period analyzed daily attendance and average length of visit at the local art museum. The results showed that when the museum was not featuring a special exhibition, attendance tended to be lower but patrons spent an average of 45 minutes longer in the museum than when it was featuring a special exhibition.	**Step 2**: Focus on *but*, which signals a contrast. When the museum has a special exhibit: Fact 1: Attendance was higher. *but* Fact 2: Patrons stayed a shorter time.
Each of the following, if true, could help to explain the differing average lengths of visits to the museum EXCEPT:	**Step 1**: A Paradox EXCEPT question: Here, the four wrong answers "help to explain" an apparent discrepancy; the correct answer will either deepen the confusion or will be irrelevant.
	Step 3: The four wrong answers *will help explain* the discrepant patterns in attendance. The correct answer will fail to give a reason why special exhibits tend to attract more visitors who stay for a shorter time.
(A) Visitors to the museum during special exhibitions tend to have narrower artistic interests, and do not view as many different exhibits during their visit.	**Step 4**: If people coming for the special exhibit have less interest in other exhibits, then there is some explanation for the shorter visits. Eliminate.
(B) A plan to extend normal museum hours during special exhibitions was considered but not enacted during the period studied.	Correct. The museum's rejected plans don't help us understand its actual attendance patterns.
(C) Many people who go to special exhibitions go simply for the prestige of having been there.	If people go to special exhibits to "see and be seen," then this would explain why they spend less time at the museum. Eliminate.
(D) Admission tickets to the special exhibitions at the museum are issued for a specific 1-hour period on a specific day.	If people have to come to special exhibits during prescribed windows of time, this would help explain why they spend less time at the museum (especially if their tickets were for just one or two hours before closing time). Eliminate.
(E) Many people who go to special exhibitions are on organized tours and do not have the opportunity to browse. *PrepTest49 Sec4 Q25*	If people have no opportunity to browse, it helps explain why they would spend less time at the museum. Eliminate.

LSAT Question	Analysis
43. A recent study of major motion pictures revealed that the vast majority of their plots were simply variations on plots that had been used many times before. Despite this fact, many people enjoy seeing several new movies each year.	**Step 2**: "Despite this fact" indicates the conflict: Fact 1: Most motion pictures have derivative plots that have been used many times before. *but* Fact 2: People enjoy seeing several new movies per year. Why would people enjoy seeing movies that just recycle well-worn plots?
Each of the following, if true, would contribute to an explanation of the apparent discrepancy in the information above EXCEPT:	**Step 1**: Paradox EXCEPT question: The four wrong answers help explain the apparent discrepancy; the correct answer does not.
	Step 3: Answers that resolve the paradox—by showing that people enjoy familiar plots, that they are unaware that plots are recycled, or that other factors are more important than plot—are *wrong* answers. The correct answer does *not* help explain the situation.
(A) Movies based on standard plots are more likely to be financially successful than are ones based on original plots.	**Step 4**: Correct. This does nothing to explain why people enjoy seeing the well-worn plots again and again.
(B) If the details of their stories are sufficiently different, two movies with the same basic plot will be perceived by moviegoers as having different plots.	This helps explain the discrepancy—people are often not aware that they've seen the plot before. Eliminate.
(C) Because of the large number of movies produced each year, the odds of a person seeing two movies with the same general plot structure in a five-year period are fairly low.	This helps explain the discrepancy—people may be unaware that plots are recycled. Eliminate.
(D) A certain aesthetic pleasure is derived from seeing several movies that develop the same plot in slightly different ways.	This helps explain the discrepancy—people may actually enjoy seeing familiar plots. Eliminate.
(E) Although most modern movie plots have been used before, most of those previous uses occurred during the 1940s and 1950s. *PrepTest59 Sec3 Q17*	This helps explain the discrepancy—unless people know very old movies, they are unlikely to be aware of similarities in plots between movies. Eliminate.

IDENTIFYING QUESTION STEMS

You've now seen the variety of ways in which the LSAT rewards both your ability to analyze and evaluate arguments, as well as your ability to make deductions from a set of statements. On Test Day, you must be able to quickly and accurately identify the question types so that you can apply all of the skills you've been mastering appropriately. LSAT experts know that a key component of success in Logical Reasoning sections is to be familiar with each question type and know immediately which skills and strategies they'll need.

Practice

For each of the following question stems, identify the question type and characterize the one right and four wrong answers.

Question Stem		My Analysis
44. If the above statements are true, then which of the following must also be true?	→	Question Type: 1 Right: 4 Wrong:
45. Which of the following principles most helps to justify the conclusion above?	→	Question Type: 1 Right: 4 Wrong:
46. Which of the following, if true, most contributes to a resolution of the apparent anomaly above?	→	Question Type: 1 Right: 4 Wrong:
47. Which of the following best expresses the argument's error in reasoning?	→	Question Type: 1 Right: 4 Wrong:
48. The argument above uses which of the following argumentative techniques?	→	Question Type: 1 Right: 4 Wrong:
49. Which of the following arguments contains an error in reasoning most similar to that in the argument above?	→	Question Type: 1 Right: 4 Wrong:

Question Stem		My Analysis
50. The argument above relies on which of the following presuppositions?	$\longrightarrow$	Question Type: 1 Right: 4 Wrong:
51. Which of the following, if true, casts the most doubt on the conclusion above?	$\longrightarrow$	Question Type: 1 Right: 4 Wrong:
52. Each of the following, if true, supports the argument EXCEPT:	$\longrightarrow$	Question Type: 1 Right: 4 Wrong:
53. The primary issue in dispute between the volunteer and the program administrator is	$\longrightarrow$	Question Type: 1 Right: 4 Wrong:
54. Each of the following contributes to an explanation of the apparent discrepancy above EXCEPT:	$\longrightarrow$	Question Type: 1 Right: 4 Wrong:
55. If the above statements are true, then all of the following must be false EXCEPT:	$\longrightarrow$	Question Type: 1 Right: 4 Wrong:

Expert Analysis

Here's how an LSAT expert would identify the question types and characterize the correct and incorrect answers for the question stems in that exercise.

Question Stem	Analysis
44. If the above statements are true, then which of the following must also be true?	Question Type: Inference
	→ 1 Right: Statement that must be true based on the stimulus
	4 Wrong: Statements that could be false based on the stimulus
45. Which of the following principles most helps to justify the conclusion above?	Question Type: Principle—but *justify* makes this similar to a Strengthen question
	→ 1 Right: A general rule that makes the conclusion more likely to follow from the evidence
	4 Wrong: General rules irrelevant to the conclusion, or rules that weaken it
46. Which of the following, if true, most contributes to a resolution of the apparent anomaly above?	Question Type: Paradox—signal is *anomaly*
	→ 1 Right: Statement that resolves the apparent contradiction
	4 Wrong: Statements that make the apparent contradiction worse or that have no effect on it
47. Which of the following best expresses the argument's error in reasoning?	Question Type: Flaw—tag is "error in reasoning"
	→ 1 Right: Description of why the conclusion does not logically follow from the evidence
	4 Wrong: Descriptions of flaw types not present in the argument, or descriptions of unflawed aspects of the argument
48. The argument above uses which of the following argumentative techniques?	Question Type: Method of Argument—tag is "argumentative technique"
	→ 1 Right: Description of the argument's structure
	4 Wrong: Descriptions of argument structures not found in the stimulus
49. Which of the following arguments contains an error in reasoning most similar to that in the argument above?	Question Type: Parallel Reasoning—"error in reasoning most similar to" indicates Parallel Flaw
	→ 1 Right: Argument with the same flaw as the one in the stimulus
	4 Wrong: Arguments with different flaw types, or unflawed arguments

Question Stem	Analysis
50. The argument above relies on which of the following presuppositions?	Question Type: Assumption—tag word is *presupposition*; *relies* signals Necessary Assumption question
	→ 1 Right: Description of the unstated fact or idea required for the conclusion to follow logically from the evidence
	4 Wrong: Restatements of evidence, statements irrelevant to the conclusion, or statements that weaken the conclusion
51. Which of the following, if true, casts the most doubt on the conclusion above?	Question Type: Weaken—tag is "casts doubt"
	→ 1 Right: Statement that makes the conclusion less likely to follow from the evidence
	4 Wrong: Statements that make the conclusion more likely to follow from the evidence or that have no effect on the conclusion
52. Each of the following, if true, supports the argument EXCEPT:	Question Type: Strengthen EXCEPT
	→ 1 Right: Statement irrelevant to the conclusion or statement that makes the conclusion less likely to follow from the evidence
	4 Wrong: Statements that make the conclusion more likely to follow from the evidence
53. The primary issue in dispute between the volunteer and the program administrator is	Question Type: Point at Issue—signal is *dispute*
	→ 1 Right: Description of the point of disagreement between the two speakers
	4 Wrong: Points of agreement between the speakers or issues about which one or both speakers have no opinion
54. Each of the following contributes to an explanation of the apparent discrepancy above EXCEPT:	Question Type: Paradox EXCEPT—key phrase is "apparent discrepancy"
	→ 1 Right: Statement that makes the apparent contradiction in the stimulus worse or that has no effect on it
	4 Wrong: Statements that resolve the apparent contradiction in the stimulus
55. If the above statements are true, then all of the following must be false EXCEPT:	Question Type: Inference EXCEPT
	→ 1 Right: Statement that could be true based on the stimulus
	4 Wrong: Statements that must be false based on the stimulus

REFLECTION

Think back over the work you've done in this chapter. Ask yourself the following questions.

· Am I able to recognize Inference questions and Principle questions calling for an inference?
· What patterns in Inference question stimuli should I be able to recognize?
· Can I remember and use the five tools that help to untangle Inference stimuli?
· Why are Extreme, 180, and Outside the Scope wrong answers so often associated with Inference questions? Can I recognize these wrong answer types when I see them?
· What do Paradox question stimuli always contain?
· Why are Keywords so helpful in untangling Paradox stimuli?
· How can I most effectively predict the correct answer to a Paradox question?

Every day, you hear people make inferences and deductions from one or more facts. The next time you encounter this in the "real world," ask yourself the following questions.

· In everyday life, we tend to use the term *inference* loosely. Sometimes we mean something closer to *guess*. Would this person's inference pass muster on the LSAT?
· If you encounter a flawed inference or deduction, does it match one of the LSAT wrong answer types? Is it, perhaps, too extreme to follow from the facts? Is it irrelevant? Or is it even contradictory to the facts given?

Likewise, if you encounter a person expressing confusion over what appears to him or her to be a paradox, pay attention.

· What are the two facts that appear to this person as contradictory?
· If someone offers an explanation, is it really a fact that helps resolve the paradox? Or is it perhaps outside the scope of the first person's question?

Practicing your LSAT skills is something you can learn to do almost any time because the skills tested on the LSAT are so central to kinds of thinking, reading, and reasoning we do every day.

SUMMARY

Congratulations! Over the last three chapters, you've learned how to answer all of the Logical Reasoning question types on the LSAT. Continue to improve your performance on Non-Argument questions with the items in the Question Pool following this section. You will, of course, encounter all of the Logical Reasoning question types—Argument-Based, Assumption Family, and Non-Argument questions—in the full sections and tests you practice between now and Test Day. Return to Chapters 8, 9, 10, and 11 from time to time to brush up on strategies that may get rusty and to refresh your memory about all of the tools and tactics you've learned.

Explanations for these questions can be found in your Online Center.

QUESTION POOLS

Inference Questions

This pool consists of Inference questions you have not seen in earlier chapters. They are arranged in reverse chronological order—from most to least recent.

1. Many scholars are puzzled about who created the seventeenth-century abridgment of Shakespeare's *Hamlet* contained in the First Quarto. Two facts about the work shed light on this question. First, the person who undertook the abridgment clearly did not possess a copy of *Hamlet*. Second, the abridgment contains a very accurate rendering of the speeches of one of the characters, but a slipshod handling of all the other parts.

   Which one of the following statements is most supported by the information above?

   (A) The abridgment was prepared by Shakespeare.
   (B) The abridgment was created to make *Hamlet* easier to produce on stage.
   (C) The abridgment was produced by an actor who had played a role in *Hamlet*.
   (D) The abridgement was prepared by a spectator of a performance of *Hamlet*.
   (E) The abridgment was produced by an actor who was trying to improve the play.

   PrepTest61 Sec4 Q5

2. Economist: If the belief were to become widespread that losing one's job is not a sign of personal shortcomings but instead an effect of impersonal social forces (which is surely correct), there would be growth in the societal demand for more government control of the economy to protect individuals from these forces, just as the government now protects them from military invasion. Such extensive government control of the economy would lead to an economic disaster, however.

   The economist's statements, if true, most strongly support which one of the following?

   (A) Increased knowledge of the causes of job loss could lead to economic disaster.
   (B) An individual's belief in his or her own abilities is the only reliable protection against impersonal social forces.
   (C) Governments should never interfere with economic forces.
   (D) Societal demand for government control of the economy is growing.
   (E) In general, people should feel no more responsible for economic disasters than for military invasions.

   PrepTest61 Sec4 Q10

3. If understanding a word always involves knowing its dictionary definition, then understanding a word requires understanding the words that occur in that definition. But clearly there are people—for example, all babies—who do not know the dictionary definitions of some of the words they utter.

   Which one of the following statements follows logically from the statements above?

   (A) Some babies utter individual words that they do not understand.
   (B) Any number of people can understand some words without knowing their dictionary definitions.
   (C) If some words can be understood without knowing their dictionary definitions, then babies understand some words.
   (D) If it is possible to understand a word without knowing its dictionary definition, then it is possible to understand a word without having to understand any other word.
   (E) If some babies understand all the words they utter, then understanding a word does not always involve knowing its dictionary definition.

   PrepTest59 Sec3 Q19

Explanations for these questions can be found in your Online Center.

Part Three: Logical Reasoning
Non-Argument Questions | **K**

4. Long-distance runners use two different kinds of cognitive strategies: "associative" and "dissociative." Associative strategies involve attending closely to physical sensations, while dissociative strategies involve mostly ignoring physical sensations. Associative strategies, unlike dissociative ones, require so much concentration that they result in mental exhaustion lasting more than a day. Since it is important for long-distance runners to enter a race mentally refreshed, _____.

Which one of the following most logically completes the argument?

(A) long-distance runners should not rely heavily on associative strategies during training the day before they run in a race

(B) unless they regularly train using associative strategies, long-distance runners should use dissociative strategies during races

(C) maximizing the benefits of training for long-distance running involves frequently alternating associative and dissociative strategies

(D) long-distance runners are about evenly divided between those who use dissociative strategies during races and those who use associative strategies during races

(E) in long-distance running, dissociative strategies are generally more effective for a day's training run than are associative strategies

PrepTest57 Sec2 Q2

5. No one with a serious medical problem would rely on the average person to prescribe treatment. Similarly, since a good public servant has the interest of the public at heart, _____.

Which one of the following statements would most reasonably complete the argument?

(A) public servants should not be concerned about the outcomes of public opinion surveys

(B) the average public servant knows more about what is best for society than the average person does

(C) public servants should be more knowledgeable about the public good than they are

(D) public servants should base decisions on something other than the average person's recommendations

(E) one is a good public servant if one is more knowledgeable about the public good than is the average person

PrepTest57 Sec2 Q18

6. Taxi drivers, whose income is based on the fares they receive, usually decide when to finish work each day by setting a daily income target; they stop when they reach that target. This means that they typically work fewer hours on a busy day than on a slow day.

The facts described above provide the strongest evidence against which one of the following?

(A) The number of hours per day that a person is willing to work depends on that person's financial needs.

(B) People work longer when their effective hourly wage is high than when it is low.

(C) Workers will accept a lower hourly wage in exchange for the freedom to set their own schedules.

(D) People are willing to work many hours a day in order to avoid a reduction in their standard of living.

(E) People who are paid based on their production work more efficiently than those who are paid a fixed hourly wage.

PrepTest57 Sec2 Q23

7. In modern "brushless" car washes, cloth strips called mitters have replaced brushes. Mitters are easier on most cars' finishes than brushes are. This is especially important with the new clear-coat finishes found on many cars today, which are more easily scratched than older finishes are.

Which one of the following is most strongly supported by the statements above, if those statements are true?

(A) When car washes all used brushes rather than mitters, there were more cars on the road with scratched finishes than there are today.

(B) Modern "brushless" car washes were introduced as a direct response to the use of clear-coat finishes on cars.

(C) Modern "brushless" car washes usually do not produce visible scratches on cars with older finishes.

(D) Brushes are more effective than mitters and are preferred for cleaning cars with older finishes.

(E) More cars in use today have clear-coat finishes rather than older finishes.

PrepTest57 Sec3 Q23

K | Part Three: Logical Reasoning
CHAPTER 11

Explanations for these questions
can be found in your Online Center.

8. Manager: I recommend that our company reconsider the decision to completely abandon our allegedly difficult-to-use computer software and replace it companywide with a new software package advertised as more flexible and easier to use. Several other companies in our region officially replaced the software we currently use with the new package, and while their employees can all use the new software, unofficially many continue to use their former software as much as possible.

Which one of the following is most strongly supported by the manager's statements?

(A) The current company software is as flexible as the proposed new software package.

(B) The familiarity that employees have with a computer software package is a more important consideration in selecting software than flexibility or initial ease of use.

(C) The employees of the manager's company would find that the new software package lacks some of the capabilities of the present software.

(D) Adopting the new software package would create two classes of employees, those who can use it and those who cannot.

(E) Many of the employees in the manager's company would not prefer the new software package to the software currently in use.

PrepTest57 Sec3 Q25

9. Some statisticians believe that the method called extreme value theory (EVT) is a powerful analytical tool. The curves generated by traditional statistical methods to analyze empirical data on human longevity predict that some humans would live beyond 130 years. According to the curves EVT generates, however, the limit on human life spans is probably between 113 and 124 years. To date, no one has lived beyond the upper limits indicated by EVT analysis.

Which one of the following can be properly inferred from the statements above?

(A) EVT is, in general, a more reliable method for projecting future trends based on past observations than are traditional statistical methods.

(B) EVT fits the data about the highest observed human life spans more closely than do traditional statistical methods.

(C) According to the findings derived through the use of EVT, it is physically impossible for any human being to live longer than 124 years.

(D) Given the results generated by EVT, there is no point in conducting research aimed at greatly extending the upper limit on human life spans.

(E) Traditional statistical methods of empirical data analysis should eventually be replaced by some version of EVT.

PrepTest51 Sec1 Q11

10. Designer: Any garden and adjoining living room that are separated from one another by sliding glass doors can visually merge into a single space. If the sliding doors are open, as may happen in summer, this effect will be created if it does not already exist and intensified if it does. The effect remains quite strong during colder months if the garden is well coordinated with the room and contributes strong visual interest of its own.

The designer's statements, if true, most strongly support which one of the following?

(A) A garden separated from an adjoining living room by closed sliding glass doors cannot be well coordinated with the room unless the garden contributes strong visual interest.

(B) In cold weather, a garden and an adjoining living room separated from one another by sliding glass doors will not visually merge into a single space unless the garden is well coordinated with the room.

(C) A garden and an adjoining living room separated by sliding glass doors cannot visually merge in summer unless the doors are open.

(D) A garden can visually merge with an adjoining living room into a single space even if the garden does not contribute strong visual interest of its own.

(E) Except in summer, opening the sliding glass doors that separate a garden from an adjoining living room does not intensify the effect of the garden and room visually merging into a single space.

PrepTest51 Sec1 Q21

Explanations for these questions can be found in your Online Center.

Part Three: Logical Reasoning
Non-Argument Questions
K

11. Expert: What criteria distinguish addictive substances from nonaddictive ones? Some have suggested that any substance that at least some habitual users can cease to use is nonaddictive. However, if this is taken to be the sole criterion of nonaddictiveness, some substances that most medical experts classify as prime examples of addictive substances would be properly deemed nonaddictive. Any adequate set of criteria for determining a substance's addictiveness must embody the view, held by these medical experts, that a substance is addictive only if withdrawal from its habitual use causes most users extreme psychological and physiological difficulty.

Which one of the following can be properly inferred from the expert's statements?

(A) If a person experiences extreme psychological and physiological difficulty in ceasing to use a substance habitually, that substance is addictive.

(B) Fewer substances would be deemed addictive than are deemed so at present if an adequate definition of "addictive" were employed.

(C) A substance that some habitual users can cease to use with little or no psychological or physiological difficulty is addictive only if that is not true for most habitual users.

(D) A chemical substance habitually used by a person throughout life without significant psychological or physiological difficulty is nonaddictive.

(E) "Addiction" is a term that is impossible to define with precision.

PrepTest51 Sec3 Q14

12. Style manual: Archaic spellings and styles of punctuation in direct quotations from older works are to be preserved if they occur infrequently and do not interfere with a reader's comprehension. However, if they occur frequently, the editor may modernize them, inserting a note with an explanation to this effect in the text, or if similar modernizing has been done in more than one quotation, inserting a general statement in the preface. On the other hand, obvious typographical errors in quotations from modern works may be corrected without explanation.

Which one of the following follows logically from the statements above?

(A) If an editor corrects the spelling of a quoted word and the word occurs only once in the text, then an explanation should appear in a note or in the text.

(B) An editor may modernize an archaic spelling of a word found in a modern work without providing an explanation.

(C) An editor should modernize an archaic spelling of a word that is quoted from an older work if the spelling interferes with reader comprehension.

(D) An editor may modernize punctuation directly quoted from an older work if that punctuation occurs frequently and interferes with reader comprehension.

(E) If an editor modernizes only one of several similar instances of quoted archaic punctuation, an explanation should appear in the preface of the work.

PrepTest51 Sec3 Q19

K | Part Three: Logical Reasoning
CHAPTER 11

Explanations for these questions can be found in your Online Center.

13. Environmentalist: Discarding old appliances can be dangerous: refrigerators contain chlorofluorocarbons; electronic circuit boards and cathode-ray tubes often contain heavy metals like lead; and old fluorescent bulbs contain mercury, another heavy metal. When landfills are operated properly, such materials pose no threat. However, when landfills are not operated properly, lead and mercury from them contaminate groundwater, for example. On the other hand, when trash is incinerated, heavy metals poison the ash and escape into the air.

The environmentalist's statements, if true, most strongly support which one of the following inferences?

(A) Old fluorescent bulbs should be recycled.
(B) Appliances containing heavy metals should not be incinerated.
(C) Chlorofluorocarbons are harmful to the atmosphere.
(D) Newer appliances are more dangerous to the environment than older ones.
(E) Appliances should be kept out of landfills.

PrepTest49 Sec2 Q20

14. Since the sweetness of sugared beverages makes athletes more likely to drink them, they can be helpful in avoiding dehydration. Furthermore, small amounts of sugar enhance the body's absorption of water and delay muscle fatigue by maintaining the body's glucose level. Still, one must use sugared beverages cautiously, for large amounts draw water from the blood to the stomach, thereby exacerbating the dehydration process.

If the statements above are true, then each of the following could also be true EXCEPT:

(A) Glucose is not the only type of sugar whose absence or scarcity in one's diet causes muscle fatigue.
(B) Problems caused by dehydration are invariably exacerbated if substances that delay muscle fatigue are consumed.
(C) Dehydrated athletes find beverages containing large amounts of sugar to be too sweet.
(D) Some situations that exacerbate the problems caused by muscle fatigue do not exacerbate those caused by dehydration.
(E) The rate at which the body absorbs water depends primarily on the amount of water already present in the blood.

PrepTest49 Sec2 Q21

15. Educator: If there is a crisis in education today, it is one of maintaining quality. People love to reduce serious learning to degrees and certificates. But one also can obtain these credentials by plodding through courses without ever learning much of value. When that happens, the credentials one receives are almost meaningless.

If the educator's statements are true, then which one of the following must be true?

(A) Increasingly, institutions are granting meaningless degrees and certificates.
(B) It has become easier for students to complete their coursework without learning anything of importance.
(C) Educational institutions should cease to grant degrees and certificates.
(D) Degrees and certificates do not guarantee that a person has acquired much worthwhile knowledge.
(E) A person benefits from an education only to the extent that he or she invests effort in it.

PrepTest49 Sec4 Q3

16. In older commercial airplanes, the design of the control panel allows any changes in flight controls made by one member of the flight crew to be immediately viewed by the other crew members. In recently manufactured aircraft, however, a crew member's flight control changes are harder to observe, thereby eliminating a routine means for performing valuable cross-checks. As a result, the flight crews operating recently manufactured airplanes must inform each other verbally about flight control changes much more frequently.

The statements above, if true, most strongly support which one of the following?

(A) How frequently an airplane's flight crew members will inform each other verbally about flight control changes depends in large part on how long it takes to perform those changes.
(B) In recently manufactured aircraft, the most valuable means available for performing cross-checks involves frequent verbal exchanges of information among the flight crew members.
(C) In older commercial airplanes, in contrast to recently manufactured airplanes, flight crew members have no need to exchange information verbally about flight control changes.
(D) The flight crew members operating a recently manufactured airplane cannot observe the flight control changes made by other crew members by viewing the control panel.
(E) How often flight crew members must share information verbally about flight control changes depends in part on what other means for performing cross-checks are available to the crew.

PrepTest49 Sec4 Q14

Explanations for these questions can be found in your Online Center.

Part Three: Logical Reasoning
Non-Argument Questions

K

Principle Questions

This pool consists of Principle questions you have not seen in earlier chapters. They are arranged in reverse chronological order—from most to least recent.

17. This year a flood devastated a small river town. Hollyville, also a river town, responded with an outpouring of aid in which a majority of its residents participated, a proportion that far surpassed that of a few years ago when Hollyville sent aid to victims of a highly publicized earthquake. This year's circumstances were a reversal of last year's, when Hollyville itself was the scene of a deadly tornado and so the recipient rather than the supplier of emergency aid.

    The situation described above most closely conforms to which one of the following generalizations?

    (A) People are more likely to aid people they know than they are to aid strangers.

    (B) Those who have received aid are more likely to be in favor of government relief programs than are those who have not.

    (C) The amount of aid that victims of a disaster receive is unrelated to the extent to which the disaster is publicized.

    (D) Once a disaster has struck them, people are more likely to aid others in need than they were before the disaster.

    (E) People are more likely to aid those who have experienced a hardship similar to one they themselves have experienced than to aid those who have experienced a dissimilar hardship.

    PrepTest59 Sec2 Q23

18. Dairy farmer: On our farm, we have great concern for our cows' environmental conditions. We have recently made improvements that increase their comfort, such as providing them with special sleeping mattresses. These changes are intended to increase blood flow to the udder. This increased blood flow would boost milk output and thus increase profits.

    Of the following propositions, which one is best illustrated by the dairy farmer's statements?

    (A) Dairy cows cannot have comfortable living conditions unless farmers have some knowledge about the physiology of milk production.

    (B) Farming practices introduced for the sake of maximizing profits can improve the living conditions of farm animals.

    (C) More than other farm animals, dairy cows respond favorably to improvements in their living environments.

    (D) The productivity of dairy farms should be increased only if the quality of the product is not compromised.

    (E) The key to maximizing profits on a dairy farm is having a concern for dairy cows' environment.

    PrepTest57 Sec2 Q10

19. Food labeling regulation: Food of a type that does not ordinarily contain fat cannot be labeled "nonfat" unless most people mistakenly believe the food ordinarily contains fat. If most people mistakenly believe that a food ordinarily contains fat, the food may be labeled "nonfat" if the label also states that the food ordinarily contains no fat.

    Which one of the following situations violates the food labeling regulation?

    (A) Although most people know that bran flakes do not normally contain fat, Lester's Bran Flakes are not labeled "nonfat."

    (B) Although most people are aware that lasagna ordinarily contains fat, Lester's Lasagna, which contains no fat, is not labeled "nonfat."

    (C) Although most garlic baguettes contain fat, Lester's Garlic Baguettes are labeled "nonfat."

    (D) Although most people are aware that applesauce does not ordinarily contain fat, Lester's Applesauce is labeled "nonfat."

    (E) Although most people mistakenly believe that salsa ordinarily contains fat, the label on Lester's Zesty Salsa says "This product, like all salsas, is nonfat."

    PrepTest57 Sec3 Q14

K

Part Three: Logical Reasoning
CHAPTER 11

Explanations for these questions
can be found in your Online Center.

20. Industrial adviser: If two new processes under consideration are not substantially different in cost, then the less environmentally damaging process should be chosen. If, however, a company already employs an environmentally damaging process and retooling for a less damaging process would involve substantial cost, then that company should retool only if retooling is either legally required or likely to bring long-term savings substantially greater than the cost.

Which one of the following judgments conforms most closely to the principles described by the industrial adviser?

(A) A new law offering companies tax credits for reducing pollution would enable a company to realize a slight long-term savings by changing to a more environmentally sound process for manufacturing dye, despite the substantial cost of retooling. In light of the new law, the company should change its process.

(B) In manufacturing pincushions, a company uses a process that, though legal, has come under heavy public criticism for the environmental damage it causes. The company should change its process to preserve its public image, despite some expected long-term losses from doing so.

(C) A company is considering two new processes for the manufacture of staples. Process A is more expensive than process B but not substantially so. However, process A is substantially less environmentally damaging than process B. The company should implement process A.

(D) Two new processes are being considered for the manufacture of ball bearings. The processes are similar, except that the chemicals used in process A will pollute a nearby river slightly more than will the chemicals for process B. Process A is also slightly cheaper than process B. The company should use process A.

(E) A company is considering changing its process for manufacturing shoelaces. The new process is cheaper and less environmentally damaging than the old. Both are legal. Changing processes would be costly, but the cost would be almost entirely recovered in long-term savings. The company should switch processes.

PrepTest51 Sec1 Q17

21. The area of mathematics called "gauge field theory," though investigated in the nineteenth century, has only relatively recently been applied to problems in contemporary quantum mechanics. Differential geometry, another area of mathematics, was investigated by Gauss in the early nineteenth century, long before Einstein determined that one of its offspring, tensor analysis, was the appropriate mathematics for exploring general relativity.

Which one of the following is best illustrated by the examples presented above?

(A) Applications of some new theories or techniques in mathematics are unrecognized until long after the discovery of those theories or techniques.

(B) Mathematicians are sometimes able to anticipate which branches of their subject will prove useful to future scientists.

(C) The discoveries of modern physics would not have been possible without major mathematical advances made in the nineteenth century.

(D) The nineteenth century stands out among other times as a period of great mathematical achievement.

(E) Mathematics tends to advance more quickly than any of the physical sciences.

PrepTest51 Sec3 Q5

Explanations for these questions can be found in your Online Center.

Part Three: Logical Reasoning
Non-Argument Questions

K

Paradox Questions

This pool consists of Paradox questions you have not seen in earlier chapters. They are arranged in reverse chronological order—from most to least recent.

22. Shark teeth are among the most common vertebrate fossils; yet fossilized shark skeletons are much less common—indeed, comparatively rare among fossilized vertebrate skeletons.

    Which one of the following, if true, most helps to resolve the apparent paradox described above?

    (A) Unlike the bony skeletons of other vertebrates, shark skeletons are composed of cartilage, and teeth and bone are much more likely to fossilize than cartilage is.

    (B) The rare fossilized skeletons of sharks that are found are often found in areas other than those in which fossils of shark teeth are plentiful.

    (C) Fossils of sharks' teeth are quite difficult to distinguish from fossils of other kinds of teeth.

    (D) Some species of sharks alive today grow and lose many sets of teeth during their lifetimes.

    (E) The physical and chemical processes involved in the fossilization of sharks' teeth are as common as those involved in the fossilization of shark skeletons.

    PrepTest61 Sec2 Q12

23. As often now as in the past, newspaper journalists use direct or indirect quotation to report unsupported or false claims made by newsmakers. However, journalists are becoming less likely to openly challenge the veracity of such claims within their articles.

    Each of the following, if true, helps to explain the trend in journalism described above EXCEPT:

    (A) Newspaper publishers have found that many readers will cancel a subscription simply because a view they take for granted has been disputed by the publication.

    (B) The areas of knowledge on which journalists report are growing in specialization and diversity, while journalists themselves are not becoming more broadly knowledgeable.

    (C) Persons supporting controversial views more and more frequently choose to speak only to reporters who seem sympathetic to their views.

    (D) A basic principle of journalism holds that debate over controversial issues draws the attention of the public.

    (E) Journalists who challenge the veracity of claims are often criticized for failing their professional obligation to be objective.

    PrepTest61 Sec2 Q19

24. Medical research has established that the Beta Diet is healthier than a more conventional diet. But on average, people who have followed the Beta Diet for several decades are much more likely to be in poor health than are people whose diet is more conventional.

    Which one of the following, if true, most helps to resolve the apparent conflict between the two statements above?

    (A) On average, people who have followed the Beta Diet for their entire lives are much more likely to have a variety of healthful habits than are people whose diet is more conventional.

    (B) The Beta Diet is used primarily as a treatment for a condition that adversely affects overall health.

    (C) People of average health who switch from a conventional diet to the Beta Diet generally find that their health improves substantially as a result.

    (D) The Beta Diet provides dramatic health benefits for some people but only minor benefits for others.

    (E) Recent research has shown that a diet high in fruits, vegetables, and skim milk is even healthier than the Beta Diet.

    PrepTest59 Sec2 Q11

25. On a short trip a driver is more likely to have an accident if there is a passenger in the car, presumably because passengers distract drivers. However, on a long trip a driver is more likely to have an accident if the driver is alone.

    Which one of the following, if true, most helps to explain the facts described above?

    (A) People are much more likely to drive alone on short trips than on long trips.

    (B) Good drivers tend to take more long trips than bad drivers.

    (C) The longer a car trip is, the more likely a passenger is to help the driver maintain alertness.

    (D) On a long trip the likelihood of an accident does not increase with each additional passenger.

    (E) Most drivers take far more short trips than long trips.

    PrepTest59 Sec3 Q4

K | Part Three: Logical Reasoning
CHAPTER 11

Explanations for these questions
can be found in your Online Center.

26. MetroBank made loans to ten small companies, in amounts ranging from $1,000 to $100,000. These ten loans all had graduated payment plans, i.e., the scheduled monthly loan payment increased slightly each month over the five-year term of the loan. Nonetheless, the average payment received by MetroBank for these ten loans had decreased by the end of the five-year term.

Which one of the following, if true, most helps to resolve the apparent discrepancy in the statements above?

(A) The number of small companies receiving new loans from MetroBank increased over the five-year term.
(B) Several of the ten small companies also borrowed money from other banks.
(C) Most banks offer a greater number of loans for under $100,000 than for over $100,000.
(D) Of the ten small companies, the three that had borrowed the largest amounts paid off their loans within three years.
(E) For some loans made by MetroBank, the monthly payment decreases slightly over the term of the loan.

PrepTest57 Sec2 Q3

27. Educators studied the performance of 200 students in a university's history classes. They found that those students who performed the best had either part-time jobs or full-time jobs, had their history classes early in the morning, and had a very limited social life, whereas those students who performed the worst had no jobs, had their history classes early in the morning, and had a very active social life.

Which one of the following, if true, most helps to explain the educators' findings?

(A) The students compensated for any study time lost due to their jobs but they did not compensate for any study time lost due to their social lives.
(B) The students who had full-time jobs typically worked late-night hours at those jobs.
(C) Better students tend to choose classes that are scheduled to meet early in the morning.
(D) A larger percentage of those students interested in majoring in history had part-time jobs than had full-time jobs.
(E) Although having a job tends to provide a release from stress, thus increasing academic performance, having a full-time job, like having an active social life, can distract a student from studying.

PrepTest57 Sec3 Q1

28. Two randomly selected groups of 30 adults each were asked to write short stories on a particular topic. One group was told that the best stories would be awarded cash prizes, while the other group was not told of any prizes. Each story was evaluated by a team of judges who were given no indication of the group from which the story came. The stories submitted by those who thought they were competing for prizes were ranked on average significantly lower than the stories from the other group.

Which one of the following, if true, most helps to explain the difference in average ranking between the two groups' stories?

(A) The cash prizes were too small to motivate an average adult to make a significant effort to produce stories of high quality.
(B) People writing to win prizes show a greater than usual tendency to produce stereotypical stories that show little creativity.
(C) Most adults show little originality in writing stories on a topic suggested by someone else.
(D) The team of judges was biased in favor of stories that they judged to be more realistic.
(E) No one explained clearly to either group what standards would be used in judging their stories.

PrepTest57 Sec3 Q4

29. In some places, iceberg lilies are the mainstay of grizzly bears' summer diets. The bears forage meadows for the lilies, uprooting them and eating their bulbs. Although the bears annually destroy a large percentage of the lilies, scientists have determined that the bears' feeding habits actually promote the survival of iceberg lilies.

Which one of the following, if true, most helps to resolve the apparent discrepancy in the statements above?

(A) When grizzly bears forage for iceberg lilies, they generally kill many more lilies than they eat.
(B) Iceberg lilies produce so many offspring that, when undisturbed, they quickly deplete the resources necessary for their own survival.
(C) A significantly smaller number of iceberg lily flowers are produced in fields where grizzly bears forage than in fields of undisturbed iceberg lilies.
(D) The geographic regions in which iceberg lilies are most prevalent are those regions populated by grizzly bears.
(E) Iceberg lilies contain plentiful amounts of some nutrients that are necessary for grizzly bears' survival.

PrepTest51 Sec1 Q3

Explanations for these questions can be found in your Online Center.

Part Three: Logical Reasoning
Non-Argument Questions

30. Last summer, after a number of people got sick from eating locally caught anchovies, the coastal city of San Martin advised against eating such anchovies. The anchovies were apparently tainted with domoic acid, a harmful neurotoxin. However, a dramatic drop in the population of *P. australis* plankton to numbers more normal for local coastal waters indicates that it is once again safe to eat locally caught anchovies.

Which one of the following, if true, would most help to explain why it is now safe to lift the advisory?

(A) *P. australis* is one of several varieties of plankton common to the region that, when ingested by anchovies, cause the latter to secrete small amounts of domoic acid.

(B) *P. australis* naturally produces domoic acid, though anchovies consume enough to become toxic only when the population of *P. australis* is extraordinarily large.

(C) Scientists have used *P. australis* plankton to obtain domoic acid in the laboratory.

(D) A sharp decline in the population of *P. australis* is typically mirrored by a corresponding drop in the local anchovy population.

(E) *P. australis* cannot survive in large numbers in seawater that does not contain significant quantities of domoic acid along with numerous other compounds.

PrepTest51 Sec1 Q22

31. Statistical studies show that last year there was the greatest drop in the violent crime rate over the course of a year since such statistics were first gathered. But they also reveal that at the same time public anxiety about violent crime substantially increased.

Which one of the following, if true, most helps to resolve the apparent discrepancy described above?

(A) Longer prison sentences were the primary cause of the decrease in the violent crime rate over the course of last year.

(B) As in the past, last year's increase in public anxiety about violent crime has been consistently underreported in the news media.

(C) Most people can realistically assess the likelihood that they will become victims of violent crime.

(D) People who feel the most anxiety about violent crime usually live in areas with relatively high violent crime rates.

(E) The proportion of violent crimes covered in the news media nearly doubled over the course of last year.

PrepTest49 Sec2 Q2

ANSWER KEY

Inference Questions

1. C
2. A
3. E
4. A
5. D
6. B
7. C
8. E
9. B
10. D
11. C
12. D
13. B
14. B
15. D
16. E

Principle Questions

17. D
18. B
19. D
20. C
21. A

Paradox Questions

22. A
23. D
24. B
25. C
26. D
27. A
28. B
29. B
30. B
31. E

Complete explanations for these questions can be found in your Online Center.

Logical Reasoning: Managing the Section

The bulk of this chapter consists of two complete Logical Reasoning sections, followed by an answer key. Complete explanations for the questions in this chapter are available in your Online Center. Taking full timed practice sections helps you maximize your score by learning to improve section management. Perfecting your timing in LSAT sections involves much more than just "getting faster." Indeed, in many cases, hurrying through (or worse, skipping) the steps of the Logical Reasoning Method may wind up costing you time by causing you to reread the stimulus or to do extra work as you evaluate the answer choices. A haphazard approach to the section can also cost you points directly when incomplete analyses or deductions lead to wrong answers.

TIMING AND SECTION MANAGEMENT

Here are a few of the principles of great section management that LSAT experts use to their advantage. Learn them and put them into practice whenever you undertake timed section or full-test practice.

Logical Reasoning Section Timing: The Basics

The facts: Every Logical Reasoning section contains 24–26 questions to be completed in 35 minutes.

The strategy: On average, then, you should take roughly 1 minute 20 seconds per question. You may be able to answer some easier questions correctly in less time. Some of the hardest or densest questions will take you longer. When you answer a question quickly, bank that time for tougher questions to come. If a question threatens to drag on for over a minute and a half, cross out those answers you've confidently eliminated, mark the question as incomplete, and move on. If you have time to come back to the question, that's great. If not, mark your score sheet with a guess from among the answer choices you were still considering. Always remember that your goal in timed section practice is to get as many correct answers as possible in 35 minutes. Don't overinvest in one or two tough questions to the detriment of your overall performance.

Efficiency, Not Speed

The facts: Rereading several times (even if you do so quickly) will cost you more time than reading strategically once. A strong prediction of the correct answer increases the likelihood that you'll spot the right choice as you evaluate the answers.

The strategy: Follow the Logical Reasoning Method. In the preceding chapters, you've seen how identifying the question, untangling the stimulus, and predicting the correct answer provide everything you need to answer questions quickly and accurately. Don't let "clock anxiety" tempt you into abandoning the most efficient approach. Being methodical *does not* mean being slow. When you have practiced enough that the Logical Reasoning Method is second nature, you'll find that it provides the shortest and most direct route to correct answers, the single goal of all the work you do on the LSAT.

Triage: Take Control of the Section

The facts: You are under no obligation to do the questions in the order in which they are presented. Typically, the Logical Reasoning sections of the LSAT follow the pattern you see in the following chart. The early questions are generally easier, although there is often one difficult question among the first 8–10 questions in the section. The latter third of the section usually contains the highest concentration of hard questions, but there are often one or two fairly easy questions near the very end of the section.

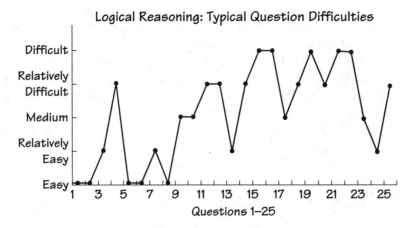

The strategy: It would be unreasonably time-consuming to try to evaluate the difficulty of 25 distinct items before starting your work on the questions. In the Logical Reasoning section, "triage" needs to be done on a question-by-question basis. Move through the section in order, but be willing to skip a question when it is to your benefit to do so. To make time-management decisions in your own best interest, you must be able to 1) identify questions quickly, 2) know your own strengths and weaknesses in Logical Reasoning, and 3) be fearless in looking for and prioritizing the questions most likely to turn into correct answers for you.

Some LSAT experts find it most helpful to manage the Logical Reasoning sections by working straight through from Question 1 to Question 25, skipping or guessing on problematic questions as they go. Others, taking their cue from the pattern in the previous chart, work from Question 1 through Question 15, and then turn to the end of the section and work backward from Question 25 to Question 16. The latter pattern ensures that the test taker will get to the easier questions likely found at the end of the section.

Regardless of any grand plan or approach you take, your battle in the Logical Reasoning sections will be won step by step, question by question. You will have to know the question types, what they ask for, and the most strategic approaches to them to maximize your score. Consistent practice will lead to real efficiency: getting as many points as you can in 35 minutes.

Skip and Guess Strategically

The facts: You do not need to answer every question to get a great score. The features of certain questions are time-consuming (e.g., long stimuli in Parallel Reasoning or Inference questions; dense Formal Logic) for most test takers. There is no bonus for solving the hardest question(s) in the section.

The strategy: Remember that you are in control of how much time and effort you dedicate to any particular question. Allowing yourself to get into an "ego battle" with particular questions—"I *will* figure this one out no matter what!"—can take precious minutes away from other questions you could be answering quickly and accurately. Be willing to skip one or two difficult or very time-consuming questions if doing so will allow you to get more questions correct subsequently. Preempt situations in which you are guessing out of frustration—"Okay, I give up. I've already given this two minutes; I'll never get it!"—by learning to guess strategically—"I'll guess on this long Method of Argument question and give myself an extra two minutes for the next two pages." In other words, guess when it is in your benefit to do so. Stay in control of the section and the test.

TAKING THE TIMING SECTION

The Logical Reasoning sections that follow were originally Sections 1 and 4 in PrepTest 65, administered in December 2011.

Proctoring

Complete these sections under timed, test-like conditions. Give yourself 35 minutes per section, and finish each in one uninterrupted sitting. If you are taking the section as part of a class, follow the proctor's instructions strictly. If you are taking the section on your own, use the LSAT Proctor Anywhere app.

Record your answer selections using one of the answer grids found at the back of this book.

Scoring

After you finish the section, record your answers in the appropriate webgrid (PrepTest 65, Section 1, or PrepTest 65, Section 4) found in your Online Center. This will make your results and percent correct easy to see, and the score report will contain links to the explanations for each question.

NOTE: Chapters 7 and 16 contain the two other scored sections from PrepTest 65. After completing those sections (under timed, proctored conditions), you may enter your answers from all four sections into the webgrid for PrepTest 65 to receive a score for the entire test.

Review

For your convenience, complete answers and explanations are included in your Online Center. When you review a section, review it completely, even those questions you got right. Check that you consistently followed the Logical Reasoning Method, identifying each question, untangling its stimulus effectively, using your analyses to predict the correct answers, and evaluating the choices quickly and accurately.

K | Part Three: Logical Reasoning
CHAPTER 12

Explanations to these questions
can be found in your Online Center.

PrepTest 65, Section 1

Time—35 minutes

25 Questions

Directions: The questions in this section are based on the reasoning contained in brief statements or passages. For some questions, more than one of the choices could conceivably answer the question. However, you are to choose the best answer; that is, the response that most accurately and completely answers the question. You should not make assumptions that are by commonsense standards implausible, superfluous, or incompatible with the passage. After you have chosen the best answer, blacken the corresponding space on your answer sheet.

1. In a recent study of more than 400 North American men and women whose previous heart attack put them at risk for a second heart attack, about half were told to switch to a "Mediterranean-type diet"—one rich in fish, vegetables, olive oil, and grains—while the other half were advised to eat a more traditional "Western" diet but to limit their fat intake. Those following the Mediterranean diet were significantly less likely than those in the other group to have a second heart attack. But the Mediterranean diet includes a fair amount of fat from fish and olive oil, so the research suggests that a diet may not have to be extremely low in fat in order to protect the heart.

Which one of the following, if true, most strengthens the argument?

(A) Research has shown that eliminating almost all fat from one's diet can be effective in decreasing the likelihood of a second heart attack.

(B) Studies suggest that the kinds of oils in the fat included in the Mediterranean diet may protect the heart against potentially fatal disruptions of heart rhythms and other causes of heart attacks.

(C) The patients who consumed the Mediterranean diet enjoyed the food and continued to follow the diet after the experiment was concluded.

(D) Many people who have had heart attacks are advised by their cardiologists to begin an exercise regimen in addition to changing their diet.

(E) Some cardiologists believe that the protection afforded by the Mediterranean diet might be enhanced by drugs that lower blood-cholesterol levels.

2. Florist: Some people like to have green carnations on St. Patrick's Day. But flowers that are naturally green are extremely rare. Thus, it is very difficult for plant breeders to produce green carnations. Before St. Patrick's Day, then, it is wise for florists to stock up on white carnations, which are fairly inexpensive and quite easy to dye green.

Which one of the following most accurately expresses the overall conclusion of the florist's argument?

(A) It is a good idea for florists to stock up on white carnations before St. Patrick's Day.

(B) Flowers that are naturally green are very rare.

(C) There are some people who like to have green carnations on St. Patrick's Day.

(D) White carnations are fairly inexpensive and can easily be dyed green.

(E) It is very difficult to breed green carnations.

3. Millions of homes are now using low-energy lighting, but millions more have still to make the switch, a fact that the government and the home lighting industry are eager to change. Although low-wattage bulbs cost more per bulb than normal bulbs, their advantages to the homeowner are enormous, and therefore everyone should use low-wattage bulbs.

Information about which one of the following would be LEAST useful in evaluating the argument?

(A) the actual cost of burning low-wattage bulbs compared to that of burning normal bulbs

(B) the profits the home lighting industry expects to make from sales of low-wattage bulbs

(C) the specific cost of a low-wattage bulb compared with that of a normal bulb

(D) the opinion of current users of low-wattage bulbs as to their effectiveness

(E) the average life of a low-wattage bulb compared with that of a normal bulb

GO ON TO THE NEXT PAGE.

Explanations to these questions can be found in your Online Center.

Part Three: Logical Reasoning
Logical Reasoning: Managing the Section

K

4. Swimming pools should be fenced to protect children from drowning, but teaching children to swim is even more important. And there is a principle involved here that applies to childrearing generally. Thus, while we should restrict children's access to the soft drinks and candies advertised on television shows directed towards children, it is even more important to teach them _____.

Which one of the following most logically completes the passage?

(A) that television can be a good source of accurate information about many things

(B) that television advertisements are deceptive and misleading

(C) how to make nutritional choices that are conducive to their well-being

(D) the importance of physical activity to health and well-being

(E) how to creatively entertain themselves without watching television

5. In its coverage of a controversy regarding a proposal to build a new freeway, a television news program showed interviews with several people who would be affected by the proposed freeway. Of the interviews shown, those conducted with people against the new freeway outnumbered those conducted with people for it two to one. The television program is therefore biased against the proposed freeway.

Which one of the following, if true, most seriously weakens the argument?

(A) Most of the people who watched the program were aware of the freeway controversy beforehand.

(B) Most viewers of television news programs do not expect those programs to be completely free of bias.

(C) In the interviews, the people against the new freeway expressed their opinions with more emotion than the people for the freeway did.

(D) Before the program aired, over twice as many people were against building the freeway than were in favor of it.

(E) The business interests of the television station that produced the program would be harmed by the construction of a new freeway.

6. Evan: I am a vegetarian because I believe it is immoral to inflict pain on animals to obtain food. Some vegetarians who share this moral reason nonetheless consume some seafood, on the grounds that it is not known whether certain sea creatures can experience pleasure or pain. But if it is truly wrong to inflict needless suffering, we should extend the benefit of the doubt to sea animals and refrain from eating seafood.

Which one of the following most closely conforms to the principle illustrated by Evan's criticism of vegetarians who eat seafood?

(A) I do not know if I have repaid Farah the money she lent me for a movie ticket. She says that she does not remember whether or not I repaid her. In order to be sure that I have repaid her, I will give her the money now.

(B) It is uncertain whether all owners of the defective vehicles know that their vehicles are being recalled by the manufacturer. Thus, we should expect that some vehicles that have been recalled have not been returned.

(C) I am opposed to using incentives such as reduced taxes to attract businesses to our region. These incentives would attract businesses interested only in short-term profits. Such businesses would make our region's economy less stable, because they have no long-term commitment to the community.

(D) Updating our computer security system could lead to new contracts. The present system has no problems, but we could benefit from emphasizing a state-of-the-art system in new proposals. If we do not get new customers, the new system could be financed through higher fees for current customers.

(E) Isabel Allende lived through the tragic events of her country's recent history; no doubt her novels have been inspired by her memories of those events. Yet Allende's characters are hopeful and full of joy, indicating that Allende's own view of life has not been negatively marked by her experiences.

GO ON TO THE NEXT PAGE.

K | Part Three: Logical Reasoning
CHAPTER 12

Explanations to these questions
can be found in your Online Center.

7. Economist: Government intervention in the free market in pursuit of socially desirable goals can affect supply and demand, thereby distorting prices. The ethics of such intervention is comparable to that of administering medicines. Most medicines have harmful as well as beneficial effects, so the use of a type of medicine is ethically justified only when its nonuse would be significantly more harmful than its use. Similarly, government intervention in the free market is justified only when it _____.

Which one of the following most logically completes the final sentence above?

(A) would likely be approved of by the majority of the affected participants
(B) has been shown to have few if any significantly harmful effects
(C) is believed unlikely to significantly exacerbate any existing problems
(D) would do less damage than would result from the government's not intervening
(E) provides a solution to some otherwise insoluble problem

8. The proportion of fat calories in the diets of people who read the nutrition labels on food products is significantly lower than it is in the diets of people who do not read nutrition labels. This shows that reading these labels promotes healthful dietary behavior.

The reasoning in the argument above is flawed in that the argument

(A) illicitly infers a cause from a correlation
(B) relies on a sample that is unlikely to be representative of the group as a whole
(C) confuses a condition that is necessary for a phenomenon to occur with a condition that is sufficient for that phenomenon to occur
(D) takes for granted that there are only two possible alternative explanations of a phenomenon
(E) draws a conclusion about the intentions of a group of people based solely on data about the consequences of their behavior

9. Some paleontologists have suggested that *Apatosaurus*, a huge dinosaur, was able to gallop. This, however, is unlikely, because galloping would probably have broken *Apatosaurus*'s legs. Experiments with modern bones show how much strain they can withstand before breaking. By taking into account the diameter and density of *Apatosaurus* leg bones, it is possible to calculate that those bones could not have withstood the strains of galloping.

Which one of the following most accurately expresses the conclusion drawn by the argument as a whole?

(A) Galloping would probably have broken the legs of *Apatosaurus*.
(B) It is possible to calculate that *Apatosaurus* leg bones could not have withstood the strain of galloping.
(C) The claim of paleontologists that *Apatosaurus* was able to gallop is likely to be incorrect.
(D) If galloping would have broken the legs of *Apatosaurus*, then *Apatosaurus* was probably unable to gallop.
(E) Modern bones are quite similar in structure and physical properties to the bones of *Apatosaurus*.

10. A new process enables ordinary table salt to be fortified with iron. This advance could help reduce the high incidence of anemia in the world's population due to a deficiency of iron in the diet. Salt is used as a preservative for food and a flavor enhancer all over the globe, and people consume salt in quantities that would provide iron in significant amounts.

Which one of the following most accurately describes the role played in the argument by the statement that people consume salt in quantities that would provide iron in significant amounts?

(A) It is the conclusion of the argument.
(B) It provides support for the conclusion of the argument.
(C) It is a claim that the argument is directed against.
(D) It qualifies the conclusion of the argument.
(E) It illustrates a principle that underlies the argument.

GO ON TO THE NEXT PAGE.

Explanations to these questions can be found in your Online Center.

Part Three: Logical Reasoning
Logical Reasoning: Managing the Section

11. Inspector: The only fingerprints on the premises are those of the owner, Mr. Tannisch. Therefore, whoever now has his guest's missing diamonds must have worn gloves.

Which one of the following exhibits a flaw in its reasoning most similar to that in the inspector's reasoning?

(A) The campers at Big Lake Camp, all of whom became ill this afternoon, have eaten food only from the camp cafeteria. Therefore, the cause of the illness must not have been something they ate.

(B) The second prototype did not perform as well in inclement weather as did the first prototype. Hence, the production of the second prototype might have deviated from the design followed for the first.

(C) Each of the swimmers at this meet more often loses than wins. Therefore, it is unlikely that any of them will win.

(D) All of Marjorie's cavities are on the left side of her mouth. Hence, she must chew more on the left side than on the right.

(E) All of these tomato plants are twice as big as they were last year. So if we grow peas, they will probably be twice as big as last year's peas.

12. Populations of a shrimp species at eleven different Indonesian coral reefs show substantial genetic differences from one reef to another. This is surprising because the area's strong ocean currents probably carry baby shrimp between the different reefs, which would allow the populations to interbreed and become genetically indistinguishable.

Which one of the following, if true, most helps to explain the substantial genetic differences among the shrimp populations?

(A) The genetic differences between the shrimp populations are much less significant than those between shrimp and any other marine species.

(B) The individual shrimp within a given population at any given Indonesian coral reef differ from one another genetically, even though there is widespread interbreeding within any such population.

(C) Before breeding, shrimp of the species examined migrate back to the coral reef at which they were hatched.

(D) Most shrimp hatched at a given Indonesian coral reef are no longer present at that coral reef upon becoming old enough to breed.

(E) Ocean currents probably carry many of the baby shrimp hatched at a given Indonesian coral reef out into the open ocean rather than to another coral reef.

GO ON TO THE NEXT PAGE.

K

Part Three: Logical Reasoning
CHAPTER 12

Explanations to these questions
can be found in your Online Center.

13. Researchers have studied the cost-effectiveness of growing halophytes—salt-tolerant plant species—for animal forage. Halophytes require more water than conventional crops, but can be irrigated with seawater, and pumping seawater into farms near sea level is much cheaper than pumping freshwater from deep wells. Thus, seawater agriculture near sea level should be cost-effective in desert regions although its yields are smaller than traditional, freshwater agriculture.

Which one of the following, if true, most strengthens the argument above?

(A) A given volume of halophytes is significantly different in nutritional value for animal forage from the same volume of conventional forage crops.

(B) Some halophytes not only tolerate seawater but require salt in order to thrive.

(C) Large research expenditures are needed to develop the strains of halophytes best suited for agricultural purposes.

(D) Costs other than the costs of irrigation are different for halophytes grown by means of seawater irrigation than for conventional crops.

(E) Pumping water for irrigation is proportionally one of the largest costs involved in growing, harvesting, and distributing any forage crop for animals.

14. Principle: If an insurance policy is written in such a way that a reasonable person seeking insurance would not read it thoroughly before signing it, then the reasonable expectations of the policyholder concerning the policy's coverage should take legal precedence over specific language in the written policy itself.

Application: The insurance company should be required to cover the hail damage to Celia's car, even though specific language in the written policy Celia signed excluded coverage for hail damage.

Which one of the following, if true, most justifies the above application of the principle?

(A) Celia is a reasonable person, and she expected the insurance policy to cover hail damage to her car.

(B) Given the way it was written, a reasonable person would not have read Celia's insurance policy thoroughly before signing it, and Celia reasonably expected the policy to cover hail damage.

(C) The insurance policy that Celia signed was written in such a way that a reasonable person would not read it thoroughly before signing it, but Celia did read the policy thoroughly before signing it.

(D) Celia did not read the insurance policy thoroughly before signing it, and a reasonable person in her position would assume that the policy would cover hail damage.

(E) Celia did not read the written insurance policy thoroughly before signing it, and a reasonable person in her position would not have done so either.

GO ON TO THE NEXT PAGE.

Explanations to these questions
can be found in your Online Center.

Part Three: Logical Reasoning
Logical Reasoning: Managing the Section

15. Researcher: Every year approximately the same number
    of people die of iatrogenic "disease"—that is, as
    a direct result of medical treatments or
    hospitalization—as die of all other causes combined.
    Therefore, if medicine could find ways of
    preventing all iatrogenic disease, the number of
    deaths per year would decrease by half.

The reasoning in the researcher's argument is flawed
because the argument fails to consider that

(A) prevention of noniatrogenic disease will have an
    effect on the occurrence of iatrogenic disease
(B) some medical treatments can be replaced by less
    invasive or damaging alternatives
(C) people who do not die of one cause may soon
    die of another cause
(D) there is no one way to prevent all cases of
    death from iatrogenic disease
(E) whenever a noniatrogenic disease occurs, there
    is a risk of iatrogenic disease

16. Activist: Any member of the city council ought either to
    vote against the proposal or to abstain. But if all
    the members abstain, the matter will be decided
    by the city's voters. So at least one member of the
    city council should vote against the proposal.

The conclusion of the activist's argument follows
logically if which one of the following is assumed?

(A) If all the members of the city council abstain in
    the vote on the proposal, the city's voters will
    definitely decide in favor of the proposal.
(B) The proposal should not be decided by the
    city's voters.
(C) No members of the city council will vote in
    favor of the proposal.
(D) If not every member of the city council abstains
    in the vote on the proposal, the matter will not
    be decided by the city's voters.
(E) If one member of the city council ought to vote
    against the proposal, the other members should
    abstain in the vote on the proposal.

17. Economist: Some critics of the media have contended
    that negative news reports on the state of the
    economy can actually harm the economy because
    such reports damage people's confidence in it,
    and this lack of confidence in turn adversely
    affects people's willingness to spend money. But
    studies show that spending trends correlate very
    closely with people's confidence in their own
    immediate economic situations. Thus these media
    critics are mistaken.

The economist's argument is flawed in that it fails to
consider the possibility that

(A) one's level of confidence in one's own economic
    situation affects how one perceives reports
    about the overall state of the economy
(B) news reports about the state of the economy are
    not always accurate
(C) people who pay no attention to economic
    reports in the media always judge accurately
    whether their own economic situation is likely
    to deteriorate or improve
(D) people who have little confidence in the overall
    economy generally take a pessimistic view
    concerning their own immediate economic
    situations
(E) an economic slowdown usually has a greater
    impact on the economic situations of individuals
    if it takes people by surprise than if people are
    forewarned

GO ON TO THE NEXT PAGE.

K Part Three: Logical Reasoning
CHAPTER 12

Explanations to these questions
can be found in your Online Center.

18. Zoologist: Every domesticated large mammal species now in existence was domesticated thousands of years ago. Since those days, people undoubtedly tried innumerable times to domesticate each of the wild large mammal species that seemed worth domesticating. Clearly, therefore, most wild large mammal species in existence today either would be difficult to domesticate or would not be worth domesticating.

The zoologist's argument requires the assumption that

(A) in spite of the difficulties encountered, at one time or another people have tried to domesticate each wild large mammal species
(B) it is not much easier today to domesticate wild large mammal species than it was in the past
(C) not all of the large mammal species that were domesticated in the past are still in existence
(D) the easier it is to domesticate a wild large mammal species, the more worthwhile it is to do so
(E) of all the domesticated large mammal species in existence today, the very first to be domesticated were the easiest to domesticate

19. Last winter was mild enough to allow most bird species to forage naturally, which explains why the proportion of birds visiting feeders was much lower than usual. The mild winter also allowed many species to stay in their summer range all winter without migrating south, thereby limiting the usual attrition accompanying migration. Hence, last year's mild winter is responsible for this year's larger-than-usual bird population.

Which one of the following, if true, would most strengthen the reasoning in the argument?

(A) Increases in bird populations sometimes occur following unusual weather patterns.
(B) When birds do not migrate south, the mating behaviors they exhibit differ from those they exhibit when they do migrate.
(C) Birds eating at feeders are more vulnerable to predators than are birds foraging naturally.
(D) Birds that remain in their summer range all winter often exhaust that range's food supply before spring.
(E) Birds sometimes visit feeders even when they are able to find sufficient food for survival by foraging naturally.

20. Journalist: Newspapers generally report on only those scientific studies whose findings sound dramatic. Furthermore, newspaper stories about small observational studies, which are somewhat unreliable, are more frequent than newspaper stories about large randomized trials, which generate stronger scientific evidence. Therefore, a small observational study must be more likely to have dramatic findings than a large randomized trial.

Which one of the following most accurately expresses a flaw in the journalist's reasoning?

(A) It casts doubt on the reliability of a study by questioning the motives of those reporting it.
(B) It fails to consider that even if a study's findings sound dramatic, the scientific evidence for those findings may be strong.
(C) It confuses a claim about scientific studies whose findings sound dramatic with a similar claim about small observational studies.
(D) It overlooks the possibility that small observational studies are far more common than large randomized trials.
(E) It fails to rule out the possibility that a study's having findings that sound dramatic is an effect rather than a cause of the study's being reported on.

21. In several countries, to slow global warming, many farmers are planting trees on their land because of government incentives. These incentives arose from research indicating that vegetation absorbs carbon dioxide that might otherwise trap heat in the atmosphere. A recent study, however, indicates that trees absorb and store carbon dioxide less effectively than native grasses. Therefore, these incentives are helping to hasten global warming.

The argument requires the assumption that

(A) trees not only absorb carbon dioxide but also emit it
(B) most farmers do not plant any trees on their land unless there is an incentive to do so
(C) land that has been deforested seldom later sustains native grasses
(D) some of the trees planted in response to the incentives are planted where native grasses would otherwise be growing
(E) few if any governments have been interested in promoting the growth of native grasses

GO ON TO THE NEXT PAGE.

Explanations to these questions can be found in your Online Center.

Part Three: Logical Reasoning
Logical Reasoning: Managing the Section   K

22. Does the position of a car driver's seat have a significant impact on driving safety? It probably does. Driving position affects both comfort and the ability to see the road clearly. A driver who is uncomfortable eventually becomes fatigued, which makes it difficult to concentrate on the road. Likewise, the better the visibility from the driver's seat, the more aware the driver can be of road conditions and other vehicles.

Which one of the following most accurately describes the role played in the argument by the claim that driving position affects both comfort and the ability to see the road clearly?

(A) It is the conclusion drawn in the argument.
(B) It is a claim that the argument shows to be inconsistent with available evidence.
(C) It is used to provide a causal explanation for an observed phenomenon.
(D) It describes evidence that the argument ultimately refutes.
(E) It is a premise offered in support of the conclusion drawn in the argument.

23. Physician: There were approximately 83,400 trampoline-related injuries last year. This suggests that trampolines are quite dangerous and should therefore be used only under professional supervision.

Trampoline enthusiast: I disagree. In the past ten years sales of home trampolines have increased much more than trampoline-related injuries have: 260 percent in sales compared with 154 percent in injuries. Every exercise activity carries risks, even when carried out under professional supervision.

The dialogue provides the most support for the claim that the physician and the trampoline enthusiast disagree over whether

(A) trampolines cause injuries to a significant number of people using them
(B) home trampolines are the main source of trampoline-related injuries
(C) the rate of trampoline-related injuries, in terms of the number of injuries per trampoline user, is declining
(D) professional supervision of trampoline use tends to reduce the number of trampoline-related injuries
(E) trampoline use is an activity that warrants mandatory professional supervision

24. Editorial: One of our local television stations has been criticized for its recent coverage of the personal problems of a local politician's nephew, but the coverage was in fact good journalism. The information was accurate. Furthermore, the newscast had significantly more viewers than it normally does, because many people are curious about the politician's nephew's problems.

Which one of the following principles, if valid, would most help to justify the reasoning in the editorial?

(A) Journalism deserves to be criticized if it does not provide information that people want.
(B) Any journalism that intentionally misrepresents the facts of a case deserves to be criticized.
(C) Any journalism that provides accurate information on a subject about which there is considerable interest is good journalism.
(D) Good journalism will always provide people with information that they desire or need.
(E) Journalism that neither satisfies the public's curiosity nor provides accurate information can never be considered good journalism.

25. Interior decorator: All coffeehouses and restaurants are public places. Most well-designed public places feature artwork. But if a public place is uncomfortable it is not well designed, and all comfortable public places have spacious interiors.

If all of the interior decorator's statements are true, then which one of the following must be true?

(A) Any restaurant that has a spacious interior is comfortable.
(B) Most public places that feature artwork are well designed.
(C) Most coffeehouses that are well designed feature artwork.
(D) Any well-designed coffeehouse or restaurant has a spacious interior.
(E) Any coffeehouse that has a spacious interior is a well-designed public place.

PrepTest65 Sec1 Qs 1–25

S T O P

IF YOU FINISH BEFORE TIME IS CALLED, YOU MAY CHECK YOUR WORK ON THIS SECTION ONLY. DO NOT WORK ON ANY OTHER SECTION IN THE TEST.

Explanations to these questions can be found in your Online Center.

PrepTest 65, Section 4

Time—35 minutes

26 Questions

Directions: The questions in this section are based on the reasoning contained in brief statements or passages. For some questions, more than one of the choices could conceivably answer the question. However, you are to choose the best answer; that is, the response that most accurately and completely answers the question. You should not make assumptions that are by commonsense standards implausible, superfluous, or incompatible with the passage. After you have chosen the best answer, blacken the corresponding space on your answer sheet.

1. When a forest is subject to acid rain, the calcium level in the soil declines. Spruce, fir, and sugar maple trees all need calcium to survive. However, sugar maples in forests that receive significant acid rain are much more likely to show signs of decline consistent with calcium deficiency than are spruces or firs in such forests.

   Which one of the following, if true, most helps to explain the greater decline among sugar maples?

   (A) Soil in which calcium levels are significantly diminished by acid rain is also likely to be damaged in other ways by acid rain.
   (B) Sugar maples that do not receive enough calcium deteriorate less rapidly than spruces or firs that do not receive enough calcium.
   (C) Spruces and firs, unlike sugar maples, can extract calcium from a mineral compound that is common in soil and is not affected by acid rain.
   (D) Sugar maples require more calcium in the spring and summer than they do in the fall and winter.
   (E) Unlike spruces or firs, most sugar maples are native to areas that receive a lot of acid rain.

2. Syndicated political columnists often use their newspaper columns to try to persuade readers to vote a certain way. However, their efforts to persuade voters rarely succeed, for by the time such a column appears, nearly all who will vote in the election will have already made a decision about which candidate to vote for.

   Which one of the following is an assumption required by the argument?

   (A) Syndicated columnists influence the votes of most of their readers who have not yet decided which candidate to vote for.
   (B) The attempts of syndicated political columnists to persuade readers to vote a certain way in an election can instead cause them to vote a different way.
   (C) People who regularly read columns by syndicated political columnists mainly read those written by columnists with whom they already largely agree.
   (D) Regular readers of columns by syndicated political columnists are less likely to be persuaded to vote a certain way by such columns than are people who seldom read such columns.
   (E) People rarely can be persuaded to change their minds about which candidate to vote for once they have made a decision.

GO ON TO THE NEXT PAGE.

Explanations to these questions can be found in your Online Center.

Part Three: Logical Reasoning
Logical Reasoning: Managing the Section

K

3. Travel industry consultant: Several airlines are increasing elbow room and leg room in business class, because surveys show that business travelers value additional space more than, say, better meals. But airlines are overconcerned about the comfort of passengers flying on business; they should instead focus on the comfort of leisure travelers, because those travelers purchase 80 percent of all airline tickets.

Which one of the following, if true, most weakens the reasoning in the travel industry consultant's argument?

(A) Business travelers often make travel decisions based on whether they feel a given airline values their business.

(B) Some airlines have indicated that they will undertake alterations in seating space throughout the entire passenger area of their planes in the near future.

(C) Sleeping in comfort during long flights is not the primary concern of leisure travelers.

(D) A far greater proportion of an airline's revenues is derived from business travelers than from leisure travelers.

(E) Most leisure travelers buy airline tickets only when fares are discounted.

4. Gaby: In school, children should be allowed fully to follow their own interests, supported by experienced teachers who offer minimal guidance. This enables them to be most successful in their adult lives.

Logan: I disagree. Schoolchildren should acquire the fundamental knowledge necessary for future success, and they learn such fundamentals only through disciplined, systematic instruction from accredited teachers.

Gaby's and Logan's comments provide most support for the claim that they disagree about

(A) the way in which schoolchildren best acquire fundamental knowledge

(B) the extent to which teachers should direct schoolchildren's education

(C) the importance of having qualified teachers involved in schoolchildren's education

(D) the sort of school environment that most fosters children's creativity

(E) the extent to which schoolchildren are interested in fundamental academic subjects

5. Judge: The case before me involves a plaintiff and three codefendants. The plaintiff has applied to the court for an order permitting her to question each defendant without their codefendants or their codefendants' legal counsel being present. Two of the codefendants, however, share the same legal counsel. The court will not order any codefendant to find new legal counsel. Therefore, the order requested by the plaintiff cannot be granted.

The conclusion of the judge's argument is most strongly supported if which one of the following principles is assumed to hold?

(A) A court cannot issue an order that forces legal counsel to disclose information revealed by a client.

(B) Defendants have the right to have their legal counsel present when being questioned.

(C) People being questioned in legal proceedings may refuse to answer questions that are self-incriminating.

(D) A plaintiff in a legal case should never be granted a right that is denied to a defendant.

(E) A defendant's legal counsel has the right to question the plaintiff.

6. The calm, shallow waters of coastal estuaries are easily polluted by nutrient-rich sewage. When estuary waters become overnutrified as a result, algae proliferate. The abundant algae, in turn, sometimes provide a rich food source for microorganisms that are toxic to fish, thereby killing most of the fish in the estuary.

Which one of the following can be properly inferred from the information above?

(A) Fish in an estuary that has been polluted by sewage are generally more likely to die from pollution than are fish in an estuary that has been polluted in some other way.

(B) In estuary waters that contain abundant algae, microorganisms that are toxic to fish reproduce more quickly than other types of microorganisms.

(C) Nutrients and other components of sewage do not harm fish in coastal estuaries in any way other than through the resulting proliferation of toxic microorganisms.

(D) Algae will not proliferate in coastal estuaries that are not polluted by nutrient-rich sewage.

(E) Overnutrifying estuary waters by sewage can result in the death of most of the fish in the estuary.

GO ON TO THE NEXT PAGE.

Part Three: Logical Reasoning
CHAPTER 12

Explanations to these questions
can be found in your Online Center.

7. The ruins of the prehistoric Bolivian city of Tiwanaku feature green andacite stones weighing up to 40 tons. These stones were quarried at Copacabana, which is across a lake and about 90 kilometers away. Archaeologists hypothesize that the stones were brought to Tiwanaku on reed boats. To show this was possible, experimenters transported a 9-ton stone from Copacabana to Tiwanaku using a reed boat built with locally available materials and techniques traditional to the area.

Which one of the following would be most useful to know in order to evaluate the support for the archaeologists' hypothesis?

(A) whether the traditional techniques for building reed boats were in use at the time Tiwanaku was inhabited
(B) whether green andacite stones quarried at the time Tiwanaku was inhabited were used at any sites near Copacabana
(C) whether reed boats are commonly used today on the lake
(D) whether the green andacite stones at Tiwanaku are the largest stones at the site
(E) whether the reed boat built for the experimenters is durable enough to remain usable for several years

8. Union member: Some members of our labor union are calling for an immediate strike. But a strike would cut into our strike fund and would in addition lead to a steep fine, causing us to suffer a major financial loss. Therefore, we must not strike now.

The union member's argument is most vulnerable to criticism on the grounds that it

(A) fails to consider that a strike might cause the union to suffer a financial loss even if no fine were imposed
(B) fails to define adequately what constitutes a major financial loss
(C) fails to consider that the benefits to be gained from a strike might outweigh the costs
(D) takes for granted that the most important factor in the labor union's bargaining position is the union's financial strength
(E) fails to establish that there will be a better opportunity to strike at a later time

9. Birds and mammals can be infected with West Nile virus only through mosquito bites. Mosquitoes, in turn, become infected with the virus when they bite certain infected birds or mammals. The virus was originally detected in northern Africa and spread to North America in the 1990s. Humans sometimes catch West Nile virus, but the virus never becomes abundant enough in human blood to infect a mosquito.

The statements above, if true, most strongly support which one of the following?

(A) West Nile virus will never be a common disease among humans.
(B) West Nile virus is most common in those parts of North America with the highest density of mosquitoes.
(C) Some people who become infected with West Nile virus never show symptoms of illness.
(D) West Nile virus infects more people in northern Africa than it does in North America.
(E) West Nile virus was not carried to North America via an infected person.

10. In trying to reduce the amount of fat in their diet, on average people have decreased their consumption of red meat by one-half in the last two decades. However, on average those who have reduced their consumption of red meat actually consume substantially more fat than those who have not.

Which one of the following, if true, most helps to resolve the apparent discrepancy described above?

(A) Many more people have reduced their consumption of red meat over the last two decades than have not.
(B) Higher prices over the last two decades have done as much to decrease the consumption of red meat as health concerns have.
(C) People who reduce their consumption of red meat tend to consume as much of other foods that are high in fat as do those who have not reduced their consumption of red meat.
(D) People who reduce their consumption of red meat tend to replace it with cheese and baked goods, which are richer in fat than red meat.
(E) Studies have shown that red meat contains slightly less fat than previously thought.

GO ON TO THE NEXT PAGE.

Explanations to these questions can be found in your Online Center.

Part Three: Logical Reasoning
Logical Reasoning: Managing the Section   K

11. Rolanda: The house on Oak Avenue has a larger yard than any other house we've looked at in Prairieview, so that's the best one to rent.

    Tom: No, it isn't. Its yard isn't really as big as it looks. Property lines in Prairieview actually start 20 feet from the street. So what looks like part of the yard is really city property.

    Rolanda: But that's true of all the other properties we've looked at too!

    Rolanda's response to Tom suggests that Tom commits which one of the following reasoning errors?

    (A) He fails to take into account the possibility that there are advantages to having a small yard.
    (B) He presumes, without providing justification, that property that belongs to the city is available for private use.
    (C) He improperly applies a generalization to an instance that it was not intended to cover.
    (D) He fails to apply a general rule to all relevant instances.
    (E) He presumes, without providing justification, that whatever is true of a part of a thing is also true of the whole.

12. The best jazz singers use their voices much as horn players use their instruments. The great Billie Holiday thought of her singing voice as a horn, reshaping melody and words to increase their impact. Conversely, jazz horn players achieve their distinctive sounds by emulating the spontaneous twists and turns of an impassioned voice. So jazz consists largely of voicelike horns and hornlike voices.

    Which one of the following most accurately describes the role played in the argument by the claim that the best jazz singers use their voices much as horn players use their instruments?

    (A) It is the argument's main conclusion and is supported by another statement, which is itself supported by a further statement.
    (B) It is the argument's only conclusion, and each of the other statements in the argument is used to support it.
    (C) It is a statement for which some evidence is provided and which in turn is used to provide support for the argument's main conclusion.
    (D) It is a statement for which no evidence is provided but which itself is used to support the argument's only conclusion.
    (E) It is a statement used to support a conclusion that in turn is used to support the argument's main conclusion.

13. Educator: Reducing class sizes in our school district would require hiring more teachers. However, there is already a shortage of qualified teachers in the region. Although students receive more individualized instruction when classes are smaller, education suffers when teachers are underqualified. Therefore, reducing class sizes in our district would probably not improve overall student achievement.

    Which one of the following is an assumption required by the educator's argument?

    (A) Class sizes in the school district should be reduced only if doing so would improve overall student achievement.
    (B) At least some qualified teachers in the school district would be able to improve the overall achievement of students in their classes if class sizes were reduced.
    (C) Students place a greater value on having qualified teachers than on having smaller classes.
    (D) Hiring more teachers would not improve the achievement of any students in the school district if most or all of the teachers hired were underqualified.
    (E) Qualified teachers could not be persuaded to relocate in significant numbers to the educator's region to take teaching jobs.

14. Geographer: Because tropical storms require heat and moisture, they form especially over ocean surfaces of at least 26 degrees Celsius (79 degrees Fahrenheit), ocean temperatures that global warming would encourage. For this reason, many early discussions of global warming predicted that it would cause more frequent and intense tropical storms. But recent research shows that this prediction is unlikely to be borne out. Other factors, such as instabilities in wind flow, are likely to counteract global warming's effects on tropical storm development.

    Which one of the following most accurately expresses the conclusion drawn in the geographer's argument?

    (A) Tropical storms are especially likely to form over warm ocean surfaces.
    (B) Contrary to early discussions, global warming is not the only factor affecting the frequency and intensity of tropical storms.
    (C) If global warming were reversed, tropical storms would be less frequent and less intense.
    (D) Instabilities in wind flow will negate the effect of global warming on the formation of tropical storms.
    (E) Global warming probably will not produce more frequent and intense tropical storms.

GO ON TO THE NEXT PAGE.

K | Part Three: Logical Reasoning
       CHAPTER 12

Explanations to these questions
can be found in your Online Center.

15. Copyright was originally the grant of a temporary
    government-supported monopoly on copying a work.
    Its sole purpose was to encourage the circulation of
    ideas by giving authors the opportunity to derive a
    reasonable financial reward from their works. However,
    copyright sometimes goes beyond its original purpose
    since sometimes _____.

    The conclusion of the argument is most strongly
    supported if which one of the following completes the
    passage?

    (A) publication of copyrighted works is not the only
        way to circulate ideas
    (B) authors are willing to circulate their works even
        without any financial reward
    (C) authors are unable to find a publisher for their
        copyrighted work
    (D) there is no practical way to enforce copyrights
    (E) copyrights hold for many years after an
        author's death

16. Critic to economist: In yet another of your bumbling
    forecasts, last year you predicted that this country's
    economy would soon go into recession if current
    economic policies were not changed. Instead,
    economic growth is even stronger this year.

    Economist: There was nothing at all bumbling about
    my warning. Indeed, it convinced the country's
    leaders to change economic policies, which is
    what prevented a recession.

    The economist responds to the critic by

    (A) indicating that the state of affairs on which the
        economist's prediction was conditioned did
        not obtain
    (B) distinguishing between a prediction that has
        not yet turned out to be correct and one that
        has turned out to be incorrect
    (C) attempting to show that the critic's statements
        are mutually inconsistent
    (D) offering a particular counterexample to a
        general claim asserted by the critic
    (E) offering evidence against one of the critic's
        factual premises

17. Watching music videos from the 1970s would give the
    viewer the impression that the music of the time was
    dominated by synthesizer pop and punk rock. But this
    would be a misleading impression. Because music videos
    were a new art form at the time, they attracted primarily
    cutting-edge musicians.

    Which one of the following arguments is most similar
    in its reasoning to that of the argument above?

    (A) Our view of pre-printing-press literature can
        never be accurate, because the surviving works
        of ancient authors are those that were deemed
        by copyists most likely to be of interest to
        future readers.
    (B) Our memory of 1960s TV shows could hardly
        be improved, because so many of the television
        programs of the era are still rerun today.
    (C) Future generations' understanding of today's
        publishing trends will be distorted if they
        judge by works published in CD-ROM format,
        since it is primarily publishers interested in
        computer games that are using CD-ROM.
    (D) Our understanding of silent films is incomplete,
        because few filmmakers of the time realized
        that the film stock they were using would
        disintegrate over time.
    (E) Our notion of fashion trends will probably be
        accurate if we rely on TV fashion programs,
        despite the fact that these programs deliberately
        select the most outrageous outfits in order to
        get the viewers' attention.

18. Hospitals, universities, labor unions, and other
    institutions may well have public purposes and be quite
    successful at achieving them even though each of their
    individual staff members does what he or she does only
    for selfish reasons.

    Which one of the following generalizations is most
    clearly illustrated by the passage?

    (A) What is true of some social organizations is not
        necessarily true of all such organizations.
    (B) An organization can have a property that not all
        of its members possess.
    (C) People often claim altruistic motives for actions
        that are in fact selfish.
    (D) Many social institutions have social consequences
        unintended by those who founded them.
    (E) Often an instrument created for one purpose
        will be found to serve another purpose just as
        effectively.

GO ON TO THE NEXT PAGE.

Explanations to these questions can be found in your Online Center.

Part Three: Logical Reasoning
Logical Reasoning: Managing the Section

19. Consumer advocate: In some countries, certain produce is routinely irradiated with gamma rays in order to extend shelf life. There are, however, good reasons to avoid irradiated foods. First, they are exposed to the radioactive substances that produce the gamma rays. Second, irradiation can reduce the vitamin content of fresh foods, leaving behind harmful chemical residues. Third, irradiation spawns unique radiolytic products that cause serious health problems, including cancer.

Each of the following, if true, weakens the consumer advocate's argument EXCEPT:

(A) Unique radiolytic products have seldom been found in any irradiated food.
(B) Cancer and other serious health problems have many causes that are unrelated to radioactive substances and gamma rays.
(C) A study showed that irradiation leaves the vitamin content of virtually all fruits and vegetables unchanged.
(D) The amount of harmful chemicals found in irradiated foods is less than the amount that occurs naturally in most kinds of foods.
(E) A study showed that the cancer rate is no higher among people who eat irradiated food than among those who do not.

20. When teaching art students about the use of color, teachers should use colored paper rather than paint in their demonstrations. Colored paper is preferable because it readily permits a repeated use of exactly the same color in different compositions, which allows for a precise comparison of that color's impact in varying contexts. With paint, however, it is difficult to mix exactly the same color twice, and the varying textures of the applied paint can interfere with the pure effect of the color itself.

Which one of the following is an assumption required by the argument?

(A) Two pieces of paper of exactly the same color will have the same effect in a given context, even if they are of different textures.
(B) A slight difference in the color of two pieces of paper is more difficult to notice than a similar difference in the color of two samples of paint.
(C) Changing light conditions have less of an effect on the apparent color of a piece of paper than on the apparent color of a sample of paint.
(D) Observing the impacts of colors across varying contexts helps students to learn about the use of color.
(E) It is important that art students understand how the effects of using colored paper in various compositions differ from those of using paint in those compositions.

21. Philosopher: To explain the causes of cultural phenomena, a social scientist needs data about several societies: one cannot be sure, for example, that a given political structure is brought about only by certain ecological or climatic factors unless one knows that there are no similarly structured societies not subject to those factors, and no societies that, though subject to those factors, are not so structured.

The claim that to explain the causes of cultural phenomena, a social scientist needs data about several societies plays which one of the following roles in the philosopher's reasoning?

(A) It describes a problem that the philosopher claims is caused by the social scientist's need for certainty.
(B) It is a premise used to support a general theoretical claim about the nature of cause and effect relationships.
(C) It is a general hypothesis that is illustrated with an example showing that there is a causal relationship between political structures and environmental conditions.
(D) It is a dilemma that, it is argued, is faced by every social scientist because of the difficulty of determining whether a given cultural phenomenon is the cause or the effect of a given factor.
(E) It is a claim that the philosopher attempts to justify by appeal to the requirements for establishing the existence of one kind of causal relationship.

22. Scientist: Physicists claim that their system of careful peer review prevents scientific fraud in physics effectively. But biologists claimed the same thing for their field 20 years ago, and they turned out to be wrong. Since then, biologists have greatly enhanced their discipline's safeguards against scientific fraud, thus preventing further major incidents. It would be conducive to progress in physics if physicists were to do the same thing.

The conclusion of the scientist's argument is most strongly supported if which one of the following is assumed?

(A) Major incidents of scientific fraud in a scientific discipline are deleterious to progress in that discipline.
(B) Very few incidents of even minor scientific fraud have occurred in biology over the last 20 years.
(C) No system of careful peer review is completely effective in preventing scientific fraud in any scientific discipline.
(D) Twenty years ago the system of peer review in biology was less effective in preventing scientific fraud than the system of peer review in physics is today.
(E) Over the years, there have been relatively few, if any, major incidents of scientific fraud in physics.

GO ON TO THE NEXT PAGE.

859

K Part Three: Logical Reasoning
CHAPTER 12

Explanations to these questions
can be found in your Online Center.

23. Biologist: Researchers believe that dogs are the
descendants of domesticated wolves that were
bred to be better companions for humans. It has
recently been found that some breeds of dog are
much more closely related genetically to wolves
than to most other breeds of dog. This shows that
some dogs are descended from wolves that were
domesticated much more recently than others.

Which one of the following principles underlies the
biologist's argument?

(A) If one breed of dog is descended from wolves
that were domesticated more recently than
were the wolves from which most other breeds
of dog are descended, the former breed may
be more closely related to wolves than those
other breeds are.

(B) If one breed of dog is more closely related to
wolves than to another breed of dog, then the
former breed of dog has more recent
undomesticated wolf ancestors than the latter
breed has.

(C) Any breed of dog descended from wolves that
were domesticated is more closely related
genetically to at least some other breeds of
dog than to wolves.

(D) If one breed of dog is more closely related to
wolves than another breed of dog is, then the
former breed of dog is more closely related to
wolves than to the latter breed of dog.

(E) Any two breeds of dog that are more closely
related to each other than to wolves are both
descended from wolves that were domesticated
long ago.

24. Paleomycologists, scientists who study ancient forms
of fungi, are invariably acquainted with the scholarly
publications of all other paleomycologists.
Professor Mansour is acquainted with the scholarly
publications of Professor DeAngelis, who is a
paleomycologist. Therefore, Professor Mansour must
also be a paleomycologist.

The flawed pattern of reasoning in the argument above
is most similar to that in which one of the following
arguments?

(A) When a flight on Global Airlines is delayed,
all connecting Global Airlines flights are also
delayed so that the passengers can make their
connections. Since Frieda's connecting flight
on Global was delayed, her first flight must
have also been a delayed Global Airlines flight.

(B) Any time that one of Global Airlines' local
ticket agents misses a shift, the other agents
on that shift need to work harder than usual.
Since none of Global's local ticket agents
missed a shift last week, the airline's local
ticket agents did not have to work harder than
usual last week.

(C) Any time the price of fuel decreases, Global
Airlines' expenses decrease and its income is
unaffected. The price of fuel decreased several
times last year. Therefore, Global Airlines
must have made a profit last year.

(D) All employees of Global Airlines can participate
in its retirement plan after they have been with
the company a year or more. Gavin has been
with Global Airlines for three years. We can
therefore be sure that he participates in
Global's retirement plan.

(E) Whenever a competitor of Global Airlines
reduces its fares, Global must follow suit or
lose passengers. Global carried more passengers
last year than it did the year before. Therefore,
Global must have reduced its fares last year to
match reductions in its competitors' fares.

GO ON TO THE NEXT PAGE.

Explanations to these questions can be found in your Online Center.

Part Three: Logical Reasoning
Logical Reasoning: Managing the Section |

25. Lutsina: Because futuristic science fiction does not need to represent current social realities, its writers can envisage radically new social arrangements. Thus it has the potential to be a richer source of social criticism than is conventional fiction.

 Priscilla: That futuristic science fiction writers more skillfully envisage radically new technologies than new social arrangements shows how writers' imaginations are constrained by current realities. Because of this limitation, the most effective social criticism results from faithfully presenting the current social realities for critical examination, as happens in conventional fiction.

 Lutsina and Priscilla disagree with each other about whether

 (A) some science fiction writers have succeeded in envisaging convincing, radically new social arrangements
 (B) writers of conventional fiction are more skillful than are writers of futuristic science fiction
 (C) futuristic science fiction has more promise as a source of social criticism than does conventional fiction
 (D) envisaging radically new technologies rather than radically new social arrangements is a shortcoming of futuristic science fiction
 (E) criticism of current social arrangements is not effective when those arrangements are contrasted with radically different ones

26. Because our club recruited the best volleyball players in the city, we will have the best team in the city. Moreover, since the best team in the city will be the team most likely to win the city championship, our club will almost certainly be city champions this year.

 The reasoning in the argument is flawed because the argument

 (A) presumes, without presenting relevant evidence, that an entity can be distinguished as the best only on the basis of competition
 (B) predicts the success of an entity on the basis of features that are not relevant to the quality of that entity
 (C) predicts the outcome of a competition merely on the basis of a comparison between the parties in that competition
 (D) presumes, without providing warrant, that if an entity is the best among its competitors, then each individual part of that entity must also be the best
 (E) concludes that because an event is the most likely of a set of possible events, that event is more likely to occur than not

 PrepTest65 Sec4 Qs 1–26

S T O P

IF YOU FINISH BEFORE TIME IS CALLED, YOU MAY CHECK YOUR WORK ON THIS SECTION ONLY.
DO NOT WORK ON ANY OTHER SECTION IN THE TEST.

ANSWER KEY

PrepTest 65, Section 1

1. B
2. A
3. B
4. C
5. D
6. A
7. D
8. A
9. C
10. B
11. A
12. C
13. E
14. B
15. C
16. B
17. D
18. B
19. C
20. D
21. D
22. E
23. E
24. C
25. D

PrepTest 65, Section 4

1. C
2. E
3. D
4. B
5. B
6. E
7. A
8. C
9. E
10. D
11. D
12. C
13. E
14. E
15. E
16. A
17. C
18. B
19. B
20. D
21. E
22. A
23. B
24. A
25. C
26. E

Complete explanations for these questions can be found in your Online Center.

Reading Comprehension

Acknowledgment is made to the following sources from which material has been adapted for use in this book:

Michael J. Balick, *Plants, People, and Culture: The Science of Ethnobotany*. ©1996 by Scientific American Library.

Jerome Barron, *Freedom of the Press for Whom? The Right of Access to Mass Media*. ©1973 by Indiana University Press.

Marion de Boo, "Dutch Farmland: Back to Nature." ©1999 by the Stanley Foundation.

Clark R. Chapman, "Bombarding Mars Lately." ©1996 by Nature Publishing Group.

James P. Draper, ed., *Black Literature Criticism*. ©1992 by Gale Research Inc.

Philip Emeagwali, "The Ways of Counting." ©1991 by the Regents of the University of Michigan.

R. Buckminster Fuller, Foreword to *Isamu Noguchi: A Sculptor's World*. ©1968 by Harper & Row, Publishers, Inc.

Garrett Hardin, *Living Within Limits: Ecology, Economics, and Population Taboos*. ©1993 by Oxford University Press.

R. H. Helmholz, "The Roman Law of Blackmail." ©2001 by The University of Chicago Press.

Huw Jones, "Fractals Before Mandelbrot: A Selective History." ©1993 by Springer-Verlag New York Inc.

Larry Katzenstein, "Good Food You Can't Get." ©July 1993 by Reader's Digest.

Robin D. G. Kelley, "But a Local Phase of a World Problem: Black History's Global Vision, 1883–1950." ©1999 by the Organization of American Historians.

Alfred Lessing, "What Is Wrong With a Forgery?" in The Forger's Art. ©1983 by The Regents of the University of California.

James Lindgren, "Unraveling the Paradox of Blackmail." ©1984 by Columbia Law Review Association, Inc.

Judith C. May, "Letters to the Editor."©1997 by The New York Times.

Declan O'Flaherty, "Computer-Generated Displays in the Courtroom: For Better or Worse?" ©1996 by Declan O'Flaherty.

Holt N. Parker, "Women Doctors in Greece, Rome, and the Byzantine Empire." ©1997-2000 by The University Press of Kentucky.

David Pitts, "The Noble Endeavor: The Creation of the Universal Declaration of Human Rights." ©2001 by U.S. Department of State, Office of International Information Programs.

"A Radical Rethink." ©2003 by The Economist Newspaper Limited.

"Revealing Ancient Bolivia." ©2002 by the Archaeological Institute of America.

Ellen Rosand, "It Bears Repeating." ©1996 by Metropolitan Opera Guild, Inc.

Christopher D. Roy, *Art and Life in Africa: Selections from the Stanley Collection, Exhibitions of 1985 and 1992*. ©1992 by the University of Iowa Museum of Art.

"Shooting at Inflation." ©1996 by The Economist Newspaper Limited.

Karl Sigmund, Ernst Fehr, and Martin A. Nowak, "The Economics of Fair Play." ©2001 by Scientific American, Inc.

David Stainforth, et al., "Climateprediction.net: Design Principles for Public Resource Modeling Research." ©November 2002 by IASTED.

Jack Stark, "Teaching Statutory Law." ©1994 by the Association of American Law Schools.

Alexander Stille, "Overload." ©1999 by Condé Nast Publications, Inc.

Lourdes Torres, "The Construction of the Self in U.S. Latina Autobiographies." ©1991 by Indiana University Press.

Michael Tracey, "The Poisoned Chalice? International Television and the Idea of Dominance." ©1985 by the American Academy of Arts and Sciences.

CHAPTER 13

The Kaplan Reading Comprehension Method

Every administration of the LSAT features one scored Reading Comprehension section. While this section typically feels the most familiar to students who are new to the LSAT, it can also be the most difficult section in which to improve.

A STRATEGIC APPROACH TO READING COMPREHENSION

What many students fail to realize is that the structure and, to some extent, content of Reading Comprehension passages remains virtually unchanged from test to test. More importantly, the questions in this section test and reward the same reading and reasoning skills on every test. LSAT experts use this predictability to their advantage, and their goal in each passage is simple: Read the passage strategically, with an eye focused on opinions and structure, and then refer back to the text to answer specific questions.

As an example, take a look at this question stem from an LSAT Reading Comprehension section:

> The information in the passage suggests that the author
> would most likely agree with which one of the following
> statements regarding training in statutory law?
>
> *PrepTest59 Sec4 Q14*

The question stem asks the reader to identify the statement with which the author would most likely agree. But, based on what information? The stem is clear: based on the information *in the passage*.

LSAT STRATEGY

LSAT experts rely only on information presented in the passages to answer Reading Comprehension questions.

In this chapter, you'll see how an expert works through a passage and the accompanying questions using the Kaplan Reading Comprehension Method. In Chapter 14, you'll see a more detailed discussion of each of the five steps involved.

Reading Comprehension as an Expert Sees It

5 –28–   (5)   (5)   5

> An LSAT expert identifies signals in question stems that indicate question type.

A proficiency in understanding, applying, and even formulating statutes—the actual texts of laws enacted by legislative bodies—is a vital aspect of the practice
(5) of law, but statutory law is often given too little attention by law schools. Much of legal education, with its focus on judicial decisions and analysis of cases, can give a law student the impression that the practice of law consists mainly in analyzing past cases to
(10) determine their relevance to a client's situation and the speculative interpretation of the law relevant to the client's legal problem.

> *too little attn to statutory law in school*

> An LSAT expert circles or underlines Keywords to identify and organize structural elements and big-picture ideas in a passage.

Students discover fairly soon, however, that much of legal work does not depend on the kind of
(15) analysis of cases that is performed in law school. For example, a lawyer representing the owner of a business can often find an explicit answer as to what the client should do about a certain tax-related matter by studying the relevant statutes. In such a case
(20) the facts are clear and the statutes' relation to them transparent, so that the client's question can be answered by direct reference to the wording of the statutes. But statutes' meanings and their applicability to relevant situations are not always so obvious, and
(25) that is one reason that the ability to interpret them accurately is an essential skill for law students to learn.
Another skill that teaching statutory law would improve is synthesis. Law professors work hard at developing their students' ability to analyze individual
(30) cases, but in so doing they favor the ability to apply the law in particular cases over the ability to understand the interrelations among laws. In contrast, the study of all the statutes of a legal system in a particular field of the law would enable students to see how these
(35) laws form a coherent whole. Students would thus be able to apply this ability to interpret and synthesize statutory law that they could then call on in legal practice. This is especially important for those law students intend to specialize in fields that rely on
(40) the mastery of a complex body of statutes, such as tax law. One possible argument against including training in statutory law as a standard part of law school curricula is that many statutes vary from region to region within a nation, so that the mastery of a set of statutes would
(45) usually not be generally applicable. There is some truth to this objection; law schools that currently provide some training in statutes generally intend it as a preparation for practice in their particular region, but for schools that are nationally oriented, this could seem
(50) to be an inappropriate investment of time and resources. But while the knowledge of a particular region's statutory law is not generally transferable to other regions, the skills acquired in mastering a particular set of statutes are, making the study of
(55) statutory law an important undertaking even for law schools with a national orientation.

> *focus on cases misleading*

> *ex lawyer and shop owner*

> *statutes not always cut and dry and you must learn to interpret them*

> *must learn statutory synthesis*

> *Margin notes summarize content and opinions for quick research while answering questions. (Hint: Don't shy away from using symbols you already use in everyday life.)*

> *Discont-regional variation prevents gen. application*

> *A u still ok for nat'lly oriented schools b/c skills are the value, not specific stat. knowledge*

9. Which one of the following most accurately expresses the main point of the passage?

(A) In spite of the reservations that nationally oriented law schools can be expected to have, law schools can serve the overall needs of law students better by implementing a standard national curriculum in statutory law.

(B) Since the skills promoted by the study of statutory law are ultimately more important than those promoted by case analysis, the relative emphasis that law schools place on these two areas should be reversed.

(C) Although statutes typically vary from region to region, law schools should provide training in statutory law in order to develop students' ability to interpret...

(D) In...the most important assets that students can have.

(E) Law schools generally are deficient in their attention to statutory law training and therefore fail to impart the skills necessary for the analysis of legal information.

> *Always circle the correct answer to a question before moving on.*

10. Which one of the following is cited in the passage as a reason that might be given for not including statutory law training in law school curricula?

(A) Such training would...the far more important...ability to analyze...

(B) Such training is n...what is already p...school education...

(C) The goals of such training can better be achieved by other means, most of which are more directly related to the actual practice of law.

(D) Such training would be irrelevant for those students who do not plan to specialize.

(E) The lack of geographic uniformity among statutory laws makes expertise in the statutes of any particular region generally nontransferable.

> In addition to question type, pay attention to key information in a question stem that tells you where or what to research.

> Circle or underline the words that clearly identify a *wrong* answer before crossing it out and evaluating the next answer choice.

5   ⑤   5 –29– 5

 inf.

> Make a note about question type near the question stem if the stem does not explicitly state what the test is asking for.

11. Which one of the following would, if true, most weaken the author's argument as expressed in the passage?

(A) Many law school administrators recommend the i...

> Cross out answer choices that are definitely incorrect, but leave challenging or ambiguous-sounding answer choices unmarked so you can reevaluate them later. Returning to debate between two potential answer choices is preferable to debating among five.

(B) Most ... profi... expe...

(C) Mos... geog... scho...

(D) The c... scho...

(E) Most ... statutory law are thoroughly familiar with only a narrow range of statutes.

12. The author discusses the skill of synthesis in the third paragraph primarily in order to

(A) identify and describe one of the benefits that the author says would result from the change that is advocated in the passage

(B) indi... oth... this...

> An LSAT expert will not hesitate to circle an answer choice that perfectly matches her prediction and then move on without reading the remaining choices. The LSAT rewards this type of bold behavior.

(C) argu... con... ear...

(D) expl... of ...

(E) prov... typ...

13. Which one of the following questions can be most clearly and directly answered by reference to information in the passage?

(A) What are some ways in which synthetic skills are strengthened or encouraged through the analysis of cases and judicial decisions?

(B) In which areas of legal practice is a proficiency in case analysis more valuable than a proficiency in statutory law?

(C) What skills are common to the study of both statutory law and judicial decisions?

(D) What are some objections that have been raised against including the regionally oriented...

(E) What is the primary ... currently offered in...

> An LSAT expert knows how to identify challenging or time-consuming questions. To maximize the number of questions you get correct, you may need to sacrifice a hard question early on to have time for two or three questions later.

14. The information in the passage suggests that the author would most likely agree with which one of the following statements regarding training in statutory law?

(A) While nationally oriented law schools have been deficient in statutory law training, most regionally oriented law schools have been equally deficient in the teaching of case law.

(B) Training in statutory law would help lawyers resolve legal questions for which the answers are not immediately apparent in the relevant statutes.

(C) Lawyers who are trained in statutory law typically also develop a higher level of efficiency in manipulating details of past cases as compared with lawyers who are not trained in this way.

(D) Courses in statutory l... focus specifically on ... region or in a particu...

> Always note words in question stems that appear in all caps. These words can be easy to overlook or forget.

(E) Lawyers who do not ... little need for trainin... brief introduction to...

15. Each of the following conforms to the kinds of educational results that the author would expect from the course of action proposed in the passage EXCEPT:

(A) skill in locating references to court decisions on an issue involving a particular statute regarding taxation

(B) an understanding of the ways in which certain underl... interrelated gr...

> After choosing an answer, circle particularly challenging questions that you may want to come back to once all the other questions in a section have been answered.

(C) a knowledge of ... formulated

(D) familiarity with ... of laws apply... region or loca...

(E) an appreciation ... involved in dr...

PrepTest59 Sec4 Qs 9–15

GO ON TO THE NEXT PAGE.

The Kaplan Reading Comprehension Method

The work modeled on the preceding pages is the result of an LSAT expert using the Kaplan Reading Comprehension Method. This approach provides a consistent, strategic way to approach each passage and every question you see in the LSAT Reading Comprehension section.

THE KAPLAN READING COMPREHENSION METHOD

Step 1: Read the Passage Strategically—Circle Keywords and jot down margin notes to summarize portions of the passage relevant to LSAT questions; summarize the author's Topic/Scope/Purpose/Main Idea.

Step 2: Read the Question Stem—Identify the question type, characterize the correct and incorrect answers, and look for clues to guide your research.

Step 3: Research the Relevant Text—Based on the clues in the question stem, consult your Roadmap; for open-ended questions, refer to your Topic/Scope/Purpose/Main Idea summaries.

Step 4: Predict the Correct Answer—Based on research, predict the meaning of the correct answer; for open-ended questions, consult your Topic/Scope/Purpose/Main Idea summaries.

Step 5: Evaluate the Answer Choices—Select the choice that matches your prediction of the correct answer, or eliminate the four wrong answer choices.

Step 1: Read the Passage Strategically

To do well in the Reading Comprehension section of the LSAT, it's imperative to read strategically.

> **Strategic reading:** focusing on Keywords and phrases to determine the structure of a passage and to identify the author's Purpose and Main Idea.

Contrast this approach to the way you typically read academic materials for a college course. You won't answer many LSAT Reading Comprehension questions by focusing on details in a passage; instead, you win points by understanding *why* details are used.

When tackling the passages in the Reading Comprehension section, experts focus on two things:

1) Creating a **Roadmap** for each passage that highlights the main points of each paragraph, as well as areas of conflict or contrast
2) Understanding a passage's **big picture** by noting the Topic, Scope, Purpose, and Main Idea of each passage

The Physical Roadmap—Keywords and Margin Notes

The LSAT expert reads with pencil in hand, allowing her to circle or underline Keywords, words that indicate the structure of the passage and the author's Purpose. Keywords fall into six categories.

LSAT STRATEGY

Strategic Reading Keywords

Emphasis/Opinion—Words that signal that an author finds a detail noteworthy or has a positive or negative opinion about the detail; any subjective or evaluative language on the author's part (e.g., *especially, crucial, unfortunately, disappointing, I suggest, it seems likely*)

Contrast—Words indicating that the author thinks two details or ideas are incompatible or illustrate conflicting points (e.g., *but, yet, despite, on the other hand*)

Logic—Words that indicate an argument, either the author's or someone else's (e.g., *thus, therefore, because*)

Illustration—Words indicating an example offered to clarify or support a point (e.g., *for example, this shows, to illustrate*)

Sequence/Chronology—Words showing steps in a process or developments over time (e.g., *traditionally, in the past, today, first, second, finally, earlier, since*)

Continuation—Words indicating that a subsequent example or detail supports the same point or illustrates the same idea (e.g., *moreover, in addition, and, also, further*)

As the LSAT expert reads a passage strategically, she also makes brief, abbreviated notes to indicate important points in the text, points to which she is likely to return when answering the questions.

The Mental Roadmap—Summarizing Topic/Scope/Purpose/Main Idea

While the expert's pencil is circling Keywords and jotting down margin notes, her mind is also keeping track of the author's big picture, building a summary of the passage as she reads. There are four concepts involved in the big picture.

LSAT STRATEGY

Reading Comprehension—The Big Picture

Topic—The overall subject of the passage

Scope—The particular aspect of the Topic on which the author focuses

Purpose—The author's reason for writing the passage (express this as a verb—e.g., *to refute*, *to outline*, *to evaluate*, *to critique*)

Main Idea—The author's conclusion or overall takeaway; if you combine the author's Purpose and Scope, you'll usually have a good sense of his Main Idea

---

On Test Day, there is no reason to write down your big-picture summaries. Just make sure you can articulate the author's Purpose and Main Idea within the Scope of the passage so that you can predict the correct answers to Global questions and Inference questions that reward an understanding of the author's overall point of view.

Try reading a passage strategically, focusing on Keywords and the big-picture summaries. Don't worry if you're not fast or confident with this approach yet. You'll have many opportunities to practice and refine this approach as you learn to master Reading Comprehension.

A proficiency in understanding, applying, and even formulating statutes—the actual texts of laws enacted by legislative bodies—is a vital aspect of the practice of law, but statutory law is often given too little
(5) attention by law schools. Much of legal education, with its focus on judicial decisions and analysis of cases, can give a law student the impression that the practice of law consists mainly in analyzing past cases to determine their relevance to a client's situation and
(10) arriving at a speculative interpretation of the law relevant to the client's legal problem.

Lawyers discover fairly soon, however, that much of their practice does not depend on the kind of painstaking analysis of cases that is performed in law
(15) school. For example, a lawyer representing the owner of a business can often find an explicit answer as to what the client should do about a certain tax-related issue by consulting the relevant statutes. In such a case the facts are clear and the statutes' relation to them
(20) transparent, so that the client's question can be answered by direct reference to the wording of the statutes. But statutes' meanings and their applicability to relevant situations are not always so obvious, and that is one reason that the ability to interpret them
(25) accurately is an essential skill for law students to learn.

Another skill that teaching statutory law would improve is synthesis. Law professors work hard at developing their students' ability to analyze individual cases, but in so doing they favor the ability to apply the
(30) law in particular cases over the ability to understand the interrelations among laws. In contrast, the study of all the statutes of a legal system in a certain small area of the law would enable the student to see how these laws form a coherent whole. Students would then be
(35) able to apply this ability to synthesize in other areas of statutory law that they encounter in their study or practice. This is especially important because most students intend to specialize in a chosen area, or areas, of the law.
(40) One possible argument against including training in statutory law as a standard part of law school curricula is that many statutes vary from region to region within a nation, so that the mastery of a set of statutes would usually not be generally applicable. There is some truth
(45) to this objection; law schools that currently provide some training in statutes generally intend it as a preparation for practice in their particular region, but for schools that are nationally oriented, this could seem to be an inappropriate investment of time and
(50) resources. But while the knowledge of a particular region's statutory law is not generally transferable to other regions, the skills acquired in mastering a particular set of statutes are, making the study of statutory law an important undertaking even for law
(55) schools with a national orientation.

On the next page, review an LSAT expert's work on that passage. In Reading Comprehension expert analyses, the Analysis column will reflect the expert's internal monologue as he reads, paraphrases, and summarizes.

PrepTest59 Sec4 Qs 9–15

A proficiency in understanding, applying, and even formulating statutes—the actual texts of laws enacted by legislative bodies—is a |vital| aspect of the practice of law, |but| statutory law is often given |too little| attention by law schools. Much of legal education, with its focus on judicial decisions and analysis of cases, can give a law student the impression that the practice of law consists mainly in analyzing past cases to determine their relevance to a client's situation and (10) arriving at a speculative interpretation of the law relevant to the client's legal problem.

Too little attn to statutory law in law school

Focus on cases misleading

Proficiency with statutes is very important for the practice of law, *but* law schools pay them little attention. Law schools focus on case law, giving students the impression that applying past cases is what legal practice is all about. **Topic:** legal education. **Scope:** the (too limited) role of statutory law. The passage is likely to further explain the importance of statutory law and may suggest how legal education should emphasize it.

Lawyers discover fairly soon, |however,| that much of their practice |does not depend| on the kind of painstaking analysis of cases that is performed in law (15) school. |For example,| a lawyer representing the owner of a business can often find an explicit answer as to what the client should do about a certain tax-related issue by consulting the relevant statutes. In such a case the facts are clear and the statutes' relation to them (20) transparent, so that the client's question can be answered by direct reference to the wording of the statutes. |But| statutes' meanings and their applicability to relevant situations are not always so obvious, and |that is one reason| that the ability to interpret them (25) accurately is an |essential| skill for law students to learn.

Ex. lawyer and shop owner

Statutes not always so cut and dry – must learn to interpret them

Despite the focus on case law in law school, lawyers in practice, soon discover statutes are crucial. A lengthy example: A lawyer uses statutes to advise a client with tax issues. Statutes are not always clear; law students should learn how to interpret them.

|Another| skill that teaching statutory law would improve is synthesis. Law professors work hard at developing their students' ability to analyze individual cases, |but| in so doing they favor the ability to apply the (30) law in particular cases over the ability to understand the interrelations among laws. |In contrast,| the study of all the statutes of a legal system in a certain small area of the law would enable the student to see how these laws form a coherent whole. Students would then be (35) able to apply this ability to synthesize in other areas of statutory law that they encounter in their study or practice. This is |especially important| |because| most students intend to specialize in a chosen area, or areas, of the law.

Must learn statutory synthesis

Seeing coherent whole is beneficial

b/c of specialization

Another statutory law skill law students should learn: synthesizing laws. Law professors emphasize application of cases *instead of* interrelationship among laws. Author: Law schools should, in contrast, teach statutory interpretation in a small area of law to teach the skill; then students will learn to apply it in other areas, and this is *especially important* because students intend to specialize in practice.

(40) |One possible argument against| including training in statutory law as a standard part of law school curricula is that many statutes vary from region to region within a nation, so that the mastery of a set of statutes would usually not be generally applicable. There is |some truth| (45) |to this objection;| law schools that currently provide some training in statutes generally intend it as a preparation for practice in their particular region, |but| for schools that are nationally oriented, this could seem to be an |inappropriate| investment of time and (50) resources. |But| while the knowledge of a particular region's statutory law is not generally transferable to other regions, the skills acquired in mastering a particular set of statutes are, making the study of statutory law an |important| undertaking |even| for law (55) schools with a national orientation.

Dissent- regional variation prevents general application

Auth – still Ok for nat'lly oriented schools b/c skills are the value, not the specific statutory knowledge

A possible argument against teaching more statutory law: Statutes vary regionally or state-to-state. The author acknowledges *some truth* to objection, particularly for national law schools. Author: *But* the objection is limited to the content of local statutes, *not* to the *skills* involved in interpreting and synthesizing statutes. Thus, the author's **Purpose** is to discuss/outline the value of increasing statutory law curriculum in law school, and his **Main Idea** is that skills acquired in studying statutory law are, even acknowledging reasonable objections, important enough to justify a greater emphasis in law school.

Steps 2 through 5: Answering Reading Comprehension Questions

After an LSAT expert has read a Reading Comprehension passage, noting the structure and summarizing the big picture, she turns to Steps 2 through 5 of the Reading Comprehension Method for a consistent, effective, and efficient approach to the questions.

Take a look at how an LSAT expert would approach the first question associated with the Statutory Law passage.

LSAT Question	Analysis
Which one of the following most accurately expresses the main point of the passage? $\longrightarrow$	**Step 2:** This asks for the Main Idea of the entire passage, so it's a Global question.
	Step 3: Consult the big picture Main Idea summary.
	Step 4: The author's Main Idea was identified in paragraph 4: Despite some objections, statutory law should be a larger focus of curriculum in both regional and national law schools. Find a match in the answer choices.
(A) In spite of the reservations that nationally oriented law schools can be expected to have, law schools can serve the overall needs of law students better by implementing a standard national curriculum in statutory law. $\longrightarrow$	**Step 5:** Author never suggests that statutory law curriculum needs to be standardized nationally. Eliminate.
(B) Since the skills promoted by the study of statutory law are ultimately more important than those promoted by case analysis, the relative emphasis that law schools place on these two areas should be reversed. $\longrightarrow$	Distortion. Although the author would like to see law schools teach more statutory law, she never suggests a flip in curriculum from case analysis to statutory law. Eliminate.
(C) Although statutes typically vary from region to region, law schools should provide training in statutory law in order to develop students' ability to synthesize legal information and interpret individual statutes. $\longrightarrow$	Correct. This matches the prediction.
(D) In the theoretical world of law school training, as opposed to the actual practice of law, a proficiency in case law is often one of the most important assets that students can have. $\longrightarrow$	While this statement might be true, it is certainly not vital enough to the passage to be the main point. The scope here is much too narrow. Eliminate.
(E) Law schools generally are deficient in their attention to statutory law training and therefore fail to impart the skills necessary for the analysis of legal information. $\longrightarrow$	Extreme. Law schools "fail to impart the skills necessary" is excessive. Eliminate.

PrepTest59 Sec4 Q9

A proficiency in understanding, applying, and even formulating statutes—the actual texts of laws enacted by legislative bodies—is a |vital| aspect of the practice of law, |but| statutory law is often given |too little|
(5) attention by law schools. Much of legal education, with its focus on judicial decisions and analysis of cases, can give a law student the impression that the practice of law consists mainly in analyzing past cases to determine their relevance to a client's situation and
(10) arriving at a speculative interpretation of the law relevant to the client's legal problem.

Too little attn to statutory law in law school

Focus on cases misleading

> Proficiency with statutes is very important for the practice of law, *but* law schools pay them little attention. Law schools focus on case law, giving students the impression that applying past cases is what legal practice is all about. **Topic:** legal education. **Scope:** the (too limited) role of statutory law. The passage is likely to further explain the importance of statutory law and may suggest how legal education should emphasize it.

Lawyers discover fairly soon, |however,| that much of their practice |does not depend| on the kind of painstaking analysis of cases that is performed in law
(15) school. |For example,| a lawyer representing the owner of a business can often find an explicit answer as to what the client should do about a certain tax-related issue by consulting the relevant statutes. In such a case the facts are clear and the statutes' relation to them
(20) transparent, so that the client's question can be answered by direct reference to the wording of the statutes. |But| statutes' meanings and their applicability to relevant situations are not always so obvious, and |that is one reason| that the ability to interpret them
(25) accurately is an |essential| skill for law students to learn.

Ex. lawyer and shop owner

Statutes not always so cut and dry – must learn to interpret them

> Despite the focus on case law in law school, lawyers in practice, soon discover statutes are crucial. A lengthy example: A lawyer uses statutes to advise a client with tax issues. Statutes are not always clear; law students should learn how to interpret them.

|Another| skill that teaching statutory law would improve is synthesis. Law professors work hard at developing their students' ability to analyze individual cases, |but| in so doing they favor the ability to apply the
(30) law in particular cases over the ability to understand the interrelations among laws. |In contrast,| the study of all the statutes of a legal system in a certain small area of the law would enable the student to see how these laws form a coherent whole. Students would then be
(35) able to apply this ability to synthesize in other areas of statutory law that they encounter in their study or practice. This is |especially important| because most students intend to specialize in a chosen area, or areas, of the law.

Must learn statutory synthesis

Seeing coherent whole is beneficial

b/c of specialization

> Another statutory law skill law students should learn: synthesizing laws. Law professors emphasize application of cases *instead of* interrelationship among laws. Author: Law schools should, in contrast, teach statutory interpretation in a small area of law to teach the skill; then students will learn to apply it in other areas, and this is *especially important* because students intend to specialize in practice.

(40) |One possible argument against| including training in statutory law as a standard part of law school curricula is that many statutes vary from region to region within a nation, so that the mastery of a set of statutes would |usually not| be generally applicable. There is |some truth|
(45) |to this objection;| law schools that currently provide some training in statutes generally intend it as a preparation for practice in their particular region, |but| for schools that are nationally oriented, this could seem to be an |inappropriate| investment of time and
(50) resources. But while the knowledge of a particular region's statutory law is not generally transferable to other regions, the skills acquired in mastering a particular set of statutes are, making the study of statutory law an |important| undertaking |even| for law
(55) schools with a national orientation.

Dissent– regional variation prevents general application

Auth – still Ok for nat'lly oriented schools b/c skills are the value, not the specific statutory knowledge

> A possible argument against teaching more statutory law: Statutes vary regionally or state-to-state. The author acknowledges *some truth* to objection, particularly for national law schools. Author: *But* the objection is limited to the content of local statutes, *not* to the *skills* involved in interpreting and synthesizing statutes. Thus, the author's **Purpose** is to discuss/outline the value of increasing statutory law curriculum in law school, and his **Main Idea** is that skills acquired in studying statutory law are, even acknowledging reasonable objections, important enough to justify a greater emphasis in law school.

THE KAPLAN READING COMPREHENSION METHOD

Step 1: Read the passage strategically.

Step 2: Identify the question type.

Step 3: Research a specific part of the passage or the big picture summaries.

Step 4: Make an informed prediction.

Step 5: Select the closest match.

Not all questions types will ask you about the entire passage. Some, like this one, will ask you about specific information included in the passage. Luckily, the LSAT is an open book test. In Step 3, refer back to the passage. Try that now.

LSAT Question	My Analysis
1. Which one of the following is cited in the passage as a reason that might be given for not including statutory law training in law school curricula? →	**Step 2:**
	Step 3:
	Step 4:
(A) Such training would divert resources away from the far more important development of the ability to analyze cases. →	**Step 5:**
(B) Such training is not essentially different from what is already provided in the core areas of law school education. →	
(C) The goals of such training can better be achieved by other means, most of which are more directly related to the actual practice of law. →	
(D) Such training would be irrelevant for those students who do not plan to specialize. →	
(E) The lack of geographic uniformity among statutory laws makes expertise in the statutes of any particular region generally nontransferable. →	

PrepTest59 Sec4 Q10

By consulting the passage before looking through answer choices, an expert is able to make an excellent prediction.

LSAT Question	Analysis
1. Which one of the following is cited in the passage as a reason that might be given for not including statutory law training in law school curricula? →	**Step 2:** "Which of the following is cited in the passage," indicates that this is a Detail question.
	Step 3: Paragraph 4 introduces a possible objection to teaching statutory law (lines 40–50): a focus on regional statutes may not be appropriate for national law schools.
	Step 4: Look for an answer choice that restates the objection raised in lines 40–50.
(A) Such training would divert resources away from the far more important development of the ability to analyze cases. →	**Step 5:** Outside the Scope. The author doesn't mention this concern at all in the passage. Eliminate.
(B) Such training is not essentially different from what is already provided in the core areas of law school education. →	180. This contradicts the primary scope of the entire passage. Eliminate.
(C) The goals of such training can better be achieved by other means, most of which are more directly related to the actual practice of law. →	"[O]ther means" are Outside the Scope, so this is unsupported by the passage. Eliminate.
(D) Such training would be irrelevant for those students who do not plan to specialize. →	Extreme/Distortion. The use of the word "irrelevant" is stronger than warranted by the passage, which notes regional differences in statutes. In Paragraph 3, the author says learning statutory analysis would benefit those who plan to specialize. Eliminate.
(E) The lack of geographic uniformity among statutory laws makes expertise in the statutes of any particular region generally nontransferable. → *PrepTest59 Sec4 Q10*	Correct. This choice hews closely to the prediction and accurately paraphrases the objection raised in Paragraph 4.

Common Reading Comprehension Wrong Answer Types

The previous question illustrated how having a solid prediction for each question is key to success in the Reading Comprehension section. But note that, as elsewhere on the LSAT, the expert has another tool for evaluating the answer choices: recognizing wrong answer types.

The common wrong answers in Reading Comprehension are generally quite similar to those in Logical Reasoning.

LSAT STRATEGY

Reading Comprehension—Wrong Answer Types

Outside the Scope—A choice containing a statement that is too broad, too narrow, or beyond the purview of the passage

Extreme—A choice containing language too emphatic (*all, never, every, none*) to be supported by the passage

Distortion—A choice that mentions details or ideas from the passage but mangles or misstates the relationship between them as given or implied by the author

180—A choice that directly contradicts what the correct answer must say

Faulty Use of Detail—A choice that accurately states something from the passage but in a manner that incorrectly answers the question

Half-Right/Half-Wrong—A choice in which one clause follows from the passage but another clause contradicts or distorts the passage

Practice

Now answer the rest of the questions associated with this passage. Refer to the Roadmap and big-picture summaries on this page, and use Steps 2 through 5 to tackle each question.

A proficiency in understanding, applying, and even formulating statutes—the actual texts of laws enacted by legislative bodies—is a vital aspect of the practice of law, but statutory law is often given too little
(5)   attention by law schools. Much of legal education, with its focus on judicial decisions and analysis of cases, can give a law student the impression that the practice of law consists mainly in analyzing past cases to determine their relevance to a client's situation and
(10)   arriving at a speculative interpretation of the law relevant to the client's legal problem.
      Lawyers discover fairly soon, however, that much of their practice does not depend on the kind of painstaking analysis of cases that is performed in law
(15)   school. For example, a lawyer representing the owner of a business can often find an explicit answer as to what the client should do about a certain tax-related issue by consulting the relevant statutes. In such a case the facts are clear and the statutes' relation to them
(20)   transparent, so that the client's question can be answered by direct reference to the wording of the statutes. But statutes' meanings and their applicability to relevant situations are not always so obvious, and that is one reason that the ability to interpret them
(25)   accurately is an essential skill for law students to learn.
      Another skill that teaching statutory law would improve is synthesis. Law professors work hard at developing their students' ability to analyze individual cases, but in so doing they favor the ability to apply the
(30)   law in particular cases over the ability to understand the interrelations among laws. In contrast, the study of all the statutes of a legal system in a certain small area of the law would enable the student to see how these laws form a coherent whole. Students would then be
(35)   able to apply this ability to synthesize in other areas of statutory law that they encounter in their study or practice. This is especially important because most students intend to specialize in a chosen area, or areas, of the law.
(40)   One possible argument against including training in statutory law as a standard part of law school curricula is that many statutes vary from region to region within a nation, so that the mastery of a set of statutes would usually not be generally applicable. There is some truth
(45)   to this objection; law schools that currently provide some training in statutes generally intend it as a preparation for practice in their particular region, but for schools that are nationally oriented, this could seem to be an inappropriate investment of time and
(50)   resources. But while the knowledge of a particular region's statutory law is not generally transferable to other regions, the skills acquired in mastering a particular set of statutes are, making the study of statutory law an important undertaking even for law
(55)   schools with a national orientation.

Too little attn to statutory law in law school

Focus on cases misleading

Ex. lawyer and shop owner

Statutes not always so cut and dry — must learn to interpret them

Must learn statutory synthesis

Seeing coherent whole is beneficial

b/c of specialization

Dissent — regional variation prevents general application

Auth — still OK for nat'lly oriented schools b/c skills are the value, not the specific statutory knowledge

---

Topic: Legal education

Scope: The limited coverage of statutory law in law school curricula

Purpose: To discuss or illustrate the value of increasing the emphasis on statutory law in law school curriculum

Main Idea: The skills gained in studying statutory law are important enough to legal practice to overcome objections and justify an increased emphasis on statutory law in law school.

LSAT Question			**My Analysis**
2.	Which one of the following would, if true, most weaken the author's argument as expressed in the passage?	→	**Step 2:**
			Step 3:
			Step 4:
(A)	Many law school administrators recommend the inclusion of statutory law training in the curricula of their schools.	→	**Step 5:**
(B)	Most lawyers easily and quickly develop proficiency in statutory law through their work experiences after law school.	→	
(C)	Most lawyers do not practice law in the same geographic area in which they attended law school.	→	
(D)	The curricula of many regionally oriented law schools rely primarily on analysis of cases.	→	
(E)	Most lawyers who have undergone training in statutory law are thoroughly familiar with only a narrow range of statutes.	→	

PrepTest59 Sec4 Q11

3.	The author discusses the skill of synthesis in the third paragraph primarily in order to	→	**Step 2:**
			Step 3:
			Step 4:
(A)	identify and describe one of the benefits that the author says would result from the change that is advocated in the passage	→	**Step 5:**
(B)	indicate that law schools currently value certain other skills over this skill and explain why this is so	→	
(C)	argue for the greater importance of this skill as compared with certain others that are discussed earlier in the passage	→	
(D)	explain why this skill is necessary for the study of statutory law	→	
(E)	provide an example of the type of problem typically encountered in the practice of law	→	

PrepTest59 Sec4 Q12

879

A proficiency in understanding, applying, and even
formulating statutes—the actual texts of laws enacted
by legislative bodies—is a vital aspect of the practice
of law, but statutory law is often given too little

(5)   attention by law schools. Much of legal education, with
its focus on judicial decisions and analysis of cases,
can give a law student the impression that the practice
of law consists mainly in analyzing past cases to
determine their relevance to a client's situation and

(10)   arriving at a speculative interpretation of the law
relevant to the client's legal problem.
       Lawyers discover fairly soon, however, that much
of their practice does not depend on the kind of
painstaking analysis of cases that is performed in law

(15)   school. For example, a lawyer representing the owner
of a business can often find an explicit answer as to
what the client should do about a certain tax-related
issue by consulting the relevant statutes. In such a case
the facts are clear and the statutes' relation to them

(20)   transparent, so that the client's question can be
answered by direct reference to the wording of the
statutes. But statutes' meanings and their applicability
to relevant situations are not always so obvious, and
that is one reason that the ability to interpret them

(25)   accurately is an essential skill for law students to learn.
       Another skill that teaching statutory law would
improve is synthesis. Law professors work hard at
developing their students' ability to analyze individual
cases, but in so doing they favor the ability to apply the

(30)   law in particular cases over the ability to understand
the interrelations among laws. In contrast, the study of
all the statutes of a legal system in a certain small area
of the law would enable the student to see how these
laws form a coherent whole. Students would then be

(35)   able to apply this ability to synthesize in other areas of
statutory law that they encounter in their study or
practice. This is especially important because most
students intend to specialize in a chosen area, or areas,
of the law.

(40)   One possible argument against including training in
statutory law as a standard part of law school curricula
is that many statutes vary from region to region within
a nation, so that the mastery of a set of statutes would
usually not be generally applicable. There is some truth

(45)   to this objection; law schools that currently provide
some training in statutes generally intend it as a
preparation for practice in their particular region, but
for schools that are nationally oriented, this could seem
to be an inappropriate investment of time and

(50)   resources. But while the knowledge of a particular
region's statutory law is not generally transferable to
other regions, the skills acquired in mastering a
particular set of statutes are, making the study of
statutory law an important undertaking even for law

(55)   schools with a national orientation.

Margin notes:
- Too little attn to statutory law in law school
- Focus on cases misleading
- Ex. lawyer and shop owner
- Statutes not always so cut and dry – must learn to interpret them
- Must learn statutory synthesis
- Seeing coherent whole is beneficial
- b/c of specialization
- Dissent – regional variation prevents general application
- Auth – still OK for nat'lly oriented schools b/c skills are the value, not the specific statutory knowledge

---

Topic: Legal education

Scope: The limited coverage of statutory law in law school curricula

Purpose: To discuss or illustrate the value of increasing the emphasis on statutory law in law school curriculum

Main Idea: The skills gained in studying statutory law are important enough to legal practice to overcome objections and justify an increased emphasis on statutory law in law school.

LSAT Question	My Analysis

4. Which one of the following questions can be most clearly and directly answered by reference to information in the passage? $\longrightarrow$

Step 2:

Step 3:

Step 4:

(A) What are some ways in which synthetic skills are strengthened or encouraged through the analysis $\longrightarrow$ of cases and judicial decisions?

Step 5:

(B) In which areas of legal practice is a proficiency in case analysis more valuable than a proficiency in $\longrightarrow$ statutory law?

(C) What skills are common to the study of both $\longrightarrow$ statutory law and judicial decisions?

(D) What are some objections that have been raised against including the study of statutes in $\longrightarrow$ regionally oriented law schools?

(E) What is the primary focus of the curriculum currently offered in most law schools? $\longrightarrow$

PrepTest59 Sec4 Q13

5. Each of the following conforms to the kinds of educational results that the author would expect from the $\longrightarrow$ course of action proposed in the passage EXCEPT:

Step 2:

Step 3:

Step 4:

(A) skill in locating references to court decisions on an issue involving a particular statute regarding $\longrightarrow$ taxation

Step 5:

(B) an understanding of the ways in which certain underlying purposes are served by an $\longrightarrow$ interrelated group of environmental laws

(C) a knowledge of how maritime statutes are $\longrightarrow$ formulated

(D) familiarity with the specific wordings of a group of laws applying to businesses in a particular $\longrightarrow$ region or locality

(E) an appreciation of the problems of wording involved in drafting antiterrorism laws $\longrightarrow$

PrepTest59 Sec4 Q15

A proficiency in understanding, applying, and even
formulating statutes—the actual texts of laws enacted
by legislative bodies—is a vital aspect of the practice
of law, but statutory law is often given too little

(5)   attention by law schools. Much of legal education, with
its focus on judicial decisions and analysis of cases,
can give a law student the impression that the practice
of law consists mainly in analyzing past cases to
determine their relevance to a client's situation and

(10) arriving at a speculative interpretation of the law
relevant to the client's legal problem.

Lawyers discover fairly soon, however, that much
of their practice does not depend on the kind of
painstaking analysis of cases that is performed in law

(15) school. For example, a lawyer representing the owner
of a business can often find an explicit answer as to
what the client should do about a certain tax-related
issue by consulting the relevant statutes. In such a case
the facts are clear and the statutes' relation to them

(20) transparent, so that the client's question can be
answered by direct reference to the wording of the
statutes. But statutes' meanings and their applicability
to relevant situations are not always so obvious, and
that is one reason that the ability to interpret them

(25) accurately is an essential skill for law students to learn.
Another skill that teaching statutory law would
improve is synthesis. Law professors work hard at
developing their students' ability to analyze individual
cases, but in so doing they favor the ability to apply the

(30) law in particular cases over the ability to understand
the interrelations among laws. In contrast, the study of
all the statutes of a legal system in a certain small area
of the law would enable the student to see how these
laws form a coherent whole. Students would then be

(35) able to apply this ability to synthesize in other areas of
statutory law that they encounter in their study or
practice. This is especially important because most
students intend to specialize in a chosen area, or areas,
of the law.

(40) One possible argument against including training in
statutory law as a standard part of law school curricula
is that many statutes vary from region to region within
a nation, so that the mastery of a set of statutes would
usually not be generally applicable. There is some truth

(45) to this objection; law schools that currently provide
some training in statutes generally intend it as a
preparation for practice in their particular region, but
for schools that are nationally oriented, this could seem
to be an inappropriate investment of time and

(50) resources. But while the knowledge of a particular
region's statutory law is not generally transferable to
other regions, the skills acquired in mastering a
particular set of statutes are, making the study of
statutory law an important undertaking even for law

(55) schools with a national orientation.

PrepTest59 Sec4 Qs 9–15

Topic: Legal education

Scope: The limited coverage of statutory law in
law school curricula

Purpose: To discuss or illustrate the value of
increasing the emphasis on statutory law in
law school curriculum

Main Idea: The skills gained in studying
statutory law are important enough to legal
practice to overcome objections and justify an
increased emphasis on statutory law in law
school.

Margin notes:

Too little attn to statutory law in law school

Focus on cases misleading

Ex. lawyer and shop owner

Statutes not always so cut and dry — must learn to interpret them

Must learn statutory synthesis

Seeing coherent whole is beneficial

b/c of specialization

Dissent -- regional variation prevents general application

Auth — still OK for nat'lly oriented schools b/c skills are the value, not the specific statutory knowledge

LSAT Question	My Analysis
6. The information in the passage suggests that the author would most likely agree with which one of the following statements regarding training in statutory law? $\longrightarrow$	**Step 2:**
	Step 3:
	Step 4:
(A) While nationally oriented law schools have been deficient in statutory law training, most regionally oriented law schools have been equally deficient in the teaching of case law. $\longrightarrow$	**Step 5:**
(B) Training in statutory law would help lawyers resolve legal questions for which the answers are not immediately apparent in the relevant statutes. $\longrightarrow$	
(C) Lawyers who are trained in statutory law typically also develop a higher level of efficiency in manipulating details of past cases as compared with lawyers who are not trained in this way. $\longrightarrow$	
(D) Courses in statutory law are less effective if they focus specifically on the statutes of a particular region or in a particular area of the law. $\longrightarrow$	
(E) Lawyers who do not specialize probably have little need for training in statutory law beyond a brief introduction to the subject. $\longrightarrow$	

PrepTest59 Sec4 Q14

Expert Analysis

Compare your work on those questions to that of an LSAT expert. In the next chapter, you'll have ample opportunity to refine your approach to each step in the Reading Comprehension Method.

LSAT Question	Analysis
2. Which one of the following would, if true, most weaken the author's argument as expressed in the passage? →	**Step 2:** The word "weaken" denotes a Logic Reasoning (Weaken) question.
	Step 3: Look at the author's main argument here since the question asks about the passage in general. Use Topic/Scope/Purpose/Main Idea summaries.
	Step 4: The author spends the entire passage arguing for more statutory law in the legal education system. He argues that this will give students a skill they do not obtain currently. Any detriment to teaching this skill weakens the author's argument.
(A) Many law school administrators recommend the inclusion of statutory law training in the curricula of their schools. →	**Step 5:** 180. This strengthens the author's argument for including statutory law. Eliminate.
(B) Most lawyers easily and quickly develop proficiency in statutory law through their work experiences after law school. →	Correct. This reduces the value of teaching the subject in law schools because a newly minted lawyer will learn these lessons in actual practice. This matches the prediction.
(C) Most lawyers do not practice law in the same geographic area in which they attended law school. →	Faulty Use of Detail. This paraphrases the objection found in paragraph 4, but the author acknowledges and overcomes this objection by focusing on the skills acquired when learning how statutes fit together. Eliminate.
(D) The curricula of many regionally oriented law schools rely primarily on analysis of cases. →	Faulty Use of Detail. This choice merely applies a fact suggested in the passage. Eliminate.
(E) Most lawyers who have undergone training in statutory law are thoroughly familiar with only a narrow range of statutes. *PrepTest59 Sec4 Q11* →	Outside the Scope. Even if this is true, the author's argument focuses on skills (not knowledge of laws) gained in statutory law training. Eliminate.

LSAT Question	**Analysis**
3. The author discusses the skill of synthesis in the third paragraph primarily in order to →	**Step 2:** The phrase "primarily in order to" signals a Logic Function question. The question asks *why* the author cites the "skill of synthesis" in paragraph 3.
	Step 3: The word *synthesis* comes up in the first sentence of the third paragraph, where it is cited as "[a]nother skill" fostered by learning statutory law in law school.
	Step 4: The word [a]*nother* signals the continuation of an argument, so this is *another* reason why statutory law should be taught in law schools.
(A) identify and describe one of the benefits that the author says would result from the change that is → advocated in the passage	**Step 5:** Correct. Synthesis is "one of the benefits" of the "change [more statutory law courses] ... advocated."
(B) indicate that law schools currently value certain other skills over this skill and explain why this → is so	Distortion. This is true according to the passage but does not describe *why* synthesis is discussed in paragraph 3. Eliminate.
(C) argue for the greater importance of this skill as compared with certain others that are discussed → earlier in the passage	Distortion. Nowhere does the author say that statutory law is *more* important than case analysis. Eliminate.
(D) explain why this skill is necessary for the study of statutory law →	Distortion. This is a skill gained by the study of statutory law, not a skill necessary *for* its study. Eliminate.
(E) provide an example of the type of problem typically encountered in the practice of law → *PrepTest59 Sec4 Q12*	Faulty Use of Detail. Mentions an example provided in paragraph 2, not paragraph 3. Eliminate.

LSAT Question	**Analysis**
4. Which one of the following questions can be most clearly and directly answered by reference to information in the passage? $\longrightarrow$	**Step 2:** A Detail question—The answer corresponds to explicit text in the passage.
	Step 3: This question does not include a research clue. Research each answer choice separately.
	Step 4: It is impossible to make an exact prediction for this open-ended question, so keep the big picture in mind: The author thinks statutory law should be taught in law schools because case analysis is insufficient to impart all required skills to budding lawyers.
(A) What are some ways in which synthetic skills are strengthened or encouraged through the analysis $\longrightarrow$ of cases and judicial decisions?	**Step 5:** Distortion. According to the author, synthesis is a skill learned by studying statutes, not through case analysis. Eliminate.
(B) In which areas of legal practice is a proficiency in case analysis more valuable than a proficiency in $\longrightarrow$ statutory law?	Outside the Scope. The passage does not address areas of law in which case analysis provides the more central skills. Eliminate.
(C) What skills are common to the study of both statutory law and judicial decisions? $\longrightarrow$	Distortion. The author emphasizes skills unique to statutory law analysis, not those it has in common with case analysis. Eliminate.
(D) What are some objections that have been raised against including the study of statutes in $\longrightarrow$ regionally oriented law schools?	Faulty Use of Detail. The only objection to increasing statutory law education was applicable to national programs, not regional ones. Eliminate.
(E) What is the primary focus of the curriculum currently offered in most law schools? *PrepTest59 Sec4 Q13* $\longrightarrow$	Correct. The author mentions in paragraph 1 that schools focus too little on statutory law and mostly use case analysis. The question in this choice can be answered directly from the passage.

LSAT Question	Analysis
5. Each of the following conforms to the kinds of educational results that the author would expect from the course of action proposed in the passage EXCEPT: →	**Step 2:** An Inference EXCEPT question—The four wrong answers will each describe a result the author would expect from his proposed change; the correct answer will either contradict the author's expectations or will be Outside the Scope.
	Step 3: Although this is an open-ended question (with no specific research clues), the first sentence of the passage states that law students currently lack proficiency in "understanding, applying, and even formulating statutes."
	Step 4: The author anticipates that statutory law training will improve students' proficiency in understanding, applying, and formulating statutes, along with the skill of synthesis (paragraph 3). These will appear in the wrong answers here.
(A) skill in locating references to court decisions on an issue involving a particular statute regarding taxation →	**Step 5:** Correct. This choice refers to cases ("court decisions") ruling on statutes. That distorts the author's point and is not, therefore, a valid inference from the passage.
(B) an understanding of the ways in which certain underlying purposes are served by an interrelated group of environmental laws →	This describes the skill of synthesizing statutes; something the author believes will result from his proposed change. Eliminate.
(C) a knowledge of how maritime statutes are formulated →	Knowledge of how statutes are formulated would be a result of training in statutory law. Eliminate.
(D) familiarity with the specific wordings of a group of laws applying to businesses in a particular region or locality →	Familiarity with specific statutes (although a minor point in the author's argument) would result from training in statutory law. Eliminate.
(E) an appreciation of the problems of wording involved in drafting antiterrorism laws →	This is a specific example of understanding how to formulate a set of statutes. Eliminate.

PrepTest59 Sec4 Q15

LSAT Question	Analysis
6. The information in the passage suggests that the author would most likely agree with which one of the following statements regarding training in statutory law? →	**Step 2:** An Inference question—The correct answer is a statement with which "the author would most likely agree" given what he wrote in the passage.
	Step 3: The question is fairly open-ended, referring to "training in statutory law," the subject of the entire passage.
	Step 4: It is difficult to predict precise wording, but the correct answer must agree with the author's position: He is in favor of statutory law training because 1) lawyers in practice regularly interpret statutes, and 2) statutory law training improves the skills of understanding and synthesizing statutes.
(A) While nationally oriented law schools have been deficient in statutory law training, most regionally oriented law schools have been equally deficient in the teaching of case law. →	**Step 5:** Half-Right/Half-Wrong. According to the author, regional schools are also deficient in statutory law training, not in case analysis. Eliminate.
(B) Training in statutory law would help lawyers resolve legal questions for which the answers are not immediately apparent in the relevant statutes. →	Correct. An accurate assessment of the author's lengthy example in paragraph 2.
(C) Lawyers who are trained in statutory law typically also develop a higher level of efficiency in manipulating details of past cases as compared with lawyers who are not trained in this way. →	Outside the Scope. The passage simply provides no support for this statement. Eliminate.
(D) Courses in statutory law are less effective if they focus specifically on the statutes of a particular region or in a particular area of the law. →	180. The author argues that the skills acquired trump the problems of regional differences in statutory law. Eliminate.
(E) Lawyers who do not specialize probably have little need for training in statutory law beyond a brief introduction to the subject. *PrepTest59 Sec4 Q14* →	Extreme. Paragraph 3 states that the skill of synthesis is especially important for those who intend to specialize; that does not mean that it is unimportant for the non-specialist. Eliminate.

REFLECTION

Most students intuitively grasp the value of a clear, helpful Roadmap when they see an LSAT expert use one to answer questions quickly and confidently. That said, most students also struggle initially to know whether they are making the "right" Roadmap for themselves and whether they are taking too much time to do so.

Here are a few guidelines and questions you can ask yourself to become a better Roadmapper.

- A Roadmap is a tool—It is either helpful or unhelpful, *not* right or wrong.

- A strong Roadmap distinguishes the parts of the text that will help you answer LSAT questions. If you circle or underline *nothing*, you're not highlighting the valuable text; if you circle or underline *everything*, you're not highlighting what's important, either.

- A helpful Roadmap shows you *where* important details are and *how* they are used, but does not attempt to restate in detail *what* the passage says.

- LSAT experts typically read and Roadmap a passage in 3–4 minutes, leaving 4½–5½ minutes to answer the questions.

As you practice making Roadmaps, reflect on how helpful they were by asking the following questions as you review the passage and questions.

- How well were you able to navigate the passage as you researched the questions? Did you know where to find the text relevant to the question?

- Could you summarize the passage accurately with a glance back over your Roadmap?

- Did you know what the author was trying to say in each paragraph?

- Did you have to reread substantial portions of the text, or could you zero in on the piece(s) you would need to answer the questions?

Sample Roadmaps

Each test taker's Roadmap will look a little different, but all effective Roadmaps share a focus on passage structure and the author's Purpose. The sample passage maps included in the book and that accompany Kaplan Reading Comprehension explanations are just that: *samples* of an expert's work. To illustrate the range of styles that effective Roadmaps might cover, the following pages present four more expert Roadmaps from the Statutory Law passage. As you review them, keep an eye on the characteristics they share as well as the differences you see among their circling, underlining, and margin notes.

TEST DAY TIP

No one other than you ever sees the Roadmap (or any other notes in your test booklet, for that matter). Don't aspire to some undefined perfection or worry that your work looks somewhat different than someone else's. Your goal is useful, accurate, succinct, and strategic scratch work.

Sample Roadmap A

A proficiency in understanding, applying, and even formulating statutes—the actual texts of laws enacted by legislative bodies—is a <u>vital aspect</u> of the practice of law, but statutory law is often <u>given too little</u>
(5) <u>attention</u> by law schools. Much of legal education, with its focus on judicial decisions and analysis of cases, can give a law student the impression that the practice of law consists mainly in analyzing past cases to determine their relevance to a client's situation and
(10) arriving at a speculative interpretation of the law relevant to the client's legal problem. }

M.l. = l.s. needs to do move taking of how to "read" laws, not just apply precedents (Not Law Reading)

Wrong impression

Lawyers discover fairly soon, however, that much of their practice does not depend on the kind of painstaking analysis of cases that is performed in law
(15) school. For example, a lawyer representing the owner of a business can often find an explicit answer as to what the client should do about a certain tax-related issue by consulting the relevant statutes. In such a case the facts are clear and the statutes' relation to them
(20) transparent, so that the client's question can be answered by direct reference to the wording of the statutes. But statutes' meanings and their applicability to relevant situations <u>are not always so obvious</u>, and that is one reason that the ability to interpret them
(25) accurately is an <u>essential skill</u> <u>for law students to learn.</u>
Another skill that teaching statutory law would improve is synthesis. Law professors work hard at developing their students' ability to analyze individual cases, but in so doing they favor the ability to apply the
(30) law in particular cases over the ability to understand the interrelations among laws. In contrast, the study of all the statutes of a legal system in a certain small area of the law would enable the student to see how these laws form a coherent whole. Students would then be
(35) able to apply this ability to synthesize in other areas of statutory law that they encounter in their study or practice. This is <u>especially important</u> because most students intend to specialize in a chosen area, or areas, of the law.
(40) One possible argument against including training in statutory law as a standard part of law school curricula is that many statutes vary from region to region within a nation, so that the mastery of a set of statutes would usually not be generally applicable. There is some truth
(45) to this objection; law schools that currently provide some training in statutes generally intend it as a preparation for practice in their particular region, but for schools that are nationally oriented, this could seem to be an inappropriate investment of time and
(50) resources. But while the knowledge of a particular region's statutory law is not generally transferable to other regions, the skills acquired in mastering a particular set of statutes are, making the study of statutory law an important undertaking even for law
(55) schools with a national orientation.

Ex. of how a lawyer needs to understand the laws' wording.

MI again

"Put it all together"

another reason for policy

Counter-Arg. Laws vary all over US; could hurt nat'l schools

Counter. Counter-Arg. Nah—learning to "read" laws is helpful everywhere

Sample Roadmap B

A <u>proficiency</u> in understanding, applying, and even formulating <u>statutes</u>—the actual texts of laws enacted by legislative bodies—is a <u>vital aspect</u> of the practice of law, but statutory law is often <u>given too little</u>
(5) <u>attention</u> by law schools. <u>Much of legal education</u>, with its focus on judicial decisions and analysis of cases, can give a law student the impression that the practice of law consists mainly in <u>analyzing past cases</u> to determine their relevance to a client's situation and
(10) arriving at a speculative interpretation of the law relevant to the client's legal problem.

Stat. law—insufficient attention in law school

Instead case analysis

Lawyers discover fairly soon, however, that much of their practice does not depend on the kind of painstaking analysis of cases that is performed in law
(15) school. <u>For example</u>, a lawyer representing the owner of a business can often find an explicit answer as to what the client should do about a certain tax-related issue by consulting the relevant statutes. In such a case the facts are clear and the statutes' relation to them
(20) transparent, so that the client's question can be answered by direct reference to the wording of the statutes. But statutes' meanings and their applicability to relevant situations <u>are not always so obvious</u>, and that is one reason that the <u>ability to interpret</u> them
(25) accurately is an <u>essential skill</u> for law students to learn.
Another skill that teaching statutory law would improve is synthesis. Law professors work hard at developing their students' ability to analyze individual cases, but in so doing they favor the ability to apply the
(30) law in particular cases over the ability to understand the interrelations among laws. In contrast, the study of all the statutes of a legal system in a certain small area of the law would enable the student to see how these laws form a coherent whole. Students would then be
(35) able to apply this ability to synthesize in other areas of statutory law that they encounter in their study or practice. This is <u>especially important because</u> most students intend to specialize in a chosen area, or areas, of the law.
(40) <u>One possible argument against</u> including training in statutory law as a standard part of law school curricula is that <u>many statutes vary from region</u> to region within a nation, so that the mastery of a set of statutes would usually not be generally applicable. <u>There is some truth</u>
(45) <u>to this objection</u>; law schools that currently provide some training in statutes generally intend it as a preparation for practice in their particular region, but for schools that are nationally oriented, this could seem to be an inappropriate investment of time and
(50) resources. But while the knowledge of a particular region's statutory law is not generally transferable to other regions, the skills acquired in mastering a particular set of statutes are, making the study of statutory law an important undertaking even for law
(55) schools with a national orientation.

Actual practice: just look up statutes

Must know how to interpret

Teaching stat. law good for synthesis

Critics

Concession

Au: skills transferable, even if statutes aren't

Sample Roadmap C

(5) A proficiency in understanding, applying, and even formulating statutes—the actual texts of laws enacted by legislative bodies—is a vital aspect of the practice of law, but statutory law is often given too little attention by law schools. Much of legal education, with its focus on judicial decisions and analysis of cases, can give a law student the impression that the practice of law consists mainly in analyzing past cases to determine their relevance to a client's situation and

L-schools need to teach statutes too!

(10) arriving at a speculative interpretation of the law relevant to the client's legal problem.

(15) Lawyers discover fairly soon, however, that much of their practice does not depend on the kind of painstaking analysis of cases that is performed in law school. For example, a lawyer representing the owner of a business can often find an explicit answer as to what the client should do about a certain tax-related issue by consulting the relevant statutes. In such a case the facts are clear and the statutes' relation to them

Legal practice not just about cases

(20) transparent, so that the client's question can be answered by direct reference to the wording of the statutes. But statutes' meanings and their applicability to relevant situations are not always so obvious, and that is one reason that the ability to interpret them

(25) accurately is an essential skill for law students to learn.

Another skill that teaching statutory law would improve is synthesis. Law professors work hard at developing their students' ability to analyze individual cases, but in so doing they favor the ability to apply the

Stat interp. would also help to synth.

(30) law in particular cases over the ability to understand the interrelations among laws. In contrast, the study of all the statutes of a legal system in a certain small area of the law would enable the student to see how these laws form a coherent whole. Students would then be

(35) able to apply this ability to synthesize in other areas of statutory law that they encounter in their study or practice. This is especially important because most students intend to specialize in a chosen area, or areas, of the law.

(40) One possible argument against including training in statutory law as a standard part of law school curricula is that many statutes vary from region to region within a nation, so that the mastery of a set of statutes would usually not be generally applicable. There is some truth

(45) to this objection; law schools that currently provide some training in statutes generally intend it as a preparation for practice in their particular region, but for schools that are nationally oriented, this could seem to be an inappropriate investment of time and

(50) resources. But while the knowledge of a particular region's statutory law is not generally transferable to other regions, the skills acquired in mastering a particular set of statutes are, making the study of statutory law an important undertaking even for law

Despite regional variance, stat. interp. skills are import.

(55) schools with a national orientation.

Sample Roadmap D

(5) A proficiency in understanding, applying, and even formulating statutes—the actual texts of laws enacted by legislative bodies—is a vital aspect of the practice of law, but statutory law is often given too little attention by law schools. Much of legal education, with its focus on judicial decisions and analysis of cases, can give a law student the impression that the practice of law consists mainly in analyzing past cases to determine their relevance to a client's situation and

Statutes: –vital –neglected by law schools

false impression

(10) arriving at a speculative interpretation of the law relevant to the client's legal problem.

(15) Lawyers discover fairly soon, however, that much of their practice does not depend on the kind of painstaking analysis of cases that is performed in law school. For example, a lawyer representing the owner of a business can often find an explicit answer as to what the client should do about a certain tax-related issue by consulting the relevant statutes. In such a case the facts are clear and the statutes' relation to them

law ≠ case analysis

(20) transparent, so that the client's question can be answered by direct reference to the wording of the statutes. But statutes' meanings and their applicability to relevant situations are not always so obvious, and that is one reason that the ability to interpret them

(25) accurately is an essential skill for law students to learn.

Another skill that teaching statutory law would improve is synthesis. Law professors work hard at developing their students' ability to analyze individual cases, but in so doing they favor the ability to apply the

(30) law in particular cases over the ability to understand the interrelations among laws. In contrast, the study of all the statutes of a legal system in a certain small area of the law would enable the student to see how these laws form a coherent whole. Students would then be

synthesis

(35) able to apply this ability to synthesize in other areas of statutory law that they encounter in their study or practice. This is especially important because most students intend to specialize in a chosen area, or areas, of the law.

(40) One possible argument against including training in statutory law as a standard part of law school curricula is that many statutes vary from region to region within a nation, so that the mastery of a set of statutes would usually not be generally applicable. There is some truth

possible arg. against auth

(45) to this objection; law schools that currently provide some training in statutes generally intend it as a preparation for practice in their particular region, but for schools that are nationally oriented, this could seem to be an inappropriate investment of time and

some truth

(50) resources. But while the knowledge of a particular region's statutory law is not generally transferable to other regions, the skills acquired in mastering a particular set of statutes are, making the study of statutory law an important undertaking even for law

but wrong

(55) schools with a national orientation.

PrepTest59 Sec4 Qs 9–15

Reading Comprehension: Passage Types and Question Types

Success in Reading Comprehension is the result of an active, methodical approach. As you read the passages, engage with the material by asking questions and attempting to determine the author's purpose. When you get to the questions, be equally strategic. Know exactly what the question is asking, then return to the passage or your Roadmap to research the correct answer.

In this chapter, we'll walk through each step of the Kaplan Method in more depth.

THE KAPLAN READING COMPREHENSION METHOD

Step 1: Read the Passage Strategically—Circle Keywords and jot down margin notes to summarize the portions of the passage relevant to LSAT questions; summarize the author's Topic/Scope/Purpose/Main Idea.

Step 2: Read the Question Stem—Identify the question type, characterize the correct and incorrect answers, and look for clues to guide your research.

Step 3: Research the Relevant Text—Based on the clues in the question stem, consult your Roadmap; for open-ended questions, refer to your Topic/Scope/Purpose/Main Idea summaries.

Step 4: Predict the Correct Answer—Based on research, predict the meaning of the correct answer; for open-ended questions, consult your Topic/Scope/Purpose/Main Idea summaries.

Step 5: Evaluate the Answer Choices—Select the choice that matches your prediction of the correct answer or eliminate the four wrong answer choices.

STRATEGIC READING AND READING COMPREHENSION PASSAGE TYPES

The first step in the Kaplan Method is to read the passage strategically. Untrained test takers read passages with little interest or curiosity and, in turn, find it difficult to identify the author's Purpose or Main Idea. In contrast, LSAT experts focus on areas of contrast and emphasis within a passage, and they always keep in mind the author's intent.

Strategic Reading and Roadmapping Skills

Roadmapping a passage is a complex task. Even for LSAT experts, Reading Comprehension passages are dense and academic. A systematic approach is invaluable for maintaining focus on the aspects of the passage that will yield points on the test.

LEARNING OBJECTIVES

In this portion of the chapter, you'll learn to:

Use Keywords

- Identify Keywords from six categories (Emphasis/Opinion, Contrast, Logic, Illustration, Sequence/Chronology, and Continuation).
- Use Keywords to accurately paraphrase the text (author's Purpose, method of argument, etc.).
- Use Keywords to accurately predict where the passage will go (Scope and Purpose of remaining paragraphs, for example).
- Use Keywords to predict points in the passage to which LSAT questions will refer.

Use Margin Notes

- Identify text that warrants a margin note.
- Capture key content in a brief, accurate margin note.

Use Big Picture Summaries—Topic/Scope/Purpose/Main Idea

- Read a passage and identify the author's Topic and Scope.
- Read a passage and identify the author's Purpose.
- Read a passage and identify the author's Main Idea.

The first two skills involved in this step—noting Keywords and jotting down margin notes—are the "physical" Roadmap you will note on the pages of your test booklet. The third skill—summarizing the big picture of the passage—is "mental," information you note in your head as you read.

Why Use Keywords?

Keywords indicate differences in opinion and structure. They help you interrogate the author as you read. Indeed, the author's selection of Keywords can change the meaning of a passage (and thus, change the correct answer to an LSAT question). Consider two facts and an LSAT-style question:

> Type X coffee beans grow at very high altitudes. Type X coffee beans produce a dark, mellow coffee when brewed.

With which one of the following statements would the author most likely agree?

> 1) Coffee beans that grow at high altitudes typically produce dark, mellow coffee when brewed.

> 2) Coffee beans that grow at high altitudes typically produce light, acidic coffee when brewed.

You cannot answer that question from the facts alone. To understand the author's point of view, you need Keywords, words only the author could add to the text. Observe:

> Type X coffee beans grow at very high altitudes, *but* produce a *surprisingly* dark, mellow coffee when brewed.

Which answer would be correct now?

Change the Keyword, and you change the correct answer on the LSAT. For example:

> Type X coffee beans grow at very high altitudes, *and so* produce a dark, mellow coffee when brewed.

For the LSAT expert, those seemingly small connecting words are the most important in the sentence because they are the words that will help distinguish right and wrong answers on the test.

Next, you'll see a full LSAT passage, highlighting the words and phrases that stand out to a strategic reader.

Read the passage below, and note how attention to structure, and not details, allows an LSAT expert to focus on the broad concepts discussed in a dense passage about a mathematical concept.

Fractal geometry is a mathematical theory devoted to the study of complex shapes called fractals. Although an exact definition of fractals has not been established, fractals commonly exhibit the property of self-similarity:

(5) the reiteration of irregular details or patterns at progressively smaller scales so that each part, when magnified, looks basically like the object as a whole. The Koch curve is a significant fractal in mathematics and examining it provides some insight into fractal

(10) geometry. To generate the Koch curve, one begins with a straight line. The middle third of the line is removed and replaced with two line segments, each as long as the removed piece, which are positioned so as to meet and form the top of a triangle. At this stage,

(15) the curve consists of four connected segments of equal length that form a pointed protrusion in the middle. This process is repeated on the four segments so that all the protrusions are on the same side of the curve, and then the process is repeated indefinitely on the

(20) segments at each stage of the construction.

Self-similarity is built into the construction process by treating segments at each stage the same way as the original segment was treated. Since the rules for getting from one stage to another are fully

(25) explicit and always the same, images of successive stages of the process can be generated by computer. Theoretically, the Koch curve is the result of infinitely many steps in the construction process, but the finest image approximating the Koch curve will be limited

(30) by the fact that eventually the segments will get too short to be drawn or displayed. However, using computer graphics to produce images of successive stages of the construction process dramatically illustrates a major attraction of fractal geometry:

(35) simple processes can be responsible for incredibly complex patterns.

A worldwide public has become captivated by fractal geometry after viewing astonishing computer-generated images of fractals; enthusiastic practitioners

(40) in the field of fractal geometry consider it a new language for describing complex natural and mathematical forms. They anticipate that fractal geometry's significance will rival that of calculus and expect that proficiency in fractal geometry will allow

(45) mathematicians to describe the form of a cloud as easily and precisely as an architect can describe a house using the language of traditional geometry. Other mathematicians have reservations about the fractal geometers' preoccupation with computer-generated

(50) graphic images and their lack of interest in theory. These mathematicians point out that traditional mathematics consists of proving theorems, and while many theorems about fractals have already been proven using the notions of pre-fractal mathematics,

(55) fractal geometers have proven only a handful of theorems that could not have been proven with pre-fractal mathematics. According to these mathematicians, fractal geometry can attain a lasting role in mathematics only if it becomes a precise

(60) language supporting a system of theorems and proofs.

PrepTest57 Sec4 Qs 20–27

An LSAT expert might not circle or underline all of the bolded text on the previous page. However, by noting the Keywords, the expert can summarize the passage and the purpose of each paragraph. This helps the expert answer the big-picture Global and Inference questions confidently and sketch out a Roadmap that will allow her to navigate back to important details when necessary.

Emphasis/Opinion and Contrast Keywords are often the most important in determining the author's point of view and purpose. Logic Keywords identify arguments (either the author's or someone else's). Other Keywords will identify examples, illustrations, and the overall structure of the passage and paragraphs.

LSAT STRATEGY

Strategic Reading Keywords

Emphasis/Opinion—Words that signal that an author finds a detail noteworthy or has a positive or negative opinion about the detail; any subjective or evaluative language on the author's part (e.g., *especially, crucial, unfortunately, disappointing, I suggest, it seems likely*)

Contrast—Words indicating that the author thinks two details or ideas are incompatible or illustrate conflicting points (e.g., *but, yet, despite, on the other hand*)

Logic—Words that indicate an argument, either the author's or someone else's (e.g., *thus, therefore, because*)

Illustration—Words indicating an example offered to clarify or support a point (e.g., *for example, this shows, to illustrate*)

Sequence/Chronology—Words showing steps in a process or developments over time (e.g., *traditionally, in the past, today, first, second, finally, earlier, since*)

Continuation—Words indicating that a subsequent example or detail supports the same point or illustrates the same idea (e.g., *moreover, in addition, and, also, further*)

In addition to circling or underlining Keywords, most LSAT experts will also jot down brief, accurate paraphrases of key content. We'll refer to these as *margin notes*.

Why Take Margin Notes?

Margin notes prompt you to make mental paraphrases of a passage as you read. This is important because, on Test Day, it is easy to lose focus and gloss over an entire paragraph or passage. Margin notes also serve as valuable reference points for locating the facts and opinions you need to answer the questions.

On the next page, you'll see the Fractal Geometry passage with the Keywords circled. Next to its first paragraph, you'll see the LSAT expert's margin notes, and you can try jotting down some of your own.

Take a look at the notes added to the first paragraph below. Add your own margin notes for paragraphs 2 and 3. Focus on opinions, contrast, and points of emphasis.

Fractal geometry is a mathematical theory devoted to the study of complex shapes called fractals. Although an exact definition of fractals has not been established, fractals commonly exhibit the property of self-similarity:

Fractal def.

(5) the reiteration of irregular details or patterns at progressively smaller scales so that each part, when magnified, looks basically like the object as a whole. The Koch curve is a significant fractal in mathematics and examining it provides some insight into fractal

Koch curve— how generated

(10) geometry. To generate the Koch curve, one begins with a straight line. The middle third of the line is removed and replaced with two line segments, each as long as the removed piece, which are positioned so as to meet and form the top of a triangle. At this stage,

(15) the curve consists of four connected segments of equal length that form a pointed protrusion in the middle. This process is repeated on the four segments so that all the protrusions are on the same side of the curve, and then the process is repeated indefinitely on the

(20) segments at each stage of the construction.

Self-similarity is built into the construction process by treating segments at each stage the same way as the original segment was treated. Since the rules for getting from one stage to another are fully

(25) explicit and always the same, images of successive stages of the process can be generated by computer. Theoretically, the Koch curve is the result of infinitely many steps in the construction process, but the finest image approximating the Koch curve will be limited

(30) by the fact that eventually the segments will get too short to be drawn or displayed. However, using computer graphics to produce images of successive stages of the construction process dramatically illustrates a major attraction of fractal geometry:

(35) simple processes can be responsible for incredibly complex patterns.

A worldwide public has become captivated by fractal geometry after viewing astonishing computer-generated images of fractals; enthusiastic practitioners

(40) in the field of fractal geometry consider it a new language for describing complex natural and mathematical forms. They anticipate that fractal geometry's significance will rival that of calculus and expect that proficiency in fractal geometry will allow

(45) mathematicians to describe the form of a cloud as easily and precisely as an architect can describe a house using the language of traditional geometry. Other mathematicians have reservations about the fractal geometers' preoccupation with computer-generated

(50) graphic images and their lack of interest in theory. These mathematicians point out that traditional mathematics consists of proving theorems, and while many theorems about fractals have already been proven using the notions of pre-fractal mathematics,

(55) fractal geometers have proven only a handful of theorems that could not have been proven with pre-fractal mathematics. According to these mathematicians, fractal geometry can attain a lasting role in mathematics only if it becomes a precise

(60) language supporting a system of theorems and proofs.

PrepTest57 Sec4 Qs 20–27

Having a strong Roadmap will allow you to research questions that refer to specific selections from the passage. Take a look at the following question stems and consider where in the passage you would find the answers to them.

Which one of the following is closest to the meaning of the phrase "fully explicit" as used in lines 24–25?

According to the description in the passage, each one of the following illustrates the concept of self-similarity EXCEPT:

The explanation of how a Koch curve is generated (lines 10–20) serves primarily to

Which one of the following does the author present as a characteristic of fractal geometry?

Each of the following statements about the Koch curve can be properly deduced from the information given in the passage EXCEPT:

The enthusiastic practitioners of fractal geometry mentioned in lines 39–40 would be most likely to agree with which one of the following statements?

PrepTest57 Sec4 Qs 21–26

The final skill you'll use in Step 1 is the "mental" aspect of strategic reading: summarizing the big picture of the passage.

Why Summarize the Author's Topic, Scope, Purpose, and Main Idea?

On most passages, anywhere from one to four of the questions ask for the author's "main idea" or "primary purpose," or ask in an open-ended way for a statement with which the author would "most likely agree." To answer these, the LSAT expert keeps track of four big picture categories as he reads.

LSAT STRATEGY

Reading Comprehension—The Big Picture

Topic—The overall subject of the passage

Scope—The particular aspect of the Topic on which the author focuses

Purpose—The author's reason for writing the passage (express this as a verb—e.g., *to refute*, *to outline*, *to evaluate*, *to critique*)

Main Idea—The author's conclusion or overall takeaway; if you combine the author's Purpose and Scope, you'll usually have a good sense of his Main Idea

---

Next, take a look at the Fractal Geometry passage with the expert's physical Roadmap. Try to summarize the big picture.

Now, as you glance back over the Roadmapped passage, summarize in your own words the Topic, Scope, Purpose, and Main Idea.

Fractal geometry is a mathematical theory devoted to the study of complex shapes called fractals. Although an exact definition of fractals has not been established, fractals commonly exhibit the property of self-similarity:
(5) the reiteration of irregular details or patterns at progressively smaller scales so that each part, when magnified, looks basically like the object as a whole. The Koch curve is a significant fractal in mathematics and examining it provides some insight into fractal
(10) geometry. To generate the Koch curve, one begins with a straight line. The middle third of the line is removed and replaced with two line segments, each as long as the removed piece, which are positioned so as to meet and form the top of a triangle. At this stage,
(15) the curve consists of four connected segments of equal length that form a pointed protrusion in the middle. This process is repeated on the four segments so that all the protrusions are on the same side of the curve, and then the process is repeated indefinitely on the
(20) segments at each stage of the construction.

Self-similarity is built into the construction process by treating segments at each stage the same way as the original segment was treated. Since the rules for getting from one stage to another are fully
(25) explicit and always the same, images of successive stages of the process can be generated by computer. Theoretically, the Koch curve is the result of infinitely many steps in the construction process, but the finest image approximating the Koch curve will be limited
(30) by the fact that eventually the segments will get too short to be drawn or displayed. However, using computer graphics to produce images of successive stages of the construction process dramatically illustrates a major attraction of fractal geometry:
(35) simple processes can be responsible for incredibly complex patterns.

A worldwide public has become captivated by fractal geometry after viewing astonishing computer-generated images of fractals; enthusiastic practitioners
(40) in the field of fractal geometry consider it a new language for describing complex natural and mathematical forms. They anticipate that fractal geometry's significance will rival that of calculus and expect that proficiency in fractal geometry will allow
(45) mathematicians to describe the form of a cloud as easily and precisely as an architect can describe a house using the language of traditional geometry. Other mathematicians have reservations about the fractal geometers' preoccupation with computer-generated
(50) graphic images and their lack of interest in theory. These mathematicians point out that traditional mathematics consists of proving theorems, and while many theorems about fractals have already been proven using the notions of pre-fractal mathematics,

(55) fractal geometers have proven only a handful of theorems that could not have been proven with pre-fractal mathematics. According to these mathematicians, fractal geometry can attain a lasting role in mathematics only if it becomes a precise
(60) language supporting a system of theorems and proofs.

PrepTest57 Sec4 Qs 20–27

Fractal def.

Koch curve— how generated

Each segment the same

Computer models simple process = complex pattern

Computer images = public interest

Some experts predict huge impact

Others doubt value

Very few new theorems proven w/fractal geo

Needs theorems & proofs

Big Picture Summaries:

Topic:

Scope:

Purpose:

Main Idea:

With the entire passage summed up in that way, consider how you would anticipate evaluating the answer choices to the following question stems.

Which one of the following most accurately expresses the main point of the passage?

The information in the passage best supports which one of the following assertions?

PrepTest57 Sec4 Qs 20 & 27

Next, you'll see the Fractal Geometry passage along with its question set just as it appeared on the test. You may try it now or come back to it after you have studied the Reading Comprehension question types and Steps 2–5 of the Reading Comprehension Method.

K

Part Four: Reading Comprehension
CHAPTER 14

Explanations for these questions
can be found in your Online Center.

Practice

Fractal geometry is a mathematical theory devoted to the study of complex shapes called fractals. Although an exact definition of fractals has not been established, fractals commonly exhibit the property of self-similarity:

(5) the reiteration of irregular details or patterns at progressively smaller scales so that each part, when magnified, looks basically like the object as a whole. The Koch curve is a significant fractal in mathematics and examining it provides some insight into fractal

(10) geometry. To generate the Koch curve, one begins with a straight line. The middle third of the line is removed and replaced with two line segments, each as long as the removed piece, which are positioned so as to meet and form the top of a triangle. At this stage,

(15) the curve consists of four connected segments of equal length that form a pointed protrusion in the middle. This process is repeated on the four segments so that all the protrusions are on the same side of the curve, and then the process is repeated indefinitely on the

(20) segments at each stage of the construction.

Self-similarity is built into the construction process by treating segments at each stage the same way as the original segment was treated. Since the rules for getting from one stage to another are fully

(25) explicit and always the same, images of successive stages of the process can be generated by computer. Theoretically, the Koch curve is the result of infinitely many steps in the construction process, but the finest image approximating the Koch curve will be limited

(30) by the fact that eventually the segments will get too short to be drawn or displayed. However, using computer graphics to produce images of successive stages of the construction process dramatically illustrates a major attraction of fractal geometry:

(35) simple processes can be responsible for incredibly complex patterns.

A worldwide public has become captivated by fractal geometry after viewing astonishing computer-generated images of fractals; enthusiastic practitioners

(40) in the field of fractal geometry consider it a new language for describing complex natural and mathematical forms. They anticipate that fractal geometry's significance will rival that of calculus and expect that proficiency in fractal geometry will allow

(45) mathematicians to describe the form of a cloud as easily and precisely as an architect can describe a house using the language of traditional geometry. Other mathematicians have reservations about the fractal geometers' preoccupation with computer-generated

(50) graphic images and their lack of interest in theory. These mathematicians point out that traditional mathematics consists of proving theorems, and while many theorems about fractals have already been proven using the notions of pre-fractal mathematics,

(55) fractal geometers have proven only a handful of theorems that could not have been proven with

pre-fractal mathematics. According to these mathematicians, fractal geometry can attain a lasting role in mathematics only if it becomes a precise

(60) language supporting a system of theorems and proofs.

1. Which one of the following most accurately expresses the main point of the passage?

    (A) Because of its unique forms, fractal geometry is especially adaptable to computer technology and is therefore likely to grow in importance and render pre-fractal mathematics obsolete.

    (B) Though its use in the generation of extremely complex forms makes fractal geometry an intriguing new mathematical theory, it is not yet universally regarded as having attained the theoretical rigor of traditional mathematics.

    (C) Fractal geometry is significant because of its use of self-similarity, a concept that has enabled geometers to generate extremely detailed computer images of natural forms.

    (D) Using the Koch curve as a model, fractal geometers have developed a new mathematical language that is especially useful in technological contexts because it does not rely on theorems.

    (E) Though fractal geometry has thus far been of great value for its capacity to define abstract mathematical shapes, it is not expected to be useful for the description of ordinary natural shapes.

2. Which one of the following is closest to the meaning of the phrase "fully explicit" as used in lines 24–25?

    (A) illustrated by an example
    (B) uncomplicated
    (C) expressed unambiguously
    (D) in need of lengthy computation
    (E) agreed on by all

3. According to the description in the passage, each one of the following illustrates the concept of self-similarity EXCEPT:

    (A) Any branch broken off a tree looks like the tree itself.

    (B) Each portion of the intricately patterned frost on a window looks like the pattern as a whole.

    (C) The pattern of blood vessels in each part of the human body is similar to the pattern of blood vessels in the entire body.

    (D) The seeds of several subspecies of maple tree resemble one another in shape despite differences in size.

    (E) The florets composing a cauliflower head resemble the entire cauliflower head.

Explanations for these questions can be found in your Online Center.

Part Four: Reading Comprehension
Reading Comprehension: Passage Types and Question Types

4. The explanation of how a Koch curve is generated (lines 10–20) serves primarily to

(A) show how fractal geometry can be reduced to traditional geometry

(B) give an example of a natural form that can be described by fractal geometry

(C) anticipate the objection that fractal geometry is not a precise language

(D) illustrate the concept of self-similarity

(E) provide an exact definition of fractals

5. Which one of the following does the author present as a characteristic of fractal geometry?

(A) It is potentially much more important than calculus.

(B) Its role in traditional mathematics will expand as computers become faster.

(C) It is the fastest-growing field of mathematics.

(D) It encourages the use of computer programs to prove mathematical theorems.

(E) It enables geometers to generate complex forms using simple processes.

6. Each of the following statements about the Koch curve can be properly deduced from the information given in the passage EXCEPT:

(A) The total number of protrusions in the Koch curve at any stage of the construction depends on the length of the initial line chosen for the construction.

(B) The line segments at each successive stage of the construction of the Koch curve are shorter than the segments at the previous stage.

(C) Theoretically, as the Koch curve is constructed its line segments become infinitely small.

(D) At every stage of constructing the Koch curve, all the line segments composing it are of equal length.

(E) The length of the line segments in the Koch curve at any stage of its construction depends on the length of the initial line chosen for the construction.

7. The enthusiastic practitioners of fractal geometry mentioned in lines 39–40 would be most likely to agree with which one of the following statements?

(A) The Koch curve is the most easily generated, and therefore the most important, of the forms studied by fractal geometers.

(B) Fractal geometry will eventually be able to be used in the same applications for which traditional geometry is now used.

(C) The greatest importance of computer images of fractals is their ability to bring fractal geometry to the attention of a wider public.

(D) Studying self-similarity was impossible before the development of sophisticated computer technologies.

(E) Certain complex natural forms exhibit a type of self-similarity like that exhibited by fractals.

8. The information in the passage best supports which one of the following assertions?

(A) The appeal of a mathematical theory is limited to those individuals who can grasp the theorems and proofs produced in that theory.

(B) Most of the important recent breakthroughs in mathematical theory would not have been possible without the ability of computers to graphically represent complex shapes.

(C) Fractal geometry holds the potential to replace traditional geometry in most of its engineering applications.

(D) A mathematical theory can be developed and find applications even before it establishes a precise definition of its subject matter.

(E) Only a mathematical theory that supports a system of theorems and proofs will gain enthusiastic support among a significant number of mathematicians.

PrepTest57 Sec4 Qs 20–27

Answer key on page 957.

Predicting How a Passage Will Develop

For the LSAT expert, strategic reading also involves predicting where the passage will go. This allows the expert to stay engaged, interrogating the author as he reads. In the following passage, only the first half of paragraph 1, along with the first sentences of paragraphs 2–4, have been reprinted. In your analysis, record what you think each paragraph will contain and where the author will go in subsequent paragraphs. Can you still determine the author's Purpose and the passage's Main Idea?

LSAT Passage	My Analysis
Specialists in international communications almost unanimously assert that the broadcasting in developing nations of television programs produced by industrialized countries amounts to cultural (5) imperialism: the phenomenon of one culture's productions overwhelming another's, to the detriment of the flourishing of the latter. This assertion assumes the automatic dominance of the imported productions and their negative effect on the domestic culture. But (10) the assertion is polemical and abstract, based on little or no research into the place held by imported programs in the economies of importing countries or in the lives of viewers. . . .	
The role of television in developing nations is far removed from what the specialists assert. . . .	
An empirical approach not unlike that of anthropologists is needed if communications specialists are to understand the impact of external (40) cultural influences on the lives of people in a society. . . .	
Communications researchers will also need to consider how to assess the position of the individual (55) viewer in their model of cultural relationships. . . .	

PrepTest51 Sec2 Qs 14–20

The Big Picture

Topic:

Scope:

Purpose:

Main Idea:

Now look at the entire passage. Were your predictions accurate?

Specialists in international communications almost unanimously assert that the broadcasting in developing nations of television programs produced by industrialized countries amounts to cultural

Specialists claim imported TV = Imperialism

(5) imperialism: the phenomenon of one culture's productions overwhelming another's, to the detriment of the flourishing of the latter. This assertion assumes

Specialists assumption

the automatic dominance of the imported productions and their negative effect on the domestic culture. But

(10) the assertion is polemical and abstract, based on little or no research into the place held by imported programs in the economies of importing countries or in the lives of viewers. This is not to deny that dominance is sometimes a risk in relationships

Author disagrees

(15) between cultures, but rather to say that the assertion lacks empirical foundation and in some cases goes against fact. For one example, imported programs rarely threaten the economic viability of the importing country's own television industry. For

Examples to support author

(20) another, imported programs do not uniformly attract larger audiences than domestically produced programs; viewers are not part of a passive, undifferentiated mass but are individuals with personal tastes, and most of them tend to prefer domestically

(25) produced television over imported television.

The role of television in developing nations is far removed from what the specialists assert. An anthropological study of one community that deals in part with residents' viewing habits where imported

Specialists wrong about role of TV

study

(30) programs are available cites the popularity of domestically produced serial dramas and points out that, because viewers enjoy following the dramas from day to day, television in the community can serve an analogous function to that of oral poetry,

Results TV like oral poetry

(35) which the residents often use at public gatherings as a daily journal of events of interest.

An empirical approach not unlike that of anthropologists is needed if communications specialists are to understand the impact of external

New approach needed

(40) cultural influences on the lives of people in a society. The first question they must investigate is: Given the evidence suggesting that the primary relationship of imported cultural productions to domestic ones is not dominance, then what model best represents the true

1st Q: if not dominance, what model?

(45) relationship? One possibility is that, rather than one culture's productions dominating another's, the domestic culture absorbs the imported productions and becomes enriched. Another is that the imported productions fuse with domestic culture only where

Absorb?

(50) the two share common aspects, such as the use of themes, situations, or character types that are relevant and interesting to both cultures.

Fuse w/ common aspects?

Communications researchers will also need to consider how to assess the position of the individual

2nd Q – How to assess individual viewers

(55) viewer in their model of cultural relationships. This model must emphasize the diversity of human responses, and will require engaging with the actual experiences of viewers, taking into account the variable contexts in which productions are

Requirements

(60) experienced, and the complex manner in which individuals ascribe meanings to those productions.

PrepTest51 Sec2 Qs 14–20

Big Picture Summaries:

Topic: TV programming in developed nations

Scope: Whether exportation of TV programming to developing nations amounts to "cultural imperialism"

Purpose: To refute specialists who insist that programming exported to developing nations dominates those nations' cultures

Main Idea: Specialists need to consider anthropological approaches and the roles of individual viewers to understand the impact of imported programming in developing nations.

Next, you'll see the TV and Developing Nations passage along with its question set just as it appeared on the test. You may try it now or come back to it after you have studied the Reading Comprehension question types and Steps 2–5 of the Reading Comprehension Method.

K | Part Four: Reading Comprehension
CHAPTER 14

Explanations for these questions
can be found in your Online Center.

Practice

Specialists in international communications almost
unanimously assert that the broadcasting in
developing nations of television programs produced
by industrialized countries amounts to cultural
(5) imperialism: the phenomenon of one culture's
productions overwhelming another's, to the detriment
of the flourishing of the latter. This assertion assumes
the automatic dominance of the imported productions
and their negative effect on the domestic culture. But
(10) the assertion is polemical and abstract, based on little
or no research into the place held by imported
programs in the economies of importing countries or
in the lives of viewers. This is not to deny that
dominance is sometimes a risk in relationships
(15) between cultures, but rather to say that the assertion
lacks empirical foundation and in some cases goes
against fact. For one example, imported programs
rarely threaten the economic viability of the
importing country's own television industry. For
(20) another, imported programs do not uniformly attract
larger audiences than domestically produced
programs; viewers are not part of a passive,
undifferentiated mass but are individuals with personal
tastes, and most of them tend to prefer domestically
(25) produced television over imported television.

The role of television in developing nations is far
removed from what the specialists assert. An
anthropological study of one community that deals in
part with residents' viewing habits where imported
(30) programs are available cites the popularity of
domestically produced serial dramas and points out
that, because viewers enjoy following the dramas
from day to day, television in the community can
serve an analogous function to that of oral poetry,
(35) which the residents often use at public gatherings as a
daily journal of events of interest.

An empirical approach not unlike that of
anthropologists is needed if communications
specialists are to understand the impact of external
(40) cultural influences on the lives of people in a society.
The first question they must investigate is: Given the
evidence suggesting that the primary relationship of
imported cultural productions to domestic ones is not
dominance, then what model best represents the true
(45) relationship? One possibility is that, rather than one
culture's productions dominating another's, the
domestic culture absorbs the imported productions
and becomes enriched. Another is that the imported
productions fuse with domestic culture only where
(50) the two share common aspects, such as the use of
themes, situations, or character types that are relevant
and interesting to both cultures.

Communications researchers will also need to
consider how to assess the position of the individual
(55) viewer in their model of cultural relationships. This
model must emphasize the diversity of human
responses, and will require engaging with the actual
experiences of viewers, taking into account the
variable contexts in which productions are
(60) experienced, and the complex manner in which
individuals ascribe meanings to those productions.

9. The primary purpose of the passage is to

(A) determine which of two hypotheses considered
by a certain discipline is correct

(B) discredit the evidence offered for a claim made
by a particular discipline

(C) argue that a certain discipline should adopt a
particular methodology

(D) examine similar methodological weaknesses in
two different disciplines

(E) compare the views of two different disciplines
on an issue

10. Which one of the following most accurately describes
the organization of the passage?

(A) The author takes issue with an assertion,
suggests reasons why the assertion is supported
by its proponents, introduces a new view that
runs counter to the assertion, and presents
examples to support the new view.

(B) The author takes issue with an assertion,
presents examples that run counter to the
assertion, suggests that a particular approach be
taken by the proponents of the assertion, and
discusses two questions that should be
addressed in the new approach.

(C) The author takes issue with an assertion,
introduces a new view that runs counter to the
assertion, presents examples that support the
new view, and gives reasons why proponents
of the assertion should abandon it and adopt
the new view.

(D) The author takes issue with an assertion,
presents examples that run counter to the
assertion, suggests a change in the approach
taken by the proponents of the assertion, and
discusses two ways in which the new approach
will benefit the proponents.

(E) The author takes issue with an assertion,
presents examples that run counter to the
assertion, introduces a new view that runs
counter to the assertion, and suggests ways in
which a compromise may be found between
the view and the assertion.

GO ON TO THE NEXT PAGE.

Explanations for these questions can be found in your Online Center.

Part Four: Reading Comprehension
Reading Comprehension: Passage Types and Question Types

K

11. Which one of the following is the most logical continuation of the last paragraph of the passage?

   (A) Lacking such an emphasis, we cannot judge conclusively the degree to which cultural relationships can be described by an abstract model.

   (B) Without such an emphasis, we can be confident that the dominance view asserted by communications specialists will survive the criticisms leveled against it.

   (C) Unless they do so, we cannot know for certain whether the model developed describes accurately the impact of external cultural influences on the lives of people.

   (D) Until they agree to do so, we can remain secure in the knowledge that communications specialists will never fully gain the scientific credibility they so passionately crave.

   (E) But even with such an emphasis, it will be the extent to which the model accurately describes the economic relationship between cultures that determines its usefulness.

12. The author most likely discusses an anthropological study in the second paragraph primarily in order to

   (A) provide to international communications specialists a model of cultural relationships

   (B) describe to international communications specialists new ways of conducting their research

   (C) highlight the flaws in a similar study conducted by international communications specialists

   (D) cite evidence that contradicts claims made by international communications specialists

   (E) support the claim that international communications specialists need to take the diversity of individual viewing habits into account

13. Which one of the following can most reasonably be concluded about the television viewers who were the subject of the study discussed in the second paragraph?

   (A) They will gradually come to prefer imported television programs over domestic ones.

   (B) They are likely someday to give up oral poetry in favor of watching television exclusively.

   (C) They would likely watch more television if they did not have oral poetry.

   (D) They enjoy domestic television programs mainly because they have little access to imported ones.

   (E) They watch television for some of the same reasons that they enjoy oral poetry.

14. According to the author, an empirical study of the effect of external cultural influences on the lives of people in a society must begin by identifying

   (A) the viewing habits and tastes of the people in the society

   (B) an accurate model of how imported cultural productions influence domestic ones

   (C) the role of the external cultural influences in the daily life of the people in the society

   (D) shared aspects of domestic and imported productions popular with mass audiences

   (E) social factors that affect how external cultural productions are given meaning by viewers

15. Suppose a study is conducted that measures the amount of airtime allotted to imported television programming in the daily broadcasting schedules of several developing nations. Given the information in the passage, the results of that study would be most directly relevant to answering which one of the following questions?

   (A) How does the access to imported cultural productions differ among these nations?

   (B) What are the individual viewing habits of citizens in these nations?

   (C) How influential are the domestic television industries in these nations?

   (D) Do imported programs attract larger audiences than domestic ones in these nations?

   (E) What model best describes the relationship between imported cultural influences and domestic culture in these nations?

PrepTest51 Sec2 Qs 14–20

LSAT Reading Comprehension Passage Types

Experts know that the LSAT generates the same types of passages on test after test. Every LSAT will have one passage from each of these four broad topics: Natural Science, Humanities, Social Science, and Law.

While that's helpful to know, it's not nearly as helpful as knowing that LSAT passages are *structured* in similar—and therefore predictable—ways. The four passage *structure* types are: Theory/Perspective, Event/Phenomenon, Biography, and Debate.

READING COMPREHENSION PASSAGE TYPES

- **Theory/Perspective**—The passage focuses on a thinker's theory or perspective on some part of the Topic; typically (though not always), the author disagrees and critiques the opponent's perspective or defends his own.

- **Event/Phenomenon**—The passage focuses on an event, a breakthrough development, or a problem that has arisen; when a solution to the problem is proposed, the author most often agrees with the solution (and that represents the passage's Main Idea).

- **Biography**—The passage discusses something about a notable person; the aspect of the person's life emphasized by the author reflects the Scope of the passage.

- **Debate**—The passage outlines two opposing positions (neither of which is the author's) on some aspect of the Topic; the author may side with one of the positions, may remain neutral, or may critique both. (This structure has been rare on recent LSATs.)

Practice

Take a look at the following passage. Read the passage strategically and Roadmap it. Then, identify the passage structure. After you're done, compare your work to that of an LSAT expert on the next page.

An effort should be made to dispel the misunderstandings that still prevent the much-needed synthesis and mutual supplementation of science and the humanities. This reconciliation should not be too
(5) difficult once it is recognized that the separation is primarily the result of a basic misunderstanding of the philosophical foundations of both science and the humanities.

Some humanists still identify science with an
(10) absurd mechanistic reductionism. There are many who feel that the scientist is interested in nothing more than "bodies in motion," in the strictly mathematical, physical, and chemical laws that govern the material world. This is the caricature of science drawn by
(15) representatives of the humanities who are ignorant of the nature of modern science and also of the scientific outlook in philosophy. For example, it is claimed that science either ignores or explains away the most essential human values. Those who believe this also
(20) assert that there are aspects of the human mind, manifest especially in the domains of morality, religion, and the arts, that contain an irreducible spiritual element and for that reason can never be adequately explained by science.
(25) Some scientists, on the other hand, claim that the humanist is interested in nothing more than emotion and sentiment, exhibiting the vagrant fancies of an undisciplined mind. To such men and women the humanities are useless because they serve no immediate
(30) and technological function for the practical survival of human society in the material world. Such pragmatists believe that the areas of morality, religion, and the arts should have only a secondary importance in people's lives.
(35) Thus there are misconceptions among humanists and scientists alike that are in need of correction. This correction leads to a much more acceptable position that could be called "scientific humanism," attempting as it does to combine the common elements of both
(40) disciplines. Both science and the humanities attempt to describe and explain. It is true that they begin their descriptions and explanations at widely separated points, but the objectives remain the same: a clearer understanding of people and their world. In achieving
(45) this understanding, science in fact does not depend exclusively on measurable data, and the humanities in fact profit from attempts at controlled evaluation. Scientific humanism can combine the scientific attitude with an active interest in the whole scale of
(50) human values. If uninformed persons insist on viewing science as only materialistic and the humanities as only idealistic, a fruitful collaboration of both fields is unlikely. The combination of science and the humanities is, however, possible, even probable, if we
(55) begin by noting their common objectives, rather than seeing only their different means.

PrepTest57 Sec4 Qs 6–12

Big Picture Summaries:
Topic:
Scope:
Purpose:
Main Idea:

Expert Analysis

The LSAT expert sees this as a Theory/Perspective passage. Compare your Roadmap to hers. While humanists and scientists disagree, the focus of this passage is not their debate, but rather their mutual misunderstandings. The author's perspective is that each side would benefit from understanding the other and learning to value the other's techniques.

LSAT Passage	Analysis
An effort should be made to dispel the misunderstandings that still prevent the much-needed synthesis and mutual supplementation of science and the humanities. This reconciliation should not be too (5) difficult once it is recognized that the separation is primarily the result of a basic misunderstanding of the philosophical foundations of both science and the humanities. *Auth: reconcile sci/hum* *Basically misunderstood*	**Step 1:** The first sentence begins with the author's clear opinion: We should (strong authorial recommendation) "dispel the misunderstandings" blocking a "much-needed" (strong Emphasis/Opinion Keyword) synthesis of science and the humanities. In other words: Science and the humanities should be brought together. Author's clear opinion provides the **Topic** (science and the humanities) and **Scope** (the gap that separates them). The next lines (4–8) reveal the author's **Purpose**: to explain that the gap is "primarily the result of" a misunderstanding of each side's underlying philosophy.
Some humanists still identify science with an (10) absurd mechanistic reductionism. There are many who feel that the scientist is interested in nothing more than "bodies in motion," in the strictly mathematical, physical, and chemical laws that govern the material world. This is the caricature of science drawn by (15) representatives of the humanities who are ignorant of the nature of modern science and also of the scientific outlook in philosophy. For example, it is claimed that science either ignores or explains away the most essential human values. Those who believe this also (20) assert that there are aspects of the human mind, manifest especially in the domains of morality, religion, and the arts, that contain an irreducible spiritual element and for that reason can never be adequately explained by science. *Humanists— sci too reductive* *Auth: they don't know real sci* *Ex.*	Paragraph 2 begins with one misunderstanding: *some humanists claim* scientists reduce everything to the mechanical laws of math, physics, and chemistry. But that's a "caricature" by those "ignorant of" what science really is, and line 17 provides an example: To the ignorant humanists, science is clueless about basic human values because science can't appreciate the "irreducible spiritual element" of the artistic and moral human mind.
(25) Some scientists, on the other hand, claim that the humanist is interested in nothing more than emotion and sentiment, exhibiting the vagrant fancies of an undisciplined mind. To such men and women the humanities are useless because they serve no immediate (30) and technological function for the practical survival of human society in the material world. Such pragmatists believe that the areas of morality, religion, and the arts should have only a secondary importance in people's lives. *Scientists— hum. is just emotion- useless*	Paragraph 3 provides the other misunderstanding: *some scientists claim* that humanists also have a blind spot. The scientists caricature humanists as emotional, sentimental, and undisciplined. Ultimately, the work produced by humanists is "useless because" it can't help our species survive.

LSAT Passage	**Analysis**

(35)   Thus there are misconceptions among humanists and scientists alike that are in need of correction. This correction leads to a much more acceptable position that could be called "scientific humanism," attempting as it does to combine the common elements of both

Auth: correct the mis-under-standing

(40) disciplines. Both science and the humanities attempt to describe and explain. It is true that they begin their descriptions and explanations at widely separated points, but the objectives remain the same: a clearer understanding of people and their world. In achieving

Find common ground

(45) this understanding, science in fact does not depend exclusively on measurable data, and the humanities in fact profit from attempts at controlled evaluation. Scientific humanism can combine the scientific attitude with an active interest in the whole scale of

(50) human values. If uninformed persons insist on viewing science as only materialistic and the humanities as only idealistic, a fruitful collaboration of both fields is unlikely. The combination of science and the humanities is, however, possible, even probable, if we

If views stay the same reconcilia-tion unlikely

(55) begin by noting their common objectives, rather than seeing only their different means.

If note common obj. combination probable

PrepTest57 Sec4 Qs 6–12

The author states that these misconceptions are "in need of correction," and then proposes a "much more acceptable position" called "scientific humanism." This new position accepts that both people of science and people of the arts want to understand the world better. Science doesn't just rely on raw data (lines 45–46), nor are humanists utterly oblivious to "controlled evaluation" (i.e., measurement). The author's **Main Idea** is then clearly stated: Studying the commonalities of both fields will produce a probable "fruitful collaboration."

You will work through this passage's questions later in this chapter.

Theory/Perspective and Event/Phenomenon are by far the most common passage types. Together, they account for over 80 percent of the Reading Comprehension passages included on recent administrations of the LSAT. The other passage types, Biography and Debate, show up infrequently.

Take a look back at a passage you've seen before. How would you categorize this passage?

Fractal geometry is a mathematical theory devoted to the study of complex shapes called fractals. Although an exact definition of fractals has not been established, fractals commonly exhibit the property of self-similarity:
(5) the reiteration of irregular details or patterns at progressively smaller scales so that each part, when magnified, looks basically like the object as a whole. The Koch curve is a significant fractal in mathematics and examining it provides some insight into fractal
(10) geometry. To generate the Koch curve, one begins with a straight line. The middle third of the line is removed and replaced with two line segments, each as long as the removed piece, which are positioned so as to meet and form the top of a triangle. At this stage,
(15) the curve consists of four connected segments of equal length that form a pointed protrusion in the middle. This process is repeated on the four segments so that all the protrusions are on the same side of the curve, and then the process is repeated indefinitely on the
(20) segments at each stage of the construction.

Self-similarity is built into the construction process by treating segments at each stage the same way as the original segment was treated. Since the rules for getting from one stage to another are fully
(25) explicit and always the same, images of successive stages of the process can be generated by computer. Theoretically, the Koch curve is the result of infinitely many steps in the construction process, but the finest image approximating the Koch curve will be limited
(30) by the fact that eventually the segments will get too short to be drawn or displayed. However, using computer graphics to produce images of successive stages of the construction process dramatically illustrates a major attraction of fractal geometry:
(35) simple processes can be responsible for incredibly complex patterns.

A worldwide public has become captivated by fractal geometry after viewing astonishing computer-generated images of fractals; enthusiastic practitioners
(40) in the field of fractal geometry consider it a new language for describing complex natural and mathematical forms. They anticipate that fractal geometry's significance will rival that of calculus and expect that proficiency in fractal geometry will allow
(45) mathematicians to describe the form of a cloud as easily and precisely as an architect can describe a house using the language of traditional geometry. Other mathematicians have reservations about the fractal geometers' preoccupation with computer-generated
(50) graphic images and their lack of interest in theory. These mathematicians point out that traditional

mathematics consists of proving theorems, and while many theorems about fractals have already been proven using the notions of pre-fractal mathematics,
(55) fractal geometers have proven only a handful of theorems that could not have been proven with pre-fractal mathematics. According to these mathematicians, fractal geometry can attain a lasting role in mathematics only if it becomes a precise
(60) language supporting a system of theorems and proofs.

PrepTest57 Sec4 Qs 20–27

Fractal def.

Koch curve—how generated

Each segment the same

Computer models simple process = complex pattern

Computer images → public interest

Some experts predict huge impact

Others doubt value

Very few new theorems proven w/fractal geo

Needs theorems & proofs

Practice

Read and Roadmap another passage. Additionally, try to identify the passage's type.

The United States government agency responsible for overseeing television and radio broadcasting, the Federal Communications Commission (FCC), had an early history of addressing only the concerns of parties
(5) with an economic interest in broadcasting—chiefly broadcasting companies. The rights of viewers and listeners were not recognized by the FCC, which regarded them merely as members of the public. Unless citizens' groups were applying for broadcasting
(10) licenses, citizens did not have the standing necessary to voice their views at an FCC hearing. Consequently, the FCC appeared to be exclusively at the service of the broadcasting industry.

A landmark case changed the course of that
(15) history. In 1964, a local television station in Jackson, Mississippi was applying for a renewal of its broadcasting license. The United Church of Christ, representing Jackson's African American population, petitioned the FCC for a hearing about the broadcasting
(20) policies of that station. The church charged that the station advocated racial segregation to the point of excluding news and programs supporting integration. Arguing that the church lacked the level of economic interest required for a hearing, the FCC rejected the
(25) petition, though it attempted to mollify the church by granting only a short-term, probationary renewal to the station. Further, the FCC claimed that since it accepted the church's contentions with regard to misconduct on the part of the broadcasters, no hearing was necessary.
(30) However, that decision raised a question: If the contentions concerning the station were accepted, why was its license renewed at all? The real reason for denying the church a hearing was more likely the prospect that citizens' groups representing community
(35) preferences would begin to enter the closed worlds of government and industry.

The church appealed the FCC's decision in court, and in 1967 was granted the right to a public hearing on the station's request for a long-term license. The
(40) hearing was to little avail: the FCC dismissed much of the public input and granted a full renewal to the station. The church appealed again, and this time the judge took the unprecedented step of revoking the station's license without remand to the FCC, ruling that the
(45) church members were performing a public service in voicing the legitimate concerns of the community and, as such, should be accorded the right to challenge the renewal of the station's broadcasting license.

The case established a formidable precedent for
(50) opening up to the public the world of broadcasting.

Subsequent rulings have supported the right of the public to question the performance of radio and television licensees before the FCC at renewal time every three years. Along with racial issues, a range of
(55) other matters—from the quality of children's programming and the portrayal of violence to equal time for opposing political viewpoints—are now discussed at licensing proceedings because of the church's intervention.

PrepTest57 Sec4 Qs 1–5

```
Big Picture Summaries:

Topic:

Scope:

Purpose:

Main Idea:
```

Expert analysis for this passage is on pages 914–915.

Expert Analysis

The LSAT expert sees this as an Event/Phenomenon passage. Compare your Roadmap to hers.

LSAT Passage	Analysis
The United States government agency responsible for overseeing television and radio broadcasting, the Federal Communications Commission (FCC), had an early history of addressing only the concerns of parties (5) with an economic interest in broadcasting—chiefly broadcasting companies. The rights of viewers and listeners were not recognized by the FCC, which regarded them merely as members of the public. Unless citizens' groups were applying for broadcasting (10) licenses, citizens did not have the standing necessary to voice their views at an FCC hearing. Consequently, the FCC appeared to be exclusively at the service of the broadcasting industry. *FCC— early only focused on broadcasters* *Citizens— no standing*	**Step 1:** Paragraph 1 introduces the **Topic** of the passage (the FCC) as well as its **Scope:** the FCC's concerns for the public regarding broadcasting license renewal. The paragraph describes the early history of the FCC: Only broadcasters' interests were considered, while the public's rights were not recognized. The only way citizens could voice their opinion was via an application for a broadcasting license.
A landmark case changed the course of that (15) history. In 1964, a local television station in Jackson, Mississippi was applying for a renewal of its broadcasting license. The United Church of Christ, representing Jackson's African American population, petitioned the FCC for a hearing about the broadcasting (20) policies of that station. The church charged that the station advocated racial segregation to the point of excluding news and programs supporting integration. Arguing that the church lacked the level of economic interest required for a hearing, the FCC rejected the (25) petition, though it attempted to mollify the church by granting only a short-term, probationary renewal to the station. Further, the FCC claimed that since it accepted the church's contentions with regard to misconduct on the part of the broadcasters, no hearing was necessary. (30) However, that decision raised a question: If the contentions concerning the station were accepted, why was its license renewed at all? The real reason for denying the church a hearing was more likely the prospect that citizens' groups representing community (35) preferences would begin to enter the closed worlds of government and industry. *Change MS UCC case with FCC* *FCC said church lacked economic interest— no hearing needed* *Issue standing for citizen groups?*	Paragraph 2 starts with strong Emphasis Keywords that call attention to a *landmark* case that *changed* history. In challenging a TV station's license renewal, the United Church of Christ "charged" that the station was racist. Lines 23–29 detail the FCC's response: "no hearing was necessary" because the FCC agreed that the UCC was right about the racist misconduct. That raised a question: Why was the station's license renewed if it was clearly misbehaving? The author responds with an opinion ("the real reason ... was more likely"): The higher-ups didn't want the community sticking its nose into the "closed worlds" of power.
The church appealed the FCC's decision in court, and in 1967 was granted the right to a public hearing on the station's request for a long-term license. The (40) hearing was to little avail; the FCC dismissed much of the public input and granted a full renewal to the station. The church appealed again, and this time the judge took the unprecedented step of revoking the station's license without remand to the FCC, ruling that the (45) church members were performing a public service in voicing the legitimate concerns of the community and, as such, should be accorded the right to challenge the renewal of the station's broadcasting license. *1st Appeal— FCC rejects church* *2nd Appeal— Judge overrules*	Paragraph 3 describes two events: First, the church's original appeal was dismissed by the FCC. But the church's second appeal was successful: A judge took the unprecedented step of revoking the station's license, claiming that church members were performing a public service.

LSAT Passage		**Analysis**

The case established a formidable precedent for
(50) opening up to the public the world of broadcasting.
Subsequent rulings have supported the right of the
public to question the performance of radio and
television licensees before the FCC at renewal time
every three years. Along with racial issues, a range of
(55) other matters—from the quality of children's
programming and the portrayal of violence to equal
time for opposing political viewpoints—are now
discussed at licensing proceedings because of the
church's intervention.

Case—strong ruling

More case support

Public role expanded

PrepTest57 Sec4 Qs 1–5

Paragraph 4's references to "formidable precedent" and "subsequent rulings" pull the passage into the present day, where the public's right to weigh in on broadcast licenses has been well established. The inquiries aren't just race-based anymore but, rather, a "range of other matters," all "because of" the UCC's heroism. The author's **Purpose** is to trace the history of the public's ability to influence broadcast licensure renewal, leading to the author's **Main Idea**—"A landmark case changed the course" of history, and a subsequent judicial ruling took the "unprecedented step" of allowing public involvement in licensing proceedings—a revolution that all dates back to a determined church in Jackson, Mississippi, in 1964.

This complete passage and its questions can be found on the following pages.

K | Part Four: Reading Comprehension
CHAPTER 14

Explanations for these questions
can be found in your Online Center.

Practice

The United States government agency responsible for overseeing television and radio broadcasting, the Federal Communications Commission (FCC), had an early history of addressing only the concerns of parties
(5) with an economic interest in broadcasting—chiefly broadcasting companies. The rights of viewers and listeners were not recognized by the FCC, which regarded them merely as members of the public. Unless citizens' groups were applying for broadcasting
(10) licenses, citizens did not have the standing necessary to voice their views at an FCC hearing. Consequently, the FCC appeared to be exclusively at the service of the broadcasting industry.

A landmark case changed the course of that
(15) history. In 1964, a local television station in Jackson, Mississippi was applying for a renewal of its broadcasting license. The United Church of Christ, representing Jackson's African American population, petitioned the FCC for a hearing about the broadcasting
(20) policies of that station. The church charged that the station advocated racial segregation to the point of excluding news and programs supporting integration. Arguing that the church lacked the level of economic interest required for a hearing, the FCC rejected the
(25) petition, though it attempted to mollify the church by granting only a short-term, probationary renewal to the station. Further, the FCC claimed that since it accepted the church's contentions with regard to misconduct on the part of the broadcasters, no hearing was necessary.
(30) However, that decision raised a question: If the contentions concerning the station were accepted, why was its license renewed at all? The real reason for denying the church a hearing was more likely the prospect that citizens' groups representing community
(35) preferences would begin to enter the closed worlds of government and industry.

The church appealed the FCC's decision in court, and in 1967 was granted the right to a public hearing on the station's request for a long-term license. The
(40) hearing was to little avail: the FCC dismissed much of the public input and granted a full renewal to the station. The church appealed again, and this time the judge took the unprecedented step of revoking the station's license without remand to the FCC, ruling that the
(45) church members were performing a public service in voicing the legitimate concerns of the community and, as such, should be accorded the right to challenge the renewal of the station's broadcasting license.

The case established a formidable precedent for
(50) opening up to the public the world of broadcasting.

Subsequent rulings have supported the right of the public to question the performance of radio and television licensees before the FCC at renewal time every three years. Along with racial issues, a range of
(55) other matters—from the quality of children's programming and the portrayal of violence to equal time for opposing political viewpoints—are now discussed at licensing proceedings because of the church's intervention.

16. Which one of the following most accurately expresses the main point of the passage?

(A) Because of the efforts of a church group in challenging an FCC decision, public input is now considered in broadcast licensing proceedings.

(B) Court rulings have forced the FCC to abandon policies that appeared to encourage biased coverage of public issues.

(C) The history of the FCC is important because it explains why government agencies are now forced to respond to public input.

(D) Because it has begun to serve the interests of the public, the FCC is less responsive to the broadcasting industry.

(E) In response to pressure from citizens' groups, the FCC has decided to open its license renewal hearings to the public.

Explanations for these questions can be found in your Online Center.

Part Four: Reading Comprehension
Reading Comprehension: Passage Types and Question Types

17. The author mentions some additional topics now discussed at FCC hearings (lines 54–59) primarily in order to

(A) support the author's claim that the case helped to open up to the public the world of broadcasting

(B) suggest the level of vigilance that citizens' groups must maintain with regard to broadcasters

(C) provide an explanation of why the public is allowed to question the performance of broadcasters on such a frequent basis

(D) illustrate other areas of misconduct with which the station discussed in the passage was charged

(E) demonstrate that the station discussed in the passage was not the only one to fall short of its obligation to the public

18. Which one of the following statements is affirmed by the passage?

(A) The broadcasting industry's economic goals can be met most easily by minimizing the attention given to the interests of viewers and listeners.

(B) The FCC was advised by broadcasters to bar groups with no economic interest in broadcasting from hearings concerning the broadcasting industry.

(C) The court ruled in the case brought by the United Church of Christ that the FCC had the ultimate authority to decide whether to renew a broadcaster's license.

(D) Before the United Church of Christ won its case, the FCC would not allow citizens' groups to speak as members of the public at FCC hearings.

(E) The case brought by the United Church of Christ represents the first time a citizens' group was successful in getting its concerns about government agencies addressed to its satisfaction.

19. Based on information presented in the passage, with which one of the following statements would the author be most likely to agree?

(A) If the United Church of Christ had not pursued its case, the FCC would not have been aware of the television station's broadcasting policies.

(B) By their very nature, industrial and business interests are opposed to public interests.

(C) The recourse of a citizens' group to the courts represents an effective means of protecting public interests.

(D) Governmental regulation cannot safeguard against individual businesses acting contrary to public interests.

(E) The government cannot be trusted to favor the rights of the public over broadcasters' economic interests.

20. The passage suggests that which one of the following has been established by the case discussed in the third paragraph?

(A) Broadcasters are legally obligated to hold regular meetings at which the public can voice its concerns about broadcasting policies.

(B) Broadcasters are now required by the FCC to consult citizens' groups when making programming decisions.

(C) Except in cases involving clear misconduct by a broadcaster, the FCC need not seek public input in licensing hearings.

(D) When evaluating the performance of a broadcaster applying for a license renewal, the FCC must obtain information about the preferences of the public.

(E) In FCC licensing proceedings, parties representing community preferences should be granted standing along with those with an economic interest in broadcasting.

PrepTest57 Sec4 Qs 1–5

Comparative Reading

One time per section, the LSAT presents a Comparative Reading selection. Instead of a single passage of 450 to 500 words, you'll see two shorter passages labeled Passage A and Passage B that together have roughly the same word count. The two passages always share the same Topic and sometimes the same Scope. The passages almost always differ, however, in Purpose and Main Idea. That doesn't mean that the two authors disagree. Indeed, many of the questions will reward you for being able to characterize what the passages share and where they differ.

LSAT STRATEGY NOTE

- Roadmap Comparative Reading passages as usual
- Think about T/S/P/MI for each
- Consider the relationship between the passages

On Comparative Reading passages, approach strategic reading and Roadmapping just as you would on regular passages with one exception: After you Roadmap the two passages, take a few seconds to catalogue their similarities and differences. Here are some helpful questions to ask about the two passages.

LSAT STRATEGY

To compare Comparative Reading passages, ask:

- Are the passages different in Scope, Purpose, or Main Idea? The answer will generally be yes; make sure to characterize the differences.
- Do the passages share common details, examples, or evidence? The answer is often yes, but beware, the two authors may reach very different conclusions or make different recommendations based on the same underlying facts.
- If either author makes a contention or recommendation, how would the other author respond to it? The test is fond of Inference questions that ask whether one author would agree or disagree with something the other said.
- Do the two passages share a common principle? If yes, paraphrase the principle; if no, characterize how the authors approach the Topic differently.

Practice

Read and Roadmap the following Comparative Reading selection. Summarize the big picture for each passage independently. Then, compare the passages.

Passage A

Recent studies have shown that sophisticated computer models of the oceans and atmosphere are capable of simulating large-scale climate trends with remarkable accuracy. But these models make use of
(5) large numbers of variables, many of which have wide ranges of possible values. Because even small differences in those values can have a significant impact on what the simulations predict, it is important to determine the impact when values differ even
(10) slightly.

Since the interactions between the many variables in climate simulations are highly complex, there is no alternative to a "brute force" exploration of all possible combinations of their values if predictions
(15) are to be reliable. This method requires very large numbers of calculations and simulation runs. For example, exhaustive examination of five values for each of only nine variables would require 2 million calculation-intensive simulation runs. Currently
(20) available individual computers are completely inadequate for such a task.

However, the continuing increase in computing capacity of the average desktop computer means that climate simulations can now be run on privately
(25) owned desktop machines connected to one another via the Internet. The calculations are divided among the individual desktop computers, which work simultaneously on their share of the overall problem. Some public resource computing projects of this kind
(30) have already been successful, although only when they captured the public's interest sufficiently to secure widespread participation.

Passage B

Researchers are now learning that many problems in nature, human society, science, and engineering are
(35) naturally "parallel"; that is, that they can be effectively solved by using methods that work simultaneously in parallel. These problems share the common characteristic of involving a large number of similar elements such as molecules, animals, even
(40) people, whose individual actions are governed by simple rules but, taken collectively, function as a highly complex system.

An example is the method used by ants to forage for food. As Lewis Thomas observed, a solitary ant is
(45) little more than a few neurons strung together by fibers. Its behavior follows a few simple rules. But when one sees a dense mass of thousands of ants, crowded together around their anthill retrieving food or repelling an intruder, a more complex picture
(50) emerges; it is as if the whole is thinking, planning, calculating. It is an intelligence, a kind of live computer, with crawling bits for wits.

We are now living through a great paradigm shift in the field of computing, a shift from sequential
(55) computing (performing one calculation at a time) to massive parallel computing, which employs thousands of computers working simultaneously to solve one computation-intensive problem. Since many computation-intensive problems are inherently
(60) parallel, it only makes sense to use a computing model that exploits that parallelism. A computing model that resembles the inherently parallel problem it is trying to solve will perform best. The old paradigm, in contrast, is subject to the speed limits
(65) imposed by purely sequential computing.

PrepTest59 Sec4 Qs 1–8

Topic:	**Topic:**
Scope:	**Scope:**
Purpose:	**Purpose:**
Main Idea:	**Main Idea:**

Compare/Contrast the passages:

Expert Analysis

Here's how an LSAT expert would Roadmap this Comparative Reading selection. Compare your work.

LSAT Passage	Analysis
Passage A	**Step 1:** This speaks of the promise of computer simulations for predicting the motions of the ocean and the atmosphere. This provides a general **Topic**, computers, and **Scope**, their use in predictions. The Keyword *but* at the beginning of the second sentence signals a potential complication. Such systems have many variables with large ranges, and even small variability can have a big impact.

Recent studies have shown that sophisticated computer models of the oceans and atmosphere are capable of simulating large-scale climate trends with remarkable accuracy. But these models make use of
(5) large numbers of variables, many of which have wide ranges of possible values. Because even small differences in those values can have a significant impact on what the simulations predict, it is important to determine the impact when values differ even
(10) slightly.

Comp models can accurately simulate climate but variable concerns

---

Since the interactions between the many variables in climate simulations are highly complex, there is no alternative to a "brute force" exploration of all possible combinations of their values if predictions
(15) are to be reliable. This method requires very large numbers of calculations and simulation runs. For example, exhaustive examination of five values for each of only nine variables would require 2 million calculation-intensive simulation runs. Currently
(20) available individual computers are completely inadequate for such a task.

To get it right need lots of calculations

Indiv. computers can't do it

Paragraph 2 discusses the complications a bit more. The only way to account for these variables is with massive numbers of calculations. The last sentence is the key: Current computers are not able to handle the task.

However, the continuing increase in computing capacity of the average desktop computer means that climate simulations can now be run on privately
(25) owned desktop machines connected to one another via the Internet. The calculations are divided among the individual desktop computers, which work simultaneously on their share of the overall problem. Some public resource computing projects of this kind
(30) have already been successful, although only when they captured the public's interest sufficiently to secure widespread participation.

Can do it w/ combined indiv. computers on internet

Public interest impt

This paragraph provides the **Purpose**: proposing a possible solution to the problem. That solution is the **Main Idea**: By linking networks of individual computers, large problems can be solved much more quickly. The last sentence says that, while this is possible, it will only become widespread when it captures the public's attention. Note the causal clause at the end of the passage as likely giving rise to a question.

Passage B

Researchers are now learning that many problems in nature, human society, science, and engineering are
(35) naturally "parallel"; that is, that they can be effectively solved by using methods that work simultaneously in parallel. These problems share the common characteristic of involving a large number of similar elements such as molecules, animals, even
(40) people, whose individual actions are governed by simple rules but, taken collectively, function as a highly complex system.

"Parallel" problems – many natural probs can be solved at same time b/c function together

Passage B begins by explaining that many systems in nature are parallel. It then defines parallel systems, the passage's **Topic**, as being made up of many similar items moving simply individually but together moving as a complicated whole. This is a relatively abstract paragraph.

LSAT Passage (cont.)	Analysis (cont.)

An example is the method used by ants to forage for food. As Lewis Thomas observed, a solitary ant is
(45) little more than a few neurons strung together by fibers. Its behavior follows a few simple rules. But when one sees a dense mass of thousands of ants, crowded together around their anthill retrieving food or repelling an intruder, a more complex picture
(50) emerges; it is as if the whole is thinking, planning, calculating. It is an intelligence, a kind of live computer, with crawling bits for wits.

Thomas – Ex. ants akin to a computer

This paragraph makes the abstraction more specific. It starts with an example, ants. Ants are simple creatures that work together to create a complicated system. The paragraph ends with a comparison between ants and computers: An ant colony is a type of living computer. A comparison is a red flag for a potential question later. More importantly, this finally sets up a relationship between both passages—they both talk about computers.

We are now living through a great paradigm shift in the field of computing, a shift from sequential
(55) computing (performing one calculation at a time) to massive parallel computing, which employs thousands of computers working simultaneously to solve one computation-intensive problem. Since many computation-intensive problems are inherently
(60) parallel, it only makes sense to use a computing model that exploits that parallelism. A computing model that resembles the inherently parallel problem it is trying to solve will perform best. The old paradigm, in contrast, is subject to the speed limits
(65) imposed by purely sequential computing.

Big shift from sequential to parallel

Auth – parallel computing is best

Paragraph 3 finally delves into the concept of parallelism in terms of computers, the **Scope**. The **Purpose** is merely to explain what the author calls a "paradigm shift in the field of computing." The **Main Idea** is that there is a shift from using one computer at a time to using many computers at once for computation-intensive problems.

PrepTest59 Sec4 Qs 1–8

Compare/Contrast the Passages: The two passages have a similar Purpose: Both passages consider parallel computing as the solution to problems. Passage B even goes so far as to say that parallel computing mimics natural systems, so its development is a natural progression.

Passage A uses weather models as its primary example, while Passage B speaks abstractly about natural systems. The specific example in Passage B is the ant colony.

Next, you'll see the Parallel Computing passage along with its question set just as it appeared on the test. You may try it now or come back to it after you have studied the Reading Comprehension question types and Steps 2–5 of the Reading Comprehension Method.

K | Part Four: Reading Comprehension
CHAPTER 14

Explanations for these questions
can be found in your Online Center.

Practice

Passage A

Recent studies have shown that sophisticated computer models of the oceans and atmosphere are capable of simulating large-scale climate trends with remarkable accuracy. But these models make use of
(5) large numbers of variables, many of which have wide ranges of possible values. Because even small differences in those values can have a significant impact on what the simulations predict, it is important to determine the impact when values differ even
(10) slightly.

Since the interactions between the many variables in climate simulations are highly complex, there is no alternative to a "brute force" exploration of all possible combinations of their values if predictions
(15) are to be reliable. This method requires very large numbers of calculations and simulation runs. For example, exhaustive examination of five values for each of only nine variables would require 2 million calculation-intensive simulation runs. Currently
(20) available individual computers are completely inadequate for such a task.

However, the continuing increase in computing capacity of the average desktop computer means that climate simulations can now be run on privately
(25) owned desktop machines connected to one another via the Internet. The calculations are divided among the individual desktop computers, which work simultaneously on their share of the overall problem. Some public resource computing projects of this kind
(30) have already been successful, although only when they captured the public's interest sufficiently to secure widespread participation.

Passage B

Researchers are now learning that many problems in nature, human society, science, and engineering are
(35) naturally "parallel"; that is, that they can be effectively solved by using methods that work simultaneously in parallel. These problems share the common characteristic of involving a large number of similar elements such as molecules, animals, even
(40) people, whose individual actions are governed by simple rules but, taken collectively, function as a highly complex system.

An example is the method used by ants to forage for food. As Lewis Thomas observed, a solitary ant is
(45) little more than a few neurons strung together by fibers. Its behavior follows a few simple rules. But when one sees a dense mass of thousands of ants, crowded together around their anthill retrieving food or repelling an intruder, a more complex picture

(50) emerges; it is as if the whole is thinking, planning, calculating. It is an intelligence, a kind of live computer, with crawling bits for wits.

We are now living through a great paradigm shift in the field of computing, a shift from sequential
(55) computing (performing one calculation at a time) to massive parallel computing, which employs thousands of computers working simultaneously to solve one computation-intensive problem. Since many computation-intensive problems are inherently
(60) parallel, it only makes sense to use a computing model that exploits that parallelism. A computing model that resembles the inherently parallel problem it is trying to solve will perform best. The old paradigm, in contrast, is subject to the speed limits
(65) imposed by purely sequential computing.

21. Which one of the following most accurately expresses the main point of passage B?

    (A) Many difficult problems in computing are naturally parallel.

    (B) Sequential computing is no longer useful because of the speed limits it imposes.

    (C) There is currently a paradigm shift occurring in the field of computing toward parallel computing.

    (D) Complex biological and social systems are the next frontier in the field of computer simulation.

    (E) Inherently parallel computing problems are best solved by means of computers modeled on the human mind.

22. The large-scale climate trends discussed in passage A are most analogous to which one of the following elements in passage B?

    (A) the thousands of computers working simultaneously to solve a calculation-intensive problem

    (B) the simple rules that shape the behavior of a single ant

    (C) the highly complex behavior of a dense mass of thousands of ants

    (D) the paradigm shift from sequential to parallel computing

    (E) the speed limits imposed by computing purely sequentially

Explanations for these questions can be found in your Online Center.

Part Four: Reading Comprehension
Reading Comprehension: Passage Types and Question Types

23. It can be inferred that the authors of the two passages would be most likely to agree on which one of the following statements concerning computing systems?

    (A) Massive, parallel computing systems are able to solve complex computation-intensive problems without having to resort to "brute force."

    (B) Computer models are not capable of simulating the behavior of very large biological populations such as insect colonies.

    (C) Parallel computing systems that link privately owned desktop computers via the Internet are not feasible because they rely too heavily on public participation.

    (D) Currently available computers are not well-suited to running simulations, even if the simulated problems are relatively simple.

    (E) Parallel computing systems employing multiple computers are the best means for simulating large-scale climate trends.

24. The author of passage A mentions public participation (lines 30–32) primarily in order to

    (A) encourage public engagement in the sort of computing model discussed in the passage

    (B) identify a factor affecting the feasibility of the computing model advocated in the passage

    (C) indicate that government support of large-scale computing efforts is needed

    (D) demonstrate that adequate support for the type of approach described in the passage already exists

    (E) suggest that a computing model like that proposed in the passage is infeasible because of forces beyond the designers' control

25. Passage B relates to passage A in which one of the following ways?

    (A) The argument in passage B has little bearing on the issues discussed in passage A.

    (B) The explanation offered in passage B shows why the plan proposed in passage A is unlikely to be implemented.

    (C) The ideas advanced in passage B provide a rationale for the solution proposed in passage A.

    (D) The example given in passage B illustrates the need for the "brute force" exploration mentioned in passage A.

    (E) The discussion in passage B conflicts with the assumptions about individual computers made in passage A.

26. The passages share which one of the following as their primary purpose?

    (A) to show that the traditional paradigm in computing is ineffective for many common computing tasks

    (B) to argue that a new approach to computing is an effective way to solve a difficult type of problem

    (C) to convince skeptics of the usefulness of desktop computers for calculation-intensive problems

    (D) to demonstrate that a new computing paradigm has supplanted the traditional paradigm for most large-scale computing problems

    (E) to describe complex and as yet unsolved problems that have recently arisen in computing

27. In calling a population of ants "an intelligence, a kind of live computer" (lines 51–52) the author of passage B most likely means that

    (A) the behavior of the colony of ants functions as a complex, organized whole

    (B) the paradigm shift taking place in computing was inspired by observations of living systems

    (C) computers are agglomerations of elements that can be viewed as being alive in a metaphorical sense

    (D) computer simulations can simulate the behavior of large biological populations with great accuracy

    (E) the simple rules that govern the behavior of individual ants have been adapted for use in computer simulations

28. The author of passage B would be most likely to agree with which one of the following statements regarding the computing system proposed in the last paragraph of passage A?

    (A) It would be a kind of live computer.

    (B) It would be completely inadequate for simulating large-scale climate trends.

    (C) It would impose strict limitations on the number of variables that could be used in any simulation it runs.

    (D) It would be likely to secure widespread public participation.

    (E) It would solve calculation-intensive problems faster than a traditional sequential computer would.

PrepTest59 Sec4 Qs 1–8

Answer key on page 957.

READING COMPREHENSION QUESTION STRATEGIES

After strategically reading a passage and creating a helpful Roadmap, an LSAT expert is ready to tackle the questions. Step 2 of the Method is vital: Identify the type of question and look for clues that dictate the appropriate strategy.

Reading Comprehension Question Types

> ### LEARNING OBJECTIVES
>
> In this portion of the chapter, you'll learn to:
>
> - Recognize Global questions
> - Recognize Inference questions
> - Recognize Detail questions
> - Recognize Logic Function questions
> - Recognize Logic Reasoning questions
> - Determine whether the question stem contains research clues

Global questions ask about the passage as a whole:

LSAT Question Stem		Analysis
Which one of the following most accurately expresses the main point of the passage? *PrepTest59 Sec4 Q9*	$\longrightarrow$	**Step 2:** "[M]ain point"—this is a Global question. Use the Main Idea summary to predict the correct answer to this question.
Which one of the following most accurately describes the organization of the passage? *PrepTest51 Sec2 Q15*	$\longrightarrow$	**Step 2:** "[O]rganization of the passage"—this question asks about the entire passage, so it's a Global question. Consult the Roadmap to determine the passage's overall structure.
The passages share which one of the following as their primary purpose? *PrepTest59 Sec4 Q6*	$\longrightarrow$	**Step 2:** "[P]rimary purpose"—this Global question asks you to identify the purpose "shared" by both passages. Use your Purpose summary to predict.

Inference questions ask for a deduction that can be made based on information in the passage.

LSAT Question Stem	Analysis
Based on the information presented in the passage, with which one of the following statements would the author be most likely to agree? *PrepTest57 Sec4 Q4* →	**Step 2:** "[M]ost likely to agree"—this is an Inference question. The stem does not provide any specific research clues, so the correct answer could be supported by any part of the passage.
Which one of the following can most reasonably be concluded about the television viewers who were the subject of the study discussed in the second paragraph? *PrepTest51 Sec2 Q18* →	**Step 2:** "[M]ost reasonably be concluded"—an Inference question. Refer back to the second paragraph and especially to the viewers who were the subject of the study.
In calling a population of ants "an intelligence, a kind of live computer" (lines 51-52) the author of passage B most likely means that *PrepTest59 Sec4 Q7* →	**Step 2:** "[M]ost likely means"—an Inference question. Reread the line reference in context and look for an answer choice that must be true based upon those statements.
Which one of the following would the author be most likely to characterize as an example of a misunderstanding of science by a humanist? *PrepTest57 Sec4 Q7* →	**Step 2:** "[M]ost likely to characterize as an example"—an Inference question. Look for the discussion of humanists' misconceptions, which are found in the second paragraph.

Detail questions ask for a specific fact mentioned in the passage.

LSAT Question Stem	Analysis
According to the author, an empirical study of the effect of external cultural influences on the lives of people in a society must begin by identifying *PrepTest51 Sec2 Q19* →	**Step 2:** "[A]ccording to the author"—this is a Detail question. Check the Roadmap to identify where the author discusses the first step in creating the study.
Which one of the following does the author present as a characteristic of fractal geometry? *PrepTest57 Sec4 Q24* →	**Step 2:** "Which of the following does the author present"—a Detail question, because it asks for a specific statement the author makes in the passage. The traits of fractals appear in the first and second paragraphs. Check there to make a prediction.

Logic Function questions ask *why* the author chose to include a specific portion of the passage. These questions provide an explicit research clue. Return to the passage and determine the context in which the statements appear.

LSAT Question Stem	Analysis
The author most likely discusses an anthropological study in the second paragraph primarily in order to *PrepTest51 Sec2 Q17* ⟶	**Step 2:** "[M]ost likely discusses" and "in order to"—this is a Logic Function question. Return to the second paragraph and read before and after the reference to the anthropological study to predict why the study is mentioned.
Which one of the following best describes one of the functions of the last paragraph in the passage? *PrepTest57 Sec4 Q10* ⟶	**Step 2:** "[B]est describes one of the functions"—this is a Logic Function question. Consult the Roadmap to determine the function of the last paragraph in relation to the rest of the passage.

Logic Reasoning questions mirror question types found in the Logical Reasoning section. Use the same approach you would employ for the corresponding question type in the Logical Reasoning section.

LSAT Question Stem	Analysis
The large-scale climate trends discussed in passage A are most analogous to which one of the following elements in passage B? *PrepTest59 Sec4 Q2* ⟶	**Step 2:** "[M]ost analogous"—this is like a Parallel Reasoning question. The research clue here is "large-scale climate trends" and "elements."
Which of the following would, if true, most weaken the author's argument as expressed in the passage? *PrepTest59 Sec4 Q11* ⟶	**Step 2:** "[M]ost weaken"—this is a Weaken question. Find the answer choice that provides the strongest counter to the author's argument.

Summary of Question Types

Question Type	Identify	Task
Global	"main point" "primary purpose" "organization" "title"	Think big picture. Review T/S/P/MI. Consult your Roadmap.
Detail	"according to" "passage states" "author mentions"	Research the relevant text. Correct answer will be a very close paraphrase of something stated in the passage.
Inference	"author implies" "passage suggests" "based on" "inferred" "likely to agree with" "author's attitude"	Research if possible. Correct answer will follow from the passage but will probably not be a close paraphrase.
Logic Function	"function" "primarily in order to" "for the purpose of"	Research the relevant text. Look at the context to determine why the author included the referenced detail.
Logic Reasoning	"supports" "undermines" "principle" "analogous"	Use the appropriate Logical Reasoning strategy.

Practice

Identify the question type indicated by each of the following question stems, and state the most effective way to research the answer.

LSAT Question Stem	My Analysis
Which one of the following would the author be most likely to characterize as an example of a misunderstanding of science by a humanist? *PrepTest57 Sec4 Q7* →	**[Sample]** **Step 2:** "[M]ost likely means"—an Inference question. Reread the line reference in context, and look for an answer choice that must be true based upon those statements.
Which one of the following best describes one of the functions of the last paragraph in the passage? *PrepTest57 Sec4 Q10* →	**[Sample]** **Step 2:** "[B]est describes one of the functions"—this is a Logic Function question. Consult the Roadmap to determine the function of the last paragraph in relation to the rest of the passage.
29. Which of the following best describes the main idea of the passage? *PrepTest57 Sec4 Q6* →	**Step 2:**
30. It can be inferred from the passage that the author would be most likely to agree with which one of the following statements? *PrepTest57 Sec4 Q8* →	**Step 2:**
31. According to the author, which one of the following is the primary cause of the existing separation between science and humanities? *PrepTest57 Sec4 Q9* →	**Step 2:**
32. The passage suggests that the author would recommend that humanists accept which one of the following modifications of their point of view? *PrepTest57 Sec4 Q11* →	**Step 2:**
33. In using the phrase "vagrant fancies of an undisciplined mind" (lines 27–28), the author suggests that humanists are sometimes considered to be *PrepTest57 Sec4 Q12* →	**Step 2:**

LSAT Question Stem	**My Analysis**
34. Which one of the following most accurately expresses the main point of the passage? *PrepTest61 Sec1 Q7* $\longrightarrow$	**Step 2:**
35. The passage provides the strongest support for inferring that Lessing holds which one of the following views? *PrepTest61 Sec1 Q8* $\longrightarrow$	**Step 2:**
36. In the first paragraph, the author refers to a highly reputed critic's persistence in believing van Meegeren's forgery to be a genuine Vermeer primarily in order to *PrepTest61 Sec1 Q9* $\longrightarrow$	**Step 2:**
37. The reaction described in which one of the following scenarios is most analogous to the reaction of the art critics mentioned in line 13? *PrepTest61 Sec1 Q10* $\longrightarrow$	**Step 2:**
38. The passage most strongly supports which one of the following statements? *PrepTest61 Sec1 Q12* $\longrightarrow$	**Step 2:**
39. Which one of the following, if true, would most strengthen Lessing's contention that a painting can display aesthetic excellence without possessing an equally high degree of artistic value? $\longrightarrow$ *PrepTest61 Sec1 Q13*	**Step 2:**

Expert Analysis

Compare your characterizations of the question stems to that of an LSAT expert.

LSAT Question Stem	Analysis
29. Which of the following best describes the main idea of the passage? *PrepTest57 Sec4 Q6*	**Step 2:** "[M]ain idea"—a Global question. Consult the big picture summary and Main Idea prediction.
30. It can be inferred from the passage that the author would be most likely to agree with which one of the following statements? *PrepTest57 Sec4 Q8*	**Step 2:** "[C]an be inferred"—an Inference question. The right answer will be supported by information presented in the passage.
31. According to the author, which one of the following is the primary cause of the existing separation between science and humanities? *PrepTest57 Sec4 Q9*	**Step 2:** "[A]ccording to the author"—a Detail question. The correct answer will be a close paraphrase of a statement in the passage.
32. The passage suggests that the author would recommend that humanists accept which one of the following modifications of their point of view? *PrepTest57 Sec4 Q11*	**Step 2:** "The passage suggests"—an Inference question. Research the passage to find the author's opinion on how humanists should change.
33. In using the phrase "vagrant fancies of an undisciplined mind" (lines 27–28), the author suggests that humanists are sometimes considered to be *PrepTest57 Sec4 Q12*	**Step 2:** "[T]he author suggests"—an Inference question. Reread the line reference in context, and look for an answer choice that must be true based on those statements.
34. Which one of the following most accurately expresses the main point of the passage? *PrepTest61 Sec1 Q7*	**Step 2:** "[M]ain point"—a Global question. Consult the Main Idea prediction.
35. The passage provides the strongest support for inferring that Lessing holds which one of the following views? *PrepTest61 Sec1 Q8*	**Step 2:** "[P]rovides the strongest support for inferring"—an Inference question. Look up references to Lessing and look for opinion Keywords.
36. In the first paragraph, the author refers to a highly reputed critic's persistence in believing van Meegeren's forgery to be a genuine Vermeer primarily in order to *PrepTest61 Sec1 Q9*	**Step 2:** "[I]n order to"—a Logic Function question. Refer back to the first paragraph and reread the reference in context. Determine why the author included it.
37. The reaction described in which one of the following scenarios is most analogous to the reaction of the art critics mentioned in line 13? *PrepTest61 Sec1 Q10*	**Step 2:** "[M]ost analogous to"—a Logic Reasoning Parallel Reasoning question. Look up the art critics' reaction in line 13, and find the choice that is structurally most similar.
38. The passage most strongly supports which one of the following statements? *PrepTest61 Sec1 Q12*	**Step 2:** "[M]ost strongly supports"—an Inference question. The correct answer will be supported by information in the passage.
39. Which one of the following, if true, would most strengthen Lessing's contention that a painting can display aesthetic excellence without possessing an equally high degree of artistic value? *PrepTest61 Sec1 Q13*	**Step 2:** "[W]ould most strengthen"—a Logic Reasoning Strengthen question. Find an answer choice that provides the most support for Lessing's view.

Researching Reading Comprehension Questions and Predicting the Correct Answer

Once you've identified the question type, it's on to Steps 3 and 4 of the Reading Comprehension Method: Research the appropriate part or parts of the passage and then predict the correct answer. These two steps are vital to Test Day success. While many students rely on their memory of the passage to answer questions, experts know that support for the correct answers can be found directly in the passage. The testmaker routinely includes distracters among the wrong answers to reward the test taker who does the research needed to avoid such traps.

LEARNING OBJECTIVES

In this part of the chapter, you'll learn to:

- Identify and employ five kinds of research clues (line reference, paragraph reference, quoted text, proper names, and content clues) in question stems to research the relevant text in a passage
- Research the relevant text and accurately predict the correct answer to Inference questions featuring referent reading clues
- Use Topic, Scope, Purpose, and Main Idea summaries to predict the correct answer to Global questions
- Use Topic, Scope, Purpose, and Main Idea summaries to predict broadly the correct answer to Inference questions lacking referent reading clues

---

Using Research Clues in the Question Stem

Some question stems will direct you back to specific parts of the passage, while other question stems ask about the passage as a whole. Still other question stems will ask about a specific part of the passage, but do not provide any clues as to where in the passage to direct your research.

LSAT STRATEGY

Reading Comprehension Research Clues

- **Line Reference**—Research around the referenced detail; look for Keywords indicating why the referenced text has been included or how it's used.
- **Paragraph References**—Consult your Roadmap to see the paragraph's scope and function.
- **Quoted Text** (often accompanied by a line reference)—Check the context of the quoted term or phrase; ask what the author meant by it in the passage.
- **Proper Nouns**—Check the context of the person, place, or thing; ask whether the author had a positive, negative, or neutral evaluation of it; ask why it was included in the passage.
- **Content Clues**—Terms, concepts, or ideas highlighted in the passage, but not included as direct quotes in the question stem; these will almost always refer you to something the author emphasized or stated an opinion on.

To prepare yourself for the following practice, review the LSAT expert's Roadmap and analysis of a passage you saw earlier in the chapter.

LSAT Passage	Analysis
An effort should be made to dispel the misunderstandings that still prevent the much-needed synthesis and mutual supplementation of science and the humanities. This reconciliation should not be too (5) difficult once it is recognized that the separation is primarily the result of a basic misunderstanding of the philosophical foundations of both science and the humanities. *Auth: reconcile sci/hum* *Basically misunderstood*	**Step 1:** The first sentence begins with the author's clear opinion: We should (strong authorial recommendation) "dispel the misunderstandings" blocking a "much-needed" (strong Emphasis/Opinion Keyword) synthesis of science and the humanities. In other words: Science and the humanities should be brought together. Author's clear opinion provides the **Topic** (science and the humanities) and **Scope** (the gap that separates them). The next lines (4–8) reveal the author's **Purpose**: to explain that the gap is "primarily the result of" a misunderstanding of each side's underlying philosophy.
Some humanists still identify science with an (10) absurd mechanistic reductionism. There are many who feel that the scientist is interested in nothing more than "bodies in motion," in the strictly mathematical, physical, and chemical laws that govern the material world. This is the caricature of science drawn by (15) representatives of the humanities who are ignorant of the nature of modern science and also of the scientific outlook in philosophy. For example, it is claimed that science either ignores or explains away the most essential human values. Those who believe this also (20) assert that there are aspects of the human mind, manifest especially in the domains of morality, religion, and the arts, that contain an irreducible spiritual element and for that reason can never be adequately explained by science. *Humanists— sci too reductive* *Auth: they don't know real sci* *Ex.*	Paragraph 2 begins with one misunderstanding: **some humanists claim** scientists reduce everything to the mechanical laws of math, physics, and chemistry. But that's a "caricature" by those "ignorant of" what science really is, and line 17 provides an example: To the ignorant humanists, science is clueless about basic human values because science can't appreciate the "irreducible spiritual element" of the artistic and moral human mind.
(25) Some scientists, on the other hand, claim that the humanist is interested in nothing more than emotion and sentiment, exhibiting the vagrant fancies of an undisciplined mind. To such men and women the humanities are useless because they serve no immediate (30) and technological function for the practical survival of human society in the material world. Such pragmatists believe that the areas of morality, religion, and the arts should have only a secondary importance in people's lives. *Scientists— hum. is just emotion— useless*	Paragraph 3 provides the other misunderstanding: *Some scientists claim* that humanists also have a blind spot. The scientists caricature humanists as emotional, sentimental, and undisciplined. Ultimately, the work produced by humanists is "useless because" it can't help our species survive.

LSAT Passage	Analysis

(35)   Thus there are misconceptions among humanists and scientists alike that are in need of correction. This *Auth: correct* correction leads to a much more acceptable position *the mis-under-* that could be called "scientific humanism," attempting *standing* as it does to combine the common elements of both

(40)   disciplines. Both science and the humanities attempt to describe and explain. It is true that they begin their descriptions and explanations at widely separated points, but the objectives remain the same: a clearer understanding of people and their world. In achieving *Find*

(45)   this understanding, science in fact does not depend *common* exclusively on measurable data, and the humanities in *ground* fact profit from attempts at controlled evaluation. Scientific humanism can combine the scientific attitude with an active interest in the whole scale of *If views*

(50)   human values. If uninformed persons insist on viewing *stay the* science as only materialistic and the humanities as *same reconcilia-* only idealistic, a fruitful collaboration of both fields is *tion unlikely* unlikely. The combination of science and the humanities is, however, possible, even probable, if we *If note*

(55)   begin by noting their common objectives, rather than *common obj.* seeing only their different means. *combination probable*

The author states that these misconceptions are "in need of correction," and then proposes a "much more acceptable position" called "scientific humanism." This new position accepts that both people of science and people of the arts want to understand the world better. Science doesn't just rely on raw data (lines 45–46), nor are humanists utterly oblivious to "controlled evaluation" (i.e., measurement). The author's **Main Idea** is then clearly stated: Studying the commonalities of both fields will produce a probable "fruitful collaboration."

PrepTest57 Sec4 Qs 6–12

Practice

Complete Steps 2–4 of the Reading Comprehension Method for each question. Question 41 is filled in as an example.

An effort should be made to dispel the misunderstandings that still prevent the much-needed synthesis and mutual supplementation of science and the humanities. This reconciliation should not be too
(5) difficult once it is recognized that the separation is primarily the result of a basic misunderstanding of the philosophical foundations of both science and the humanities.

Auth: reconcile sci/hum

Basically misunderstood

Some humanists still identify science with an
(10) absurd mechanistic reductionism. There are many who feel that the scientist is interested in nothing more than "bodies in motion," in the strictly mathematical, physical, and chemical laws that govern the material world. This is the caricature of science drawn by
(15) representatives of the humanities who are ignorant of the nature of modern science and also of the scientific outlook in philosophy. For example, it is claimed that science either ignores or explains away the most essential human values. Those who believe this also
(20) assert that there are aspects of the human mind, manifest especially in the domains of morality, religion, and the arts, that contain an irreducible spiritual element and for that reason can never be adequately explained by science.

Humanists— sci too reductive

Auth: they don't know real sci

(25) Some scientists, on the other hand, claim that the humanist is interested in nothing more than emotion and sentiment, exhibiting the vagrant fancies of an undisciplined mind. To such men and women the humanities are useless because they serve no immediate
(30) and technological function for the practical survival of human society in the material world. Such pragmatists believe that the areas of morality, religion, and the arts should have only a secondary importance in people's lives.

Scientists— hum. is just emotion— useless

(35) Thus there are misconceptions among humanists and scientists alike that are in need of correction. This correction leads to a much more acceptable position that could be called "scientific humanism," attempting as it does to combine the common elements of both
(40) disciplines. Both science and the humanities attempt to describe and explain. It is true that they begin their descriptions and explanations at widely separated points, but the objectives remain the same: a clearer understanding of people and their world. In achieving
(45) this understanding, science in fact does not depend exclusively on measurable data, and the humanities in fact profit from attempts at controlled evaluation. Scientific humanism can combine the scientific attitude with an active interest in the whole scale of
(50) human values. If uninformed persons insist on viewing science as only materialistic and the humanities as

Auth: correct the mis-under standing

Find common ground

If views stay the same reconcilia- tion unlikely

only idealistic, a fruitful collaboration of both fields is unlikely. The combination of science and the humanities is, however, possible, even probable, if we
(55) begin by noting their common objectives, rather than seeing only their different means.

Auth: reconcile sci/hum

If note common obj. combination probable

PrepTest57 Sec4 Qs 6–12

40. Which one of the following best describes the main idea of the passage?

Step 2:

Step 3:

Step 4:

Ex.

41. Which one of the following would the author be most likely to characterize as an example of a misunderstanding of science by a humanist?

[Sample]

Step 2: "[M]ost likely to characterize" indicates an Inference question. Example of a misunderstanding of science by a humanist" is a research clue. Find the part of the passage that describes how humanists misrepresent the views of scientists.

Step 3: Paragraph 2 discusses humanists' misconceptions of scientists, and lines 10–14 summarize the misconception: Humanists think of scientists as data pushers, soulless, and non-spiritual.

Step 4: Find an answer choice that describes science as embodying an "absurd mechanistic reductionism."

42. It can be inferred from the passage that the author would be most likely to agree with which one of the following statements?

Step 2:

Step 3:

Step 4:

43. According to the author, which one of the following is the primary cause of the existing separation between science and the humanities?

Step 2:

Step 3:

Step 4:

44. Which one of the following best describes one of the functions of the last paragraph in the passage?

Step 2:

Step 3:

Step 4:

45. The passage suggests that the author would recommend that humanists accept which one of the following modifications of their point of view?

Step 2:

Step 3:

Step 4:

46. In using the phrase "vagrant fancies of an undisciplined mind" (lines 27–28), the author suggests that humanists are sometimes considered to be

Step 2:

Step 3:

Step 4:

PrepTest57 Sec4 Qs 6–12

Expert Analysis

Here's how an LSAT expert completed Steps 2–4 on those question stems. Compare your work.

Analysis	Analysis

40. Which one of the following best describes the main idea of the passage?

Step 2: Identify the Question Type

"[M]ain idea of the passage"—a Global question.

Step 3: Research the Relevant Text

Consult the Roadmap and Main Idea prediction.

Step 4: Make a Prediction

Main idea: Scientists and humanists must correct their misunderstandings and synthesize the approaches of their fields.

42. It can be inferred from the passage that the author would be most likely to agree with which one of the following statements?

Step 2: Identify the Question Type

"[C]an be inferred" and "author would most likely to agree" both indicate this is an Inference question.

Step 3: Research the Relevant Text

No specific research clue. Focus on author's opinion and purpose.

Step 4: Make a Prediction

The question asks what the author would agree with. Paraphrase the author's Purpose and Main Idea: both scientists and humanists are guilty of misunderstanding the other, and the two groups should resolve their differences.

43. According to the author, which one of the following is the primary cause of the existing separation between science and the humanities?

Step 2: Identify the Question Type

"[A]ccording to the author"—a Detail question.

Step 3: Research the Relevant Text

The phrase "primary cause of ... separation" leads to paragraph 1, where the author discusses why science and the humanities have yet to synthesize.

Step 4: Make a Prediction

Lines 5–8 directly state that the science-humanities split is "primarily the result of" a basic misunderstanding of each discipline's theoretical underpinnings by the other. Find an answer choice that most closely states that misunderstanding.

44. Which one of the following best describes one of the functions of the last paragraph in the passage?

Step 2: Identify the Question Type

"[B]est describes one of the functions"—a Logic Function question.

Step 3: Research the Relevant Text

The last paragraph is the focus of this question stem. Use the Roadmap to determine what function the last paragraph plays in relation to the entire passage.

Step 4: Make a Prediction

Paragraph 4 offers "a much more acceptable position" that incorporates both disciplines' "common elements." The author's purpose in this paragraph is to offer his case for synthesizing science and humanism.

Analysis	Analysis
45. The passage suggests that the author would recommend that humanists accept which one of the following modifications of their point of view?	46. In using the phrase "vagrant fancies of an undisciplined mind" (lines 27–28), the author suggests that humanists are sometimes considered to be

Step 2: Identify the Question Type	**Step 2: Identify the Question Type**
"[T]he passage suggests" -- an Inference question.	"[T]he author suggests"—an Inference question.
Step 3: Research the Relevant Text	**Step 3: Research the Relevant Text**
The words "author would recommend" points to paragraph 4, where the author makes recommendations concerning the synthesis of science and humanism.	Lines 27–28 are clearly relevant, because they're directly referenced in the question stem.
Step 4: Make a Prediction	**Step 4: Make a Prediction**
The lines that deal directly with humanists' role in bridging the divide are 46–47, in which the author points out that humanists benefit from controlled evaluation, a philosophical approach they hang around the necks of scientists as a shortcoming. So, the author would likely suggest that humanists make room in their viewpoint for more "scientific" approaches to their discipline.	Having just explained how scientists are wrongly caricatured as soulless stiffs, the author uses lines 27–28 to expose an equally egregious misrepresentation. But it's the following lines (29–31) that convey the widespread misconception that those vagrant, undisciplined fantasies are "useless" for "practical survival." Make a prediction: Humanists are considered to be impractical.

PrepTest57 Sec4 Qs 6, 8–12

Keep those predictions in mind. You'll soon be using them to evaluate the answer choices.

Evaluating Reading Comprehension Answer Choices

Many test takers struggle to get through the Reading Comprehension section in the time allowed. One factor contributing to the time crunch is the tendency to read through answer choices multiple times in the hope that somehow the correct answer will reveal itself. LSAT experts follow a different approach: After having made a prediction in Step 4, they confidently and quickly select the answer choice that is the closest match.

LEARNING OBJECTIVES

In this portion of the chapter, you'll learn to:

- Use a prediction of the correct answer to evaluate the answer choices
- Use the Topic, Scope, Purpose, and Main Idea summaries to evaluate the answer choices
- Evaluate answer choices by efficiently checking them against the passage text

Try that now with the same questions you just worked with.

K | Part Four: Reading Comprehension
CHAPTER 14

Explanations for these questions
can be found in your Online Center.

Practice

Now, apply the predictions from the previous exercise to evaluate the answer choices from this passage.

An effort should be made to dispel the misunderstandings that still prevent the much-needed synthesis and mutual supplementation of science and the humanities. This reconciliation should not be too

(5) difficult once it is recognized that the separation is primarily the result of a basic misunderstanding of the philosophical foundations of both science and the humanities.

Some humanists still identify science with an

(10) absurd mechanistic reductionism. There are many who feel that the scientist is interested in nothing more than "bodies in motion," in the strictly mathematical, physical, and chemical laws that govern the material world. This is the caricature of science drawn by

(15) representatives of the humanities who are ignorant of the nature of modern science and also of the scientific outlook in philosophy. For example, it is claimed that science either ignores or explains away the most essential human values. Those who believe this also

(20) assert that there are aspects of the human mind, manifest especially in the domains of morality, religion, and the arts, that contain an irreducible spiritual element and for that reason can never be adequately explained by science.

(25) Some scientists, on the other hand, claim that the humanist is interested in nothing more than emotion and sentiment, exhibiting the vagrant fancies of an undisciplined mind. To such men and women the humanities are useless because they serve no immediate

(30) and technological function for the practical survival of human society in the material world. Such pragmatists believe that the areas of morality, religion, and the arts should have only a secondary importance in people's lives.

(35) Thus there are misconceptions among humanists and scientists alike that are in need of correction. This correction leads to a much more acceptable position that could be called "scientific humanism," attempting as it does to combine the common elements of both

(40) disciplines. Both science and the humanities attempt to describe and explain. It is true that they begin their descriptions and explanations at widely separated points, but the objectives remain the same: a clearer understanding of people and their world. In achieving

(45) this understanding, science in fact does not depend exclusively on measurable data, and the humanities in fact profit from attempts at controlled evaluation. Scientific humanism can combine the scientific attitude with an active interest in the whole scale of

(50) human values. If uninformed persons insist on viewing science as only materialistic and the humanities as only idealistic, a fruitful collaboration of both fields is unlikely. The combination of science and the humanities is, however, possible, even probable, if we

(55) begin by noting their common objectives, rather than seeing only their different means.

40. Which one of the following best describes the main idea of the passage?

(A) Scientists' failure to understand humanists hinders collaborations between the two groups.

(B) The materialism of science and the idealism of the humanities have both been beneficial to modern society.

(C) Technological development will cease if science and the humanities remain at odds with each other.

(D) The current relationship between science and the humanities is less cooperative than their relationship once was.

(E) A synthesis of science and the humanities is possible and much-needed.

41. Which one of the following would the author be most likely to characterize as an example of a misunderstanding of science by a humanist?

(A) Science encourages the view that emotions are inexplicable.

(B) Science arises out of practical needs but serves other needs as well.

(C) Science depends exclusively on measurable data to support its claims.

(D) Science recognizes an irreducible spiritual element that makes the arts inexplicable.

(E) Science encourages the use of description in the study of human values.

42. It can be inferred from the passage that the author would be most likely to agree with which one of the following statements?

(A) Scientific humanism is characterized by the extension of description and explanation from science to the humanities.

(B) A clearer understanding of people is an objective of humanists that scientists have not yet come to share.

(C) Controlled measures of aesthetic experience are of little use in the study of the humanities.

(D) Humanists have profited from using methods generally considered useful primarily to scientists.

(E) Fruitful collaboration between scientists and humanists is unlikely to become more common.

Explanations for these questions can be found in your Online Center.

Part Four: Reading Comprehension
Reading Comprehension: Passage Types and Question Types | K

43. According to the author, which one of the following is the primary cause of the existing separation between science and the humanities?

    (A) inflammatory claims by scientists regarding the pragmatic value of the work of humanists
    (B) misunderstandings of the philosophical foundations of each by the other
    (C) the excessive influence of reductionism on both
    (D) the predominance of a concern with mechanics in science
    (E) the failure of humanists to develop rigorous methods

44. Which one of the following best describes one of the functions of the last paragraph in the passage?

    (A) to show that a proposal introduced in the first paragraph is implausible because of information presented in the second and third paragraphs
    (B) to show that the views presented in the second and third paragraphs are correct but capable of reconciliation
    (C) to present information supporting one of two opposing views presented in the second and third paragraphs
    (D) to present an alternative to views presented in the second and third paragraphs
    (E) to offer specific examples of the distinct views presented in the second and third paragraphs

45. The passage suggests that the author would recommend that humanists accept which one of the following modifications of their point of view?

    (A) a realization that the scientist is less interested in describing "bodies in motion" than in constructing mathematical models of the material world
    (B) an acknowledgement that there is a spiritual element in the arts that science does not account for
    (C) an acceptance of the application of controlled evaluation to the examination of human values
    (D) a less strident insistence on the primary importance of the arts in people's lives
    (E) an emphasis on developing ways for showing how the humanities support the practical survival of mankind

46. In using the phrase "vagrant fancies of an undisciplined mind" (lines 27–28), the author suggests that humanists are sometimes considered to be

    (A) wildly emotional
    (B) excessively impractical
    (C) unnecessarily intransigent
    (D) justifiably optimistic
    (E) logically inconsistent

PrepTest57 Sec4 Qs 6–12

Practice: Steps 1–5

Now, try each step of the Reading Comprehension Method on a new selection. Start by reading and Roadmapping the passage.

It is commonly assumed that even if some forgeries have aesthetic merit, no forgery has as much as an original by the imitated artist would. Yet even the most prominent art specialists can be duped by a
(5) talented artist turned forger into mistaking an almost perfect forgery for an original. For instance, artist Han van Meegeren's *The Disciples at Emmaus* (1937)—painted under the forged signature of the acclaimed Dutch master Jan Vermeer (1632–1675)—
(10) attracted lavish praise from experts as one of Vermeer's finest works. The painting hung in a Rotterdam museum until 1945, when, to the great embarrassment of the critics, van Meegeren revealed its origin. Astonishingly, there was at least one highly
(15) reputed critic who persisted in believing it to be a Vermeer even after van Meegeren's confession.

Given the experts' initial enthusiasm, some philosophers argue that van Meegeren's painting must have possessed aesthetic characteristics that, in a
(20) Vermeer original, would have justified the critics' plaudits. Van Meegeren's *Emmaus* thus raises difficult questions regarding the status of superbly executed forgeries. Is a forgery inherently inferior as art? How are we justified, if indeed we are, in revising
(25) downwards our critical assessment of a work unmasked as a forgery? Philosopher of art Alfred Lessing proposes convincing answers to these questions.

A forged work is indeed inferior as art, Lessing
(30) argues, but not because of a shortfall in aesthetic qualities strictly defined, that is to say, in the qualities perceptible on the picture's surface. For example, in its composition, its technique, and its brilliant use of color, van Meegeren's work is flawless, even
(35) beautiful. Lessing argues instead that the deficiency lies in what might be called the painting's intangible qualities. All art, explains Lessing, involves technique, but not all art involves origination of a new vision, and originality of vision is one of the
(40) fundamental qualities by which artistic, as opposed to purely aesthetic, accomplishment is measured. Thus Vermeer is acclaimed for having inaugurated, in the seventeenth century, a new way of seeing, and for pioneering techniques for embodying this new way of
(45) seeing through distinctive treatment of light, color, and form.

Even if we grant that van Meegeren, with his undoubted mastery of Vermeer's innovative techniques, produced an aesthetically superior
(50) painting, he did so about three centuries after Vermeer developed the techniques in question. Whereas Vermeer's origination of these techniques in the seventeenth century represents a truly impressive and historic achievement, van Meegeren's production

(55) of *The Disciples at Emmaus* in the twentieth century presents nothing new or creative to the history of art. Van Meegeren's forgery therefore, for all its aesthetic merits, lacks the historical significance that makes Vermeer's work artistically great.

PrepTest61 Sec1 Qs 7–13

Big Picture Summaries:

Topic:

Scope:

Purpose:

Main Idea:

Expert analysis for this passage is on pages 942–943.

This chapter continues on the next page ▶ ▶ ▶

Compare your Roadmap to that of an LSAT expert.

LSAT Passage	Analysis

It is commonly assumed that even if some forgeries have aesthetic merit, no forgery has as much as an original by the imitated artist would. Yet even the most prominent art specialists can be duped by a
(5) talented artist turned forger into mistaking an almost perfect forgery for an original. For instance, artist Han van Meegeren's *The Disciples at Emmaus* (1937)—painted under the forged signature of the acclaimed Dutch master Jan Vermeer (1632–1675)—
(10) attracted lavish praise from experts as one of Vermeer's finest works. The painting hung in a Rotterdam museum until 1945, when, to the great embarrassment of the critics, van Meegeren revealed its origin. Astonishingly, there was at least one highly
(15) reputed critic who persisted in believing it to be a Vermeer even after van Meegeren's confession.

Common view – forgery never equal to original

but even experts get fooled

Ex. HvM not Vermeer

Paragraph 1 opens with "is commonly assumed," so the author will likely introduce a counterpoint. The **Topic**, introduced in the first sentence, is artistic forgeries. The common assumption is that no matter how aesthetically pleasing a forgery might be, it never has the aesthetic merit of an original work. The author's response is a cautionary tale: "even the most prominent art specialists can be duped." He provides the example of a 1937 forgery by Han van Meegeren, who signed the painting as Jan Vermeer, a Dutch master from the seventeenth century.

Given the experts' initial enthusiasm, some philosophers argue that van Meegeren's painting must have possessed aesthetic characteristics that, in a
(20) Vermeer original, would have justified the critics' plaudits. Van Meegeren's *Emmaus* thus raises difficult questions regarding the status of superbly executed forgeries. Is a forgery inherently inferior as art? How are we justified, if indeed we are, in revising
(25) downwards our critical assessment of a work unmasked as a forgery? Philosopher of art Alfred Lessing proposes convincing answers to these questions.

Forgery success leads to difficult questions

Auth – pro Lessing's answers

The success of van Meegeren's forgery tricking even art experts prompted some philosophers to challenge the common assumption mentioned in paragraph 1. The author then raises two questions:

Are forgeries inherently inferior; and is there justification for thinking less of a work once determined a forgery?

The passage's **Scope** emerges as Lessing is introduced—the author believes Lessing provides "convincing" answers to these questions.

A forged work is indeed inferior as art, Lessing
(30) argues, but not because of a shortfall in aesthetic qualities strictly defined, that is to say, in the qualities perceptible on the picture's surface. For example, in its composition, its technique, and its brilliant use of color, van Meegeren's work is flawless, even
(35) beautiful. Lessing argues instead that the deficiency lies in what might be called the painting's intangible qualities. All art, explains Lessing, involves technique, but not all art involves origination of a new vision, and originality of vision is one of the
(40) fundamental qualities by which artistic, as opposed to purely aesthetic, accomplishment is measured. Thus Vermeer is acclaimed for having inaugurated, in the seventeenth century, a new way of seeing, and for pioneering techniques for embodying this new way of
(45) seeing through distinctive treatment of light, color, and form.

Lessing – forgery is not less b/c of technique but b/c of intangibles

Ex. originality/ vision

Lessing's answer, the author says at the opening of paragraph 3, is that forgeries are inferior, but not because of what's visible. For Lessing, the forgery's inferiority stems from its "intangible qualities," its lack of originality and vision. The author attributes these "intangible" qualities to Vermeer, giving him credit for pioneering a "new way of seeing" and new artistic techniques in the seventeenth century.

LSAT Passage (cont.)	Analysis (cont.)

 [Even if] we grant that van Meegeren, with his undoubted mastery of Vermeer's innovative techniques, produced an aesthetically superior
(50) painting, he did so about three centuries after Vermeer developed the techniques in question. [Whereas] Vermeer's origination of these techniques in the seventeenth century represents a truly impressive and historic achievement, van Meegeren's production
(55) of *The Disciples at Emmaus* in the twentieth century presents [nothing] new or creative to the history of art. Van Meegeren's forgery [therefore,] for all its aesthetic merits, [lacks] the historical significance that makes Vermeer's work artistically great.

Auth — even if great technique, forgers still don't provide works of hist. signif.

PrepTest61 Sec1 Qs 7–13

In the final paragraph, the author applies Lessing's criteria to the van Meegeren forgery. Van Meegeren's work, technically brilliant though it may be, is inferior because it adds "nothing new or creative to the world of art."

The author's **Purpose** is not to contradict the assumption but actually to explain why it's true. The **Main Idea** simply summarizes Lessing's analysis: Forgeries are inferior because they lack the intangible originality and vision of originals, not due to any technical deficiency.

Complete Steps 2–4 of the Reading Comprehension Method for each question.

It is commonly assumed that even if some forgeries have aesthetic merit, no forgery has as much as an original by the imitated artist would. Yet even the most prominent art specialists can be duped by a
(5) talented artist turned forger into mistaking an almost perfect forgery for an original. For instance, artist Han van Meegeren's *The Disciples at Emmaus* (1937)—painted under the forged signature of the acclaimed Dutch master Jan Vermeer (1632–1675)—
(10) attracted lavish praise from experts as one of Vermeer's finest works. The painting hung in a Rotterdam museum until 1945, when, to the great embarrassment of the critics, van Meegeren revealed its origin. Astonishingly, there was at least one highly
(15) reputed critic who persisted in believing it to be a Vermeer even after van Meegeren's confession.

Given the experts' initial enthusiasm, some philosophers argue that van Meegeren's painting must have possessed aesthetic characteristics that, in a
(20) Vermeer original, would have justified the critics' plaudits. Van Meegeren's *Emmaus* thus raises difficult questions regarding the status of superbly executed forgeries. Is a forgery inherently inferior as art? How are we justified, if indeed we are, in revising
(25) downwards our critical assessment of a work unmasked as a forgery? Philosopher of art Alfred Lessing proposes convincing answers to these questions.

A forged work is indeed inferior as art, Lessing
(30) argues, but not because of a shortfall in aesthetic qualities strictly defined, that is to say, in the qualities perceptible on the picture's surface. For example, in its composition, its technique, and its brilliant use of color, van Meegeren's work is flawless, even
(35) beautiful. Lessing argues instead that the deficiency lies in what might be called the painting's intangible qualities. All art, explains Lessing, involves technique, but not all art involves origination of a new vision, and originality of vision is one of the
(40) fundamental qualities by which artistic, as opposed to purely aesthetic, accomplishment is measured. Thus Vermeer is acclaimed for having inaugurated, in the seventeenth century, a new way of seeing, and for pioneering techniques for embodying this new way of
(45) seeing through distinctive treatment of light, color, and form.

Even if we grant that van Meegeren, with his undoubted mastery of Vermeer's innovative techniques, produced an aesthetically superior
(50) painting, he did so about three centuries after Vermeer developed the techniques in question. Whereas Vermeer's origination of these techniques in the seventeenth century represents a truly impressive and historic achievement, van Meegeren's production
(55) of *The Disciples at Emmaus* in the twentieth century

presents nothing new or creative to the history of art. Van Meegeren's forgery therefore, for all its aesthetic merits, lacks the historical significance that makes Vermeer's work artistically great.

47. Which one of the following most accurately expresses the main point of the passage?

Step 2:

Step 3:

Step 4:

48. The passage provides the strongest support for inferring that Lessing holds which one of the following views?

Step 2:

Step 3:

Step 4:

Handwritten margin notes:

Common view – forgery never equal to original but even experts get fooled

Ex. HvM not Vermeer

Forgery success leads to difficult questions

Auth – pro Lessing's answers

Lessing – forgery is not less b/c of technique but b/c of intangibles

Ex. originality/ vision

Auth – even if great technique, forgers still don't provide works of hist. signif.

49. In the first paragraph, the author refers to a highly reputed critic's persistence in believing van Meegeren's forgery to be a genuine Vermeer primarily in order to

Step 2:

Step 3:

Step 4:

50. The reaction described in which one of the following scenarios is most analogous to the reaction of the art critics mentioned in line 13?

Step 2:

Step 3:

Step 4:

51. The passage provides the strongest support for inferring that Lessing holds which one of the following views?

Step 2:

Step 3:

Step 4:

52. The passage most strongly supports which one of the following statements?

Step 2:

Step 3:

Step 4:

53. Which one of the following, if true, would most strengthen Lessing's contention that a painting can display aesthetic excellence without possessing an equally high degree of artistic value?

Step 2:

Step 3:

Step 4:

PrepTest61 Sec1 Qs 7–13

K | Part Four: Reading Comprehension
CHAPTER 14

Explanations for these questions
can be found in your Online Center.

Now, apply your predictions from the previous page to evaluate the answer choices from this passage.

It is commonly assumed that even if some forgeries have aesthetic merit, no forgery has as much as an original by the imitated artist would. Yet even the most prominent art specialists can be duped by a
(5) talented artist turned forger into mistaking an almost perfect forgery for an original. For instance, artist Han van Meegeren's *The Disciples at Emmaus* (1937)—painted under the forged signature of the acclaimed Dutch master Jan Vermeer (1632–1675)—
(10) attracted lavish praise from experts as one of Vermeer's finest works. The painting hung in a Rotterdam museum until 1945, when, to the great embarrassment of the critics, van Meegeren revealed its origin. Astonishingly, there was at least one highly
(15) reputed critic who persisted in believing it to be a Vermeer even after van Meegeren's confession.

Given the experts' initial enthusiasm, some philosophers argue that van Meegeren's painting must have possessed aesthetic characteristics that, in a
(20) Vermeer original, would have justified the critics' plaudits. Van Meegeren's *Emmaus* thus raises difficult questions regarding the status of superbly executed forgeries. Is a forgery inherently inferior as art? How are we justified, if indeed we are, in revising
(25) downwards our critical assessment of a work unmasked as a forgery? Philosopher of art Alfred Lessing proposes convincing answers to these questions.

A forged work is indeed inferior as art, Lessing
(30) argues, but not because of a shortfall in aesthetic qualities strictly defined, that is to say, in the qualities perceptible on the picture's surface. For example, in its composition, its technique, and its brilliant use of color, van Meegeren's work is flawless, even
(35) beautiful. Lessing argues instead that the deficiency lies in what might be called the painting's intangible qualities. All art, explains Lessing, involves technique, but not all art involves origination of a new vision, and originality of vision is one of the
(40) fundamental qualities by which artistic, as opposed to purely aesthetic, accomplishment is measured. Thus Vermeer is acclaimed for having inaugurated, in the seventeenth century, a new way of seeing, and for pioneering techniques for embodying this new way of
(45) seeing through distinctive treatment of light, color, and form.

Even if we grant that van Meegeren, with his undoubted mastery of Vermeer's innovative techniques, produced an aesthetically superior
(50) painting, he did so about three centuries after Vermeer developed the techniques in question. Whereas Vermeer's origination of these techniques in the seventeenth century represents a truly impressive and historic achievement, van Meegeren's production
(55) of *The Disciples at Emmaus* in the twentieth century

presents nothing new or creative to the history of art. Van Meegeren's forgery therefore, for all its aesthetic merits, lacks the historical significance that makes Vermeer's work artistically great.

47. Which one of the following most accurately expresses the main point of the passage?

(A) *The Disciples at Emmaus*, van Meegeren's forgery of a Vermeer, was a failure in both aesthetic and artistic terms.

(B) The aesthetic value of a work of art is less dependent on the work's visible characteristics than on certain intangible characteristics.

(C) Forged artworks are artistically inferior to originals because artistic value depends in large part on originality of vision.

(D) The most skilled forgers can deceive even highly qualified art experts into accepting their work as original.

(E) Art critics tend to be unreliable judges of the aesthetic and artistic quality of works of art.

48. The passage provides the strongest support for inferring that Lessing holds which one of the following views?

(A) The judgments of critics who pronounced *The Disciples at Emmaus* to be aesthetically superb were not invalidated by the revelation that the painting is a forgery.

(B) The financial value of a work of art depends more on its purely aesthetic qualities than on its originality.

(C) Museum curators would be better off not taking art critics' opinions into account when attempting to determine whether a work of art is authentic.

(D) Because it is such a skilled imitation of Vermeer, *The Disciples at Emmaus* is as artistically successful as are original paintings by artists who are less significant than Vermeer.

(E) Works of art that have little or no aesthetic value can still be said to be great achievements in artistic terms.

Explanations for these questions
can be found in your Online Center.

Part Four: Reading Comprehension
Reading Comprehension: Passage Types and Question Types | **K**

49. In the first paragraph, the author refers to a highly reputed critic's persistence in believing van Meegeren's forgery to be a genuine Vermeer primarily in order to

(A) argue that many art critics are inflexible in their judgments
(B) indicate that the critics who initially praised *The Disciples at Emmaus* were not as knowledgeable as they appeared
(C) suggest that the painting may yet turn out to be a genuine Vermeer
(D) emphasize that the concept of forgery itself is internally incoherent
(E) illustrate the difficulties that skillfully executed forgeries can pose for art critics

50. The reaction described in which one of the following scenarios is most analogous to the reaction of the art critics mentioned in line 13?

(A) lovers of a musical group contemptuously reject a tribute album recorded by various other musicians as a second-rate imitation
(B) art historians extol the work of a little-known painter as innovative until it is discovered that the painter lived much more recently than was originally thought
(C) diners at a famous restaurant effusively praise the food as delicious until they learn that the master chef is away for the night
(D) literary critics enthusiastically applaud a new novel until its author reveals that its central symbols are intended to represent political views that the critics dislike
(E) movie fans evaluate a particular movie more favorably than they otherwise might have because their favorite actor plays the lead role

51. The passage provides the strongest support for inferring that Lessing holds which one of the following views?

(A) It is probable that many paintings currently hanging in important museums are actually forgeries.
(B) The historical circumstances surrounding the creation of a work are important in assessing the artistic value of that work.
(C) The greatness of an innovative artist depends on how much influence he or she has on other artists.
(D) The standards according to which a work is judged to be a forgery tend to vary from one historical period to another.
(E) An artist who makes use of techniques developed by others cannot be said to be innovative.

52. The passage most strongly supports which one of the following statements?

(A) In any historical period, the criteria by which a work is classified as a forgery can be a matter of considerable debate.
(B) An artist who uses techniques that others have developed is most likely a forger.
(C) A successful forger must originate a new artistic vision.
(D) Works of art created early in the career of a great artist are more likely than those created later to embody historic innovations.
(E) A painting can be a forgery even if it is not a copy of a particular original work of art.

53. Which one of the following, if true, would most strengthen Lessing's contention that a painting can display aesthetic excellence without possessing an equally high degree of artistic value?

(A) Many of the most accomplished art forgers have had moderately successful careers as painters of original works.
(B) Reproductions painted by talented young artists whose traditional training consisted in the copying of masterpieces were often seen as beautiful, but never regarded as great art.
(C) While experts can detect most forgeries, they can be duped by a talented forger who knows exactly what characteristics experts expect to find in the work of a particular painter.
(D) Most attempts at art forgery are ultimately unsuccessful because the forger has not mastered the necessary techniques.
(E) The criteria by which aesthetic excellence is judged change significantly from one century to another and from one culture to another.

PrepTest61 Sec1 Qs 7–13

FULL PASSAGE PRACTICE

Congratulations. You're now prepared to tackle LSAT Reading Comprehension passages as an expert does. You've learned the skills and strategies associated with each step in the Reading Comprehension Method.

From this point on in the chapter, and in the passages and questions you'll practice in Chapter 15, we'll remove the boxes and hints we've used earlier to prompt you to follow the Reading Comprehension Method. Gone too are the LSAT experts' Roadmaps. Even though there are no boxes, continue to use the Reading Comprehension Method. Remember, the LSAT experts whose work you've been reviewing have done dozens, if not hundreds, of these passages, and hundreds, if not thousands, of these questions. To reach their level of proficiency, you need to practice diligently.

For your convenience, the Reading Comprehension Method is reprinted again here. The passages and question sets on the following pages are laid out exactly as they were on the original tests. You'll find an answer key at the end of the chapter and complete explanations in your Online Center.

THE KAPLAN READING COMPREHENSION METHOD

Step 1: Read the Passage Strategically—Circle Keywords and jot down margin notes to summarize the portions of the passage relevant to LSAT questions; summarize the author's Topic/Scope/Purpose/Main Idea.

Step 2: Read the Question Stem—Identify the question type, characterize the correct and incorrect answers, and look for clues to guide your research.

Step 3: Research the Relevant Text—Based on the clues in the question stem, consult your Roadmap; for open-ended questions, refer to your Topic/Scope/Purpose/Main Idea summaries.

Step 4: Predict the Correct Answer—Based on research, predict the meaning of the correct answer; for open-ended questions, consult your Topic/Scope/Purpose/Main Idea summaries.

Step 5: Evaluate the Answer Choices—Select the choice that matches your prediction of the correct answer, or eliminate the four wrong answer choices.

K | Part Four: Reading Comprehension
CHAPTER 14

Explanations for these questions
can be found in your Online Center.

The Universal Declaration of Human Rights (UDHR), approved by the United Nations General Assembly in 1948, was the first international treaty to expressly affirm universal respect for human rights.

(5) Prior to 1948 no truly international standard of humanitarian beliefs existed. Although Article 1 of the 1945 UN Charter had been written with the express purpose of obligating the UN to "encourage respect for human rights and for fundamental

(10) freedoms for all without distinction as to race, sex, language, or religion," there were members of delegations from various small countries and representatives of several nongovernmental organizations who felt that the language of Article 1

(15) was not strong enough, and that the Charter as a whole did not go far enough in its efforts to guarantee basic human rights. This group lobbied vigorously to strengthen the Charter's human rights provisions and proposed that member states be

(20) required "to take separate and joint action and to co-operate with the organization for the promotion of human rights." This would have implied an obligation for member states to act on human rights issues. Ultimately, this proposal and others like it were not

(25) adopted; instead, the UDHR was commissioned and drafted.

The original mandate for producing the document was given to the UN Commission on Human Rights in February 1946. Between that time and the General

(30) Assembly's final approval of the document, the UDHR passed through an elaborate eight-stage drafting process in which it made its way through almost every level of the UN hierarchy. The articles were debated at each stage, and all 30 articles were

(35) argued passionately by delegates representing diverse ideologies, traditions, and cultures. The document as it was finally approved set forth the essential principles of freedom and equality for everyone— regardless of sex, race, color, language, religion,

(40) political or other opinion, national or social origin, property, birth or other status. It also asserted a number of fundamental human rights, including among others the right to work, the right to rest and leisure, and the right to education.

(45) While the UDHR is in many ways a progressive document, it also has weaknesses, the most regrettable of which is its nonbinding legal status. For all its strong language and high ideals, the UDHR remains a resolution of a purely programmatic nature.

(50) Nevertheless, the document has led, even if belatedly, to the creation of legally binding human rights

conventions, and it clearly deserves recognition as an international standard-setting piece of work, as a set of aspirations to which UN member states are

(55) intended to strive, and as a call to arms in the name of humanity, justice, and freedom.

54. By referring to the Universal Declaration of Human Rights as "purely programmatic" (line 49) in nature, the author most likely intends to emphasize

(A) the likelihood that the document will inspire innovative government programs designed to safeguard human rights

(B) the ability of the document's drafters to translate abstract ideals into concrete standards

(C) the compromises that went into producing a version of the document that would garner the approval of all relevant parties

(D) the fact that the guidelines established by the document are ultimately unenforceable

(E) the frustration experienced by the document's drafters at stubborn resistance from within the UN hierarchy

55. The author most probably quotes directly from both the UN Charter (lines 8–11) and the proposal mentioned in lines 20–22 for which one of the following reasons?

(A) to contrast the different definitions of human rights in the two documents

(B) to compare the strength of the human rights language in the two documents

(C) to identify a bureaucratic vocabulary that is common to the two documents

(D) to highlight what the author believes to be the most important point in each document

(E) to call attention to a significant difference in the prose styles of the two documents

56. The author's stance toward the Universal Declaration of Human Rights can best be described as

(A) unbridled enthusiasm
(B) qualified approval
(C) absolute neutrality
(D) reluctant rejection
(E) strong hostility

Explanations for these questions can be found in your Online Center.

Part Four: Reading Comprehension
Reading Comprehension: Passage Types and Question Types

57. According to the passage, each of the following is true of the Universal Declaration of Human Rights EXCEPT:

   (A) It asserts a right to rest and leisure.
   (B) It was drafted after the UN Charter was drafted.
   (C) The UN Commission on Human Rights was charged with producing it.
   (D) It has had no practical consequences.
   (E) It was the first international treaty to explicitly affirm universal respect for human rights.

58. The author would be most likely to agree with which one of the following statements?

   (A) The human rights language contained in Article 1 of the UN Charter is so ambiguous as to be almost wholly ineffectual.
   (B) The weaknesses of the Universal Declaration of Human Rights generally outweigh the strengths of the document.
   (C) It was relatively easy for the drafters of the Universal Declaration of Human Rights to reach a consensus concerning the contents of the document.
   (D) The drafters of the Universal Declaration of Human Rights omitted important rights that should be included in a truly comprehensive list of basic human rights.
   (E) The Universal Declaration of Human Rights would be truer to the intentions of its staunchest proponents if UN member countries were required by law to abide by its provisions.

59. Suppose that a group of independent journalists has uncovered evidence of human rights abuses being perpetrated by a security agency of a UN member state upon a group of political dissidents. Which one of the following approaches to the situation would most likely be advocated by present-day delegates who share the views of the delegates and representatives mentioned in lines 11–14?

   (A) The UN General Assembly authenticates the evidence and then insists upon prompt remedial action on the part of the government of the member state.
   (B) The UN General Assembly stipulates that any proposed response must be unanimously accepted by member states before it can be implemented.
   (C) The UN issues a report critical of the actions of the member state in question and calls for a censure vote in the General Assembly.
   (D) The situation is regarded by the UN as an internal matter that is best left to the discretion of the government of the member state.
   (E) The situation is investigated further by nongovernmental humanitarian organizations that promise to disclose their findings to the public via the international media.

PrepTest61 Sec1 Qs 1–6

Answer key on page 957.

K

Part Four: Reading Comprehension
CHAPTER 14

Explanations for these questions
can be found in your Online Center.

The Japanese American sculptor Isamu Noguchi (1904–1988) was an artist who intuitively asked—and responded to—deeply original questions. He might well have become a scientist within a standard
(5) scientific discipline, but he instead became an artist who repeatedly veered off at wide angles from the well-known courses followed by conventionally talented artists of both the traditional and modern schools. The story behind one particular sculpture
(10) typifies this aspect of his creativeness.

By his early twenties, Noguchi's sculptures showed such exquisite comprehension of human anatomy and deft conceptual realization that he won a Guggenheim Fellowship for travel in Europe. After
(15) arriving in Paris in 1927, Noguchi asked the Romanian-born sculptor Constantin Brancusi if he might become his student. When Brancusi said no, that he never took students, Noguchi asked if he needed a stonecutter. Brancusi did. Noguchi cut and
(20) polished stone for Brancusi in his studio, frequently also polishing Brancusi's brass and bronze sculptures. Noguchi, with his scientist's mind, pondered the fact that sculptors through the ages had relied exclusively upon negative light—that is, shadows—for their
(25) conceptual communication, precisely because no metals, other than the expensive, nonoxidizing gold, could be relied upon to give off positive-light reflections.

Noguchi wanted to create a sculpture that was purely reflective. In 1929, after returning to the
(30) United States, he met the architect and philosopher R. Buckminster Fuller, offering to sculpt a portrait of him. When Fuller heard of Noguchi's ideas regarding positive-light sculpture, he suggested using chrome-nickel steel, which Henry Ford, through automotive
(35) research and development, had just made commercially available for the first time in history. Here, finally, was a permanently reflective surface, economically available in massive quantities.

In sculpting his portrait of Fuller, Noguchi did not
(40) think of it as merely a shiny alternate model of traditional, negative-light sculptures. What he saw was that completely reflective surfaces provided a fundamental invisibility of surface like that of utterly still waters, whose presence can be apprehended only
(45) when objects—a ship's mast, a tree, or sky—are reflected in them. Seaplane pilots making offshore landings in dead calm cannot tell where the water is and must glide in, waiting for the unpredictable touchdown. Noguchi conceived a similarly invisible sculpture,
(50) hidden in and communicating through the reflections of images surrounding it. Then only the distortion of familiar shapes in the surrounding environment could be seen by the viewer. The viewer's awareness of the "invisible" sculpture's presence and dimensional
(55) relationships would be derived only secondarily.

Even after this stunning discovery, Noguchi remained faithful to his inquisitive nature. At the moment when his explorations had won critical recognition of the genius of his original and
(60) fundamental conception, Noguchi proceeded to the next phase of his evolution.

60. In saying that "no metals, other than the expensive, nonoxidizing gold, could be relied upon to give off positive-light reflections" (lines 25–27), the author draws a distinction between

(A) a metal that can be made moderately reflective in any sculptural application and metals that can be made highly reflective but only in certain applications

(B) a naturally highly reflective metal that was technically suited for sculpture and other highly reflective metals that were not so suited

(C) metals that can be made highly reflective but lose their reflective properties over time and a metal that does not similarly lose its reflective properties

(D) a highly reflective sculptural material that, because it is a metal, is long lasting and nonmetallic materials that are highly reflective but impermanent

(E) a highly reflective metal that was acceptable to both traditional and modern sculptors and highly reflective metals whose use in sculpture was purely experimental

61. The passage provides information sufficient to answer which one of the following questions?

(A) In what way did Noguchi first begin to acquire experience in the cutting and polishing of stone for use in sculpture?

(B) In the course of his career, did Noguchi ever work in any art form other than sculpture?

(C) What are some materials other than metal that Noguchi used in his sculptures after ending his association with Brancusi?

(D) During Noguchi's lifetime, was there any favorable critical response to his creation of a positive-light sculpture?

(E) Did Noguchi at any time in his career consider creating a transparent or translucent sculpture lighted from within?

Explanations for these questions can be found in your Online Center.

Part Four: Reading Comprehension
Reading Comprehension: Passage Types and Question Types

62. The passage offers the strongest evidence that the author would agree with which one of the following statements?

(A) Noguchi's work in Paris contributed significantly to the art of sculpture in that it embodied solutions to problems that other sculptors, including Brancusi, had sought unsuccessfully to overcome.

(B) Noguchi's scientific approach to designing sculptures and to selecting materials for sculptures is especially remarkable in that he had no formal scientific training.

(C) Despite the fact that Brancusi was a sculptor and Fuller was not, Fuller played a more pivotal role than did Brancusi in Noguchi's realization of the importance of negative light to the work of previous sculptors.

(D) Noguchi was more interested in addressing fundamental aesthetic questions than in maintaining a consistent artistic style.

(E) Noguchi's work is of special interest for what it reveals not only about the value of scientific thinking in the arts but also about the value of aesthetic approaches to scientific inquiry.

63. In which one of the following is the relation between the two people most analogous to the relation between Ford and Noguchi as indicated by the passage?

(A) A building-materials dealer decides to market a new type of especially durable simulated-wood flooring material after learning that a famous architect has praised the material.

(B) An expert skier begins experimenting with the use of a new type of material in the soles of ski boots after a shoe manufacturer suggests that that material might be appropriate for that use.

(C) A producer of shipping containers begins using a new type of strapping material, which a rock-climbing expert soon finds useful as an especially strong and reliable component of safety ropes for climbing.

(D) A consultant to a book editor suggests the use of a new type of software for typesetting, and after researching the software the editor decides not to adopt it but finds a better alternative as a result of the research.

(E) A friend of a landscaping expert advises the use of a certain material for the creation of retaining walls and, as a result, the landscaper explores the use of several similar materials.

64. The passage most strongly supports which one of the following inferences?

(A) Prior to suggesting the sculptural use of chrome-nickel steel to Noguchi, Fuller himself had made architectural designs that called for the use of this material.

(B) Noguchi believed that the use of industrial materials to create sculptures would make the sculptures more commercially viable.

(C) Noguchi's "invisible" sculpture appears to have no shape or dimensions of its own, but rather those of surrounding objects.

(D) If a positive-light sculpture depicting a person in a realistic manner were coated with a metal subject to oxidation, it would eventually cease to be recognizable as a realistic likeness.

(E) The perception of the shape and dimensions of a negative-light sculpture does not depend on its reflection of objects from the environment around it.

65. Which one of the following inferences about the portrait of Fuller does the passage most strongly support?

(A) The material that Noguchi used in it had been tentatively investigated by other sculptors but not in direct connection with its reflective properties.

(B) It was similar to at least some of the sculptures that Noguchi produced prior to 1927 in that it represented a human form.

(C) Noguchi did not initially think of it as especially innovative or revolutionary and thus was surprised by Fuller's reaction to it.

(D) It was produced as a personal favor to Fuller and thus was not initially intended to be noticed and commented on by art critics.

(E) It was unlike the sculptures that Noguchi had helped Brancusi to produce in that the latter's aesthetic effects did not depend on contrasts of light and shadow.

66. Which one of the following would, if true, most weaken the author's position in the passage?

(A) Between 1927 and 1929, Brancusi experimented with the use of highly reflective material for the creation of positive-light sculptures.

(B) After completing the portrait of Fuller, Noguchi produced only a few positive-light sculptures and in fact changed his style of sculpture repeatedly throughout his career.

(C) When Noguchi arrived in Paris, he was already well aware of the international acclaim that Brancusi's sculptures were receiving at the time.

(D) Many of Noguchi's sculptures were, unlike the portrait of Fuller, entirely abstract.

(E) Despite his inquisitive and scientific approach to the art of sculpture, Noguchi neither thought of himself as a scientist nor had extensive scientific training.

Part Four: Reading Comprehension
CHAPTER 14

Explanations for these questions
can be found in your Online Center.

The following passages are adapted from critical essays on the American writer Willa Cather (1873–1947).

Passage A

When Cather gave examples of high quality in fiction, she invariably cited Russian writers Ivan Turgenev or Leo Tolstoy or both. Indeed, Edmund Wilson noted in 1922 that Cather followed
(5) the manner of Turgenev, not depicting her characters' emotions directly but telling us how they behave and letting their "inner blaze of glory shine through the simple recital." Turgenev's method was to select details that described a character's appearance and
(10) actions without trying to explain them. A writer, he said, "must be a psychologist—but a secret one; he must know and feel the roots of phenomena, but only present the phenomena themselves." Similarly, he argued that a writer must have complete knowledge
(15) of a character so as to avoid overloading the work with unnecessary detail, concentrating instead on what is characteristic and typical.

Here we have an impressionistic aesthetic that anticipates Cather's: what Turgenev referred to as
(20) secret knowledge Cather called "the thing not named." In one essay she writes that "whatever is felt upon the page without being specifically named there—that, one might say, is created." For both writers, there is the absolute importance of selection and simplification;
(25) for both, art is the fusing of the physical world of setting and actions with the emotional reality of the characters. What synthesizes all the elements of narrative for these writers is the establishment of a prevailing mood.

Passage B

(30) In a famous 1927 letter, Cather writes of her novel *Death Comes for the Archbishop*, "Many [reviewers] assert vehemently that it is not a novel. Myself, I prefer to call it a narrative." Cather's preference anticipated an important reformulation of
(35) the criticism of fiction: the body of literary theory, called "narratology," articulated by French literary theorists in the 1960s. This approach broadens and simplifies the fundamental paradigms according to which we view fiction: they ask of narrative only that
(40) it be narrative, that it tell a story. Narratologists tend *not* to focus on the characteristics of narrative's dominant modern Western form, the "realistic novel": direct psychological characterization, realistic treatment of time, causal plotting, logical closure.
(45) Such a model of criticism, which takes as its object "narrative" rather than the "novel," seems exactly appropriate to Cather's work.

Indeed, her severest critics have always questioned precisely her capabilities as a *novelist*. Morton Zabel
(50) argued that "[Cather's] themes...could readily fail to find the structure and substance that might have given them life or redeemed them from the tenuity of a sketch"; Leon Edel called one of her novels "two inconclusive fragments." These critics and others like
(55) them treat as failures some of the central features of Cather's impressionistic technique: unusual treatment of narrative time, unexpected focus, ambiguous conclusions, a preference for the bold, simple, and stylized in character as well as in landscape. These
(60) "non-novelistic" structures indirectly articulate the essential and conflicting forces of desire at work throughout Cather's fiction.

67. If the author of passage A were to read passage B, he or she would be most likely to agree with which one of the following?

(A) Though Cather preferred to call *Death Comes for the Archbishop* a narrative rather than a novel, she would be unlikely to view most of her other novels in the same way.

(B) The critics who questioned Cather's abilities as a novelist focused mostly on her failed experiments and ignored her more aesthetically successful novels.

(C) A model of criticism that takes narrative rather than the novel as its object is likely to result in flawed interpretations of Cather's work.

(D) Critics who questioned Cather's abilities as a novelist fail to perceive the extent to which Cather actually embraced the conventions of the realistic novel.

(E) Cather's goal of representing the "thing not named" explains her preference for the bold, simple, and stylized in the presentation of character.

68. Passage B indicates which one of the following?

(A) Narratologists point to Cather's works as prime examples of pure narrative.

(B) Cather disliked the work of many of the novelists who preceded her.

(C) Cather regarded at least one of her works as not fitting straightforwardly into the category of the novel.

(D) Cather's unusual treatment of narrative time was influenced by the Russian writers Turgenev and Tolstoy.

(E) Cather's work was regarded as flawed by most contemporary critics.

Explanations for these questions can be found in your Online Center.

Part Four: Reading Comprehension
Reading Comprehension: Passage Types and Question Types

69. It can be inferred that both authors would be most likely to regard which one of the following as exemplifying Cather's narrative technique?

(A) A meticulous inventory of the elegant furniture and décor in a character's living room is used to indicate that the character is wealthy.

(B) An account of a character's emotional scars is used to explain the negative effects the character has on his family.

(C) A description of a slightly quivering drink in the hand of a character at a dinner party is used to suggest that the character is timid.

(D) A chronological summary of the events that spark a family conflict is used to supply the context for an in-depth narration of that conflict.

(E) A detailed narration of an unprovoked act of violence and the reprisals it triggers is used to portray the theme that violence begets violence.

70. Which one of the following most accurately states the main point of passage B?

(A) Cather's fiction is best approached by focusing purely on narrative, rather than on the formal characteristics of the novel.

(B) Most commentators on Cather's novels have mistakenly treated her distinctive narrative techniques as aesthetic flaws.

(C) Cather intentionally avoided the realistic psychological characterization that is the central feature of the modern Western novel.

(D) Cather's impressionistic narratives served as an important impetus for the development of narratology in the 1960s.

(E) Cather rejected the narrative constraints of the realistic novel and instead concentrated on portraying her characters by sketching their inner lives.

71. It is most likely that the authors of the two passages would both agree with which one of the following statements?

(A) More than her contemporaries, Cather used stream-of-consciousness narration to portray her characters.

(B) Cather's works were not intended as novels, but rather as narratives.

(C) Narratology is the most appropriate critical approach to Cather's work.

(D) Cather's technique of evoking the "thing not named" had a marked influence on later novelists.

(E) Cather used impressionistic narrative techniques to portray the psychology of her characters.

72. Both authors would be likely to agree that which one of the following, though typical of many novels, would NOT be found in Cather's work?

(A) Description of the salient features of the setting, such as a chair in which a character often sits.

(B) A plot that does not follow chronological time, but rather moves frequently between the novel's past and present.

(C) Description of a character's physical appearance, dress, and facial expressions.

(D) Direct representation of dialogue between the novel's characters, using quotation marks to set off characters' words.

(E) A narration of a character's inner thoughts, including an account of the character's anxieties and wishes.

73. A central purpose of each passage is to

(A) describe the primary influences on Cather's work

(B) identify some of the distinctive characteristics of Cather's work

(C) explain the critical reception Cather's work received in her lifetime

(D) compare Cather's novels to the archetypal form of the realistic novel

(E) examine the impact of European literature and literary theory on Cather's work

PrepTest57 Sec4 Qs 13–19

REFLECTION

Congratulations on your newfound Reading Comprehension abilities. Take a few moments and reflect on how you reached the levels you've demonstrated on those last passages and questions. Ask yourself the following questions.

- How is LSAT Reading Comprehension reading different than reading for school or pleasure? Why is it referred to as strategic reading?
- What does it mean to be an active reader? How do you interrogate the author as you read?
- What role do Keywords play in strategic reading?
- Why is it helpful to jot down brief paraphrases of crucial text?
- Why do you summarize the passage's Topic and Scope and the author's Purpose and Main Idea?
- What are the distinguishing characteristics of the Reading Comprehension question types?
- How do you spot and use research clues in the question stems?
- How can you most appropriately predict the answers to Global and open-ended Inference questions?
- What are the common wrong answer types associated with Reading Comprehension questions?

While these questions will help you reflect on your performance in the Reading Comprehension section, you can actually practice Reading Comprehension skills all the time. Over the coming days and weeks, make a point of reading material that is academic and written at roughly the same level as LSAT Reading Comprehension passages. As you do, interrogate the author. Spot Keywords and summarize the authors' purposes and points of view. Try imagining, or even writing, LSAT questions to accompany the outside reading you do. The more you "think like the testmaker," the closer you are to true LSAT mastery.

ANSWER KEY

Fractal Geometry (pp. 902–903)

1. B
2. C
3. D
4. D
5. E
6. A
7. E
8. D

TV and Developing Nations (pp. 906–907)

9. C
10. B
11. C
12. D
13. E
14. B
15. A

FCC and UCC (pp. 916–917)

16. A
17. A
18. D
19. C
20. E

Parallel Computing (pp. 922–923)

21. C
22. C
23. E
24. B
25. C
26. B
27. A
28. E

Science and Humanities (pp. 938–939)

40. E
41. C
42. D
43. B
44. D
45. C
46. B

The Value of Forgeries (pp. 946–947)

47. C
48. A
49. E
50. C
51. B
52. E
53. B

Universal Declaration of Human Rights (UDHR) (pp. 950–951)

54. D
55. B
56. B
57. D
58. E
59. A

Isamu Noguchi Sculpture (pp. 952–953)

60. C
61. D
62. D
63. C
64. E
65. B
66. A

Willa Cather (pp. 954–955)

67. E
68. C
69. C
70. A
71. E
72. E
73. B

Complete explanations for these questions can be found in your Online Center.

CHAPTER 15

Reading Comprehension Practice

The earlier chapters in the Reading Comprehension section covered the Reading Comprehension Method and demonstrated the skills and strategies rewarded by the testmaker in this section of the test. This chapter gives you the opportunity to work with full passages and their associated question sets. It contains the ten passages from PrepTests 49, 51, 57, 59, and 61 that were not in Chapters 13 or 14.

NOTES ON READING COMPREHENSION PRACTICE

Use the Reading Comprehension Method consistently. Continue to use the Reading Comprehension Method as you practice full passages. Pay close attention to your work in each step. Some students underestimate the importance of reading strategically; others overlook the crucial roles played by researching the text and predicting the correct answer. Each step in the method is vital to your progress on the Reading Comprehension section.

THE KAPLAN READING COMPREHENSION METHOD

Step 1: Read the Passage Strategically

Step 2: Read the Question Stem

Step 3: Research the Relevant Text

Step 4: Predict the Correct Answer

Step 5: Evaluate the Answer Choices

Review your work thoroughly. Complete explanations for the passages and questions in this chapter are found in your Online Center. Review them completely, even if you get all of the questions correct. Each question's difficulty—from ★ (easiest) to ★★★★ (hardest)—is indicated in the explanations.

Practice and timing. On Test Day, you will have about 8 ½ minutes per passage. As you work on individual passages, however, keep your focus on the successful implementation of the method. Your greatest gains in speed will come with familiarity, practice, and (ironically) patience. When you practice full tests or 35-minute Reading Comprehension sections, time yourself strictly.

QUESTION POOL

Try out some practice on passages that have not appeared in earlier chapters. These passages are arranged chronologically, from most to least recent.

Passage A

One function of language is to influence others' behavior by changing what they know, believe, or desire. For humans engaged in conversation, the perception of another's mental state is perhaps the
(5) most common vocalization stimulus.

While animal vocalizations may have evolved because they can potentially alter listeners' behavior to the signaler's benefit, such communication is—in contrast to human language—inadvertent, because
(10) most animals, with the possible exception of chimpanzees, cannot attribute mental states to others. The male *Physalaemus* frog calls because calling causes females to approach and other males to retreat, but there is no evidence that he does so because he attributes knowledge
(15) or desire to other frogs, or because he knows his calls will affect their knowledge and that this knowledge will, in turn, affect their behavior. Research also suggests that, in marked contrast to humans, nonhuman primates do not produce vocalizations in response to perception
(20) of another's need for information. Macaques, for example, give alarm calls when predators approach and coo calls upon finding food, yet experiments reveal no evidence that individuals were more likely to call about these events when they were aware of them but their offspring
(25) were clearly ignorant; similarly, chimpanzees do not appear to adjust their calling to inform ignorant individuals of their own location or that of food. Many animal vocalizations whose production initially seems goal-directed are not as purposeful as they first appear.

Passage B

(30) Many scientists distinguish animal communication systems from human language on the grounds that the former are rigid responses to stimuli, whereas human language is spontaneous and creative.

In this connection, it is commonly stated that no
(35) animal can use its communication system to lie. Obviously, a lie requires intention to deceive: to judge whether a particular instance of animal communication is truly prevarication requires knowledge of the animal's intentions. Language philosopher H. P. Grice explains
(40) that for an individual to mean something by uttering *x*, the individual must intend, in expressing *x*, to induce an audience to believe something and must also intend the utterance to be recognized as so intended. But conscious intention is a category of mental experience
(45) widely believed to be uniquely human. Philosopher Jacques Maritain's discussion of the honeybee's elaborate "waggle-dance" exemplifies this view. Although bees returning to the hive communicate to other bees the distance and direction of food sources,
(50) such communication is, Maritain asserts, merely a

conditioned reflex: animals may use communicative signs but lack conscious intention regarding their use.

But these arguments are circular: conscious intention is ruled out a priori and then its absence
(55) taken as evidence that animal communication is fundamentally different from human language. In fact, the narrowing of the perceived gap between animal communication and human language revealed by recent research with chimpanzees and other animals
(60) calls into question not only the assumption that the difference between animal and human communication is qualitative rather than merely quantitative, but also the accompanying assumption that animals respond mechanically to stimuli, whereas humans speak with
(65) conscious understanding and intent.

1. Both passages are primarily concerned with addressing which one of the following questions?

    (A) Are animals capable of deliberately prevaricating in order to achieve specific goals?

    (B) Are the communications of animals characterized by conscious intention?

    (C) What kinds of stimuli are most likely to elicit animal vocalizations?

    (D) Are the communication systems of nonhuman primates qualitatively different from those of all other animals?

    (E) Is there a scientific consensus about the differences between animal communication systems and human language?

2. In discussing the philosopher Maritain, the author of passage B seeks primarily to

    (A) describe an interpretation of animal communication that the author believes rests on a logical error

    (B) suggest by illustration that there is conscious intention underlying the communicative signs employed by certain animals

    (C) present an argument in support of the view that animal communication systems are spontaneous and creative

    (D) furnish specific evidence against the theory that most animal communication is merely a conditioned reflex

    (E) point to a noted authority on animal communication whose views the author regards with respect

Explanations for these questions can be found in your Online Center.

Part Four: Reading Comprehension
Reading Comprehension Practice

3. The author of passage B would be most likely to agree with which one of the following statements regarding researchers who subscribe to the position articulated in passage A?

   (A) They fail to recognize that humans often communicate without any clear idea of their listeners' mental states.

   (B) Most of them lack the credentials needed to assess the relevant experimental evidence correctly.

   (C) They ignore well-known evidence that animals do in fact practice deception.

   (D) They make assumptions about matters that should be determined empirically.

   (E) They falsely believe that all communication systems can be explained in terms of their evolutionary benefits.

4. Which one of the following assertions from passage A provides support for the view attributed to Maritain in passage B (lines 50–52)?

   (A) One function of language is to influence the behavior of others by changing what they think.

   (B) Animal vocalizations may have evolved because they have the potential to alter listeners' behavior to the signaler's benefit.

   (C) It is possible that chimpanzees may have the capacity to attribute mental states to others.

   (D) There is no evidence that the male *Physalaemus* frog calls because he knows that his calls will affect the knowledge of other frogs.

   (E) Macaques give alarm calls when predators approach and coo calls upon finding food.

5. The authors would be most likely to disagree over

   (A) the extent to which communication among humans involves the ability to perceive the mental states of others

   (B) the importance of determining to what extent animal communication systems differ from human language

   (C) whether human language and animal communication differ from one another qualitatively or merely in a matter of degree

   (D) whether chimpanzees' vocalizations suggest that they may possess the capacity to attribute mental states to others

   (E) whether animals' vocalizations evolved to alter the behavior of other animals in a way that benefits the signaler

6. Passage B differs from passage A in that passage B is more

   (A) optimistic regarding the ability of science to answer certain fundamental questions

   (B) disapproving of the approach taken by others writing on the same general topic

   (C) open-minded in its willingness to accept the validity of apparently conflicting positions

   (D) supportive of ongoing research related to the question at hand

   (E) circumspect in its refusal to commit itself to any positions with respect to still-unsettled research questions

   PrepTest61 Sec1 Qs 14–19

K

Part Four: Reading Comprehension

CHAPTER 15

Explanations for these questions
can be found in your Online Center.

In contrast to the mainstream of U.S. historiography during the late nineteenth and early twentieth centuries, African American historians of the period, such as George Washington Williams and
(5) W. E. B. DuBois, adopted a transnational perspective. This was true for several reasons, not the least of which was the necessity of doing so if certain aspects of the history of African Americans in the United States were to be treated honestly.

(10)   First, there was the problem of citizenship. Even after the adoption in 1868 of the Fourteenth Amendment to the U.S. Constitution, which defined citizenship, the question of citizenship for African Americans had not been genuinely resolved. Because
(15) of this, emigrationist sentiment was a central issue in black political discourse, and both issues were critical topics for investigation. The implications for historical scholarship and national identity were enormous. While some black leaders insisted on their right to U.S.
(20) citizenship, others called on black people to emigrate and find a homeland of their own. Most African Americans were certainly not willing to relinquish their claims to the benefits of U.S. citizenship, but many had reached a point of profound pessimism and had
(25) begun to question their allegiance to the United States.

     Mainstream U.S. historiography was firmly rooted in a nationalist approach during this period; the glorification of the nation and a focus on the nation-state as a historical force were dominant. The
(30) expanding spheres of influence of Europe and the United States prompted the creation of new genealogies of nations, new myths about the inevitability of nations, their "temperaments," their destinies. African American intellectuals who
(35) confronted the nationalist approach to historiography were troubled by its implications. Some argued that imperialism was a natural outgrowth of nationalism and its view that a state's strength is measured by the extension of its political power over colonial territory;
(40) the scramble for colonial empires was a distinct aspect of nationalism in the latter part of the nineteenth century.

     Yet, for all their distrust of U.S. nationalism, most early black historians were themselves engaged in a
(45) sort of nation building. Deliberately or not, they contributed to the formation of a collective identity, reconstructing a glorious African past for the purposes of overturning degrading representations of blackness and establishing a firm cultural basis for a
(50) shared identity. Thus, one might argue that black historians' internationalism was a manifestation of a kind of nationalism that posits a diasporic community, which, while lacking a sovereign territory or official language, possesses a single culture, however
(55) mythical, with singular historical roots. Many members of this diaspora saw themselves as an oppressed "nation" without a homeland, or they imagined Africa as home. Hence, these historians understood their task to be the writing of the history

(60) of a people scattered by force and circumstance, a history that began in Africa.

7. Which one of the following most accurately expresses the main idea of the passage?

(A)   Historians are now recognizing that the major challenge faced by African Americans in the late nineteenth and early twentieth centuries was the struggle for citizenship.

(B)   Early African American historians who practiced a transnational approach to history were primarily interested in advancing an emigrationist project.

(C)   U.S. historiography in the late nineteenth and early twentieth centuries was characterized by a conflict between African American historians who viewed history from a transnational perspective and mainstream historians who took a nationalist perspective.

(D)   The transnational perspective of early African American historians countered mainstream nationalist historiography, but it was arguably nationalist itself to the extent that it posited a culturally unified diasporic community.

(E)   Mainstream U.S. historians in the late nineteenth and early twentieth centuries could no longer justify their nationalist approach to history once they were confronted with the transnational perspective taken by African American historians.

8. Which one of the following phrases most accurately conveys the sense of the word "reconstructing" as it is used in line 47?

(A)   correcting a misconception about
(B)   determining the sequence of events in
(C)   investigating the implications of
(D)   rewarding the promoters of
(E)   shaping a conception of

9. Which one of the following is most strongly supported by the passage?

(A)   Emigrationist sentiment would not have been as strong among African Americans in the late nineteenth century had the promise of U.S. citizenship been fully realized for African Americans at that time.

(B)   Scholars writing the history of diasporic communities generally do not discuss the forces that initially caused the scattering of the members of those communities.

(C)   Most historians of the late nineteenth and early twentieth centuries endeavored to make the histories of the nations about which they wrote seem more glorious than they actually were.

(D)   To be properly considered nationalist, a historical work must ignore the ways in which one nation's foreign policy decisions affected other nations.

(E)   A considerable number of early African American historians embraced nationalism and the inevitability of the dominance of the nation-state.

Explanations for these questions can be found in your Online Center.

Part Four: Reading Comprehension
Reading Comprehension Practice
K

10. As it is described in the passage, the transnational approach employed by African American historians working in the late nineteenth and early twentieth centuries would be best exemplified by a historical study that

   (A) investigated the extent to which European and U.S. nationalist mythologies contradicted one another

   (B) defined the national characters of the United States and several European nations by focusing on their treatment of minority populations rather than on their territorial ambitions

   (C) recounted the attempts by the United States to gain control over new territories during the late nineteenth and early twentieth centuries

   (D) considered the impact of emigrationist sentiment among African Americans on U.S. foreign policy in Africa during the late nineteenth century

   (E) examined the extent to which African American culture at the turn of the century incorporated traditions that were common to a number of African cultures

11. The passage provides information sufficient to answer which one of the following questions?

   (A) Which African nations did early African American historians research in writing their histories of the African diaspora?

   (B) What were some of the African languages spoken by the ancestors of the members of the African diasporic community who were living in the United States in the late nineteenth century?

   (C) Over which territories abroad did the United States attempt to extend its political power in the latter part of the nineteenth century?

   (D) Are there textual ambiguities in the Fourteenth Amendment that spurred the conflict over U.S. citizenship for African Americans?

   (E) In what ways did African American leaders respond to the question of citizenship for African Americans in the latter part of the nineteenth century?

12. The author of the passage would be most likely to agree with which one of the following statements?

   (A) Members of a particular diasporic community have a common country of origin.

   (B) Territorial sovereignty is not a prerequisite for the project of nation building.

   (C) Early African American historians who rejected nationalist historiography declined to engage in historical myth-making of any kind.

   (D) The most prominent African American historians in the late nineteenth and early twentieth centuries advocated emigration for African Americans.

   (E) Historians who employed a nationalist approach focused on entirely different events from those studied and written about by early African American historians.

13. The main purpose of the second paragraph of the passage is to

   (A) explain why early African American historians felt compelled to approach historiography in the way that they did

   (B) show that governmental actions such as constitutional amendments do not always have the desired effect

   (C) support the contention that African American intellectuals in the late nineteenth century were critical of U.S. imperialism

   (D) establish that some African American political leaders in the late nineteenth century advocated emigration as an alternative to fighting for the benefits of U.S. citizenship

   (E) argue that the definition of citizenship contained in the Fourteenth Amendment to the U.S. Constitution is too limited

14. As it is presented in the passage, the approach to history taken by mainstream U.S. historians of the late nineteenth and early twentieth centuries is most similar to the approach exemplified in which one of the following?

   (A) An elected official writes a memo suggesting that because a particular course of action has been successful in the past, the government should continue to pursue that course of action.

   (B) A biographer of a famous novelist argues that the precocity apparent in certain of the novelist's early achievements confirms that her success was attributable to innate talent.

   (C) A doctor maintains that because a certain medication was developed expressly for the treatment of an illness, it is the best treatment for that illness.

   (D) A newspaper runs a series of articles in order to inform the public about the environmentally hazardous practices of a large corporation.

   (E) A scientist gets the same result from an experiment several times and therefore concludes that its chemical reactions always proceed in the observed fashion.

PrepTest61 Sec1 Qs 20–27

K | Part Four: Reading Comprehension
CHAPTER 15

Explanations for these questions
can be found in your Online Center.

In an experiment, two strangers are given the opportunity to share $100, subject to the following constraints: One person—the "proposer"—is to suggest how to divide the money and can make only
(5) one such proposal. The other person—the "responder"—must either accept or reject the offer without qualification. Both parties know that if the offer is accepted, the money will be split as agreed, but if the offer is rejected, neither will receive
(10) anything.

This scenario is called the Ultimatum Game. Researchers have conducted it numerous times with a wide variety of volunteers. Many participants in the role of the proposer seem instinctively to feel that
(15) they should offer 50 percent to the responder, because such a division is "fair" and therefore likely to be accepted. Two-thirds of proposers offer responders between 40 and 50 percent. Only 4 in 100 offer less than 20 percent. Offering such a small amount is
(20) quite risky; most responders reject such offers. This is a puzzle: Why would anyone reject an offer as too small? Responders who reject an offer receive nothing, so if one assumes—as theoretical economics traditionally has—that people make economic
(25) decisions primarily out of rational self-interest, one would expect that an individual would accept any offer.

Some theorists explain the insistence on fair divisions in the Ultimatum Game by citing our
(30) prehistoric ancestors' need for the support of a strong group. Small groups of hunter-gatherers depended for survival on their members' strengths. It is counterproductive to outcompete rivals within one's group to the point where one can no longer depend
(35) on them in contests with other groups. But this hypothesis at best explains why proposers offer large amounts, not why responders reject low offers.

A more compelling explanation is that our emotional apparatus has been shaped by millions of
(40) years of living in small groups, where it is hard to keep secrets. Our emotions are therefore not finely tuned to one-time, strictly anonymous interactions. In real life we expect our friends and neighbors to notice our decisions. If people know that someone is
(45) content with a small share, they are likely to make that person low offers. But if someone is known to angrily reject low offers, others have an incentive to make that person high offers. Consequently, evolution should have favored angry responses to low offers; if
(50) one regularly receives fair offers when food is divided, one is more likely to survive. Because one-shot interactions were rare during human evolution, our emotions do not discriminate between one-shot and repeated interactions. Therefore, we respond
(55) emotionally to low offers in the Ultimatum Game because we instinctively feel the need to reject dismal offers in order to keep our self-esteem. This

self-esteem helps us to acquire a reputation that is beneficial in future encounters.

15. Which one of the following most accurately summarizes the main idea of the passage?

(A) Contrary to a traditional assumption of theoretical economics, the behavior of participants in the Ultimatum Game demonstrates that people do not make economic decisions out of rational self-interest.

(B) Although the reactions most commonly displayed by participants in the Ultimatum Game appear to conflict with rational self-interest, they probably result from a predisposition that had evolutionary value.

(C) Because our emotional apparatus has been shaped by millions of years of living in small groups in which it is hard to keep secrets, our emotions are not finely tuned to one-shot, anonymous interactions.

(D) People respond emotionally to low offers in the Ultimatum Game because they instinctively feel the need to maintain the strength of the social group to which they belong.

(E) When certain social and evolutionary factors are taken into account, it can be seen that the behavior of participants in the Ultimatum Game is motivated primarily by the need to outcompete rivals.

16. The passage implies that the Ultimatum Game is

(A) one that requires two strangers to develop trust in each other
(B) responsible for overturning a basic assumption of theoretical economics
(C) a situation that elicits unpredictable results
(D) a type of one-shot, anonymous interaction
(E) proof that our emotional apparatus has been shaped by millions of years of living in small groups

17. The author's primary purpose in the passage is to

(A) survey existing interpretations of the puzzling results of an experiment
(B) show how two theories that attempt to explain the puzzling results of an experiment complement each other
(C) argue that the results of an experiment, while puzzling, are valid
(D) offer a plausible explanation for the puzzling results of an experiment
(E) defend an experiment against criticism that methodological flaws caused its puzzling results

Explanations for these questions can be found in your Online Center.

Part Four: Reading Comprehension
Reading Comprehension Practice |

18. Which one of the following sentences would most logically conclude the final paragraph of the passage?

    (A) Contrary to the assumptions of theoretical economics, human beings do not act primarily out of self-interest.

    (B) Unfortunately, one-time, anonymous interactions are becoming increasingly common in contemporary society.

    (C) The instinctive urge to acquire a favorable reputation may also help to explain the desire of many proposers in the Ultimatum Game to make "fair" offers.

    (D) High self-esteem and a positive reputation offer individuals living in small groups many other benefits as well.

    (E) The behavior of participants in the Ultimatum Game sheds light on the question of what constitutes a "fair" division.

19. In the context of the passage, the author would be most likely to consider the explanation in the third paragraph more favorably if it were shown that

    (A) our prehistoric ancestors often belonged to large groups of more than a hundred people

    (B) in many prehistoric cultures, there were hierarchies within groups that dictated which allocations of goods were to be considered fair and which were not

    (C) it is just as difficult to keep secrets in relatively large social groups as it is in small social groups

    (D) it is just as counterproductive to a small social group to allow oneself to be outcompeted by one's rivals within the group as it is to outcompete those rivals

    (E) in many social groups, there is a mutual understanding among the group's members that allocations of goods will be based on individual needs as opposed to equal shares

PrepTest59 Sec4 Qs 23–27

K

Part Four: Reading Comprehension

CHAPTER 15

Explanations for these questions can be found in your Online Center.

The work of South African writer Ezekiel Mphahlele has confounded literary critics, especially those who feel compelled to draw a sharp distinction between autobiography and fiction. These critics point
(5) to Mphahlele's best-known works—his 1959 autobiography *Down Second Avenue* and his 1971 novel *The Wanderers*—to illustrate the problem of categorizing his work. While his autobiography traces his life from age five until the beginning of his
(10) self-imposed 20-year exile at age thirty-eight, *The Wanderers* appears to pick up at the beginning of his exile and go on from there. Critics have variously decried the former as too fictionalized and the latter as too autobiographical, but those who focus on
(15) traditional labels inevitably miss the fact that Mphahlele manipulates different prose forms purely in the service of the social message he advances.

Even where critics give him a favorable reading, all too often their reviews carry a negative subtext.
(20) For example, one critic said of *The Wanderers* that if anger, firsthand experiences, compassion, and topicality were the sole requirements for great literature, the novel might well be one of the masterpieces of this declining part of the twentieth
(25) century. And although this critic may not have meant to question the literary contribution of the novel, there are those who are outright dismissive of *The Wanderers* because it contains an autobiographical framework and is populated with real-world
(30) characters. Mphahlele briefly defends against such charges by pointing out the importance of the fictional father-son relationship that opens and closes the novel. But his greater concern is the social vision that pervades his work, though it too is prone to
(35) misunderstandings and underappreciation. Mphahlele is a humanist and an integrationist, and his writings wonderfully articulate his vision of the future; but critics often balk at this vision because Mphahlele provides no road maps for bringing such a future
(40) about.

Mphahlele himself shows little interest in establishing guidelines to distinguish autobiography from fiction. Though he does refer to *Down Second Avenue* as an autobiography and *The Wanderers* as a
(45) novel, he asserts that no novelist can write complete fiction or absolute fact. It is the nature of writing, at least the writing he cares about, that the details must be drawn from the writer's experiences, and thus are in some sense fact, but conveyed in such a way as to
(50) maximize the effectiveness of the social message contained in the work, and thus inevitably fiction. As he claims, the whole point of the exercise of writing has nothing to do with classification; in all forms writing is the transmission of ideas, and important
(55) ideas at that: "Whenever you write prose or poetry or drama you are writing a social criticism of one kind

or another. If you don't, you are completely irrelevant—you don't count."

20. Based on the passage, with which one of the following statements would Mphahlele be most likely to agree?

(A) All works of literature should articulate a vision of the future.
(B) It is not necessary for a writer to write works to fit predetermined categories.
(C) Literary categories are worth addressing only when literary works are being unjustifiably dismissed.
(D) Most works of literature that resemble novels could accurately be classified as autobiographies.
(E) The most useful categories in literature are those that distinguish prose from poetry and poetry from drama.

21. The passage states that Mphahlele believes which one of the following?

(A) Writing should provide a guide for achieving social change.
(B) Writing should have as its goal the transmission of ideas.
(C) Writing is most effective when it minimizes the use of real people and events to embellish a story.
(D) Good writing is generally more autobiographical than fictional.
(E) Fiction and autobiography are clearly identifiable literary forms if the work is composed properly.

22. In lines 18–25, the author uses the phrase "negative subtext" in reference to the critic's comment to claim that

(A) the critic believes that Mphahlele himself shows little interest in establishing guidelines that distinguish fact from fiction in literature
(B) the comment is unfairly one-sided and gives no voice to perspectives that Mphahlele might embrace
(C) the requirement of firsthand experiences mentioned in the comment is in direct contradiction to the requirements of fiction
(D) the requirements for great literature mentioned in the comment are ill conceived, thus the requirements have little bearing on what great literature really is
(E) the requirements for great literature mentioned in the comment are not the sole requirements, thus Mphahlele's work is implied by the critic not to be great literature

Explanations for these questions can be found in your Online Center.

Part Four: Reading Comprehension
Reading Comprehension Practice | K

23. According to the passage, critics offer which one of the following reasons for their dismissal of *The Wanderers*?

   (A) It should not have been populated with real-world characters.
   (B) It should have been presented as an autobiography.
   (C) It does not clearly display Mphahlele's vision.
   (D) It intends to deliver controversial social criticisms.
   (E) It places too much emphasis on relationships.

24. The author quotes Mphahlele (lines 55–58) primarily in order to

   (A) demonstrate Mphahlele's eloquence as a writer
   (B) provide a common goal of writing among novelists
   (C) further elaborate the kind of writing Mphahlele values
   (D) introduce the three literary forms Mphahlele uses to write social criticism
   (E) show that Mphahlele makes no distinction among prose, poetry, and drama

25. Which one of the following aspects of Mphahlele's work does the author of the passage appear to value most highly?

   (A) his commitment to communicating social messages
   (B) his blending of the categories of fiction and autobiography
   (C) his ability to redefine established literary categories
   (D) his emphasis on the importance of details
   (E) his plan for bringing about the future he envisions

26. Which one of the following is most strongly suggested by the information in the passage?

   (A) Mphahlele's stance as a humanist and an integrationist derives from an outlook on writing that recognizes a sharp distinction between fiction and autobiography.
   (B) The social vision contained in a work is irrelevant to critics who feel compelled to find distinct categories in which to place literary works.
   (C) Critics are concerned with categorizing the works they read not as a means to judge the quality of the works but as a way of discovering tendencies within literary traditions.
   (D) If Mphahlele were to provide direction as to how his vision of the future might be realized, more critics might find this vision acceptable.
   (E) For a work to be classified as a novel, it must not contain any autobiographical elements.

PrepTest51 Sec2 Qs 1–7

A vigorous debate in astronomy centers on an epoch in planetary history that was first identified by analysis of rock samples obtained in lunar missions. Scientists discovered that the major craters on the
(5) Moon were created by a vigorous bombardment of debris approximately four billion years ago—the so-called late heavy bombardment (LHB). Projectiles from this bombardment that affected the Moon should also have struck Earth, a likelihood with profound
(10) consequences for the history of Earth since, until the LHB ended, life could not have survived here.

   Various theoretical approaches have been developed to account for both the evidence gleaned from samples of Moon rock collected during lunar
(15) explorations and the size and distribution of craters on the Moon. Since the sizes of LHB craters suggest they were formed by large bodies, some astronomers believe that the LHB was linked to the disintegration of an asteroid or comet orbiting the Sun. In this view,
(20) a large body broke apart and peppered the inner solar system with debris. Other scientists disagree and believe that the label "LHB" is in itself a misnomer. These researchers claim that a cataclysm is not necessary to explain the LHB evidence. They claim
(25) that the Moon's evidence merely provides a view of the period concluding billions of years of a continuous, declining heavy bombardment throughout the inner solar system. According to them, the impacts from the latter part of the bombardment were
(30) so intense that they obliterated evidence of earlier impacts. A third group contends that the Moon's evidence supports the view that the LHB was a sharply defined cataclysmic cratering period, but these scientists believe that because of its relatively brief
(35) duration, this cataclysm did not extend throughout the inner solar system. They hold that the LHB involved only the disintegration of a body within the Earth-Moon system, because the debris from such an event would have been swept up relatively quickly.
(40)   New support for the hypothesis that a late bombardment extended throughout the inner solar system has been found in evidence from the textural features and chemical makeup of a meteorite that has been found on Earth. It seems to be a rare example of
(45) a Mars rock that made its way to Earth after being knocked from the surface of Mars. The rock has recently been experimentally dated at about four billion years old, which means that, if the rock is indeed from Mars, it was knocked from the planet at
(50) about the same time that the Moon was experiencing the LHB. This tiny piece of evidence suggests that at least two planetary systems in the inner solar system experienced bombardment at the same time. However, to determine the pervasiveness of the LHB, scientists
(55) will need to locate many more such rocks and perhaps obtain surface samples from other planets in the inner solar system.

27. Which one of the following most accurately expresses the main point of the passage?

(A) The LHB is an intense meteorite bombardment that occurred about four billion years ago and is responsible for the cratering on the Moon and perhaps on other members of the inner solar system as well.

(B) Astronomers now believe that they may never collect enough evidence to determine the true nature of the LHB.

(C) If scientists continue to collect new clues at their current rate, the various LHB hypotheses can soon be evaluated and a clear picture will emerge.

(D) The Moon's evidence shows that the LHB was linked to a small body that disintegrated while in solar orbit and sprayed the inner solar system with debris.

(E) New evidence has been found that favors the view that the LHB was widespread, but before competing theories of the LHB can be excluded, more evidence needs to be gathered.

28. The author's attitude toward arguments that might be based on the evidence of the rock mentioned in the passage as being from Mars (lines 44–46) can most accurately be described as

(A) ambivalence because the theory of the rock's migration to Earth is at once both appealing and difficult to believe

(B) caution because even if the claims concerning the rock's origins can be proven, it is unwise to draw general conclusions without copious evidence

(C) skepticism because it seems unlikely that a rock could somehow make its way from Mars to Earth after being dislodged

(D) curiosity because many details of the rock's interplanetary travel, its chemical analysis, and its dating analysis have not yet been published

(E) outright acceptance because the origins of the rock have been sufficiently corroborated

Explanations for these questions can be found in your Online Center.

Part Four: Reading Comprehension
Reading Comprehension Practice

29. The author mentions that the LHB "should also have struck Earth" (lines 8–9) primarily to

    (A) support a particular theory of the extent of the LHB
    (B) question the lack of LHB evidence found on Earth
    (C) advocate certain scientific models for the origins of life on Earth
    (D) provide a reason why scientists are interested in studying the LHB
    (E) introduce additional support for the dating of the LHB

30. The author implies that all theoretical approaches to the LHB would agree on which one of the following?

    (A) the approximate duration of the LHB
    (B) the origin of the debris involved in the LHB
    (C) the idea that cratering decreased significantly after the LHB
    (D) the idea that the LHB destroyed the life that existed on Earth four billion years ago
    (E) the approximate amount of debris involved in the LHB

31. According to the passage, the third group of scientists (line 31) believes that the LHB

    (A) affected only the Moon
    (B) was so brief that its extent had to be fairly localized
    (C) consisted of so little debris that it was absorbed quickly by the planets in the inner solar system
    (D) occurred more recently than four billion years ago
    (E) may have lasted a long time, but all its debris remained within the Earth-Moon system

32. Which one of the following, if true, would lend the most support to the view that the LHB was limited to Earth and the Moon?

    (A) An extensive survey of craters on Mars shows very little evidence for an increase in the intensity of projectiles striking Mars during the period from three billion to five billion years ago.
    (B) Scientists discover another meteorite on Earth that they conclude had been knocked from the surface of the Moon during the LHB.
    (C) A re-analysis of Moon rocks reveals that several originated on Earth during the LHB.
    (D) Based on further testing, scientists conclude that the rock believed to have originated on Mars actually originated on the Moon.
    (E) Excavations on both Earth and the Moon yield evidence that the LHB concluded billions of years of heavy bombardment.

    PrepTest51 Sec2 Qs 8–13

K

Part Four: Reading Comprehension
CHAPTER 15

Explanations for these questions
can be found in your Online Center.

Computers have long been utilized in the sphere
of law in the form of word processors, spreadsheets,
legal research systems, and practice management
systems. Most exciting, however, has been the
(5) prospect of using artificial intelligence techniques to
create so-called legal reasoning systems—computer
programs that can help to resolve legal disputes by
reasoning from and applying the law. But the
practical benefits of such automated reasoning
(10) systems have fallen short of optimistic early
predictions and have not resulted in computer systems
that can independently provide expert advice about
substantive law. This is not surprising in light of the
difficulty in resolving problems involving the
(15) meaning and applicability of rules set out in a legal
text.
        Early attempts at automated legal reasoning
focused on the doctrinal nature of law. They viewed
law as a set of rules, and the resulting computer
(20) systems were engineered to make legal decisions by
determining the consequences that followed when its
stored set of legal rules was applied to a collection of
evidentiary data. Such systems underestimated the
problems of interpretation that can arise at every
(25) stage of a legal argument. Examples abound of
situations that are open to differing interpretations:
whether a mobile home in a trailer park is a house or
a motor vehicle, whether a couple can be regarded as
married in the absence of a formal legal ceremony,
(30) and so on. Indeed, many notions invoked in the text
of a statute may be deliberately left undefined so as
to allow the law to be adapted to unforeseen
circumstances. But in order to be able to apply legal
rules to novel situations, systems have to be equipped
(35) with a kind of comprehensive knowledge of the
world that is far beyond their capabilities at present
or in the foreseeable future.
        Proponents of legal reasoning systems now argue
that accommodating reference to, and reasoning from,
(40) cases improves the chances of producing a successful
system. By focusing on the practice of reasoning
from precedents, researchers have designed systems
called case-based reasoners, which store individual
example cases in their knowledge bases. In contrast
(45) to a system that models legal knowledge based on a
set of rules, a case-based reasoner, when given a
concrete problem, manipulates the cases in its
knowledge base to reach a conclusion based on a
similar case. Unfortunately, in the case-based systems
(50) currently in development, the criteria for similarity
among cases are system dependent and fixed by the
designer, so that similarity is found only by testing
for the presence or absence of predefined factors.
This simply postpones the apparently intractable
(55) problem of developing a system that can discover for
itself the factors that make cases similar in relevant
ways.

33. Which one of the following most accurately expresses
the main point of the passage?

(A) Attempts to model legal reasoning through
computer programs have not been successful
because of problems of interpreting legal
discourse and identifying appropriate
precedents.

(B) Despite signs of early promise, it is now
apparent that computer programs have little
value for legal professionals in their work.

(C) Case-based computer systems are vastly superior
to those computer systems based upon the
doctrinal nature of the law.

(D) Computers applying artificial intelligence
techniques show promise for revolutionizing
the process of legal interpretation in the
relatively near future.

(E) Using computers can expedite legal research,
facilitate the matching of a particular case to a
specific legal principle, and even provide
insights into possible flaws involving legal
reasoning.

34. The logical relationship of lines 8–13 of the passage to
lines 23–25 and 49–53 of the passage is most
accurately described as

(A) a general assertion supported by two specific
observations

(B) a general assertion followed by two arguments,
one of which supports and one of which
refutes the general assertion

(C) a general assertion that entails two more specific
assertions

(D) a theoretical assumption refuted by two specific
observations

(E) a specific observation that suggests two
incompatible generalizations

35. In the passage as a whole, the author is primarily
concerned with

(A) arguing that computers can fundamentally
change how the processes of legal
interpretation and reasoning are conducted in
the future

(B) indicating that the law has subtle nuances that
are not readily dealt with by computerized
legal reasoning programs

(C) demonstrating that computers are approaching
the point where they can apply legal precedents
to current cases

(D) suggesting that, because the law is made by
humans, computer programmers must also
apply their human intuition when designing
legal reasoning systems

(E) defending the use of computers as essential and
indispensable components of the modern legal
profession

Explanations for these questions can be found in your Online Center.

Part Four: Reading Comprehension
Reading Comprehension Practice | K

36. The passage suggests that the author would be most likely to agree with which one of the following statements about computerized automated legal reasoning systems?

    (A) These systems have met the original expectations of computer specialists but have fallen short of the needs of legal practitioners.
    (B) Progress in research on these systems has been hindered, more because not enough legal documents are accessible by computer than because theoretical problems remain unsolved.
    (C) These systems will most likely be used as legal research tools rather than as aids in legal analysis.
    (D) Rule systems will likely replace case-based systems over time.
    (E) Developing adequate legal reasoning systems would require research breakthroughs by computer specialists.

37. It can be most reasonably inferred from the passage's discussion of requirements for developing effective automated legal reasoning systems that the author would agree with which one of the following statements?

    (A) Focusing on the doctrinal nature of law is the fundamental error made by developers of automated legal systems.
    (B) Contemporary computers do not have the required memory capability to store enough data to be effective legal reasoning systems.
    (C) Questions of interpretation in rule-based legal reasoning systems must be settled by programming more legal rules into the systems.
    (D) Legal statutes and reasoning may involve innovative applications that cannot be modeled by a fixed set of rules, cases, or criteria.
    (E) As professionals continue to use computers in the sphere of law they will develop the competence to use legal reasoning systems effectively.

38. Based on the passage, which one of the following can be most reasonably inferred concerning case-based reasoners?

    (A) The major problem in the development of these systems is how to store enough cases in their knowledge bases.
    (B) These systems are more useful than rule systems because case-based reasoners are based on a simpler view of legal reasoning.
    (C) Adding specific criteria for similarity among cases to existing systems would not overcome an important shortcoming of these systems.
    (D) These systems can independently provide expert advice about legal rights and duties in a wide range of cases.
    (E) These systems are being designed to attain a much more ambitious goal than had been set for rule systems.

39. Which one of the following is mentioned in the passage as an important characteristic of many statutes that frustrates the application of computerized legal reasoning systems?

    (A) complexity of syntax
    (B) unavailability of relevant precedents
    (C) intentional vagueness and adaptability
    (D) overly narrow intent
    (E) incompatibility with previous statutes

40. The examples of situations that are open to differing interpretations (lines 25–30) function in the passage to

    (A) substantiate the usefulness of computers in the sphere of law
    (B) illustrate a vulnerability of rule systems in computerized legal reasoning
    (C) isolate issues that computer systems are in principle incapable of handling
    (D) explain how legal rules have been adapted to novel situations
    (E) question the value of reasoning from precedents in interpreting legal rules

PrepTest51 Sec2 Qs 21–28

K

Part Four: Reading Comprehension
CHAPTER 15

Explanations for these questions
can be found in your Online Center.

The use of computer-generated visual displays in courtrooms is growing as awareness of their ability to recreate crime scenes spreads. Displays currently in use range from still pictures in series that mimic

(5) simple movement to sophisticated simulations based on complex applications of rules of physics and mathematics. By making it possible to slow or stop action, to vary visual perspectives according to witnesses' vantage points, or to highlight or enlarge

(10) images, computer displays provide litigators with tremendous explanatory advantages. Soon, litigators may even have available graphic systems capable of simulating three dimensions, thus creating the illusion that viewers are at the scene of a crime or accident,

(15) directly experiencing its occurrence. The advantages of computer-generated displays derive from the greater psychological impact they have on juries as compared to purely verbal presentations; studies show that people generally retain about 85 percent of visual

(20) information but only 10 percent of aural information. This is especially valuable in complex or technical trials, where juror interest and comprehension are generally low. In addition, computers also allow litigators to integrate graphic aids seamlessly into

(25) their presentations.

Despite these benefits, however, some critics are urging caution in the use of these displays, pointing to a concomitant potential for abuse or unintentional misuse, such as the unfair manipulation of a juror's

(30) impression of an event. These critics argue further that the persuasive and richly communicative nature of the displays can mesmerize jurors and cause them to relax their normal critical faculties. This potential for distortion is compounded when one side in a trial

(35) does not use the technology—often because of the considerable expense involved—leaving the jury susceptible to prejudice in favor of the side employing computer displays. And aside from the risk of intentional manipulation of images or deceitful use

(40) of capacities such as stop-action and highlighting, there is also the possibility that computer displays can be inherently misleading. As an amalgamation of data collection, judgment, and speculation, the displays may in some instances constitute evidence unsuitable

(45) for use in a trial.

To avoid misuse of this technology in the courtroom, practical steps must be taken. First, counsel must be alert to the ever-present danger of its misuse; diligent analyses of the data that form the

(50) basis for computer displays should be routinely performed and disclosed. Judges, who have the discretion to disallow displays that might unfairly prejudice one side, must also be vigilant in assessing the displays they do allow. Similarly, judges should

(55) forewarn jurors of the potentially biased nature of computer-generated evidence. Finally, steps should be taken to ensure that if one side utilizes computer technology, the opposing side will also have access to it. Granting financial aid in these circumstances

(60) would help create a more equitable legal arena in this respect.

41. Which one of the following most accurately states the main point of the passage?

(A) Those involved in court trials that take advantage of computer-generated displays as evidence need to take steps to prevent the misuse of this evidence.

(B) The use of computer-generated displays has grown dramatically in recent years because computer aids allow litigators to convey complex information more clearly.

(C) The persuasive nature of computer-generated displays requires that the rules governing the use of these displays be based on the most sophisticated principles of jurisprudence.

(D) Litigators' prudent use of computer-generated displays will result in heightened jury comprehension of complex legal issues and thus fairer trials.

(E) Any disadvantages of computer-generated visual displays can be eliminated by enacting a number of practical procedures to avoid their intentional misuse.

42. Which one of the following most accurately describes the organization of the passage?

(A) The popularity of a new technology is lamented; criticisms of the technology are voiced; corrective actions to stem its use are recommended.

(B) A new technology is endorsed; specific examples of its advantages are offered; ways to take further advantage of the technology are presented.

(C) A new technology is presented as problematic; specific problems associated with its use are discussed; alternative uses of the technology are proposed.

(D) A new technology is introduced as useful; potential problems associated with its use are identified; recommendations for preventing these problems are offered.

(E) A new technology is described in detail; arguments for and against its use are voiced; recommendations for promoting the widespread use of the technology are advanced.

Explanations for these questions can be found in your Online Center.

Part Four: Reading Comprehension
Reading Comprehension Practice

43. As described in the passage, re-creating an accident with a computer-generated display is most similar to which one of the following?

(A) using several of a crime suspect's statements together to suggest that the suspect had a motive

(B) using an author's original manuscript to correct printing errors in the current edition of her novel

(C) using information gathered from satellite images to predict the development of a thunderstorm

(D) using a video camera to gather opinions of passersby for use in a candidate's political campaign advertisements

(E) using detailed geological evidence to design a museum exhibit depicting a recent volcanic eruption

44. Based on the passage, with which one of the following statements regarding the use of computer displays in courtroom proceedings would the author be most likely to agree?

(A) The courts should suspend the use of stop-action and highlighting techniques until an adequate financial aid program has been established.

(B) Computer-generated evidence should be scrutinized to ensure that it does not rely on excessive speculation in depicting the details of an event.

(C) Actual static photographs of a crime scene are generally more effective as displays than are computer displays.

(D) Verbal accounts by eyewitnesses to crimes should play a more vital role in the presentation of evidence than should computer displays.

(E) Computer displays based on insufficient or inaccurate input of data would not seem realistic and would generally not persuade jurors effectively.

45. The author states which one of the following about computer displays used in trial proceedings?

(A) Despite appearances, computer displays offer few practical advantages over conventional forms of evidence.

(B) Most critics of computer-generated evidence argue for banning such evidence in legal proceedings.

(C) Judges should forewarn jurors of the potentially biased nature of computer-generated displays.

(D) Computer displays are used primarily in technical trials, in which jury interest is naturally low.

(E) Litigators who utilize computer-generated displays must ensure that the opposing side has equal access to such technology.

46. The author mentions each of the following as an advantage of using computer displays in courtroom proceedings EXCEPT:

(A) They enable litigators to slow or stop action.

(B) They can aid jurors in understanding complex or technical information.

(C) They make it possible to vary visual perspectives.

(D) They allow litigators to integrate visual materials smoothly into their presentations.

(E) They prevent litigators from engaging in certain kinds of unjustified speculation.

PrepTest49 Sec3 Qs 1–6

Explanations for these questions
can be found in your Online Center.

Through the last half century, the techniques used
by certain historians of African art for judging the
precise tribal origins of African sculptures on the
basis of style have been greatly refined. However, as
(5) one recent critic of the historians' classificatory
assumptions has put it, the idea that the distribution
of a particular style is necessarily limited to the area
populated by one tribe may be "a dreadful
oversimplification . . . a decided falsification of the
(10) very life of art in Africa."

Objects and styles have often been diffused
through trade, most notably by workshops of artists
who sell their work over a large geographical area.
Styles cannot be narrowly defined as belonging
(15) uniquely to a particular area; rather, there are
important "centers of style" throughout Africa where
families, clans, and workshops produce sculpture and
other art that is dispersed over a large, multitribal
geographical area. Thus, a family of artists belonging
(20) to a single ethnic group may produce sculpture on
commission for several neighboring tribes. While this
practice contributes to a marked uniformity of styles
across a large area, the commissioned works must
nevertheless be done to some extent in the style of
(25) the tribe commissioning the work. This leads to much
confusion on the part of those art historians who
attempt to assign particular objects to individual
groups on the basis of style.

One such center of style is located in the village
(30) of Ouri, in central Burkina Faso, where members of
the Konaté family continue a long tradition of
sculpture production not only for five major
neighboring ethnic groups, but in recent times also
for the tourist trade in Ouagadougou. The Konaté
(35) sculptors are able to distinguish the characteristics of
the five styles in which they carve, and will point to
the foliate patterns that radiate from the eyes of a
Nuna mask, or the diamond-shaped mouth of many
Ko masks, as characteristics of a particular tribal style
(40) that must be included to satisfy their clients.
Nevertheless, their work is consistent in its
proportions, composition, color, and technique. In
fact, although the Konaté sculptors can identify the
styles they carve, the characteristic patterns are so
(45) subtly different that few people outside of the area
can distinguish Nuna masks from Ko masks.

Perhaps historians of African art should ask if
objects in similar styles were produced in centers of
style, where artists belonging to one ethnic group
(50) produced art for all of their neighbors. Perhaps it is
even more important to cease attempting to break
down large regional styles into finer and finer tribal
styles and substyles, and to recognize that artists in
Africa often do not produce work only in their own
(55) narrowly defined ethnic contexts. As the case of the
Konaté sculptors makes clear, one cannot readily tell
which group produced an object by analyzing fine
style characteristics.

47. Which one of the following titles most completely and
accurately describes the contents of the passage?

(A) *African Centers of Style: Their Implications for
Art Historians' Classifications of African Art*

(B) *African Art Redefined: The Impact of the
Commercialization of Sculpture and the Tourist
Demand on Style*

(C) *Characteristics of African Sculpture: Proportion,
Composition, Color, and Technique*

(D) *Style Versus Technique: The Case Against
Historians of African Art*

(E) *Konaté Sculptors: Pioneers of the African Art
Trade*

48. Based on the passage, the art historians mentioned in
line 2 would be most likely to agree with which one of
the following statements?

(A) Understanding the nature of centers of style is a
key to better classification of African art.

(B) Similarities among African masks can be due to
standard techniques used in carving the eyes
and mouths of the masks.

(C) Some subtly distinguished substyles should not
be distinguished from large regional styles.

(D) It is a fairly recent practice for African mask
sculptors to produce masks for tribes of which
they are not members.

(E) The tribal origin of African sculptures is
important to their classification.

49. According to the passage, which one of the following
is a feature that Konaté sculptors can identify as a
requirement of a particular tribal style?

(A) horizontal incisions
(B) eye position
(C) top attachments
(D) bottom decorations
(E) mouth shape

Explanations for these questions can be found in your Online Center.

Part Four: Reading Comprehension
Reading Comprehension Practice

50. The author's primary purpose in the passage is to

(A) classify a set of artistic styles according to a newly proposed set of principles

(B) provide evidence that the elements of a particular group of artistic works have been misclassified

(C) explain the principles used by a group of historians to classify certain kinds of artistic works

(D) reveal the underlying assumptions of a traditional approach to the classification of certain kinds of artistic works

(E) argue that a particular approach to classifying certain kinds of artistic works is mistaken

51. The passage provides the most support for which one of the following inferences?

(A) Some of the sculptures that the Konaté family produces are practically indistinguishable from those produced by certain other sculptors far from Burkina Faso.

(B) The carving styles used by some members of the Konaté family are distinctly different from those used by other members.

(C) Other families of sculptors in Burkina Faso collaborate with the Konaté family in producing masks.

(D) The Konaté family produces masks for some African ethnic groups other than the Nuna and Ko groups.

(E) The village of Ouri where the Konaté family produces sculptures is the oldest center of style in Burkina Faso.

52. Which one of the following does the author attribute to the Konaté sculptors?

(A) use of nontraditional materials in sculptures

(B) production of sculptures in several distinct styles that are nevertheless very similar to one another

(C) stylistic innovations that have influenced the work of other sculptors in a large geographical area

(D) adoption of a carving style that was previously used only by members of a different tribe

(E) introduction of the practice of producing sculptures for neighboring groups

53. Which one of the following most accurately expresses what the author means by "centers of style" (line 16)?

(A) geographical areas in which masks and similar sculptures are for the most part interchangeable among a number of closely connected tribes who use them

(B) locations in which works of art are produced by sculptors using a particular style who then instruct other artists throughout large surrounding geographical areas

(C) locations in which stylistically consistent but subtly varied works of art are produced and distributed to ethnically varied surrounding areas

(D) large geographical areas throughout which the various tribes produce works of art that differ subtly along ethnic lines but are so similar that they are very difficult for outside observers to distinguish from one another

(E) locations in which sculptures and similar works of art are traditionally produced by a diverse community of artists who migrate in from various tribes of surrounding areas

PrepTest49 Sec3 Qs 7–13

Explanations for these questions can be found in your Online Center.

Surviving sources of information about women doctors in ancient Greece and Rome are fragmentary: some passing mentions by classical authors, scattered references in medical works, and about 40
(5) inscriptions on tombs and monuments. Yet even from these fragments we can piece together a picture. The evidence shows that in ancient Greece and Rome there were, in fact, female medical personnel who were the ancient equivalent of what we now call
(10) medical doctors. So the history of women in medicine by no means begins in 1849 with Dr. Elizabeth Blackwell, the first woman to earn an M.D. in modern times, or even in 1321 with Francesca de Romana's licensure to practice general medicine, the
(15) earliest known officially recorded occurrence of this sort.

The very nature of the scant evidence tells us something. There is no list of women doctors in antiquity, no direct comment on the fact that there
(20) were such people. Instead, the scattering of references to them indicates that, although their numbers were probably small, women doctors were an unremarkable part of ancient life. For example, in *The Republic* (421 B.C.), the earliest known source attesting to the
(25) existence of women doctors in Greece, Plato argues that, for the good of the state, jobs should be assigned to people on the basis of natural aptitude, regardless of gender. To support his argument he offers the example that some women, as well as some
(30) men, are skilled in medicine, while others are not. Here, Plato is not trying to convince people that there ought to be women doctors. Rather, he is arguing for an ideal distribution of roles within the state by pointing to something that everyone could already
(35) see—that there were female doctors as well as male.

Moreover, despite evidence that some of these women doctors treated mainly female patients, their practice was clearly not limited to midwifery. Both Greek and Latin have distinct terms for midwife and
(40) doctor, and important texts and inscriptions refer to female practitioners as the latter. Other references provide evidence of a broad scope of practice for women doctors. The epitaph for one named Domnina reads: "You delivered your homeland from disease."
(45) A tribute to another describes her as "savior of all through her knowledge of medicine."

Also pointing to a wider medical practice are the references in various classical medical works to a great number of women's writings on medical
(50) subjects. Here, too, the very nature of the evidence tells us something, for Galen, Pliny the elder, and other ancient writers of encyclopedic medical works quote the opinions and prescriptions of male and female doctors indiscriminately, moving from one to
(55) the other and back again. As with the male doctors they cite, these works usually simply give excerpts from the female authority's writing without biographical information or special comment.

54. Which one of the following most accurately states the main point of the passage?

(A) There is a range of textual evidence indicating that the existence and professional activity of women doctors were an accepted part of everyday life in ancient Greece and Rome.

(B) Some scholars in ancient Greece and Rome made little distinction in their writings between learned women and learned men, as can especially be seen in those scholars' references to medical experts and practitioners.

(C) Although surviving ancient Greek and Roman texts about women doctors contain little biographical or technical data, important inferences can be drawn from the very fact that those texts pointedly comment on the existence of such doctors.

(D) Ancient texts indicate that various women doctors in Greece and Rome were not only practitioners but also researchers who contributed substantially to the development of medical science.

(E) Scholars who have argued that women did not practice medicine until relatively recently are mistaken, insofar as they have misinterpreted textual evidence from ancient Greece and Rome.

55. Which one of the following does the author mention in the passage?

(A) diseases that were not curable in ancient times but are readily cured by modern medicine

(B) a specialized field of medicine that was not practiced by women in ancient Greece and Rome

(C) a scholar who has argued that Francesca de Romana was the first female doctor in any Western society

(D) the extent to which medical doctors in ancient Greece and Rome were trained and educated

(E) ancient writers whose works refer explicitly to the writings of women

Explanations for these questions can be found in your Online Center.

Part Four: Reading Comprehension
Reading Comprehension Practice

56. The primary function of the third paragraph of the passage is to

  (A) provide additional support for the argument presented in the first paragraph

  (B) suggest that the implications of the argument presented in the first paragraph are unnecessarily broad

  (C) acknowledge some exceptions to a conclusion defended in the second paragraph

  (D) emphasize the historical importance of the arguments presented in the first two paragraphs

  (E) describe the sources of evidence that are cited in the first two paragraphs in support of the author's main conclusion

57. Which one of the following could most logically be appended to the end of the final paragraph?

  (A) So it is only by combining the previously mentioned fragments of ancient writings that historians have been able to construct a fairly complete account of some of these women's lives.

  (B) That there were women doctors apparently seemed unremarkable to these writers who cited their works, just as it did to Plato.

  (C) Although the content of each of these excerpts is of limited informative value, the very range of topics that they cover suggests that Plato's claims about women doctors should be reevaluated.

  (D) These texts indicate that during a certain period of ancient Greek and Roman history there were female medical scholars, but it is unclear whether at that time there were also female medical practitioners.

  (E) Nevertheless, these writers' evenhanded treatment of male and female medical researchers must be interpreted partly in light of the conflicting picture of ancient medical practice that emerges from the fragmentary earlier writings.

58. Which one of the following most accurately describes the author's attitude toward the sources of information mentioned in lines 1–5?

  (A) wary that they might be misinterpreted due to their fragmentary nature

  (B) optimistic that with a more complete analysis they will yield answers to some crucial lingering questions

  (C) hopeful that they will come to be accepted generally by historians as authentic documents

  (D) confident that they are accurate enough to allow for reliable factual inferences

  (E) convinced of their appropriateness as test cases for the application of a new historical research methodology

59. The tribute quoted in lines 45–46 is offered primarily as evidence that at least some women doctors in ancient times were

  (A) acknowledged as authorities by other doctors

  (B) highly educated

  (C) very effective at treating illness

  (D) engaged in general medical practice

  (E) praised as highly as male doctors

60. The passage most strongly supports which one of the following inferences about women in ancient Greece and Rome?

  (A) Those who became doctors usually practiced medicine for only a short time.

  (B) Those who were not doctors were typically expected to practice medicine informally within their own families.

  (C) There is no known official record that any of them were licensed to practice general medicine.

  (D) There is no reliable evidence that any of them who practiced general medicine also worked as a midwife.

  (E) Some of those who practiced medicine were posthumously honored for nonmedical civic accomplishments.

PrepTest49 Sec3 Qs 14–20

K

Part Four: Reading Comprehension
CHAPTER 15

Explanations for these questions
can be found in your Online Center.

Every culture that has adopted the cultivation of
maize—also known as corn—has been radically
changed by it. This crop reshaped the cultures of the
Native Americans who first cultivated it, leading to
(5) such developments as the adoption of agrarian and in
some cases urban lifestyles, and much of the
explosion of European populations after the fifteenth
century was driven by the introduction of maize
together with another crop from the Americas,
(10) potatoes. The primary reason for this plant's profound
influence is its sheer productivity. With maize, ancient
agriculturalists could produce far more food per acre
than with any other crop, and early Central
Americans recognized and valued this characteristic
(15) of the plant. But why are maize and a few similar
crops so much more bountiful than others? Modern
biochemistry has revealed the physical mechanism
underlying maize's impressive productivity.

To obtain the hydrogen they use in the production
(20) of carbohydrates through photosynthesis, all plants
split water into its constituent elements, hydrogen and
oxygen. They use the resultant hydrogen to form one
of the molecules they need for energy, but the oxygen
is released into the atmosphere. During
(25) photosynthesis, carbon dioxide that the plant takes in
from the atmosphere is used to build sugars within
the plant. An enzyme, rubisco, assists in the sugar-
forming chemical reaction. Because of its importance
in photosynthesis, rubisco is arguably the most
(30) significant enzyme in the world. Unfortunately, though,
when the concentration of oxygen relative to carbon
dioxide in a leaf rises to a certain level, as can happen
in the presence of many common atmospheric conditions,
oxygen begins to bind competitively to the enzyme,
(35) thus interfering with the photosynthetic reaction.

Some plants, however, have evolved a
photosynthetic mechanism that prevents oxygen from
impairing photosynthesis. These plants separate the
places where they split water atoms into hydrogen
(40) and oxygen from the places where they build sugars
from carbon dioxide. Water molecules are split, as in
all plants, in specialized chlorophyll-containing
structures in the green leaf cells, but the rubisco is
sequestered within airtight tissues in the center of the
(45) leaf. The key to the process is that in these plants,
oxygen and all other atmospheric gases are excluded
from the cells containing rubisco. These cells, called
the bundle sheath cells, surround the vascular
structures of the leaf—structures that function
(50) analogously to human blood vessels. Carbon dioxide,
which cannot enter these cells as a gas, first
undergoes a series of reactions to form an
intermediary, nongas molecule named C-4 for the
four carbon atoms it contains. This molecule enters
(55) the bundle sheath cells and there undergoes reactions
that release the carbon dioxide that will fuel the
production of carbohydrates (e.g., sugars). Taking its
name from the intermediary molecule, the entire
process is called C-4 photosynthesis. Such C-4 plants
(60) as sugar cane, rice, and maize are among the world's
most productive crops.

61. Which one of the following most accurately states the
main point of the passage?

(A) The greater productivity of maize, as compared
with many other crops, is due to its C-4
photosynthetic process, in which the reactions
that build sugars are protected from the effects
of excess oxygen.

(B) Because of their ability to produce greater
quantities and higher qualities of nutrients,
those plants, including maize, that use a C-4
photosynthetic process have helped to shape
the development of many human cultures.

(C) C-4 photosynthesis, which occurs in maize,
involves a complex sequence of chemical
reactions that makes more efficient use of
available atmospheric hydrogen than do
photosynthetic reactions in non-C-4 plants.

(D) The presence of the enzyme rubisco is a key
factor in the ability of C-4 plants, including
maize, to circumvent the negative effects of
gases such as oxygen on the production of
sugars in photosynthesis.

(E) Some of the world's most productive crop
plants, including maize, have evolved
complex, effective mechanisms to prevent
atmospheric gases that could bind
competitively to rubisco from entering the
plants' leaves.

62. Which one of the following most accurately describes
the organization of the material presented in the second
and third paragraphs of the passage?

(A) The author suggests that the widespread
cultivation of a particular crop is due to its
high yield, explains its high yield by describing
the action of a particular enzyme in that crop,
and then outlines the reasons for the evolution
of that enzyme.

(B) The author explains some aspects of a
biochemical process, describes a naturally
occurring hindrance to that process, and then
describes an evolutionary solution to that
hindrance in order to explain the productivity
of a particular crop.

(C) The author describes a problem inherent in
certain biochemical processes, scientifically
explains two ways in which organisms solve
that problem, and then explains the
evolutionary basis for one of those solutions.

(D) The author describes a widespread cultural
phenomenon involving certain uses of a type of
plant, explains the biochemical basis of the
phenomenon, and then points out that certain
other plants may be used for similar purposes.

(E) The author introduces a natural process,
describes the biochemical reaction that is
widely held to be the mechanism underlying
the process, and then argues for an alternate
evolutionary explanation of that process.

Explanations for these questions can be found in your Online Center.

Part Four: Reading Comprehension
Reading Comprehension Practice

63. Assuming that all other relevant factors remained the same, which one of the following, if it developed in a species of plant that does not have C-4 photosynthesis, would most likely give that species an advantage similar to that which the author attributes to C-4 plants?

    (A) Water is split into its constituent elements in specialized chlorophyll-containing structures in the bundle sheath cells.
    (B) An enzyme with which oxygen cannot bind performs the role of rubisco.
    (C) The vascular structures of the leaf become impermeable to both carbon dioxide gas and oxygen gas.
    (D) The specialized chlorophyll-containing structures in which water is split surround the vascular structures of the leaf.
    (E) An enzyme that does not readily react with carbon dioxide performs the role of rubisco in the green leaf cells.

64. The author's reference to "all other atmospheric gases" in line 46 plays which one of the following roles in the passage?

    (A) It indicates why certain atmospheric conditions can cause excess oxygen to build up and thus hinder photosynthesis in non-C-4 plants as described in the previous paragraph.
    (B) It supports the claim advanced earlier in the paragraph that oxygen is not the only atmospheric gas whose presence in the leaf can interfere with photosynthesis.
    (C) It supports the conclusion that non-C-4 photosynthesis makes use of several atmospheric gases that C-4 photosynthesis does not use.
    (D) It explains why carbon dioxide molecules undergo the transformations described later in the paragraph before participating in photosynthesis in C-4 plants.
    (E) It advances a broader claim that oxygen levels remain constant in C-4 plants in spite of changes in atmospheric conditions.

65. The passage contains information sufficient to justify inferring which one of the following?

    (A) In rice plants, atmospheric gases are prevented from entering the structures in which water is split into its constituent elements.
    (B) In rice plants, oxygen produced from split water molecules binds to another type of molecule before being released into the atmosphere.
    (C) Rice is an extremely productive crop that nourishes large segments of the world's population and is cultivated by various widely separated cultures.
    (D) In rice plants, rubisco is isolated in the bundle sheath cells that surround the vascular structures of the leaves.
    (E) Although rice is similar to maize in productivity and nutritive value, maize is the more widely cultivated crop.

66. The author of the passage would be most likely to agree with which one of the following statements?

    (A) Maize's impressive productivity cannot be understood without an understanding of its cultural influences.
    (B) Maize is an example of a plant in which oxygen is not released as a by-product of photosynthesis.
    (C) Maize's high yields are due not only to its use of C-4 but also to its ability to produce large quantities of rubisco.
    (D) Until maize was introduced to Europeans by Native Americans, European populations lacked the agricultural techniques required for the cultivation of C-4 plants.
    (E) Maize's C-4 photosynthesis is an example of an effective evolutionary adaptation that has come to benefit humans.

67. The passage provides the most support for which one of the following statements?

    (A) In many plants, rubisco is not isolated in airtight tissues in the center of the leaf.
    (B) A rubisco molecule contains four carbon atoms.
    (C) Rubisco is needed in photosynthesis to convert carbon dioxide to a nongas molecule.
    (D) In maize, rubisco helps protect against the detrimental effects of oxygen buildup in the leaves.
    (E) Rubisco's role in the C-4 process is optimized when oxygen levels are high relative to carbon dioxide levels.

PrepTest49 Sec3 Qs 21–27

ANSWER KEY

Passage 1–Can Animals Lie?

1. B
2. A
3. D
4. D
5. C
6. B

Passage 2–African American Historiography

7. D
8. E
9. A
10. E
11. E
12. B
13. A
14. B

Passage 3–Ultimatum Game

15. B
16. D
17. D
18. C
19. D

Passage 4–Ezekiel Mphahlele's Writing

20. B
21. B
22. E
23. A
24. C
25. A
26. D

Passage 5–The Late Heavy Bombardment

27. E
28. B
29. D
30. C
31. B
32. A

Passage 6–Automated Legal Reasoning

33. A
34. A
35. B
36. E
37. D
38. C
39. C
40. B

Passage 7–Computer-Generated Displays

41. A
42. D
43. E
44. B
45. C
46. E

Passage 8–Centers of Style

47. A
48. E
49. E
50. E
51. D
52. B
53. C

Passage 9–Ancient Female Doctors

54. A
55. E
56. A
57. B
58. D
59. D
60. C

Passage 10–Corn Productivity

61. A
62. B
63. B
64. D
65. D
66. E
67. A

Complete explanations for these questions can be found in your Online Center.

Reading Comprehension: Managing the Section

The bulk of this chapter consists of a complete Reading Comprehension section, followed by an answer key. Complete explanations can be found in your Online Center. Taking full timed practice sections helps you maximize your score by learning to improve section management. Perfecting your timing in LSAT sections involves much more than just "getting faster." Indeed, in many cases, hurrying through the strategic reading and Roadmap step of the Reading Comprehension Method may wind up costing you time by causing you to reread parts of the passage multiple times as you work through the question set. Even worse, failing to summarize the author's Purpose and Main Point or having a poor grasp of a passage's organization could lead you to wrong answers, costing you points directly.

TIMING AND SECTION MANAGEMENT

Here are a few of the principles of great section management that LSAT experts use to their advantage. Learn them and put them into practice whenever you undertake a timed section or full-test practice.

Reading Comprehension Section Timing: The Basics

The facts: Every Reading Comprehension section has four passages, each with 5–8 questions for a total of 26–28 questions to be completed in 35 minutes.

The strategy: On average, then, you should take 8–9 minutes for each passage. Of that time, you'll usually take 3–4 minutes reading strategically and Roadmapping the passage. You'll use the remaining 4–5 minutes to answer the questions. Don't rush Step 1 of the Reading Comprehension Method. Approached strategically, the easiest passages may take less than eight minutes—bank that time for the longer and tougher ones. When a passage threatens to drag on much longer than nine minutes, however, be prepared to guess on its toughest questions and move on with ample time to read the next passage and answer its questions.

Efficiency, Not Speed

The facts: You have less time per question in Reading Comprehension than you do in any other section of the LSAT. A good Roadmap will allow you to locate key details quickly, and understanding the passage's Scope and the author's Purpose and Main Idea should help you efficiently answer a handful of other questions.

The strategy: Follow the Reading Comprehension Method. In the preceding chapters, you've seen how strategic reading and a solid Roadmap reveal the pieces of the passage and the ideas you need to know to answer questions quickly and accurately. Don't let "clock anxiety" tempt you into abandoning the most efficient approach to the Reading Comp section. Being methodical does not mean being slow. When you have practiced enough that the Reading Comprehension Method is second nature, you'll find that it provides the shortest and most direct route to correct answers, the single goal of all the work you do on the LSAT.

Triage: Take Control of the Section

The facts: You are under no obligation to do the passages or questions in the order in which they are presented. The first passage in the section is most often the easiest for most test takers. Either the third or fourth passage is most often the hardest for most test takers.

The strategy: Triage is a term used in the medical profession to refer to the process of determining priorities in an emergency. You can "triage" the Reading Comprehension section by looking for and prioritizing the passages and questions most likely to turn into correct answers for you. Some LSAT experts triage the section by taking a minute or less at the start of the section to look at all four passages and choose an optimal order in which to address them. These experts prioritize passages that, at a glance, have simple prose, clear organization, and/or familiar topics. Other experts follow a predetermined order (1-2-4-3 is a reasonable rule of thumb), but they are willing to skip and come back to a passage or to rearrange their order of attack immediately upon determining that a passage is particularly abstruse or confusing.

Similarly, you can triage the questions within a passage's question set. A passage's Global question is usually the first in the set and should be answered while the Topic/Scope/Purpose/Main Idea summaries are fresh in your mind. By the way, when a passage has two Global questions, the second is usually near the end of the question set; it's worth your while to check for a second Global question because you can answer it with a nearly identical prediction. After that, you may choose to tackle questions with clear research clues in their question stems. These will guide you back to specific details in the passage; these details, as you know from earlier chapters, are usually associated with Keywords that indicate the author's purpose or opinion. Open-ended questions can be time-consuming. Be as strategic as possible with them by eliminating answer choices that conflict with the author's point of view or fall clearly outside the scope of the passage.

Whether you are triaging a section or a set of questions, follow the best practices of a great doctor triaging an emergency: Be decisive and remember that you are in control of the situation.

Skip and Guess Strategically

The facts: You do not need to answer every question to get a great score. Time-consuming questions (e.g., "The passage supports each of the following EXCEPT" questions) are scattered throughout the section. There is no bonus for answering the hardest question(s) in the section.

The strategy: Remember that you are in control of how much time and effort you dedicate to any particular passage or question. Allowing yourself to get into an "ego battle" with particular passages or questions—"I *will* figure this one out no matter what!"—can take time away from other questions you could answer quickly and accurately. Be willing to skip one or two difficult or very time-consuming questions if doing so will allow you to get more questions correct on subsequent passages. Preempt situations in which you are guessing out of frustration—"Okay, I give up. I've already given this two minutes; I'll never get it!"—by learning to guess strategically—"I'll guess on this lengthy Inference question and give myself an extra two minutes for the next two passages." In other words, guess when it is to your benefit to do so. Stay in control of the section and the test.

TAKING THE TIMING SECTION

The Reading Comprehension section that follows was originally Section 3 in PrepTest 65, administered in December 2011.

Proctoring

Complete this section under timed, test-like conditions. Give yourself 35 minutes for the section and finish it in one uninterrupted sitting. If you are taking the section as part of a class, follow the proctor's instructions strictly. If you are taking the section on your own, use the LSAT Proctor Anywhere app.

Record your answer selections using one of the answer grids found at the back of this book.

Scoring

After you finish the section, record your answers in the appropriate webgrid (PrepTest 65, Section 3) found in your Online Center. This will make your results and percent correct easy to see, and the score report will contain links to the explanations for each question.

NOTE: Chapters 7 and 16 contain the other three scored sections from PrepTest 65. After completing those sections (under timed, proctored conditions), you may enter your answers from all four sections into the webgrid for PrepTest 65 to receive a score for the entire test.

Review

For your convenience, complete Answers and Explanations are also available as a PDF file in your Online Center. Whether you review the section online or with the PDF, review it completely, even those questions you got right. In addition to reading over the explanations for the right and wrong answers, check to see that you consistently followed the Reading Comprehension Method, read each passage strategically, created a helpful Roadmap, identified each question type, researched and predicted effectively, and answered the questions as efficiently as possible.

K

Part Four: Reading Comprehension
CHAPTER 16

Explanations for these questions
can be found in your Online Center.

PrepTest 65, Section 3

Time—35 minutes
27 Questions

Directions: Each set of questions in this section is based on a single passage or a pair of passages. The questions are to be answered on the basis of what is <u>stated</u> or <u>implied</u> in the passage or pair of passages. For some of the questions, more than one of the choices could conceivably answer the question. However, you are to choose the <u>best</u> answer; that is, the response that most accurately and completely answers the question, and blacken the corresponding space on your answer sheet.

In the 1980s there was a proliferation of poetry collections, short stories, and novels published by women of Latin American descent in the United States. By the end of the decade, another genre of
(5) U.S. Latina writing, the autobiography, also came into prominence with the publication of three notable autobiographical collections: *Loving in the War Years: Lo Que Nunca Pasó Por Sus Labios*, by Cherríe Moraga; *Getting Home Alive*, by Aurora Levins
(10) Morales and Rosario Morales; and *Borderlands/ La Frontera*, by Gloria Anzaldúa.

These collections are innovative at many levels. They confront traditional linguistic boundaries by using a mix of English and Spanish, and they each
(15) address the politics of multiple cultural identities by exploring the interrelationships among such factors as ethnicity, gender, and language. This effort manifests itself in the generically mixed structure of these works, which combine essays, sketches, short stories, poems,
(20) and journal entries without, for the most part, giving preference to any of these modes of presentation.

In *Borderlands/La Frontera*, Anzaldúa presents her personal history and the history of the Mexican American community to which she belongs by
(25) juxtaposing narrative sequences and poetry. Moraga's *Loving in the War Years* is likewise characterized by a mixture of genres, and, as she states in her introduction, the events in her life story are not arranged chronologically, but rather in terms of her
(30) political development. According to one literary critic who specializes in the genre of autobiography, this departure from chronological ordering represents an important difference between autobiographies written by women and those traditionally written by men.
(35) *Getting Home Alive* departs even further from the conventions typical of autobiography by bringing together the voices of two people, a mother and her daughter, each of whom authors a portion of the text. The narratives and poems of each author are not
(40) assigned to separate sections of the text, but rather are woven together, with a piece by one sometimes commenting on a piece by the other. While this ordering may seem fragmentary and confusing, it is in fact a fully intentional and carefully designed
(45) experiment with literary structure. In a sense, this mixing of structures parallels the content of these autobiographies: the writers employ multigeneric and multivocal forms to express the complexities inherent in the formation of their identities.
(50) Rather than forcing their personal histories to conform to existing generic parameters, these writers have revolutionized the genre of autobiography,

redrawing the boundaries of this literary form to make it more amenable to the expression of their own
(55) experiences. In doing so, they have shown a strong determination to speak for themselves in a world that they feel has for too long taken their silence for granted.

1. Which one of the following most accurately expresses the main point of the passage?

   (A) Certain Latina writers who formerly wrote mostly poetry and fiction have found through experimentation that the genre of autobiography suits their artistic purposes especially well.

   (B) Latina autobiographers writing in the late 1980s set aside some standard conventions of autobiography in an effort to make the genre more suitable for the expression of their personal histories.

   (C) There is a great diversity of styles and narrative strategies among recent traditional and nontraditional Latina autobiographers.

   (D) Through recent experimentation in autobiography, Latina writers have shown that nonfictional narrative can be effectively combined with other genres in a single literary work.

   (E) Recent writings by Latina authors have prompted some literary critics who specialize in autobiography to acknowledge that differences in gender and ethnicity often underlie differences in writing styles.

2. According to the passage, which one of the following was a motivating factor in certain Latina authors' decisions regarding the structure of their autobiographical writings?

   (A) the importance of chronological ordering to those authors' artistic goals

   (B) those authors' stated intention of avoiding certain nonnarrative genres

   (C) those authors' preference to avoid overt political expression

   (D) the complexities of identity formation faced by those authors

   (E) those authors' judgment that poetry should not be a narrative medium

GO ON TO THE NEXT PAGE.

Explanations for these questions can be found in your Online Center.

Part Four: Reading Comprehension
Reading Comprehension: Managing the Section

3. The author's discussion of *Getting Home Alive* serves primarily to

(A) distinguish one type of experimental autobiography from two other types by Latina writers

(B) explain how certain Latina autobiographers combine journal entries and poems in their works

(C) demonstrate that the use of multiple voices is a common feature of Latina autobiography

(D) show why readers have difficulty understanding certain autobiographies by Latina writers

(E) illustrate the extent of certain Latina autobiographers' experimentation with form and structure

4. The passage indicates which one of the following about the Latina autobiographies that the author discusses?

(A) Each contains some material that would ordinarily be regarded as belonging to a genre of literature other than autobiography.

(B) Each quotes from previously unpublished private journals or other private documents.

(C) Each contains analysis of the ways in which its content was influenced by its author's cultural background.

(D) Each contains writings that were produced by more than one author.

(E) Each includes explanations of the methodologies that its author, or authors, used in writing the autobiography.

5. Based on the passage, the author's attitude regarding *Getting Home Alive*, by Aurora Levins Morales and Rosario Morales, can be most accurately described as

(A) disappointment in scholars' failure to recognize it as an appropriate sequel to its authors' purely fictional and poetic works

(B) expectation that readers in general might not readily recognize that there is a clear purpose for its unconventional organization

(C) surprise that academic commentators have treated it as having significance as a historical document

(D) confidence that it will be widely recognized by scholars as a work of both history and literary criticism

(E) insistence that it should be credited with having helped to broaden critics' understanding of what counts as autobiography

6. The author most likely intends to include which one of the following principles among the "existing generic parameters" referred to in line 52?

(A) The events presented in an autobiography should be arranged sequentially according to when they actually happened.

(B) When different modes of presentation are combined in one literary work, no one mode should be given preference.

(C) Autobiographical writing should not have political overtones.

(D) Sketches and poems collected together in a single work need not be separated by genre within that work.

(E) Personal experiences can be represented in a compelling way in any literary genre.

7. Which one of the following would, if true, most undermine the author's claim in lines 51–56 about the effect that the Latina autobiographies discussed had on the genre of autobiography?

(A) Few autobiographical works published after 1985 have been recognized for their effective use of chronologically linear prose as a means of portraying the complexities of membership in multiple cultures.

(B) Few critically acclaimed books written by Latina authors have been autobiographical collections consisting partly or wholly of essays, poems, short stories, sketches, and journal entries.

(C) Many autobiographies have been written by authors in the United States since 1985, and some of these present a unified, chronologically linear prose narrative in a single language.

(D) Several nineteenth-century autobiographies that are generally unknown among contemporary critics of twentieth-century autobiography are characterized by generically mixed structure and multiple authorship.

(E) Several multigeneric, nonautobiographical collections consisting at least partly of poetry, short stories, or essays by Latina authors have been published since 1985, and many of these have been critically acclaimed for their innovative structures.

GO ON TO THE NEXT PAGE.

Part Four: Reading Comprehension
CHAPTER 16

Explanations for these questions can be found in your Online Center.

While recent decades have seen more information recorded than any other era, the potential for losing this information is now greater than ever. This prospect is of great concern to archivists, who are charged with
(5) preserving vital records and documents indefinitely. One archivist notes that while the quantity of material being saved has increased exponentially, the durability of recording media has decreased almost as rapidly. The clay tablets that contain the laws of ancient
(10) Mesopotamia, for example, are still displayed in museums around the world, and many medieval manuscripts written on animal parchment still look as though they were copied yesterday, whereas books printed on acidic paper as recently as the 1980s are
(15) already unreadable. Black-and-white photographs will last for a couple of centuries, but most color photographs become unstable within 40 years, and videotapes last only about 20 years.

Computer technology would seem to offer
(20) archivists an answer, as maps, photographs, films, videotapes, and all forms of printed material may now be transferred to and stored electronically on computer disks or tape, occupying very little space. But as the pace of technological change increases, so too does
(25) the speed with which each new generation of technology supplants the last. For example, many documents and images transferred in the 1980s to optical computer disks—then the cutting edge of technology—may not now be retrievable because
(30) they depend on computer software and hardware that are no longer available. And recent generations of digital storage tape are considered safe from deterioration for only ten years. Yet, even as some archivists are reluctant to become dependent on
(35) ever-changing computer technology, they are also quickly running out of time.

Even if viable storage systems are developed— new computer technologies are emerging that may soon provide archivists with the information storage
(40) durability they require—decisions about what to keep and what to discard will have to be made quickly, as materials recorded on conventional media continue to deteriorate. Ideally, these decisions should be informed by an assessment of the value of each document.
(45) Printed versions of ancient works by Homer and Virgil, for example, survived intact because their enduring popularity resulted in multiple copies of the works being made at different historical moments. But many great works, including those of Plato, were
(50) lost for several centuries and are known today only because random copies turned up in the archives of medieval monasteries or in other scholarly collections. Undoubtedly, many important works have not survived at all. The danger now is not so much that some recent
(55) masterpiece will be lost for an extended period of time, but rather that the sheer volume of accumulated records stored on nondurable media will make it virtually impossible for archivists to sort the essential from the dispensable in time to save it.

8. Which one of the following most accurately expresses the main point of the passage?

(A) The increasing volume of information being stored and the decreasing durability of modern storage media are making it more and more difficult for archivists to carry out their charge.

(B) Modern data storage-and-retrieval techniques have enabled archivists to distinguish essential from dispensable information with greater efficiency than ever before.

(C) Many archivists have come to believe that documents and images preserved on conventional storage media are likely to endure longer than those recorded on electronic storage media.

(D) Given the limitations on the capacity of modern storage media, it is increasingly important for archivists to save only those documents that they believe to have genuine value.

(E) Modern electronic media enable us to record and store information so easily that much of what is stored is not considered by archivists to be essential or valuable.

9. The passage provides information sufficient to answer which one of the following questions?

(A) Are there any copies of the works of Homer and Virgil stored on parchment?

(B) Why is information stored on acidic paper more unstable than information stored on digital storage tape?

(C) When were optical storage disks a state-of-the-art storage medium?

(D) Approximately how many of the original clay tablets recording Mesopotamian law are still in existence?

(E) How were the works of Plato originally recorded?

GO ON TO THE NEXT PAGE.

Explanations for these questions can be found in your Online Center.

Part Four: Reading Comprehension
Reading Comprehension: Managing the Section

K

10. The passage most strongly suggests that the author holds which one of the following views?

   (A) Archivists have little choice but to become dependent on computer technology to store information.

   (B) Archivists should wait for truly durable data storage systems to be developed before electronically storing any more vital information.

   (C) The problems concerning media durability facing most archivists would diminish greatly if their information were not stored electronically at all.

   (D) Storing paintings, photographs, and other images presents greater overall problems for archivists than storing text does.

   (E) Generally, the more information one attempts to store in a given amount of space, the less durable the storage of that information will be.

11. Which one of the following describes the author's primary purpose in mentioning the fact that a wide variety of images and documents can now be stored electronically (lines 19–23)?

   (A) to provide evidence to justify the assertion made in the first sentence of the passage

   (B) to identify an ostensible solution to the problem raised in the first paragraph

   (C) to argue a point that is rejected in the last sentence of the passage

   (D) to offer an additional example of the problem stated at the end of the first paragraph

   (E) to suggest that the danger described in the last paragraph has been exaggerated

12. The passage provides the most support for inferring which one of the following statements?

   (A) Information stored electronically is more vulnerable than information stored on paper to unauthorized use or theft.

   (B) Much of the information stored on optical computer disks in the 1980s was subsequently transferred to digital storage tape.

   (C) The high cost of new electronic data storage systems is prohibiting many archivists from transferring their archives to computer disks and tape.

   (D) Media used recently to store information electronically may ultimately be less durable than older, conventional media such as photographs and videotapes.

   (E) The percentage of information considered essential by archivists has increased proportionally as the amount of information stored has increased.

13. The passage most strongly suggests that the author holds which one of the following views?

   (A) Future electronic information storage systems will not provide archivists with capabilities any more viable in the long term than those available today.

   (B) As much information should be stored by archivists as possible, as there is no way to predict which piece of information will someday be considered a great work.

   (C) The general public has been misled by manufacturers as to the long-term storage capabilities of electronic information storage systems.

   (D) Distinguishing what is dispensable from what is essential has only recently become a concern for archivists.

   (E) Value judgments made by today's archivists will influence how future generations view and understand the past.

GO ON TO THE NEXT PAGE.

K | Part Four: Reading Comprehension
CHAPTER 16

Explanations for these questions
can be found in your Online Center.

*The following passages are adapted from articles
recently published in North American law review
journals.*

Passage A

In Canadian and United States common law,
blackmail is unique among major crimes: no one has
yet adequately explained why it ought to be illegal.
The heart of the problem—known as the blackmail
(5) paradox—is that two acts, each of which is legally
permissible separately, become illegal when combined.
If I threaten to expose a criminal act or embarrassing
private information unless I am paid money, I have
committed blackmail. But the right to free speech
(10) protects my right to make such a disclosure, and, in
many circumstances, I have a legal right to seek
money. So why is it illegal to combine them?

The lack of a successful theory of blackmail has
damaging consequences: drawing a clear line between
(15) legal and illegal acts has proved impossible without
one. Consequently, most blackmail statutes broadly
prohibit behavior that no one really believes is criminal
and rely on the good judgment of prosecutors not to
enforce relevant statutes precisely as written.

(20) It is possible, however, to articulate a coherent
theory of blackmail. The key to the wrongness of the
blackmail transaction is its triangular structure. The
blackmailer obtains what he wants by using a
supplementary leverage, leverage that depends upon
(25) a third party. The blackmail victim pays to avoid
being harmed by persons other than the blackmailer.
For example, when a blackmailer threatens to turn in
a criminal unless paid money, the blackmailer is
bargaining with the state's chip. Thus, blackmail is
(30) criminal because it involves the misuse of a third party
for the blackmailer's own benefit.

Passage B

Classical Roman law had no special category
for blackmail; it was not necessary. Roman jurists
began their evaluation of specific categories of
(35) actions by considering whether the action caused
harm, not by considering the legality or illegality of
the action itself.

Their assumption—true enough, it seems—was
that a victim of blackmail would be harmed if shameful
(40) but private information were revealed to the world.
And if the shame would cause harm to the person's
status or reputation, then prima facie the threatened
act of revelation was unlawful. The burden of proof
shifted to the possessor of the information: the party
(45) who had or threatened to reveal shameful facts had
to show positive cause for the privilege of revealing
the information.

In short, assertion of the truth of the shameful
fact being revealed was not, in itself, sufficient to
(50) constitute a legal privilege. Granted, truth was not
wholly irrelevant; false disclosures were granted even
less protection than true ones. But even if it were true,
the revelation of shameful information was protected

only if the revelation had been made for a legitimate
purpose and dealt with a matter that the public
(55) authorities had an interest in having revealed. Just
because something shameful happened to be true did
not mean it was lawful to reveal it.

14. Which one of the following is the central topic of
each passage?

(A) why triangular transactions are illegal
(B) the role of the right to free speech in a given
legal system
(C) how blackmail has been handled in a given
legal system
(D) the history of blackmail as a legal concept
(E) why no good explanation of the illegality of
blackmail exists

15. In using the phrase "the state's chip" (line 30), the
author of passage A most clearly means to refer to
a government's

(A) legal authority to determine what actions
are crimes
(B) legitimate interest in learning about crimes
committed in its jurisdiction
(C) legitimate interest in preventing crimes before
they occur
(D) exclusive reliance on private citizens as a
source of important information
(E) legal ability to compel its citizens to testify in
court regarding crimes they have witnessed

16. Which one of the following statements is most strongly
supported by information given in the passages?

(A) In Roman law, there was no blackmail paradox
because free speech protections comparable to
those in Canadian and U.S. common law were
not an issue.
(B) Blackmail was more widely practiced in Roman
antiquity than it is now because Roman law did
not specifically prohibit blackmail.
(C) In general, Canadian and U.S. common law
grant more freedoms than classical Roman
law granted.
(D) The best justification for the illegality of
blackmail in Canadian and U.S. common law
is the damage blackmail can cause to the
victim's reputation.
(E) Unlike Roman law, Canadian and U.S.
common law do not recognize the interest of
public authorities in having certain types of
information revealed.

GO ON TO THE NEXT PAGE.

Explanations for these questions can be found in your Online Center.

Part Four: Reading Comprehension
Reading Comprehension: Managing the Section

17. Which one of the following is a statement that is true of blackmail under Canadian and U.S. common law, according to passage A, but that would not have been true of blackmail in the Roman legal context, according to passage B?

    (A) It combines two acts that are each legal separately.
    (B) It is a transaction with a triangular structure.
    (C) The laws pertaining to it are meant to be enforced precisely as written.
    (D) The blackmail victim pays to avoid being harmed by persons other than the blackmailer.
    (E) Canadian and U.S. common law have no special category pertaining to blackmail.

18. Based on what can be inferred from the passages, which one of the following acts would have been illegal under Roman law, but would not be illegal under Canadian and U.S. common law?

    (A) bribing tax officials in order to avoid paying taxes
    (B) revealing to public authorities that a high-ranking military officer has embezzled funds from the military's budget
    (C) testifying in court to a defendant's innocence while knowing that the defendant is guilty
    (D) informing a government tax agency that one's employers have concealed their true income
    (E) revealing to the public that a prominent politician had once had an adulterous affair

19. The relationship between the ways in which Canadian and U.S. common law and classical Roman law treat blackmail, as described in the passages, is most analogous to the relationship between which one of the following pairs?

    (A) One country legally requires anyone working as a carpenter to be licensed and insured; another country has no such requirement.
    (B) One country makes it illegal to use cell phones on trains; another country makes it illegal to use cell phones on both trains and buses.
    (C) One country legally allows many income tax deductions and exemptions; another country legally allows relatively few deductions and exemptions.
    (D) One country makes it illegal for felons to own guns; another country has no such ban because it makes gun ownership illegal for everyone but police and the military.
    (E) One country makes it illegal to drive motorcycles with racing-grade engines on its roads; another country legally permits such motorcycles but fines riders who commit traffic violations higher amounts than it does other motorists.

GO ON TO THE NEXT PAGE.

K | Part Four: Reading Comprehension
CHAPTER 16

Explanations for these questions can be found in your Online Center.

As part of an international effort to address environmental problems resulting from agricultural overproduction, hundreds of thousands of acres of surplus farmland throughout Europe will be taken out
(5) of production in coming years. Restoring a natural balance of flora to this land will be difficult, however, because the nutrients in soil that has been in constant agricultural use are depleted. Moreover, much of this land has been heavily fertilized, and when such land
(10) is left unplanted, problem weeds like thistles often proliferate, preventing many native plants from establishing themselves. While the quickest way to restore heavily fertilized land is to remove and replace the topsoil, this is impractical on a large scale such as
(15) that of the European effort. And while it is generally believed that damaged ecological systems will restore themselves very gradually over time, a study underway in the Netherlands is investigating the possibility of artificially accelerating the processes through which
(20) nature slowly reestablishes plant diversity on previously farmed land.

In the study, a former cornfield was raked to get rid of cornstalks and weeds, then divided into 20 plots of roughly equal size. Control plots were replanted
(25) with corn or sown with nothing at all. The remaining plots were divided into two groups: plots in one group were sown with a mixture of native grasses and herbs; those in the other group received the same mixture of grasses and herbs together with clover and toadflax.
(30) After three years, thistles have been forced out of the plots where the broadest variety of species was sown and have also disappeared from mats of grass in the plots sown with fewer seed varieties. On the control plots that were left untouched, thistles have become dominant.
(35) On some of the plots sown with seeds of native plant species, soil from nearby land that had been taken out of production 20 years earlier was scattered to see what effect introducing nematodes, fungi, and other beneficial microorganisms associated with later
(40) stages of natural soil development might have on the process of native plant repopulation. The seeds sown on these enriched plots have fared better than seeds sown on the unenriched plots, but still not as well as those growing naturally on the nearby land. Researchers
(45) have concluded that this is because fields farmed for many years are overrun with aggressive disease organisms, while, for example, beneficial mycorrhiza— fungi that live symbiotically on plant roots and strengthen them against the effects of disease
(50) organisms—are lacking. These preliminary results suggest that restoring natural plant diversity to overfarmed land hinges on restoring a natural balance of microorganisms in the soil. In other words, diversity underground fosters diversity aboveground. Researchers
(55) now believe that both kinds of diversity can be restored more quickly to damaged land if beneficial microorganisms are "sown" systematically into the soil along with a wide variety of native plant seeds.

20. Which one of the following most accurately expresses the central idea of the passage?

(A) The rehabilitation of land damaged by agricultural overproduction can be accelerated by means of a two-pronged strategy aimed at restoring biological diversity.

(B) Restoring plant diversity to overused farmland requires many years and considerable effort.

(C) The damaging effects of long-term agricultural overproduction argue for the modification of current agricultural practices.

(D) Soil on farmland damaged by overproduction will gradually replenish and restore itself over time if left untouched.

(E) Agricultural overproduction tends to encourage the proliferation of disease organisms in the soil as well as problem weeds.

21. Which one of the following most accurately describes the organization of the passage?

(A) A study is described, the results of the study are scrutinized, and the results are judged to be inconclusive but promising.

(B) A hypothesis is presented, evidence both supporting and undermining the hypothesis is given, and a modification of the hypothesis is argued for.

(C) A study is evaluated, a plan of action based on the study's findings is suggested, and conclusions are drawn concerning the likely effectiveness of the plan.

(D) A goal is stated, studies are discussed that argue for modifying the goal's objectives, and a methodology is detailed to achieve the revised goal.

(E) A problem is presented, a study addressing the problem is described, and a course of action based on the study's findings is given.

22. The passage offers which one of the following as an explanation for why native plant varieties grew better when sown on land that had been out of production for 20 years than when sown on the plots enriched with soil taken from that land?

(A) Land that has been farmed for many years lacks certain key nutrients.

(B) Land that has been farmed for many years is usually overrun with harmful and aggressive organisms.

(C) Land that has been farmed for many years has usually been subjected to overfertilization.

(D) The soil that was taken from the land that had been out of production was lacking in fungi and other beneficial organisms.

(E) The soil that was taken from the land that had been out of production contained harmful organisms that attack plant roots.

GO ON TO THE NEXT PAGE.

Explanations for these questions can be found in your Online Center.

Part Four: Reading Comprehension
Reading Comprehension: Managing the Section | **K**

23. Based on the passage, which one of the following is most likely to be true of any soil used to replace topsoil in the process mentioned in the first paragraph?

    (A) Thistles cannot grow in it.
    (B) It does not contain significant amounts of fungi.
    (C) It contains very few seeds of native grasses and herbs.
    (D) It does not contain large amounts of fertilizer.
    (E) It was never used for growing corn or other commercial crops.

24. The author's reference to the belief that "damaged ecological systems will restore themselves very gradually over time" (lines 16–17) primarily serves to

    (A) introduce a long-held belief that the Netherlands study is attempting to discredit
    (B) cite the justification generally used by people favoring intense agricultural production
    (C) suggest that the consequences of agricultural overproduction are not as dire as people generally believe
    (D) present the most common perception of why agricultural overproduction is problematic
    (E) describe the circumstances surrounding and motivating the Netherlands study

25. In which one of the following circumstances would it be LEAST advantageous to use the methods researched in the Netherlands study in order to restore to its natural state a field that has been in constant agricultural use?

    (A) The field's natural nutrients have been depleted through overproduction.
    (B) The field's topsoil can easily be removed and replaced.
    (C) The field has been heavily fertilized for many decades.
    (D) The field has the potential to support commercial grass plants such as rye.
    (E) The field is adjacent to other fields where corn is growing and will continue to be grown.

26. It can be inferred from the passage that if the disease organisms mentioned in line 48 were eliminated in a plot of land that had been in constant agricultural use, which one of the following would be the most likely to occur?

    (A) Populations of symbiotic mycorrhiza that live in the soil would initially decline.
    (B) Unwanted plant species like thistles would be unable to survive.
    (C) The chance of survival of a beneficial native plant would increase.
    (D) The number of all types of beneficial microorganisms would increase in the long term.
    (E) Populations of other types of disease organisms would increase proportionally.

27. Which one of the following is most analogous to the process, described in the last paragraph, by which the spread of thistles can be curtailed?

    (A) A newspaper works to prevent Party A from winning a majority of seats in the legislature by publishing editorials encouraging that party's supporters to switch their allegiance and vote for candidates from a rival party.
    (B) A newspaper works to prevent Party A from winning a majority of seats in the legislature by publishing editorials defending candidates from a rival party against attacks by certain broadcast journalists.
    (C) A newspaper works to prevent Party A from winning a majority of seats in the legislature by publishing editorials intended to discourage supporters of Party A from voting in the upcoming election.
    (D) A newspaper works to prevent Party A from winning a majority of seats in the legislature by publishing editorials attacking certain public figures who support candidates from Party A.
    (E) A newspaper works to prevent Party A from winning a majority of seats in the legislature by publishing editorials intended to create antagonism between two factions within that party.

S T O P

IF YOU FINISH BEFORE TIME IS CALLED, YOU MAY CHECK YOUR WORK ON THIS SECTION ONLY.
DO NOT WORK ON ANY OTHER SECTION IN THE TEST.

ANSWER KEY

Passage 1—Latina Autobiography in the 1980s

1. B
2. D
3. E
4. A
5. B
6. A
7. D

Passage 2—The Archivist's Dilemma

8. A
9. C
10. A
11. B
12. D
13. E

Passage 3—Blackmail in Two Legal Contexts

14. C
15. B
16. A
17. A
18. E
19. D

Passage 4—Restoring Europe's Farmland

20. A
21. E
22. B
23. D
24. E
25. B
26. C
27. B

Complete explanations for these questions can be found in your Online Center.

PART FIVE

Countdown to Test Day

CHAPTER 17

Test Day

Is it starting to feel like your whole life is a buildup to the LSAT? You've known about it for years, worried about it for months, and now spent weeks (at least) in solid preparation for it. As the test gets closer, you may find your anxiety building. Don't worry; after the preparation you've done, you're in good shape for the test. The key to calming any pre-test jitters is to be prepared for the road to Test Day and beyond.

THE WEEK BEFORE THE TEST

Your goal during the week before the LSAT is to set yourself up for success on Test Day. Up until this point, you have been working to build your LSAT potential, but Test Day is about achievement.

LSAT STRATEGY

Things to Do Leading Up to Test Day:

- Get your body on schedule for the time of the test, and do LSAT questions at that same time of day.
- Eat, sleep, and exercise.
- Visit your test site.
- Get your passport-style photo taken professionally.
- Print out and double-check your admissions ticket.
- Check www.lsac.org for the most recent Test Day guidelines.
- Decide whether you want to take the test or withdraw.

Planning Your Remaining Study Time:

- Balance stress management and study.
- Study areas of greatest strength, not only areas of greatest opportunity.
- The majority of your work should be under timed conditions—either Timing or Endurance.
- Still review the Answers and Explanations for every practice problem.
- Remember that you are going to law school.

Recent Trends

A review of the most recently administered LSATs gives a good indication of what you are likely to see on Test Day.

Logical Reasoning Question Frequency by # of Questions/Test

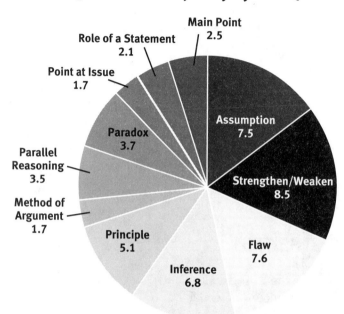

Released LSATs 2009–2013

Reading Comprehension Passage Structure Frequency by Approximate Percentage

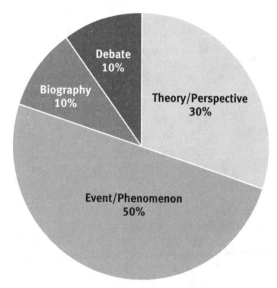

Released LSATs 2009–2013

Reading Comprehension Question Frequency by # of Questions/Test

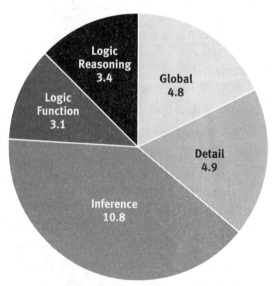

Released LSATs 2009–2013

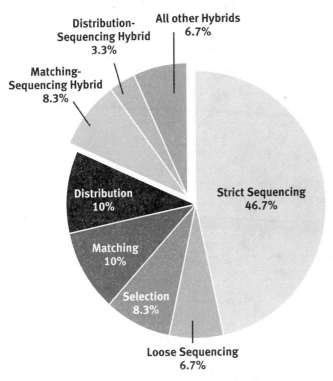

Logic Games Game Type Frequency by Percentage

Distribution-Sequencing Hybrid 3.3%

All other Hybrids 6.7%

Matching-Sequencing Hybrid 8.3%

Distribution 10%

Strict Sequencing 46.7%

Matching 10%

Selection 8.3%

Loose Sequencing 6.7%

Released LSATs 2009–2013

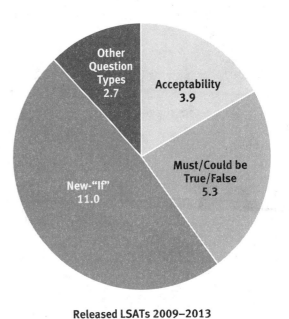

Logic Games Question Type Frequency by # of Questions/Test

Other Question Types 2.7

Acceptability 3.9

New-"If" 11.0

Must/Could be True/False 5.3

Released LSATs 2009–2013

Most Challenging Section (as reported by students immediately after the test)

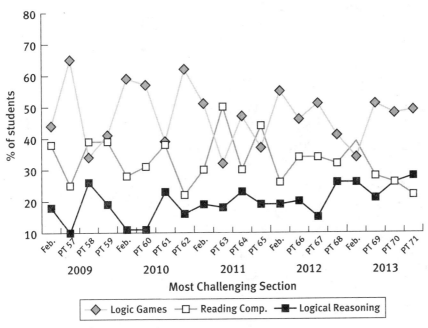

Most Challenging Section

◆ Logic Games   □ Reading Comp.   ■ Logical Reasoning

Source: Kaplan Test Day student surveys

THE DAY BEFORE THE TEST

The day before the test is as important as the six days before it. The first instinct of most test takers is to cram as much as possible in hopes of grabbing a few last-second points. But the LSAT isn't a test that can be crammed for. You should think of Test Day as game day. Make sure you can hit your potential when it counts. Relax the day before the test so that you can hit peak performance on the test.

LSAT STRATEGY

The day before the test:

· Relax! Read a book, watch a movie, take a walk, or go shopping.
· Don't take any full-length tests, and preferably don't study at all.
· Get all of your materials together—your admission ticket, passport photo, plastic bag, snack, watch, and so on.
· Eat a full meal for dinner and get plenty of sleep.

LSAT FACTS

The following items are required for admission on Test Day:

· Admissions ticket
· A passport photo affixed to your admissions ticket
· Government-issued ID
· Regular No. 2 pencils (no mechanical pencils)

LSAT STRATEGY

Kaplan recommends you bring the following items with you on Test Day:

· 1-gallon ziplock bag (necessary to store items somewhere other than your desktop)
· A nondigital timing device (i.e., an analog watch)
· A snack for the break (avoid sugary snacks, if possible)
· Bottled beverage
· Eraser (or pencils with quality erasers)
· Pencil sharpener (or just lots of pencils)
· Pain reliever (e.g., aspirin)
· Tissues
· A positive, upbeat attitude!

THE MORNING OF THE TEST

On the morning of the exam, you should obviously get up early to give yourself time to wake up and eat breakfast. Leave early for the test center. A relaxed morning is a much better start than a frantic, stressful one.

LSAT STRATEGY

On the morning of the test:

- Get up early and plan accordingly for commute/traffic/parking.
- Eat an appropriate breakfast.
- Dress in layers (but do not wear a hooded sweatshirt).
- Gather your allowable items into a one-gallon ziplock plastic bag.

When gathering your items into your plastic bag, avoid bringing anything on this list of prohibited items. (This list is not exhaustive, so check the LSAC website for the most up-to-date information.)

LSAT FACTS

The following items are prohibited:

- Cell phones (Leave it at home or in the car.)
- Electronic devices of any kind, including tablets and digital watches
- Ear plugs
- Backpacks or purses
- Mechanical pencils
- Papers or books
- Hats and hooded sweatshirts

AT THE TEST SITE AND DURING THE TEST

Aim to arrive at your testing facility at least 30 minutes before the test is scheduled to begin. Arriving early is not just about being prompt, it's also important to have a game plan for what to do at the testing facility before the exam starts.

LSAT STRATEGY

At the Testing Facility on Test Day:

- Arrive 30 minutes early.
- Find and use the drinking fountains and bathroom.
- Get into "LSAT mode" by reviewing previous work (discard papers before checking in).
- Enter the testing room a few minutes before the test is set to begin.
- Use the time before the test begins to mentally prepare yourself for the test.

LSAT STRATEGY

What to Expect:

- Stress levels will be high.
- It will be cold or hot.
- Students will talk unproductively during the break.
- You will be successful.

LSAT STRATEGY

Three Essential Takeaways from Your Kaplan LSAT Training:

- Every question has one right answer and four terrible ones.
- When applicable, strive to predict an answer to all LR and RC questions before evaluating the answer choices.
- Invest the proper time to set up a Logic Game or Roadmap a passage; it will pay dividends in the questions.

LSAT STRATEGY

Taking the Test:

- Look forward, not backward—always keep moving through the test and focus on the section you're currently in, not sections you've already done or will do in the future.
- Fill in every bubble.
- Grid appropriately.
- When the proctor says stop, it means stop.
- Relax during the break. Avoid the temptation to try for an unethical advantage by talking about the test to other test takers.
- Don't worry about how you're scoring. Don't try to figure out which section is the experimental one. Focus only on what's in front of you.

LSAT STRATEGY

Staying Calm:

- The LSAT is scored on a curve; if something seems challenging, it will likely be challenging for everyone.
- No single question will make or break your score. Keep moving; the questions will be there to return to if you have time later.
- If you lose focus, don't keep rereading the same question; move to a different question and start fresh. Upon return to a question, it may seem more manageable.
- If you panic, stop, put your pencil down, and take a few slow deep breaths. You're prepared for the test, and if today's not your day, you can always take the test again.

Kaplan Test Day Survey Results

After each test administration, Kaplan surveys our students on various aspects of the Test Day experience. Here are some results from a recent administration:

Did the desk surface give you enough room to work?

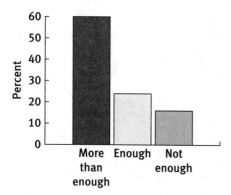

On a scale of 1 to 5, with 5 being the best, how comfortable and quiet was your testing environment?

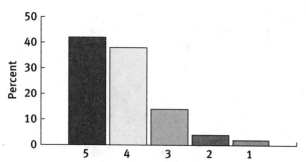

On a scale of 1 to 5, with 5 being the best, how would you rate the effectiveness of proctoring?

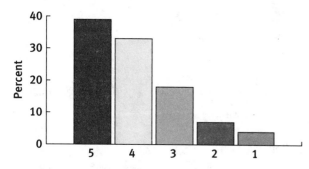

On a scale of 1 to 5, with 5 being the best, how would you rate the overall quality of the experience at your test site?

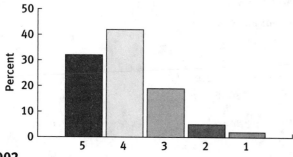

> *"I am so glad you recommended that we to drive to the site one week beforehand. I did it the Saturday prior to the test and figured out the difficult parking situation. I was able to get into the classrooms and make note of the possible types of desks I would be working on—a major plus as I had one of the smaller desk options! I felt more comfortable knowing the environment that I would be working in on that day."*

Takeaway: If you take away the anxiety of the unknowns, then you can just focus on the test.

> *"A girl taking the exam passed out during the first five minutes of the first section. She fell on her face and many people taking the test were very concerned because she was unconscious for a few minutes. The proctors called 911 and spoke on the phone during the test. The whole ordeal lasted about ten minutes but they never stopped timing."*

Takeaway: If there is a problem that can be corrected then and there, do not hesitate to speak up. If something significant occurs, like the situation above, that affects your score, contact the LSAC, and calmly and factually explain the situation. They won't change your score, but they may provide some recourse.

> *"Absolutely loved my test site. The proctors and administration were so great, the rooms were quiet and clean."*

Takeaway: Most LSAT administrations run without any problems. Do not let horror stories of bad proctoring experiences cloud your expectations. Focus on what you can control.

> *"A lot of people took the test today, but I felt confident that I was the most prepared because some people asked really dumb questions like if the writing sample was optional."*

Takeaway: Your experience at Kaplan has prepared you well—all that's left is for you to perform your best!

AFTER THE TEST

If it turns out that Test Day doesn't go *exactly* as planned, that's all right—it rarely, if ever, does, and the LSAT does not require perfection. All of your fellow test takers will likely experience some level of self-doubt as well; that's fairly typical. It is, however, important to know whether a Test Day experience included one of the rare anomolies that actually warrants canceling your score. Most of you will be able to skip this section and move on to life after the LSAT.

Should You Cancel Your Score?

LSAT STRATEGY

Benefits to not canceling your score:

- No matter how you "feel," you don't know for sure how you did. You may have done much better than you think.
- You will have access to the answers you selected during Test Day, which will be an excellent review tool.
- Law schools by and large are not averaging scores, so a single lower score won't be all that detrimental.
- A cancellation still counts against your limit of taking the test three times in two years, so if you end up needing to re-take the exam, there's less pressure next time out because at least you have a baseline score on record.

LSAT STRATEGY

Situations that would NOT warrant a score cancellation:

- Minor distractions in the testing facility (pencil tapping, coughing, temperature, etc.)
- You didn't get to finish or forgot to bubble the last few questions in a section or two
- Small-scale time issues related to the five-minute warning, where clocks were positioned, whether or not the times were written on the board (they aren't required to be, and often aren't)

Situations that would warrant a score cancellation:

- Needing to leave the room for an extended time during the test
- A significant gridding mistake affecting a large portion of an entire section
- Large-scale time issues caused by either the proctor or poor personal time management; for example, a shortened section or a complete breakdown in timing, causing a large number of unanswered questions in a section

---

Post-LSAT Festivities

After weeks or months of preparation it's finally over. What do you do now?

- Congratulate yourself!
- Celebrate responsibly!
- Reach out to thank those who made a difference to you during the process.
- After some rest, get started writing your personal statement, requesting letters of recommendation, and gathering your transcripts.

Everyone at Kaplan is proud of you. You are on a path to success starting with your performance on the LSAT, and then your education as a law student and practice as a lawyer. Congratulations on your journey!

PART SIX

Practice Tests

Practice Tests

One of the most difficult aspects of the LSAT is its length—a full 3.5 hours of testing time (and much more when you count breaks and delays). Building your test-taking stamina is critical to performing well on Test Day.

As you prepare for the LSAT, taking full-length exams is the best way to build your endurance and get feedback on your progress. Four PrepTests are provided in this book:

> PrepTest 63 (June 2011)

> PrepTest 55 (October 2008)

> PrepTest 53 (December 2007)

> PrepTest 47 (October 2005)

When the LSAC releases a previously-administered LSAT, it does not include the Experimental section. The four tests included here are all four-section tests. If you'd like to make your practice as test-like as possible, add a full section from a different exam to function as an "Experimental" section. This extra section will not count toward your score, but it will give you a better feel for what it is like to focus for five straight multiple-choice sections. If you opt to just do the four sections of the PrepTest it will still be valuable Endurance practice and a good gauge of where you're currently scoring. Alternatively, you can also break apart any of these four tests and use them as Timing practice to work on your pacing like you did in Chapters 7, 12, and 16.

Once you've decided how to use the material, complete all sections under timed conditions. If you do not have live proctoring opportunities available, we recommend downloading our proctoring app: "LSAT Proctor Anywhere."

We'd also recommend including the Writing Sample as a timed section at the end of full-length practice if you have the opportunity. Although the Writing Sample is unscored and it is the least important part of the LSAT, schools do use it to help them choose between students with very similar records.

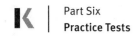
TIMING

The timing for the LSAT is as follows:

1st Section:	35 minutes
2nd Section:	35 minutes
3rd Section:	35 minutes
Break:	10–15 minutes
4th Section:	35 minutes
5th Section:	35 minutes
Writing Sample:	35 minutes

Note: If you're just taking the four-section PrepTest without adding an Experimental section, do two scored sections before the break and two scored sections after the break.

We recommend starting with the most recent tests, which are listed first; these are more likely to reflect what will be on your LSAT.

There are several answer grids approximating what you will see on Test Day in the back of this book. If you need additional grids, you'll find a PDF of the grid online that can be printed out. Mark you answer choices on the grid as you complete the exam.

After you've completed the test, enter your answers from the grid in your Online Center to see your test score, compare your scores from test to test, and see detailed analysis of your performance on specific question and game types.

PrepTest 63

PrepTest 63 (June 2011)

SECTION I

Time—35 minutes

25 Questions

<u>Directions:</u> The questions in this section are based on the reasoning contained in brief statements or passages. For some questions, more than one of the choices could conceivably answer the question. However, you are to choose the <u>best</u> answer; that is, the response that most accurately and completely answers the question. You should not make assumptions that are by commonsense standards implausible, superfluous, or incompatible with the passage. After you have chosen the best answer, blacken the corresponding space on your answer sheet.

1. Backyard gardeners who want to increase the yields of their potato plants should try growing stinging nettles alongside the plants, since stinging nettles attract insects that kill a wide array of insect pests that damage potato plants. It is true that stinging nettles also attract aphids, and that many species of aphids are harmful to potato plants, but that fact in no way contradicts this recommendation, because _____.

   Which one of the following most logically completes the argument?

   (A) stinging nettles require little care and thus are easy to cultivate
   (B) some types of aphids are attracted to stinging nettle plants but do not damage them
   (C) the types of aphids that stinging nettles attract do not damage potato plants
   (D) insect pests typically cause less damage to potato plants than other harmful organisms do
   (E) most aphid species that are harmful to potato plants cause greater harm to other edible food plants

2. Jocko, a chimpanzee, was once given a large bunch of bananas by a zookeeper after the more dominant members of the chimpanzee's troop had wandered off. In his excitement, Jocko uttered some loud "food barks." The other chimpanzees returned and took the bananas away. The next day, Jocko was again found alone and was given a single banana. This time, however, he kept silent. The zookeeper concluded that Jocko's silence was a stratagem to keep the other chimpanzees from his food.

   Which one of the following, if true, most seriously calls into question the zookeeper's conclusion?

   (A) Chimpanzees utter food barks only when their favorite foods are available.
   (B) Chimpanzees utter food barks only when they encounter a sizable quantity of food.
   (C) Chimpanzees frequently take food from other chimpanzees merely to assert dominance.
   (D) Even when they are alone, chimpanzees often make noises that appear to be signals to other chimpanzees.
   (E) Bananas are a food for which all of the chimpanzees at the zoo show a decided preference.

3. A recent survey quizzed journalism students about the sorts of stories they themselves wished to read. A significant majority said they wanted to see stories dealing with serious governmental and political issues and had little tolerance for the present popularity of stories covering lifestyle trends and celebrity gossip. This indicates that today's trends in publishing are based on false assumptions about the interests of the public.

   Which one of the following most accurately describes a flaw in the argument's reasoning?

   (A) It takes what is more likely to be the effect of a phenomenon to be its cause.
   (B) It regards the production of an effect as incontrovertible evidence of an intention to produce that effect.
   (C) It relies on the opinions of a group unlikely to be representative of the group at issue in the conclusion.
   (D) It employs language that unfairly represents those who are likely to reject the argument's conclusion.
   (E) It treats a hypothesis as fact even though it is admittedly unsupported.

GO ON TO THE NEXT PAGE.

4. Electric bug zappers, which work by attracting insects to light, are a very effective means of ridding an area of flying insects. Despite this, most pest control experts now advise against their use, recommending instead such remedies as insect-eating birds or insecticide sprays.

Which one of the following, if true, most helps to account for the pest control experts' recommendation?

(A) Insect-eating birds will take up residence in any insect-rich area if they are provided with nesting boxes, food, and water.

(B) Bug zappers are less effective against mosquitoes, which are among the more harmful insects, than they are against other harmful insects.

(C) Bug zappers use more electricity but provide less light than do most standard outdoor light sources.

(D) Bug zappers kill many more beneficial insects and fewer harmful insects than do insect-eating birds and insecticide sprays.

(E) Developers of certain new insecticide sprays claim that their products contain no chemicals that are harmful to humans, birds, or pets.

5. Gardener: The design of Japanese gardens should display harmony with nature. Hence, rocks chosen for placement in such gardens should vary widely in appearance, since rocks found in nature also vary widely in appearance.

The gardener's argument depends on assuming which one of the following?

(A) The selection of rocks for placement in a Japanese garden should reflect every key value embodied in the design of Japanese gardens.

(B) In the selection of rocks for Japanese gardens, imitation of nature helps to achieve harmony with nature.

(C) The only criterion for selecting rocks for placement in a Japanese garden is the expression of harmony with nature.

(D) Expressing harmony with nature and being natural are the same thing.

(E) Each component of a genuine Japanese garden is varied.

6. Small experimental vacuum tubes can operate in heat that makes semiconductor components fail. Any component whose resistance to heat is greater than that of semiconductors would be preferable for use in digital circuits, but only if that component were also comparable to semiconductors in all other significant respects, such as maximum current capacity. However, vacuum tubes' maximum current capacity is presently not comparable to that of semiconductors.

If the statements above are true, which one of the following must also be true?

(A) Vacuum tubes are not now preferable to semiconductors for use in digital circuits.

(B) Once vacuum tubes and semiconductors have comparable maximum current capacity, vacuum tubes will be used in some digital circuits.

(C) The only reason that vacuum tubes are not now used in digital circuits is that vacuum tubes' maximum current capacity is too low.

(D) Semiconductors will always be preferable to vacuum tubes for use in many applications other than digital circuits.

(E) Resistance to heat is the only advantage that vacuum tubes have over semiconductors.

7. The cause of the epidemic that devastated Athens in 430 B.C. can finally be identified. Accounts of the epidemic mention the hiccups experienced by many victims, a symptom of no known disease except that caused by the recently discovered Ebola virus. Moreover, other symptoms of the disease caused by the Ebola virus are mentioned in the accounts of the Athenian epidemic.

Each of the following, if true, weakens the argument EXCEPT:

(A) Victims of the Ebola virus experience many symptoms that do not appear in any of the accounts of the Athenian epidemic.

(B) Not all of those who are victims of the Ebola virus are afflicted with hiccups.

(C) The Ebola virus's host animals did not live in Athens at the time of the Athenian epidemic.

(D) The Ebola virus is much more contagious than the disease that caused the Athenian epidemic was reported to have been.

(E) The epidemics known to have been caused by the Ebola virus are usually shorter-lived than was the Athenian epidemic.

GO ON TO THE NEXT PAGE.

8. Letter to the editor: Your article was unjustified in criticizing environmentalists for claiming that more wolves on Vancouver Island are killed by hunters than are born each year. You stated that this claim was disproven by recent studies that indicate that the total number of wolves on Vancouver Island has remained roughly constant for 20 years. But you failed to account for the fact that, fearing the extinction of this wolf population, environmentalists have been introducing new wolves into the Vancouver Island wolf population for 20 years.

Which one of the following most accurately expresses the conclusion of the argument in the letter to the editor?

(A) Environmentalists have been successfully maintaining the wolf population on Vancouver Island for 20 years.

(B) As many wolves on Vancouver Island are killed by hunters as are born each year.

(C) The population of wolves on Vancouver Island should be maintained by either reducing the number killed by hunters each year or introducing new wolves into the population.

(D) The recent studies indicating that the total number of wolves on Vancouver Island has remained roughly constant for 20 years were flawed.

(E) The stability in the size of the Vancouver Island wolf population does not warrant the article's criticism of the environmentalists' claim.

9. Computer scientist: For several decades, the number of transistors on new computer microchips, and hence the microchips' computing speed, has doubled about every 18 months. However, from the mid-1990s into the next decade, each such doubling in a microchip's computing speed was accompanied by a doubling in the cost of producing that microchip.

Which one of the following can be properly inferred from the computer scientist's statements?

(A) The only effective way to double the computing speed of computer microchips is to increase the number of transistors per microchip.

(B) From the mid-1990s into the next decade, there was little if any increase in the retail cost of computers as a result of the increased number of transistors on microchips.

(C) For the last several decades, computer engineers have focused on increasing the computing speed of computer microchips without making any attempt to control the cost of producing them.

(D) From the mid-1990s into the next decade, a doubling in the cost of fabricating new computer microchips accompanied each doubling in the number of transistors on those microchips.

(E) It is unlikely that engineers will ever be able to increase the computing speed of microchips without also increasing the cost of producing them.

GO ON TO THE NEXT PAGE.

10. Ms. Sandstrom's newspaper column describing a strange natural phenomenon on the Mendels' farm led many people to trespass on and extensively damage their property. Thus, Ms. Sandstrom should pay for this damage if, as the Mendels claim, she could have reasonably expected that the column would lead people to damage the Mendels' farm.

The argument's conclusion can be properly inferred if which one of the following is assumed?

(A) One should pay for any damage that one's action leads other people to cause if one could have reasonably expected that the action would lead other people to cause damage.

(B) One should pay for damage that one's action leads other people to cause only if, prior to the action, one expected that the action would lead other people to cause that damage.

(C) It is unlikely that the people who trespassed on and caused the damage to the Mendels' property would themselves pay for the damage they caused.

(D) Ms. Sandstrom knew that her column could incite trespassing that could result in damage to the Mendels' farm.

(E) The Mendels believe that Ms. Sandstrom is able to form reasonable expectations about the consequences of her actions.

11. Meyer was found by his employer to have committed scientific fraud by falsifying data. The University of Williamstown, from which Meyer held a PhD, validated this finding and subsequently investigated whether he had falsified data in his doctoral thesis, finding no evidence that he had. But the university decided to revoke Meyer's PhD anyway.

Which one of the following university policies most justifies the decision to revoke Meyer's PhD?

(A) Anyone who holds a PhD from the University of Williamstown and is found to have committed academic fraud in the course of pursuing that PhD will have the PhD revoked.

(B) No PhD program at the University of Williamstown will admit any applicant who has been determined to have committed any sort of academic fraud.

(C) Any University of Williamstown student who is found to have submitted falsified data as academic work will be dismissed from the university.

(D) Anyone who holds a PhD from the University of Williamstown and is found to have committed scientific fraud will have the PhD revoked.

(E) The University of Williamstown will not hire anyone who is under investigation for scientific fraud.

12. Aerobics instructor: Compared to many forms of exercise, kickboxing aerobics is highly risky. Overextending when kicking often leads to hip, knee, or lower-back injuries. Such overextension is very likely to occur when beginners try to match the high kicks of more skilled practitioners.

Which one of the following is most strongly supported by the aerobics instructor's statements?

(A) Skilled practitioners of kickboxing aerobics are unlikely to experience injuries from overextending while kicking.

(B) To reduce the risk of injuries, beginners at kickboxing aerobics should avoid trying to match the high kicks of more skilled practitioners.

(C) Beginners at kickboxing aerobics will not experience injuries if they avoid trying to match the high kicks of more skilled practitioners.

(D) Kickboxing aerobics is more risky than forms of aerobic exercise that do not involve high kicks.

(E) Most beginners at kickboxing aerobics experience injuries from trying to match the high kicks of more skilled practitioners.

13. A large company has been convicted of engaging in monopolistic practices. The penalty imposed on the company will probably have little if any effect on its behavior. Still, the trial was worthwhile, since it provided useful information about the company's practices. After all, this information has emboldened the company's direct competitors, alerted potential rivals, and forced the company to restrain its unfair behavior toward customers and competitors.

Which one of the following most accurately expresses the overall conclusion drawn in the argument?

(A) Even if the company had not been convicted of engaging in monopolistic practices, the trial probably would have had some effect on the company's behavior.

(B) The light shed on the company's practices by the trial has emboldened its competitors, alerted potential rivals, and forced the company to restrain its unfair behavior.

(C) The penalty imposed on the company will likely have little or no effect on its behavior.

(D) The company's trial on charges of engaging in monopolistic practices was worthwhile.

(E) The penalty imposed on the company in the trial should have been larger.

GO ON TO THE NEXT PAGE.

14. Waller: If there were really such a thing as extrasensory perception, it would generally be accepted by the public since anyone with extrasensory powers would be able to convince the general public of its existence by clearly demonstrating those powers. Indeed, anyone who was recognized to have such powers would achieve wealth and renown.

Chin: It's impossible to demonstrate anything to the satisfaction of all skeptics. So long as the cultural elite remains closed-minded to the possibility of extrasensory perception, the popular media reports, and thus public opinion, will always be biased in favor of such skeptics.

Waller's and Chin's statements commit them to disagreeing on whether

(A) extrasensory perception is a real phenomenon
(B) extrasensory perception, if it were a real phenomenon, could be demonstrated to the satisfaction of all skeptics
(C) skeptics about extrasensory perception have a weak case
(D) the failure of the general public to believe in extrasensory perception is good evidence against its existence
(E) the general public believes that extrasensory perception is a real phenomenon

15. Counselor: Hagerle sincerely apologized to the physician for lying to her. So Hagerle owes me a sincere apology as well, because Hagerle told the same lie to both of us.

Which one of the following principles, if valid, most helps to justify the counselor's reasoning?

(A) It is good to apologize for having done something wrong to a person if one is capable of doing so sincerely.
(B) If someone tells the same lie to two different people, then neither of those lied to is owed an apology unless both are.
(C) Someone is owed a sincere apology for having been lied to by a person if someone else has already received a sincere apology for the same lie from that same person.
(D) If one is capable of sincerely apologizing to someone for lying to them, then one owes that person such an apology.
(E) A person should not apologize to someone for telling a lie unless he or she can sincerely apologize to all others to whom the lie was told.

16. A survey of address changes filed with post offices and driver's license bureaus over the last ten years has established that households moving out of the city of Weston outnumbered households moving into the city two to one. Therefore, we can expect that next year's census, which counts all residents regardless of age, will show that the population of Weston has declined since the last census ten years ago.

Which one of the following, if true, most helps to strengthen the argument?

(A) Within the past decade many people both moved into the city and also moved out of it.
(B) Over the past century any census of Weston showing a population loss was followed ten years later by a census showing a population gain.
(C) Many people moving into Weston failed to notify either the post office or the driver's license bureau that they had moved to the city.
(D) Most adults moving out of Weston were parents who had children living with them, whereas most adults remaining in or moving into the city were older people who lived alone.
(E) Most people moving out of Weston were young adults who were hoping to begin a career elsewhere, whereas most adults remaining in or moving into the city had long-standing jobs in the city.

17. Psychologist: People tend to make certain cognitive errors when they predict how a given event would affect their future happiness. But people should not necessarily try to rid themselves of this tendency. After all, in a visual context, lines that are actually parallel often appear to people as if they converge. If a surgeon offered to restructure your eyes and visual cortex so that parallel lines would no longer ever appear to converge, it would not be reasonable to take the surgeon up on the offer.

The psychologist's argument does which one of the following?

(A) attempts to refute a claim that a particular event is inevitable by establishing the possibility of an alternative event
(B) attempts to undermine a theory by calling into question an assumption on which the theory is based
(C) argues that an action might not be appropriate by suggesting that a corresponding action in an analogous situation is not appropriate
(D) argues that two situations are similar by establishing that the same action would be reasonable in each situation
(E) attempts to establish a generalization and then uses that generalization to argue against a particular action

GO ON TO THE NEXT PAGE.

18. Principle: Even if an art auction house identifies the descriptions in its catalog as opinions, it is guilty of misrepresentation if such a description is a deliberate attempt to mislead bidders.

    Application: Although Healy's, an art auction house, states that all descriptions in its catalog are opinions, Healy's was guilty of misrepresentation when its catalog described a vase as dating from the mid-eighteenth century when it was actually a modern reproduction.

    Which one of the following, if true, most justifies the above application of the principle?

    (A) An authentic work of art from the mid-eighteenth century will usually sell for at least ten times more than a modern reproduction of a similar work from that period.

    (B) Although pottery that is similar to the vase is currently extremely popular among art collectors, none of the collectors who are knowledgeable about such pottery were willing to bid on the vase.

    (C) The stated policy of Healy's is to describe works in its catalogs only in terms of their readily perceptible qualities and not to include any information about their age.

    (D) Some Healy's staff members believe that the auction house's catalog should not contain any descriptions that have not been certified to be true by independent experts.

    (E) Without consulting anyone with expertise in authenticating vases, Healy's described the vase as dating from the mid-eighteenth century merely in order to increase its auction price.

19. Anthropologist: It was formerly believed that prehistoric *Homo sapiens* ancestors of contemporary humans interbred with Neanderthals, but DNA testing of a Neanderthal's remains indicates that this is not the case. The DNA of contemporary humans is significantly different from that of the Neanderthal.

    Which one of the following is an assumption required by the anthropologist's argument?

    (A) At least some Neanderthals lived at the same time and in the same places as prehistoric *Homo sapiens* ancestors of contemporary humans.

    (B) DNA testing of remains is significantly less reliable than DNA testing of samples from living species.

    (C) The DNA of prehistoric *Homo sapiens* ancestors of contemporary humans was not significantly more similar to that of Neanderthals than is the DNA of contemporary humans.

    (D) Neanderthals and prehistoric *Homo sapiens* ancestors of contemporary humans were completely isolated from each other geographically.

    (E) Any similarity in the DNA of two species must be the result of interbreeding.

20. Council member: The profits of downtown businesses will increase if more consumers live in the downtown area, and a decrease in the cost of living in the downtown area will guarantee that the number of consumers living there will increase. However, the profits of downtown businesses will not increase unless downtown traffic congestion decreases.

    If all the council member's statements are true, which one of the following must be true?

    (A) If downtown traffic congestion decreases, the number of consumers living in the downtown area will increase.

    (B) If the cost of living in the downtown area decreases, the profits of downtown businesses will increase.

    (C) If downtown traffic congestion decreases, the cost of living in the downtown area will increase.

    (D) If downtown traffic congestion decreases, the cost of living in the downtown area will decrease.

    (E) If the profits of downtown businesses increase, the number of consumers living in the downtown area will increase.

GO ON TO THE NEXT PAGE.

21. On the Discount Phoneline, any domestic long-distance call starting between 9 A.M. and 5 P.M. costs 15 cents a minute, and any other domestic long-distance call costs 10 cents a minute. So any domestic long-distance call on the Discount Phoneline that does not cost 10 cents a minute costs 15 cents a minute.

The pattern of reasoning in which one of the following arguments is most similar to that in the argument above?

(A) If a university class involves extensive lab work, the class will be conducted in a laboratory; otherwise, it will be conducted in a normal classroom. Thus, if a university class does not involve extensive lab work, it will not be conducted in a laboratory.

(B) If a university class involves extensive lab work, the class will be conducted in a laboratory; otherwise, it will be conducted in a normal classroom. Thus, if a university class is not conducted in a normal classroom, it will involve extensive lab work.

(C) If a university class involves extensive lab work, the class will be conducted in a laboratory; otherwise, it will be conducted in a normal classroom. Thus, if a university class is conducted in a normal classroom, it will not be conducted in a laboratory.

(D) If a university class involves extensive lab work, the class will be conducted in a laboratory; otherwise, it will be conducted in a normal classroom. Thus, if a university class involves extensive lab work, it will not be conducted in a normal classroom.

(E) If a university class involves extensive lab work, the class will be conducted in a laboratory; otherwise, it will be conducted in a normal classroom. Thus, if a university class is not conducted in a normal classroom, it will be conducted in a laboratory.

22. One child pushed another child from behind, injuring the second child. The first child clearly understands the difference between right and wrong, so what was done was wrong if it was intended to injure the second child.

Which one of the following principles, if valid, most helps to justify the reasoning in the argument?

(A) An action that is intended to harm another person is wrong only if the person who performed the action understands the difference between right and wrong.

(B) It is wrong for a person who understands the difference between right and wrong to intentionally harm another person.

(C) Any act that is wrong is done with the intention of causing harm.

(D) An act that harms another person is wrong if the person who did it understands the difference between right and wrong and did not think about whether the act would injure the other person.

(E) A person who does not understand the difference between right and wrong does not bear any responsibility for harming another person.

23. Researcher: Each subject in this experiment owns one car, and was asked to estimate what proportion of all automobiles registered in the nation are the same make as the subject's car. The estimate of nearly every subject has been significantly higher than the actual national statistic for the make of that subject's car. I hypothesize that certain makes of car are more common in some regions of the nation than in other regions; obviously, that would lead many people to overestimate how common their make of car is nationally. That is precisely the result found in this experiment, so certain makes of car must indeed be more common in some areas of the nation than in others.

Which one of the following most accurately expresses a reasoning flaw in the researcher's argument?

(A) The argument fails to estimate the likelihood that most subjects in the experiment did not know the actual statistics about how common their make of car is nationwide.

(B) The argument treats a result that supports a hypothesis as a result that proves a hypothesis.

(C) The argument fails to take into account the possibility that the subject pool may come from a wide variety of geographical regions.

(D) The argument attempts to draw its main conclusion from a set of premises that are mutually contradictory.

(E) The argument applies a statistical generalization to a particular case to which it was not intended to apply.

GO ON TO THE NEXT PAGE.

24. In university towns, police issue far more parking citations during the school year than they do during the times when the students are out of town. Therefore, we know that most parking citations in university towns are issued to students.

Which one of the following is most similar in its flawed reasoning to the flawed reasoning in the argument above?

(A) We know that children buy most of the snacks at cinemas, because popcorn sales increase as the proportion of child moviegoers to adult moviegoers increases.

(B) We know that this houseplant gets more of the sunlight from the window, because it is greener than that houseplant.

(C) We know that most people who go to a university are studious because most of those people study while they attend the university.

(D) We know that consumers buy more fruit during the summer than they buy during the winter, because there are far more varieties of fruit available in the summer than in the winter.

(E) We know that most of the snacks parents buy go to other people's children, because when other people's children come to visit, parents give out more snacks than usual.

25. Counselor: Those who believe that criticism should be gentle rather than harsh should consider the following: change requires a motive, and criticism that is unpleasant provides a motive. Since harsh criticism is unpleasant, harsh criticism provides a motive. Therefore, only harsh criticism will cause the person criticized to change.

The reasoning in the counselor's argument is most vulnerable to criticism on the grounds that the argument

(A) infers that something that is sufficient to provide a motive is necessary to provide a motive

(B) fails to address the possibility that in some cases the primary goal of criticism is something other than bringing about change in the person being criticized

(C) takes for granted that everyone who is motivated to change will change

(D) confuses a motive for doing something with a motive for avoiding something

(E) takes the refutation of an argument to be sufficient to show that the argument's conclusion is false

S T O P

IF YOU FINISH BEFORE TIME IS CALLED, YOU MAY CHECK YOUR WORK ON THIS SECTION ONLY.
DO NOT WORK ON ANY OTHER SECTION IN THE TEST.

SECTION II

Time—35 minutes

23 Questions

Directions: Each group of questions in this section is based on a set of conditions. In answering some of the questions, it may be useful to draw a rough diagram. Choose the response that most accurately and completely answers each question and blacken the corresponding space on your answer sheet.

Questions 1–5

Each of seven candidates for the position of judge—Hamadi, Jefferson, Kurtz, Li, McDonnell, Ortiz, and Perkins—will be appointed to an open position on one of two courts—the appellate court or the trial court. There are three open positions on the appellate court and six open positions on the trial court, but not all of them will be filled at this time. The judicial appointments will conform to the following conditions:

Li must be appointed to the appellate court.

Kurtz must be appointed to the trial court.

Hamadi cannot be appointed to the same court as Perkins.

1. Which one of the following is an acceptable set of appointments of candidates to courts?

   (A) appellate: Hamadi, Ortiz
       trial: Jefferson, Kurtz, Li, McDonnell, Perkins
   (B) appellate: Hamadi, Li, Perkins
       trial: Jefferson, Kurtz, McDonnell, Ortiz
   (C) appellate: Kurtz, Li, Perkins
       trial: Hamadi, Jefferson, McDonnell, Ortiz
   (D) appellate: Li, McDonnell, Ortiz
       trial: Hamadi, Jefferson, Kurtz, Perkins
   (E) appellate: Li, Perkins
       trial: Hamadi, Jefferson, Kurtz, McDonnell, Ortiz

2. Which one of the following CANNOT be true?

   (A) Hamadi and McDonnell are both appointed to the appellate court.
   (B) McDonnell and Ortiz are both appointed to the appellate court.
   (C) Ortiz and Perkins are both appointed to the appellate court.
   (D) Hamadi and Jefferson are both appointed to the trial court.
   (E) Ortiz and Perkins are both appointed to the trial court.

3. Which one of the following CANNOT be true?

   (A) Jefferson and McDonnell are both appointed to the appellate court.
   (B) Jefferson and McDonnell are both appointed to the trial court.
   (C) McDonnell and Ortiz are both appointed to the trial court.
   (D) McDonnell and Perkins are both appointed to the appellate court.
   (E) McDonnell and Perkins are both appointed to the trial court.

4. If Ortiz is appointed to the appellate court, which one of the following must be true?

   (A) Hamadi is appointed to the appellate court.
   (B) Jefferson is appointed to the appellate court.
   (C) Jefferson is appointed to the trial court.
   (D) Perkins is appointed to the appellate court.
   (E) Perkins is appointed to the trial court.

5. Which one of the following, if substituted for the condition that Hamadi cannot be appointed to the same court as Perkins, would have the same effect on the appointments of the seven candidates?

   (A) Hamadi and Perkins cannot both be appointed to the appellate court.
   (B) If Hamadi is not appointed to the trial court, then Perkins must be.
   (C) If Perkins is appointed to the same court as Jefferson, then Hamadi cannot be.
   (D) If Hamadi is appointed to the same court as Li, then Perkins must be appointed to the same court as Kurtz.
   (E) No three of Hamadi, Kurtz, Li, and Perkins can be appointed to the same court as each other.

GO ON TO THE NEXT PAGE.

Questions 6–10

Exactly six members of a skydiving team—Larue, Ohba, Pei, Treviño, Weiss, and Zacny—each dive exactly once, one at a time, from a plane, consistent with the following conditions:

    Treviño dives from the plane at some time before Weiss does.

    Larue dives from the plane either first or last.

    Neither Weiss nor Zacny dives from the plane last.

    Pei dives from the plane at some time after either Ohba or Larue but not both.

6. Which one of the following could be an accurate list of the members in the order in which they dive from the plane, from first to last?

    (A)   Larue, Treviño, Ohba, Zacny, Pei, Weiss
    (B)   Larue, Treviño, Pei, Zacny, Weiss, Ohba
    (C)   Weiss, Ohba, Treviño, Zacny, Pei, Larue
    (D)   Treviño, Weiss, Pei, Ohba, Zacny, Larue
    (E)   Treviño, Weiss, Zacny, Larue, Pei, Ohba

7. Which one of the following must be true?

    (A)   At least two of the members dive from the plane after Larue.
    (B)   At least two of the members dive from the plane after Ohba.
    (C)   At least two of the members dive from the plane after Pei.
    (D)   At least two of the members dive from the plane after Treviño.
    (E)   At least two of the members dive from the plane after Weiss.

8. If Larue dives from the plane last, then each of the following could be true EXCEPT:

    (A)   Treviño dives from the plane fourth.
    (B)   Weiss dives from the plane fourth.
    (C)   Ohba dives from the plane fifth.
    (D)   Pei dives from the plane fifth.
    (E)   Zacny dives from the plane fifth.

9. If Zacny dives from the plane immediately after Weiss, then which one of the following must be false?

    (A)   Larue dives from the plane first.
    (B)   Treviño dives from the plane third.
    (C)   Zacny dives from the plane third.
    (D)   Pei dives from the plane fourth.
    (E)   Zacny dives from the plane fourth.

10. If Treviño dives from the plane immediately after Larue, then each of the following could be true EXCEPT:

    (A)   Ohba dives from the plane third.
    (B)   Weiss dives from the plane third.
    (C)   Zacny dives from the plane third.
    (D)   Pei dives from the plane fourth.
    (E)   Weiss dives from the plane fourth.

GO ON TO THE NEXT PAGE.

Questions 11–17

A company's six vehicles—a hatchback, a limousine, a pickup, a roadster, a sedan, and a van—are serviced during a certain week—Monday through Saturday—one vehicle per day. The following conditions must apply:

> At least one of the vehicles is serviced later in the week than the hatchback.
> The roadster is serviced later in the week than the van and earlier in the week than the hatchback.
> Either the pickup and the van are serviced on consecutive days, or the pickup and the sedan are serviced on consecutive days, but not both.
> The sedan is serviced earlier in the week than the pickup or earlier in the week than the limousine, but not both.

11. Which one of the following could be the order in which the vehicles are serviced, from Monday through Saturday?

   (A)   the hatchback, the pickup, the sedan, the limousine, the van, the roadster
   (B)   the pickup, the sedan, the van, the roadster, the hatchback, the limousine
   (C)   the pickup, the van, the sedan, the roadster, the limousine, the hatchback
   (D)   the van, the roadster, the pickup, the hatchback, the sedan, the limousine
   (E)   the van, the sedan, the pickup, the roadster, the hatchback, the limousine

12. Which one of the following CANNOT be the vehicle serviced on Thursday?

   (A)   the hatchback
   (B)   the limousine
   (C)   the pickup
   (D)   the sedan
   (E)   the van

13. If neither the pickup nor the limousine is serviced on Monday, then which one of the following must be true?

   (A)   The hatchback and the limousine are serviced on consecutive days.
   (B)   The hatchback and the sedan are serviced on consecutive days.
   (C)   The van is serviced on Monday.
   (D)   The limousine is serviced on Saturday.
   (E)   The pickup is serviced on Saturday.

14. If the limousine is not serviced on Saturday, then each of the following could be true EXCEPT:

   (A)   The limousine is serviced on Monday.
   (B)   The roadster is serviced on Tuesday.
   (C)   The hatchback is serviced on Wednesday.
   (D)   The roadster is serviced on Wednesday.
   (E)   The sedan is serviced on Wednesday.

15. If the sedan is serviced earlier in the week than the pickup, then which one of the following could be true?

   (A)   The limousine is serviced on Wednesday.
   (B)   The sedan is serviced on Wednesday.
   (C)   The van is serviced on Wednesday.
   (D)   The hatchback is serviced on Friday.
   (E)   The limousine is serviced on Saturday.

16. If the limousine is serviced on Saturday, then which one of the following must be true?

   (A)   The pickup is serviced earlier in the week than the roadster.
   (B)   The pickup is serviced earlier in the week than the sedan.
   (C)   The sedan is serviced earlier in the week than the roadster.
   (D)   The hatchback and the limousine are serviced on consecutive days.
   (E)   The roadster and the hatchback are serviced on consecutive days.

17. Which one of the following could be the list of the vehicles serviced on Tuesday, Wednesday, and Friday, listed in that order?

   (A)   the pickup, the hatchback, the limousine
   (B)   the pickup, the roadster, the hatchback
   (C)   the sedan, the limousine, the hatchback
   (D)   the van, the limousine, the hatchback
   (E)   the van, the roadster, the limousine

GO ON TO THE NEXT PAGE.

Questions 18–23

A street entertainer has six boxes stacked one on top of the other and numbered consecutively 1 through 6, from the lowest box up to the highest. Each box contains a single ball, and each ball is one of three colors—green, red, or white. Onlookers are to guess the color of each ball in each box, given that the following conditions hold:

    There are more red balls than white balls.
    There is a box containing a green ball that is lower in the stack than any box that contains a red ball.
    There is a white ball in a box that is immediately below a box that contains a green ball.

18. If there are exactly two white balls, then which one of the following boxes could contain a green ball?

  (A)   box 1
  (B)   box 3
  (C)   box 4
  (D)   box 5
  (E)   box 6

19. If there are green balls in boxes 5 and 6, then which one of the following could be true?

  (A)   There are red balls in boxes 1 and 4.
  (B)   There are red balls in boxes 2 and 4.
  (C)   There is a white ball in box 1.
  (D)   There is a white ball in box 2.
  (E)   There is a white ball in box 3.

20. The ball in which one of the following boxes must be the same color as at least one of the other balls?

  (A)   box 2
  (B)   box 3
  (C)   box 4
  (D)   box 5
  (E)   box 6

21. Which one of the following must be true?

  (A)   There is a green ball in a box that is lower than box 4.
  (B)   There is a green ball in a box that is higher than box 4.
  (C)   There is a red ball in a box that is lower than box 4.
  (D)   There is a red ball in a box that is higher than box 4.
  (E)   There is a white ball in a box that is lower than box 4.

22. If there are red balls in boxes 2 and 3, then which one of the following could be true?

  (A)   There is a red ball in box 1.
  (B)   There is a white ball in box 1.
  (C)   There is a green ball in box 4.
  (D)   There is a red ball in box 5.
  (E)   There is a white ball in box 6.

23. If boxes 2, 3, and 4 all contain balls that are the same color as each other, then which one of the following must be true?

  (A)   Exactly two of the boxes contain a green ball.
  (B)   Exactly three of the boxes contain a green ball.
  (C)   Exactly three of the boxes contain a red ball.
  (D)   Exactly one of the boxes contains a white ball.
  (E)   Exactly two of the boxes contain a white ball.

S T O P

IF YOU FINISH BEFORE TIME IS CALLED, YOU MAY CHECK YOUR WORK ON THIS SECTION ONLY.
DO NOT WORK ON ANY OTHER SECTION IN THE TEST.

SECTION III
Time—35 minutes
26 Questions

Directions: The questions in this section are based on the reasoning contained in brief statements or passages. For some questions, more than one of the choices could conceivably answer the question. However, you are to choose the best answer; that is, the response that most accurately and completely answers the question. You should not make assumptions that are by commonsense standards implausible, superfluous, or incompatible with the passage. After you have chosen the best answer, blacken the corresponding space on your answer sheet.

1. Commentator: In last week's wreck involving one of Acme Engines' older locomotives, the engineer lost control of the train when his knee accidentally struck a fuel shut-down switch. Acme claims it is not liable because it never realized that the knee-level switches were a safety hazard. When asked why it relocated knee-level switches in its newer locomotives, Acme said engineers had complained that they were simply inconvenient. However, it is unlikely that Acme would have spent the $500,000 it took to relocate switches in the newer locomotives merely because of inconvenience. Thus, Acme Engines should be held liable for last week's wreck.

   The point that Acme Engines spent $500,000 relocating knee-level switches in its newer locomotives is offered in the commentator's argument as

   (A) proof that the engineer is not at all responsible for the train wreck
   (B) a reason for believing that the wreck would have occurred even if Acme Engines had remodeled their older locomotives
   (C) an explanation of why the train wreck occurred
   (D) evidence that knee-level switches are not in fact hazardous
   (E) an indication that Acme Engines had been aware of the potential dangers of knee-level switches before the wreck occurred

2. Artist: Almost everyone in this country really wants to be an artist even though they may have to work other jobs to pay the rent. After all, just about everyone I know hopes to someday be able to make a living as a painter, musician, or poet even if they currently work as dishwashers or discount store clerks.

   The reasoning in the artist's argument is flawed in that the argument

   (A) contains a premise that presupposes the truth of the conclusion
   (B) presumes that what is true of each person in a country is also true of the country's population as a whole
   (C) defends a view solely on the grounds that the view is widely held
   (D) bases its conclusion on a sample that is unlikely to accurately represent people in the country as a whole
   (E) fails to make a needed distinction between wanting to be an artist and making a living as an artist

3. The qwerty keyboard became the standard keyboard with the invention of the typewriter and remains the standard for typing devices today. If an alternative known as the Dvorak keyboard were today's standard, typists would type significantly faster. Nevertheless, it is not practical to switch to the Dvorak keyboard because the cost to society of switching, in terms of time, money, and frustration, would be greater than the benefits that would be ultimately gained from faster typing.

   The example above best illustrates which one of the following propositions?

   (A) Often it is not worthwhile to move to a process that improves speed if it comes at the expense of accuracy.
   (B) People usually settle on a standard because that standard is more efficient than any alternatives.
   (C) People often remain with an entrenched standard rather than move to a more efficient alternative simply because they dislike change.
   (D) The emotional cost associated with change is a factor that sometimes outweighs financial considerations.
   (E) The fact that a standard is already in wide use can be a crucial factor in making it a more practical choice than an alternative.

GO ON TO THE NEXT PAGE.

4. Sam: Mountain lions, a protected species, are preying on bighorn sheep, another protected species. We must let nature take its course and hope the bighorns survive.

   Meli: Nonsense. We must do what we can to ensure the survival of the bighorn, even if that means limiting the mountain lion population.

   Which one of the following is a point of disagreement between Meli and Sam?

   (A) Humans should not intervene to protect bighorn sheep from mountain lions.
   (B) The preservation of a species as a whole is more important than the loss of a few individuals.
   (C) The preservation of a predatory species is easier to ensure than the preservation of the species preyed upon.
   (D) Any measures to limit the mountain lion population would likely push the species to extinction.
   (E) If the population of mountain lions is not limited, the bighorn sheep species will not survive.

5. Parent: Pushing very young children into rigorous study in an effort to make our nation more competitive does more harm than good. Curricula for these young students must address their special developmental needs, and while rigorous work in secondary school makes sense, the same approach in the early years of primary school produces only short-term gains and may cause young children to burn out on schoolwork. Using very young students as pawns in the race to make the nation economically competitive is unfair and may ultimately work against us.

   Which one of the following can be inferred from the parent's statements?

   (A) For our nation to be competitive, our secondary school curriculum must include more rigorous study than it now does.
   (B) The developmental needs of secondary school students are not now being addressed in our high schools.
   (C) Our country can be competitive only if the developmental needs of all our students can be met.
   (D) A curriculum of rigorous study does not adequately address the developmental needs of primary school students.
   (E) Unless our nation encourages more rigorous study in the early years of primary school, we cannot be economically competitive.

6. A transit company's bus drivers are evaluated by supervisors riding with each driver. Drivers complain that this affects their performance, but because the supervisor's presence affects every driver's performance, those drivers performing best with a supervisor aboard will likely also be the best drivers under normal conditions.

   Which one of the following is an assumption on which the argument depends?

   (A) There is no effective way of evaluating the bus drivers' performance without having supervisors ride with them.
   (B) The supervisors are excellent judges of a bus driver's performance.
   (C) For most bus drivers, the presence of a supervisor makes their performance slightly worse than it otherwise would be.
   (D) The bus drivers are each affected in roughly the same way and to the same extent by the presence of the supervisor.
   (E) The bus drivers themselves are able to deliver accurate assessments of their driving performance.

7. Economic growth accelerates business demand for the development of new technologies. Businesses supplying these new technologies are relatively few, while those wishing to buy them are many. Yet an acceleration of technological change can cause suppliers as well as buyers of new technologies to fail.

   Which one of the following is most strongly supported by the information above?

   (A) Businesses supplying new technologies are more likely to prosper in times of accelerated technological change than other businesses.
   (B) Businesses that supply new technologies may not always benefit from economic growth.
   (C) The development of new technologies may accelerate economic growth in general.
   (D) Businesses that adopt new technologies are most likely to prosper in a period of general economic growth.
   (E) Economic growth increases business failures.

GO ON TO THE NEXT PAGE.

8. Energy analyst: During this record-breaking heat wave, air conditioner use has overloaded the region's electrical power grid, resulting in frequent power blackouts throughout the region. For this reason, residents have been asked to cut back voluntarily on air conditioner use in their homes. But even if this request is heeded, blackouts will probably occur unless the heat wave abates.

Which one of the following, if true, most helps to resolve the apparent discrepancy in the information above?

(A) Air-conditioning is not the only significant drain on the electrical system in the area.

(B) Most air-conditioning in the region is used to cool businesses and factories.

(C) Most air-conditioning systems could be made more energy efficient by implementing simple design modifications.

(D) Residents of the region are not likely to reduce their air conditioner use voluntarily during particularly hot weather.

(E) The heat wave is expected to abate in the near future.

9. Long-term and short-term relaxation training are two common forms of treatment for individuals experiencing problematic levels of anxiety. Yet studies show that on average, regardless of which form of treatment one receives, symptoms of anxiety decrease to a normal level within the short-term-training time period. Thus, for most people the generally more expensive long-term training is unwarranted.

Which one of the following, if true, most weakens the argument?

(A) A decrease in symptoms of anxiety often occurs even with no treatment or intervention by a mental health professional.

(B) Short-term relaxation training conducted by a more experienced practitioner can be more expensive than long-term training conducted by a less experienced practitioner.

(C) Recipients of long-term training are much less likely than recipients of short-term training to have recurrences of problematic levels of anxiety.

(D) The fact that an individual thinks that a treatment will reduce his or her anxiety tends, in and of itself, to reduce the individual's anxiety.

(E) Short-term relaxation training involves the teaching of a wider variety of anxiety-combating relaxation techniques than does long-term training.

10. Editorial: Many critics of consumerism insist that advertising persuades people that they need certain consumer goods when they merely desire them. However, this accusation rests on a fuzzy distinction, that between wants and needs. In life, it is often impossible to determine whether something is merely desirable or whether it is essential to one's happiness.

Which one of the following most accurately expresses the conclusion drawn in the editorial's argument?

(A) The claim that advertising persuades people that they need things that they merely want rests on a fuzzy distinction.

(B) Many critics of consumerism insist that advertising attempts to blur people's ability to distinguish between wants and needs.

(C) There is nothing wrong with advertising that tries to persuade people that they need certain consumer goods.

(D) Many critics of consumerism fail to realize that certain things are essential to human happiness.

(E) Critics of consumerism often use fuzzy distinctions to support their claims.

11. People who browse the web for medical information often cannot discriminate between scientifically valid information and quackery. Much of the quackery is particularly appealing to readers with no medical background because it is usually written more clearly than scientific papers. Thus, people who rely on the web when attempting to diagnose their medical conditions are likely to do themselves more harm than good.

Which one of the following is an assumption the argument requires?

(A) People who browse the web for medical information typically do so in an attempt to diagnose their medical conditions.

(B) People who attempt to diagnose their medical conditions are likely to do themselves more harm than good unless they rely exclusively on scientifically valid information.

(C) People who have sufficient medical knowledge to discriminate between scientifically valid information and quackery will do themselves no harm if they rely on the web when attempting to diagnose their medical conditions.

(D) Many people who browse the web assume that information is not scientifically valid unless it is clearly written.

(E) People attempting to diagnose their medical conditions will do themselves more harm than good only if they rely on quackery instead of scientifically valid information.

GO ON TO THE NEXT PAGE.

12. When adults toss balls to very young children they generally try to toss them as slowly as possible to compensate for the children's developing coordination. But recent studies show that despite their developing coordination, children actually have an easier time catching balls that are thrown at a faster speed.

Which one of the following, if true, most helps to explain why very young children find it easier to catch balls that are thrown at a faster speed?

(A) Balls thrown at a faster speed, unlike balls thrown at a slower speed, trigger regions in the brain that control the tracking of objects for self-defense.

(B) Balls that are tossed more slowly tend to have a higher arc that makes it less likely that the ball will be obscured by the body of the adult tossing it.

(C) Adults generally find it easier to catch balls that are thrown slowly than balls that are thrown at a faster speed.

(D) Children are able to toss balls back to the adults with more accuracy when they throw fast than when they throw the ball back more slowly.

(E) There is a limit to how fast the balls can be tossed to the children before the children start to have more difficulty in catching them.

13. Like a genetic profile, a functional magnetic-resonance image (fMRI) of the brain can contain information that a patient wishes to keep private. An fMRI of a brain also contains enough information about a patient's skull to create a recognizable image of that patient's face. A genetic profile can be linked to a patient only by referring to labels or records.

The statements above, if true, most strongly support which one of the following?

(A) It is not important that medical providers apply labels to fMRIs of patients' brains.

(B) An fMRI has the potential to compromise patient privacy in circumstances in which a genetic profile would not.

(C) In most cases patients cannot be reasonably sure that the information in a genetic profile will be kept private.

(D) Most of the information contained in an fMRI of a person's brain is also contained in that person's genetic profile.

(E) Patients are more concerned about threats to privacy posed by fMRIs than they are about those posed by genetic profiles.

14. Council member: I recommend that the abandoned shoe factory be used as a municipal emergency shelter. Some council members assert that the courthouse would be a better shelter site, but they have provided no evidence of this. Thus, the shoe factory would be a better shelter site.

A questionable technique used in the council member's argument is that of

(A) asserting that a lack of evidence against a view is proof that the view is correct

(B) accepting a claim simply because advocates of an opposing claim have not adequately defended their view

(C) attacking the proponents of the courthouse rather than addressing their argument

(D) attempting to persuade its audience by appealing to their fear

(E) attacking an argument that is not held by any actual council member

15. It was misleading for James to tell the Core Curriculum Committee that the chair of the Anthropology Department had endorsed his proposal. The chair of the Anthropology Department had told James that his proposal had her endorsement, but only if the draft proposal she saw included all the recommendations James would ultimately make to the Core Curriculum Committee.

The argument relies on which one of the following assumptions?

(A) If the chair of the Anthropology Department did not endorse James's proposed recommendations, the Core Curriculum Committee would be unlikely to implement them.

(B) The chair of the Anthropology Department would have been opposed to any recommendations James proposed to the Core Curriculum Committee other than those she had seen.

(C) James thought that the Core Curriculum Committee would implement the proposed recommendations only if they believed that the recommendations had been endorsed by the chair of the Anthropology Department.

(D) James thought that the chair of the Anthropology Department would have endorsed all of the recommendations that he proposed to the Core Curriculum Committee.

(E) The draft proposal that the chair of the Anthropology Department had seen did not include all of the recommendations in James's proposal to the Core Curriculum Committee.

GO ON TO THE NEXT PAGE.

16. Travaillier Corporation has recently hired employees with experience in the bus tour industry, and its executives have also been negotiating with charter bus companies that subcontract with bus tour companies. But Travaillier has traditionally focused on serving consumers who travel primarily by air, and marketing surveys show that Travaillier's traditional consumers have not changed their vacation preferences. Therefore, Travaillier must be attempting to enlarge its consumer base by attracting new customers.

Which one of the following, if true, would most weaken the argument?

(A) In the past, Travaillier has found it very difficult to change its customers' vacation preferences.
(B) Several travel companies other than Travaillier have recently tried and failed to expand into the bus tour business.
(C) At least one of Travaillier's new employees not only has experience in the bus tour industry but has also designed air travel vacation packages.
(D) Some of Travaillier's competitors have increased profits by concentrating their attention on their customers who spend the most on vacations.
(E) The industry consultants employed by Travaillier typically recommend that companies expand by introducing their current customers to new products and services.

17. Educator: Traditional classroom education is ineffective because education in such an environment is not truly a social process and only social processes can develop students' insights. In the traditional classroom, the teacher acts from outside the group and interaction between teachers and students is rigid and artificial.

The educator's conclusion follows logically if which one of the following is assumed?

(A) Development of insight takes place only if genuine education also occurs.
(B) Classroom education is effective if the interaction between teachers and students is neither rigid nor artificial.
(C) All social processes involve interaction that is neither rigid nor artificial.
(D) Education is not effective unless it leads to the development of insight.
(E) The teacher does not act from outside the group in a nontraditional classroom.

18. The probability of avoiding heart disease is increased if one avoids fat in one's diet. Furthermore, one is less likely to eat fat if one avoids eating dairy foods. Thus the probability of maintaining good health is increased by avoiding dairy foods.

The reasoning in the argument is most vulnerable to criticism on which one of the following grounds?

(A) The argument ignores the possibility that, even though a practice may have potentially negative consequences, its elimination may also have negative consequences.
(B) The argument fails to consider the possibility that there are more ways than one of decreasing the risk of a certain type of occurrence.
(C) The argument presumes, without providing justification, that factors that carry increased risks of negative consequences ought to be eliminated.
(D) The argument fails to show that the evidence appealed to is relevant to the conclusion asserted.
(E) The argument fails to consider that what is probable will not necessarily occur.

19. Professor: One cannot frame an accurate conception of one's physical environment on the basis of a single momentary perception, since each such glimpse occurs from only one particular perspective. Similarly, any history book gives only a distorted view of the past, since it reflects the biases and prejudices of its author.

The professor's argument proceeds by

(A) attempting to show that one piece of reasoning is incorrect by comparing it with another, presumably flawed, piece of reasoning
(B) developing a case for one particular conclusion by arguing that if that conclusion were false, absurd consequences would follow
(C) making a case for the conclusion of one argument by showing that argument's resemblance to another, presumably cogent, argument
(D) arguing that because something has a certain group of characteristics, it must also have another, closely related, characteristic
(E) arguing that a type of human cognition is unreliable in one instance because it has been shown to be unreliable under similar circumstances

GO ON TO THE NEXT PAGE.

20. To date, most of the proposals that have been endorsed by the Citizens League have been passed by the city council. Thus, any future proposal that is endorsed by the Citizens League will probably be passed as well.

The pattern of reasoning in which one of the following arguments is most similar to that in the argument above?

(A) Most of the Vasani grants that have been awarded in previous years have gone to academic biologists. Thus, if most of the Vasani grants awarded next year are awarded to academics, most of these will probably be biologists.

(B) Most of the individual trees growing on the coastal islands in this area are deciduous. Therefore, most of the tree species on these islands are probably deciduous varieties.

(C) Most of the editors who have worked for the local newspaper have not been sympathetic to local farmers. Thus, if the newspaper hires someone who is sympathetic to local farmers, they will probably not be hired as an editor.

(D) Most of the entries that were received after the deadline for last year's photography contest were rejected by the judges' committee. Thus, the people whose entries were received after the deadline last year will probably send them in well before the deadline this year.

(E) Most of the stone artifacts that have been found at the archaeological site have been domestic tools. Thus, if the next artifact found at the site is made of stone, it will probably be a domestic tool.

21. Chemist: The molecules of a certain weed-killer are always present in two forms, one the mirror image of the other. One form of the molecule kills weeds, while the other has no effect on them. As a result, the effectiveness of the weed-killer in a given situation is heavily influenced by which of the two forms is more concentrated in the soil, which in turn varies widely because local soil conditions will usually favor the breakdown of one form or the other. Thus, much of the data on the effects of this weed-killer are probably misleading.

Which one of the following, if true, most strengthens the chemist's argument?

(A) In general, if the molecules of a weed-killer are always present in two forms, then it is likely that weeds are killed by one of those two forms but unaffected by the other.

(B) Almost all of the data on the effects of the weed-killer are drawn from laboratory studies in which both forms of the weed-killer's molecules are equally concentrated in the soil and equally likely to break down in that soil.

(C) Of the two forms of the weed-killer's molecules, the one that kills weeds is found in most local soil conditions to be the more concentrated form.

(D) The data on the effects of the weed-killer are drawn from studies of the weed-killer under a variety of soil conditions similar to those in which the weed-killer is normally applied.

(E) Data on the weed-killer's effects that rely solely on the examination of the effects of only one of the two forms of the weed-killer's molecules will almost certainly be misleading.

GO ON TO THE NEXT PAGE.

22. Principle: A police officer is eligible for a Mayor's Commendation if the officer has an exemplary record, but not otherwise; an officer eligible for the award who did something this year that exceeded what could be reasonably expected of a police officer should receive the award if the act saved someone's life.

Conclusion: Officer Franklin should receive a Mayor's Commendation but Officer Penn should not.

From which one of the following sets of facts can the conclusion be properly drawn using the principle?

(A) In saving a child from drowning this year, Franklin and Penn both risked their lives beyond what could be reasonably expected of a police officer. Franklin has an exemplary record but Penn does not.

(B) Both Franklin and Penn have exemplary records, and each officer saved a child from drowning earlier this year. However, in doing so, Franklin went beyond what could be reasonably expected of a police officer; Penn did not.

(C) Neither Franklin nor Penn has an exemplary record. But, in saving the life of an accident victim, Franklin went beyond what could be reasonably expected of a police officer. In the only case in which Penn saved someone's life this year, Penn was merely doing what could be reasonably expected of an officer under the circumstances.

(D) At least once this year, Franklin has saved a person's life in such a way as to exceed what could be reasonably expected of a police officer. Penn has not saved anyone's life this year.

(E) Both Franklin and Penn have exemplary records. On several occasions this year Franklin has saved people's lives, and on many occasions this year Franklin has exceeded what could be reasonably expected of a police officer. On no occasions this year has Penn saved a person's life or exceeded what could be reasonably expected of an officer.

23. Essayist: It is much less difficult to live an enjoyable life if one is able to make lifestyle choices that accord with one's personal beliefs and then see those choices accepted by others. It is possible for people to find this kind of acceptance by choosing friends and associates who share many of their personal beliefs. Thus, no one should be denied the freedom to choose the people with whom he or she will associate.

Which one of the following principles, if valid, most helps to justify the essayist's argument?

(A) No one should be denied the freedom to make lifestyle choices that accord with his or her personal beliefs.

(B) One should associate with at least some people who share many of one's personal beliefs.

(C) If having a given freedom could make it less difficult for someone to live an enjoyable life, then no one should be denied that freedom.

(D) No one whose enjoyment of life depends, at least in part, on friends and associates who share many of the same personal beliefs should be deliberately prevented from having such friends and associates.

(E) One may choose for oneself the people with whom one will associate, if doing so could make it easier to live an enjoyable life.

24. Physician: The rise in blood pressure that commonly accompanies aging often results from a calcium deficiency. This deficiency is frequently caused by a deficiency in the active form of vitamin D needed in order for the body to absorb calcium. Since the calcium in one glass of milk per day can easily make up for any underlying calcium deficiency, some older people can lower their blood pressure by drinking milk.

The physician's conclusion is properly drawn if which one of the following is assumed?

(A) There is in milk, in a form that older people can generally utilize, enough of the active form of vitamin D and any other substances needed in order for the body to absorb the calcium in that milk.

(B) Milk does not contain any substance that is likely to cause increased blood pressure in older people.

(C) Older people's drinking one glass of milk per day does not contribute to a deficiency in the active form of vitamin D needed in order for the body to absorb the calcium in that milk.

(D) People who consume high quantities of calcium together with the active form of vitamin D and any other substances needed in order for the body to absorb calcium have normal blood pressure.

(E) Anyone who has a deficiency in the active form of vitamin D also has a calcium deficiency.

GO ON TO THE NEXT PAGE.

25. Political philosopher: A just system of taxation would require each person's contribution to correspond directly to the amount the society as a whole contributes to serve that person's interests. For purposes of taxation, wealth is the most objective way to determine how well the society has served the interest of any individual. Therefore, each person should be taxed solely in proportion to her or his income.

The flawed reasoning in the political philosopher's argument is most similar to that in which one of the following?

(A) Cars should be taxed in proportion to the danger that they pose. The most reliable measure of this danger is the speed at which a car can travel. Therefore, cars should be taxed only in proportion to their ability to accelerate quickly.

(B) People should be granted autonomy in proportion to their maturity. A certain psychological test was designed to provide an objective measure of maturity. Therefore, those scoring above high school level on the test should be granted complete autonomy.

(C) Everyone should pay taxes solely in proportion to the benefits they receive from government. Many government programs provide subsidies for large corporations. Therefore, a just tax would require corporations to pay a greater share of their income in taxes than individual citizens pay.

(D) Individuals who confer large material benefits upon society should receive high incomes. Those with high incomes should pay correspondingly high taxes. Therefore, we as a society should place high taxes on activities that confer large benefits upon society.

(E) Justice requires that health care be given in proportion to each individual's need. Therefore, we need to ensure that the most seriously ill hospital patients are given the highest priority for receiving care.

26. A recent poll showed that almost half of the city's residents believe that Mayor Walker is guilty of ethics violations. Surprisingly, however, 52 percent of those surveyed judged Walker's performance as mayor to be good or excellent, which is no lower than it was before anyone accused him of ethics violations.

Which one of the following, if true, most helps to explain the surprising fact stated above?

(A) Almost all of the people who believe that Walker is guilty of ethics violations had thought, even before he was accused of those violations, that his performance as mayor was poor.

(B) In the time since Walker was accused of ethics violations, there has been an increase in the percentage of city residents who judge the performance of Walker's political opponents to be good or excellent.

(C) About a fifth of those polled did not know that Walker had been accused of ethics violations.

(D) Walker is currently up for reelection, and anticorruption groups in the city have expressed support for Walker's opponent.

(E) Walker has defended himself against the accusations by arguing that the alleged ethics violations were the result of honest mistakes by his staff members.

S T O P

IF YOU FINISH BEFORE TIME IS CALLED, YOU MAY CHECK YOUR WORK ON THIS SECTION ONLY.
DO NOT WORK ON ANY OTHER SECTION IN THE TEST.

SECTION IV

Time—35 minutes

27 Questions

<u>Directions:</u> Each set of questions in this section is based on a single passage or a pair of passages. The questions are to be answered on the basis of what is <u>stated</u> or <u>implied</u> in the passage or pair of passages. For some of the questions, more than one of the choices could conceivably answer the question. However, you are to choose the <u>best</u> answer; that is, the response that most accurately and completely answers the question, and blacken the corresponding space on your answer sheet.

In Alaska, tradition is a powerful legal concept, appearing in a wide variety of legal contexts relating to natural-resource and public-lands activities. Both state and federal laws in the United States assign
(5) privileges and exemptions to individuals engaged in "traditional" activities using otherwise off-limits land and resources. But in spite of its prevalence in statutory law, the term "tradition" is rarely defined. Instead, there seems to be a presumption that its
(10) meaning is obvious. Failure to define "tradition" clearly in written law has given rise to problematic and inconsistent legal results.

One of the most prevalent ideas associated with the term "tradition" in the law is that tradition is based
(15) on long-standing practice, where "long-standing" refers not only to the passage of time but also to the continuity and regularity of a practice. But two recent court cases involving indigenous use of sea otter pelts illustrate the problems that can arise in the application
(20) of this sense of "traditional."

The hunting of sea otters was initially prohibited by the Fur Seal Treaty of 1910. The Marine Mammal Protection Act (MMPA) of 1972 continued the prohibition, but it also included an Alaska Native
(25) exemption, which allowed takings of protected animals for use in creating authentic native articles by means of "traditional native handicrafts." The U.S. Fish and Wildlife Service (FWS) subsequently issued regulations defining authentic native articles as those
(30) "commonly produced" before 1972, when the MMPA took effect. Not covered by the exemption, according to the FWS, were items produced from sea otter pelts, because Alaska Natives had not produced such handicrafts "within living memory."
(35) In 1986, FWS agents seized articles of clothing made from sea otter pelts from Marina Katelnikoff, an Aleut. She sued, but the district court upheld the FWS regulations. Then in 1991 Katelnikoff joined a similar suit brought by Boyd Dickinson, a Tlingit from whom
(40) articles of clothing made from sea otter pelts had also been seized. After hearing testimony establishing that Alaska Natives had made many uses of sea otters before the occupation of the territory by Russia in the late 1700s, the court reconsidered what constituted a
(45) traditional item under the statute. The court now held that the FWS's regulations were based on a "strained interpretation" of the word "traditional," and that the reference to "living memory" imposed an excessively restrictive time frame. The court stated, "The fact that
(50) Alaskan natives were prevented, by circumstances beyond their control, from exercising a tradition for a

given period of time does not mean that it has been lost forever or that it has become any less a 'tradition.' It defies common sense to define 'traditional' in such
(55) a way that only those traditions that were exercised during a comparatively short period in history could qualify as 'traditional.'"

1. Which one of the following most accurately expresses the main point of the passage?

(A) Two cases involving the use of sea otter pelts by Alaska Natives illustrate the difficulties surrounding the application of the legal concept of tradition in Alaska.

(B) Two court decisions have challenged the notion that for an activity to be considered "traditional," it must be shown to be a long-standing activity that has been regularly and continually practiced.

(C) Two court cases involving the use of sea otter pelts by Alaska Natives exemplify the wave of lawsuits that are now occurring in response to changes in natural-resource and public-lands regulations.

(D) Definitions of certain legal terms long taken for granted are being reviewed in light of new evidence that has come from historical sources relating to Alaska Native culture.

(E) Alaskan state laws and U.S. federal laws are being challenged by Alaska Natives because the laws are not sufficiently sensitive to indigenous peoples' concerns.

GO ON TO THE NEXT PAGE.

2. The court in the 1991 case referred to the FWS's interpretation of the term "traditional" as "strained" (line 46) because, in the court's view, the interpretation

(A) ignored the ways in which Alaska Natives have historically understood the term "traditional"
(B) was not consonant with any dictionary definition of "traditional"
(C) was inconsistent with what the term "traditional" is normally understood to mean
(D) led the FWS to use the word "traditional" to describe a practice that should not have been described as such
(E) failed to specify which handicrafts qualified to be designated as "traditional"

3. According to the passage, the court's decision in the 1991 case was based on which one of the following?

(A) a narrow interpretation of the term "long-standing"
(B) a common-sense interpretation of the phrase "within living memory"
(C) strict adherence to the intent of FWS regulations
(D) a new interpretation of the Fur Seal Treaty of 1910
(E) testimony establishing certain historical facts

4. The passage most strongly suggests that the court in the 1986 case believed that "traditional" should be defined in a way that

(A) reflects a compromise between the competing concerns surrounding the issue at hand
(B) emphasizes the continuity and regularity of practices to which the term is applied
(C) reflects the term's usage in everyday discourse
(D) encourages the term's application to recently developed, as well as age-old, activities
(E) reflects the concerns of the people engaging in what they consider to be traditional activities

5. Which one of the following is most strongly suggested by the passage?

(A) Between 1910 and 1972, Alaska Natives were prohibited from hunting sea otters.
(B) Traditional items made from sea otter pelts were specifically mentioned in the Alaska Native exemption of the MMPA.
(C) In the late 1700s, Russian hunters pressured the Russian government to bar Alaska Natives from hunting sea otters.
(D) By 1972, the sea otter population in Alaska had returned to the levels at which it had been prior to the late 1700s.
(E) Prior to the late 1700s, sea otters were the marine animal most often hunted by Alaska Natives.

6. The author's reference to the Fur Seal Treaty (line 22) primarily serves to

(A) establish the earliest point in time at which fur seals were considered to be on the brink of extinction
(B) indicate that several animals in addition to sea otters were covered by various regulatory exemptions issued over the years
(C) demonstrate that there is a well-known legal precedent for prohibiting the hunting of protected animals
(D) suggest that the sea otter population was imperiled by Russian seal hunters and not by Alaska Natives
(E) help explain the evolution of Alaska Natives' legal rights with respect to handicrafts defined as "traditional"

7. The ruling in the 1991 case would be most relevant as a precedent for deciding in a future case that which one of the following is a "traditional" Alaska Native handicraft?

(A) A handicraft no longer practiced but shown by archaeological evidence to have been common among indigenous peoples several millennia ago
(B) A handicraft that commonly involves taking the pelts of more than one species that has been designated as endangered
(C) A handicraft that was once common but was discontinued when herd animals necessary for its practice abandoned their local habitat due to industrial development
(D) A handicraft about which only a very few indigenous craftspeople were historically in possession of any knowledge
(E) A handicraft about which young Alaska Natives know little because, while it was once common, few elder Alaska Natives still practice it

GO ON TO THE NEXT PAGE.

The literary development of Kate Chopin, author of *The Awakening* (1899), took her through several phases of nineteenth-century women's fiction. Born in 1850, Chopin grew up with the sentimental novels that
(5) formed the bulk of the fiction of the mid–nineteenth century. In these works, authors employed elevated, romantic language to portray female characters whose sole concern was to establish their social positions through courtship and marriage. Later, when she
(10) started writing her own fiction, Chopin took as her models the works of a group of women writers known as the local colorists.

After 1865, what had traditionally been regarded as "women's culture" began to dissolve as women
(15) entered higher education, the professions, and the political world in greater numbers. The local colorists, who published stories about regional life in the 1870s and 1880s, were attracted to the new worlds opening up to women, and felt free to move within these worlds
(20) as artists. Like anthropologists, the local colorists observed culture and character with almost scientific detachment. However, as "women's culture" continued to disappear, the local colorists began to mourn its demise by investing its images with mythic significance.
(25) In their stories, the garden became a paradisal sanctuary; the house became an emblem of female nurturing; and the artifacts of domesticity became virtual totemic objects.

Unlike the local colorists, Chopin devoted herself
(30) to telling stories of loneliness, isolation, and frustration. But she used the conventions of the local colorists to solve a specific narrative problem: how to deal with extreme psychological states without resorting to the excesses of the sentimental novels she read as a youth.
(35) By reporting narrative events as if they were part of a region's "local color," Chopin could tell rather shocking or even melodramatic tales in an uninflected manner.

Chopin did not share the local colorists' growing nostalgia for the past, however, and by the 1890s she
(40) was looking beyond them to the more ambitious models offered by a movement known as the New Women. In the form as well as the content of their work, the New Women writers pursued freedom and innovation. They modified the form of the sentimental
(45) novel to make room for interludes of fantasy and parable, especially episodes in which women dream of an entirely different world than the one they inhabit. Instead of the crisply plotted short stories that had been the primary genre of the local colorists, the New
(50) Women writers experimented with impressionistic methods in an effort to explore hitherto unrecorded aspects of female consciousness. In *The Awakening*, Chopin embraced this impressionistic approach more fully to produce 39 numbered sections of uneven
(55) length unified less by their style or content than by their sustained focus on faithfully rendering the workings of the protagonist's mind.

8. Which one of the following statements most accurately summarizes the content of the passage?

(A) Although Chopin drew a great deal of the material for *The Awakening* from the concerns of the New Women, she adapted them, using the techniques of the local colorists, to recapture the atmosphere of the novels she had read in her youth.

(B) Avoiding the sentimental excesses of novels she read in her youth, and influenced first by the conventions of the local colorists and then by the innovative methods of the New Women, Chopin developed the literary style she used in *The Awakening*.

(C) With its stylistic shifts, variety of content, and attention to the internal psychology of its characters, Chopin's *The Awakening* was unlike any work of fiction written during the nineteenth century.

(D) In *The Awakening*, Chopin rebelled against the stylistic restraint of the local colorists, choosing instead to tell her story in elevated, romantic language that would more accurately convey her protagonist's loneliness and frustration.

(E) Because she felt a kinship with the subject matter but not the stylistic conventions of the local colorists, Chopin turned to the New Women as models for the style she was struggling to develop in *The Awakening*.

9. With which one of the following statements about the local colorists would Chopin have been most likely to agree?

(A) Their idealization of settings and objects formerly associated with "women's culture" was misguided.

(B) Their tendency to observe character dispassionately caused their fiction to have little emotional impact.

(C) Their chief contribution to literature lay in their status as inspiration for the New Women.

(D) Their focus on regional life prevented them from addressing the new realms opening up to women.

(E) Their conventions prevented them from portraying extreme psychological states with scientific detachment.

GO ON TO THE NEXT PAGE.

10. According to the passage, which one of the following conventions did Chopin adopt from other nineteenth-century women writers?

(A) elevated, romantic language
(B) mythic images of "women's culture"
(C) detached narrative stance
(D) strong plot lines
(E) lonely, isolated protagonists

11. As it is used by the author in line 14 of the passage, "women's culture" most probably refers to a culture that was expressed primarily through women's

(A) domestic experiences
(B) regional customs
(C) artistic productions
(D) educational achievements
(E) political activities

12. The author of the passage describes the sentimental novels of the mid–nineteenth century in lines 3–9 primarily in order to

(A) argue that Chopin's style represents an attempt to mimic these novels
(B) explain why Chopin later rejected the work of the local colorists
(C) establish the background against which Chopin's fiction developed
(D) illustrate the excesses to which Chopin believed nostalgic tendencies would lead
(E) prove that women's literature was already flourishing by the time Chopin began to write

13. The passage suggests that one of the differences between *The Awakening* and the work of the New Women was that *The Awakening*

(A) attempted to explore aspects of female consciousness
(B) described the dream world of female characters
(C) employed impressionism more consistently throughout
(D) relied more on fantasy to suggest psychological states
(E) displayed greater unity of style and content

14. The primary purpose of the passage is to

(A) educate readers of *The Awakening* about aspects of Chopin's life that are reflected in the novel
(B) discuss the relationship between Chopin's artistic development and changes in nineteenth-century women's fiction
(C) trace the evolution of nineteenth-century women's fiction using Chopin as a typical example
(D) counter a claim that Chopin's fiction was influenced by external social circumstances
(E) weigh the value of Chopin's novels and stories against those of other writers of her time

15. The work of the New Women, as it is characterized in the passage, gives the most support for which one of the following generalizations?

(A) Works of fiction written in a passionate, engaged style are more apt to effect changes in social customs than are works written in a scientific, detached style.
(B) Even writers who advocate social change can end up regretting the change once it has occurred.
(C) Changes in social customs inevitably lead to changes in literary techniques as writers attempt to make sense of the new social realities.
(D) Innovations in fictional technique grow out of writers' attempts to describe aspects of reality that have been neglected in previous works.
(E) Writers can most accurately depict extreme psychological states by using an uninflected manner.

GO ON TO THE NEXT PAGE.

Until the 1950s, most scientists believed that the geology of the ocean floor had remained essentially unchanged for many millions of years. But this idea became insupportable as new discoveries were made.
(5) First, scientists noticed that the ocean floor exhibited odd magnetic variations. Though unexpected, this was not entirely surprising, because it was known that basalt—the volcanic rock making up much of the ocean floor—contains magnetite, a strongly magnetic
(10) mineral that was already known to locally distort compass readings on land. This distortion is due to the fact that although some basalt has so-called "normal" polarity—that is, the magnetite in it has the same polarity as the earth's present magnetic field—other
(15) basalt has reversed polarity, an alignment opposite that of the present field. This occurs because in magma (molten rock), grains of magnetite—behaving like little compass needles—align themselves with the earth's magnetic field, which has reversed at various
(20) times throughout history. When magma cools to form solid basalt, the alignment of the magnetite grains is "locked in," recording the earth's polarity at the time of cooling.

As more of the ocean floor was mapped, the
(25) magnetic variations revealed recognizable patterns, particularly in the area around the other great oceanic discovery of the 1950s: the global mid-ocean ridge, an immense submarine mountain range that winds its way around the earth much like the seams of a baseball.
(30) Alternating stripes of rock with differing polarities are laid out in rows on either side of the mid-ocean ridge: one stripe with normal polarity and the next with reversed polarity. Scientists theorized that mid-ocean ridges mark structurally weak zones where the ocean
(35) floor is being pulled apart along the ridge crest. New magma from deep within the earth rises easily through these weak zones and eventually erupts along the crest of the ridges to create new oceanic crust. Over millions of years, this process, called ocean floor spreading,
(40) built the mid-ocean ridge.

This theory was supported by several lines of evidence. First, at or near the ridge crest, the rocks are very young, and they become progressively older away from the crest. Further, the youngest rocks all
(45) have normal polarity. Finally, because geophysicists had already determined the ages of continental volcanic rocks and, by measuring the magnetic orientation of these same rocks, had assigned ages to the earth's recent magnetic reversals, they were able to compare
(50) these known ages of magnetic reversals with the ocean floor's magnetic striping pattern, enabling scientists to show that, if we assume that the ocean floor moved away from the spreading center at a rate of several centimeters per year, there is a remarkable correlation
(55) between the ages of the earth's magnetic reversals and the striping pattern.

16. Which one of the following most accurately expresses the main idea of the passage?

(A) In the 1950s, scientists refined their theories concerning the process by which the ocean floor was formed many millions of years ago.

(B) The discovery of basalt's magnetic properties in the 1950s led scientists to formulate a new theory to account for the magnetic striping on the ocean floor.

(C) In the 1950s, two significant discoveries led to the transformation of scientific views about the geology of the oceans.

(D) Local distortions to compass readings are caused, scientists have discovered, by magma that rises through weak zones in the ocean floor to create new oceanic crust.

(E) The discovery of the ocean floor's magnetic variations convinced scientists of the need to map the entire ocean floor, which in turn led to the discovery of the global mid-ocean ridge.

17. The author characterizes the correlation mentioned in the last sentence of the passage as "remarkable" in order to suggest that the correlation

(A) indicates that ocean floor spreading occurs at an extremely slow rate

(B) explains the existence of the global mid-ocean ridge

(C) demonstrates that the earth's magnetic field is considerably stronger than previously believed

(D) provides strong confirmation of the ocean floor spreading theory

(E) reveals that the earth's magnetic reversals have occurred at very regular intervals

18. According to the passage, which one of the following is true of magnetite grains?

(A) In the youngest basalt, they are aligned with the earth's current polarity.

(B) In magma, most but not all of them align themselves with the earth's magnetic field.

(C) They are not found in other types of rock besides basalt.

(D) They are about the size of typical grains of sand.

(E) They are too small to be visible to the naked eye.

GO ON TO THE NEXT PAGE.

19. If the time intervals between the earth's magnetic field reversals fluctuate greatly, then, based on the passage, which one of the following is most likely to be true?

(A) Compass readings are most likely to be distorted near the peaks of the mid-ocean ridge.
(B) It is this fluctuation that causes the ridge to wind around the earth like the seams on a baseball.
(C) Some of the magnetic stripes of basalt on the ocean floor are much wider than others.
(D) Continental rock is a more reliable indicator of the earth's magnetic field reversals than is oceanic rock.
(E) Within any given magnetic stripe on the ocean floor, the age of the basalt does not vary.

20. Which one of the following would, if true, most help to support the ocean floor spreading theory?

(A) There are types of rock other than basalt that are known to distort compass readings.
(B) The ages of the earth's magnetic reversals have been verified by means other than examining magnetite grains in rock.
(C) Pieces of basalt similar to the type found on the mid-ocean ridge have been found on the continents.
(D) Along its length, the peak of the mid-ocean ridge varies greatly in height above the ocean floor.
(E) Basalt is the only type of volcanic rock found in portions of the ocean floor nearest to the continents.

21. Which one of the following is most strongly supported by the passage?

(A) Submarine basalt found near the continents is likely to be some of the oldest rock on the ocean floor.
(B) The older a sample of basalt is, the more times it has reversed its polarity.
(C) Compass readings are more likely to become distorted at sea than on land.
(D) The magnetic fields surrounding magnetite grains gradually weaken over millions of years on the ocean floor.
(E) Any rock that exhibits present-day magnetic polarity was formed after the latest reversal of the earth's magnetic field.

GO ON TO THE NEXT PAGE.

Passage A

Central to the historian's profession and scholarship has been the ideal of objectivity. The assumptions upon which this ideal rests include a commitment to the reality of the past, a sharp separation
(5) between fact and value, and above all, a distinction between history and fiction.

According to this ideal, historical facts are prior to and independent of interpretation: the value of an interpretation should be judged by how well it accounts
(10) for the facts; if an interpretation is contradicted by facts, it should be abandoned. The fact that successive generations of historians have ascribed different meanings to past events does not mean, as relativist historians claim, that the events themselves lack fixed
(15) or absolute meanings.

Objective historians see their role as that of a neutral judge, one who must never become an advocate or, worse, propagandist. Their conclusions should display the judicial qualities of balance and
(20) evenhandedness. As with the judiciary, these qualities require insulation from political considerations, and avoidance of partisanship or bias. Thus objective historians must purge themselves of external loyalties; their primary allegiance is to objective historical truth
(25) and to colleagues who share a commitment to its discovery.

Passage B

The very possibility of historical scholarship as an enterprise distinct from propaganda requires of its practitioners that self-discipline that enables them to
(30) do such things as abandon wishful thinking, assimilate bad news, and discard pleasing interpretations that fail elementary tests of evidence and logic.

Yet objectivity, for the historian, should not be confused with neutrality. Objectivity is perfectly
(35) compatible with strong political commitment. The objective thinker does not value detachment as an end in itself but only as an indispensable means of achieving deeper understanding. In historical scholarship, the ideal of objectivity is most compellingly embodied in
(40) the *powerful argument*—one that reveals by its every twist and turn its respectful appreciation of the alternative arguments it rejects. Such a text attains power precisely because its author has managed to suspend momentarily his or her own perceptions so as
(45) to anticipate and take into account objections and alternative constructions—not those of straw men, but those that truly issue from the rival's position, understood as sensitively and stated as eloquently as the rival could desire. To mount a telling attack on a
(50) position, one must first inhabit it. Those so habituated to their customary intellectual abode that they cannot even explore others can never be persuasive to anyone but fellow habitués.

Such arguments are often more faithful to the
(55) complexity of historical interpretation—more faithful even to the irreducible plurality of human perspectives— than texts that abjure position-taking altogether. The powerful argument is the highest fruit of the kind of thinking I would call objective, and in it neutrality

(60) plays no part. Authentic objectivity bears no resemblance to the television newscaster's mechanical gesture of allocating the same number of seconds to both sides of a question, editorially splitting the difference between them, irrespective of their perceived merits.

22. Both passages are concerned with answering which one of the following questions?

(A) What are the most serious flaws found in recent historical scholarship?
(B) What must historians do in order to avoid bias in their scholarship?
(C) How did the ideal of objectivity first develop?
(D) Is the scholarship produced by relativist historians sound?
(E) Why do the prevailing interpretations of past events change from one era to the next?

23. Both passages identify which one of the following as a requirement for historical research?

(A) the historian's willingness to borrow methods of analysis from other disciplines when evaluating evidence
(B) the historian's willingness to employ methodologies favored by proponents of competing views when evaluating evidence
(C) the historian's willingness to relinquish favored interpretations in light of the discovery of facts inconsistent with them
(D) the historian's willingness to answer in detail all possible objections that might be made against his or her interpretation
(E) the historian's willingness to accord respectful consideration to rival interpretations

GO ON TO THE NEXT PAGE.

24. The author of passage B and the kind of objective historian described in passage A would be most likely to disagree over whether

  (A) detachment aids the historian in achieving an objective view of past events

  (B) an objective historical account can include a strong political commitment

  (C) historians today are less objective than they were previously

  (D) propaganda is an essential tool of historical scholarship

  (E) historians of different eras have arrived at differing interpretations of the same historical events

25. Which one of the following most accurately describes an attitude toward objectivity present in each passage?

  (A) Objectivity is a goal that few historians can claim to achieve.

  (B) Objectivity is essential to the practice of historical scholarship.

  (C) Objectivity cannot be achieved unless historians set aside political allegiances.

  (D) Historians are not good judges of their own objectivity.

  (E) Historians who value objectivity are becoming less common.

26. Both passages mention propaganda primarily in order to

  (A) refute a claim made by proponents of a rival approach to historical scholarship

  (B) suggest that scholars in fields other than history tend to be more biased than historians

  (C) point to a type of scholarship that has recently been discredited

  (D) identify one extreme to which historians may tend

  (E) draw contrasts with other kinds of persuasive writing

27. The argument described in passage A and the argument made by the author of passage B are both advanced by

  (A) citing historical scholarship that fails to achieve objectivity

  (B) showing how certain recent developments in historical scholarship have undermined the credibility of the profession

  (C) summarizing opposing arguments in order to point out their flaws

  (D) suggesting that historians should adopt standards used by professionals in certain other fields

  (E) identifying what are seen as obstacles to achieving objectivity

S T O P

IF YOU FINISH BEFORE TIME IS CALLED, YOU MAY CHECK YOUR WORK ON THIS SECTION ONLY.
DO NOT WORK ON ANY OTHER SECTION IN THE TEST.

Wait for the supervisor's instructions before you open the page to the topic.
Please print and sign your name and write the date in the designated spaces below.

Time: 35 Minutes

General Directions

You will have 35 minutes in which to plan and write an essay on the topic inside. Read the topic and the accompanying directions carefully. You will probably find it best to spend a few minutes considering the topic and organizing your thoughts before you begin writing. In your essay, be sure to develop your ideas fully, leaving time, if possible, to review what you have written. **Do not write on a topic other than the one specified. Writing on a topic of your own choice is not acceptable.**

No special knowledge is required or expected for this writing exercise. Law schools are interested in the reasoning, clarity, organization, language usage, and writing mechanics displayed in your essay. How well you write is more important than how much you write.

Confine your essay to the blocked, lined area on the front and back of the separate Writing Sample Response Sheet. Only that area will be reproduced for law schools. Be sure that your writing is legible.

Both this topic sheet and your response sheet must be turned over to the testing staff before you leave the room.

Topic Code	Print Your Full Name Here		
_____	Last	First	M.I.

Date	Sign Your Name Here
/ /	

Scratch Paper
Do not write your essay in this space.

LSAT Writing Sample Topic

The biggest newspaper in a large market is deciding whether to continue to write all of its local stories in-house or to contract out much of this work off-site to local freelancers. The largest section of the newspaper is devoted to local coverage. Using the facts below, write an essay in which you argue for one choice over the other based on the following two criteria:

- The newspaper wants to maximize the quality of its local coverage.
- The newspaper wants to minimize the costs of producing local stories.

Writing all local stories in-house requires maintaining an extensive staff for this purpose. This involves expenditures for salaries, benefits, and overhead. Staff must also be reimbursed for employee business expenses associated with gathering stories. The day-to-day management of personnel frictions in a sizable staff can be challenging. Training and communicating with in-house staff is direct. This allows for the effective adoption and maintenance of strict standards. Different approaches and innovation tend to be discouraged.

Contracting out much of the responsibility for local coverage would tend to encourage different approaches and innovation. It would free up some staff time for potentially more rewarding work such as conducting in-depth investigations of local concerns. The only compensation for the freelancers contracted for local coverage would be a fixed amount for each accepted story, depending on its length after editing by in-house staff. There would be a high turnover of these freelancers. Their loyalty to the company would be relatively low. Hiring replacements would require staff time. Training and communicating with freelancers would be relatively difficult. This includes efforts to inculcate and enforce strict standards.

Scratch Paper
Do not write your essay in this space.

LAST NAME (Print)   MI   FIRST NAME (Print)

SIGNATURE

Writing Sample Response Sheet

DO NOT WRITE
IN THIS SPACE

Begin your essay in the lined area below.
Continue on the back if you need more space.

Directions:

1. Use the Answer Key on the next page to check your answers.

2. Use the Scoring Worksheet below to compute your raw score.

3. Use the Score Conversion Chart to convert your raw score into the 120–180 scale.

Scoring Worksheet

1. Enter the number of questions you answered correctly in each section.

                        Number
                        Correct

   SECTION I . . . . _____

   SECTION II . . . . . . _____

   SECTION III . . . . . _____

   SECTION IV . . . . . _____

2. Enter the sum here: _____
                        This is your Raw Score.

Conversion Chart

For Converting Raw Score to the 120–180 LSAT Scaled Score
LSAT PrepTest 63

Reported Score	Raw Score Lowest	Raw Score Highest
180	100	101
179	99	99
178	98	98
177	97	97
176	—*	—*
175	96	96
174	95	95
173	94	94
172	93	93
171	92	92
170	90	91
169	89	89
168	88	88
167	86	87
166	85	85
165	83	84
164	82	82
163	80	81
162	78	79
161	77	77
160	75	76
159	73	74
158	71	72
157	69	70
156	67	68
155	66	66
154	64	65
153	62	63
152	60	61
151	58	59
150	56	57
149	54	55
148	53	53
147	51	52
146	49	50
145	47	48
144	46	46
143	44	45
142	42	43
141	41	41
140	39	40
139	38	38
138	36	37
137	35	35
136	33	34
135	32	32
134	30	31
133	29	29
132	28	28
131	27	27
130	25	26
129	24	24
128	23	23
127	22	22
126	21	21
125	20	20
124	19	19
123	18	18
122	—*	—*
121	17	17
120	0	16

*There is no raw score that will produce this scaled score for this form.

SECTION I

1.	C	8.	E	15.	C	22.	B
2.	B	9.	D	16.	D	23.	B
3.	C	10.	A	17.	C	24.	E
4.	D	11.	D	18.	E	25.	A
5.	B	12.	B	19.	C		
6.	A	13.	D	20.	B		
7.	B	14.	D	21.	E		

SECTION II

1.	E	8.	C	15.	A	22.	C
2.	B	9.	D	16.	B	23.	D
3.	A	10.	A	17.	B		
4.	C	11.	B	18.	B		
5.	E	12.	E	19.	C		
6.	B	13.	C	20.	E		
7.	D	14.	E	21.	A		

SECTION III

1.	E	8.	B	15.	E	22.	A
2.	D	9.	C	16.	E	23.	C
3.	E	10.	A	17.	D	24.	A
4.	A	11.	B	18.	A	25.	A
5.	D	12.	A	19.	C	26.	A
6.	D	13.	B	20.	E		
7.	B	14.	B	21.	B		

SECTION IV

1.	A	8.	B	15.	D	22.	B
2.	C	9.	A	16.	C	23.	C
3.	E	10.	C	17.	D	24.	B
4.	B	11.	A	18.	A	25.	B
5.	A	12.	C	19.	C	26.	D
6.	E	13.	C	20.	B	27.	E
7.	C	14.	B	21.	A		

PrepTest 55

PrepTest 55 (October 2008)

SECTION I
Time—35 minutes
25 Questions

Directions: The questions in this section are based on the reasoning contained in brief statements or passages. For some questions, more than one of the choices could conceivably answer the question. However, you are to choose the best answer; that is, the response that most accurately and completely answers the question. You should not make assumptions that are by commonsense standards implausible, superfluous, or incompatible with the passage. After you have chosen the best answer, blacken the corresponding space on your answer sheet.

1. The editor of a magazine has pointed out several errors of spelling and grammar committed on a recent TV program. But she can hardly be trusted to pass judgment on such matters: similar errors have been found in her own magazine.

   The flawed reasoning in the argument above is most similar to that in which one of the following?

   (A) Your newspaper cannot be trusted with the prerogative to criticize the ethics of our company: you misspelled our president's name.
   (B) Your news program cannot be trusted to judge our hiring practices as unfair: you yourselves unfairly discriminate in hiring and promotion decisions.
   (C) Your regulatory agency cannot condemn our product as unsafe: selling it is allowed under an existing-product clause.
   (D) Your coach cannot be trusted to judge our swimming practices: he accepted a lucrative promotional deal from a soft-drink company.
   (E) Your teen magazine should not run this feature on problems afflicting modern high schools: your revenue depends on not alienating the high school audience.

2. Soaking dried beans overnight before cooking them reduces cooking time. However, cooking without presoaking yields plumper beans. Therefore, when a bean dish's quality is more important than the need to cook that dish quickly, beans should not be presoaked.

   Which one of the following is an assumption required by the argument?

   (A) Plumper beans enhance the quality of a dish.
   (B) There are no dishes whose quality improves with faster cooking.
   (C) A dish's appearance is as important as its taste.
   (D) None of the other ingredients in the dish need to be presoaked.
   (E) The plumper the bean, the better it tastes.

3. Durth: Increasingly, businesses use direct mail advertising instead of paying for advertising space in newspapers, in magazines, or on billboards. This practice is annoying and also immoral. Most direct mail advertisements are thrown out without ever being read, and the paper on which they are printed is wasted. If anyone else wasted this much paper, it would be considered unconscionable.

   Which one of the following most accurately describes Durth's method of reasoning?

   (A) presenting a specific counterexample to the contention that direct mail advertising is not immoral
   (B) asserting that there would be very undesirable consequences if direct mail advertising became a more widespread practice than it is now
   (C) claiming that direct mail advertising is immoral because one of its results would be deemed immoral in other contexts
   (D) basing a conclusion on the claim that direct mail advertising is annoying to those who receive it
   (E) asserting that other advertising methods do not have the negative effects of direct mail advertising

GO ON TO THE NEXT PAGE.

4. Among the various models of Delta vacuum cleaners, one cannot accurately predict how effectively a particular model cleans simply by determining how powerful its motor is. The efficiency of dust filtration systems varies significantly, even between models of Delta vacuum cleaners equipped with identically powerful motors.

The argument's conclusion is properly drawn if which one of the following is assumed?

(A) For each Delta vacuum cleaner, the efficiency of its dust filtration system has a significant impact on how effectively it cleans.

(B) One can accurately infer how powerful a Delta vacuum cleaner's motor is from the efficiency of the vacuum cleaner's dust filtration system.

(C) All Delta vacuum cleaners that clean equally effectively have identically powerful motors.

(D) For any two Delta vacuum cleaners with equally efficient dust filtration systems, the one with the more powerful motor cleans more effectively.

(E) One cannot accurately assess how effectively any Delta vacuum cleaner cleans without knowing how powerful that vacuum cleaner's motor is.

5. Many scientists believe that bipedal locomotion (walking on two feet) evolved in early hominids in response to the move from life in dense forests to life in open grasslands. Bipedalism would have allowed early hominids to see over tall grasses, helping them to locate food and to detect and avoid predators. However, because bipedalism also would have conferred substantial advantages upon early hominids who never left the forest—in gathering food found within standing reach of the forest floor, for example—debate continues concerning its origins. It may even have evolved, like the upright threat displays of many large apes, because it bettered an individual's odds of finding a mate.

Which one of the following statements is most supported by the information above?

(A) For early hominids, forest environments were generally more hospitable than grassland environments.

(B) Bipedal locomotion would have helped early hominids gather food.

(C) Bipedal locomotion actually would not be advantageous to hominids living in open grassland environments.

(D) Bipedal locomotion probably evolved among early hominids who exclusively inhabited forest environments.

(E) For early hominids, gathering food was more relevant to survival than was detecting and avoiding predators.

6. Mathematics teacher: Teaching students calculus before they attend university may significantly benefit them. Yet if students are taught calculus before they are ready for the level of abstraction involved, they may abandon the study of mathematics altogether. So if we are going to teach pre-university students calculus, we must make sure they can handle the level of abstraction involved.

Which one of the following principles most helps to justify the mathematics teacher's argument?

(A) Only those who, without losing motivation, can meet the cognitive challenges that new intellectual work involves should be introduced to it.

(B) Only those parts of university-level mathematics that are the most concrete should be taught to pre-university students.

(C) Cognitive tasks that require exceptional effort tend to undermine the motivation of those who attempt them.

(D) Teachers who teach university-level mathematics to pre-university students should be aware that students are likely to learn effectively only when the application of mathematics to concrete problems is shown.

(E) The level of abstraction involved in a topic should not be considered in determining whether that topic is appropriate for pre-university students.

GO ON TO THE NEXT PAGE.

7. In 1955, legislation in a certain country gave the government increased control over industrial workplace safety conditions. Among the high-risk industries in that country, the likelihood that a worker will suffer a serious injury has decreased since 1955. The legislation, therefore, has increased overall worker safety within high-risk industries.

Which one of the following, if true, most weakens the argument above?

(A) Because of technological innovation, most workplaces in the high-risk industries do not require as much unprotected interaction between workers and heavy machinery as they did in 1955.

(B) Most of the work-related injuries that occurred before 1955 were the result of worker carelessness.

(C) The annual number of work-related injuries has increased since the legislation took effect.

(D) The number of work-related injuries occurring within industries not considered high-risk has increased annually since 1955.

(E) Workplace safety conditions in all industries have improved steadily since 1955.

8. Economist: Historically, sunflower seed was one of the largest production crops in Kalotopia, and it continues to be a major source of income for several countries. The renewed growing of sunflowers would provide relief to Kalotopia's farming industry, which is quite unstable. Further, sunflower oil can provide a variety of products, both industrial and consumer, at little cost to Kalotopia's already fragile environment.

The economist's statements, if true, most strongly support which one of the following?

(A) Kalotopia's farming industry will deteriorate if sunflowers are not grown there.

(B) Stabilizing Kalotopia's farming industry would improve the economy without damaging the environment.

(C) Kalotopia's farming industry would be better off now if it had never ceased to grow any of the crops that historically were large production crops.

(D) A crop that was once a large production crop in Kalotopia would, if it were grown there again, benefit that country's farmers and general economy.

(E) Sunflower seed is a better crop for Kalotopia from both the environmental and the economic viewpoints than are most crops that could be grown there.

9. Several major earthquakes have occurred in a certain region over the last ten years. But a new earthquake prediction method promises to aid local civil defense officials in deciding exactly when to evacuate various towns. Detected before each of these major quakes were certain changes in the electric current in the earth's crust.

Which one of the following, if true, most weakens the argument?

(A) Scientists do not fully understand what brought about the changes in the electric current in the earth's crust that preceded each of the major quakes in the region over the last ten years.

(B) Most other earthquake prediction methods have been based on a weaker correlation than that found between the changes in the electric current in the earth's crust and the subsequent earthquakes.

(C) The frequency of major earthquakes in the region has increased over the last ten years.

(D) There is considerable variation in the length of time between the changes in the electric current and the subsequent earthquakes.

(E) There is presently only one station in the region that is capable of detecting the electric current in the earth's crust.

10. Unlike many machines that are perfectly useful in isolation from others, fax machines must work with other fax machines. Thus, in the fax industry, the proliferation of incompatible formats, which resulted from the large number of competing manufacturers, severely limited the usefulness—and hence the commercial viability—of fax technology until the manufacturers agreed to adopt a common format for their machines.

The information above provides the most support for which one of the following propositions?

(A) Whenever machines are dependent on other machines of the same type, competition among manufacturers is damaging to the industry.

(B) In some industries it is in the interest of competitors to cooperate to some extent with one another.

(C) The more competitors there are in a high-tech industry, the more they will have to cooperate in determining the basic design of their product.

(D) Some cooperation among manufacturers in the same industry is more beneficial than is pure competition.

(E) Cooperation is beneficial only in industries whose products depend on other products of the same type.

GO ON TO THE NEXT PAGE.

11. In comparing different methods by which a teacher's performance can be evaluated and educational outcomes improved, researchers found that a critique of teacher performance leads to enhanced educational outcomes if the critique is accompanied by the information that teacher performance is merely one of several factors that, in concert with other factors, determines the educational outcomes.

Which one of the following best illustrates the principle illustrated by the finding of the researchers?

(A) Children can usually be taught to master subject matter in which they have no interest if they believe that successfully mastering it will earn the respect of their peers.

(B) People are generally more willing to accept a negative characterization of a small group of people if they do not see themselves as members of the group being so characterized.

(C) An actor can more effectively evaluate the merits of her own performance if she can successfully convince herself that she is really evaluating the performance of another actor.

(D) The opinions reached by a social scientist in the study of a society can be considered as more reliable and objective if that social scientist is not a member of that society.

(E) It is easier to correct the mistakes of an athlete if it is made clear to him that the criticism is part of an overarching effort to rectify the shortcomings of the entire team on which he plays.

12. Critic: A novel cannot be of the highest quality unless most readers become emotionally engaged with the imaginary world it describes. Thus shifts of narrative point of view within a novel, either between first and third person or of some other sort, detract from the merit of the work, since such shifts tend to make most readers focus on the author.

Which one of the following is an assumption necessary for the critic's conclusion to be properly drawn?

(A) Most readers become emotionally engaged with the imaginary world described by a novel only if the novel is of the highest quality.

(B) A novel is generally not considered to be of high quality unless it successfully engages the imagination of most readers.

(C) Most readers cannot become emotionally involved with a novel's imaginary world if they focus on the author.

(D) Most readers regard a novel's narrative point of view as representing the perspective of the novel's author.

(E) Shifts in narrative point of view serve no literary purpose.

13. People aged 46 to 55 spend more money per capita than people of any other age group. So it is puzzling that when companies advertise consumer products on television, they focus almost exclusively on people aged 25 and under. Indeed, those who make decisions about television advertising think that the value of a television advertising slot depends entirely on the number of people aged 25 and under who can be expected to be watching at that time.

Which one of the following, if true, most helps to explain the puzzling facts stated above?

(A) The expense of television advertising slots makes it crucial for companies to target people who are most likely to purchase their products.

(B) Advertising slots during news programs almost always cost far less than advertising slots during popular sitcoms whose leading characters are young adults.

(C) When television executives decide which shows to renew, they do so primarily in terms of the shows' ratings among people aged 25 and under.

(D) Those who make decisions about television advertising believe that people older than 25 almost never change their buying habits.

(E) When companies advertise consumer products in print media, they focus primarily on people aged 26 and over.

14. Eighteenth-century moralist: You should never make an effort to acquire expensive new tastes, since they are a drain on your purse and in the course of acquiring them you may expose yourself to sensations that are obnoxious to you. Furthermore, the very effort that must be expended in their acquisition attests their superfluity.

The moralist's reasoning is most vulnerable to criticism on the grounds that the moralist

(A) draws a conclusion that simply restates a claim presented in support of that conclusion

(B) takes for granted that the acquisition of expensive tastes will lead to financial irresponsibility

(C) uses the inherently vague term "sensations" without providing a definition of that term

(D) mistakes a cause of acquisition of expensive tastes for an effect of acquisition of such tastes

(E) rejects trying to achieve a goal because of the cost of achieving it, without considering the benefits of achieving it

GO ON TO THE NEXT PAGE.

15. Zack's Coffeehouse schedules free poetry readings almost every Wednesday. Zack's offers half-priced coffee all day on every day that a poetry reading is scheduled.

Which one of the following can be properly inferred from the information above?

(A) Wednesday is the most common day on which Zack's offers half-priced coffee all day.
(B) Most free poetry readings given at Zack's are scheduled for Wednesdays.
(C) Free poetry readings are scheduled on almost every day that Zack's offers half-priced coffee all day.
(D) Zack's offers half-priced coffee all day on most if not all Wednesdays.
(E) On some Wednesdays Zack's does not offer half-priced coffee all day.

16. Philosopher: An event is intentional if it is a human action performed on the basis of a specific motivation. An event is random if it is not performed on the basis of a specific motivation and it is not explainable by normal physical processes.

Which one of the following inferences conforms most closely to the philosopher's position?

(A) Tarik left the keys untouched on the kitchen counter, but he did not do so on the basis of a specific motivation. Therefore, the keys' remaining on the kitchen counter was a random event.
(B) Ellis tore the envelope open in order to read its contents, but the envelope was empty. Nevertheless, because Ellis acted on the basis of a specific motivation, tearing the envelope open was an intentional event.
(C) Judith's hailing a cab distracted a driver in the left lane. She performed the action of hailing the cab on the basis of a specific motivation, so the driver's becoming distracted was an intentional event.
(D) Yasuko continued to breathe regularly throughout the time that she was asleep. This was a human action, but it was not performed on the basis of a specific motivation. Therefore, her breathing was a random event.
(E) Henry lost his hold on the wrench and dropped it because the handle was slippery. This was a human action and is explainable by normal physical processes, so it was an intentional event.

17. It is a mistake to conclude, as some have, that ancient people did not know what moral rights were simply because no known ancient language has an expression correctly translatable as "a moral right." This would be like saying that a person who discovers a wild fruit tree and returns repeatedly to harvest from it and study it has no idea what the fruit is until naming it or learning its name.

Which one of the following is an assumption required by the argument?

(A) To know the name of something is to know what that thing is.
(B) People who first discover what something is know it better than do people who merely know the name of the thing.
(C) The name or expression that is used to identify something cannot provide any information about the nature of the thing that is identified.
(D) A person who repeatedly harvests from a wild fruit tree and studies it has some idea of what the fruit is even before knowing a name for the fruit.
(E) One need not know what something is before one can name it.

18. There is little plausibility to the claim that it is absurd to criticize anyone for being critical. Obviously, people must assess one another and not all assessments will be positive. However, there is wisdom behind the injunction against being judgmental. To be judgmental is not merely to assess someone negatively, but to do so prior to a serious effort at understanding.

Which one of the following most accurately expresses the main conclusion drawn in the argument?

(A) To be judgmental is to assess someone negatively prior to making a serious effort at understanding.
(B) It is absurd to criticize anyone for being critical.
(C) There is some plausibility to the claim that it is absurd to criticize anyone for being critical.
(D) Not all assessments people make of one another will be positive.
(E) There is wisdom behind the injunction against being judgmental.

GO ON TO THE NEXT PAGE.

19. Even those who believe that the art of each age and culture has its own standards of beauty must admit that some painters are simply superior to others in the execution of their artistic visions. But this superiority must be measured in light of the artist's purposes, since the high merits, for example, of Jose Rey Toledo's work and his extraordinary artistic skills are not in doubt, despite the fact that his paintings do not literally resemble what they represent.

The claim that some painters are superior to others in the execution of their artistic visions plays which one of the following roles in the argument?

(A) It is a hypothesis that the argument attempts to refute.

(B) It is a generalization, one sort of objection to which the argument illustrates by giving an example.

(C) It is a claim that, according to the argument, is to be understood in a manner specified by the conclusion.

(D) It is a claim that the argument derives from another claim and that it uses to support its conclusion.

(E) It is a generalization that the argument uses to justify the relevance of the specific example it cites.

20. A study of rabbits in the 1940s convinced many biologists that parthenogenesis—reproduction without fertilization of an egg—sometimes occurs in mammals. However, the study's methods have since been shown to be flawed, and no other studies have succeeded in demonstrating mammalian parthenogenesis. Thus, since parthenogenesis is known to occur in a wide variety of nonmammalian vertebrates, there must be something about mammalian chromosomes that precludes the possibility of parthenogenesis.

A flaw in the reasoning of the argument is that the argument

(A) takes for granted that something that has not been proven to be true is for that reason shown to be false

(B) infers that a characteristic is shared by all nonmammalian vertebrate species merely because it is shared by some nonmammalian vertebrate species

(C) rules out an explanation of a phenomenon merely on the grounds that there is another explanation that can account for the phenomenon

(D) confuses a necessary condition for parthenogenesis with a sufficient condition for it

(E) assumes that the methods used in a study of one mammalian species were flawed merely because the study's findings cannot be generalized to all other mammalian species

21. Advertiser: Most TV shows depend on funding from advertisers and would be canceled without such funding. However, advertisers will not pay to have their commercials aired during a TV show unless many people watching the show buy the advertised products as a result. So if people generally fail to buy the products advertised during their favorite shows, these shows will soon be canceled. Thus, anyone who feels that a TV show is worth preserving ought to buy the products advertised during that show.

The advertiser's reasoning most closely conforms to which one of the following principles?

(A) If a TV show that one feels to be worth preserving would be canceled unless one took certain actions, then one ought to take those actions.

(B) If a TV show would be canceled unless many people took certain actions, then everyone who feels that the show is worth preserving ought to take those actions.

(C) If a TV show is worth preserving, then everyone should take whatever actions are necessary to prevent that show from being canceled.

(D) If one feels that a TV show is worth preserving, then one should take at least some actions to reduce the likelihood that the show will be canceled.

(E) If a TV show would be canceled unless many people took certain actions, then those who feel most strongly that it is worth preserving should take those actions.

GO ON TO THE NEXT PAGE.

22. Psychologist: It is well known that becoming angry often induces temporary incidents of high blood pressure. A recent study further showed, however, that people who are easily angered are significantly more likely to have permanently high blood pressure than are people who have more tranquil personalities. Coupled with the long-established fact that those with permanently high blood pressure are especially likely to have heart disease, the recent findings indicate that heart disease can result from psychological factors.

Which one of the following would, if true, most weaken the psychologist's argument?

(A) Those who are easily angered are less likely to recover fully from episodes of heart disease than are other people.

(B) Medication designed to control high blood pressure can greatly affect the moods of those who use it.

(C) People with permanently high blood pressure who have tranquil personalities virtually never develop heart disease.

(D) Those who discover that they have heart disease tend to become more easily frustrated by small difficulties.

(E) The physiological factors that cause permanently high blood pressure generally make people quick to anger.

23. A professor of business placed a case-study assignment for her class on her university's computer network. She later found out that instead of reading the assignment on the computer screen, 50 out of the 70 students printed it out on paper. Thus, it is not the case that books delivered via computer will make printed books obsolete.

Which one of the following, if true, most strengthens the argument?

(A) Several colleagues of the professor have found that, in their non-business courses, several of their students behave similarly in relation to assignments placed on the computer network.

(B) Studies consistently show that most computer users will print reading material that is more than a few pages in length rather than read it on the computer screen.

(C) Some people get impaired vision from long periods of reading printed matter on computer screens, even if they use high quality computer screens.

(D) Scanning technology is very poor, causing books delivered via computer to be full of errors unless editors carefully read the scanned versions.

(E) Books on cassette tape have only a small fraction of the sales of printed versions of the same books, though sales of videos of books that have been turned into movies remain strong.

GO ON TO THE NEXT PAGE.

24. Advertisement: Researchers studied a group of people trying to lose weight and discovered that those in the group who lost the most weight got more calories from protein than from carbohydrates and ate their biggest meal early in the day. So anyone who follows our diet, which provides more calories from protein than from anything else and which requires that breakfast be the biggest meal of the day, is sure to lose weight.

The reasoning in the advertisement is most vulnerable to criticism on the grounds that the advertisement overlooks the possibility that

(A) eating foods that derive a majority of their calories from carbohydrates tends to make one feel fuller than does eating foods that derive a majority of their calories from protein

(B) a few of the people in the group studied who lost significant amounts of weight got nearly all of their calories from carbohydrates and ate their biggest meal at night

(C) the people in the group studied who increased their activity levels lost more weight, on average, than those who did not, regardless of whether they got more calories from protein or from carbohydrates

(D) some people in the group studied lost no weight yet got more calories from protein than from carbohydrates and ate their biggest meal early in the day

(E) people who eat their biggest meal at night tend to snack more during the day and so tend to take in more total calories than do people who eat their biggest meal earlier in the day

25. Some twentieth-century art is great art. All great art involves original ideas, and any art that is not influential cannot be great art.

Each of the following statements follows logically from the set of statements above EXCEPT:

(A) Some influential art involves original ideas.

(B) Some twentieth-century art involves original ideas.

(C) Only art that involves original ideas is influential.

(D) Only art that is influential and involves original ideas is great art.

(E) Some twentieth-century art is influential and involves original ideas.

S T O P

IF YOU FINISH BEFORE TIME IS CALLED, YOU MAY CHECK YOUR WORK ON THIS SECTION ONLY.
DO NOT WORK ON ANY OTHER SECTION IN THE TEST.

SECTION II
Time—35 minutes
27 Questions

Directions: Each set of questions in this section is based on a single passage or a pair of passages. The questions are to be answered on the basis of what is stated or implied in the passage or pair of passages. For some of the questions, more than one of the choices could conceivably answer the question. However, you are to choose the best answer; that is, the response that most accurately and completely answers the question, and blacken the corresponding space on your answer sheet.

Often when a highly skilled and experienced employee leaves one company to work for another, there is the potential for a transfer of sensitive information between competitors. Two basic principles
(5) in such cases appear irreconcilable: the right of the company to its intellectual property—its proprietary data and trade secrets—and the right of individuals to seek gainful employment and to make free use of their abilities. Nevertheless, the courts have often tried to
(10) preserve both parties' legal rights by refusing to prohibit the employee from working for the competitor, but at the same time providing an injunction against disclosure of any of the former employer's secrets. It has been argued that because such measures help
(15) generate suspicions and similar psychological barriers to full and free utilization of abilities in the employee's new situation, they are hardly effective in upholding the individual's rights to free employment decisions. But it is also doubtful that they are effective in
(20) preserving trade secrets.

It is obviously impossible to divest oneself of that part of one's expertise that one has acquired from former employers and coworkers. Nor, in general, can one selectively refrain from its use, given that it has
(25) become an integral part of one's total intellectual capacity. Nevertheless, almost any such information that is not public knowledge may legitimately be claimed as corporate property: normal employment agreements provide for corporate ownership of all
(30) relevant data, including inventions, generated by the employee in connection with the company's business.

Once an employee takes a position with a competitor, the trade secrets that have been acquired by that employee may manifest themselves clearly and
(35) consciously. This is what court injunctions seek to prohibit. But they are far more likely to manifest themselves subconsciously and inconspicuously—for example, in one's daily decisions at the new post, or in the many small contributions one might make to a large
(40) team effort—often in the form of an intuitive sense of what to do or to avoid. Theoretically, an injunction also prohibits such inadvertent "leakage." However, the former employer faces the practical problem of securing evidence of such leakage, for little will
(45) usually be apparent from the public activities of the new employer. And even if the new employee's activities appear suspicious, there is the further problem of distinguishing trade secrets from what may be legitimately asserted as technological skills
(50) developed independently by the employee or already

possessed by the new employer. This is a major stumbling block in the attempt to protect trade secrets, since the proprietor has no recourse against others who independently generate the same information. It is
(55) therefore unlikely that an injunction against disclosure of trade secrets to future employers actually prevents any transfer of information except for the passage of documents and other concrete embodiments of the secrets.

1. Which one of the following most accurately expresses the main point of the passage?

(A) There are more effective ways than court injunctions to preserve both a company's right to protect its intellectual property and individuals' rights to make free use of their abilities.

(B) Court injunctions must be strengthened if they are to remain a relevant means of protecting corporations' trade secrets.

(C) Enforcement of court injunctions designed to protect proprietary information is impossible when employees reveal such information to new employers.

(D) Court injunctions prohibiting employees from disclosing former employers' trade secrets to new employers probably do not achieve all of their intended objectives.

(E) The rights of employees to make full use of their talents and previous training are being seriously eroded by the prohibitions placed on them by court injunctions designed to prevent the transfer of trade secrets.

GO ON TO THE NEXT PAGE.

2. Given the passage's content and tone, which one of the following statements would most likely be found elsewhere in a work from which this passage is an excerpt?

(A) Given the law as it stands, corporations concerned about preserving trade secrets might be best served by giving their employees strong incentives to stay in their current jobs.

(B) While difficult to enforce and interpret, injunctions are probably the most effective means of halting the inadvertent transfer of trade secrets while simultaneously protecting the rights of employees.

(C) Means of redress must be made available to companies that suspect, but cannot prove, that former employees are revealing protected information to competitors.

(D) Even concrete materials such as computer disks are so easy to copy and conceal that it will be a waste of time for courts to try to prevent the spread of information through physical theft.

(E) The psychological barriers that an injunction can place on an employee in a new workplace are inevitably so subtle that they have no effect on the employee.

3. The author's primary purpose in the passage is to

(A) suggest that injunctions against the disclosure of trade secrets not only create problems for employees in the workplace, but also are unable to halt the illicit spread of proprietary information

(B) suggest that the information contained in "documents and other concrete embodiments" is usually so trivial that injunctions do little good in protecting intellectual property

(C) argue that new methods must be found to address the delicate balance between corporate and individual rights

(D) support the position that the concept of protecting trade secrets is no longer viable in an age of increasing access to information

(E) argue that injunctions are not necessary for the protection of trade secrets

4. The passage provides the most support for which one of the following assertions?

(A) Injunctions should be imposed by the courts only when there is strong reason to believe that an employee will reveal proprietary information.

(B) There is apparently no reliable way to protect both the rights of companies to protect trade secrets and the rights of employees to seek new employment.

(C) Employees should not be allowed to take jobs with their former employers' competitors when their new job could compromise trade secrets of their former employers.

(D) The multiplicity of means for transferring information in the workplace only increases the need for injunctions.

(E) Some companies seek injunctions as a means of punishing employees who take jobs with their competitors.

5. With which one of the following statements regarding documents and other concrete embodiments mentioned in line 58 would the author be most likely to agree?

(A) While the transfer of such materials would be damaging, even the seemingly innocuous contributions of an employee to a competitor can do more harm in the long run.

(B) Such materials are usually less informative than what the employee may recollect about a previous job.

(C) Injunctions against the disclosure of trade secrets should carefully specify which materials are included in order to focus on the most damaging ones.

(D) Large-scale transfer of documents and other materials cannot be controlled by injunctions.

(E) Such concrete materials lend themselves to control and identification more readily than do subtler means of transferring information.

6. In the passage, the author makes which one of the following claims?

(A) Injunctions against the disclosure of trade secrets limit an employee's chances of being hired by a competitor.

(B) Measures against the disclosure of trade secrets are unnecessary except in the case of documents and other concrete embodiments of the secrets.

(C) Employees who switch jobs to work for a competitor usually unintentionally violate the law by doing so.

(D) Employers are not restricted in the tactics they can use when seeking to secure protected information from new employees.

(E) What may seem like intellectual theft may in fact be an example of independent innovation.

GO ON TO THE NEXT PAGE.

The following passages concern a plant called purple loosestrife. Passage A is excerpted from a report issued by a prairie research council; passage B from a journal of sociology.

Passage A

Purple loosestrife (*Lythrum salicaria*), an aggressive and invasive perennial of Eurasian origin, arrived with settlers in eastern North America in the early 1800s and has spread across the continent's

(5) midlatitude wetlands. The impact of purple loosestrife on native vegetation has been disastrous, with more than 50 percent of the biomass of some wetland communities displaced. Monospecific blocks of this weed have maintained themselves for at least 20 years.

(10) Impacts on wildlife have not been well studied, but serious reductions in waterfowl and aquatic furbearer productivity have been observed. In addition, several endangered species of vertebrates are threatened with further degradation of their

(15) breeding habitats. Although purple loosestrife can invade relatively undisturbed habitats, the spread and dominance of this weed have been greatly accelerated in disturbed habitats. While digging out the plants can temporarily halt their spread, there has been little

(20) research on long-term purple loosestrife control. Glyphosate has been used successfully, but no measure of the impact of this herbicide on native plant communities has been made.

With the spread of purple loosestrife growing

(25) exponentially, some form of integrated control is needed. At present, coping with purple loosestrife hinges on early detection of the weed's arrival in areas, which allows local eradication to be carried out with minimum damage to the native plant community.

Passage B

(30) The war on purple loosestrife is apparently conducted on behalf of nature, an attempt to liberate the biotic community from the tyrannical influence of a life-destroying invasive weed. Indeed, purple loosestrife control is portrayed by its practitioners as

(35) an environmental initiative intended to save nature rather than control it. Accordingly, the purple loosestrife literature, scientific and otherwise, dutifully discusses the impacts of the weed on endangered species—and on threatened biodiversity

(40) more generally. Purple loosestrife is a pollution, according to the scientific community, and all of nature suffers under its pervasive influence.

Regardless of the perceived and actual ecological effects of the purple invader, it is apparent that

(45) popular pollution ideologies have been extended into the wetlands of North America. Consequently, the scientific effort to liberate nature from purple loosestrife has failed to decouple itself from its philosophical origin as an instrument to control nature

(50) to the satisfaction of human desires. Birds, particularly game birds and waterfowl, provide the

bulk of the justification for loosestrife management. However, no bird species other than the canvasback has been identified in the literature as endangered by

(55) purple loosestrife. The impact of purple loosestrife on furbearing mammals is discussed at great length, though none of the species highlighted (muskrat, mink) can be considered threatened in North America. What is threatened by purple loosestrife is the

(60) economics of exploiting such preferred species and the millions of dollars that will be lost to the economies of the United States and Canada from reduced hunting, trapping, and recreation revenues due to a decline in the production of the wetland

(65) resource.

7. Both passages explicitly mention which one of the following?

   (A) furbearing animals
   (B) glyphosate
   (C) the threat purple loosestrife poses to economies
   (D) popular pollution ideologies
   (E) literature on purple loosestrife control

8. Each of the passages contains information sufficient to answer which one of the following questions?

   (A) Approximately how long ago did purple loosestrife arrive in North America?
   (B) Is there much literature discussing the potential benefit that hunters might derive from purple loosestrife management?
   (C) What is an issue regarding purple loosestrife management on which both hunters and farmers agree?
   (D) Is the canvasback threatened with extinction due to the spread of purple loosestrife?
   (E) What is a type of terrain that is affected in at least some parts of North America by the presence of purple loosestrife?

9. It can be inferred that the authors would be most likely to disagree about which one of the following?

   (A) Purple loosestrife spreads more quickly in disturbed habitats than in undisturbed habitats.
   (B) The threat posed by purple loosestrife to local aquatic furbearer populations is serious.
   (C) Most people who advocate that eradication measures be taken to control purple loosestrife are not genuine in their concern for the environment.
   (D) The size of the biomass that has been displaced by purple loosestrife is larger than is generally thought.
   (E) Measures should be taken to prevent other non-native plant species from invading North America.

GO ON TO THE NEXT PAGE.

10. Which one of the following most accurately describes the attitude expressed by the author of passage B toward the overall argument represented by passage A?

(A) enthusiastic agreement
(B) cautious agreement
(C) pure neutrality
(D) general ambivalence
(E) pointed skepticism

11. It can be inferred that both authors would be most likely to agree with which one of the following statements regarding purple loosestrife?

(A) As it increases in North America, some wildlife populations tend to decrease.
(B) Its establishment in North America has had a disastrous effect on native North American wetland vegetation in certain regions.
(C) It is very difficult to control effectively with herbicides.
(D) Its introduction into North America was a great ecological blunder.
(E) When it is eliminated from a given area, it tends to return to that area fairly quickly.

12. Which one of the following is true about the relationship between the two passages?

(A) Passage A presents evidence that directly counters claims made in passage B.
(B) Passage B assumes what passage A explicitly argues for.
(C) Passage B displays an awareness of the arguments touched on in passage A, but not vice versa.
(D) Passage B advocates a policy that passage A rejects.
(E) Passage A downplays the seriousness of claims made in passage B.

13. Which one of the following, if true, would cast doubt on the argument in passage B but bolster the argument in passage A?

(A) Localized population reduction is often a precursor to widespread endangerment of a species.
(B) Purple loosestrife was barely noticed in North America before the advent of suburban sprawl in the 1950s.
(C) The amount by which overall hunting, trapping, and recreation revenues would be reduced as a result of the extinction of one or more species threatened by purple loosestrife represents a significant portion of those revenues.
(D) Some environmentalists who advocate taking measures to eradicate purple loosestrife view such measures as a means of controlling nature.
(E) Purple loosestrife has never become a problem in its native habitat, even though no effort has been made to eradicate it there.

GO ON TO THE NEXT PAGE.

With their recognition of Maxine Hong Kingston as a major literary figure, some critics have suggested that her works have been produced almost *ex nihilo*, saying that they lack a large traceable body of direct
(5) literary antecedents especially within the Chinese American heritage in which her work is embedded. But these critics, who have examined only the development of written texts, the most visible signs of a culture's narrative production, have overlooked Kingston's
(10) connection to the long Chinese tradition of a highly developed genre of song and spoken narrative known as "talk-story" (*gong gu tsai*).

Traditionally performed in the dialects of various ethnic enclaves, talk-story has been maintained within
(15) the confines of the family and has rarely surfaced into print. The tradition dates back to Sung dynasty (A.D. 970–1279) storytellers in China, and in the United States it is continually revitalized by an overlapping sequence of immigration from China.
(20) Thus, Chinese immigrants to the U.S. had a fully established, sophisticated oral culture, already ancient and capable of producing masterpieces, by the time they began arriving in the early nineteenth century. This transplanted oral heritage simply embraced new
(25) subject matter or new forms of Western discourse, as in the case of Kingston's adaptations written in English.

Kingston herself believes that as a literary artist she is one in a long line of performers shaping a recalcitrant history into talk-story form. She
(30) distinguishes her "thematic" storytelling memory processes, which sift and reconstruct the essential elements of personally remembered stories, from the memory processes of a print-oriented culture that emphasizes the retention of precise sequences of
(35) words. Nor does the entry of print into the storytelling process substantially change her notion of the character of oral tradition. For Kingston, "writer" is synonymous with "singer" or "performer" in the ancient sense of privileged keeper, transmitter, and creator of stories
(40) whose current stage of development can be frozen in print, but which continue to grow both around and from that frozen text.

Kingston's participation in the tradition of talk-story is evidenced in her book *China Men*, which
(45) utilizes forms typical of that genre and common to most oral cultures including: a fixed "grammar" of repetitive themes; a spectrum of stock characters; symmetrical structures, including balanced oppositions (verbal or physical contests, antithetical characters,
(50) dialectical discourse such as question-answer forms and riddles); and repetition. In *China Men*, Kingston also succeeds in investing idiomatic English with the allusive texture and oral-aural qualities of the Chinese language, a language rich in aural and visual puns,
(55) making her work a written form of talk-story.

14. Which one of the following most accurately states the main point of the passage?

(A) Despite some critics' comments, Kingston's writings have significant Chinese American antecedents, which can be found in the traditional oral narrative form known as talk-story.

(B) Analysis of Kingston's writings, especially *China Men*, supports her belief that literary artists can be performers who continue to reconstruct their stories even after they have been frozen in print.

(C) An understanding of Kingston's work and of Chinese American writers in general reveals that critics of ethnic literatures in the United States have been mistaken in examining only written texts.

(D) Throughout her writings Kingston uses techniques typical of the talk-story genre, especially the retention of certain aspects of Chinese speech in the written English text.

(E) The writings of Kingston have rekindled an interest in talk-story, which dates back to the Sung dynasty, and was extended to the United States with the arrival of Chinese immigrants in the nineteenth century.

15. Which one of the following can be most reasonably inferred from the passage?

(A) In the last few years, written forms of talk-story have appeared in Chinese as often as they have in English.

(B) Until very recently, scholars have held that oral storytelling in Chinese ethnic enclaves was a unique oral tradition.

(C) Talk-story has developed in the United States through a process of combining Chinese, Chinese American, and other oral storytelling forms.

(D) Chinese American talk-story relies upon memory processes that do not emphasize the retention of precise sequences of words.

(E) The connection between certain aspects of Kingston's work and talk-story is argued by some critics to be rather tenuous and questionable.

GO ON TO THE NEXT PAGE.

16. It can be inferred from the passage that the author uses the phrase "personally remembered stories" (line 32) primarily to refer to

(A) a literary genre of first-person storytelling
(B) a thematically organized personal narrative of one's own past
(C) partially idiosyncratic memories of narratives
(D) the retention in memory of precise sequences of words
(E) easily identifiable thematic issues in literature

17. In which one of the following is the use of cotton fibers or cotton cloth most analogous to Kingston's use of the English language as described in lines 51–55?

(A) Scraps of plain cotton cloth are used to create a multicolored quilt.
(B) The surface texture of woolen cloth is simulated in a piece of cotton cloth by a special process of weaving.
(C) Because of its texture, cotton cloth is used for a certain type of clothes for which linen is inappropriate.
(D) In making a piece of cloth, cotton fiber is substituted for linen because of the roughly similar texture of the two materials.
(E) Because of their somewhat similar textures, cotton and linen fibers are woven together in a piece of cloth to achieve a savings in price over a pure linen cloth.

18. The passage most clearly suggests that Kingston believes which one of the following about at least some of the stories contained in her writings?

(A) Since they are intimately tied to the nature of the Chinese language, they can be approximated, but not adequately expressed, in English.
(B) They should be thought of primarily as ethnic literature and evaluated accordingly by critics.
(C) They will likely be retold and altered to some extent in the process.
(D) Chinese American history is best chronicled by traditional talk-story.
(E) Their significance and beauty cannot be captured at all in written texts.

19. The author's argument in the passage would be most weakened if which one of the following were true?

(A) Numerous writers in the United States have been influenced by oral traditions.
(B) Most Chinese American writers' work is very different from Kingston's.
(C) Native American storytellers use narrative devices similar to those used in talk-story.
(D) *China Men* is for the most part atypical of Kingston's literary works.
(E) Literary critics generally appreciate the authenticity of Kingston's work.

20. The author's specific purpose in detailing typical talk-story forms (lines 43–51) is to

(A) show why Kingston's book *China Men* establishes her as a major literary figure
(B) support the claim that Kingston's use of typically oral techniques makes her work a part of the talk-story tradition
(C) dispute the critics' view that Chinese American literature lacks literary antecedents
(D) argue for Kingston's view that the literary artist is at best a "privileged keeper" of stories
(E) provide an alternative to certain critics' view that Kingston's work should be judged primarily as literature

21. Which one of the following most accurately identifies the attitude shown by the author in the passage toward talk-story?

(A) scholarly appreciation for its longstanding artistic sophistication
(B) mild disappointment that it has not distinguished itself from other oral traditions
(C) tentative approval of its resistance to critical evaluations
(D) clear respect for the diversity of its ancient sources and cultural derivations
(E) open admiration for the way it uses song to express narrative

GO ON TO THE NEXT PAGE.

In economics, the term "speculative bubble" refers to a large upward move in an asset's price driven not by the asset's fundamentals—that is, by the earnings derivable from the asset—but rather by
(5) mere speculation that someone else will be willing to pay a higher price for it. The price increase is then followed by a dramatic decline in price, due to a loss in confidence that the price will continue to rise, and the "bubble" is said to have burst. According to
(10) Charles Mackay's classic nineteenth-century account, the seventeenth-century Dutch tulip market provides an example of a speculative bubble. But the economist Peter Garber challenges Mackay's view, arguing that there is no evidence that the Dutch tulip
(15) market really involved a speculative bubble.

By the seventeenth century, the Netherlands had become a center of cultivation and development of new tulip varieties, and a market had developed in which rare varieties of bulbs sold at high prices. For
(20) example, a Semper Augustus bulb sold in 1625 for an amount of gold worth about U.S.$11,000 in 1999. Common bulb varieties, on the other hand, sold for very low prices. According to Mackay, by 1636 rapid price rises attracted speculators, and prices of many
(25) varieties surged upward from November 1636 through January 1637. Mackay further states that in February 1637 prices suddenly collapsed; bulbs could not be sold at 10 percent of their peak values. By 1739, the prices of all the most prized kinds of bulbs had fallen
(30) to no more than one two-hundredth of 1 percent of Semper Augustus's peak price.

Garber acknowledges that bulb prices increased dramatically from 1636 to 1637 and eventually reached very low levels. But he argues that this
(35) episode should not be described as a speculative bubble, for the increase and eventual decline in bulb prices can be explained in terms of the fundamentals. Garber argues that a standard pricing pattern occurs for new varieties of flowers. When a particularly
(40) prized variety is developed, its original bulb sells for a high price. Thus, the dramatic rise in the price of some original tulip bulbs could have resulted as tulips in general, and certain varieties in particular, became fashionable. However, as the prized bulbs become
(45) more readily available through reproduction from the original bulb, their price falls rapidly; after less than 30 years, bulbs sell at reproduction cost. But this does not mean that the high prices of original bulbs are irrational, for earnings derivable from the millions
(50) of bulbs descendent from the original bulbs can be very high, even if each individual descendent bulb commands a very low price. Given that an original bulb can generate a reasonable return on investment even if the price of descendent bulbs decreases
(55) dramatically, a rapid rise and eventual fall of tulip bulb prices need not indicate a speculative bubble.

22. Which one of the following most accurately expresses the main point of the passage?

(A) The seventeenth-century Dutch tulip market is widely but mistakenly believed by economists to provide an example of a speculative bubble.

(B) Mackay did not accurately assess the earnings that could be derived from rare and expensive seventeenth-century Dutch tulip bulbs.

(C) A speculative bubble occurs whenever the price of an asset increases substantially followed by a rapid and dramatic decline.

(D) Garber argues that Mackay's classic account of the seventeenth-century Dutch tulip market as a speculative bubble is not supported by the evidence.

(E) A tulip bulb can generate a reasonable return on investment even if the price starts very high and decreases dramatically.

23. Given Garber's account of the seventeenth-century Dutch tulip market, which one of the following is most analogous to someone who bought a tulip bulb of a certain variety in that market at a very high price, only to sell a bulb of that variety at a much lower price?

(A) someone who, after learning that many others had withdrawn their applications for a particular job, applied for the job in the belief that there would be less competition for it

(B) an art dealer who, after paying a very high price for a new painting, sells it at a very low price because it is now considered to be an inferior work

(C) someone who, after buying a box of rare motorcycle parts at a very high price, is forced to sell them at a much lower price because of the sudden availability of cheap substitute parts

(D) a publisher who pays an extremely high price for a new novel only to sell copies at a price affordable to nearly everyone

(E) an airline that, after selling most of the tickets for seats on a plane at a very high price, must sell the remaining tickets at a very low price

GO ON TO THE NEXT PAGE.

24. The passage most strongly supports the inference that Garber would agree with which one of the following statements?

   (A) If speculative bubbles occur at all, they occur very rarely.

   (B) Many of the owners of high-priced original tulip bulbs could have expected to at least recoup their original investments from sales of the many bulbs propagated from the original bulbs.

   (C) If there is not a speculative bubble in a market, then the level of prices in that market is not irrational.

   (D) Most people who invested in Dutch tulip bulbs in the seventeenth century were generally rational in all their investments.

   (E) Mackay mistakenly infers from the fact that tulip prices dropped rapidly that the very low prices that the bulbs eventually sold for were irrational.

25. The passage states that Mackay claimed which one of the following?

   (A) The rapid rise in price of Dutch tulip bulbs was not due to the fashionability of the flowers they produced.

   (B) The prices of certain varieties of Dutch tulip bulbs during the seventeenth century were, at least for a time, determined by speculation.

   (C) The Netherlands was the only center of cultivation and development of new tulip varieties in the seventeenth century.

   (D) The very high prices of bulbs in the seventeenth-century Dutch tulip market were not irrational.

   (E) Buyers of rare and very expensive Dutch tulip bulbs were ultimately able to derive earnings from bulbs descendent from the original bulbs.

26. The main purpose of the second paragraph is to

   (A) present the facts that are accepted by all experts in the field

   (B) identify the mistake that one scholar alleges another scholar made

   (C) explain the basis on which one scholar makes an inference with which another scholar disagrees

   (D) undermine the case that one scholar makes for the claim with which another scholar disagrees

   (E) outline the factual errors that led one scholar to draw the inference that he drew

27. The phrase "standard pricing pattern" as used in line 38 most nearly means a pricing pattern

   (A) against which other pricing patterns are to be measured

   (B) that conforms to a commonly agreed-upon criterion

   (C) that is merely acceptable

   (D) that regularly recurs in certain types of cases

   (E) that serves as an exemplar

S T O P

IF YOU FINISH BEFORE TIME IS CALLED, YOU MAY CHECK YOUR WORK ON THIS SECTION ONLY.
DO NOT WORK ON ANY OTHER SECTION IN THE TEST.

SECTION III
Time—35 minutes
25 Questions

Directions: The questions in this section are based on the reasoning contained in brief statements or passages. For some questions, more than one of the choices could conceivably answer the question. However, you are to choose the best answer; that is, the response that most accurately and completely answers the question. You should not make assumptions that are by commonsense standards implausible, superfluous, or incompatible with the passage. After you have chosen the best answer, blacken the corresponding space on your answer sheet.

1. Aristophanes' play *The Clouds*, which was written when the philosopher Socrates was in his mid-forties, portrays Socrates as an atheistic philosopher primarily concerned with issues in natural science. The only other surviving portrayals of Socrates were written after Socrates' death at age 70. They portrayed Socrates as having a religious dimension and a strong focus on ethical issues.

    Which one of the following, if true, would most help to resolve the apparent discrepancy between Aristophanes' portrayal of Socrates and the other surviving portrayals?

    (A) Aristophanes' portrayal of Socrates in *The Clouds* was unflattering, whereas the other portrayals were very flattering.
    (B) Socrates' philosophical views and interests changed sometime after his mid-forties.
    (C) Most of the philosophers who lived before Socrates were primarily concerned with natural science.
    (D) Socrates was a much more controversial figure in the years before his death than he was in his mid-forties.
    (E) Socrates had an influence on many subsequent philosophers who were primarily concerned with natural science.

2. Board member: The J Foundation, a philanthropic organization, gave you this grant on the condition that your resulting work not contain any material detrimental to the J Foundation's reputation. But your resulting work never mentions any of the laudable achievements of our foundation. Hence your work fails to meet the conditions under which the grant was made.

    The reasoning in the board member's argument is vulnerable to criticism on the grounds that the argument

    (A) takes for granted that a work that never mentions any laudable achievements cannot be of high intellectual value
    (B) confuses a condition necessary for the receipt of a grant with a condition sufficient for the receipt of a grant
    (C) presumes, without providing justification, that a work that does not mention a foundation's laudable achievements is harmful to that foundation's reputation
    (D) fails to consider that recipients of a grant usually strive to meet a foundation's conditions
    (E) fails to consider the possibility that the work that was produced with the aid of the grant may have met all conditions other than avoiding detriment to the J Foundation's reputation

3. Psychiatrist: Breaking any habit is difficult, especially when it involves an addictive substance. People who break a habit are more likely to be motivated by immediate concerns than by long-term ones. Therefore, people who succeed in breaking their addiction to smoking cigarettes are more likely to be motivated by the social pressure against smoking—which is an immediate concern—than by health concerns, since _____.

    The conclusion of the psychiatrist's argument is most strongly supported if which one of the following completes the argument?

    (A) a habit that involves an addictive substance is likely to pose a greater health threat than a habit that does not involve any addictive substance
    (B) for most people who successfully quit smoking, smoking does not create an immediate health concern at the time they quit
    (C) some courses of action that exacerbate health concerns can also relieve social pressure
    (D) most people who succeed in quitting smoking succeed only after several attempts
    (E) everyone who succeeds in quitting smoking is motivated either by social pressure or by health concerns

GO ON TO THE NEXT PAGE.

4. Cassie: In order to improve the quality of customer service provided by our real estate agency, we should reduce client loads—the number of clients each agent is expected to serve at one time.

   Melvin: Although smaller client loads are desirable, reducing client loads at our agency is simply not feasible. We already find it very difficult to recruit enough qualified agents; recruiting even more agents, which would be necessary in order to reduce client loads, is out of the question.

   Of the following, which one, if true, is the logically strongest counter that Cassie can make to Melvin's argument?

   (A) Since reducing client loads would improve working conditions for agents, reducing client loads would help recruit additional qualified agents to the real estate agency.
   (B) Many of the real estate agency's current clients have expressed strong support for efforts to reduce client loads.
   (C) Several recently conducted studies of real estate agencies have shown that small client loads are strongly correlated with high customer satisfaction ratings.
   (D) Hiring extra support staff for the real estate agency's main office would have many of the same beneficial effects as reducing client loads.
   (E) Over the last several years, it has become increasingly challenging for the real estate agency to recruit enough qualified agents just to maintain current client loads.

5. The star-nosed mole has a nose that ends in a pair of several-pointed stars, or tentacles that are crucial for hunting, as moles are poor-sighted. These tentacles contain receptors that detect electric fields produced by other animals, enabling the moles to detect and catch suitable prey such as worms and insects.

   Which one of the following is most strongly supported by the information above?

   (A) Both worms and insects produce electric fields.
   (B) The star-nosed mole does not rely at all on its eyesight for survival.
   (C) The star-nosed mole does not rely at all on its sense of smell when hunting.
   (D) Only animals that hunt have noses with tentacles that detect electric fields.
   (E) The star-nosed mole does not produce an electric field.

6. In her recent book a psychologist described several cases that exhibit the following pattern: A child, denied something by its parent, initiates problematic behavior such as screaming; the behavior escalates until finally the exasperated parent acquiesces to the child's demand. At this point the child, having obtained the desired goal, stops the problematic behavior, to the parent's relief. This self-reinforcing pattern of misbehavior and accommodation is repeated with steadily increasing levels of misbehavior by the child.

   The cases described by the psychologist illustrate each of the following generalizations EXCEPT:

   (A) A child can develop problematic behavior patterns as a result of getting what it wants.
   (B) A child and parent can mutually influence each other's behavior.
   (C) Parents, by their choices, can inadvertently increase their child's level of misbehavior.
   (D) A child can unintentionally influence a parent's behavior in ways contrary to the child's intended goals.
   (E) A child can get what it wants by doing what its parent doesn't want it to do.

7. Scientist: In our study, chemical R did not cause cancer in laboratory rats. But we cannot conclude from this that chemical R is safe for humans. After all, many substances known to be carcinogenic to humans cause no cancer in rats; this is probably because some carcinogens cause cancer only via long-term exposure and rats are short lived.

   Which one of the following most precisely describes the role played in the scientist's argument by the statement that chemical R did not cause cancer in laboratory rats?

   (A) It is cited as evidence against the conclusion that chemical R is safe for humans.
   (B) It is advanced to support the contention that test results obtained from laboratory rats cannot be extrapolated to humans.
   (C) It illustrates the claim that rats are too short lived to be suitable as test subjects for the carcinogenic properties of substances to which humans are chronically exposed.
   (D) It is used as evidence to support the hypothesis that chemical R causes cancer in humans via long-term exposure.
   (E) It is cited as being insufficient to support the conclusion that chemical R is safe for humans.

GO ON TO THE NEXT PAGE.

8. Department store manager: There is absolutely no reason to offer our customers free gift wrapping again this holiday season. If most customers take the offer, it will be expensive and time-consuming for us. On the other hand, if only a few customers want it, there is no advantage in offering it.

Which one of the following is an assumption required by the department store manager's argument?

(A) Gift wrapping would cost the store more during this holiday season than in previous holiday seasons.

(B) Anything that slows down shoppers during the holiday season costs the store money.

(C) It would be to the store's advantage to charge customers for gift wrapping services.

(D) It would be expensive to inform customers about the free gift wrapping service.

(E) Either few customers would want free gift wrapping or most customers would want it.

9. Among people who have a history of chronic trouble falling asleep, some rely only on sleeping pills to help them fall asleep, and others practice behavior modification techniques and do not take sleeping pills. Those who rely only on behavior modification fall asleep more quickly than do those who rely only on sleeping pills, so behavior modification is more effective than are sleeping pills in helping people to fall asleep.

Which one of the following, if true, most weakens the argument?

(A) People who do not take sleeping pills spend at least as many total hours asleep each night as do the people who take sleeping pills.

(B) Most people who have trouble falling asleep and who use behavior modification techniques fall asleep more slowly than do most people who have no trouble falling asleep.

(C) Many people who use only behavior modification techniques to help them fall asleep have never used sleeping pills.

(D) The people who are the most likely to take sleeping pills rather than practice behavior modification techniques are those who have previously had the most trouble falling asleep.

(E) The people who are the most likely to practice behavior modification techniques rather than take sleeping pills are those who prefer not to use drugs if other treatments are available.

10. Lawyer: This witness acknowledges being present at the restaurant and watching when my client, a famous television personality, was assaulted. Yet the witness claims to recognize the assailant, but not my famous client. Therefore, the witness's testimony should be excluded.

The lawyer's conclusion follows logically if which one of the following is assumed?

(A) If a witness claims to recognize both parties involved in an assault, then the witness's testimony should be included.

(B) There are other witnesses who can identify the lawyer's client as present during the assault.

(C) It is impossible to determine whether the witness actually recognized the assailant.

(D) The testimony of a witness to an assault should be included only if the witness claims to recognize both parties involved in the assault.

(E) It is unlikely that anyone would fail to recognize the lawyer's client.

11. Biologist: Many paleontologists have suggested that the difficulty of adapting to ice ages was responsible for the evolution of the human brain. But this suggestion must be rejected, for most other animal species adapted to ice ages with no evolutionary changes to their brains.

The biologist's argument is most vulnerable to criticism on which one of the following grounds?

(A) It fails to address adequately the possibility that even if a condition is sufficient to produce an effect in a species, it may not be necessary to produce that effect in that species.

(B) It fails to address adequately the possibility that a condition can produce a change in a species even if it does not produce that change in other species.

(C) It overlooks the possibility that a condition that is needed to produce a change in one species is not needed to produce a similar change in other species.

(D) It presumes without warrant that human beings were presented with greater difficulties during ice ages than were individuals of most other species.

(E) It takes for granted that, if a condition coincided with the emergence of a certain phenomenon, that condition must have been causally responsible for the phenomenon.

GO ON TO THE NEXT PAGE.

12. The total number of book titles published annually in North America has approximately quadrupled since television first became available. Retail sales of new titles, as measured in copies, increased rapidly in the early days of television, though the rate of increase has slowed in recent years. Library circulation has been flat or declining in recent years.

Which one of the following is most strongly supported by the information above?

(A) Television has, over the years, brought about a reduction in the amount of per capita reading in North America.

(B) The introduction of television usually brings about a decrease in library use.

(C) Book publishers in North America now sell fewer copies per title than they sold in the early days of television.

(D) The availability of television does not always cause a decline in the annual number of book titles published or in the number of books sold.

(E) The introduction of television expanded the market for books in North America.

13. Botanist: It has long been believed that people with children or pets should keep poinsettia plants out of their homes. Although this belief has been encouraged by child-rearing books, which commonly list poinsettias as poisonous and therefore dangerous, it is mistaken. Our research has shown, conclusively, that poinsettias pose no risk to children or pets.

Which one of the following most accurately expresses the conclusion drawn in the botanist's argument?

(A) Child-rearing books should encourage people with children to put poinsettias in their homes.

(B) Poinsettias are not dangerously poisonous.

(C) According to many child-rearing books, poinsettias are dangerous.

(D) The belief that households with children or pets should not have poinsettias is mistaken.

(E) Poinsettias pose no risk to children or pets.

14. Archaeologist: An ancient stone building at our excavation site was composed of three kinds of stone—quartz, granite, and limestone. Of these, only limestone occurs naturally in the area. Most of the buildings at the site from the same time period had limestone as their only stone component, and most were human dwellings. Therefore, the building we are studying probably was not a dwelling.

Which one of the following, if true, would most strengthen the archaeologist's reasoning?

(A) Most of the buildings that were used as dwellings at the site were made, at least in part, of limestone.

(B) Most of the buildings at the site that were not dwellings were made, at least in part, from types of stone that do not occur naturally in the area.

(C) Most of the buildings that were built from stones not naturally occurring in the area were not built with both quartz and granite.

(D) Most of the buildings at the site were used as dwellings.

(E) No quartz has been discovered on the site other than that found in the building being studied.

GO ON TO THE NEXT PAGE.

15. Theodore will be able to file his tax return on time only in the event that he has an accountant prepare his tax return and the accountant does not ask Theodore for any additional documentation of his business expenses. If he does have an accountant prepare his return, the accountant will necessarily ask Theodore to provide this additional documentation. Therefore, Theodore will not be able to file on time.

The pattern of reasoning in which one of the following arguments most closely parallels the pattern of reasoning in the argument above?

(A) Given the demands of Timothy's job, his next free evening will occur next Friday. Since he spent a lot of money on his last evening out, he will probably decide to spend his next free evening at home. Therefore, Timothy will probably be at home next Friday evening.

(B) Tovah cannot attend the concert next week if she is away on business. If she misses that concert, she will not have another opportunity to attend a concert this month. Since she will be away on business, Tovah will not be able to attend a concert this month.

(C) Mark's children will not be content this weekend unless he lets them play video games some of the time. Mark will let them play video games, but only at times when he has no other activities planned. Therefore, unless Mark and his children take a break from planned activities, Mark's children will not be content this weekend.

(D) If Teresa is not seated in first class on her airline flight, she will be seated in business class. Therefore, since she cannot be seated in first class on that flight, she will necessarily be seated in business class.

(E) Susannah will have a relaxing vacation only if her children behave especially well and she does not start to suspect that they are planning some mischief. Since she will certainly start to suspect that they are planning some mischief if they behave especially well, Susannah's vacation cannot possibly be relaxing.

16. When a threat to life is common, as are automobile and industrial accidents, only unusual instances tend to be prominently reported by the news media. Instances of rare threats, such as product tampering, however, are seen as news by reporters and are universally reported in featured stories. People in general tend to estimate the risk of various threats by how frequently those threats come to their attention.

If the statements above are true, which one of the following is most strongly supported on the basis of them?

(A) Whether governmental action will be taken to lessen a common risk depends primarily on the prominence given to the risk by the news media.

(B) People tend to magnify the risk of a threat if the threat seems particularly dreadful or if those who would be affected have no control over it.

(C) Those who get their information primarily from the news media tend to overestimate the risk of uncommon threats relative to the risk of common threats.

(D) Reporters tend not to seek out information about long-range future threats but to concentrate their attention on the immediate past and future.

(E) The resources that are spent on avoiding product tampering are greater than the resources that are spent on avoiding threats that stem from the weather.

GO ON TO THE NEXT PAGE.

17. Real estate agent: Upon selling a home, the sellers are legally entitled to remove any items that are not permanent fixtures. Legally, large appliances like dishwashers are not permanent fixtures. However, since many prospective buyers of the home are likely to assume that large appliances in the home would be included with its purchase, sellers who will be keeping the appliances are morally obliged either to remove them before showing the home or to indicate in some other way that the appliances are not included.

Which one of the following principles, if valid, most helps to justify the real estate agent's argumentation?

(A) If a home's sellers will be keeping any belongings that prospective buyers of the home might assume would be included with the purchase of the home, the sellers are morally obliged to indicate clearly that those belongings are not included.

(B) A home's sellers are morally obliged to ensure that prospective buyers of the home do not assume that any large appliances are permanent fixtures in the home.

(C) A home's sellers are morally obliged to include with the sale of the home at least some of the appliances that are not permanent fixtures but were in the home when it was shown to prospective buyers.

(D) A home's sellers are morally obliged not to deliberately mislead any prospective buyers of their home about which belongings are included with the sale of the home and which are not.

(E) If a home's sellers have indicated in some way that a large appliance is included with the home's purchase, then they are morally obliged not to remove that appliance after showing the home.

18. Many parents rigorously organize their children's activities during playtime, thinking that doing so will enhance their children's cognitive development. But this belief is incorrect. To thoroughly structure a child's playtime and expect this to produce a creative and resourceful child would be like expecting a good novel to be produced by someone who was told exactly what the plot and characters must be.

The argument is most vulnerable to criticism on which one of the following grounds?

(A) It takes for granted that if something is conducive to a certain goal it cannot also be conducive to some other goal.

(B) It overlooks the possibility that many children enjoy rigorously organized playtime.

(C) It takes a necessary condition for something's enhancing a child's creativity and resourcefulness to be a sufficient condition for its doing so.

(D) It fails to consider the possibility that being able to write a good novel requires something more than creativity and resourcefulness.

(E) It fails to consider the possibility that something could enhance a child's overall cognitive development without enhancing the child's creativity and resourcefulness.

19. Bureaucrat: The primary, constant goal of an ideal bureaucracy is to define and classify all possible problems and set out regulations regarding each eventuality. Also, an ideal bureaucracy provides an appeal procedure for any complaint. If a complaint reveals an unanticipated problem, the regulations are expanded to cover the new issue, and for this reason an ideal bureaucracy will have an ever-expanding system of regulations.

Which one of the following is an assumption the bureaucrat's argument requires?

(A) An ideal bureaucracy will provide an appeal procedure for complaints even after it has defined and classified all possible problems and set out regulations regarding each eventuality.

(B) For each problem that an ideal bureaucracy has defined and classified, the bureaucracy has received at least one complaint revealing that problem.

(C) An ideal bureaucracy will never be permanently without complaints about problems that are not covered by that bureaucracy's regulations.

(D) An ideal bureaucracy can reach its primary goal if, but only if, its system of regulations is always expanding to cover problems that had not been anticipated.

(E) Any complaint that an ideal bureaucracy receives will reveal an unanticipated problem that the bureaucracy is capable of defining and classifying.

GO ON TO THE NEXT PAGE.

20. Scientists studying a common type of bacteria have discovered that most bacteria of that type are in hibernation at any given time. Some microbiologists have concluded from this that bacteria in general are usually in hibernation. This conclusion would be reasonable if all types of bacteria were rather similar. But, in fact, since bacteria are extremely diverse, it is unlikely that most types of bacteria hibernate regularly.

Which one of the following most accurately expresses the overall conclusion of the argument?

(A) Bacteria of most types are usually in hibernation.

(B) It is probably not true that most types of bacteria hibernate regularly.

(C) If bacteria are extremely diverse, it is unlikely that most types of bacteria hibernate regularly.

(D) The conclusion that bacteria in general are usually in hibernation would be reasonable if all types of bacteria were rather similar.

(E) It is likely that only one type of bacteria hibernates regularly.

21. Any student who is not required to hand in written homework based on the reading assignments in a course will not complete all of the reading assignments. Even highly motivated students will neglect their reading assignments if they are not required to hand in written homework. Therefore, if the students in a course are given several reading assignments and no written assignments, no student in that course will receive a high grade for the course.

The conclusion of the argument follows logically if which one of the following is assumed?

(A) No student who completes anything less than all of the reading assignments for a course will earn a high grade for that course.

(B) Any student who completes all of the reading and written assignments for a course will earn a high grade in that course.

(C) All highly motivated students who complete all of the reading assignments for a course will receive high grades for that course.

(D) If highly motivated students are required to hand in written homework on their reading assignments, then they will complete all of their reading assignments.

(E) Some highly motivated students will earn high grades in a course if they are required to hand in written homework on their reading assignments.

22. In a study, one group of volunteers was fed a high-protein, low-carbohydrate diet; another group was fed a low-protein, high-carbohydrate diet. Both diets contained the same number of calories, and each volunteer's diet prior to the experiment had contained moderate levels of proteins and carbohydrates. After ten days, those on the low-carbohydrate diet had lost more weight than those on the high-carbohydrate diet. Thus, the most effective way to lose body fat is to eat much protein and shun carbohydrates.

Which one of the following, if true, most weakens the argument above?

(A) A low-protein, high-carbohydrate diet causes the human body to retain water, the added weight of which largely compensates for the weight of any body fat lost, whereas a high-protein, low-carbohydrate diet does not.

(B) Many people who consume large quantities of protein nevertheless gain significant amounts of body fat.

(C) A high-protein, low-carbohydrate diet will often enable the human body to convert some body fat into muscle, without causing any significant overall weight loss.

(D) In the experiment, the volunteers on the high-carbohydrate diet engaged in regular exercise of a kind known to produce weight loss, and those on the low-carbohydrate diet did not.

(E) Many of the volunteers who had been on the low-carbohydrate diet eventually regained much of the weight they had lost on the diet after returning to their normal diets.

GO ON TO THE NEXT PAGE.

23. Essayist: Computers have the capacity to represent and to perform logical transformations on pieces of information. Since exactly the same applies to the human mind, the human mind is a type of computer.

The flawed pattern of reasoning in which one of the following most closely resembles the flawed pattern of reasoning in the essayist's argument?

(A) Often individual animals sacrifice their lives when the survival of their offspring or close relatives is threatened. It is probable, therefore, that there is a biological basis for the fact that human beings are similarly often willing to sacrifice their own well-being for the good of their community.

(B) In the plastic arts, such as sculpture or painting, no work can depend for its effectiveness upon a verbal narrative that explains it. Since the same can be said of poetry, we cannot consider this characteristic as a reasonable criterion for distinguishing the plastic arts from other arts.

(C) In any organism, the proper functioning of each component depends upon the proper functioning of every other component. Thus, communities belong to the category of organisms, since communities are invariably characterized by this same interdependence of components.

(D) Some vitamins require the presence in adequate amounts of some mineral in order to be fully beneficial to the body. Thus, since selenium is needed to make vitamin E fully active, anyone with a selenium deficiency will have a greater risk of contracting those diseases from which vitamin E provides some measure of protection.

(E) Friendship often involves obligations whose fulfillment can be painful or burdensome. The same can be said of various forms of cooperation that cannot strictly be called friendship. Thus cooperation, like friendship, can require that priority be given to goals other than mere self-interest.

24. It is popularly believed that a poem has whatever meaning is assigned to it by the reader. But objective evaluation of poetry is possible only if this popular belief is false; for the aesthetic value of a poem cannot be discussed unless it is possible for at least two readers to agree on the correct interpretation of the poem.

Which one of the following is an assumption required by the argument?

(A) Only if they find the same meaning in a poem can two people each judge that it has aesthetic value.

(B) If two readers agree about the meaning of a given poem, that ensures that an objective evaluation of the poem can be made.

(C) Discussion of a poem is possible only if it is false that a poem has whatever meaning is assigned to it by the reader.

(D) A given poem can be objectively evaluated only if the poem's aesthetic value can be discussed.

(E) Aesthetic evaluation of literature is best accomplished through discussion by more than two readers.

25. Dean: The mathematics department at our university has said that it should be given sole responsibility for teaching the course Statistics for the Social Sciences. But this course has no more mathematics in it than high school algebra does. The fact that a course has mathematics in it does not mean that it needs to be taught by a mathematics professor, any more than a course approaching its subject from a historical perspective must be taught by a history professor. Such demands by the mathematics department are therefore unjustified.

The dean's argument is most vulnerable to criticism on the grounds that it

(A) presumes, without providing justification, that expertise in a subject does not enable one to teach that subject well

(B) purports to refute a view by showing that one possible reason for that view is insufficient

(C) presumes, without providing justification, that most students are as knowledgeable about mathematics as they are about history

(D) fails to establish that mathematics professors are not capable of teaching Statistics for the Social Sciences effectively

(E) presumes, without providing justification, that any policies that apply to history courses must be justified with respect to mathematics courses

S T O P

IF YOU FINISH BEFORE TIME IS CALLED, YOU MAY CHECK YOUR WORK ON THIS SECTION ONLY.
DO NOT WORK ON ANY OTHER SECTION IN THE TEST.

SECTION IV
Time—35 minutes
23 Questions

<u>Directions</u>: Each group of questions in this section is based on a set of conditions. In answering some of the questions, it may be useful to draw a rough diagram. Choose the response that most accurately and completely answers each question and blacken the corresponding space on your answer sheet.

Questions 1–6

There are exactly six law students—Gambini, Little, Mitchum, Richardson, Saito, and Veracruz—in a trial advocacy class. The class is divided into three trial teams—team 1, team 2, and team 3—of exactly two students each. Each student is on exactly one of the teams. Each student prepares exactly one of either the opening argument or the final argument for his or her team. The teams must be formed according to the following specifications:

Mitchum is on the same team as either Gambini or Veracruz.
Little prepares an opening argument.
Either Gambini or Richardson, but not both, prepares a final argument.

1. Which one of the following could be the composition of each team and the argument each student prepares?

   (A) team 1: Little, opening; Gambini, final
       team 2: Veracruz, opening; Mitchum, final
       team 3: Saito, opening; Richardson, final
   (B) team 1: Mitchum, opening; Gambini, final
       team 2: Veracruz, opening; Little, final
       team 3: Richardson, opening; Saito, final
   (C) team 1: Richardson, opening; Gambini, final
       team 2: Mitchum, opening; Saito, final
       team 3: Little, opening; Veracruz, final
   (D) team 1: Gambini, opening; Mitchum, final
       team 2: Little, opening; Richardson, final
       team 3: Veracruz, opening; Saito, final
   (E) team 1: Gambini, opening; Mitchum, final
       team 2: Richardson, opening; Saito, final
       team 3: Little, opening; Veracruz, final

2. If Gambini is on the same team as Mitchum, and if Gambini prepares the final argument for that team, then which one of the following could be true?

   (A) Little is on the same team as Veracruz, who prepares the opening argument for the team.
   (B) Richardson is on the same team as Saito, who prepares the opening argument for the team.
   (C) Richardson is on the same team as Saito, who prepares the final argument for the team.
   (D) Saito is on the same team as Veracruz, who prepares the opening argument for the team.
   (E) Saito is on the same team as Veracruz, who prepares the final argument for the team.

3. Which one of the following could be true?

   (A) Gambini, who prepares a final argument, is on the same team as Richardson.
   (B) Gambini, who prepares a final argument, is on the same team as Veracruz.
   (C) Gambini, who prepares an opening argument, is on the same team as Little.
   (D) Little, who prepares an opening argument, is on the same team as Mitchum.
   (E) Mitchum, who prepares an opening argument, is on the same team as Saito.

4. If Richardson is on the same team as Veracruz, then for exactly how many of the students can it be determined which of the arguments he or she prepares?

   (A) one
   (B) two
   (C) three
   (D) four
   (E) five

5. If Little is on the same team as Richardson, then which one of the following must be true?

   (A) Saito is on the same team as Veracruz.
   (B) Gambini is on the same team as Mitchum.
   (C) Mitchum prepares a final argument.
   (D) Veracruz prepares a final argument.
   (E) Gambini prepares an opening argument.

6. If Saito prepares an opening argument, then which one of the following pairs of students could be on the same team as each other?

   (A) Gambini and Little
   (B) Gambini and Saito
   (C) Little and Veracruz
   (D) Mitchum and Veracruz
   (E) Richardson and Veracruz

GO ON TO THE NEXT PAGE.

Questions 7–12

While on vacation, Sukanya receives several e-mail messages from work, each message from one of three associates: Hilary, Jerome, and Lula. Sukanya receives at least one and no more than two messages from each of them. Sukanya receives each message on the day it is sent. No more than one message is sent each day. The messages are received in a manner consistent with the following:

The first message is not from Lula.
Both the first and last messages are from the same person.
Exactly once Sukanya receives a message from Jerome on the day after receiving one from Hilary.
Of the first three messages, exactly one is from Jerome.

7. Which one of the following could be an accurate list of the e-mail messages Sukanya receives, identified by the person each message is from and listed in the order she receives them?

(A) Lula, Hilary, Jerome, Hilary, Jerome, Lula
(B) Jerome, Lula, Hilary, Lula, Jerome
(C) Jerome, Lula, Hilary, Jerome, Hilary
(D) Jerome, Lula, Hilary, Hilary, Jerome
(E) Hilary, Lula, Lula, Jerome, Jerome, Hilary

8. What is the maximum possible number of e-mail messages Sukanya receives after Jerome's first message but before Hilary's first message?

(A) zero
(B) one
(C) two
(D) three
(E) four

9. If Sukanya receives exactly four e-mail messages, then which one of the following must be true?

(A) Exactly one of the messages is from Lula.
(B) Exactly two of the messages are from Jerome.
(C) The second message is from Lula.
(D) The third message is from Hilary.
(E) The fourth message is from Jerome.

10. Which one of the following e-mail messages CANNOT be from Lula?

(A) the second message
(B) the third message
(C) the fourth message
(D) the fifth message (if there is a fifth one)
(E) the sixth message (if there is a sixth one)

11. If Sukanya receives six e-mail messages, the fifth of which is from Lula, which one of the following must be true?

(A) The first message is from Jerome.
(B) The second message is from Lula.
(C) The third message is from Hilary.
(D) The fourth message is from Jerome.
(E) The sixth message is from Lula.

12. If Sukanya receives two e-mail messages from Lula, what is the maximum possible number of e-mail messages Sukanya receives after Lula's first message but before Lula's last message?

(A) zero
(B) one
(C) two
(D) three
(E) four

GO ON TO THE NEXT PAGE.

Questions 13–18

Mercotek carried out a study to compare the productivity of its night shift with that of its day shift. Every week the company's six crews—F, G, H, R, S, and T—were ranked from first (most productive) to sixth (least productive). There were no ties. For any given week, either G and T were the two night-shift crews or else S and H were—the four other crews were the day-shift crews for that week. The following relationships held for every week of the study:

F is more productive than G.
R is more productive than S.
R is more productive than T.
S is more productive than H.
G is more productive than T.

13. Which one of the following could be an accurate ranking of all the crews, in order from first to sixth, for a given week of the study?

(A) F, G, T, R, S, H
(B) F, R, G, T, H, S
(C) G, R, T, S, H, F
(D) R, F, G, S, H, T
(E) R, S, H, T, F, G

14. If F is ranked third for a given week of the study, then which one of the following could also be true of that week?

(A) G ranks second.
(B) H ranks fourth.
(C) R ranks second.
(D) S ranks fourth.
(E) T ranks fourth.

15. Which one of the following CANNOT be the crew ranked fifth for any given week of the study?

(A) G
(B) H
(C) R
(D) S
(E) T

16. For any given week of the study, the ranking of all the crews is completely determined if which one of the following is true?

(A) F ranks second that week.
(B) G ranks fifth that week.
(C) H ranks third that week.
(D) R ranks third that week.
(E) S ranks third that week.

17. If the night-shift crews rank fifth and sixth for a given week of the study, then which one of the following could also be true of that week?

(A) G ranks fourth.
(B) H ranks fifth.
(C) R ranks third.
(D) S ranks fourth.
(E) T ranks fifth.

18. Which one of the following is a complete and accurate list of the crews that CANNOT be ranked third for any given week of the study?

(A) G, H, S
(B) R, T
(C) F, T
(D) G, T
(E) T

GO ON TO THE NEXT PAGE.

Questions 19–23

A shuttle van stops exactly four times—once at Fundy, once at Los Altos, once at Mineola, and once at Simcoe—not necessarily in that order. The van starts with exactly four passengers on board—Greg, Jasmine, Rosa, and Vijay—each of whom gets off at a different stop. The following conditions hold:

Los Altos is the first or second stop.
Rosa is still on board when the van reaches Mineola.
Jasmine is on board longer than Vijay.
If Jasmine is still on board when the van reaches Fundy, then Greg is still on board when the van reaches Simcoe; otherwise, Greg is not still on board when the van reaches Simcoe.

19. Which one of the following could be a complete and accurate matching of stops, listed in the order in which the van stops at them, to the passengers who get off at them?

(A) Los Altos: Greg
  Mineola: Vijay
  Fundy: Jasmine
  Simcoe: Rosa
(B) Simcoe: Vijay
  Mineola: Greg
  Fundy: Rosa
  Los Altos: Jasmine
(C) Los Altos: Jasmine
  Mineola: Vijay
  Fundy: Greg
  Simcoe: Rosa
(D) Los Altos: Rosa
  Mineola: Vijay
  Fundy: Jasmine
  Simcoe: Greg
(E) Los Altos: Vijay
  Fundy: Jasmine
  Mineola: Rosa
  Simcoe: Greg

20. If Mineola is the first stop, which one of the following is a complete and accurate list of the passengers who could possibly get off there?

(A) Rosa
(B) Greg, Rosa
(C) Greg, Vijay
(D) Greg, Rosa, Vijay
(E) Jasmine, Rosa, Vijay

21. If Fundy is the first stop, then which one of the following could accurately list the passengers in order from first to last off?

(A) Greg, Vijay, Jasmine, Rosa
(B) Rosa, Vijay, Greg, Jasmine
(C) Vijay, Greg, Rosa, Jasmine
(D) Vijay, Jasmine, Greg, Rosa
(E) Vijay, Rosa, Jasmine, Greg

22. Which one of the following must be true if Greg is still on board both when the van reaches Los Altos and when it reaches Simcoe, not necessarily in that order, assuming he is the second one off the van?

(A) Vijay is on board when the van reaches Simcoe.
(B) Vijay is on board when the van reaches Los Altos.
(C) Rosa is on board when the van reaches Simcoe.
(D) Rosa is on board when the van reaches Fundy.
(E) Jasmine is on board when the van reaches Mineola.

23. If Greg is not on board when the van reaches Simcoe, then which one of the following must be false?

(A) Greg is on board when the van reaches Fundy.
(B) Jasmine is on board when the van reaches Mineola.
(C) Rosa is on board when the van reaches Fundy.
(D) Vijay is on board when the van reaches Fundy.
(E) Vijay is on board when the van reaches Mineola.

S T O P

IF YOU FINISH BEFORE TIME IS CALLED, YOU MAY CHECK YOUR WORK ON THIS SECTION ONLY.
DO NOT WORK ON ANY OTHER SECTION IN THE TEST.

Wait for the supervisor's instructions before you open the page to the topic.
Please print and sign your name and write the date in the designated spaces below.

Time: 35 Minutes

General Directions

You will have 35 minutes in which to plan and write an essay on the topic inside. Read the topic and the accompanying directions carefully. You will probably find it best to spend a few minutes considering the topic and organizing your thoughts before you begin writing. In your essay, be sure to develop your ideas fully, leaving time, if possible, to review what you have written. **Do not write on a topic other than the one specified. Writing on a topic of your own choice is not acceptable.**

No special knowledge is required or expected for this writing exercise. Law schools are interested in the reasoning, clarity, organization, language usage, and writing mechanics displayed in your essay. How well you write is more important than how much you write.

Confine your essay to the blocked, lined area on the front and back of the separate Writing Sample Response Sheet. Only that area will be reproduced for law schools. Be sure that your writing is legible.

Both this topic sheet and your response sheet must be turned over to the testing staff before you leave the room.

Topic Code	Print Your Full Name Here		
_____	Last	First	M.I.

Date	Sign Your Name Here
/ /	

Scratch Paper
Do not write your essay in this space.

LSAT Writing Sample Topic

Directions: The scenario presented below describes two choices, either one of which can be supported on the basis of the information given. Your essay should consider both choices and argue <u>for</u> one and <u>against</u> the other, based on the two specified criteria and the facts provided. There is no "right" or "wrong" choice: a reasonable argument can be made for either.

Aña Rodriguez is a shy five-year-old girl. The Rodriguez family must send Aña to either Mercer Preschool or Butte Preschool. The Rodriguezes are equally satisfied with the quality of the teachers and the facilities at both schools. Using the facts below, write an essay in which you argue for one preschool over the other based on the following two criteria:

- The preschool must provide a stimulating social environment for Aña.
- The preschool must be conveniently located.

Aña is an only child who lives on a block with no other children her age. Two children Aña occasionally plays with at the local playground would be in her class at Mercer. The class size at Mercer is eight children. Mercer occupies its students' time, for the most part, with activities for the entire class. There is little unstructured time. Mercer is within easy walking distance of the Rodriguez home. Parking near Mercer is nearly impossible. After the infrequent winter snowstorms, snow is typically left to melt rather than shoveled. Walking can be difficult at such times.

Aña's best friend will be attending Butte. Aña knows none of the other children who would be in her class. The class size at Butte is 12 children. Most of the students' time is not formally structured. The children are free to participate in a number of optional activities with or without their classmates. The few structured activities all involve small groups of two or three children. Butte is a 10-minute drive, or 20-minute bus ride, from the Rodriguez house. Parking is always available since Butte has its own lot. Aña's younger cousin Pablo, who lives on her block, will be attending a different class at Butte.

Scratch Paper
Do not write your essay in this space.

LAST NAME (Print)　　　MI　　FIRST NAME (Print)

SIGNATURE

Writing Sample Response Sheet

DO NOT WRITE
IN THIS SPACE

Begin your essay in the lined area below.
Continue on the back if you need more space.

Directions:

1. Use the Answer Key on the next page to check your answers.

2. Use the Scoring Worksheet below to compute your raw score.

3. Use the Score Conversion Chart to convert your raw score into the 120–180 scale.

Scoring Worksheet

1. Enter the number of questions you answered correctly in each section.

	Number Correct
SECTION I	_____
SECTION II	_____
SECTION III	_____
SECTION IV	_____

2. Enter the sum here: _____

    This is your Raw Score.

Conversion Chart

For Converting Raw Score to the 120–180 LSAT Scaled Score

LSAT PrepTest 55

Reported Score	Raw Score Lowest	Raw Score Highest
180	99	100
179	98	98
178	97	97
177	96	96
176	—*	—*
175	95	95
174	94	94
173	—*	—*
172	93	93
171	92	92
170	91	91
169	90	90
168	89	89
167	87	88
166	86	86
165	85	85
164	83	84
163	82	82
162	81	81
161	79	80
160	77	78
159	76	76
158	74	75
157	72	73
156	70	71
155	69	69
154	67	68
153	65	66
152	63	64
151	61	62
150	59	60
149	58	58
148	56	57
147	54	55
146	52	53
145	50	51
144	48	49
143	47	47
142	45	46
141	43	44
140	41	42
139	40	40
138	38	39
137	36	37
136	35	35
135	33	34
134	32	32
133	30	31
132	29	29
131	27	28
130	26	26
129	25	25
128	24	24
127	22	23
126	21	21
125	20	20
124	19	19
123	18	18
122	17	17
121	16	16
120	0	15

*There is no raw score that will produce this scaled score for this form.

SECTION I

1.	B	8.	D	15.	D	22.	E
2.	A	9.	D	16.	B	23.	B
3.	C	10.	B	17.	D	24.	D
4.	A	11.	E	18.	E	25.	C
5.	B	12.	C	19.	C		
6.	A	13.	D	20.	A		
7.	A	14.	E	21.	B		

SECTION II

1.	D	8.	E	15.	D	22.	D
2.	A	9.	B	16.	C	23.	D
3.	A	10.	E	17.	B	24.	B
4.	B	11.	A	18.	C	25.	B
5.	E	12.	C	19.	D	26.	C
6.	E	13.	A	20.	B	27.	D
7.	A	14.	A	21.	A		

SECTION III

1.	B	8.	E	15.	E	22.	A
2.	C	9.	D	16.	C	23.	C
3.	B	10.	D	17.	A	24.	D
4.	A	11.	B	18.	E	25.	B
5.	A	12.	D	19.	C		
6.	D	13.	D	20.	B		
7.	E	14.	B	21.	A		

SECTION IV

1.	D	8.	C	15.	C	22.	C
2.	C	9.	A	16.	C	23.	D
3.	A	10.	E	17.	C		
4.	B	11.	D	18.	E		
5.	E	12.	B	19.	E		
6.	C	13.	D	20.	D		
7.	D	14.	B	21.	D		

PrepTest 53

PrepTest 53 (December 2007)

SECTION I

Time—35 minutes

25 Questions

Directions: The questions in this section are based on the reasoning contained in brief statements or passages. For some questions, more than one of the choices could conceivably answer the question. However, you are to choose the best answer; that is, the response that most accurately and completely answers the question. You should not make assumptions that are by commonsense standards implausible, superfluous, or incompatible with the passage. After you have chosen the best answer, blacken the corresponding space on your answer sheet.

1. Consumer advocate: Businesses are typically motivated primarily by the desire to make as great a profit as possible, and advertising helps businesses to achieve this goal. But it is clear that the motive of maximizing profits does not impel businesses to present accurate information in their advertisements. It follows that consumers should be skeptical of the claims made in advertisements.

Each of the following, if true, would strengthen the consumer advocate's argument EXCEPT:

(A) Businesses know that they can usually maximize their profits by using inaccurate information in their advertisements.

(B) Businesses have often included inaccurate information in their advertisements.

(C) Many consumers have a cynical attitude toward advertising.

(D) Those who create advertisements are less concerned with the accuracy than with the creativity of advertisements.

(E) The laws regulating truth in advertising are not applicable to many of the most common forms of inaccurate advertising.

2. Elaine: The purpose of art museums is to preserve artworks and make them available to the public. Museums, therefore, should seek to acquire and display the best examples of artworks from each artistic period and genre, even if some of these works are not recognized by experts as masterpieces.

Frederick: Art museums ought to devote their limited resources to acquiring the works of recognized masters in order to ensure the preservation of the greatest artworks.

Elaine's and Frederick's statements provide the most support for the claim that they would disagree about whether

(A) many artistic masterpieces are not recognized as such by art experts

(B) museums should seek to represent all genres of art in their collections

(C) art museums should seek to preserve works of art

(D) an art museum ought to acquire an unusual example of a period or genre if more characteristic examples are prohibitively expensive

(E) all of the artworks that experts identify as masterpieces are actually masterpieces

3. Science columnist: It is clear why humans have so many diseases in common with cats. Many human diseases are genetically based, and cats are genetically closer to humans than are any other mammals except nonhuman primates. Each of the genes identified so far in cats has an exact counterpart in humans.

Which one of the following, if true, most weakens the science columnist's explanation for the claim that humans have so many diseases in common with cats?

(A) Cats have built up resistance to many of the diseases they have in common with humans.

(B) Most diseases that humans have in common with cats have no genetic basis.

(C) Cats have more diseases in common with nonhuman primates than with humans.

(D) Many of the diseases humans have in common with cats are mild and are rarely diagnosed.

(E) Humans have more genes in common with nonhuman primates than with cats.

4. This region must find new ways to help business grow. After all, shoe manufacturing used to be a major local industry, but recently has experienced severe setbacks due to overseas competition, so there is a need for expansion into new manufacturing areas. Moreover, our outdated public policy generally inhibits business growth.

Which one of the following most accurately expresses the main conclusion drawn in the argument?

(A) The region needs to find new ways to enhance business growth.

(B) Shoe manufacturing is no longer a major source of income in the region.

(C) Shoe manufacturing in the region has dramatically declined due to overseas competition.

(D) Business in the region must expand into new areas of manufacturing.

(E) Outdated public policy inhibits business growth in the region.

GO ON TO THE NEXT PAGE.

5. As a result of modern medicine, more people have been able to enjoy long and pain-free lives. But the resulting increase in life expectancy has contributed to a steady increase in the proportion of the population that is of advanced age. This population shift is creating potentially devastating financial problems for some social welfare programs.

Which one of the following propositions is most precisely exemplified by the situation presented above?

(A) Technical or scientific innovation cannot be the solution to all problems.

(B) Implementing technological innovations should be delayed until the resulting social changes can be managed.

(C) Every enhancement of the quality of life has unavoidable negative consequences.

(D) All social institutions are affected by a preoccupation with prolonging life.

(E) Solving one set of problems can create a different set of problems.

6. Since Jackie is such a big fan of Moral Vacuum's music, she will probably like The Cruel Herd's new album. Like Moral Vacuum, The Cruel Herd on this album plays complex rock music that employs the acoustic instrumentation and harmonic sophistication of early sixties jazz. The Cruel Herd also has very witty lyrics, full of puns and sardonic humor, like some of Moral Vacuum's best lyrics.

Which one of the following, if true, most strengthens the argument?

(A) Jackie has not previously cared for The Cruel Herd, but on the new album The Cruel Herd's previous musical arranger has been replaced by Moral Vacuum's musical arranger.

(B) Though The Cruel Herd's previous albums' production quality was not great, the new album is produced by one of the most widely employed producers in the music industry.

(C) Like Moral Vacuum, The Cruel Herd regularly performs in clubs popular with many students at the university that Jackie attends.

(D) All of the music that Jackie prefers to listen to on a regular basis is rock music.

(E) Jackie's favorite Moral Vacuum songs have lyrics that are somber and marked by a strong political awareness.

7. Superconductors are substances that conduct electricity without resistance at low temperatures. Their use, however, will never be economically feasible, unless there is a substance that superconducts at a temperature above minus 148 degrees Celsius. If there is such a substance, that substance must be an alloy of niobium and germanium. Unfortunately, such alloys superconduct at temperatures no higher than minus 160 degrees Celsius.

If the statements above are true, which one of the following must also be true?

(A) The use of superconductors will never be economically feasible.

(B) If the alloys of niobium and germanium do not superconduct at temperatures above minus 148 degrees Celsius, then there are other substances that will do so.

(C) The use of superconductors could be economically feasible if there is a substance that superconducts at temperatures below minus 148 degrees Celsius.

(D) Alloys of niobium and germanium do not superconduct at temperatures below minus 160 degrees Celsius.

(E) No use of alloys of niobium and germanium will ever be economically feasible.

8. Doctor: In three separate studies, researchers compared children who had slept with night-lights in their rooms as infants to children who had not. In the first study, the children who had slept with night-lights proved more likely to be nearsighted, but the later studies found no correlation between night-lights and nearsightedness. However, the children in the first study were younger than those in the later studies. This suggests that if night-lights cause nearsightedness, the effect disappears with age.

Which one of the following, if true, would most weaken the doctor's argument?

(A) A fourth study comparing infants who were currently sleeping with night-lights to infants who were not did not find any correlation between night-lights and nearsightedness.

(B) On average, young children who are already very nearsighted are no more likely to sleep with night-lights than young children who are not already nearsighted.

(C) In a study involving children who had not slept with night-lights as infants but had slept with night-lights when they were older, most of the children studied were not nearsighted.

(D) The two studies in which no correlation was found did not examine enough children to provide significant support for any conclusion regarding a causal relationship between night-lights and nearsightedness.

(E) In a fourth study involving 100 children who were older than those in any of the first three studies, several of the children who had slept with night-lights as infants were nearsighted.

GO ON TO THE NEXT PAGE.

9. Global surveys estimate the earth's population of nesting female leatherback turtles has fallen by more than two-thirds in the past 15 years. Any species whose population declines by more than two-thirds in 15 years is in grave danger of extinction, so the leatherback turtle is clearly in danger of extinction.

Which one of the following is an assumption that the argument requires?

(A) The decline in the population of nesting female leatherback turtles is proportional to the decline in the leatherback turtle population as a whole.

(B) If the global population of leatherback turtles falls by more than two-thirds over the next 15 years, the species will eventually become extinct.

(C) The global population of leatherback turtles consists in roughly equal numbers of females and males.

(D) Very few leatherback turtles exist in captivity.

(E) The only way to ensure the continued survival of leatherback turtles in the wild is to breed them in captivity.

10. Public health experts have waged a long-standing educational campaign to get people to eat more vegetables, which are known to help prevent cancer. Unfortunately, the campaign has had little impact on people's diets. The reason is probably that many people simply dislike the taste of most vegetables. Thus, the campaign would probably be more effective if it included information on ways to make vegetables more appetizing.

Which one of the following, if true, most strengthens the argument?

(A) The campaign to get people to eat more vegetables has had little impact on the diets of most people who love the taste of vegetables.

(B) Some ways of making vegetables more appetizing diminish vegetables' ability to help prevent cancer.

(C) People who find a few vegetables appetizing typically do not eat substantially more vegetables than do people who dislike the taste of most vegetables.

(D) People who dislike the taste of most vegetables would eat many more vegetables if they knew how to make them more appetizing.

(E) The only way to make the campaign to get people to eat more vegetables more effective would be to ensure that anyone who at present dislikes the taste of certain vegetables learns to find those vegetables appetizing.

11. Pure science—research with no immediate commercial or technological application—is a public good. Such research requires a great amount of financial support and does not yield profits in the short term. Since private corporations will not undertake to support activities that do not yield short-term profits, a society that wants to reap the benefits of pure science ought to use public funds to support such research.

The claim about private corporations serves which one of the following functions in the argument?

(A) It expresses the conclusion of the argument.

(B) It explains what is meant by the expression "pure research" in the context of the argument.

(C) It distracts attention from the point at issue by introducing a different but related goal.

(D) It supports the conclusion by ruling out an alternative way of achieving the benefits mentioned.

(E) It illustrates a case where unfortunate consequences result from a failure to accept the recommendation offered.

12. Melinda: Hazard insurance decreases an individual's risk by judiciously spreading the risk among many policyholders.

Jack: I disagree. It makes sense for me to buy fire insurance for my house, but I don't see how doing so lessens the chances that my house will burn down.

Jack's response most clearly trades on an ambiguity in which one of the following expressions used by Melinda?

(A) judiciously spreading
(B) many policyholders
(C) risk
(D) decreases
(E) hazard insurance

GO ON TO THE NEXT PAGE.

13. Some doctors believe that a certain drug reduces the duration of episodes of vertigo, claiming that the average duration of vertigo for people who suffer from it has decreased since the drug was introduced. However, during a recent three-month shortage of the drug, there was no significant change in the average duration of vertigo. Thus, we can conclude that the drug has no effect on the duration of vertigo.

Which one of the following is an assumption required by the argument?

(A) If a drug made a difference in the duration of vertigo, a three-month shortage of that drug would have caused a significant change in the average duration of vertigo.

(B) If there were any change in the average duration of vertigo since the introduction of the drug, it would have demonstrated that the drug has an effect on the duration of vertigo.

(C) A period of time greater than three months would not have been better to use in judging whether the drug has an effect on the duration of vertigo.

(D) Changes in diet and smoking habits are not responsible for any change in the average duration of vertigo since the introduction of the drug.

(E) There are various significant factors other than drugs that decrease the duration of vertigo for many people who suffer from it.

14. It has been suggested that a television set should be thought of as nothing more than "a toaster with pictures" and that since we let market forces determine the design of kitchen appliances we can let them determine what is seen on television. But that approach is too simple. Some governmental control is needed, since television is so important politically and culturally. It is a major source of commercial entertainment. It plays an important political role because it is the primary medium through which many voters obtain information about current affairs. It is a significant cultural force in that in the average home it is on for more than five hours a day.

Which one of the following most accurately expresses the role played in the argument by the claim that television is so important politically and culturally?

(A) It states a view that the argument as a whole is designed to discredit.

(B) It is an intermediate conclusion that is offered in support of the claim that a television set should be thought of as nothing more than "a toaster with pictures" and for which the claim that we can let market forces determine what is seen on television is offered as support.

(C) It is a premise that is offered in support of the claim that we let market forces determine the design of kitchen appliances.

(D) It is an intermediate conclusion that is offered in support of the claim that some governmental control of television is needed and for which the claim that the television is on for more than five hours a day in the average home is offered as partial support.

(E) It is a premise that is offered in support of the claim that television is the primary medium through which many voters obtain information about current affairs.

GO ON TO THE NEXT PAGE.

15. Earthworms, vital to the health of soil, prefer soil that is approximately neutral on the acid-to-alkaline scale. Since decomposition of dead plants makes the top layer of soil highly acidic, application of crushed limestone, which is highly alkaline, to the soil's surface should make the soil more attractive to earthworms.

Which one of the following is an assumption on which the argument depends?

(A) As far as soil health is concerned, aiding the decomposition of dead plants is the most important function performed by earthworms.

(B) After its application to the soil's surface, crushed limestone stays in the soil's top layer long enough to neutralize some of the top layer's acidity.

(C) Crushed limestone contains available calcium and magnesium, both of which are just as vital as earthworms to healthy soil.

(D) By itself, acidity of soil does nothing to hasten decomposition of dead plants.

(E) Alkaline soil is significantly more likely to benefit from an increased earthworm population than is highly acidic soil.

16. Jurist: A nation's laws must be viewed as expressions of a moral code that transcends those laws and serves as a measure of their adequacy. Otherwise, a society can have no sound basis for preferring any given set of laws to all others. Thus, any moral prohibition against the violation of statutes must leave room for exceptions.

Which one of the following can be properly inferred from the jurist's statements?

(A) Those who formulate statutes are not primarily concerned with morality when they do so.

(B) Sometimes criteria other than the criteria derived from a moral code should be used in choosing one set of laws over another.

(C) Unless it is legally forbidden ever to violate some moral rules, moral behavior and compliance with laws are indistinguishable.

(D) There is no statute that a nation's citizens have a moral obligation to obey.

(E) A nation's laws can sometimes come into conflict with the moral code they express.

17. An association between two types of conditions does not establish that conditions of one type cause conditions of the other type. Even persistent and inviolable association is inconclusive; such association is often due to conditions of both types being effects of the same kind of cause.

Which one of the following judgments most closely conforms to the principle stated above?

(A) Some people claim that rapid growth of the money supply is what causes inflation. But this is a naive view. What these people do not realize is that growth in the money supply and inflation are actually one and the same phenomenon.

(B) People who have high blood pressure tend to be overweight. But before we draw any inferences, we should consider that an unhealthy lifestyle can cause high blood pressure, and weight gain can result from living unhealthily.

(C) In some areas, there is a high correlation between ice cream consumption and the crime rate. Some researchers have proposed related third factors, but we cannot rule out that the correlation is purely coincidental.

(D) People's moods seem to vary with the color of the clothes they wear. Dark colors are associated with gloomy moods, and bright colors are associated with cheerful moods. This correlation resolves nothing, however. We cannot say whether it is the colors that cause the moods or the converse.

(E) Linguists propose that the similarities between Greek and Latin are due to their common descent from an earlier language. But how are we to know that the similarities are not actually due to the two languages having borrowed structures from one another, as with the languages Marathi and Telegu?

GO ON TO THE NEXT PAGE.

18. Salesperson: When a salesperson is successful, it is
      certain that that person has been in sales for at
      least three years. This is because to succeed as a
      salesperson, one must first establish a strong
      client base, and studies have shown that anyone
      who spends at least three years developing a
      client base can eventually make a comfortable
      living in sales.

The reasoning in the salesperson's argument is
vulnerable to criticism on the grounds that it fails to
consider the possibility that

(A) salespeople who have spent three years
       developing a client base might not yet be
       successful in sales
(B) some salespeople require fewer than three years
       in which to develop a strong client base
(C) a salesperson who has not spent three years
       developing a client base may not succeed in sales
(D) it takes longer than three years for a salesperson
       to develop a strong client base
(E) few salespeople can afford to spend three years
       building a client base

19. People who have habitually slept less than six hours a
      night and then begin sleeping eight or more hours a
      night typically begin to feel much less anxious.
      Therefore, most people who sleep less than six hours a
      night can probably cause their anxiety levels to fall by
      beginning to sleep at least eight hours a night.

The reasoning in which one of the following arguments
is most similar to that in the argument above?

(A) When a small company first begins to advertise
       on the Internet, its financial situation generally
       improves. This shows that most small
       companies that have never advertised on the
       Internet can probably improve their financial
       situation by doing so.
(B) Certain small companies that had never
       previously advertised on the Internet have found
       that their financial situations began to improve
       after they started to do so. So most small
       companies can probably improve their financial
       situations by starting to advertise on the Internet.
(C) It must be true that any small company that
       increases its Internet advertising will improve its
       financial situation, since most small companies
       that advertise on the Internet improved their
       financial situations soon after they first began to
       do so.
(D) Usually, the financial situation of a small
       company that has never advertised on the
       Internet will improve only if that company starts
       to advertise on the Internet. Therefore, a typical
       small company that has never advertised on the
       Internet can probably improve its financial
       situation by doing so.
(E) A small company's financial situation usually
       improves soon after that company first begins to
       advertise on the Internet. Thus, most small
       companies that have never advertised on the
       Internet could probably become financially
       strong.

GO ON TO THE NEXT PAGE.

20. Biologist: Lions and tigers are so similar to each other anatomically that their skeletons are virtually indistinguishable. But their behaviors are known to be quite different: tigers hunt only as solitary individuals, whereas lions hunt in packs. Thus, paleontologists cannot reasonably infer solely on the basis of skeletal anatomy that extinct predatory animals, such as certain dinosaurs, hunted in packs.

The conclusion is properly drawn if which one of the following is assumed?

(A) The skeletons of lions and tigers are at least somewhat similar in structure in certain key respects to the skeletons of at least some extinct predatory animals.

(B) There have existed at least two species of extinct predatory dinosaurs that were so similar to each other that their skeletal anatomy is virtually indistinguishable.

(C) If skeletal anatomy alone is ever an inadequate basis for inferring a particular species' hunting behavior, then it is never reasonable to infer, based on skeletal anatomy alone, that a species of animals hunted in packs.

(D) If any two animal species with virtually indistinguishable skeletal anatomy exhibit quite different hunting behaviors, then it is never reasonable to infer, based solely on the hunting behavior of those species, that the two species have the same skeletal anatomy.

(E) If it is unreasonable to infer, solely on the basis of differences in skeletal anatomy, that extinct animals of two distinct species differed in their hunting behavior, then the skeletal remains of those two species are virtually indistinguishable.

21. The trees always blossom in May if April rainfall exceeds 5 centimeters. If April rainfall exceeds 5 centimeters, then the reservoirs are always full on May 1. The reservoirs were not full this May 1 and thus the trees will not blossom this May.

Which one of the following exhibits a flawed pattern of reasoning most similar to the flawed pattern of reasoning in the argument above?

(A) If the garlic is in the pantry, then it is still fresh. And the potatoes are on the basement stairs if the garlic is in the pantry. The potatoes are not on the basement stairs, so the garlic is not still fresh.

(B) The jar reaches optimal temperature if it is held over the burner for 2 minutes. The contents of the jar liquefy immediately if the jar is at optimal temperature. The jar was held over the burner for 2 minutes, so the contents of the jar must have liquefied immediately.

(C) A book is classified "special" if it is more than 200 years old. If a book was set with wooden type, then it is more than 200 years old. This book is not classified "special," so it is not printed with wooden type.

(D) The mower will operate only if the engine is not flooded. The engine is flooded if the foot pedal is depressed. The foot pedal is not depressed, so the mower will operate.

(E) If the kiln is too hot, then the plates will crack. If the plates crack, then the artisan must redo the order. The artisan need not redo the order. Thus, the kiln was not too hot.

22. Doctor: Being overweight has long been linked with a variety of health problems, such as high blood pressure and heart disease. But recent research conclusively shows that people who are slightly overweight are healthier than those who are considerably underweight. Therefore, to be healthy, it suffices to be slightly overweight.

The argument's reasoning is flawed because the argument

(A) ignores medical opinions that tend to lead to a conclusion contrary to the one drawn

(B) never adequately defines what is meant by "healthy"

(C) does not take into account the fact that appropriate weight varies greatly from person to person

(D) holds that if a person lacks a property that would suffice to make the person unhealthy, then that person must be healthy

(E) mistakes a merely relative property for one that is absolute

GO ON TO THE NEXT PAGE.

23. Robust crops not only withstand insect attacks more successfully than other crops, they are also less likely to be attacked in the first place, since insects tend to feed on weaker plants. Killing insects with pesticides does not address the underlying problem of inherent vulnerability to damage caused by insect attacks. Thus, a better way to reduce the vulnerability of agricultural crops to insect pest damage is to grow those crops in good soil—soil with adequate nutrients, organic matter, and microbial activity.

Which one of the following is an assumption on which the argument depends?

(A) The application of nutrients and organic matter to farmland improves the soil's microbial activity.

(B) Insects never attack crops grown in soil containing adequate nutrients, organic matter, and microbial activity.

(C) The application of pesticides to weak crops fails to reduce the extent to which they are damaged by insect pests.

(D) Crops that are grown in good soil tend to be more robust than other crops.

(E) Growing crops without the use of pesticides generally produces less robust plants than when pesticides are used.

24. People perceive color by means of certain photopigments in the retina that are sensitive to certain wavelengths of light. People who are color-blind are unable to distinguish between red and green, for example, due to an absence of certain photopigments. What is difficult to explain, however, is that in a study of people who easily distinguish red from green, 10 to 20 percent failed to report distinctions between many shades of red that the majority of the subjects were able to distinguish.

Each of the following, if true, helps to explain the result of the study cited above EXCEPT:

(A) People with abnormally low concentrations of the photopigments for perceiving red can perceive fewer shades of red than people with normal concentrations.

(B) Questions that ask subjects to distinguish between different shades of the same color are difficult to phrase with complete clarity.

(C) Some people are uninterested in fine gradations of color and fail to notice or report differences they do not care about.

(D) Some people are unable to distinguish red from green due to an absence in the retina of the photopigment sensitive to green.

(E) Some people fail to report distinctions between certain shades of red because they lack the names for those shades.

25. Occultist: The issue of whether astrology is a science is easily settled: it is both an art and a science. The scientific components are the complicated mathematics and the astronomical knowledge needed to create an astrological chart. The art is in the synthesis of a multitude of factors and symbols into a coherent statement of their relevance to an individual.

The reasoning in the occultist's argument is most vulnerable to criticism on the grounds that the argument

(A) presumes, without providing justification, that any science must involve complicated mathematics

(B) incorrectly infers that a practice is a science merely from the fact that the practice has some scientific components

(C) denies the possibility that astrology involves components that are neither artistic nor scientific

(D) incorrectly infers that astronomical knowledge is scientific merely from the fact that such knowledge is needed to create an astrological chart

(E) presumes, without providing justification, that any art must involve the synthesis of a multitude of factors and symbols

S T O P

IF YOU FINISH BEFORE TIME IS CALLED, YOU MAY CHECK YOUR WORK ON THIS SECTION ONLY.
DO NOT WORK ON ANY OTHER SECTION IN THE TEST.

SECTION II

Time—35 minutes

23 Questions

<u>Directions:</u> Each group of questions in this section is based on a set of conditions. In answering some of the questions, it may be useful to draw a rough diagram. Choose the response that most accurately and completely answers each question and blacken the corresponding space on your answer sheet.

<u>Questions 1–5</u>

Five performers—Traugott, West, Xavier, Young, and Zinser—are recruited by three talent agencies—Fame Agency, Premier Agency, and Star Agency. Each performer signs with exactly one of the agencies and each agency signs at least one of the performers. The performers' signing with the agencies is in accord with the following:

    Xavier signs with Fame Agency.
    Xavier and Young do not sign with the same agency as each other.
    Zinser signs with the same agency as Young.
    If Traugott signs with Star Agency, West also signs with Star Agency.

1. Which one of the following could be a complete and accurate list of the performers who sign with each agency?

  (A) Fame Agency: Xavier
       Premier Agency: West
       Star Agency: Traugott, Young, Zinser
  (B) Fame Agency: Xavier
       Premier Agency: Traugott, West
       Star Agency: Young, Zinser
  (C) Fame Agency: Xavier
       Premier Agency: Traugott, Young
       Star Agency: West, Zinser
  (D) Fame Agency: Young, Zinser
       Premier Agency: Xavier
       Star Agency: Traugott, West
  (E) Fame Agency: Xavier, Young, Zinser
       Premier Agency: Traugott
       Star Agency: West

2. Which one of the following could be true?

  (A) West is the only performer who signs with Star Agency.
  (B) West, Young, and Zinser all sign with Premier Agency.
  (C) Xavier signs with the same agency as Zinser.
  (D) Zinser is the only performer who signs with Star Agency.
  (E) Three of the performers sign with Fame Agency.

3. Which one of the following must be true?

  (A) West and Zinser do not sign with the same agency as each other.
  (B) Fame Agency signs at most two of the performers.
  (C) Fame Agency signs the same number of the performers as Star Agency.
  (D) Traugott signs with the same agency as West.
  (E) West does not sign with Fame Agency.

4. The agency with which each of the performers signs is completely determined if which one of the following is true?

  (A) Traugott signs with Fame Agency.
  (B) Traugott signs with Star Agency.
  (C) West signs with Premier Agency.
  (D) Xavier signs with Fame Agency.
  (E) Zinser signs with Premier Agency.

5. If Zinser signs with Star Agency, which one of the following must be false?

  (A) Premier Agency signs exactly one performer.
  (B) Star Agency signs exactly three of the performers.
  (C) Traugott signs with Star Agency.
  (D) West signs with Star Agency.
  (E) None of the other performers signs with the same agency as Xavier.

GO ON TO THE NEXT PAGE.

Questions 6–11

A competition is being held to select a design for Yancy College's new student union building. Each of six architects— Green, Jackson, Liu, Mertz, Peete, and Valdez—has submitted exactly one design. There are exactly six designs, and they are presented one at a time to the panel of judges, each design being presented exactly once, consistent with the following conditions:

> Mertz's design is presented at some time before Liu's and after Peete's.
> Green's design is presented either at some time before Jackson's or at some time after Liu's, but not both.
> Valdez's design is presented either at some time before Green's or at some time after Peete's, but not both.

6. Which one of the following could be the order in which the designs are presented, from first to last?

(A) Jackson's, Peete's, Mertz's, Green's, Valdez's, Liu's
(B) Peete's, Jackson's, Liu's, Mertz's, Green's, Valdez's
(C) Peete's, Mertz's, Jackson's, Liu's, Green's, Valdez's
(D) Peete's, Mertz's, Valdez's, Green's, Liu's, Jackson's
(E) Valdez's, Liu's, Jackson's, Peete's, Mertz's, Green's

7. Mertz's design CANNOT be presented

(A) sixth
(B) fifth
(C) fourth
(D) third
(E) second

8. If Liu's design is presented sixth, then which one of the following must be true?

(A) Green's design is presented at some time before Jackson's.
(B) Jackson's design is presented at some time before Mertz's.
(C) Peete's design is presented at some time before Green's.
(D) Peete's design is presented at some time before Valdez's.
(E) Valdez's design is presented at some time before Green's.

9. If Jackson's design is presented at some time before Mertz's, then each of the following could be true EXCEPT:

(A) Jackson's design is presented second.
(B) Peete's design is presented third.
(C) Peete's design is presented fourth.
(D) Jackson's design is presented fifth.
(E) Liu's design is presented fifth.

10. Which one of the following designs CANNOT be the design presented first?

(A) Green's
(B) Jackson's
(C) Liu's
(D) Peete's
(E) Valdez's

11. Which one of the following could be an accurate partial list of the architects, each matched with his or her design's place in the order in which the designs are presented?

(A) first: Mertz; fourth: Liu; fifth: Green
(B) second: Green; third: Peete; fourth: Jackson
(C) second: Mertz; fifth: Green; sixth: Jackson
(D) fourth: Peete; fifth: Liu; sixth: Jackson
(E) fourth: Valdez; fifth: Green; sixth: Liu

GO ON TO THE NEXT PAGE.

Questions 12–17

Detectives investigating a citywide increase in burglaries questioned exactly seven suspects—S, T, V, W, X, Y, and Z—each on a different one of seven consecutive days. Each suspect was questioned exactly once. Any suspect who confessed did so while being questioned. The investigation conformed to the following:

T was questioned on day three.
The suspect questioned on day four did not confess.
S was questioned after W was questioned.
Both X and V were questioned after Z was questioned.
No suspects confessed after W was questioned.
Exactly two suspects confessed after T was questioned.

12. Which one of the following could be true?

(A) X was questioned on day one.
(B) V was questioned on day two.
(C) Z was questioned on day four.
(D) W was questioned on day five.
(E) S was questioned on day six.

13. If Z was the second suspect to confess, then each of the following statements could be true EXCEPT:

(A) T confessed.
(B) T did not confess.
(C) V did not confess.
(D) X confessed.
(E) Y did not confess.

14. If Y was questioned after V but before X, then which one of the following could be true?

(A) V did not confess.
(B) Y confessed.
(C) X did not confess.
(D) X was questioned on day four.
(E) Z was questioned on day two.

15. Which one of the following suspects must have been questioned before T was questioned?

(A) V
(B) W
(C) X
(D) Y
(E) Z

16. If X and Y both confessed, then each of the following could be true EXCEPT:

(A) V confessed.
(B) X was questioned on day five.
(C) Y was questioned on day one.
(D) Z was questioned on day one.
(E) Z did not confess.

17. If neither X nor V confessed, then which one of the following must be true?

(A) T confessed.
(B) V was questioned on day two.
(C) X was questioned on day four.
(D) Y confessed.
(E) Z did not confess.

GO ON TO THE NEXT PAGE.

Questions 18–23

The three highest-placing teams in a high school debate tournament are the teams from Fairview, Gillom, and Hilltop high schools. Each team has exactly two members. The individuals on these three teams are Mei, Navarro, O'Rourke, Pavlovich, Sethna, and Tsudama. The following is the case:

Sethna is on the team from Gillom High.
Tsudama is on the second-place team.
Mei and Pavlovich are not on the same team.
Pavlovich's team places higher than Navarro's team.
The team from Gillom High places higher than the team from Hilltop High.

18. Which one of the following could be an accurate list of the members of each of the three highest-placing teams?

(A) first place: Mei and O'Rourke
second place: Pavlovich and Sethna
third place: Navarro and Tsudama
(B) first place: Mei and Pavlovich
second place: Sethna and Tsudama
third place: Navarro and O'Rourke
(C) first place: Navarro and Sethna
second place: Pavlovich and Tsudama
third place: Mei and O'Rourke
(D) first place: O'Rourke and Pavlovich
second place: Navarro and Tsudama
third place: Mei and Sethna
(E) first place: Pavlovich and Sethna
second place: O'Rourke and Tsudama
third place: Mei and Navarro

19. If Pavlovich is on the team from Hilltop High, then which one of the following could be true?

(A) O'Rourke is on the first-place team.
(B) Pavlovich is on the first-place team.
(C) Mei is on the second-place team.
(D) Navarro is on the second-place team.
(E) Sethna is on the second-place team.

20. If O'Rourke is on the second-place team, then which one of the following could be true?

(A) Mei is on the team from Gillom High.
(B) Navarro is on the team from Fairview High.
(C) O'Rourke is on the team from Gillom High.
(D) Pavlovich is on the team from Hilltop High.
(E) Tsudama is on the team from Gillom High.

21. If Pavlovich and Tsudama are teammates, then for how many of the individuals can it be exactly determined where his or her team places?

(A) two
(B) three
(C) four
(D) five
(E) six

22. If Mei is on a team that places higher than the Hilltop team, then which one of the following could be true?

(A) The Fairview team places first.
(B) The Gillom team places second.
(C) Navarro is on the second-place team.
(D) O'Rourke is on the first-place team.
(E) Pavlovich is on the first-place team.

23. Sethna's teammate could be any one of the following EXCEPT:

(A) Mei
(B) Navarro
(C) O'Rourke
(D) Pavlovich
(E) Tsudama

S T O P

IF YOU FINISH BEFORE TIME IS CALLED, YOU MAY CHECK YOUR WORK ON THIS SECTION ONLY.
DO NOT WORK ON ANY OTHER SECTION IN THE TEST.

SECTION III
Time—35 minutes
25 Questions

Directions: The questions in this section are based on the reasoning contained in brief statements or passages. For some questions, more than one of the choices could conceivably answer the question. However, you are to choose the best answer; that is, the response that most accurately and completely answers the question. You should not make assumptions that are by commonsense standards implausible, superfluous, or incompatible with the passage. After you have chosen the best answer, blacken the corresponding space on your answer sheet.

1. At many electronics retail stores, the consumer has the option of purchasing product warranties that extend beyond the manufacturer's warranty. However, consumers are generally better off not buying extended warranties. Most problems with electronic goods occur within the period covered by the manufacturer's warranty.

    Which one of the following, if true, most strengthens the argument?

    (A)   Problems with electronic goods that occur after the manufacturer's warranty expires are generally inexpensive to fix in comparison with the cost of an extended warranty.
    (B)   Because problems are so infrequent after the manufacturer's warranty expires, extended warranties on electronic goods are generally inexpensive.
    (C)   Most of those who buy extended warranties on electronic goods do so because special circumstances make their item more likely to break than is usually the case.
    (D)   Some extended warranties on electronic goods cover the product for the period covered by the manufacturer's warranty as well as subsequent years.
    (E)   Retail stores sell extended warranties in part because consumers who purchase them are likely to purchase other products from the same store.

2. Since the 1970s, environmentalists have largely succeeded in convincing legislators to enact extensive environmental regulations. Yet, as environmentalists themselves not only admit but insist, the condition of the environment is worsening, not improving. Clearly, more environmental regulations are not the solution to the environment's problems.

    The argument's reasoning is flawed because the argument

    (A)   attacks the environmentalists themselves instead of their positions
    (B)   presumes, without providing warrant, that only an absence of environmental regulations could prevent environmental degradation
    (C)   fails to consider the possibility that the condition of the environment would have worsened even more without environmental regulations
    (D)   fails to justify its presumption that reducing excessive regulations is more important than preserving the environment
    (E)   fails to consider the views of the environmentalists' opponents

GO ON TO THE NEXT PAGE.

3. Although it is unwise to take a developmental view of an art like music—as if Beethoven were an advance over Josquin, or Miles Davis an advance over Louis Armstrong—there are ways in which it makes sense to talk about musical knowledge growing over time. We certainly know more about certain sounds than was known five centuries ago; that is, we understand how sounds that earlier composers avoided can be used effectively in musical compositions. For example, we now know how the interval of the third, which is considered dissonant, can be used in compositions to create consonant musical phrases.

Which one of the following most accurately expresses the main conclusion of the argument?

(A) Sounds that were never used in past musical compositions are used today.
(B) Sounds that were once considered dissonant are more pleasing to modern listeners.
(C) It is inappropriate to take a developmental view of music.
(D) It is unwise to say that one composer is better than another.
(E) Our understanding of music can improve over the course of time.

4. A recent test of an electric insect control device discovered that, of the more than 300 insects killed during one 24-hour period, only 12 were mosquitoes. Thus this type of device may kill many insects, but will not significantly aid in controlling the potentially dangerous mosquito population.

Which one of the following, if true, most seriously weakens the argument?

(A) A careful search discovered no live mosquitoes in the vicinity of the device after the test.
(B) A very large proportion of the insects that were attracted to the device were not mosquitoes.
(C) The device is more likely to kill beneficial insects than it is to kill harmful insects.
(D) Many of the insects that were killed by the device are mosquito-eating insects.
(E) The device does not succeed in killing all of the insects that it attracts.

5. Brain-scanning technology provides information about processes occurring in the brain. For this information to help researchers understand how the brain enables us to think, however, researchers must be able to rely on the accuracy of the verbal reports given by subjects while their brains are being scanned. Otherwise brain-scan data gathered at a given moment might not contain information about what the subject reports thinking about at that moment, but instead about some different set of thoughts.

Which one of the following most accurately expresses the main conclusion of the argument?

(A) It is unlikely that brain-scanning technology will ever enable researchers to understand how the brain enables us to think.
(B) There is no way that researchers can know for certain that subjects whose brains are being scanned are accurately reporting what they are thinking.
(C) Because subjects whose brains are being scanned may not accurately report what they are thinking, the results of brain-scanning research should be regarded with great skepticism.
(D) Brain scans can provide information about the accuracy of the verbal reports of subjects whose brains are being scanned.
(E) Information from brain scans can help researchers understand how the brain enables us to think only if the verbal reports of those whose brains are being scanned are accurate.

GO ON TO THE NEXT PAGE.

6. Ornithologist: This bird species is widely thought to subsist primarily on vegetation, but my research shows that this belief is erroneous. While concealed in a well-camouflaged blind, I have observed hundreds of these birds every morning over a period of months, and I estimate that over half of what they ate consisted of insects and other animal food sources.

The reasoning in the ornithologist's argument is most vulnerable to criticism on the grounds that the argument

(A) assumes, without providing justification, that the feeding behavior of the birds observed was not affected by the ornithologist's act of observation

(B) fails to specify the nature of the animal food sources, other than insects, that were consumed by the birds

(C) adopts a widespread belief about the birds' feeding habits without considering the evidence that led to the belief

(D) neglects the possibility that the birds have different patterns of food consumption during different parts of the day and night

(E) fails to consider the possibility that the birds' diet has changed since the earlier belief about their diet was formed

7. Educator: Only those students who are genuinely curious about a topic can successfully learn about that topic. They find the satisfaction of their curiosity intrinsically gratifying, and appreciate the inherent rewards of the learning process itself. However, almost no child enters the classroom with sufficient curiosity to learn successfully all that the teacher must instill. A teacher's job, therefore, _____.

Which one of the following most logically completes the educator's argument?

(A) requires for the fulfillment of its goals the stimulation as well as the satisfaction of curiosity

(B) necessitates the creative use of rewards that are not inherent in the learning process itself

(C) is to focus primarily on those topics that do not initially interest the students

(D) is facilitated by students' taking responsibility for their own learning

(E) becomes easier if students realize that some learning is not necessarily enjoyable

8. Environmentalist: When bacteria degrade household cleaning products, vapors that are toxic to humans are produced. Unfortunately, household cleaning products are often found in landfills. Thus, the common practice of converting landfills into public parks is damaging human health.

Which one of the following is an assumption the environmentalist's argument requires?

(A) In at least some landfills that have been converted into public parks there are bacteria that degrade household cleaning products.

(B) Converting a landfill into a public park will cause no damage to human health unless toxic vapors are produced in that landfill and humans are exposed to them.

(C) If a practice involves the exposure of humans to vapors from household cleaning products, then it causes at least some damage to human health.

(D) When landfills are converted to public parks, measures could be taken that would prevent people using the parks from being exposed to toxic vapors.

(E) If vapors toxic to humans are produced by the degradation of household cleaning products by bacteria in any landfill, then the health of at least some humans will suffer.

9. Tea made from camellia leaves is a popular beverage. However, studies show that regular drinkers of camellia tea usually suffer withdrawal symptoms if they discontinue drinking the tea. Furthermore, regular drinkers of camellia tea are more likely than people in general to develop kidney damage. Regular consumption of this tea, therefore, can result in a heightened risk of kidney damage.

Which one of the following, if true, most seriously weakens the argument?

(A) Several other popular beverages contain the same addictive chemical that is found in camellia tea.

(B) Addictive chemicals are unlikely to cause kidney damage solely by virtue of their addictive qualities.

(C) Some people claim that regular consumption of camellia tea helps alleviate their stress.

(D) Most people who regularly drink camellia tea do not develop kidney damage.

(E) Many people who regularly consume camellia tea also regularly consume other beverages suspected of causing kidney damage.

GO ON TO THE NEXT PAGE.

10. Artist: Avant-garde artists intend their work to challenge a society's mainstream beliefs and initiate change. And some art collectors claim that an avant-garde work that becomes popular in its own time is successful. However, a society's mainstream beliefs do not generally show any significant changes over a short period of time. Therefore, when an avant-garde work becomes popular it is a sign that the work is not successful, since it does not fulfill the intentions of its creator.

The reference to the claim of certain art collectors plays which one of the following roles in the artist's argument?

(A) It serves to bolster the argument's main conclusion.

(B) It identifies a view that is ultimately disputed by the argument.

(C) It identifies a position supported by the initial premise in the argument.

(D) It provides support for the initial premise in the argument.

(E) It provides support for a counterargument to the initial premise.

11. A recent epidemiological study found that businesspeople who travel internationally on business are much more likely to suffer from chronic insomnia than are businesspeople who do not travel on business. International travelers experience the stresses of dramatic changes in climate, frequent disruption of daily routines, and immersion in cultures other than their own, stresses not commonly felt by those who do not travel. Thus, it is likely that these stresses cause the insomnia.

Which one of the following would, if true, most strengthen the reasoning above?

(A) Most international travel for the sake of business occurs between countries with contiguous borders.

(B) Some businesspeople who travel internationally greatly enjoy the changes in climate and immersion in another culture.

(C) Businesspeople who already suffer from chronic insomnia are no more likely than businesspeople who do not to accept assignments from their employers that require international travel.

(D) Experiencing dramatic changes in climate and disruption of daily routines through international travel can be beneficial to some people who suffer from chronic insomnia.

(E) Some businesspeople who once traveled internationally but no longer do so complain of various sleep-related ailments.

12. Many mountain climbers regard climbing Mount Everest as the ultimate achievement. But climbers should not attempt this climb since the risk of death or serious injury in an Everest expedition is very high. Moreover, the romantic notion of gaining "spiritual discovery" atop Everest is dispelled by climbers' reports that the only profound experiences they had at the top were of exhaustion and fear.

Which one of the following principles, if valid, most helps to justify the reasoning above?

(A) Projects undertaken primarily for spiritual reasons ought to be abandoned if the risks are great.

(B) Dangerous activities that are unlikely to result in significant spiritual benefits for those undertaking them should be avoided.

(C) Activities that are extremely dangerous ought to be legally prohibited unless they are necessary to produce spiritual enlightenment.

(D) Profound spiritual experiences can be achieved without undergoing the serious danger involved in mountain climbing.

(E) Mountain climbers and other athletes should carefully examine the underlying reasons they have for participating in their sports.

13. Each of the smallest particles in the universe has an elegantly simple structure. Since these particles compose the universe, we can conclude that the universe itself has an elegantly simple structure.

Each of the following arguments exhibits flawed reasoning similar to that in the argument above EXCEPT:

(A) Each part of this car is nearly perfectly engineered. Therefore this car is nearly perfect, from an engineering point of view.

(B) Each part of this desk is made of metal. Therefore this desk is made of metal.

(C) Each brick in this wall is rectangular. Therefore this wall is rectangular.

(D) Each piece of wood in this chair is sturdy. Therefore this chair is sturdy.

(E) Each sentence in this novel is well constructed. Therefore this is a well-constructed novel.

GO ON TO THE NEXT PAGE.

14. Criminologist: A judicial system that tries and punishes criminals without delay is an effective deterrent to violent crime. Long, drawn-out trials and successful legal maneuvering may add to criminals' feelings of invulnerability. But if potential violent criminals know that being caught means prompt punishment, they will hesitate to break the law.

Which one of the following, if true, would most seriously weaken the criminologist's argument?

(A) It is in the nature of violent crime that it is not premeditated.

(B) About one-fourth of all suspects first arrested for a crime are actually innocent.

(C) Many violent crimes are committed by first-time offenders.

(D) Everyone accused of a crime has the right to a trial.

(E) Countries that promptly punish suspected lawbreakers have lower crime rates than countries that allow long trials.

15. Journalist: Many people object to mandatory retirement at age 65 as being arbitrary, arguing that people over 65 make useful contributions. However, if those who reach 65 are permitted to continue working indefinitely, we will face unacceptable outcomes. First, young people entering the job market will not be able to obtain decent jobs in the professions for which they were trained, resulting in widespread dissatisfaction among the young. Second, it is not fair for those who have worked 40 or more years to deprive others of opportunities. Therefore, mandatory retirement should be retained.

The journalist's argument depends on assuming which one of the following?

(A) Anyone who has worked 40 years is at least 65 years old.

(B) All young people entering the job market are highly trained professionals.

(C) It is unfair for a person not to get a job in the profession for which that person was trained.

(D) If people are forced to retire at age 65, there will be much dissatisfaction among at least some older people.

(E) If retirement ceases to be mandatory at age 65, at least some people will choose to work past age 65.

16. Editorial: Contrary to popular belief, teaching preschoolers is not especially difficult, for they develop strict systems (e.g., for sorting toys by shape), which help them to learn, and they are always intensely curious about something new in their world.

Which one of the following, if true, most seriously weakens the editorial's argument?

(A) Preschoolers have a tendency to imitate adults, and most adults follow strict routines.

(B) Children intensely curious about new things have very short attention spans.

(C) Some older children also develop strict systems that help them learn.

(D) Preschoolers ask as many creative questions as do older children.

(E) Preschool teachers generally report lower levels of stress than do other teachers.

17. Lawyer: A body of circumstantial evidence is like a rope, and each item of evidence is like a strand of that rope. Just as additional pieces of circumstantial evidence strengthen the body of evidence, adding strands to the rope strengthens the rope. And if one strand breaks, the rope is not broken nor is its strength much diminished. Thus, even if a few items of a body of circumstantial evidence are discredited, the overall body of evidence retains its basic strength.

The reasoning in the lawyer's argument is most vulnerable to criticism on the grounds that the argument

(A) takes for granted that no items in a body of circumstantial evidence are significantly more critical to the strength of the evidence than other items in that body

(B) presumes, without providing justification, that the strength of a body of evidence is less than the sum of the strengths of the parts of that body

(C) fails to consider the possibility that if many items in a body of circumstantial evidence were discredited, the overall body of evidence would be discredited

(D) offers an analogy in support of a conclusion without indicating whether the two types of things compared share any similarities

(E) draws a conclusion that simply restates a claim presented in support of that conclusion

GO ON TO THE NEXT PAGE.

18. Ethicist: Many environmentalists hold that the natural environment is morally valuable for its own sake, regardless of any benefits it provides us. However, even if nature has no moral value, nature can be regarded as worth preserving simply on the grounds that people find it beautiful. Moreover, because it is philosophically disputable whether nature is morally valuable but undeniable that it is beautiful, an argument for preserving nature that emphasizes nature's beauty will be less vulnerable to logical objections than one that emphasizes its moral value.

The ethicist's reasoning most closely conforms to which one of the following principles?

(A) An argument in favor of preserving nature will be less open to logical objections if it avoids the issue of what makes nature worth preserving.

(B) If an argument for preserving nature emphasizes a specific characteristic of nature and is vulnerable to logical objections, then that characteristic does not provide a sufficient reason for preserving nature.

(C) If it is philosophically disputable whether nature has a certain characteristic, then nature would be more clearly worth preserving if it did not have that characteristic.

(D) Anything that has moral value is worth preserving regardless of whether people consider it to be beautiful.

(E) An argument for preserving nature will be less open to logical objections if it appeals to a characteristic that can be regarded as a basis for preserving nature and that philosophically indisputably belongs to nature.

19. An editor is compiling a textbook containing essays by several different authors. The book will contain essays by Lind, Knight, or Jones, but it will not contain essays by all three. If the textbook contains an essay by Knight, then it will also contain an essay by Jones.

If the statements above are true, which one of the following must be true?

(A) If the textbook contains an essay by Lind, then it will not contain an essay by Knight.

(B) The textbook will contain an essay by only one of Lind, Knight, and Jones.

(C) The textbook will not contain an essay by Knight.

(D) If the textbook contains an essay by Lind, then it will also contain an essay by Jones.

(E) The textbook will contain an essay by Lind.

20. The ability of mammals to control their internal body temperatures is a factor in the development of their brains and intelligence. This can be seen from the following facts: the brain is a chemical machine, all chemical reactions are temperature dependent, and any organism that can control its body temperature can assure that these reactions occur at the proper temperatures.

Which one of the following is an assumption on which the argument depends?

(A) Organisms unable to control their body temperatures do not have the capacity to generate internal body heat without relying on external factors.

(B) Mammals are the only animals that have the ability to control their internal body temperatures.

(C) The brain cannot support intelligence if the chemical reactions within it are subject to uncontrolled temperatures.

(D) The development of intelligence in mammals is not independent of the chemical reactions in their brains taking place at the proper temperatures.

(E) Organisms incapable of controlling their internal body temperatures are subject to unpredictable chemical processes.

21. People who object to the proposed hazardous waste storage site by appealing to extremely implausible scenarios in which the site fails to contain the waste safely are overlooking the significant risks associated with delays in moving the waste from its present unsafe location. If we wait to remove the waste until we find a site certain to contain it safely, the waste will remain in its current location for many years, since it is currently impossible to guarantee that any site can meet that criterion. Yet keeping the waste at the current location for that long clearly poses unacceptable risks.

The statements above, if true, most strongly support which one of the following?

(A) The waste should never have been stored in its current location.

(B) The waste should be placed in the most secure location that can ever be found.

(C) Moving the waste to the proposed site would reduce the threat posed by the waste.

(D) Whenever waste must be moved, one should limit the amount of time allotted to locating alternative waste storage sites.

(E) Any site to which the waste could be moved will be safer than its present site.

GO ON TO THE NEXT PAGE.

22. A recent survey indicates that the average number of books read annually per capita has declined in each of the last three years. However, it also found that most bookstores reported increased profits during the same period.

Each of the following, if true, helps to resolve the survey's apparently paradoxical results EXCEPT:

(A) Recent cutbacks in government spending have forced public libraries to purchase fewer popular contemporary novels.

(B) Due to the installation of sophisticated new antitheft equipment, the recent increase in shoplifting that has hit most retail businesses has left bookstores largely unaffected.

(C) Over the past few years many bookstores have capitalized on the lucrative coffee industry by installing coffee bars.

(D) Bookstore owners reported a general shift away from the sale of inexpensive paperback novels and toward the sale of lucrative hardback books.

(E) Citing a lack of free time, many survey respondents indicated that they had canceled magazine subscriptions in favor of purchasing individual issues at bookstores when time permits.

23. Naturalist: A species can survive a change in environment, as long as the change is not too rapid. Therefore, the threats we are creating to woodland species arise not from the fact that we are cutting down trees, but rather from the rate at which we are doing so.

The reasoning in which one of the following is most similar to that in the naturalist's argument?

(A) The problem with burning fossil fuels is that the supply is limited; so, the faster we expend these resources, the sooner we will be left without an energy source.

(B) Many people gain more satisfaction from performing a job well—regardless of whether they like the job—than from doing merely adequately a job they like; thus, people who want to be happy should choose jobs they can do well.

(C) Some students who study thoroughly do well in school. Thus, what is most important for success in school is not how much time a student puts into studying, but rather how thoroughly the student studies.

(D) People do not fear change if they know what the change will bring; so, our employees' fear stems not from our company's undergoing change, but from our failing to inform them of what the changes entail.

(E) Until ten years ago, we had good soil and our agriculture flourished. Therefore, the recent decline of our agriculture is a result of our soil rapidly eroding and there being nothing that can replace the good soil we lost.

GO ON TO THE NEXT PAGE.

24. Professor: A person who can select a beverage from among 50 varieties of cola is less free than one who has only these 5 choices: wine, coffee, apple juice, milk, and water. It is clear, then, that meaningful freedom cannot be measured simply by the number of alternatives available; the extent of the differences among the alternatives is also a relevant factor.

The professor's argument proceeds by

(A) supporting a general principle by means of an example

(B) drawing a conclusion about a particular case on the basis of a general principle

(C) supporting its conclusion by means of an analogy

(D) claiming that whatever holds for each member of a group must hold for the whole group

(E) inferring one general principle from another, more general, principle

25. Principle: Meetings should be kept short, addressing only those issues relevant to a majority of those attending. A person should not be required to attend a meeting if none of the issues to be addressed at the meeting are relevant to that person.

Application: Terry should not be required to attend today's two o'clock meeting.

Which one of the following, if true, most justifies the stated application of the principle?

(A) The only issues on which Terry could make a presentation at the meeting are issues irrelevant to at least a majority of those who could attend.

(B) If Terry makes a presentation at the meeting, the meeting will not be kept short.

(C) No issue relevant to Terry could be relevant to a majority of those attending the meeting.

(D) If Terry attends the meeting a different set of issues will be relevant to a majority of those attending than if Terry does not attend.

(E) The majority of the issues to be addressed at the meeting are not relevant to Terry.

S T O P

IF YOU FINISH BEFORE TIME IS CALLED, YOU MAY CHECK YOUR WORK ON THIS SECTION ONLY.
DO NOT WORK ON ANY OTHER SECTION IN THE TEST.

SECTION IV

Time—35 minutes

27 Questions

<u>Directions:</u> Each set of questions in this section is based on a single passage or a pair of passages. The questions are to be answered on the basis of what is <u>stated</u> or <u>implied</u> in the passage or pair of passages. For some of the questions, more than one of the choices could conceivably answer the question. However, you are to choose the <u>best</u> answer; that is, the response that most accurately and completely answers the question, and blacken the corresponding space on your answer sheet.

Asian American poetry from Hawaii, the Pacific island state of the United States, is generally characterizable in one of two ways: either as portraying a model multicultural paradise, or as
(5) exemplifying familiar Asian American literary themes such as generational conflict. In this light, the recent work of Wing Tek Lum in *Expounding the Doubtful Points* is striking for its demand to be understood on its own terms. Lum offers no romanticized notions of
(10) multicultural life in Hawaii, and while he does explore themes of family, identity, history, and literary tradition, he does not do so at the expense of attempting to discover and retain a local sensibility. For Lum such a sensibility is informed by the fact
(15) that Hawaii's population, unlike that of the continental U.S., has historically consisted predominantly of people of Asian and Pacific island descent, making the experience of its Asian Americans somewhat different than that of mainland
(20) Asian Americans.

In one poem, Lum meditates on the ways in which a traditional Chinese lunar celebration he is attending at a local beach both connects him to and separates him from the past. In the company of new
(25) Chinese immigrants, the speaker realizes that while ties to the homeland are comforting and necessary, it is equally important to have "a sense of new family" in this new land of Hawaii, and hence a new identity—one that is sensitive to its new environment.
(30) The role of immigrants in this poem is significant in that, through their presence, Lum is able to refer both to the traditional culture of his ancestral homeland as well as to the flux within Hawaiian society that has been integral to its heterogeneity. Even in a laudatory
(35) poem to famous Chinese poet Li Po (701–762 A.D.), which partly serves to place Lum's work within a distinguished literary tradition, Lum refuses to offer a stereotypical nostalgia for the past, instead pointing out the often elitist tendencies inherent in the work of
(40) some traditionally acclaimed Chinese poets.

Lum closes his volume with a poem that further points to the complex relationships between heritage and local culture in determining one's identity. Pulling together images and figures as vastly
(45) disparate as a famous Chinese American literary character and an old woman selling bread, Lum avoids an excessively romantic vision of U.S. culture, while simultaneously acknowledging the dream of this culture held by many newly arrived immigrants.
(50) The central image of a communal pot where each

person chooses what she or he wishes to eat but shares with others the "sweet soup / spooned out at the end of the meal" is a hopeful one; however, it also appears to caution that the strong cultural
(55) emphasis in the U.S. on individual drive and success that makes retaining a sense of homeland tradition difficult should be identified and responded to in ways that allow for a healthy new sense of identity to be formed.

1. Which one of the following most accurately expresses the main point of the passage?

(A) The poetry of Lum departs from other Asian American poetry from Hawaii in that it acknowledges its author's heritage but also expresses the poet's search for a new local identity.

(B) Lum's poetry is in part an expression of the conflict between a desire to participate in a community with shared traditions and values and a desire for individual success.

(C) Lum writes poetry that not only rejects features of the older literary tradition in which he participates but also rejects the popular literary traditions of Hawaiian writers.

(D) The poetry of Lum illustrates the extent to which Asian American writers living in Hawaii have a different cultural perspective than those living in the continental U.S.

(E) Lum's poetry is an unsuccessful attempt to manage the psychological burdens of reconciling a sense of tradition with a healthy sense of individual identity.

GO ON TO THE NEXT PAGE.

2. Given the information in the passage, which one of the following is Lum most likely to believe?

(A) Images in a poem should be explained in that poem so that their meaning will be widely understood.

(B) The experience of living away from one's homeland is necessary for developing a healthy perspective on one's cultural traditions.

(C) It is important to reconcile the values of individual achievement and enterprise with the desire to retain one's cultural traditions.

(D) One's identity is continually in transition and poetry is a way of developing a static identity.

(E) One cannot both seek a new identity and remain connected to one's cultural traditions.

3. The author of the passage uses the phrase "the flux within Hawaiian society" (line 33) primarily in order to

(A) describe the social tension created by the mix of attitudes exhibited by citizens of Hawaii

(B) deny that Hawaiian society is culturally distinct from that of the continental U.S.

(C) identify the process by which immigrants learn to adapt to their new communities

(D) refer to the constant change to which the culture in Hawaii is subject due to its diverse population

(E) emphasize the changing attitudes of many immigrants to Hawaii toward their traditional cultural norms

4. According to the passage, some Asian American literature from Hawaii has been characterized as which one of the following?

(A) inimical to the process of developing a local sensibility

(B) centered on the individual's drive to succeed

(C) concerned with conflicts between different age groups

(D) focused primarily on retaining ties to one's homeland

(E) tied to a search for a new sense of family in a new land

5. The author of the passage describes *Expounding the Doubtful Points* as "striking" (lines 7–8) primarily in order to

(A) underscore the forceful and contentious tone of the work

(B) indicate that the work has not been properly analyzed by literary critics

(C) stress the radical difference between this work and Lum's earlier work

(D) emphasize the differences between this work and that of other Asian American poets from Hawaii

(E) highlight the innovative nature of Lum's experiments with poetic form

6. With which one of the following statements regarding Lum's poetry would the author of the passage be most likely to agree?

(A) It cannot be used to support any specific political ideology.

(B) It is an elegant demonstration of the poet's appreciation of the stylistic contributions of his literary forebears.

(C) It is most fruitfully understood as a meditation on the choice between new and old that confronts any human being in any culture.

(D) It conveys thoughtful assessments of both his ancestral homeland tradition and the culture in which he is attempting to build a new identity.

(E) It conveys Lum's antipathy toward tradition by juxtaposing traditional and nontraditional images.

GO ON TO THE NEXT PAGE.

In England the burden of history weighs heavily on common law, that unwritten code of time-honored laws derived largely from English judicial custom and precedent. Students of contemporary British law are
(5) frequently required to study medieval cases, to interpret archaic Latin maxims, or to confront doctrinal principles whose validity is based solely on their being part of the "timeless reason" of the English legal tradition. Centuries-old custom serves as
(10) the basis both for the divisions of law school subject matter and for much of the terminology of legal redress. Connected not only with legal history but also with the cultural history of the English people, common law cannot properly be understood without
(15) taking a long historical view.

Yet the academic study of jurisprudence has seldom treated common law as a constantly evolving phenomenon rooted in history; those interpretive theories that do acknowledge the antiquity of
(20) common law ignore the practical contemporary significance of its historical forms. The reasons for this omission are partly theoretical and partly political. In theoretical terms, modern jurisprudence has consistently treated law as a unified system of
(25) rules that can be studied at any given moment in time as a logical whole. The notion of jurisprudence as a system of norms or principles deemphasizes history in favor of the coherence of a system. In this view, the past of the system is conceived as no more than
(30) the continuous succession of its states of presence. In political terms, believing in the logic of law is a necessary part of believing in its fairness; even if history shows the legal tradition to be far from unitary and seldom logical, the prestige of the legal
(35) institution requires that jurisprudence treat the tradition as if it were, in essence, the application of known rules to objectively determined facts. To suggest otherwise would be dispiriting for the student and demoralizing for the public.
(40) Legal historian Peter Goodrich has argued, however, that common law is most fruitfully studied as a continually developing tradition rather than as a set of rules. Taking his cue from the study of literature, Goodrich sees common law as a sort of
(45) literary text, with history and tradition serving as the text's narrative development. To study the common law historically, says Goodrich, is to study a text in which fiction is as influential as analysis, perception as significant as rule, and the play of memory as
(50) strong as the logic of argument. The concept of tradition, for Goodrich, implies not only the preservation and transmission of existing forms, but also the continuous rewriting of those forms to adapt them to contemporary legal circumstances.

7. Which one of the following statements best expresses the main idea of the passage?

(A) The residual influences of common law explain not only the divisions of subject matter but also the terminology associated with many legal procedures.

(B) In the academic study of jurisprudence, theoretical interpretations of common law have traditionally been at odds with political interpretations of common law.

(C) Common law, while often treated as an oral history of the English people, would, according to one scholar, be more fruitfully studied as a universally adaptable and constantly changing system of rules.

(D) Although obviously steeped in history and tradition, common law has seldom been studied in relation to its development, as one theorist proposes that it be understood.

(E) Although usually studied as a unitary and logical system of rules and norms, the history of common law shows that body of law to be anything but consistent and fair.

8. It can be inferred that the author of the passage believes which one of the following about the history of law in relation to modern jurisprudence?

(A) Modern jurisprudence misinterprets the nature of the legal tradition.

(B) The history of law proves the original forms of common law to be antiquated and irrelevant to modern jurisprudence.

(C) The history of law, if it is to be made applicable to modern jurisprudence, is best studied as a system of rules rather than as a literary text.

(D) Mainstream theories of modern jurisprudence overlook the order and coherence inherent in legal history.

(E) Mainstream theories of modern jurisprudence, by and large devoid of a sense of legal history, are unnecessarily dispiriting to students and the public alike.

GO ON TO THE NEXT PAGE.

9. Which one of the following would best exemplify the kind of interpretive theory referred to in the first sentence of the second paragraph of the passage?

(A) a theory that traced modern customs involving property ownership to their origins in medieval practice

(B) a theory that relied on a comparison between modern courtroom procedures and medieval theatrical conventions

(C) a theory that analyzed medieval marriage laws without examining their relationship to modern laws

(D) a theory that compared the development of English common law in the twentieth century with simultaneous developments in German common law without examining the social repercussions of either legal system

(E) a theory that compared rules of evidence in civil courts with those in criminal courts

10. It can be inferred from the passage that Peter Goodrich would be most likely to agree with which one of the following statements concerning common law?

(A) Common law is more fruitfully studied as a relic of the history of the English people than as a legal code.

(B) The "text" of common law has degenerated from an early stage of clarity to a current state of incoherence.

(C) Without the public's belief in the justness of common law, the legal system cannot be perpetuated.

(D) While rich in literary significance, the "text" of common law has only a very limited applicability to modern life.

(E) The common law "text" inherited by future generations will differ from the one currently in use.

11. Which one of the following best defines the word "political" as it is used in the second paragraph of the passage?

(A) concerned with the ways by which people seek to advance themselves in a profession

(B) concerned with the covert and possibly unethical methods by which governments achieve their goals

(C) having to do with the maintenance of ethical standards between professions and the citizenry

(D) having to do with the maintenance of an institution's effectiveness

(E) having to do with the manner in which institutions are perceived by radical theorists

12. The passage states that students of British law are frequently required to study

(A) histories of English politics
(B) episodes of litigation from the Middle Ages
(C) treatises on political philosophy
(D) histories of ancient Roman jurisprudence
(E) essays on narrative development

13. Which one of the following best describes the author's opinion of most modern academic theories of common law?

(A) They are overly detailed and thus stultifying to both the student and the public.

(B) They lack an essential dimension that would increase their accuracy.

(C) They overemphasize the practical aspects of the common law at the expense of the theoretical.

(D) They excuse students of the law from the study of important legal disputes of the past.

(E) They routinely treat the study of the law as an art rather than as a science.

14. The primary purpose of the passage is to

(A) explain a paradoxical situation and discuss a new view of the situation

(B) supply a chronological summary of the history of an idea

(C) trace the ideas of an influential theorist and evaluate the theorist's ongoing work

(D) contrast the legal theories of past eras with those of today and suggest how these theories should be studied

(E) advocate a traditional school of thought while criticizing a new trend

GO ON TO THE NEXT PAGE.

The passages discuss relationships between business interests and university research.

Passage A

     As university researchers working in a "gift economy" dedicated to collegial sharing of ideas, we have long been insulated from market pressures. The recent tendency to treat research findings as
(5) commodities, tradable for cash, threatens this tradition and the role of research as a public good.

     The nurseries for new ideas are traditionally universities, which provide an environment uniquely suited to the painstaking testing and revision of
(10) theories. Unfortunately, the market process and values governing commodity exchange are ill suited to the cultivation and management of new ideas. With their shareholders impatient for quick returns, businesses are averse to wide-ranging experimentation. And, what
(15) is even more important, few commercial enterprises contain the range of expertise needed to handle the replacement of shattered theoretical frameworks.

     Further, since entrepreneurs usually have little affinity for adventure of the intellectual sort, they can
(20) buy research and bury its products, hiding knowledge useful to society or to their competitors. The growth of industrial biotechnology, for example, has been accompanied by a reduction in the free sharing of research methods and results—a high price to pay for
(25) the undoubted benefits of new drugs and therapies.

     Important new experimental results once led university scientists to rush down the hall and share their excitement with colleagues. When instead the rush is to patent lawyers and venture capitalists, I
(30) worry about the long-term future of scientific discovery.

Passage B

     The fruits of pure science were once considered primarily a public good, available for society as a whole. The argument for this view was that most of
(35) these benefits were produced through government support of universities, and thus no individual was entitled to restrict access to them.

     Today, however, the critical role of science in the modern "information economy" means that what was
(40) previously seen as a public good is being transformed into a market commodity. For example, by exploiting the information that basic research has accumulated about the detailed structures of cells and genes, the biotechnology industry can derive profitable
(45) pharmaceuticals or medical screening technologies. In this context, assertion of legal claims to "intellectual property"—not just in commercial products but in the underlying scientific knowledge—becomes crucial.

     Previously, the distinction between a scientific
(50) "discovery" (which could not be patented) and a technical "invention" (which could) defined the limits of industry's ability to patent something. Today, however, the speed with which scientific discoveries can be turned into products and the large profits

(55) resulting from this transformation have led to a blurring of both the legal distinction between discovery and invention and the moral distinction between what should and should not be patented.

     Industry argues that if it has supported—either in
(60) its own laboratories or in a university—the makers of a scientific discovery, then it is entitled to seek a return on its investment, either by charging others for using the discovery or by keeping it for its own exclusive use.

15. Which one of the following is discussed in passage B but not in passage A?

   (A) the blurring of the legal distinction between discovery and invention

   (B) the general effects of the market on the exchange of scientific knowledge

   (C) the role of scientific research in supplying public goods

   (D) new pharmaceuticals that result from industrial research

   (E) industry's practice of restricting access to research findings

16. Both passages place in opposition the members of which one of the following pairs?

   (A) commercially successful research and commercially unsuccessful research

   (B) research methods and research results

   (C) a marketable commodity and a public good

   (D) a discovery and an invention

   (E) scientific research and other types of inquiry

GO ON TO THE NEXT PAGE.

17. Both passages refer to which one of the following?

   (A)   theoretical frameworks
   (B)   venture capitalists
   (C)   physics and chemistry
   (D)   industrial biotechnology
   (E)   shareholders

18. It can be inferred from the passages that the authors believe that the increased constraint on access to scientific information and ideas arises from

   (A)   the enormous increase in the volume of scientific knowledge that is being generated
   (B)   the desire of individual researchers to receive credit for their discoveries
   (C)   the striving of commercial enterprises to gain a competitive advantage in the market
   (D)   moral reservations about the social impact of some scientific research
   (E)   a drastic reduction in government funding for university research

19. Which one of the following statements is most strongly supported by both passages?

   (A)   Many scientific researchers who previously worked in universities have begun to work in the biotechnology industry.
   (B)   Private biotechnology companies have invalidly patented the basic research findings of university researchers.
   (C)   Because of the nature of current scientific research, patent authorities no longer consider the distinction between discoveries and inventions to be clear-cut.
   (D)   In the past, scientists working in industry had free access to the results of basic research conducted in universities.
   (E)   Government-funded research in universities has traditionally been motivated by the goals of private industry.

GO ON TO THE NEXT PAGE.

Sometimes there is no more effective means of controlling an agricultural pest than giving free rein to its natural predators. A case in point is the cyclamen mite, a pest whose population can be
(5) effectively controlled by a predatory mite of the genus *Typhlodromus*. Cyclamen mites infest strawberry plants; they typically establish themselves in a strawberry field shortly after planting, but their populations do not reach significantly damaging
(10) levels until the plants' second year. *Typhlodromus* mites usually invade the strawberry fields during the second year, rapidly subdue the cyclamen mite populations, and keep them from reaching significantly damaging levels.
(15)   *Typhlodromus* owes its effectiveness as a predator to several factors in addition to its voracious appetite. Its population can increase as rapidly as that of its prey. Both species reproduce by parthenogenesis—a mode of reproduction in which unfertilized eggs
(20) develop into fertile females. Cyclamen mites lay three eggs per day over the four or five days of their reproductive life span; *Typhlodromus* lay two or three eggs per day for eight to ten days. Seasonal synchrony of *Typhlodromus* reproduction with the
(25) growth of prey populations and ability to survive at low prey densities also contribute to the predatory efficiency of *Typhlodromus*. During winter, when cyclamen mite populations dwindle to a few individuals hidden in the crevices and folds of leaves
(30) in the crowns of the strawberry plants, the predatory mites subsist on the honeydew produced by aphids and white flies. They do not reproduce except when they are feeding on the cyclamen mites. These features, which make *Typhlodromus* well-suited for
(35) exploiting the seasonal rises and falls of its prey, are common among predators that control prey populations.
    Greenhouse experiments have verified the importance of *Typhlodromus* predation for keeping
(40) cyclamen mites in check. One group of strawberry plants was stocked with both predator and prey mites; a second group was kept predator-free by regular application of parathion, an insecticide that kills the predatory species but does not affect the cyclamen
(45) mite. Throughout the study, populations of cyclamen mites remained low in plots shared with *Typhlodromus*, but their infestation attained significantly damaging proportions on predator-free plants.
(50)   Applying parathion in this instance is a clear case in which using a pesticide would do far more harm than good to an agricultural enterprise. The results were similar in field plantings of strawberries, where cyclamen mites also reached damaging levels when
(55) predators were eliminated by parathion, but they did not attain such levels in untreated plots. When cyclamen mite populations began to increase in an untreated planting, the predator populations quickly responded to reduce the outbreak. On average,
(60) cyclamen mites were about 25 times more abundant in the absence of predators than in their presence.

20. Which one of the following most accurately expresses the main point of the passage?

(A) Control of agricultural pests is most effectively and safely accomplished without the use of pesticides, because these pesticides can kill predators that also control the pests.

(B) Experimental verification is essential in demonstrating the effectiveness of natural controls of agricultural pests.

(C) The relationship between *Typhlodromus* and cyclamen mites demonstrates how natural predation can keep a population of agricultural pests in check.

(D) Predation by *Typhlodromus* is essential for the control of cyclamen mite populations in strawberry fields.

(E) Similarity in mode and timing of reproduction is what enables *Typhlodromus* effectively to control populations of cyclamen mites in fields of strawberry plants.

21. Based on the passage, the author would probably hold that which one of the following principles is fundamental to long-term predatory control of agricultural pests?

(A) The reproduction of the predator population should be synchronized with that of the prey population, so that the number of predators surges just prior to a surge in prey numbers.

(B) The effectiveness of the predatory relationship should be experimentally demonstrable in greenhouse as well as field applications.

(C) The prey population should be able to survive in times of low crop productivity, so that the predator population will not decrease to very low levels.

(D) The predator population's level of consumption of the prey species should be responsive to variations in the size of the prey population.

(E) The predator population should be vulnerable only to pesticides to which the prey population is also vulnerable.

22. Which one of the following is mentioned in the passage as a factor contributing to the effectiveness of *Typhlodromus* as a predator?

(A) its ability to withstand most insecticides except parathion

(B) its lack of natural predators in strawberry fields

(C) its ability to live in different climates in different geographic regions

(D) its constant food supply in cyclamen mite populations

(E) its ability to survive when few prey are available

GO ON TO THE NEXT PAGE.

23. Suppose that pesticide X drastically slows the reproductive rate of cyclamen mites and has no other direct effect on cyclamen mites or *Typhlodromus*. Based on the information in the passage, which one of the following would most likely have occurred if, in the experiments mentioned in the passage, pesticide X had been used instead of parathion, with all other conditions affecting the experiments remaining the same?

(A) In both treated and untreated plots inhabited by both *Typhlodromus* and cyclamen mites, the latter would have been effectively controlled.

(B) Cyclamen mite populations in all treated plots from which *Typhlodromus* was absent would have been substantially lower than in untreated plots inhabited by both kinds of mites.

(C) In the treated plots, slowed reproduction in cyclamen mites would have led to a loss of reproductive synchrony between *Typhlodromus* and cyclamen mites.

(D) In the treated plots, *Typhlodromus* populations would have decreased temporarily and would have eventually increased.

(E) In the treated plots, cyclamen mite populations would have reached significantly damaging levels more slowly, but would have remained at those levels longer, than in untreated plots.

24. It can be inferred from the passage that the author would be most likely to agree with which one of the following statements about the use of predators to control pest populations?

(A) If the use of predators to control cyclamen mite populations fails, then parathion should be used to control these populations.

(B) Until the effects of the predators on beneficial insects that live in strawberry fields are assessed, such predators should be used with caution to control cyclamen mite populations.

(C) Insecticides should be used to control certain pest populations in fields of crops only if the use of natural predators has proven inadequate.

(D) If an insecticide can effectively control pest populations as well as predator populations, then it should be used instead of predators to control pest populations.

(E) Predators generally control pest populations more effectively than pesticides because they do not harm the crops that their prey feed on.

25. The author mentions the egg-laying ability of each kind of mite (lines 20–23) primarily in order to support which one of the following claims?

(A) Mites that reproduce by parthenogenesis do so at approximately equal rates.

(B) Predatory mites typically have a longer reproductive life span than do cyclamen mites.

(C) *Typhlodromus* can lay their eggs in synchrony with cyclamen mites.

(D) *Typhlodromus* can reproduce at least as quickly as cyclamen mites.

(E) The egg-laying rate of *Typhlodromus* is slower in the presence of cyclamen mites than it is in their absence.

26. Which one of the following would, if true, most strengthen the author's position regarding the practical applicability of the information about predatory mites presented in the passage?

(A) The individual *Typhlodromus* mites that have the longest reproductive life spans typically also lay the greatest number of eggs per day.

(B) The insecticides that are typically used for mite control on strawberry plants kill both predatory and nonpredatory species of mites.

(C) In areas in which strawberry plants become infested by cyclamen mites, winters tend to be short and relatively mild.

(D) *Typhlodromus* are sometimes preyed upon by another species of mites that is highly susceptible to parathion.

(E) *Typhlodromus* easily tolerate the same range of climatic conditions that strawberry plants do.

27. Information in the passage most strongly supports which one of the following statements?

(A) Strawberry crops can support populations of both cyclamen mites and *Typhlodromus* mites without significant damage to those crops.

(B) For control of cyclamen mites by another mite species to be effective, it is crucial that the two species have the same mode of reproduction.

(C) Factors that make *Typhlodromus* effective against cyclamen mites also make it effective against certain other pests of strawberry plants.

(D) When *Typhlodromus* is relied on to control cyclamen mites in strawberry crops, pesticides may be necessary to prevent significant damage during the first year.

(E) Strawberry growers have unintentionally caused cyclamen mites to become a serious crop pest by the indiscriminate use of parathion.

S T O P

IF YOU FINISH BEFORE TIME IS CALLED, YOU MAY CHECK YOUR WORK ON THIS SECTION ONLY.
DO NOT WORK ON ANY OTHER SECTION IN THE TEST.

Wait for the supervisor's instructions before you open the page to the topic.
Please print and sign your name and write the date in the designated spaces below.

Time: 35 Minutes

General Directions

You will have 35 minutes in which to plan and write an essay on the topic inside. Read the topic and the accompanying directions carefully. You will probably find it best to spend a few minutes considering the topic and organizing your thoughts before you begin writing. In your essay, be sure to develop your ideas fully, leaving time, if possible, to review what you have written. **Do not write on a topic other than the one specified. Writing on a topic of your own choice is not acceptable.**

No special knowledge is required or expected for this writing exercise. Law schools are interested in the reasoning, clarity, organization, language usage, and writing mechanics displayed in your essay. How well you write is more important than how much you write.

Confine your essay to the blocked, lined area on the front and back of the separate Writing Sample Response Sheet. Only that area will be reproduced for law schools. Be sure that your writing is legible.

Both this topic sheet and your response sheet must be turned over to the testing staff before you leave the room.

Topic Code	Print Your Full Name Here		
_____	Last	First	M.I.

Date	Sign Your Name Here
/ /	

Scratch Paper
Do not write your essay in this space.

LSAT Writing Sample Topic

<u>Directions</u>: The scenario presented below describes two choices, either one of which can be supported on the basis of the information given. Your essay should consider both choices and argue <u>for</u> one and <u>against</u> the other, based on the two specified criteria and the facts provided. There is no "right" or "wrong" choice: a reasonable argument can be made for either.

Dennis, a photographer and local historian, has been commissioned to write a book about the preservation of photographs. He has worked out two different approaches to completing the book, which must be finished in two years. Using the facts below, write an essay in which you argue for one approach over the other based on the following two criteria:

- Dennis would like to improve his knowledge of photographic preservation through practical, hands-on experience.
- Dennis wants to produce a draft of the book as soon as possible.

One approach is for Dennis to take a two-year, part-time position at the photographic archives of a prestigious portrait gallery. He would help people locate visual images for publication, exhibition, research, or personal use from the archives. He would also perform various administrative tasks. Over the two-year period, Dennis would learn a great deal about the methodologies and techniques relating to photographic preservation through routine contact with professional archivists and visiting researchers. He would also enjoy extensive access to the portrait gallery's resources during that time.

Alternatively, Dennis can take a one-year, full-time position with the local public archives, which has a vast collection of photographs from the surrounding region dating back to 1865. Dennis would be helping to complete the cataloging and scanning of those photographs for inclusion in an online system. His extensive responsibilities would include entering historic photographs into a web-based database, determining the street address or location of scenes depicted in the photographs, transferring historic photographic negatives to acid-free storage, and retouching scanned images. He would work alongside skilled archivists and would gain a working knowledge of photographic conservation-preservation procedures.

Scratch Paper
Do not write your essay in this space.

LAST NAME (Print)　　　　　　　　　　　MI　　FIRST NAME (Print)

SIGNATURE

Writing Sample Response Sheet

DO NOT WRITE
IN THIS SPACE

**Begin your essay in the lined area below.
Continue on the back if you need more space.**

Directions:

1. Use the Answer Key on the next page to check your answers.

2. Use the Scoring Worksheet below to compute your raw score.

3. Use the Score Conversion Chart to convert your raw score into the 120–180 scale.

Scoring Worksheet

1. Enter the number of questions you answered correctly in each section.

Number Correct

SECTION I . . . . _____

SECTION II . . . . _____

SECTION III . . . . . . _____

SECTION IV . . . . . . _____

2. Enter the sum here: _____

This is your Raw Score.

Conversion Chart

For Converting Raw Score to the 120–180 LSAT Scaled Score

LSAT PrepTest 53

Reported Score	Raw Score Lowest	Raw Score Highest
180	98	100
179	97	97
178	96	96
177	—*	—*
176	95	95
175	94	94
174	93	93
173	92	92
172	91	91
171	90	90
170	89	89
169	88	88
168	87	87
167	86	86
166	84	85
165	83	83
164	81	82
163	80	80
162	78	79
161	77	77
160	75	76
159	73	74
158	71	72
157	70	70
156	68	69
155	66	67
154	64	65
153	62	63
152	61	61
151	59	60
150	57	58
149	55	56
148	53	54
147	52	52
146	50	51
145	48	49
144	46	47
143	45	45
142	43	44
141	41	42
140	40	40
139	38	39
138	36	37
137	35	35
136	33	34
135	32	32
134	30	31
133	29	29
132	28	28
131	26	27
130	25	25
129	24	24
128	22	23
127	21	21
126	20	20
125	19	19
124	18	18
123	17	17
122	16	16
121	15	15
120	0	14

*There is no raw score that will produce this scaled score for this form.

SECTION I

1.	C	8.	D	15.	B	22.	E
2.	B	9.	A	16.	E	23.	D
3.	B	10.	D	17.	B	24.	D
4.	A	11.	D	18.	B	25.	B
5.	E	12.	C	19.	A		
6.	A	13.	A	20.	C		
7.	A	14.	D	21.	A		

SECTION II

1.	B	8.	A	15.	E	22.	E
2.	A	9.	D	16.	A	23.	B
3.	B	10.	C	17.	D		
4.	B	11.	B	18.	E		
5.	C	12.	B	19.	A		
6.	C	13.	E	20.	B		
7.	A	14.	A	21.	C		

SECTION III

1.	A	8.	A	15.	E	22.	B
2.	C	9.	E	16.	B	23.	D
3.	E	10.	B	17.	A	24.	A
4.	A	11.	C	18.	E	25.	C
5.	E	12.	B	19.	A		
6.	D	13.	B	20.	D		
7.	A	14.	A	21.	C		

SECTION IV

1.	A	8.	A	15.	A	22.	E
2.	C	9.	C	16.	C	23.	A
3.	D	10.	E	17.	D	24.	C
4.	C	11.	D	18.	C	25.	D
5.	D	12.	B	19.	D	26.	E
6.	D	13.	B	20.	C	27.	A
7.	D	14.	A	21.	D		

PrepTest 47

PrepTest 47 (October 2005)

SECTION I

Time—35 minutes

26 Questions

Directions: The questions in this section are based on the reasoning contained in brief statements or passages. For some questions, more than one of the choices could conceivably answer the question. However, you are to choose the best answer; that is, the response that most accurately and completely answers the question. You should not make assumptions that are by commonsense standards implausible, superfluous, or incompatible with the passage. After you have chosen the best answer, blacken the corresponding space on your answer sheet.

1. While it might be expected that those neighborhoods most heavily patrolled by police have the least crime, the statistical evidence overwhelmingly supports the claim that such neighborhoods have the most crime. This shows that the presence of police does not decrease crime in a neighborhood.

The reasoning in the argument is flawed because the argument

(A) attempts to support its conclusion by making an appeal to emotions

(B) fails to consider the possibility that criminals may commit crimes in more than one neighborhood

(C) draws a general conclusion from too small a sample of data

(D) fails to consider the possibility that police presence in a particular area is often a response to the relatively high crime rate in that area

(E) takes for granted that public resources devoted to police presence could be allocated in another manner that would be a stronger deterrent to crime

2. Despite increasing international efforts to protect the natural habitats of endangered species of animals, the rate at which these species are becoming extinct continues to rise. It is clear that these efforts are wasted.

Which one of the following, if true, most weakens the argument?

(A) Scientists are better able to preserve the habitats of endangered species now than ever before.

(B) Species that would have become extinct have been saved due to the establishment of animal refuges.

(C) Scientists estimate that at least 2000 species become extinct every year.

(D) Many countries do not recognize the increased economic benefit of tourism associated with preserved natural habitats.

(E) Programs have been proposed that will transfer endangered species out of habitats that are in danger of being destroyed.

3. When a lawmaker spoke out against a research grant awarded to a professor in a university's psychology department as a foolish expenditure of public money, other professors in that department drafted a letter protesting the lawmaker's interference in a field in which he was not trained. The chair of the psychology department, while privately endorsing the project, refused to sign the protest letter on the ground that she had previously written a letter applauding the same legislator when he publicized a senseless expenditure by the country's military.

Which one of the following principles, if established, provides the strongest justification for the department chair's refusal, on the ground she gives, to sign the protest letter?

(A) A person should not publicly criticize the actions of a lawmaker in different cases without giving careful consideration to the circumstances of each particular case.

(B) The chair of an academic department has an obligation to ensure that public funds allocated to support projects within that department are spent wisely.

(C) A person who has praised a lawmaker for playing a watchdog role in one case should not criticize the lawmaker for attempting to play a watchdog role in another case that involves the person's professional interests.

(D) Since academic institutions accept public funds but do not pay taxes, a representative of an academic institution should not publicly pass judgment on the actions of government officials.

(E) Academic institutions have the same responsibility as military institutions have to spend public money wisely.

GO ON TO THE NEXT PAGE.

4. Aaron: A prominent judge, criticizing "famous lawyers who come before courts ill-prepared to argue their cases," recently said, "This sort of cavalier attitude offends the court and can do nothing but harm to the client's cause." I find the judge's remarks irresponsible.

Belinda: I find it natural and an admirable display of candor. Letting people know of the damage their negligence causes is responsible behavior.

The point at issue between Aaron and Belinda is whether

(A) ill-prepared lawyers damage their clients' causes
(B) the judge's criticism of lawyers is irresponsible
(C) a lawyer's being ill-prepared to argue a client's case constitutes negligence
(D) famous lawyers have a greater responsibility to be well prepared than do lawyers who are not famous
(E) it is to be expected that ill-prepared lawyers would offend the court in which they appear

5. The human emotional response presents an apparent paradox. People believe that they can be genuinely moved only by those things and events that they believe to be actual, yet they have genuine emotional responses to what they know to be fictional.

Which one of the following situations most closely conforms to the principle cited above?

(A) Fred was watching a horror movie. Although he did not expect to be bothered by make-believe monsters, he nonetheless felt frightened when they appeared on the screen.
(B) Tamara was reading Hamlet. Although she knew that it was a work of fiction, she still made statements such as "Hamlet was born in Denmark" and "Hamlet was a prince."
(C) Raheem thought that his sister was in the hospital. Although he was mistaken, he was nevertheless genuinely worried when he believed she was there.
(D) Jeremy was upset by the actions that a writer attributed to a secret organization, although he considered it unlikely that the writer's account was accurate.
(E) Sandy was watching a film about World War II. Although the film's details were accurate, it was nevertheless difficult for Sandy to maintain interest in the characters.

6. Recent investigations of earthquakes have turned up a previously unknown type of seismic shock, known as a displacement pulse, which is believed to be present in all earthquakes. Alarmingly, high-rise buildings are especially vulnerable to displacement pulses, according to computer models. Yet examination of high-rises within cities damaged by recent powerful earthquakes indicates little significant damage to these structures.

Which one of the following, if true, contributes to a resolution of the apparent paradox?

(A) Displacement pulses travel longer distances than other types of seismic shock.
(B) Scientific predictions based on computer models often fail when tested in the field.
(C) While displacement pulses have only recently been discovered, they have accompanied all earthquakes that have ever occurred.
(D) The displacement pulses made by low- and medium-intensity earthquakes are much less powerful than those made by the strongest earthquakes.
(E) Computer models have been very successful in predicting the effects of other types of seismic shock.

7. Terry: Months ago, I submitted a claim for my stolen bicycle to my insurance company. After hearing nothing for several weeks, I contacted the firm and found they had no record of my claim. Since then, I have resubmitted the claim twice and called the firm repeatedly, but I have yet to receive a settlement. Anyone can make mistakes, of course, but the persistence of the error makes me conclude that the company is deliberately avoiding paying up.

Which one of the following principles is violated by Terry's reasoning?

(A) Consumers should avoid attributing dishonesty to a corporation when the actions of the corporation might instead be explained by incompetence.
(B) Consumers should attempt to keep themselves informed of corporate behavior that directly affects their interests.
(C) In judging the quality of service of a corporation, a consumer should rely primarily on the consumer's own experience with the corporation.
(D) In judging the morality of a corporation's behavior, as opposed to that of an individual, mitigating circumstances are irrelevant.
(E) Corporations ought to make available to a customer any information the customer requests that is relevant to the customer's interests.

GO ON TO THE NEXT PAGE.

8. Fortune-teller: Admittedly, the claims of some self-proclaimed "psychics" have been shown to be fraudulent, but the exposure of a few charlatans cannot alter the fundamental fact that it has not been scientifically proven that there is no such thing as extrasensory perception (ESP). Furthermore, since the failed attempts to produce such a proof have been so numerous, one must conclude that some individuals do possess ESP.

The reasoning in the fortune-teller's argument is most vulnerable to criticism on the grounds that the argument

(A) takes for granted that proof that many people lack a characteristic does not establish that everyone lacks that characteristic

(B) takes for granted that the number of unsuccessful attempts to prove a claim is the only factor relevant to whether one should accept that claim

(C) overlooks the possibility that some of the scientific studies mentioned reached inaccurate conclusions about whether ESP exists

(D) takes for granted that there is no scientific way to determine whether some individuals possess ESP

(E) takes for granted that the fact that a claim has not been demonstrated to be false establishes that it is true

9. Film historians have made two major criticisms of Depression-era filmmakers: first, that they were too uncritical of the economic status quo; and second, that they self-indulgently created films reflecting their own dreams and desires. However, these filmmakers made their movies with an eye to profit, and so they provided what their audiences most wanted in a film: a chance to imagine being wealthy enough not to have a care in the world. Thus, the second criticism cannot be accurate.

The conclusion of the argument follows logically if which one of the following is assumed?

(A) To avoid self-indulgence, filmmakers should take a critical stance toward the existing economic system and should allow audiences to form their own personal aspirations.

(B) It is unjustified to demand of all filmmakers that their films engage in criticism of the economic status quo.

(C) The people who regularly went to movies during the Depression were those likely to have been most satisfied with the economic status quo.

(D) Depression-era filmmakers who did not make films for profit could not take radical critical stances toward then-current economic and political issues.

(E) It cannot be self-indulgent for a filmmaker to give an audience what it most wants.

10. Editorial: Many observers note with dismay the decline in the number of nongovernmental, voluntary community organizations. They argue that this decline is caused by the corresponding growth of government services once provided by these voluntary community groups. But this may not be true. The increase in government services may coincide with a decrease in volunteerism, but the former does not necessarily cause the latter; the latter may indeed cause the former.

The editorial undermines the conclusion of the causal argument by

(A) showing that there is no causality involved
(B) offering a counterexample to the alleged correlation
(C) proving that no generalization can properly be drawn about people's motives for volunteering
(D) offering an alternate explanation of the correlation cited
(E) proving that governments must do what community organizations fail to do

11. In contemplating major purchases, businesses often consider only whether there is enough money left from monthly revenues after paying monthly expenses to cover the cost of the purchase. But many expenses do not occur monthly; taking into account only monthly expenses can cause a business to overexpand. So the use of a cash-flow statement is critical for all businesses.

Which one of the following, if true, most strengthens the argument?

(A) Only a cash-flow statement can accurately document all monthly expenses.

(B) Any business that has overexpanded can benefit from the use of a cash-flow statement.

(C) When a business documents only monthly expenses it also documents only monthly revenue.

(D) A cash-flow statement is the only way to track both monthly expenses and expenses that are not monthly.

(E) When a business takes into account all expenses, not just monthly ones, it can make better decisions.

GO ON TO THE NEXT PAGE.

12. All known living things are made of the same basic kinds of matter, are carbon based, and are equipped with genetic codes. So human life has the same origin as all other known life.

The conclusion follows logically if which one of the following is assumed?

(A) Without the existence of other life forms, human life would never have come into existence.

(B) There are not any living beings that have genetic codes but are not carbon based.

(C) There can never be any living thing that does not have a genetic code.

(D) Many yet-to-be-discovered types of living things will also be carbon based.

(E) Any two living things made of the same basic kinds of matter have the same origin.

13. All societies recognize certain rules to be so crucial that they define those rules as duties, such as rules restricting violence and those requiring the keeping of agreements. Contained in the notion of a duty is the idea that its fulfillment is so fundamental to a properly functioning society that persons obligated by it cannot be excused on the ground that its fulfillment would be harmful to their self-interest. This shows that _____.

Which one of the following most reasonably completes the argument?

(A) all societies overrate the benefits of certain rules, such as those governing the keeping of agreements

(B) all societies have certain rules that no people are capable of following

(C) all societies recognize the possibility of clashes between individual self-interest and the performance of duty

(D) a properly functioning society will recognize that some duties take priority over others

(E) societies have no right to expect people always to perform their duties

14. Linguist: Regional dialects, many of which eventually become distinct languages, are responses by local populations to their own particular communicative needs. So even when the unification of the world economy forces the adoption of a universal language for use in international trade, this language itself will inevitably develop many regional dialects.

Which one of the following is an assumption that the linguist's argument requires?

(A) No two local populations have the same communicative needs as each other.

(B) In some regions of the world, at least some people will not engage in international trade after the unification of the world economy.

(C) A universal language for use in international trade will not arise unless the world economy is unified.

(D) When the unification of the world economy forces the adoption of a universal language for use in international trade, many regional dialects of other languages will be eradicated.

(E) After the unification of the world economy, there will be variation among many different local populations in their communicative needs in international trade.

GO ON TO THE NEXT PAGE.

15. Often, a product popularly believed to be the best of its type is no better than any other; rather, the product's reputation, which may be independent of its quality, provides its owner with status. Thus, although there is no harm in paying for status if that is what one wants, one should know that one is paying for prestige, not quality.

Which one of the following arguments is most similar in its reasoning to the argument above?

(A) Often, choosing the best job offer is a matter of comparing the undesirable features of the different jobs. Thus, those who choose a job because it has a desirable location should know that they might be unhappy with its hours.

(B) Most people have little tolerance for boastfulness. Thus, although one's friends may react positively when hearing the details of one's accomplishments, it is unlikely that their reactions are entirely honest.

(C) Those beginning a new hobby sometimes quit it because of the frustrations involved in learning a new skill. Thus, although it is fine to try to learn a skill quickly, one is more likely to learn a skill if one first learns to enjoy the process of acquiring it.

(D) Personal charm is often confused with virtue. Thus, while there is nothing wrong with befriending a charming person, anyone who does so should realize that a charming friend is not necessarily a good and loyal friend.

(E) Many theatrical actors cannot enjoy watching a play because when they watch others, they yearn to be on stage themselves. Thus, although there is no harm in yearning to perform, such performers should, for their own sakes, learn to suppress that yearning.

16. Essayist: Many people are hypocritical in that they often pretend to be more morally upright than they really are. When hypocrisy is exposed, hypocrites are embarrassed by their moral lapse, which motivates them and others to try to become better people. On the other hand, when hypocrisy persists without exposure, the belief that most people are good is fostered, which motivates most people to try to be good.

The essayist's statements, if true, most strongly support which one of the following?

(A) The existence of hypocrisy encourages people to believe that no one is morally blameless.

(B) The existence of hypocrisy encourages people to make efforts to live by moral standards.

(C) The existence of hypocrisy in some people encourages others to fall into moral lapses.

(D) The hiding of hypocrisy is a better way of motivating people to try to be good than is the exposing of it.

(E) There is no stronger motivator for people to try to be good than the exposing of hypocrisy.

17. "Multiple use" refers to the utilization of natural resources in combinations that will best meet the present and future needs of the public. Designating land as a wilderness area does not necessarily violate the multiple-use philosophy, for even when such use does not provide the greatest dollar return, it can provide the greatest overall benefit from that site.

Which one of the following is an assumption required by the argument?

(A) Natural resources should be used in combinations that will most greatly benefit present and future generations.

(B) Designating a wilderness area prevents any exploitation of natural resources in that area.

(C) The present and future needs of the public would best be met by designating greater numbers of wilderness areas.

(D) The multiple-use philosophy takes into account some nonfinancial needs of the public.

(E) The multiple-use philosophy holds that the future needs of the public are more important than the present ones.

GO ON TO THE NEXT PAGE.

18. In the troposphere, the lowest level of the earth's atmosphere, the temperature decreases as one progresses straight upward. At the top, the air temperature ranges from –50 degrees Celsius over the poles to –85 degrees Celsius over the equator. At that point the stratosphere begins, and the temperature stops decreasing and instead increases as one progresses straight upward through the stratosphere. The stratosphere is warmed by ozone. When an ozone particle absorbs a dose of ultraviolet sunlight, heat is generated.

If the statements above are true, which one of the following must also be true?

(A) The troposphere over the poles is thicker than the troposphere over the equator.

(B) It is warmer at the top of the stratosphere over the poles than it is at the top of the stratosphere over the equator.

(C) The temperature in the middle part of the stratosphere over the North Pole is at least as great as the temperature in the middle part of the stratosphere over the equator.

(D) The temperature at any point at the top of the stratosphere is at least as great as the temperature at the top of the troposphere directly beneath that point.

(E) Depletion of the earth's ozone layer would increase the air temperature in the stratosphere and decrease the air temperature in the troposphere.

19. There have been no new cases of naturally occurring polio in North America in recent years. Yet there are approximately 12 new cases of polio each year in North America, all caused by the commonly administered live oral polio vaccine (OPV). Substituting inactivated polio vaccine (IPV) for most childhood polio immunizations would cut the number of cases of vaccination-caused polio about in half. Clearly it is time to switch from OPV to IPV as the most commonly used polio vaccine for North American children.

Which one of the following, if true, most weakens the argument?

(A) If IPV replaces OPV as the most commonly used polio vaccine, at least a few new cases of naturally occurring polio in North America will result each year.

(B) The vast majority of cases of polio caused by OPV have occurred in children with preexisting but unsuspected immunodeficiency disorders.

(C) A child's risk of contracting polio from OPV has been estimated at 1 in 8.7 million, which is significantly less than the risk of being struck by lightning.

(D) Although IPV is preferred in some European nations, most countries with comprehensive child immunization programs use OPV.

(E) IPV, like most vaccines, carries a slight risk of inducing seizures in children with neurological diseases such as epilepsy.

20. Professor: Each government should do all that it can to improve the well-being of all the children in the society it governs. Therefore, governments should help finance high-quality day care since such day care will become available to families of all income levels if and only if it is subsidized.

Which one of the following is an assumption on which the professor's argument depends?

(A) Only governments that subsidize high-quality day care take an interest in the well-being of all the children in the societies they govern.

(B) Government subsidy of high-quality day care would not be so expensive that it would cause a government to eliminate benefits for adults.

(C) High-quality day care should be subsidized only for those who could not otherwise afford it.

(D) At least some children would benefit from high-quality day care.

(E) Government is a more efficient provider of certain services than is private enterprise.

GO ON TO THE NEXT PAGE.

21. Opposition leader: Our country has the least fair court system of any country on the continent and ought not to be the model for others. Thus, our highest court is the least fair of any on the continent and ought not to be emulated by other countries.

The flawed reasoning in which one of the following arguments is most similar to that in the opposition leader's argument?

(A) The residents of medium-sized towns are, on average, more highly educated than people who do not live in such towns. Therefore, Maureen, who was born in a medium-sized town, is more highly educated than Monica, who has just moved to such a town.

(B) At a certain college, either philosophy or engineering is the most demanding major. Therefore, either the introductory course in philosophy or the introductory course in engineering is the most demanding introductory-level course at that college.

(C) For many years its superior engineering has enabled the Lawson Automobile Company to make the best racing cars. Therefore, its passenger cars, which use many of the same parts, are unmatched by those of any other company.

(D) Domestic cats are closely related to tigers. Therefore, even though they are far smaller than tigers, their eating habits are almost the same as those of tigers.

(E) If a suit of questionable merit is brought in the first district rather than the second district, its chances of being immediately thrown out are greater. Therefore, to have the best chance of winning the case, the lawyers will bring the suit in the second district.

22. Columnist: There are certain pesticides that, even though they have been banned for use in the United States for nearly 30 years, are still manufactured there and exported to other countries. In addition to jeopardizing the health of people in these other countries, this practice greatly increases the health risk to U.S. consumers, for these pesticides are often used on agricultural products imported into the United States.

Which one of the following, if true, most seriously weakens the columnist's argument?

(A) Trace amounts of some of the pesticides banned for use in the United States can be detected in the soil where they were used 30 years ago.

(B) Most of the pesticides that are manufactured in the United States and exported are not among those banned for use in the United States.

(C) The United States is not the only country that manufactures and exports the pesticides that are banned for use in the United States.

(D) The banned pesticides pose a greater risk to people in the countries in which they are used than to U.S. consumers.

(E) There are many pesticides that are banned for use in other countries that are not banned for use in the United States.

23. Columnist: Neuroscientists have found that states of profound creativity are accompanied by an increase of theta brain waves, which occur in many regions of the brain, including the hippocampus. They also found that listening to music increases theta waves dramatically. Thus, one can attain a state of profound creativity merely by listening to a tape of recorded music.

The columnist's reasoning is most vulnerable to criticism on the grounds that it

(A) takes for granted that there is a causal connection between the hippocampus and being in a state of profound creativity

(B) fails to consider that music is not necessary for one to be in a state of profound creativity

(C) does not rule out the possibility that listening to music by means other than a tape recording also increases theta waves

(D) ignores the possibility that an increase in theta waves may not always be accompanied by a state of profound creativity

(E) provides insufficient reasons to believe that people who are not in states of profound creativity have low levels of theta brain waves

GO ON TO THE NEXT PAGE.

24. Consumer advocate: The manufacturer's instructions for assembling a product should be written in such a way that most consumers would find it much easier to put the product together if the instructions were available than if they were not.

Which one of the following, if true, would provide the strongest reason for thinking that the principle advanced by the consumer advocate cannot always be followed?

(A) The typical consumer who assembles a product does so using the manufacturer's instructions, but still has great difficulty.

(B) Often the store at which a consumer purchases an unassembled product will offer, for a fee, to assemble the product and deliver it.

(C) For the typical product, most consumers who assemble it do so very easily and without ever consulting the manufacturer's instructions.

(D) Usually a consumer who is trying to assemble a product using the manufacturer's instructions has no difficulty understanding the instructions.

(E) Some consumers refer to the manufacturer's instructions for assembling a product only if they have difficulty assembling the product.

25. Claude: Because of the relatively high number of middle-aged people in the workforce, there will be fewer opportunities for promotion into upper-management positions. Since this will decrease people's incentive to work hard, economic productivity and the quality of life will diminish.

Thelma: This glut of middle-aged workers will lead many people to form their own companies. They will work hard and thus increase economic productivity, improving the quality of life even if many of the companies ultimately fail.

On the basis of their statements, Claude and Thelma are committed to agreeing about which one of the following?

(A) The quality of life in a society affects that society's economic productivity.

(B) The failure of many companies will not necessarily have a negative effect on overall economic productivity.

(C) How hard a company's employees work is a function of what they think their chances for promotion are in that company.

(D) The number of middle-aged people in the workforce will increase in the coming years.

(E) Economic productivity will be affected by the number of middle-aged people in the workforce.

26. Researchers gave 100 first-graders after-school lessons in handwriting. They found that those whose composition skills had improved the most had learned to write letters the most automatically. This suggests that producing characters more automatically frees up mental resources for other activities.

Which one of the following, if true, most strengthens the argument?

(A) Among the first-graders who received the after-school lessons in handwriting, those who practiced the most learned to write letters the most automatically.

(B) The first-graders who wrote letters the most automatically before receiving the after-school lessons in handwriting showed the greatest improvement in their composition skills over the course of the lessons.

(C) Over the course of the lessons, the first-graders who showed greater improvement in their ability to write letters automatically also generally showed greater improvement in their composition skills.

(D) Before receiving the after-school lessons in handwriting, the 100 first-graders who received the lessons were representative of first-graders more generally, with respect to their skills in both handwriting and composition.

(E) Among the first-graders who received the lessons in handwriting, those who started out with strong composition skills showed substantial improvement in how automatically they could write letters.

S T O P

IF YOU FINISH BEFORE TIME IS CALLED, YOU MAY CHECK YOUR WORK ON THIS SECTION ONLY.
DO NOT WORK ON ANY OTHER SECTION IN THE TEST.

SECTION II

Time—35 minutes

26 Questions

<u>Directions:</u> Each passage in this section is followed by a group of questions to be answered on the basis of what is <u>stated</u> or <u>implied</u> in the passage. For some of the question, more than one of the choices could conceivably answer the question. However, you are to choose the <u>best</u> answer; that is, the response that most accurately and completely answers the question, and blacken the corresponding space on your answer sheet.

In 1963, a three-week-long demonstration for jobs at the construction site of the Downstate Medical Center in Brooklyn, New York, became one of the most significant and widely publicized campaigns of
(5) the civil rights movement in the United States. An interdenominational group made up mostly of locally based African American ministers, who had remained politically moderate until then, organized and led hundreds of people in an aggressive protest. Their
(10) efforts relied mainly on the participation and direct financial support of the ministers' own congregations and other congregations throughout Brooklyn. The goal of this campaign was to build a mass movement that would force changes in government policies as
(15) well as in trade union hiring practices, both of which they believed excluded African Americans from construction jobs.

Inspired by the emergence of African American religious leaders as key figures elsewhere in the civil
(20) rights movement, and reasoning that the ministers would be able to mobilize large numbers of people from their congregations and network effectively with other religious leaders throughout the city, the Congress of Racial Equality (CORE), a national civil
(25) rights organization, had decided to ask the ministers to lead the Downstate campaign. However, by organizing a civil disobedience campaign, the ministers were jeopardizing one of the very factors that had led CORE to seek their involvement: their
(30) positions as politically moderate community leaders. Urban African American ministers and churches had been working for decades with community and government organizations to address the social, political, and economic concerns of their
(35) communities, and ministers of African American congregations in Brooklyn had often acted as mediators between their communities and the government. Many of them also worked for major political parties and ran for political office themselves.
(40) By endorsing and leading the Downstate protest, the ministers were risking their political careers and their reputations within their communities for effecting change through established political channels.

The Downstate campaign ended with an
(45) agreement between the ministers and both government and union officials. This agreement did not include new legislation or a commitment to a specific numerical increase in jobs for African Americans, as the protestors had demanded. But even
(50) though some civil rights activists therefore considered the agreement incomplete, government officials did pledge to enforce existing antidiscrimination legislation. Moreover, the Downstate campaign effectively aroused public concern for the previously
(55) neglected problem of discrimination in the construction industry. It also drew public attention, which had hitherto focused on the progress of the civil rights movement primarily in the southern United States, to the additional need to alleviate
(60) discrimination in the North. Finally, throughout the campaign, the ministers managed to maintain their moderate political ties. The dual role played by the ministers—activists who nonetheless continued to work through established political channels—served
(65) as a model for future ministers who sought to initiate protest actions on behalf of their communities.

1. It can be reasonably inferred from the passage that the author's attitude is most favorable toward which one of the following?

(A) the ways in which the Downstate campaign altered the opinions of union leaders
(B) the impact that the Downstate campaign had on the implementation of new anti-discrimination legislation
(C) CORE's relationship to the demonstrators in the Downstate campaign
(D) the effects that the Downstate campaign had on public awareness
(E) the way in which the leaders of the Downstate campaign negotiated the agreement that ended the campaign

GO ON TO THE NEXT PAGE.

2. Which one of the following assertions about the results of the Downstate campaign does the author affirm in the passage?

   (A)   It achieved all of its participants' goals for changes in union policy but not all of its participants' goals for government action.

   (B)   It directly achieved neither all of its participants' goals for government action nor all of its participants' goals for changes in union hiring policies.

   (C)   It achieved all of its participants' goals for changes in government policies, but did not achieve all of its participants' goals for union commitment to hiring policies.

   (D)   It achieved all of its particular goals for government action immediately, but only gradually achieved some of its participants' desired effects on public opinion.

   (E)   It eventually achieved all of its participants' particular goals for both government action and establishment of union hiring policies, but only after extended effort and significant risk.

3. The primary function of the reference to past activities of ministers and churches (lines 31–38) is to

   (A)   demonstrate that the tactics used by the leaders of the Downstate campaign evolved naturally out of their previous political activities

   (B)   explain why the leaders of the Downstate campaign decided to conduct the protest in the way they did

   (C)   provide examples of the sorts of civil rights activities that the leaders of CORE had promoted

   (D)   indicate how the Downstate campaign could have accomplished its goals by means other than those used

   (E)   underscore the extent to which the Downstate campaign represented a change in approach for its leaders

4. Which one of the following does the author affirm in the passage?

   (A)   CORE was one of several civil rights organizations that challenged the hiring practices of the construction industry.

   (B)   The Downstate campaign relied primarily on CORE and other national civil rights organizations for most of its support.

   (C)   After the Downstate campaign, concern for discrimination in the construction industry was directed primarily toward the northern United States.

   (D)   Many ministers of African American congregations in Brooklyn had sought election to political office.

   (E)   In response to the Downstate campaign, union officials pledged to adopt specific numerical goals for the hiring of African Americans.

5. The passage most clearly suggests that which one of the following is true of the group of ministers who led the Downstate campaign?

   (A)   The Downstate campaign did not signal a significant change in their general political and social goals.

   (B)   After the Downstate campaign, they went on to organize various other similar campaigns.

   (C)   They had come together for the purpose of addressing problems in the construction industry well before CORE's involvement in the Downstate campaign.

   (D)   They were criticized both by CORE and by other concerned organizations for their incomplete success in the Downstate campaign.

   (E)   Prior to the Downstate campaign, many of them had not been directly involved in civil rights activities.

GO ON TO THE NEXT PAGE.

The Cultural Revolution of 1966 to 1976, initiated by Communist Party Chairman Mao Zedong in an attempt to reduce the influence of China's intellectual elite on the country's institutions, has had
(5) lasting repercussions on Chinese art. It intensified the absolutist mind-set of Maoist Revolutionary Realism, which had dictated the content and style of Chinese art even before 1966 by requiring that artists "truthfully" depict the realities of socialist life in
(10) China. Interest in nonsocial, nonpolitical subjects was strictly forbidden, and, during the Cultural Revolution, what constituted truth was entirely for revolutionary forces to decide—the only reality artists could portray was one that had been thoroughly
(15) colored and distorted by political ideology.

Ironically, the same set of requirements that constricted artistic expression during the Cultural Revolution has had the opposite effect since; many artistic movements have flourished in reaction to the
(20) monotony of Revolutionary Realism. One of these, the Scar Art movement of the 1980s, was spearheaded by a group of intellectual painter who had been trained in Maoist art schools and then exiled to rural areas during the Cultural Revolution.
(25) In exile, these painters were for perhaps the first time confronted with the harsh realities of rural poverty and misery—aspects of life in China that their Maoist mentors would probably have preferred they ignore. As a result of these experiences, they developed a
(30) radically new approach to realism. Instead of depicting the version of reality sanctioned by the government, the Scar Art painters chose to represent the "scarred reality" they had seen during their exile. Their version of realist painting emphasized the day-
(35) to-day hardships of rural life. While the principles of Revolutionary Realism had insisted that artists choose public, monumental, and universal subjects, the Scar artists chose instead to focus on the private, the mundane, and the particular; where the principles of
(40) Revolutionary Realism had demanded that they depict contemporary Chinese society as outstanding or perfect, the Scar artists chose instead to portray the bleak realities of modernization.

As the 1980s progressed, the Scar artists' radical
(45) approach to realism became increasingly co-opted for political purposes, and as this political cast became stronger and more obvious, many artists abandoned the movement. Yet a preoccupation with rural life persisted, giving rise to a related development known
(50) as the Native Soil movement, which focused on the native landscape and embodied a growing nostalgia for the charms of peasant society in the face of modernization. Where the Scar artists had reacted to the ideological rigidity of the Cultural Revolution by
(55) emphasizing the damage inflicted by modernization,

the Native Soil painters reacted instead by idealizing traditional peasant life. Unfortunately, in the end Native Soil painting was trivialized by a tendency to romanticize certain qualities of rural Chinese society
(60) in order to appeal to Western galleries and collectors.

6. Which one of the following titles most accurately captures the main point of the passage?

(A) "Painting and Politics: A Survey of Political Influences on Contemporary Chinese Art"
(B) "How Two Movements in Chinese Painting Transformed the Cultural Revolution"
(C) "Scarred Reality: A Look into Chinese Rural Life in the Late Twentieth Century"
(D) "The Rise of Realism in Post-Maoist Art in China"
(E) "The Unforeseen Artistic Legacy of China's Cultural Revolution"

7. Which one of the following works of art would be most compatible with the goals and interests of Scar Art as described in the passage?

(A) a painting of a village scene in which peasants commemorate a triumph over cruel political officials
(B) a painting symbolically representing the destruction caused by a large fire
(C) a painting depicting the weary face of a poorly clothed peasant toiling in a grain mill
(D) a painting caricaturing Mao Zedong as an overseer of farm workers
(E) a painting of two traditionally dressed peasant children walking in a summer wheat field

8. Which one of the following statements about realism in Chinese art can most reasonably be inferred from the passage?

(A) The artists who became leaders of the Native Soil movement practiced a modified form of realism in reaction against the styles and techniques of Scar Art.
(B) Chinese art has encompassed conflicting conceptions of realism derived from contrasting political and artistic purposes.
(C) The goals of realism in Chinese art have been effectively furthered by both the Scar Art movement and the Native Soil movement.
(D) Until the development of the Scar Art movement, interest in rural life had been absent from the types of art that prevailed among Chinese realist painters.
(E) Unlike the art that was predominant during the Cultural Revolution, Scar Art was not a type of realist art.

GO ON TO THE NEXT PAGE.

9. It can be inferred from the passage that the author would be LEAST likely to agree with which one of the following statements regarding the Cultural Revolution?

    (A) It had the ironic effect of catalyzing art movements at odds with its policies.
    (B) The art that was endorsed by its policies was less varied and interesting than Chinese art since the Cultural Revolution.
    (C) Much of the art that it endorsed did not accurately depict the realities of life in China but rather a politically motivated idealization.
    (D) Its effects demonstrate that restrictive policies generally foster artistic growth more than liberal policies do.
    (E) Its impact has continued to be felt in the Chinese art world years after it ended.

10. The primary function of the first paragraph is to

    (A) introduce the set of political and artistic ideas that spurred the development of two artistic movements described in the subsequent paragraphs
    (B) acknowledge the inescapable melding of political ideas and artistic styles in China
    (C) explain the transformation of Chinese society that came about as a result of the Cultural Revolution
    (D) present a hypothesis about realism in Chinese art that is refuted by the ensuing discussion of two artistic movements
    (E) show that the political realism practiced by the movements discussed in the ensuing paragraphs originated during the Cultural Revolution

11. It can be inferred from the passage that the author would be most likely to agree with which one of the following views of the Native Soil movement?

    (A) Its development was the inevitable consequence of the Scar Art movement's increasing politicization.
    (B) It failed to earn the wide recognition that Scar Art had achieved.
    (C) The rural scenes it depicted were appealing to most people in China.
    (D) Ironically, it had several key elements in common with Revolutionary Realism, in opposition to which it originally developed.
    (E) Its nostalgic representation of rural life was the means by which it stood in opposition to Revolutionary Realism.

GO ON TO THE NEXT PAGE.

Individual family members have been assisted in resolving disputes arising from divorce or separation, property division, or financial arrangements, through court-connected family mediation programs, which
(5) differ significantly from court adjudication. When courts use their authority to resolve disputes by adjudicating matters in litigation, judges' decisions are binding, subject only to appeal. Formal rules govern the procedure followed, and the hearings are
(10) generally open to the public. In contrast, family mediation is usually conducted in private, the process is less formal, and mediators do not make binding decisions. Mediators help disputing parties arrive at a solution themselves through communication and
(15) cooperation by facilitating the process of negotiation that leads to agreement by the parties.

Supporters of court adjudication in resolving family disputes claim that it has numerous advantages over family mediation, and there is some validity to
(20) this claim. Judges' decisions, they argue, explicate and interpret the broader social values involved in family disputes, and family mediation can neglect those values. Advocates of court adjudication also argue that since the dynamics of power in disputes
(25) are not always well understood, mediation, which is based on the notion of relatively equal parties, would be inappropriate in many situations. The court system, on the other hand, attempts to protect those at a disadvantage because of imbalances in bargaining
(30) power. Family mediation does not guarantee the full protection of an individual's rights, whereas a goal of the court system is to ensure that lawyers can secure all that the law promises to their clients. Family mediation also does not provide a formal record of
(35) the facts and principles that influence the settlement of a dispute, so if a party to a mediated agreement subsequently seeks modification of the judgment, the task of reconstructing the mediation process is especially difficult. Finally, mediated settlements
(40) divert cases from judicial consideration, thus eliminating the opportunity for such cases to refine the law through the ongoing development of legal precedent.

But in the final analysis, family mediation is
(45) better suited to the unique needs of family law than is the traditional court system. Proponents of family mediation point out that it constitutes a more efficient and less damaging process than litigation. By working together in the mediation process, family members
(50) can enhance their personal autonomy and reduce government intervention, develop skills to resolve future disputes, and create a spirit of cooperation that can lead to greater compliance with their agreement. The family mediation process can assist in resolving
(55) emotional as well as legal issues and thus may reduce

stress in the long term. Studies of family mediation programs in several countries report that the majority of participants reach a full or partial agreement and express positive feelings about the process, perceiving
(60) it to be more rational and humane than the court system.

12. Which one of the following most accurately expresses the main point of the passage?

(A) Recent studies show that family mediation is preferred by family members for resolving family disputes because it is more rational and humane than the court adjudication process.

(B) Even though a majority of participants in family mediation programs are satisfied with the settlements they reach, the use of court adjudication in resolving family disputes has several advantages over the use of mediation.

(C) When given the option, family members involved in disputes have typically elected to use family mediation rather than court adjudication to settle their disputes.

(D) While court adjudication of family disputes has certain advantages, family mediation serves the needs of family members better because it enhances autonomy and encourages greater communication and cooperation in reaching an agreement.

(E) Although supporters of court adjudication argue that family mediation does not contribute to the development and refinement of legal precedent, they fail to recognize that most family disputes can be resolved without appeal to legal precedents.

13. Which one of the following most accurately expresses the primary purpose of the sentence at lines 30–33?

(A) to illustrate that court adjudication can have certain benefits that family mediation may lack

(B) to present material that reveals the inherent limitations of the court adjudication model

(C) to prove that the assumptions implicit in court adjudication and family mediation are irreconcilable

(D) to present an alternative judicial option that combines the benefits of both court adjudication and family mediation

(E) to suggest that lawyers are essential for the protection of individual rights during disputes

GO ON TO THE NEXT PAGE.

14. Based on the passage, which one of the following relationships is most analogous to that between the mediator and the family members involved in a dispute?

   (A) A labor relations specialist assists a group of auto assembly workers and the plant's management in reaching an agreeable salary increase for the workers.

   (B) A drama teacher decides on the school's annual production based on the outcome of a majority vote by the student body.

   (C) A group director solicits feedback from staff prior to implementing a new computer system designed to be more efficient.

   (D) An administrative assistant records the minutes of an office meeting in order to improve interoffice communications.

   (E) A judge meets privately with the opposing counsel of two parties after rendering a decision in a case.

15. According to the passage, proponents of family mediation note that the family mediation process

   (A) is more time-consuming than court adjudication

   (B) almost always results in full agreement among the parties

   (C) attempts to protect those at a disadvantage because of unequal bargaining power

   (D) is most effective in resolving disputes involved in divorce and separation

   (E) helps develop the conflict-resolving skills of the parties in a dispute

16. It can most reasonably be inferred from the passage that the author would agree with which one of the following statements regarding the differences between court adjudication and family mediation?

   (A) The differences are minimal and would rarely lead to substantially different settlements of similar disputes.

   (B) The two processes are so different that the attitudes of the participants toward the outcomes reached can vary significantly depending on which process is used.

   (C) The main difference between family mediation and court adjudication is that while family mediation is less damaging, court adjudication is more efficient.

   (D) Family mediation led by expert mediators differs much less from court adjudication than does mediation led by mediators who have less expertise.

   (E) While family mediation differs significantly from court adjudication, these differences do not really make one or the other better suited to the needs of family law.

17. According to the passage, proponents of court adjudication of family disputes would be most likely to agree with which one of the following?

   (A) Court adjudication of family disputes usually produces a decision that satisfies all parties to the dispute equally.

   (B) Family mediation fails to address the underlying emotional issues in family disputes.

   (C) Settlements of disputes reached through family mediation are not likely to guide the resolution of similar future disputes among other parties.

   (D) Court adjudication presumes that the parties to a dispute have relatively equal bargaining power.

   (E) Court adjudication hearings for family disputes should always be open to the public.

18. The author's primary purpose in the passage is to

   (A) document the evolution of a particular body of law and its various conflict-resolution processes

   (B) describe how societal values are embedded in and affect the outcome of two different processes for resolving disputes

   (C) explain why one method of conflict resolution is preferable to another for a certain class of legal disputes

   (D) show how and why legal precedents in a certain branch of the law can eventually alter the outcomes of future cases

   (E) demonstrate that the court system too often disregards the needs of individuals involved in disputes

GO ON TO THE NEXT PAGE.

Until recently, biologists were unable to explain the fact that pathogens—disease-causing parasites—have evolved to incapacitate, and often overwhelm, their hosts. Such behavior is at odds with the

(5) prevailing view of host-parasite relations—that, in general, host and parasite ultimately develop a benign coexistence. This view is based on the idea that parasites that do not harm their hosts have the best chance for long-term survival: they thrive because

(10) their hosts thrive. Some biologists, however, recently have suggested that if a pathogen reproduced so extensively as to cause its host to become gravely sick, it could still achieve evolutionary success if its replication led to a level of transmission into new

(15) hosts that exceeded the loss of pathogens resulting from the host's incapacitation. This scenario suggests that even death-causing pathogens can achieve evolutionary success.

One implication of this perspective is that a

(20) pathogen's virulence—its capacity to overcome a host's defenses and incapacitate it—is a function of its mode of transmission. For example, rhinoviruses, which cause the common cold, require physical proximity for transmission to occur. If a rhinovirus

(25) reproduces so extensively in a solitary host that the host is too unwell to leave home for a day, the thousands of new rhinoviruses produced that day will die before they can be transmitted. So, because it is transmitted directly, the common cold is unlikely to

(30) disable its victims.

The opposite can occur when pathogens are transported by a vector—an organism that can carry and transmit an infectious agent. If, for example, a pathogen capable of being transported by a mosquito

(35) reproduces so extensively that its human host is immobilized, it can still pass along its genes if a mosquito bites the host and transmits this dose to the next human it bites. In such circumstances the virulence is likely to be more severe, because the

(40) pathogen has reproduced to such concentration in the host that the mosquito obtains a high dose of the pathogen, increasing the level of transmission to new hosts.

While medical literature generally supports the

(45) hypothesis that vector-borne pathogens tend to be more virulent than directly transmitted pathogens—witness the lethal nature of malaria, yellow fever, typhus, and sleeping sickness, all carried by biting insects—a few directly transmitted pathogens such as

(50) diphtheria and tuberculosis bacteria can be just as lethal. Scientists call these "sit and wait" pathogens, because they are able to remain alive outside their hosts until a new host comes along, without relying on a vector. Indeed, the endurance of these pathogens,

(55) many of which can survive externally for weeks or months before transmission into a new host—compared, for instance, to an average rhinovirus life span of hours—makes them among the most dangerous of all pathogens.

19. Which one of the following most accurately summarizes the main idea of the passage?

(A) A new hypothesis about the host-incapacitating behavior of some pathogens suggests that directly transmitted pathogens are just as virulent as vector-borne pathogens, due to the former's ability to survive outside a host for long periods of time.

(B) A new hypothesis about the host-incapacitating behavior of some pathogens suggests that, while most pathogens reproduce so extensively as to cause their hosts to become gravely sick or even to die, some eventually develop a benign coexistence with their hosts.

(C) A new hypothesis about the host-incapacitating behavior of some pathogens suggests that they are able to achieve reproductive success because they reproduce to a high level of concentration in their incapacitated hosts.

(D) A new hypothesis about the host-incapacitating behavior of some pathogens suggests that they are generally able to achieve reproductive success unless their reproduction causes the death of the host.

(E) A new hypothesis about the host-incapacitating behavior of some pathogens suggests that pathogen virulence is generally a function of their mode of transmission, with vector-borne pathogens usually more virulent than directly transmitted pathogens, except for those directly transmitted pathogens able to endure outside their hosts.

20. According to the passage, the prevailing view of the host-parasite relationship is that, in general,

(A) the host is ultimately harmed enough to prevent the parasite from thriving

(B) a thriving parasite will eventually incapacitate its host

(C) a parasite must eventually be transmitted to a new host in order to survive

(D) the parasite eventually thrives with no harm to its host

(E) ultimately the host thrives only if the parasite thrives

21. With which one of the following statements about the prevailing view of host-parasite relations would the biologists mentioned in line 10 be most likely to agree?

(A) The view contradicts most evidence of actual host-parasite relations.

(B) The view suggests that even death-causing pathogens can achieve evolutionary success.

(C) The view presumes the existence of a type of parasite behavior that does not exist.

(D) The view ignores the possibility that there is more than one way to achieve evolutionary success.

(E) The view erroneously assumes that hosts never harm the parasites that feed off them.

GO ON TO THE NEXT PAGE.

22. The examples of diphtheria and tuberculosis bacteria provide the most support for which one of the following conclusions about the dangerousness of pathogens?

(A) The most dangerous pathogens are those with the shortest life spans outside a host.

(B) Those pathogens with the greatest endurance outside a host are among the most dangerous.

(C) Those pathogens transported by vectors are always the most dangerous.

(D) The least dangerous pathogens are among those with the longest life spans outside a host.

(E) Those pathogens transmitted directly are always the least dangerous.

23. Which one of the following, if true, would most seriously challenge the position of the biologists mentioned in line 10?

(A) Most pathogens capable of causing their hosts' deaths are able to achieve reproductive success.

(B) Most pathogens transmitted from incapacitated hosts into new hosts are unable to overwhelm the new hosts.

(C) Most pathogens that do not incapacitate their hosts are unable to achieve reproductive success.

(D) Most hosts that become gravely sick are infected by pathogens that reproduce to relatively high concentrations.

(E) Most pathogens transmitted from incapacitated hosts are unable to reproduce in their new hosts.

24. Which one of the following most accurately describes the organization of the passage?

(A) introduction of a scientific anomaly; presentation of an explanation for the anomaly; mention of an implication of the explanation; discussion of two examples illustrating the implication; discussion of exceptions to the implication

(B) introduction of a scientific anomaly; presentation of an explanation for the anomaly; discussion of two examples illustrating the explanation; discussion of exceptions to the explanation; mention of an implication of the explanation

(C) introduction of a scientific anomaly; presentation of an explanation for the anomaly; discussion of two examples illustrating the explanation; mention of an implication of the explanation; discussion of examples illustrating the implication

(D) introduction of a scientific anomaly; presentation of an implication of the anomaly; discussion of two examples illustrating the implication; discussion of exceptions to the implication

(E) introduction of a scientific anomaly; discussion of two examples illustrating the anomaly; presentation of an explanation for the anomaly; discussion of examples illustrating the explanation

25. The passage implies that which one of the following is a reason that rhinoviruses are unlikely to be especially virulent?

(A) They immobilize their hosts before they have a chance to reproduce extensively enough to pass directly to new hosts.

(B) They cannot survive outside their hosts long enough to be transmitted from incapacitated hosts to new hosts.

(C) They cannot reproduce in numbers sufficient to allow vectors to obtain high enough doses to pass to new hosts.

(D) They cannot survive long enough in an incapacitated host to be picked up by vectors.

(E) They produce thousands of new rhinoviruses each day.

26. The primary purpose of the passage is to

(A) compare examples challenging the prevailing view of host-parasite relations with examples supporting it

(B) argue that the prevailing view of host-parasite relations is correct but is based on a mistaken rationale

(C) offer a modification to the prevailing view of host-parasite relations

(D) attack evidence that supports the prevailing view of host-parasite relations

(E) examine the origins of the prevailing view of host-parasite relations

S T O P

IF YOU FINISH BEFORE TIME IS CALLED, YOU MAY CHECK YOUR WORK ON THIS SECTION ONLY.
DO NOT WORK ON ANY OTHER SECTION IN THE TEST.

SECTION III

Time—35 minutes

26 Questions

Directions: The questions in this section are based on the reasoning contained in brief statements or passages. For some questions, more than one of the choices could conceivably answer the question. However, you are to choose the best answer; that is, the response that most accurately and completely answers the question. You should not make assumptions that are by commonsense standards implausible, superfluous, or incompatible with the passage. After you have chosen the best answer, blacken the corresponding space on your answer sheet.

1. Although fiber-optic telephone cable is more expensive to manufacture than copper telephone cable, a telephone network using fiber-optic cable is less expensive overall than a telephone network using copper cable. This is because copper cable requires frequent amplification of complex electrical signals to carry them for long distances, whereas the pulses of light that are transmitted along fiber-optic cable can travel much farther before amplification is needed.

    The above statements, if true, most strongly support which one of the following?

    (A) The material from which fiber-optic cable is manufactured is more expensive than the copper from which copper cable is made.

    (B) The increase in the number of transmissions of complex signals through telephone cables is straining those telephone networks that still use copper cable.

    (C) Fiber-optic cable can carry many more signals simultaneously than copper cable can.

    (D) Signals transmitted through fiber-optic cable travel at the same speed as signals transmitted through copper cable.

    (E) The cost associated with frequent amplification of signals traveling through copper cable exceeds the extra manufacturing cost of fiber-optic cable.

2. Being near woodlands, the natural habitat of bees, promotes the health of crops that depend on pollination. Bees, the most common pollinators, visit flowers far from woodlands less often than they visit flowers close to woodlands.

    Which one of the following, if true, most strengthens the argument?

    (A) The likelihood that a plant is pollinated increases as the number of visits from pollinators increases.

    (B) Many bees live in habitats other than woodlands.

    (C) Woodlands are not the natural habitat of all pollinators.

    (D) Some pollinators visit flowers far from their habitats more often than they visit flowers close to their habitats.

    (E) Many crops that are not near woodlands depend on pollination.

3. According to the rules of the university's housing lottery, the only students guaranteed dormitory rooms are fourth-year students. In addition, any fourth-year student on the dean's list can choose a dormitory room before anyone who is not a fourth-year student.

    Which one of the following inferences is most strongly supported by the rules described above?

    (A) Benizer is a fourth-year student who is not on the dean's list, so she is not guaranteed a dormitory room.

    (B) Ivan and Naomi are both fourth-year students but only Naomi is on the dean's list. Therefore, Ivan can choose a dormitory room before Naomi.

    (C) Halle, a third-year student, is on the dean's list. Thus, she is guaranteed a dormitory room.

    (D) Gerald and Katrina are both on the dean's list but only Gerald is a fourth-year student. Thus, Gerald can choose a dormitory room before Katrina.

    (E) Anissa is a fourth-year student who is on the dean's list. Thus, since Jehan is a second-year student who is also on the dean's list, he can choose a dormitory room before Anissa.

GO ON TO THE NEXT PAGE.

4. To the editor:

For generations, magnificent racehorses have been bred in our area. Our most valuable product, however, has been generations of children raised with the character that makes them winners in the contests of life. Gambling is wrong, and children raised in an atmosphere where the goal is to get something for nothing will not develop good character. Those who favor developing good character in children over gambling on horses should vote against allowing our first racetrack to be built.

L.E.

Which one of the following, if true, most weakens L.E.'s argument?

(A) If good character is developed in children early, the children continue to have good character in different environments.

(B) In other areas with gambling, parents are able to raise children of good character.

(C) In most areas with horse racing, the percentage of adults who gamble increases gradually from year to year.

(D) Children whose parents gamble do not necessarily gamble when they become adults.

(E) Where voters have had the opportunity to vote on horse racing, they have consistently approved it.

5. Azadeh: The recent increase in the amount of organically produced food indicates that consumers are taking a greater interest in the environment. Thus, there is new hope for a healthier planet.

Ben: No, Azadeh, if you interviewed people who buy organic produce, you'd see that they're actually as selfish as everyone else, since they're motivated only by worries about their own health.

Azadeh's and Ben's statements provide the most support for holding that they disagree about whether

(A) it is likely that a healthy planet can be maintained if most people continue in their present eating habits

(B) people can become healthier by increasing their consumption of organic foods

(C) people ought to be more concerned about the environment than they currently are

(D) the rise in organic food production shows people to have a greater concern for the environment than they had before

(E) people can be persuaded to have a greater concern for the environment than they now have

6. Citizen: The primary factor determining a dog's disposition is not its breed, but its home environment. A bad owner can undo generations of careful breeding. Legislation focusing on specific breeds of dogs would not address the effects of human behavior in raising and training animals. As a result, such breed-specific legislation could never effectively protect the public from vicious dogs. Moreover, in my view, the current laws are perfectly adequate.

Which one of the following most accurately expresses the conclusion drawn by the citizen?

(A) The public would not be effectively protected from violent dogs by breed-specific legislation.

(B) A good home environment is more important than breeding to a dog's disposition.

(C) The home environment of dogs would not be regulated by breed-specific legislation.

(D) Irresponsible dog owners are capable of producing dogs with bad dispositions regardless of generations of careful breeding.

(E) The vicious-dog laws that are currently in effect do not address the effects of human behavior in raising and training dogs.

7. Legislator: To keep our food safe, we must prohibit the use of any food additives that have been found to cause cancer.

Commentator: An absolute prohibition is excessive. Today's tests can detect a single molecule of potentially cancer-causing substances, but we know that consuming significantly larger amounts of such a chemical does not increase one's risk of getting cancer. Thus, we should instead set a maximum acceptable level for each problematic chemical, somewhat below the level at which the substance has been shown to lead to cancer but above zero.

Of the following, which one, if true, is the logically strongest counter the legislator can make to the commentator's argument?

(A) The level at which a given food additive has been shown to lead to cancer in children is generally about half the level at which it leads to cancer in adults.

(B) Consuming small amounts of several different cancer-causing chemicals can lead to cancer even if consuming such an amount of any one cancer-causing chemical would not.

(C) The law would prohibit only the deliberate addition of cancer-causing chemicals and would not require the removal of naturally occurring cancer-causing substances.

(D) For some food additives, the level at which the substance has been shown to lead to cancer is lower than the level at which the additive provides any benefit.

(E) All food additives have substitutes that can be used in their place.

GO ON TO THE NEXT PAGE.

8. Consumer advocate: There is ample evidence that the model of car one drives greatly affects the chances that one's car will be stolen. The model of car stolen most often in our country last year, for example, was also the model stolen most often in the preceding year.

The consumer advocate's reasoning is most vulnerable to criticism on the grounds that it

(A) fails to address adequately the possibility that the model of car that was stolen most often last year was the most common model of car in the consumer advocate's country
(B) fails to address adequately the possibility that the age of a car also greatly affects its chances of being stolen
(C) fails to address adequately the possibility that the car model that was stolen most often last year was stolen as often as it was because it has a very high resale value
(D) presumes, without providing justification, that someone considering whether or not to steal a particular car considers only what model the car is
(E) presumes, without providing justification, that the likelihood of a car's being stolen should override other considerations in deciding which car one should drive

9. Laird: Pure research provides us with new technologies that contribute to saving lives. Even more worthwhile than this, however, is its role in expanding our knowledge and providing new, unexplored ideas.

Kim: Your priorities are mistaken. Saving lives is what counts most of all. Without pure research, medicine would not be as advanced as it is.

Laird and Kim disagree on whether pure research

(A) derives its significance in part from its providing new technologies
(B) expands the boundaries of our knowledge of medicine
(C) should have the saving of human lives as an important goal
(D) has its most valuable achievements in medical applications
(E) has any value apart from its role in providing new technologies to save lives

10. Naturalist: To be dependable, the accounting framework used by national economists to advise the government must take into account all of our nation's assets; but the current accounting framework used by our national economists assigns no value to government-owned natural resources, which are clearly assets.

The naturalist's statements, if true, most strongly support which one of the following?

(A) Economists' indifference toward the destruction of natural resources will lead policymakers to make poor decisions.
(B) Naturalists and economists disagree about whether natural resources have value.
(C) The accounting framework used by national economists is not reliable.
(D) Natural resources are a vital economic asset for every nation.
(E) Changes in the environment have a value that is not represented in any accounting framework.

11. Carrots are known to be one of the best sources of naturally occurring vitamin A. However, although farmers in Canada and the United States report increasing demand for carrots over the last decade, the number of people diagnosed with vitamin A deficiency in these countries has also increased in that time.

Each of the following, if true of Canada and the United States over the last decade, helps to resolve the apparent discrepancy described above EXCEPT:

(A) The population has significantly increased in every age group.
(B) The purchase of peeled and chopped carrots has become very popular, though carrots are known to lose their vitamins quickly once peeled.
(C) Certain cuisines that have become popular use many more vegetable ingredients, including carrots, than most cuisines that were previously popular.
(D) Carrot consumption has increased only among those demographic groups that have historically had low vitamin A deficiency rates.
(E) Weather conditions have caused a decrease in the availability of carrots.

GO ON TO THE NEXT PAGE.

12. Critics have argued that because Freudianism holds that people have unconscious desires that can defeat their attempts to follow rational life plans, it is incompatible with the predominantly rationalistic spirit of Western philosophical and psychological thought. But it is a central tenet of Freudianism that through psychoanalysis one can become conscious of one's previously unconscious desires, enabling one to avoid being defeated by them. Therefore, _____.

Which one of the following most logically completes the argument?

(A) Freudianism does not run counter to the rationalistic mainstream of Western philosophical and psychological thought

(B) Freudianism holds that people can always achieve happiness through psychoanalysis

(C) Freudianism may be the beginning of a new trend in Western philosophical and psychological thought

(D) psychoanalysis provides one with a rational life plan

(E) Freudianism reflects the predominantly rationalistic spirit of Western philosophical and psychological thought more than any other psychological theory

13. Writer: In the diplomat's or lawyer's world, a misinterpreted statement can result in an international incident or an undeserved prison term. Thus, legal and diplomatic language is stilted and utterly without literary merit, since by design it prevents misinterpretation, which in these areas can have severe consequences.

The writer's argument requires assuming which one of the following?

(A) Language that has literary value is more likely to be misunderstood than language without literary value.

(B) Literary documents are generally less important than legal or diplomatic documents.

(C) Lawyers and diplomats are much less likely to be misunderstood than are novelists.

(D) The issues that are of interest to lawyers and diplomats are of little interest to others.

(E) People express themselves more cautiously when something important is at stake.

14. Overexposure to certain wavelengths of strong sunlight is the main cause of melanoma, a virulent form of skin cancer. For this reason, doctors now urge everyone to put adequate sunblock on skin exposed to strong sunlight. Adequate sunblock, according to doctors, is any preparation that prevents sunburn even if the person is exposed to strong sunlight for a significant length of time.

Which one of the following, if true, most weakens the recommendation that people wear adequate sunblock?

(A) There is no evidence that there are wavelengths of sunlight that lead to both sunburn and melanoma.

(B) There are people who have allergic reactions to certain chemicals found in many sunblocks.

(C) Many sunblocks need repeated applications to remain effective for a significant length of time.

(D) Toxins contained in certain chemical compounds also cause melanoma.

(E) Sunburns appear immediately after exposure to the sun but melanoma appears years after repeated exposures.

15. In a study, parents were asked to rate each television program that their children watched. The programs were rated for violent content on a scale of one to five, with "one" indicating no violence and "five" indicating a great deal. The number of times their children were disciplined in school was also recorded. Children who watched programs with an average violence rating of three or higher were 50 percent more likely to have been disciplined than other children.

Each of the following, if true, helps to explain the statistical relationship described above EXCEPT:

(A) Children who are excited by violent action programs on television tend to become bored with schoolwork and to express their boredom in an unacceptable fashion.

(B) When parents watch violent programs on television with their children, those children become more likely to regard antisocial behavior as legitimate.

(C) Parents who rated their children's television viewing low on violence had become desensitized to the violence on television by watching too much of it.

(D) Children learn from violent programs on television to disrespect society's prohibitions of violence and, as a result, are more likely than other children to disrespect the school disciplinary codes.

(E) Parents who do not allow their children to watch programs with a high level of violence are more likely than other parents to be careful about other aspects of their children's behavior.

GO ON TO THE NEXT PAGE.

16. In the last election, 89 percent of reporters voted for the incumbent. The content of news programs reveals that reporters allowed the personal biases reflected in this voting pattern to affect their news coverage: 54 percent of coverage concerning the challenger was negative, compared with only 30 percent of that concerning the incumbent.

The argument is logically most vulnerable to criticism on the grounds that it

(A) presumes, without providing justification, that both candidates received equal amounts of coverage overall

(B) ignores the possibility that there was more negative news worthy of reporting concerning the challenger than there was concerning the incumbent

(C) presumes, without providing justification, that allowing biases to influence reporting is always detrimental to the resulting news coverage

(D) ignores the possibility that the electorate's voting behavior is not significantly affected by the content of coverage of candidates

(E) ignores the possibility that reporters generally fear losing access to incumbents more than they fear losing access to challengers

17. Art critic: Abstract paintings are nonrepresentational, and so the only measure of their worth is their interplay of color, texture, and form. But for a painting to spur the viewer to political action, instances of social injustice must be not only represented, but also clearly comprehensible as such. Therefore, abstract painting can never be a politically significant art form.

Which one of the following is an assumption that is required by the art critic's argument?

(A) Abstract painting cannot stimulate people to act.

(B) Unless people view representations of social injustice, their political activity is insignificant.

(C) Only art that prompts people to counter social injustice is significant art.

(D) Paintings that fail to move a viewer to political action cannot be politically significant.

(E) The interplay of color, texture, and form is not a measure of the worth of representational paintings.

18. North Americans who travel to Europe for the first time should include significant time in Italy on their itinerary. To develop an appreciation of a continent that goes beyond the mere accumulation of impressions, one needs to acquire a thorough knowledge of at least one country, and North Americans seem to find it easier to get to know Italy than other European countries.

Which one of the following best illustrates the principle illustrated by the argument above?

(A) A person who wants to learn to play the piano should study classical music, because though it is more difficult to play than is popular music, mastery of its techniques enables one to quickly master popular pieces.

(B) To overcome a fear of water that prevents one from swimming, one should paddle about in shallow water with a trusted friend who is a good swimmer.

(C) Edith Wharton is the most accessible of the classical U.S. writers. So in order to provide a superb introduction to U.S. literature, a class should emphasize her work while also studying the works of others.

(D) One can appreciate Taiko-drumming only if one understands how physically demanding it is. Thus, one should see Taiko-drumming and not just hear it in order to appreciate it fully.

(E) One should travel through North America by train rather than by automobile, because train travel imparts the same sense of open space as does automobile travel, while also affording one the full leisure to attend to the scenery.

GO ON TO THE NEXT PAGE.

19. Although high cholesterol levels have been associated with the development of heart disease, many people with high cholesterol never develop heart disease, while many without high cholesterol do. Recently, above average concentrations of the blood particle lipoprotein(a) were found in the blood of many people whose heart disease was not attributable to other causes. Dietary changes that affect cholesterol levels have no effect on lipoprotein(a) levels. Hence, there is no reason for anyone to make dietary changes for the sake of preventing heart disease.

Which one of the following most accurately describes a flaw in the argument?

(A) It fails to consider the possibility that lipoprotein(a) raises cholesterol levels.

(B) It provides no evidence for a link between lipoprotein(a) and heart disease.

(C) It presents but ignores evidence that, for some people, high cholesterol contributes to heart disease.

(D) It fails to consider the possibility that poor diets cause some people to develop health problems other than heart disease.

(E) It offers no explanation for why some people with high cholesterol levels never develop heart disease.

20. Philosopher: It is absurd to argue that people are morally obligated to act in a certain way simply because not acting in that way would be unnatural. An unnatural action is either a violation of the laws of nature or a statistical anomaly. There is no possibility of acting as one cannot, nor does the mere fact that something is not usually done provide any good reason not to do it.

Which one of the following most accurately describes a technique used in the philosopher's argument?

(A) undermining a concept by showing that its acceptance would violate a law of nature

(B) stating the definition of a key term of the argument

(C) using statistical findings to dispute a claim

(D) undermining a claim by showing that the claim is self-contradictory

(E) using empirical evidence to support one definition of a key term of the argument over another

21. Clearly, fitness consultants who smoke cigarettes cannot help their clients become healthier. If they do not care about their own health, they cannot really care for their clients' health, and if they do not care for their clients' health, they cannot help them to become healthier.

The conclusion follows logically if which one of the following is assumed?

(A) Anyone who does not care for his or her own health cannot help others become healthier.

(B) Anyone who cares about the health of others can help others become healthier.

(C) Anyone who does not care for the health of others cannot help them become healthier.

(D) Anyone who does not smoke cares about the health of others.

(E) Anyone who cares about his or her own health does not smoke.

GO ON TO THE NEXT PAGE.

22. If one does not have enough information to make a well-informed decision, one should not make a decision solely on the basis of the information one does possess. Instead, one should continue to seek information until a well-informed decision can be made.

Of the following, which one most closely conforms to the principle stated above?

(A) Economists should not believe the predictions of an economic model simply because it is based on information about the current economy. Many conflicting models are based on such information, and they cannot all be accurate.

(B) When deciding which career to pursue, one needs to consider carefully all of the information one has. One should not choose a career solely on the basis of financial compensation; instead, one should consider other factors such as how likely one is to succeed at the career and how much one would enjoy it.

(C) Though a researcher may know a great deal about a topic, she or he should not assume that all information relevant to the research is already in her or his possession. A good researcher always looks for further relevant information.

(D) When one wants to buy a reliable car, one should not choose which car to buy just on the inadequate basis of one's personal experience with cars. Rather, one should study various models' reliability histories that summarize many owners' experiences.

(E) When there is not enough information available to determine the meaning of a line of poetry, one should not form an opinion based on the insufficient information. Instead, one should simply acknowledge that it is impossible to determine what the line means.

23. Television network executive: Some scientists have expressed concern about the numerous highly popular television programs that emphasize paranormal incidents, warning that these programs will encourage superstition and thereby impede the public's scientific understanding. But these predictions are baseless. Throughout recorded history, dramatists have relied on ghosts and spirits to enliven their stories, and yet the scientific understanding of the populace has steadily advanced.

The television network executive's argument is most vulnerable to criticism on which one of the following grounds?

(A) It fails to consider that one phenomenon can steadily advance even when it is being impeded by another phenomenon.

(B) It takes for granted that if a correlation has been observed between two phenomena, they must be causally connected.

(C) It fails to consider that the occurrence of one phenomenon can indirectly affect the pervasiveness of another even if the former does not impede the latter.

(D) It fails to consider that just because one phenomenon is known to affect another, the latter does not also affect the former.

(E) It takes for granted that the contention that one phenomenon causes another must be baseless if the latter phenomenon has persisted despite steady increases in the pervasiveness of the former.

24. Police commissioner: Last year our city experienced a 15 percent decrease in the rate of violent crime. At the beginning of that year a new mandatory sentencing law was enacted, which requires that all violent criminals serve time in prison. Since no other major policy changes were made last year, the drop in the crime rate must have been due to the new mandatory sentencing law.

Which one of the following, if true, most seriously weakens the police commissioner's argument?

(A) Studies of many other cities have shown a correlation between improving economic conditions and decreased crime rates.

(B) Prior to the enactment of the mandatory sentencing law, judges in the city had for many years already imposed unusually harsh penalties for some crimes.

(C) Last year, the city's overall crime rate decreased by only 5 percent.

(D) At the beginning of last year, the police department's definition of "violent crime" was broadened to include 2 crimes not previously classified as "violent."

(E) The city enacted a policy 2 years ago requiring that 100 new police officers be hired in each of the 3 subsequent years.

GO ON TO THE NEXT PAGE.

25. A corporation created a new division. To staff it, applicants were rigorously screened and interviewed. Those selected were among the most effective, efficient, and creative workers that the corporation had ever hired. Thus, the new division must have been among the most effective, efficient, and creative divisions the corporation had ever created.

The flawed pattern of reasoning in which one of the following is most similar to that in the argument above?

(A) In order to obtain the best players for its country's Olympic team, a committee reviewed the performance of its country's teams. After reviewing statistics and reading reports, the committee chose one player from each of the six best teams, thus assuring that the six best players in the country had been chosen.

(B) Several salespeople were given incentives to recruit the largest number of new customers in one month. To monitor the incentive program, the boss interviewed one of the salespeople and found that the salesperson had already exceeded the minimum goals of the program. Thus the incentive program was indeed effective.

(C) A law firm decided to add a department devoted to family law. To obtain the best employees it could, the firm studied the credentials and composition of several other firms well known to have successful staffs working in family law. Eventually, the firm hired a staff of new lawyers and support personnel having training and aptitudes as much like those of the studied firms as possible. Thus the law firm must have created one of the best family-law departments.

(D) To put together this year's two All-Star Teams, the best players in the league were selected. Half of them were put on Team One, and half were put on Team Two. Since each player on the two teams was one of the best players in the league this year, it follows that the two All-Star Teams are the two best teams this year.

(E) Various schools chose teams of students to compete in a debate tournament. Each school's team presented a position and rebutted the others' positions. After the initial scores were in, the ten top teams competed against each other. Since one team eventually emerged with the highest average score, it was clearly the best team.

26. Students in a college ethics class were asked to judge whether two magazines had been morally delinquent in publishing a particular classified advertisement that was highly offensive in its demeaning portrayal of some people. They were told only that the first magazine had undertaken to screen all classified advertisements and reject for publication those it found offensive, whereas the second magazine's policy was to publish any advertisement received from its subscribers. Most students judged the first magazine, but not the second, to have been morally delinquent in publishing the advertisement.

Which one of the following principles, if established, provides the strongest justification for the judgment that the first magazine and not the second was morally delinquent?

(A) It is wrong to publish messages that could cause direct or indirect harm to innocent people.

(B) Anyone regularly transmitting messages to the public has a moral responsibility to monitor the content of those messages.

(C) If two similar agents commit two similar actions, those agents should be held to the same standard of accountability.

(D) Failure to uphold a moral standard is not necessarily a moral failing except for those who have specifically committed themselves to upholding that standard.

(E) A magazine should not be considered at fault for publishing a classified advertisement if that advertisement would not be offensive to any of the magazine's subscribers.

S T O P

IF YOU FINISH BEFORE TIME IS CALLED, YOU MAY CHECK YOUR WORK ON THIS SECTION ONLY.
DO NOT WORK ON ANY OTHER SECTION IN THE TEST.

SECTION IV

Time—35 minutes

22 Questions

<u>Directions:</u> Each group of questions in this section is based on a set of conditions. In answering some of the questions, it may be useful to draw a rough diagram. Choose the response that most accurately and completely answers each question and blacken the corresponding space on your answer sheet.

<u>Questions 1–5</u>

Exactly seven products—P, Q, R, S, T, W, and X—are each to be advertised exactly once in a section of a catalog. The order in which they will be displayed is governed by the following conditions:

Q must be displayed in some position before W.
R must be displayed immediately before X.
T cannot be displayed immediately before or
   immediately after W.
S must be displayed either first or seventh.
Either Q or T must be displayed fourth.

1. Which one of the following CANNOT be the product that is displayed first?

   (A)   P
   (B)   Q
   (C)   R
   (D)   T
   (E)   X

2. If X is displayed immediately before Q, then which one of the following could be true?

   (A)   T is displayed first.
   (B)   R is displayed fifth.
   (C)   Q is displayed last.
   (D)   Q is displayed second.
   (E)   P is displayed second.

3. If P is displayed second, then which one of the following could be displayed third?

   (A)   R
   (B)   S
   (C)   T
   (D)   W
   (E)   X

4. Which one of the following could be true?

   (A)   Q is displayed fifth.
   (B)   Q is displayed seventh.
   (C)   R is displayed third.
   (D)   W is displayed third.
   (E)   X is displayed fifth.

5. If R is displayed sixth, then which one of the following must be displayed fifth?

   (A)   P
   (B)   Q
   (C)   T
   (D)   W
   (E)   X

GO ON TO THE NEXT PAGE.

Questions 6–11

A lighting control panel has exactly seven switches, numbered from 1 to 7. Each switch is either in the on position or in the off position. The circuit load of the panel is the total number of its switches that are on. The control panel must be configured in accordance with the following conditions:

> If switch 1 is on, then switch 3 and switch 5 are off.
> If switch 4 is on, then switch 2 and switch 5 are off.
> The switch whose number corresponds to the circuit load of the panel is itself on.

6. Which one of the following could be a complete and accurate list of the switches that are on?

   (A)   switch 2, switch 3, switch 4, switch 7
   (B)   switch 3, switch 6, switch 7
   (C)   switch 2, switch 5, switch 6
   (D)   switch 1, switch 3, switch 4
   (E)   switch 1, switch 5

7. If switch 1 and switch 3 are both off, then which one of the following could be two switches that are both on?

   (A)   switch 2 and switch 7
   (B)   switch 4 and switch 6
   (C)   switch 4 and switch 7
   (D)   switch 5 and switch 6
   (E)   switch 6 and switch 7

8. If exactly two of the switches are on, then which one of the following switches must be off?

   (A)   switch 3
   (B)   switch 4
   (C)   switch 5
   (D)   switch 6
   (E)   switch 7

9. If switch 6 and switch 7 are both off, then what is the maximum circuit load of the panel?

   (A)   one
   (B)   two
   (C)   three
   (D)   four
   (E)   five

10. If switch 5 and switch 6 are both on, then which one of the following switches must be on?

   (A)   switch 1
   (B)   switch 2
   (C)   switch 3
   (D)   switch 4
   (E)   switch 7

11. What is the maximum circuit load of the panel?

   (A)   three
   (B)   four
   (C)   five
   (D)   six
   (E)   seven

GO ON TO THE NEXT PAGE.

Questions 12–17

In Crescentville there are exactly five record stores, whose names are abbreviated S, T, V, X, and Z. Each of the five stores carries at least one of four distinct types of music: folk, jazz, opera, and rock. None of the stores carries any other type of music. The following conditions must hold:

Exactly two of the five stores carry jazz.

T carries rock and opera but no other type of music.

S carries more types of music than T carries.

X carries more types of music than any other store in Crescentville carries.

Jazz is among the types of music S carries.

V does not carry any type of music that Z carries.

12. Which one of the following could be true?

   (A) S carries folk and rock but neither jazz nor opera.
   (B) T carries jazz but neither opera nor rock.
   (C) V carries folk, rock, and opera, but not jazz.
   (D) X carries folk, rock, and jazz, but not opera.
   (E) Z carries folk and opera but neither rock nor jazz.

13. Which one of the following could be true?

   (A) S, V, and Z all carry folk.
   (B) S, X, and Z all carry jazz.
   (C) Of the five stores, only S and V carry jazz.
   (D) Of the five stores, only T and X carry rock.
   (E) Of the five stores, only S, T, and V carry opera.

14. If exactly one of the stores carries folk, then which one of the following could be true?

   (A) S and V carry exactly two types of music in common.
   (B) T and S carry exactly two types of music in common.
   (C) T and V carry exactly two types of music in common.
   (D) V and X carry exactly two types of music in common.
   (E) X and Z carry exactly two types of music in common.

15. Which one of the following must be true?

   (A) T carries exactly the same number of types of music as V carries.
   (B) V carries exactly the same number of types of music as Z carries.
   (C) S carries at least one more type of music than Z carries.
   (D) Z carries at least one more type of music than T carries.
   (E) X carries exactly two more types of music than S carries.

16. If V is one of exactly three stores that carry rock, then which one of the following must be true?

   (A) S and Z carry no types of music in common.
   (B) S and V carry at least one type of music in common.
   (C) S and Z carry at least one type of music in common.
   (D) T and Z carry at least one type of music in common.
   (E) T and V carry at least two types of music in common.

17. If S and V both carry folk, then which one of the following could be true?

   (A) S and T carry no types of music in common.
   (B) S and Z carry no types of music in common.
   (C) T and Z carry no types of music in common.
   (D) S and Z carry two types of music in common.
   (E) T and V carry two types of music in common.

GO ON TO THE NEXT PAGE.

Questions 18–22

Maggie's Deli is open exactly five days every week. Monday through Friday. Its staff, each of whom works on at least one day each week, consists of exactly six people—Janice, Kevin, Nan, Ophelia, Paul, and Seymour. Exactly three of them— Janice, Nan, and Paul—are supervisors. The deli's staffing is consistent with the following:

> Each day's staff consists of exactly two people, at least one of whom is a supervisor.
> Tuesday's and Wednesday's staffs both include Ophelia.
> Of the days Nan works each week, at least two are consecutive.
> Seymour does not work on any day before the first day Paul works that week.
> Any day on which Kevin works is the first day during the week that some other staff member works.

18. Which one of the following could be an accurate staffing schedule?

(A) Monday: Janice, Kevin
     Tuesday: Nan, Ophelia
     Wednesday: Nan, Paul
     Thursday: Kevin, Paul
     Friday: Janice, Seymour
(B) Monday: Paul, Seymour
     Tuesday: Ophelia, Paul
     Wednesday: Nan, Ophelia
     Thursday: Kevin, Nan
     Friday: Janice, Seymour
(C) Monday: Janice, Kevin
     Tuesday: Nan, Ophelia
     Wednesday: Nan, Ophelia
     Thursday: Kevin, Paul
     Friday: Paul, Seymour
(D) Monday: Janice, Kevin
     Tuesday: Janice, Ophelia
     Wednesday: Nan, Ophelia
     Thursday: Nan, Seymour
     Friday: Kevin, Paul
(E) Monday: Paul, Seymour
     Tuesday: Ophelia, Paul
     Wednesday: Nan, Ophelia
     Thursday: Janice, Kevin
     Friday: Nan, Paul

19. If Kevin and Paul work Thursday, who must work Friday?

(A) Janice
(B) Kevin
(C) Nan
(D) Paul
(E) Seymour

20. Each of the following could be true EXCEPT:

(A) Janice works Monday and Tuesday.
(B) Kevin and Paul work Friday.
(C) Seymour works Monday and Friday.
(D) Janice and Kevin work Thursday.
(E) Paul works Monday and Friday.

21. Which one of the following CANNOT be the pair of staff that works Monday?

(A) Janice and Seymour
(B) Kevin and Paul
(C) Paul and Seymour
(D) Nan and Ophelia
(E) Janice and Nan

22. Which one of the following could be true?

(A) Nan works Wednesday and Friday only.
(B) Seymour works Monday and Paul works Tuesday.
(C) Kevin works Monday, Wednesday, and Friday.
(D) Nan works Wednesday with Ophelia and Thursday with Kevin.
(E) Ophelia and Kevin work Tuesday.

S T O P

IF YOU FINISH BEFORE TIME IS CALLED, YOU MAY CHECK YOUR WORK ON THIS SECTION ONLY.
DO NOT WORK ON ANY OTHER SECTION IN THE TEST.

Wait for the supervisor's instructions before you open the page to the topic.
Please print and sign your name and write the date in the designated spaces below.

Time: 35 Minutes

General Directions

You will have 35 minutes in which to plan and write an essay on the topic inside. Read the topic and the accompanying directions carefully. You will probably find it best to spend a few minutes considering the topic and organizing your thoughts before you begin writing. In your essay, be sure to develop your ideas fully, leaving time, if possible, to review what you have written. **Do not write on a topic other than the one specified. Writing on a topic of your own choice is not acceptable.**

No special knowledge is required or expected for this writing exercise. Law schools are interested in the reasoning, clarity, organization, language usage, and writing mechanics displayed in your essay. How well you write is more important than how much you write.

Confine your essay to the blocked, lined area on the front and back of the separate Writing Sample Response Sheet. Only that area will be reproduced for law schools. Be sure that your writing is legible.

Both this topic sheet and your response sheet must be turned over to the testing staff before you leave the room.

Topic Code	Print Your Full Name Here		
_____	Last	First	M.I.

Date	Sign Your Name Here
/ /	

Scratch Paper
Do not write your essay in this space.

LSAT Writing Sample Topic

Directions: The scenario presented below describes two choices, either one of which can be supported on the basis of the information given. Your essay should consider both choices and argue <u>for</u> one and <u>against</u> the other, based on the two specified criteria and the facts provided. There is no "right" or "wrong" choice: a reasonable argument can be made for either.

The Poplar Valley Civic Association (PVCA) needs to raise money to buy new playground equipment for the local park. Board members have narrowed their fundraising options to a raffle or a pancake breakfast. Write an essay in which you argue for one option over the other, keeping in mind the following two criteria:

- The PVCA wants to raise at least enough money to pay for the fundraiser itself and the new playground equipment.
- The PVCA wants to use the event to foster cohesion in the community.

If the PVCA holds a raffle, tickets will be sold by community volunteers for a drawing to be held at the town's annual picnic. PVCA board members will be charged with soliciting prize donations from local businesses. The town's bike shop has already pledged a pair of bikes if the raffle is held. A local travel agency donated a cruise for a similar raffle last year. Local restaurants are also likely prospects. The number of tickets sold will depend not only on the attractiveness of the prizes but on the diligence of volunteer ticket sellers, who will need to canvass the neighborhood and their workplaces systematically for buyers. The cost of printing tickets and holding the raffle will be nominal, so almost all of the money raised could be used to buy equipment.

If the PVCA opts for the pancake breakfast, printed invitations will be mailed to all households in the community. The mailing itself will be fairly expensive, given the cost of postage, but response rates for such solicitations are usually high, and many people end up donating more than the actual cost of tickets. The breakfast will be held on a weekend morning in the elementary school cafeteria, using community volunteers to do the cooking, serving, setup, and cleanup. The cafeteria's kitchen is fully equipped. A local caterer has already volunteered to donate the batter, syrup, and paper products; otherwise, the cost of supplies for the breakfast would be considerably higher than the minimal costs for the raffle.

Scratch Paper
Do not write your essay in this space.

LAST NAME (Print)　　　　　　　　　　　MI　　FIRST NAME (Print)

SIGNATURE

Writing Sample Response Sheet

DO NOT WRITE
IN THIS SPACE

**Begin your essay in the lined area below.
Continue on the back if you need more space.**

Directions:

1. Use the Answer Key on the next page to check your answers.

2. Use the Scoring Worksheet below to compute your raw score.

3. Use the Score Conversion Chart to convert your raw score into the 120–180 scale.

Scoring Worksheet

1. Enter the number of questions you answered correctly in each section.

      Number Correct

   SECTION I . . . . _____

   SECTION II . . . . _____

   SECTION III . . . . . . _____

   SECTION IV . . . . . . _____

2. Enter the sum here: _____

   This is your Raw Score.

Conversion Chart

For Converting Raw Score to the 120–180 LSAT Scaled Score
LSAT PrepTest 47

Reported Score	Raw Score Lowest	Raw Score Highest
180	99	100
179	98	98
178	97	97
177	96	96
176	__*	__*
175	95	95
174	94	94
173	93	93
172	92	92
171	91	91
170	90	90
169	89	89
168	88	88
167	87	87
166	85	86
165	84	84
164	83	83
163	81	82
162	80	80
161	78	79
160	77	77
159	75	76
158	73	74
157	72	72
156	70	71
155	68	69
154	66	67
153	65	65
152	63	64
151	61	62
150	59	60
149	57	58
148	55	56
147	54	54
146	52	53
145	50	51
144	48	49
143	46	47
142	45	45
141	43	44
140	41	42
139	40	40
138	38	39
137	36	37
136	35	35
135	33	34
134	32	32
133	30	31
132	29	29
131	27	28
130	26	26
129	25	25
128	24	24
127	22	23
126	21	21
125	20	20
124	19	19
123	18	18
122	17	17
121	16	16
120	0	15

*There is no raw score that will produce this scaled score for this form.

SECTION I

1.	D	8.	E	15.	D	22.	C
2.	B	9.	E	16.	B	23.	D
3.	C	10.	D	17.	D	24.	C
4.	B	11.	D	18.	D	25.	E
5.	A	12.	E	19.	A	26.	C
6.	B	13.	C	20.	D		
7.	A	14.	E	21.	B		

SECTION II

1.	D	8.	B	15.	E	22.	B
2.	B	9.	D	16.	B	23.	E
3.	E	10.	A	17.	C	24.	A
4.	D	11.	E	18.	C	25.	B
5.	A	12.	D	19.	E	26.	C
6.	E	13.	A	20.	D		
7.	C	14.	A	21.	D		

SECTION III

1.	E	8.	A	15.	C	22.	D
2.	A	9.	D	16.	B	23.	A
3.	D	10.	C	17.	D	24.	E
4.	B	11.	C	18.	C	25.	D
5.	D	12.	A	19.	C	26.	D
6.	A	13.	A	20.	B		
7.	B	14.	A	21.	E		

SECTION IV

1.	E	8.	B	15.	C	22.	B
2.	A	9.	C	16.	C		
3.	C	10.	C	17.	B		
4.	A	11.	C	18.	C		
5.	D	12.	E	19.	E		
6.	B	13.	D	20.	B		
7.	A	14.	B	21.	A		

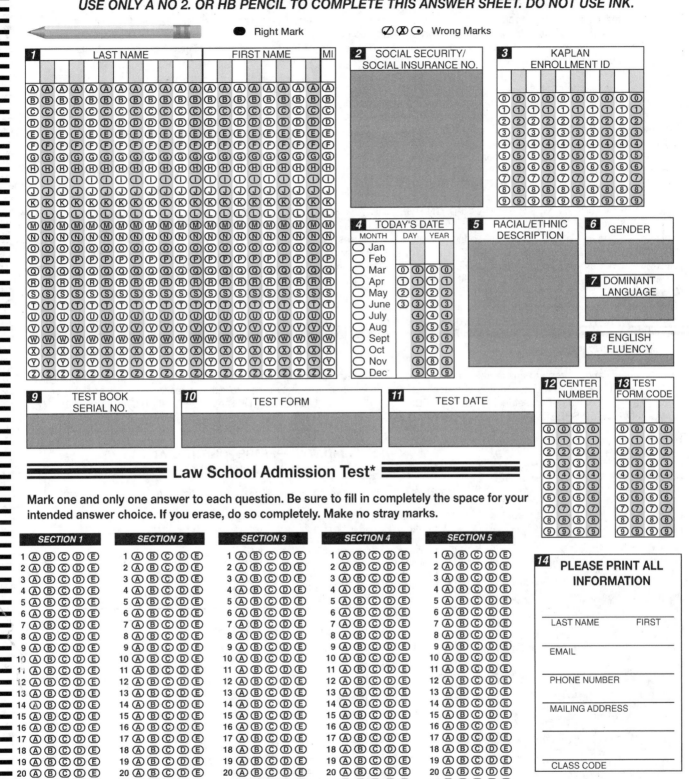

USE ONLY A NO 2. OR HB PENCIL TO COMPLETE THIS ANSWER SHEET. DO NOT USE INK.

● Right Mark ⊘ ⊗ ⊙ Wrong Marks

1 LAST NAME / FIRST NAME / MI

2 SOCIAL SECURITY/ SOCIAL INSURANCE NO.

3 KAPLAN ENROLLMENT ID

4 TODAY'S DATE

MONTH	DAY	YEAR
○ Jan		
○ Feb		
○ Mar		
○ Apr		
○ May		
○ June		
○ July		
○ Aug		
○ Sept		
○ Oct		
○ Nov		
○ Dec		

5 RACIAL/ETHNIC DESCRIPTION

6 GENDER

7 DOMINANT LANGUAGE

8 ENGLISH FLUENCY

9 TEST BOOK SERIAL NO.

10 TEST FORM

11 TEST DATE

12 CENTER NUMBER

13 TEST FORM CODE

═══ Law School Admission Test* ═══

Mark one and only one answer to each question. Be sure to fill in completely the space for your intended answer choice. If you erase, do so completely. Make no stray marks.

SECTION 1 / SECTION 2 / SECTION 3 / SECTION 4 / SECTION 5

(Questions 1–30, answer choices A B C D E for each section)

14 PLEASE PRINT ALL INFORMATION

LAST NAME   FIRST

EMAIL

PHONE NUMBER

MAILING ADDRESS

CLASS CODE

KAPLAN TEST PREP

www.kaptest.com/lsat
1-800-KAP-TEST

LSAT is a registered trademark of the
Law School Admissions Council, Inc.

SCANTRON Mark Reflex® EM-284925-2:654321   LL3225A

General Directions for the LSAT* Answer Sheet

The actual testing time for this portion of the test will be 2 hours 55 minutes. There are five sections, each with a time limit of 35 minutes. The supervisor will tell you when to begin and end each section. If you finish a section before time is called, you may check your work on that section <u>only</u>; do not turn to any other section of the test book and do not work on any other section either in the test book or on the answer sheet.

There are several different types of questions on the test, and each question type has its own directions. <u>Be sure you understand the directions for each question type before attempting to answer any questions in that section.</u>

Not everyone will finish all the questions in the time allowed. Do not hurry, but work steadily and as quickly as you can without sacrificing accuracy. You are advised to use your time effectively. If a question seems too difficult, go on to the next one and return to the difficult question after completing the section. MARK THE BEST ANSWER YOU CAN FOR EVERY QUESTION. NO DEDUCTIONS WILL BE MADE FOR WRONG ANSWERS. YOUR SCORE WILL BE BASED ONLY ON THE NUMBER OF QUESTIONS YOU ANSWER CORRECTLY.

ALL YOUR ANSWERS MUST BE MARKED ON THE ANSWER SHEET. Answer spaces for each question are lettered to correspond with the letters of the potential answers to each question in the test book. After you have decided which of the answers is correct, blacken the corresponding space on the answer sheet. BE SURE THAT EACH MARK IS BLACK AND COMPLETELY FILLS THE ANSWER SPACE. Give only one answer to each question. If you change an answer, be sure that all previous marks are <u>erased completely</u>. Since the answer sheet is machine scored, incomplete erasures may be interpreted as intended answers. ANSWERS RECORDED IN THE TEST BOOK WILL NOT BE SCORED.

There may be more questions noted on this answer sheet than there are questions in a section. Do not be concerned but be certain that the section and number of the question you are answering matches the answer sheet section and question number. Additional answer spaces in any answer sheet section should be left blank. Begin your next section in the number one answer space for that section.

Kaplan takes various steps to ensure that answer sheets are returned from test centers in a timely manner for processing. In the unlikely event that an answer sheet(s) is not received, Kaplan will permit the examinee to either retest at no additional fee or to receive a refund of his or her test fee. THESE REMEDIES ARE THE EXCLUSIVE REMEDIES AVAILABLE IN THE UNLIKELY EVENT THAT AN ANSWER SHEET IS NOT RECEIVED BY KAPLAN.

Score Cancellation

Complete this section only if you are absolutely certain you want to cancel your score. A CANCELLATION REQUEST CANNOT BE RESCINDED. IF YOU ARE AT ALL UNCERTAIN, YOU SHOULD <u>NOT</u> COMPLETE THIS SECTION.

To cancel your score from this administration, you **must**:

A. fill in both ovals here..... ○ ○

B. read the following statement. Then sign your name and enter the date.
YOUR SIGNATURE ALONE IS NOT SUFFICIENT FOR SCORE CANCELLATION. BOTH OVALS MUST BE FILLED IN FOR SCANNING EQUIPMENT TO RECOGNIZE YOUR REQUEST FOR SCORE CANCELLATION.

I certify that I wish to cancel my test score from this administration. I understand that my request is irreversible and that my score will not be sent to me or to the law schools to which I apply.

_____
Sign your name in full

_____
Date

HOW DID YOU PREPARE FOR THE LSAT*?
(Select all that apply.)

Responses to this item are voluntary and will be used for statistical research purposes only.

○ By attending a Kaplan LSAT* prep course or tutoring program
○ By attending a non-Kaplan prep course or tutoring program (Please specify:_____)
○ By using a Kaplan LSAT* prep book
○ By using a non-Kaplan prep book (Please specify: _____)
○ By working through the sample questions and free sample tests provided by the LSAC
○ By working through official LSAT* PrepTests and/or other LSAC test prep products
○ Other preparation (Please specify: _____)
○ No preparation

CERTIFYING STATEMENT

Please write (DO NOT PRINT) the following statement. Sign and date.

I certify that I am the examinee whose name appears on this answer sheet and that I am here to take the LSAT for the sole purpose of being considered for application to law school. I further certify that I will neither assist nor receive assistance from any other candidate, and I agree not to copy or retain examination questions or to transmit them to or discuss them with any other person in any form.

_____
_____
_____
_____
_____
_____
_____
_____
_____
_____

SIGNATURE: _____ TODAY'S DATE: _____/_____/_____
                                        MONTH DAY YEAR

***LSAT is a registered trademark of the Law School Admissions Council, Inc.**

USE ONLY A NO 2. OR HB PENCIL TO COMPLETE THIS ANSWER SHEET. DO NOT USE INK.

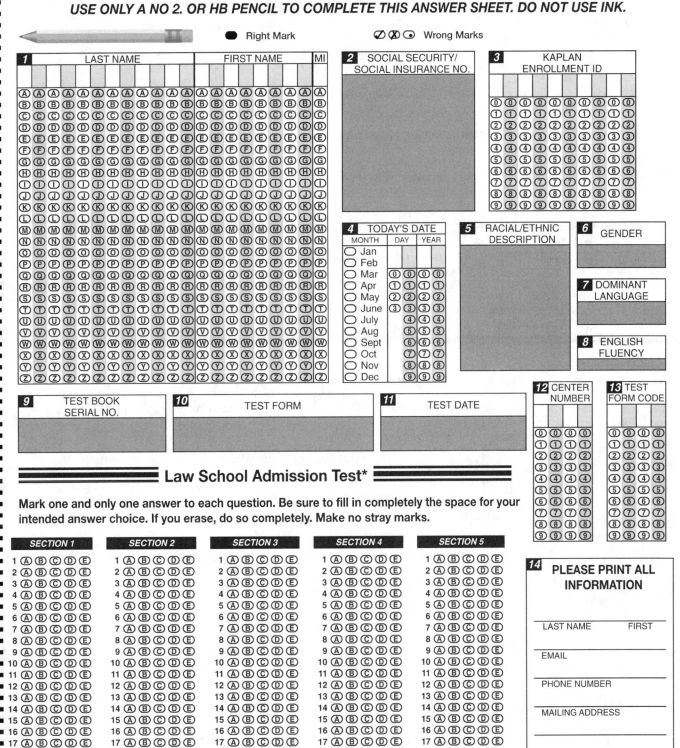

● Right Mark   ⊘⊗⊙ Wrong Marks

1 LAST NAME | FIRST NAME | MI

2 SOCIAL SECURITY/ SOCIAL INSURANCE NO.

3 KAPLAN ENROLLMENT ID

4 TODAY'S DATE
MONTH | DAY | YEAR
- Jan
- Feb
- Mar
- Apr
- May
- June
- July
- Aug
- Sept
- Oct
- Nov
- Dec

5 RACIAL/ETHNIC DESCRIPTION

6 GENDER

7 DOMINANT LANGUAGE

8 ENGLISH FLUENCY

9 TEST BOOK SERIAL NO.

10 TEST FORM

11 TEST DATE

12 CENTER NUMBER

13 TEST FORM CODE

Law School Admission Test*

Mark one and only one answer to each question. Be sure to fill in completely the space for your intended answer choice. If you erase, do so completely. Make no stray marks.

SECTION 1	SECTION 2	SECTION 3	SECTION 4	SECTION 5
1 Ⓐ Ⓑ Ⓒ Ⓓ Ⓔ	1 Ⓐ Ⓑ Ⓒ Ⓓ Ⓔ	1 Ⓐ Ⓑ Ⓒ Ⓓ Ⓔ	1 Ⓐ Ⓑ Ⓒ Ⓓ Ⓔ	1 Ⓐ Ⓑ Ⓒ Ⓓ Ⓔ
2 Ⓐ Ⓑ Ⓒ Ⓓ Ⓔ	2 Ⓐ Ⓑ Ⓒ Ⓓ Ⓔ	2 Ⓐ Ⓑ Ⓒ Ⓓ Ⓔ	2 Ⓐ Ⓑ Ⓒ Ⓓ Ⓔ	2 Ⓐ Ⓑ Ⓒ Ⓓ Ⓔ
3 Ⓐ Ⓑ Ⓒ Ⓓ Ⓔ	3 Ⓐ Ⓑ Ⓒ Ⓓ Ⓔ	3 Ⓐ Ⓑ Ⓒ Ⓓ Ⓔ	3 Ⓐ Ⓑ Ⓒ Ⓓ Ⓔ	3 Ⓐ Ⓑ Ⓒ Ⓓ Ⓔ
4 Ⓐ Ⓑ Ⓒ Ⓓ Ⓔ	4 Ⓐ Ⓑ Ⓒ Ⓓ Ⓔ	4 Ⓐ Ⓑ Ⓒ Ⓓ Ⓔ	4 Ⓐ Ⓑ Ⓒ Ⓓ Ⓔ	4 Ⓐ Ⓑ Ⓒ Ⓓ Ⓔ
5 Ⓐ Ⓑ Ⓒ Ⓓ Ⓔ	5 Ⓐ Ⓑ Ⓒ Ⓓ Ⓔ	5 Ⓐ Ⓑ Ⓒ Ⓓ Ⓔ	5 Ⓐ Ⓑ Ⓒ Ⓓ Ⓔ	5 Ⓐ Ⓑ Ⓒ Ⓓ Ⓔ
6 Ⓐ Ⓑ Ⓒ Ⓓ Ⓔ	6 Ⓐ Ⓑ Ⓒ Ⓓ Ⓔ	6 Ⓐ Ⓑ Ⓒ Ⓓ Ⓔ	6 Ⓐ Ⓑ Ⓒ Ⓓ Ⓔ	6 Ⓐ Ⓑ Ⓒ Ⓓ Ⓔ
7 Ⓐ Ⓑ Ⓒ Ⓓ Ⓔ	7 Ⓐ Ⓑ Ⓒ Ⓓ Ⓔ	7 Ⓐ Ⓑ Ⓒ Ⓓ Ⓔ	7 Ⓐ Ⓑ Ⓒ Ⓓ Ⓔ	7 Ⓐ Ⓑ Ⓒ Ⓓ Ⓔ
8 Ⓐ Ⓑ Ⓒ Ⓓ Ⓔ	8 Ⓐ Ⓑ Ⓒ Ⓓ Ⓔ	8 Ⓐ Ⓑ Ⓒ Ⓓ Ⓔ	8 Ⓐ Ⓑ Ⓒ Ⓓ Ⓔ	8 Ⓐ Ⓑ Ⓒ Ⓓ Ⓔ
9 Ⓐ Ⓑ Ⓒ Ⓓ Ⓔ	9 Ⓐ Ⓑ Ⓒ Ⓓ Ⓔ	9 Ⓐ Ⓑ Ⓒ Ⓓ Ⓔ	9 Ⓐ Ⓑ Ⓒ Ⓓ Ⓔ	9 Ⓐ Ⓑ Ⓒ Ⓓ Ⓔ
10 Ⓐ Ⓑ Ⓒ Ⓓ Ⓔ	10 Ⓐ Ⓑ Ⓒ Ⓓ Ⓔ	10 Ⓐ Ⓑ Ⓒ Ⓓ Ⓔ	10 Ⓐ Ⓑ Ⓒ Ⓓ Ⓔ	10 Ⓐ Ⓑ Ⓒ Ⓓ Ⓔ
11 Ⓐ Ⓑ Ⓒ Ⓓ Ⓔ	11 Ⓐ Ⓑ Ⓒ Ⓓ Ⓔ	11 Ⓐ Ⓑ Ⓒ Ⓓ Ⓔ	11 Ⓐ Ⓑ Ⓒ Ⓓ Ⓔ	11 Ⓐ Ⓑ Ⓒ Ⓓ Ⓔ
12 Ⓐ Ⓑ Ⓒ Ⓓ Ⓔ	12 Ⓐ Ⓑ Ⓒ Ⓓ Ⓔ	12 Ⓐ Ⓑ Ⓒ Ⓓ Ⓔ	12 Ⓐ Ⓑ Ⓒ Ⓓ Ⓔ	12 Ⓐ Ⓑ Ⓒ Ⓓ Ⓔ
13 Ⓐ Ⓑ Ⓒ Ⓓ Ⓔ	13 Ⓐ Ⓑ Ⓒ Ⓓ Ⓔ	13 Ⓐ Ⓑ Ⓒ Ⓓ Ⓔ	13 Ⓐ Ⓑ Ⓒ Ⓓ Ⓔ	13 Ⓐ Ⓑ Ⓒ Ⓓ Ⓔ
14 Ⓐ Ⓑ Ⓒ Ⓓ Ⓔ	14 Ⓐ Ⓑ Ⓒ Ⓓ Ⓔ	14 Ⓐ Ⓑ Ⓒ Ⓓ Ⓔ	14 Ⓐ Ⓑ Ⓒ Ⓓ Ⓔ	14 Ⓐ Ⓑ Ⓒ Ⓓ Ⓔ
15 Ⓐ Ⓑ Ⓒ Ⓓ Ⓔ	15 Ⓐ Ⓑ Ⓒ Ⓓ Ⓔ	15 Ⓐ Ⓑ Ⓒ Ⓓ Ⓔ	15 Ⓐ Ⓑ Ⓒ Ⓓ Ⓔ	15 Ⓐ Ⓑ Ⓒ Ⓓ Ⓔ
16 Ⓐ Ⓑ Ⓒ Ⓓ Ⓔ	16 Ⓐ Ⓑ Ⓒ Ⓓ Ⓔ	16 Ⓐ Ⓑ Ⓒ Ⓓ Ⓔ	16 Ⓐ Ⓑ Ⓒ Ⓓ Ⓔ	16 Ⓐ Ⓑ Ⓒ Ⓓ Ⓔ
17 Ⓐ Ⓑ Ⓒ Ⓓ Ⓔ	17 Ⓐ Ⓑ Ⓒ Ⓓ Ⓔ	17 Ⓐ Ⓑ Ⓒ Ⓓ Ⓔ	17 Ⓐ Ⓑ Ⓒ Ⓓ Ⓔ	17 Ⓐ Ⓑ Ⓒ Ⓓ Ⓔ
18 Ⓐ Ⓑ Ⓒ Ⓓ Ⓔ	18 Ⓐ Ⓑ Ⓒ Ⓓ Ⓔ	18 Ⓐ Ⓑ Ⓒ Ⓓ Ⓔ	18 Ⓐ Ⓑ Ⓒ Ⓓ Ⓔ	18 Ⓐ Ⓑ Ⓒ Ⓓ Ⓔ
19 Ⓐ Ⓑ Ⓒ Ⓓ Ⓔ	19 Ⓐ Ⓑ Ⓒ Ⓓ Ⓔ	19 Ⓐ Ⓑ Ⓒ Ⓓ Ⓔ	19 Ⓐ Ⓑ Ⓒ Ⓓ Ⓔ	19 Ⓐ Ⓑ Ⓒ Ⓓ Ⓔ
20 Ⓐ Ⓑ Ⓒ Ⓓ Ⓔ	20 Ⓐ Ⓑ Ⓒ Ⓓ Ⓔ	20 Ⓐ Ⓑ Ⓒ Ⓓ Ⓔ	20 Ⓐ Ⓑ Ⓒ Ⓓ Ⓔ	20 Ⓐ Ⓑ Ⓒ Ⓓ Ⓔ
21 Ⓐ Ⓑ Ⓒ Ⓓ Ⓔ	21 Ⓐ Ⓑ Ⓒ Ⓓ Ⓔ	21 Ⓐ Ⓑ Ⓒ Ⓓ Ⓔ	21 Ⓐ Ⓑ Ⓒ Ⓓ Ⓔ	21 Ⓐ Ⓑ Ⓒ Ⓓ Ⓔ
22 Ⓐ Ⓑ Ⓒ Ⓓ Ⓔ	22 Ⓐ Ⓑ Ⓒ Ⓓ Ⓔ	22 Ⓐ Ⓑ Ⓒ Ⓓ Ⓔ	22 Ⓐ Ⓑ Ⓒ Ⓓ Ⓔ	22 Ⓐ Ⓑ Ⓒ Ⓓ Ⓔ
23 Ⓐ Ⓑ Ⓒ Ⓓ Ⓔ	23 Ⓐ Ⓑ Ⓒ Ⓓ Ⓔ	23 Ⓐ Ⓑ Ⓒ Ⓓ Ⓔ	23 Ⓐ Ⓑ Ⓒ Ⓓ Ⓔ	23 Ⓐ Ⓑ Ⓒ Ⓓ Ⓔ
24 Ⓐ Ⓑ Ⓒ Ⓓ Ⓔ	24 Ⓐ Ⓑ Ⓒ Ⓓ Ⓔ	24 Ⓐ Ⓑ Ⓒ Ⓓ Ⓔ	24 Ⓐ Ⓑ Ⓒ Ⓓ Ⓔ	24 Ⓐ Ⓑ Ⓒ Ⓓ Ⓔ
25 Ⓐ Ⓑ Ⓒ Ⓓ Ⓔ	25 Ⓐ Ⓑ Ⓒ Ⓓ Ⓔ	25 Ⓐ Ⓑ Ⓒ Ⓓ Ⓔ	25 Ⓐ Ⓑ Ⓒ Ⓓ Ⓔ	25 Ⓐ Ⓑ Ⓒ Ⓓ Ⓔ
26 Ⓐ Ⓑ Ⓒ Ⓓ Ⓔ	26 Ⓐ Ⓑ Ⓒ Ⓓ Ⓔ	26 Ⓐ Ⓑ Ⓒ Ⓓ Ⓔ	26 Ⓐ Ⓑ Ⓒ Ⓓ Ⓔ	26 Ⓐ Ⓑ Ⓒ Ⓓ Ⓔ
27 Ⓐ Ⓑ Ⓒ Ⓓ Ⓔ	27 Ⓐ Ⓑ Ⓒ Ⓓ Ⓔ	27 Ⓐ Ⓑ Ⓒ Ⓓ Ⓔ	27 Ⓐ Ⓑ Ⓒ Ⓓ Ⓔ	27 Ⓐ Ⓑ Ⓒ Ⓓ Ⓔ
28 Ⓐ Ⓑ Ⓒ Ⓓ Ⓔ	28 Ⓐ Ⓑ Ⓒ Ⓓ Ⓔ	28 Ⓐ Ⓑ Ⓒ Ⓓ Ⓔ	28 Ⓐ Ⓑ Ⓒ Ⓓ Ⓔ	28 Ⓐ Ⓑ Ⓒ Ⓓ Ⓔ
29 Ⓐ Ⓑ Ⓒ Ⓓ Ⓔ	29 Ⓐ Ⓑ Ⓒ Ⓓ Ⓔ	29 Ⓐ Ⓑ Ⓒ Ⓓ Ⓔ	29 Ⓐ Ⓑ Ⓒ Ⓓ Ⓔ	29 Ⓐ Ⓑ Ⓒ Ⓓ Ⓔ
30 Ⓐ Ⓑ Ⓒ Ⓓ Ⓔ	30 Ⓐ Ⓑ Ⓒ Ⓓ Ⓔ	30 Ⓐ Ⓑ Ⓒ Ⓓ Ⓔ	30 Ⓐ Ⓑ Ⓒ Ⓓ Ⓔ	30 Ⓐ Ⓑ Ⓒ Ⓓ Ⓔ

14 PLEASE PRINT ALL INFORMATION

LAST NAME   FIRST

EMAIL

PHONE NUMBER

MAILING ADDRESS

CLASS CODE

KAPLAN⟩ TEST PREP

www.kaptest.com/lsat
1-800-KAP-TEST

LSAT is a registered trademark of the Law School Admissions Council, Inc.

SCANTRON Mark Reflex® EM-284925-2:654321   LL3225A

General Directions for the LSAT* Answer Sheet

The actual testing time for this portion of the test will be 2 hours 55 minutes. There are five sections, each with a time limit of 35 minutes. The supervisor will tell you when to begin and end each section. If you finish a section before time is called, you may check your work on that section <u>only</u>; do not turn to any other section of the test book and do not work on any other section either in the test book or on the answer sheet.

There are several different types of questions on the test, and each question type has its own directions. <u>Be sure you understand the directions for each question type before attempting to answer any questions in that section.</u>

Not everyone will finish all the questions in the time allowed. Do not hurry, but work steadily and as quickly as you can without sacrificing accuracy. You are advised to use your time effectively. If a question seems too difficult, go on to the next one and return to the difficult question after completing the section. MARK THE BEST ANSWER YOU CAN FOR EVERY QUESTION. NO DEDUCTIONS WILL BE MADE FOR WRONG ANSWERS. YOUR SCORE WILL BE BASED ONLY ON THE NUMBER OF QUESTIONS YOU ANSWER CORRECTLY.

ALL YOUR ANSWERS MUST BE MARKED ON THE ANSWER SHEET. Answer spaces for each question are lettered to correspond with the letters of the potential answers to each question in the test book. After you have decided which of the answers is correct, blacken the corresponding space on the answer sheet. BE SURE THAT EACH MARK IS BLACK AND COMPLETELY FILLS THE ANSWER SPACE. Give only one answer to each question. If you change an answer, be sure that all previous marks are <u>erased completely</u>. Since the answer sheet is machine scored, incomplete erasures may be interpreted as intended answers. ANSWERS RECORDED IN THE TEST BOOK WILL NOT BE SCORED.

There may be more questions noted on this answer sheet than there are questions in a section. Do not be concerned but be certain that the section and number of the question you are answering matches the answer sheet section and question number. Additional answer spaces in any answer sheet section should be left blank. Begin your next section in the number one answer space for that section.

Kaplan takes various steps to ensure that answer sheets are returned from test centers in a timely manner for processing. In the unlikely event that an answer sheet(s) is not received, Kaplan will permit the examinee to either retest at no additional fee or to receive a refund of his or her test fee. THESE REMEDIES ARE THE EXCLUSIVE REMEDIES AVAILABLE IN THE UNLIKELY EVENT THAT AN ANSWER SHEET IS NOT RECEIVED BY KAPLAN.

Score Cancellation

Complete this section only if you are absolutely certain you want to cancel your score. A CANCELLATION REQUEST CANNOT BE RESCINDED. IF YOU ARE AT ALL UNCERTAIN, YOU SHOULD <u>NOT</u> COMPLETE THIS SECTION.

To cancel your score from this administration, you <u>must</u>:

A. fill in both ovals here..... ◯ ◯

B. read the following statement. Then sign your name and enter the date. **YOUR SIGNATURE ALONE IS NOT SUFFICIENT FOR SCORE CANCELLATION. BOTH OVALS MUST BE FILLED IN FOR SCANNING EQUIPMENT TO RECOGNIZE YOUR REQUEST FOR SCORE CANCELLATION.**

I certify that I wish to cancel my test score from this administration. I understand that my request is irreversible and that my score will not be sent to me or to the law schools to which I apply.

Sign your name in full
_____

Date
_____

HOW DID YOU PREPARE FOR THE LSAT*?
(Select all that apply.)

Responses to this item are voluntary and will be used for statistical research purposes only.

- ◯ By attending a Kaplan LSAT* prep course or tutoring program
- ◯ By attending a non-Kaplan prep course or tutoring program (Please specify:_____)
- ◯ By using a Kaplan LSAT* prep book
- ◯ By using a non-Kaplan prep book (Please specify: _____)
- ◯ By working through the sample questions and free sample tests provided by the LSAC
- ◯ By working through official LSAT* PrepTests and/or other LSAC test prep products
- ◯ Other preparation (Please specify: _____)
- ◯ No preparation

CERTIFYING STATEMENT

Please write (DO NOT PRINT) the following statement. Sign and date.

I certify that I am the examinee whose name appears on this answer sheet and that I am here to take the LSAT for the sole purpose of being considered for application to law school. I further certify that I will neither assist nor receive assistance from any other candidate, and I agree not to copy or retain examination questions or to transmit them to or discuss them with any other person in any form.

_____

_____

_____

_____

_____

_____

_____

_____

_____

SIGNATURE: _____ TODAY'S DATE: _____ / _____ / _____
                                                        MONTH   DAY   YEAR

*LSAT is a registered trademark of the Law School Admissions Council, Inc.

USE ONLY A NO 2. OR HB PENCIL TO COMPLETE THIS ANSWER SHEET. DO NOT USE INK.

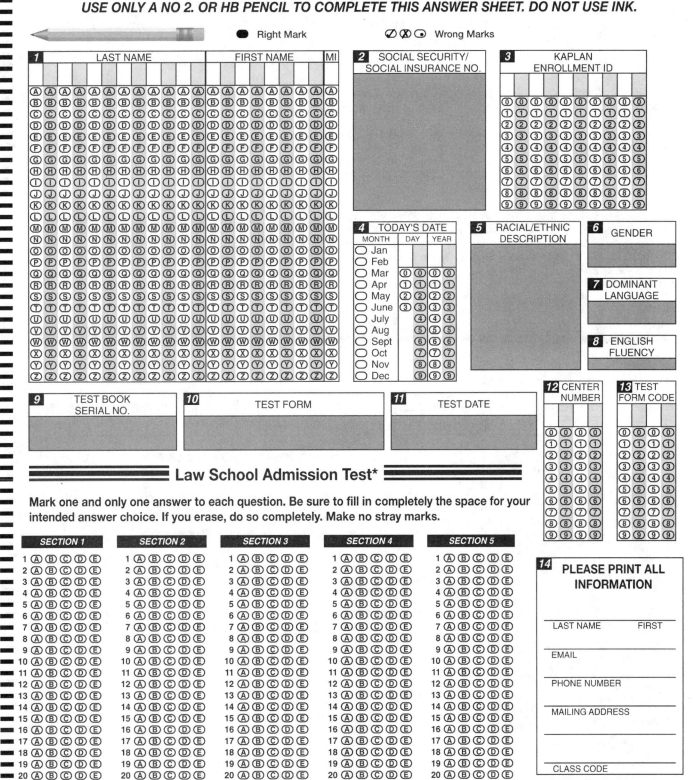

● Right Mark   ⊘ ⊗ ⊙ Wrong Marks

1 LAST NAME   FIRST NAME   MI

2 SOCIAL SECURITY/ SOCIAL INSURANCE NO.

3 KAPLAN ENROLLMENT ID

4 TODAY'S DATE
MONTH   DAY   YEAR
○ Jan
○ Feb
○ Mar
○ Apr
○ May
○ June
○ July
○ Aug
○ Sept
○ Oct
○ Nov
○ Dec

5 RACIAL/ETHNIC DESCRIPTION

6 GENDER

7 DOMINANT LANGUAGE

8 ENGLISH FLUENCY

9 TEST BOOK SERIAL NO.

10 TEST FORM

11 TEST DATE

12 CENTER NUMBER

13 TEST FORM CODE

=== **Law School Admission Test*** ===

Mark one and only one answer to each question. Be sure to fill in completely the space for your intended answer choice. If you erase, do so completely. Make no stray marks.

SECTION 1 / **SECTION 2** / **SECTION 3** / **SECTION 4** / **SECTION 5**

(Questions 1–30, each with answer choices Ⓐ Ⓑ Ⓒ Ⓓ Ⓔ)

14 PLEASE PRINT ALL INFORMATION

LAST NAME   FIRST

EMAIL

PHONE NUMBER

MAILING ADDRESS

CLASS CODE

KAPLAN TEST PREP

www.kaptest.com/lsat
1-800-KAP-TEST

LSAT is a registered trademark of the Law School Admissions Council, Inc.

SCANTRON   Mark Reflex® EM-284925-2:654321   LL3225A

General Directions for the LSAT* Answer Sheet

The actual testing time for this portion of the test will be 2 hours 55 minutes. There are five sections, each with a time limit of 35 minutes. The supervisor will tell you when to begin and end each section. If you finish a section before time is called, you may check your work on that section <u>only</u>; do not turn to any other section of the test book and do not work on any other section either in the test book or on the answer sheet.

There are several different types of questions on the test, and each question type has its own directions. <u>Be sure you understand the directions for each question type before attempting to answer any questions in that section.</u>

Not everyone will finish all the questions in the time allowed. Do not hurry, but work steadily and as quickly as you can without sacrificing accuracy. You are advised to use your time effectively. If a question seems too difficult, go on to the next one and return to the difficult question after completing the section. MARK THE BEST ANSWER YOU CAN FOR EVERY QUESTION. NO DEDUCTIONS WILL BE MADE FOR WRONG ANSWERS. YOUR SCORE WILL BE BASED ONLY ON THE NUMBER OF QUESTIONS YOU ANSWER CORRECTLY.

ALL YOUR ANSWERS MUST BE MARKED ON THE ANSWER SHEET. Answer spaces for each question are lettered to correspond with the letters of the potential answers to each question in the test book. After you have decided which of the answers is correct, blacken the corresponding space on the answer sheet. BE SURE THAT EACH MARK IS BLACK AND COMPLETELY FILLS THE ANSWER SPACE. Give only one answer to each question. If you change an answer, be sure that all previous marks are <u>erased completely</u>. Since the answer sheet is machine scored, incomplete erasures may be interpreted as intended answers. ANSWERS RECORDED IN THE TEST BOOK WILL NOT BE SCORED.

There may be more questions noted on this answer sheet than there are questions in a section. Do not be concerned but be certain that the section and number of the question you are answering matches the answer sheet section and question number. Additional answer spaces in any answer sheet section should be left blank. Begin your next section in the number one answer space for that section.

Kaplan takes various steps to ensure that answer sheets are returned from test centers in a timely manner for processing. In the unlikely event that an answer sheet(s) is not received, Kaplan will permit the examinee to either retest at no additional fee or to receive a refund of his or her test fee. THESE REMEDIES ARE THE EXCLUSIVE REMEDIES AVAILABLE IN THE UNLIKELY EVENT THAT AN ANSWER SHEET IS NOT RECEIVED BY KAPLAN.

Score Cancellation

Complete this section only if you are absolutely certain you want to cancel your score. A CANCELLATION REQUEST CANNOT BE RESCINDED. IF YOU ARE AT ALL UNCERTAIN, YOU SHOULD <u>NOT</u> COMPLETE THIS SECTION.

To cancel your score from this administration, you **must**:

A. fill in both ovals here..... ◯ ◯

B. read the following statement. Then sign your name and enter the date. **YOUR SIGNATURE ALONE IS NOT SUFFICIENT FOR SCORE CANCELLATION. BOTH OVALS MUST BE FILLED IN FOR SCANNING EQUIPMENT TO RECOGNIZE YOUR REQUEST FOR SCORE CANCELLATION.**

I certify that I wish to cancel my test score from this administration. I understand that my request is irreversible and that my score will not be sent to me or to the law schools to which I apply.

_____
Sign your name in full

_____
Date

HOW DID YOU PREPARE FOR THE LSAT*?
(Select all that apply.)

Responses to this item are voluntary and will be used for statistical research purposes only.

◯ By attending a Kaplan LSAT* prep course or tutoring program
◯ By attending a non-Kaplan prep course or tutoring program (Please specify:_____)
◯ By using a Kaplan LSAT* prep book
◯ By using a non-Kaplan prep book (Please specify: _____)
◯ By working through the sample questions and free sample tests provided by the LSAC
◯ By working through official LSAT* PrepTests and/or other LSAC test prep products
◯ Other preparation (Please specify: _____)
◯ No preparation

CERTIFYING STATEMENT

Please write (DO NOT PRINT) the following statement. Sign and date.

I certify that I am the examinee whose name appears on this answer sheet and that I am here to take the LSAT for the sole purpose of being considered for application to law school. I further certify that I will neither assist nor receive assistance from any other candidate, and I agree not to copy or retain examination questions or to transmit them to or discuss them with any other person in any form.

_____
_____
_____
_____
_____
_____
_____
_____
_____

SIGNATURE:_____ TODAY'S DATE: _____/_____/_____
                                                              MONTH DAY YEAR

*LSAT is a registered trademark of the Law School Admissions Council, Inc.

USE ONLY A NO 2. OR HB PENCIL TO COMPLETE THIS ANSWER SHEET. DO NOT USE INK.

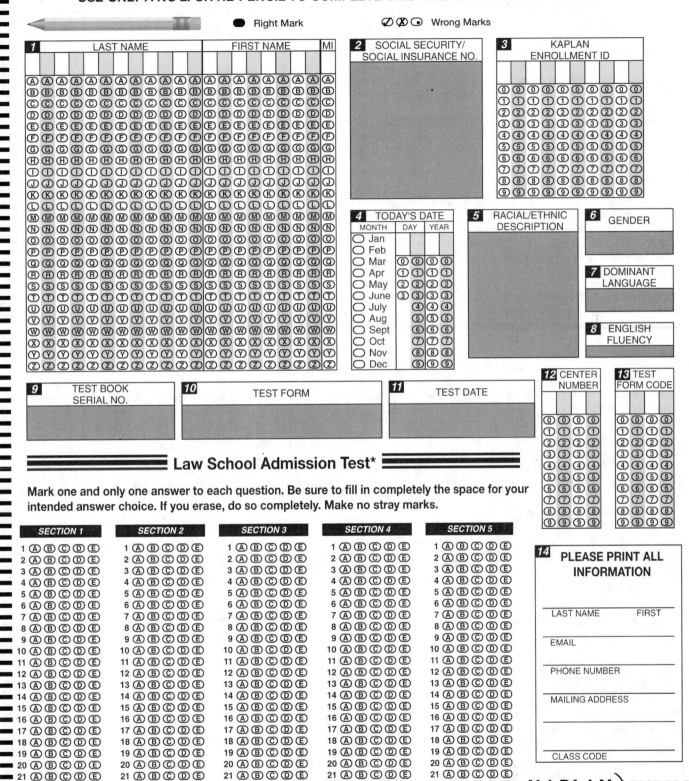

● Right Mark ⊘ ⊗ ⊙ Wrong Marks

Law School Admission Test*

Mark one and only one answer to each question. Be sure to fill in completely the space for your intended answer choice. If you erase, do so completely. Make no stray marks.

14 PLEASE PRINT ALL INFORMATION

LAST NAME   FIRST

EMAIL

PHONE NUMBER

MAILING ADDRESS

CLASS CODE

KAPLAN TEST PREP

www.kaptest.com/lsat
1-800-KAP-TEST

LSAT is a registered trademark of the
Law School Admissions Council, Inc.

SCANTRON Mark Reflex® EM-284925-2:654321   LL3225A

General Directions for the LSAT* Answer Sheet

The actual testing time for this portion of the test will be 2 hours 55 minutes. There are five sections, each with a time limit of 35 minutes. The supervisor will tell you when to begin and end each section. If you finish a section before time is called, you may check your work on that section <u>only</u>; do not turn to any other section of the test book and do not work on any other section either in the test book or on the answer sheet.

There are several different types of questions on the test, and each question type has its own directions. <u>Be sure you understand the directions for each question type before attempting to answer any questions in that section.</u>

Not everyone will finish all the questions in the time allowed. Do not hurry, but work steadily and as quickly as you can without sacrificing accuracy. You are advised to use your time effectively. If a question seems too difficult, go on to the next one and return to the difficult question after completing the section. MARK THE BEST ANSWER YOU CAN FOR EVERY QUESTION. NO DEDUCTIONS WILL BE MADE FOR WRONG ANSWERS. YOUR SCORE WILL BE BASED ONLY ON THE NUMBER OF QUESTIONS YOU ANSWER CORRECTLY.

ALL YOUR ANSWERS MUST BE MARKED ON THE ANSWER SHEET. Answer spaces for each question are lettered to correspond with the letters of the potential answers to each question in the test book. After you have decided which of the answers is correct, blacken the corresponding space on the answer sheet. BE SURE THAT EACH MARK IS BLACK AND COMPLETELY FILLS THE ANSWER SPACE. Give only one answer to each question. If you change an answer, be sure that all previous marks are <u>erased completely</u>. Since the answer sheet is machine scored, incomplete erasures may be interpreted as intended answers. ANSWERS RECORDED IN THE TEST BOOK WILL NOT BE SCORED.

There may be more questions noted on this answer sheet than there are questions in a section. Do not be concerned but be certain that the section and number of the question you are answering matches the answer sheet section and question number. Additional answer spaces in any answer sheet section should be left blank. Begin your next section in the number one answer space for that section.

Kaplan takes various steps to ensure that answer sheets are returned from test centers in a timely manner for processing. In the unlikely event that an answer sheet(s) is not received, Kaplan will permit the examinee to either retest at no additional fee or to receive a refund of his or her test fee. THESE REMEDIES ARE THE EXCLUSIVE REMEDIES AVAILABLE IN THE UNLIKELY EVENT THAT AN ANSWER SHEET IS NOT RECEIVED BY KAPLAN.

Score Cancellation

Complete this section only if you are absolutely certain you want to cancel your score. A CANCELLATION REQUEST CANNOT BE RESCINDED. IF YOU ARE AT ALL UNCERTAIN, YOU SHOULD <u>NOT</u> COMPLETE THIS SECTION.

To cancel your score from this administration, you **must**:

A. fill in both ovals here..... ○ ○

B. read the following statement. Then sign your name and enter the date. **YOUR SIGNATURE ALONE IS NOT SUFFICIENT FOR SCORE CANCELLATION. BOTH OVALS MUST BE FILLED IN FOR SCANNING EQUIPMENT TO RECOGNIZE YOUR REQUEST FOR SCORE CANCELLATION.**

I certify that I wish to cancel my test score from this administration. I understand that my request is irreversible and that my score will not be sent to me or to the law schools to which I apply.

_____
Sign your name in full

_____
Date

HOW DID YOU PREPARE FOR THE LSAT*?
(Select all that apply.)

Responses to this item are voluntary and will be used for statistical research purposes only.

○ By attending a Kaplan LSAT* prep course or tutoring program
○ By attending a non-Kaplan prep course or tutoring program (Please specify:_____)
○ By using a Kaplan LSAT* prep book
○ By using a non-Kaplan prep book (Please specify: _____)
○ By working through the sample questions and free sample tests provided by the LSAC
○ By working through official LSAT* PrepTests and/or other LSAC test prep products
○ Other preparation (Please specify: _____)
○ No preparation

CERTIFYING STATEMENT

Please write (DO NOT PRINT) the following statement. Sign and date.

I certify that I am the examinee whose name appears on this answer sheet and that I am here to take the LSAT for the sole purpose of being considered for application to law school. I further certify that I will neither assist nor receive assistance from any other candidate, and I agree not to copy or retain examination questions or to transmit them to or discuss them with any other person in any form.

_____
_____
_____
_____
_____
_____
_____
_____
_____

SIGNATURE:_____   TODAY'S DATE: _____/_____/_____
                                                                         MONTH   DAY   YEAR

***LSAT is a registered trademark of the Law School Admissions Council, Inc.**

USE ONLY A NO 2. OR HB PENCIL TO COMPLETE THIS ANSWER SHEET. DO NOT USE INK.

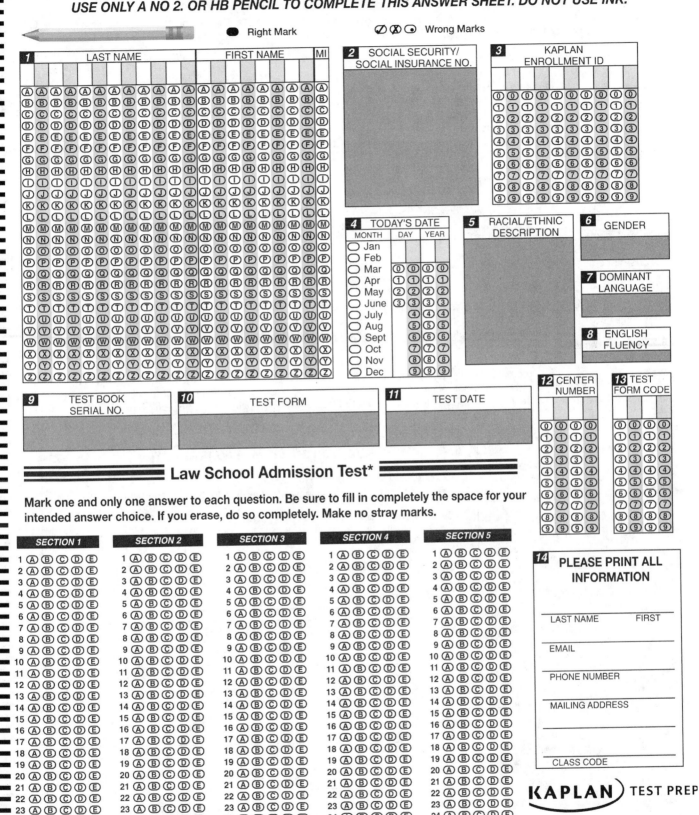

● Right Mark   ⊘ ⊗ ⊙ Wrong Marks

1 LAST NAME | FIRST NAME | MI

2 SOCIAL SECURITY/ SOCIAL INSURANCE NO.

3 KAPLAN ENROLLMENT ID

4 TODAY'S DATE
MONTH | DAY | YEAR
Jan, Feb, Mar, Apr, May, June, July, Aug, Sept, Oct, Nov, Dec

5 RACIAL/ETHNIC DESCRIPTION

6 GENDER

7 DOMINANT LANGUAGE

8 ENGLISH FLUENCY

9 TEST BOOK SERIAL NO.

10 TEST FORM

11 TEST DATE

12 CENTER NUMBER

13 TEST FORM CODE

Law School Admission Test*

Mark one and only one answer to each question. Be sure to fill in completely the space for your intended answer choice. If you erase, do so completely. Make no stray marks.

SECTION 1 — 1–30 Ⓐ Ⓑ Ⓒ Ⓓ Ⓔ
SECTION 2 — 1–30 Ⓐ Ⓑ Ⓒ Ⓓ Ⓔ
SECTION 3 — 1–30 Ⓐ Ⓑ Ⓒ Ⓓ Ⓔ
SECTION 4 — 1–30 Ⓐ Ⓑ Ⓒ Ⓓ Ⓔ
SECTION 5 — 1–30 Ⓐ Ⓑ Ⓒ Ⓓ Ⓔ

14 PLEASE PRINT ALL INFORMATION

LAST NAME   FIRST

EMAIL

PHONE NUMBER

MAILING ADDRESS

CLASS CODE

KAPLAN TEST PREP

www.kaptest.com/lsat
1-800-KAP-TEST

LSAT is a registered trademark of the Law School Admissions Council, Inc.

SCANTRON   Mark Reflex® EM-284925-2:654321   LL3225A

General Directions for the LSAT* Answer Sheet

The actual testing time for this portion of the test will be 2 hours 55 minutes. There are five sections, each with a time limit of 35 minutes. The supervisor will tell you when to begin and end each section. If you finish a section before time is called, you may check your work on that section only; do not turn to any other section of the test book and do not work on any other section either in the test book or on the answer sheet.

There are several different types of questions on the test, and each question type has its own directions. Be sure you understand the directions for each question type before attempting to answer any questions in that section.

Not everyone will finish all the questions in the time allowed. Do not hurry, but work steadily and as quickly as you can without sacrificing accuracy. You are advised to use your time effectively. If a question seems too difficult, go on to the next one and return to the difficult question after completing the section. MARK THE BEST ANSWER YOU CAN FOR EVERY QUESTION. NO DEDUCTIONS WILL BE MADE FOR WRONG ANSWERS. YOUR SCORE WILL BE BASED ONLY ON THE NUMBER OF QUESTIONS YOU ANSWER CORRECTLY.

ALL YOUR ANSWERS MUST BE MARKED ON THE ANSWER SHEET. Answer spaces for each question are lettered to correspond with the letters of the potential answers to each question in the test book. After you have decided which of the answers is correct, blacken the corresponding space on the answer sheet. BE SURE THAT EACH MARK IS BLACK AND COMPLETELY FILLS THE ANSWER SPACE. Give only one answer to each question. If you change an answer, be sure that all previous marks are erased completely. Since the answer sheet is machine scored, incomplete erasures may be interpreted as intended answers. ANSWERS RECORDED IN THE TEST BOOK WILL NOT BE SCORED.

There may be more questions noted on this answer sheet than there are questions in a section. Do not be concerned but be certain that the section and number of the question you are answering matches the answer sheet section and question number. Additional answer spaces in any answer sheet section should be left blank. Begin your next section in the number one answer space for that section.

Kaplan takes various steps to ensure that answer sheets are returned from test centers in a timely manner for processing. In the unlikely event that an answer sheet(s) is not received, Kaplan will permit the examinee to either retest at no additional fee or to receive a refund of his or her test fee. THESE REMEDIES ARE THE EXCLUSIVE REMEDIES AVAILABLE IN THE UNLIKELY EVENT THAT AN ANSWER SHEET IS NOT RECEIVED BY KAPLAN.

Score Cancellation

Complete this section only if you are absolutely certain you want to cancel your score. A CANCELLATION REQUEST CANNOT BE RESCINDED. IF YOU ARE AT ALL UNCERTAIN, YOU SHOULD NOT COMPLETE THIS SECTION.

To cancel your score from this administration, you **must**:

A. fill in both ovals here..... ○ ○

B. read the following statement. Then sign your name and enter the date.
YOUR SIGNATURE ALONE IS NOT SUFFICIENT FOR SCORE CANCELLATION. BOTH OVALS MUST BE FILLED IN FOR SCANNING EQUIPMENT TO RECOGNIZE YOUR REQUEST FOR SCORE CANCELLATION.

I certify that I wish to cancel my test score from this administration. I understand that my request is irreversible and that my score will not be sent to me or to the law schools to which I apply.

_____
Sign your name in full

_____
Date

HOW DID YOU PREPARE FOR THE LSAT*?
(Select all that apply.)

Responses to this item are voluntary and will be used for statistical research purposes only.

○ By attending a Kaplan LSAT* prep course or tutoring program
○ By attending a non-Kaplan prep course or tutoring program (Please specify:_____)
○ By using a Kaplan LSAT* prep book
○ By using a non-Kaplan prep book (Please specify: _____)
○ By working through the sample questions and free sample tests provided by the LSAC
○ By working through official LSAT* PrepTests and/or other LSAC test prep products
○ Other preparation (Please specify: _____)
○ No preparation

CERTIFYING STATEMENT

Please write (DO NOT PRINT) the following statement. Sign and date.

I certify that I am the examinee whose name appears on this answer sheet and that I am here to take the LSAT for the sole purpose of being considered for application to law school. I further certify that I will neither assist nor receive assistance from any other candidate, and I agree not to copy or retain examination questions or to transmit them to or discuss them with any other person in any form.

_____
_____
_____
_____
_____
_____
_____
_____
_____
_____

SIGNATURE: _____ TODAY'S DATE: _____/_____/_____
                                                                      MONTH DAY YEAR

*LSAT is a registered trademark of the Law School Admissions Council, Inc.